Quick Tax Facts

Patient Protection, Health Care Reconciliation, and HIRE Acts of 2010

Key Provisions at a Glance

The chart below summarizes the key tax provisions of the Patient Protection and Affordable Care Act, as amended by the Health Care and Education Reconciliation Act of 2010, and the Hiring Incentives to Restore Employment Act. See the explanations in CCH's *2010 Tax Legislation, Patient Protection and Affordable Care, Health Care Reconciliation, HIRE and Other Recent Tax Acts: Law, Explanation and Analysis*, for a complete discussion.

Individuals

Provision	In Effect	Impact
Gross Income Exclusion for Repayments under State Loan Programs for Health Care Professionals	After 12/31/08	Provides an exclusion from gross income for repayments under state loan repayment or forgiveness programs for student loans of certain health care professionals.
Adoption Credit and Adoption Assistance Programs	After 12/31/09	Increases the dollar limitations for the adoption credit and adoption assistance program exclusion to $13,170.
Charitable Contributions for Haiti Earthquake Relief	After 1/11/10 and before 3/1/10	Allows individuals to claim a charitable deduction on their 2009 return for cash contributions relating to Haiti earthquake relief.
Medical Benefits for Children under Age 27	3/30/10	Extends certain medical tax benefits to children under age 27.
Excise Tax on Tanning Salons	Services performed on or after 7/1/10	Imposes a 10 percent tax on amounts paid for indoor salon tanning services.
Limitation on Distributions from Health Accounts	After 12/31/10	Includes in gross income distributions from an Archer medical savings account or health savings account to pay for over-the-counter medicines.
Additional Tax on HSA and Archer MSA Distributions	After 12/31/10	Increases the additional tax on distributions made from a health savings account or Archer medical savings account not used for qualified medical expenses to 20 percent of the amount includible in gross income.
Additional Medicare Tax on High-Income Taxpayers	After 12/31/12	Imposes an additional 0.9 percent hospital insurance tax on individuals who receive wages and self-employment income in excess of $200,000 ($250,000 in the case of joint filers; $125,000 in the case of a married individual filing separately).
Additional Medicare Tax on Investment income	After 12/31/12	Imposes a 3.8 percent Medicare tax on a portion of the net investment income of individuals, estates and trusts.
Itemized Deductions for Medical Expenses	After 12/31/12	Increases the threshold for the itemized deduction for unreimbursed medical expenses to 10 percent of adjusted gross income (AGI).
Penalty for Failing to Carry Health Insurance	After 12/31/13	Imposes a penalty on applicable individuals who fail to have minimum essential health care coverage for themselves and their dependents.
Health Insurance Premium Assistance Credit	Tax years ending after 12/31/13	Provides a refundable health insurance premium assistance credit to individuals with household income between 100 percent and 400 percent of the federal poverty line.

CCH

Businesses

Provision	In Effect	Impact
Code Sec. 179 Expense Election	2010	Extends the increased Code Sec. 179 expensing limits of $250,000 for the dollar limitation and $800,000 for the investment limitation for 2010.
Small Employer Health Insurance Credit	2010 – 2013	Allows eligible small employers to claim a 35 percent credit (25 percent in the case of tax-exempt eligible small employers) for premiums paid toward health coverage for its employees. After 2013, employers must participate in an insurance exchange to claim the credit and other modifications and restrictions apply.
Employer Payroll Tax Holiday	After 3/18/10 through 12/31/10	Provides qualified employers an exemption from paying its share of OASDI taxes for newly-hired workers who were formerly unemployed.
Employee Retention Credit	After 3/18/10 through 12/31/10	Allows qualified employers to claim a credit (up to $1,000) for retaining qualified newly-hired workers for at least one year.
Simple Cafeteria Plans	After 12/31/10	Allows certain small employers to choose to provide a simple cafeteria plan for their employees under which the nondiscrimination rules for regular cafeteria plans would be treated as satisfied.
Limitation on Deduction for Employee Remuneration	After 12/31/12	Limits the deduction for employee remuneration paid by certain health insurance providers for individuals paid in excess of $500,000.
Shared Responsibility Payment for Employers Regarding Health Coverage	After 12/31/13	Imposes a shared responsibility assessable payment on certain large employers that fail to offer health care coverage.
Free Choice Vouchers	After 12/31/13	Requires employers offering health care coverage through employer-sponsored plans to provide free choice vouchers to qualified employees.

Reporting Requirements & Other Provisions

Provision	In Effect	Impact
Failure to Report Information or File Return for Certain Foreign Trusts Penalty	Notices and returns required to be filed after 12/31/09	Increases the minimum penalty for failure to report information or file returns with respect to foreign trusts to $10,000.
Underpayments Attributable to Undisclosed Foreign Financial Assets Penalty	After 3/18/10	Imposes a 40 percent accuracy-related penalty for underpayments attributable to a transaction involving undisclosed foreign financial assets.
Statute of Limitations for Omission of Income in Connection with Foreign Assets	Returns filed after 3/18/10	Extends the statute of limitations for assessments to six years if there is an omission of gross income in excess of $5,000 attributable to a foreign financial asset.
Inclusion of Cost of Employer-Sponsored Health Coverage on W-2	After 12/31/10	Requires employers to disclose the total cost of employer-sponsored health insurance coverage on the employee's Form W-2.
Health Care Coverage Reporting	After 12/31/13	Requires information reporting by providers regarding health care coverage.

2010 TAX LEGISLATION

Patient Protection and Affordable Care
Health Care Reconciliation
HIRE
and Other Recent Tax Acts

Law, Explanation and Analysis

CCH Editorial Staff Publication

.CCH
a Wolters Kluwer business

This publication is designed to provide accurate and authoritative information in regard to the subject matter covered. It is sold with the understanding that the publisher is not engaged in rendering legal, accounting, or other professional service. If legal advice or other expert assistance is required, the services of a competent professional person should be sought.

ISBN 978-0-8080-2414-9

4025 W. Peterson Ave.
Chicago, IL 60646-6085
1 800 248 3248
www.CCHGroup.com

No claim is made to original government works; however, within this Product or Publication, the following are subject to CCH's copyright: (1) the gathering, compilation, and arrangement of such government materials; (2) the magnetic translation and digital conversion of data, if applicable; (3) the historical, statutory and other notes and references; and (4) the commentary and other materials.

Printed in the United States of America

Patient Protection and Affordable Care Act, as amended by the Health Care and Reconciliation Act of 2010, the Hiring Incentives to Restore Employment (HIRE) Act, and Other Recent Tax Legislation

Health Care Reform, Job Stimulus and More!

In a flurry of activity early in the year, Congress passed a series of bills covering a range of issues, but all with a significant impact on the federal tax law. From massive health care reform, to employment, to smaller measures designed to encourage charitable giving, the new laws present a host of planning opportunities for tax practitioners and their clients.

The Road to Health Care Reform

After nearly a year of hearings, heated debate, town hall meetings, polls, and votes, Congress has passed comprehensive health care reform legislation. The Patient Protection and Affordable Care Act (the Patient Protection Act) (P.L. 111-148), as amended by the Health Care and Education Reconciliation Act of 2010 (2010 Reconciliation Act) (P.L. 111-152), is designed to effectuate fundamental reforms to the United States health care system. Almost all individuals not covered by Medicaid or Medicare would be required to obtain health care coverage or pay penalties. Employer-provided coverage would generally satisfy the universal coverage requirement. Lower-income individuals, as well as some middle-class families, would receive a credit or voucher to help pay for health insurance, which can be used at one of the American Health Benefits Exchanges that are required to be established by every state. Employers electing not to offer qualifying coverage would be subject to an additional tax to help finance the health care coverage for their employees. Exceptions would be made for small businesses.

The new law includes over $400 billion in revenue raisers and new taxes on employers and individuals, including a 40-percent surtax on high-end employer-sponsored health plans, an increase in the employee portion of the Medicare tax to 2.35 percent for couples with adjusted gross incomes (AGI) over $250,000 a year and individuals with AGI over $200,000, new fees on certain health-related industries, an increase in the threshold for the deduction of eligible unreimbursed medical expenses from 7.5% to 10% of AGI starting in 2013, and more.

Pursuant to the Patient Protection Act, the IRS is responsible for overseeing a significant part of health care reform, such as the administration of additional taxes on individuals and employers, determinations of various exemptions from those taxes, and oversight of new information reporting requirements. Many of the new requirements have phased-in and delayed effective dates, giving the IRS and taxpayers a window of time to prepare.

The road to reach this point and enact this comprehensive health care reform has required an unprecedented series of compromises by Congress and intervention by President Obama. On November 7, 2009, the House passed the Affordable Health Care for America Act of 2009 (H.R. 3962). The 2,000+ page bill proposed an overhaul of the health insurance industry, included a public option, and broadly expanded the number of Americans who would be covered under some kind of insurance. The proposal also included a new surtax on higher-income individuals at a cost of more than $400 billion over 10 years to help pay for nearly universal coverage.

Health care reform took another major step forward on November 18, 2009, when Senate Democratic leaders unveiled the Patient Protection and Affordable Care Act (H.R. 3590). The bill blended proposals passed earlier by the Senate Finance Committee (SFC) and the Senate Health, Education, Labor, and Pensions (HELP) Committee. The $849 billion package, with $370 billion in revenue raisers, was drafted not only with an eye toward garnering the 60 votes necessary for full Senate approval but also in preparation for conference committee negotiations. Although the Senate bill was similar in scope to the House-passed Affordable Health Care for America Act (H.R. 3962), there were significant differences between the two bills. Most notably, the Senate bill lacked a public option. The Senate in dramatic fashion passed the Patient Protection and Affordable Care Act (H.R. 3590), on December 24, 2009, by a vote of 60 to 39. The Senate vote paved the way for a conference between the House and Senate in early 2010.

The hopes of President Obama and Democratic leaders for a quick conference to reconcile the differences between the House and Senate passed health care reform bills were dashed on January 19, 2010, when Republican Scott Brown won the special election in Massachusetts for the Senate seat formerly held by the late Ted Kennedy. As a result, Senate democrats lost the 60-seat super majority required to defeat a filibuster in the Senate. With near unanimous Republican opposition in the Senate to a public option and the House-passed bill, and significant opposition from House Representatives who argued that the Senate-passed bill did not go far enough, a compromise seemed unlikely.

Faced with the realization that a compromise was improbable, Democratic leaders resorted to a series of parliamentarian maneuvers to enact final health care reform. House leaders agreed to bring the Senate passed Patient Protection Act to the floor. In effort to address those objectionable portions of the legislation, House leaders unveiled the 2010 Reconciliation Act. The 2010 Reconciliation Act serves as "sidecar" bill, allowing the House to move changes to the Patient Protection Act using the budget reconciliation rules. The budget reconciliation process allows the Senate to pass the package with only 51 votes, rather than a 60-vote super-majority.

The House passed the Patient Protection Act, along with the 2010 Reconciliation Act, on March 21, 2010. President Obama signed the Patient Protection Act into law on March 23, 2010. The Senate subsequently began debate on the 2010 Reconciliation Act on March 23, 2010. After defeating numerous amendments and points of order, the Senate passed the 2010 Reconciliation Act on March 25, 2010. However, prior to passage, the Senate parliamentarian sustained objections to two sections of the bill related to student loans. As a result, the House was required to take a second vote. The House passed the amended, Senate-passed version on March 25, 2010. On March 30, 2010, President Obama signed the 2010 Reconciliation Act into law.

Tax Breaks for Businesses and Foreign Asset Disclosure Requirements

Congress took a brief respite from health care reform negotiations in February and turned its attention to addressing the still weak U.S. job market, unemployment benefits and victims of the recent earthquake in Haiti. The Senate passed, on February 24, 2010, the Hiring Incentives to Restore Employment (HIRE) Act (P.L. 111-147). The House of Representatives subsequently amended the Senate-passed bill to fully offset the cost and passed the measure on March 4, 2010, necessitating another vote by the Senate. The Senate passed the final, House-amended version on March 17, 2010. President Obama signed the legislation into law on March 18, 2010.

The HIRE Act provides additional tax breaks for businesses to encourage hiring and imposes a number of potential burdens with respect to reporting and disclosure of foreign assets. In addition to continuing a few other employment-related tax breaks, such as Code Sec. 179 expensing and COBRA premium assistance, the new payroll tax holiday and retention credit and their interaction with the work opportunity credit will give employers additional factors to consider in their hiring decisions.

The new reporting and disclosure requirements with respect to foreign assets are significant. Direct reporting responsibilities are imposed on foreign financial institutions with the threat of withholding used as the tool to achieve compliance. Disclosure and reporting responsibilities imposed on individuals with respect to foreign assets and trusts are also extended to U.S. persons formed or availed of to avoid the disclosure and reporting requirements. This continues a trend of requiring significant additional disclosures in tax returns to assist the IRS in controlling noncompliance and giving the IRS the tools to further reduce the tax gap with respect to reporting income from foreign assets.

Temporary Extension of Unemployment Funding and COBRA

President Obama, on March 2, 2010, signed the Temporary Extension Act of 2010 (P.L. 111-144). The new law provides a 30-day funding extension for unemployment compensation, COBRA premiums, Medicare physician payments and therapy caps. It also temporarily funds surface transportation and flood insurance programs, small business loan guarantees, federal poverty guidelines and retransmission of television broadcasts.

Charitable Donations to Earthquake Victims

On January 22, 2010, President Obama signed into law P.L. 111-126, which allows taxpayers who make monetary contributions to the victims of the earthquake in Haiti after January 11, 2010, and before March 1, 2010, to claim an itemized charitable contribution deduction on their 2009 federal tax return. The House of Representatives unanimously passed legislation on January 20, 2010. The Senate approved the measure by unanimous consent one day later on January 21, 2010.

About This Work and CCH

Following the passage of the Patient Protection and Affordable Care Act (P.L. 111-148), as amended by the Health Care and Education Reconciliation Act of 2010 (P.L. 111-152), the Hiring Incentives to Restore Employment Act (P.L. 111-147), the Temporary Extension Act of 2010 (P.L. 111-144) and P.L. 111-126, CCH is providing practitioners with a single integrated law and explanation of the tax provisions of these Acts. As always, CCH Tax and Accounting remains dedicated to responding to the needs of tax professionals in helping them quickly understand and work with these new laws as they take effect. Other products and tax services relating to the new legislation can be found at CCH's website http://tax.cchgroup.com.

Contributors

Jean Baxley, J.D., LL.M.
Crowell & Moring
Washington, D.C.

Elizabeth Thomas Dold, J.D., LL.M.
Groom Law Group
Washington, D.C.

Charles R. Goulding, J.D., CPA, MBA
Energy Tax Savers Inc.
Syosset, New York

Robert S. Keebler, CPA, MST, AEP
(Distinguished)
Baker Tilly Virchow Krause, LLP
Appleton, Wisconsin

Paul C. Lau, CPA, CMA, CFM
Blackman Kallick
Chicago, Illinois

Mark A. Luscombe, J.D., LL.M, CPA
CCH, a Wolters Kluwer business
Riverwoods, Illinois

Peter J. Melcher, MBA, J.D., LL.M.
Baker Tilly Virchow Krause, LLP
Appleton, Wisconsin

Michael Miller
Roberts & Holland LLP
New York, New York

Vincent O'Brien, CPA
Vincent J. O'Brien, CPA, PC
Lynbrook, New York

Pam Perdue, J.D.
Summers Compton & Wells P.C.
St. Louis, Missouri

Michael Schlesinger, J.D., LL.M.
Schlesinger and Sussman
New York, New York

Sandy Soltis, CPA, CFP
Blackman Kallick
Chicago, Illinois

Michel Stein, J.D., LL.M.
Hochman, Salkin, Rettig, Toscher & Perez
Beverly Hills, California

Steven Toscher, J.D.
Hochman, Salkin, Rettig, Toscher & Perez
Beverly Hills, California

CCH appreciates the contributions of our expert authors for their insight and practical analysis of the new law. The analysis provided by these experts is not intended as or written for use by any taxpayer to avoid penalties. The analysis is not intended as legal advice. Taxpayers should seek advice based on their own particular circumstances from an independent tax advisor.

CCH Tax and Accounting Publishing
EDITORIAL STAFF

¶1 Features of This Publication

This publication is your complete guide to the tax provisions of the *Patient Protection and Affordable Care Act* (P.L. 111-148), as amended by the *Health Care and Education Reconciliation Act of 2010* (P.L. 111-152); *Hiring Incentives to Restore Employment Act* (P.L. 111-147); *Temporary Extension Act of 2010* (P.L. 111-144); and *Legislation to Accelerate the Income Tax Benefits for Charitable Cash Contributions for the Relief of Victims of the Earthquake in Haiti* (P.L. 111-126).

The core portion of this publication contains the CCH Explanations of these Acts. The explanations outline all of the tax law changes and what they mean for you and your clients. The explanations also feature practical guidance, examples, planning opportunities and strategies, as well as pitfalls to be avoided as a result of the law changes. In addition, a chapter is included with explanations of relevant non-tax provisions of the heath care legislation.

The publication also contains numerous other features designed to help you locate and understand the changes made by these Acts. These features include cross references to related materials, detailed effective dates, and numerous finding tables and indexes. A more detailed description of these features appears below.

HIGHLIGHTS

Highlights are quick summaries of the major provisions of the *Patient Protection and Affordable Care Act* (P.L. 111-148), as amended by the *Health Care and Education Reconciliation Act of 2010* (P.L. 111-152), and the *Hiring Incentives to Restore Employment Act* (P.L. 111-147). The Highlights are arranged by taxpayer type and area of interest, such as health care coverage requirements, tax credits and deductions for individuals and businesses, and foreign asset reporting requirements. At the end of each summary is a paragraph reference to the more detailed CCH Explanation on that topic, giving you an easy way to find the portions of the publication that are of most interest to you. *Highlights begin at ¶5.*

TAXPAYERS AFFECTED

The first chapter of the publication, *Taxpayers Affected*, contains a detailed look at how the new laws impact specific categories of taxpayers. This chapter provides a quick reference for readers who want to know the immediate impact that the laws will have on their clients. *Taxpayers Affected begins at ¶101.*

CCH EXPLANATIONS

CCH Explanations are designed to give you a complete, accessible understanding of the new laws. Explanations are arranged by subject for ease of use. There are two main finding devices you can use to locate explanations on a given topic. These are:

- A detailed table of contents at the beginning of the publication listing all of the CCH Explanations of the new laws;

- A table of contents preceding each chapter.

Each CCH Explanation contains special features to aid in your complete understanding of the new laws. These include:

- A summary at the beginning of each explanation providing a brief overview of the new laws;

- A background or prior law discussion that puts the law changes into perspective;

- Editorial aids, including examples, cautions, planning notes, elections, comments, compliance tips, and key rates and figures, that highlight the impact of the new laws;

- Charts and examples illustrating the ramifications of specific law changes;

- Captions at the end of each explanation identifying the Code sections added, amended or repealed, as well as the Act sections containing the changes;

- Cross references to the law and committee report paragraphs related to the explanation;

- A line highlighting the effective date of each law change, marked by an arrow symbol; and

- References at the end of the discussion to related information in the Standard Federal Tax Reporter, Tax Research Consultant and Practical Tax explanations.

The CCH Explanations begin at ¶205.

AMENDED CODE PROVISIONS

Changes to the Internal Revenue Code made by the *Patient Protection and Affordable Care Act* (P.L. 111-148), as amended by the *Health Care and Education Reconciliation Act of 2010* (P.L. 111-152); the *Hiring Incentives to Restore Employment Act* (P.L. 111-147); *Temporary Extension Act of 2010* (P.L. 111-144); and *Legislation to Accelerate the Income Tax Benefits for Charitable Cash Contributions for the Relief of Victims of the Earthquake in Haiti* (P.L. 111-126), appear under the heading "Code Sections Added, Amended or Repealed." *Any changed or added law text is set out in italics.* Deleted Code text, or the Code provision prior to amendment, appears in the Amendment Notes following each reconstructed Code provision. An effective date for each Code change is also provided.

The amendment notes contain cross references to the corresponding committee reports and the CCH Explanations that discuss the new laws. *The text of the Code relating to the Patient Protection and Affordable Care Act (P.L. 111-148), as amended by the Health Care and Education Reconciliation Act of 2010 (P.L. 111-152), begins at ¶5001. The text of the Code relating to the Hiring Incentives to Restore Employment Act (P.L. 111-147), Temporary Extension Act of 2010 (P.L. 111-144), and P.L. 111-126 begins at ¶6001.*

Sections of the Act that do not amend the Internal Revenue Code, appear in full text following "Code Sections Added, Amended or Repealed." *The text of these provisions relating to the Patient Protection and Affordable Care Act (P.L. 111-148), as amended by the Health Care and Education Reconciliation Act of 2010 (P.L. 111-152), appears in Act Section order beginning at ¶7003. The text of these provisions relating to the Hiring Incentives to Restore Employment Act (P.L. 111-147), appears in Act Section order beginning at ¶7203. The text of these provisions relating to the Temporary Extension Act of*

2010 (P.L. 111-144), *appears in Act Section order beginning at ¶7303. The text of these provisions relating to the P.L. 111-126 appears in Act Section order beginning at ¶7350.*

COMMITTEE REPORTS

The Joint Committee on Taxation (JCT) Technical Explanation of the Revenue Provisions of the "Reconciliation Act of 2010," as amended, in combination with the "Patient Protection and Affordable Care Act" (JCX-18-10), explains the intent of Congress regarding the provisions of the *Patient Protection and Affordable Care Act* (P.L. 111-148), as amended by the *Health Care and Education Reconciliation Act of 2010* (P.L. 111-152). There was no conference report issued for the *Patient Protection and Affordable Care Act* (P.L. 111-148), as amended by the *Health Care and Education Reconciliation Act of 2010* (P.L. 111-152). The relevant portions of the Technical Explanation from the JCT are included in this section to aid the reader's understanding, but may not be cited as the official House, Senate or Conference Committee Report accompanying the *Patient Protection and Affordable Care Act* (P.L. 111-148), as amended by the *Health Care and Education Reconciliation Act of 2010* (P.L. 111-152). At the end of each section, references are provided to the corresponding CCH explanations and the Internal Revenue Code provisions. *The pertinent sections of the Technical Explanation relating to the Patient Protection and Affordable Care Act (P.L. 111-148), as amended by the Health Care and Education Reconciliation Act of 2010 (P.L. 111-152), appear in Act Section order beginning at ¶10,001.*

The Joint Committee on Taxation (JCT), Technical Explanation of the Revenue Provisions Contained in Senate Amendment 3310, the Hiring Incentives to Restore Employment Act, Under Consideration by the Senate (JCX-4-10), February 23, 2010, explains the intent of Congress regarding the revenue provisions of the *Hiring Incentives to Restore Employment Act* (P.L. 111-147). There was no conference report issued for the *Hiring Incentives to Restore Employment Act* (P.L. 111-147). The relevant portions of the Technical Explanation of the Revenue Provisions from the JCT are included in this section to aid the reader's understanding, but may not be cited as the official House, Senate or Conference Committee Report accompanying the *Hiring Incentives to Restore Employment Act* (P.L. 111-147). At the end of each section, references are provided to the corresponding CCH explanations and the Internal Revenue Code provisions. *The pertinent sections of the Technical Explanation relating to the Hiring Incentives to Restore Employment Act (P.L. 111-147), appear in Act Section order beginning at ¶11,001.*

The Joint Committee on Taxation (JCT), Technical Explanation of H.R. 4462: A Bill to Accelerate the Income Tax Benefits for Charitable Cash Contributions for the Relief of Victims of the Earthquake in Haiti (JCX-4-10), January 20, 2010, explains the intent of Congress regarding the revenue provisions of the *Legislation to Accelerate the Income Tax Benefits for Charitable Cash Contributions for the Relief of Victims of the Earthquake in Haiti* (P.L. 111-126). There was no conference report issued for the *Legislation to Accelerate the Income Tax Benefits for Charitable Cash Contributions for the Relief of Victims of the Earthquake in Haiti* (P.L. 111-126). The relevant portions of the Technical Explanation of the Revenue Provisions from the JCT are included in this section to aid the reader's understanding, but may not be cited as the official House, Senate or Conference Committee Report accompanying the *Legislation to Accelerate the Income Tax Benefits for Charitable Cash Contributions for the Relief of Victims of the Earthquake in Haiti*(P.L. 111-126). At the end of each section, references are provided to the corresponding CCH explanations and the Internal Revenue Code provisions. *The pertinent sections of the Technical Explanation relating to P.L. 111-126 appear in Act Section order beginning at ¶12,001.*

EFFECTIVE DATES

A table listing the major effective dates provides a reference bridge between Code Sections and Act Sections. The tables also indicate the retroactive or prospective nature of the law. *The effective dates table for the Patient Protection and Affordable Care Act (P.L. 111-148), as amended by the Health Care and Education Reconciliation Act of 2010 (P.L. 111-152), begins at ¶20,001. The effective dates table for the Hiring Incentives to Restore Employment Act (P.L. 111-147), begins at ¶20,005. The effective dates table for the Temporary Extension Act of 2010 (P.L. 111-144), begins at ¶20,010.*

SPECIAL FINDING DEVICES

Other special tables and finding devices in this book include:

- A table cross-referencing Code Sections to the CCH Explanations (*see ¶25,001*);
- A table showing all Code Sections added, amended or repealed (*see ¶25,005*);
- A table showing provisions of other acts that were amended (*see ¶25,010*);
- A table of Act Sections not amending the Internal Revenue Code (*see ¶25,015*); and
- An Act Section amending Code Section table (*see ¶25,020*).

CLIENT LETTERS

Sample client letters allow you to quickly communicate the changes made by the *Patient Protection and Affordable Care Act (P.L. 111-148)*, as amended by the *Health Care and Education Reconciliation Act of 2010* (P.L. 111-152), and the *Hiring Incentives to Restore Employment Act (P.L. 111-147)* to clients and customers (*see ¶27,005*).

¶1

¶2 Table of Contents

Other Tables

APPENDICES

¶3 Detailed Table of Contents

CHAPTER 2. HEALTH CARE: INDIVIDUALS

CHAPTER 3. HEALTH CARE: BUSINESSES

CHAPTER 4. HEALTH CARE: REPORTING REQUIREMENTS AND OTHER PROVISIONS

¶3

CHAPTER 5. HEALTH CARE: NONTAX PROVISIONS

CHAPTER 6. HIRE: BUSINESSES AND INDIVIDUALS

CHAPTER 7. HIRE: FOREIGN ACCOUNT TAX COMPLIANCE

¶3

¶5 Highlights

HEALTH CARE—INDIVIDUALS

¶205 **Failure to carry health insurance.** Beginning in 2014, individuals must make a "shared responsibility payment" if they do not have health insurance for themselves and their dependents.

¶210 **Premium assistance credit.** Beginning in 2014, taxpayers with household income between 100 percent and 400 percent of the federal poverty line can qualify for a refundable health insurance premium assistance credit.

¶215 **Medical deduction threshold.** The threshold for the itemized deduction for unreimbursed medical expenses is increased from 7.5 percent of adjusted gross income (AGI) to 10 percent of AGI for regular income tax purposes, for tax years beginning after December 31, 2012.

¶220 **Over-the-counter medicines.** Qualified medical expenses for purposes of the rules on HSAs, Archer MSAs, health FSAs, and HRAs no longer include over-the-counter medicines and drugs.

¶225 **HSA and MSA distributions.** The additional tax on distributions from HSAs and Archer MSAs not used for qualified medical expenses is increased to 20 percent.

¶230 **Additional health insurance tax.** Individuals are subject to an additional hospital insurance tax on wages and self-employment income in excess of $200,000 ($250,000 in the case of a joint return) for tax years beginning after December 31, 2012.

¶232 **Medicare tax on investment income.** A 3.8 percent Medicare tax is imposed on a portion of the net investment income of individuals, estates and trusts for tax years beginning after 2012.

¶235 **Tanning salons.** A 10 percent tax is imposed on amounts paid for indoor tanning services.

¶240 **Adoption credit and adoption assistance.** The dollar limitations for the adoption assistance program exclusion and the adoption credit have been increased by $1,000, and the adoption credit has been made refundable.

¶242 **Medical benefits for children under 27.** A child who is under the age of 27 is a dependent of a taxpayer for purposes of the exclusion for reimbursements for medical care expenses under an employer-provided accident or health plan and other purposes related to medical benefits.

¶245 **Student loan repayment programs.** Individuals can exclude repayments under state loan repayment or forgiveness programs that are intended to provide for the increased availability of health care services in underserved or health professional shortage areas from gross income.

¶250 **Health care benefits of Tribe members.** The recipient can exclude qualified health care benefits provided to a member of an Indian tribe, the member's spouse, or the member's dependents from the gross income.

HEALTH CARE—BUSINESSES

¶305 **Large employers' responsibility for health coverage.** Large employers who fail to comply with requirements concerning health coverage for full-time employees for months beginning after December 31, 2013, are subject to a penalty tax.

¶310 **Small employer health insurance credit.** An eligible small employer may claim a tax credit for premiums it pays toward health coverage for its employees in tax years beginning in 2010 through 2013.

¶315 **Free choice vouchers.** An employer who offers minimum essential coverage to its employees consisting of coverage through an eligible employer-sponsored plan and pays any portion of the plan's costs shall provide free choice vouchers to its qualified employees.

¶320 **Health plans offered through cafeteria plans.** A cafeteria plan may not provide a health plan that is offered through the American Health Benefit Exchange unless the employer is a qualified employer for purposes of the Exchange.

¶325 **Health FSAs offered through cafeteria plans.** Health FSAs offered as a part of a cafeteria plan must limit contributions through salary reductions to $2,500 for tax years beginning after December 31, 2012.

¶330 **Simple cafeteria plans.** Certain small employers may choose to provide a simple cafeteria plan for their employees, under which the nondiscrimination rules of a classic cafeteria plan are treated as satisfied.

¶335 **Retiree prescription drug plans.** The rule that allows an employer, as a plan sponsor, to disregard the value of any qualified retiree prescription drug plan subsidy in calculating its business deduction for retiree prescription drug costs is repealed for tax years beginning after December 31, 2012.

¶340 **Excessive remuneration by health insurance providers.** The deduction for employee remuneration paid by certain health insurance providers to specified employees is limited.

¶342 **Economic substance doctrine.** The common-law economic substance doctrine has been codified.

¶343 **Underpayment penalty.** The accuracy-related penalty has been expanded to include understatements attributable to any disallowance of claimed tax benefits by reason of a transaction lacking economic substance.

¶345 **"Cadillac" health plans.** A 40 percent excise tax will be imposed on insurers to the extent that the aggregate value of employer-sponsored health coverage for an employee exceeds a threshold amount starting in 2018.

¶350 **Drug and insurance companies.** Annual fees are imposed on manufacturers and importers of branded prescription drugs and providers of health insurance for U.S. health risks, and a 2.3 percent excise tax is imposed on sales of medical devices.

¶355 **Credit for therapeutic discovery projects.** A 50 percent tax credit is provided as part of the investment credit for eligible taxpayers' qualified investment with respect to any qualifying therapeutic discovery project made in a tax year beginning in 2009 or 2010.

¶357 **Cellulosic biofuel producer credit for black liquor.** Black liquor has been excluded from the cellulosic biofuel producer credit.

¶360 **Tax treatment of certain organizations.** The special deduction from regular tax that Blue Cross and Blue Shield organizations, and other qualifying health insurance organizations are allowed under Code Sec. 833 is modified to provide that these organizations are only entitled to this special tax treatment if 85 percent or more of their insurance premium revenues are spent on clinical services.

¶365 **Corporate estimated taxes.** The estimated tax payment required to be made by a large corporation in July, August, or September of 2014 has been increased to 173.50 percent of the amount otherwise due.

HEALTH CARE—REPORTING REQUIREMENTS AND OTHER PROVISIONS

¶405 **Reporting of employer-provided health coverage on W-2.** Employers are required to disclose the total cost of employer-sponsored health insurance coverage provided to their employees annually on the employee's Form W-2 starting with the 2011 plan year.

¶410   Health care coverage reporting. Any person who provides minimum essential health care coverage to an individual during a calendar year is required to file a return reporting such coverage in the form and manner described by the Secretary of the Treasury and provide a statement to the covered individual for calendar years beginning after 2013.

¶415   Reporting by employers. Beginning in 2014, applicable employers are required to report to the Secretary of the Treasury and provide statements to employees concerning coverage offered to full-time employees and their dependents.

¶420   Reporting payments to corporations. The reporting requirement exception for certain payments made to a corporation in the course of a trade or business is eliminated.

¶425   IRS disclosure to HHS. The IRS is permitted to disclose to the Department of Health and Human Services certain return information to verify cost sharing reduction or premium tax credit amounts and facilitate eligibility determinations for other programs.

¶430   SSA access to taxpayer information. The Social Security Administration (SSA) has access to certain information about taxpayers to assist it in reducing the Part D premium subsidy for high-income beneficiaries.

¶435   Nonprofit health insurance issuers. Qualified nonprofit health insurance issuers receiving grants or loans under the Consumer Operated and Oriented Plan (CO-OP) program can be tax exempt.

¶440   Tax-exempt hospitals. Hospitals have to satisfy four requirements to maintain their Code Sec. 501(c)(3) tax-exempt status.

¶445   Patient-Centered Outcomes Research Trust Fund. The Patient-Centered Outcomes Research Trust Fund is funded for comparative effectiveness research, and fees are imposed on insurers of health plans and employer sponsors of self-insured health plans to help fund it.

¶450   Community Living Assistance Services and Support Program The newly established Community Living Assistance Services and Support (CLASS) program is treated for tax purposes in the same manner as a qualified long-term care insurance contract for qualified long-term care services.

¶455   Group health plans. Group health plans are subject to new requirements, including extension of dependent coverage, mandatory coverage of preventive health services, prohibition of lifetime or annual limits on the dollar value of benefits and unreasonable annual limits, and rescission.

¶5

HIRE ACT—BUSINESSES AND INDIVIDUALS

¶605   **Employer's payroll tax holiday and retention credit.** For the remainder of 2010, employers do not have to pay their share of OASDI or railroad retirement taxes for newly hired workers who were unemployed. Employers can also claim a credit of up to $1,000 for retaining new workers for at least one year.

¶610   **Code Sec. 179 expensing.** The increase in the Code Sec. 179 expensing allowance (to a $250,000 dollar limitation and $800,000 investment limitation) that applies to tax years beginning in 2008 and 2009 is extended to tax years beginning in 2010.

¶615   **COBRA premium assistance.** The eligibility period for the 65 percent COBRA premium assistance is extended through March 31, 2010, and eligibility for the subsidy is extended to certain individuals who lose their group health care coverage as a result of a reduction in hours of employment, followed by an involuntary termination of employment.

¶620   **Credit for tax credit bond issuers.** Issuers of specified tax credit bonds can elect to claim a refundable tax credit in lieu of the credit that would ordinarily be allowed to the purchasers.

¶625   **Qualified school construction bonds.** The allocation of a state's volume limitation is determined by the state education agency and any unused amounts allocated to large local education agencies by the IRS can be carried over.

¶630   **Large corporation's estimated tax payments.** Corporations with at least $1 billion in assets must increase their estimated tax payments for July, August, and September of 2014, 2015, and 2019 to 156.25 percent, 121.50 percent, and 106.50 percent, respectively, of the amount otherwise due.

¶635   **Haiti contributions.** Calendar-year taxpayers can claim charitable contribution deductions on their 2009 returns for cash contributions made after January 11, 2010, and before March 1, 2010, for the benefit of victims of the 2010 earthquake in Haiti.

HIRE ACT—FOREIGN ACCOUNT TAX COMPLIANCE

¶705   **Payments to foreign financial institutions and other entities.** Generally, a withholding agent must deduct and withhold a tax equal to 30 percent on certain payments made to a foreign financial institution or to a non-financial foreign entity, unless reporting requirements are met.

¶710   **Foreign financial assets.** Individuals holding interests in specified foreign financial assets with an aggregate value of more than $50,000 must comply with disclosure requirements, or be subject to a penalty, unless the failure to comply is due to reasonable cause.

¶5

¶715   **Underpayments attributable to nondisclosure.** A 40-percent accuracy-related penalty is imposed for underpayments attributable to transactions involving undisclosed foreign financial assets required to be disclosed under any of several disclosure requirements.

¶720   **Omission of income in connection with foreign assets** The statute of limitations for assessments is extended to six years if there is an omission of gross income in excess of $5,000 attributable to a foreign financial asset. The three-year limitations period is suspended for failure to timely provide information with respect to PFICs.

¶725   **PFICs.** U.S. shareholders of PFICs must file annual information returns.

¶730   **E-filing of foreign withholding returns.** The IRS may require financial institutions to file returns with respect to withheld taxes for which the institution is liable as a withholding agent under the nonresident alien and foreign corporation withholding rules or under the new foreign account withholding rules electronically.

¶735   **Foreign trusts.** The circumstances under which a foreign trust will be treated as having a U.S. beneficiary, and thus be treated as a grantor trust, have been clarified. If any U.S. person who transfers property to the trust is involved in any agreement or understanding that may result in trust income or corpus being paid or accumulated to or for the benefit of a U.S. person, that agreement or understanding is treated as a term of the trust.

¶740   **Uncompensated use of trust property.** The uncompensated use of foreign trust property by a U.S. grantor or beneficiary or a related U.S. person is treated as a distribution by the trust for nongrantor trust income tax purposes. The loan of cash or marketable securities by a foreign trust, or the use of any other property of the trust, to or by any U.S. person is also treated as paid or accumulated for the benefit of a U.S. person for purposes of the grantor trust rules.

¶745   **Owners of foreign trusts.** A U.S. person who is treated as the owner of any portion of a foreign trust under the grantor trust rules must submit any information required by the IRS with respect to the foreign trust.

¶750   **Foreign trust reporting penalty.** The minimum amount of the penalty for failure to report information or file returns with respect to foreign trusts is increased to $10,000, but if the aggregate penalties imposed exceed the gross reportable amount, the excess must be refunded to the taxpayer.

¶5

¶755   **Dividend-equivalent payments.** Dividend equivalent payments received by foreign persons are treated as U.S.-source dividends for many purposes.

¶760   **Registered bond requirements.** Exceptions to the registered bond requirements for foreign-targeted obligations are repealed for most purposes.

¶765   **Worldwide interest allocation** Implementation of the elections to allocate interest expense on a worldwide basis and expand a financial institution group of a worldwide affiliated group are delayed for three years, to take effect for tax years beginning after December 31, 2020.

Health Care and HIRE: Taxpayers Affected

PATIENT PROTECTION AND AFFORDABLE CARE ACT AS AMENDED BY HEALTH CARE AND RECONCILIATION ACT OF 2010

HIRING INCENTIVES TO RESTORE EMPLOYMENT ACT

HIRE—INDIVIDUALS

HIRE—BUSINESSES

HIRE—EXEMPT ORGANIZATIONS, GOVERN-MENT, AND FOREIGN ENTITIES

PATIENT PROTECTION AND AFFORDABLE CARE ACT AS AMENDED BY HEALTH CARE AND RECONCILIATION ACT OF 2010

¶101 Overview

Although the primary thrust of the Patient Protection and Affordable Care Act (P.L. 111-148) as amended by the Health Care and Reconciliation Act of 2010 (P.L. 111-152) is health insurance reform, the Internal Revenue Code plays several key functions in achieving that goal. First, the Internal Revenue Code provides "carrots" to lower income individuals and small businesses in the form of tax breaks for health care expenses in order to help work toward the goal of universal health coverage. Second, the Internal Revenue Code also provides "sticks" in the form of penalties imposed on individuals and businesses that do not obtain health coverage for themselves or their employees. Third, the Internal Revenue Code is used to raised revenue to help pay for the overall cost of health insurance reform. Fourth, many requirements are placed on health insurance providers. Fifth, many additional burdens are placed on the IRS to help enforce the components of this legislation.

HEALTH CARE—INDIVIDUALS

¶102 Effect on Individuals Generally

The Patient Protection and Affordable Care Act (P.L. 111-148), as amended by the Health Care and Reconciliation Act of 2010 (P.L. 111-152), is designed to encourage all individuals to be covered under a health care plan providing at least minimum essential coverage. The Acts accomplish this objective by requiring the 40 percent of Americans not presently covered under an employment-based plan to purchase insurance either from a private insurer or through one of the new American Health Benefit Exchanges (AHBE) to be established by the states. Those who can afford such coverage, but do not purchase it, are subject to a penalty. Those who cannot afford coverage may be eligible for premium assistance credits, while those who cannot afford the plans provided by their employers may be eligible for a free choice voucher to help them purchase insurance through their state's AHBE.

The Health Care and Reconciliation Act of 2010 broadens the definition of dependents to include children under age 27 for purposes of the general exclusion for reimbursements for medical care expenses under an employer-provided accident or health plan, and certain other purposes. Beginning in 2011, individuals whose employers offer health insurance coverage will see the total cost of such coverage reported on their W-2 wage statements. Members of Indian tribes who receive health care through the tribe alone or in conjunction with the Indian Health Service will not have to include the health benefits they, their spouses and dependents receive in income.

To help offset the cost of these changes, higher income employees and self-employed individuals will be subject to an additional hospital services insurance (Medicare) tax. In addition, pursuant to the Health Care and Reconciliation Act of 2010, a 3.8 percent unearned income Medicare contribution tax will be imposed on net investment income beginning in 2013. Itemized medical expenses will become deductible only to the extent they exceed ten percent of adjusted gross income

After more than a decade of attempts by Congress to bring nationwide uniformity to the application of the economic substance doctrine, the Health Care and Reconciliation Act of 2010 codifies the doctrine and clarifies that it involves a conjunctive analysis – there must be an inquiry regarding the objective effects of the transaction on the taxpayer's economic position as well as an inquiry regarding the taxpayer's subjective motives for engaging in the transaction. A stiff 20 percent "strict liability" penalty is imposed for underpayments attributable to the disallowance of claimed tax benefits by reason of a transaction lacking economic substance, and an even stiffer 40 percent penalty applies to nondisclosed noneconomic substance transactions.

Under the Patient Protection and Affordable Care Act distributions from health accounts, such as Health Savings Accounts (HSAs) and Archer Medical Savings Accounts (MSAs), will be taxable to the extent used to pay for over-the-counter medication, and all distributions that are not used for qualified medical expenses will subject the account holder to a higher 20 percent additional tax. Starting in 2013, an FSA will not be a qualified benefit under a cafeteria plan unless the plan provides for a $2,500 maximum salary reduction contribution to the FSA (adjusted annually for inflation starting in 2014). Those who use tanning salons will pay a ten percent excise tax on the tanning services they receive.

Recognizing that any improvement in health care also requires better access to health care professionals in presently underserved communities, the Patient Protection and Affordable Care Act provides that physicians and other health professionals will not be taxed when their student loans are repaid or forgiven under a broader range of state programs. Parents who adopt are provided an increased credit and amount of excludable adoption assistance payments.

¶102

¶103 Effect on Individuals Without Health Care Coverage

Mandatory coverage.—An important objective of the Patient Protection and Affordable Care Act is to require the 40-50 million individuals living in the U.S. who currently do not have health coverage, but who annually receive more than $116 billion worth of health care, to purchase minimum essential coverage. Beginning in 2014, individuals who do not have minimum coverage for themselves and their dependents become liable for a shared responsibility payment civil penalty.

For 2014 the monthly penalty will not exceed the greater of $285 ($95 × 3) (the "flat dollar amount") or 1 percent of household income over the filing threshold (the "percentage of income"), with the flat dollar amount increasing to $2,085, and the percentage of income increasing to 2.5% by 2016. After 2016, the flat dollar amount is increased for inflation. Household income is defined for this purpose as modified adjusted gross income increased by foreign earned income and tax-exempt interest. (¶205).

Prisoners, undocumented aliens, health care sharing ministry members and those certified as being opposed to having coverage on religious grounds are exempt from the requirement. The penalty will not apply to individuals who fall below the filing threshold, are members of an Indian tribe, have only a short-term gap in coverage, establish hardship, or live outside the U.S.

To encourage the purchase of minimum essential coverage, the Secretary of the Treasury will send written notification by June 30 to every individual filer who lacks such coverage explaining the services available through the American Health Benefit Exchange in the filer's state (¶410).

¶104 Effect on Individuals with Health Care Coverage

Any person who provides minimum essential health care coverage to an individual during a calendar year is required to file a return reporting such coverage in the form and manner described by the Secretary of the Treasury. Individuals with health care coverage will annually receive a written statement from the provider of such coverage detailing the contents of the informational return (¶410).

¶105 Effect on Lower Income Individuals

Premium assistance credit for low income individuals.—Individuals whose incomes are up to four times the federal poverty line (or up to approximately $88,000 for a family of four), are not receiving Medicare, Medicaid, military or Peace Corp health coverage, and cannot otherwise afford to purchase health insurance may benefit from the Patient Protection and Affordable Care Act's refundable health insurance premium assistance credit. Such low income individuals will be eligible for a premium credit if they purchase one of four levels of qualified health plan coverage accessed through the new state American Health Benefit Exchanges (AHBE).

To be eligible for the credit lower income individuals will be required to pay between two and 9.5 percent of their annual incomes for health insurance premiums (¶210).

Disclosure of tax return information to determine eligibility for premium assistance and other health benefits.—While the IRS is generally prohibited from disclosing or sharing tax return information, the Patient Protection and Affordable Care Act permits it to disclose to the Department of Health and Human Services (HHS) a taxpayer's identity, filing status, number of dependents and modified gross income information so that HHS may verify cost sharing reduction or premium tax credit amounts, and determine the taxpayer's eligibility for other programs such as Medicaid. HHS is, in turn, permitted to share the disclosed information with a state AHBE for the same purposes (¶425).

¶106 Effect on Higher Income Individuals

Hospital services insurance tax.—As one of the revenue offsets against expenditures resulting from the Patient Protection and Affordable Care Act, and to help finance Medicare, the combined employer and employee portions of the Medicare payroll tax, and the total hospital services insurance tax imposed on self-employed individuals, will increase from 2.9 percent to 3.8 percent on wages and self-employed income in excess of $200,000 ($250,000 for joint filers, $125,000 in the case of a married taxpayer filing separately) (¶230).

Disclosures in connection with Medicare Part D subsidy reductions.—Beginning in 2011, the Medicare Part D (Voluntary Prescription Drug Benefit Program) subsidy will be reduced for those whose incomes exceed the Medicare Part B (which pays for physician services, lab and X-ray services, durable medical equipment, and outpatient and other services) threshold.

The Patient Protection and Affordable Care Act allows the IRS to disclose income information to the Social Security Administration in connection with the Part D subsidy reduction, similar to the IRS' current authority to disclose such information in connection with adjusting the Part B subsidy (¶430).

¶107 Effect on Individuals with Investment Income

Unearned income Medicare contributions tax—The Health Care and Reconciliation Act of 2010 imposes an annual 3.8 percent "unearned income Medicare contribution" tax annually beginning in 2013 on the lesser of: (1) net investment income from interest, dividends, annuities, royalties, rents and certain other income and gains not generated in the ordinary course of an active trade or business, or which is generated in a trade or business of trading financial instruments or commodities or (2) modified adjusted gross income (which includes, for this purpose, foreign earned income net of certain expenses) in excess of $200,000 ($250,000 for joint filers and surviving spouses, $125,000 in the case of married taxpayers filing separately) (¶232).

The definition of net investment income excludes distributions from most qualified plans and amounts subject to self-employment tax. In the case of the disposition of a partnership interest, or stock in an S corporation, net investment income includes gain or loss only if it would be taken into account by the partner or shareholder had the entity sold all its properties for fair market value immediately before the disposition. Thus, only net gain or loss attributable to property held by the entity, and not attributable to an active trade or business, is included.

Similar rules apply to estates and trusts with respect to their undistributed net investment income. They become subject to a 3.8 percent unearned income Medicare contribution on the lesser of: (1) their undistributed net investment income or (2) the excess of their adjusted gross income over the dollar amount at which the highest income tax bracket applicable to an estate or trust begins.

¶108   Effect on Individuals Who Engage in Transactions Lacking a Substantial Non-tax Purpose

Congress has, since 1999, been concerned that the IRS was being hamstrung in its use of the common law economic substance doctrine to combat abusive transactions because of a split in the Circuit Courts of Appeal over the proper application of the doctrine. There have been repeated attempts by members of Congress to pass legislation that would create a single, uniform test for determining whether a transaction has economic substance.

The positive potential revenue effect of codifying the doctrine has also presented a tempting opportunity to offset expenditures. Under the Health Care and Reconciliation Act of 2010 taxpayers who engage in any transaction that has tax savings as its primary objective, and that lacks other non-tax objectives, may be subject to both the common law economic substance doctrine and the new codified economic substance doctrine (¶342).

For any transaction to which the economic substance doctrine is relevant, such transaction will only be treated as having economic substance if, apart from the Federal income tax effects, it changes in a meaningful way the taxpayer's economic position, and the taxpayer has a substantial purpose for entering into the transaction. For individual taxpayers, the codified doctrine will only apply to transactions entered into in connection with a trade or business or activity engaged in for the production of income.

A 20 percent penalty is imposed for an underpayment attributable to any disallowance of claimed tax benefits by reason of a transaction lacking economic substance under the codified doctrine, or failing to meet the requirements of any similar rule of law. The penalty is increased to 40 percent for an underpayment attributable to a "nondisclosed noneconomic substance transaction." A nondisclosed nonecomonic substance transaction is any portion of a transaction lacking economic substance with respect to which the relevant facts affecting the tax treatment are not adequately disclosed in the return or in a statement attached to the return (¶343).

¶109 Effect on Individuals Covered by an Employer-Sponsored Plan

The W-2 Wage and Tax Statements employees receive will, starting in 2011, show the full cost (both the employer and the employee paid portions) of employer sponsored health care coverage. This will not include any long-term care coverage, accident or disability insurance coverage or salary reduction contributions to flexible spending arrangements, Health Savings Accounts or Archer Medical Savings Accounts (¶405).

¶110 Effect on Individuals Not Covered by an Employer-Sponsored Plan

Free choice vouchers.—Employees whose employers offer minimum essential health coverage and pay at least a portion of the cost for it, but whose incomes make it impossible or impractical for them to participate in such plan, will receive a free choice voucher from their employers equal to the monthly amount the employer would have paid had the employee participated in the plan (¶315).

The employer will receive a compensation deduction, while the employee will not be taxed to the extent the voucher is applied toward the cost of the monthly premium of any qualified health plan purchased through one of the state American Health Benefit Exchanges.

¶111 Effect on Members of Indian Tribes

Qualified health care benefits received by members of an Indian tribe, their spouses and dependents are excluded from the recipient's gross income. This includes benefits provided directly or indirectly by the Indian Health Service through a grant, contract or compact with an Indian tribe or tribal organization, medical care provided by the tribe, and coverage under accident or health insurance plans that the tribe offers to its members (¶250).

¶112 Effect on Individuals With Young Adult Children

The Health Care and Reconciliation Act of 2010 provides that children under age 27 are considered dependents of a taxpayer for purposes of the general exclusion from gross income for reimbursements for medical care expenses of an employee, spouse, and dependents under an employer-provided accident or health plan, the deduction for the health insurance costs of a self-employed person, spouse, and dependents, the rule that allows a qualified pension or annuity plan to provide benefits for sickness, accident, hospitalization, and medical expenses to retired employees, spouses, and dependents, and the rule that treats a voluntary employee benefits association that provides sick and accident benefits to its members and their dependents as a tax-exempt organization (¶242).

¶113 Effect on Itemizers of Medical Expense Deductions

Ten percent threshold for itemized medical expenses.—While the Patient Protection and Affordable Care Act is designed to encourage obtaining health care coverage, it reduces the ability to deduct any unreimbursed medical care expenses. Starting in 2013, the threshold for the itemized deduction of such expenses increases from 7.5 percent to 10 percent of adjusted gross income. For AMT purposes, the threshold remains at 10 percent. For 2013-2016 the increased threshold will not apply to taxpayers or their spouses who are age 65 or older before the end of the applicable tax year (¶215).

¶114 Effect on Health Account Holders

Starting in 2011, individuals who have Health Savings Accounts (HSAs) or Archer Medical Savings Accounts (MSAs) will no longer be permitted to take distributions in order to pay for over-the-counter medications (there is a special exception for insulin) with pre-tax dollars. Any amounts used to pay for these over-the-counter items will be included in gross income (¶220).

Similarly, individuals who have Health Flexible Spending Arrangements or Health Reimbursement Arrangements will not have excludible income for any reimbursement for over-the-counter medicines. At the same time, those who have HSAs and MSAs and take distributions that are not used for qualified medical expenses will, instead of paying the current 10 and 15 percent additional tax, respectively, pay a 20 percent additional tax (¶225).

Effective for tax years beginning after December 31, 2012, an FSA will not be a qualified benefit under a cafeteria plan unless the plan provides for a $2,500 maximum salary reduction contribution to the FSA. Beginning in 2014 the $2,500 limitation is adjusted annually for inflation (¶325).

¶115 Effect on Individuals Who Adopt

To encourage adoption, the maximum adoption credit is increased by $1,000 and made refundable. The amount of excludable qualified adoption assistance payments paid by employers is increased by the same amount, as is the credit and exclusion for special needs children (no proof of actual adoption expenses is required in adopting such children). These increases will be indexed for inflation in future years. However, under sunset provisions originally enacted as part of the Economic Growth and Tax Relief Reconciliation Act of 2001, but extended by the Patient Protection and Affordable Care Act, the amount of the credit and exclusion will be reduced in 2012 (¶240).

¶116 Effect on Health Professionals With Student Loan Debt

In addition to increasing the number of individuals covered by a plan of health insurance, another objective of the Patient Protection and Affordable Care Act is to encourage increased availability of health care in areas that are underserved or there is a shortage of health care professionals. An existing program under the National Health Service Corps Loan Program, and state programs under the Public Health Services Act, provide forgiveness or repayment of student loan debt incurred by health care professionals who agree to agree to work in certain locations or for certain employers. The repayment or forgiveness of the student loans does not result in taxable income to the health care professional. The Patient Protection and Affordable Care Act expands the exclusion to include other state loan repayment and forgiveness programs with similar objectives (¶245).

¶117 Effect on Individuals Who Use Indoor Tanning Salons

Although the Senate initially seemed ready to impose a tax on cosmetic surgery, after significant lobbying efforts by organizations such as the American Society of Aesthetic Plastic Surgery and American Society of Plastic Surgeons, it settled instead on imposing a tax on tanning services. Patrons of indoor tanning salons will pay a 10 percent excise tax on ultraviolet lamp tanning services they receive after July 1. The excise tax is collected by the tanning salon owner, who must remit the tax on a quarterly basis. If the owner fails to remit the 10 percent excise tax, the owner becomes liable for it (¶235).

HEALTH CARE—BUSINESSES

¶118 Effect on Businesses Generally

Employers are given many responsibilities in the Patient Protection and Affordable Care Act (P.L. 111-148) to help achieve health insurance reform. These range from providing greater health insurance coverage and helping to pay for that coverage to providing the information necessary to enforce the requirements of the new legislation. Health insurance providers also have many new requirements imposed by the legislation, including limits on executive compensation, taxes and fees, and reporting obligations.

Businesses generally are affected by expanded information reporting requirements. Information reporting is expanded by requiring that all payments made by a payer to a corporation totaling $600 or more in any tax year must be reported to the IRS on an information return (¶420).

Under the Health Care and Reconciliation Act of 2010, the economic substance doctrine for business transactions and claims for refund has been codified (¶342). The accuracy-related penalty has been expanded to apply to understatements attributable to applications of the economic substance doctrine (¶343).

¶119 Effect on Employers

Penalty taxes.—A penalty tax is imposed on employers with 50 or more full-time employees for failure to offer full-time employees an opportunity to enroll in minimum essential coverage under an employer-sponsored health plan. A penalty tax is also imposed if employees qualify for a premium tax credit or cost-sharing reductions or if employees are subject to extended waiting periods (¶305).

Medicare tax withholding.—Employers are required to withhold additional Medicare tax on high-income taxpayers and report net premiums written to the IRS (¶230).

Excise tax on "Cadillac" plans.—Employers are required to calculate the excise tax applicable to high coverage "Cadillac" health plans and report amounts to the IRS and each coverage provider. A penalty is provided for calculation errors (¶345).

Expanded W-2 reporting.—Employers are required to include on Form W-2 the total cost of employer-sponsored health insurance coverage (¶405).

Minimum coverage report.—Large employers are required to report to the IRS and to the individuals involved whether they offer minimum essential coverage. A large employer is defined as an employer with an average of at least 50 full-time employees. Penalties are provided for failure to correctly report (¶415).

Free choice vouchers.—Employers are required to provide free choice vouchers to qualified employees if the employer offers minimum essential health care coverage to employees through an eligible employer-sponsored plan for which the employer pays a portion of the plan costs. Qualified employees are those whose health care expenses constitute too large a percentage of their incomes (¶¶210 and 315).

Exclusion of over-the-counter medicines.—The definition of qualified medical expenses regarding distributions from Health Spending Accounts (HSAs), Archer Medical Savings Accounts (MSAs), Health Flexible Spending Accounts (FSAs), and Health Reimbursement Arrangements (HRAs) is modified to exclude over-the-counter medicines (¶220).

Limits on FSAs.—Health flexible spending arrangements (FSAs) in tax years after December 31, 2012 must limit contributions through salary reductions to $2,500, adjusted for inflation for tax years after December 31, 2013 (¶325).

Expanded adoption assistance.—A dollar limitation for employer-sponsored adoption assistance programs is increased by $1,000 and the sunset of the tax provision is postponed for one year (¶240).

Children under age 27 dependents.—Children under age 27 are considered dependents for purposes of the general exclusion for reimbursed employee medical expenses and medical expenses of retirees under qualified pension or annuity plans (¶242).

Business deduction to consider retiree drug subsidy.—Employers, as plan sponsors, may no longer disregard the value of any qualified retiree prescription drug plan subsidy in calculating the employer's business deduction for retiree prescription drug costs (¶335). For many employers, this may significantly increase the expense of self-insuring retiree prescription drug costs.

Payroll deduction for CLASS program.—Employers are required to do payroll deduction for enrollment in the Community Living Assistance Services and Support (CLASS) program (¶450).

¶120 Effect on Small Employers

A small employer with 25 or fewer full-time employees and average compensation of $50,000 or less may be eligible for up to a 35 percent tax credit for premiums paid toward employee health coverage. The percentage increases to 50 percent for two years after 2013 if the employer participates in an insurance exchange (¶310). A five-percent owner and related individuals are not considered employees for this purpose.

An employer must be a qualified employer for purposes of the American Health Benefit Exchange in order for an employer cafeteria plan to include a health plan. A qualified employer for tax years beginning after December 31, 2013 is an employer who employed an average of at least one, but not more than 100, employees on business days during the preceding calendar year and employs at least one employee on the first day of the plan year (¶320).

An employer that, during either of the two preceding years, employed an average of 100 or fewer employees on business days may choose to provide a simple cafeteria plan for employees that permits greater flexibility under the nondiscrimination rules (¶320).

¶121 Effect on Seasonal Employers

Special rules apply to determine whether seasonal employers qualify for the small employer health insurance credit (¶310) and whether reporting on health insurance coverage is required (¶415).

¶122 Effect on Self-Employed Persons

Self-employed coverage under any group health plan is subject to the excise tax on employer-sponsored health coverage if a deduction is allowable under Code Sec. 162(I) for any portion of the cost of the coverage (¶345).

Self-employed persons and related individuals are not considered an employee for purposes of the small employer health insurance credit (¶310).

Self-employed persons are subject to the additional Medicare tax on high-income individuals (¶230, ¶232).

Children under age 27 are considered dependents for purposes of the deduction for self-employed health insured costs (¶242).

¶123 Effect on Agricultural Employers

Agricultural employers are subject to special rules in determining whether they are liable for the shared responsibility penalty tax (¶305).

¶124 Effect on Construction Industry Employers

Construction industry employers are subject to special rules in determining whether they are liable for the shared responsibility penalty tax (¶305).

¶125 Effect on Corporations

Information reporting is expanded by requiring that all payments made by a payer to a corporation totaling $600 or more in any calendar year must be reported to the IRS on an information return (¶420).

Controlled groups of corporations are treated as a single employer for purposes of the shared responsibility penalty tax (¶305), the small employer health insurance credit (¶310), and the excise tax on high coverage "Cadillac" health plans (¶345).

Corporate estimated tax payments have been accelerated in 2014 (¶365).

¶126 Effect on S Corporations

A two-percent shareholder of an S Corporation and related individuals are not considered employees for purposes of the small employer health insurance credit (¶310).

Passive trade or business activities in an S Corporation may be subject to the Medicare tax on investment income (¶232).

¶127 Effect on Partnerships

Partners of partnerships and members of Limited Liability Companies (LLCs) are subject to the additional Medicare tax on high-income individuals (¶230).

Partnerships are not eligible for the tax credit for therapeutic discovery projects if any partner would not be qualified (¶355)

Controlled groups of partnerships are treated as a single employer for purposes of the shared responsibility penalty tax (¶305), the small employer health insurance credit (¶310), and the excise tax on high coverage "Cadillac" health plans (¶345).

Passive trade or business activities in a partnership may be subject to the Medicare tax on investment income (¶232).

¶128 Effect on Real Estate Investment Trusts (REITs)

Special rules for calculating the small business health insurance credit apply to Real Estate Investment Trusts (REITs) (¶310).

¶129 Effect on Regulated Investment Companies (RICs)

Special rules for calculating the small business health insurance credit apply to Regulated Investment Companies (RICs) (¶310).

¶130 Effect on Controlled Groups

Controlled groups of corporations, partnerships and proprietorships under common control, and affiliated service groups are treated as a single employer for purposes of the shared responsibility penalty tax (¶305), the small employer health insurance credit (¶310), and the excise tax on high coverage "Cadillac" health plans (¶345).

¶131 Effect on Health Insurance Providers

Deduction limit on compensation.—A $500,000 deduction limitation is placed on employee and director remuneration paid by certain health insurance providers. For tax years beginning after December 31, 2012, health insurance providers are subject to the restrictions only if not less than 25 percent of the gross premiums from providing health insurance coverage is from essential health benefits coverage. There is also a limitation for deferred compensation (¶340).

Excise tax on "Cadillac" plans.—A 40 percent excise tax is imposed on health insurers if the aggregate value of coverage of an employer-sponsored health plan exceeds certain threshold amounts – a "Cadillac" plan. The threshold amounts are increased for certain high cost states. There are also additional annual limits for certain retirees and high risk professions. Health insurance providers may include plan administrators and employers in the case of contributions to an employer-sponsored Health Savings Account (HSA) or Archer Medical Savings Account (MSA) (¶345).

Fees on net premiums.—New annual fees are imposed on the net premiums written by certain U.S. health insurance providers (¶350). A partial exclusion is provided for certain exempt activities.

Code Sec. 833 deductions.—In order to qualify for the special deduction under Code Sec. 833, Blue Cross and Blue Shield and other qualifying health organizations must spend 85 percent or more of their insurance premium revenues on clinical services (¶360).

Coverage reporting.—Any person who provides minimum essential health care coverage is required to file a return reporting such coverage to the IRS and to the individual (¶410).

¶132 Effect on Health Insurance Policy Issuers

Fees are imposed on health insurance policy issuers to fund a new Patient-Centered Outcomes Research Trust Fund (PCORTF) for competitive effectiveness research (¶445).

¶133 Effect on Sponsors of Self-employed Health Plans

Fees are imposed on sponsors of self-employed health plans to fund a new Patient-Centered Outcomes Research Trust Fund (PCORTF) for competitive effectiveness research (¶445).

¶134 Effect on Group Health Plans

Group health plans are subject to new requirements with respect to coverage, acceptable limits, and rescission (¶455).

¶135 Effect on Manufacturers and Importers of Branded Prescription Drugs

New annual fees are imposed on manufacturers and importers of branded prescription drugs (¶350).

¶136 Effect on Manufacturers and Importers of Medical Devices

New excise taxes are imposed on manufacturers and importers of medical devices (¶350).

¶137 Effect on Developers of Therapeutic Projects

A new 50 percent tax credit is provided for eligible investments with respect to qualifying therapeutic discovery projects. An eligible taxpayer must employ no more than 250 employees (¶355).

¶138 Effect on Paper Producers

Black liquor is excluded from the cellulosic biofuels production credit (¶357).

¶139 Effect on Indoor Tanning Facilities

Indoor tanning facilities must collect and remit a ten percent excise tax imposed on the amounts paid for indoor tanning services (¶235).

¶140 Effect on Estates and Trusts

Estates and trusts must apportion the small business health insurance credit between the estate or trust and its beneficiaries based on the income allocated to each (¶310).

A 3.8 percent Medicare tax on a portion of net investment income is imposed on estates and trusts (¶232).

HEALTH CARE—TAX-EXEMPT ENTITIES

¶141 Effect on Tax-Exempt Entities

The Patient Protection and Affordable Care Act affects the health care activities of tax-exempt entities and the health coverage for their employees. Tax-exempt entities are not eligible for the tax credit for therapeutic discovery projects (¶355).

¶142 Effect on Tax-Exempt Cooperative Small Employers

A tax-exempt cooperative small employer with 25 or fewer full-time employees and average compensation of $50,000 or less may be eligible for up to a 25 percent tax credit for premiums paid toward employee health coverage. The percentage increases to 35 percent for two years after 2013 if the employer participates in an insurance exchange. Cooperatives also have special rules for calculating the credit (¶310).

¶143 Effect on Nonprofit Health Insurance Issuers and Reinsurers

A partial exemption from the fees imposed on the net premiums of health insurance providers is provided for certain exempt activities (¶350).

Tax-exempt status is available to qualified nonprofit health insurance issuers receiving grants or loans under the Consumer Operated and Oriented Plan (CO-OP). Tax-exempt status may also extend to reinsurance entities established by or under contract with the states (¶435).

¶144 Effect on Voluntary Employee Benefit Associations (VEBAs)

Children under age 27 are to be considered dependents of the members of Voluntary Employee Benefit Associations (VEBAs) that provide sick and accident benefits (¶242).

¶145 Effect on Nonprofit Charitable Hospitals

Additional requirements are imposed on hospitals to maintain tax-exempt status. An excise tax is provided for failure to meet the requirements (¶440).

¶146 Effect on Tax-Exempt Trusts

Certain tax-exempt trusts are not subject to the Medicare tax on investment income (¶232).

¶147 Effect on Patient-Centered Outcomes Research Trust Fund (PCORTF)

A new Patient-Centered Outcomes Research Trust Fund (PCORTF) for comparative effectiveness research is established and funded (¶445).

¶148 Effect on Community Living Assistance Services and Support (CLASS) Program

A new Community Living Assistance Services and Support (CLASS) Program is to be treated for tax purposes in the same manner as a qualified long-term care insurance contract for qualified long-term care services (¶450). A CLASS Independence Advisory Council is also established.

¶144

HEALTH CARE—GOVERNMENT ENTITIES

¶149 Effect on Government Entities

The Patient Protection and Affordable Care Act imposes many new responsibilities on government bodies. Required returns and statements with respect to health insurance coverage provided by a government unit or agency must be made by the officer or employee who entered into the agreement to provide the coverage or the person otherwise designated (¶410).

Government entities are not eligible for the tax credit for therapeutic discovery projects (¶355).

¶150 Effect on Government Health Plans

Employer-sponsored health insurance coverage for civilian employees by federal, state and local governments, or any agency thereof, is subject to the excise tax on employer-sponsored coverage (¶345).

Fees are imposed on certain government health plans to fund a new Patient-Centered Outcomes Research Trust Fund (PCORTF) (¶445).

¶151 Effect on Secretary of Treasury and IRS

Penalty taxes.—The Treasury and IRS are given a number of responsibilities under the Patient Protection and Affordable Care Act. The IRS is to administer the penalty imposed on individuals without health insurance, however criminal prosecutions and use of liens and levies are prohibited (¶205). The IRS is also to give notice of, and demand payment for, the shared responsibility penalty tax on larger employers (¶305).

Health insurance credits.—The IRS is authorized to issue any regulations necessary to carry out the premium assistance credit rules (¶210) and the small business health insurance credit (¶310).

Tanning service excise tax.—The IRS is to issue regulations with respect to the remission of the tanning services excise tax (¶235).

Therapeutic discovery project.—The IRS is to set up the qualifying therapeutic discovery project and to consider applications and make awards (¶355).

Lack of coverage notice.—The IRS, in consultation with Department of Health and Human Services, is required to send notice to each individual return filer who is not enrolled in minimum essential coverage (¶410).

¶151

Fees on medical devices, drugs and insurance providers.—The IRS is to provide guidance on the annual fees on: (1) sales of branded prescription drugs and medical devices and (2) premiums of health insurance providers, and guidance on apportionment of aggregates fees (¶ 350).

Form for health coverage reporting.—The IRS is to develop a form for larger employers to report health insurance coverage (¶ 415).

Sharing return information with HHS.—The IRS is permitted to disclose to the Department of Health and Human Services certain taxpayer return information in order to verify cost sharing reduction or premium tax credit amounts and facilitate eligibility determinations for other programs (¶ 425).

Sharing return information with SSA.—The IRS is given authority to provide to the Social Security Administration certain taxpayer information to assist in reducing the Part D premium subsidy for high-income beneficiaries (¶ 430).

CLASS program.—The IRS is to establish procedures for enrollment in the Community Living Assistance Services and Support (CLASS) program and to manage the CLASS Independence Fund (¶ 450). The IRS is also required to submit annual reports to Congress on the CLASS program.

¶152 Effect on Department of Health and Human Services

The IRS, in consultation with the Department of Health and Human Services, is required to send notice to each individual return filer who is not enrolled in minimum essential coverage (¶ 410).

The IRS is permitted to disclose to the Department of Health and Human Services certain taxpayer return information in order to verify cost sharing reduction or premium tax credit amounts and facilitate eligibility determinations for other programs (¶ 425). Discrepancies between this information and state Exchange reported information may be disclosed to the Exchange.

¶153 Effect on Social Security Administration

The Social Security Administration is given access to certain taxpayer information to assist in reducing the Part D premium subsidy for high-income beneficiaries (¶ 430).

¶154 Effect on Secretary of Labor

The Secretary of Labor is required to conduct a study to determine whether employees' wages are reduced by reason of the shared responsibility penalty credit (¶ 305).

¶155 Effect on Secretary of Veterans Affairs

The Secretary of Veterans Affairs is directed to study the effect of new fees on the cost of medical care provided to veterans and veterans' access to medical devices and branded prescription drugs (¶350).

¶156 Effect on Controller General

The Controller General is directed to conduct a study on the affordability of health insurance coverage (¶210).

¶157 Effect on States

Under the Patient Protection and Affordable Care Act, states must establish American Health Benefit Exchanges (AHBEs), and qualified individuals and small businesses purchasing coverage within an AHBE may qualify for a premium assistance credit (¶205).

Beginning in 2017, a state may allow large group markets to offer health insurance under the new AHBEs (¶320).

Repayments under state loan repayment or forgiveness programs designed to improve health care services are excluded from income (¶245).

¶158 Effect on Indian Tribes and Tribal Organizations

Qualified health care benefits provided by an Indian tribe or tribal organization to its members and the member's spouse and dependents are excluded from gross income (¶250).

HIRING INCENTIVES TO RESTORE EMPLOYMENT ACT

¶159 Overview

Jobs take center stage.—With the debate over health care reform still raging, Congress has at least temporarily turned its attention to jobs and the economy. On March 4, the House passed the Hiring Incentives to Restore Employment Act (P.L. 111-147), which had previously passed the Senate in February. However, the House added certain provisions to the measure, sending it back to the Senate where it was finally approved on March 17.

The main thrust of the HIRE act is on job creation and retention as evidenced by provisions that grant payroll tax forgiveness and provide a credit for retention of employees (¶605), extend Code Sec. 179 expensing by businesses (¶610), and make changes in tax credit bonds (¶620) and qualified school construction bonds (¶625). Revenue raisers are directed at U.S. taxpayers failing to report interests in foreign trusts and other assets (¶705 through ¶760), acceleration of corporate estimated tax payments for large corporations (¶630), and a delay in implementation of the worldwide allocation of interest expense deduction for worldwide affiliated groups (¶765).

Passage of the HIRE Act followed on the heels of the President signing the Temporary Extension Act of 2010 (P.L. 111-144), on March 2, after a hold on the legislation by Senator Bunning (R. Kentucky) had been resolved. That legislation includes a 30-day extension of eligibility for COBRA premium assistance (¶615), along with certain other items including unemployment insurance, certain surface transportation programs covered by the Highway Trust Fund, and an increase in physician reimbursement under Medicare.

HIRE—INDIVIDUALS

¶160 Effect on Individuals Generally

Although not aimed primarily at individuals, provisions of the Hiring Incentives to Restore Employment Act (P.L. 111-147) that grant payroll tax forgiveness and provide a credit for retention of employees (¶605) will have at least an indirect impact on individuals seeking new employment or interested in retaining current employment.

On the revenue side, individuals with interests in foreign trusts and certain foreign assets will find themselves subject to new rules on withholding (¶705), new reporting requirements (¶710 and ¶745), and penalties for failure to comply (¶715 and ¶750).

Although an extension of eligibility for COBRA premium assistance was not included in the HIRE Act, separately, Congress passed and, on March 2, the President signed the Temporary Extension Act of 2010 (P.L. 111-144), which extends such eligibility through March 31, 2010 (¶615). Separately, on January 22, the President signed P.L. 111-126, which allows donors to accelerate the benefits of a charitable cash donation for the relief of victims of the January 12 earthquake in Haiti (¶635). Accordingly, donors can claim a qualifying donation on their 2009 tax return.

¶161 Effect on Owners and Beneficiaries of Foreign Trusts

Revenue raisers look to foreign shores.—In the search for revenue offsets to counter the business tax breaks included in the Hiring Incentives to Restore Employment Act (P.L. 111-147), Congress decided to include a number of provisions aimed at disclosure and reporting of interests in foreign trusts and other accounts similar to those that had previously been included in the House tax extenders bill (H.R. 4213).

Specifically, with respect to foreign trusts, the HIRE Act clarifies that an amount is treated as accumulated for the benefit of a U.S. person even if that person's interest in the trust is contingent (¶735). In addition, the HIRE Act would take a broader approach to treating foreign trusts as having a U.S. beneficiary in cases involving discretionary authority over such trusts. The HIRE Act would create a presumption that a foreign trust has a U.S. beneficiary if a U.S. person directly or indirectly transfers property to such a trust, unless the U.S. person submits information demonstrating that no part of the trust's income or corpus will paid to, or accumulated for, the benefit of a U.S. person either during the tax year or at the termination of the trust (¶735).

Additional provisions applicable to foreign trusts would deem the uncompensated use of trust property as a distribution to the U.S. grantor or beneficiary (¶740). However, the use of property at fair market value or a loan that is repaid at a market rate of interest would not constitute a distribution for purposes of this provision. A reporting requirement would be imposed on U.S. persons treated as the owners of foreign trusts under the grantor trust rules (¶745) and a minimum penalty of $10,000 would be imposed for failure to comply with the reporting requirement (¶750).

Separately, new rules require withholding agents to withhold 30 percent of "withholdable payments" (e.g. dividends, rent, salaries, wages, etc.) from sources within the U.S. made to a foreign financial institution or non-financial foreign entity, unless specific reporting requirements are met (¶705). These rules would effectively require the foreign entities to provide withholding agents with the name, address, and taxpayer identification number of any U.S. individual who is a "substantial owner" of the foreign entity. In the case of a foreign trust, that term would include a U.S. person treated as an owner under the grantor trust rules or U.S. person with a 10-percent beneficial interest in the trust.

¶162 Effect on Owners of Foreign Assets

Reporting and disclosure requirements tightened.—Reporting requirements are imposed by the Hiring Incentives to Restore Employment Act (P.L. 111-147) on U.S. persons who hold interests in foreign bank accounts or securities with an aggregate value greater than $50,000 (¶710). With respect to foreign bank accounts, the disclosure must include the account number, the name and address of the institution, and the maximum value of the account during the tax year. Similarly, for stocks and other securities, disclosure would include the name of the issuer and the asset's maximum value during the tax year. A minimum penalty of $10,000 would be imposed for failure to comply with the disclosure requirements with an additional penalty imposed if the failure continues for more than 90 days after notification.

Penalties imposed. limitations period extended.—The HIRE Act would also impose a new 40-percent accuracy-related penalty on underpayments attributable to failure to disclose interests in foreign bank accounts or other entities (¶715). In addition, the HIRE Act calls for a new six-year statute of limitations for assessments on understatements attributable to interests in foreign bank accounts or other entities, if there is an omission of gross income in excess of $5,000 that is attributable to an asset subject to the new foreign asset reporting requirements (¶720). Finally, the existing three-year limitations period will be suspended for failure to provide timely information reporting.

¶163 Effect on Shareholders in Passive Foreign Investment Companies (PFICs)

The Hiring Incentives to Restore Employment Act (P.L. 111-147) would require U.S. persons who are shareholders in passive foreign investment companies (PFICs) to satisfy annual information reporting requirements (¶725). Due to other information reporting requirements imposed by the HIRE Act it is anticipated that the IRS will use its regulatory authority to avoid duplicate reporting.

¶164 Effect on Investors in Tax Credit and Tax-Exempt Bonds

Refundable credit.—The Hiring Incentives to Restore Employment Act (P.L. 111-147) provides issuers of certain tax credit bonds with an election to claim a refundable credit in lieu of the credit that would normally belong to purchasers of the bonds, similar to that offered to issuers of Build America Bonds (¶620). The types of bonds covered by the provision would include clean renewable energy bonds (CREBs), qualified energy conservation bonds (QECs), qualified zone academy bonds (QZABs), and qualified school construction bonds (QSCBs).

School bond rules clarified.—A technical correction dealing with QSCBs clarifies that the limitation on the amount of such bonds allocated to a particular state is to be allocated to issuers within that state by the state education agency or another agency authorized by state law to make the allocation (¶625). Also, rules allowing the carryover of any unused QSCB limitation by a state or an Indian tribal government also apply to the 40-percent of the limitation allocated among the largest school districts.

Foreign registration exceptions repealed.—Separately, the HIRE Act repeals the foreign targeted obligation exception to the registration requirements for U.S. Treasury obligations. Accordingly, to qualify for a Code Sec. 163 deduction on the interest paid or accrued with respect to an obligation designed to be sold only to a non-U.S. person, the obligation must now be in registered form (¶760). Similar changes are made with respect to provisions governing state and local bonds and the exclusion for portfolio interest.

¶165 Effect on Recipients of Substitute Dividends

Treated as dividends from U.S. sources.—Under a provision of the Hiring Incentives to Restore Employment Act (P.L. 111-147), substitute dividends and dividend equivalents received by foreign persons will be treated as dividends from U.S. sources for certain purposes including the withholding rules applicable to foreign persons (¶755). This treatment would cover any payments made under a securities lending or sale and repurchase transaction or under a notional principal contract that is contingent on or determined by reference to a dividend payment from sources within the U.S.

¶166 Effect on Charitable Donors

P.L. 111-126 allows donors to accelerate the benefits of a charitable cash donation for the relief of victims of the January 12 earthquake in Haiti (¶635). Accordingly, donors can claim a qualifying donation on their 2009 tax return. To qualify for this treatment the donation must have been made after January 11, 2010, and before March 1, 2010. A telephone bill showing the name of the charitable organization, as well as the amount and date of the contribution, will satisfy the recordkeeping requirements.

HIRE—BUSINESSES

¶167 Effect on Businesses Generally

The HIRE Act focuses its main tax breaks on businesses to try to promote hiring. The revenue raising offsets to pay for these tax breaks largely focus on disclosure and reporting with respect to foreign assets and accounts. These revenue raising provisions generally have an impact on businesses as well as individuals.

From date of hire after February 3, 2010, through the remainder of 2010, qualified employers do not have to pay their share of Old Age Survivors and Disability Insurance (OASDI) taxes after March 18, 2010 for newly hired workers who were previously unemployed during the preceding 60-day period (¶605). An employer must opt out of the payroll tax holiday in order to claim the work opportunity credit for that employee.

Employers can claim up to a $1,000 credit for retaining new workers for at least 52 weeks (¶605).

If a U.S. person transfers property to a trust, there is a rebuttable presumption that the trust has a U.S. beneficiary for purposes of treating the foreign trust as a grantor trust. If any person has discretion to make a trust distribution, a foreign trust is treated as having a U.S. beneficiary unless none of the potential recipients are U.S. persons. If a U.S. person who transfers property to the trust is involved in any agreement that may result in trust income or corpus being paid or accumulated to or for a U.S. person, such agreement will be considered a term of the trust (¶735).

The uncompensated use of foreign trust property by a U.S. person related to either a U.S. grantor or a U.S. beneficiary is treated as a distribution by the trust for nongrantor trust income tax purposes. The use of any other property of the trust for or by any U.S. person is treated as paid or accumulated for the benefit of a U.S. person for purposes of applying the grantor trust income tax rules (¶740). A U.S. person who is treated as the owner of any portion of a foreign trust under the grantor trust rules is required to submit to the IRS any information the IRS may require with respect to the trust (¶745). Penalties have been increased for failure to report information or file returns with respect to foreign trusts (¶750).

U.S. shareholders of passive foreign investment companies must file an annual information return with the IRS (¶725).

¶167

The three-year limitations period is suspended for failure to timely file these information returns (¶720).

Under the Temporary Extension Act of 2010 (P.L. 111-144), the eligibility for former employees to receive 65 percent COBRA premium assistance is extended through March 31, 2010 (¶615).

¶168 Effect on Small Business

The Code Sec. 179 expense and investment limitations have been extended through 2010. The Code Sec. 179 amounts are no longer adjusted for inflation (¶610).

¶169 Effect on Domestic Businesses

New disclosure requirements.—The IRS is authorized to apply the new disclosure requirements with respect to foreign assets to any domestic entity if that entity is formed or availed of for purposes of holding, directly or indirectly, specified foreign assets (¶710). A U. S. person who fails to meet the new disclosure requirements is subject to a 40-percent accuracy-related penalty (¶715).

Statute of limitations.—The statute of limitations for tax assessments is extended to six years if there is an omission of gross income in excess of $5,000 attributable to a foreign financial asset (¶720). The three-year statute is suspended if the new disclosure requirements are not timely filed.

¶170 Effect on Foreign Businesses

A non-financial foreign entity that is a beneficial owner of a withholdable payment must certify that it has no substantial U.S. owners or provide identifying information for each substantial U.S. owner (¶705).

¶171 Effect on Corporations

A corporation is a U.S. owned foreign entity for purposes of the foreign account withholding and disclosure rules if a specified U.S. person owns, directly or indirectly, more than 10 percent of the corporate stock by vote or value (¶705). The 10-percent level is reduced to 0 if the corporation is engaged in investing or trading.

Large corporations with assets of not less than $1 billion are subject to an acceleration of estimated tax due dates in 2014, 2015, and 2019 (¶630).

¶172 Effect on Foreign Corporations

Dividend equivalent payments.—Dividend equivalent payments received by foreign persons that are treated as U.S.-source dividends are expanded to include securities lending and sale-repurchase transactions and notional principal contracts where the payment (directly or indirectly) is contingent upon, or determined by reference to, the payment of a dividend from U.S. sources (¶755). The Treasury is also given authority to expand the definition to include substantially similar transactions. Rules are also provided where there is a chain of dividend equivalent transactions.

Exclusion from reporting requirements.—Foreign corporations under Code Sec. 1471(e)(2)(B) are excluded from the definition of an expanded affiliated group under the definition of a specified U.S. person for purposes of the foreign financial institution reporting requirements (¶705).

¶173 Effect on Publicly-Traded Corporations

A publicly-traded corporation is excepted from the definition of a specified U.S. person for purposes of the foreign financial institution reporting requirements (¶705).

¶174 Effect on Affiliated Groups

A member of an expanded affiliated group is excepted from the definition of a specified U.S. person for purposes of the foreign financial institution reporting requirements. An expanded affiliated group is defined as an affiliated group with one or more chains of includible corporations connected through stock ownership with a common parent that is an includible corporation provided certain more than 50 percent ownership requirements are met (¶705). The definition of an expanded affiliated group does not apply to insurance companies subject to tax under Code Sec. 801 or to foreign corporations. A partnership or other non-corporate entity is treated as a member of an expanded affiliated group if the entity is controlled by members of such expanded affiliated group.

Application of the one-time election for worldwide affiliated groups to allocate interest expense on a worldwide basis is delayed for two years to tax years beginning after December 31, 2019 (¶765).

¶175 Effect on Partnerships

Treatment for foreign withholding and disclosure rules.—A partnership is a U.S. owned foreign entity for purposes of the foreign account withholding and disclosure rules if a specified U.S. person directly or indirectly owns more than 10 percent of the profits or capital interests of the partnership (¶705). The 10-percent limit is reduced to zero if the partnership is engaged in investing or trading.

¶175

Statute of limitations.—The new six-year statute of limitations for omission of income attributable to foreign assets and the existing exception for substantial omissions of income also applies to partnerships (¶720).

Deemed as member of affiliated group.—A partnership or other non-corporate entity is treated as a member of an expanded affiliated group under the definition of a specified U.S. person for purposes of the foreign financial institution reporting requirements if the entity is controlled by members of such expanded affiliated group (¶705).

¶176 Effect on REITs

A Real Estate Investment Trust (REIT) is excepted from the definition of a specified U.S. person for purposes of the foreign financial institution reporting requirements (¶705).

¶177 Effect on Financial Entities

Electronic filing.—The IRS may require financial institutions to electronically file certain returns related to withholding on foreign transfers (¶730). A failure to file penalty is authorized

Information reporting.—Foreign financial institutions must provide, with respect to each U.S. account, identifying information for each account holder that is a specified U.S. or substantial U.S. owner, the account number, account balance, and gross receipts and withdrawals from the account (¶705).

Withholding requirements.—A withholding agent is required to withhold 30 percent on any withholdable payment made to a foreign financial institution or a non-financial foreign entity unless specific reporting requirements are met (¶705). An agreement with the IRS may waive the withholding requirement.

¶178 Effect on Banks

A bank is excepted from the definition of a specified U.S. person for purposes of the foreign financial institution reporting requirements (¶705).

¶179 Effect on RICs

A Regulated Investment Company (RIC) is excepted from the definition of a specified U.S. person for purposes of the foreign financial institution reporting requirements (¶705).

¶180 Effect on Investing and Trading Entities

A corporation, partnership or trust engaged in investing or trading is a U.S. owned foreign entity for purposes of the foreign accounts withholding and disclosure rules regardless of the ownership by a specified U.S. person (¶705).

¶181 Effect on Passive Foreign Investment Companies

U.S. shareholders of passive foreign investment companies must file an annual information return with the IRS (¶725).

¶182 Effect on Common Trust Funds

A common trust fund is excepted form the definition of a specified U.S. person for purposes of the foreign financial institution reporting requirements (¶705).

¶183 Effect on Insurance Companies

Insurance companies subject to tax under Code Sec. 801 are excluded from the definition of an expanded affiliated group for purposes of determining who is a specified U.S. person under the foreign financial institution reporting requirements (¶705).

HIRE—EXEMPT ORGANIZATIONS, GOVERNMENT, AND FOREIGN ENTITIES

¶184 Effect on Tax-Exempt Entities

Foreign reporting requirements.—A tax-exempt entity is excepted from the definition of a specified U.S. person for purposes of the foreign financial institution reporting requirements (¶705).

Payroll tax relief and employee retention credit.—Tax-exempt entities qualify for the new payroll tax holiday and employee retention credit (¶605).

¶185 Effect on Government Entities

No payroll tax relief or retention credit.—Government employees, whether federal or state, generally do not qualify for the payroll tax holiday or retention credit (¶605). Public college and university employees are an exception.

¶185

Exceptions to registered bond requirements repealed.—Certain foreign-related exemptions to the registered bond requirements are repealed, expanding the bonds required to be registered (¶760).

Refundable credit on tax credit bonds.—Issuers of certain tax credit bonds can elect a refundable tax credit of 45 percent (or 65 percent for small issuers) of interest paid to purchasers in lieu of the credit normally allowed to purchasers. These bonds include new clean renewable energy bonds, qualified energy conservation bonds, qualified zone academy bonds, and qualified school construction bonds (¶620).

Qualified school construction bonds.—Qualified school construction bonds are allocated within a state to the state education agency or other agency authorized under state law to make the allocation (¶625). The amounts so allocated are also allowed under the carryover provisions of current law.

¶186 Effect on U.S. Possessions

Retention credit extended to possessions.—A House amendment to the Hiring Incentives to Restore Employment Act (P.L. 111-147) effectively extends the worker retention credit (¶605) to businesses in U.S. possessions, including the Commonwealth of Puerto Rico and the Northern Mariana Islands.

¶187 Effect on Public Colleges and Universities

Public colleges and universities qualify for the new payroll tax holiday and employee retention credit (¶605).

¶188 Effect on Foreign Trusts

Trust owners and beneficiaries targeted.—Foreign trusts will be impacted at least indirectly by provisions aimed primarily at trust owners and beneficiaries. For example, the Hiring Incentives to Restore Employment Act (P.L. 111-147) clarifies that an amount will be treated as accumulated for the benefit of a U.S. person even if that person's interest in the trust is contingent (¶735). In addition, the HIRE Act would treat foreign trusts as having a U.S. beneficiary in cases involving discretionary authority over such trusts. The HIRE Act would create a presumption that a foreign trust has a U.S. beneficiary if a U.S. person directly or indirectly transfers property to such a trust, unless the U.S. person submits information demonstrating that no part of the trust's income or corpus will paid to, or accumulated for, the benefit of a U.S. person either during the tax year or at the termination of the trust (¶735).

Use of trust property examined.—Additional provisions applicable to foreign trusts would deem the uncompensated use of trust property as a distribution to the U.S. grantor or beneficiary (¶740). However, the use of property at fair market value or a loan that is repaid at a market rate of interest would not constitute a distribution for purposes of this provision. A reporting requirement would be imposed on the U.S.

owners of foreign trusts (¶745). and a minimum penalty would be imposed for failure to comply with the reporting requirement (¶750).

New withholding rules added.—New rules require withholding agents to withhold 30 percent of "withholdable payments" (e.g. dividends, rent, salaries, wages, etc.) from sources within the U.S. made to a foreign financial institution or non-financial foreign entity, unless specific reporting requirements are met (¶705). These rules would effectively require the foreign entities to provide withholding agents with the name, address, and taxpayer identification number of any U.S. individual who is a "substantial owner" of the foreign entity. In the case of a foreign trust, that term would include someone treated as an owner under the grantor trust rules or someone with a 10-percent beneficial interest in the trust.

¶189 Effect on Foreign Governments, International Organizations, and Foreign Central Banks

Foreign governments, international organizations and foreign central banks of issue are excepted from the withholding requirements for payments to non-financial foreign entities (¶705).

Health Care: Individuals

¶205 Penalty for Failing to Carry Health Insurance

SUMMARY OF NEW LAW

Beginning in 2014, individuals must make a "shared responsibility payment" if they do not have minimum essential health insurance for themselves and their dependents.

BACKGROUND

The United States federal government has never provided universal health care, or required individuals to have health insurance. About 60 percent of Americans under the age of 65 have employment-based health insurance, with premiums often paid or subsidized by the employer. Most Americans who are at least 65 years old qualify for Medicare, a social insurance program that is partially financed by special payroll

BACKGROUND

taxes on workers and employers. Many other Americans obtain health insurance through government programs like veterans' care, Medicaid or the State Children's Health Insurance Program (SCHIP). Finally, an estimated 40-50 million Americans are uninsured.

The cost of providing care to uninsured and under-insured Americans contributes to the rapidly rising cost of health care and health insurance. In 2008, uninsured Americans received about $116 billion worth of health care. They paid for about one-third; governments and charities paid for about a quarter; and the remainder was uncompensated care. These uncompensated costs are recouped via higher charges for all health care services, which has the effect of increasing insurance premiums. One study concluded that in 2008, this "stealth premium" increased annual insurance premiums by $1,017 for family coverage, and by $368 for individual coverage (Hidden Health Tax: Americans Pay a Premium, Families USA, May 2009, at www.familiesusa.org).

Some governments have attempted to expand coverage by requiring individuals to carry health insurance. On the international front, Switzerland and the Netherlands have both achieved nearly universal health insurance coverage by means of extensive programs that include individual mandates. However, more than 95 percent of their populations were insured before the mandates went into effect. Closer to home, Massachusetts began a health care reform program in 2006 that imposed an individual mandate beginning in 2008. In 2009, just 2.6 percent of the State's population was uninsured, the lowest uninsured rate in the country. While these kinds of programs seem to expand health insurance coverage, there is some question as to their effectiveness in holding down costs and increasing access to actual health care (Individual Mandate: A Background Report, at www.library.ca.gov; The Swiss and Dutch Health Insurance Systems: Universal Coverage and Regulated Competitive Insurance Markets, at www.commonwealthfund.org).

Some individuals have left the traditional insurance market altogether and, instead, joined health care sharing ministries (HCSM). An HCSM is a nonprofit religious organization that acts as a quasi-insurer for members who share their medical expenses. HCSMs currently share more than $60 million per year in medical expenses for more than 100,000 members in all 50 States. Typically, HCSM members contribute a set amount to the organization each month, based on the member's chosen deductible and family size. Some HCSMs direct their members to send their contributions directly to other members who have incurred covered expenses, who then use the funds to pay their medical providers. Other HCSMs collect the contributions and distribute them to members with covered expenses, or to the medical providers who furnished covered care. Some HCSMs even have networks of preferred providers that offer discounts to the HCSM or its members. Most HCSMs require members to prove they belong to a Christian church. Some also require members to pledge to abstain from tobacco, excessive alcohol, illegal drugs, and sex outside marriage; and refuse to cover costs they perceive to be related to such behaviors. Applicants might also be required to obtain a health screening, so that the HCSM can exclude coverage for pre-existing conditions. HCSMs may resemble traditional insurance, but they are largely unregulated, they are not required to have reserves to cover unexpectedly large

¶205

BACKGROUND

expenses, and they do not participate in State guaranty funds that assume the claims of insolvent insurers (Alliance of Health Care Sharing Ministries, at www.healthcaresharing.org; A Christian Approach to Covering Healthcare, U.S. News and World Report, June 25, 2008, at http://health.usnews.com/articles/ health/2008/06/25/a-christian-approach-to-covering-healthcare.html?PageNr=1; Ministries Offer Bill-Sharing as Insurance Alternative, at http://www.ama-assn.org/ amednews/2008/07/07/bisa0707.htm).

NEW LAW EXPLAINED

Penalty imposed on individuals without health insurance.—Beginning in 2014, a penalty is imposed on applicable individuals for each month they fail to have "minimum essential health coverage" for themselves and their dependents (Code Sec. 5000A, as added and amended by the Patient Protection and Affordable Care Act (PPACA) (P.L. 111-148)). This penalty is also referred to as a "shared responsibility payment".

Taxpayers affected. Generally, all persons are applicable individuals with respect to any month and subject to the penalty unless they fall into one of these four categories (Code Sec. 5000A(d)(1) as added by PPACA):

(1) Prisoners—Persons are not applicable individuals for any month if they are incarcerated for the month, other than incarceration pending the disposition of charges (Code Sec. 5000A(d)(4), as added by PPACA).

(2) Undocumented aliens—Persons are not applicable individuals for any month if, for that month, they are not citizens or nationals of the United States, or aliens lawfully present in the United States (Code Sec. 5000A(d)(3), as added by PPACA).

(3) Health care sharing ministry members—Persons are not applicable individuals in any month in which they are members of a health care sharing ministry (HCSM) that satisfies the following tests:

 (a) the HCSM must be a tax-exempt organization under Code Sec. 501(c)(3) (a public charity);

 (b) its members must share a common set of ethical or religious beliefs, and share medical expenses among themselves in accordance with those beliefs and without regard to the State in which a member resides or is employed;

 (c) its members must retain their memberships even after they develop medical conditions;

 (d) it (or a predecessor) must have been in existence at all times since December 31, 1999, and its members must have shared their medical expenses continuously and without interruption since at least December 31, 1999; and

 (e) it must conduct an annual audit that is performed by an independent CPA firm in accordance with generally accepted accounting principles (GAAP), and the audit must be made available to the public upon request (Code Sec. 5000A(d)(2)(B), as added by PPACA).

NEW LAW EXPLAINED

(4) Religious conscience—Persons are not applicable individuals in any month in which an American Health Benefit Exchange certifies that they are exempt from the penalty because they are members of, and adherents of the established tenets or teachings of, a recognized religious sect or division that causes them to be conscientiously opposed to accepting the benefits of any private or public insurance that makes payments because of death, disability, old age or retirement; or that makes payments toward the cost of, or provides services for, medical care (Code Sec. 5000A(d)(2)(A), as added and amended by PPACA). For a discussion of the establishment and requirements of the Exchanges, see ¶ 505. For a discussion of the general procedures that will be established for religious conscience exception, see ¶ 515.

Comment: These last two categories are both characterized as religious exemptions (Code Sec. 5000A(d)(2), as added by PPACA). The exemption for HCSM members is largely limited to Christians, since most (probably all) existing HCSM are Christian organizations, and a new HCSM cannot qualify for the exemption. The religious conscience exception is the same test used for exemption from self-employment taxes under Code Sec. 1402(g)(1)).

Exemptions. Persons who are applicable individuals are nonetheless exempt from the penalty under the following circumstances:

- Unaffordable coverage—The penalty does not apply to an applicable individual who cannot afford coverage (Code Sec. 5000A(e)(1), as added and amended by PPACA). This exemption is discussed in the "Exceptions—filing threshold and unaffordable coverage" section below.

- Filing threshold—The penalty does not apply to applicable individuals whose household income is below their income thresholds for filing income tax returns (Code Sec. 5000A(e)(2), as added by PPACA and amended by the Health Care and Education Reconciliation Act of 2010 (P.L. 111-152)). This exemption is discussed in the "Exceptions—filing threshold and unaffordable coverage" section below.

- Native Americans—The penalty does not apply to an applicable individual during any month in which the individual is a member of an Indian tribe, as defined for purposes of the Indian employment credit under Code Sec. 45A(c)(6) (i.e., an Indian tribe, band, nation, pueblo, or other organized group or community that is recognized as eligible for the special programs and services provided by the United States to Indians because of their status as Indians) (Code Sec. 5000A(e)(3), as added by PPACA).

- Short lapses—The penalty does not apply for any month if the last day of that month occurs during a period in which the applicable individual lacked minimum essential coverage (defined below) for a period of less than three months. This three-month period is determined without regard to calendar year(s), and the Treasury Secretary is authorized to prescribe rules for collecting the penalty when a continuous period of inadequate coverage includes more than one tax year. Once the period of inadequate coverage meets the three-month threshold, the penalty is imposed for the entire period; thus, the penalty does not apply until a taxpayer goes three consecutive months without adequate coverage, but it is then imposed

¶205

NEW LAW EXPLAINED

from the beginning of that three-month period. The waiver of the penalty applies only to an applicable individual's first underinsured period during a calendar year; it does not apply to any subsequent periods during the same year (Code Sec. 5000A(e)(4), as added by PPACA).

Example 1: Jason is a calendar-year taxpayer. During 2015, he is uninsured from January 1 until February 19. On February 20, he obtains health insurance through his new employer. However, he loses his job and his insurance on March 31, and is uninsured from April 1 through July 31. He is insured again from August 1 through September 30, but is uninsured for the rest of the year. The penalty waiver for a short lapse applies to his first uninsured period (January 1 through February 19). It does not apply to his second uninsured period (April 1 through July 31) because it is not a short lapse; thus, the penalty applies for that entire four-month period. The short lapse waiver does not apply to his third uninsured period (October 1 through December 31) because it already applied to a period during the calendar year. Thus, the penalty applies for April, May, June, July, October, November and December.

Note that Jason's second uninsured period is longer than his first; thus, he would be better off applying the penalty waiver to that second period. It does not appear that he has that option, however, as the statute provides that when there are multiple short-lapse periods in the same calendar year, the waiver "shall only apply to months in the first of such periods" (Code Sec. 5000A(e)(4)(B)(iii), as added by PPACA).

- Hardships—The penalty does not apply if the Secretary of Health and Human Services determines that the individual has suffered a hardship with respect to the capability to obtain coverage under a qualified health plan for the month (Code Sec. 5000A(e)(5), as added by PPACA).

- Dependents—As discussed below, dependents are effectively exempt from paying the penalty, because it is imposed instead on the taxpayer who claims the dependency exemption (Code Sec. 5000A(b)(3)(A), as added by PPACA).

- Individuals outside the U.S.—Certain persons who reside in U.S. territories or outside the United States are effectively exempt from the penalty, because they are treated as having minimum essential coverage during any month:

  — in which they are bona fide residents of any U.S. possession, or

  — that occurs during the residency period that qualifies them for the foreign earned income exclusion (Code Sec. 5000A(f)(4), as added by PPACA).

  Comment: To be a bona fide resident of a U.S. possession for a tax year, an individual must be present in the possession for at least 183 days during the year, must not have a tax home outside that possession during the year, and must not have a closer connection to the United States or a foreign country than to the possession (Code Sec. 937(a)). Individuals generally qualify for the foreign earned income exclusion if they are bona fide residents of a foreign country or

NEW LAW EXPLAINED

countries during an uninterrupted period that includes an entire tax year, or are present in a foreign country or countries for at least 330 full days during any period of 12 consecutive months (Code Sec. 911(d)(1)).

Comment: An American Benefit Exchange is allowed to offer catastrophic health plans to individuals who are certified by the Secretary of Health and Human Services (HHS) as exempt from the penalty under the unaffordable and hardship exceptions (Act Sec. 1302(e)(2)(B) of PPACA). For a general discussion of federal program that will be implemented to provide procedures for determining eligibility for Exchange participation and individual exemptions from minimum essential coverage, see ¶315. For a discussion of catastrophic plans than may be offered through an Exchange, see ¶530.

Liability for penalty. The penalty is imposed on applicable individuals who do not have minimum essential coverage for one or more months during any calendar year beginning after 2013 (Code Sec. 5000A(b)(1), as added and amended by PPACA). The penalty is included with the taxpayer's income tax return for the tax year that includes the month for which the penalty is imposed (Code Sec. 5000A(b)(2), as added by PPACA). Two special rules also apply.

- Dependents—If a taxpayer claims an applicable individual as a dependent, the taxpayer (rather than the dependent) is liable for any penalty that would otherwise be imposed on the dependent during the taxpayer's tax year (Code Sec. 5000A(b)(3)(A), as added by PPACA).

- Spouses—Married taxpayers who file a joint return are jointly liable for the penalty that is imposed on either one of them for any month during the tax year (Code Sec. 5000A(b)(3)(B), as added by PPACA).

    Gray Area: In applying the penalty, the statute does not define "for any month." Presumably, the IRS will determine whether this means the penalty applies if there is no essential minimum coverage for the entire month, at least half of the month, on the first day of the month, on the last day of the month, etc.

Example 2: Helen is a college student who lives with her father during 2014. She is covered by his health insurance as long as she is a full-time student, but when she graduates on May 23, she is dropped from his policy. For several months, she works part-time and temporary jobs that do not offer her health insurance, and she does not obtain her own insurance through an Exchange or on the private market. On October 5, she starts working full-time and also obtains insurance through her new employer. Since she was uninsured during June through September, the penalty is imposed for at least those four months (and possibly longer, depending on what "for the month" means). However, if Helen's father claims her dependency exemption on his 2014 return, the penalty is imposed on him, rather than on Helen.

Comment: One of the non-tax-related changes made by the Patient Protection Act requires insurers that provide coverage for dependent children to continue such coverage until the dependent turns 26 years old (see ¶455). Generally, this

¶205

NEW LAW EXPLAINED

change has no effect on the definition of "dependent" with respect to the tax treatment of the cost of the coverage. However, children under the age of 27 may be considered dependents of a taxpayer for purposes of the general exclusion for medical care expenses of an employee, the deduction for the health insurance costs of a self-employed person, and the rules allowing for health benefits to be provided by qualified pension or annuity retirement plan or voluntary employee benefits association. For a discussion of tax treatment of adult dependents, see ¶242.

Administration. The penalty must be paid upon notice and demand by the Treasury Secretary, and is generally assessed and collected in the same manner as most other assessable penalties under the Internal Revenue Code (Code Sec. 5000A(g)(1), as added by PPACA). However, enforcement of the penalty is limited in two ways:

- Crimes—Taxpayers are not subject to any criminal prosecution or penalty for failing to timely pay the penalty (Code Sec. 5000A(g)(2)(A), as added by PPACA).

- Collection—The IRS cannot use liens or levies to collect any unpaid penalty (Code Sec. 5000A(g)(2)(B), as added by PPACA).

    Comment: Every person who provides minimum essential coverage to an individual during the calendar year must file information returns with the IRS reporting such coverage. In addition, the IRS is required to send a written notification to each individual who files an individual tax return and who is not enrolled in minimum essential coverage of the services available through their State Exchanges. For discussion of these reporting requirements, see ¶410.

Amount of penalty. The penalty is equal to the lesser of:

- the sum of the monthly penalty amounts for the tax year, or

- the amount of the national average premium for qualified health plans that: (i) offer a bronze-level of coverage through an Exchange; (ii) provide coverage for families the size of the taxpayer's family; and (iii) are offered through Exchanges for plan years beginning in the calendar year with or within which the tax year ends (Code Sec. 5000A(c)(1), as added and amended by PPACA). For a discussion of the required contents of an essential benefits coverage and the different levels of coverage, see ¶530.

The *monthly penalty* with respect to any taxpayer who fails to have minimum essential coverage is equal to $1/12$ of the greater of:

- the flat dollar amount, which is equal to the applicable dollar amount for each of the individuals who were not properly insured by the taxpayer, up to a maximum of 300 percent of the applicable dollar amount, or

- the applicable percentage of income (Code Sec. 5000A(c)(2), as added and amended by PPACA). These terms are all defined below.

The *flat dollar amount* is the sum of the applicable dollar amounts for each of the applicable individuals who lack minimum essential coverage, and whom the taxpayer is required to insure (that is, the taxpayer, the taxpayer's spouse on a joint return, and the taxpayer's dependents). However, the flat dollar amount cannot

¶205

NEW LAW EXPLAINED

exceed 300 percent of the applicable dollar amount (Code Sec. 5000A(c)(2)(A), as added and amended by PPACA).

Key Rates and Figures: The *applicable dollar amount* is generally $695 (Code Sec. 5000A(c)(3)(A), as added by PPACA and amended by the 2010 Reconciliation Act), phased in and adjusted as follows:

— For 2014, the applicable dollar amount is $95 (Code Sec. 5000A(c)(3)(B), as added and amended by PPACA).

— For 2015, the applicable dollar amount is $325 (Code Sec. 5000A(c)(3)(B), as added and amended PPACA and amended by the 2010 Reconciliation Act).

— For 2016, the applicable dollar amount is $695 (Code Sec. 5000A(c)(3)(A), as added by PPACA and amended by the 2010 Reconciliation Act).

— For calendar years beginning after 2016, the $695 applicable dollar amount is increased for inflation, with each adjustment rounded down to the lowest multiple of $50 (Code Sec. 5000A(c)(3)(D), as added by PPACA and amended by the 2010 Reconciliation Act).

— The applicable dollar amount is halved for any month in which the applicable individual is under the age of 18 at the beginning of the month (Code Sec. 5000A(c)(3)(C), as added by PPACA). However, this adjustment is ignored for purposes of the rule that limits the flat dollar amount to 300 percent of the applicable dollar amount (Code Sec. 5000A(c)(2), as added and amended by PPACA).

The *percentage of income* is an amount equal to the following percentage of the excess of the taxpayer's household income (as defined below) over the taxpayer's filing threshold for the tax year:

— 1.0 percent for tax years beginning in 2014;

— 2.0 percent for tax years beginning in 2015, and

— 2.5 percent for tax years beginning after 2015 (Code Sec. 5000A(c)(2)(B), as added and amended by PPACA, and amended by the 2010 Reconciliation Act).

Example 3: The Johnsons are married and file a joint return for 2014. They are applicable individuals who are not exempt from the penalty for failure to maintain minimum essential coverage. Their household income is $45,000, and their filing threshold is $23,900. They and their four dependents are all uninsured for the entire calendar year. One dependent is an adult, and the other three are under the age of 18 for the entire year. The Johnsons' shared responsibility payment is calculated as follows:

• They are jointly and severally liable for the penalty for themselves and their four uninsured dependents.

• For purposes of the flat dollar penalty, the applicable dollar amount for 2014 is $95. This amount is halved for applicable individuals under the age of 18.

¶205

NEW LAW EXPLAINED

> Thus, the Johnsons' total penalty would be $427.50 ($95 for each of the three adults, and $47.50 for each of the three children). However, the flat dollar amount is limited to 300 percent of the applicable dollar amount, with no adjustment for individuals under 18. Thus, the Johnsons' flat dollar penalty is $285 ($95 ×3).
>
> - The Johnsons' household income exceeds their filing threshold by $21,100 ($45,000 − $23,900). Thus, their percentage of income penalty is $211 (1.0 percent of $21,100).
>
> - The Johnsons' actual penalty is the lesser of (i) their monthly penalty amount, which is $285 (the greater of $285 or $211) or (ii) the average national annual premium for qualified health plans that offer bronze-level of coverage for a family of six through an Exchange. They must include the penalty amount with their 2014 return.

Comment: The more rapid increase in the applicable dollar penalties over the percentage-of-income penalties will also increase the disparity between the two amounts. For instance, assume the same facts above except it is 2016, when the applicable dollar amount is $695, the Johnsons' initial penalty would be $3,127.50; their flat dollar amount would be $2,085 (300 percent of $695); and their percentage-of-income penalty would be $527.50. Thus, their monthly penalty amounts would be $2,085.

Minimum essential coverage. For purposes of the penalty, minimum essential coverage is coverage under any of the following (Code Sec. 5000A(f)(1), as added by PPACA).

- Government sponsored program—This includes Medicare, Medicaid, the Children's Health Insurance Program (CHIP), TRICARE for Life, the veteran's health care program, or the health plan for Peace Corps volunteers.

- Eligible employer-sponsored plan—This is a group health plan or group health insurance coverage offered by an employer to the employee through the small or large group market within a State (including grandfathered health plans, or a governmental plan (plans for employees of governments, certain international organizations, Indian tribes, or railroad employee) (Code Sec. 5000A(f)(2), as added by PPACA). A *group market* is the health insurance market under which individuals obtain health insurance coverage, directly or through an arrangement, on behalf of themselves and their dependents through a group health plan maintained by an employer (Act Sec. 1302(a)(1) of PPACA). The large group market comprises health plans maintained by large employers (generally those with more than 100 employees), while the small group market comprises health plans maintained by small employers (generally those with no more than 100 employees; however, each State can elect to reduce this 100-employee threshold to 50 employees) (Act Sec. 1302(a)(3) and (b) of PPACA).

- Individual market plan—The individual market is the market for health insurance coverage offered to individuals other than in connection with a group health plan (Act Sec. 1304(a)(2) of PPACA).

NEW LAW EXPLAINED

- Grandfathered plan—A grandfathered plan is basically a group health plan or health insurance coverage that is in effect on March 23, 2010, the date of enactment of the Patient Protection Act (Act Sec. 1251 of PPACA). For a discussion of grandfathered plans, see ¶535.

- Other coverage—Other health coverage can include plans or programs, such as a State health benefit risk pool, that the Secretary of Health and Human Services, in coordination with the Treasury Secretary, recognizes for this purpose.

  Comment: This definition of "minimum essential coverage" is used for several other provisions of the Patient Protection Act including determining an individual's qualification for a refundable health insurance premium assistance credit (see ¶210).

Minimum essential coverage does not include health insurance coverage that consists of excepted benefits (Code Sec. 5000A(f)(3), as added by PPACA). For this purpose, excepted benefits generally means coverage:

- only for accident or disability income insurance, or any combination thereof;
- liability insurance, including general liability insurance and automobile liability insurance, and coverage issued as a supplement to liability insurance;
- workers' compensation or similar insurance;
- automobile medical payment insurance;
- credit-only insurance;
- coverage for on-site medical clinics; or
- other similar insurance coverage, specified in regulations, under which benefits for medical care are secondary or incidental to other insurance benefits.

If benefits are provided under a separate policy, certificate or insurance contract, then excepted benefits also include:

- limited scope dental or vision benefits, benefits for long-term care, nursing home care, home health care, community-based care, or any combination thereof, and other similar, limited benefits as specified in regulations;
- coverage only for a specified disease or illness;
- hospital indemnity or other fixed indemnity insurance; and
- Medicare supplemental health insurance, coverage supplemental to the medical and dental coverage provided to the military under chapter 55 of title 10, and similar supplemental coverage provided to coverage under a group health plan (Sec. 2791 of the Public Health Service Act).

  Comment: A large employer that does not offer its employees minimum essential coverage may be liable for its own shared responsibility payment (Code Sec. 4980H, as added and amended by PPACA, and amended by the 2010 Reconciliation Act). See ¶305.

Exceptions—filing threshold and unaffordable coverage. As mentioned above, the penalty for failure to maintain minimum essential coverage does not apply to applicable individuals whose household incomes are below their filing thresholds, or

NEW LAW EXPLAINED

who cannot afford coverage (Code Sec. 5000A(e), as added and amended by PPACA, and by the 2010 Reconciliation Act). Both exceptions are dependent on determining the applicable individual's household income.

Generally, *household income* is the sum of the taxpayer's modified adjusted gross income (AGI), plus the modified AGI of all other individuals who are taken into account in determining the taxpayer's family size and were required to file an income tax return for the tax year (Code Sec. 5000A(c)(4), as added by PPACA and amended by 2010 Reconciliation Act). An applicable individual's *family size* is equal to the number of personal exemptions the taxpayer is allowed for the tax year. Thus, household income is the aggregate modified AGI of the taxpayer (and spouse, if the couple files a joint return) plus the modified AGI of the taxpayer's dependents whose taxable incomes exceed their applicable filing thresholds for the tax year (including children subject to the "kiddie tax" whose unearned income was not reported on the parent's return).

> **Comment:** Modified AGI for this purposes is the taxpayer's AGI increased by any tax-exempt interest the taxpayer receives or accrues during the tax year, plus any excluded foreign earned income or housing costs excluded under Code Sec. 911.

Filing threshold—The penalty does not apply to an applicable individual for any month in a calendar year if the individual's household income for that year is less than the amount of gross income the taxpayer must have in order to be required to file a return (Code Sec. 5000A(e)(2), as added by PPACA and amended by 2010 Reconciliation Act).

> **Comment:** The filing threshold depends on the taxpayer's filing status and is adjusted each year for inflation. Note that this exception compares the aggregate *modified AGI* of all the members of the taxpayer's *household* to a filing threshold based on an *individual* taxpayer's *gross income* (or a married couple's combined income on a joint return).

Unaffordable coverage—The penalty does not apply to individuals for months in which they cannot afford coverage (Code Sec. 5000A(e)(1)(A), as added by PPACA). Coverage is unaffordable for a month if the applicable individual's required contribution (determined on an annual basis) for that month exceeds eight percent of the individual's household income for the tax year. In other words, an individual who spends eight percent or less of household income for health insurance is exempt from the penalty.

> **Caution:** For purposes of the unaffordable coverage exception, the definition of "household income" is modified in two respects. First, it is household income for the most recent tax year for which the government determines information is available. Second, it is increased by any portion of the required contribution made through a salary reduction agreement and excluded from the individual's gross income (for instance, health insurance premiums paid through a cafeteria plan).

> **Comment:** For plan years beginning after 2014, the eight-percent-of-household-income limit is replaced by the percentage that the Secretary of HHS determines

NEW LAW EXPLAINED

reflects the excess of the rate of premium growth between the preceding calendar year and 2013, over the rate of income growth for that period (Code Sec. 5000A(e)(1)(D), as added by PPACA).

The *required contribution* depends on where the applicable individual can get insurance.

- If the individual is eligible to purchase minimum essential coverage through an eligible-employer sponsored plan, the required contribution is the portion of the annual premium that the individual would pay, through salary reduction or otherwise, for self-only coverage (Code Sec. 5000A(e)(1)(B)(i), as added by PPACA).

- Otherwise, the required contribution is (i) the annual premium for the lowest cost bronze plan available in the individual market through the State Exchange in the rating area in which the individual resides (see ¶530), regardless of whether the individual actually purchases a qualified health plan through the Exchange, (ii) reduced by the individual's premium assistance credit for the tax year (see ¶210), determined as if the individual was covered by a qualified health plan offered through the Exchange for the entire tax year (Code Sec. 5000A(e)(1)(B)(ii), as added by PPACA).

If an applicable individual is eligible for employer coverage because of a relationship to an employee, affordability is determined by reference to the required contribution of that employee (Code Sec. 5000A(e)(1)(C), as added and amended by PPACA). For instance, if a child is eligible for minimum essential coverage through a noncustodial parent's employer, affordability is determined by reference to the noncustodial parent, even though the custodial parent probably claims the child's dependency exemption and, therefore, is liable for the penalty with respect to the child.

> **Comment:** If self-only coverage is affordable to an employee, but family coverage is unaffordable, the employee is subject to the penalty if the employee does not maintain minimum essential coverage. However, since family coverage is unaffordable, any individual eligible for employer coverage due to a relationship with the employee is exempt from the penalty (Joint Committee on Taxation, *Technical Explanation of the Revenue Provisions of the "Reconciliation Act of 2010," as amended, in combination with the "Patient Protection and Affordable Care Act"* JCX-18-10, March 21, 2010).

> **Caution:** Note that the individual mandate uses eight percent of household income as the ceiling for affordable coverage, while a taxpayer might have to spend 9.5 percent of household income on premiums before qualifying for the premium assistance credit (see ¶210).

> **Example 4:** Ellen's household income is 315 percent of the federal poverty line; thus, she must spend 9.5 percent of her household income on health plan premiums before she can qualify for the premium credit. Her employer offers Ellen self-only coverage that would cost her five percent of her household income, and family coverage that would cost her 10 percent of her household

NEW LAW EXPLAINED

income. She is not eligible for the premium credit because self-only coverage costs less than 9.5 percent of her household income. She is subject to the individual responsibility penalty, because the self-only plan costs less than eight percent of her household income. Although family coverage costs more than 9.5 percent of income, Ellen's family does not qualify for a tax credit regardless of whether Ellen does or does not purchase self-only coverage through her employer. However, her family is exempt from the individual mandate penalty because self-only coverage is affordable to Ellen, but the family coverage is not considered affordable (Joint Committee on Taxation, *Technical Explanation of the Revenue Provisions of the "Reconciliation Act of 2010," as amended, in combination with the "Patient Protection and Affordable Care Act"* (JCX-18-10), March 21, 2010).

Comment: The Patient Protection Act notes that the poorer health and shorter life spans suffered by uninsured Americans cost the economy up to $207 billion per year, providing health care to the uninsured cost $43 billion in 2008, and medical expenses are a factor in 62 percent of personal bankruptcies. Congress believes that the individual mandate to purchase health insurance will add millions of new consumers to the health insurance market, and achieve near-universal insurance coverage by building upon and strengthening the employer-based health insurance system. This is supposed to increase the supply of and demand for health care services, provide greater financial security for families, minimize adverse selection and broaden the insurance risk pool to include healthy individuals, which will lower health insurance premiums and reduce the administrative costs for private health insurance from their current rate of 26 -30 percent of premiums in the individual and small group market (Act Sec. 1501(a) of PPACA, as amended).

▶ **Effective date.** The addition of Code Sec. 5000A applies to tax years ending after December 31, 2013 (Act Sec. 1501(d) of the Patient Protection and Affordable Care Act (PPACA) (P.L. 111-148)). The amendments to Code Sec. 5000A(b)(1), (c), (d)(2)(A) and(e)(1)(C) are effective on March 23, 2010, the date of enactment of PPACA. The amendments to Code Sec. 5000A(c)(2)(B), (c)(3), (c)(4) and (e)(2) are effective on March 30, 2010, the date of enactment of the Health Care and Education Reconciliation Act of 2010 (P.L. 111-152).

Law source: Law at ¶5235 and ¶7009. Committee Report at ¶10,080.

— Act Secs. 1501(b), 10106(b), 10106(c), and 10106(d) of the Patient Protection and Affordable Care Act (PPACA) (P.L. 111-148), adding and amending Code Sec. 5000A;

— Act Sec. 1002(a) of the Health Care and Education Reconciliation Act of 2010 (P.L. 111-152), amending Code Sec. 5000A(c)(2)(B) and (c)(3);

— Act Sec. 1002(b) of 2010 Reconciliation Act, striking Code Sec. 5000A(c)(4)(D), and amending Code Sec. 5000A(e)(2);

— Act Sec. 1004(a) of 2010 Reconciliation Act , amending Code Sec. 5000A(c)(4).

— Act Sec. 1501(d) of PPACA, providing the effective date.

NEW LAW EXPLAINED

Reporter references: For further information, consult the following CCH reporters.

— Tax Research Consultant, FILEIND: 15,052.25

— Practical Tax Explanation, § 1,025

¶210 Health Insurance Premium Assistance Refundable Credit

SUMMARY OF NEW LAW

Beginning in 2014, taxpayers with household income between 100 percent and 400 percent of the federal poverty line can (FPL) qualify for a refundable health insurance premium assistance credit.

BACKGROUND

The Internal Revenue Code provides only three possible tax benefits for taxpayers who pay health insurance premiums. First, individual taxpayers can claim an itemized deduction for medical expenses they pay for themselves, their spouses, and their dependents, to the extent those expenses exceed a certain percentage of their adjusted gross income (AGI) and are not compensated by insurance or otherwise (Code Sec. 213). Deductible expenses include premiums paid for medical insurance. For a discussion of the AGI threshold for claiming itemized deductions of medical expenses, see ¶215.

Second, in calculating their AGI, self-employed individuals can deduct 100 percent of amounts paid for health insurance for themselves, their spouses, and their dependents (Code Sec. 162(l)). The deductible amount is limited to the taxpayer's earned income, which is generally the individual's net earnings from self-employment with respect to a trade or business. No deduction is permitted if the self-employed person is eligible to participate in any subsidized employer-sponsored health plan. Deductible amounts may not be treated as medical expenses for purposes of the AGI threshold for medical expense deductions. For a discussion of who may be claimed as a dependent in deducting health insurance premiums by a self-employed individual, see ¶242.

Finally, eligible individuals are allowed a refundable tax credit equal to 65 percent of the amount paid during eligible coverage months for qualifying health insurance coverage for themselves and their qualifying family members (Code Sec. 35(a)). The credit is increased to 80 percent of the amount paid in the case of eligible coverage months beginning on or after May 1, 2009, and before January 1, 2011 (Code Sec. 35(a), as amended by the TAA Health Coverage Improvement Act of 2009 (P.L.111-5)). The credit, which is referred to as the Health Coverage Tax Credit (HCTC), is available only to individuals receiving trade adjustment assistance (TAA) and retirees age 55 or older receiving benefits from the Pension and Benefit Guaran-

BACKGROUND

tee Corporation (PBGC). Trade adjustment assistance (TAA) is generally paid to workers who become unemployed due to increases in imports, especially imports from Mexico and Canada, or because of a shift of production to Mexico or Canada. The credit is not available to unemployed individuals paying for health insurance under COBRA who do not fall within one of these two narrow categories. The HCTC credit amount is not taken into account in determining any deduction for medical insurance premiums under Code Secs. 213 or 162(l).

NEW LAW EXPLAINED

Refundable health insurance premium assistance credit created.—Effective for tax years ending after December 31, 2013, certain individuals who purchase qualified health care coverage through an American Health Benefit Exchange are entitled to a refundable income tax credit equal to the premium assistance credit amount (Code Sec. 36B(a), as added by the Patient Protection and Affordable Care Act (PPACA) (P.L. 111-148)).

> **Comment:** By January 1, 2014, each State must establish an American Health Benefit Exchange and Small Business Health Options Program (SHOP Exchange) to provide qualified individuals and qualified small business employers access to qualified health plans. For a discussion of the establishment and requirements of the Exchanges, see ¶505. The Exchanges will have four levels of essential benefits coverage available to participants at either a "bronze," "silver," "gold," or "platinum" level. The bronze level plans must provide benefits that are actuarially equivalent to 60 percent of the full actuarial value of the benefits provided under the plan. The percentage increases to 70 percent for silver level plans, 80 percent for gold level plans, and 90 percent for platinum level plans. For a discussion of the required contents of an essential benefits coverage, see ¶530.

> For those purchasing coverage within an Exchange, the refundable premium assistance credit can limit the out-of-pocket expense for silver level health plans (Code Sec. 36B(a) and (b)(3)(B), as added by PPACA). For example, some taxpayers can have the credit paid in advance directly to the insurer, to reduce a taxpayer's out-of-pocket premium cost. For a discussion of the advance payment of the premium credit, see ¶525. Taxpayers who purchase silver-level coverage may also qualify for cost-sharing subsidies to help pay for deductibles, copayments, etc. For a discussion of the cost-sharing subsidy rules, see ¶520. Eligibility for these benefits is limited to qualified individual who enroll in qualified plans (discussed below).

Eligibility for premium credit. A taxpayer must satisfy the following criteria to be eligible for the premium assistance credit:

(1) The taxpayer must be a qualified individual, which means an individual seeking to enroll in a qualified health plan in the individual market offered through an Exchange, and residing in the State that established the Exchange (Act Sec. 1312(f)(1)(A) of PPACA). For a discussion of the requirements to be a qualified

NEW LAW EXPLAINED

individual eligible to enroll in a qualified health plan through an Exchange, see ¶510.

(a) An individual is not treated as a qualified individual if: (1) at the time of enrollment, the individual is incarcerated other than incarceration pending the disposition of charges; or (2) the individual is not a U.S. citizen or national or an alien lawfully present in the United States. An individual is treated as lawfully present if the individual is, and can reasonably be expected to be for the entire period of enrollment for which the premium assistance credit is being claimed, a citizen or national of the United States or an alien lawfully present in the United States (Code Sec. 36B(e)(2), as added by PPACA).

(b) A qualified health plan is a health plan that is certified as eligible to be offered via an Exchange. However, a catastrophic plan is not a qualified health plan for purposes of the premium assistance credit (Code Sec. 36B(c)(3)(A), as added by PPACA). For a discussion of the certification of qualified health plans by an Exchange, see ¶505. For a discussion of catastrophic plans that may be offered through an Exchange, see ¶530.

(2) The taxpayer's household income must be at least 100 percent, but not more than 400 percent, of the federal poverty line (FPL) for a family of the size involved (Code Sec. 36B(c)(1)(A), as added and amended by PPACA).

(a) An alien lawfully present in the United States, but ineligible for Medicaid (Medicaid requires five year residency for lawful aliens), who has household income not greater than 100 percent of the FPL for a family of the size involved is eligible for the premium assistance credit and will be treated as having a household income equal to 100 percent of the FPL for a family of the size involved (Code Sec. 36B(c)(1)(B), as added by PPACA).

(b) For purposes of determining what percentage a taxpayer's household income bears to the FPL for a family of the size involved, if any individual for whom the taxpayer can claim a personal exemption is an undocumented alien (including the taxpayer or spouse), the undocumented alien is not counted in family size. The taxpayer's household income is equal to the product of the taxpayer's household income and a fraction, with the numerator being the FPL for the taxpayer's family size excluding the undocumented alien, and the denominator being the FPL for the taxpayer's family size including the undocumented alien. A comparable method yielding the same result may be used to determine what percentage a taxpayer's household income bears to the FPL (Code Sec. 36B(e)(1)(B), as added by PPACA).

(c) The term poverty line has the meaning given that term in section 2110(c)(5) of the Social Security Act, which is the official poverty line defined by the Office of Management and Budget based on the most recent data available from the Bureau of the Census (Code Sec. 36B(d)(3)(A), as added by PPACA). The Secretary of Health and Human Services will annually, or at any shorter interval determined feasible and advisable, revise the poverty line. The poverty line used for the premium assistance credit is the most

¶210

NEW LAW EXPLAINED

recently published poverty line as of the first day of the regular enrollment period for a qualified health plan offered through an Exchange during the calendar year (Code Sec. 36B(d)(3)(B), as added by PPACA).

(3) Taxpayers who are married at the end of the tax year must file a joint return Code Sec. 36B(c)(1)(C), as added by PPACA).

(4) An individual who can be claimed as another taxpayer's dependent is not eligible for the premium assistance credit (Code Sec. 36B(c)(1)(D), as added by PPACA).

Calculation of income for determining premium credit eligibility. Family size is the number of individuals for whom the taxpayer is allowed a personal exemption for the tax year (Code Sec. 36B(d)(1), as added by PPACA).

> **Comment:** An undocumented alien is not counted in family size for purposes of determining what percentage a taxpayer's household income bears to the FPL (Code Sec. 36B(e)(1)(B), as added by PPACA).

Household income includes the modified adjusted gross income (AGI) of the taxpayer and all individuals for whom the taxpayer can claim a personal exemption and who must file a tax return for the tax year (Code Sec. 36B(d)(2)(A), as added by PPACA, and amended by the Health Care and Education Reconciliation Act of 2010 (P.L. 111-152)). Modified AGI means the taxpayer's AGI increased by any amount of foreign earned income and foreign housing expenses excluded from gross income under Code Sec. 911, and any amount of tax exempt interest (Code Sec. 36B(d)(2)(B), as added by PPACA and amended by the 2010 Reconciliation Act).

> **Comment:** If an undocumented alien is a member of the taxpayer's household, the taxpayer's household income is equal to the product of the taxpayer's household income and a fraction, with the numerator being the FPL for the taxpayer's family size excluding the undocumented alien, and the denominator being the FPL for the taxpayer's family size including the undocumented alien (Code Sec. 36B(e)(1)(B), as added by PPACA).

The Secretary of Health and Human Services (HHS), in consultation with the IRS, will provide rules for calculating family size and household income that will be least burdensome to individuals who enroll in qualified health plans through an Exchange and are, therefore, eligible for the premium assistance credit (Code Sec. 36B(e)(3), as added by PPACA). For a discussion of the general procedures that will be established by the HHS for determining eligibility for premium tax credits, including a taxpayer's household income, family size, and citizenship/immigration status, see ¶515.

Calculation of premium credit. The *premium assistance credit amount* for any tax year is the sum of the premium assistance amounts for all of the taxpayer's coverage months during the tax year (Code Sec. 36B(b)(1), as added by PPACA).

> **Comment:** The premium assistance credit operates on a sliding scale that begins at two percent of income for taxpayers at 100 percent of the FPL and phases out at 9.5 percent of income for those at 300-400 percent of the FPL. For instance, if the credit were in effect for 2010, the premium for the second lowest cost silver health plan for family coverage would be $11,500, and if a family of four had household income of $88,000 (approximately 400 percent of the current FPL), the

¶210

NEW LAW EXPLAINED

credit would be $3,140 ($11,500 - $8,360 ($88,000 x .095)) since the taxpayer would be expected to pay 9.5 percent of income, or $8,360, for health insurance premiums. In contrast, if the family's household income was $29,000 (approximately 133 percent of the current FPL), the credit would be $10,920 ($11,500 - $580 ($29,000 x .02)) because the taxpayer would be expected to pay only two percent of income, or $580, for health insurance premiums.

There is a cliff effect to the sliding scale which perhaps is best illustrated by the fact that an extra dollar of income could make a taxpayer ineligible for Medicaid (no premium cost) and required to pay two percent of income for health insurance premiums. Similarly, an extra dollar of income could move the taxpayer to the next highest percentage. For example, a family with income at 133 percent of FPL would be required to pay two percent of income for health insurance premiums, but at income of 133.01 percent of FPL, the percentage would jump to three percent.

The *premium assistance amount* for any coverage month is the lesser of:

- the monthly premium for the month for one or more qualified health plans offered in the individual market Exchange within a State covering the taxpayer, the taxpayer's spouse, or any dependent of the taxpayer who is enrolled through an Exchange established by the State, *or*

- the excess, if any, of the *adjusted monthly premium* for that month for the *applicable second lowest cost silver plan* with respect to the taxpayer over an amount equal to 1/12th of the product of the *applicable percentage* and the taxpayer's household income for the tax year (Code Sec. 36B(b)(2), as added by PPACA).

The term *coverage month* means any month in which the taxpayer, the taxpayer's spouse, or any dependent is covered by a qualified health plan enrolled in through an Exchange and the premium is paid by the taxpayer or through advance payment of the premium assistance credit (Code Sec. 36B(c)(2)(A), as added by PPACA). The term coverage month does not include any month that the individual is eligible for minimum essential coverage outside the individual market (Code Sec. 36B(c)(2)(B)(i), as added by PPACA). For this purpose, minimum essential coverage includes coverage which would not subject to the taxpayer to a penalty for failing to have such coverage other than coverage through the Exchange (i.e., government-sponsored coverage, employer-sponsored coverage, grandfathered plans etc.) (Code Secs. 36B(c)(2)(B), (c)(3)(B) and 5000A(f)(1), as added by PPACA). For discussion of what constitutes minimum essential coverage, see ¶205. For a discussion of grandfathered health plans, see ¶535.

However, for purposes of the premium assistance credit, an employee is not considered eligible for minimum essential coverage under an employer-sponsored plan, including a grandfathered health plan, if the employee's required contribution would exceed 9.5 percent of the employee's household income. This rule also applies to any individual who would be eligible to enroll in an employer-sponsored plan by reason of relationship to the employee (Code Sec. 36B(c)(2)(C)(i), as added by PPACA and amended by the 2010 Reconciliation Act). In addition, an employer-sponsored plan that provides less than 60 percent coverage for total allowed costs does not provide

NEW LAW EXPLAINED

minimum essential coverage because it does not provide minimum value (Code Sec. 36B(c)(2)(C)(ii), as added by PPACA).

Neither of these exceptions apply if the employee, or any individual eligible for an employer-sponsored plan by reason of relationship to the employee, is covered by the employer-sponsored or grandfathered plan (Code Sec. 36B(c)(2)(C)(iii), as added by PPACA). After 2014, the employee's contribution limit of 9.5 percent is subject to adjustment to reflect the excess of premium growth over income growth for the preceding calendar year (Code Sec. 36B(c)(2)(C)(iv), as added and amended by PPACA, and amended by the 2010 Reconciliation Act; Code Sec. 36B(b)(3)(A)(ii), as added and amended by PPAC, and amended by the 2010 Reconciliation Act). After 2018, an additional adjustment involving the consumer price index rate of growth for the preceding calendar year may be required (Code Sec. 36B(b)(3)(A)(ii), as added and amended by PPACA, and amended by the 2010 Reconciliation Act).

The term coverage month also does not include any month that an individual has a Free Choice Voucher (Code Sec. 36B(c)(2)(D), as added by PPACA). Generally, Free Choice Vouchers must be provided to qualified employees by employers offering minimum essential coverage to employees through an eligible employer-sponsored plan for which the employer pays a portion of the plan costs (Act Sec. 10108(a) and (b) of PPACA). For this purposes, a qualified employee is any employee whose required contribution for minimum essential coverage through an employer-sponsored plan exceeds eight percent of the employee's household income for the tax year, but does not exceed 9.8 percent of his household income, whose household income is not greater that 400 percent of the FPL, and who does not participate in the employer-sponsored plan (Act Sec. 10108(c) of PPACA). For a discussion of Free Choice Vouchers, see ¶315.

> **Comment:** Presumably, Act Sec. 10108(c) of PPACA will be amended to reflect that an employee's required contribution for minimum essential coverage through an employer-sponsored plan will be limited to 9.5 percent of his household income in keeping with the amendment to Code Sec. 36B(b)(3)(A) made by the 2010 Reconciliation Act that sets the maximum premium percentage at 9.5 percent.

The *applicable second lowest cost silver plan* is the second lowest cost silver plan of the individual market Exchange in the rating area where the taxpayer resides that is offered through the same Exchange offering the qualified health plan providing: (1) self-only coverage for single taxpayers with no dependents or those who purchase self-only coverage; and (2) family coverage for all other taxpayers (Code Sec. 36B(b)(3)(B), as added by PPACA).

The *adjusted monthly premium* for an applicable second lowest cost silver plan is the monthly premium that would have been charged for the plan if each individual covered under a qualified health plan were covered by that silver plan, and the premium was adjusted only for the age of each individual pursuant to section 2701 of the Public Health Service Act (Code Sec. 36B(b)(3)(C), as added by PPACA). If any qualified health plan offers benefits beyond the essential health benefits that it must provide, the portion of the premium that is for the additional benefits is not taken into account in determining the monthly premium or the adjusted monthly premium

NEW LAW EXPLAINED

(Code Sec. 36B(b)(3)(D), as added by PPACA). If an individual enrolls in both a qualified health plan and a limited scope dental plan that provides pediatric dental benefits, however, the premium for the dental benefits is treated as a premium payable for a qualified health plan since pediatric dental benefits must be provided by a qualified health plan (Code Sec. 36B(b)(3)(E), as added by PPACA).

The *applicable percentage* is between 2.0 and 9.5 percent of a taxpayer's household income for any tax year with respect to a taxpayer whose household income is between 100 and 400 percent of the federal poverty line (FPL) for that tax year (Code Sec. 36B(b)(3)(A)(i), as added by PPACA, and amended by the 2010 Reconciliation Act). The applicable percentage for any taxpayer whose household income is within an income tier specified in the following table increases, on a sliding scale in a linear manner, from the initial premium percentage to the final premium percentage specified for that income tier.

Applicable Percentage
Effective on March 30, 2010

In the case of household income (expressed as a percent of poverty line) within the following income tier:	The initial premium percentage is—	The final premium percentage is—
Up to 133%	2.0%	2.0%
133% up to 150%	3.0%	4.0%
150% up to 200%	4.0%	6.3%
200% up to 250%	6.3%	8.05%
250% up to 300%	8.05%	9.5%
300% up to 400%	9.5%	9.5%

For tax years beginning after 2014, the initial and final applicable percentages, as in effect for the preceding calendar year, are subject to adjustment to reflect the excess of premium growth over income growth for the preceding calendar year. After 2018, an additional adjustment may be required to reflect any excess of the estimated premium growth over the consumer price index rate of growth for the preceding calendar year. However, the additional adjustment applies to a calendar year only if the aggregate amount of premium assistance credits and cost-sharing reductions under Act Sec. 1402 of the Patient Protection Act, exceeds 0.504 percent of the gross domestic product for the preceding calendar year (Code Sec. 36B(b)(3)(A)(ii), as added and amended by PPACA, and amended by the 2010 Reconciliation Act). For a discussion of the cost-sharing reductions (i.e., subsidies) that individuals who enroll in a qualified health plan at the silver coverage level in an Exchange may be eligible for, see ¶520.

If any individual for whom a taxpayer can claim a personal exemption is an undocumented alien (including the taxpayer or spouse), the aggregate amount of premiums taken into account for purposes of computing the premium assistance credit must be reduced by the portion of the premiums attributable to the undocumented alien (Code Sec. 36B(e)(1)(A), as added by PPACA).

¶210

NEW LAW EXPLAINED

> **Comment:** According to the Joint Committee on Taxation, an eligible individual enrolls in a health plan through an exchange and reports his or her income to the exchange. The premium assistance tax credit is based on that income and paid by the Treasury directly to the insurance plan in which the individual is enrolled (Joint Committee on Taxation, *Technical Explanation of the Revenue Provisions of the "Reconciliation Act of 2010," as amended, in combination with the "Patient Protection and Affordable Care Act"* (JCX-18-10), March 21, 2010). Presumably, this procedure precludes taxpayers from having to attempt the complex computation of the premium assistance credit.

Advance payment of credit. The premium assistance credit must be reduced, but not below zero, by the amount of any advance payment of the credit (Code Sec. 36B(f)(1), as added by PPACA).

> **Comment:** In order to reduce the premiums payable by individuals eligible for the premium assistance credit, the Patient Protection Act provides for advance determination of credit eligibility and advance payments of qualified health plan premiums by the Secretary of the Treasury to the health plan issuers. For a discussion of the advance payment of the premium assistance credit, see ¶ 525.

If the advance payments for a tax year exceed the premium assistance credit allowed, the excess is an increase to the tax imposed for the tax year (Code Sec. 36B(f)(2)(A), as added by PPACA). For any taxpayer whose household income is less than 400 percent of the FPL for the family size involved, the increase in tax is limited to $400 ($250 for unmarried taxpayers) (Code Sec. 36B(f)(2)(B)(i), as added by PPACA). The $400 and $250 limitations on the tax increase are subject to cost of living adjustments after 2014, rounded to the next lowest multiple of $50 if the adjustment is not a multiple of $50 (Code Sec. 36B(f)(2)(B)(ii), as added by PPACA).

> **Comment:** The amount of the premium assistance tax credit, or any refund resulting from the credit, is not includable in income for purposes of determining an individual's eligibility for benefits or assistance under any federal program or under any state or local program financed in whole or in part with federal funds (Act Sec. 1415(1) of PPACA). Furthermore, such credit or refund amounts are not taken into account as resources for the month of receipt and the following two months. Any advance payment of the credit is treated as made to the qualified health plan in which the individual is enrolled, and not to the individual (Act Sec. 1415(2) of PPACA).

Each Exchange must provide the following information to the Secretary of the Treasury and to the taxpayer with respect to any health plan provided through the Exchange:

- the level of coverage (bronze, silver, gold or platinum) provided to the taxpayer, and the period the coverage was in effect;

- the total premium for the coverage, excluding any applicable premium assistance tax credit or cost-sharing reductions;

- the aggregate amount of any advance payment of the premium assistance tax credit or cost-sharing reductions;

NEW LAW EXPLAINED

- the name, address, and taxpayer identification number (TIN) of the primary insured, and the name and TIN of each additional individual covered under the policy;

- any information provided to the Exchange, including any change of circumstances, necessary to determine eligibility for, and the amount of, the premium assistance tax credit; and

- information necessary to determine whether a taxpayer received any excess advance payments (Code Sec. 36B(f)(3), as added and amended by the 2010 Reconciliation Act).

    Comment: The purpose of the information requirement is to limit excess advance premium assistance credit payments that subject the taxpayer to an increase in tax. The requirement also extends to entities that the State contracts with to establish or help operate its Exchange (Code Sec. 36B(f)(3), as added and amended by the Amendment to the 2010 Reconciliation Act).

Guidance. The IRS is authorized to issue any necessary regulations to carry out the premium assistance credit rules, including coordination of the credit with the advance payment of the credit, and changes in taxpayer filing status after an advance payment determination is made (Code Sec. 36B(g), as added by PPACA).

Within five years after March 23, 2010, the Comptroller General must conduct a study on the affordability of health insurance coverage that includes:

(1) the impact of the Code Sec. 36B premium assistance credit and the small employers tax credit for employee health insurance expenses under Code Sec. 45R on maintaining and expanding health insurance coverage for individuals (for a discussion of the small employers tax credit underCode Sec. 45R , see ¶310);

(2) the availability of affordable health benefit plans, including whether 9.5 percent of household income is the appropriate level for determining whether employer-provided coverage is affordable for the employee; and

(3) the ability of individuals to maintain essential health benefit coverage (Act Sec. 1401(c) of PPACA).

The Comptroller General must submit a report on the study to the Committee on Ways and Means, the Committee on Education and Labor, and the Committee on Energy and Commerce of the House of Representatives, and the Committee on Finance and the Committee on Health, Education, Labor and Pensions of the Senate, and include any legislative recommendations (Act Sec. 1401(c) of PPACA).

No deduction is allowed for the portion of premiums paid by the taxpayer for coverage of one or more individuals under a qualified health plan that is equal to the premium assistance credit determined for the tax year (Code Sec. 280C(g), as added by PPACA).

▶ **Effective date.** Generally, the amendments made by this provision apply to tax years ending after December 31, 2013 (Act Secs. 1401(e) and 10108(h)(2) of the Patient Protection and Affordable Care Act (PPACA) (P.L. 111-148)). However, the amendments to Code Sec. 36B(b)(3)(A)(ii), (c)(1)(A), (c)(2)(C)(iv) and Code Sec. 6211(b)(4)(A) are effective

¶210

NEW LAW EXPLAINED

on March 23, 2010, the date of enactment of the Patient Protection Act. The amendments to Code Sec. 36B(b)(3)(A), (c)(2)(C), Code Sec. 36B(d)(2), and the addition of Code Sec. 36B(f)(3), are effective on March 30, 2010, the date of enactment of the Health Care and Education Reconciliation Act of 2010 (P.L. 111-152)).

Law source: Law at ¶5045, ¶5150, and ¶5275. Committee Report at ¶10,030 and ¶10,360.

— Act Secs. 1401(a), 10105(a), (b) and (c), and 10108(h)(1) of the Patient Protection and Affordable Care Act (PPACA) (P.L. 111-148), adding and amending Code Sec. 36B;

— Act Sec. 1401(b) adding Code Sec. 280C(g);

— Act Sec. 1401(c);

— Act Secs. 1401(d) and 10105(d) amending Code Sec. 6211(b)(4)(A) and 31 U.S.C. Sec. 1324(b)(2);

— Act Sec. 1001(a) of the Health Care and Education Reconciliation Act of 2010 (P.L. 111-152), amending Code Sec. 36B(b)(3)(A) and (c)(2)(C);

— Act Sec. 1004(a)(1)(A) and (a)(2)(A) of 2010 Reconciliation Act , amending Code Sec. 36B(d)(2);

— Act Sec. 1004(c), adding Code Sec. 36B(f)(3).

— Act Secs. 1401(e) and 10108(h)(2), providing the effective date.

Reporter references: For further information, consult the following CCH reporters.

— Tax Research Consultant, INDIV: 57,000

— Practical Tax Explanation, § 12,001

¶215 Itemized Deduction for Medical Expenses

SUMMARY OF NEW LAW

For tax years beginning after December 31, 2012, the threshold to claim an itemized deduction for unreimbursed medical expenses is increased from 7.5 percent of adjusted gross income (AGI) to 10 percent of AGI for regular income tax purposes.

BACKGROUND

An itemized deduction is allowed for unreimbursed expenses paid for the medical care of the taxpayer or the taxpayer's spouse or dependents (Code Sec. 213(a)). Expenses paid for medical care include amounts paid for the diagnosis, cure, mitigation, treatment, or prevention of disease, and for treatments affecting any part or function of the body (Code Sec. 213(d)). Only payments for legal medical services rendered by physicians, surgeons, dentists, and other medical practitioners qualify as medical expenses. Amounts paid for equipment, supplies, and diagnostic devices may be deductible if needed for medical care. Medical care expenses must be incurred primarily to alleviate or prevent a physical or mental defect or illness and do not include expenses that are merely beneficial to general health, such as vitamins or

BACKGROUND

a vacation. Medical expenses also include premiums paid for insurance that covers the expenses of medical care and amounts paid for transportation to get medical care. Amounts paid for long-term care services and limited amounts paid for any qualified long-term care insurance contract are medical expenses. The cost of medicine and drugs is deductible only for medicine and drugs that require a prescription, except for insulin.

For regular income tax purposes, individuals are allowed an itemized deduction for unreimbursed medical expenses, but only to the extent that the expenses exceed 7.5 percent of adjusted gross income (AGI) (Code Sec. 213(a)). This deduction is available both to insured and uninsured individuals. Thus, for example, an individual with employer-provided health insurance (or certain other forms of tax-subsidized health benefits) may claim the itemized deduction for the individual's medical expenses not covered by that insurance if the 7.5 percent AGI threshold is met. The medical deduction encompasses health insurance premiums to the extent that they have not been excluded from taxable income through the employer exclusion or self-insured deduction. For purposes of the alternative minimum tax (AMT), medical expenses are deductible only to the extent that they exceed 10 percent of AGI (Code Sec. 56(b)(1)(B)).

NEW LAW EXPLAINED

Medical expense deduction threshold increased.—The threshold to claim an itemized deduction for unreimbursed medical expenses is increased from 7.5 percent of adjusted gross income (AGI) to 10 percent of AGI for regular income tax purposes, for tax years beginning after December 31, 2012 (Code Sec. 213(a), as amended by the Patient Protection and Affordable Care Act (PPACA) (P.L. 111-148)).

> **Example:** Rich has adjusted gross income of $50,000 in 2012 and in 2013. His unreimbursed medical expenses are $5,000 for each year. In 2012, Rich can deduct $1,250 ($5,000 - $3,750 ($50,000 x 7.5 percent)) in medical expenses. In 2013, however, he cannot deduct any of his medical expenses ($5,000 - $5,000 ($50,000 x 10 percent)).

Taxpayers (or their spouses) who are age 65 and older before the close of the tax year are exempt from the increased threshold and continue to be eligible to claim the medical expense deduction if their medical expenses exceed 7.5 percent of AGI. This temporary waiver applies to tax years beginning after December 31, 2012, and ending before January 1, 2017 (Code Sec. 213(f), as added by PPACA).

The alternative minimum tax (AMT) treatment of the itemized deduction for medical expenses is not changed. Thus, medical expenses are deductible only to the extent that they exceed 10 percent of AGI, even if the taxpayer (or their spouse) is age 65 or older before the close of the tax year (Code Sec. 56(b)(1)(B), as amended by PPACA).

> **State Tax Consequences:** The increased threshold for the itemized deduction for unreimbursed medical expenses from 7.5 percent of AGI to 10 percent of AGI

NEW LAW EXPLAINED

for regular income tax purposes, will impact States that adopt federal itemized deductions but that do not conform by the time the increase takes effect. Such States may allow a subtraction from federal AGI for the difference between federal and State allowable medical expenses. States, like Indiana and Pennsylvania that do not allow itemized deductions or deductions for medical expenses or States like California, Minnesota, and Oregon that do not adopt Code Sec. 139A, will not be affected by the increase. The increase will also not affect States like Alabama, Arizona, and New Jersey that allow a deduction for medical expenses, but that do not adopt the federal threshold amount.

Practical Analysis: Vincent O'Brien, President of Vincent J. O'Brien, CPA, PC, Lynbrook, New York, observes that a growing number of taxpayers each year are subject to the alternative minimum tax. Such taxpayers are already subject to the 10-percent-of-adjusted-gross-income deduction threshold when computing their deductible medical expenses. As a result, this provision will have no effect on the federal tax liability for such taxpayers.

However, it may affect their state income tax liability, depending on where they reside and/or have income. Some states allow an itemized deduction for medical expenses on their state income tax returns that equals the deduction for medical expenses on federal Schedule A, *Itemized Deductions.*

Therefore, even if a taxpayer is subject to the alternative minimum tax for federal income tax purposes, the taxpayer's medical expenses for estate purposes may still have been determined using the amount listed on federal Schedule A that was computed with the 7.5-percent deduction threshold. When the deduction threshold is raised to 10 percent for regular tax purposes, this will also decrease the allowable medical expenses deductible for such taxpayers on their state returns.

Taxpayers that are not subject to the alternative minimum tax will now be subject to the higher (10 percent) deduction threshold for the first time. This makes planning medical expenses more important. While many medical expenses cannot (or should not) be timed for tax-deduction purposes, to the extent that taxpayers have discretion over when they incur and pay medical expenses, batching such expenses into one tax year makes it more likely that they will exceed the deduction threshold for that year. This is especially true when planning medical procedures that will occur around the end of a tax year.

In addition, if expenses for medical procedures that are performed during the tax year are charged to a credit card, the expenses are deductible in the current tax year, even if the credit card bill is paid in January (or later) during the following tax year.

▶ **Effective date.** The provision applies to tax years beginning after December 31, 2012 (Act Sec. 9013(d) of the Patient Protection and Affordable Care Act (PPACA) (P.L. 111-148)).

Law source: Law at ¶5080 and ¶5135. Committee Report at ¶10,280.

— Act Sec. 9013(a) of the Patient Protection and Affordable Care Act (PPACA) (P.L. 111-148), amending Code Sec. 213(a);

— Act Sec. 9013(b), adding Code Sec. 213(f);

NEW LAW EXPLAINED

— Act Sec. 9013(c), amending Code Sec. 56(b)(1)(B);

— Act Sec. 9013(d), providing the effective date.

Reporter references: For further information, consult the following CCH reporters.

— Standard Federal Tax Reporter, ¶12,543.01

— Tax Research Consultant, INDIV:42,300

— Practical Tax Explanation, §7201

¶220 Limitation of Distributions from Health Accounts for Over-the-Counter Medicines

SUMMARY OF NEW LAW

The cost incurred for a medicine or drug will be treated as a qualified medical expense for purposes of reimbursement through a health flexible spending arrangement (health FSA) or health reimbursement arrangement (HRA), as well as a distribution from a health savings account (HSA) or Archer medical savings accounts (MSA), *only* if the medicine is a prescribed drug or is insulin. Thus, the cost of over-the-counter medicines may not be reimbursed with excludible income, unless the medicine is prescribed by a physician.

BACKGROUND

Most employers provide group health coverage through accident and health plans for employees, including hospital, surgical, major medical, dental and disability protection. Premiums for such coverage may be paid by the employer, by the employee or partially by each. Generally, the amount of premiums paid by the employer is deductible by the employer. Amounts paid directly or indirectly to the employee to reimburse him for medical care expenses for himself, his spouse or dependents are excludable from the employee's gross income. (Code Sec. 105(b)). For this purpose, medical care has the same meaning as used for an individual to claim an itemized deduction for medical expenses and includes expenses paid for the diagnosis, cure, mitigation, treatment, or prevention of disease, and for treatments affecting any part or function of the body (Code Sec. 213(d)). It also includes the cost of medicine and drugs but if only if such medicine or drug is prescribed by a doctor or is insulin. Thus, amounts paid directly or indirectly to an employee through an employer-provided health plan for over-the-counter medicine may not be excluded from gross income of the employee.

However, reimbursements through a health flexible spending arrangement (FSA), health reimbursement arrangement (HRA), or other employer health plan for the cost of most nonprescription drugs are not included in gross income if properly substantiated by the employee. A health FSA or HRA is an employer-established benefit plan

BACKGROUND

that may be offered in conjunction with other employer-provided benefits as part of a cafeteria plan. The plans provide a reimbursement account or other arrangement under which an employee is reimbursed for qualified medical expenses that are not covered by insurance. FSAs are generally funded through voluntary salary reduction agreements between employees and their employers. Contributions to a Health FSA and all distributions to pay qualified medical expenses including over-the-counter medicine are excludable from income. Generally, amounts in the account at the end of the plan year cannot be carried over to the next year. However, the plan can provide for a grace period of up to 2-1/2 months after the end of the plan year. HRAs, on the other hand, must be funded solely through employer contributions. But like FSAs, distributions from an HRA paid to reimburse employees for qualified medical expenses including over-the-counter medicine may be excluded from the employee's gross income. Amounts that remain in an employee's HRA at the end of the year can generally be carried over to the next year.

Health savings accounts (HSAs) and Archer medical savings accounts (MSAs) provide tax-favored treatment for amounts that are contributed and used to pay the qualified medical expenses of the account beneficiary, his or her spouse, or dependent (Code Secs. 220 and 223). An HSA or Archer MSA account beneficiary is the person on whose behalf the account was established, who is covered under a high deductible health plan. Within limits, contributions are deductible from the account beneficiary's income and an employer's contributions on behalf of an employee (if any) are not wages includible in gross income. Distributions are excludable from gross income if they are made for qualified medical expenses. Generally, these are the same as medical expenses that can be claimed as an itemized deduction by an individual. However, nonprescription drugs may be considered qualified medical expenses and distributions for such items may be excluded from gross income. Distributions that are not for qualified medical expenses are included in gross income and subject to an additional penalty.

NEW LAW EXPLAINED

Distributions and reimbursements for medicines limited.—The definition of qualified medical expenses, for purposes of reimbursements from health flexible spending arrangements (health FSAs) or health reimbursement arrangements (HRAs), and distributions from health savings accounts (HSAs) or Archer medical savings accounts (Archer MSAs), has been modified to include amounts paid for medicine or a drug *only* if such medicine or drug is a prescribed drug (determined without regard to whether such drug is available without a prescription) or is insulin. Therefore, reimbursements for over-the-counter medicines through a health FSA, HRA, or other employer-provided accident or health plan under Code Sec. 105 may not be excluded from the employee's gross income (Code Sec. 106, as amended by the Patient Protection and Affordable Care Act (PPACA) (P.L. 111-148)). Also, distributions from a HSA or Archer MSA to pay for over-the-counter medicines may not be excluded from the employee's gross income and will be subject to the additional penalty (Code Secs. 220(d)(2)(A) and 223(d)(2), as

¶220

NEW LAW EXPLAINED

amended by PPACA). This modification conforms to the definition for purposes of the itemized deductions for medical expenses.

Comment: Beginning in 2011, the additional tax on distributions from a HSA or Archer MSA is 20 percent of the amount includible in income (see ¶225).

Practical Analysis: Pam Perdue, Of Counsel with Summers, Compton, Wells & Hamburg in St. Louis, Missouri, notes that when the IRS ruled in Rev. Rul. 2003-102 that Health FSAs could be drafted to allow for the reimbursement of certain over-the-counter medicines, it was at a time when one of the most widely used allergy medicines was being made available over the counter. The change to allow FSAs to reimburse over the counter medicines presented a cheaper alternative for those relying upon allergy or other medicines to treat chronic conditions. It meant that the employee had a tax-effective means to purchase the necessary medicines without the cost of a doctor's visit, and generally at a lower price.

Restricting coverage once again to medicines subject to a prescription means that the cheaper option no longer exists. This change, coupled with the lowering of the maximum FSA limit, will result in a significant erosion in the purchasing power of Health FSAs.

From the perspective of the employer, the fact that the change is effective with respect to expenses incurred after December 31, 2010, will mean that the employers will need to communicate the change to employees fairly quickly.

State Tax Consequences: The exclusion of over-the-counter medicines and drugs from qualified medical expenses for purposes of the rules on HSAs, Archer MSAs, health FSAs, and HRAs will not affect those States, like California and Alabama that do not recognize HSAs. Some States, such as Pennsylvania, that refer to qualified medical expenses under federal law, will be affected by this change unless/until the State updates its Code conformity date.

▶ **Effective date.** The provision regarding distributions from savings accounts applies to amounts paid with respect to tax years beginning after December 31, 2010. The provision regarding reimbursements for medicine restricted to prescribed drugs and insulin applies to expenses incurred in tax years beginning after December 31, 2010 (Act Sec. 9003(d) of the Patient Protection and Affordable Care Act (PPACA) (P.L. 111-148)).

Law source: Law at ¶5085, ¶5140, and ¶5145. Committee Report at ¶10,180.

— Act Sec. 9003(a) of the Patient Protection and Affordable Care Act (PPACA) (P.L. 111-148), amending Code Sec. 223(d)(2)(A);

— Act Sec. 9003(b), amending Code Sec. 220(d)(2)(A);

— Act Sec. 9003(c), adding Code Sec. 106(f);

— Act Sec. 9003(d), providing the effective date.

Reporter references: For further information, consult the following CCH reporters.

— Standard Federal Tax Reporter, ¶6702.032

— Tax Research Consultant, COMPEN:51,202

— Practical Tax Explanation, §7235

¶220

¶225 Additional Tax on HSA and Archer MSA Distributions

SUMMARY OF NEW LAW

The additional tax on distributions from health savings accounts (HSAs) and Archer medical savings accounts (MSAs) not used for qualified medical expenses is increased to 20 percent of the amount of the distribution included in gross income.

BACKGROUND

Health savings accounts (HSAs) and Archer medical savings accounts (MSAs) provide tax-favored treatment for amounts that are contributed and used to pay the qualified medical expenses of the account beneficiary, his or her spouse, or dependent (Code Secs. 220 and 223). An HSA or Archer MSA account beneficiary is the person on whose behalf the account was established, and who is covered under a high deductible health plan. Within limits, contributions by the beneficiary to his or her account may be deducted and an employer's contributions on behalf of an employee (if any) are not wages includible in gross income. Distributions are excludable from gross income if they are made for qualified medical expenses of the account beneficiary, his or her spouse or dependents. Distributions from an HSA that are not used for qualified medical expenses are included in beneficiary's gross income and subject to an additional penalty of 10 percent of the amount included in income unless made after the beneficiary's death, or disability. Distributions from an Archer MSA that are not used for qualified medical expenses are included in beneficiary's gross income and subject to an additional penalty of 15 percent of the amount included in income unless made after the beneficiary's death, or disability. For this purpose, a qualified medical expense has the same meaning as used for an individual to claim an itemized deduction for medical expenses. It includes expenses paid for the diagnosis, cure, mitigation, treatment, or prevention of disease, and for treatments affecting any part or function of the body (Code Sec. 213(d)).

> **Comment:** Effective for distributions from an HSA or Archer MSA after December 31, 2010, qualified medical expenses includes the cost of any medicine or drug *only* if it is prescribed by a physician or is insulin (see ¶220).

NEW LAW EXPLAINED

Additional tax on HSA and Archer MSA distributions not used for qualified medical expenses increased.—The additional tax on distributions made from HSAs not used for qualified medical expenses is increased from 10 percent to 20 percent of the amount includible in gross income (Code Sec. 223(f)(4)(A)), as amended by the Patient Protection and Affordable Care Act (PPACA) (P.L. 111-148). Similarly, the additional tax on distributions made from Archer MSAs not used for qualified medical

NEW LAW EXPLAINED

expenses is increased from 15 percent to 20 percent of the amount includible in gross income (Code Sec. 220(f)(4)(A), as amended by PPACA).

> **State Tax Consequences:** The increase in the tax imposed on nonqualified distributions from HSAs and Archer MSAs will not impact State taxation.

▶ **Effective date.** The provision applies to distributions made after December 31, 2010 (Act Sec. 9004(c) of the Patient Protection and Affordable Care Act (PPACA) (P.L. 111-148)).

Law source: Law at ¶5140 and ¶5145. Committee Report at ¶10,190.

— Act Sec. 9004(a) of the Patient Protection and Affordable Care Act (PPACA) (P.L. 111-148), amending Code Sec. 223(f)(4)(A);

— Act Sec. 9004(b), amending Code Sec. 220(f)(4)(A);

— Act Sec. 9004(c), providing the effective date.

Reporter references: For further information, consult the following CCH reporters.

— Standard Federal Tax Reporter, ¶12,675.03 and ¶12,785.037

— Tax Research Consultant, INDIV: 42,460.10 and PLANIND: 6,258.05

— Practical Tax Explanation, §20,530

¶230 Additional Medicare Tax on Wages and Self-Employment Income

SUMMARY OF NEW LAW

An additional 0.9 percent Medicare tax is imposed on the wages and self-employment income of certain high-income taxpayers received with respect to employment for tax years beginning after December 31, 2012.

BACKGROUND

The Federal Insurance Contributions Act (FICA), imposes two taxes on employers and employees. The first finances the federal old-age, survivors and disability insurance (OASDI) program, more commonly known as Social Security. The second is to finance hospital and hospital service insurance (HI) for those 65 years of age or older, more familiarly known as Medicare.

The employee's portion of the Social Security tax is 6.2 percent of the employee's wages, up to the Social Security wage base (Code Sec. 3101(a)). The employer's portion also equals 6.2 percent of the employee's wages, up to the Social Security wage base (Code Sec. 3111(a)). Thus, the equivalent of 12.4 percent of the employee's wages is contributed to the OASDI fund. The wage limit for the Social Security portion of the FICA tax is $106,800 for 2010 (Notice 2009-80, I.R.B. 2009-51, as corrected by Announcement 2009-92, I.R.B. 2009-52). The Medicare tax on an employee's wages also consists of an employee's portion and an employer's portion. The

BACKGROUND

employee's portion is 1.45 percent of the employee's wages (Code Sec. 3101(b)). The employer's portion of the Medicare tax also equals 1.45 percent of the employee's wages (Code Sec. 3111(b)). Thus, the equivalent of 2.9 percent of the employee's wages is contributed to Medicare.

Individuals engaged in trade or business as sole proprietors or partners must pay self-employment tax on net earnings from self-employment. Self-employment tax has two components. The OASDI component (Social Security) is imposed on net self-employment earnings up to the social security wage base. The HI component (Medicare) is imposed on net earnings from self-employment without limitation. The Social Security rate for 2010 is 12.4 percent of the first $106,800 of net earnings from self-employment (Code Sec. 1401(a); Notice 2009-80, as corrected by Announcement 2009-92). The Medicare rate is 2.90 percent of all net earnings from self-employment (Code Sec. 1401(b)). Thus, the combined self-employment tax rate is 15.3 percent (12.40 plus 2.90). A self-employed individual is permitted to deduct one-half of the self-employment tax liability for the year as a business expense in arriving at adjusted gross income (AGI) (Code Sec. 164(f)). Alternately, such individual is allowed to reduce self-employment income by an amount equal to one half of the combined self-employment tax rate, or 7.65 percent (1/2 of 15.3 percent) multiplied by the taxpayer's self-employment income (Code Sec. 1402(a)(12)).

NEW LAW EXPLAINED

Additional Medicare tax imposed on high-income taxpayers.—In addition to the 1.45 percent employee portion of the HI (Medicare) tax imposed on wages, a 0.9 percent Medicare tax is imposed on every taxpayer (other than a corporation, estate or trust) who receives wages with respect to employment during any tax year beginning after December 31, 2012, in excess of $200,000 ($250,000 in the case of a joint return, $125,000 in the case of a married taxpayer filing separately) (Code Sec. 3101(b)(2), as added and amended by the Patient Protection and Affordable Care Act (PPACA) (P.L. 111-148), and amended by the Health Care and Education Reconciliation Act of 2010 (P.L. 111-152)).

Comment: For this purpose, the term "employment" is as defined under Code Sec. 3121(b) and generally includes any service, of whatever nature, performed by an employee for the person employing him, irrespective of the citizenship or residence of either. The additional Medicare tax means that the portion of wages received in connection with employment in excess of $200,000 ($250,000 for joint filers, $125,000 in the case of married taxpayer filing separately) will, after the effective date, be subject to a 2.35 percent employee portion of the Medicare tax, or a total Medicare rate (employer and employee portions) of 3.8 percent.

Practice Pointer: Unlike the general 1.45 percent Medicare tax on wages, the additional 0.9 percent tax is on the combined wages of the employee and the employee's spouse, in the case of a joint return (Joint Committee on Taxation, *Technical Explanation of the Revenue Provisions of the "Reconciliation Act of 2010," as amended, in combination with the "Patient Protection and Affordable Care Act"* (JCX-18-10), March 21, 2010).

¶230

NEW LAW EXPLAINED

The obligation to withhold the additional Medicare tax is only imposed on an employer if the employee receives wages from the employer in excess of $200,000 (Code Sec. 3102(f)(1), as added by PPACA). The employer is permitted to disregard the amount of wages received by the taxpayer's spouse.

> **Example:** Employer Inc. employs Wally Worker. Wally receives $150,000 in wages from Employer. Wally also receives $60,000 in wages at a second job for a different employer. Wally's spouse, with whom Wally does not file a joint return, earns $100,000 in wages. Employer is not required to withhold the additional HI tax on Wally's wages because Wally does not receive more than $200,000 of wages from Employer.

If the additional HI tax is not withheld by the employer, the employee is responsible for paying such tax (Code Sec. 3102(f)(2), as added by PPACA). However, if an employer required to deduct and withhold the additional HI tax fails to do so, and the employee pays the additional tax, the employer will not be obligated for the additional HI tax but remains subject to penalties and additions to tax for failing to withhold (Code Sec. 3102(f)(3), as added by PPACA).

> **Comment:** The employee is personally liable for the additional 0.9 percent Medicare tax to the extent it is not withheld by the employer. This contrasts with the employee portion of the general Medicare tax of 1.45 percent of wages for which the employee generally has no direct liability (Joint Committee on Taxation, *Technical Explanation of the Revenue Provisions of the "Reconciliation Act of 2010", as amended, in combination with the "Patient Protection and Affordable Care Act"* (JCX-18-10), March 21, 2010).

Underpayment of estimated tax penalty. For purposes of applying the underpayment of estimated tax penalty under Code Sec. 6654, the additional 0.9 percent tax imposed on wages in excess of $200,000 ($250,000 in the case of a joint return, $125,000 in the case of a married taxpayer filing separately) is treated as a tax to which the penalty may apply (Code Sec. 6654(m), as added by 2010 Reconciliation Act).

Self-employed individuals. Taxpayers other than corporations, estates and trusts are also subject to a new 0.9 percent tax on self employment income in excess of $200,000 ($250,000 in the case of a joint return, $125,000 in the case of a married taxpayer filing separately) for tax years beginning after December 31, 2012 (Code Sec. 1401(b)(2)(A), as added by PPACA and amended by 2010 Reconciliation Act). To coordinate the additional tax with FICA, the $200,000/$250,0000 (joint return)/$1250,000 (married filing separately) figures are reduced, but not below zero, by the amount of the taxpayer's "wages taken into account in determining the tax imposed under section 3121(b)(2) . . . " (Code Sec. 1401(b)(2)(B), as added by PPACA and amended by 2010 Reconciliation Act).

> **Caution:** The text of the Patient Protection Act refers to Code Sec. 3121(b)(2), but it appears that this reference is intended to be to Code Sec. 3101(b)(2).

¶230

NEW LAW EXPLAINED

The one-half of self-employment taxes that are deductible under Code Sec. 164(f) does not include the additional Medicare tax (Code Sec. 164(f), as amended by PPACA). Similarly, taxpayers who alternately elect to reduce self-employment income by an amount equal to one half of the combined self-employment tax rate, pursuant to Code Sec. 1402(a)(12), do not include the additional Medicare tax in the rate used to make such computation (Code Sec. 1402(a)(12)(B), as added by PPACA).

> **Practical Analysis:** Pam Perdue, Of Counsel with Summers, Compton, Wells & Hamburg in St. Louis, Missouri, observes that the additional Medicare tax on high earners, coupled with the rollback of the Bush tax cuts, will likely send many small business owners scrambling for ways to avoid current income. This might include increased retirement plan savings and/or consideration of Subchapter S status.

> **Practical Analysis:** Vincent O'Brien, President of Vincent J. O'Brien, CPA, PC, Lynbrook, New York, observes that this change has far-reaching effects on tax planning and compliance issues for practitioners and taxpayers.
>
> Prior to this provision, the Medicare tax needed to be addressed on individual income tax returns only when a taxpayer had self-employment income from a sole proprietorship or from ownership interests in a partnership (or limited liability company that is taxed as a partnership). Now, the extra portion of the employee share of the Medicare tax may not always be withheld by a taxpayer's employer, and it will become necessary to plan for and compute this portion of the Medicare tax when preparing personal income tax returns for any individuals who have sufficient salary and wages, even if they do not have self-employment income.
>
> Since this tax will have to be paid as part of the Form 1040, practitioners will need to assist clients in monitoring the tax and adjusting their withholding and/or estimated tax payments accordingly. (In addition, the new 3.8-percent Medicare tax separately imposed on the unearned income of taxpayers who exceed applicable thresholds will also require similar planning and adjustments to the withholding and/or estimated tax payments of affected taxpayers.)
>
> The new provision also increases the importance of properly planning the form of business organization for the operation of trades or businesses. Payroll taxes (or self-employment taxes) have always been an important consideration in this planning process. Now, every dollar of income that is subject to the payroll (or self-employment) tax will be subject to an additional 0.9 percent of tax, to the extent that the taxpayer (and spouse, if applicable) exceeds the new threshold. Therefore, considerations related to the payroll or self-employment tax become even more critical.
>
> In many cases, choosing an S corporation through which to conduct a trade or business can result in minimizing payroll (or self-employment) taxes for the owner. Assuming that an owner materially participates in a business, after the S corporation owner is paid a reasonable salary, profit that is reported to the owner on Schedule K-1, *Shareholder's Share of Income, Deductions, Credits, etc.*, is subject to income

¶230

NEW LAW EXPLAINED

tax, but it is not subject to the self-employment tax. On the contrary, if the same trade or business were to be organized as a partnership (or limited liability company that is taxed as a partnership), the profit that is reported to the owner on Schedule K-1 is subject to income tax and to the self-employment tax as well.

Practical Analysis: Robert Keebler, a Partner with Baker Tilly Virchow, Krause & Company, LLP, Appleton, Wisconsin, notes that the 0.9-percent increase in the payroll tax is likely to encourage planners to create more S corporations than LLCs.

In the proper situation, taxable earnings for payroll taxes can be replaced with active S corporation income that will not be subject to this 0.9-percent tax.

This payroll tax increase will also encourage taxpayers to borrow inside entities generating interest deductions against business income.

For most taxpayers, very little planning is available; however, for very high income taxpayers, shifting wages to a return on an active investment will be the most viable planning available.

Practical Analysis: Michael Schlesinger, Partner in the law firm of Schlesinger & Sussman, New York, New York and Clifton, New Jersey, notes that a quick read of Congress's imposition of additional Medicare tax on wages and self-employment income clearly illustrates that it is a complex provision; however, if Congress does not change the law, any shareholder-employee of an S corporation can easily reduce its effect by taking distributions in excess of the threshold limits ($200,000 for single individuals; $250,000 for joint returns and $125,000 for marrieds filing separately). While shareholder-employees are required to take a reasonable salary, presently, there is no clear standard as to what this means. The IRS has suggested for the last couple of years that Congress pass a law for S corporations to eliminate this "tax planning device" and either put S corporation shareholders for self-employment tax in the same position as partners or close to it. But, despite IRS statistics detailing the abuse occurring, Congress has yet to act. It remains to be seen what will happen in the future.

Another troubling point is Code Sec. 3102(f)(2) holds the employee personally responsible if the employer fails to collect this additional tax. Hopefully this means that the employee will be liable only if the employer fails to withhold the tax, not if the employer withholds but does not remit.

▶ **Effective date.** The provision applies with respect to remuneration received, and tax years beginning, after December 31, 2012 (Act Secs. 9015(c) and 10906(c) of the Patient Protection and Affordable Care Act (PPACA) (P.L. 111-148) and Act Sec. 1402(b)(3) of the Health Care and Education Reconciliation Act of 2010 (P.L. 111-152).

Law source: Law at ¶5125, ¶5180, ¶5185, ¶5190, ¶5195, and ¶5227. Committee Report at ¶10,300.

¶230

NEW LAW EXPLAINED

— Act Secs. 9015(a)(1) and 10906(a) of the Patient Protection and Affordable Care Act (PPACA) (P.L. 111-148) amending and redesignating Code Sec. 3101(b) as Code Sec. 3101(b)(1), deleting Code Sec. 3101(b)(1)-(6), and adding and amending Code Sec. 3101(b)(2);

— Act Sec. 1402(b)(1)(A) of the Health Care and Education Reconciliation Act of 2010 (P.L. 111-152), amending Code Sec. 3101(b)(2), as added and amended by PPACA;

— Act Sec. 9015(a)(2) of PPACA adding Code Sec. 3102(f);

— Act Secs. 9015(b)(1) and 10906(b) of PPACA amending and redesignating Code Sec. 1401(b) as Code Sec. 1401(b)(1), and adding and amending Code Sec. 1401(b)(2);

— Act Sec. 1402(b)(1)(B) of the 2010 Reconciliation Act amending Code Sec. 1401(b)(2), as added by PPACA;

— Act Secs. 9015(b)(2)(A) of PPACA amending Code Sec. 164(f);

— Act Secs. 9015(b)(2)(B) of PPACA amending Code Sec. 1402(a)(12)(B);

— Act Sec. 1402(b)(2) of the 2010 Reconciliation Act redesignating Code Sec. 6654(m) as Code Sec. 6654(n) and adding new Code Sec. 6654(m);

— Act Secs. 9015(c) and 10906(c) of PPACA and Act Sec. 1402(b)(3) of the 2010 Reconciliation Act providing the effective date.

Reporter references: For further information, consult the following CCH reporters.

— Standard Federal Tax Reporter, ¶32,543.07

— Tax Research Consultant, INDIV: 63,060

— Practical Tax Expert, §22,205.10, §22,205.15 and §23,105

¶232 Medicare Contribution Tax on Unearned Income

SUMMARY OF NEW LAW

Effective for tax years beginning after December 31, 2012, a 3.8 percent Medicare tax is imposed on the lesser of an individual's net investment income for the tax year or modified AGI in excess of $200,000 ($250,000 in the case of joint filers and surviving spouses, and $125,000 in the case of a married taxpayer filing separately).

BACKGROUND

The Federal Insurance Contributions Act (FICA), imposes two taxes on employers and employees. The first finances the federal old-age, survivors and disability insurance (OASDI) program, more commonly known as Social Security. The second is to finance hospital and hospital service insurance (HI) for those 65 years of age or older, more familiarly known as Medicare.

The Medicare tax on an employee's wages consists of an employee's portion and an employer's portion. The employee's portion is 1.45 percent of the employee's wages (Code Sec. 3101(b)). The employer's portion of the HI tax also equals 1.45 percent of

BACKGROUND

the employee's wages (Code Sec. 3111(b)). Thus, the equivalent of 2.9 percent of the employee's wages is contributed to Medicare. However, under the Patient Protection and Affordable Care Act (PPACA) (P.L. 111-148) an additional 0.9 percent Medicare tax is imposed on the employee portion for individuals who have wages in excess of $200,000 ($250,000 in the case of married taxpayer's filing jointly, $125,000 in the case of a married taxpayer filing separately) (see ¶230).

Individuals engaged in trade or business as sole proprietors or partners must pay self-employment tax on net earnings from self-employment. Self-employment tax has two components. The OASDI component (Social Security) is imposed on net self-employment earnings up to the Social Security wage base. The HI component (Medicare) is imposed on net earnings from self-employment without limitation. The Medicare rate is 2.90 percent of all net earnings from self-employment (Code Sec. 1401(b)). However, under the Patient Protection Act, an additional 0.9 percent Medicare tax is imposed on self-employment income in excess of $200,000 ($250,000 in the case of married taxpayer's filing jointly, $125,000 in the case of a married taxpayer filing separately) (see ¶230).

A self-employed individual is permitted to deduct one-half of the self-employment tax liability for the year as a business expense in arriving at adjusted gross income (AGI) (Code Sec. 164(f)). Alternately, such individual is allowed to reduce self-employment income by an amount equal to one half of the combined self-employment tax rate, or 7.65 percent (1/2 of 15.3 percent) multiplied by the taxpayer's self-employment income (Code Sec. 1402(a)(12)).

The Medicare tax has only been imposed on wages and net earnings from self-employment. No Medicare tax has been imposed on investment income.

NEW LAW EXPLAINED

Medicare tax on unearned income.—A 3.8 percent Medicare contribution tax is imposed on the lesser of: (1) an individual's net investment income for the tax year, or (2) any excess of modified adjusted gross income (AGI) for the tax year over a threshold amount (Code Sec. 1411(a)(1), as added by the Health Care and Education Reconciliation Act of 2010 (P.L. 111-152). The new tax applies to all tax years beginning after 2012.

Net investment income. Net investment income is the excess of the sum of the following items less any otherwise allowable deductions properly allocable to such income or gain:

- gross income from interest, dividends, annuities, royalties and rents unless such income derived is in the ordinary course of any trade or business (for this purpose, income derived in the ordinary course of a trade or business excludes any trade or business that is either a passive activity of the taxpayer (within the meaning of Code Sec. 469), or involves trading in financial instruments and commodities (as defined in Code Sec. 475(e)(2)) (collectively referred to in this explanation as a passive trade or business));

NEW LAW EXPLAINED

- other gross income from any passive trade or business; and

- net gain included in computing taxable income that is attributable to the disposition of property other than property held in any trade or business that is not a passive trade or business (Code Sec. 1411(c)(1) and (2), as added by the 2010 Reconciliation Act).

> **Comment:** Gross income does not include items such as interest on tax-exempt bonds, veterans' benefits, and excluded gain from the sale of a principal residence, that are otherwise excluded from income (Joint Committee on Taxation, *Technical Explanation of the Revenue Provisions of the "Reconciliation Act of 2010," as amended, in combination with the "Patient Protection and Affordable Care Act"* (JCX-18-10), March 21, 2010).

Example 1: Deidre is a limited partner in the RE partnership that operates an equipment leasing business. RE also owns non-dividend paying stock that it holds solely for future capital appreciation. The stock was purchased with borrowed funds for which RE incurs an annual interest expense. Deidre does not materially participate in any of RE's activities. In 2013, Deidre's distributive share of RE's rental income from its equipment leasing business is $60,000, which is her only source of investment income in that year. In 2013, Deidre's distributive share of RE's interest expense incurred in connection with its ownership of the stock is $20,000. All of Deidre's 2013 gross income for purposes of the unearned income Medicare contribution tax is derived from rents. Her share of RE's interest expense would not be considered allocable to such gross income and, therefore, may not be used in computing her net investment income for the year.

Net investment income includes any income, gain, or loss that is attributable to an investment of working capital (Code Sec. 1411(c)(3), as added by the 2010 Reconciliation Act). It does not, however, include any distribution from qualified employee benefit plans or arrangements as described in Code Secs. 401(a), 403(a) or (b), 408, 408A, or 457(b) (Code Sec. 1411(c)(5), as added by the 2010 Reconciliation Act). It also does not include any item taken into account in determining self-employment income for the tax year on which an individual pays hospital insurance (HI or Medicare) tax (see ¶ 230) (Code Sec. 1411(c)(6), as added by the 2010 Reconciliation Act).

> **Comment:** In the case of a trade or business, the unearned income Medicare contribution tax applies if it is a passive trade or business with respect to the taxpayer. It does not, however, apply to other trades or businesses conducted by a sole proprietor, partnership, or S corporation (Joint Committee on Taxation, *Technical Explanation of the Revenue Provisions of the "Reconciliation Act of 2010," as amended, in combination with the "Patient Protection and Affordable Care Act"* (JCX-18-10), March 21, 2010).

NEW LAW EXPLAINED

Example 2: Alan is a 50 percent partner of the AB Partnership that conducts two separate activities: heavy equipment leasing and the manufacturing of widgets. Alan does not satisfy any of the standards for material participation with respect to the heavy equipment leasing business, but actively participates in the widget manufacturing business. In 2014, AB generates $100,000 of gross rental income from the equipment leasing business and $50,000 of gross income from the widget manufacturing business. In 2014, AB has $20,000 of business deductions that offset the equipment leasing income, and $10,000 of business deductions that offset the widget manufacturing business. Alan has $500,000 of modified AGI in 2014. Alan is subject to the unearned income Medicare contribution tax on his $40,000 share of AB net rental income (1/2 of the difference between the $100,000 gross income and the $20,000 deductions) attributable to the equipment leasing business. He does not incur the unearned income Medicare contribution tax with respect to his distributive share of the widget manufacturing income.

The net gain component of the computation only includes that portion of the gain or loss on the disposition of an interest in a partnership or S corporation that equals the amount of the net gain or loss that would be taken into account by the partner or shareholder if all property of the partnership or S corporation were sold at fair market value immediately before the disposition of the interest (Code Sec. 1411(c)(4), as added by the 2010 Reconciliation Act).

> **Comment:** In the case of disposition of an interest in a partnership or S corporation, only net gain or loss attributable to property held by the entity which is not property attributable to an active trade or business is taken into account.

Example 3: Assume the same facts as in the above example. In 2017, Alan sells his interest in the AB partnership to Cathy for $300,000, at a time when his basis in his partnership interest (outside basis) is $100,000. At that time AB has only two categories of assets: the equipment leasing assets that have a basis to AB of $120,000 and a fair market value of $300,000, and the widget manufacturing assets that have a basis to AB of $60,000 and a fair market value of $150,000. If AB were to sell the equipment leasing assets, Alan's share of the gain (ignoring any depreciation recapture) would be $90,000 (1/2 of the difference between the $300,000 fair market value and $120,000 adjusted basis). Thus, $90,000 of Alan's $200,000 of gain ($300,000 sales prices less $100,000 basis) on the sale of his AB partnership interest to Cathy would be subject to the unearned income Medicare contribution tax. The gain Alan would recognize if AB were to sell the widget manufacturing assets is not taken into account.

Modified AGI. For purposes of calculating the new 3.8 percent unearned income Medicare contribution tax, modified AGI means an individual's AGI for the tax year increased by otherwise excludable foreign earned income or foreign housing costs under Code Sec. 911 (as reduced by any deduction, exclusions, or credits properly

NEW LAW EXPLAINED

allocable to or chargeable against such foreign earned income) (Code Sec. 1411(d), as added by the 2010 Reconciliation Act).

Threshold amount. The threshold amount is $200,000 ($250,000 in the case of joint filers and surviving spouses, and $125,000 in the case of a married taxpayer filing separately) (Code Sec. 1411(b), as added by the 2010 Reconciliation Act).

Example 4: Ila and Ian, a married couple who file a joint return, collectively earn $270,000 in wages, and have $80,000 of net investment income, in 2013. Their modified AGI is $350,000. For 2013, the couple will incur a 3.8 percent unearned income Medicare contribution tax on the lesser of their: (1) $80,000 of net investment income, or (2) $100,000 of modified AGI in excess of the $250,000 threshold for married taxpayers filing jointly. Thus, Ila and Ian will incur a $3,040 (3.8 percent x $80,000) unearned income Medicare contribution tax in 2013.

Example 5: In 2013, Rodney, a single taxpayer, receives no wages or self-employment income. He does, however, earn $3.2 million in net investment income from a stock and bond portfolio that is not part of a qualified employee benefit plan. This is the total amount of Rodney's modified AGI for 2013. Rodney will incur a 3.8 percent unearned income Medicare contribution tax on the lesser of his: (1) $3.2 million net investment income, or (2) $3 million modified AGI in excess of the $200,000 threshold amount for a single taxpayer. Thus, Rodney will incur a $114,000 (3.8 percent x 3,000,000) unearned income Medicare contribution tax in 2013.

Estates and trusts. Estates and trusts also must pay a 3.8 percent unearned income Medicare contribution tax on the lesser of; (1) their undistributed net investment income for the tax year, or (2) any excess of their AGI (as determined under Code Sec. 67(e)) over the dollar amount at which the highest tax bracket for estates and trusts begins for the tax year (Code Sec. 1411(a)(2), as added by the 2010 Reconciliation Act).

Exclusions. The new 3.8 percent unearned income Medicare contribution tax does not apply to nonresident aliens or a trust whose unexpired interests are devoted to religious, charitable, scientific, literary, and/or educational purposes, and/or to foster national or international amateur sports competition (provided no part of its activities involve the provision of athletic facilities or equipment), and/or to the prevention of cruelty to children or animals (Code Sec. 1411(e), as added by the 2010 Reconciliation Act).

Estimated tax penalty. The provisions of the failure to pay estimated tax penalty, and the computation of tax on which such penalty is computed are amended to reflect the additional unearned income Medicare contribution tax contained in Code Sec. 1411 (Code Sec. 6654(a) and (f), as amended by the 2010 Reconciliation Act).

NEW LAW EXPLAINED

Practical Analysis: Michael Schlesinger, Partner in the law firm of Schlesinger & Sussman, New York, New York and Clifton, New Jersey, observes that, when investors have a chance to study the Patient Protection and 2010 Reconciliation Acts, they will realize that the tax-exempt bond market will start to rebound. Why, the Committee Reports in footnote 285 have exempted tax-exempt bonds. Family partnerships and S corporations will probably see a rebound and be utilized by parents who have "Medicare" net investment income. The parents' goal will be to run their Medicare net investment income through the family vehicles transferring ownership interests to their children so that they can shelter some of the net investment income from this Medicare tax. In this way, not only will they avoid a 3.8-percent nondeductible tax but they will also accomplish some estate planning as well, assuming Congress give guidance regarding estate and gift taxes. Parents just have to make sure that they can satisfy the standards of *A. Strangi Est. II* [85 TCM 1331, Dec. 55,160(M), TC Memo. 2003-145, *aff'd* CA-5, 2005-2 USTC ¶60,506, 417 F3d 468 (2005)] and its ilk, such as having the children represented by counsel, not running afoul of Code Sec. 2036, etc.

Practical Analysis: Robert Keebler, a Partner with Baker Tilly Virchow, Krause & Company, LLP, Appleton, Wisconsin, notes the following:

- Act Sec. 1411 likely affects passive real estate interests.
- The threshold amount includes IRA income although IRAs are not "net investment" income.
- For retired clients whose threshold amount will naturally exceed $250K or $200K. (single) Roth conversions will have additional merit.
- Insurance and deferred annuities will have more merit.
- The threshold for trusts is the income level where the 39.6-percent bracket begins.
- Charitable lead trusts will have more merit.
- Charitable reminder trusts will have merit to help avoid spikes in income.
- Installment sales may have more merit to smooth income.
- Municipal bonds will continue to be popular.
- Strategies will develop to create investment interest deductions.

The good news is that the surtax does not apply to IRA or qualified plan distributions. On the other hand, IRA and plan distributions (distributions) will count in determining the base over which the surtax is imposed, in essence making the distributions subject, at least in part, to the surtax.

In January 2011, the highest marginal rate is scheduled to increase from 35 percent to 39.6 percent, an increase of 4.6 percent. In January 2013, the 3.8-percent surtax will begin increasing the highest marginal rate from 39.6 percent to 43.4 percent; a significant increase from where we stand today.

¶232

NEW LAW EXPLAINED

Planning for the surtax involves two steps:

1. Reduce investment income.

2. Reduce modified adjusted gross income (MAGI) to below the threshold amount.

Roth conversions in 2010 present an opportunity to help a large group of clients that will be subject to the new health care surtax on investment income. This benefit occurs not by reducing investment income but also by reducing MAGI and therefore reducing the amount subject to the surtax. For taxpayers with total income below $250,000, the threshold amount, or total active investment income and non-IRA income above the threshold amount, conversion to a Roth IRA will not yield additional "surtax" benefits.

> Example: John, a married person, earns board of directors' fees of $250,000 and has no adjustments to MAGI. In this case, 100 percent of John's investment income will be subject to the new health care surtax and planning must focus on reducing investment income.

Taxpayers whose wage, active investment and other non-IRA income is likely to be below the threshold amount of $250,000 but whose IRA and qualified plan income increases the taxpayer's income to greater than the threshold amount may realize additional benefits from a Roth conversion related to this new health care surtax. In a case such as this, conversion to a Roth IRA would avoid distributions that would increase taxpayer's MAGI causing additional investment income to be subject to the surtax.

> Example: Linda, a retired plastic surgeon, and her husband Joseph, a retired CPA, earn dividends and interest of $250,000 and have no adjustments to MAGI. In this case, none of their investment income will be subject to the surtax. However, beginning in 2013 they are required to begin required minimum distributions from their large IRAs. Assume the IRA distributions are $100,000, which increases their MAGI to $350,000. In this case $100,000 ($350,000 – $250,000) will be subject to the surtax resulting in a tax liability of $3,800.

> If in 2010 they convert to a Roth IRA, there would be no RMDs, and the health care surtax would not apply. Further, even if they took a Roth distribution, the distribution would not count toward the computation of MAGI and not result in income subject to the surtax.

Mathematical Analysis

The complexity of the Roth conversion is increased exponentially by the surtax and must be taken into account. The first step will be to bifurcate the traditional IRA into two tranches; the portion that will increase MAGI over the threshold amount and the portion that will not affect the surtax. Once this occurs, the planner must run the numbers on both conversions independently. Preliminary calculations suggest that for clients in the "bubble" category, those with usual income below the threshold but whose income would exceed the threshold if they receive required minimum distributions from a traditional IRA or qualified plan would increase their wealth transfer potential by over 20 percent if they convert to a Roth IRA, even if the taxes on conversion are funded from within the IRA itself.

NEW LAW EXPLAINED

▶ **Effective date.** The provision applies to tax years beginning after December 31, 2012 (Act Sec. 1402(a)(4) of the Health Care and Education Reconciliation Act of 2010 (P.L. 111-152).

Law source: Law at ¶5180, ¶5187, and ¶5277. Committee Report at ¶10,410.

— Act Sec. 1402(a)(1) of the Health Care and Education Reconciliation Act of 2010 (P.L. 111-152), adding Code Sec. 1411;

— Act Sec. 1402(a)(2), amending Code Sec. 6654(a) and (f);

— Act Sec. 1402(a)(4), providing the effective date.

Reporter references: For further information, consult the following CCH reporters.

— Standard Federal Tax Reporter, ¶32,543.07

— Tax Research Consultant, INDIV: 63,060

— Practical Tax Expert, § 22,205.10, § 22,205.15 and § 23,105

¶235 Excise Tax on Indoor Tanning Salon Services

SUMMARY OF NEW LAW

A 10 percent excise tax is imposed on amounts paid for indoor tanning services (whether paid by insurance or otherwise) performed on or after July 1, 2010.

BACKGROUND

In addition to tax imposed on income, the Internal Revenue Code imposes a number of excise taxes on commodities and services provided by a select group of trades— notably, the fuel industry, the trucking industry, the airline industry, telecommunications providers, the coal industry, the tire industry, and manufacturers of certain sporting goods and vaccines. Because federal excise taxes are usually assessed at a point in the stream of commerce at least one or two steps higher than the retail level, consumers are often unaware that they are paying federal excise tax on a particular good or service (or unaware that the cost of the tax has been passed down to them through an increased retail price on the item being sold). Currently, there is no excise taxes imposed on the users of indoor tanning facilities.

Federal excise taxes can be split into two general categories: (1) those that impose tax when an item is manufactured or first sold by the producer; and (2) those that impose tax when a commodity or service is used, sometimes without regard to the value of the commodity or services provided. Thus, taxation can be based on sales prices or surtax added to the price of a commodity (i.e., loosely called a "manufacturers tax") or based on usage by the customer. A manufacturer's excise tax is usually collected when the commodity is sold by the producer or imported into the United States. The advantage of taxing at the production or importation level is that the tax is easier to administer, and the revenue is easier to collect.

¶235

Excise tax imposed on patrons of indoor tanning salons.—A 10-percent excise tax is imposed on each individual for whom "indoor tanning services" performed (Code Sec. 5000B(a), as added by Act Sec. 10907(b) of the Patient Protection and Affordable Care Act (PPACA) (P.L. 111-148)). The tax is imposed on the full amount of the charge for the service and is imposed regardless of who pays the ultimate cost of the service, whether insurance or otherwise. While the tax is imposed on the patron of the indoor tanning salon, it is the salon owner who is required to collect the taxes and remit them to the IRS on a quarterly basis (Code Sec. 5000B(c), as added by PPACA). To the extent the salon owner fails to collect the tax at the time payment is made for the tanning service, the salon owner becomes liable for the 10-percent tax.

> **Compliance Note:** The IRS is given discretion in determining how and when a remittance of the tax is to be made.

For purposes of new excise tax, an "indoor tanning service" is defined as a service employing any electronic product designed to incorporate 1 or more ultraviolet lamps and intended for the irradiation of an individual by ultraviolet radiation, with wavelengths in air between 200 and 400 nanometers, to induce skin tanning (Code Sec. 5000B(b)(1), as added by PPACA). An exception to this definition is made for phototherapy services performed by licensed medical professionals (Code Sec. 5000B(b)(2), as added by PPACA).

▶ **Effective date.** The provision shall apply to services performed on or after July 1, 2010 (Act Sec. 9017(c) of the Patient Protection and Affordable Care Act (PPACA) (P.L. 111-148) and as amended by Act Sec. 10907(d), providing the effective date.

Law source: Law at ¶5240. Committee Report at ¶10,320.

— Act Secs. 9017 and 10907(b) of the Patient Protection and Affordable Care Act (PPACA) (P.L. 111-148), adding and amending Code Sec. 5000B;

— Act Secs. 9017(c) and 10907(d), providing the effective date.

Reporter references: For further information, consult the following CCH reporters.

— Tax Research Consultant, EXCISE: 100

¶240 Adoption Credit and Adoption Assistance Programs

SUMMARY OF NEW LAW

For 2010, the dollar limitation for the adoption credit and income exclusion for employer-paid or employer-reimbursed adoption expenses through a qualified adoption assistance program is increased by $1,000 to $13,170 per eligible child (including a special needs child). In addition, the adoption credit has been made refundable.

BACKGROUND

There are two related tax provisions to assist families who adopt children: a nonrefundable tax credit and an income exclusion for employer-paid or employer-reimbursed adoption expenses through a qualified adoption assistance program (Code Secs. 23 and 137). A qualified adoption assistance program is a separate written plan of an employer, for the exclusive benefit of its employees, which provides adoption assistance. The plan must meet requirements similar to those that apply to educational assistance programs under Code Sec. 127(b) regarding eligibility, principal shareholders or owners, funding, and notification of employees. Both the tax credit and the exclusion may apply to the same adoption, but not for the same expenses. In addition, a taxpayer may not claim the tax credit or the exclusion for any expense for which another deduction or credit is allowed. Further, no credit is allowed for any expense to the extent the taxpayer receives funds under any federal, State, or local program.

For 2010, the credit and income exclusion apply for the first $12,170 of qualified adoption expenses for each eligible child (including a special needs child). Qualified expenses are taken into account for purposes of the credit in the tax year following the tax year that they are paid or incurred. However, expenses paid or incurred in the tax year that the adoption becomes final may be taken into account in that tax year. For 2010, the amount of the credit and exclusion is phased out ratably for taxpayers with modified adjusted gross income (AGI) between $182,520 and $222,520. Modified AGI for this purpose is the taxpayer's AGI plus any amount of foreign earned income and foreign housing expenses otherwise excluded from income, any income from U.S. possessions otherwise excluded from income, and all employer payments and reimbursements for adoption expenses whether or not they are taxable to the employee.

Qualified adoption expenses include reasonable and necessary adoption fees, court costs, attorney fees, and other expenses that are directly related to, and the principal purpose of which is, the legal adoption by the taxpayer of an eligible child. All reasonable and necessary expenses required by a State as a condition of adoption are qualified adoption expenses. For example, expenses may include the cost of construction, renovations, alterations or purchases specifically required by the State to meet the needs of the child. However, the increase in the basis of the property that would result from such an expenditure must be reduced by the amount of the credit or exclusion. Qualified adoption expenses may not be incurred in violation of State or federal law or be reimbursed under an employer or other program. Expenses incurred in carrying out a surrogate parenting arrangement or in adopting a spouse's child do not qualify for the credit. Qualified adoption expenses do not include expenses for a child who is not a citizen or resident of the United States unless the adoption is finalized. Any expense paid or incurred before the tax year in which a foreign adoption becomes final is treated as if it were paid or incurred in the year the adoption becomes final.

An eligible child for purposes of the adoption credit and exclusion is an individual who has not attained the age of 18 as of the time of the adoption or who is physically or mentally incapable of caring for himself or herself. The credit or exclusion is also is allowed for the adoption of a special needs child, regardless of actual expenses

BACKGROUND

incurred by the parents. A child with special needs is one whom a State has determined both cannot and should not be returned home to his parents and cannot be placed with adoptive parents without providing some adoption assistance. In either case, the child must be a citizen or resident of the United States (Code Sec. 23(d)(3)).

For tax years before 2010, the adoption credit, like all nonrefundable tax credits, can offset alternative minimum tax (AMT) liability. Code Sec. 26(a)(2). In 2010, the adoption credit can continue to offset AMT liability, but the credit cannot exceed the excess of the taxpayer's regular income tax liability and AMT liability over the sum of the nonrefundable personal credits allowed to the taxpayer (other than the adoption credit, the residential energy efficient property credit, and the foreign tax credit). Code Sec. 26(b)(4). The taxpayer may carry forward any excess for up to five years and add the amount to the adoption credit allowed for that year. Code Sec. 23(c)(1). Credits are treated as used on a first-in, first-out basis.

> **Comment:** In order to comply with the deficit reduction and budget scoring provisions of Congressional Budget Act of 1974 (P.L. 93-344), the Economic Growth and Tax Relief Reconciliation Act of 2001 (EGTRRA) (P.L.107-16) provides that all provisions of, and amendments made by, EGTRRA shall not apply to tax, plan or limitation years beginning after December 31, 2010 (Act Sec. 901(a)(1) of EGTRRA). The Code will thereafter be applied and administered as if these provisions and amendments had not been enacted (Act Sec. 901(b) of EGTRRA). EGTRRA increased the amount allowed for the adoption credit and for employer adoption assistance programs. Before the changes made by EGTRRA, the amounts allowed were $5,000 ($6,000 for a special-needs child). Accordingly, for 2011 and later tax years, the amount of the credit and the exclusion is limited to $5,000 or $6,000 in the case of a special-needs child.

NEW LAW EXPLAINED

Adoption credit and adoption assistance program expanded.—For 2010, the dollar limitation for the adoption credit and income exclusion for employer-paid or employer-reimbursed adoption expenses through a qualified adoption assistance program is increased by $1,000 to $13,170 (Code Secs. 36C(b)(1) and 137(b)(1), as amended by the Patient Protection and Affordable Care Act (PPACA) (P.L. 111-148)). The increased amount includes the credit and exclusion amounts for special needs children (Code Secs. 36C(a)(3) and 137(a)(2), as amended by PPACA). The increased amounts will indexed for inflation for tax years beginning after December 31, 2010 (Code Secs. 36C(h) and 137(f), as amended by PPACA).

> **State Tax Consequences:** The increase in the dollar limitation for the exclusion of adoption assistance program payments to $13,170 will impact States that conform to Code Sec. 137, but because of their Code conformity dates will not adopt the increase. Because the exclusion applies to tax years after 2009, States that allow the federal exclusion will most likely conform when they update their Code conformity dates. However, States like California that do not annually update their conformity dates will most likely require an addition for the

¶240

NEW LAW EXPLAINED

difference between the allowable federal and State exclusions. Also, the increase may affect States like California that provide an adoption credit and require any deduction for adoption expenses to be reduced by the amount of the credit.

Caution: The EGTRRA sunset provision, which would have reduced the amount of credit and exclusion allowable to previous levels, is extended, so that now the reduced amounts will apply for tax years beginning after December 31, 2011 (Act Sec. 10909(c) of PPACA).

In addition to the increase in the limit for 2010 and 2011, the adoption credit has been made refundable (Code Sec. 36C, as redesignated and amended by PPACA). Accordingly, the credit is no longer allowed under Code Sec. 23, but the law under which it is allowed has been redesignated as Code Sec. 36C (Act Sec. 10909(b)(1) of PPACA).

▶ **Effective date.** The amendments made by this section apply to tax years beginning after December 31, 2009 (Act Sec. 10909(d) of the Patient Protection and Affordable Care Act (PPACA) (P.L. 111-148)).

Law source: Law at ¶5005, ¶5010, ¶5015, ¶5020, ¶5025, ¶5030, ¶5035, ¶5040, ¶5050, ¶5100, ¶5165, ¶5170, ¶5175, ¶5275, and ¶7054. Committee Report at ¶10,390.

— Act Sec. 10909(a)(1) of the Patient Protection and Affordable Care Act (PPACA) (P.L. 111-148), amending Code Sec. 23(a)(3), (b)(1), and (h), as redesignated as Code Sec. 36C(a)(3), (b)(1), and (h) by Act Sec. 10909(b)

— Act Sec. 10909(a)(2), amending Code Sec. 137(a)(2), (b)(1), and (f)

— Act Secs. 10909(c) and (d), providing the effective date.

Reporter references: For further information, consult the following CCH reporters.

— Standard Federal Tax Reporter, ¶3725.01, ¶7625.01

— Tax Research Consultant, COMPEN: 36,650, INDIV: 57,350, PLANIND: 3,060

— Practical Tax Explanation, § 12,301, § 20,201

¶242 Medical Benefits for Children Under Age 27

SUMMARY OF NEW LAW

Children under the age of 27 will be considered dependents of a taxpayer for purposes of the general exclusion for reimbursements for medical care expenses of an employee, spouse, and dependents under an employer-provided accident or health plan (Code Sec. 105(b)), the deduction for the health insurance costs of a self-employed person, spouse, and dependents (Code Sec. 162(l)), the rule that allows a qualified pension or annuity plan to provide benefits for sickness, accident, hospitalization, and medical expenses to retired employees, spouses, and dependents (Code Sec. 401(h)), and the rule that treats a voluntary employee benefits association (VEBA) that provides sick and accident benefits to its members and their dependents as a tax-exempt organization (Code Sec. 501(c)(9)).

BACKGROUND

The Internal Revenue Code provides a number of tax benefits related to the provision of medical care to individuals, their spouses, and their dependents. In general, a dependent for these purposes is defined by reference to the rules in Code Sec. 152 relating to dependency exemptions. Under these rules, a child is a dependent for whom a dependency exemption may be claimed only if he or she is a qualifying child (Code Sec. 152(c)) or a qualifying relative (Code Sec. 152(d)).

In general, a qualifying child must:

- have a specified relationship to the taxpayer;
- live with the taxpayer for more than one-half of the year;
- provide only one-half or less of his or her own support;
- be under the age of 19 at the end of the year, or, if a full-time student, under the age of 24; and
- not file a joint return except to claimed a refund.

If the preceding requirements for qualifying child status are not satisfied, it may be possible to claim a child as a dependent under the rules for a qualifying relative. In order to be considered a qualifying relative for whom a dependency exemption may be claimed a child must:

- have a specified relationship to the taxpayer;
- have gross income less than the exemption amount for the year;
- receive over one-half of his or her support from the taxpayer; and
- is not a qualifying child of another taxpayer.

It is not necessary for a qualifying relative to live with the taxpayer and no age restrictions apply. Other requirements for qualifying child and qualifying relative status apply.

Employer-financed accident or health insurance. Employees may exclude from gross income the value of employer-provided health coverage for themselves, their spouses, and their dependents under an accident or health plan (Code Sec. 106). Gross income also does not include amounts received by an employee through employer-financed accident or health insurance for amounts that reimburse the employee for expenses incurred for the medical care of the employee, the employee's spouse, or the employee's dependents (as defined in Code Sec. 152, determined without regard to subsections (b)(1), (b)(2), and (d)(1)(B) thereof). Any child to whom Code Sec. 152(e) applies (relating to special rules for divorced parents) is treated as a dependent of both parents (Code Sec. 105(b)). The exclusion does not apply to amounts deducted as medical expenses in any prior tax year (Reg. § 1.105-2). Payments from an accident and health plan are also excludable from an employee's income to the extent that the plan providing the benefits is funded by the employee (Reg. § 1.105-1(c)).

Health insurance costs of the self-employed. Self-employed persons may deduct from gross income 100 percent of amounts paid during the year for health insurance for themselves, their spouses, and their dependents (Code Sec. 162(l)(1)). The deduction cannot exceed the taxpayer's net earned income derived from the trade or

BACKGROUND

business for which the insurance plan was established, minus the deductions for 50 percent of the self-employment tax and/or the deduction for contributions to qualified retirement plans, self-employed SEP or SIMPLE plans. Amounts eligible for the deduction do not include amounts paid during any month, or part of a month, that the self-employed individuals were able to participate in a subsidized health plan maintained by their employers or their spouses' employers (Code Sec. 162(l)(2)(B)).

Pension plan providing medical benefits to retirees. A qualified pension or annuity plan can provide benefits for sickness, accident, hospitalization, and medical expenses of retired employees, their spouses, and their dependents if: (1) the benefits are subordinate to the retirement benefits provided; (2) a separate account is established and maintained for these benefits; and (3) the employer's contributions to the separate account are reasonable and ascertainable. The benefits are not considered subordinate to the retirement benefits if the aggregate contributions for medical benefits, when added to contributions for life insurance protection under the plan, exceed 25 percent of the total contributions to the plan, other than contributions to fund past service credits, after the date on which the account is established (Code Sec. 401(h)). A dependent is a person for whom a dependency exemption may be claimed (Reg. § 1.401-14(b)(4)).

Voluntary employees' beneficiary association. A tax-exempt 501(a) organization includes a voluntary employees' beneficiary association (VEBA) that provides for the payment of life, sick, accident, or other benefits to the members of such association or their dependents or designated beneficiaries, if no part of the net earnings of such association inures (other than through such payments) to the benefit of any private shareholder or individual (Code Sec. 501(c)(9)). Dependent means the member's spouse, any child of the member or the member's spouse who is a minor or a student, any other minor child residing with the member, and any other individual who an association, relying on information furnished to it by a member, in good faith believes a dependency exemption may be claimed (Reg. § 1.501(c)(9)-3).

NEW LAW EXPLAINED

Certain medical care tax benefits extended to children under age 27.—A child who is under the age of 27 will be considered a dependent of a taxpayer for purposes of the general exclusion for reimbursements for medical care expenses under an employer-provided accident or health plan, the self-employed health insurance deduction, the rule that allows a qualified pension or annuity plan to provide benefits for sickness, accident, hospitalization, and medical expenses to retired employees, their spouses, and their dependents, and the rule that treats a voluntary employee benefits association (VEBA) that provides sick and accident benefits to its members and their dependents as a tax-exempt organization (Code Secs. 105(b), 162(l), 401(h), and 501(c)(9) as amended by the Health Care and Education Reconciliation Act of 2010 (P.L. 111-152)).

Exclusion for employer-provided accident and health insurance. The exclusion from gross income for reimbursements made under an employer-provided accident or health insurance plan for medical care expenses of an employee, employee's spouse, or

NEW LAW EXPLAINED

employee's dependents is extended to apply to any child of the employee who as of the end of the tax year has not attained the age of 27 (Code Sec. 105(b), as amended by the 2010 Reconciliation Act).

> **Comment:** It is no longer necessary for the child of the employee to be a dependent of the employee in order for this exclusion to apply. Thus, if the child is age 26 or less at the end of the tax year, the exclusion applies even if the child provides more than one-half of his or her own support, earns more income than the exemption amount, does not live with the taxpayer, or any other restriction which prevents the employee from claiming a dependency exemption for the child either under qualifying child or qualifying relative rules.

A child for purposes of this provision is defined by reference to Code Sec. 152(f)(1). Thus, a child includes:

- a son, daughter, stepson, or stepdaughter of the taxpayer;
- a foster child placed with the taxpayer by an authorized placement agency or by judgment, decree, or other order of any court of competent jurisdiction; and
- a legally adopted child of the taxpayer or a child who has been lawfully placed with the taxpayer for legal adoption.

> **Comment:** This provision only amends Code Sec. 105(b), relating to the exclusion for reimbursements under an employer's accident or health insurance plan. The provision is also intended to exclude the value of employer-provided coverage under an accident or health plan for injuries or sickness of a child under the age of 27 (i.e., the provision also applies to the Code Sec. 106 exclusion mentioned in the Background section above) (Joint Committee on Taxation, *Technical Explanation of the Revenue Provisions of the "Reconciliation Act of 2010," as amended, in combination with the "Patient Protection and Affordable Care Act"* (JCX-18-10), March 21, 2010).

Self-employed health insurance deduction. The deduction for health insurance costs of a self-employed individual is extended to apply to any child of a taxpayer who is under the age of 27 at the end of the tax year regardless of whether or not such child is a dependent of the taxpayer (Code Sec. 162(l)(1), as amended by the 2010 Reconciliation Act). A child for this purpose is defined by reference to Code Sec. 152(f)(1). However, the self-employed taxpayer may not claim the deduction for the cost of health care insurance if the taxpayer is eligible to participate in any subsidized health plan maintained by any employer of a taxpayer's dependent or a child of the taxpayer who is under age 27 at the end of the tax year (Code Sec. 162(l)(2)(B), as amended by the 2010 Reconciliation Act).

> **Comment:** Current law does not allow the deduction for the health care costs of a self-employed individual if he or she can participate in a health plan maintained by an employer (i.e., the self-employed individual has another job) or an employer of the self-employed individual's spouse. Now the deduction is also denied if the self-employed individual can participate in a subsidized plan maintained by an employer of a dependent or a child under the age of 27 at the end of the tax year.

¶242

NEW LAW EXPLAINED

Medical and other benefits for retired employees. A child under age 27 at the end of a calendar year is considered a dependent for purposes of the rule which allows a qualified pension or annuity plan to provide benefits for sickness, accident, hospitalization, and medical expenses to retired employees, their spouses, and their dependents if the benefits are subordinate to the retirement benefits and certain other conditions are met. A child for this purpose is also defined by reference to Code Sec. 152(f)(1) (see above) (Code Sec. 401(h), as amended by the 2010 Reconciliation Act).

Voluntary employees' beneficiary association (VEBA). A child under the age of 27 is considered a dependent of a VEBA member for purposes of the rule that treats a VEBA as a tax-exempt entity if it provides sick and accident benefits to its members and their dependents (Code Sec. 501(c)(9), as amended by the 2010 Reconciliation Act). A child for purposes of this law change is defined by reference to Code Sec. 152(f)(1). Thus, it is no longer necessary that the child actually satisfy the rules for claiming a dependency exemption.

> **Comment:** As noted, in addition to sick and accident benefits, a VEBA may also provide life and other benefits to its members and dependents. The new law only treats children under the age of 27 as dependents with respect to the provision of sick and accident benefits. Furthermore, unlike the other provisions discussed in this paragraph, the new law does not specifically provide that the child needs to be less than age 27 at the end of the calendar year in the case of such benefits provided by a VEBA.

Practical Analysis: Michael Schlesinger, Partner in the law firm of Schlesinger & Sussman, New York, New York and Clifton, New Jersey, notes that, in terms of operation of Code Secs. 105(b) and 162(l), an interesting situation arises with S corporations if an S corporation establishes an accident and health insurance plan where the S corporation pays the premiums for accident and health insurance for a more-than-two-percent shareholder-employee. The employee has to include the value of the premiums in gross income; however, Code Sec. 162(l) allows a deduction to the shareholder for the premiums. Accordingly, the expanded definition of deduction for health insurance premiums and children under 27 years of age applies to the more-than-two-percent S corporate shareholder.

> **Comment:** In addition to the change in treatment of adult dependents for certain tax benefits, the Patient Protection and Affordable Care Act of 2010 (PPACA) (P.L. 111-148) requires insurers that provide group health coverage for dependent children to continue such coverage until the dependent turns 26 years old. For a discussion of group health plan reforms including the change in treatment of dependents, see ¶455.

▶ **Effective date.** No effective is provided. The provision is therefore considered effective on March 30, 2010, the date of enactment of the Health Care and Education Reconciliation Act of 2010 (P.L. 111-152).

¶242

NEW LAW EXPLAINED

Law source: Law at ¶5083, ¶5120, ¶5153, and ¶5155. Committee Report at ¶10,400.

— Act Sec.1004(d)(1) of the Health Care and Education Reconciliation Act of 2010 (P.L. 111-152), amending Code Sec. 105(b);

— Act Sec.1004(d)(2), amending Code Sec. 162(l)(1);

— Act Sec.1004(d)(3), amending Code Sec. 162(l)(2)(B);

— Act Sec.1004(d)(4), amending Code Sec. 501(c)(9);

— Act Sec. 1004(d)(5), amending Code Sec. 401(h).

Reporter references: For further information, consult the following CCH reporters.

— Standard Federal Tax Reporter, ¶6702.01; ¶22,628.01; ¶18,105.01; ¶8522.03

— Tax Research Consultant, COMPEN:45,056; COMPEN: 54,056; RETIRE: 9,412; COMP: 45,250

— Practical Tax Explanation, §20,315.10; §20,910.35b; §24,240.10; §5,401

¶245   Exclusion for Assistance Provided to Participants in State Student Loan Repayment Programs for Certain Health Professionals

SUMMARY OF NEW LAW

Repayments under State loan repayment or forgiveness programs that are intended to provide for the increased availability of health care services in underserved or health professional shortage areas (as determined by the State) are excluded from gross income.

BACKGROUND

In order to ensure professional participation in public service activities, many educational organizations sponsor programs that offer students an opportunity to partially or completely discharge their student loans by working for a period of time in a public service organization. Generally, the gross income of a taxpayer includes the amount of any debt that is discharged or forgiven. However, taxpayers whose student loans are forgiven (in whole or in part) because they worked for a certain time period in a designated profession for any of a broad class of employers generally do not have to include the discharged amount in income (Code Sec. 108(f)(1)). For purposes of the exclusion, a student loan is any loan to an individual to assist in attending an educational organization that qualifies for a tax exemption. Specifically, the loan must be made by one of the following lenders:

- the United States or one of its instrumentalities or agencies;

- a State, territory or possession of the United States, or the District of Columbia, or any political subdivision;

BACKGROUND

- a State, county or municipal hospital that is controlled by an exempt public benefit corporation and whose employees are deemed public employees under State law;
- any exempt educational organization that receives the funds from which the loans are made from one of the entities listed above; or
- an exempt educational organization under a program that is designed to encourage its students to serve in occupations with unmet needs or in areas with unmet needs and under which the services provided by the students or former students are for or under the direction of a governmental unit or a tax-exempt organization.

The exclusion applies to forgiveness of loans made by educational organizations and tax-exempt organizations to refinance any existing student loans, and not just loans made by educational organizations, but only if made under a program of the refinancing organization that requires the student to fulfill a public service requirement under the direction of a governmental entity or tax-exempt organization. However, the exclusion does not apply to a discharge of a loan by an exempt organization under its own program or from funds provided by another organization, if the discharge is on account of services performed for either organization.

Participants in the National Health Service Corps (NHSC) Loan Program may receive repayment of part of their education loans and tax assistance. Participants are required to provide medical service in a geographic area identified by the Public Health Service as having a shortage of health care professionals. States may also provide for education loan repayment programs for persons who agree to provide primary health services in health professional shortage areas. Under the Public Health Service Act, such programs may receive federal grants with respect to such repayment programs if certain requirements are met. Any amounts received by participants in the NHSC loan repayment program and State programs eligible for funds under the Public Health Service Act are excluded from gross income (Code Sec. 108(f)(4)).

NEW LAW EXPLAINED

Repayments under State loan programs for health care professionals not included in gross income.—In addition to repayments under the National Health Service Corps Loan Program and State repayment programs under the Public Health Service Act, repayments under other State loan repayment or forgiveness programs that are intended to provide for the increased availability of health care services in underserved or health professional shortage areas (as determined by the State) are also excluded from gross income for tax years beginning after 2008 (Code Sec. 108(f)(4), as amended by Patient Protection and Affordable Care Act (PPACA) (P.L. 111-148)).

> **State Tax Consequences:** Because the exclusion of repayments under State loan repayment or forgiveness programs that are intended to provide for the increased availability of health care services in underserved or health professional shortage areas applies to amounts received in tax years after 2008, many States will not conform for the 2009 tax year without further legislation. However,

NEW LAW EXPLAINED

because 2009 State income tax forms or instructions, which are already available, will not require an addition of the federally excluded amounts, it is unclear whether the States will allow the exclusion. Taxpayers and tax professionals should look for guidance from the States regarding resolution of this issue.

▶ **Effective date.** The amendment made by this provision applies to amounts received by an individual in tax years beginning after December 31, 2008 (Act Sec. 10908(b) of the Patient Protection and Affordable Care Act (PPACA) (P.L. 111-148)).

Law source: Law at ¶5090. Committee Report at ¶10,380.

— Act Sec. 10908(a) of the Patient Protection and Affordable Care Act of (PPACA) (P.L. 111-148), amending Code Sec. 108(f)(4);

— Act Sec. 10908(b), providing the effective date.

Reporter references: For further information, consult the following CCH reporters.

— Standard Federal Tax Reporter, ¶7010.049

— Tax Research Consultant, INDIV:60,054.10

— Practical Tax Explanation, § 3420.25

¶250 Exclusion of Qualified Health Care Benefits of Indian Tribe Members

SUMMARY OF NEW LAW

Qualified health care benefits provided to the member of an Indian tribe, the member's spouse, or the member's dependents are excluded from the recipient's gross income.

BACKGROUND

The Federal government provides health care to American Indians and Alaska Natives based on its trust responsibility found in the U.S. Constitution and affirmed by treaties, federal court decisions, and federal law. Today, health care is provided to 1.9 million American Indians and Alaska Natives primarily residing on or near Indian reservations located in 35 States.

Due to the underfunding by the Federal government of the Indian Health Service, many Indian tribes and tribal organizations have purchased health insurance for their members or paid for their actual health care expenses. In the absence of an employment relationship between a member and the tribe, the IRS may consider the value of these benefits as taxable income to the person receiving them. In recent non-binding guidance, the IRS has required individuals participating in State-sponsored health-related assistance programs to satisfy a financial means test (Chief Counsel Advice 200648027 (July 25, 2006)).

NEW LAW EXPLAINED

Exclusion from gross income of health benefits provided by Indian tribal governments.—The value of any qualified Indian health care benefit is excluded from gross income (Code Sec. 139D, as added by the Patient Protection and Affordable Care Act (PPACA) (P.L. 111-148)). For this purpose, a qualified Indian health care benefit includes:

- any health service or benefit provided or purchased, directly or indirectly, by the Indian Health Service through a grant, contract, or compact with an Indian tribe or tribal organization, or through a third-party program funded by the Indian Health Service;

- medical care provided or purchased by, or amounts to reimburse for such medical care provided by, an Indian tribe or tribal organization for, or to, a member of an Indian tribe, including a member's spouse or dependent;

- coverage under an accident or health insurance (or an arrangement having the effect of accident or health insurance), or an accident or health plan, provided by an Indian tribe or tribal organization for medical care to a member of an Indian tribe, including a member's spouse or dependent; and

- any other medical care provided by an Indian tribe or tribal organization that supplements, replaces, or substitutes for a program or service relating to medical care provided by the Federal government to Indian tribes or their members (Code Sec. 139D(b), as added by PPACA).

To deny a double tax benefit, this exclusion does not apply to the amount of a qualified Indian health care benefit that is not includible in the gross income of the beneficiary under another Code provision. Similarly, the exclusion does not apply to the amount of a qualified benefit for which the beneficiary may claim a deduction under another provision of the Code (Code Sec. 139D(d), as added by PPACA).

> **State Tax Consequences:** The exclusion of qualified Indian health care benefits from gross income under new Code Sec. 139D will impact States, like New Jersey, that do not use federal adjusted gross income (AGI) as a starting point for calculating State taxable income or States that, because of their Code conformity dates, will not adopt the new provision without further legislation. Also, because it is a new code section, States like Alabama that conform to the IRC on a provision-by-provision basis will not conform without further legislation. For these States, such benefits will be included in gross income.

Indian tribe defined. An Indian tribe is defined for this purpose the same as for the Indian employment credit under Code Sec. 45A(c)(6). It includes any Indian tribe, band, nation, pueblo, or other organized group or community, including any Alaska Native village, or regional or village corporation, as defined in, or established pursuant to, the Alaska Native Claims Settlement Act (43 U.S.C. 1601 et seq.) which is recognized as eligible for the special programs and services provided by the United States to Indians because of their status as Indians (Code Sec. 139D(c)(1), as added by PPACA).

¶250

NEW LAW EXPLAINED

Tribal organization defined. A tribal organization is defined by reference to section 4(l) of the Indian Self-Determination and Education Assistance Act (P.L. 93-638) (25 USC 450(b)). Thus, a tribal organization means the recognized governing body of any Indian tribe; any legally established organization of Indians which is controlled, sanctioned, or chartered by such governing body or which is democratically elected by the adult members of the Indian community to be served by such organization and which includes the maximum participation of Indians in all phases of its activities. However, in any case where a contract is let or grant made to an organization to perform services benefiting more than one Indian tribe, the approval of each such Indian tribe is a prerequisite to the letting or making of such contract or grant (Code Sec. 139D(c)(2), as added by PPACA).

Medical care defined. The term medical care has the same meaning as used for an individual to claim an itemized deduction for medical expenses and includes expenses paid for the diagnosis, cure, mitigation, treatment, or prevention of disease, and for treatments affecting any part or function of the body (as well as transportation primarily for and essential to medical care) (Code Sec. 139D(c)(3), as added by PPACA). In addition, medical care includes qualified long-term care services (as defined in Code Sec. 7702B(c)) and insurance covering medical care or for eligible long-term care premiums for any qualified long-term care insurance contract (as defined in Code Sec. 7702B(b)).

Accident or health insurance and accident or health plan. The terms accident or health insurance and accident or health plan have the same meaning as when used in Code Sec. 105 (Code Sec. 139(D)(c)(4), as added by PPACA).

Dependent defined. A dependent as the same meaning as provided in Code Sec. 152 without regard to the rules that provide: (1) an individual who is a dependent of another taxpayer is treated as having no dependents and an individual is not a dependent of another taxpayer if he or she files a joint return (Code Sec. 139D(c)(5), as added by PPACA). In addition, the determination of whether a qualifying relative is a taxpayer's dependent is made without regard to the rule that requires that the taxpayer provides over one-half the qualifying relative's support.

No inference regarding prior law treatment. The provision shall not be construed to create an inference regarding the treatment of benefits provided before March 23, 2010, or to benefits that are not within the scope of the provision (Act Section 9021(d) of PPACA).

▶ **Effective date.** The provision applies to benefits and coverage provided after March 23, 2010, the date of enactment (Act Section 9021(c) of the Patient Protection and Affordable Care Act (PPACA) (P.L. 111-148)).

Law source: Law at ¶5110 and ¶7039. Committee Report at ¶10,330.

— Act Sec. 9021(a) of the Patient Protection and Affordable Care Act (PPACA) (P.L. 111-148), adding Code Sec. 139D;

— Act Sec. 9021(c), providing the effective date;

— Act Sec. 9021(d), adding provision relating to no inference regarding prior law treatment.

¶250

NEW LAW EXPLAINED

Reporter references: For further information, consult the following CCH reporters.
— Standard Federal Tax Reporter, ¶6702.01
— Tax Research Consultant, COMPEN: 45,154 and INDIV: 33,500
— Practical Tax Explanation, §20,301

Health Care: Businesses

¶305 Shared Responsibility for Employers Regarding Health Coverage

SUMMARY OF NEW LAW

Large employers who fail to offer their full-time employees the opportunity to enroll in minimum essential coverage under an eligible employer-sponsored plan for any month and have at least one full-time employee enrolled for that month in a qualified health plan for which a premium tax credit or cost-sharing reduction is allowed or

SUMMARY OF NEW LAW

paid for the employee are subject to an assessable payment. An assessable payment is also imposed on large employers who offer coverage, but have one or more full-time employees enrolled in a qualified health plan for which a premium tax credit or cost-sharing reduction is allowed or paid for these employees.

BACKGROUND

Employers are not required to provide health care benefits to their employees under federal law. However, most large employers and many small businesses provide such benefits. The employer's cost in providing health care benefits is generally deductible as a Code Sec. 162 ordinary and necessary business expense for compensation, though special rules may apply if the benefits are provided through a funded welfare benefit plan. Employees are allowed to exclude from gross income the value of the employer-provided health coverage under an accident or health plan as well as the value of any medical care received under such a plan (Code Secs. 105(b) and 106).

One way that employers can offer employer-provided health insurance coverage for purposes of the tax exclusion is to offer to reimburse employees for the premiums for health insurance purchased by employees in the individual health insurance market. The payment or reimbursement of employees' substantiated individual health insurance premiums is excludible from employees' gross income (Rev. Rul. 61-146, 1961-2 CB 25). Proposed regulations provide that this reimbursement for individual health insurance premiums can also be paid through salary reduction under a cafeteria plan (Proposed Reg. § 1.125-1(m)). This offer to reimburse individual health insurance premiums constitutes a group health plan.

Although employers are not required to provide health coverage, those who do must comply with a number of plan requirements imposed by the Employee Retirement Income Security Act of 1974 (ERISA), such as reporting and disclosure requirements, procedures for appealing denied benefit claims, health care continuation coverage (COBRA), limitations on the use of pre-existing condition exclusions, and others. Group health plans that fail to comply with some of these requirements are subject to an excise tax in the amount of $100 per day per failure during the period of noncompliance. The excise tax is imposed on the employer sponsoring the plan, or on the plan itself in the case of a multi-employer plan (Code Secs. 4980B and 4980D). The excise tax imposed under these rules is not deductible by the employers (Code Sec. 275(a)(6)).

Under Medicaid, states may establish "premium assistance" programs, which pay a Medicaid beneficiary's share of premiums for employer-sponsored health coverage. Besides being available to the beneficiary through his or her employer, the coverage must be comprehensive and cost-effective for the state. An individual's enrollment in an employer plan is considered cost-effective if paying the premiums, deductibles, coinsurance and other cost-sharing obligations of the employer plan is less expensive than the state's expected cost of directly providing Medicaid-covered services. States are also required to provide coverage for those Medicaid-covered services that are not

BACKGROUND

included in the private plans. As of 2007, approximately 12 states had Medicaid premium assistance programs as authorized under current law.

NEW LAW EXPLAINED

Shared responsibility assessable payment imposed on certain large employers.—An assessable payment is imposed on an applicable large employer that:

- fails to offer to its full-time employees (and their dependents) the opportunity to enroll in minimum essential coverage under an eligible employer-sponsored health plan for any month, and

- has at least one full-time employee who has been certified to the employer as having enrolled for that month in a qualified health plan through offered through a Health Insurance Exchange with respect to which an applicable premium tax credit or cost-sharing reduction is allowed or paid for the employee (Code Sec. 4980H(a), as added by the Patient Protection and Affordable Care Act (PPACA) (P.L. 111-148)).

> **Comment:** By January 1, 2014, each State must establish an American Health Benefit Exchange and Small Business Health Options Program (SHOP Exchange) to provide qualified individuals and qualified small business employers access to qualified health plans. For a discussion of the establishment and requirements of the Exchanges, see ¶505. Individuals who are eligible for participation in a qualified health plan through an Exchange, may also be eligible for a premiums assistance tax credit (see ¶210) and cost-sharing subsidy (see ¶520). The Exchange is required to certify to an employer if it has an employee enrolled in a qualified health plan through the Exchange.

The assessable payment is equal to the product of the applicable payment amount, which is $1/12$ of $2,000 for any month (i.e., $166.67 per month), and the number of full-time employees for the month (Code Sec. 4980H(c)(1), as added by PPACA, and amended and redesignated by the Health Care and Education Reconciliation Act of 2010 (P.L. 111-152)). After 2014, the $2,000 amount will be adjusted for inflation (see "*Indexing,*" below). However, in computing the assessable payment, the number of the employer's full-time employees for any month is reduced by 30 (Code Sec. 4980H(c)(2)(D)(i)(I), as added and amended by PPACA, and amended and redesignated by the 2010 Reconciliation Act).

Example 1: In 2014, Gama Corp. fails to offer minimum essential coverage and has 90 full-time employees, 10 of whom receive a premium tax credit for the year for enrolling in a state exchange offered plan. For 60 of its full-time employees (90 full-time employees, less 30), Gama owes $2,000 per employee, for a total assessable payment of $120,000 ($2,000 x 60 full-time employees), which is assessed on a monthly basis.

In the case where certain persons under common control are treated as a single employer for purposes of determining if the employer is an applicable large employer

NEW LAW EXPLAINED

(see the discussion in *"Definitions"*, below), only one 30-employee reduction is allowed for all such persons (e.g., one 30-employee reduction per controlled group of employers). The reduction is allocated among these persons ratably based on the number of full-time employees employed by each person (Code Sec. 4980H(c)(2)(D)(ii), as added and amended by PPACA, and amended and redesignated by the 2010 Reconciliation Act).

For purposes of these rules, an eligible employer-sponsored plan is defined the same as for the individual requirement to maintain minimum essential health coverage. It includes a group health plan or group health insurance coverage offered by an employer that is a governmental plan, or any other plan or coverage offered in the small or large group market within a state. For further discussion of an eligible employer-sponsored plan and minimum essential coverage, see ¶ 205.

Large employers offering health coverage. An assessable payment is also imposed on an applicable large employer that:

- offers to its full-time employees (and their dependents) the opportunity to enroll in minimum essential coverage under a Code Sec. 5000A(f)(2) eligible employer-sponsored plan for any month, but

- has one or more full-time employees who have been certified for that month in a qualified health plan offered through a Health Insurance Exchange with respect to which an applicable premium tax credit or cost-sharing reduction is allowed or paid for the employee (Code Sec. 4980H(b)(1), as added by PPACA, and amended and redesignated by the 2010 Reconciliation Act).

The assessable payment in this case is equal to the product of the number of the full-time employees receiving a premium tax credit or cost-sharing subsidy for the purchase of health insurance through a state exchange for the month and an amount equal to $1/12$ of $3,000 for any month (i.e., $250 per month). After 2014, the $3,000 amount will be adjusted for inflation (see *"Indexing,"* below).

However, the aggregate amount of the assessable payment imposed on an offering employer with respect to all certified employees for any month is limited to the product of the applicable payment amount ($1/12$ of $2,000 per month) and the number of all full-time employees during that month (Code Sec. 4980H(b)(2), as added by PPACA, and redesignated by the 2010 Reconciliation Act). After 2014, the $2,000 amount will be adjusted for inflation (see *"Indexing,"* below). For purposes of this calculation, the number of full-time employees for any month is reduced by 30 (Code Sec. 4980H(c)(2)(D)(i)(II), as added and amended by PPACA, and amended and redesignated by the 2010 Reconciliation Act).

> **Comment:** Thus, in calculating the overall limitation, all full-time employees of the employer are taken into account, regardless of how many employees are receiving a premium tax credit or cost-sharing reduction. The number of full-time employees is then reduced by 30, and the resulting number of full-time employees (that is, the number of full-time employees in excess of the 30-employee threshold) is multiplied by the applicable payment amount ($1/12$ of $2,000 per month) to determine the overall limitation. The overall limitation, therefore,

¶305

NEW LAW EXPLAINED

is determined in the same way as the assessable payment imposed for a failure to provide health coverage (see above).

Example 2: In 2014, Omega Corp. offers health coverage and has 100 full-time employees, 10 of whom receive a tax credit for the year for enrolling in a state exchange offered plan. For each employee receiving a tax credit, Omega owes $3,000, for a total assessable payment of $30,000 ($3,000 x 10 employees). The maximum amount of the assessable payment for Omega is capped at the amount of the assessable payment that it would have been assessed for a failure to provide coverage, or $140,000 ($2,000 x 70 full-time employees (100 full-time employees, less 30)). Since the calculated assessable payment ($30,000) is less than the overall limitation ($140,000), Omega owes the $30,000 assessable payment, which is assessed on a monthly basis.

In the case where certain persons under common control are treated as a single employer for purposes of determining if the employer is an applicable large employer (see the discussion in *"Definitions"*, below), only one 30-employee reduction is allowed for all such persons in calculating the overall limitation on the assessable payment. The reduction is allocated among these persons ratably based on the number of full-time employees employed by each person (Code Sec. 4980H(c)(2)(D)(ii), as added and amended by PPACA, and amended and redesignated by the 2010 Reconciliation Act).

An assessable payment is not imposed on an offering employer for any month with respect to any employee to whom the employer provides a free choice voucher under Act Sec. 10108 of the Patient Protection Act (Code Sec. 4980H(b)(3), as added by PPACA, and redesignated by the 2010 Reconciliation Act). See ¶ 315 for a discussion of the free choice voucher rules.

Comment: A Medicaid-eligible individual can always choose to leave the employer's coverage and enroll in Medicaid, and an employer will not be subject to an assessable payment for any employees enrolled in Medicaid (Joint Committee on Taxation, *Technical Explanation of the Revenue Provisions of the "Reconciliation Act of 2010," as amended, in combination with the "Patient Protection and Affordable Care Act"* (JCX-18-10)).

Definitions. An *applicable large employer*, with respect to a calendar year, is an employer who employed an average of at least 50 full-time employees on business days during the preceding calendar year (Code Sec. 4980H(c)(2)(A), as added by PPACA, and redesignated by the 2010 Reconciliation Act). An exemption applies to an employer if:

- its workforce exceeds 50 full-time employees for 120 or fewer days during the calendar year, and
- the employees in excess of 50 employed during the 120-day period are seasonal workers (Code Sec. 4980H(c)(2)(B)(i), as added by PPACA, and redesignated by the 2010 Reconciliation Act). Thus, such an employer is not subject to the shared responsibility assessable payment.

¶305

NEW LAW EXPLAINED

A seasonal worker is a worker who performs labor or services on a seasonal basis, as defined by the Secretary of Labor, including workers covered by 29 C.F.R. §500.20(s)(1), and retail workers employed exclusively during holiday seasons (Code Sec. 4980H(c)(2)(B)(ii), as added by PPACA, and redesignated by the 2010 Reconciliation Act). Under 29 C.F.R. §500.20(s)(1), labor is performed on a seasonal basis if, ordinarily, the employment pertains to or is of the kind exclusively performed at certain seasons or periods of the year and which, from its nature, may not be continuous or carried on throughout the year. A worker who moves from one seasonal activity to another, while employed in agriculture or performing agricultural labor, is employed on a seasonal basis even though he may continue to be employed during a major portion of the year.

In determining the employer's size, all persons treated as a single employer under the aggregation rules of Code Sec. 414(b), (c), (m), or (o) are treated as one employer. These include controlled groups of corporations, partnerships and proprietorships under common control, and affiliated service groups (Code Sec. 4980H(c)(2)(C), as added by PPACA, and redesignated by the 2010 Reconciliation Act). In addition, if the employer was not in existence throughout the preceding calendar year, the determination of whether that employer is an applicable large employer is based on the average number of employees that it is reasonably expected the employer will employ on business days in the current calendar year. Moreover, any references to an employer for purposes of the applicable large employer definition include references to the employer's predecessors.

Solely for purposes of determining if it is an applicable large employer, an employer must also include, in addition to its full-time employees for any month, a number of full-time equivalent employees determined by dividing the aggregate number of hours of service of employees who are not full-time employees for the month, by 120 (Code Sec. 4980H(c)(2)(E), as added and redesignated by the 2010 Reconciliation Act).

Example 3: Assume that Diva Corp. has, in addition to full-time employees, five part-time employees for the month. The part-time workers' aggregate number of hours of service for the month is 480. Based on the service hours of its part-time workers, Diva must add four full-time equivalent employees (480 aggregate hours of service / 120) to the number of its full-time employees for that month in determining if it is an applicable large employer.

Comment: Even though the number of full-time employees during any month may be reduced by 30 for purposes of calculating the assessable payment imposed on a non-offering employer and the overall limitation on the assessable payment imposed on an offering employer (see the discussions above), an employer may not reduce the number of its full-time employees by 30 in determining if it is an applicable large employer.

A *full-time employee* with respect to any month is an employee who is employed on average at least 30 hours of service per week (Code Sec. 4980H(c)(4)(A), as added by PPACA, and redesignated by the 2010 Reconciliation Act). The Secretary of the Treasury, in consultation with the Secretary of Labor, is authorized to prescribe

NEW LAW EXPLAINED

regulations, rules, and other guidance necessary to determine the hours of service of an employee, including rules for the application of the "full-time employee" definition to employees who are not compensated on an hourly basis (Code Sec. 4980H(c)(4)(B), as added by PPACA, and redesignated by the 2010 Reconciliation Act).

An *applicable premium tax credit and cost-sharing reduction* includes:

(1) any premium assistance tax credit allowed (see ¶210);

(2) any cost-sharing reduction for individuals enrolled in qualified health plans (see ¶520); and

(3) any advance payment of the premium tax credit or cost-sharing reduction (see ¶525) (Code Sec. 4980H(c)(3), as added by PPACA, and redesignated by the 2010 Reconciliation Act).

Any other term used in the employer shared responsibility provision that is not specifically defined there, but that is also used in the Patient Protection Act, will have the same meaning as when used in the Patient Protection Act (Code Sec. 4980H(c)(6), as added by PPACA, and redesignated by the 2010 Reconciliation Act).

Indexing. For calendar years after 2014, the $2,000 amount used in determining the applicable payment amount and the $3,000 amount used in determining the assessable payment imposed on applicable large employers offering coverage will be increased for inflation. The increase will equal the product of the relevant dollar amount ($2,000 or $3,000) and the premium adjustment percentage for the calendar year, and will be rounded down to the next lowest multiple of $10 (Code Sec. 4980H(c)(5), as added by PPACA, and amended and redesignated by the 2010 Reconciliation Act).

For this purpose, the premium adjustment percentage for any calendar year is the percentage (if any) by which the average per capita premium for health insurance coverage in the United States for the preceding calendar year (as estimated by the Secretary of Health and Human Services no later than October 1 of such preceding calendar year) exceeds the average per capita premium for 2013 (as determined by the Secretary of Health and Human Services, see ¶530) (Act Sec. 1302(c)(4) of PPACA).

Disallowance of deduction, administration and procedure. An employer may not deduct the assessable payment imposed under these rules (Code Sec. 4980H(c)(7), as added by PPACA, and redesignated by the 2010 Reconciliation Act; Code Sec. 275(a)(6)).

> **Comment:** Code Sec. 275(a)(6) generally denies a deduction for certain excise taxes imposed under a number of chapters of the Code, including chapter 43 (Qualified Pension, etc., Plans) where new Code Sec. 4980H has been added.

An employer must pay the assessable payment upon notice and demand by the Secretary of the Treasury. The payment is assessed and collected in the same manner as an assessable penalty under subchapter B of chapter 68 of the Internal Revenue Code (Code Secs. 6671-6725) (Code Sec. 4980H(d)(1), as added by PPACA, and redesignated by the 2010 Reconciliation Act).

NEW LAW EXPLAINED

> **Comment:** The Joint Committee on Taxation indicates that the restrictions on assessment under Code Sec. 6213 do not apply to the assessable payment imposed under new Code Sec. 4980H (Joint Committee on Taxation, *Technical Explanation of the Revenue Provisions of the "Reconciliation Act of 2010," as amended, in combination with the "Patient Protection and Affordable Care Act"* (JCX-18-10)).

The Secretary of the Treasury may provide for the payment of the assessable payment on an annual, monthly, or other periodic basis (Code Sec. 4980H(d)(2), as added by PPACA, and redesignated by the 2010 Reconciliation Act). In addition, the Secretary of the Treasury is authorized to prescribe rules, regulations, or other guidance for the repayment of the assessable payment (including interest) where:

- it is based on the allowance or payment of an applicable premium tax credit or cost-sharing reduction with respect to an employee,
- such allowance or payment is subsequently disallowed, and
- the assessable payment would not have been required but for such allowance or payment (Code Sec. 4980H(d)(3), as added by PPACA, and redesignated by the 2010 Reconciliation Act).

> **Comment:** Code Sec. 4980H uses the term "assessable payment" throughout the provision, except for two places where it specifically refers to the assessable payment as a "tax" and one place where it refers to it as "assessable penalties." The assessable payment has also been referred to as a "tax" and "shared responsibility penalty" in other parts of the Patient Protection Act. In addition, the Joint Committee on Taxation describes the assessable payment as a penalty that is an excise tax and refers to it as both a "penalty" and an "excise tax" (Joint Committee on Taxation, *Technical Explanation of the Revenue Provisions of the "Reconciliation Act of 2010," as amended, in combination with the "Patient Protection and Affordable Care Act"* (JCX-18-10)). Regardless of how the assessable payment is referred to (as a "tax" or as a "penalty"), the legislation makes it clear that it is not deductible by the employer (similar to the excise taxes imposed by other provisions in chapter 43 of the Code) and that it is assessed and collected in the same manner as assessable penalties.

Study and report on effect of assessable payment on workers' wages. The Secretary of Labor will conduct a study to determine whether employees' wages are reduced by reason of the application of the Code Sec. 4980H assessable payment. The Secretary of Labor will make the determination based on the National Compensation Survey published by the Bureau of Labor Statistics, and will report the study results to the House Ways and Means Committee and the Senate Finance Committee (Act Sec. 1513(c) of PPACA).

Practical Analysis: Pam Perdue, Of Counsel with Summers, Compton, Wells & Hamburg in St. Louis, Missouri, comments that, despite the nondeductible penalty, some employers, particularly smaller employers, may calculate that they are still better off financially by dropping group coverage, particularly if premium costs continue to rise.

NEW LAW EXPLAINED

> It should be noted that, unlike the case with seasonal employees, the provision does not provide an exception for temporary workers. This, coupled with the Act's restrictions on waiting periods, may make it difficult for an employer to avoid the penalties with respect to temporary employees not falling within the definition of seasonal employees.
>
> Some employers may be tempted by these provisions to attempt to structure more independent contractor relationships in the hopes of avoiding these shared responsibility provisions.

▶ **Effective date.** The provision applies to months beginning after December 31, 2013 (Act Secs. 1513(d), 10106(f)(3) and 10108(i)(1)(B) of the Patient Protection and Affordable Care Act (PPACA) (P.L. 111-148)). No specific effective date is provided by the Health Care and Education Reconciliation Act of 2010 (P.L. 111-152). The amendments made by the 2010 Reconciliation Act are, therefore, considered effective on March 30, 2010, the date of enactment.

Law source: Law at ¶5225 and ¶7018. Committee Report at ¶10,100.

— Act Secs. 1513(a), 10106(e), (f)(1), (2), and 10108(i)(1)(A) of the Patient Protection and Affordable Care Act (PPACA) (P.L. 111-148), adding and amending Code Sec. 4980H;

— Act Sec. 1513(b) and (c);

— Act Secs. 1513(d), 10106(f)(3) and 10108(i)(1)(B), providing the effective date;

— Act Sec. 1003 of the Health Care and Education Reconciliation Act of 2010 (P.L. 111-152), amending Code Sec. 4980H.

Reporter references: For further information, consult the following CCH reporters.

— Standard Federal Tax Reporter, ¶34,612.01

— Tax Research Consultant, COMPEN: 45,200

— Practical Tax Explanation, §20,701

¶310 Small Employer Health Insurance Credit

SUMMARY OF NEW LAW

An eligible small employer may claim a 35-percent tax credit (25 percent in the case of a tax-exempt eligible small employer) for premiums it pays toward health coverage for its employees in tax years beginning in 2010 through 2013. An eligible small employer is an employer that has no more than 25 full-time employees and the average annual compensation of these employees is not greater than $50,000. The credit is reduced by 6.667 percent for each full-time employee in excess of 10 employees and by 4 percent for each $1,000 that average annual compensation paid to the employees exceeds $25,000. In tax years that begin after 2013, an employer must participate in an insurance exchange in order to claim the credit, and other modifications and restrictions on the credit apply.

BACKGROUND

Employers may generally deduct, as an ordinary and necessary business expense, the cost of providing health coverage for employees (Code Sec. 162). The value of employer-provided health insurance is not subject to employer paid Federal Insurance Contributions Act (FICA) tax. Employees may exclude from gross income the value of employer-provided coverage under an accident or health plan (Code Sec. 106). An exclusion from gross income also applies to the value of medical care provided under an accident or health plan to the employee and the employee's spouse and dependents (Code Sec. 105(b)). Employees who participate in a cafeteria plan are able to pay premiums on a pre-tax basis through salary reduction (Code Sec. 125).

NEW LAW EXPLAINED

Credit for employee health insurance expenses of eligible small employers.—An eligible small employer may claim a tax credit in tax years beginning after 2009 if it makes nonelective contributions that pay for at least one-half of the cost of health insurance premiums for the coverage of its participating employees (Code Sec. 45R, as added by the Patient Protection and Affordable Care Act (PPACA) (P.L. 111-148)).

The amount of the credit for employee health insurance expenses of an eligible small employer in tax years beginning in 2010 through 2013 is equal to 35 percent of the *lesser* of:

(1) the total amount of nonelective contributions the employer makes on behalf of its employees during the tax year under a contribution arrangement for the payment of premiums for qualified health insurance coverage (as defined in Code Sec. 9832(b)(1)) of its employees, or

(2) the total amount of nonelective contributions that would have been made during the tax year if each employee taken into account in item (1) had enrolled in a qualified health plan that had a premium equal to the amount that the Secretary of Health and Human Services determines is the average premium for the small group market in the state in which the employer is offering health insurance coverage (or the area within the state that is specified by the Secretary of Health and Human Services) (Code Sec. 45R(a), (b) and (g), as added by PPACA).

Comment: In effect, this limitation prevents an employer from claiming the credit on the portion of employer-paid premiums that exceeds the average premium charges in the state's small group market.

Health insurance credit amount for tax years beginning after 2013. An eligible small employer may claim a health insurance credit for any tax year beginning after 2013 during the credit period (Code Sec. 45R(a), as added by PPACA). The credit period is the two-consecutive-tax-year period beginning with the first tax year in which the employer or any predecessor offers one or more qualified health plans to its employees through a Health Benefit Exchange (Code Sec. 45R(e)(2), as added by PPACA). No credit period is treated as beginning with a tax year beginning before 2014 (Code Sec. 45R(g)(1), as added by PPACA).

NEW LAW EXPLAINED

Comment: The health insurance credit may only be claimed for two additional tax years in tax years that begin after 2013 (e.g., for 2014 and 2015 in the case of a calendar-year eligible small employer) and only if the eligible small employer offers one or more qualified health plans through an Exchange during those years. The Exchange referred to is required to be established by each State by January 1, 2014. Specifically, each State must establish an American Health Benefit Exchange and Small Business Health Options Program (SHOP Exchange) to provide qualified individuals and qualified small business employers access to qualified health plans. For a discussion of the establishment and requirements of the Exchanges, see ¶505.

The credit amount for a tax year beginning after 2013 is equal to 50 percent of the *lesser* of:

(1) the total amount of nonelective contributions the employer makes on behalf of its employees during the tax year under a contribution arrangement for premiums for qualified health plans offered to its employees through an Exchange, or

(2) the total amount of nonelective contributions that would have been made during the tax year if each employee taken into account in item (1) had enrolled in a qualified health plan that had a premium equal to the average premium for the small group market in the rating area in which the employee enrolls for coverage (Code Sec. 45R(b), as added by PPACA).

Comment: As in the case of tax years beginning in 2010 through 2013, the credit in tax years beginning after 2013 may not be claimed on excessive premiums.

Contribution arrangement defined. The employer must make nonelective contributions through an "arrangement." In the case of a tax year beginning in 2010 through 2013, the arrangement must require an employer to make a nonelective contribution on behalf of each employee who enrolls in a qualified health plan offered to employees by the employer in an amount equal to a uniform percentage, but not less than 50 percent, of the premium cost of the qualified health plan (Code Sec. 45R(d)(4) and (g)(3), as added by PPACA). An employer contribution is considered a nonelective contribution so long as it is *not* made through a salary reduction arrangement (Code Sec. 45R(e)(3), as added by PPACA). For tax years beginning after 2013, the arrangement must offer the insurance through an Exchange. For earlier tax years, the arrangement may, but is not required to, offer the insurance through an Exchange (Code Sec. 45R(d)(4) and (g)(3), as added by PPACA).

Credit phaseout. The credit is reduced (but not below zero) by the sum of:

(1) The product of:

(a) the credit amount, and

(b) the number of the employer's full-time equivalent employees for the tax year in excess of 10, divided by 15; and

NEW LAW EXPLAINED

(2) The product of:

    (a) the credit amount, and

    (b) the employer's average annual wages in excess of the applicable dollar amount for the tax year ($25,000 in tax years beginning in 2010-2013), divided by the applicable dollar amount (Code Sec. 45R(c), as added by PPACA).

Comment: The reduction of the credit amount required by item (1), above, for having more than 10 full-time equivalent employees is in effect equal to 6.667 percent for each qualified employee in excess of 10. Thus, if an employer has 25 or more full-time employees, the credit is reduced to zero (6.667 percent times 15 employees (the number in excess of 10) equals a 100 percent reduction). The credit may not be claimed even if the average annual wages for the year do not exceed the $25,000 applicable dollar amount.

Example 1: Kindly Inc. computes its 2010 credit amount without regard to the credit phaseout as $90,000. If it has 20 employees, the credit is reduced by $60,000 (((20 - 10) ÷ 15) × $90,000 = $60,000). The reduction is equal to 66.67 percent (6.667 percent × 10 (excess number of employees) = 66.67 percent) of $90,000 or $60,000. The credit amount that may be claimed is $30,000 ($90,000 - $60,000), assuming no further reduction is required because the average annual wages exceed the $25,000 applicable dollar amount.

Comment: The reduction of the credit amount required for item (2), above, for having average annual wages in excess of the $25,000 applicable dollar amount is, in effect, equal to 4 percent for each $1,000 of wages in excess of $25,000. Thus, if average annual wages are $50,000 or greater, the credit amount is reduced to zero (4 percent × 25 equals a 100% reduction) even if the employer has fewer than 25 full-time employees.

Example 2: Assume that the average compensation paid by Kindly Inc. in Example 1, above, to its 20 employees is $27,000 and, therefore, exceeds the applicable dollar amount by $2,000. An additional reduction in the credit amount is required. The additional reduction is equal to $7,200 ($90,000 credit amount × ($2,000 (the excess compensation over the applicable dollar amount) ÷ $25,000) (the applicable dollar amount) = $7,200) or eight percent of the credit amount. Taking the additional $7,200 reduction into account, Kindly Inc. may claim a $22,800 small employer health insurance credit ($90,000 - $60,000 - $7,200 = $22,800).

The following table shows the percentage by which the credit amount should be reduced if an employer has more than 10 full-time equivalent employees. Note that any amount that remains after this reduction is subject to an additional reduction if the employee's average annual wages exceed the $25,000 applicable dollar amount.

¶310

NEW LAW EXPLAINED

Table 1 – Credit Amount Reduction for Employers With More Than 10 Full-Time Equivalent Employees

Number of Full-Time Equivalent Employees	*Credit Amount Reduction Percentage*
1-10	0.00%
11	6.667%
12	13.334%
13	20.00%
14	26.668%
15	33.335%
16	40.002%
17	46.669%
18	53.336%
19	60.003%
20	66.670%
21	73.337%
22	80.004%
23	86.671%
24	93.338%
25 or more	100%

The following table shows the percentage by which the credit amount is reduced for each $1,000 of compensation in excess of the $25,000 applicable dollar amount.

Table 2 – Credit Amount Reduction for Employers With Average Annual Full-Time Employee Compensation in Excess of $25,000

Average Annual Compensation*	*Credit Amount Reduction Percentage*
$25,000 or less	0.00%
$26,000	4%
$27,000	8%
$28,000	12%
$29,000	16%
$30,000	20%
$31,000	24%
$32,000	28%
$33,000	32%
$34,000	36%
$35,000	40%
$36,000	44%
$37,000	48%
$38,000	52%
$39,000	56%
$40,000	60%
$41,000	64%
$42,000	68%
$43,000	72%
$44,000	76%
$45,000	80%

¶310

NEW LAW EXPLAINED

Average Annual Compensation*	Credit Amount Reduction Percentage
$46,000	84%
$47,000	88%
$48,000	92%
$49,000	96%
$50,000 or more	100%

* If an employer's average annual wages are not a multiple of $1,000, average annual wages are rounded to the next lowest multiple of $1,000 (Code Sec. 45R(d)(3)(A), as added by PPACA).

Eligible small employer defined. An employer determines its status as an eligible small employer each tax year. An employer is an eligible small employer if the following conditions are satisfied during the tax year:

- it has 25 or fewer full-time equivalent employees;

- the average annual wages of these employees is not greater than twice the applicable dollar amount for the tax year ($25,000 in tax years beginning in 2010 through 2013); and

- the employer has a qualified health care arrangement in effect (Code Sec. 45R(d)(1), as added by PPACA).

> **Comment:** Although an eligible small employer includes a taxpayer with exactly 25 full-time employees or who pays average compensation of exactly $50,000, the credit is completely phased out under the phaseout rules described above if an employer has 25 or more full-time equivalent employees or pays $50,000 (or more) in average annual wages.

Full-time equivalent employee defined. The number of full-time equivalent employees of an employer during a tax year is equal to the total number of hours for which employees were paid wages by the employer divided by 2,080. The result, if not a whole number, is rounded to the next lowest whole number (Code Sec. 45R(d)(2)(A), as added by PPACA).

In making this computation, only the first 2,080 hours of each employee's wages are taken into account. Hours in excess of this amount are not counted (Code Sec. 45R(d)(2)(B), as added by PPACA).

> **Comment:** 2,080 hours is the number of hours in a 52-week work year assuming a 40-hour work week ($52 \times 40 = 2,080$). An employee's hours in excess of this amount (i.e., overtime hours) are not taken into account in determining the number of full-time equivalent employees.

The Secretary of Treasury, in consultation with the Secretary of Labor, will prescribe rules to determine hours of service, including rules for employees who are not paid on an hourly basis (Code Sec. 45R(d)(2)(C), as added by PPACA).

Certain persons treated as single employer. All persons treated as a single employer under Code Sec. 414(b), (c), (m), or (o) are treated as one employer (Code Sec. 45R(e)(5)(A), as added by PPACA).

NEW LAW EXPLAINED

Special rule for seasonal employees. For purposes of determining average annual wages and the number of full-time equivalent employees, hours of service worked by, and wages paid to, a seasonal worker are not taken into account unless the worker works for the employer on more than 120 days during the tax year (Code Sec. 45R(d)(5)(A), as added by PPACA).

> **Comment:** The 120-day test is applied by taking into account any day of work regardless of the number of hours worked on that day.

A seasonal worker is defined as a worker who performs labor or services on a seasonal basis as defined by the Secretary of Labor and includes workers covered by 29 C.F.R. § 500.20(s)(1) and retail workers employed exclusively during holiday seasons.

Average annual wages. The amount of the average annual wages is equal to the aggregate amount of wages paid by the employer to employees during the tax year divided by the number of full-time equivalent employees of the employer during the tax year. If this amount is not a multiple of $1,000, it is rounded to the next lowest multiple of $1,000 (Code Sec. 45R(d)(3), as added by PPACA).

Applicable dollar amount. The applicable dollar amount is $25,000 for tax years beginning in 2010, 2011, 2012, and 2013. In each tax year beginning in a calendar year after 2013, the applicable dollar amount is adjusted for inflation (Code Sec. 45R(d)(3)(B), as added and amended by PPACA).

> **Comment:** The unamended version of Code Sec. 45R(d)(2)(C), as added by Act Sec. 1421 of the Patient Protection Act provides that the dollar amount for tax years beginning in 2011 through 2013 is $20,000. Act Sec. 10105(e)(1) of the Patient Protection Act amended Code Sec. 45R(d)(2)(C) to increase the dollar amount to $25,000 and extend the applicability of the credit to tax years beginning in 2010.

Employee defined. For all purposes of the credit, the following individuals are not considered employees (Code Sec. 45R(e)(1), as added by PPACA):

(1) Any employee within the meaning of Code Sec. 401(c)(1) (i.e., a self-employed individual);

(2) Any 2-percent shareholder (as defined in Code Sec. 1372(b)) of an eligible small business which is an S corporation;

(3) Any 5-percent owner (as defined in Code Sec. 416(i)(1)(B)(i) of an eligible small business; or

(4) Any individual who bears any of the relationships described in Code Sec. 152(d)(2)(A)-(G) to an individual described in items (1), (2) or (3), above, or is a dependent described in Code Sec. 152(d)(2)(H) of such an individual.

Leased employees (as defined in Code Sec. 414(a)) are considered employees (Code Sec. 45R(e)(1), as added by PPACA).

Wages defined. Wages for purposes of the provision are defined by reference to Code Sec. 3121(a), relating to the definition of wages for purposes of the Federal Insurance Contributions Act (FICA) but without regard to any dollar limitation (Code Sec. 45R(e)(4), as added by PPACA).

NEW LAW EXPLAINED

Additional rules. The following special rules described in Code Sec. 52 relating to the work opportunity credit (Code Sec. 51) apply to the small employer health insurance credit (Code Sec. 45R(e)(5)(B), as added by PPACA).

• No credit is allowed to a tax-exempt organization, other than a cooperative described in Code Sec. 521, which is exempt from income tax (Code Sec. 52(c));

• An estate or trust must apportion the credit between itself and its beneficiaries based on income allocable to each (Code Sec. 52(d));

• In computing the credit, a regulated investment company (RIC), real estate investment trust (REIT), and cooperative organization (Code Sec. 1381(a)) must apply rules similar to the rules provided in Code Sec. 46(e) and (h), as in effect prior to the date of enactment of the Revenue Reconciliation Act of 1990 (P.L. 101-508) (Code Sec. 52(e)).

Special computation rules for tax-exempt eligible small employers. The credit percentage for a tax-exempt eligible small employer is 25 percent for a tax year that begins in 2010, 2011, 2012, or 2013 and 35 percent for a tax year that begins after 2013 (Code Sec. 45R(b) and (g)(2)(A), as added by PPACA). A tax-exempt eligible small employer is an eligible small employer, as defined above, that is a Code Sec. 501(c) organization that is exempt from tax under Code Sec. 501(a) (Code Sec. 45R(f)(2), as added by PPACA). If the credit exceeds the amount of payroll taxes of the organization during the calendar year in which the tax year begins, then the credit amount is limited to the amount of the payroll taxes (Code Sec. 45R(f)(1), as added by PPACA).

> **Caution:** Code Sec. 45R(e)(5)(B), as added by the Patient Protection Act, provides that rules similar to Code Sec. 52(c) apply. Since Code Sec. 52(c) denies the credit to tax-exempt organizations, it appears that this reference to Code Sec. 52(c) is erroneous.

Payroll taxes are defined as amounts required to be withheld from the tax-exempt organization's employees under Code Sec. 3401(a), Code Sec. 3101(b), and amounts of the taxes imposed on the tax-exempt organization under Code Sec. 3111(b) (Code Sec. 45R(f)(3)(A), as added by PPACA). The special rule contained in Code Sec. 24(d)(2)(C), which treats amounts paid pursuant to an agreement entered into by American employers with respect to foreign affiliates that are the equivalent of social security taxes imposed by Code Sec. 3101 or railroad retirement taxes (Code Sec. 3201(a)) applies (Code Sec. 45R(f)(3)(B), as added by PPACA).

Insurance definitions. Any term used in new Code Sec. 45R which is also used in the Public Health Service Act or subtitle A of title I of the Patient Protection Act has the same meaning as provided in those laws (Code Sec. 45R(h), as added by PPACA).

Regulations. The IRS is granted authority to issue regulations necessary to implement Code Sec. 45R, including regulations to prevent the use of successor entities to avoid the two-year limitation on the credit period for tax years beginning after 2013 and to prevent the use of multiple entities to avoid the Code Sec. 45R(c) credit phaseout rules that are based on number of employees and average wages (Code Sec. 45R(i), as added by PPACA).

Credit is component of general business credit. The small employer health insurance credit is a component of the general business credit (Code Sec. 38(b)(36), as

NEW LAW EXPLAINED

added by PPACA). The general business credit may be carried back one tax year and forward 20 tax years.

Credit allowed in full against alternative minimum tax. The small employer health insurance credit is treated as a specified credit (Code Sec. 38(c)(4)(B)(vi), as added by PPACA). Consequently, it may be claimed in full against both regular and alternative minimum tax (AMT) liabilities. This rule is effective for credits in tax years beginning after December 31, 2010, and to carrybacks of such credits.

Deduction for premiums is reduced by credit amount. The deduction for employer-paid premiums for qualified health plans or, in the case of tax years beginning in 2010 through 2013, for health insurance coverage, is reduced by the amount of the small employer health insurance credit determined with respect to those premiums (Code Sec. 280C(h), as added and amended by PPACA).

Deduction for expiring credits. Any portion of the small employer health insurance credit that is not claimed by the expiration of the 20-year carryforward period may be claimed as a deduction in the first tax year after expiration of the carryforward period (Code Sec. 199(c)(14), as added by PPACA).

▶ **Effective date.** The small employer health insurance credit and related amendments apply to amounts paid or incurred in tax years beginning after December 31, 2009 (Act Sec. 1421(f)(1) of the Patient Protection and Affordable Care Act (PPACA) (P.L. 111-148), as amended by Act Sec. 10105(e)(4) and Act Sec. 10105(e)(5)). The provision treating the credit as a specified credit is effective for credits in tax years beginning after December 31, 2009, and to carrybacks of such credits (Act Sec. 1421(f)(2) of PPACA, as amended by Act Sec. 10105(e)(4)).

Law source: Law at ¶5055, ¶5060, ¶5130, and ¶5150. Committee Report at ¶10,070.

— Act Sec. 1421(a) of the Patient Protection and Affordable Care Act (PPACA) (P.L. 111-148), adding Code Sec. 45R;

— Act Sec. 10105(e)(1), amending Code Sec. 45R(d)(3), as added by Act Sec. 1421(a);

— Act Sec. 10105(e)(2), amending Code Sec. 45R(g), as added by Act Sec. 1421(a);

— Act Sec. 1421(b), adding Code Sec. 38(b)(36);

— Act Sec. 1421(c), adding Code Sec. 38(c)(4)(B)(vi);

— Act Sec. 1421(d)(1), adding Code Sec. 280C(h);

— Act Sec. 10105(e)(3), amending Code Sec. 280C(h), as added by Act Sec. 1421(d)(1);

— Act Sec. 1421(d)(2), adding Code Sec. 196(c)(14);

— Act Sec. 1421(f), as amended by Act Sec. 10105(e)(4), and Act Sec. 10105(e)(5), providing the effective dates.

Reporter references: For further information, consult the following CCH reporters.

— Standard Federal Tax Reporter, ¶6702.01

— Tax Research Consultant, COMPEN: 45,154

— Practical Tax Explanation, §20,301

¶310

¶315 Free Choice Vouchers

SUMMARY OF NEW LAW

An employer who offers minimum essential coverage to its employees consisting of coverage through an eligible employer-sponsored plan and pays any portion of the plan's costs shall provide free choice vouchers to its qualified employees. Qualified employees are those who do not participate in a health plan offered by the employer and meet other requirements. The free choice voucher amount is generally equal to the monthly portion of the cost of the eligible employer-sponsored plan that would have been paid by the employer if the employee were covered under the plan.

BACKGROUND

Employers are not required to provide health care benefits to their employees under federal law. However, most large employers and many small businesses provide such benefits. There is no tax credit available for an employer that provides health coverage for its employees. The employer's cost in providing such benefits is generally deductible as a Code Sec. 162 ordinary and necessary business expense for compensation, though special rules may apply if the benefits are provided through a funded welfare benefit plan. Employees are allowed to exclude from gross income the value of the employer-provided health coverage under an accident or health plan as well as the value of any medical care received under such a plan (Code Secs. 105(b) and 106).

Although employers are not required to provide health coverage, those who choose to do so must comply with a number of plan requirements imposed by the Employee Retirement Income Security Act of 1974 (ERISA), such as reporting and disclosure requirements, health care continuation coverage (COBRA), limitations on the use of pre-existing condition exclusions, and others. Group health plans that fail to comply with some of these requirements are subject to an excise tax in the amount of $100 per day per failure during the period of noncompliance. The excise tax is imposed on the employer sponsoring the plan (Code Secs. 4980B and 4980D).

Wages paid to employees are subject to the Federal Insurance Contributions Act (FICA) tax, which funds the social security and medicare programs. Both the employer and the employee must pay their share of the FICA tax. For purposes of determining the amount of the FICA tax due, wages generally include all remuneration for employment, including the cash value of any remuneration paid in a form other than cash. However, the general definition of wages is subject to various special rules and exceptions (Code Sec. 3121(a)).

Federal law does not require individuals to have health insurance. Massachusetts is the only state that imposes a tax penalty on certain individuals who do not meet a state health insurance requirement.

¶310

Free choice vouchers provided to qualified employees by offering employers.—
An employer who offers minimum essential coverage to its employees consisting of
coverage through an eligible employer-sponsored plan and pays any portion of the
plan's costs (an offering employer) shall provide free choice vouchers to its qualified
employees (Act Sec. 10108(a) and (b) of the Patient Protection and Affordable Care Act
(PPACA) (P.L. 111-148)).

A qualified employee with respect to any plan year of an offering employer is an
employee:

- whose required contribution for minimum essential coverage through an eligible
  employer-sponsored plan
  - exceeds eight percent of the employee's household income for the tax year that
    ends with or within the plan year (such household income is determined on the
    basis of the individual's household income for the most recent tax year for which
    the Secretary of Labor, after consultation with the Secretary of the Treasury,
    determines information is available); and
  - does not exceed 9.8 percent of the employee's household income for the tax year;
- whose household income for the tax year is not greater than 400 percent of the
  poverty line for a family of the size involved; and
- who does not participate in a health plan offered by the offering employer (Act Sec.
  10108(c)(1) of PPACA).

In the case of any calendar year beginning after 2014, the Secretary of Health and
Human Services will adjust the eight percent and 9.8 percent figures for the calendar
year to reflect the rate of premium growth between the preceding calendar year and
2013 over the rate of income growth for that period (Act Sec. 10108(c)(2) of PPACA).

For purposes of the qualified employee definition, the required contribution for minimum essential coverage is determined under the requirements for an individual to
maintain minimum essential coverage (see ¶ 205). In the case of an individual eligible to
purchase minimum essential coverage consisting of coverage through an eligible
employer-sponsored plan, the required contribution is the portion of the annual premium that would be paid by the individual for self-only coverage. In the case of an
individual eligible to purchase minimum essential coverage under a health plan offered
through a Health Benefit Exchange within a state, the required contribution is generally
the annual premium for the lowest cost bronze plan available from the Exchange in the
state in the rating area in which the individual resides, reduced by the amount of the
premium assistance tax credit, for the tax year. For a discussion of the premium
assistance tax credit, see ¶ 210.

> **Comment:** By January 1, 2014, each State must establish an American Health
> Benefit Exchange and Small Business Health Options Program (SHOP Exchange)
> to provide qualified individuals and qualified small business employers access
> to qualified health plans. For a discussion of the establishment and requirements
> of the Exchanges, see ¶505. The Exchanges will have four levels of essential
> benefits coverage available to participants at either a "bronze," "silver," "gold,"

NEW LAW EXPLAINED

or "platinum" level. The bronze level plans must provide benefits that are actuarially equivalent to 60 percent of the full actuarial value of the benefits provided under the plan. The percentage increases to 70 percent for silver level plans, 80 percent for gold level plans, and 90 percent for platinum level plans. For a discussion of the required contents of an essential benefits coverage, see ¶530.

The amount of any free choice voucher provided by the employer is equal to the monthly portion of the cost of the eligible employer-sponsored plan that would have been paid by the employer if the employee were covered under the plan with respect to which the employer pays the largest portion of the plan's cost. Such amount is equal to the amount the employer would pay for an employee with self-only coverage unless the employee elects family coverage (in which case this amount is the amount the employer would pay for family coverage). The cost of any health plan is determined under rules similar to the rules of Act Sec. 2204 of the Public Health Service Act, except that such amount is adjusted for age and category of enrollment in accordance with regulations established by the Secretary of Health and Human Services (Act Sec. 10108(d)(1) of PPACA).

The amount of any free choice voucher is credited by an Exchange to the monthly premium of any qualified health plan in the Exchange in which the qualified employee is enrolled, and the offering employer pays any credited amounts to the Exchange. If the amount of the free choice voucher exceeds the amount of the premium of the qualified health plan in which the qualified employee is enrolled for the month, the excess is paid to the employee (Act Sec. 10108(d)(2) and (3) of PPACA).

> **Comment:** Any term used in the free choice voucher provision that is also used in new Code Sec. 5000A, as added by the Patient Protection Act, has the meaning given to that term under Code Sec. 5000A (Act Sec. 10108(e) of PPACA).

The amount of any free choice voucher provided by an employer is excluded from the employee's gross income to the extent that the amount of the voucher does not exceed the amount paid for a qualified health plan (see ¶530) (Code Sec. 139D, as added by PPACA). An employer is allowed a deduction for the amount of any free choice voucher provided, which is treated as an amount paid for compensation for personal services actually rendered (Code Sec. 162(a), as amended by PPACA).

For a discussion of the coordination of the free choice voucher rules with the new Code Sec. 36B premium assistance credit, see ¶210. For a discussion of the coordination of the free choice voucher rules with the new Code Sec. 4980H employer shared responsibility penalty, see ¶305. For a discussion of the coordination of the free choice voucher rules with the employer's new Code Sec. 6056 information reporting requirements, see ¶415.

▶ **Effective date.** No specific effective date is provided by the Act for the free choice voucher rules. These rules are, therefore, considered effective on March 23, 2010, the date of enactment. The rules for excluding free choice vouchers from an employee's income under new Code Sec. 139D and the rules allowing a deduction to an employer for the amount of the provided free choice vouchers under Code Sec. 162 apply to vouchers provided after

¶315

NEW LAW EXPLAINED

December 31, 2013 (Act Sec. 10108(f)(3) and (g)(2) of the Patient Protection and Affordable Care Act (PPACA) (P.L. 111-148)).

Law source: Law at ¶5115, ¶5120, ¶5225, and ¶7045. Committee Report at ¶10,370.

— Act Sec. 10108(a), (b), (c), (d) and (e) of the Patient Protection and Affordable Care Act (PPACA) (P.L. 111-148);

— Act Sec. 10108(f)(1), adding Code Sec. 139D;

— Act Sec. 10108(g)(1), amending Code Sec. 162;

— Act Sec. 10108(f)(3) and (g)(2), providing the effective date.

Reporter references: For further information, consult the following CCH reporters.

— Standard Federal Tax Reporter, ¶6803.01, ¶8636.01

— Tax Research Consultant, COMPEN: 45,150, COMPEN: 45,200

— Practical Tax Explanation, § 9410.05 and § 20,301

¶320 Exchange-Participating Qualified Health Plans Offered Through Cafeteria Plans

SUMMARY OF NEW LAW

A cafeteria plan may not provide a health plan that is offered through the American Health Benefit Exchange unless the employer is a qualified employer for purposes of the Exchange.

BACKGROUND

Generally, all forms of income and compensation, from whatever source derived, are included in the taxable income of the recipient, unless a specific exclusion of the income exists (Code Sec. 61). This includes any benefits that may be received by an employee from an employer as compensation. There are several exceptions to this rule. For example, amounts received by an employee from an employer as part of an accident or health plan and amounts employers contribute to the cost of accident and health plans covering employees are excluded from income under Code Secs. 105 and 106, respectively.

There are many other exclusions provided by the Internal Revenue Code related to employee benefits. One such exception applies to benefits received through a cafeteria plan under Code Sec. 125. A cafeteria plan is an employer-sponsored plan under which employees have the option of selecting benefits or cash. Employees can select the qualified benefits that fit their situations and receive taxable cash payments in lieu of receiving benefits that they do not select.

BACKGROUND

Generally, only benefits for which an exclusion is already granted by the Internal Revenue Code can be offered as "qualified benefits" as a part of a cafeteria plan. Some of the "qualified benefits" that can be offered as part of a cafeteria plan include:

- Nontaxable group-term life insurance on the life of an employee in an amount that is less than or equal to $50,000;
- Excludable accident and health plan and benefits;
- Dependent care assistance;
- Disability benefits;
- Adoption assistance;
- Premiums for life insurance on the life or lives of a spouse or dependent with a benefit of up to $2,000; and
- Contributions to Health Savings Accounts (HSAs) (Code Sec. 125(f); Proposed Reg. § 1.125-1(a)(3); Notice 89-110, 1989-2 CB 447).

NEW LAW EXPLAINED

"Qualified benefit" generally does not include certain exchange-participating qualified health plans.—Effective for tax years beginning after December 31, 2013, a cafeteria plan cannot offer a qualified health plan offered through an American Health Benefit Exchange (Code Sec. 125(f)(3)(A), as added by the Patient Protection and Affordable Care Act (PPACA) (P.L. 111-148)).

> **Comment:** By January 1, 2014, each State must establish an American Health Benefit Exchange and Small Business Health Options Program (SHOP Exchange) to provide qualified individuals and qualified small business employers access to qualified health plans. For a discussion of the establishment and requirements of the Exchanges, see ¶505. The Exchanges will have four levels of essential benefits coverage available to participants at either a "bronze," "silver," "gold," or "platinum" level. The bronze level plans must provide benefits that are actuarially equivalent to 60 percent of the full actuarial value of the benefits provided under the plan. The percentage increases to 70 percent for silver level plans, 80 percent for gold level plans, and 90 percent for platinum level plans. For a discussion of the required contents of an essential benefits coverage, see ¶530.

A "qualified health plan" is one that:

- has in effect a certification that such plan meets the criteria for certification issued or recognized by each Exchange through which such plan is offered;
- provides the essential health benefits package; and
- is offered by a health insurance issuer that (a) is licensed and in good standing to offer health insurance coverage in each state in which the issuer offers health insurance coverage under the Patient Protection Act, (b) agrees to offer at least one qualified health plan in the silver level and at least one plan in the gold level in each exchange, (c) agrees to charge the same premium rate for each qualified

NEW LAW EXPLAINED

health plan of the issuer without regard to whether the plan is offered directly from the issuer or through an agent and (d) complies with regulations developed under Act Sec. 1311(d) of the Patient Protection Act and any other applicable exchange regulations (Act Sec. 1301(a) of PPACA).

> **Comment:** A "qualified health plan" also includes one offered through the Consumer Operated and Oriented Plan (CO-OP) program or a community health insurance option (Act Secs. 1322 and 1323 of PPACA).

There is an exception to this prohibition in the case of Exchange-eligible employers offering employees the opportunity to enroll in a qualified health plan through an Exchange (Code Sec. 125(f)(3)(B), as added by PPACA). An Exchange-eligible employer is, in tax years beginning after December 31, 2013, a small employer electing to make all of its full-time employees eligible for one or more qualified health plans offered in the small group market through an Exchange (Act Sec. 1312(f)(2)(A) of PPACA). A small employer is an employer who employed an average of at least one, but not more than 100, employees on business days during the preceding calendar year and employs at least one employee on the first day of the plan year (Act Sec. 1304(b)(2) of PPACA). The "small group market" is the health insurance market under which employees obtain health insurance coverage through a group health plan maintained by a small employer (Act Sec. 1304(a)(3) of PPACA). This exception allows Exchange-eligible employers in the small group market to offer "qualified health plans" through an exchange as a part of a cafeteria plan in tax years beginning after December 31, 2013.

Beginning in 2017, a state may allow issuers of health insurance coverage in large group markets to offer health insurance under the American Health Benefit Exchange, thereby making it possible for all employers to be Exchange-eligible employers (Act Sec. 1312(f)(2)(B) of PPACA). A large employer is any employer who employed an average of more than 100 employees in the preceding calendar year and employs at least one employee on the first day of the plan year (Act Sec. 1304(b)(1) of PPACA). This expanded exception allows all Exchange-eligible employers to offer "qualified health plans" as a part of cafeteria plans beginning in 2017, but only if the state allows large employers to participate in the Exchange.

▶ **Effective date.** The provision applies to tax years beginning after December 31, 2013 (Act Sec. 1515(c) of the Patient Protection and Affordable Care Act (PPACA) (P.L. 111-148)).

Law source: Law at ¶5095. Committee Report at ¶10,120.

— Act Sec. 1515(a) of the Patient Protection and Affordable Care Act (PPACA) (P.L. 111-148), adding Code Sec. 125(f)(3);

— Act Sec. 1515(b), amending Code Sec. 125(f);

— Act Sec. 1515(c), providing the effective date.

Reporter references: For further information, consult the following CCH reporters.

— Standard Federal Tax Reporter, ¶7324.021

— Tax Research Consultant, COMPEN: 51,104

— Practical Tax Explanation, §20,815

¶325 Health Flexible Spending Accounts Offered in Cafeteria Plans

SUMMARY OF NEW LAW

Health flexible spending arrangements (health FSAs) offered as a part of a cafeteria plan must limit contributions through salary reductions to $2,500.

BACKGROUND

Generally, all forms of income and compensation, from whatever source derived, are included in the taxable income of the recipient, unless a specific exclusion of the income exists (Code Sec. 61). There are several exceptions to this rule that do provide such exclusions. One such exception is a cafeteria plan under Code Sec. 125. A cafeteria plan is an employer-sponsored plan under which employees have the option of selecting benefits or cash. Employees can choose which of the offered benefits fits their situations and receive taxable cash payments in lieu of the un-selected benefits. Benefits provided under a cafeteria plan may be funded through employer contributions, employee salary reductions, or a combination of both.

One such benefit that can be provided under a cafeteria plan is a flexible spending arrangement. A flexible spending arrangement (FSA) is a benefit under which participants are given an account that is credited with employer contributions or pre-tax employee salary reductions. The amounts in the account can then be used for dependent care services or health care service expenses, depending on whether the plan is a dependent care FSA or a health FSA. A health FSA must qualify as a health or accident plan under Code Secs. 105 and 106, and can only be used to pay for expenses that would qualify for a deduction for medical services under Code Sec. 213.

Health FSAs have become a very popular method for employees to lower their income tax by paying for common medical expenses, everything from doctor co-pays to aspirin, with pre-tax income. Generally speaking, there is no limit on the amount which an employee can elect to contribute to a health FSA through salary reductions, other than those that may be imposed by the employer's plan.

NEW LAW EXPLAINED

Limitation on FSAs offered as part of cafeteria plans.—Effective for tax years beginning after December 31, 2012, a health flexible spending arrangement (FSA) will not be a qualified benefit under a cafeteria plan unless the plan provides for a $2,500 maximum salary reduction contribution to the FSA (Code Sec. 125(i)(1), as added by Act Secs. 9005 and 10902 of the Patient Protection and Affordable Care Act (PPACA) (P.L. 111-148), as amended by Act Sec. 1403(a) of the Health Care and Education Reconciliation Act of 2010 (P.L. 111-152)). If the plan does allow salary reductions in

NEW LAW EXPLAINED

excess of $2,500, then an employee will be subject to tax on distributions from the health FSA, thereby eliminating any of the tax benefits of health FSA contributions.

State Tax Consequences: The limitation of FSA contributions to $2,500 for tax years after 2012 will not impact states that conform to the federal exclusion by the time the provision takes effect. Because most states start their tax calculations with federal adjustable gross income, there should be no impact on those states. States that do not conform may allow an exclusion from taxation for amounts above the federal limitation as well.

Effective for tax years beginning after December 31, 2013, the $2,500 limitation is adjusted annually for inflation. Any inflation adjustment that is not a multiple of $50 is rounded down to the next lowest multiple of $50 (Code Sec. 125(i)(2), as added by Act Sec. 10902 of PPACA and amended by Act Sec 1403(b) of the 2010 Reconciliation Act).

Practical Analysis: Pam Perdue, Of Counsel with Summers, Compton, Wells & Hamburg in St. Louis, Missouri, notes that the fact that the maximum contribution limit of $2,500 is scheduled to increase based upon the CPI-U, that is, the consumer price index for all urban consumers, may well mean that once this reduced limit does in fact start to rise, increases will in no way keep pace with the actual increase in health care cost. This is because the CPI includes many items that have historically risen at a much slower pace than the cost of health care. If the reform fails to halt that trend, the increases in the FSA limit will fail to keep pace with the actual increase in the cost of health care.

Implementation of a limit means that employers must communicate the new limit and then quickly adopt procedures and make software changes necessary to ensure compliance.

▶ **Effective date.** The amendments apply to tax years beginning after December 31, 2012 (Act Secs. 9005(b) and 10902(b) of the Patient Protection and Affordable Care Act (PPACA) (P.L. 111-148), as amended by Act Sec. 1403(a) of the Health Care and Education Reconciliation Act of 2010 (P.L. 111-152)).

Law source: Law at ¶5095. Committee Report at ¶10,200.

— Act Sec. 9005(a)(1) of the Patient Protection and Affordable Care Act (PPACA) (P.L. 111-148), redesignating Code Sec. 125(i) and (j) as Code Sec. 125(j) and (k), respectively;

— Act Sec. 9005(a)(2) of PPACA, adding Code Sec. 125(i);

— Act Sec. 10902(a) of PPACA, as amended by Act Sec. 1403(b) of the Health Care and Education Reconciliation Act of 2010 (P.L. 111-152), amending Code Sec. 125(i), as added by Act Sec. 9005(a)(2) of PPACA;

— Act Secs. 9005(b) and 10902(b) of PPACA, as amended by Act Sec. 1403(a) of the 2010 Reconciliation Act, providing the effective date.

Reporter references: For further information, consult the following CCH reporters.

— Standard Federal Tax Reporter, ¶7324.04 and ¶7324.042

— Tax Research Consultant, COMPEN: 51,200

— Practical Tax Explanation, §20,815.15

¶330 Simple Cafeteria Plans

SUMMARY OF NEW LAW

Certain small employers may choose to provide a simple cafeteria plan for their employees, under which the nondiscrimination rules of a classic cafeteria plan are treated as satisfied.

BACKGROUND

Generally, all forms of income and compensation, from whatever source derived, are included in the taxable income of the recipient, unless a specific exclusion of the income exists (Code Sec. 61). This includes noncash benefits received from an employer. However, there are many specific exclusions provided by the Internal Revenue Code for various benefits received by employees, such as (among others) employer contributions for accident and health plans (Code Sec. 106), dependent care assistance (Code Sec. 129) or group-term life insurance (Code Sec. 79). Where an employer provides these benefits to employees, the employees are subject to tax on the full amounts of benefits they can elect to receive (subject to the exclusions), regardless of whether the employees actually elect to receive the benefits.

Another avenue of providing excludable benefits to employees is through the implementation of a cafeteria plan under Code Sec. 125. A cafeteria plan is an employer-sponsored plan under which employees have the option of selecting benefits or cash. Employees can choose which of the offered benefits fits their situations and receive taxable cash payments in lieu of the unselected benefits.

A cafeteria plan must be a written plan and may not discriminate in favor of highly compensated participants. A highly compensated participant is: (1) an officer or spouse or dependent of an officer of the employer, (2) a stockholder or spouse or dependent of a stockholder owning more than five percent (determined by voting power or value) of all classes of the stock of the employer, or (3) a highly compensated employee or spouse or dependent of a highly compensated employee (Code Sec. 125(e)). An individual is highly compensated for purposes of these nondiscrimination rules if he or she had compensation in excess of an annually-adjusted amount ($110,000 in 2010) (Code Sec. 414(q); Notice 2009-94, 2009-50 I.R.B. 848). A cafeteria plan discriminates in favor of highly compensated participants if the plan provides greater benefits to those employees in comparison to non-highly compensated employees. This can be determined based upon either the benefits available to be elected by the participants, by the benefits actually elected by the participants or by the amount contributed by the employer for the benefits (Proposed Reg. § 1.125-7(c)).

Additionally, a cafeteria plan may not favor key employees. A key employee is an officer with compensation in excess of an inflation-adjusted amount ($160,000 for 2010), a five-percent owner or a one-percent owner with compensation in excess of $150,000 (not adjusted for inflation) (Code Sec. 125(b)(2); Code Sec. 416(i)(1); Notice

BACKGROUND

2009-94, 2009-50 I.R.B. 848). A cafeteria plan favors key employees if more than 25 percent of the nontaxable qualified benefits provided under the plan are provided to key employees (Code Sec. 125(b)(2)).

A violation of the nondiscrimination rules with regard to either highly compensated participants or key employees does not invalidate the cafeteria plan for all participants. However, it does invalidate the protections of a cafeteria plan for the highly compensated participants or key employees. In such an instance, the highly compensated participants or key employees will be subject to tax on the benefits they receive under the plan (Code Sec. 125(b)(1), (2)). Because of this risk of increased tax for highly compensated participants and key employees, small employers, who may have a higher percentage of these employees compared to larger employers, may not be able to offer cafeteria plans to their employees.

NEW LAW EXPLAINED

Small employers can provide simple cafeteria plans.—In years beginning after December 31, 2010, certain small employers' cafeteria plans can qualify as simple cafeteria plans, under which the applicable nondiscrimination requirements of a classic cafeteria plan are treated as satisfied (Code Sec. 125(j)(1), as added by the Patient Protection and Affordable Care Act (PPACA) (P.L. 111-148)). A simple cafeteria plan is a cafeteria plan established and maintained by an eligible employer that meets certain contribution, eligibility and participation requirements (Code Sec. 125(j)(2), as added by PPACA).

An applicable nondiscrimination requirement that will be deemed as met by an employer establishing a simple cafeteria plan is any nondiscrimination requirement applicable to a classic cafeteria plan under Code Sec. 125(b), group-term life insurance under Code Sec. 79(d), an accident and health plan under Code Sec. 105(h), or a dependent care assistance program under Code Sec. 129(d)(2), (3), (4) or (8) (Code Sec. 125(j)(6), as added by PPACA).

> **Comment:** Small employers may find it difficult to justify providing a classic cafeteria plan to employees if it requires diminishing benefits enjoyed by owner-employees to satisfy the nondiscrimination requirements of a classic cafeteria plan. Through the establishment of a simple cafeteria plan, employers can retain potentially discriminatory benefits for highly compensated and key employees (subject to some restrictions relating to contributions, discussed below) while allowing other employees to enjoy the benefits of a cafeteria plan without worrying about running afoul of the nondiscrimination requirements of a classic cafeteria plan.

An employer eligible to establish a simple cafeteria plan is any employer that, during either of the two preceding years, employed an average of 100 or fewer employees on business days. For purposes of this rule, a year may only be taken into account if the employer was in existence throughout the year (Code Sec. 125(j)(5)(A), as added by PPACA). If an employer was not in existence throughout the preceding year, the employer may nonetheless be considered as an eligible employer if it reasonably

NEW LAW EXPLAINED

expects to average 100 or fewer employees on business days during the current year (Code Sec. 125(j)(5)(B), as added by PPACA).

If an employer has 100 or fewer employees for any year and establishes a simple cafeteria plan for that year, then it can be treated as meeting the requirement for any subsequent year even if the employer employs more than 100 employees in the subsequent year (Code Sec. 125(j)(5)(C)(i), as added by PPACA). However, this exception does not apply if the employer employs an average of 200 or more employees during the subsequent year (Code Sec. 125(j)(5)(C)(ii), as added by PPACA).

> **Comment:** This provision allows small but growing employers to continue to offer simple cafeteria plan benefits to employees without the concern of having to meet the discrimination requirements by having to switch to a classic cafeteria plan. Without this exception, the establishment of simple cafeteria plans could create a disincentive to increased hiring.

A simple cafeteria plan must also meet rigid contribution requirements on the part of the employer. The contribution requirements are met if the employer is required by the plan, regardless of whether a qualified employee makes any salary reduction contribution, to make a contribution to provide qualified benefits on behalf of each qualified employee, in an amount equal to: (1) a uniform percentage (not less than two percent) of the employee's compensation for the year, or (2) an amount not less than the lesser of: (a) six percent of the employee's compensation for the plan year or (b) twice the amount of the salary reduction contributions of each qualified employee (Code Sec. 125(j)(3)(A), as added by PPACA).

If the employer bases the satisfaction of the contribution requirements on the second option, it will not be treated as met if the rate of contributions with respect to any salary reduction contribution of a highly compensated or key employee is greater than that with respect to any other employee (Code Sec. 125(j)(3)(B), as added by PPACA). Beyond this prohibition, the established contribution requirements are not to be treated as prohibiting an employer from making contributions to provide qualified benefits under the plan in addition to the required contributions.

For purposes of the contribution requirements, a salary reduction contribution is any amount contributed to the plan at the election of the employee and not includable in the employee's gross income under the cafeteria plan provisions (Code Sec. 125(j)(3)(D)(i), as added by PPACA). The terms "highly compensated employee" and "key employee" retain their definitions under the classic cafeteria plan provisions. A "qualified employee" is any employee who is not a highly compensated or key employee.

Employee eligibility and participation requirements. A simple cafeteria plan must also satisfy minimum eligibility and participation requirements. The requirements are met if all employees who had at least 1,000 hours of service for the preceding plan year are eligible to participate and if each employee eligible to participate may elect any benefit under the plan, subject to terms and conditions applicable to all participants (Code Sec. 125(j)(4)(A), as added by PPACA).

NEW LAW EXPLAINED

An employer may elect to exclude from the plan, regardless of the satisfaction of the 1,000 hour requirement, employees who have not attained the age of 21 before the close of the plan year, who have less than one year of service with the employer as of any day during the plan year, who are covered under a collective bargaining agreement if there is evidence that the benefits covered under the plan were the subject of good faith bargaining between employee representatives and the employer, or are nonresident aliens working outside the United States whose income did not come from a U.S. source (Code Sec. 125(j)(4)(B), as added by PPACA).

References to employers with regard to simple cafeteria plans include references to predecessors of such employers (Code Sec. 125(j)(5)(D)(i), as added by PPACA). This means that, among other considerations, for purposes of determining the qualification of a business that has recently changed ownership, the fact that the previous owner had 100 or fewer employees in a preceding year can be used to determine eligibility of the current ownership to establish a simple cafeteria plan. Also, any person treated as a single employer for purposes of the Work Opportunity Credit under Code Sec. 52(a) or (b) or for purposes of deferred compensation rules under Code Sec. 414(n) or (o) shall be treated as one person for purposes of simple cafeteria plans (Code Sec. 125(j)(5)(D)(ii), as added by PPACA).

▶ **Effective date.** The provision applies to years beginning after December 31, 2010 (Act Sec. 9022(b) of the Patient Protection and Affordable Care Act (PPACA) (P.L. 111-148)).

Law source: Law at ¶5095. Committee Report at ¶10,340.

— Act Sec. 9022(a) of the Patient Protection and Affordable Care Act (PPACA) (P.L. 111-148), redesignating Code Sec. 125(j) and (k) as Code Sec. 125(k) and (l), respectively, and adding Code Sec. 125(j);

— Act Sec. 9022(b), providing the effective date.

Reporter references: For further information, consult the following CCH reporters.

— Standard Federal Tax Reporter, ¶7324.01

— Tax Research Consultant, COMPEN: 51,000

— Practical Tax Explanation, §20,801

¶335 Elimination of Deduction for Federal Subsidies for Certain Retiree Prescription Drug Plans

SUMMARY OF NEW LAW

The rule that allows an employer, as a plan sponsor, to disregard the value of any qualified retiree prescription drug plan subsidy in calculating the employer's business deduction for retiree prescription drug costs is repealed.

BACKGROUND

A business that provides a qualified retiree prescription drug plan to its retired employees is eligible for a special subsidy payment each year from the federal government based on the cost of providing such coverage (Section 1860D-22 of the Social Security Act (SSA) (P.L. 108-173)). The amount of the subsidy is 28 percent of allowable retiree drug costs between $250 and $5,000. These dollar amounts are indexed annually for inflation. For 2010, the amount of the subsidy is 28 percent of allowable retiree drug costs between $310 and $6,300 (Centers for Medicare & Medicaid Services (CMS) Retiree Drug Subsidy Program Announcement, April 21, 2009 (http://rds.cms.hhs.gov/news/announcements/cost_threshold10.htm)). The subsidy payment is excludable from income for both regular tax and alternative minimum tax (including the adjustment for current earnings) purposes (Code Secs. 56(g)(4)(B) and 139A).

A "qualified retiree prescription drug plan" is employment-based retiree health coverage that has an actuarial value at least equal to the Medicare Part D standard plan for the risk pool and that meets certain other disclosure and recordkeeping requirements (Section 1860D-22(a)(2) of SSA). "Employment-based retiree health coverage" is health insurance or other coverage of health care costs, whether provided by voluntary insurance coverage, or pursuant to statutory or contractual obligation, for Medicare Part D eligible individuals (including spouses and dependents of such individuals) under group health plans based on their status as retired participants in such plans (Section 1860D-22(c)(1) of SSA). A "qualified retiree," for these purposes, is an individual who is eligible for Medicare but not enrolled in either a Medicare Part D prescription drug plan or a Medicare Advantage-Prescription Drug plan, but who is covered under a qualified retiree prescription drug plan. "Allowable retiree drug costs," in general, are, with respect to prescription drug costs under a qualified retiree prescription drug plan, the part of the actual costs paid by the plan sponsor on behalf of a qualifying retiree under the plan.

> **Comment:** According to the Joint Committee on Taxation, *Technical Explanation of the Revenue Provisions of the "Reconciliation Act of 2010," as amended, in combination with the "Patient Protection and Affordable Care Act"* (JCX-18-10), March 21, 2010, "[f]or purposes of calculating allowable retiree costs, actual costs paid are net of discounts, chargebacks, and average percentage rebates, and exclude administrative costs."

Employer's deduction. The value of any qualified retiree prescription drug plan subsidy received by an employer is disregarded in calculating the employer's business deduction for prescription drug costs (Code Sec. 139A). Therefore, an employer can claim a deduction for prescription drug expenses incurred even though the employer also received an excludable subsidy related to the same expenses (Joint Committee on Taxation, *Technical Explanation of the Revenue Provisions of the "Reconciliation Act of 2010," as amended, in combination with the "Patient Protection and Affordable Care Act"* (JCX-18-10), March 21, 2010). This is an exception to the general rule disallowing a deduction under any Code provision for any expense or amount that would otherwise be allowable as a deduction if such expense or amount is allocable to a class or classes of exempt income (Code Sec. 265(a); Reg. § 1.265-1(a)).

¶335

NEW LAW EXPLAINED

Deduction repealed for expenses allocable to Medicare Part D subsidy. The provision that allows an employer to disregard the value of any qualified retiree prescription drug plan subsidy in calculating the employer's business deduction for retiree prescription drug costs is repealed, effective for tax years beginning after December 31, 2012 (Code Sec. 139A, as amended by the Patient Protection and Affordable Care Act (PPACA) (P.L. 111-148); Act Sec. 9012(b) of PPACA, as amended by Act Sec. 1407 of the Health Care and Education Reconciliation Act of 2010 (P.L. 111-152)). Thus, the amount otherwise allowable as a business deduction for retiree prescription drug expenses is reduced by the amount of the excludable subsidy payments received.

> **State Tax Consequences:** The repeal of the provision that allows an employer to disregard the value of any qualified retiree prescription drug plan subsidy in calculating the employer's business deduction for retiree prescription drug costs, effective for tax years beginning after 2012, will impact states that adopt Code Sec. 162, but that have Code conformity dates that would not include this amendment, unless their conformity dates are updated to include the amendment. States that annually update their conformity dates will most likely adopt the amendment by the time it takes effect. Those states that do not conform may allow a subtraction for the amount of subsidy used to reduce the federal deduction.

> **Practical Analysis:** Mark Luscombe, Principal Analyst for the Tax and Accounting Group at CCH, a Wolters Kluwer business, points out that this provision is already having a significant impact on the financial statements of employers self-insuring retiree health coverage. Several major corporations have announced multi-million dollar hits to earnings as a result of this change. The debate remains, however, as to whether the provision is only eliminating a double benefit that those companies had been receiving in the past.

▶ **Effective date.** This provision is effective for tax years beginning after December 31, 2012 (Act Sec. 9012(b) of the Patient Protection and Affordable Care Act (PPACA) (P.L. 111-148), as amended by Act Sec. 1407 of the Health Care and Education Reconciliation Act of 2010 (P.L. 111-152)).

Law source: Law at ¶5105. Committee Report at ¶10,270.

— Act Sec. 9012(a) of the Patient Protection and Affordable Care Act (PPACA) (P.L. 111-148), amending Code Sec. 139A;

— Act Sec. 9012(b) of PPACA, as amended by Act Sec. 1407 of the Health Care and Education Reconciliation Act of 2010 (P.L. 111-152), providing the effective date.

Reporter references: For further information, consult the following CCH reporters.

— Standard Federal Tax Reporter, 7649A.01

— Tax Research Consultant, INDIV: 33,050

¶340 Limitation on Excessive Employee Remuneration

SUMMARY OF NEW LAW

The deduction for employee remuneration paid by certain health insurance providers is limited. The limitation applies to certain individuals who are paid in excess of $500,000 in tax years beginning after December 31, 2012.

BACKGROUND

A publicly held corporation may not deduct applicable employee remuneration in excess of $1 million for covered employees (Code Sec. 162(m)(1)). Generally, "covered employees" include the chief executive officer of the corporation and the four most highly compensated employees of the corporation other than the chief executive officer (CEO), whose compensation is required to be reported to the shareholders by the Securities Exchange Act of 1934 (Code Sec. 162(m)(3)). "Applicable employee remuneration" generally includes the taxable wages paid to the employee, but excludes commissions and other performance-based compensation (Code Sec. 162(m)(4)).

A $500,000 deduction limit applies to compensation paid to "covered executives" by certain employers who participated in the Troubled Asset Relief Program (TARP) (Code Sec. 162(m)(5)(A)). Covered executives include the CEO, the chief financial officer (CFO), and the three most highly compensated employees of the employer, other than the CEO or CFO (Code Sec. 162(m)(5)(D)). Subject to limited exceptions, recipients of assistance under TARP cannot pay or accrue any bonus, retention award, or executive compensation while any obligation arising from such assistance remains outstanding (Act Sec. 7001 of the American Recovery and Reinvestment Act of 2009 (P.L. 111-5)).

NEW LAW EXPLAINED

New limitations on employee remuneration.—In a disqualified tax year, applicable individual remuneration for services performed is not deductible above the amount of $500,000 (Code Sec. 162(m)(6)(A)(i), as added by the Patient Protection and Affordable Care Act (PPACA) (P.L. 111-148)). A disqualified tax year is any tax year for which the employer is a covered health insurance provider (Code Sec. 162(m)(6)(B), as added by PPACA). An applicable individual is an officer, director, or employee of a covered health insurance provider. Any individual who provides services for or on behalf of the covered health insurance provider is also an applicable individual (Code Sec. 162(m)(6)(F), as added by PPACA). Applicable individual remuneration means the aggregate amount of remuneration for a disqualified tax year that would be deductible except for this new limitation. Applicable individual remuneration does not include deferred deduction remuneration (Code Sec. 162(m)(6)(D), as added by PPACA).

For tax years beginning after December 31, 2009, and before January 1, 2013, a covered health insurance provider is an employer which is a health insurance issuer (Code Sec.

NEW LAW EXPLAINED

9832(b)(2)) and which receives premiums from providing health insurance coverage (Code Sec. 9832(b)(1)). For tax years beginning after December 31, 2012, a covered health insurance provider is an employer which is a health insurance issuer that receives gross premiums from providing health insurance coverage such that not less than 25 percent of those gross premiums is from essential health benefits coverage (Code Sec. 5000A(f)(1); Code Sec. 162(m)(6)(C)(i), as added by PPACA).

Two or more persons who are treated as a single employer under the aggregation rules (Code Sec. 414(b), (c), (m), or (o)) are treated as a single employer for the purpose of this limitation except that the brother/sister controlled group and combined group rules (Code Sec. 1563(a)(2) and (3)) are disregarded (Code Sec. 162(m)(6)(C)(ii), as added by PPACA).

There is a separate limitation for deferred deduction remuneration for a tax year beginning after December 31, 2012, for services performed by an applicable individual during any disqualified tax year beginning after December 31, 2009. The deduction is limited to the amount that the remuneration exceeds $500,000 reduced, but not below zero, by the sum of two items. The first item is the applicable individual remuneration for the disqualified tax year. The second item is the portion of deferred deduction remuneration taken into account in a preceding tax year (or the portion that would have been taken into account if the limitation were applicable to a tax year beginning after December 31, 2009) (Code Sec. 162(m)(6)(A)(ii), as added by PPACA). Deferred deduction remuneration is remuneration that would be applicable individual remuneration for services performed in a disqualified tax year where the deduction (without regard to this new limitation) is allowable in a subsequent tax year (Code Sec. 162(m)(6)(E), as added by PPACA).

Coordination rules apply that are based on the disallowed golden parachute payment rule (Code Sec. 162(m)(4)(F)) and the rule on stock compensation excise tax (Code Sec. 162(m)(4)(G)) (Code Sec. 162(m)(6)(G), as added by PPACA).

> **State Tax Consequences:** The limitation on the deduction for employee remuneration paid by certain health insurance providers that applies to certain individuals who are paid in excess of $500,000 in tax years beginning after December 31, 2012, will impact states that have not conformed to the limitation by the time it takes effect. In such states, a subtraction may be allowed for amounts exceeding the federal limitation.

▶ **Effective date.** The amendment made by this section applies to tax years beginning after December 31, 2009, with respect to services performed after that date (Act Sec. 9014(b) of the Patient Protection and Affordable Care Act (PPACA) (P.L. 111-148)).

Law source: Law at ¶5120. Committee Report at ¶10,290.

— Act Sec. 9014(a) of the Patient Protection and Affordable Care Act (PPACA) (P.L. 111-148), adding Code Sec. 162(m)(6);

— Act Sec. 9014(b), providing the effective date.

Reporter references: For further information, consult the following CCH reporters.

— Standard Federal Tax Reporter, ¶8636.0252, ¶8636.0267

— Tax Research Consultant, COMPEN: 12,350

— Practical Tax Explanation, §9,310.05, §9,310.30

¶342 Economic Substance Doctrine

SUMMARY OF NEW LAW

The economic substance doctrine, a common law doctrine under which the tax benefits of a transaction are not allowed if the transaction does not have economic substance or lacks a business purpose, has been codified.

BACKGROUND

In order to be respected, a transaction must have economic significance apart from the benefit achieved solely by tax reduction. A transaction has economic substance if it is rationally related to a useful non-tax purpose that is plausible in light of the taxpayer's conduct and economic situation, and the transaction has a reasonable possibility of profit. A transaction's economic substance is determined by analyzing the subjective intent of the taxpayer entering into the transaction and the objective economic substance of the transaction.

The economic substance doctrine represents a judicial effort to enforce the statutory purpose of the Internal Revenue Code. Courts use the doctrine to prevent taxpayers from subverting the legislative intent in enacting particular Code sections by engaging in transactions that are fictitious or lack economic reality simply to reap a tax benefit (*Coltec Indus. Inc. v. U.S*, 2006-2 USTC ¶ 50,389, 454 F3d 1340 (Fed. Cir. 2006)). However, the various U.S. Courts of Appeals differ on whether the economic substance analysis requires the application of a two-prong test, or is a facts and circumstances analysis regarding whether the transaction had a practical economic effect, taking into account both subjective and objective aspects of the transaction.

The two-prong test requires an analysis of whether there was a business purpose other than obtaining tax benefits, and an objective analysis of whether a reasonable expectation of a profit exists. Some courts have held that a transaction will lack economic substance only if the taxpayer lacked a nontax business purpose and the transaction had no objective economic substance (*Rice's Toyota World, Inc. v. Comm'r*, 85-1 USTC ¶ 9123, 752 F2d 89 (4th Cir. 1985)). Thus, these courts invalidate a transaction only if it lacked economic substance *and* the taxpayer's sole motive was tax avoidance.

Other federal courts have held that for a transaction to be valid it must be compelled by business or regulatory realities (have economic substance) and the taxpayer must have subjective motives for the transaction independent of tax considerations. This "conjunctive" approach requires that the taxpayer demonstrate both aspects in order for the transaction to be respected (*Klamath Strategic Investment Fund, LLC. v. Comm'r*, 2009-1 USTC ¶ 50,395, 568 F3d 537 (5th Cir. 2009)).

Still other federal courts have rejected the two-prong test. One court concluded that "consideration of business purpose and economic substance are simply more precise factors to consider in the [determination of] whether the transaction had any practical

BACKGROUND

economic effects other than the creation of income tax losses" (*J.S. James v. Comm'r*, 90-1 USTC ¶50,185, 899 F2d 905 (10th Cir. 1990)).

NEW LAW EXPLAINED

Economic substance doctrine codified for certain transactions.—For any transaction to which the economic substance doctrine is relevant, such transaction will only be treated as having economic substance if, apart from the federal income tax effects, it changes in a meaningful way the taxpayer's economic position, and the taxpayer has a substantial purpose for entering into the transaction (Code Sec. 7701(o)(1), as added by the Health Care and Education Reconciliation Act of 2010 (P.L. 111-152)). The term "transaction" includes, for this purpose, a series of transactions (Code Sec. 7701(o)(5)(D), as added by the 2010 Reconciliation Act).

The term "economic substance doctrine" refers to the common law doctrine under which tax benefits under the income tax provisions of the Internal Revenue Code are not allowed for transactions lacking economic substance or a business purpose (Code Sec. 7701(o)(5)(A), as added by the 2010 Reconciliation Act). For individual taxpayers, the codified economic substance doctrine will only apply to transactions entered into in connection with a trade or business or activity engaged in for the production of income (Code Sec. 7701(o)(5)(B), as added by the 2010 Reconciliation Act).

A state or local income tax effect that is related to a federal income tax effect is, for this purpose, treated as a federal income tax effect (Code Sec. 7701(o)(3), as added by the 2010 Reconciliation Act). A federal accounting benefit which has its origin in a reduction of federal income tax is not considered a substantial purpose for entering into a transaction (Code Sec. 7701(o)(4), as added by the 2010 Reconciliation Act).

> **Comment:** The codified standard clarifies that the economic substance doctrine involves a conjunctive analysis requiring an inquiry regarding the objective effects of the transaction on the taxpayer's economic position, as well as an inquiry regarding the taxpayer's subjective motives for engaging in the transaction. This eliminates the disparity among the Federal circuit courts concerning application of the doctrine (Joint Committee on Taxation, *Technical Explanation of the Revenue Provisions of the "Reconciliation Act of 2010", as amended, in combination with the "Patient Protection and Affordable Care Act"* (JCX-18-10), March 21, 2010).

The profit potential of a transaction will be considered in applying the economic substance test only if the present value of the reasonably expected pre-tax profit from the transaction (taking into account fees, other transaction expenses and, in appropriate cases as set forth in future regulations, foreign taxes) is substantial in relation to the present value of the expected net tax benefits that would be allowed if the

NEW LAW EXPLAINED

transaction were respected (Code Sec. 7701(o)(2)(A) and (B), as added by the 2010 Reconciliation Act).

> **Planning Note:** A taxpayer may rely on factors other than profit potential to demonstrate that a transaction results in a meaningful change in the taxpayer's economic position, or that the taxpayer has a substantial non-federal income tax purpose for entering into such transaction. The taxpayer is not required to show a minimum return to satisfy the profit potential test, but if the taxpayer relies on a profit potential, the present value of the reasonably expected pre-tax profit must be substantial in relation to the present value of the expected net tax benefits that would be allowed if the transaction were respected.

> **Comment:** While codification of the economic substance doctrine is designed to provide a uniform definition for all cases to which it applies, it is not designed to alter the flexibility of the courts in other respects including the courts' ability to aggregate, disaggregate, or otherwise recharacterize a transaction when applying the doctrine (Joint Committee on Taxation, *Technical Explanation of the Revenue Provisions of the "Reconciliation Act of 2010", as amended, in combination with the "Patient Protection and Affordable Care Act"* (JCX-18-10), March 21, 2010).

Codification of the economic substance doctrine is not intended to impact the determination of whether the doctrine is relevant to a particular transaction (Code Sec. 7701(o)(5)(C), as added by the 2010 Reconciliation Act).

> **Comment:** Current standards will still be used to determine when to use an economic substance analysis. Codification of the economic substance doctrine is also not intended to alter the tax treatment of certain basic business transactions, such as whether to capitalize a business enterprise with debt or equity or whether to use a U.S. or foreign corporation to make a foreign investment, that have been respected under longstanding judicial or administrative practice, even if the choice between meaningful economic alternatives is based in whole or in part on comparative tax advantages (Joint Committee on Taxation, *Technical Explanation of the Revenue Provisions of the "Reconciliation Act of 2010", as amended, in combination with the "Patient Protection and Affordable Care Act"* (JCX-18-10), March 21, 2010).

Practical Analysis: Steven Toscher, J.D., and Michel R. Stein, J.D., LL.M., Principals at Hochman, Salkin, Rettig, Toscher & Perez, P.C., of Beverly Hills, California, observe that, while the goal of the codification of the economic substance doctrine was to end the conflict in existing judicial formulations of the doctrine and raise revenue, the new provision may do neither.

While the codification is broader than some judicial formulations, it may be more restrictive than existing law. The new legislation has shifted the doctrine from a common-law concept to a more restrictive Code-based limitation and may in fact narrow the application of the doctrine.

Practical Analysis: Peter Melcher, Senior Manager with Baker Tilly Virchow, Krause & Company, LLP, Appleton, Wisconsin, explains that the economic substance doctrine was developed by the courts to prevent avoidance of the substantive provisions of the Code and can traced back at least as far as *Weiss v. Stearn*, SCt, 1 USTC ¶94, 265 US 242, 44 SCt 490 (1924). In *Frank Lyon Co.*, SCt, 78-1 USTC ¶9370, 435 US 561, 98 SCt 1291 (1978), the U.S. Supreme Court indicated that the doctrine has both an objective and a subjective prong. Under the objective prong, the question is generally whether the transaction has profit potential. Under the subjective prong, the question is whether the taxpayer was motivated to enter into the transaction by a business purpose other than obtaining tax benefits.

The courts subsequently applied this two-prong test in different ways. Some applied a disjunctive analysis under which a transaction was respected if it had *either* an objective or subjective business purpose. (*See, for example, Rice's Toyota World*, CA-4, 85-1 USTC ¶9123, 752 F2d 89 (1982).) Others applied a conjunctive analysis under which a transaction was respected only if it satisfied *both* the objective and subjective prongs. (*See, for example, Dow Chem. Co.*, CA-6, 2006-2 USTC ¶50,126, 435 F3d 594 (2006).) To confuse the issue further, some courts ruled that profit potential could be minimal compared with the economic benefit of a transaction. (*See, for example, ACM Partnership*, Dec. 51,922(M), 73 TCM 2189, TC Memo. 1997-115.)

Clarification or Extension of Prior Law?

Although sometimes referred to as a clarification of existing law, new Code Sec. 7701(o) is really a resolution of the disputed issues in favor of the IRS. Not only does Code Sec. 7701(o) adopt the conjunctive analysis (Code Sec. 7701(o)(1)), but it also requires that the pre-tax profit potential be substantial compared with the pre-tax value of the tax benefit (Code Sec. 7701(o)(2)). On the surface it might appear that the purpose of the new law is to make it more likely that the IRS can prevail in court on its economic substance argument by implementing a more favorable test, but a more likely reason is that it believes the law will deter aggressive tax planning, much like Circular 230.

Quantifying Profit Potential

It is interesting to note that an earlier version of the bill quantified the amount of required profit potential, setting it at the risk-free rate of return on capital. Note that the interest rate on three-month Treasury Bills is often used as a proxy for the risk-free rate. Not including a bright-line rate might make it difficult to determine what is meant by substantial pre-tax profit potential.

Perverse Incentives from the Penalties?

The statute imposes strict liability for a transaction that lacks economic substance and the penalties are substantial—20 percent, increasing to 40 percent if the transaction is not disclosed (see ¶343). The ABA Section of Taxation expressed concern that this may encourage disclosure of transactions that are of no interest to the IRS while discouraging disclosure of more questionable transactions. There is no downside to disclosing a transaction that a taxpayer feels reasonably confident about and it could reduce penalties from 40 percent to 20 percent. Conversely, for aggressive transactions, the 40-percent penalty may discourage taxpayers from disclosing questionable transactions. If the taxpayer believes there is a significant risk that the

NEW LAW EXPLAINED

transaction lacks economic substance, it may decide that the benefit of avoiding detection outweighs the reduction in the penalty from 40 percent to 20 percent.

No Application to Estate and Gift Tax

New Code Sec. 7701(o)(5)(A) provides that "the term economic analysis means the common law doctrine under which benefits under subtitle A with respect to a transaction are not allowable if the transaction does not have economic substance or lacks a business purpose." Note that subtitle A (Code Secs. 1–1563) applies only to income tax. Moreover, new Code Sec. 7701(o)(5)(B) provides that "in the case of an individual, paragraph (1) shall apply only to transactions entered into in connection with a trade or business or an activity engaged in for the production of income." Thus, it is clear that Code Sec. 7701(o) does not apply to the estate or gift tax. This is not to say that the common law economic substance doctrine does not apply to the estate and gift tax, however. *B.R. Brown*, CA-9, 2003-1 USTC ¶60,462, 329 F3d 664 (2003), makes it clear that substance over form principles apply to the estate and gift tax, albeit in a somewhat different way than they apply to the income tax.

▶ **Effective date.** The provision applies to transactions entered into after March 30, 2010, the date of enactment (Act Sec. 1409 (e)(1) of the Health Care and Education Reconciliation Act of 2010 (P.L. 111-152)).

Law source: Law at ¶5287. Committee Report at ¶10,440.

— Act Sec. 1409(a) of the Health Care and Education Reconciliation Act of 2010 (P.L. 111-152), redesignating Code Sec. 7701(o) as (p) and adding new Code Sec. 7701(o);

— Act Sec. 1409(e)(1), providing the effective date.

Reporter references: For further information, consult the following CCH reporters.

— Standard Federal Tax Reporter, ¶621.05

— Tax Research Consultant, SALES: 3,154

— Practical Tax Explanation, §4,140

— Federal Estate and Gift Tax Reporter, ¶4955.10

¶343 Penalties for Underpayments Attributable to Transactions Lacking Economic Substance

SUMMARY OF NEW LAW

The scope of the Code Sec. 6662 accuracy-related penalty has been expanded to include understatements attributable to any disallowance of claimed tax benefits by reason of a transaction lacking economic substance.

¶343

BACKGROUND

An accuracy-related penalty applies to the portion of any underpayment that is attributable to: (1) negligence, (2) any substantial understatement of income tax, (3) any substantial valuation misstatement, (4) any substantial overstatement of pension liabilities, or (5) any substantial estate or gift tax valuation understatement (Code Sec. 6662). If the correct income tax liability exceeds that reported by the taxpayer by the greater of 10 percent of the correct tax or $5,000 (or, in the case of corporations, by the lesser of: (a) 10 percent of the correct tax (or $10,000 if greater) or (b) $10 million), then a substantial understatement exists and a penalty may be imposed equal to 20 percent of the underpayment of tax attributable to the understatement.

The accuracy-related penalty generally is abated in cases in which the taxpayer can demonstrate that there was "reasonable cause" for the underpayment and that the taxpayer acted in good faith (Code Sec. 6664(c)). Reasonable cause will be found when a taxpayer reasonably relies in good faith on a professional tax advisor's opinion, which is based on any analysis of the pertinent facts and authorities and which unambiguously concludes that there is a greater than 50-percent likelihood that the tax treatment of the item will be upheld if challenged.

A separate accuracy-related penalty applies to any "listed transaction" and to any other "reportable transaction" that is not a listed transaction, if a significant purpose of such transaction is the avoidance or evasion of federal income tax (Code Sec. 6662A). For this purpose, a reportable transaction is a transaction that the Treasury Secretary determines is required to be disclosed because it has the potential for tax avoidance or evasion. A listed transaction is a reportable transaction which is the same as, or substantially similar to, a transaction specifically identified by the Treasury Secretary as a tax avoidance transaction for purposes of the reporting disclosure requirements.

In general, a 20-percent accuracy-related penalty is imposed on any understatement attributable to an adequately disclosed listed transaction or reportable transaction. The penalty is not imposed, however, if the relevant facts affecting the tax treatment were adequately disclosed, there is or was substantial authority for the claimed tax treatment, and the taxpayer reasonably believed, based on the facts and law as they exist at the time that the return in question is filed or in reliance on professional advice, that the claimed tax treatment was more likely than not the proper treatment. If, however, the taxpayer does not adequately disclose the transaction, the taxpayer generally will be subject to an increased penalty equal to 30 percent of the understatement, and there is no exception even if there was substantial authority for the claimed tax treatment and the taxpayer reasonably believed such treatment was more likely than not proper. This creates a "strict liability" standard.

To the extent a penalty on an understatement is imposed under Code Sec. 6662A, that same amount of understatement is not also subject to the accuracy-related penalty under Code Sec. 6662. The Code Sec. 6662 penalty also does not apply to any portion of an underpayment on which a fraud penalty is imposed.

Under Code Sec. 6676, if a claim for refund or credit with respect to income tax (other than a claim relating to the earned income tax credit) is made for an excessive amount, the person making such claim is subject to a penalty in an amount equal to

BACKGROUND

20 percent of the excessive amount unless there was a reasonable basis for the claim. For this purpose, "excessive amount" means the excess of the amount of the claim for refund sought for any tax year over the amount of such claim allowable for the year.

NEW LAW EXPLAINED

Penalties for underpayments attributable to transactions lacking economic substance.—A 20-percent penalty is imposed for an underpayment attributable to any disallowance of claimed tax benefits by reason of a transaction lacking economic substance, as defined in new Code Sec. 7701(o), or failing to meet the requirements of any similar rule of law (Code Sec. 6662(b)(6), as added by the Health Care and Education Reconciliation Act of 2010 (P.L. 111-152)). The penalty is increased to 40 percent for an underpayment attributable to a "nondisclosed noneconomic substance transaction" (Code Sec. 6662(i)(1), as added by the 2010 Reconciliation Act).

A nondisclosed nonecomonic substance transaction is any portion of a transaction lacking economic substance with respect to which the relevant facts affecting the tax treatment are not adequately disclosed in the return or in a statement attached to the return (Code Sec. 6662(i)(2), as added by the 2010 Reconciliation Act).

> **Comment:** In general, in any case in which a court determines that the economic substance doctrine is relevant, a transaction has economic substance only if: (1) the transaction changes in a meaningful way (apart from federal income tax effects) the taxpayer's economic position, and (2) the taxpayer has a substantial purpose (apart from federal income tax effects) for entering into such transaction (Code Sec. 7701(o), as added by the 2010 Reconciliation Act; see ¶342). The 20-percent and 40-percent penalties will apply to a transaction that is disregarded using the same factors and analysis required in determining that a transaction lacks economic substance, even if a different term is used to describe the doctrine (Joint Committee on Taxation, *Technical Explanation of the Revenue Provisions of the "Reconciliation Act of 2010", as amended, in combination with the "Patient Protection and Affordable Care Act"* (JCX-18-10), March 21, 2010).

> **Comment:** The determination of whether a position is a nondisclosed noneconomic substance transaction will generally be based on the return as originally filed or as amended by the taxpayer prior to being contacted by the IRS. Thus, no amendment or supplement to a tax return will be taken into account in determining whether a position has been disclosed if it is filed after the taxpayer has been contacted for audit or such other date that the Treasury Secretary may specify (Code Sec. 6662(i)(3), as added by the 2010 Reconciliation Act)

No exceptions, including the reasonable cause exception, are available to the imposition of the penalty for any underpayment, or reportable transaction understatement, attributable to a transaction lacking economic substance (Code Sec. 6664(c)(2) and (d)(2), as added by the 2010 Reconciliation Act).

> **Comment:** Outside opinions or in-house analysis will not, therefore, protect a taxpayer from imposition of a penalty if it is determined that the transaction

¶343

NEW LAW EXPLAINED

lacks economic substance or fails to meet the requirements of any similar rule of law (Joint Committee on Taxation, *Technical Explanation of the Revenue Provisions of the "Reconciliation Act of 2010", as amended, in combination with the "Patient Protection and Affordable Care Act"* (JCX-18-10), March 21, 2010).

The Code Sec. 6662A accuracy-related penalty on understatements with respect to reportable transactions will not be imposed if the 40-percent penalty is imposed on an underpayment attributable to one or more nondisclosed noneconomic substance transactions (Code Sec. 6662A(e)(2)(B), as amended by the 2010 Reconciliation Act).

Comment: The new penalty for an underpayment attributable to any disallowance of claimed tax benefits by reason of a transaction lacking economic substance also will not apply to any portion of an underpayment on which a fraud penalty is imposed (Joint Committee on Taxation, *Technical Explanation of the Revenue Provisions of the "Reconciliation Act of 2010", as amended, in combination with the "Patient Protection and Affordable Care Act"* (JCX-18-10), March 21, 2010).

Claims for refund lacking economic substance. A claim for refund or credit that is excessive under Code Sec. 6676 due to its lacking economic substance or failing to meet the requirements of any similar rule of law is subject to a 20-percent penalty, and will be treated as lacking a reasonable basis for purposes of trying to avoid such penalty (Code Sec. 6676(c), as added by the 2010 Reconciliation Act).

Comment: A taxpayer submitting an excessive claim for refund which is not based on a noneconomic substance transaction will continue to be eligible to try to establish that there was a reasonable basis for the claim in order to avoid the 20-percent penalty under Code Sec. 6676.

▶ **Effective date.** The provision applies to transactions entered into after March 30, 2010, the date of enactment (Act Sec. 1409(e)(1) of the Health Care and Education Reconciliation Act of 2010 (P.L. 111-152)). The provisions made by Act Sec. 1409(b) and 1409(c)(1) apply to underpayments attributable to transactions entered into after March 30, 2010 (Act Sec. 1409(e)(2)). The provisions made by Act Sec. 1409(c)(2) apply to understatements attributable to transactions entered into after March 30, 2010 (Act Sec. 1409(e)(3)). The provisions made by Act Sec. 1409(d) apply to refunds and credits attributable to transactions entered into after March 30, 2010 (Act Sec. 1409(e)(4)).

Law source: Law at ¶5278, ¶5279, ¶5279A, and ¶5279C. Committee Report at ¶10,440.

— Act Sec. 1409(b) of the Health Care and Education Reconciliation Act of 2010, adding Code Sec. 6662(b)(6) and (i) and amending Code Sec. 6662A(e)(2)(B);

— Act Sec. 1409(c)(1), redesignating Code Sec. 6664(c)(2) and (3) as (3) and (4) respectively, amending Code Sec. 6664(c)(4)(A) as redesignated, and adding new Code Sec. 6664(c)(2);

— Act Sec. 1409(c)(2), redesignating Code Sec. 6662(d)(2) and (3) as (3) and (4) respectively, amending Code Sec. 6664(d)(4) as redesignated, and adding new Code Sec. 6662(d)(2);

— Act Sec. 1409(d), redesignating Code Sec. 6676(c) as (d), and adding new Code Sec. 6676(c);

— Act Sec. 1409(e)(2), (3) and (4), providing the effective dates.

NEW LAW EXPLAINED

Reporter references: For further information, consult the following CCH reporters.
— Standard Federal Tax Reporter, ¶39,652.01
— Tax Research Consultant, PENALTY: 3,108
— Practical Tax Explanation, § 40,210.20
— Federal Estate and Gift Tax Reporter, ¶21,790.01

¶345 Excise Tax on High Cost Employer-Sponsored Health Coverage

SUMMARY OF NEW LAW

A 40-percent excise tax will be imposed on health coverage providers starting in 2018 to the extent that the aggregate value of employer-sponsored health coverage for an employee exceeds a threshold amount. This is the tax on so-called "Cadillac" health plans.

BACKGROUND

Employer-offered group health plans are highly regulated, and the regulations are generally enforced through excise taxes. For example, excise taxes are imposed for failure to comply with continuation of benefits (i.e., COBRA) requirements (Code Sec. 4980B), group health plan portability requirements (Code Sec. 4980D), and comparable health savings account contribution requirements (Code Sec. 4980G). Until now, however, health coverage itself has not been taxed. Indeed, it has been a highly tax-favored employee benefit.

NEW LAW EXPLAINED

Excise tax imposed on high cost employer-sponsored health coverage.—A 40-percent excise tax will be imposed on health coverage providers starting in 2018 to the extent that the aggregate value of employer-sponsored health coverage for an employee exceeds a threshold amount (Code Sec. 4980I, as added by the Patient Protection and Affordable Care Act (PPACA) (P.L. 111-148), and amended by the Health Care and Education Reconciliation Act of 2010 (P.L. 111-152)).

The tax is imposed with respect to coverage for a tax period if: (1) an employee is covered under any applicable employer-sponsored coverage of an employer at any time during the tax period, and (2) there is any "excess benefit" with respect to the coverage. The tax is 40 percent of the excess benefit (Code Sec. 4980I(a), as added by PPACA). A tax period for these purposes is the calendar year, or a shorter period if the Secretary of the Treasury so prescribes (Code Sec. 4980I(f)(8), as added by PPACA). The tax is not deductible for federal income tax purposes (Code Sec. 275(a)(6); Code Sec. 4980I(f)(10), as added by PPACA). "Employee" for these purposes includes former

NEW LAW EXPLAINED

employees, surviving spouses, or other primary insured individuals (Code Sec. 4980I(d)(3), as added by the 2010 Reconciliation Act).

Taxable excess benefit. The tax is on the excess benefit, which is the sum of the monthly excess amounts during the tax period (Code Sec. 4980I(b)(1), as added by PPACA). A monthly excess amount is the excess of: (a) the aggregate cost of the applicable employer-sponsored coverage of the employee for the month, over (b) an amount equal to 1/12 of the annual limitation for the calendar year in which the month occurs (Code Sec. 4980I(b)(2), as added by PPACA).

Annual limitation for calculating excess benefit. The annual limitation for any calendar year is the statutory dollar limit for that year as adjusted for inflation (Code Sec. 4980I(b)(3)(A), as added by PPACA), and for certain other factors. The annual limitation applicable for any month depends on the type of coverage provided as of the beginning of the month (Code Sec. 4980I(b)(3)(B), as added by PPACA and amended by the 2010 Reconciliation Act). An employee is treated as having self-only coverage for these purposes, unless: (1) the coverage is provided under a multiemployer plan (Code Sec. 4980I(b)(3)(B), as added by PPACA and amended by the 2010 Reconciliation Act); or (2) the employee is enrolled in coverage other than self-only coverage in a group health plan that provides minimum essential coverage to the employee and at least one other beneficiary and these benefits do not vary based on whether the covered individual is the employee or another beneficiary (Code Sec. 4980I(f)(1); Code Sec. 5000A(f), as added by PPACA).

The dollar limits for determining the tax thresholds are:

- $10,200 (for 2018) multiplied by the health cost adjustment percentage for an employee with self-only coverage, and

- $27,500 (for 2018) multiplied by the health cost adjustment percentage for an employee with coverage other than self-only coverage.

  Comment: The $10,200 and $27,500 amounts are just starting points for determining the thresholds for taxing excess benefits.

Health cost adjustment percentages. The health cost adjustment percentages, which are applied to the $10,200 and $27,500 amounts, are designed to capture upward deviations in the rise of the cost of good health care coverage between 2010 and 2018 as compared to an expected change (i.e., 55 percent). The percentage equals 100 percent plus:

- the excess (if any) of the percentage by which the per employee cost for providing coverage under the Blue Cross/Blue Shield standard benefit option under the Federal Employees Health Benefits Plan for plan year 2018 (determined by using the benefit package for such coverage in 2010) exceeds such cost for plan year 2010,

- over 55 percent (Code Sec. 4980I(b)(3)(C)(ii), as added by the 2010 Reconciliation Act).

¶345

NEW LAW EXPLAINED

> **Example 1:** Suppose the per employee cost of the Blue Cross/Blue Shield standard benefit option under the Federal Employees Health Benefits Plan for self-only coverage goes up by 80 percent between 2010 and 2018 (controlling for the same 2010 benefits package). The adjustment percentage for coverage under self-only plans is 135 percent (100 + (80 − 55)).

> **Comment:** Note that the adjustment percentage is not reduced below 100 percent if the cost goes up by less than 55 percent.

The health cost adjustment percentage is determined for employees with self-only coverage by taking only self-only coverage into account, and it is determined for employees with coverage other than self-only coverage by taking only coverage other than self-only coverage into account (Code Sec. 4980I(b)(3)(C)(i), as added by PPACA and amended by the 2010 Reconciliation Act).

Employer-specific age and gender adjustment to the threshold amounts. An employer-specific adjustment is made each tax period to the threshold amounts so that an employer with a workforce that is more expensive to insure due to age or gender characteristics will not be put at a disadvantage. The threshold dollar limits for any tax period (i.e., the $10,200 and $27,500 amounts as adjusted by the applicable health cost percentage in 2018, and inflation thereafter) are increased by an amount equal to the excess (if any) of: (a) the premium cost of the Blue Cross/Blue Shield standard benefit option under the Federal Employees Health Benefits Plan for the type of coverage provided such individual in such taxable period if priced for the age and gender characteristics of all employees of the individual's employer, over (b) that premium cost for the provision of such coverage under such option in such taxable period if priced for the age and gender characteristics of the national workforce (Code Sec. 4980I(b)(3)(C)(iii), as added by the 2010 Reconciliation Act).

> **Example 2:** Suppose in 2018, Acme Corporation's workforce is older than the average age of the national workforce. The threshold amounts that would otherwise apply to Acme's employees to calculate the excess benefit will be adjusted upwards. The amount is determined by taking the premium cost of the Blue Cross/Blue Shield standard benefit option for federal employees in 2018 priced for the age and gender characteristics of Acme's workforce in 2018, and subtracting the premium cost if the Blue Cross/Blue Shield plan were priced for the age and gender characteristic of the national workforce. Suppose the premium difference for a self-only plan is $1,000, and $2,500 for plans that are not self-only plans. $1,000 is added to the threshold amounts for employees with self-only coverage, and $2,500 is added for employees with coverage from plans that are not self-only.

Additions to thresholds for coverage of retirees and high risk professions. More generous thresholds apply for coverage of individuals who: (1) have attained age 55, receive retiree coverage, and are not eligible for Medicare, or (2) participate in a plan sponsored by an employer, the majority of whose employees are engaged in high risk

NEW LAW EXPLAINED

professions, which include law enforcement officers, firefighters, members of a rescue squad or ambulance crew, longshore workers, and individuals engaged in the construction, mining, agriculture (not including food processing), forestry, and fishing industries, or are employed to repair or install electrical or telecommunications lines (Code Sec. 4980I(f)(2), (3), as added by PPACA). In either of those cases:

- the $10,200 amount (as adjusted by the health cost adjustment percentage) is increased by $1,650, and

- the $27,500 amount (as adjusted by the health cost adjustment percentage) is increased by $3,450 (Code Sec. 4980I(b)(3)(C)(iv), as added by PPACA and amended by the 2010 Reconciliation Act).

An individual cannot qualify for more than one such increase, even if the individual qualifies both as a retiree and as engaged in a high risk profession.

Example 3: In 2018, Fern Rodriguez is 60 years old, receives retiree benefits, and has self-only coverage. Suppose the adjustment percentage is 110 percent. Suppose also there is no adjustment for the age or gender characteristics of her employer's workforce. The threshold amount for her coverage for 2018 is ($10,200 × 110 percent) plus $1,650, or $12,870.

Inflation adjustments. The threshold amounts, as determined for 2018 (including the adjustments for the health care adjustment percentage, and the adjustments for retirees and individuals in high risk occupations), are indexed to the Consumer Price Index for Urban Consumers (CPI-U) as determined by the Department of Labor beginning in 2019. For 2019 only, an additional one percent is added to the cost of living adjustment (Code Sec. 4980I(b)(3)(C)(v), as added by PPACA, and amended by the 2010 Reconciliation Act).

Paying the tax. A coverage provider must pay the tax on its applicable share of the excess benefit with respect to an employee for any tax period (Code Sec. 4980I(c)(1), as added by PPACA). A coverage provider for these purposes includes:

- The health insurer, if the applicable employer-sponsored coverage consists of coverage under a group health plan which provides health insurance coverage;

- The employer, in the case of contributions to an employer-sponsored Health Savings Account (HSA) or Medical Savings Account (MSA); and

- The person that administers plan benefits (including the plan sponsor if the plan sponsor administers benefits under the plan (Code Sec. 4980I(f)(6), as added by PPACA) in the case of any other applicable employer-sponsored coverage (Code Sec. 4980I(c)(2), as added by PPACA).

Accordingly, the plan administrator pays the excise tax in the case of a self-insured group health plan, a Health Flexible Spending Account (Health FSA), or a Health Reimbursement Arrangement (HRA). On the other hand, the employer pays the excise tax where the employer acts as plan administrator to a self-insured group health plan, a

NEW LAW EXPLAINED

Health FSA, or an HRA, and with respect to employer contributions to an HSA. A plan sponsor for these purposes includes the employer or employee organization that established and maintains the plan. In the case of a plan established or maintained by multiple employers or by one or more employers with one or more employee organizations, the committee or board that established or maintains the plan is the plan sponsor (Code Sec. 4980I(f)(7), as added by PPACA; ERISA Sec. 3(16)(B)).

> **Comment:** Placing the tax on coverage providers will provide an incentive for them to cap their rates at the threshold amounts.

> **Example 4:** For 2018, the cost of applicable employer-sponsored coverage provided by the provider is $30,000, and the aggregate cost of all applicable employer-sponsored coverage provided to the employee is $35,000. If the total excess benefit is $7,500, the provider's applicable share is $6,429 (($30,000 / $35,000) × $7,500).

Employer's responsibility to calculate the tax and applicable shares. An employer must: (a) calculate for each tax period the amount of the excess benefit subject to the tax and the applicable share of the excess benefit for each coverage provider, and (b) notify the Treasury Secretary and each coverage provider of the amount determined for the provider (Code Sec. 4980I(c)(4)(A), as added by PPACA). In the case of coverage through a multiemployer plan (as defined in Code Sec. 414(f)), the plan sponsor must make the calculations and provide the required notice (Code Sec. 4980I(c)(4)(B), as added by PPACA).

> **Example 5:** For 2018, employee Jennifer Jackson elects family coverage under a fully-insured health care policy covering major medical and dental with a value of $35,000. Suppose her adjusted threshold amount is $27,500 for 2018. The amount subject to the excise tax is $7,500 ($35,000 less the threshold of $27,500). The employer reports $7,500 as taxable to the insurer, which calculates and remits the excise tax to the IRS.

> **Example 6:** For 2018, employee Randy Segal elects family coverage under a fully-insured major medical policy with a value of $30,000 and a separate fully-insured dental policy with a value of $2,000. Randy also contributes $3,000 to a Health FSA. Randy has an aggregate health insurance coverage value of $33,000 (the dental plan is not counted as coverage subject to tax). Suppose the adjusted threshold amount is $27,500 for 2018. The amount subject to the excise tax is $5,500 ($33,000 less the threshold of $27,500). The employer reports $5,000 ($5,500 × $30,000 / $33,000) as taxable to the major medical insurer which then calculates and remits the excise tax to the IRS. If the employer uses a third-party administrator for the Health FSA, the employer reports $500 ($5,500 ×

NEW LAW EXPLAINED

> $3,000/$33,000) to the administrator and the administrator calculates and re-mits the excise tax to the IRS.

Coverage subject to tax. Applicable employer-sponsored coverage subject to the excise tax includes coverage under any group health plan made available to the employee by an employer which is excludable from the employee's gross income, or would be so excludable if it were employer-provided coverage, including coverage in the form of reimbursements under a Health FSA or an HRA, employer contributions to an HSA, and coverage for dental, vision, and other supplementary health insurance coverage (Code Sec. 4980I(d)(1)(A), as added by PPACA; Code Sec. 106). It does not include employer-sponsored coverage for:

- separate dental or vision coverage;
- fixed indemnity health coverage purchased by the employee with after-tax dollars (Code Sec. 4980I(d)(1)(B)(i), as added by PPACA and amended by the 2010 Reconciliation Act; Code Sec. 162(l));
- disability benefits or long term care under an accident or health plan;
- liability insurance (including general liability insurance and auto liability insurance), or coverage issued as a supplement to liability insurance;
- workers' compensation or similar insurance;
- automobile medical payment insurance;
- credit-only insurance; and
- other similar insurance coverage under which benefits for medical care are secondary or incidental to other insurance benefits (Code Sec. 4980I(d)(1)(B)(iii), as added by PPACA and amended by 2010 Reconciliation Act; Code Sec. 9832(c)(1) and (3); Reg. § 54.9831-1(c)(3)).

Fixed indemnity coverage pays fixed dollar amounts based on the occurrence of qualifying events, including but not limited to the diagnosis of a specific disease, an accidental injury, or a hospitalization, provided that the coverage is not coordinated with other health coverage.

Coverage paid by employee. Employer-sponsored health insurance coverage is health coverage offered by an employer to an employee without regard to whether the employer pays for the coverage (in which case it is excludable from the employee's gross income), or the employee pays for the coverage with his or her own after-tax dollars (Code Sec. 4980I(d)(1)(C), as added by PPACA).

Coverage for self-employed. For a self-employed individual, coverage under any group health plan providing health insurance coverage is treated as applicable employer-sponsored coverage if a deduction is allowable under Code Sec. 162(l) with respect to all or any portion of the cost of the coverage (Code Sec. 4980I(d)(1)(D), as added by PPACA).

NEW LAW EXPLAINED

Coverage by government plans. Applicable employer-sponsored coverage includes coverage under any group health plan established and maintained for its civilian employees by the federal, state, and local governments, or by any agency or instrumentality of any such government (Code Sec. 4980I(d)(1)(E), as added by PPACA).

Determining cost of coverage. The aggregate value of all employer-sponsored health insurance coverage, including dental, vision, and other supplementary health insurance coverage, is generally calculated in the same manner as the applicable premiums for the tax year for the employee determined under the rules for COBRA continuation coverage. If the plan provides for the same COBRA continuation coverage premium for both individual coverage and family coverage, the plan would have to calculate separate individual and family premiums for this purpose. In determining the coverage value for retirees, employers can elect to treat retirees who retire before age 65 together with those who retire at or after age 65 (Code Sec. 4980I(d)(2)(A), as added by PPACA; Code Sec. 4980B(f)(4)).

> **Comment:** The applicable premium under COBRA for any period of continuation coverage is the cost to the plan for such period of coverage for similarly situated non-COBRA beneficiaries with respect to whom a qualifying event has not occurred, and is determined without regard to whether the cost is paid by the employer or employee. Special rules apply for determining the applicable premium in the case of self-insured plans (Code Sec. 4980B(f)(4)).

Cost of Health FSAs and HSAs. The cost of the coverage of a Health FSA is the dollar amount of the aggregate salary reduction contributions for the year. To the extent that the FSA provides for reimbursement in excess of this amount, the value of the coverage generally is determined in the same manner as the applicable premium for COBRA continuation coverage. If the plan provides for the same COBRA continuation coverage premium for both individual coverage and family coverage, the plan would be required to calculate separate individual and family premiums for this purpose (Code Sec. 4980I(d)(2)(B), as added by PPACA; Code Sec. 106(c)(2)). For HSAs and MSAs, the cost of the coverage equals the amount of employer contributions under the arrangement (Code Sec. 4980I(d)(2)(C), as added by PPACA).

Cost allocation on a monthly basis. If cost is determined on other than a monthly basis, the cost shall be allocated to months in a tax period on such basis as the Secretary may prescribe (Code Sec. 4980I(d)(2)(D), as added by PPACA).

Penalty for failure to properly calculate excess benefit. If the employer reports to insurers and plan administrators (as well as the IRS) a lower amount of insurance cost subject to the excise tax than required, the employer is subject to a penalty equal to any additional excise tax that each such insurer and administrator would have owed if the employer had reported correctly, increased for interest from the date that the tax was otherwise due to the date paid by the employer (Code Sec. 4980I(e)(1), as added by PPACA). This may occur, for example, if the employer undervalues the aggregate premium and thereby lowers the amount subject to the excise tax for all insurers and plan administrators (including the employer when acting as plan administrator of a self-insured plan).

¶345

NEW LAW EXPLAINED

This penalty may be waived if the employer can show that the failure is due to reasonable cause and not to willful neglect (Code Sec. 4980I(e)(2)(C), as added by PPACA). The penalty is in addition to the amount of excise tax owed, which may not be waived.

The penalty is not to be imposed if the employer or plan sponsor neither knew, nor exercising reasonable diligence would have known, that such failure existed (Code Sec. 4980I(e)(2)(A), as added by PPACA). Nor is it imposed if the failure was due to reasonable cause and not willful neglect, and the failure is corrected during the 30-day period beginning on the first date that the employer knew, or exercising reasonable diligence would have known, that such failure existed (Code Sec. 4980I(e)(2)(B), as added by PPACA).

Aggregation of employers. The employer aggregation rules for controlled groups of corporations, partnerships or proprietorships under common control, affiliated service groups, and leased employees apply to the excise tax on high cost plans (Code Sec. 4980I(f)(9), as added by PPACA; Code Sec. 414(b), (c), (m) and (o)).

Practical Analysis: Jean Baxley, Of Counsel at Crowell & Moring of Washington, D.C., notes that employers and plan sponsors (in the case of multiemployer plans) are responsible for determining the amount of any excess benefit subject to the excise tax. Cost forms the basis for this determination, and the fact that HSA and MSA amounts are included in the computation, complicates the computation of any excess benefit.

Liability for any applicable excise tax may need to be allocated among up to three types of coverage providers—health insurance issuers, employers and plan administrators. Responsibility for the correct computation of taxable excess benefits falls on the employer or plan sponsor. To the extent such computation understates the taxable excess benefit, a penalty plus underpayment interest applies. The Act places responsibility for the penalty only on the employer or the plan sponsor (and not on the insurer, if any).

Liability for any applicable excise tax may need to be allocated among up to three types of coverage providers—health insurance issuers, employers and plan administrators. Responsibility for the correct computation of taxable excess benefits falls on the employer or plan sponsor. To the extent such computation understates the taxable excess benefit, a penalty plus underpayment interest applies. The Act places responsibility for the penalty only on the employer or the plan sponsor (and not on the insurer, if any).

▶ **Effective date.** The excise tax applies to tax years beginning after December 31, 2017 (Act Secs. 9001(c) and 10901(c) of the Patient Protection and Affordable Care Act (PPACA) (P.L. 111-148)), and Act Sec. 1401(b) of the Health Care and Education Reconciliation Act of 2010 (P.L. 111-152).

NEW LAW EXPLAINED

Law source: Law at ¶5230. Committee Report at ¶10,160.

— Act Sec. 9001(a), as amended by Act Sec. 10901(a), of the Patient Protection and Affordable Care Act P.L. 111-148), as amended by Act Sec. 1401(a) of the Health Care and Education Reconciliation Act of 2010 (P.L. 111-152), adding Code Sec. 4980I;

— Act Secs. 9001(c) and 10901(c), of PPACA, and Act Sec. 1401(b) of the 2010 Reconciliation Act providing the effective date.

Reporter references: For further information, consult the following CCH reporters.

— Standard Federal Tax Reporter, ¶34,601.01, ¶34,612.01 and ¶34,619Z.01

— Tax Research Consultant, COMPEN: 45,200

— Practical Tax Explanation, §20,305, §20,515.35 and §20,701

¶350 Fees on Manufacturers and Importers of Prescription Drugs and Health Insurance Providers and Excise Tax on Sales of Medical Devices

SUMMARY OF NEW LAW

New annual fees are imposed on manufacturers and importers of branded prescription drugs and providers of health insurance for U.S. health risks. A 2.3 percent excise tax is imposed on sales of medical devices.

BACKGROUND

An excise tax is imposed on certain vaccines that are used by a manufacturer, producer or importer of the vaccine prior to sale of the product and vaccines that are shipped to a U.S. possession (Code Sec. 4131). A "taxable vaccine" is any vaccine that is manufactured or produced in the United States, or entered into the United States for consumption, use or warehousing, and that is included in a list of taxable vaccines (Code Sec. 4132). However, no excise tax or fee is currently imposed under the Internal Revenue Code on companies that manufacture or import branded prescription drugs or medical devices for sale in the United States.

Special rules are used to determine the taxable income of insurance companies (Code Secs. 801-848). An excise tax is imposed on premiums paid to foreign insurers and reinsurers covering U.S. risks, but no annual fee is currently imposed under the Internal Revenue Code on providers of health insurance.

NEW LAW EXPLAINED

New annual fees imposed on drug manufacturers and importers and health insurance providers; new excise tax imposed on sales of medical devices.—New annual fees are imposed on manufacturers and importers on U.S. sales of branded prescription drugs (Act Sec. 9008 of the Patient Protection and Affordable Care Act (PPACA) (P.L. 111-148), as amended by Act Sec. 1404 of the Health Care and Education Reconciliation Act of 2010 (P.L. 111-152)). New annual fees are also imposed on the net premiums written by certain providers of health insurance for U.S. health risks (Act Sec. 9010 of PPACA, as amended by Act Sec. 10905 of PPACA and Act Sec. 1406 of the 2010 Reconciliation Act). A new excise tax is imposed on sales of certain medical devices (Code Sec. 4191, as added by the 2010 Reconciliation Act).

Fee on sales of branded drugs. A new fee is imposed on any manufacturer or importer of certain branded prescription drugs or biologics offered for sale in the United States. The fee applies to both domestic and foreign manufacturers and importers of such products (Act Sec. 9008(a) and (d) of PPACA, as amended by Act Sec. 1404 of the 2010 Reconciliation Act).

The aggregate fee imposed on all covered entities is $2.5 billion for 2011, $2.8 billion for 2012, $2.8 billion for 2013, $3 billion for 2014, $3 billion for 2015, $3 billion for 2016, $4 billion for 2017, $4.1 billion for 2018, and $2.8 billion for 2019 and following years (Act Sec. 9008(b)(4) of PPACA, as added by Act Sec. 1404(a)(2)(B) of the 2010 Reconciliation Act). The Secretary of the Treasury will annually apportion the fee based on each entity's relative market share of covered domestic sales of branded prescription drugs for the prior year (Act Sec. 9008(b) of PPACA, as amended by Act Sec. 1404(a)(2) of the 2010 Reconciliation Act). Domestic sales included are only those that are made to or funded by specified government programs, such as Medicare, Medicaid, the Veterans Administration, the Department of Defense, and TRICARE. Sales of orphan drugs for which a credit under Code Sec. 45C was allowed for any tax year are excluded (Act Sec. 9008(e) of PPACA).

Each covered entity's fee is due no later than the annual payment date for each calendar year beginning after 2010 (Act Sec. 9008(a)(1) of PPACA, as amended by Act Sec. 1404(a)(1) of the 2010 Reconciliation Act). The annual payment date is determined by the Secretary of the Treasury, but cannot be later than September 30 of such calendar year. If more than one person is liable for the fee with respect to a single covered entity, all such persons will be jointly and severally liable for payment of the fee (Act Sec. 9008(d)(3) of PPACA, as added by Act Sec. 1404(a)(3) of the 2010 Reconciliation Act).

> **Comment:** The fees collected from manufacturers and importers of branded prescription drugs will be credited to the Medicare Part B trust fund (Joint Committee on Taxation, *Technical Explanation of the Revenue Provisions of the "Reconciliation Act of 2010," as amended, in combination with the "Patient Protection and Affordable Care Act"* (JCX-18-10), March 21, 2010).

The Secretary of the Treasury is directed to publish guidance necessary to carry out the purposes of the provision on the annual fee on branded prescription drugs (Act Sec. 9008(i) of PPACA).

NEW LAW EXPLAINED

Fee on net health insurance premiums. A new fee is imposed on providers of insurance for any "United States health risk", which means the health risk of any individual who is a U.S. citizen, a resident of the United States (as defined by Code Sec. 7701(b)(1)(A), or located in the United States (Act Sec. 9010(a), (c) and (d) of PPACA, as amended by Act Sec. 10905 of PPACA and Act Sec. 1406 of the 2010 Reconciliation Act).

The aggregate fee imposed on all covered entities is $8 billion for 2014, $11.3 billion for 2015, $11.3 billion for 2016, $13.9 billion for 2017, and $14.3 billion for 2018. For 2019 and following years, the aggregate fee is indexed to the rate of premium growth (Act Sec. 9010(b) and (e) of PPACA, as amended by Act Sec. 10905(a) and (b) of PPACA and Act Sec. 1406(a)(4) of the 2010 Reconciliation Act). The Secretary of the Treasury will annually apportion the fee based on each entity's relative market share of net premiums written for the prior year. In determining the net premiums written that are taken into account, certain dollar limits apply, and net premiums written that are attributable to exempt activities of a tax-exempt health organization may be partially excluded (Act Sec. 9010(b) of PPACA, as amended by Act Sec. 10905(a) of PPACA and Act Sec. 1406(a)(2) of the 2010 Reconciliation Act).

The fee applies to covered entities providing health insurance for any U.S. health risk during the calendar year in which the fee is due. Covered entities can include insurance companies that are subject to federal income tax, organizations exempt from tax under Code Sec. 501(a), foreign insurers providing health insurance for U.S. health risks, and insurers providing health insurance for U.S. health risks under Medicare Advantage, Medicare Part D or Medicaid (Joint Committee on Taxation, *Technical Explanation of the Revenue Provisions of the "Reconciliation Act of 2010," as amended, in combination with the "Patient Protection and Affordable Care Act"* (JCX-18-10), March 21, 2010). However, there are many exceptions to what is considered a covered entity. Federal, state, and other government entities are excluded. Employers that self-insure their employees' health risks are not subject to the fee. In addition, certain nonprofit organizations and voluntary employees' beneficiary associations (VEBAs) are exempt from the fee (Act Sec. 9010(c) of PPACA, as amended by Act Sec. 10905(c) of PPACA and Act Sec. 1406(a)(3) of the 2010 Reconciliation Act).

For purposes of the fee, "health insurance" does not include insurance coverage for long-term care, disability, accidents, specified illnesses, hospital indemnity or other fixed indemnity insurance, or Medicare supplemental health insurance (as defined in Sec. 1882(g)(1) of the Social Security Act) (Act Sec. 9010(h)(3) of PPACA, as amended by Act Sec. 10905(d) of PPACA).

Each covered entity's fee is due no later than the annual payment date for each calendar year beginning after 2013. The annual payment date is determined by the Secretary of the Treasury, but cannot be later than September 30 of such calendar year (Act Sec. 9010(a) of PPACA, as amended by Act Sec. 10905(f)(1) of PPACA and Act Sec. 1406(a)(1) of the 2010 Reconciliation Act).

Covered entities must report their net premiums written for the calendar year with respect to health insurance for any U.S. health risk to the Secretary of the Treasury. The report must be made at the time and in the manner determined by the Secretary of the Treasury (Act Sec. 9010(g)(1) of PPACA). A penalty is imposed on the failure to

NEW LAW EXPLAINED

file a required report, unless the failure is shown to be due to reasonable cause. The penalty is equal to: (a) $10,000, plus (b) the lesser of $1,000 per day during which such failure continues or the amount of the fee imposed for which the report was required. The penalty will be treated as a penalty for purposes of Subtitle F of the Internal Revenue Code and must be paid on notice and demand and in the same manner as a tax. Only civil actions for refund of the penalty under the procedures of Subtitle F shall apply (Act Sec. 9010(g)(2) of PPACA). The reported information shall not be treated as taxpayer information under Code Sec. 6103 (Act Sec. 9010(g)(4) of PPACA).

In addition, an accuracy-related penalty applies to any understatement of the amount of net premiums written, which is the difference between the amount of net premiums written that were reported by the covered entity and the amount of net premiums written that should have been reported (Act Sec. 9010(g)(3) of PPACA, as added by Act Sec. 1406(a)(5) of the 2010 Reconciliation Act). This penalty is subject to the provisions of Subtitle F of the Internal Revenue Code that apply to assessable penalties.

The Secretary of the Treasury is directed to publish guidance necessary to carry out the purposes of the provision on the annual fee on net health insurance premiums (Act Sec. 9010(i) of PPACA, as amended by Act Sec. 10905(e) of PPACA). The Secretary of the Treasury is also directed to prescribe regulations that are necessary or appropriate to prevent avoidance of the purposes of the provision, such as regulations covering inappropriate actions taken to qualify as an exempt entity.

Excise tax on sales of medical devices. A new excise tax is imposed on any manufacturer, producer or importer of certain medical devices that is equal to 2.3 percent of the price for which the medical device is sold (Code Sec. 4191(a), as added by the 2010 Reconciliation Act). The excise tax applies to sales after December 31, 2012 (Act Sec. 1405(c) of the 2010 Reconciliation Act).

> **Comment:** The Patient Protection Act originally included an annual fee on manufacturers and importers of medical devices. The 2010 Reconciliation Act repealed the annual fee and replaced it with an excise tax (Act Sec. 9009 of PPACA, prior to repeal by Act Sec. 1405(d) of the 2010 Reconciliation Act; Joint Committee on Taxation, *Technical Explanation of the Revenue Provisions of the "Reconciliation Act of 2010," as amended, in combination with the "Patient Protection and Affordable Care Act"* (JCX-18-10), March 21, 2010).

For purposes of the excise tax, a taxable medical device means any device regulated by the Food and Drug Administration (FDA) (as defined in 21 U.S.C. § 321) and intended for humans. However, sales of products intended for use on animals, eyeglasses, contact lenses, hearing aids, and any other medical device determined to be of a type that is generally purchased by the general public at retail for individual use are not subject to the excise tax (Code Sec. 4191(a)(2), as added by the 2010 Reconciliation Act). It is anticipated that the Secretary of the Treasury will publish a list of medical device classifications that are of a type generally purchased by the general public at retail for individual use (Joint Committee on Taxation, *Technical Explanation of the Revenue Provisions of the "Reconciliation Act of 2010," as amended, in combination with the "Patient Protection and Affordable Care Act"* (JCX-18-10), March 21, 2010).

¶350

NEW LAW EXPLAINED

The excise tax on sales of medical devices shall not apply to the sale by the manufacturer of a medical device for use by the purchaser for further manufacture or for resale by the purchaser to a second purchaser for use by the second purchaser in further manufacture. The excise tax also shall not apply to the sale by the manufacturer of a medical device for export or for resale by the purchaser to a second purchaser for export (Code Sec. 4221(a), as amended by the 2010 Reconciliation Act). Overpayments of the excise tax on sales of medical devices may be allowed as a credit or refund in certain circumstances (Code Sec. 6416(b)(2), as amended by the 2010 Reconciliation Act).

Tax treatment of fees. Neither the annual fee on branded prescription drug sales or the annual fee on certain health insurance providers may be deducted for federal income tax purposes. They are to be treated as nondeductible taxes under Code Sec. 275. In addition, the annual fees are treated as excise taxes for purposes of Subtitle F of the Internal Revenue Code, so that only civil actions for refund of such taxes can be pursued (Act Secs. 9008(f) and 9010(f) of PPACA).

Study and report on effect on veterans. The Secretary of Veterans Affairs is directed to conduct a study on the effect of the new fees on the cost of medical care provided to veterans and veterans' access to medical devices and branded prescription drugs. The Secretary of Veterans Affairs must report the results of this study to the House Ways and Means Committee and the Senate Finance Committee no later than December 31, 2012 (Act Sec. 9011 of PPACA).

Practical Analysis: Charles Goulding, President and founder of Energy Tax Savers, notes that, although in reviewing this provision on a stand-alone basis it might appear that U.S. tax policy is completely favoring generics over branded drugs, there are interrelated changes in the Health Care Reform Act impacting both branded and generic drug makers. As a starting point, one needs to realize that although more prescriptions are written for generics, total sales for branded drugs are much higher because the individual prescription sales prices are much higher. Branded drug makers would now get a very valuable 12 years of patent exclusivity versus generics when selling biologic drugs. Although biologic drugs are currently a small portion of branded drug makers' total product sales, they are the fastest growing sales segment. Both branded drugs and generics would increase the rebates or discounts provided to Medicaid, their biggest customer.

▶ **Effective date.** The section on the imposition of an annual fee on drug manufacturers and importers applies to calendar years beginning after December 31, 2010 (Act Sec. 9008(j) of the Patient Protection and Affordable Care Act (PPACA) (P.L. 111-148), as amended by Act Sec. 1404(a)(4) of the Health Care and Education Reconciliation Act of 2010 (P.L. 111-152)). The section on the imposition of an annual fee on health insurance providers applies to calendar years beginning after December 31, 2013 (Act Sec. 9010(j) of PPACA, as amended by Act Sec. 1406(a)(6) of the 2010 Reconciliation Act). The excise tax on sales of medical devices applies to sales after December 31, 2012 (Act Sec. 1405(c) of the 2010 Reconciliation Act).

¶350

NEW LAW EXPLAINED

Law source: Law at ¶5197, ¶5198, ¶5276, ¶7030, ¶7033, ¶7036, ¶7048, ¶7051, ¶7109, and ¶7112. Committee Report at ¶10,230, ¶10,240, ¶10,250, ¶10,260 and ¶10,420.

— Act Sec. 9008 of the Patient Protection and Affordable Care Act (PPACA) (P.L. 111-148), as amended by Act Sec. 1404 of the Health Care and Education Reconciliation Act of 2010 (P.L. 111-152);

— Act Sec. 9009 of PPACA was repealed by Act Sec. 1405(d) of the 2010 Reconciliation Act;

— Act Sec. 9010 of PPACA, as amended by Act Sec. 10905 of PPACA and Act Sec. 1406 of the 2010 Reconciliation Act;

— Act Sec. 9011 of PPACA;

— Act Sec. 1405(a) of the 2010 Reconciliation Act, adding Code Sec. 4191;

— Act Sec. 1405(b) of the 2010 Reconciliation Act, amending Code Secs. 4221(a) and 6416(b)(2);

— Act Sec. 9008(j) of PPACA, as amended by Act Sec. 1404(a)(4) of the 2010 Reconciliation Act, Act Sec. 9010(j) of PPACA, as amended by Act Sec. 1406(a)(6) of the 2010 Reconciliation Act, and Act Sec. 1405(c) of the 2010 Reconciliation Act providing the effective dates.

Reporter references: For further information, consult the following CCH reporters.

— Standard Federal Tax Reporter, ¶14,502.01 and ¶26,135.01

— Tax Research Consultant, BUSEXP: 21,350 and EXCISE: 6,160.10

— Practical Tax Explanation, §9,940.10, §50,210 and §51,405

¶355 Credit for Therapeutic Discovery Projects

SUMMARY OF NEW LAW

A 50-percent tax credit is provided for eligible taxpayers' qualified investment with respect to any qualifying therapeutic discovery project of the taxpayer made in a tax year beginning in 2009 or 2010. The credit is part of the investment credit and is available only for qualifying therapeutic discovery projects certified by the Secretary of the Treasury under a qualifying therapeutic discovery projects program established by the Secretary, in consultation with the Secretary of Health and Human Services. The total amount of credits allocated under the program is limited to $1 billion. A grant for qualified investments in therapeutic discovery projects in lieu of the tax credit is also available.

BACKGROUND

A taxpayer's allowable research credit generally is equal to 20 percent (14 percent in the case of the alternative simplified credit) of the amount by which the taxpayer's qualified research expenses for a tax year exceed its base amount for that year (Code Sec. 41). Consequently, the research credit is generally available with respect to incremental increases in qualified research.

BACKGROUND

A separate 20-percent research tax credit is also available for the excess of 100 percent of corporate cash expenses paid for basic research conducted by universities and certain nonprofit scientific research organizations, over the sum of: (1) the greater of two minimum basic research floors, plus (2) an amount reflecting any decrease in nonresearch giving to universities by the corporation as compared to such giving during a fixed base period, as adjusted for inflation. This credit computation is referred to as the "university basic research credit"(Code Sec. 41(e)).

Qualified research expenses eligible for the tax research credit consist of: (1) taxpayer's in-house expenses for wages and supplies attributable to qualified research; (2) certain time-sharing costs for computer use in qualified research; and (3) 65 percent of amounts paid or incurred by the taxpayer to certain other persons for qualified research conducted on the taxpayer's behalf (contract research expenses). Despite the limitation for contract research expenses, qualified research expenses include 100 percent of amounts paid or incurred by the taxpayer to an eligible small business, university or federal laboratory for qualified energy research (Code Sec. 41(b)).

A 50-percent credit is also allowed for expenses related to human clinical testing of drugs for the treatment of certain rare diseases and conditions that afflict less than 200,000 persons in the United States (Code Sec. 45C).

Under current law, there is no credit specifically designed to promote investment in new therapies for diseases.

NEW LAW EXPLAINED

Credit added for investment in qualifying therapeutic discovery project.—A tax credit is allowed for 50 percent of an eligible taxpayer's qualified investment for the tax year with respect to any qualifying therapeutic discovery project of the taxpayer (Code Sec. 48D, as added by the Patient Protection and Affordable Care Act (PPACA) (P.L. 111-148)). The credit is part of the investment credit and the basis of any property that is part of a qualifying therapeutic discovery project is included in the credit base for purposes of applying the investment credit at-risk limitation rules under Code Sec. 49 (Code Secs. 46(6) and 49(a)(1)(C)(vi), as added by PPACA).

An eligible taxpayer is a taxpayer that employs no more that 250 employees in all businesses of the taxpayer at the time the taxpayer submits its application for the credit under Code Sec. 48D(d)(2) (Code Sec. 48D(c)(2), as added by PPACA).

> **Comment:** For purposes of the definition of an eligible taxpayer, all persons treated as a single employer under Code Sec. 52(a) (controlled group of corporations) or 52(b) (partnerships, proprietorships which are under common control) or Code Sec. 414(m) (affiliated service groups) or 414(o) (separate organizations, employee leasing arrangements) are treated as a single employer under Code Sec. 48D(c)(2).

The qualified investment for any tax year is the total amount of the costs paid or incurred in that year for expenses necessary for and directly related to the conduct of a qualifying therapeutic discovery project (Code Sec. 48D(b)(1), as added by PPACA).

¶355

NEW LAW EXPLAINED

An investment is a qualified investment only if it is made in a tax year beginning in 2009 or 2010 (Code Sec. 48D(b)(5), as added by PPACA). In the case of costs that are paid for property subject to an allowance for depreciation, project expenditure rules similar to the rules of Code Sec. 46(c)(4) and (d) (as in effect prior to the enactment of the Revenue Reconciliation Act of 1990 (P.L. 101-508)) are applied. (Code Sec. 48D(b)(4) as added by PPACA). The amount treated as a qualified investment may not exceed the amount certified by the IRS as eligible for the credit (Code Sec. 48D(b)(2), as added by PPACA). The qualified investment does not take into account any cost for:

- remuneration paid to the chief executive officer and the four highest paid officers other than the chief executive officer (i.e., remuneration described in Code Sec. 162(m)(3));
- interest expenses;
- facility maintenance expenses;
- any service cost under Reg. § 1.263A-1(e)(4); or
- any other expense appropriate to carry out the purposes of the qualifying therapeutic discovery project (Code Sec. 48D(b)(3), as added by PPACA).

Facility maintenance expenses are costs paid or incurred to maintain a facility, including mortgage or rent payments, insurance payments, utility and maintenance costs and the costs of employing maintenance personnel (Code Sec. 48D(c)(3), as added by PPACA).

A qualifying therapeutic discovery project is a project that is designed to:

- treat or prevent diseases or conditions by conducting pre-clinical activities, clinical trials and clinical studies or carrying out research protocols, for the purpose of securing governmental approval of a product,
- diagnose diseases or conditions or to determine molecular factors related to diseases or conditions by developing molecular diagnostics to guide therapeutic decisions, or
- develop a product, process or technology to further the delivery or administration of therapeutics (Code Sec. 48D(c)(1), as added by PPACA).

Qualifying therapeutic discovery project program. Within 60 days of enactment of Code Sec. 48D, the Secretary of Treasury, with the assistance of the Secretary of Health and Human Services, will set up a qualifying therapeutic discovery project program to consider applications and award certifications for qualified investments eligible for credits under Code Sec. 48D (Code Sec. 48D(d)(1)(A), as added by PPACA). The total amount of credits to be allocated cannot exceed $1 billion for the two-year period beginning in 2009 (Code Sec. 48D(d)(1)(B), as added by PPACA). Applicants for certification must submit an application containing required information. The application will be approved or denied within 30 days of its submission. An application for certification may include a request for an allocation of credits for more than one of the years for which the credits are available (Code Sec. 48D(d)(2), as added by PPACA).

NEW LAW EXPLAINED

Selection criteria. In determining the projects with respect to which qualified investments may be certified for credits, the IRS will take into account only those projects that show reasonable potential:

- to result in new therapies to treat areas of unmet medical need or to prevent, detect or treat chronic or acute diseases and conditions;

- to reduce long-term health care costs in the United States; or

- to significantly advance the goal of curing cancer within the 30-year period beginning on the date on which the qualifying therapeutic discovery project program is established (Code Sec. 48D(d)(3)(A), as added by PPACA).

In addition, the IRS will also take into consideration which projects have the greatest potential to create high quality, high paying jobs in the United States and to advance U.S. competitiveness in the fields of life, biological and medical sciences (Code Sec. 48D(d)(3)(B), as added by PPACA).

Disclosure of allocations. Upon making a certification under the program, the IRS will publicly disclose the identity of the applicant and the amount of the credit awarded to that applicant (Code Sec. 48D(d)(4), as added by PPACA).

Basis adjustment. If a credit is allocated under the qualifying therapeutic discovery project program for an expenditure for property subject to an allowance for depreciation, the basis of that property is reduced by the amount of the credit (Code Sec. 48D(e)(1), as added by PPACA).

Denial of double benefit. No credit is allowed under the program for any investment for which bonus depreciation is allowed under Code Secs. 168(k), 1400L(b)(1) or 1400N(d)(1) (Code Sec. 48D(e)(2)(A), as added by PPACA). Furthermore, no deduction is allowed for the portion of the expenses otherwise allowable as a deduction taken into account in determining the credit under the program for the tax year which is equal to the amount of the credit determined for such tax year under Code Sec. 48D(a) attributable to such portion. This provision does not apply to expenses related to depreciable property, the basis of which was reduced under Code Sec. 48D(e)(1) or which are described in Code Sec. 280C(g), discussed below (Code Sec. 48D(e)(2)(B), as added by PPACA). Finally, any expenses taken into account under the program for a tax year may not be taken into account in determining the credit allowable under Code Secs. 41 (research credit) or 45C (orphan drug credit). However, any expenses for any tax year which are qualified research expenses under Code Sec. 41(b) are taken into account in determining base period research expenses for purposes of applying Code Sec. 41 to subsequent tax years (Code Sec. 48D(e)(2)(C), as added by PPACA).

Rule to prevent double tax benefit with respect to research and orphan drug credit expenses. To prevent any double benefits that may arise from claiming this credit, Code Sec. 280C is amended to disallow a deduction for that portion of the qualified investment related to a qualifying therapeutic discovery project otherwise allowable as a deduction for the tax year which: (1) would be qualified research expenses (as defined in Code Sec. 41(b)), basic research expenses (as defined in Code Sec. 41(e)(2)) or qualified clinical testing expenses (as defined in Code Sec. 45C(b) relating to the orphan drug credit) if the credit under Code Secs. 41 or 45C were allowed with

NEW LAW EXPLAINED

respect to such expenses, and (2) is equal to the amount of the credit determined under Code Sec. 48D(a), reduced by the amount disallowed as a deduction under Code Sec. 48D(e)(2)(B) (see "Denial of double tax benefit," above) and the amount of any basis reduction of depreciable property by the amount of the credit that is required under Code Sec. 48D(e)(1), as discussed above (Code Sec. 280C(g)(1), as added by PPACA).

If the taxpayer capitalizes the expenses described above rather than deducting them, a similar rule applies. In the case of qualified research expenses (as defined in Code Sec. 41(b)), basic research expenses (as defined in Code Sec. 41(e)(2)) or qualified clinical testing expenses (as defined in Code Sec. 45C(b)) that are taken into account in determining the credit under Code Sec. 48D, if the amount of the portion of the credit with respect to those expenses exceeds the amount allowable as a deduction for such expenses (determined without regard to Code Sec. 280C(g)(1)), the amount chargeable to capital account for the tax year for such expenses is reduced by the amount of such excess (Code Sec. 280C(g)(2), as added by PPACA).

Controlled groups. In the case of a corporation that is a member of a controlled group of corporations, or a trade or business that is treated as being under common control with other trades or businesses, then in determining the amount of the credit, all members of the same controlled group of corporations or all trades or businesses which are under common control are treated as a single taxpayer. The credit allowable to each such member or person is its proportionate share of the qualifying therapeutic discovery project expenses paid or incurred giving rise to the credit (Code Sec. 280C(g)(3), as added by PPACA).

Coordination with Department of Treasury grants. In the case of an investment with respect to which a person receives a Department of the Treasury grant under Act Sec. 9023(e) of the Patient Protection Act, no credit is allowed with respect to the investment for the tax year in which the grant is made or any subsequent tax year (Code Sec. 48D(f)(1), as added by PPACA). If a credit was allowed with respect to an investment for any tax year ending before a grant is made, then

- the tax imposed on the taxpayer for the tax year in which the grant is made is increased by the amount of the credit that was allowed under Code Sec. 38,

- the general business credit carryforwards under Code Sec. 39 are adjusted so as to recapture the portion of the disallowed credit, and

- the amount of the grant is determined without regard to any reduction in the basis of any depreciable property by reason of such credit (Code Sec. 48D(f)(2), as added by PPACA).

Any grant is not includible in the gross income of the taxpayer (Code Sec. 48D(f)(3), as added by PPACA).

Grant in lieu of tax credit. Act Sec. 9023(e) of the Patient Protection Act provides the procedures and rules with respect to grants for qualified investments in therapeutic discovery projects. Generally, grants are available for persons who make qualified investments in qualifying therapeutic discovery projects in the amount of 50 percent of such investment if a timely application is filed. To qualify for the grant, the investment must be made in tax years beginning in 2009 or 2010. For a tax year that

NEW LAW EXPLAINED

begins in 2009, an application for certification for a credit under Code Sec. 48D is treated as an application for a grant if the taxpayer makes an express election to do so on the certification application. For a tax year beginning in 2010, the application for a grant must be submitted no earlier than the day after the last day of such tax year and no later than the due date (including extensions) for filing the tax return for such year (Act Sec. 9023(e)(2)(B) of PPACA). The Secretary of the Treasury will provide the form of application and the information required to be included in the application (Act Sec. 9023(e)(2)(C) of PPACA). Grant amounts will be paid to applicants during the 30-day period beginning on the later of the date of the application for the grant or the date on which the qualified investment is made (Act Sec. 9023(e)(3) of PPACA).

> **Caution:** Act Sec. 9023(e)(11) of PPACA provides that the IRS may not make any grant unless the application is *received* before January 1, 2013. This provision appears to conflict with the preceding provision which requires a grant application for a tax year beginning in 2010 (the last grant year) to be *submitted* no later than the due date of the return for the 2010 tax year.

> **Comment:** The term "qualified investment" with respect to a grant in lieu of tax credits means a qualified investment that is certified under Code Sec. 48D(d) for purposes of the credit under Code Sec. 48D (Act Sec. 9023(e)(4) of PPACA). In the case of investments of on ongoing nature, the IRS will issue regulations to determine the date on which a qualified investment is considered made for purposes of determining the time for payment (Act Sec. 9023(e)(3)(B) of PPACA).

Grants made under Act Sec. 9023(e) of PPACA are subject to rules similar to the rules in Code Sec. 50 (i.e., investment tax credit recapture rules). In applying those rules, any increase in tax due to a qualified investment ceasing to be a qualified investment will be imposed on the person to whom the grant was made (Act Sec. 9023(e)(5)(A) of PPACA). Also, if the amount of a grant exceeds the amount allowable, the excess will be recaptured in full as if the investment to which such excess portion of the grant relates had ceased to be a qualified investment immediately after the grant was made (Act Sec. 9023(e)(5)(B)(i) of PPACA). Under no circumstances will the amount of the grant, the identity of the person to whom the grant was made or a description of the investment with respect to which the grant was made be treated as return information under Code Sec. 6103 (Act Sec. 9023(e)(5)(B)(ii) of PPACA).

> **Comment:** The exclusion of such information from treatment as "return information" means it is not protected from disclosure.

No grants under Act Sec. 9023(e) of PPACA will be made to:

- any federal, state or local government or to any political subdivision, agency or instrumentality of such government;
- any organization described in Code Sec. 501(c) and exempt from tax under Code Sec. 501(a);
- any entity referred to in Code Sec. 54(j)(4) (clean renewable energy bond lenders, cooperative electric companies or governmental bodies); or
- any partnership or other passthrough entity if any partner (or other holder of an equity or profits interest) is described in the above three categories (Act Sec. 9023(e)(6) of PPACA).

NEW LAW EXPLAINED

In the case of a partnership or other passthrough entity described above, partners and other holders of any equity or profits interest are required to provide to the partnership or entity any information required by the Secretary necessary to carry out the purposes of the provision (Act Sec. 9023(e)(6) of PPACA).

Several other provisions of Act Sec. 9023(e) of PPACA provide that:

- Any reference to the Secretary of the Treasury includes the Secretary's delegate (Act Sec. 9023(e)(7) of PPACA).

- Any term used in Act Sec. 9023(e) of PPACA, which is also used in Code Sec. 48D, has the same meaning with respect to the act section as when used in the code section (Act Sec. 9023(e)(8) of PPACA).

- No credit is allowed under Code Sec. 46(6) by reason of Code Sec. 48D for any investment for which a grant is awarded under Act Sec. 9023(e) of PPACA (Act Sec. 9023(e)(9) of PPACA) (i.e., the taxpayer may not claim the Code Sec. 48D credit if a grant is received).

- Sums necessary to carry out Act Sec. 9023 of PPACA are appropriated to the Secretary (Act Sec. 9023(e)(10) of PPACA).

Practical Analysis: Charles Goulding, President and founder of Energy Tax Savers, notes that the new credit for investments creating new medical therapies is designed to encourage investments in new leading edge medical therapies that prevent, diagnose and treat acute and chronic diseases. Unlike the traditional R&D tax credits that reward demonstrated innovation, this credit is designed to jump-start medical breakthroughs at the front end by providing a credit for hiring scientists and conducting clinical studies. These types of investments are often resource constrained and frequently occur as part of University-supported efforts that often have limited grant funding. Even when innovation appears promising, the necessary clinical studies are extremely expensive, so this credit is aimed at the heart of the cost barrier constraints.

Businesses eligible for the new medical therapy credit should use this new credit for qualifying activities that are not eligible for the traditional R&D tax credit and then continue to use the R&D credit for qualifying expenses related to the R&D tax credit.

▶ **Effective date.** The amendments made by Act Sec. 9023(a) through (d) apply to amounts paid or incurred after December 31, 2008, in tax years beginning after such date (Act Sec. 9023(f) of the Patient Protection and Affordable Care Act (PPACA) (P.L. 111-148)).

Law source: Law at ¶5065, ¶5070, ¶5075, and ¶5150. Committee Report at ¶10,350.

— Act Sec. 9023(a) of the Patient Protection and Affordable Care Act (PPACA) (P.L. 111-148), adding Code Sec. 48D;
— Act Sec. 9023(b), adding Code Sec. 46(6);
— Act Sec. 9023(c)(1), adding Code Sec. 49(a)(1)(C)(vi);
— Act Sec. 9023(c)(2), adding Code Sec. 280C(g); and
— Act Sec. 9023(f), providing the effective date.

¶355

NEW LAW EXPLAINED

Reporter references: For further information, consult the following CCH reporters.

— Standard Federal Tax Reporter, ¶4580.01

— Tax Research Consultant, BUSEXP: 51,050

— Practical Tax Explanation, § 13,701

¶357 Black Liquor Carve-Out for Cellulosic Biofuel Producer Credit

SUMMARY OF NEW LAW

Black liquor has been excluded from the cellulosic biofuel producer credit.

BACKGROUND

Although the primary biofuel produced by the agricultural sector is ethanol, with corn being the main feedstock, cellulose-based feedstocks are also viable as feedstocks both for alcohol fuels and non-alcohol fuels. Cellulose is the structural component of the primary cell wall of green plants (*Congressional Research Service Report for Congress—Cellulosic Biofuels: Analysis of Policy Issues for Congress*, November 9, 2009).

The cellulosic biofuel producer credit, a $1.01 per gallon nonrefundable income tax credit for the production of qualified cellulosic biofuel, was added as a component of the Code Sec. 40 alcohol fuels credit by the Heartland, Habitat, Harvest, and Horticulture Act of 2008 (P.L. 110-246). If the cellulosic biofuel is alcohol, whether ethanol or methanol, the $1.01 per gallon credit is reduced by any alcohol credit amount. For cellulosic biofuel that is ethanol, the credit amount is also reduced by any small ethanol producers credit that was allowed (see Form 6478, Alcohol and Cellulosic Biofuel Fuels Credit). The cellulosic biofuel producer credit applies to qualified cellulosic biofuel produced after December 31, 2008, but before January 1, 2013 (Code Sec. 40(b)(6)(H) and (e)(3)).

Cellulosic biofuel is defined as any liquid fuel that: (1) is produced from any lignocellulosic or hemicellulosic matter that is available on a renewable or recurring basis, (2) meets Environmental Protection Agency (EPA) registration requirements for fuel and fuel additives established under section 211 of the Clean Air Act, and (3) if alcohol, is not alcohol of less than 150 proof (Code Sec. 40(b)(6)(E)(i)); Instructions to Form 6478). Renewable sources of lignocellulosic or hemicellulosic matter include dedicated energy crops and trees, wood and wood residues, plants, grasses, agricultural residues, fibers, animal wastes and other waste materials, and municipal solid waste (Conference Committee Report to P.L. 110-246, H.R. Conf. Rep. No. 110-627).

Qualified cellulosic biofuel production is defined as cellulosic biofuel produced by the taxpayer during the tax year that: (1) is sold to another person: (a) for production of a qualified cellulosic biofuel mixture in the other person's trade or business (other than casual off-farm production), (b) for use by the other person as a fuel in a trade or

BACKGROUND

business, or (c) who sells that cellulosic biofuel at retail to another person and places it in the other person's fuel tank; or (2) is used by the taxpayer for any purpose described in item (1).

Black liquor is a by-product of the kraft process for making paper—a by-product that paper companies have produced and used to run their recovery boilers since the 1930s. Black liquor's water, sediment and ash content is significantly above that of other fuels (see Joint Committee on Taxation, *Technical Explanation of the Revenue Provisions of the "Reconciliation Act of 2010," as amended, in combination with the "Patient Protection and Affordable Care Act"* (JCX-18-10), March 21, 2010).

In spring of 2009, an animated debate was sparked by the revelation that paper companies were claiming billions of dollars for the alternative fuel mixture credit under Code Sec. 6426(e) by adding small amounts of diesel fuel to black liquor (see Joint Committee on Taxation, *Description of Revenue Provisions Contained in the President's Fiscal Year 2010 Budget Proposal; Part Two: Business Tax Provisions* (JCS-3-09), September 2009).

Opponents of allowing black liquor to earn the alternative fuel mixture credit asserted that it represented an unintended windfall to certain paper mills but did not increase the production of renewable fuels because paper mills have produced and used black liquor for decades. Also, there were questions about whether the payments to U.S. paper companies constituted an unfair trade subsidy in violation of the North American Free Trade Agreement (NAFTA). Canadian interests expressed the view that the alternative fuel payments were a U.S. government subsidy to their U.S. competitors (see Joint Committee on Taxation, *Description of Revenue Provisions Contained in the President's Fiscal Year 2010 Budget Proposal; Part Two: Business Tax Provisions* (JCS-3-09), September 2009). Supporters of allowing the credit for black liquor said that it was keeping the U.S. paper industry afloat during very trying economic times.

The debate only intensified when the IRS, in an informal Chief Counsel Advice (CCA 200941011), announced that black liquor also qualified for the $1.01 per gallon cellulosic biofuel producer credit. The advice noted, however, that black liquor cannot qualify for both the alternative fuel mixture credit and the cellulosic biofuel producer credit. While the alternative fuel mixture credit expired at the close of 2009 (though is likely to be renewed with an exclusion for black liquor), the cellulosic biofuel producer credit remains in effect until 2013.

NEW LAW EXPLAINED

Black liquor excluded from the cellulosic biofuel producer credit.—Paper companies are now barred from claiming the $1.01 per gallon cellulosic biofuel producer credit under Code Sec. 40(b)(6) for "black liquor" (Code Sec. 40(b)(6)(E)(iii), as added by the Health Care and Education Reconciliation Act of 2010 P.L. 111-152)).

The mechanism for closing down the $1.01 per gallon credit for black liquor is a provision that limits the amount of water, sediment and ash in qualified fuels. Specifically, cellulosic biofuel is now defined to exclude any fuel if: (1) more than 4 percent of

NEW LAW EXPLAINED

it, by weight, is any combination of water and sediment, or (2) its ash content is more than 1 percent by weight.

> **Comment:** Black liquor's water, sediment and ash content is significantly above that of other fuels. Water content includes both free water and water in solution with dissolved solids. Sediment consists of solid particles that are dispersed in the liquid fuel. Ash is the residue remaining after combustion.

Water content is determined by distillation using ASTM (American Society for Testing and Materials International) method D95, or a similar method suitable to the fuel being tested. Sediment is determined by centrifuge or extraction using ASTM method D1796 or D473, or a similar method that reports sediment content in weight percent. As for ash, ASTM D3174 or a similar method of combustion suitable for the fuel being tested may be used in determining the residue remaining after combustion (Joint Committee on Taxation, *Technical Explanation of the Revenue Provisions of the "Reconciliation Act of 2010," as amended, in combination with the "Patient Protection and Affordable Care Act"* (JCX-18-10), March 21, 2010).

This change is estimated to raise $23.6 billion over 10 years.

▶ **Effective date.** This provision applies to fuels sold or used on or after January 1, 2010 (Act Sec. 1408(b) of the Health Care and Education Reconciliation Act of 2010 (P.L. 111-152)).

Law source: Law at ¶5057. Committee Report at ¶10,430.

— Act Sec. 1408(a) of the Health Care and Education Reconciliation Act of 2010 (P.L. 111-152), adding Code Sec. 40(b)(6)(E)(iii);

— Act Sec. 1408(b), providing the effective date.

Reporter references: For further information, consult the following CCH reporters.

— Standard Federal Tax Reporter, ¶4304.01

— Tax Research Consultant, EXCISE: 24,374

— Practical Tax Explanation, § 14,205

— Federal Excise Tax Reporter, ¶2215.08 and ¶49,250.04

¶360 Modification of Tax Treatment of Certain Health Organizations

SUMMARY OF NEW LAW

The special deduction from regular tax that Blue Cross and Blue Shield organizations, and other qualifying health insurance organizations, are allowed under Code Sec. 833 is modified to provide that these organizations will only be entitled to this special tax treatment if 85 percent or more of their insurance premium revenues are spent on clinical services.

BACKGROUND

A Blue Cross or Blue Shield organization that was in existence on August 16, 1986 and was also a tax-exempt organization for its last tax year prior to January 1, 1987, is entitled to a special tax deduction under Code Sec. 833 (Code Sec. 833(c)(2)). In addition, other health insurance organizations may qualify for this special tax deduction. Such an organization will qualify if: (1) its activities were substantially all involved with providing health insurance with at least 10 percent of the health insurance provided to individuals and small groups (not counting medicare supplemental coverage); (2) its insurance policies covering individuals provide full coverage of preexisting conditions of high-risk individuals without a price differential (with a reasonable waiting period); (3) its coverage is provided without regard to age, income, or employment status of individuals under 65 years of age, and with at least 35 percent of insurance premiums determined on a community rated basis; and (4) its net earnings do not inure to the benefit of any private shareholder or individual (Code Sec. 833(c)(3)).

The Code Sec. 833 special rules provide that Blue Cross and Blue Shield organizations (and other qualifying health insurance organizations) are: (1) treated as stock insurance companies; (2) allowed a deduction (not to exceed taxable income) equal to 25 percent of the year's annual claims and liabilities under cost-plus contracts and administrative expenses related to such claims and contracts less the prior year's surplus for regular tax; and (3) exempt from the provisions concerning unearned premiums of property and casualty insurance companies (Code Secs. 833(b) and 833(c)). This special deduction from regular tax allowed to these organizations may not be claimed against AMTI (Code Sec. 56(c)(3)).

NEW LAW EXPLAINED

Modification of tax treatment of certain health organizations.—The new law provides that the special tax treatment that Blue Cross, Blue Shield, or other health insurance organizations that qualify for the special Code Sec. 833 tax treatment previously received will no longer apply unless the health insurance organization's percentage of total premium revenue expended on reimbursement of clinical services provided to enrollees during the tax year (as reported under section 2718 of the Public Health Service Act) is 85 percent or more (Code Sec. 833(c)(5), as added by the Patient Protection and Affordable Care Act (PPACA) (P.L. 111-148)).

> **State Tax Consequences:** The new requirement that provides that, in order to receive special tax treatment, Blue Cross, Blue Shield, or other health insurance organizations that qualify for the special Code Sec. 833 tax treatment must expend at least 85 percent of their total premium revenue on reimbursement of clinical services during the tax year will not affect most states, because most states either do not incorporate the federal tax provisions regarding insurance companies and/or subject insurance companies to a gross premiums tax in lieu of other state taxes.

▶ **Effective date.** The provision applies to tax years beginning after December 31, 2009 (Act Sec. 9016(b) of the Patient Protection and Affordable Care Act (PPACA) (P.L. 111-148)).

NEW LAW EXPLAINED

Law source: Law at ¶5160. Committee Report at ¶10,310.

— Act Sec. 9016(a) of the Patient Protection and Affordable Care Act (PPACA) (P.L. 111-148), adding Code Sec. 833(c)(5);

— Act Sec. 9016(b), providing the effective date.

Reporter references: For further information, consult the following CCH reporters.

— Standard Federal Tax Reporter, ¶26,171.01

— Tax Research Consultant, EXEMPT: 15,160.10

— Practical Tax Explanation, § 15,130.10

Health Care: Reporting Requirements and Other Provisions

¶405 Inclusion of Cost of Employer-Sponsored Health Coverage on W-2

SUMMARY OF NEW LAW

Employers are required to disclose the aggregate cost of employer-sponsored health insurance coverage provided to their employees on the employee's Form W-2. Contributions to any health savings account (HSA) or Archer medical savings account (MSA) of the employee or the employee's spouse or salary reduction contributions to a flexible spending arrangement under a cafeteria plan will not be included. This employer disclosure requirement begins with the Form W-2 for the 2011 tax year.

BACKGROUND

Employers are required to provide each employee with a Form W-2, Wage and Tax Statement, on an annual basis, generally on or before January 31 of the following year. Form W-2 is a written statement that contains information with respect to wages and tax withholdings. This information includes:

- the name of the employer;
- the name of the employee (and his social security account number, if wages have been paid);
- the total amount of wages as defined in Code Sec. 3401(a);
- the total amount deducted and withheld as tax under Code Sec. 3402;
- the total amount of wages as defined in Code Sec. 3121(a);
- the total amount deducted and withheld as tax under Code Sec. 3101;
- the total amount paid to the employee under Code Sec. 3507 with respect to advance payment of earned income credit;
- the total amount of elective deferrals under Code Sec. 402(g)(3) and compensation deferred under Code Sec. 457, including any designated Roth contributions under Code Sec 402(A);
- the total amount incurred for dependent care assistance with respect to that employee under a dependent care assistance program;
- in the case of an employee who is a member of the U.S. Armed Forces, the employee's earned income determined for purposes of the Code Sec. 32 earned income credit;
- the amount contributed to any Archer medical savings account of that employee or the employee's spouse;
- the amount contributed to any health savings account of that employee or the employee's spouse; and
- the total amount of deferrals for the year under a nonqualified deferred compensation plan under Code Sec. 409A(d) (Code Sec. 6051(a)).

Special rules also apply with respect to compensation paid to members of the military and uniformed services, Peace Corps volunteers, and employees receiving tips in the course of their employment.

There is no requirement that the employer report the total value of employer-sponsored health insurance coverage on the Form W-2. However, some employers voluntarily report the amount of salary reduction under a cafeteria plan that results in tax-free benefits to the employee in box 14 of Form W-2. The portion of the employer sponsored coverage that is paid for by the employee with after-tax contributions is included on the Form W-2.

NEW LAW EXPLAINED

Employers required to disclose cost of employer-sponsored health coverage on Form W-2.—Employers are required to disclose the aggregate cost of "applicable

NEW LAW EXPLAINED

employer-sponsored coverage" provided to employees annually on the employee's Form W-2 (Code Sec. 6051(a)(14), as added by the Patient Protection and Affordable Care Act (PPACA) (P.L. 111-148)). Regardless of whether the employee or employer pays for the coverage, the aggregate cost of the coverage reported is determined under rules similar to those used in Code Sec. 4980B(f)(4) to determine the applicable premiums for purposes of the COBRA continuation coverage requirements of group health plans (Code Sec. 6051(a)(14), as added by PPACA).

For purposes of the new reporting requirement, "applicable employer-sponsored coverage" means, with respect to any employee, coverage under any group health plan made available to the employee by the employer which is excludable from the employee's gross income under Code Sec. 106 or would be so excludable if it were considered employer-provided coverage under Code Sec. 106 (Code Sec. 4980I(d)(1)(A), as added by PPACA).

Coverage is treated as applicable employer-sponsored coverage regardless of whether the employer or employee pays for the coverage. Applicable employer-sponsored coverage does not include coverage for long-term care, accidents, or disability income insurance. Nor does it include coverage that applies to only a specified disease or illness, hospital indemnity, or other fixed indemnity insurance, the payment for which is not excludable from gross income and deductible under Code Sec. 162(l) (Code Sec. 4980I(d)(1)(B) and (C), as added by PPACA).

Applicable employer-sponsored coverage includes coverage under any group health plan established and maintained by the U.S. government, the government of any state or its political subdivision, by any agency or instrumentality of such government. In the case of qualifying self-employed individuals (i.e., individuals treated as employees under Code Sec. 401(c)(1)), coverage under any group health plan providing health insurance coverage will be treated as applicable employer-sponsored coverage if a deduction is allowable under Code Sec. 162(l) with respect to all or any portion of the cost of such coverage (Code Sec. 4980I(d)(1)(D) and (E), as added by PPACA).

> **Comment:** Code Sec. 4980I, as added by PPACA and amended by the Health Care and Education Reconciliation Act of 2010 P.L. 111-152), imposes an excise tax on high cost employer-sponsored health coverage. For a discussion of this excise tax, see ¶435.

Applicable employer-sponsored coverage does *not* include any salary reduction contributions to a flexible spending arrangement under a cafeteria plan or contributions to an Archer medical savings account or health savings account of the employee or the employee's spouse (Code Sec. 6051(a)(14), as added by PPACA).

> **Comment:** This provision only requires disclosure of the aggregate cost of employer-sponsored health insurance coverage by the employer. It does not require a specific breakdown of the various types of medical coverage. Thus, if an employee enrolls in employer-sponsored health insurance coverage under a medical plan, a dental plan and a vision plan, the employer must report the total cost of all of these health related insurance policies. The disclosure requirement begins with the Forms W-2 for the 2011 tax year.

¶405

NEW LAW EXPLAINED

▶ **Effective date.** The provision applies to tax years beginning after December 31, 2010 (Act Sec. 9002(b) of the Patient Protection and Affordable Care Act (PPACA) (P.L. 111-148).

Law source: Law at ¶5255. Committee Report at ¶10,170.

— Act Sec. 9002(a) of the Patient Protection and Affordable Care Act (PPACA) (P.L. 111-148), amending Code Sec. 6051(a)(12) and (a)(13), and adding Code Sec. 6051(a)(14);

— Act Sec. 9002(b), providing the effective date.

Reporter references: For further information, consult the following CCH reporters.

— Standard Federal Tax Reporter, ¶36,425.01

— Tax Research Consultant, PAYROLL: 3,356.05

— Practical Tax Explanation, §22,110.10

¶410 Health Care Coverage Reporting

SUMMARY OF NEW LAW

Any person who provides minimum essential health care coverage to an individual during a calendar year is required to file a return reporting such coverage in the form and manner prescribed by the Secretary of the Treasury. Such a person is also required to furnish a written statement to the individual with respect to whom information is reported, detailing the contents of the information return.

BACKGROUND

The Code imposes a variety of information reporting requirements on participants in certain transactions (Code Secs. 6031 through 6060). For example, every person engaged in a trade or business generally is required to file information returns for each calendar year for payments of $600 or more made in the course of the payor's trade or business (Code Sec. 6041).

A penalty applies for failing to timely file an information return or including incorrect or incomplete information on an information return. The amount of the penalty ranges from $15 to $50 for each return with respect to which such a failure occurs, depending on how soon the failure is corrected, up to a maximum total penalty of $250,000 for all failures during a calendar year (Code Sec. 6721). Similarly, failures to furnish correct information statements to recipients of payments for which information reporting is required is subject to a penalty of $50 for each statement, up to a maximum penalty of $100,000 for all failures during a calendar year (Code Sec. 6722). The information returns and payee statements that are subject to these penalties are described in Code Sec. 6724(d)(1) and (2), respectively.

In addition, a failure to comply with various other information reporting requirements results in a penalty of $50 for each failure up to a maximum penalty of $100,000 for all such failures during the calendar year (Code Sec. 6723).

BACKGROUND

Federal law does not presently require individuals to have health insurance or require employers to provide health insurance to their employees. Further, individuals, employers and health insurance coverage providers are not subject to any reporting requirements with respect to health care coverage.

NEW LAW EXPLAINED

Information reporting required for health insurance coverage.—Every person who provides minimum essential health care coverage to an individual during a calendar year is required to file a return reporting such coverage, at such time as the Secretary of the Treasury may prescribe (Code Sec. 6055(a), as added by the Patient Protection and Affordable Care Act (PPACA) (P.L. 111-148)).

> **Comment:** Beginning in 2014, applicable individuals are required to ensure that they and their dependents have minimum essential health coverage, and a penalty is imposed on applicable individuals who fail to do so. For discussion of the penalty and the definition of minimum essential coverage, see ¶205.

The required return must be in the form as the Secretary of the Treasury may prescribe, and must contain:

- the name, address and taxpayer identification number (TIN) of the primary insured;
- the name and TIN of each other individual obtaining coverage under the policy;
- the dates during which the insured was covered under minimum essential coverage during the calendar year, and
- such other information as the Secretary of the Treasury may require (Code Sec. 6055(b)(1), as added by PPACA).

In the case of minimum essential coverage that consists of health insurance coverage, the required return must also include information concerning whether the coverage is a qualified health plan offered through an Health Benefit Exchange, and, in the case of a qualified health plan, the amount of any advance payment of any cost-sharing reduction or any premium assistance tax credit, with respect to such coverage (Code Sec. 6055(b)(1)(B)(iii), as added by PPACA).

> **Comment:** By January 1, 2014, each State must establish an American Health Benefit Exchange and Small Business Health Options Program (SHOP Exchange) to provide qualified individuals and qualified small business employers access to qualified health plans. For a discussion of the establishment and requirements of the Exchanges, see ¶505. Individuals who are eligible for participation in a qualified health plan through an Exchange, may also be eligible for a premiums assistance tax credit (see ¶210) and cost-sharing subsidy (see ¶520). The Exchange is required to certify to an employer if it has an employee enrolled in a qualified health plan through the Exchange.

If the provided minimum essential coverage consists of health insurance coverage of a health insurance issuer provided through a group health plan of an employer, the return must include the name, address and employer identification number of the

NEW LAW EXPLAINED

employer maintaining the plan, and the portion of the premium, if any, required to be paid by the employer. If the coverage is a qualified health plan in the small group market offered through an Exchange, the return must also include such other information as the Secretary of the Treasury may require for administration of the new credit for employee health insurance expenses of small employers under Code Sec. 45R, as added and amended by PPACA (Code Sec. 6055(b)(2), as added by PPACA). For a discussion of the small employer health insurance credit, see ¶310.

A person required to file a return under these rules is also required to furnish a written statement to each individual whose name is reported on the return, showing the name, address and phone number of the person required to make the return, and the information required to be shown on the return with respect to that individual (Code Sec. 6055(c)(1), as added by PPACA). The statement must be furnished on or before January 31 of the year following the calendar year for which the information return was required to be made (Code Sec. 6055(c)(2), as added by PPACA).

If coverage is provided by a governmental unit, an agency or instrumentality of a governmental unit or an agency, the required returns and statements must be made by the officer or employee who enters into the agreement to provide the coverage, or by the person appropriately designated for purposes of this reporting requirement (Code Sec. 6055(d), as added by PPACA).

Failure to file an information return reporting health insurance coverage or failure to include correct or complete information on such a return is subject to the existing penalties for failure to file correct information returns under Code Sec. 6721 (Code Sec. 6724(d)(1)(B)(xxiv), as added by PPACA). Similarly, the present-law penalties for failure to furnish correct payee statements under Code Sec. 6722 apply to failure to furnish statements to individuals with respect to whom information is reported or failure to include correct or complete information on such statements (Code Sec. 6724(d)(2)(GG), as added by PPACA).

The Secretary of the Treasury, in consultation with the Secretary of Health and Human Services, is required to send a written notification to each individual who files an individual income tax return and who is not enrolled in minimum essential coverage. The notification must be sent no later than June 30 of each year, and must contain information on the services available through the Exchange operating in the state in which the individual resides (Act Sec. 1502(c) of PPACA).

▶ **Effective date.** The provision applies to calendar years beginning after 2013 (Act Sec. 1502(e) of the Patient Protection and Affordable Care Act (PPACA) (P.L. 111-148)).

Law source: Law at ¶5235, ¶5260, ¶5280 and ¶7015. Committee Report at ¶10,090.

— Act Sec. 1502(a) of the Patient Protection and Affordable Care Act (PPACA) (P.L. 111-148), adding Code Sec. 6055;

— Act Sec. 1502(b), amending Code Sec. 6724(d)(1)(B) and (d)(2);

— Act Sec. 1502(c) and (d);

— Act Sec. 1502(e), providing the effective date.

¶410

NEW LAW EXPLAINED

Reporter references: For further information, consult the following CCH reporters.

— Standard Federal Tax Reporter, ¶ 40,220.01, ¶ 40,285.025 and ¶ 40,285.03

— Tax Research Consultant, FILEBUS: 9,350, PENALTY: 3,202 and PENALTY: 3,204

— Practical Tax Explanation, § 39,101 and § 40,305.05

¶ 415 Reporting of Employer Health Insurance Coverage

SUMMARY OF NEW LAW

Beginning in 2014, certain large employers and employers offering minimum essential coverage through eligible employer-sponsored plans will be required to report to the Secretary of the Treasury whether they offer full time employees and their dependents the opportunity to enroll in minimum essential coverage under an eligible employer sponsored plan and provide details regarding the coverage offered and other required information. Such employers will also be required to furnish a written statement to each full-time employee with respect to whom information is reported, detailing the contents of the information return.

BACKGROUND

The Code imposes a variety of information reporting requirements on participants in certain transactions (Code Secs. 6031 through 6060). For example, every person engaged in a trade or business generally is required to file information returns for each calendar year for payments of $600 or more made in the course of the payor's trade or business (Code Sec. 6041).

A penalty applies for failing to timely file an information return or including incorrect or incomplete information on an information return. The amount of the penalty ranges from $15 to $50 for each return with respect to which such a failure occurs, depending on how soon the failure is corrected, up to a maximum total penalty of $250,000 for all failures during a calendar year (Code Sec. 6721). Similarly, failures to furnish correct information statements to recipients of payments for which information reporting is required are subject to a penalty of $50 for each statement, up to a maximum penalty of $100,000 for all failures during a calendar year (Code Sec. 6722). The information returns and payee statements that are subject to these penalties are described in Code Sec. 6724(d)(1) and (2), respectively.

In addition, a failure to comply with various other information reporting requirements results in a penalty of $50 for each failure up to a maximum penalty of $100,000 for all such failures during the calendar year (Code Sec. 6723).

Federal law does not presently require employers to provide health insurance to their employees, or to report on whether or not they provide health insurance coverage.

Applicable large employers and offering employers required to report on health insurance coverage.—Applicable large employers that are subject to the Code Sec. 4980H rules for shared responsibility regarding health coverage and certain employers that offer minimum essential coverage to their employees through an eligible employer-sponsored plan ("offering employers"), are required to file a return reporting on such coverage at such time as the Secretary of the Treasury may prescribe (Code Sec. 6056(a), as added and amended by the Patient Protection and Affordable Care Act (PPACA) (P.L. 111-148)). For a discussion of the Code Sec. 4980H shared responsibility for employers regarding health coverage, see ¶ 305.

An applicable large employer for this purpose is, with respect to a calendar year, an employer who employed an average of at least 50 full-time employees on business days during the preceding calendar year. An exemption applies to employers whose workforce exceeds 50 full-time employees for 120 or fewer days during the calendar year, provided that the employees in excess of 50 for the 120-day period are seasonal workers. Solely for purposes of determining if it is an applicable large employer, an employer must also include, in addition to its full-time employees, a number of full-time equivalent employees determined by dividing the aggregate number of hours of service of employees who are not full-time employees for the month, by 120 (Code Sec. 4980H(c)(2), as added and amended by PPACA, and as amended and redesignated by the Health Care and Education Reconciliation Act of 2010 (P.L. 111-152)).

An offering employer for purposes of this reporting requirement is any employer who offers minimum essential coverage to its employees consisting of coverage through an eligible employer-sponsored plan, and pays any portion of the costs of such plan, if the required contribution of any employee exceeds eight percent of the wages paid to such employee (Code Sec. 6056(f)(1)(A), as added by PPACA; Act Sec. 10108(b) of PPACA). For this purpose, wages are defined in Code Sec. 3121(a), and the required contribution is determined under Code Sec. 5000A(e)(1)(B)(i), as added by PPACA. See ¶ 205 for a discussion of the required contribution under these rules. The eight percent figure will be adjusted in calendar years beginning after 2014 to reflect the rate of premium growth between the preceding calendar year and 2013 over the rate of income growth for such period (Code Sec. 6056(f)(1)(B), as added by PPACA). Any other term used by these reporting rules will have the meaning given such term by the Code Sec. 4980H employer shared responsibility rules (Code Sec. 6056(f)(2), as added by PPACA).

The required return must be in the form as the Secretary of the Treasury may prescribe, and must contain the name, date, employer identification number of the employer, and a certification as to whether the employer offers to its full-time employees (and their dependents) the opportunity to enroll in minimum essential coverage under an eligible employer-sponsored plan (Code Sec. 6056(b)(1) and (b)(2), as added and amended by PPACA). For this purpose, an eligible employer-sponsored plan is defined in Code Sec. 5000A(f)(2), as added by PPACA, and includes a group health plan or group health insurance coverage offered by an employer that is a governmental plan, or any other plan or coverage offered in the small or large group market within a state. For further discussion of eligible employer-sponsored plans, see ¶ 205.

¶415

NEW LAW EXPLAINED

If an employer certifies that it offered its full-time employees and their dependents the opportunity to enroll in minimum essential coverage under an eligible employer-sponsored plan, the return must also report:

- in the case of an applicable large employer, the length of any waiting period with respect to such coverage;

- the months during the calendar year for which coverage was available;

- the monthly premium for the lowest cost option in each of the enrollment categories under the plan;

- the employer's share of the total allowed costs of benefits provided under the plan; and

- in the case of an offering employer, the option for which the employer pays the largest portion of the cost of the plan and the portion of the cost paid by the employer in each of the enrollment categories under that option (Code Sec. 6056(b)(2)(C), as added and amended by PPACA).

  Comment: The waiting period for this purpose is defined in Sec. 2701(b)(4) of the Public Health Service Act and means, with respect to a group health plan and an individual who is a potential participant or beneficiary in the plan, the period that must pass with respect to the individual before the individual is eligible to be covered for benefits under the terms of the plan.

The required return must also state the number of full-time employees for each month during the calendar year, the name, address and taxpayer identification number of each full-time employee during the calendar year, and the months, if any, during which such employee and any dependents were covered under a health benefits plan. The return must further provide any other information required by the Secretary of the Treasury (Code Sec. 6056(b)(2), as added and amended by PPACA).

The Secretary of the Treasury has the authority to review the accuracy of the information provided pursuant to the new reporting requirements, including the applicable large employer's share under of the total allowed costs of benefits provided under the plan (Code Sec. 6056(b), as added and amended by PPACA).

A person required to file a return under these rules is also required to furnish a written statement to each full-time employee whose name is required to be reported on the return, showing the name, address and phone number of the person required to make the return, and the information required to be shown on the return with respect to such an employee (Code Sec. 6056(c)(1), as added by PPACA). The required statement must be furnished on or before January 31 of the year following the calendar year for which the information return was required to be made (Code Sec. 6056(c)(2), as added by PPACA).

If the applicable large employer or offering employer is a governmental unit, an agency or instrumentality of a governmental unit or an agency, the required returns and statements must be made by the person appropriately designated for purposes of this reporting requirement (Code Sec. 6056(e), as added by PPACA).

NEW LAW EXPLAINED

To the maximum extent feasible, the Secretary of the Treasury may provide that a return or statement required under these rules may be provided as part of a return or statement required under Code Sec. 6051 (regarding employment tax information returns and statements for employees), or Code Sec. 6055, as added by PPACA (regarding the new information reporting requirements for health care coverage, discussed at ¶410) (Code Sec. 6056(d)(1), as added by PPACA). In the case of an applicable large employer or offering employer offering health insurance coverage of a health insurance issuer, the employer may enter into an agreement with the issuer to include the required information with the return and statement required to be provided by the issuer under Code Sec. 6055, as added by PPACA (Code Sec. 6056(d)(2), as added and amended by PPACA).

Failure to file an information return reporting on health insurance coverage or failure to include correct or complete information on the return is subject to the existing penalties for failure to file correct information returns under Code Sec. 6721 (Code Sec. 6724(d)(1)(B)(xxv), as added and amended by PPACA). Similarly, the present-law penalties for failure to furnish correct payee statements under Code Sec. 6722 apply to failure to furnish statements to individuals with respect to whom information is reported or failure to include correct or complete information on such statements (Code Sec. 6724(d)(2)(HH), as added and amended by PPACA).

▶ **Effective date.** The provision applies to periods beginning after December 31, 2013 (Act Secs. 1514(d) and 10108(j)(4) of the Patient Protection and Affordable Care Act (PPACA) (P.L. 111-148)).

Law source: Law at ¶5265 and ¶5280. Committee Report at ¶10,110.

— Act Secs. 1514(a), 10106(g) and 10108(j)(1), (2) and (3)(A)-(D) of the Patient Protection and Affordable Care Act (PPACA) (P.L. 111-148), adding and amending Code Sec. 6056;

— Act Secs. 1514(b) and 10108(j)(3)(E), (F), amending Code Sec. 6724(d)(1)(B) and (d)(2);

— Act Sec. 1514(c);

— Act Secs. 1514(d) and 10108(j)(4), providing the effective dates.

Reporter references: For further information, consult the following CCH reporters.

— Standard Federal Tax Reporter, ¶40,220.01, ¶40,285.025 and ¶40,285.03

— Tax Research Consultant, FILEBUS: 9,350, PENALTY: 3,202 and PENALTY: 3,204

— Practical Tax Explanation, § 39,101 and § 40,305.05

¶420 Reporting Requirements on Payments to Corporations

SUMMARY OF NEW LAW

The exception to the reporting requirement for payments of $600 or more made to a corporation in the course of a trade or business, is eliminated, other than for corporations exempt from tax under Code Sec. 501(a).

BACKGROUND

A variety of information reporting requirements are imposed on participants in certain transactions (Code Secs. 6031 through 6060). One of the principal methods of improving tax compliance with respect to a form of income is to require information reporting by the third-party payer. When such payers are required to provide the IRS with information with respect to taxable payments, the likelihood that the recipient will properly include the payment in income greatly increases.

The chief provision governing information reporting by payors require information returns by all persons engaged in a trade or business who make payments in any tax year aggregating $600 or more in the course of that trade or business to a single payee (Code Sec. 6041(a)). The phrase "all persons engaged in a trade or business" includes not only persons in business for gain or profit, but also nonprofit organizations and exempt organizations (Reg. § 1.6041-1(b)(1)).

The reporting obligation applies if the total of all payments made by the payor in any tax year is $600 or more, even though the amount for any class of payment by itself is less than $600. Payments that must be reported are:

- salaries, wages, commissions, fees, incentive awards and other forms of compensation, and

- interest, rents, royalties, annuities, pensions, and other gains, profits and income.

The information return is generally submitted electronically as a Form-1099 or Form-1096. Certain payments to beneficiaries or employees may, however, require use of Forms W-3 or W-2, respectively (Reg. § 1.6041-1(a)(2)).

Payments to a corporation are generally excepted from these reporting obligations by the regulations (Reg. § 1-6041-3(p)). This exception does not apply, however, to payments made for attorneys' fees, and amounts paid to a corporation that provides medical or health care services (unless made to a hospital or extended care facility that is either tax-exempt or owned and operated by the federal government or by any unit of a state or local government) or bills or collects payments for these services. Payments to certain exempt organizations, governmental entities, international organizations, or retirement plans are also excepted from reporting by Reg. § 1-6041-3(p).

In 1982, Congress expanded the reporting requirements previously encompassed by Code Sec. 6041 by enacting Code Sec. 6041A. Code Sec. 6041A(a) requires certain service recipients to report payments of $600 of more to a service provider. Until final regulations are issued under Code Sec. 6041A, information returns are not required for payments described in Code Sec. 6041A(a) that are exempt from reporting under Reg. § 1-6041-3 (Notice 2001-38, 2001-1 CB 1334).

NEW LAW EXPLAINED

Reporting of payments to corporations required.—The exception to the general information reporting requirement for payments of $600 or more made to corporations in the course of a trade or business is eliminated, other than for corporations exempt from tax under Code Sec. 501(a) (Code Sec. 6041(h), as added by the Patient Protection and Affordable Care Act (PPACA) (P.L. 111-148)). This rule applies notwithstanding any

NEW LAW EXPLAINED

regulations prescribed by the Secretary of the Treasury before March 23, 2010, the date of enactment of the Patient Protection Act. Thus, if all payments made by a payor in the course of its trade or business to a corporation total $600 or more in any tax year, the payor must file the appropriate information return reporting those payments.

> **Practical Analysis:** The regulatory exception for payments to exempt or governmental organizations, international organizations and retirement plans is not affected by this provision. It is unclear how payments for services, reportable under Code Sec. 6041A(a), but made exempt by Notice 2001-38, will be impacted by the amendment to Code Sec. 6041(a).

The class of payments with respect to which reporting is required has also been expanded to include all amounts paid in consideration for property, and other gross proceeds for both property and services (Code Sec. 6041(a), as amended by PPACA). The amount of such gross proceeds is required to be shown on the information return.

The Secretary of the Treasury is authorized to promulgate regulations necessary to carry out the purposes of Code Sec. 6041, as amended by PPACA, including rules to avoid duplicative information reporting of transactions (Code Sec. 6041(i), as added by PPACA).

Caution: Failure to comply with these requirements may result in the imposition of penalties, which may include a penalty for failure to file the information return (Code Sec. 6721); a penalty for failure to furnish payee statements (Code Sec. 6722); or failure to comply with other various reporting requirements (Code Sec. 6723).

Comment: The U.S. Department of the Treasury Report, *Update on Reducing the Federal Tax Gap and Improving Voluntary Compliance*, states that these information reports will serve as reminders to the corporate recipients to include these amounts in gross receipts and will make these amounts visible to the IRS for targeted compliance programs.

▶ **Effective date.** The provision applies to payments made after December 31, 2011 (Act Sec. 9006(c) of Patient Protection and Affordable Care Act (PPACA) (P.L. 111-148)).

Law source: Law at ¶5250. Committee Report at ¶10,210.

— Act Sec. 9006(a) of the Patient Protection and Affordable Care Act (PPACA) (P.L. 111-148), adding Code Sec. 6041(h) and (i);

— Act Sec. 9006(b), amending Code Sec. 6041(a);

— Act Sec. 9006(c), providing the effective date.

Reporter references: For further information, consult the following CCH reporters.

— Standard Federal Tax Reporter, ¶35,836.021 and ¶35,836.03

— Tax Research Consultant, FILEBUS: 9,200 and FILEBUS: 9,206

— Practical Tax Explanation, §39,105.15

¶420

¶425 Disclosures to Carry Out Eligibility Requirements for Certain Programs

SUMMARY OF NEW LAW

The IRS is permitted to disclose to the Department of Health and Human Services certain return information in order to verify cost sharing reduction or premium tax credit amounts and facilitate eligibility determinations for other programs.

BACKGROUND

The IRS is generally prohibited from disclosing taxpayer returns and return information except to the extent authorized under the Internal Revenue Code (Code Sec. 6103). "Return information," for these purposes, is broadly defined and includes, among other things, a taxpayer's identity (name, mailing address, taxpayer identification number, or any combination of the three), the nature, source, or amount of his income, payments, receipts, deductions, exemptions, credits, assets, liabilities, net worth, tax liability, tax withheld, deficiencies, overassessments, or tax payments, whether the taxpayer's return was, is being, or will be examined or subject to other investigation or processing, or any other data, received by, recorded by, prepared by, furnished to, or collected by the IRS with respect to a return or with respect to the determination of the existence, or possible existence, of liability (or amount of liability) of a person for any tax, penalty, interest, fine, forfeiture, or other imposition, or offense. However, it does not include data in a form which cannot be associated with, or otherwise identify, a particular taxpayer (Code Sec. 6103(b)(2), (b)(6)).

There are a number of exceptions to the general prohibition on disclosure of returns and return information. For example, pursuant to Code Sec. 6103(l)(20), the IRS may disclose to the Social Security Administration certain return information of a taxpayer whose Medicare premium may be subject to adjustment. Also, pursuant to Code Sec. 6103(l)(7), agencies administering certain federally-assisted programs may receive certain return information for the purposes of determining program eligibility or benefits amounts (Code Sec. 6103(l)(7)). The IRS and the recipients of disclosed information are subject to procedural requirements and recordkeeping safeguards with respect to returns and return information (Code Sec. 6103(p)). Information recipients are required to (1) establish a system of records to keep track of disclosure requests, the date of requests and the reason for the request; (2) establish a secure area for storing the information; and (3) restrict access to the information. Further, disclosed information must be returned to the IRS or made undisclosable.

The unauthorized disclosure of returns or return information is a felony subject to a possible $5,000 fine or five years of imprisonment, or both (Code Sec. 7213(a)). The unauthorized inspection of such returns or return information carries up to a $1,000 fine or one year of imprisonment, or both (Code Sec. 7213A). Further, a taxpayer can bring a civil action for damages for the unauthorized disclosure or inspection of any return or return information (Code Sec. 7431(a)(2)).

Disclosures of taxpayer information permitted to carry out eligibility requirements for certain programs.—The IRS is permitted to disclosure certain return information with respect to program eligibility determinations and verification of for the premium assistance tax credit or cost sharing reduction amounts provided to qualified individuals through a Health Insurance Exchange (Code Sec. 6103(l)(21), as added by the Patient Protection and Affordable Care Act (PPACA) (P.L. 111-148), and amended by the Health Care and Education Reconciliation Act of 2010 (P.L. 111-152)). Upon written request from the Secretary of Health and Human Services, the Secretary of the Treasury or his delegate (Treasury) shall disclose to officers, employees, and contractors of the Department of Health and Human Services (HHS) certain return information of any taxpayer whose income is relevant in determining:

- any premium assistant tax credit (see ¶ 210);
- any cost-sharing reduction (see ¶ 520); or
- eligibility for participation in a State Medicaid program, a State's children's health insurance program (CHIP), or a basic health program under Act Sec. 1331 of the Patient Protection Act (regarding state flexibility to establish basic health programs for low-income individuals not eligible for Medicaid) (Code Sec. 6103(a)(3), as amended by PPACA; Code Sec. 6103(l)(21)(A), as added by PPACA).

> **Comment:** By January 1, 2014, each State must establish an American Health Benefit Exchange and Small Business Health Options Program (SHOP Exchange) to provide qualified individuals and qualified small business employers access to qualified health plans. For a discussion of the establishment and requirements of the Exchanges, see ¶505. Individuals who are eligible for participation in a qualified health plan through an Exchange, may also be eligible for a premium assistance tax credit and cost-sharing subsidy.

The return information to be disclosed is limited to the taxpayer's identity, filing status, the number of individuals for whom the taxpayer may claim an exemption deduction under Code Sec. 151 (including the taxpayer and spouse), the modified adjusted gross income (MAGI) (as defined in new Code Sec. 36B) of the taxpayer and the MAGI of each of these individuals who are required to file a return of tax imposed by chapter 1 for the tax year, and the tax year with respect to which the information relates, or if such information is not available (Code Sec. 6103(l)(21)(A), as added by the Patient Protection Act and amended by the 2010 Reconciliation Act). The Treasury may also prescribe by regulations for the disclosure of other information that might indicate whether the taxpayer is eligible for any premium tax credit or any cost-sharing reduction and the amount thereof (Code Sec. 6103(l)(21)(A)(v), as added by PPACA).

The Secretary of Health and Human Services may disclose to an Exchange established under the Patient Protection Act or its contractors, or to a state agency administering a state program described in the bulleted list above, or its contractors, any inconsistency between the information provided by the Exchange or state agency

NEW LAW EXPLAINED

and the information provided to HHS under Code Sec. 6103(l)(21)(A) (Code Sec. 6103(l)(21)(B), as added by PPACA).

The return information that is disclosed may be used by officers, employees, and contractors of HHS, an Exchange, or a state agency only for the purposes of, and to the extent necessary in: (1) establishing eligibility for participation in the Exchange, and verifying the appropriate amount of, any premium tax credit or any cost-sharing reduction, and (2) determining eligibility for participation in the state programs described above (Code Sec. 6103(l)(21)(C), as added by PPACA).

The procedural and recordkeeping safeguards under Code Sec. 6103(p) must also be complied with, and the unauthorized disclosure or inspection of a return or return information is subject to civil sanctions and is punishable by fine, imprisonment, or both (Code Secs. 6103(p)(4) and 7213(a)(2), as amended by PPACA; Code Sec. 7213A).

> **Comment:** Act Sec. 1414(a)(2) of the Patient Protection Act also amends section 205(c)(2)(C) of the Social Security Act by authorizing the Secretary of Health and Human Services, and the Exchanges, to collect and use the names and Social Security account numbers of individuals as required to administer the provisions of, and the amendments made by, the Patient Protection Act.

▶ **Effective date.** No specific effective date is provided by the Patient Protection and Affordable Care Act (PPACA) (P.L. 111-148), or by the Health Care and Education Reconciliation Act of 2010 (P.L. 111-152). The provision is, therefore, generally considered effective on March 23, 2010, the date of enactment of the Patient Protection Act. However, the authorization under Code Sec. 6103(l)(21)(A)(iv) for disclosure of "modified adjusted gross" income, rather than "modified gross" income, is considered effective on March 30, 2010, the date of enactment of the 2010 Reconciliation Act.

Law source: Law at ¶5270, ¶5285 and ¶7012. Committee Reports at ¶10,050 and ¶10,400.

— Act Sec. 1414(a)(1) of the Patient Protection and Affordable Care Act (PPACA) (P.L. 111-148), adding Code Sec. 6103(l)(21);

— Act Sec. 1004(a)(1)(B) of the Health Care and Education Reconciliation Act of 2010 (P.L. 111-152), amending Code Sec. 6103(l)(21)(A)(iv);

— Act Sec. 1414(a)(2) of PPACA;

— Act Sec. 1414(b) and (c) of PPACA, amending Code Sec. 6103(a) and Code Sec. 6103(p)(4);

— Act Sec. 1414(d) of PPACA, amending Code Sec. 7213(a).

Reporter references: For further information, consult the following CCH reporters.

— Standard Federal Tax Reporter, ¶36,894.0277 and ¶41,353.01

— Tax Research Consultant, IRS: 9,254 and IRS: 66,360

— Practical Tax Explanation, §39,065

— Federal Estate and Gift Tax Reporter, ¶20,435.01

¶425

¶430 Disclosures for Purposes of Reducing the Part D Premium Subsidy for High-Income Beneficiaries

SUMMARY OF NEW LAW

The Social Security Administration (SSA) now has access to certain information about taxpayers to assist it in reducing the Part D premium subsidy for high-income beneficiaries.

BACKGROUND

The Medicare Prescription Drug, Improvement, and Modernization Act (MMA) of 2003 (P.L. 108-173) added section 1860D-31, the Medicare Prescription Drug Discount Card and Transitional Assistance Program. Its purpose was to endorse certain prescription drug discount card programs that would provide prescription drug discounts to eligible individuals through card sponsors. The Discount Card Program was transitional, giving immediate help to Medicare beneficiaries during calendar years 2004 and 2005, in anticipation of Medicare Part D, The Voluntary Prescription Drug Benefit Program, which was also enacted by MMA and went into effect in 2006.

Medicare Part B pays for physician services, lab and X-ray services, durable medical equipment, and outpatient and other services. Those enrolled in the Part B program are charged a monthly premium. The standard beneficiary premium is set to cover 25 percent of the costs of the Part B program, and the federal government pays the remainder. Beginning in 2007, Medicare beneficiaries whose income is greater than certain legislated threshold amounts pay a higher premium on a sliding scale—the "premium adjustment." For example, in 2010, Medicare beneficiaries whose income is greater than $85,000 for an individual and $170,000 for beneficiaries who file a joint return pay a higher premium (Sec. 1839(i) of the Social Security Act).

Under Code Sec. 6103, returns and return information are confidential and may not be disclosed by the IRS. But Code Sec. 6103 also provides a number of exceptions to the general rule of nondisclosure. For example, certain return information may be disclosed for purposes of establishing the appropriate amount of any Medicare Part B premium subsidy adjustment (Joint Committee on Taxation, *Technical Explanation of the Revenue Provisions of the "Reconciliation Act of 2010," as amended, in combination with the "Patient Protection and Affordable Care Act"* (JCX-18-10), March 21, 2010).

Specifically, the IRS, upon written request, and solely for the purpose of establishing the appropriate amount of any Medicare Part B premium adjustment, can provide limited information to the SSA regarding a taxpayer whose Medicare premium may be subject to adjustment. For this purpose, the IRS can provide: (1) taxpayer identity information; (2) filing status; (3) adjusted gross income; (4) amounts excluded from gross income under various provisions; (5) tax-exempt interest received or accrued during the tax year; (6) the tax year to which the previous information relates; and (7) other relevant information related to the liability of the taxpayer as prescribed by regulation (Code Sec. 6103(l)(20)).

BACKGROUND

Similarly, under MMA, Part D beneficiary premiums account for 25.5 percent of expected total Part D premium costs for standard coverage. Medicare pays the remainder. Unlike Part B, however, beneficiary subsidies under Part D are not subject to income thresholds or means testing; therefore, the premium subsidy is not reduced for high-income beneficiaries.

NEW LAW EXPLAINED

SSA to use taxpayer information for purposes of reducing the Part D premium subsidy for high-income beneficiaries.—Starting in 2011, the Medicare portion or premium subsidy amount has been reduced for certain beneficiaries of the Voluntary Prescription Drug Benefit Program under Medicare Part D—namely, for beneficiaries whose modified adjusted gross income (MAGI) (as defined by the Social Security Act) exceeds the thresholds used under Part B (Act Sec. 3308(a) of the Patient Protection and Affordable Care Act (PPACA) (P.L. 111-148), amending Section 1860D-13 of the Social Security Act (42 U.S.C. 1395w-113)). The 2009 thresholds for MAGI were $85,000 for an individual tax return and $170,000 for a joint return (generally based on 2007 returns).

The implementation of the income-related reduction in the Part D premium subsidy amount would be similar to the implementation of the income-related reductions in Part B premium subsidies. Thus, the Medicare portion will decrease based on percentages used to decrease the Part B premium subsidy. As a result, similar to Part B, the beneficiary share of total Part D costs will increase as MAGI of individuals or joint filers increases, but within set ranges of MAGI.

In connection with the Part D beneficiary premium increases, the IRS has broader authority to disclose income information to the Social Security Administration (SSA). In addition to disclosing information in connection with adjusting the Part B subsidy, the IRS may now disclose the same information in connection with the Part D beneficiary premium increases. The return information may be used by officers, employees, and contractors of the SSA only as needed to establish the right amount of any Medicare Part D premium subsidy adjustment (Joint Committee on Taxation, *Technical Explanation of the Revenue Provisions of the "Reconciliation Act of 2010," as amended, in combination with the "Patient Protection and Affordable Care Act"* (JCX-18-10), March 21, 2010). Also, the information listed in Code Sec. 6103(l)(20) now may be used to resolve taxpayer appeals with respect to any premium adjustment or increase under Part B or Part D (Code Sec. 6103(l)(20), as amended by PPACA).

Finally, with respect to information that the IRS has disclosed to the SSA in connection with any premium adjustment or increase, Code Sec. 6103(l)(20) has been amended to allow the SSA, in turn, to disclose information as follows:

- disclosure of the taxpayer identity information and the amount of the premium subsidy adjustment or increased premium amount to the Centers for Medicare and Medicaid Services in order to collect the premium subsidy amount or premium increase;

¶430

NEW LAW EXPLAINED

- disclosure of the taxpayer identity information and the amount of the premium subsidy adjustment or increased premium amount to the Office of Personnel Management and the Railroad Retirement Board in order to collect the premium subsidy amount or increased premium amount;

- disclosure of return information to the Department of Health and Human Services in order to resolve administrative appeals of premium subsidy adjustments or increased premiums; and

- disclosure of return information to the Department of Justice for use in judicial proceedings in order to carry out the purposes of establishing premium adjustments or increases (Code Sec. 6103(l)(20), as amended by PPACA).

▶ **Effective date.** No specific effective date is provided by the Act. The provision, therefore, is considered effective on March 23, 2010, the date of enactment.

Law source: Law at ¶5270. Committee Report at ¶10,140.

— Act Sec. 3308(b)(2) of the Patient Protection and Affordable Care Act (PPACA) (P.L. 111-148), amending Code Sec. 6103(l)(20).

Reporter references: For further information, consult the following CCH reporters.

— Standard Federal Tax Reporter, ¶36,894.0277

— Tax Research Consultant, IRS: 9,254.05

¶435 Exempt Status Available to Nonprofit Health Insurance Issuers

SUMMARY OF NEW LAW

Tax exempt status under Code Sec. 501(a) has been made available to qualified nonprofit health insurance issuers (as defined by Act Sec. 1322 of the Patient Protection and Affordable Care Act of 2010) receiving grants or loans under the Consumer Operated and Oriented Plan (CO-OP) program.

BACKGROUND

Tax-exempt status is available to various classes of nonprofit organizations (corporations, trusts, community funds, social clubs, civic groups) by way of Code Sec. 501(a). The most common basis for invoking tax-exempt status falls under Code Sec. 501(c)(3)'s broad category of exemptions for religious, charitable, scientific, literary and educational organizations, but many other types of nonprofits are exempted under Code Sec. 501(a). Generally, there are three public sectors to our society—the governmental, the for-profit (or business) sector, and the not-for-profit (or nonprofit) sector. The rationale for granting exempt status differs for differing types of organizations, but the distinguishing feature of nonprofit organizations is that the basis for their tax-exempt status is their pledge to serve the welfare or convenience of a wide

BACKGROUND

class of individuals or organizations, rather than to enrich the individuals running the organizations, such as employees or shareholders. Qualification and operational requirements differ by type of exempt organization, as do the reporting requirements.

NEW LAW EXPLAINED

New category of exempt organization established.—Tax-exempt status under Code Sec. 501(a) has been made available to qualified nonprofit health insurance issuers (as defined by Act Sec. 1322 of the Patient Protection and Affordable Care Act (PPACA) (P.L. 111-148)) receiving grants or loans under the Consumer Operated and Oriented Plan (CO-OP) program. The grants or loans must be received pursuant to the Act Sec. 1322 provisions of Patient Protection Act, for such periods as the issuer is in compliance with the requirements of that section and any other agreements the issuer has made with respect to such grants or loans (Code Sec. 501(c)(29)(A), as added by PPACA). For a discussion of the CO-OP program, see ¶ 540.

The CO-OP program has been designed to encourage the creation of qualified nonprofit health insurance issuers that will offer qualified health plans to individuals in the states in which the issuers are licensed to offer such insurance plans (Act Sec. 1322(a)(2) of PPACA). Any such qualified nonprofit health insurance issuer must give notice to the Secretary of the Treasury (in a manner to be described by regulation) that it is applying for recognition of exempt status under Code Sec. 501(c)(29). In addition, the issuer cannot:

- participate or intervene in any political campaign (including the publishing or distributions of political statements) on behalf of, or in opposition to, any candidate for public office;

- in any substantial manner participate in activities relating to the carrying on of propaganda or otherwise attempting to influence legislation; and

- no part of the net earnings of the issuer may inure to the benefit of any private shareholder or individual.

The third prohibition, above, against inurement will not apply to an issuer when all the profits of the issuer are required to be used to lower the premiums, improve the benefits, or for other programs designed to improve the quality of the health care delivered to its members (Act Sec. 1322(c)(4) of PPACA). The tax on excess benefit transactions under Code Sec. 4958 will apply to Code Sec. 501(c)(29) organizations in the same manner as it applies to organizations exempt under Code Sec. 501(c)(3) and 501(c)(4) (Code Sec. 4958(e)(1) as amended by PPACA).

An organization that becomes a qualified nonprofit health insurance issuer under Code Sec. 529(c)(29) must include the following information on their returns filed pursuant to Code Sec. 6033(a):

- the amount of reserves on hand, and

- the amount of reserves required by each state in which the issuer is licensed to issue qualified health plans (Code Sec. 6033(m), as added by PPACA).

¶435

NEW LAW EXPLAINED

State Tax Consequences: The new requirements for exempt nonprofit status for certain hospitals may affect states that adopt Code Sec. 501, but because of their Code conformity dates may not impose the additional requirements for tax-exempt status. However, most states broadly provide that organizations that qualify for tax-exempt status for federal tax purposes will also qualify for tax-exempt status for state tax purposes. These states will not be impacted by the new requirements. States, like California, that have provisions that are similar, but not identical, to the federal provisions governing tax-exempt status, may allow hospitals that do not meet the additional federal requirements to be tax-exempt for state tax purposes. Such hospitals would have to apply for the state tax exemption.

Reinsurance. As part of the transition to the health insurance system envisioned by Congress (as effectuated by PPACA), each state must either establish or enter into contracts with reinsurance entities to carry out the reinsurance program under Act Sec. 1341 of the Patient Protection Act by January 1, 2014 (Act Sec. 1341(a) of PPACA). These state programs must be maintained to collect payments and make payments to the health insurance issuers that cover high risk individuals in the individual market during the three-year period beginning January 1, 2014 (Act Sec. 1341(b)(1) of PPACA).

Applicable reinsurance entities, for this purpose, are also tax-exempt entities (Act Sec. 1341(c)(3) of PPACA). States are permitted to have more than one such applicable reinsurance entity, and states are also permitted to enter into agreements under which reinsurance entities may carry out such programs on a multi-state basis for the states entering into the agreement (Act Sec. 1341(c)(2) of PPACA).

Practical Analysis: Jean Baxley, Of Counsel at Crowell & Moring of Washington, D.C., notes that the Act does not touch on the treatment, for federal income tax purposes, of the amounts paid by health insurance issuers to "applicable reinsurance entities" established by the Act, i.e., whether the payments are for reinsurance or deductible as general business expenses, or are contributions to the capital of the applicable reinsurance entities. The payments would seem to be premiums paid for reinsurance to the extent reinsurance coverage is obtained, which would decrease life insurance gross income under Code Sec. 803(a) for health insurance issuers that are taxed as life insurance companies for federal income tax purposes, and decrease premiums earned under Code Sec. 832(b)(4) for health insurance issuers that are taxed as property and casualty companies for federal income tax purposes.

Health insurance issuers in the individual coverage market that cover "high risk individuals," as that term is defined in regulations to be issued by the Secretary of Health and Human Services, may receive reinsurance payments from the tax-exempt "applicable reinsurance entities" established in the Act. The character of this income to health insurance issuers is not prescribed in the Act, but presumably the payments would be treated as reinsurance proceeds.

The amount a health insurance issuer will be required to pay to the applicable reinsurance entity may be payable in advance or periodically throughout the year

NEW LAW EXPLAINED

> under the regulations to be issued by the Secretary of Heath and Human Services. This flexibility may lead to issues regarding timing of deductions for health insurance issuers that make these payments.

▶ **Effective date.** No specific effective date is provided by the Act. These rules are, therefore, considered effective on March 23, 2010, the date of enactment.

Law source: Law at ¶5155, ¶5215, ¶5245, ¶7006 and ¶7042. Committee Report at ¶10,020.

— Act Sec. 1322(h)(1) of the Patient Protection and Affordable Care Act (PPACA) (P.L. 111-148), adding Code Sec. 501(c)(29);

— Act Sec. 1322(h)(3), amending Code Sec. 4958(e)(1);

— Act Sec. 1322(h)(2), redesignating former Code Sec. 6033(m) as Code Sec. 6033(n) and adding new Code Sec. 6033(m);

— Act Secs. 1341(c) and 10104(r).

Reporter references: For further information, consult the following CCH reporters.

— Standard Federal Tax Reporter, ¶22,604.01, ¶34,255.026, ¶35,425.021

— Tax Research Consultant, EXEMPT: 100, EXEMPT: 6,056.25, EXEMPT: 9,102

— Practical Tax Explanation, § 33,001, § 33,705.30

¶440 Additional Requirements for Charitable Hospitals

SUMMARY OF NEW LAW

Four additional requirements have been imposed on charitable hospitals that must be met in order for the hospitals to maintain their Code Sec. 501(c)(3) tax-exempt status.

BACKGROUND

Charitable organizations, i.e., organizations described in Code Sec. 501(c)(3), generally are exempt from federal income tax, are eligible to receive tax deductible contributions, have access to tax-exempt financing through state and local governments, and generally are exempt from state and local taxes. A charitable organization must operate primarily in pursuit of one or more tax-exempt purposes constituting the basis of its tax exemption. The Internal Revenue Code specifies such purposes as religious, charitable, scientific, educational, literary, testing for public safety, to foster international amateur sports competition, or for the prevention of cruelty to children or animals. In general, an organization is organized and operated for charitable purposes if it provides relief for the poor and distressed or the underprivileged.

The Code does not provide a per se exemption for hospitals. Rather, a hospital qualifies for exemption if it is organized and operated for a charitable purpose and otherwise meets the requirements of Code Sec. 501(c)(3). The promotion of health has

BACKGROUND

been recognized by the IRS as a charitable purpose that is beneficial to the community as a whole. It includes not only the establishment or maintenance of charitable hospitals, but also clinics, homes for the aged, and other providers of health care.

Since 1969, the IRS has applied a "community benefit" standard for determining whether a hospital is charitable. According to Rev. Rul. 69-545, community benefit can include, for example: maintaining an emergency room open to all persons regardless of ability to pay; having an independent board of trustees composed of representatives of the community; operating with an open medical staff policy, with privileges available to all qualifying physicians; providing charity care; and utilizing surplus funds to improve the quality of patient care, expand facilities, and advance medical training, education and research. Beginning in 2009, hospitals generally are required to submit information on community benefit on their annual information returns filed with the IRS. There are no sanctions short of revocation of tax-exempt status for hospitals that fail to satisfy the community benefit standard.

Exempt organizations are required to file an annual information return, stating specifically the items of gross income, receipts, disbursements, and such other information as the IRS may prescribe. Code Sec. 501(c)(3) organizations that are classified as public charities must file Form 990, Return of Organization Exempt From Income Tax, which requests information specific to Code Sec. 501(c)(3) organizations. Additionally, an organization that operates at least one facility that is, or is required to be, licensed, registered, or similarly recognized by a state as a hospital must complete Schedule H (Form 990), which requests information regarding charity care, community benefits, bad debt expense, and certain management company and joint venture arrangements of a hospital.

NEW LAW EXPLAINED

Additional requirements imposed on charitable hospitals.—The Patient Protection and Affordable Care Act establishes four new requirements applicable to Code Sec. 501(c)(3) hospitals (Code Sec. 501(r)(1), as added by the Patient Protection and Affordable Care Act (PPACA) (P.L. 111-148)). The new requirements are in addition to, and not in lieu of, the requirements otherwise applicable to an organization described in Code Sec. 501(c)(3). The requirements generally apply to any Code Sec. 501(c)(3) organization that operates at least one hospital facility (Code Sec. 501(r)(2)(A), as added by PPACA). For purposes of the provision, a hospital facility generally includes: (1) any facility that is, or is required to be, licensed, registered, or similarly recognized by a state as a hospital; and (2) any other facility or organization the Secretary of the Treasury (the "Secretary") determines has the provision of hospital care as its principal purpose. An organization is required to comply with the following requirements with respect to each hospital facility operated by such organization (Code Sec. 501(r)(2)(B), as added by PPACA).

> **Comment:** The requirements appear to reflect concerns that have arisen in recent years about whether nonprofit hospitals are providing adequate public benefits to justify their tax-exempt status, according to the Congressional Research Ser-

NEW LAW EXPLAINED

vice ("501(c)(3) Hospitals and the Community Benefit Standard" (November 10, 2009)).

Community health needs assessment. First, each hospital facility is required to conduct a community health needs assessment at least once every three tax years and adopt an implementation strategy to meet the community needs identified through such an assessment (Code Sec. 501(r)(3), as added by PPACA). The assessment process must take into account input from persons who represent the broad interests of the community served by the hospital, including those with special knowledge or expertise of public health issues. Each hospital facility is required to make the assessment widely available.

Financial assistance policy. Second, each hospital facility is required to adopt, implement, and widely publicize a written financial assistance policy (Code Sec. 501(r)(4)(A), as added by PPACA). The financial assistance policy must indicate the eligibility criteria for financial assistance and whether such assistance includes free or discounted care. For those eligible for discounted care, the policy must indicate the basis for calculating the amounts that will be billed to such patients. The policy must also indicate how to apply for such assistance. If a hospital does not have a separate billing and collections policy, the financial assistance policy must also indicate what actions the hospital may take in the event of nonpayment, including collections action and reporting to credit agencies.

Each hospital facility is required to adopt and implement a written policy to provide, without discrimination, emergency medical treatment to individuals regardless of their eligibility under the financial assistance policy (Code Sec. 501(r)(4)(B), as added by PPACA).

Limitation on charges. Third, each hospital facility is permitted to bill patients who qualify for financial assistance no more than the amount generally billed to insured patients (Code Sec. 501(r)(5), as added by PPACA). A hospital facility may not use gross charges (i.e., "chargemaster" rates) when billing individuals who qualify for financial assistance.

> **Comment:** The limitation on what could be charged by a charitable hospital for emergency or other medically necessary care was originally "the lowest amounts charged." Americans for Tax Reform has said that the change to "the amount generally billed" makes the limitation less onerous on hospitals.

> **Comment:** It is intended that amounts billed to those who qualify for financial assistance may be based on either the best, or an average of the three best, negotiated commercial rates, or Medicare rates.

Billing and collection requirements. Fourth, a hospital facility (or its affiliates) may not undertake certain extraordinary collection actions (even if otherwise permitted by law) against a patient without first making reasonable efforts to inform the patient about the hospital's financial assistance policy and to determine whether the patient is eligible for assistance under the policy (Code Sec. 501(r)(6), as added by PPACA).

> **Comment:** Such extraordinary collection actions include lawsuits, liens on residences, arrests, body attachments, or other similar collection processes (Commit-

NEW LAW EXPLAINED

tee Report for Senate Finance Healthcare Reform, America's Healthy Future Act of 2009 (October 19, 2009)).

The IRS is directed to issue guidance concerning what attempts to determine eligibility for financial assistance constitute reasonable attempts (Code Sec. 501(r)(7), as added by PPACA).

Comment: It is intended that, for this purpose, "reasonable attempts" include notification by the hospital of its financial assistance policy upon admission and in written and oral communications with the patient regarding the patient's bill, including invoices and telephone calls, before collection action or reporting to credit rating agencies is initiated (Committee Report for Senate Finance Healthcare Reform, America's Healthy Future Act of 2009 (October 19, 2009)).

Excise tax for failure to meet hospital exemption requirements. If a hospital organization must meet the additional requirements under Code Sec. 501(r), and fails to meet the community health needs assessments requirements under Code Sec. 501(r)(3), an excise tax is imposed on the hospital (Code Sec. 4959, as added by PPACA). The tax on the organization is $50,000 for any applicable tax year. For example, if a facility does not complete a community health needs assessment in tax years one, two or three, it is subject to the penalty in year three. If it then fails to complete a community health needs assessment in year four, it is subject to another penalty in year four (for failing to satisfy the requirement during the three-year period beginning with tax year two and ending with tax year four).

Mandatory review of tax exemption for hospitals. The Secretary of the Treasury will review at least once, every three years, the community benefit activities of each hospital organization to which Code Sec. 501(r) applies (Act Sec. 9007(c) of PPACA).

Additional reporting requirements. A hospital must disclose, in its annual information report to the IRS (Form 990 and related schedules), how it is addressing the needs identified in the community health needs assessment and, if all identified needs are not addressed, the reasons why (e.g., lack of financial or human resources) (Code Sec. 6033(b)(15)(A), as added by PPACA). The Patient Protection Act also requires each organization to which Code Sec. 501(r)(3) applies to file with its annual information return a copy of its audited financial statements (or, in the case of an organization the financial statements of which are included in a consolidated financial statement with other organizations, such consolidated financial statements) (Code Sec. 6033(b)(15)(B), as added by PPACA).

Reports. The Patient Protection Act requires the Secretary, in consultation with the Secretary of Health and Human Services, to report annually to Congress the levels of charity care, bad debt expenses, unreimbursed costs of means-tested government programs, and unreimbursed costs of non-means tested government programs incurred by private tax-exempt, taxable, and governmental hospitals, as well as the cost of community benefit activities incurred by private tax-exempt hospitals (Act Sec. 9007(e)(1) of PPACA).

In addition, the Secretary, in consultation with the Secretary of Health and Human Services, must conduct a study of the trends in these amounts with the results of the

NEW LAW EXPLAINED

study provided to Congress five years from March 23, 2010 (Act Sec. 9007(e)(2) of PPACA).

> **Comment:** In a January 7, 2010, letter to Speaker of the House Nancy Pelosi (D-Calif.) and Majority Leader Harry Reid (D-Nev.), the American Hospital Association (AHA) wrote that they do not believe that the new requirements for charitable hospitals and their ability to maintain tax exemption are necessary, and the AHA urged removal of the provisions from the final health reform conference report.

Practical Analysis: Charles Goulding, President and founder of Energy Tax Savers, observes that, in recent years, there has been concern that certain charitable or not-for-profit hospitals have not been providing the charitable medical services that their privileged not-for-profit status was predicated on, particularly if they are perceived not to be serving the local community. Not-for-profit status typically impacts numerous taxes, including federal, state and city incomes taxes; property taxes; and sales taxes. In certain localities, a not-for-profit hospital may be the largest enterprise, employer and land owner. With the budget constraints impacting all levels of government, there are multiple tax authorities interested in the tax status of these hospitals.

Not-for-profit hospitals will need to establish tax documentation processes to substantiate their continuing right to not-for-profit status. This documentation should be aimed at supporting both federal tax–exempt status and local law–exempt status based on their state charter and state not-for-profit law requirements. Internal control processes should be aimed at achieving perfect reporting compliance so that any inadvertent omission or late filing isn't used to put tax status at issue.

There are some large hospital organizations with a mix of for profit and not-for-profit organizations. When serving overlapping communities, these organizations may have the flexibility to rebalance patient services to ensure compliance with the developing hospital not-for-profit status compliance requirements.

▶ **Effective date.** The additional requirements imposed on charitable hospitals generally apply to tax years beginning after March 23, 2010, the date of enactment (Act Secs. 9007(f)(1) and 10903(b) of the Patient Protection and Affordable Care Act (PPACA) (P.L. 111-148)). The requirements of Code Sec. 501(r)(3) apply to tax years beginning after the date which is two years after March 23, 2010, the date of enactment (Act Sec. 9007(f)(2) of PPACA). The excise tax for failure to meet the exemption requirements applies to failures occurring after March 23, 2010, the date of enactment (Act Sec. 9007(f)(3) of PPACA).

Law source: Law at ¶5155, ¶5220, ¶5245 and ¶7027. Committee Report at ¶10,220.

— Act Sec. 9007(a) of the Patient Protection and Affordable Care Act (PPACA) (P.L. 111-148), redesignating Code Sec. 501(r) as Code Sec. 501(s) and adding a new Code Sec. 501(r);

— Act Sec. 9007(b), adding Code Sec. 4959;

— Act Secs. 9007(c) and (e);

— Act Sec. 9007(d), amending Code Sec. 6033(b);

— Act Sec. 10903(a), amending Code Sec. 501(r)(5);

— Act Secs. 9007(f) and 10903(b), providing the effective dates.

¶440

NEW LAW EXPLAINED

Reporter references: For further information, consult the following CCH reporters.

— Standard Federal Tax Reporter, ¶22,609.022

— Tax Research Consultant, EXEMPT: 3,150

— Practical Tax Explanation, §33,105

¶445   Patient-Centered Outcomes Research Trust Fund Established and Funded

SUMMARY OF NEW LAW

The Patient-Centered Outcomes Research Trust Fund (PCORTF) is funded for comparative effectiveness research. Fees are imposed on insurers of health plans and employer sponsors of self-insured health plans to help fund the PCORTF.

BACKGROUND

From time to time, Congress establishes trust funds for special purposes. For example, there is the Black Lung Disability Trust Fund (Code Sec. 9501), the Airport and Airway Trust Fund (Code Sec. 9502), and the Highway Trust Fund (Code Sec. 9503). In general, these trust funds are funded by fees, excise taxes, penalties, or appropriations.

Employer-offered group health plans are highly regulated, and these regulations are generally enforced through excise taxes. For example, taxes are imposed for failure to comply with continuation of benefits (i.e., COBRA) requirements (Code Sec. 4980B), group health plan portability requirements (Code Sec. 4980D), and comparable health savings account contribution requirements (Code Sec. 4980G). These excise taxes on health insurers and plans are compliance-driven rather than imposed with an eye toward raising revenue for a specific purpose.

NEW LAW EXPLAINED

Patient-Centered Outcomes Research Trust Fund established and funded in part by health plan fees.—The Secretary of Health and Human Services (HHS Secretary) must establish a Patient-Centered Outcomes Research Institute (Institute) to conduct, support, and synthesize research with respect to the outcomes, effectiveness, and appropriateness of health care services and procedures in order to identify the manner in which diseases, disorders, and other health conditions can most effectively and appropriately be prevented, diagnosed, treated, and managed clinically (Sec. 1181 of the Social Security Act, as added by the Patient Protection and Affordable Care Act (PPACA) (P.L. 111-148)). To fund the Institute, the Treasury Department is directed to establish the "Patient-Centered Outcomes Research Trust Fund" (PCORTF), with the

NEW LAW EXPLAINED

Secretary of the Treasury as trustee (Code Sec. 9511(a),as added by PPACA). The PCORTF is to be funded in part by fees imposed on health plans. The Institute is a tax-exempt organization (Code Sec. 501(l)(4), as added by PPACA).

Appropriations to PCORTF. The following amounts are appropriated to the PCORTF: $10,000,000 for fiscal year 2010; $50,000,000 for fiscal year 2011; and $150,000,000 for fiscal year 2012. For each fiscal year beginning with fiscal year 2013 and ending with 2019, the amount appropriated to the PCORTF is:

- an amount equal to the "net revenues" received in the Treasury from the fees imposed on health insurance and self-insured plans under new Code Secs. 4375, 4376 and 4377 (as added by PPACA) for such fiscal year, and
- $150 million (Code Sec. 9511(b), as added by PPACA).

  Comment: The Senate changed the name, but this provision is the comparative effectiveness research initiative put forth in the House version of the health bill. Although this appears to be the source for the "death panel" uproar, the Institute will basically just be conducting research to identify the most cost-effective treatments.

"Net revenues" for purposes of item (1), above, means the amount, as estimated by the Treasury Secretary, equaling the excess of the fees received in the Treasury on account of the new fees on insured and self-insured health plans, over the decrease in income tax revenue resulting from taxpayers deducting the fees as ordinary and necessary business expenses against income (Code Sec. 9511(e), as added by PPACA).

The fixed dollar amounts (e.g., $150 million in 2013) are to be funded out of general revenue, and additional amounts are to be transferred from the Federal Hospital Insurance Trust Fund, the Federal Supplementary Medical Insurance Trust Fund, and from the Medicare Prescription Drug Account. No amount may be appropriated or transferred to PCORTF on and after the date of any expenditure which is not expressly permitted (Code Sec. 9511(b), as added by PPACA).

Amounts in PCORTF are available to the Patient-Centered Outcomes Research Institute without the need for further appropriations (Code Sec. 9511(d)(1) as added by PPACA). The Secretary of the Treasury, as the PCORTF trustee, must transfer 20 percent of the amounts appropriated or credited to the PCORTF for each of fiscal years 2011 through 2019 to the HHS Secretary to carry out the purposes of the Institute, and these amounts shall remain available until spent. Of these amounts, the HHS Secretary shall distribute 80 percent to the Office of Communication and Knowledge Transfer of the Agency for Healthcare Research and Quality, and 20 percent to the HHS Secretary to disseminate information generated by the Institute (Code Sec. 9511(d)(2), as added by PPACA; Sec. 937 of the Public Health Services Act).

No amounts are to be transferred to the PCORTF after September 30, 2019, and any amounts in the fund after that date, are to be transferred to the general fund of the Treasury (Code Sec. 9511(f), as added by PPACA).

Imposition of fee on issuers of health insurance policies. The Patient Protection Act imposes on each "specified health insurance policy" for each policy year ending after

NEW LAW EXPLAINED

September 30, 2012, a fee equal to the product of $2 ($1 for policy years ending in fiscal 2013) multiplied by the average number of lives covered under the policy (Code Sec. 4375(a), as added by PPACA). For policy years ending in any fiscal year beginning after September 30, 2014, the $2 amount is adjusted for increases in projected per capita health care spending (Code Sec. 4375(d), as added by PPACA). The issuer of the policy pays the fee (Code Sec. 4375(b), as added by PPACA).

A "specified health insurance policy" is any accident or health insurance policy (including a policy under a group health plan) issued with respect to individuals residing in the United States (including possessions) (Code Secs. 4375(c)(1) and 4377(a)(3), as added by PPACA). Certain policies, however, are exempt if substantially all of their coverage is of excepted benefits described in Code Sec. 9832(c) (Code Sec. 4375(c)(2), as added by PPACA). Excepted benefits include coverage for only accident or disability; liability insurance (including general liability and auto liability insurance); workers' compensation or similar insurance; auto medical payment insurance; coverage for on-site medical clinics; limited scope dental or vision benefits; benefits for long-term care, nursing home care, community based care; coverage only for a specified disease or illness; hospital indemnity or other fixed indemnity insurance; and Medicare supplemental coverage. Pre-paid health coverage arrangements are treated as specified health insurance policies and the person agreeing to provide coverage is treated as the issuer (Code Sec. 4375(c)(3), as added by PPACA).

The fee on issuers of health insurance policies does not apply to policy years ending after September 30, 2019 (Code Sec. 4375(e), as added by PPACA).

Imposition of fee on sponsors of self-insured health plans. A fee is imposed on "applicable self-insured health plans" for each plan year ending after September 30, 2012. The fee equals the product of $2 ($1 for policy years ending in fiscal 2013) multiplied by the average number of lives covered under the policy (Code Sec. 4376(a), as added by PPACA). The $2 amount is adjusted in the future for increases in health care spending (Code Sec. 4376(d), as added by PPACA). The fee is imposed on the plan sponsor (Code Sec. 4376(b)(1), as added by PPACA). Further, the fee does not apply to plan years ending after September 30, 2019 (Code Sec. 4376(e), as added by PPACA).

A "plan sponsor" for these purposes is the employer in the case of a plan established or maintained by a single employer, and the employee organization in the case of a plan established or maintained by an employee organization. In the case of: (1) a plan established or maintained by two or more employers or jointly by one or more employers and one or more employee organizations, (2) a multiple employer welfare arrangement, or (3) a Code Sec. 501(c)(9) voluntary employees' beneficiary association (VEBA), the sponsor is the association, committee, joint board of trustees, or other similar group of representatives of the parties who establish or maintain the plan. In the case of a rural electric cooperative or a rural telephone cooperative, the plan sponsor is the cooperative or association (Code Sec. 4376(b)(2), as added by PPACA).

An "applicable self-insured health plan" is any plan for providing accident or health coverage if any portion of the plan's coverage is provided other than through an

NEW LAW EXPLAINED

insurance policy, and the plan is established or maintained by on or more of the following:

- by one or more employers for the benefit of their employees or former employees;
- by one or more employee organizations for the benefit of their members or former members;
- jointly by one or more employers and one or more employee organizations for the benefit of employees or former employees;
- by a Code Sec. 501(c)(9) voluntary employees' beneficiary association (VEBA);
- by any Code Sec. 501(c)(6) organization; or
- in the case of a plan not described in any of the other categories, by a multiple employer welfare arrangement (as defined in ERISA Sec. 3(40)), a rural electric cooperative (as defined in ERISA Sec. 3(40)(B)(iv)), or a rural telephone cooperative association (as defined in ERISA Sec. 3(40)(B)(v)) (Code Sec. 4376(c), as added by PPACA).

"Accident and health coverage" means any coverage which, if provided by an insurance policy, would cause the policy to be a Code Sec. 4375(c) specified health insurance policy (see above) (Code Sec. 4377(a)(1), as added by PPACA).

Fees on government plans. Governmental entities are not exempt from these fees except in the case of certain exempt governmental programs. Exempt governmental programs include Medicare, Medicaid, SCHIP, and any program established by federal law for proving medical care (other than through insurance policies) to members of the Armed Forces, veterans, or members of Indian tribes (Code Sec. 4377(b), as added by PPACA).

Procedure. For purposes of the procedure and administration rules, the fee on insured and self-insured plans is treated as a tax (Code Sec. 4377(c), as added by PPACA).

No need to pay collected fees over to U.S. possessions. No amount collected from the fee on health insurance and self-insurance plans needs to be "covered over" (i.e., paid by the Treasury) to any possession of the United States (Code Sec. 4377(d), as added by PPACA). Thus, these fees are not treated in a manner similar to fees on certain shipments to the United States from Puerto Rico or the Virgin Islands that are required to be covered over to the treasuries of these possessions (Code Sec. 7652).

Practical Analysis: Charles Goulding, President and founder of Energy Tax Savers, notes that, in its simplest terms, Comparative Effective Research is the process of how to make the best effective choices when trying to determine the best overall strategy for allocating limited resources. So in the health care arena, a classic example is: Should our country allocate more money on prevention or on cures? These are critical determinations with human impacts. For example, a medical device manufacturer might want to see more money spent on improved devices for knee alignments, and another medical device maker might want to see more money spent on improved diabetes insulin devices. At the prevention level, another group

NEW LAW EXPLAINED

might feel that more money should be spent on obesity issues, thereby reducing the need for both more knee and insulin devices.

This provision adds substantial amounts to funding that Congress has already provided in this area. As part of the economic stimulus legislation, $1.1 billion was provided over 10 years for health care research and quality, including $400 million for the U.S. National Institutes of Health to create a new agency for Health Care Research and Quality, a Federal coordinating council on comparative effectiveness research and the commissioning of an Institute of Medicine study on priorities for cost-benefit research.

Major funding commitments aimed at shaping policy in an area impacting one sixth of the U.S. economy are by definition going to have a substantial impact on business and tax policy. The industry winners of these policy choices are going to benefit from increased funding and will be the areas where new employment and R&D funding is going to occur and where new employment and R&D tax credits will be relevant. The industry losers initially will have to go their own way, regroup, adapt to the new environment and utilize the same kinds of tax incentives for the remaining opportunities they identify.

▶ **Effective date.** No effective date is provided by the Act. The provisions, therefore, are considered effective on March 23, 2010.

Law source: Law at ¶5155, ¶5200, ¶5205, ¶5210, ¶5290, and ¶7021. Committee Report at ¶10,150.

— Act Sec. 6301(a) of the Patient Protection and Affordable Care Act (PPACA) (P.L. 111-148), adding Sec. 1181 of the Social Security Act;

— Act Sec. 6301(e)(1), adding Code Sec. 9511;

— Act Sec. 6301(e)(2), adding Code Secs. 4375, 4376 and 4377;

— Act Sec. 6301(f), adding Code Sec. 501(l)(4).

Reporter references: For further information, consult the following CCH reporters.

— Standard Federal Tax Reporter, ¶34,612.01

— Tax Research Consultant, COMPEN: 45,200 and EXCISE: 100

— Practical Tax Explanation, §20,325

¶450 Tax Treatment of Community Living Assistance Services and Supports (CLASS) Program

SUMMARY OF NEW LAW

The newly established Community Living Assistance Services and Supports (CLASS) program will be treated for tax purposes in the same manner as a qualified long-term care insurance contract for qualified long-term care services. The CLASS program is a consumer-funded and voluntary long-term insurance program, under which premi-

SUMMARY OF NEW LAW

ums are paid through a payroll deduction and cash benefits are provided for the purchase of community living assistance services and supports by individuals with functional limitations.

BACKGROUND

Presently, there are 10 million Americans in need of long-term services and supports. As the baby boomers age into retirement, these numbers will more than double. Most private-sector disability or long-term care insurance provides limited benefits coverage.

Medicare, a government run insurance program, provides coverage for persons age 65 and older and some persons with disabilities, but does not cover long-term care or custodial care in a nursing home facility. Medicare may pay for home health care, including personal services provided by home health aides where a person is homebound needing part-time skilled nursing care or physical or other therapy services. Disabled persons under age 65 are only eligible to receive Medicare benefits after they have received Social Security disability benefits for at least two years.

Medicaid, a joint federal and state program administered by the individual states, is the "safety net" to meet the cost of long-term needs care once those needs become too substantial for informal care, and individuals have exhausted their own assets to pay for formal care. Medicaid was created with the purpose of assisting states in providing medical long-term care assistance to people who meet certain eligibility criteria. Each state sets its own guidelines regarding eligibility and services. Medicaid may pay for home health services including skilled nursing care, home health care, personal care, chore services, and medical equipment.

Because most group medical plans and individual policies do not provide for long-term health care coverage, an individual later in life may consider purchasing a long-term care insurance policy. There are many different types of policies offered. One such type is the qualified long-term care insurance contract for qualified long-term care services (Code Sec. 7702B).

Generally, a qualified long-term care insurance contract is treated as an accident and health insurance contract and, thus, amounts received under a long-term care insurance contract are excluded from gross income as amounts received for personal injuries or sickness. As adjusted for inflation, this exclusion is capped at $280 on per diem contracts in 2009 and at $290 in 2010 (Rev. Proc. 2008-66, 2008-45 I.R.B. 1107; Rev. Proc. 2009-50, 2009-45 I.R.B. 617). Payments exceeding the per diem limitation are generally included in income. Because of this tax treatment, employees generally will not realize income on premiums paid by their employers for such coverage, and premium payments made by an individual will be considered medical expenses. However, employer-provided, long-term care insurance premiums are not excludable from an employee's income if provided through a cafeteria or other flexible spending arrangement. The deduction of the applicable percentage of health insurance expenses of self-employed individuals under Code Sec. 162(l) applies to long-term care insurance premiums. In addition, long-term care expenses that are paid out-of-pocket

¶450

BACKGROUND

qualify for the itemized medical expense deduction under Code Sec. 213(a) (Code Sec. 7702B(a) and (d)).

A qualified long-term care insurance contract is any insurance contract that provides only coverage of qualified long-term care services and meets the following requirements:

- the contract is guaranteed renewable;
- the contract does not provide for a cash surrender value or other money that can be paid, assigned, pledged, or borrowed;
- refunds, other than refunds paid upon the death of the insured or complete surrender or cancellation of the contract, and dividends may only be used to reduce future premiums or to increase future benefits;
- the contract does not pay or reimburse expenses that are reimbursable under Medicare, except when Medicare is a secondary payor or when the contract makes payments per diem or on another periodic basis without regard to actual expense; and
- the required consumer protection provisions are included in the contract (Code Sec. 7702B(b)).

Qualified long-term care services include necessary diagnostic, preventive, therapeutic, curing, treating, mitigating, and rehabilitative services, and maintenance or personal care services that are required by a chronically ill individual and provided pursuant to a plan of care prescribed by a licensed health care practitioner (Code Sec. 7702B(c)(1)).

A chronically ill individual is any person certified within the preceding 12-month period by a licensed health care practitioner as: (1) being unable to perform at least two activities of daily living for a period of at least 90 days due to a loss of functional capacity; (2) having a level of disability, as designated by regulations to be promulgated, similar to that described in (1); or (3) requiring substantial supervision to protect the person from threats to health and safety because of severe cognitive impairment. Activities of daily living are eating, toileting, transferring, bathing, dressing, and continence. A contract will not be treated as a long-term insurance contract unless at least five of these activities are taken into account in determining whether an individual is chronically ill (Code Sec. 7702B(c)(2)).

Maintenance or personal care services include any care that has the primary purpose of providing needed assistance for any of the disabilities that result in the individual being considered chronically ill. This also includes protection from threats to health and safety due to severe cognitive impairment (Code Sec. 7702B(c)(3)).

For tax years beginning after 2009, if long-term health care coverage (whether or not qualified) is provided by a rider on or as part of a life-insurance or annuity contract, the portion of the contract that provides the coverage is treated as a separate long-term health insurance contract for all purposes of the Code. The portion that provides long-term health care coverage refers to only the terms and benefits under a life insurance contract or annuity contract that are in addition to the terms and benefits under the contract without regard to long-term care coverage. In addition, no

¶450

BACKGROUND

itemized medical expense deduction may be claimed for any payment made for coverage under a qualified long-term care insurance contract if the payment is made as a charge against the cash surrender value of a life insurance contract or the cash value of an annuity contract. Certain annuity contracts are excluded from the application of this rule (Code Sec. 7702B(e)).

A state long-term care plan arrangement is treated as a qualified long-term care insurance contract if the terms of the arrangement would otherwise satisfy the qualification requirements for a long-term care insurance contract. A state long-term care plan is any plan:

- established by a state or instrumentality of a state;

- that provides coverage only for long-term care services; and

- under which coverage is only extended to employees and former employees of a state (including political subdivisions and state instrumentalities), their spouses and relatives of the employees or their spouses (as defined in Code Sec. 152(d)(2)(A) through (G)) (Code Sec. 7702B(f)).

NEW LAW EXPLAINED

CLASS program treated as a qualified long-term care insurance contract for tax purposes.—The Community Living Assistance Services and Supports (CLASS) program has been added as Title XXXII of the Public Health Service Act (PHSA) (42 U.S.C. 201), and will be treated for federal tax purposes in the same manner as a qualified long-term care insurance contract for qualified long-term care services (PHSA Sec. 3210, as added by the Patient Protection and Affordable Care Act (PPACA) (P.L. 111-148)).

> **Comment:** Thus, payments received under the CLASS program may be excluded from income and premium payments may be considered deductible medical expenses.

Overview of the CLASS program. The CLASS program was established by Title VIII of the Patient Protection Act (which is referred to as the "CLASS Act") to create a national voluntary insurance program for purchasing community living assistance services and supports that will provide individuals having functional limitations with tools they need to maintain their independence, and will alleviate burdens on family caregivers. The CLASS program also provides a financing mechanism that supports personal choice and independence to live in the community, and establishes an infrastructure that will help address the nation's community living assistance services and supports needs (PHSA Sec. 3201, as added by PPACA).

CLASS Independence Benefit Plan. Under the CLASS Act, the Secretary of Health and Human Services (HHS), in consultation with appropriate actuaries and other experts, is charged with developing at least three actuarially sound benefit plans as alternatives for consideration for designation as the CLASS Independence Benefit Plan. The HHS Secretary must designate a benefit plan as the CLASS Independence Benefit Plan by October 1, 2012 (PHSA Sec. 3203(a)(3), as added by PPACA). Each of the alternative plans developed must be designed to provide eligible beneficiaries

NEW LAW EXPLAINED

with the required benefits (see "*CLASS program benefits*," below) consistent with the following requirements (PHSA Sec. 3203(a)(1), as added by PPACA):

- *Premiums.* The HHS Secretary will establish yearly premiums based on an actuarial analysis of the 75-year costs of the program that ensures solvency throughout such 75-year period.
- *Vesting.* There is a five-year vesting period for benefit eligibility.
- *Benefit triggers.* To obtain benefits, it must be determined that an individual has a functional limitation, as certified by a licensed health care practitioner, that is expected to last for a continuous period of more than 90 days. This generally means that the individual must:

  — be unable to perform at least the minimum number of activities of daily living as are required under the plan for the provision of benefits without substantial assistance from another individual;

  — require substantial supervision to protect the individual from threats to health and safety due to substantial cognitive impairment; or

  — have a level of functional limitation similar to the levels described in (A) or (B) above.

- *Cash benefit.* The amount of the benefit received cannot be less than an average of $50 per day, and can vary based on a scale of functional ability, with no less than two and no more than six benefit level amounts. The benefit is paid on a daily or weekly basis and there is no lifetime or aggregate limit.

Generally, the amount of the monthly premium determined for an individual upon enrollment in the CLASS program will remain the same for as long as the individual is an active enrollee. However, the premium may be adjusted if required for the CLASS program's solvency. Any resulting increase in such cases will not apply to the monthly premium of any active enrollee who is not actively employed, has attained age 65 and has paid premiums for at least 20 years. In addition, the premium may be recalculated in the case of a reenrollment of an individual after a 90-day period during which the individual failed to pay the monthly premium, and may be increased by a penalty amount in the case of a reenrollment after a five-year lapse. In determining the monthly premiums, administrative costs may be taken into account, but are limited to an amount not to exceed three percent of all premiums paid during the year (PHSA Sec. 3203(b) of PPACA). The HHS Secretary is authorized to establish procedures for self-attestation and income verification (PHSA Sec. 3203(c) of PPACA).

Enrollment and disenrollment requirements. The HHS Secretary, in coordination with the Secretary of the Treasury, will establish procedures for automatic enrollment of individuals in the CLASS program by an employer under rules similar to the rules for automatic enrollment of employees under plans described in Code Secs. 401(k), 403(b) or 457. These procedures will also provide an alternative enrollment process for an individual who is self-employed, has more than one employer or whose employer does not elect to participate in the automatic enrollment process (PHSA Sec. 3204(a), as added by PPACA).

¶450

NEW LAW EXPLAINED

An individual may enroll in the CLASS program if he or she—

- has attained age 18;
- receives wages or income on which tax is imposed under Code Sec. 3101(a) or 3201(a), or is self employed and his or her income is subject to tax under Code Sec. 1401(a);
- is actively employed;
- is not a patient in a hospital or nursing facility, an intermediate care facility for the mentally retarded, or an institution for mental diseases and receiving medical assistance under Medicaid; and
- is not confined in a jail, prison, other penal institution or correctional facility, or by court order pursuant to conviction of a criminal offense or in connection with a verdict or finding based on factors such as mental disease, a mental defect, or mental incompetence (PHSA Sec. 3204(c), as added by PPACA).

An individual may elect to waive enrollment in the CLASS program at any time (PHSA Sec. 3204(b), as added by PPACA).

The monthly premium for the enrollment in the CLASS program will be generally deducted from the individual's wages or self-employment income by employers who elect to deduct and withhold such premiums on behalf of the enrolled employees. An alternative procedure for payment will also be established for individuals who do not have an employer electing to deduct and withhold premiums, or who do not earn wages or derive self-employment income (PHSA Sec. 3204(e), as added by PPACA). Each calendar year the Treasury Secretary will deposit into the CLASS Independence Fund an amount equal to the premiums collected during the year, and the deposited amount will be transferred in at least monthly payments to the CLASS Independence Fund based on estimates by the HHS Secretary, subject to subsequent necessary adjustments (PHSA Sec. 3204(f), as added by PPACA).

An individual who, in the year of the initial eligibility, has not enrolled in the program, may be eligible to elect to enroll in the program during an open enrollment period under procedures established by the HHS Secretary, in coordination with the Treasury Secretary. The open enrollment period will be specific to that individual and may not occur more frequently than biennially after the date on which the individual first elected to waive enrollment in the CLASS program. An individual will only be permitted to disenroll from the program during an annual disenrollment period (PHSA Sec. 3204(g), as added by PPACA).

CLASS program benefits. Active enrollees may apply for receipt of benefits under the CLASS Independence Benefit Plan according to procedures established by the HHS Secretary. By January 1, 2012, the HHS Secretary is required, among other things, to establish an Eligibility Assessment System, which will provide eligibility assessments of active enrollees who apply for receipt of benefits. The HHS Secretary is also authorized to issue regulations to develop an expedited nationally equitable eligibility determination process, an appeals process, and a redetermination process, which will determine, among other things, whether an active enrollee is eligible for a cash benefit under the program, and, if so, the amount of the cash benefit. In addition, the HHS Secretary will provide procedures under which a benefits appli-

NEW LAW EXPLAINED

cant is guaranteed the right to appeal an adverse determination (PHSA Sec. 3205(a), as added by PPACA).

An eligible beneficiary will receive the following benefits under the plan:

• cash benefits;

• advocacy services; and

• advice and assistance counseling.

The cash benefit will be not less than an average of $50 per day for the first year in which beneficiaries receive benefits under the plan. For any subsequent year, the cash benefit will be not less than the average per day dollar limit applicable for the preceding year, increased by the percentage increase in the consumer price index for all urban consumers (United States city average) over the previous year (PHSA Sec. 3205(b), as added by PPACA).

The HHS Secretary must establish procedures for administering the payment of benefits to eligible beneficiaries under the plan, including the payment of the cash benefit into a Life Independence Account set up on behalf of each eligible beneficiary. Special payment rules are provided for beneficiaries enrolled in Medicaid, who will be generally allowed to retain a certain percentage of the cash benefit, with the remainder applied to the cost of the beneficiary's care or assistance. Generally, benefits will be paid to, or on behalf of, an eligible beneficiary beginning with the first month in which an application for such benefits is approved. Eligible beneficiaries may elect to defer benefits and receive a lump-sum payment of the deferred benefits. The applicable period for determining an eligible beneficiary's applicable annual benefit and amount of any accrued benefit is the 12-month period that starts with the first month in which the beneficiary began to receive the benefits and each 12-month period thereafter. An eligible beneficiary must periodically recertify his or her continued eligibility for receiving benefits by submitting medical evidence and records of expenditures attributable to the aggregate cash benefit received during the preceding year (PHSA Sec. 3205(c), as added by PPACA).

Benefits paid under the CLASS program will be disregarded when determining or continuing the beneficiary's eligibility for receiving benefits under any other federal, state, or locally funded assistance program (PHSA Sec. 3205(f), as added by PPACA). In addition, such benefits may be used to compensate a family caregiver for providing community living assistance services and supports to an eligible beneficiary (PHSA Sec. 3205(g), as added by PPACA).

CLASS Independence Fund. A CLASS Independence Fund is established in the U.S. Treasury, and the Treasury Secretary will serve as the Managing Trustee of the Fund. The Fund will consist of premiums paid by CLASS program enrollees, and accrued benefits recouped in the event of a beneficiary's death or the beneficiary's failure to receive the benefits before the end of the 12-month period in which the benefits accrued. The Fund will also include amounts remaining after the investment of the payments plus any income derived from the investments. The amounts in the Fund will remain available without fiscal year limitation to be invested on behalf of the CLASS program enrollees, to pay the administrative expenses related to the Fund,

NEW LAW EXPLAINED

and to pay cash benefits to eligible beneficiaries under the CLASS Independence Benefit Plan (PHSA Sec. 3206(a), as added by PPACA).

The CLASS Independence Fund will have a Board of Trustees composed of the Secretary of the Treasury, the Secretary of Labor, and the HHS Secretary, and two members of the public who will be nominated by the President for a four-year term and will be subject to confirmation by the Senate. The Board of Trustees will be responsible for: (1) holding the CLASS Independence Fund; (2) reporting to Congress not later than April 1st of each year on the operation and status of the Fund during the preceding fiscal year and on its expected operation and status during the current fiscal year and the next two fiscal year; (3) reporting to Congress immediately whenever the Board believes that the amount of the Fund is not actuarially sound in regards to premium and income projections; (4) reviewing the general policies followed in managing the Fund and recommending changes in the policies, including necessary changes in the provisions of law that govern how the Fund is to be managed (PHSA Sec. 3206(c), as added by PPACA).

CLASS Independence Advisory Council. The CLASS Act also establishes the CLASS Independence Advisory Council, which will consist of not more than 15 individuals who are not otherwise employed by the federal government and who are appointed by the President. The Council members will generally serve overlapping three-year terms, and cannot serve for more than two consecutive terms. The majority of the appointees must represent individuals who participate or are likely to participate in the CLASS program, and must include representatives of various categories. The Council will advise the HHS Secretary on general policy in the administration of the CLASS program and in the formation of regulations, which will include the development of the CLASS Independent Benefit Plan, the determination of monthly premiums and the financial solvency of the program (PHSA Sec. 3207, as added by PPACA).

Annual reports on CLASS program. Beginning January 1, 2014, the HHS Secretary must submit an annual report to Congress on the CLASS program, that must generally provide information on the total number of enrollees and eligible beneficiaries, the total amount of cash benefits paid during the fiscal year, any identified instances of fraud or abuse, and recommendations necessary to improve the program (PHSA Sec. 3208(d), as added by PPACA).

In addition, the HHS Inspector General must submit an annual report to the HHS Secretary and Congress discussing the overall progress of the CLASS program and the existence of waste, fraud, and abuse in the program (PHSA Sec. 3209, as added by PPACA).

Definitions. For purposes of the CLASS program rules, an "active enrollee" means an individual who is enrolled in the CLASS program and who has paid any premiums due to maintain such enrollment. An "eligible beneficiary" is any individual who is an active enrollee in the CLASS program and who, as of the date on which the individual is determined to have a functional limitation that is expected to last for a continuous period of more than 90 days:

NEW LAW EXPLAINED

- has paid premiums for enrollment for at least 60 months;
- has earned, regarding at least three calendar years that occur during the first 60 months for which the individual has paid premiums for enrollment, at least an amount equal to the amount of wages and self-employment income that an individual must have in order to be credited with a quarter of coverage under Section 213(d) of the Social Security Act for that year; and
- has paid premiums for enrollment for at least 24 consecutive months, if a lapse in premium payments of more than three months has occurred during the period that begins on the date of the individual's enrollment and ends on the date of such determination.

Definitions of other terms used in the CLASS program rules are also provided, including "actively employed," "activities of daily living," "poverty line" and others (PHSA Sec. 3202, as added by PPACA).

▶ **Effective date.** The amendments made by Act Sec. 8002(a), (b) and (d) take effect on January 1, 2011 (Act Sec. 8002(e) of the Patient Protection and Affordable Care Act (PPACA) (P.L. 111-148)).

Law source: Law at ¶7024.

— Act Sec. 8002(a) of the Patient Protection and Affordable Care Act (PPACA) (P.L. 111-148), adding Sections 3201 through 3210 of the Public Health Service Act (PHSA) (42 U.S.C. 201);

— Act Sec. 10801(a), amending PHSA Secs. 3203 and 3204;

— Act Sec. 8002(e), providing the effective date.

Reporter references: For further information, consult the following CCH reporters.

— Standard Federal Tax Reporter, ¶43,168.01

— Tax Research Consultant, COMPEN: 45,066

— Practical Tax Explanation, §7,240.15, §7,252

¶455 Market Reforms and Improved Coverage

SUMMARY OF NEW LAW

Group health plans and health insurance issuers offering group or individual health insurance coverage are subject to new requirements, including (among other things) extension of dependent coverage, mandatory coverage of preventive health services, prohibition of lifetime or annual limits on the dollar value of benefits, unreasonable annual limits, and rescission. These new requirements have been incorporated into Chapter 100 of the Internal Revenue Code

BACKGROUND

Group health care plans and issuers of insurance under such plans are subject to certain portability and coverage requirements that appear in Title XXVII, Part A, Group Market Reforms, of the Public Health Service Act (PHSA). Similar or identical

BACKGROUND

provisions are found in Title 29 of the United States Code (Labor), and the Internal Revenue Code (IRC). These provisions were originally added by the Health Insurance and Portability and Accountability Act of 1996 (HIPAA) (P.L. 104-191). In the PHSA, Part A includes four subparts:

- Subpart 1, Portability, Access, and Renewability Requirements: PHSA Sec. 2701, 42 U.S.C. § 300gg (portability requirements); PHSA Sec. 2702, 42 U.S.C. § 300gg-1 (prohibition of discrimination for health status);

- Subpart 2, Other Requirements: PHSA Sec. 2704, 42 U.S.C. § 300gg-4 (mothers and newborns); PHSA Sec. 2705, 42 U.S.C. § 300gg-5 (mental health benefit parity); PHSA Sec. 2706, 42 U.S.C. § 300gg-6 (reconstructive surgery following mastectomies); PHSA Sec. 2707, 42 U.S.C. § 300gg-7 (coverage of students on medically necessary leave of absence);

- Subpart 3, Provisions Applicable only to Health Insurance Issuers: PHSA Sec. 2711, 42 U.S.C. § 300gg-11 (guaranteed availability of coverage for employers in the group market), PHSA Sec. 2712, 42 U.S.C. § 300gg-12 (guaranteed renewability of coverage for employers in the group market), PHSA Sec. 2713, 42 U.S.C. § 300gg-13 (disclosure of information); and

- Subpart 4, Exclusion of Plans; Enforcement; Preemption: PHSA Sec. 2721, 42 U.S.C. § 300gg-21 (exclusion of certain plans), PHSA Sec. 2722, 42 U.S.C. § 300gg-22 (enforcement), and PHSA Sec. 2723, 42 U.S.C. § 300gg-23 (preemption).

Some of these provisions appear in virtually identical form in Chapter 100, Group Health Plan Requirements, of the IRC (as well as in Title 29 of the United States Code (Labor)). The major difference is that the IRC provisions apply only to group plans while the PHSA provisions apply to both group plans and insurance issuers that provide coverage through such plans. IRC Chapter 100 has three subchapters:

- Subchapter A, Requirements Relating to Portability, Access, and Renewability, which includes Code Secs. 9801 (portability), 9802 (nondiscrimination), and 9803 (guaranteed renewability in multemployer plans);

- Subchapter B, Other Requirements, which includes Code Secs. 9811 (mothers and newborns), 9812 (mental health parity), 9813 (dependent students on leave);

- Subchapter C, General Provisions, Codes Secs. 9831 (exceptions), 9832 (definitions), 9833 (regulations), 9834 (enforcement).

The IRS has enforcement authority over employers and plans for compliance with the provisions of Chapter 100. Failure of a group health plan to comply with these requirements can result in imposition of an excise tax of $100 for each day in the noncompliance period for each individual for whom such failure relates. The tax is generally imposed on the employer, but under certain circumstances it is imposed on the plan. There are exceptions for small employer plans; for noncompliance that was undiscovered despite the exercise of reasonable diligence, and for noncompliance that is corrected within 30 days of becoming known (Code Secs. 9834, 4980D).

The PHSA delegates enforcement authority over health insurance issuers is delegated under the PHSA to the states. If a state does not exercise this authority, the Secretary of Health and Human Services is authorized to impose penalties against issuers. The

BACKGROUND

maximum penalty is $100 for each day for each individual with respect to which the noncompliance occurred. Exceptions are made if the noncompliance was not discovered despite the exercise of reasonable diligence, or if it is corrected within 30 days of becoming known (PHSA Sec. 2722, 42 U.S.C. § 300gg-22).

A self-insured medical reimbursement plan cannot discriminate in favor of highly compensated individuals as to eligibility or benefits (Code Sec. 105(h)(2)). Highly compensated individuals for this purpose are: the five highest paid officers of the employer; shareholders who own more than 10 percent (by value) of the employer's stock; and individuals who are among the highest paid 25 percent of all employees, other than those who can be excluded from the plan (Code Sec. 105(h)(5)). A plan is treated as nondiscriminatory as to eligibility if:

- the plan benefits 70 percent or more of all employees, or 80 percent or more of all eligible employees if 70 percent or more of all employees are eligible to benefit, or

- the employees qualify under a classification set up by the employer and found by the IRS not to be discriminatory in favor of highly compensated individuals (Code Sec. 105(h)(3), Reg. § 1.105-11).

All benefits provided to highly compensated individuals must be offered to all other participants (Code Sec. 105(h)(4)). Employers that are members of a controlled group, are under common control, or are part of an affiliated group are treated as a single employer for these purposes (Code Sec. 104(h)(8)).

NEW LAW EXPLAINED

Market reforms of PHSA incorporated into IRC.—The provisions of Part A, Title XXVII, of the Public Health Service Act (PHSA), as amended by the Patient Protection and Affordable Care Act (PPACA) (P.L. 111-148), apply to group health plans, and health insurance issuers providing health insurance coverage in connection with group health plans, as if those provisions were included in subchapter B of Chapter 100 of the Internal Revenue Code (IRC). The PHSA provisions trump other IRC provisions to the extent there is a conflict (Code Sec. 9815(a), as added by PPACA).

> **Comment:** On its face, Code Sec. 9815, by importing Part A into Chapter 100 of the IRC, imports all the new market requirements for group health plans and issuers of group plan insurance, as well as for issuers of individual insurance. Still, there is no change in the enforcement provisions, and the name of IRC chapter 100 is still entitled "Group Health Plan Requirements," so it does not appear that the IRS will have any enforcement authority over insurance issuers or over the individual insurance market.

Health care coverage improvements. Amendments to PHSA Title XXVII, Part A, subpart 1, subject group health plans and health insurance issuers offering group or individual coverage to several new requirements intended to improve health care coverage. The new requirements are effective for plan years beginning on or after September 23, 2010, the date that is six months after the date of enactment of the Patient Protection Act (Act Sec. 1004 of PPACA):

NEW LAW EXPLAINED

- *No lifetime or annual limits.* Lifetime or annual limits on the dollar value of benefits for any participant or beneficiary are prohibited. A transition rule applies for plan years beginning prior to January 1, 2014, during which a restricted annual limit is permitted on the dollar value of benefits regarding the scope of essential health benefits under Act Sec. 1302(b) of the Patient Protection Act. Per beneficiary lifetime or annual limits are not prohibited on benefits that are not essential health benefits to the extent that such limits are otherwise permitted under federal or state law (PHSA Sec. 2711 as added by PPACA)).

  Comment: "Essential health benefits" include ambulatory patient services; emergency services; hospitalization; maternity and newborn care; mental health and substance use disorder services; prescription drugs; rehabilitative and habilitative services and devices; laboratory services; preventive and wellness services and chronic disease management; and pediatric services (Act Sec. 1302(b) of PPACA).

- *No rescission.* Rescission with respect to an enrollee once the enrollee is covered is prohibited, unless the individual has committed fraud or made an intentional misrepresentation of material facts prohibited by the plan or coverage terms. The enrollee must be given prior notice of cancellation (PHSA Sec. 2712 as added by PPACA).

- *Preventive health services.* Plans and issuers must provide coverage (without any cost sharing) for certain preventive health services including, at minimum, (1) evidence-based items or services that have in effect a rating of A or B in the current recommendations of the United States Preventive Services Task Force (USPSTF); (2) immunizations recommended by the Advisory Committee on Immunization Practices of the Centers for Disease Control and Prevention; (3) for infants, children, and adolescents, evidence-informed preventive care and screenings provided for in the comprehensive guidelines supported by the Health Resources and Services Administration (HRSA); and (4) with respect to women, any additional preventive care and screenings as provided for in comprehensive guidelines supported by the HRSA. The current recommendations of the USPSTF regarding breast cancer screening, mammography, and prevention are considered the most current other than those issued in or around November, 2009. Intervals are to be set by the Secretary of Health and Human Services (HHS). The Secretary may develop guidelines to permit group health plans and health insurance issuers to offer coverage using value-based insurance designs (PHSA Sec. 2713, as added by PPACA).

- *Extension of dependent coverage.* Dependent coverage must be extended by group health plans and health insurance issuers offering group or individual health insurance coverage that provide dependent coverage of children. The plan or issuer must continue to make such coverage available for an adult child until the child turns 26 years of age. This rule does not extend to a child of a child receiving dependent coverage (PHSA Sec. 2714, as added by PPACA, and amended by the Health Care and Education Reconciliation Act of 2010 (P.L. 111-152)).

- *Development and use of uniform explanation of coverage documents.* Within 24 months of March 23, 2010, the date of enactment of the Patient Protection Act, health

NEW LAW EXPLAINED

insurance issuers (including a group health plan that is not a self-insured plan) offering health insurance coverage within the United States (or in the case of a self-insured group health plan the plan sponsor or designated administrator) must provide, prior to any enrollment restriction, a summary of benefits and coverage explanation pursuant to the standards developed by the HHS Secretary to (1) an applicant at the time of application; (2) an enrollee prior to the time of enrollment or reenrollment; and (3) a policyholder or certificate holder at the time of issuance of the policy or delivery of the certificate. An entity that willfully fails to provide the required information will be subject to a fine of up to $1,000 per failure (PHSA Sec. 2715, as added by PPACA).

- *Transparency in coverage.* Group plans and health insurance issuers must submit to the American Health Benefit Exchange accurate information required for certification as a qualified health plan under Act Sec. 1311(e)(3). Plans and issuers must also submit this information to the HHS Secretary and the state insurance commissioner, and must make it available to the public. Required information includes: (1) claims payment policies and practices; (2) periodic financial disclosures; (3) data on enrollment and disenrollment; (4) data on the number of claims denied; (5) data on rating practices; (6) information on cost-sharing and payments for out-of-network coverage; (7) information on enrollee and participant rights; and (8) other information deemed appropriate by the HHS Secretary. A plan or coverage that is not offered through an Exchange is not required to submit the information to an Exchange (PHSA Sec. 2715A, as added by PPACA).

- *Discrimination in favor of highly compensated individuals prohibited.* A group health plan (other than a self-insured plan) must satisfy the requirements of Code Sec. 105(h)(2), which prohibit discrimination in favor of highly compensated individuals regarding eligibility to participate and benefits. These rules already apply to self-insured medical reimbursement plans under Code Sec. 105(h)(2). In addition, rules similar to those in Code Sec. 105(h)(3) (nondiscriminatory eligibility classifications), Code Sec. 105(h)(4) (nondiscriminatory benefits), and Code Sec. 105(h)(8) (aggregation) will apply. The definition of highly paid individual is taken from Code Sec. 105(h)(5). This provision specifically does not apply to self-insured group health plans (PHSA Sec. 2716 and Code Sec. 9815(b), as added by PPACA);

- *Ensuring quality care.* Annual reporting requirements to the HHS Secretary and enrollees are to be developed by the HHS Secretary over the 24 months after March 23, 2010, and imposed on group health plan and a health insurance issuers with respect to benefits and reimbursement structures. The reporting will focus on efforts to improve health outcomes, implement activities to prevent hospital readmissions, implement activities to improve patient safety and reduce medical errors, and implement wellness and prevention programs. Second Amendment gun rights are protected, with limitations on collecting, storing and disclosing information, increasing premiums, denying health insurance coverage, and reducing or withholding discounts, rebates or rewards, based on lawful ownership, use, possession or storage of firearms or ammunition (PHSA Sec. 2717, as added by PPACA);

¶455

NEW LAW EXPLAINED

- *Making sure enrollees get value.* Except for self-insured plans, issuers and group plans must provide annual reports concerning the proportion of premiums spent on (1) reimbursement for clinical services, (2) activities that improve health care quality, and (3) all other non-claims costs, including an explanation of the nature of such costs. The report must identify the ratio of the incurred loss (or incurred claims) plus the loss adjustment expense (or change in contract reserves) to earned premiums. Starting no later than January 1, 2011, issuers and plans must provide annual rebates of excess costs to their enrollees. These provisions specifically do not apply to self-insured group health plans (PHSA Sec. 2718, Code Sec. 9815(b), as added by PPACA);

- *Appeals process.* Issuers and group health plans must have an effective appeals process for coverage determinations and claims. At a minimum, the plan or issuer must (1) have in effect an internal claims appeal process; (2) provide notice to enrollees of available internal and external appeals processes, and the availability of any applicable office of health insurance consumer assistance or ombudsman to assist enrollees with the appeals processes; and (3) allow enrollees to review their files, present evidence and testimony as part of the appeals process, and receive continued coverage pending the outcome of the appeals. Plans and issuers must also provide an external review process that includes consumer protections. The appeals process will be subject to external review by state commissioners (PHSA Sec. 2719, as added by PPACA).

- *Patient protections.* Issuers and group health plans are subject to requirements for providing patients with a choice of doctors within the plan, coverage of emergency services (no prior approval, and the same requirements applying to both participating and nonparticipating health care providers), access to pediatric care, and to obstetrical or gynecological care (PHSA Sec. 2719A, as added by PPACA).

  Comment: PHSA Secs. 2711, 2712, 2714, 2715 and 2718 also affect grandfathered plans in the individual and group health markets. See ¶535 for further discussion.

Health insurance market reforms. Amendments to PHSA Title XXVII, Part A, subpart 2, impose new requirements on group health plans and/or health insurance issuers offering group or individual coverage intended to improve health insurance coverage. The new requirements are effective for plan years beginning on or after January 1, 2014 (Act Sec. 1255 of PPACA):

- *Fair premiums.* Limits on the range of health insurance premiums an issuer can charge, with adjustments available only for age, area, tobacco use and family or individual coverage (PHSA Sec. 2701, as added by PPACA);

- *Guaranteed availability of coverage.* An issuer that offers coverage in the individual or group market in a state must accept every employer and individual in that state that applies for such coverage. The issuer can establish special enrollment periods, however (PHSA Sec. 2702, as added by PPACA);

- *Guaranteed renewability of coverage.* If a health insurance issuer offers health insurance coverage in the individual or group market, the issuer must renew or

NEW LAW EXPLAINED

continue in force such coverage at the option of the plan sponsor or the individual, as applicable (PHSA Sec. 2703, as added by PPACA);

- *Portability requirements.* The PHSA has long had portability requirements for group plans and their insurers. The PHSA is amended so that the requirements apply to individual health insurance rather than just to group plans and insurance provided for group plans (PHSA Sec. 2704, as renumbered and amended by PPACA). The IRC has a nearly identical provision, Code Sec. 9801, which applies only to group health plans. As of January 1, 2014, PHSA Sec. 2704 will extend these rules under the IRC to insurers in the individual and group markets.

- *Nondiscrimination for health status.* The PHSA already has health status nondiscrimination requirements for group plans and their insurers. The PHSA provision is amended to extend these requirements to the individual health insurance market (PHSA Sec. 2705, as renumbered and amended by PPACA). Code Sec. 9802 is similar, but applies only to group health plans. As of January 1, 2014, PHSA Sec. 2705 will extend these rules under the IRC to insurers in the individual and group markets.

- *Nondiscrimination for health care providers.* Discrimination is prohibited against any health care provider who is acting within the scope of that provider's license or certification under applicable state law (PHSA Sec. 2706, as added by PPACA).

- *Comprehensive coverage.* Plans and their insurers must meet certain requirements with respect to coverage of essential health benefits, limits on cost-sharing, and provision of child-only plans (PHSA Sec. 2707, as added by PPACA).

- *Excessive waiting.* Plans and insurers cannot impose waiting periods that exceed 90 days (PHSA Sec. 2708, as added by PPACA).

- *Coverage for individuals participating in clinical trials.* An issuer or group plan cannot: (1) deny an individual participation in a clinical trial; (2) deny (or limit or impose additional conditions on) coverage of routine patient costs for items and services furnished in connection with participation in the trial; or (3) discriminate against the individual on the basis of the individual's participation in such trial (PHSA Sec. 2709, as added by PPACA).

The remainder of Part A includes a range of existing sections, some of which are already mirrored in the IRC (though only applicable to group health plans). These are renumbered by the Patient Protection Act, and are now apparently treated as applying as if they were in the IRC. These include the following:

- Requirements for mothers and newborns (PHSA Sec. 2725, as renumbered by PPACA). This is already mirrored in Code Sec. 9811.

- Parity in mental health and substance abuse disorder benefits (PHSA Sec. 2726, as renumbered by PPACA). This almost identical to Code Sec. 9812, which applies only to group health plans.

- Reconstructive surgery following mastectomies, PHSA Sec. 2727, as renumbered by PPACA).

¶455

NEW LAW EXPLAINED

- Coverage of students on medically necessary leave of absence (PHSA Sec. 2728, as renumbered by PPACA). This is almost identical to Code Sec. 9813, which applies only to group health plans.

- Guaranteed availability of coverage for employers in the group market (PHSA Sec. 2731, as renumbered by PPACA).

- Guaranteed renewability of coverage for employers in the group market (PHSA Sec. 2732, as renumbered by PPACA).

- Disclosure of information (PHSA Sec. 2733, as renumbered by PPACA).

- Exclusion of certain plans (PHSA Sec. 2735, as renumbered by PPACA). There is some overlap with Code Sec. 9831.

- Enforcement (PHSA Sec. 2736, as renumbered by PPACA).

- Preemption (PHSA Sec. 2737, as renumbered by PPACA).

  Comment: PHSA Secs. 2704 and 2708 also affect grandfathered plans in the individual and group health markets. See ¶535 for further discussion.

▶ **Effective date.** No effective date is provided for Code Sec. 9815, the provision is therefore considered effective on March 23, 2010, the date of enactment of Patient Protection and Affordable Care Act (PPACA) (P.L. 111-148). The amendments to Act Secs. 2711-2719A of the Public Health Service Act (PHSA) are effective for plan years beginning on or after September 23, 2010, six months after the date of enactment of the Patient Protection Act. The amendments to PHSA Secs 2701-2709 are effective for plan years beginning on or after January 1, 2014.

Law source: Law at ¶5295. Committee Report at ¶10,130.

— Act Sec. 1562(f) of the Patient Protection and Affordable Care Act (PPACA) (P.L. 111-148), as redesignated by Act Sec. 10107, adding Code Sec. 9815;

— Act Sec. 1001, adding and amending Public Health Service Act (PHSA) Secs. 2711-2719A;

— Act Sec. 1201, adding and amending PHSA Secs. 2701-2708;

— Act Sec. 10101, amending PHSA Secs. 2711, 2715, 2716, 2718, 2719, and adding 2715A and 2719A;

— Act Sec. 10103, amending PHSA Secs. 2701, 2708, and adding 2709;

— Act Secs. 1004 and 1255, as redesignated by Act Sec. 10103, providing the effective dates; and

— Act Secs. 1004(d)(3)(B) and 2301(b) of the Health Care and Education Reconciliation Act of 2010 (P.L. 111-152), amending PHSA Sec. 2714.

Reporter references: For further information, consult the following CCH reporters.

— Standard Federal Tax Reporter, ¶34,612.01, ¶44,053.01, ¶44,058.01, ¶44,063.01, ¶44,086.01, ¶44,088.01¶44,089G.01, ¶44,091.01, ¶44,093.01, ¶44,095.01 and ¶44,099.01

— Tax Research Consultant, COMPEN: 45,100 and COMPEN: 45,200

— Practical Tax Explanation, §20,325 and §20,330.10

Health Care: Nontax Provisions

5

>>>→ *Caution: The explanation below reflects certain nontax provisions of the Patient Protection and Affordable Care Act (P.L. 111-148) and the Health Care and Education Reconciliation Act of 2010 (P.L. 111-152). While the issues discussed do not have a direct effect on federal taxes, this explanation is helpful in understanding several tax-related explanations that appear in preceding chapters of this publication.*

¶505 Establishment of Health Insurance Exchanges

SUMMARY OF NEW LAW

States must establish American Health Benefit Exchanges and Small Business Health Options Program (SHOP) Exchanges to be administered by a governmental agency or nonprofit organization. Under these Exchanges, individuals and small businesses with 100 or fewer employees can purchase qualified coverage, though, eventually, states may allow businesses with more than 100 employees to purchase coverage in the SHOP Exchange. States may form regional Exchanges or allow more than one Exchange to operate in a State as long as each Exchange serves a distinct geographic area.

BACKGROUND

Individuals who do not receive health insurance through work and who cannot buy insurance through the individual market, because of pre-existing conditions and other barriers, currently have few options. Employees of small businesses lack access to affordable quality health insurance as well.

There is no existing exchange provision in federal law. The American Health Benefit Exchange provisions, however, are similar to the Massachusetts Connector, which also acts as an intermediary that assists individuals in acquiring health insurance. Signed into law on April 12, 2006, the Massachusetts health care reform law includes a Health Connector, which collects funds to provide coverage under the State reform law (http://www.mahealthconnector.org/).

NEW LAW EXPLAINED

Health Insurance Exchanges required to be established by each State.—By January 1, 2014, each State must establish an American Health Benefit Exchange for that State that would facilitate the purchase of qualified health plans by qualified individuals (Act Sec. 1311(b) of the Patient Protection and Affordable Care Act (PPACA) (P.L. 111-148)). Each State is also required to establish a Small Business Health Options Program (SHOP) Exchange designed to assist qualified small employers in the State (i.e., with 100 or fewer employees) in enrolling their employees in qualified health plans in the State's small group market (Act Sec. 1311(b)(1)(C) of PPACA). Beginning in 2017, a State may allow businesses with more than 100 employees to purchase coverage in the SHOP Exchange. A State may elect to provide for only one State Exchange that would provide both American Health Benefit Exchange services and SHOP Exchange services to both qualified individuals and qualified small employers. This can be done only if the single Exchange has adequate resources to assist individuals and small employers (Act Sec. 1311(b)(2) of PPACA).

An Exchange may operate in more than one State (i.e., a regional or interstate Exchange) if: (1) each State in which the Exchange operates permits it to do so, and (2) the Secretary of Health and Human Services (HHS) approves the regional or interstate Exchange. Also, a State may establish one or more subsidiary Exchanges if each subsidiary Exchange serves a geographically distinct area. However, the area served by each subsidiary Exchange must be at least as large as a rating area described in Act Sec. 2701(a) of the Public Health Service.

A State may elect to authorize an Exchange established by the State to enter into an agreement with an eligible entity to carry out one or more Exchange responsibilities. An "eligible entity" is defined as either:

- a person that (a) is incorporated, (b) has demonstrated experience on a State or regional basis in the individual and small group health insurance markets and in benefits coverage; and (c) is not a health insurance issuer or that is treated under as a member of the same controlled group of corporations (or under common control with) as a health insurance issuer; or
- the State Medicaid agency (Act Sec. 1311(f) of PPACA).

NEW LAW EXPLAINED

Requirements for Exchanges. The Exchanges will be administered by a governmental agency or nonprofit organization. Exchanges must also comply with a number of other rules (discussed below), relating to coverage offerings, required benefits, and other provisions (Act Sec. 1311(d)(1) of PPACA). Exchanges must consult with stakeholders in carrying out its activities. These stakeholders include health care consumers who enroll in qualified health plans; individuals and entities experienced in facilitating enrollment in qualified health plans; representatives of small businesses and self-employed individuals; State Medicaid offices; and advocates for enrolling hard-to-reach populations (Act Sec. 1311(d)(6) of PPACA).

At minimum, an Exchange must:

- implement procedures for the certification, recertification, and decertification of health plans as qualified health plans;

- provide for the operation of a toll-free telephone hotline to respond to assistance requests;

- maintain an Internet website through which enrollees and prospective enrollees of qualified health plans may obtain standardized comparative information on health plans;

- assign a rating to each qualified health plan offered through the Exchange;

- utilize a standardized format for presenting health benefits plan options in the Exchange, including the use of the uniform outline of coverage;

- inform individuals of eligibility requirements for the Medicaid program, the Children's Health Insurance Program (CHIP), or any applicable State or local public program, and, if through screening of the application by the Exchange, it determines that such individuals are eligible for any such program, enroll such individuals in such program;

- establish and make available by electronic means a calculator to determine the actual cost of coverage after the application of any premium assistance tax credit (see ¶ 210) and any cost-sharing reduction (see ¶ 520);

- subject to the procedures for determining eligibility (see ¶ 515), grant a certification attesting that, for purposes of the individual responsibility penalty for failure to maintain minimum essential health coverage (see ¶ 205), an individual is exempt from the requirement or from the penalty imposed because (a) there is no affordable qualified health plan available through the Exchange or the individual's employer covering the individual; or (b) the individual meets the requirements for any other exemption from the individual responsibility requirement or penalty;

- transfer to the Secretary of the Treasury:

  — a list of the individuals who are issued a certification of an exemption from the penalty for failing to carry health insurance (see ¶ 205) (including the name and taxpayer identification number of each individual);

  — the name and taxpayer identification number of each individual who was an employee of an employer but who was determined to be eligible for the premium

NEW LAW EXPLAINED

assistance tax credit (see ¶ 210) because the employer did not provide minimum essential coverage or the employer provided the minimum essential coverage but it was determined to either be unaffordable to the employee or did not provide the required minimum actuarial value; and

— the name and taxpayer identification number of each individual who notifies the Exchange that they have changed employers and of each individual who ceases coverage under a qualified health plan during a plan year (and the effective date of such cessation);

• provide each employer with the name of each of its employees who ceases coverage under a qualified health plan during a plan year (and the effective date of such cessation); and

• establish the Navigator program (described below) (Act Sec. 1311(d)(4) of PPACA).

Exchanges are required to publish the average costs of licensing, regulatory fees, and any other payments required by the Exchange, as well as the Exchange's administrative costs. This information should be published on an Internet website to help educate consumers on such costs. Such information shall also include information as to monies lost to waste, fraud, and abuse (Act Sec. 1311(d)(7) of PPACA).

Exchange coverage offerings. An Exchange must make qualified health plans available to qualified individuals and qualified employers. An Exchange is barred from making available any health plans that are not qualified. For a discussion of the certification of a qualified health plan, see ¶ 505. For a discussion of the essential health benefits that a qualified health plan must offer, see the discussion below and ¶ 530. However, each Exchange must require plan issuers providing limited scope dental benefits (Code Sec. 9832(c)(2)(A)) to offer the plan through the Exchange. This can be done either separately or in connection with a qualified health plan if the plan provides pediatric dental benefits (Act Sec. 1311(d)(2) of PPACA).

Exchanges may make available a qualified health plan notwithstanding any provision of law that may require benefits other than the essential health benefits specified. Further, a State may require that a qualified health plan offered in the State offer benefits in addition to the essential health benefits. However, in this instance, the State must assume the cost by: (1) making payments to an qualified individual enrolled in a qualified health plan offered in such State, or (2) making payments directly to the qualified health plan in which such individual is enrolled, on behalf of the individual. This is intended to defray the cost of any additional benefits (Act Sec. 1311(d)(3) of PPACA, as amended by 10104(e)(1)).

Exchange's certification of qualified health plans. The Patient Protection Act allows for Exchanges to certify health plans as qualified health plans. This certification may be done if:

• the health plan meets the rules for certification by the Department of Health and Human Services (HHS); and

NEW LAW EXPLAINED

- the Exchange determines that making such health plan available through the Exchange is in the interests of qualified individuals and qualified employers in the State or States in which the Exchange operates.

However, an Exchange may not exclude a health plan due to the fact that the health plan is a fee-for-service plan or through the imposition of premium price controls. Nor may a health plan be excluded on the basis that the plan provides treatments necessary to prevent patients' deaths in circumstances the Exchange determines are inappropriate or too costly.

The Exchange must require health plans seeking certification to submit a justification for any premium increase prior to implementation of the increase. These plans must prominently post such information on their web sites. The Exchange shall take this information, and the information and the recommendations provided to the Exchange by the State (relating to patterns or practices of excessive or unjustified premium increases) into consideration when determining whether to make the health plan available through the Exchange. The Exchange must also take into account any excess of premium growth outside the Exchange as compared to the rate of such growth inside the Exchange, including information reported by the State (Act Sec. 1311(e) of PPACA).

Coverage transparency. The Exchange must require health plans seeking certification as qualified health plans to submit to the Exchange, the HHS Secretary, and the State insurance commissioner (and make available to the public), accurate and timely disclosure of the following information:

- claims payment policies and practices;
- periodic financial disclosures;
- data on enrollment;
- data on disenrollment;
- data on the number of claims that are denied;
- data on rating practices;
- information on cost-sharing and payments with respect to any out-of-network coverage;
- information on enrollee and participant rights; and
- any other information considered to be appropriate by the HHS Secretary.

  Comment: The information required to be submitted under the coverage transparency rule must be provided in plain language. The term "plain language" is defined as language that the intended audience, including individuals with limited English proficiency, can readily understand and use because that language is concise, well-organized, and follows other best practices of plain language writing. The Secretaries of HHS and Labor must jointly develop and issue guidance on best practices of plain language writing.

The Patient Protection Act imposes additional rules relating to cost-sharing transparency as well. Specifically, the Exchange must require health plans seeking certification as qualified health plans to permit individuals to learn the amount of cost-

NEW LAW EXPLAINED

sharing (including deductibles, copayments, and coinsurance), under the individual's plan or coverage, that the person would be responsible for paying. This applies with regard to the furnishing of a specific item or service by a participating provider in a timely manner at the request of the individual. At a minimum, this information must be made available to the individual through an Internet web site and also via other means, for individuals without Internet access.

The Secretary of Labor must "update and harmonize" its rules regarding the accurate and timely disclosure to participants by group health plans of plan disclosure, plan terms and conditions, and periodic financial disclosure (Act Sec. 1311(e)(3) of PPACA, as added by Act Sec. 10104(f)(2)).

HHS certification of qualified health plans. The HHS Secretary must establish criteria, by regulation, for certifying health plans as qualified health plans, for purposes of the Exchange rules. At a minimum, these criteria must:

- meet marketing requirements, and not use marketing practices or benefit designs that discourage plan enrollment by individuals with significant health needs;

- ensure a sufficient choice of providers (consistent with network adequacy provisions under Act Sec. 2702(c) of the Public Health Service Act) and provide information both to enrollees and prospective enrollees on the availability of in-network and out-of-network providers;

- include within health insurance plan networks those essential community providers, where available, that serve predominately low-income, medically-underserved individuals (but this is not to be construed as requiring any health plan to provide coverage for any specific medical procedure);

- be accredited with respect to local performance on clinical quality measures, patient experience ratings, as well as consumer access, utilization management, quality assurance, provider credentialing, complaints and appeals, network adequacy and access, and patient information programs by HHS-recognized accreditation entity or receive this performance accreditation within a period established by an Exchange for such accreditation that is applicable to all qualified health plans;

- implement a quality improvement strategy;

- utilize a uniform enrollment form (either electronically or paper-based) that qualified individuals and qualified employers may use in enrolling in qualified health plans offered through an Exchange;

- utilize the standard format established for presenting health benefits plan options; and

- provide information to enrollees and prospective enrollees, and to each Exchange in which the plan is offered, on any Public Health Service Act-endorsed quality measures for health plan performance (Act Sec. 1311(c)(1) of PPACA).

The Act also clarifies that nothing in the provision regarding community providers is to be construed as requiring a qualified health plan to contract with a community provider if that provider refuses to accept the health plan's payment rates that are generally applicable (Act Sec. 1311(c)(2) of PPACA).

¶505

NEW LAW EXPLAINED

Rating system. The HHS Secretary must develop a rating system that would rate qualified health plans offered through an Exchange in each benefits level on the basis of the relative quality and price. The Exchange must include the quality rating in the information provided to individuals and employers through the Internet portal (Act Sec. 1331(c)(3) of PPACA). The HHS Secretary is required to operate, maintain, and update an Internet portal to assist States in developing and maintaining their own Internet portals for Exchanges.

Also, the HHS Secretary must make available, for use by the Exchanges, a model template for an Internet portal. This may be used to direct qualified individuals and qualified employers to qualified health plans, as well as assist these individuals and employers in determining whether they are eligible to participate in an Exchange or eligible for a premium assistance tax credit (see ¶205) or cost-sharing reduction (see ¶520). This Internet portal also would be used to present standardized information (including quality ratings) regarding qualified health plans offered through an Exchange to assist consumers in making easy health insurance choices (Act Sec. 1331(c)(5) of PPACA).

This template must include access, with regard to each qualified health plan offered through the Exchange in each rating area, to the uniform outline of coverage the plan is required to provide, under Act Sec. 2716 of the Public Health Service Act and to a copy of the plan's written policy (Act Sec. 1331(c)(5) of PPACA).

> **Comment:** The HHS Secretary must develop an enrollee satisfaction survey system that would evaluate the level of enrollee satisfaction with qualified health plans offered through an Exchange. This is to be done for each qualified health plan that had more than 500 enrollees in the previous year. The Exchange would need to include enrollee satisfaction information in the information provided to individuals and employers through the Internet portal. This would make it easier for individuals to easily compare enrollee satisfaction levels between comparable plans (Act Sec. 1331(c)(4) of PPACA).

Exchange enrollment periods. Under the Patient Protection Act, the HHS Secretary must require an Exchange to provide for:

- an initial open enrollment, as determined by July 1, 2012, by the HHS Secretary;

- annual open enrollment periods, as determined by the HHS Secretary for calendar years after the initial enrollment period;

- special enrollment periods as available for group health plans under Code Sec. 9801; and

- special monthly enrollment periods for Indians (Act Sec. 1331(c)(6) of PPACA).

Quality rewards via market-based incentives. Quality of a health plan offered through an Exchange is to be rewarded through market-based incentives. A strategy for this is a payment structure that provides increased reimbursement or other incentives for:

- the improvement of health outcomes by implementing activities that include quality reporting, effective case management, care coordination, chronic disease management, medication and care compliance initiatives, including through the

¶505

NEW LAW EXPLAINED

use of the medical home model, for treatment or services under the plan or coverage;

- the implementation of activities to prevent hospital readmissions through a comprehensive program for hospital discharge that includes patient-centered education and counseling, comprehensive discharge planning, and post discharge reinforcement by an appropriate health care professional;

- the implementation of activities to improve patient safety and reduce medical errors through the appropriate use of best clinical practices, evidence based medicine, and health information technology under the plan or coverage;

- the implementation of wellness and health promotion activities; and

- the implementation of activities to reduce health and health care disparities, including through the use of language services, community outreach, and cultural competency training.

The HHS Secretary is required to develop guidelines, in consultation with health care quality experts and stakeholders. Periodic reporting to the applicable Exchange of the activities that a qualified health plan has conducted to implement a quality strategy described is also required (Act Sec. 1311(g) of PPACA, as amended by Act Sec. 10104(g)(3)).

Quality improvements. Beginning on January 1, 2015, unless the HHS Secretary authorizes an exception, a qualified health plan may contract with:

- a hospital with greater than 50 beds (or number adjusted by HHS) only if the hospital uses a specified patient safety evaluation system, and implements a mechanism to ensure that each patient receives a comprehensive program for hospital discharge that includes patient-centered education and counseling, comprehensive discharge planning, and post discharge reinforcement by an appropriate health care professional; or

- a health care provider only if the provider implements mechanisms to improve health care quality as required by the HHS Secretary (Act Sec 1311(h) of PPACA).

Funding limitations. In establishing an Exchange, a State must ensure that each Exchange is self-sustaining beginning on January 1, 2015. This provision allows an Exchange to charge assessments or user fees to participating health insurance issuers, or to otherwise generate funding, in order to support its operations. However, in carrying out its activities, an Exchange may not use any funds intended for the administrative and operational expenses of the Exchange for staff retreats, promotional giveaways, excessive executive compensation, or promotion of federal or State legislative and regulatory modifications (Act Sec. 1311(d)(5) of PPACA).

Assistance to States in establishing Exchanges. The HHS Secretary is authorized to make grant awards to states by March 23, 2011 (one year after the date of enactment of PPACA), to help states pay costs associated with establishing Exchanges. These State grants are renewable if the Secretary determines that the State is making adequate progress towards establishing an Exchange, implementing reforms, and meeting other HHS-established benchmarks (Act Sec. 1311(a) of PPACA). State grants may not be awarded after January 1, 2015 (Act Sec. 1311(a)(4)(B) of PPACA). The

NEW LAW EXPLAINED

HHS Secretary must provide technical assistance to states in order to facilitate small business participation in SHOP Exchanges (Act Sec. 1311(a)(5) of PPACA).

Navigators. An Exchange must establish a navigator program under which it awards grants to entities to carry out certain duties. To be eligible to receive a grant, an entity must demonstrate to the Exchange that the entity has existing relationships (or could readily establish relationships), with employers and employees, consumers (including uninsured and underinsured consumers), or self-employed individuals likely to be qualified to enroll in a qualified health plan.

Eligible entities may include trade, industry, and professional associations, commercial fishing industry organizations, ranching and farming organizations, community and consumer-focused nonprofit groups, chambers of commerce, unions, resource partners of the Small Business Administration, other licensed insurance agents and brokers, and other entities that are capable of carrying out required duties and can meet required standards and provide required information.

An entity that serves as a navigator must:

- conduct public education activities to raise awareness of the availability of qualified health plans;
- distribute fair and impartial information regarding qualified health plan enrollment, and the availability of premium tax credits and cost-sharing reductions;
- facilitate enrollment in qualified health plans;
- provide referrals to any applicable office of health insurance consumer assistance or health insurance ombudsman or any other appropriate State agency or agencies, for any enrollee with a grievance, complaint, or question regarding his or her health plan, coverage, or a determination under such plan or coverage; and
- provide information in a manner that is culturally and linguistically appropriate to the needs of the population being served by the Exchange or Exchanges.

The HHS Secretary must establish standards for navigators. These standards are to include provisions to ensure that any private or public entity that is selected as a navigator is qualified, and licensed if appropriate, to engage in the navigator activities, and to avoid conflicts of interest. Under the standards, a navigator cannot be a health insurance issuer; or receive any consideration directly or indirectly from any health insurance issuer in connection with the enrollment of any qualified individuals or employees of a qualified employer in a qualified health plan.

The HHS Secretary, in collaboration with States, must develop standards to ensure that information made available by navigators is fair, accurate, and impartial. Grants are to be made from the operational funds of the Exchange and not federal funds received by the State to establish the Exchange (Act Secs. 1311(i) and 10104(h) of PPACA).

Mental health parity applicability. Mental health parity rules, under Public Health Service Act Sec. 2726, apply to qualified health plans in the same manner and to the same extent as such section applies to health insurance issuers and group health plans (Act Sec. 1311(j) of PPACA).

NEW LAW EXPLAINED

Conflicts with HHS rules. An Exchange may not establish rules that conflict with or prevent the application of regulations issued by the HHS Secretary (Act Sec. 1311(k) of PPACA).

▶ **Effective date.** No effective date is provided by the Act. The provision is therefore considered effective on March 23, 2010, the date of enactment.

— Act Sec. 1311 of the Patient Protection and Affordable Care Act (PPACA) (P.L. 111-148), as amended by Act Secs. 10104(e)-(h).

➽→ *Caution: The explanation below reflects certain nontax provisions of the Patient Protection and Affordable Care Act (P.L. 111-148) and the Health Care and Education Reconciliation Act of 2010 (P.L. 111-152). While the issues discussed do not have a direct effect on federal taxes, this explanation is helpful in understanding several tax-related explanations that appear in preceding chapters of this publication.*

¶510 Health Insurance Exchange Eligibility Rules

SUMMARY OF NEW LAW

Rules governing eligibility rules for both individuals and for employers under the Health Insurance Exchanges are provided.

BACKGROUND

There is no specific existing provision in federal law for eligibility to participate in an Health Insurance Exchange established under the Patient Protection Act. However, the Health Insurance Portability and Accountability Act (HIPAA) does provide some limited eligibility provisions, as follows:

- HIPAA's nondiscrimination provisions generally prohibit a group health plan or group health insurance issuer from using health factors to deny employees and their dependents eligibility for benefits.

- Under HIPAA, plans and insurers must allow a "special enrollment" for employees and/or their dependents who are eligible for, but not enrolled in, the group health plan in two situations: (1) when the individuals are losing other coverage (including COBRA, or due to reaching a health plan's lifetime limits), and (2) in cases of marriage or birth/adoption of a new dependent.

NEW LAW EXPLAINED

Health Insurance Exchange eligibility rules clarified for individuals and employers.—A qualified individual may enroll in any qualified health plan under the American Health Benefit Exchange that is available to the individual in the State he or she resides

NEW LAW EXPLAINED

and for which the individual is eligible (Act Sec. 1312(a)(1), of the Patient Protection and Affordable Care Act (PPACA) (P.L. 111-148), as amended by Act Sec. 10104(i)(1)). A qualified employer may provide support for employee coverage under a qualified health plan provided through a under a Small Business Health Options Program (SHOP) Exchange. This is done by an employer selecting any level of coverage permissible to be made available to employees under an Exchange. Within the level chosen by an employer, each employee may choose to enroll in a qualified health plan offering coverage at that level (Act Sec. 1312(a)(2) of PPACA). For a discussion of the establishment of American Health Benefit and SHOP Exchanges, see ¶ 505. For a discussion of the essential health benefits that must be provided by a qualified plan, and the level of coverage, see ¶ 530)

Qualified individuals. For this purpose, a "qualified individual" is defined as someone who is seeking to enroll in a qualified health plan in the individual market offered through an Exchange, and resides in the State that established the Exchange. Individuals who are incarcerated, other than those whose incarceration is pending the disposition of charges, are not to be treated as qualified individuals (Act Sec. 1312(f)(1), as amended by Act Sec. 10104(i)(3) of PPACA).

A person is not considered a "qualified individual" if he or she is not (or is not reasonably expected to be) for the entire enrollment period, an U.S. citizen or national, or an alien lawfully present in the United States. A person who does not come within this definition is not a qualified individual and may not be covered under a qualified health plan in the individual market that is offered through an Exchange (Act Sec. 1312(f)(3) of PPACA).

> **Comment:** A qualified individual who is enrolled in a qualified health plan may pay any applicable premium owed by that person to the insurance issuer that has issued the qualified health plan (Act Sec. 1312(b) of PPACA).

Qualified employers. A "qualified employer" is a small employer that elects to make all of its full-time employees eligible for one or more qualified health plans offered in the small group market through an Exchange (Act Sec. 1312(f)(2)(A) of PPACA). Beginning in 2017, each State may allow health insurance coverage issuers to offer qualified health plans in the large group market through an Exchange. The Patient Protection Act makes it clear that it is not to be construed as requiring an issuer to offer such plans through an Exchange.

If a State chooses to allow issuers to offer qualified health plans in the large group market through an Exchange, the Patient Protection Act clarifies that the term "qualified employer" includes a large employer that elects to make all of its full-time employees eligible for one or more qualified health plans offered in the large group market through an Exchange (Act Sec. 1312(f)(2)(B) of PPACA).

Single risk pool. Under the Patient Protection Act, health insurance issuers are to consider all enrollees in all qualified health plans, other than certain grandfathered plans, offered by the issuer in the individual market to be members of a single risk pool. This includes those enrollees who do not enroll in such plans through the Exchange (Act Sec. 1312(c)(1) of PPACA). Similarly, health insurance issuers must consider all enrollees in all health plans offered by the issuer in the small group

¶510

NEW LAW EXPLAINED

market to be members of a single risk pool, including those who do not enroll in such plans through the Exchange. Grandfathered health plans are also exempted from this requirement for the small group market (Act Sec. 1312(c)(2) of PPACA). For a discussion of grandfathered plans, see ¶535.

A State is allowed to require the individual and small group insurance markets within the State to be merged if the State deems this to be appropriate (Act Sec. 1312(c)(3) of PPACA). As for grandfathered health plans, any State law requiring the inclusion of a grandfathered health plan in a single risk pool (such as the individual market single risk pool and the small group market single risk pool) does not apply (Act Sec. 1312(c)(4) of PPACA).

> **Comment:** Nothing in this portion of the Patient Protection Act is to be construed as terminating, abridging or otherwise limiting the operation of any State law requirements regarding any health plans or policies that are offered outside of an Exchange, to offer benefits (Act Sec. 1312(d)(2) of PPACA).

Voluntary nature of Exchanges. The Patient Protection Act makes clear that nothing is to be construed as restricting the choice of a qualified individual to enroll or not to enroll in a qualified health plan or to participate in a Exchange (Act Sec. 1312(d)(3) of PPACA). However, for a catastrophic plan, a qualified individual may enroll only if eligible to enroll in a plan under the Exchange.

Similarly, nothing is to be interpreted as prohibiting a qualified employer from selecting for its employers, a health plan offered outside of the Exchange (Act Sec. 1312(d)(1) of PPACA). Also, nothing is to be construed as prohibiting a health insurance issuer from offering a health plan to a qualified individual or qualified employer outside of the Exchanges.

Enrollment. An Exchange, or a qualified health plan offered under an Exchange, may not impose a penalty or other fee on an individual who cancels enrollment in a plan because he or she becomes eligible for minimum essential coverage (other than under a grandfathered plan) (see ¶205), or such coverage becomes affordable.

The HHS Secretary must establish procedures so that States may allow agents or brokers to enroll individuals and employers in any qualified health plans in the individual or small group markets as soon as the plan is offered via an Exchange within the State. States may also allow agents and brokers to assist individuals in applying for premium tax credits and cost-sharing reductions for plans sold through an Exchange (Act Sec. 1312(e), as amended by Act Sec. 10104(i)(2) of PPACA).

Special rules for Members of Congress. The only health plans that the federal government may offer to Members of Congress (i.e., members of the House or the Senate) and their congressional staffs are those that are created under the Patient Protection Act or offered through an Exchange. Staffers include full and part-time employees employed by the Member's official office either in Washington, DC, or outside of Washington, DC. (Act Sec. 1312(d)(3)(D) of PPACA).

▶ **Effective date.** No effective date is provided by the Act. The provision is therefore considered to be effective on March 23, 2010, the date of enactment.

— Act Sec. 1312 of the Patient Protection and Affordable Care Act (PPACA) (P.L. 111-148), as amended by Act Sec. 10104(i).

¶510

»»→ *Caution: The explanation below reflects certain nontax provisions of the Patient Protection and Affordable Care Act (P.L. 111-148) and the Health Care and Education Reconciliation Act of 2010 (P.L. 111-152). While the issues discussed do not have a direct effect on federal taxes, this explanation is helpful in understanding several tax-related explanations that appear in preceding chapters of this publication.*

¶515 Procedures for Determining Eligibility for Exchange Participation, Tax Credits, and Cost-Sharing Reductions

SUMMARY OF NEW LAW

General procedures are established for determining eligibility for Exchange participation, premium tax credits, reduced cost-sharing, and individual responsibility exemptions. An applicant's citizenship/immigration status, income, and family size will be verified against federal records.

BACKGROUND

By January 1, 2014, each State must establish an American Health Benefit Exchange and Small Business Health Options Program (SHOP Exchange) to provide qualified individuals and qualified small business employers access to qualified health plans. For a discussion of the establishment and requirements of the Exchanges (see ¶505). Individuals who are eligible for participation in a qualified health plan through an Exchange, may also be eligible for a premiums assistance tax credit (see ¶210) and cost-sharing subsidy (see ¶520). Currently, there is no federal law to establish procedures for determining an individuals's eligibility to participate in an Exchange, the premium assistance tax credit, or the cost-sharing subsidies. In addition, there is no federal law to establish procedures for determining if an individual may be exempted from the penalty for failure to maintain minimum essential health care coverage (see ¶205).

NEW LAW EXPLAINED

Procedures for eligibility determinations outlined.—As part of the establishment of Health Insurance Exchanges and the requirement that individuals maintain minimum essential health care coverage, the Secretary of Health and Human Services (HHS) must establish a program for determining (Act Sec. 1411(a) of the Patient Protection and Affordable Care Act (PPACA) (P.L. 111-148)):

- whether an individual to be covered by an Exchange-offered qualified health plan in the individual market, or claiming a premium assistance tax credit (see ¶210) or reduced cost-sharing ¶520), is a U.S. citizen or national, or an alien lawfully present in the United States;

NEW LAW EXPLAINED

- whether an individual claiming a premium assistance tax credit or reduced cost-sharing meets income and coverage requirements, and the amount of the credit or reduced cost-sharing;

- whether an individual's employer-sponsored health coverage is "unaffordable"; and

- whether to grant certification of exemption for an individual from the requirement to maintain minimum essential health coverage, or applicable penalty (see ¶205).

Applicant information. Applicants must furnish the following information in order to make these determinations:

- *Applicants for enrollment in Exchange-offered qualified health plans in the individual market:* Name, address, and date of birth of each individual to be covered by the plan (*i.e.,* enrollee) (Act Sec. 1411(b)(1) of PPACA).

- *Enrollees with eligibility based on attestation of citizenship:* Social Security number (Act Sec. 1411(b)(2)(A)) of PPACA).

- *Enrollees with eligibility based on attestation of immigration status:* Social Security number (if applicable) and identifying information regarding immigration status (Act Sec. 1411(b)(2)(B) of PPACA).

- *Enrollees claiming premium tax credits or reduced cost-sharing:* Income and family size information for the tax year ending with (or within) the second calendar year preceding the calendar year in which the plan year begins. This information includes: taxpayer identity information, filing status, number of individuals for which a personaly or dependency exemption is claimed, modified adjusted gross income (AGI), the tax year to which the information relates, and other information prescribed by regulation (Act Sec. 1411(b)(3)(A) PPACA). Information regarding changed circumstances (for individuals with significant reductions in income or changes in marital status or family size, as well as those who were not required to file a tax return for the relevant tax year) may also be required (Act Sec. 1411(b)(3)(B) of PPACA). For a discussion of the disclosure of tax return information by the IRS to carry out eligibility requirements, see ¶425.

- *Enrollees claiming premium tax credits and reduced cost-sharing based on employer-sponsored coverage that lacks minimum essential coverage or affordable minimum essential coverage:* Employer's name, address and employer identification number; whether the enrollee is a full-time employee, and whether the employer provides minimum essential coverage; if minimum essential coverage is provided, the lowest cost option and the required contribution under the employer plan; and, if the employer's minimum essential coverage is unaffordable, information regarding income, family size and changed circumstances. If an enrollee changes (or adds) employment while in a qualified health plan for which the credit or reduction is allowed, he or she must provide such information regarding the new employer (Act Sec. 1411(b)(4) of PPACA).

NEW LAW EXPLAINED

- *Individuals seeking exemption from the individual responsibility requirement:* Individuals claiming exemption due to lack of affordable coverage or household income less than 100 percent of the poverty line must furnish information regarding income, family size, changed circumstances and employer-sponsored coverage. The HHS Secretary must prescribe required information for those seeking exemption as a member of a religious sect or division, as a member of a health care sharing ministry, as an Indian, or for a hardship (Act Sec. 1411(b)(5) of PPACA).

Verification. Exchanges will transfer applicant-provided information to the HHS Secretary for verification. In turn, the Secretary will (Act Sec. 1411(c) of PPACA):

- submit information regarding citizenship/immigration status (including attestation of the individual) to the Social Security Commissioner and/or Secretary of Homeland Security for comparison with federal records; and

- submit information regarding eligibility for premium tax credits and cost-sharing reductions to the Treasury Secretary for verification of household income and family size.

Verifications and determinations among federal officials will be done via an online system or other approved method (Act Sec. 1411(c)(4) of PPACA). Results must be reported back to the HHS Secretary, who will notify the Exchange (Act Sec. 1411(e) of PPACA). Note that the Secretary may change procedures to reduce administrative costs and burdens on applicants. The HHS Secretary will check the accuracy of information not required to be verified by another federal official, and may delegate this responsibility to the Exchange (Act Sec. 1411(d) of PPACA).

> **Comment:** Critics have alleged that IRS disclosure of taxpayer information for the purpose of verifying eligibility for premium credits and cost-sharing could infringe on individual privacy rights.

If applicant-provided information relating to enrollment, premium tax credits and cost-sharing reductions is positively verified, the HHS Secretary will notify the Treasury Secretary of the amount of any advance payment to be made (see ¶525). Similarly, if applicant-provided information relating to exemption from the individual responsibility requirement is positively verified, the HHS Secretary will issue a certification of exemption (Act Sec. 1411(e)(2) of PPACA).

Inconsistencies. If citizenship/lawful presence is not positively verified with the Social Security Commissioner or Secretary of Homeland Security, the applicant's eligibility will be determined under procedures used for Medicaid (Act Sec. 1411(e)(3) of PPACA).

> **Comment:** A streamlined verification process is used for individuals declaring they are citizens or nationals of the United States for purposes of establishing eligibility for Medicaid or the Children's Health Insurance Program (CHIP). In lieu of providing documentation, a State may submit, at least monthly, the names and Social Security numbers of newly enrolled individuals to the Social Security Commissioner, for comparison with the agency's records. The State

NEW LAW EXPLAINED

may enter into an agreement with the Social Security Commissioner to electronically submit the information, or to use another method. This provision was added by the Children's Health Insurance Program Reauthorization Act of 2009 (P.L. 111-3), and took effect on January 1, 2010.

The HHS Secretary will notify the Exchange of inconsistencies with other information. In response, the Exchange will first contact the applicant to confirm the accuracy of the information, and take other actions to be identified by the Secretary. If still unresolved, the Exchange must notify the applicant of the inconsistency and provide him or her with the opportunity to present "satisfactory documentary evidence" or resolve the issue with the verifier during a 90-day period beginning when the notice is sent. The Secretary may extend this 90-day period for enrollments occurring in 2014 (Act Sec. 1411(e)(4)(A) of PPACA).

During this 90-day period, the Exchange has several responsibilities (not involving citizenship/immigration status) (Act Sec. 1411(e)(4)(B) of PPACA):

- before the close of the 90-day period, the Exchange must make any determinations based on information contained on the application;

- if, at the close of the 90-day period, an inconsistency is unresolved regarding premium tax credits or cost-sharing reductions, the Exchange must notify the applicant of the credit or reduction amount (if any) based on federal records;

- if the HHS Secretary notifies the Exchange that an enrollee is eligible for a premium tax credit or cost-sharing reduction due to a lack of minimum essential coverage through an employer (or unaffordable coverage), the Exchange must notify the employer of this fact and that the employer may be liable for a tax (for a discussion the employer requirement for providing minimum health care coverage, see ¶305);

- if, at the close of the 90-day period, an inconsistency remains concerning exemption from the individual responsibility requirement, the Exchange must notify the applicant that certification for exemption will not be issued; and

- the Exchange also must notify each individual receiving an inconsistency notice about the appeals process (Act Sec. 1411(e)(4)(C) of PPACA).

Appeals. The HHS Secretary, in consultation with the Treasury Secretary, the Secretary of Homeland Security and the Social Security Commissioner, must establish procedures for hearing and deciding on appeals of verification determinations, and periodically redetermining eligibility in appropriate circumstances (Act Sec. 1411(f)(1) of PPACA).

The HHS Secretary must establish a separate appeals process for employers notified that they may be liable for a tax for not providing minimum essential coverage or affordable coverage. The process must allow the employer to present information, including evidence of the employer-sponsored plan and employer contributions. It also must allow the employer access to the data used for the determination, as permissible by law. An employer generally is not entitled to an employee's tax return

¶515

NEW LAW EXPLAINED

information, but may be notified of the employee's name and whether his or her income is above or below the affordability threshold. An employee can provide a waiver, however, allowing the employer to access to his or her tax return information (Act Sec. 1411(f)(2) of PPACA).

Confidentiality. Applicants are required to provide only the information necessary to authenticate identity, determine eligibility, and figure the amount of the premium tax credit or cost-sharing reduction. Individuals receiving such information may not disclose it for unauthorized purposes (Act Sec. 1411(g) of PPACA).

Penalties. Individuals who violate these provisions are subject to civil penalties, in addition to other applicable penalties, as follows (Act Sec. 1411(h) of PPACA):

- up to $25,000, for providing incorrect information on an application due to "negligence or disregard" of the rules and regulations (to be waived if the HHS Secretary determines that there was reasonable cause and that the individual acted in good faith);

- up to $250,000, for knowingly and willfully providing false or fraudulent information; and

- up to $25,000, for knowingly and willfully using or disclosing information, in violation of the confidentiality provisions.

The HHS Secretary (or U.S. Attorney General) may not put a lien or levy on property for failure to pay a penalty (Act Sec. 1411(h)(3) of PPACA).

Employer responsibility study. The HHS Secretary, in consultation with the Treasury Secretary, must conduct a study of the procedures necessary to protect the following rights (Act Sec. 1411(i)(1) of PPACA):

- employees' right to keep their tax return information confidential;

- employees' right to enroll in a qualified health plan through an Exchange if their employers do not provide affordable coverage;

- employers' right to adequate due process; and

- employers' right to access information to accurately determine payments assessed on them.

Study results, and recommendations for legislative changes, must be submitted to the Senate Committee on Finance, the Senate Committee on Health, Education, Labor and Pensions, the House Committee on Education and Labor, and the House Ways and Means Committee by January 1, 2013 (Act Sec. 1411(i)(2) of PPACA).

▶ **Effective date.** No specific effective date is provided by the Act. The provision is, therefore, considered effective on March 23, 2010, the date of enactment.

— Act Sec. 1411 of the Patient Protection and Affordable Care Act (PPACA) (P.L. 111-148).

>>>→ *Caution: The explanation below reflects certain nontax provisions of the Patient Protection and Affordable Care Act (P.L. 111-148) and the Health Care and Education Reconciliation Act of 2010 (P.L. 111-152). While the issues discussed do not have a direct effect on federal taxes, this explanation is helpful in understanding several tax-related explanations that appear in preceding chapters of this publication.*

¶520 Cost-Sharing Reductions

SUMMARY OF NEW LAW

Individuals who enroll in a qualified health plan at the silver coverage level in an Health Insurance Exchange may be eligible for cost-sharing reductions (*i.e.*, subsidies) if their household income does not exceed 400 percent of the poverty line. Reductions decrease annual out-of-pocket limits and, for lower-income individuals, further increase a plan's share of total allowed benefits costs. The federal government will pay plan issuers for the value of the reductions they make.

BACKGROUND

Beginning in 2014, a penalty is imposed on applicable individuals for each month they fail to have "minimum essential health coverage" for themselves and their dependents (see ¶205). This penalty is also referred to as a "shared responsibility payment." As is the case with premiums, there is no end in sight to escalating deductibles, coinsurance, and copayments, all elements of cost-sharing contained in most health insurance plans. Even Americans who do have health insurance may be unable to afford the cost-sharing required to actually obtain covered services. A report by the Congressional Research Service points out that premium credits, without cost-sharing assistance, would provide many individuals with health insurance that they could not afford to *use*.

NEW LAW EXPLAINED

Cost-sharing reduced for eligible insureds.—Low-to moderate-income individuals who enroll in an qualified health plan providing silver level coverage through an Health Insurance Exchange may be eligible for cost-sharing reductions. "Cost-sharing" includes deductibles, coinsurance, copayments, and similar charges, as well as qualified medical expenses for essential health benefits covered under the plan. It does not include premiums, balance billing amounts for non-network providers, or spending for noncovered services (Act Sec. 1302(c)(3)(A) of PPACA).

> **Comment:** By January 1, 2014, each State must establish an American Health Benefit Exchange and Small Business Health Options Program (SHOP Exchange) to provide qualified individuals and qualified small business employers access to qualified health plans. For a discussion of the establishment and requirements of the Exchanges (see ¶505). The Exchanges will have four levels of essential benefits coverage available to participants at either a "bronze," "silver," "gold,"

NEW LAW EXPLAINED

or "platinum" level. The bronze level plans must provide benefits that are actuarially equivalent to 60 percent of the full actuarial value of the benefits provided under the plan. The percentage increases to 70 percent for silver level plans, 80 percent for gold level plans, and 90 percent for platinum level plans. For a discussion of the required contents of an essential benefits coverage, see ¶530. Individuals who are eligible for participation in a qualified health plan through an Exchange, may be eligible for a premiums assistance tax credit (see ¶210) and the cost-sharing subsidy.

To qualify for the cost-sharing reduction, household income must exceed 100 percent, but may not exceed 400 percent, of the poverty line (for the family size involved). Individuals meeting these criteria are considered "eligible insureds" (Act Sec. 1402(b) of the Patient Protection and Affordable Care Act (PPACA) (P.L. 111-148)).

> **Comment:** Limiting cost-sharing reductions to those with household incomes that do not exceed 400 percent of the applicable poverty line targets the financial assistance to low-and moderate- income individuals and families. There does not appear to be any sort of asset test used to help determine eligibility.

> **Caution:** Be aware that there are two slightly different versions of the federal poverty measure: (1) "poverty thresholds," which are updated annually by the U.S. Census Bureau; and (2) "poverty guidelines," which are issued annually by the U.S. Department of Health and Human Services (HHS). The Act refers to the "poverty line," which most likely means the HHS poverty guidelines, published annually in the *Federal Register*.

> **Example:** Applying the 2009 poverty guidelines, which have been extended until at least March 31, 2010, an individual in the contiguous United States with income over $10,830 and up to $43,320 (400 percent of the poverty guideline) would meet the income criterion for the cost-sharing reduction. Similarly, a family of four with household income over $22,050 and up to $88,200 would meet the criterion. The poverty guidelines are typically adjusted annually, so the figures will be higher in 2014 when the Exchanges to become operational.

An alien who is lawfully present in the United States with household income that does not exceed 100 percent of the applicable poverty line, and who is ineligible for Medicaid due to alien status, is treated as having household income equal to 100 percent of the poverty line for purposes of the cost-sharing reduction (Act Sec. 1402(b) of PPACA).

> **Caution:** To be considered an "eligible insured" for the cost-sharing reduction, the law states that household income must "exceed" 100 percent of the applicable poverty line. Treating income for this group of aliens as "equal to" 100 percent would technically exclude them. The language may be corrected in the future, as this most likely was not Congress' intent.

Determining the reduction. Cost-sharing reductions work by lowering the annual out-of-pocket limit for eligible insureds, on a sliding scale, by the following amounts (Act Sec. 1402(c)(1)(A) of PPACA):

NEW LAW EXPLAINED

- two-thirds, if household income is greater than 100 percent, but not more than 200 percent, of the applicable poverty line;
- one-half, if household income is greater than 200 percent, but not more than 300 percent, of the applicable poverty line; and
- one-third, if household income is greater than 300 percent, but not more than 400 percent, of the applicable poverty line.

> **Comment:** Beginning in 2014, the out-of-pocket limit, or "annual limitation on cost-sharing," will be the out-of-pocket limit in effect for health savings accounts (HSAs) for the year. For 2015 and later years, the limit for self-only coverage will be adjusted based on a percentage of average per capita health insurance premium increases, and the limit for family coverage will be twice the amount for self-only coverage (Act Sec. 1302(c)(1) of PPACA). See ¶530 for more information about the cost-sharing limit.

> **Comment:** Financial assistance for cost-sharing becomes more limited as income increases.

Lower-income insureds are eligible for additional reductions. The HHS Secretary will establish procedures for qualified health plan issuers to further reduce cost-sharing so that the plan's share of total allowed costs of benefits under the plan (*i.e.*, actuarial value percentage) is increased to:

- 94 percent, if household income is not less than 100 percent, but is not more than 150 percent, of the applicable poverty line;
- 87 percent, if household income exceeds 150 percent, but is not more than 200 percent, of the applicable poverty line; and
- 73 percent, if household income exceeds 200 percent, but is not more than 250 percent, of the applicable poverty line (Act Sec. 1402(c)(2) of PPACA) as amended by the Health Care and Education Reconciliation Act of 2010 (P.L. 111-152)).

> **Comment:** Liability for these lower-income individuals will range from an average of six percent to 27 percent of the costs for covered benefits under the plan.

The HHS Secretary also will ensure that the initial reductions (lower out-of-pocket limits) do not increase the plan's actuarial value beyond the percentage limits above. For this purpose, the actuarial value limit applicable to eligible insureds with household income that exceeds 250 percent, but is not more than 400 percent, of the applicable poverty line is 70 percent (Act Sec. 1402(c)(1)(B) of PPACA, as amended by the 2010 Reconciliation Act).

Process. The HHS Secretary will notify qualified health plan issuers of enrolled insureds who are eligible for cost-sharing reductions, and issuers will reduce cost-sharing under the plan (Act Sec. 1402(a) of PPACA). Issuers must notify the Secretary of the cost-sharing reductions they make, and the Secretary will make periodic and timely payments to the issuer for the value of the reductions. The Secretary may establish a capitated payment system with appropriate risk adjustments (Act Sec. 1402(c)(3) of PPACA).

Special rules. Unique rules apply to benefits in excess of essential heath benefits, to pediatric dental benefits, and to Indians:

¶520

NEW LAW EXPLAINED

- Cost-sharing reductions do not apply to benefits offered in addition to the essential health benefits required to be provided by the plan, whether offered by a qualified health plan or required by a State (Act Sec. 1402(c)(4) of PPACA).

- If an individual enrolls in both a qualified health plan and a stand-alone dental plan that provides pediatric dental benefits for any plan year, the portion of any cost-sharing reduction allocable, per regulations, to pediatric dental benefits included in the health plan's required essential benefits does not apply (Act Sec. 1402(c)(5) of PPACA).

- Plan issuers must eliminate *any* cost-sharing under the plan for Indians who are enrolled in any qualified health plan in the individual market through an Exchange, if their household income does not exceed 300 percent of the poverty line. Also, if an Indian enrolled in a qualified health plan is furnished an item or service directly by an Indian health provider or through referral under contract health services, cost-sharing may not be imposed for the item or service, and a plan issuer may not reduce payment to such entity by the amount of cost-sharing that would otherwise be due from the Indian. The HHS Secretary will pay the issuer an amount that reflects the increased actuarial value of the plan (Act Sec. 1402(d) of PPACA).

  Comment: An "Indian" means a person who is a member of an Indian tribe, that is any band, nation, or other organized group or community, including any Alaska Native village or regional or village corporation, that is recognized as eligible for special programs and services provided by the United States because of their status as Indians (25 U.S.C. § 450b).

Illegal immigrants. Cost-sharing reductions do not apply to eligible insureds who are not lawfully present in the United States. An individual is considered "lawfully present" only if he or she is, and is reasonably expected to be for the entire cost-sharing reduction period, a U.S. citizen or national, or an alien who is lawfully present in the United States (Act Sec. 1402(e) of PPACA).

When figuring reductions for a taxpayer, household income (relative to the poverty line) must be determined under a method that:

- subtracts the unlawfully present individual from the family size; and

- multiplies household income by a fraction where the numerator is the poverty line for the taxpayer's family size after subtracting the unlawfully present individual, and the denominator is the poverty line before the subtraction.

A comparable method that reaches the same result also may be used. The HHS Secretary, in consultation with the Treasury Secretary, will prescribe rules setting forth the methods by which calculations of family size and household income may be made (see ¶515) (Act Sec. 1402(e) of PPACA).

Limitations. Cost-sharing reductions are limited to coverage months for which a premium assistance tax credit is allowed to the insured (or applicable taxpayer on behalf of the insured) (see ¶210). Also, data for determining eligibility for cost-sharing reductions is based on the tax year for which advanced determinations are made (see ¶525), rather than the tax year for which premium credits are allowed (Act Sec. 1402(f) of PPACA).

NEW LAW EXPLAINED

▶ **Effective date.** No specific effective date is provided for this provision. Therefore, Act Secs. 1402(a) and (b) are considered effective on March 23, 2010, the date of enactment of the Patient Protection and Affordable Care Act (PPACA) (P.L. 111-148). Act Sec. 1402(c) is considered effective on March 30, 2010, the date of enactment of the Health Care and Education Reconciliation Act of 2010 (P.L. 111-152).

— Act Secs. 1402(a) and (b) of the Patient Protection and Affordable Care Act (PPACA) (P.L. 111-148);

— Act Sec. 1402(c), as amended by Act Sec. 1001(b) of the Health Care and Education Reconciliation Act of 2010 (P.L. 111-152);

— Act Secs. 1402(d), (e) and (f).

>>>→ *Caution: The explanation below reflects certain nontax provisions of the Patient Protection and Affordable Care Act (P.L. 111-148) and the Health Care and Education Reconciliation Act of 2010 (P.L. 111-152). While the issues discussed do not have a direct effect on federal taxes, this explanation is helpful in understanding several tax-related explanations that appear in preceding chapters of this publication.*

¶525 Advance Determinations and Payments

SUMMARY OF NEW LAW

Income eligibility for purposes of premium tax credits and cost-sharing reductions (*i.e.*, subsidies) may be determined in advance, upon request of an Health Benefit Exchange. The Treasury Secretary will make advance payments of the credits and reductions to qualified health plan issuers, providing up-front savings to eligible insured individuals.

BACKGROUND

By January 1, 2014, each State must establish an American Health Benefit Exchange and Small Business Health Options Program (SHOP Exchange) to provide qualified individuals and qualified small business employers access to qualified health plans. For a discussion of the establishment and requirements of the Exchanges (see ¶505). Individuals who are eligible for participation in a qualified health plan through an Exchange, may also be eligible for a premiums assistance tax credit (see ¶210) and cost-sharing subsidy (see ¶520). Some tax credits, like the Health Coverage Tax Credit (HCTC) and a portion of the Earned Income Credit, are available on an *advance* basis. This allows taxpayers to receive benefits from the credit throughout the year without having to wait and claim it on their income tax returns.

Advance determinations and payments permitted.—A program, allowing advance determinations of income eligibility for purposes of premium assistance tax credit and cost-sharing reductions, must be established by the Secretary of Health and Human Services (HHS) (Act Sec. 1412(a) of the Patient Protection and Affordable Care Act (PPACA) (P.L. 111-148)). For a discussion about the premium assistance tax credit, see ¶ 210. For a discussion of the cost-sharing reductions, see ¶ 520.

Advance determinations will be made during an individual's annual open enrollment period in a qualified health plan, and will be based on an individual's household income for the most recent tax year for which the HHS Secretary determines information is available (Act Sec. 1412(b) of PPACA). When information on an application form demonstrates a significant change in circumstances (such as a 20-percent drop in income or a filing for unemployment benefits) or when a tax return was not required for the relevant tax year, procedures will allow advance determinations to be based on alternative measures of income.

Payments. For premium assistance tax credits, the HHS Secretary will notify the Treasury Secretary and the applicable Exchange of the advance determination. The Treasury Secretary will make the advance payment to the qualified health plan issuer on a monthly or other periodic basis (Act Sec. 1412(c) of PPACA). The issuer will then:

- reduce the insured's premium by the amount of the advance payment;
- notify the Exchange and the HHS Secretary of the reduction;
- include the premium reduction in each billing statement;
- notify the HHS Secretary if an insured fails to pay premiums; and
- allow a three-month grace period for nonpayment, before discontinuing coverage.

For cost-sharing reductions, the HHS Secretary similarly will notify the Treasury Secretary and the applicable Exchange of the advance determination. The Treasury Secretary will make the advance payment of cost-sharing reductions to the qualified health plan issuer at the time and in the amount specified in the notice.

The HHS Secretary also must notify the Treasury Secretary of employers that do not provide minimum essential coverage or affordable coverage, enabling one or more employees to qualify for premium tax credits and cost-sharing reductions (Act Sec. 1412(a) of PPACA). For a discussion the assessable penalty imposed on an employer for failing to provide minimum health care coverage, see ¶ 305.

Illegal immigrants. No federal payments, credits or cost-sharing reductions can be made for individuals who are not lawfully present in the United States (Act Sec. 1413(d) of PPACA).

State flexibility. Premium assistance tax redits or cost-sharing reductions do not preclude states from making payments to, or on behalf of, an individual for health coverage offered through an Exchange (Act Sec. 1412(e) of PPACA).

▶ **Effective date.** No specific effective date is provided by the Act. The provision is, therefore, considered effective on March 23, 2010, the date of enactment.

— Act Sec. 1412 of the Patient Protection and Affordable Care Act (PPACA) (P.L. 111-148).

>>>→ *Caution: The explanation below reflects certain nontax provisions of the Patient Protection and Affordable Care Act (P.L. 111-148) and the Health Care and Education Reconciliation Act of 2010 (P.L. 111-152). While the issues discussed do not have a direct effect on federal taxes, this explanation is helpful in understanding several tax-related explanations that appear in preceding chapters of this publication.*

¶530 Contents of Essential Health Benefits Package

SUMMARY OF NEW LAW

The essential health benefits package offered by qualified health benefit plan through a Health Insurance Exchange must include specific categories of benefits, meet certain cost-sharing standards, and provide certain levels of coverage. The scope of benefits provided must equal benefits provided under a "typical" employer-sponsored plan. Required levels of coverage range from "bronze" (60 percent of the value of plan benefits) to "platinum" (90 percent of the value). Plans offering "catastrophic" coverage may be offered in the individual market (generally only to those under age 30).

BACKGROUND

Beginning in 2014, States must establish American Health Benefit Exchanges and Small Business Health Options Program (SHOP) Exchanges to be administered by a governmental agency or nonprofit organization. Under these Exchanges, individuals and small businesses with 100 or fewer employees can purchase qualified coverage, though, eventually, states may allow businesses with more than 100 employees to purchase coverage in the SHOP Exchange. States may form regional Exchanges or allow more than one Exchange to operate in a State as long as each Exchange serves a distinct geographic area. For a discussion of the establishment of the Exchanges, see ¶505.

Only "qualified health benefit plans" may be sold via an Exchange. A "qualified health plan" is a health plan that is:

- certified as eligible to be offered via an Exchange;

- offered by a duly licensed health insurance issuer that has agreed to offer plans that meet certain cost-sharing requirements; and

- provides a specific package of health benefits at certain coverage levels, coupled with prescribed cost-sharing amounts (this package is referred to as the "essential health benefits package").

Certain plans not offered through an Exchange will generally also be treated as qualified health plans. These include nonprofit plans offered through the CO-OP program (see ¶540), multi-state plans (see ¶545), and qualified direct primary care medical home plans. All qualified health plans may vary premiums as appropriate by rating area, in accord with rules under the Public Health Service Act.

Certain coverage must be included in the essential health benefits package.— Beginning in 2014, an essential health benefits package provided by a qualified health plan through a Health Insurance Exchange generally must (1) offer coverage for specific categories of benefits; (2) meet certain cost-sharing standards; and (3) provide certain levels of coverage (Act Sec. 1302(a) of the Patient Protection and Affordable Care Act (PPACA) (P.L. 111-148)).

Minimum items and services to be covered. In the essential health benefits package, minimum coverage must include, the following items and services (Act Sec. 1302(b)(1) of PPACA):

- ambulatory patient services;
- emergency services;
- hospitalization;
- maternity and newborn care;
- mental health and substance use disorder services;
- prescription drugs;
- rehabilitative and habilitative services and devices;
- laboratory services;
- preventive and wellness services (including chronic disease management); and
- pediatric services (including oral and vision care).

Note that health plans may provide benefits in addition to those included in the essential health benefits package (Act Sec. 1302(b)(5) of PPACA). However, the scope of benefits offered in an essential health benefits package must be equivalent to the scope of benefits provided under the "typical" employer-sponsored plan. The Chief Actuary of the Centers for Medicare & Medicaid Services must certify that this standard is met and this certification must be reported to Congress by the Secretary of Health and Human Services (HHS) (Act Sec. 1302(b)(2) of PPACA).

> **Comment:** What is the scope of benefits provided in a "typical" employer-sponsored plan? In order to find out, the Act requires the Labor Department to conduct a survey of employer-sponsored plans (including multi-employer plans) (Act Sec. 1302(b)(2) of PPACA).

Designing the benefits package. The Act grants the HHS Secretary some discretion to determine the specific elements of the essential health benefits package. When designing the benefits package, however, the Secretary must factor in the following considerations (Act Sec. 1302(b)(4) of PPACA).

- Balance of benefits—The package must reflect an appropriate balance among the essential benefits.
- No discriminatory design decisions—The package may not be designed (e.g., with respect to coverage decisions or reimbursement rates) in ways that discriminate against individuals because of their age, disability or expected length of life.

¶530

NEW LAW EXPLAINED

- Consider diverse health needs—The package should reflect the health needs of women, children, persons with disabilities, and other diverse segments of the population.

- Denial of benefits—Essential health benefits cannot be denied to individuals based on the individual's age, life expectancy, current or predicted disability, degree of medical dependency, or quality of life.

- Emergency room services—The package must provide coverage for emergency room services in situations where the service provider does not have a contractual relationship with the plan. Cost-sharing for such out-of-network service may not exceed what would apply if the service were performed in-network.

- Stand-alone dental benefits—If a stand-alone dental plan is offered through an Exchange, other health plans offered through that exchange need not provide for the pediatric dental care that is otherwise required as an essential benefit.

Periodic review and revision of the benefits package. The HHS Secretary must periodically review the essential health benefits package and provide a report to Congress. Required elements in the review include an assessment of whether and how the benefits package needs to be modified and an assessment of how any potential change in the mix of benefits required will affect both cost and actuarial limitations (Act Sec. 1302(b)(4)(G) of PPACA). Periodic updates of the benefits package must address the conclusions reached in the review (Act Sec. 1302(b)(4)(H) of PPACA). In addition, the CMS Chief Actuary must certify that a revised package still meets the "typicality" requirement (Act Sec. 1302(b)(2) of PPACA).

> **Comment:** The HHS Secretary must provide notice and an opportunity for public hearing both when designing the original package and when revising the package (Act Sec. 1302(b)(3) of PPACA).

Cost-sharing. Limits are placed on the cost-sharing that may be required with respect to the essential health benefits package offered by any qualified health plan. Cost-sharing includes deductibles, copayments, or coinsurance, but does not include premiums or spending for non-covered services (Act Sec. 1302(c)(3) of PPACA). In 2014, total cost-sharing may not exceed the amount applicable out-of-pocket limit for health savings accounts (HSAs) for self-only and family coverage for taxable years beginning in 2014 (Act Sec. 1302(c)(1)(A) of PPACA).

> **Comment:** For 2015 and thereafter, the amount applicable for self-only coverage is increased by the product of the 2014 limit and the premium adjustment percentage. The premium adjustment percentage for a calendar year is the percentage by which the average per capita premium in the United States for the preceding calendar year exceeds the average per capita premium for 2013. For other coverage, the indexed amount for self-only coverage is doubled (Act Sec. 1302(c)(1)(B) and (c)(4) of PPACA). The average per capita premium must be determined by the Secretary no later than October 1 of the preceding year. The indexed amount will be rounded if necessary to the next lowest multiple of $50.

Generally, deductibles under a plan offered in the small employer group market must not exceed $2,000 for self-only coverage ($4,000 for other coverage). These amounts may be increased by the maximum amount of reimbursement reasona-

NEW LAW EXPLAINED

bly available to a flexible spending account (FSA) participant. In addition, these amounts will be indexed annually, using the premium adjustment percentage used to adjust cost-sharing limits. Note that these limits may not affect the actuarial value of any health plan (including a plan in the bronze level) (Act Sec. 1302(c)(2)(A)—(C) of PPACA).

Levels of coverage. Qualified health plans must provide coverage of the essential benefits at either the "bronze," "silver," "gold," or "platinum" levels. For bronze level plans, the level of coverage must provide benefits that are actuarially equivalent to 60 percent of the full actuarial value of the benefits provided under the plan. For silver level plans, the percentage increases to 70 percent. For gold and platinum level plans, the percentage increases to 80 percent and 90 percent, respectively (Act Sec. 1302(d)(1) of PPACA).

The HHS Secretary must issue regulations regarding the determination of actuarial value for this purpose (Act Sec. 1302(d)(2)(A) of PPACA). Because actuarial estimates can differ, the Secretary must also develop guidelines to provide for a *de minimis* variation (Act Sec. 1302(d)(3) of PPACA). Regulations must also be issued allowing employer contributions to an HSA to be taken into account in determining coverage levels for employer plans (Act Sec. 1302(d)(2)(B) of PPACA, as amended by Act Sec. 10104(b)).

An exception to the general rule regarding the level of coverage that must be provided is available for certain plans offering "catastrophic" coverage. These plans may only be offered in the individual market, and enrollees in such plans must be either under age 30 or exempt from the individual requirement to maintain minimum health care coverage (see ¶205) (Act Secs. 1302(e)(2) and (3) of PPACA).

To fall within the exception, the catastrophic plan must be designed so that it provides the essential health benefits listed above, but provides no benefits for any plan year until the individual's share of the cost has matched the out-of-pocket limits for HSAs (excluding coverage for preventive health services). In addition, coverage must be provided for at least three primary care visits (Act Sec. 1302(e)(1) of PPACA).

If an insurer offers a qualified health plan through an Exchange at a given level of coverage (e.g., bronze, silver, gold, or platinum), it must also offer that plan, with the given level of coverage, as a plan in which all enrollees are individuals under the age of 21 (as of the beginning of the plan year). These child-only plans are treated as qualified health plans (Act Sec. 1302(f) of PPACA).

Treatment of payments to federally-qualified health centers. If an enrollee of a qualified health plan is provided services or items from a federally-qualified health center (FQHC), then the entity providing the plan must pay the FQHC at least the amount it would have received from Medicare or Medicaid for providing the item or service (Act Sec. 1302(g) of PPACA).

   Comment: According to CMS, FQHCs include providers such as community health centers, public housing centers, and outpatient health programs

NEW LAW EXPLAINED

funded by the Indian Health Service ("Fact Sheet: Federally Qualified Health Center," http://www.cms.hhs.gov).

▶ **Effective date.** No specific effective date is provided by the Act. The provision is, therefore, considered effective on March 23, 2010, the date of enactment.

— Act Sec. 1302 of the Patient Protection and Affordable Care Act (PPACA) (P.L. 111-148), providing general requirements for the essential health benefits package

»»→ Caution: The explanation below reflects certain nontax provisions of the Patient Protection and Affordable Care Act (P.L. 111-148) and the Health Care and Education Reconciliation Act of 2010 (P.L. 111-152). While the issues discussed do not have a direct effect on federal taxes, this explanation is helpful in understanding several tax-related explanations that appear in preceding chapters of this publication.

¶535 Grandfathered Plans in the Individual and Group Health Markets

SUMMARY OF NEW LAW

Individuals may keep their individual and group health plans that were in effect upon enactment of the Patient Protection and Affordable Care Act (PPACA) (P.L. 111-148), and these plans are exempt from many of the individual and group market reforms that take effect in 2014.

BACKGROUND

Federal regulation of the private health insurance market has been narrow in scope and applicable mostly to employer-sponsored health insurance. Existing regulations include a variety of standards under the Internal Revenue Code and the Employee Retirement Income Security Act (ERISA) of 1974. Similar standards for State and local government health care plans exist under the Public Health Service Act. These standards include the following:

- COBRA Continuation of Coverage (Code Sec. 4980B, ERISA Secs. 601 through 608, PHSA Secs. 2201-2207);

- Health Insurance Portability and Accountability Act (HIPAA) Portability, Access, and Renewability Provisions (Code Secs. 9801 through 9803, ERISA Secs. 701 through 706, PHSA Secs. 2701-2702, 2711-2713, 2721-23); and

- Mental Health Parity Act (Code Sec. 9812, ERISA Sec. 712, PHSA Sec. 2705).

Beyond these standards, regulation of the private health insurance market previously has been primarily done at the State level. State regulatory authority is broad in scope

BACKGROUND

and includes requirements related to the issuance and renewal of coverage, benefits, rating, consumer protections, and other issues.

NEW LAW EXPLAINED

Certain individual and group health plans grandfathered.—Individuals who are enrolled in a group health plan or individual health coverage on March 23, 2010, the date of enactment of the Patient Protection and Affordable Care Act (PPACA) (P.L. 111-148) may not be required to terminate that coverage (Act. Sec. 1251(a)(1) of PPACA). Any group health plan or health insurance coverage to which this provision applies is considered a "grandfathered health plan."

A "grandfathered health plan" is generally not subject to the provisions of the Patient Protection Act amending the Public Health Service Act (Act Sec. 1251(a) of the PPACA). However, grandfathered plans are subject to the following provisions (Act. Sec 1251(a)(4) of PPACA, as added by Act Sec. 2301 of the Health Care and Education Reconciliation Act of 2010 (P.L. 111-152)):

- PHSA Sec. 2708, relating to excessive waiting periods (effective for plan years beginning on or after January 1, 2014);

- PHSA Sec. 2711 relating to lifetime limits (effective for plan years beginning on or after September 23, 2010, the date that is six months after the date of enactment of PPACA);

- PHSA Sec. 2712, relating to rescissions (effective for plan years beginning on or after September 23, 2010, the date that is six months after the date of enactment of PPACA);

- PHSA Sec. 2714, relating to extension of dependent coverage (effective for plan years beginning on or after September 23, 2010, the date that is six months after the date of enactment of PPACA).

- PHSA Sec. 2711 relating to annual limits (effective for plan years beginning on or after September 23, 2010, the date that is six months after the date of enactment of PPACA);

- PHSA Sec. 2704, relating to pre-existing condition exclusions (effective for plan years beginning on or after January 1, 2014);

- PHSA Sec. 2714, relating to extension of dependent coverage in a grandfathered group health plan, but only if the dependent is not eligible to enroll in an eligible employer-sponsored health plan (effective for plan years beginning before January 1, 2014).

NEW LAW EXPLAINED

Grandfathered plans also must comply with these reform provisions for plan years beginning on or after March 23, 2010 (Act Sec. 1251(a)(3) of PPACA, as amended by Act Sec. 10103(d)):

- requirements to provide uniform explanations of coverage and standardized definitions (Act. Sec. 1001 of PPACA, adding PHSA Sec. 2715); and
- requirements to provide loss-ratio reports and rebate premiums if loss ratios fall below 80 percent (Act. Sec. 1001 of PPACA, adding PHSA Sec. 2718).

Family members, new employees. As long as the terms of the group plan or insurance coverage allow it, family members of an individual may enroll in a grandfathered plan in which that individual is enrolled (Act Sec. 1251(b) of PPACA). This rule applies if the individual was enrolled in the grandfathered plan on the date of enactment and the coverage is later renewed. A grandfathered group health plan may provide for the enrollment of new employees and their families (Act Sec. 1251(c) of PPACA).

> **Comment:** Although the law does not require individuals to terminate their existing coverages, the law also does not prevent a group health plan or insurance coverage from changing those grandfathered plans. Thus, whether an individual can maintain her existing coverage will depend in large part on whether the plan sponsor or insurer continues to provide that type of grandfathered plan.

Collective Bargaining Agreements. Group health coverage that was subject to a collective bargaining agreement ratified before the enactment of the Patient Protection Act is not covered by the Act's market reforms until the collective bargaining agreement terminates (Act Sec. 1251(d) of PPACA). A collective bargaining agreement that is modified to conform to any of these provisions will be considered to remain in effect and will not be treated as being terminated.

▶ **Effective date.** This provision is effective for plan years beginning on or after January 1, 2014 (Act Sec. 1253 of Patient Protection and Affordable Care Act (PPACA) (P.L. 111-148)).

— Act Secs. 1251 and 10103(d) of the Patient Protection and Affordable Care Act (PPACA) (P.L. 111-148);

— Act Sec. 2301 of the Health Care and Education Reconciliation Act (P.L. 111-152), amending Act. Sec 1251(a) of PPACA;

— Act Sec. 1253, providing the effective date.

>>>→ *Caution: The explanation below reflects certain nontax provisions of the Patient Protection and Affordable Care Act (P.L. 111-148) and the Health Care and Education Reconciliation Act of 2010 (P.L. 111-152). While the issues discussed do not have a direct effect on federal taxes, this explanation is helpful in understanding several tax-related explanations that appear in preceding chapters of this publication.*

¶540 Nonprofit Health Insurance Issuers ("CO-OP Program")

SUMMARY OF NEW LAW

The Secretary of Health and Human Services must establish a Consumer Operated and Oriented Plan (the "CO-OP" program) under which grants and loans may be made to assist in the creation (or expansion) of qualified nonprofit health insurance issuers. These issuers will offer qualified health plans in the individual and small group markets of Health Insurance Exchanges. The Secretary must, by July 1, 2013, award and begin the distribution of six billion dollars appropriated to fund the grants and loans.

BACKGROUND

A premise underlying the health care reform debate is the perception that private, for-profit insurers have not succeeded in providing sufficiently broad access to health insurance at affordable prices. Thus, one aspect of the debate has centered on the search for an organizational model that would serve as an alternative to private insurance. The hotly-debated "public option" is one example of such an alternative. Another is the not-for-profit health insurance cooperative, which received significant attention in Congress during the health care debate as a less-controversial alternative to the public option. Not-for-profit cooperatives have existed for years to produce a variety of goods and services. Cooperatives exist in some states to provide electricity to rural areas. Health insurance cooperatives have also existed for years. Current examples include HealthPartners in Minnesota (www.healthpartners.com) and the Group Health Cooperative (http://www.ghc.org) based in Seattle, Washington.

NEW LAW EXPLAINED

CO-OP Program must be established to provide start-up funds for eligible nonqualified health insurance cooperatives.—The Secretary of Health and Human Services (HHS) is required to establish a Consumer Operated and Oriented Plan (the "CO-OP" program) under which grants and loans may be made to assist in the creation (or expansion) of qualified nonprofit health insurance issuers. These nonprofits will offer qualified health plans through the American Health Benefit Exchanges and Small Business Health Options Program (SHOP) Exchanges in States in which they are

¶540

NEW LAW EXPLAINED

licensed (Act Sec. 1322(a) of the Patient Protection and Affordable Care Act (PPACA) (P.L. 111-148)). For a discussion of the establishment of the Exchanges, see ¶ 505. If certain conditions are met, the nonprofits will be treated as tax-exempt organizations. For a discussion of the tax-exempt status available to nonprofit health insurance issuers, see ¶ 435.

Establishment of program. As part of the CO-OP program, certain grants and loans are authorized to assist entities with their start-up costs, and help them comply with State solvency requirements (Act Sec. 1322(b)(1) of PPACA). In awarding the grants and loans, the Secretary must adhere to certain guidelines (Act Sec. 1322(b)(2)(A) of PPACA).

- CO-OP Advisory Board—The Secretary must take into account the recommendations of a CO-OP Advisory Board (described below).

- Priority applicants—Although the Secretary generally has discretion in the awarding of grants and loans, priority must be given to nonprofit issuers that operate on a Statewide basis, use an integrated delivery system, or have significant support from the private sector.

- Nonprofit representation in every State—The Secretary of Health and Human Services (HHS) must ensure that funding is available to establish at least one qualified nonprofit issuer in each State (additional issuers may be established in any State given sufficient funding). If one or more States are left without a nonprofit issuer, the Secretary may use funds to either encourage the establishment of a nonprofit issuer in a such a State, or to expand the reach of a nonprofit issuer established in another State (Act Sec. 1322(b)(2)(B) of PPACA).

In addition, the HHS Secretary must require each nonprofit issuer receiving a grant or loan to agree to do the following (Act Sec. 1322(b)(2)(C) of PPACA):

- satisfy the requirements for qualified nonprofit health insurance issuers, as well as other provisions of the agreement with the Secretary; and

- refrain from using the grants or loans to fund legislative lobbying or other marketing efforts.

Nonprofits that violate these requirements and fail to correct their errors within a reasonable period must repay to the Secretary 110 percent of the aggregate amount of the grants or loans (plus interest). In addition, the Secretary must notify the Treasury Secretary of any violation that results in the termination of the nonprofit issuer's tax-exempt status (Act Sec. 1322(b)(2)(C)(iii) of PPACA).

Establishment of program: Limits on Secretary. The Secretary's power to engage in certain activities is expressly limited. The Secretary is prohibited from participating in negotiations between nonprofit issuers and health care facilities or providers, or establishing or maintaining prices for reimbursement of any benefits covered by the issuers. In addition, the Secretary may not "interfere" with competition with respect to the nonprofit issuers (Act Sec. 1322(f) of PPACA).

¶540

NEW LAW EXPLAINED

Procedures for award and repayment of grants and loans. The Secretary may award up to $6 billion to nonprofit issuers under the CO-OP program (Act Sec. 1322(g) of PPACA). The award and distribution of the grants and loans must begin no later than July 1, 2013 (Act Sec. 1322(b)(2)(D) of PPACA). In addition, no later than July 1, 2013, but before awarding any grants or loans, the Secretary must issue regulations providing for the repayment of the funds, taking into account State solvency regulations and other related issues. Loans must be repaid within five years, while grants must be repaid within 15 years (Act Sec. 1322(b)(3) of PPACA, as added by Act Sec. 10104(l) of PPACA).

Advisory Board. No later than June 23, 2010 (three months after the date of enactment of the Patient Protection Act), the Comptroller General must appoint 15 individuals to serve as members of a temporary CO-OP program advisory board (Act Sec. 1322(b)(4) of PPACA). The purpose of the board is to make recommendations to the Secretary regarding those applying for the receipt of the grants and loans. Members of the board serve without pay but are entitled to travel expenses.

Those appointed must meet qualifications set forth in Social Security Act Sec. 1805(c)(2). Specifically, appointees must include, among others, individuals with national recognition for their expertise in health finance and economics, actuarial science, health facility management, health plans and integrated delivery systems and other related fields. Appointees must be selected so that different professions and geographic regions (including both urban and rural) are represented on the board. Board members must also meet ethical standards that guard against insurance industry interference. The Board is also governed by the provisions of the Federal Advisory Committee Act, which is intended to ensure that advice offered by such committees is objective and available to the public.

The Advisory Board will terminate on the earlier of the date it completes its duties or December 15, 2015.

Definition of qualified nonprofit health insurance issuer. Only qualified nonprofit health insurance issuers are eligible for grants and loans under the CO-OP program. Such issuers must meet the following requirements (Act Sec. 1322(c) of PPACA).

- Nonprofit, member organization—The issuer must be structured under State law as a nonprofit, member corporation engaged in the issuance of qualified health plans through the individual and/or small business Exchanges in each State in which it is licensed (Act Sec. 1322(c)(1) of PPACA).

- Recently-created organization—An issuer may not have offered insurance on or before July 16, 2009, and it may not be an affiliate of or successor to such an insurance company (Act Sec. 1322(c)(2)(A) of PPACA). In addition, a nonprofit issuer may not begin operation in a given State until that State has in effect the market reforms required by the Act (Act Sec. 1322(c)(6) of PPACA).

- No State sponsorship—The issuer may not be sponsored by a State or local government (Act Sec. 1322(c)(2)(B) of PPACA).

NEW LAW EXPLAINED

- Governance requirements—The issuer's governing documents must incorporate conflict of interest and other ethical standards designed to protect against the "involvement and interference" of the insurance industry. In addition, decisions regarding the governance of the issuer must be subject to a majority vote of its members. In accordance with guidance to be issued by the Secretary, the issuer must operate with a "strong consumer focus" (Act Sec. 1322(c)(3) of PPACA).

- Use of profits—Any profits made by the issuer must be funneled back into the issuer's operations, either to lower premiums or to improve the quality of health care delivered to its members (Act Sec. 1322(c)(4) of PPACA).

- State insurance requirements—An issuer must comply with all State laws that other issuers of qualified health plans must follow, including solvency and licensure requirements (Act Sec. 1322(c)(5) of PPACA).

Private purchasing councils. Qualified nonprofit health insurance issuers participating in the CO-OP program may establish a "private purchasing council." Participants in a purchasing council may enter into collective purchasing agreements that may offer administrative efficiencies and cost savings. Claims administration, health information technology and actuarial services are examples of the types of items and services that may be obtained by the purchasing council (Act Sec. 1322(d)(1) of PPACA).

> **Comment:** Note that the purchasing council may not set payment rates for health care providers (Act Sec. 1322(d)(2) of PPACA). In addition, a purchasing council is governed by the federal antitrust laws (Act Sec. 1322(d)(3) of PPACA).

> **Comment:** Representatives of any branch of government, or of an established insurance company, are prohibited from serving on the board of directors of a nonprofit issuer or with a private purchasing council (Act Sec. 1322(e) of PPACA).

GAO study. The GAO must conduct an ongoing study on the effect on competition, including market concentration, of the changes made by the Act, including an analysis of new health insurance issuers. The GAO must then report to Congress on the results of the study, beginning no later than December 31, 2014, and continuing in each even-numbered year thereafter. Recommendations for any changes needed to increase competition in the health insurance market should be included (Act Sec. 1322(i) of PPACA).

▶ **Effective date.** No specific effective date is provided by the Act. The provision is, therefore, considered effective on March 23, 2010, the date of enactment.

— Act Sec. 1322 of the Patient Protection and Affordable Care Act (PPACA) (P.L. 111-148), providing for the establishment of the program;

¶540

>>→ *Caution: The explanation below reflects certain nontax provisions of the Patient Protection and Affordable Care Act (P.L. 111-148) and the Health Care and Education Reconciliation Act of 2010 (P.L. 111-152). While the issues discussed do not have a direct effect on federal taxes, this explanation is helpful in understanding several tax-related explanations that appear in preceding chapters of this publication.*

¶545 Multi-State Plans

SUMMARY OF NEW LAW

At least two multi-state qualified health plans must be available as part of the Health Insurance Exchange in each State. The multi-state plans will provide coverage in the individual and small employer markets. The Director of the Office of Personnel Management will enter into contracts with private insurers to offer the multi-state plans.

BACKGROUND

By January 1, 2014, each State must establish an American Health Benefit Exchange and Small Business Health Options Program (SHOP Exchange) to provide qualified individuals and qualified small business employers access to qualified health plans. For a discussion of the establishment and requirements of the Exchanges, see ¶505. Under these Exchanges, individuals and small businesses with 100 or fewer employees can purchase qualified coverage, though, eventually, states may allow businesses with more than 100 employees to purchase coverage in the SHOP Exchange. States may form regional Exchanges or allow more than one Exchange to operate in a State as long as each Exchange serves a distinct geographic area.

NEW LAW EXPLAINED

Multi-State plan option must be provided as part of State Exchanges.—At least two multi-state qualified health plans must be available as part of the American Health Benefit Exchange and Small Business Health Options Program (SHOP) Exchanges established in each State. For a discussion of the establishment of the Exchanges, see ¶ 505. The Director of the Office of Personnel Management will enter into contracts with private insurers to offer the multi-state plans. The multi-state plans will provide coverage in the individual and small employer markets (Act Sec. 1334(a)(1) of the Patient Protection and Affordable Care Act (PPACA) (P.L. 111-148), as added by Act Sec. 10104(q)). At least one multi-state plan offered within each Exchange must be offered by a non-profit entity (Act Sec. 1334(a)(3) of PPACA, as added by Act Sec. 10104(q)).

OPM powers and duties. The Director has the following powers and duties with respect to the establishment of multi-state plans.

NEW LAW EXPLAINED

- Contract terms—The Director may enter into contracts with health insurance issuers without regard to federal competitive bidding statutes (Act Sec. 1334(a)(1) of PPACA, as added by Act Sec. 10104(q)). Each contract must be for a uniform term of at least one year and may be automatically renewable. The Director must ensure that health benefits coverage is provided in accordance with the rules under the Public Health Service Act regarding preexisting condition exclusions (Act Sec. 1334(a)(2) of PPACA, as added by Act Sec. 10104(q)).

- Administration—The Director must administer such contracts in a manner similar to the Director's administration of contracts with carriers under the Federal Employees Health Benefit Program ("FEHBP"). This includes negotiating with each multi-state plan regarding the plan's medical loss ratio, profit margin, premiums and other similar terms and conditions (Act Sec. 1334(a)(4) of PPACA, as added by Act Sec. 10104(q)). The Director may prohibit the offering of any multi-state health plan that does not meet such terms and conditions (Act Sec. 1334(a)(5) of PPACA, as added by Act Sec. 10104(q)).

- Treatment of abortion services—The Director must ensure that at least one multi-state plan offered in each State Exchange does not provide coverage for abortion services for which public funding is prohibited (Act Sec. 1334(a)(6) of PPACA, as added by Act Sec. 10104(q)).

- Contract disputes—The Director may not withdraw approval of a multi-state plan contract without notice to the issuer and an opportunity for a hearing (Act Sec. 1334(a)(7) of PPACA, as added by Act Sec. 10104(q)).

Certification and eligibility of multi-state plans. Generally, a qualified multi-state health plan is deemed to meet the certification requirements for participation in the Exchanges (Act Sec. 1334(d) of PPACA, as added by Act Sec. 10104(q)). For a discussion of the certification process, see ¶ 505. In order to issue a multi-state plan, a health insurance issuer must agree to meet the requirements for multi-state qualified plans, and must be properly licensed in each State (so long as State standards and requirements do not conflict with the Patient Protection Act or the provisions of part A of Title XXVII of the Public Health Service Act). The issuer must also meet the minimum standards for offering Federal Employees Health Benefit Plans (FEHBPs). The Director may establish other requirements in consultation with the Secretary of Health and Human Services (Act Sec. 1334(b) of PPACA, as added by Act Sec. 10104(q)).

> **Comment:** The Director may contract with multi-state plans that are not yet operational in all 50 States so long as the following phase-in schedule is followed. In the first year in which the plan is offered, the issuer must offer the plan in 60 percent of the States, with the required percentage increasing to 70 percent in the second year; 85 percent in the third year; and 100 percent in the fourth year (Act Sec. 1334(e) of PPACA, as added by Act Sec. 10104(q)).

Requirements for multi-state qualified plans. Multi-State qualified plans must meet the following requirements (Act Sec. 1334(c)(1) of PPACA, as added by Act Sec. 10104(q)):

NEW LAW EXPLAINED

- Essential benefits—The plan must offer in each State a uniform benefits package that meets the essential benefits requirements (see ¶530).

- Levels of coverage—The plan must offer the varied levels of coverage (e.g., bronze, silver, etc.) and meet all other requirements of qualified health plans under the Patient Protection Act (see ¶530).

- Rating requirements—Generally, the plan must comply with the rating requirements set forth in part A of Title XXVII of the PHSA. However, if a State maintains an age rating requirement that is lower than 3:1, the plan must comply with the State's more protective age rating requirement before it may be offered in the State (Act Sec. 1334(c)(5) of PPACA, as added by Act Sec. 10104(q)).

- Community rating—The issuer must offer the plan in all geographic regions and in all States adopting adjusted community ratings prior to March 23, 2010, the date of enactment of the Patient Protection Act.

Additional benefits offered by States. States may require that benefits in addition to those required as essential benefits be offered to enrollees by a multi-state plan (Act Sec. 1334(c)(2) of PPACA, as added by Act Sec. 10104(q) of PPACA). Such a State must assume the cost of any such additional benefits by making payments either to the individual enrollees or directly to the multi-state plan on behalf of such enrollees (Act Sec. 1334(c)(4) of PPACA, as added by Act Sec. 10104(q)).

Enrollee eligibility for tax credit. Individuals enrolled in a multi-state qualified plan are eligible for both premium assistance tax credit and cost sharing reduction assistance (Act Sec. 1334(c)(3) of PPACA, as added by Act Sec. 10104(q) of PPACA). The amount of the tax credit is not affected by a State decision to offer additional benefits. For a discussion of the premium assistance tax credit, see ¶210. For a discussion of the cost sharing reduction assistance, see ¶520.

Relationship to FEHBP. The multi-state plan option is modeled to some extent on the existing Federal Employees Health Benefit Plan. Thus, the requirements governing FEHBPs also apply to multi-state qualified health plans, so long as they do not conflict with the requirements of the Patient Protection Act (Act Sec. 1334(f) of PPACA, as added by Act Sec. 10104(q) of PPACA). However, the Director must take specific steps to ensure that implementation of the multi-state health plan does not interfere with the FEHBP.

Accordingly, the Director may not allocate fewer resources to the administration of the FEHBP, and may establish separate units within the OPM to administer the multi-state plans. Enrollees in the multi-state health plan must be treated as a separate risk pool. Carriers participating in the FEHBP are not required to offer a multi-state qualified health plan. Finally, premiums paid for coverage under a multi-state qualified health plan may not be considered to be federal funds (Act Sec. 1334(g) of PPACA, as added by Act Sec. 10104(q) of PPACA).

OPM to establish Advisory Board. The Director must establish an advisory board to provide recommendations relating to the implementation of the multi-state plans. A "significant percentage" of board members must be either enrollees in the multi-state plans or their representatives (Act Sec. 1334(h) of PPACA, as added by Act Sec. 10104(q) of PPACA).

NEW LAW EXPLAINED

Appropriations. Funds are authorized to be appropriated to implement this section (Act Sec. 1334(i) of PPACA, as added by Act Sec. 10104(q)).

▶ **Effective date.** No specific effective date is provided by the Act. The provision is, therefore, considered effective on March 23, 2010, the date of enactment.

— Act Sec. 1334 of the Patient Protection and Affordable Care Act (PPACA) (P.L. 111-148), as added by Act Sec. 10104(q).

HIRE: Businesses and Individuals 6

¶605 Employer's Payroll Tax Holiday and Retention Credit

SUMMARY OF NEW LAW

For the remainder of 2010, employers do not have to pay their share of OASDI or railroad retirement taxes for newly hired workers who were formerly unemployed. Employers can also claim a credit of up to $1,000 for retaining each of these new workers for at least one year.

BACKGROUND

Two parallel tax systems fund retirement and disability benefits for most workers: the Federal Insurance Contributions Act (FICA, Code Secs. 3101 - 3128) and the Railroad Retirement Tax Act (RRTA, Code Secs. 3201 - 3241). The effect on employers is virtually identical under both systems, but they are structured somewhat differently.

FICA imposes two taxes on most employers and employees:

- old-age, survivors and disability insurance (OASDI) taxes to fund social security benefits (Code Sec. 3111(a)), and

- hospital insurance (HI) taxes to fund medical benefits (Code Sec. 3111(b)).

FICA taxes total 15.3 percent of most wages paid for covered employment, with the employer paying one-half and the employee paying one-half; thus, the employer and the employee each pay FICA tax equal to 7.65 percent of the employee's covered

BACKGROUND

wages. An employer under FICA is the person for whom an individual performs any service as an employee (Code Sec. 3401(d)). FICA taxes are not progressive. They are imposed at a flat rate generally beginning with the first dollar an employee earns, and the OASDI tax does not apply to wages that exceed an inflation-adjusted ceiling. Thus, during 2010:

- the employer pays OASDI tax equal to 6.2 percent of an employee's taxable wages up to $106,800 (Code Sec. 3111(a); Notice 2009-80), and

- the employer pays HI tax equal to 1.45 percent of all of the employee's total taxable wages (Code Sec. 3111(b)).

Covered employment comprises most forms of employment, except for:

- Americans who work outside the United States for non-American employers (Code Sec. 3121(b));

- foreign temporary agricultural workers (Code Sec. 3121(b)(1));

- compensation for certain services performed for the worker's own parent or child (Code Sec. 3121(b)(3));

- particular types of federal workers and office-holders (Code Sec. 3121(b)(5) and (6));

- most state and city workers who are not covered by retirement systems (Code Sec. 3121(b)(7)):

- some religious workers (Code Sec. 3121(b)(8));

- certain students who work for schools and hospitals (Code Sec. 3121(b)(10) and (13));

- workers for foreign governments and international organizations (Code Sec. 3121(b)(11) and (15));

- sharecroppers (Code Sec. 3121(b)(16));

- fishing boat crew members who are compensated only by a portion of the catch (Code Sec. 3121(b)(20)); and

- domestic services performed by persons under the age of 18 (Code Sec. 3121(b)(21)).

In addition, FICA taxes apply only to compensation above certain thresholds for childcare, domestic services and casual labor (Code Sec. 3121(a)(7)); agricultural labor (Code Sec. 3121(a)(8)); home workers (Code Sec. 3121(a)(10)); and workers for tax-exempt organizations (Code Sec. 3121(a)(16)). Reported cash tips of less than $20 per month are also exempt from FICA (Code Sec. 3121(a)(12)(B)).

Employers must deposit FICA taxes on a monthly or semiweekly basis, depending on the employer's prior deposit history (Reg. § 31.6302-1). Employers who fail to comply with FICA reporting, remittance and record-keeping requirements can be liable for interest, additional taxes and penalties (Code Secs. 6601, 6651, 6656, 6657, 6662, 6672 and 6701).

RRTA replaces the social security system for railroad workers. RRTA taxes are divided into two tiers. The first tier is based on combined railroad retirement and

BACKGROUND

social security credits, using social security benefit formulas. The second tier is based on railroad service only and is comparable to the pensions paid over and above social security benefits in other heavy industries. The employer's Tier 1 tax on compensation paid to employees is equal to the amount the employer would pay under FICA (that is, 7.65 percent of the employee's covered compensation) (Code Sec. 3221(a)).

An RRTA employer is a railroad carrier or any company that (i) is directly or indirectly owned or controlled by or under common control with a railroad carrier, and (ii) operates any equipment or facility or performs any service (except trucking service, casual service, and the casual operation of equipment or facilities) in connection with the transportation of passengers or property by railroad, or the receipt, delivery, elevation, transfer in transit, refrigeration or icing, storage, or handling of property transported by railroad. Employers do not include street, interurban or electric railways that are not operated as part of a general steam-railroad system of transportation; or companies engaged in mining coal, supplying coal to an employer if delivery is not beyond the mine tipple, and operating equipment or facilities in these activities (Code Sec. 3231(a); Reg. §31.3231(a)-1). Employees under RRTA include any individual who is in the service of one or more employers, including as an officer of an employer (Code Sec. 3231(b); Reg. §31.3231(b)-1).

Taxable wages under FICA, and *taxable compensation* under RRTA, comprise all current compensation paid to an employee by the employer for covered employment, including tips and gratuities; commissions that are part of compensation; bonuses; gifts from employers to employees; most awards and prizes; reimbursements of employee business expenses under nonaccountable plans; standby pay; back pay awards; dismissal pay; supplemental unemployment benefits; employee FICA taxes paid by the employer; dividends recharacterized as compensation; and the cash value of all remuneration paid in any medium other than cash. Taxable wages do not include some employee achievement awards; reimbursements of employee business expenses under accountable plans; reimbursements of moving expenses that the employer reasonably believes are deductible by the employee; scholarships and fellowships; most employer contributions to health savings accounts (HSAs) and Archer medical savings accounts (MSAs); and dividends paid to an employee stock option plan (ESOP) (Code Secs. 3401(a), 3121(a), 3231(e) and 3306(b)).

Work opportunity credit. Employers may claim a work opportunity credit for employees who are members of several targeted groups, such as unemployed veterans, people with disabilities, residents of disadvantaged communities, and recipients of particular government benefits (Code Sec. 51). A qualified employee must be certified as eligible for the credit by a state employment security agency (Code Sec. 51(d)(13)), and must work at least 120 hours for the employer claiming the credit (Code Sec. 51(i)(3)(B)). The credit is generally equal to 40 percent of the employee's first-year wages up to $6,000, for a maximum credit of $2,400 (Code Sec. 51(b)). The maximum credit is reduced for summer youth employees (Code Sec. 51(d)(7)(B)) and employees who work for fewer than 400 hours (Code Sec. 51(i)(3)(A)); and it is increased for qualified veterans with service-connected disabilities (Code Sec. 51(b)(3)) and long-term family aid recipients (Code Sec. 51(e)). Employers must reduce their deduction for wage or salary expenses paid during the tax year by the full amount allowable as

BACKGROUND

a work opportunity credit (Code Sec. 280C(a)). An employer may elect not to claim the work opportunity credit (Code Sec. 51(j)).

An employer cannot claim the credit for employing *related individuals*, such as:

- individuals who are related to the employer, to a shareholder who owns more than 50 percent of a corporate employer's stock, or to an individual who owns more than 50 percent of the capital and profit interests in a noncorporate employer;

- individuals who are dependents of the employer, or of a 50-percent shareholder in a corporate employer; and

- individuals who are grantors, beneficiaries or fiduciaries (or dependents of grantors, beneficiaries or fiduciaries) of an employer that is an estate or trust (Code Sec. 51(i)(1)).

Related persons are the employer's (or shareholder's or owner's) children and their descendants (that is, grandchildren, great-grandchildren, etc.); siblings and their descendants (that is, brothers, sisters, nieces and nephews); parents and ancestors (that is, grandparents, great-grandparents, etc.); stepchildren, stepparents and stepsiblings; in-laws; spouse; and household members (Reg. § 1.51-1(e)).

General business credit. The work opportunity credit is one of several credits that is combined into the general business credit (Code Sec. 38). A taxpayer's current year business credit is the sum of its current year general business credits, plus business credit carryforwards and carrybacks (Code Sec. 38(a)). The credit is generally limited to the taxpayer's net income tax over the greater of its tentative minimum tax, or 25 percent of the taxpayer's net regular tax liability in excess of $25,000 (Code Sec. 38(c)). The excess business credit generally must be carried back one year, and then can be carried forward for 20 years (Code Sec. 39(a)(1)).

NEW LAW EXPLAINED

Employers get a payroll tax holiday for hiring unemployed workers, and a tax credit for retaining them.—A qualified employer is provided an exemption from having to pay its share of old-age, survivors and disability insurance (OASDI) taxes for a qualified individual's employment from the day after March 18, 2010 through December 31, 2010 (Code Sec. 3111(d), as added by Hiring Incentives to Restore Employment (HIRE) Act (P.L. 111-147)). Similarly, a qualified railroad employer is provided an exemption from having to pay its share of Railroad Retirement Tax Act (RRTA) Tier 1 taxes for a qualified individual's employment from the day after March 18, 2010, through December 31, 2010 (Code Sec. 3221(c), as added by the 2010 HIRE Act). In both cases, the employer can also claim a credit of up to $1,000 for retaining a newly hired worker for at least 52 consecutive weeks (Act Sec. 102 of the 2010 HIRE Act).

Generally, a *qualified employer* eligible for the exemption is any employer other than the United States, any State, any local government, or any instrumentality of the preceding. However, a qualified employer will include any public higher education institution (Code Secs. 3111(d)(2) and 3221(c)(2), as added by the 2010 HIRE Act).

¶605

NEW LAW EXPLAINED

A *qualified individual* is any individual who:

- begins employment with a qualified employer after February 3, 2010, and before January 1, 2011;
- certifies, by signed affidavit under penalties of perjury, that they have not been employed for more than 40 hours during the 60-day period ending on the date the employment with the qualified employer begins;
- is not hired to replace another employee of the qualified employer, unless the other employee voluntarily quit or was fired with cause; and
- is not related to the employer in a way that would make him or her ineligible for the work opportunity credit (Code Secs. 3111(d)(3) and 3221(c)(3), as added by the 2010 HIRE Act).

> **Comment:** According to the Joint Committee on Taxation, it is intended that the third requirement above will be satisfied when a qualified employer hires an otherwise qualified individual to replace an individual whose employment was terminated for cause or due to other facts and circumstances. For example, an employer that reopens a factory that was closed due to lack of demand may rehire qualified individuals who had worked for the employer but were terminated when the factory was closed. In contrast, an employer who terminates the employment of an individual not for cause, but in order to take advantage of these incentives, is not eligible for the payroll tax holiday or the retention credit (Joint Committee on Taxation, Technical Explanation of the Hiring Incentives to Restore Employment Act (JCX-4-10)).

> **Compliance Tip:** The IRS is developing a form that employees can use to certify that they have not been employed for more than 40 hours during the 60 days before their hiring date (IRS News Release IR-2010-33, March 18, 2010).

Payroll tax forgiveness. The waiver of the employer's share of OASDI or RRTA tax applies automatically if the qualified employer pays the qualified individual wages (under FICA) or compensation (under RRTA) for services performed in the employer's trade or business (or, if the employer is a tax-exempt organization, in furtherance of activities related to its exempt purpose) (Code Secs. 3111(d)(1) and 3221(c)(1), as added by the 2010 HIRE Act). A qualified employer that does not want to use the payroll tax holiday must elect out of the waiver, under procedures to be provided by the Secretary of the Treasury and the IRS (Code Secs. 3111(d)(4) and 3221(c)(4), as added by the 2010 HIRE Act). A qualified employer who fails to elect out of the payroll tax forgiveness cannot claim the work opportunity credit with respect to a qualified individual for one year after that individual's hire date (Code Sec. 51(c)(5), as added by the 2010 HIRE Act).

> **Caution:** The first date on which a qualified individual can begin employment (February 4, 2010) is earlier than the date on which the payroll tax holiday becomes effective (March 18, 2010).

> **Comment:** The payroll tax holiday will not affect the worker's future social security or RRTA benefits, because additional appropriations to the social security and RRTA trust funds will replace the lost OASDI and RRTA taxes (Act Secs. 101(c) and (d)(2) of the 2010 HIRE Act; IRS News Release IR-2010-33, March 18, 2010).

NEW LAW EXPLAINED

Technically, the waiver does not apply during the first quarter of 2010. Instead, the amount of OASDI or RRTA taxes that would have been waived during the first quarter is treated as a payment of the employer's payroll taxes for the second calendar quarter of 2010, made on the date those payroll taxes are due (Code Secs. 3111(d)(5) and 3221(c)(5), as added by the 2010 HIRE Act).

> **Comment:** Presumably, this provision recognizes that independent payroll processors and computerized payroll software will not have time to incorporate the payroll tax holiday into calculations of payroll tax liabilities for the first quarter of 2010.

> **Compliance Tip:** Employers must still withhold and pay over the employee's share of OASDI or RRTA Tier 1 taxes, as well as the employer's and employee's share of health insurance (HI) taxes (IRS News Release IR-2010-33, March 18, 2010).

Retention credit. For each retained worker, a qualified employer's general business credit is increased by the lesser of:

- $1,000, or
- 6.2 percent of the retained worker's wages during a 52-week consecutive period (Act Sec. 102(a) of the 2010 HIRE Act).

> **Comment:** This means that the credit for any worker paid more than $16,130 per year is $1,000. Annual compensation of $16,130 amounts to about $7.75 per hour for a full-time employee, slightly more than the current federal minimum wage of $7.25 per hour.

A retained worker is a qualified individual (as defined above) who:

- was employed by the qualified employer on any date during a tax year ending after March 18, 2010;
- continued in that employment for a period of at least 52 consecutive weeks; and
- earned wages during the last 26 weeks of that period equal to at least 80 percent of the wages for the first 26 weeks of the period (Act Sec. 102(b) of the 2010 HIRE Act).

The credit applies for the first tax year in which the retained worker satisfies the 52-week test (Act Sec. 102(a)(2) of the 2010 HIRE Act). It cannot be carried back to any tax year beginning before March 18, 2010 (Act Sec. 102(c) of the 2010 HIRE Act).

> **Comment:** It appears that a period of employment that qualifies for the payroll tax holiday also counts toward the 52-week period required for the retention credit. Imagine, for instance, that Acme Corp. hires Brianna, a qualified individual, on April 1, 2010, and she works for Acme until May 15, 2011, earning a total of $18,000 in wages. Acme is entitled to the payroll tax holiday with respect to her wages from April 1 through December 31, 2010; and to a $1,000 retention credit as of April 1, 2011.

> **State Tax Consequences:** Generally, states do not incorporate federal tax credits. Therefore, the business credit for the retention of certain newly hired individ-

NEW LAW EXPLAINED

uals and the credit for certain qualified tax credit bonds, will not impact the states.

U.S. possessions. The retention credit is effectively extended to U.S. possessions which, for this purpose, include the Commonwealth of Puerto Rico and the Commonwealth of the Northern Mariana Islands (Act Sec. 102(d)(3)(A) of the 2010 HIRE Act).

- Payments by Treasury to mirror code possessions.—The U.S. Treasury will pay each mirror code possession an amount equal to that possession's loss caused by the retention credit. The amount is based on information provided by the government of the possession (Act Sec. 102(d)(1)(A) of the 2010 HIRE Act). A mirror code possession is one that determines the income tax liability of its residents by reference to U.S. income tax laws as if the possession were the United States (Act Sec. 102(d)(3)(B) of the 2010 HIRE Act).

- Payments by Treasury to non-mirror code possessions.—The U.S. Treasury will pay each non-mirror code possession an amount estimated to be equal to the aggregate benefits that would have been provided to its residents by reason of the retention credit if the possession had a mirror code tax system. In order to receive payment, the possession must have a plan, approved by the Treasury Secretary, to promptly distribute the payment to its residents (Act Sec. 102(d)(1)(B) of the 2010 HIRE Act).

- Restriction on retention-credit claims against U.S. tax liability.—A taxpayer who is allowed a retention credit against taxes imposed by a possession, or who is eligible for a retention credit-related payment from a non-mirror code possession, cannot claim a retention credit against U.S. income tax liability (Act Sec. 102(d)(2) of the 2010 HIRE Act).

- Treatment of Treasury payments to possessions.—For purposes of the rules permitting the U.S. Treasury to disburse refunds arising from tax credits, payments made under these provisions are treated as refunds due from the retention credit (Act Sec. 102(d)(3)(C) of the 2010 HIRE Act; see Act Sec. 1001(b)(3)(C) of the American Recovery and Reinvestment Tax Act of 2009 (P.L. 111-5)).

    Comment: Mirror code possessions are the United States Virgin Islands, Guam, and the Commonwealth of the Northern Mariana Islands. Non-mirror code possessions are Puerto Rico and American Samoa (Conference Report on P.L. 111-5, American Recovery and Reinvestment Act of 2009, (H. Rept. 111-16)).

    Comment: These same provisions apply to U.S. possessions for purposes of the Code Sec. 6428 recovery credit (which most taxpayers received in the form of rebates during 2008) and the Code Sec. 36A Making Work Pay credit.

    Planning Note: Employers that want to maximize the retention credit must consider several factors. First, the credit applies to part-time workers as well as full-time workers; and to each retained employee, rather than the employer's aggregate payroll costs. Thus, an employer that needs one full-time worker might be better off hiring two (or more) part-time workers instead, in order to multiply its retention credit. This factor is somewhat balanced by the fact that the credit applies only to employees who stay with the employer for at least 52 weeks. Imagine, for instance, that Acme Corp. hires four part-time workers

NEW LAW EXPLAINED

instead of one full-time worker, in the hope of quadrupling its retention credit. If all four of those workers leave Acme over the next year, as better jobs become available with other employers, Acme ends up with no retention credit at all (to say nothing of all the resources wasted in hiring and training the departed employees). On the other hand, as long as at least one employee stays for a year, Acme is no worse off than if it had hired one full-time worker to begin with.

Employers should also consider how they can receive the maximum tax benefit for hiring a worker who qualifies for both the work opportunity credit and these hiring and retention incentives. Since the employer must opt out of the automatic payroll holiday in order to claim the work opportunity credit, these calculations and predictions should be performed before the employee is hired.

- The work opportunity is a tax credit that reduces the employer's tax liability. Thus, it does not provide any tax benefit until the employer files its tax return. Alternatively, the payroll tax holiday offers more immediate tax relief, by reducing the amount of the employer's payroll tax deposits.

- The work opportunity credit is generally calculated as 40 percent of a qualified worker's wages up to $6,000. Thus, for most workers, the maximum credit is $2,400. Savings from the payroll tax holiday are more variable, depending on the qualified individual's wages. For example, assume that the payroll tax forgiveness applies to a particular worker from March through December, or for 10 months. If the worker earns the maximum wages subject to OASDI ($106,800) during those 10 months, the employer saves more than $6,600 in payroll taxes. In contrast, if the worker makes only $10,000 during that period, the employer saves only about $620.

- The work opportunity credit kicks in quickly—a partial credit applies after the employee works 120 hours, and the full credit applies after just 400 hours. Thus, if an employee makes at least $6,000 for 10 weeks of full-time work and is then terminated, the employer can still claim the full $2,400 credit. On the other hand, the retention credit does not apply until the employer has employed the worker for a full 52 weeks. In addition, the payroll tax holiday applies only as long as the qualified individual works for the employer. For example, if a worker makes $6,000 over 10 weeks and is then terminated, the employer's payroll tax savings amount to only about $372, and there is no retention credit.

- The work opportunity credit does not require any consistency in a worker's pay or work schedule. For instance, as long as the worker earns at least $6,000 and works at least 400 hours of work during the first year, the employer is entitled to the $2,400 credit, regardless of how that work and that pay are distributed over the course of the year. In other words, the employer can vary the worker's schedule and pay as much as the worker will tolerate. The retention credit applies only if in the second half of the 52-week period, the worker earns at least 80 percent of what the worker earned during the first half. For instance, if the employer pays the worker $10 per hour for full-time (40 hours per week) work in the first six months, the worker's pay must average $320 per week over the next six months.

NEW LAW EXPLAINED

- To receive the work opportunity credit, the employer must obtain certification from a state employment security agency to show that the employee belongs to a targeted group. The payroll tax holiday and the retention credit requirements are simpler—the employer must simply obtain the worker's own affidavit stating that the worker was unemployed for the requisite period. In addition, the holiday applies automatically, unless the employer elects out of it.

Practical Analysis: Elizabeth Thomas Dold, a Principal at Groom Law Group of Washington, D.C., notes that Form 941 is once again the mechanism for tax relief, only this time it is relief from the employer's portion of the FICA taxes (but not federal unemployment taxes (FUTA)) rather than the COBRA subsidy. A number of important steps must take place in order to be entitled to the relief:

1. Ascertain who is a "qualified employer" who is eligible for the relief. This excludes governmental employers other than a public institution of higher education. What might be difficult is the process where multiple EINs and entities are involved—including parent, subsidiary, payroll agent, common paymaster, *etc.*

2. Ascertain who is a "qualified individual." This includes an individual who (a) performs services for a trade of business or if a tax-exempt business under Code Sec. 501(a) or performs services in furtherance of the activities related to the purpose or function constituting the basis of the employer's exemption; (b) hired on or after February 4, 2010, through December 31, 2010; (c) certifies by signed affidavit, under penalties of perjury, that such individual has not been employed for more than 40 hours during the 60-day period ending on the date such individual begins such employment; (d) is not employed by the qualified employer to replace another employee of such employer unless such other employee separated from employment voluntarily or for cause; and (e) is not a related individual described in Code Sec. 51(i)(1). We understand that the IRS is preparing a sample employee certification for this purpose, but it is unclear (a) if electronic signature will be permissible; (b) what requirements to file or otherwise retain these records; or (c) if it will also include the employer representations (otherwise a separate document should be retained in the files in the event of audit)—unrelated worker, performs services in trade or business or in furtherance of tax-exempt status, not an improper replacement employee, *etc.*

3. Update all payroll systems to track immediately wages paid to "qualified individuals" from "qualified employers" effective March 19, 2010, through year-end. This would include regular and supplemental wages, 401(k) and 403(b) deferrals, *etc.*, up to the social security wage base. (System changes, unfortunately, do not happen overnight and have costs involved with any change.)

4. Take a credit on Form 941/944 for the applicable period or otherwise elect out of the relief (presumably a partial waiver would also be permissible). For the relief for the first quarter, employers will obtain the credit with the second quarter return. Presumably, if the employer has not completed steps 1 through 3 by the quarterly deadlines, it can file Form 941-X (944-X, annual) to obtain the credit through the three-year statute of limitations period. However, this is complicated

NEW LAW EXPLAINED

by the election-out provision, which allows the employer to forgo the payroll holiday in favor of the existing work opportunity credit.

The increased business credit is processed through the employer's tax return (*e.g.*, Form 1120) and not through payroll returns, which is helpful for payroll processers. However, payroll still needs to take steps 1 through 2 above, and track wages to determine who was employed for a period of not less than 52 consecutive weeks, and whose wages for such employment during the last 26 weeks of such period equaled at least 80 percent of such wages for the first 26 weeks of such period. Presumably, this credit is not available to tax-exempt employers.

▶ **Effective date.** The payroll tax forgiveness applies to wages and compensation paid after March 18, 2010 (Act Sec. 101(e) of the Hiring Incentives to Restore Employment (HIRE) Act (P.L. 111-147)). No specific effective date is provided for the retention credit by the Act. The provision is, therefore, effective on March 18, 2010.

Law source: Law at ¶6010, ¶6105, ¶6110, ¶7206 and ¶7209. Committee Report at ¶11,010 and ¶11,020.

— Act Sec. 101(a) of the Hiring Incentives to Restore Employment (HIRE) Act (P.L. 111-147), adding Code Sec. 3111(d);

— Act Sec. 101(b), adding Code Sec. 51(c)(5);

— Act Sec. 101(d), redesignating Code Sec. 3221(c) as Code Sec. 3221(d) and adding new Code Sec. 3221(c);

— Act Sec. 102;

— Act Sec. 101(e), providing the effective date.

Reporter references: For further information, consult the following CCH reporters.

— Standard Federal Tax Reporter, ¶4803 and ¶33,506.021

— Tax Research Consultant, BUSEXP: 54,250 and PAYROLL: 9,050

— Practical Tax Explanation, § 13,805 and § 22,201

¶610 Code Sec. 179 Expense Election for 2010

SUMMARY OF NEW LAW

The increased Code Sec. 179 expense allowance provided for tax years beginning in 2008 and 2009 is extended one additional year. Thus, for the years beginning in 2010, the Code Sec. 179 dollar limitation is $250,000, and the investment limitation is $800,000.

BACKGROUND

An expense deduction is provided for taxpayers (other than estates, trusts or certain noncorporate lessors) who elect to treat the cost of qualifying property, called section 179 property, as an expense rather than a capital expenditure (Code Sec. 179). Section 179 property is depreciable tangible personal property that is purchased for use in the active conduct of a trade or business (Code Sec. 179(d)(1)).

A dollar limit is placed on the maximum amount of section 179 property a taxpayer may expense during the year. For tax years beginning before 2007 and after 2010, the dollar limitation is $25,000. For tax years beginning in 2007 and 2010, the dollar limitation has been increased to $125,000 (Code Sec. 179(b)(1)). The $25,000 and $125,000 figures are adjusted for inflation (Code Sec. 179(b)(5)), and the inflation-adjusted dollar limitation for 2010 is $134,000 (Rev. Proc. 2009-50, I.R.B. 2009-45). For tax years beginning in 2008 and 2009, the annual dollar limitation is increased to $250,000, which amount is not indexed for inflation (Code Sec. 179(b)(7)).

The annual dollar limitation is reduced dollar for dollar by the cost of section 179 property placed in service during the tax year in excess of an investment limitation of $200,000 for tax years beginning before 2007 and after 2010, and $500,000 for tax years beginning in 2007 and 2010. These limits are indexed annually for inflation (Code Sec. 179(b)(5)), and the inflation-adjusted investment limitation for 2010 is $530,000 (Rev. Proc. 2009-50, I.R.B. 2009-45). For tax years beginning in 2008 and 2009, the dollar limitation is $800,000, but is not indexed for inflation (Code Sec. 179(b)(7)).

NEW LAW EXPLAINED

Increased expensing limitations extended to 2010; inflation adjustment eliminated.—The increased Code Sec. 179 expensing limits of $250,000 for the dollar limitation and $800,000 for the investment limitation have been extended to tax years beginning in 2010 (Code Sec. 179(b)(1) and (2), as amended by Act Sec. 201(a)(1) and (2) of the Hiring Incentives to Restore Employment (HIRE) Act (P.L. 111-147)). In addition, the provision in the law which provided that the dollar and investment limitations will be indexed for inflation (other than for 2008 and 2009) has been eliminated (Act Sec. 201(a)(3)).

> **Caution:** Without further legislation, the dollar and investment limitations for tax years that begin in 2011 will be $25,000 and $200,000, respectively, and will not be indexed for inflation going forward.

> **State Tax Consequences:** The extension through 2010 of the Code Sec. 179 $250,000 expense allowance and $800,000 limitation amount will not impact states, including California, Florida, Indiana, New Jersey, and Wisconsin that have decoupled from the federal expensing allowance and limitation. For states like Connecticut, Illinois, Massachusetts, and Michigan that adopt the federal allowance and limitation amounts, whether they adopt this amendment will depend on their Code conformity dates. Those states that update their Code conformity dates annually will most likely conform during their next legislative sessions. However, more states (such as Florida) have been decoupling from the

NEW LAW EXPLAINED

increased expense allowances and limitations to alleviate further state revenue shortfalls.

Practical Analysis: Vincent O'Brien, President of Vincent J. O'Brien, CPA, PC, Lynbrook, New York, observes that business owners who had planned to make capital expenditures after 2010 may consider accelerating those purchases so that they occur prior to the end of 2010, since the Code Sec. 179 dollar limit is scheduled to fall dramatically from $250,000 to $25,000, beginning in 2011.

While it seems unthinkable that Congress would allow the Code Sec. 179 dollar limit to return to the $25,000 level, there is no guarantee that the dollar limit will be increased above this amount. Even if Congress ultimately decides to make the limit higher, it may take a significant amount of time after the expiration occurs for such a law to be crafted and passed. Such a delay could cause business owners to face a long period of uncertainty as to what the dollar limit will be. This underscores the benefit of completing purchases during 2010.

When planning the timing of purchases eligible for the Code Sec. 179 deduction, there is another consideration for business owners that have ownership interests in more than one flow-through entity (such as an S corporation, a partnership, or a limited liability company that is taxed as a partnership). Such business owners must carefully plan when electing to use the Code Sec. 179 deduction in more than one entity.

When more than one entity reports a Code Sec. 179 deduction to the same individual on a Schedule K-1, in 2010, the individual is limited to deducting only $250,000 on his or her individual income tax return, regardless of the number of entities that report Code Sec. 179 deductions to the individual. If the sum of the Code Sec. 179 deductions reported to the individual exceeds the $250,000 limit, the individual is barred from using the excess deduction in the current tax year and in all future tax years. Furthermore, the individual must reduce his or her basis in the ownership interests of all of the entities by the total amount of the Code Sec. 179 deductions reported on Schedule K-1, including the amount that could not be used due to the $250,000 limitation.

Practical Analysis: Michael Schlesinger, a Partner in Schlesinger & Sussman of New York, New York and author of PRACTICAL GUIDE TO S CORPORATIONS (4th edition), notes that whenever Congress needs a quick fix to stimulate the economy, it runs to Code Sec. 179, playing with its qualifications. The current extension is a perfect example where Congress has just decided to continue Code Sec. 179's current deduction for another year. However, as everyone knows, with quick fixes there are problems. This is certainly evident in Code Sec. 179. For instance, while Code Sec. 179 has been around for years in various forms, one thing is consistent—the inability of estates and trusts to utilize Code Sec. 179 as is evidenced by Code Sec. 179(d)(4). Where this prohibition is painfully illustrated is with S corporations. If an S corporation has an estate and/or a trust for a shareholder, Reg. §1.179-1(f)(3) provides that the trust or estate may not deduct its allocable share of the Code Sec.

NEW LAW EXPLAINED

179 expense elected by the S corporation, and the S corporation's basis in Code Sec. 179 property shall not be reduced to reflect any portion of the Code Sec. 179 expense that is allocable to the trust or estate. However, the S corporation may claim a depreciation deduction under Code Sec. 168 or a Code Sec. 38 credit (if available) with respect to any depreciable basis resulting from the trust or estate's inability to claim its allocable portion of the Code Sec. 179 expense.

Other examples which require planning due to Congress' restrictions follow:

- Congress only extended Code Sec. 179's provisions for another year. On the face of it, this extension is good in that this gives taxpayers approximately .75 years to plan. However, if they do not have sufficient taxable income to utilize Code Sec. 179's immediate write off, then they are trapped by Code Sec. 179(b)(3)'s carryforward provisions, which, in a nutshell, provide that any unused deductions can be carried forward but the amount to be expensed in a carryforward year is limited to the maximum annual dollar cost ceiling, investment limitation or, if lesser, Code Sec. 179(b)(3)'s income limitation. Thus, in 2011, unless Congress changes the provisions, Code Sec. 179(b)(1)'s expense dollar limitation cannot exceed $25,000 instead of the current $250,000, and the beginning of Code Sec. 179(b)(2)'s phase out starts at $200,000, not $800,000 as it is currently.

- If an S corporate shareholder plans to dispose of his or her stock where gain or loss is not recognized in whole or in part (including transfers of an S corporate interest at death) and the shareholder has not been able to fully utilize his or her Code Sec. 179 deduction due to Code Sec. 179's income limitation, Reg. § 1.179-3(h)(2) states that immediately before the transfer of the shareholder's stock in the S corporation, the shareholder's basis is increased by the amount of the shareholder's outstanding carryover of disallowed deduction with respect to his or her S corporate interest.

- Reg. § 1.179-2(b)(4) states that Code Sec. 179's dollar limitation (Code Sec. 179(b)(1)'s current limit is $250,000) applies to the S corporation as well as to each S corporate shareholder. In applying the dollar limitation to a taxpayer that is a S corporate shareholder in one or more S corporations, the S corporate shareholder's share of Code Sec. 179 expenses allocated to the S corporate shareholder from each S corporation is aggregated with any non-S corporation Code Sec. 179 expenses of the taxpayer for the tax year. So, assume that a calendar-year S corporation owned equally by two individual shareholders, Mike and Laurie, purchases $250,000 of Code Sec. 179 property on January 1, 2010, and elects to expense all of it. On December 31, 2010, Mike individually for his sole proprietorship purchases $200,000 of Code Sec. 179 property. Mike cannot take a Code Sec. 179 deduction of $325,000 ($125,000 from the passthrough of 50% of the S corporation's Code Sec. 179 deduction and $200,000 from his proprietorship) on his 2010 Form 1040; rather, he can only take under Code Sec. 179(b)(1) a maximum of $250,000. Accordingly, $75,000 of a Code Sec. 179 deduction is wasted due to bad timing of purchases.

- Code Sec. 179(d)(6) prescribes that members of a controlled group cannot expense totally more than $250,000 in a tax year. Code Sec. 179(d)(7) states that for purposes of determining a control group for Code Sec. 179 purposes, the

NEW LAW EXPLAINED

group is determined using a "more than 50%" ownership test rather than "at least an 80%" one. So, if an S corporation owns more than 50% of the stock of another corporation, then care must be practiced so as not to run afoul of Code Sec. 179(b)(1)'s dollar limitation.

It is to be noted that Congress is still wrestling with provisions for estate and gift tax, which, when enacted, could affect planning possibilities for Code Sec. 179. Thus, future planning for Code Sec. 179 has to incorporate these possibilities and at this juncture, it is impossible to project what Congress might do.

▶ **Effective date.** The amendments made by this section apply to tax years beginning after December 31, 2009 (Act Sec. 201(b) of the Hiring Incentives to Restore Employment (HIRE) Act (P.L. 111-147)).

Law source: Law at ¶6040. Committee Report at ¶11,030.

— Act Sec. 201(a)(1) of the Hiring Incentives to Restore Employment (HIRE) Act (P.L. 111-147), amending Code Sec. 179(b)(1);

— Act Sec. 201(a)(2), amending Code Sec. 179(b)(2);

— Act Sec. 201(a)(3) and (4), striking Code Sec. 179(b)(5) and (7), and redesignating Code Sec. 179(b)(6) as Code Sec. 179(b)(5);

— Act Sec. 201(b), providing the effective date.

Reporter references: For further information, consult the following CCH reporters.

— Standard Federal Tax Reporter, ¶12,126.01

— Tax Research Consultant, DEPR: 12,000

— Practical Tax Explanation, §9,801

¶615 COBRA Premium Assistance

SUMMARY OF NEW LAW

The eligibility period for an assistance eligible individual to receive the 65 percent COBRA premium assistance is extended through March 31, 2010. In addition, eligibility for the subsidy is extended to certain individuals who lose their group health care coverage as a result of a reduction in hours of employment, followed by an involuntary termination of employment.

BACKGROUND

A group health plan must offer each qualified beneficiary, who would otherwise lose coverage under the plan as a result of a qualifying event, an opportunity to elect, within the election period, continuation coverage under the plan (otherwise known as COBRA continuation coverage). An excise tax is imposed on the employer (or plan

BACKGROUND

in the case of a multiemployer plan) and persons legally responsible for administering or providing benefits under the plan if this requirement is not satisfied (Code Sec. 4980B). A qualified beneficiary is any individual who is covered under a group health plan on the day before a qualifying event by virtue of being, on that day, a covered employee, the spouse, or the dependent child of a covered employee (Reg. §54.4980B-3). A qualifying event with respect to any covered employee, is a certain event that, but for the COBRA rules, would result in a qualified beneficiary's loss of group health plan coverage. For example, termination of a covered employee's employment, or a reduction in the employee's hours, would be qualifying events.

> **Comment:** The plan may require the payment of premiums for the COBRA continuation coverage. The premiums may not exceed 102 percent of the premium paid, by either the employer or employee, for a similarly situated beneficiary currently covered by the plan for the same period of coverage.

A temporary reduction in premiums for COBRA continuation coverage is available to an assistance eligible individual who loses group health coverage as a result of the covered employee's involuntary termination from employment (Act Sec. 3001 of Division B of the American Recovery and Reinvestment Act of 2009 (P.L. 111-5)). Specifically, the assistance eligible individual is treated for COBRA purposes as having paid the full premium required for COBRA continuation coverage if the individual pays 35 percent of the premium (Act Sec. 3001(a)(1)(A) of the 2009 Recovery Act). In effect, the individual gets a 65-percent reduction in COBRA premiums and such assistance may be excluded from gross income (Code Sec. 139C).

For this purpose, an assistance eligible individual is any qualified beneficiary under a group health plan who at any time during the period beginning on September 1, 2008, and ending on February 28, 2010, is eligible for COBRA continuation coverage and elects such coverage (Act Sec. 3001(a)(3) of the 2009 Recovery Act). The qualifying event for which the beneficiary would otherwise lose group health plan coverage must be the involuntary termination of the covered employee's employment during the period. Thus, if COBRA continuation coverage is based on a qualifying event other than the employee's involuntary termination, then the qualified beneficiary is not an assistance eligible individual and not eligible for COBRA premium assistance.

Similarly, if COBRA continuation coverage is based on a qualifying event which occurs before the covered employee's involuntary termination, then the involuntary termination does not cause the qualified beneficiary to become an assistance eligible individual. However, the IRS has provided that, if in anticipation of an involuntary termination of a covered employee, the employer takes action that results in a loss of coverage for a qualified beneficiary (for example, a reduction in hours for the covered employee in anticipation of involuntary termination), the action causing the loss of coverage prior to the involuntary termination will be disregarded in determining whether involuntary termination is the qualifying event that results in eligibility for COBRA continuation coverage (Notice 2009-27, Q&A 15, 2009-16 I.R.B. 383).

> **Comment:** The eligibility period for COBRA premium assistance originally ended on December 31, 2009. The Department of Defense Appropriations Act of 2010 (P.L. 111-118) extended the eligibility period through February 28, 2010.

BACKGROUND

Duration of subsidy. The 65-percent premium reduction or subsidy for COBRA continuation coverage terminates with the first month beginning on or after the earlier of:

- the date that is 15 months after the first day of the first month for which the subsidy applies;

- the end of the maximum required period of COBRA continuation coverage for the beneficiary; or

- the date the assistance eligible individual is eligible for coverage under Medicare or any other employer-sponsored health plan (Act Sec. 3001(a)(2) of 2009 Recovery Act, as amended by the 2010 Defense Act).

The maximum time an assistance eligible individual can receive premium assistance was extended from nine to 15 months by the 2010 Defense Act. If an eligible individual's reduced premium period expired (after receiving it for nine months), he or she can get the subsidy for an additional six months, provided he or she otherwise remains an assistance eligible individual. Such individuals are considered to be in a transition period and will have additional time to pay any unpaid premiums related to the extension. To continue coverage, such individuals must pay 35 percent of the unpaid premiums retroactively by the later of February 17, 2010, or 30 days after the plan administrator provides notice of the extension (Act Sec. 3001(a)(16) of the 2009 Recovery Act, as added by the 2010 Defense Act). For this purpose, an individual's transition period begins immediately after the end of the maximum number of months (generally nine) of premium reduction was available prior to the amendments made by the 2010 Defense Act (December 19, 2009).

Subsidy reimbursement. The person to whom COBRA premiums are payable (i.e., the employer, the plan, or the insurer) is reimbursed for the 65 percent that is not paid by the assistance eligible individual through a credit against its payroll taxes (Code Sec. 6432). If the reimbursement due exceeds the amount of such taxes, the excess will be paid as a refund. However, no refund will be made with respect to any assistance eligible individual until after the employer, plan, or insurer has received the reduced premium from the assistance eligible individual. Each person entitled to a reimbursement must submit a report including:

- an attestation of involuntary termination of employment for each covered employee on the basis of whose termination a claim for reimbursement is made;

- a report of the amount of payroll taxes offset for the reporting period and the estimated offsets of such taxes for the subsequent reporting period; and

- a report containing the taxpayer identification numbers (TINs) of all covered employees, the amount of subsidy reimbursed with respect to each covered employee and qualified beneficiaries, and a designation with respect to each covered employee as to whether the subsidy reimbursement is for coverage of one individual or two or more individuals.

COBRA premium assistance extended and modified.—The definition of assistance eligible individual is modified by extending the eligibility period through March 31, 2010, and providing that a qualifying event that triggers eligibility for premium assistance may include a reduction of the covered employee's hours of employment that is followed by an involuntary termination of the covered employee's employment during the eligibility period (Act Sec. 3001(a)(3) of the American Recovery and Reinvestment Act of 2009 (P.L. 111-5), as amended by the Temporary Extension Act of 2010 (P.L. 111-144)). Thus, an assistance eligible individual is any qualified beneficiary if:

- at any time during the period beginning on September 1, 2008, and ending on March 31, 2010, the qualified beneficiary is eligible for COBRA continuation coverage;
- the beneficiary elects COBRA continuation coverage; and
- the qualifying event for which the beneficiary would otherwise lose health plan coverage (i) is the involuntary termination of employment of the covered employee during the eligibility period, or (ii) consists of a reduction of hours of employment of the covered employee, followed by his or her involuntary termination of employment during that period.

> **State Tax Consequences:** The 30-day extension includes the exclusion from gross income for COBRA premium assistance received by qualified beneficiaries. The extension of the exclusion will impact states that do not adopt federal tax law as currently amended or that only incorporate specific Code sections. For such states, the amounts excluded from federal adjusted gross income would have to be added back for state income tax purposes.

Special rules for reduction of hours. A special rule applies to a qualified beneficiary who is an assistance eligible individual as a result of a reduction in hours of employment of a covered employee during the eligibility period, followed by an involuntary termination of employment occurring on or after March 2, 2010, and before April 1, 2010 (Act Sec. 3001(a)(17) of the 2009 Recovery Act, as added by the 2010 Temporary Extension Act). If the qualified beneficiary did not make (or made and then discontinued) a COBRA coverage election based on the reduction in hours of employment for the covered employee, the subsequent involuntary termination of employment of the employee will be treated as the qualifying event for purposes of electing COBRA coverage. As a result, the individual will be entitled to a new COBRA notice and a new election period. The plan administrator must provide to the qualified beneficiary the new COBRA notice during the 60-day period beginning on the date of the covered employee's termination of employment. The notification must include information on the special rules, including the fact that nothing will be construed as requiring the beneficiary to make a payment for COBRA continuation coverage between the reduction of hours of employment for the covered employee and his or her involuntary termination of employment.

> **Caution:** Despite the new COBRA notice and election period, the COBRA continuation coverage period for the qualified beneficiary is determined as though the qualifying event were the reduction of hours of employment for the

NEW LAW EXPLAINED

covered employee and not his or her involuntary termination. For example, assume a covered employee under a group health plan experiences a reduction of hours of employment on October 15, 2009, that results in the loss of health coverage. While the employee is eligible for COBRA continuation coverage as a qualified beneficiary, he or she does not elect such coverage. If the employee is involuntarily terminated on March 15, 2010, he or she would be entitled to new notification of electing COBRA continuation coverage. However, if the individual elects coverage this time, his or her coverage period begins on October 15, 2009 and not March 15, 2010. Thus, if the employee is eligible for a 17 month period of COBRA continuation coverage, the coverage would expire on March 15, 2011.

Employer documentation of involuntary termination. For purposes of reimbursing the person to whom COBRA premiums are payable for the 65-percent subsidy (the employer, plan, or insurer), the qualifying event for an assistance eligible individual will be deemed to be the covered employee's involuntary termination of employment if the employer:

- determines that the COBRA qualifying event for the assistance eligible individual was the involuntary termination of employment of the covered employee based on a reasonable interpretation of the COBRA premium assistance provisions; and

- the employer maintains supporting documentation (including its own attestation that the covered employee was involuntarily terminated) (Code Sec. 6432(e), as added by 2010 Temporary Extension Act).

    Comment: A qualified beneficiary may request that the U.S. Department of Labor (DOL) (or, in the case of government employees, the Department of Health and Human Services (DHHS)) review a denial of treatment as an assistance eligible individual. The DOL or DHHS must make a determination of the individual's eligibility within 15 business days after receipt of the individual's application. In addition, the DOL, DHHS, or the affected individual can bring a civil action in federal court to enforce a determination of whether the individual is an assistance eligible individual. The DOL or DHHS may also assess a penalty against a plan sponsor or health insurance issuer of up to $110 per day for each failure to comply with its determination that an individual is eligible, after the tenth day after the sponsor or insurance issuer receives the DOL's or DHHS's determination (Act Sec. 3001(a)(5) of the 2009 Recovery Act, as amended by 2010 Temporary Extension Act).

    Comment: Appeals to the DOL must be submitted on the DOL application form. The form is available at *www.dol.gov/COBRA* and can be completed online or mailed or faxed as indicated in the instructions.

Transition rules. For purposes of the transitions rules applicable due to the extension of the COBRA premium assistance to a maximum of 15 months, an assistance eligible individual may continue coverage if they pay 35 percent of the unpaid premiums by the later of: (i) February 17, 2010, (ii) 30 days after the plan administrator provides notice of the extension, or (iii) the date on which coverage ceased under the plan by reason of a failure to timely make payment of any premium required under the plan with respect to the qualified beneficiary (Act Sec. 3001(a)(16)(A) of the 2009 Recovery Act, as added by the Department of Defense Appropriations Act of 2010 (P.L.

NEW LAW EXPLAINED

111-118), and amended by the 2010 Temporary Extension Act). The beneficiary's transition period begins immediately after the covered employee experiences an involuntary termination of employment prior to December 19, 2009 (Act Sec. 3001(a)(16)(C) of the 2009 Recovery Act, as added by the 2010 Defense Act, and amended by the 2010 Temporary Extension Act).

> **Practical Analysis:** Vincent O'Brien, President of Vincent J. O'Brien, CPA, PC, Lynbrook, New York, observes that the federal COBRA continuation of coverage rules affect employers with at least 20 employees. Such employers must also offer COBRA premium assistance to eligible former employees.
>
> In addition, many states have "mini-COBRA" requirements that affect employers with fewer than 20 employees and require such employers to provide coverage comparable to the federal COBRA continuation coverage for former employees. Employers who are not subject to the federal COBRA requirement should determine if their state requires them to offer continuation of coverage. If an employer is subject to a state's mini-COBRA requirement, the employer must also offer premium assistance to eligible former employees.

▶ **Effective date.** Generally, the amendments of this provision take effect as if included in Act Sec. 3001 of Division B of the American Recovery and Reinvestment Act of 2009 (P.L. 111-5) to which they relate (Act Sec. 3(c) of the Temporary Extension Act of 2010 (P.L. 111-144)). However:

- the amendments clarifying COBRA continuation coverage resulting from the reduction in hours of employment apply to periods of coverage beginning after March 2, 2010, the date of enactment (Act Sec. 3(c)(1) of the 2010 Temporary Extension Act);

- the amendments clarifying the transition rules related to the extension of the duration of COBRA continuation coverage to a maximum of 15 months take effect on February 17, 2009 (Act Sec. 3(c)(2) of the Temporary Extension Act); and

- the amendments clarifying the period of COBRA premium assistance and enforcement take effect on March 2, 2010, the date of enactment (Act Sec. 3(c)(3) of the 2010 Temporary Extension Act).

Law source: Law at ¶6005, ¶6020, ¶6150, ¶6180, and ¶7306.

— Act Sec. 3(a) and 3(b)(1) of the Temporary Extension Act of 2010 (P.L. 111-144), amending Act Sec. 3001(a)(3) and adding Act Sec. 3001(a)(17) of Division B of the American Recovery and Reinvestment Act of 2009 (P.L. 111-5);

— Act Sec. 3(b)(2), amending Act Sec. 3001(a)(16) of the 2009 Recovery Act, as added by Act Sec. 1010(c) of the Department of Defense Appropriations Act of 2010 (P.L. 111-118);

— Act Sec. 3(b)(3) and (b)(4), amending Act Sec. 3001(a)(2)(A)(ii)(I) and 3001(a)(5), respectively, of the 2009 Recovery Act;

— Act Sec. 3(b)(5), amending Code Secs. 35(g)(9), 139C, 6432(a), 6432(c)(3), 6720C(a); and redesignating former Code Sec. 6432(e) and (f) as Code Sec. 6432(f) and (g), respectively, and adding new Code Sec. 6432(e);

— Act Sec. 3(c), providing the effective dates.

NEW LAW EXPLAINED

Reporter references: For further information, consult the following CCH reporters.
— Standard Federal Tax Reporter, ¶34,601.021, ¶38,940.01.
— Tax Research Consultant, COMPEN: 45,206, INDIV: 57,600.
— Practical Tax Explanation, §4085, §20,743.

¶620 Refundable Credit for Issuers of Specified Tax Credit Bonds

SUMMARY OF NEW LAW

Issuers of specified tax credit bonds can elect to claim a refundable tax credit generally equal to the amount of interest that is payable or would be payable to purchasers of the bonds. This credit for issuers is in lieu of the credit that would ordinarily be allowed to the purchasers.

BACKGROUND

The Internal Revenue Code has long contained provisions making the interest on qualifying state and local bonds exempt from federal income tax, thereby providing an indirect federal subsidy for state and local government operations and activities (Code Sec. 103). State and local bonds are classified generally as either governmental bonds or private activity bonds. Governmental bonds are primarily used to finance governmental functions or are repaid with government funds. For private activity bonds, the state or local government merely serves as a conduit to provide financing to nongovernmental entities, such as private businesses or individuals. Both types of exempt bonds are subject to a number of restrictions intended to ensure that their proceeds are indeed used for public purposes.

A tax credit bond provides a different way for the federal government to subsidize specific projects. Generally, a tax credit bond is not interest-bearing obligation but rather a taxpayer holding the bond on an allowance date during the tax year receives a federal income tax credit equal to the interest the bond would otherwise pay (Code Sec. 54A). The annual amount of the credit is determined by multiplying the outstanding face amount of the bond by the bond's applicable credit rate, which is the rate the IRS estimates will permit issuance of the bonds without discount and interest cost to the qualified issuer. The credit accrues quarterly and must be included in the bondholders gross income. However, the amount of the credit is limited to the amount of the purchaser's regular tax liability plus alternative minimum tax (AMT) liability, meaning that the credit is not refundable.

The current types of tax credit bonds include:

- qualified forestry conservation bonds under Code Sec. 54B;
- new clean renewable energy bonds (CREBs) under Code Sec. 54C;

BACKGROUND

- qualified energy conservation bonds (QECs) under Code Sec. 54D;
- qualified zone academy bonds (QZABs) issued after October 3, 2008, under Code Sec. 54E; and
- qualified school construction bonds (QSCBs) under Code Sec. 54F.

   Comment: In the case of CREBs and QECs, the amount of the credit that can be claimed by the purchaser is limited to 70 percent of the amount of the credit that would permit issuance of such bonds without discount and interest cost to the issuer.

The American Recovery and Reinvestment Tax Act (P.L. 111-5) added a new kind of tax credit bond. An issuer of an otherwise tax-exempt bond issued prior to January 1, 2011, may make an irrevocable election to have the bond treated as a Build America Bond under Code Sec. 54AA. If the election is made, the bond is treated as a taxable governmental bond in which the interest is subsidized by the Federal government in one of two ways. First, a Build American Bond may provide holders with taxable interest payments, plus a federal tax credit equal to 35 percent of the interest payment ("tax-credit build America bonds"). Alternatively, if the bond is a qualified bond it may provide holders with taxable interest payments, but the issuer may elect to claim a tax credit equal to 35 percent of the interest payment ("direct-pay build America bonds"). Thus, these qualified bonds allow issuing state or local governments to receive a direct payment from the federal government in the form of the federal tax credit that would have otherwise been delivered to the bondholder. For this purpose, a qualified direct-pay bond is any build America bond issued as part of an issue if 100 percent of the excess of available project proceeds of such issue over the amounts in a reasonably required reserve with respect to such issue are to be used for capital expenses.

   Compliance Tip: Subject to updated IRS reporting forms or procedures, an issuer of Build America Bonds makes the direct-pay election on its books and records on or before the bond issue date (Notice 2009-26, I.R.B. 2009-16, 833).

NEW LAW EXPLAINED

Issuers of specified tax credit bonds can elect to claim credit.—Issuers of specified tax credit bonds can irrevocably elect to claim a refundable credit in lieu of the credit that would ordinarily belong to the purchasers of the bonds (Code Sec. 6431(f), as added by the Hiring Incentives to Restore Employment (HIRE) Act (P.L. 111-147)). The election can apply to tax credit bonds originally issued at any time after March 18, 2010 (Code Sec. 6431(f)(1)(B), as added by the 2010 HIRE Act). For this purpose, specified tax credit bonds include:

- new clean renewable energy bonds (CREBs) under Code Sec. 54C;
- qualified energy conservation bonds (QECBs) under Code Sec. 54D;
- qualified zone academy bonds (QZABs) under Code Sec. 54E; and
- qualified school construction bonds (QSCBs) under Code Sec. 54F (Code Sec. 6431(f)(3), as added by the 2010 HIRE Act).

NEW LAW EXPLAINED

> **Comment:** The new provision essentially allows issuers of these specified tax credit bonds to make the same election that issuers of Build America Bonds are allowed to make under Code Sec. 54AA(g). However, unlike the direct-pay election for Build America Bonds, this election is not limited to bonds issued before January 1, 2011 (Code Sec. 6431(f)(1)(B), as added by the 2010 HIRE Act).

An issuer making the election generally receives a credit with respect to any interest payment due under a specified bond equal to the lesser of:

- the amount of interest payable under such bond on the bond's interest payment date; or
- the amount of interest which would have been payable under such bond on the bond's interest payment date if the interest were determined at the applicable credit rate that would permit issuance of such bonds without discount and interest cost to the issuer (Code Sec. 6431(f)(1)(C), as added by the 2010 HIRE Act).

In the case of new clean renewable energy bonds (CREBs) under Code Sec. 54C and qualified energy conservation bonds (QESBs) under Code Sec. 54D, the credit amount determined in the second alternative, above, is limited to 70 percent of the amount of interest determined. This limited amount is determined without regard to the 70 percent limitation on the amount of credit that can be claimed by holders of these bonds. (Code Sec. 6431(f)(2), as added by the 2010 HIRE Act).

> **Comment:** The 70 percent limitation on the credit for electing issuers mirrors the 70 percent limitation on the amount of the credit that can be claimed by holders of new CREBs and QESBs under Code Secs. 54C(b) and 54D(b), respectively.

As is the case with qualified Build America Bonds, purchasers of these qualified tax credit bonds are not allowed a tax credit for the bonds, and they must include the bond interest in income (Code Sec. 6431(f)(1)(D) and (E), as added by the 2010 HIRE Act). Any credit received by the issuer is not included in income, but any deduction allowed by the issuer for interest paid must be reduced by the amount of credit received with respect to that interest (Code Sec. 6431(f)(1)(F) and (G), as added by the 2010 HIRE Act).

▶ **Effective date.** The amendment made by this provision applies to bonds issued after March 18, 2010 (Act Sec. 301(c)(1) of the Hiring Incentives to Restore Employment (HIRE) Act of 2010 (P.L. 111-147)).

Law source: Law at ¶6145. Committee Report at ¶11,040.

— Act Sec. 301(a) of the Hiring Incentives to Restore Employment (HIRE) Act (P.L. 111-147), adding Code Sec. 6431(f);

— Act Sec. 301(c)(1), providing the effective date.

Reporter references: For further information, consult the following CCH reporters.

— Standard Federal Tax Reporter, ¶4888.01 and ¶38,933.01

— Tax Research Consultant, BUSEXP: 55,814

— Practical Tax Explanation, § 14,505 and § 14,515

¶625 Qualified School Construction Tax Credit Bonds

SUMMARY OF NEW LAW

The allocation of a state's volume limitation is to be determined by the state education agency and any unused amounts allocated to large local education agencies by the IRS can be carried over.

BACKGROUND

The Internal Revenue Code has long contained provisions making the interest on qualifying state and local bonds exempt from federal income tax, thereby providing an indirect federal subsidy for state and local government operations and activities (Code Sec. 103). Recently, a newer form of federal subsidization of state and local activities has been provided through tax credit bonds. Tax credit bonds are not interest-bearing obligations. Instead, a taxpayer holding a tax credit bond on an allowance date is allowed a credit against federal income tax that is intended to be equivalent to the interest that the bond would otherwise pay. The bondholder must include the amount of the credit in gross income as interest income. The credit effectively replaces the interest that would be paid on an exempt bond, allowing the issuer to borrow interest-free. In return, the issuer must follow certain requirements with regard to the form of the bonds and the use of the proceeds (Code Sec. 54A).

The American Recovery and Reinvestment Tax Act of 2009 (P.L. 111-5) added a new type of tax credit bond to the Code that applies specifically to the construction and operation of public schools. Qualified school construction bonds (QSCBs) under Code Sec. 54F provide a federal subsidy to help state and local governments finance public school construction, rehabilitation, and repair. A bond is a QSCB if:

- 100 percent of the available project proceeds of the bond issue are to be used for the construction, rehabilitation, or repair of a public school facility or to acquire land on which a facility funded by the same issue is to be built;

- the bond is issued by a state or local government within the jurisdiction of which the school is located; and

- the issuer designates the bond as a QSCB (Code Sec. 54F(a)).

There is national volume cap or limit on the amount of QSCBs that may be issued for the year. The limit is $11 billion for 2009 and $11 billion for 2010 (Code Sec. 54F(c)). An additional $200 million is allocated in each of those years for Indian tribes (Code Sec. 54D(f)(4)). The IRS allocates 40 percent of the annual cap among large local educational agencies and the remaining 60 percent among the State governments (including the District of Columbia and U.S. possessions). The limitation amount allocated to each State then is allocated by the State government to bond issuers within the State (Code Sec. 54F(d)). Unused allocations to states and Indian tribes (but not to large local education agencies) can be carried over to the state's (or the tribe's) allocation for the next calendar year (Code Sec. 54(e)).

Allocation and carry-over of qualified school construction bonds limitation modified.—The portion of the qualified school construction bond (QSCB) volume cap that the IRS allocates to a state is further allocated within that state by the State education agency or other agency that is authorized under State law to make the allocation (Code Sec. 54F(d)(1), as amended by the Hiring Incentives to Restore Employment (HIRE) Act (P.L. 111-147)).

> **Comment:** This change is intended to provide allocations within a state with some insulation from political pressures, by removing the allocation authority from the state in general and vesting it instead with the state governmental body that is in the best position to allocate the limitation properly. This puts the process of allocating the limitation on QSCBs in line with other similar tax credit bond provisions, such as qualified zone academy bonds (QZABs) under Code Sec. 54E.

Also, the provision allowing for the carryover of unused amounts allocated to States and Indian schools is expanded to apply to unused amounts allocated to large local education agencies (Code Sec. 54F(e), as amended by the 2010 HIRE Act).

▶ **Effective date.** The amendments made by this provision apply to obligations issued after February 17, 2009 (Act Sec. 301(c)(2) of the Hiring Incentives to Restore Employment (HIRE) Act (P.L. 111-147); Act Sec. 1521(c) of the American Recovery and Reinvestment Tax Act of 2009 (P.L.111-5)).

Law source: Law at ¶6015. Committee Report at ¶11,040.

— Act Sec. 301(b)(1) of the Hiring Incentives to Restore Employment (HIRE) Act P.L. 111-147, amending Code Sec. 54F(d)(1);

— Act Sec. 301(b)(2), amending Code Sec. 54F(e);

— Act Sec. 301(c)(2), providing the effective date.

Reporter references: For further information, consult the following CCH reporters.

— Standard Federal Tax Reporter, ¶4928.04

— Tax Research Consultant, BUSEXP: 55,812

— Practical Tax Explanation, § 14,510.30

¶630 Corporate Estimated Tax Payments

SUMMARY OF NEW LAW

The estimated tax payment required to be made by certain large corporations in July, August, or September of 2014, 2015, and 2019 have been increased to 173.50 percent, 121.50 percent, and 106.50 percent, respectively, of the amount otherwise due.

BACKGROUND

Generally, a corporation is required to make quarterly estimated tax payments during its tax year based on its income tax liability (Code Sec. 6655). For a corporation whose tax year is a calendar year, these estimated tax payments must be made by April 15, June 15, September 15, and December 15. For corporations using a fiscal year, the corresponding months are substituted for these dates. Thus, a fiscal-year corporation pays estimated tax installments for a tax year on the 15th day of the fourth, sixth, ninth and twelfth months of the year.

The Corporate Estimated Tax Shift Act of 2009 (P.L. 111-42) increased the estimated tax payment required to be made in July, August, or September of 2014 by a corporation with assets of $1 billion or more (determined as of the end of the preceding tax year) to 100.25 percent of the amount otherwise due. The next required installment of estimated tax was reduced accordingly to reflect the increase. The estimated tax payment was further increased by 33 percentage points to 133.25 percent of the amount otherwise due (Worker, Homeownership, and Business Assistance Act of 2009 (P.L. 111-92)) and then by 1.5 percentage point to 134.75 percent of the amount otherwise due (P.L. 111-124). The next required installment of estimated tax is reduced accordingly to reflect these increases.

NEW LAW EXPLAINED

Certain payments of corporate estimated taxes increased.—The estimated tax payment required to be made in July, August, or September of 2014, 2015, and 2019, by a corporation with assets of $1 billion or more (determined as of the end of the preceding tax year) has been increased. Specifically, the estimated tax payment required to be made in July, August, or September of 2014, is increased by 23 percentage points from the amount otherwise required to be paid and then increased by an additional 15.75 percentage points from the amount otherwise required to be paid (Act Sec. 561 of the Hiring Incentives to Restore Employment (HIRE) Act (P.L. 111-147) and Act Sec. 1410 of the Health Care and Education Tax Credits Reconciliation Act of 2010 (P.L. 111-152), amending Act Sec. 202(b)(1) of Corporate Estimated Tax Shift Act of 2009 (P.L. 111-42), as amended by the Worker, Homeownership, and Business Assistance Act of 2009 (P.L. 111-92 and P.L. 111-124)). The estimated tax payment required to be made in July, August, or September of 2015, is also increased by 21.5 percentage points from the amount otherwise required to be paid. The estimated tax payment required to be made in July, August, or September of 2019, is increased by 6.5 percentage points from the amount otherwise required to be paid. Thus, affected corporations must pay an estimated tax payment of:

- 173.50 percent of the amount otherwise due in July, August, or September of 2014;

- 121.5 percent of the amount otherwise due in July, August, or September of 2015; and

- 106.5 percent of the amount otherwise due in July, August, or September of 2019.

In each year, the next required installment of estimated tax is reduced accordingly to reflect the increase.

¶630

NEW LAW EXPLAINED

Comment: Because the federal government's fiscal year begins October 1st, the effect of the provision is to shift revenues from one fiscal year to another in order to meet budgetary requirements.

▶ **Effective date.** No specific effective date is provided by the Acts. Thus, the increases in the estimated tax payments required to be made in July, August, or September of 2014, 2015, and 2019, as a result of the Hiring Incentives to Restore Employment (HIRE) Act (P.L. 111-147) are considered effective on March 18, 2010, the date of enactment. The increase in the estimated tax payment required to be made in July, August, or September of 2014, as a result of the Health Care and Education Tax Credits Reconciliation Act of 2010 (P.L. 111-152) is considered effective on March 30, 2010, the date of enactment.

Law source: Law at ¶7215. Committee Report at ¶14,450.

— Act Sec. 561 of the Hiring Incentives to Restore Employment (HIRE) Act (P.L. 111-147); and

— Act Sec. 1410 of the Health Care and Education Tax Credits Reconciliation Act of 2010 (P.L. 111-152).

Reporter references: For further information, consult the following CCH reporters.

— Standard Federal Tax Reporter, ¶39,575.01

— Tax Research Consultant, FILEBUS: 6,054.05

— Practical Tax Explanation, §26,015.10

¶635 Charitable Contributions for Earthquake Relief

SUMMARY OF NEW LAW

Calendar-year taxpayers may claim a charitable contribution deduction on their 2009 returns for cash contributions made after January 11, 2010, and before March 1, 2010, to help Haiti recover from the devastating earthquake that occurred on January 12, 2010.

BACKGROUND

Generally, a taxpayer may claim an income tax deduction for contributions to certain charitable organizations (Code Sec. 170). An individual taxpayer deducts charitable contributions in the year in which they are paid, regardless of when the amounts were pledged. The deduction for an individual donor's aggregate charitable contributions within a single tax year is limited to 50 percent of the donor's contribution base: adjusted gross income (AGI) computed without regard to the charitable deduction and without regard to any net operating loss (NOL). Corporations that pay pledged amounts within two and a half months after the end of the corporation's tax year end, can elect to deduct the charitable contribution in the preceding year. A corporation's charitable contribution deduction is limited to 10 percent of the corporation's taxable income, with some adjustments. When an individual or a corporate donor's charita-

BACKGROUND

ble contribution exceeds the applicable percentage limits, excess contributions can be carried forward and deducted over the five following years.

Any taxpayer who claims a charitable contribution deduction is required to substantiate that contributions were actually made in the amounts claimed on the taxpayer's tax return. Donors of charitable contributions of cash, checks, or other monetary gifts must retain certain written records of the gift, regardless of the amount. Taxpayers making a charitable contribution of $250 or more have additional substantiation requirements that must be satisfied prior to claiming a charitable deduction. Specifically, the donor must receive a contemporaneous written acknowledgment of the contribution from the donee organization. The acknowledgment must include:

- the amount of cash and a description, but not the value, of any property contributed;

- whether the donee organization provided any goods or services in consideration for property contributed; and

- a description and good-faith estimate of the value of any goods or services (other than intangible religious benefits) provided to the taxpayer in exchange for a contribution.

    Comment: If the goods and services provided in exchange include intangible religious benefits, a statement is needed to that effect.

NEW LAW EXPLAINED

Charitable deductions for contributions Haiti earthquake relief may be claimed on 2009 return.—Calendar-year taxpayers who make qualified contributions after January 11, 2010, and before March 1, 2010, to charities engaged in relief efforts related to the earthquake that occurred in Haiti on January 12, 2010, may treat such contributions as having been made on December 31, 2009 (Act Sec. 1(a) of P.L. 111-126). Thus, taxpayers may claim a deduction for a qualified Haiti earthquake contribution on their 2009 returns filed in 2010. Alternatively, taxpayers may claim the deduction on their 2010 returns filed in 2011. However, taxpayers may not claim the deduction in both years.

    Planning Note: For taxpayers using the calendar year, the tax benefit of a charitable contribution made in January or February often is not realized until the following year when the tax return is filed. Thus, under this provision, taxpayers may realize the tax benefit of qualifying contributions immediately on their 2009 tax return. However, taxpayers should make their best estimate whether it would be more advantageous for them to take the deduction on their 2009 or 2010 return. This determination should be based on which year the taxpayer will itemize and whether deductible contributions will be greater in one year than the other. If a taxpayer fails to take the Haitian charitable contribution deduction on their 2009 return, they may still take that deduction on their 2010 return provided the taxpayer itemizes rather than taking the standard deduction.

NEW LAW EXPLAINED

Only cash contributions made specifically for the relief of victims in areas affected by the earthquake in Haiti on January 12, 2010, qualify for the accelerated deduction and only if a charitable deduction would otherwise be allowed for the contribution (Act Sec. 1(b) of P.L. 111-126). In IRS News Release IR-2010-12, the IRS clarified that cash contributions for this purposes means deductible contributions may be made by text message, check, credit card, or debit card. Contributions of property, such as food, do not qualify for the accelerated deduction.

Like other charitable contributions, taxpayers claiming a deduction for a contribution of money, regardless of amount, must maintain as a record of the contribution a bank record or a written communication from the donee showing the name of the donee organization, the date of the contribution, and the amount of the contribution. The additional substantiation requirements also apply in the case of charitable contributions with a value of $250 or more. No charitable deduction is allowed for any contribution of $250 or more unless the taxpayer substantiates the contribution by a contemporaneous written acknowledgment of the contribution by the donee organization. However, contributions made by text message may be documented by the taxpayer's telephone bill, which must show the name of the donee organization, the date of the contribution, and the amount of the contribution (Act Sec. 1(c) of P.L. 111-126).

Effective date. No specific effective date is provided by the Act. The provision is, therefore, considered effective on January 22, 2010, the date of enactment.

Law source: Law at ¶7350. Committee Report at ¶12,010.

— Act Sec. 1 of P.L. 111-126.

Reporter references: For further information, consult the following CCH reporters.

— Standard Federal Tax Reporter, ¶11,620.057

— Tax Research Consultant, INDIV: 51,400, INDIV: 51,402, INDIV: 51,454.05

— Practical Tax Explanation, §7,501

HIRE: Foreign Account Tax Compliance

7

¶705 Expanded Withholding Rules and Additional Reporting Requirements for Foreign Financial Institutions and Non-Financial Foreign Entities

SUMMARY OF NEW LAW

Generally, a withholding agent must deduct and withhold a tax equal to 30 percent on any withholdable payment (interest, dividends, rents, salaries, wages, premiums, annuities, compensations, and other fixed or determinable annual or periodical gains, profits and income from sources within the United States) made to a foreign financial institution or to a non-financial foreign entity, unless specific reporting requirements are met. With respect to each U.S. account maintained by the foreign financial institution, the institution must provide identifying information for each account holder that is a specified U.S. person or substantial U.S. owner, the account number, the account balance, and gross receipts and withdrawals from the account. A non-financial foreign entity that is a beneficial owner of a withholdable payment must certify that it has no substantial U.S. owners or provide identifying information for each substantial U.S. owner.

BACKGROUND

Payments of U.S. source fixed or determinable annual or periodical (FDAP) income, including interest, dividends, and similar types of investment income, made to foreign persons are subject to U.S. withholding tax at a 30-percent rate, unless the withholding agent can establish that the beneficial owner of the amount is eligible for an exemption from withholding or a reduced rate of withholding under an income tax treaty (Code Secs. 871, 881, 1441 and 1442). Interest is from U.S. sources if it is paid by the United States or an agency, a state or political subdivision, the District of Columbia, or a resident or domestic corporation (Code Sec. 861(a)). Dividend income is sourced with reference to the payor's place of incorporation (Code Sec. 861(a)(2)). Rental income is sourced by location or place of use of the leased property, and royalties are sourced where the property from which the royalties are generated is used (Code Sec. 861(a)(4)). The principal statutory exemptions from 30-percent withholding tax are interest on bank deposits, portfolio interest and capital gains (Code Secs. 871(h) and 881(c)).

A system of self-certification is used to administer the U.S. withholding tax rules. A nonresident investor who seeks withholding tax relief for U.S. source investment income must provide certification on the appropriate IRS Form W-8 to the withholding agent to establish foreign status and eligibility for an exemption or reduced rate. A withholding agent making payments of U.S. source amounts to a foreign person is required to report the payments, including any U.S. tax withheld, to the IRS on Forms 1042 and 1042-S by March 15 of the year following the year that the payment is made (Reg. § 1.1461-1(b) and (c)).

If a withholding agent withholds more than is required, the payee may file a claim for refund. Whenever there is an overpayment of tax, the IRS is generally required to pay

BACKGROUND

interest to a taxpayer (Code Sec. 6611). There is an overpayment on the date of payment of the first amount which, when added to any previous payments, is in excess of the tax liability due (including any interest, addition to the tax, or additional amount) (Reg. §301.6611-1(b)). The IRS is not required to pay interest if it refunds or credits the amount due within 45 days of the filing of the return (Code Sec. 6611(e)). This grace period allows the IRS time to transmit refund information to the Treasury's Financial Management Service for issuance of the refund check.

Every person engaged in a trade or business in the United States must file with the IRS an information return on Form 1099 for payments totaling at least $600 that it makes to a U.S. person in the course of its trade or business (Code Sec 6041). The Form 1099 information reporting requirement is linked to the backup withholding rules of Code Sec. 3406. To avoid 28-percent backup withholding, a U.S. person must furnish the payor with Form W-9 establishing that the payee is a U.S. person (Reg. §32.3406(d)-1 and Reg. §32.3406(h)-3). The combination of reporting and backup withholding is meant to ensure that U.S. persons pay tax on investment income. Amounts paid to foreign persons are generally exempt from Form 1099 information reporting because they are subject to the nonresident withholding provisions.

To the extent that the nonresident withholding rules apply to a foreign financial institution, they may be modified by qualified intermediary (QI) agreements between the institutions and the IRS. A QI is a foreign financial institution or foreign clearing organization that has entered into a withholding and reporting agreement (QI agreement) with the IRS (Reg. §1.1441-1(e)(5)(ii)).

All QIs are withholding agents for purposes of the nonresident withholding and reporting rules and payors for purposes of the backup withholding and Form 1099 information reporting rules. Under a QI agreement, however, a QI may choose not to assume primary responsibility for nonresident withholding. The QI is then required to provide a U.S. withholding agent with Form W-8IMY certifying the status of its unnamed non-U.S. account holders and is not required to withhold or report the payments on Form 1042-S. Similarly, a QI may choose not to assume primary responsibility for Form 1099 reporting and backup withholding. In this instance, the QI is not required to backup withhold or file Form 1099, but must provide the U.S. payor with Form W-9 for each U.S. recipient account holder.

A foreign financial institution that becomes a QI and elects to assume primary withholding responsibility is subject to all obligations imposed on U.S. withholding agents or payors and must provide U.S. withholding agents with withholding rates to enable the U.S. agents to appropriately withhold and report on payments made through the QI. If a U.S. non-exempt recipient fails to provide a Form W-9, the QI must disclose the recipient's name, address and taxpayer identification number (TIN) to the withholding agent. However, if the QI is prohibited under local law from making such disclosures, the QI is not required to disclose the information as long as the QI backup withholds.

A foreign financial institution that becomes a QI and elects primary withholding responsibility is not required to forward beneficial ownership information regarding its customers to a U.S. financial institution or other withholding agent of U.S. source investment type income to establish the customer's eligibility for an exemption from,

BACKGROUND

or reduced rate of, U.S. withholding tax. Instead, the QI is permitted to establish for itself the eligibility of its customers for an exemption or reduced rate, based on a Form W-8 and information as to residence obtained under the know-your-customer (KYC) rules to which the QI is subject in its home jurisdiction, as approved by the IRS or as specified in the QI agreement (Rev. Proc. 2000-12, 2000-1 CB 387).

A QI must use its best efforts to obtain documentation regarding the status of account holders and must adhere to the KYC rules in the QI agreement. A QI must also apply presumption rules unless a payment can be reliably associated with valid documentation from the account holder.

A QI may treat an account holder as a foreign beneficial owner of an amount if the account holder provides a valid Form W-8 or other valid documentary evidence supporting foreign status. If the appropriate documentation has been provided, the QI may treat the account holder as entitled to a reduced rate of withholding if all requirements for the reduced rate are satisfied. However, the QI cannot reduce the withholding rate if the QI knows the account holder is not the beneficial owner of a payment to the account. If the foreign account holder is the beneficial owner of a payment, the QI can shield the account holder's identity from U.S. custodians and the IRS. If a foreign account holder is a nominee and not the beneficial owner of a payment, the account holder must provide the QI with Form W-IMY for itself and specific information about each beneficial owner to which the payment relates. A QI that receives this information may shield the account holder's identity from a U.S. custodian, but not from the IRS.

If an account holder is a U.S. person, the account holder must provide the QI with Form W-9 supporting U.S. status. Absent receipt of Form W-9, the QI must follow the presumption rules in the QI agreement to determine whether nonresident 30-percent withholding, or 28-percent backup withholding, is required. A reduced rate of nonresident withholding may not be applied based on the presumption rules.

Pursuant to the QI agreement presumption rules, U.S. source investment income paid to an offshore account is presumed paid to an undocumented foreign account holder and is subject to 30-percent withholding. Most U.S. source deposit interest and interest or original issue discount (OID) on short-term obligations paid to an offshore account, however, is presumed made to an undocumented U.S. non-exempt account holder and is subject to 28-percent backup withholding. Foreign source income and broker proceeds paid to an offshore account are presumed paid to a U.S. exempt recipient and, therefore, are exempt from both nonresident and backup withholding.

A QI must file Form 1042 by March 15 of the year following any calendar year in which the QI acts as a QI. A QI is not required to file Forms 1042-S for amounts paid to each separate account holder, but instead must file a separate Form 1042-S for each type of reporting pool (income that falls within a particular withholding rate or within a particular income, exemption or recipient code). Similarly, the QI has specific Form 1099 filing requirements.

The U.S. KYC rules require financial institutions to develop and maintain a written customer identification program, and anti-money laundering policies and procedures. A customer identification program at a minimum requires the financial institution to collect the name, date of birth (for individuals), address, and identifica-

BACKGROUND

tion number for new customers. Financial institutions must perform customer due diligence. Enhanced due diligence requirements apply if the account or financial institution has a higher risk profile. Financial institutions are required to verify enough customer information to enable the financial institution to form a "reasonable belief that it knows the true identity of each customer."

The European Union (EU) Third Money Laundering Directive also applies to a broad range of persons including credit institutions and financial institutions, as well as to persons acting in the exercise of certain professional activities. It requires systems, policies and procedures for customer due diligence, reporting and recordkeeping, risk assessment, compliance and communication. The required customer due diligence measures go further than the KYC rules in the United States by requiring identification and verification of the beneficial owner and an understanding of the ownership and control structure. EU member states generally must require identification of the customer and any beneficial owners before a business relationship can be established. In addition, the EU Third Money Laundering Directive requires ongoing account monitoring during the course of the relationship to ensure that the transactions conducted are consistent with the customer and the business risk profile. Records must be maintained for up to five years after the customer relationship ends.

With regard to U.S. source investment income, the nonresident withholding rules apply broadly to any financial institution or other payor, including foreign financial institutions (Reg. § 1.1441-7(a)). However, the withholding requirements are difficult to enforce with regard to foreign financial institutions unless these institutions have some connection to the United States, e.g., the foreign institution is doing business in the United States, or the institution is a foreign subsidiary of a U.S. financial institution.

NEW LAW EXPLAINED

Expanded disclosure by foreign financial institutions and non-financial foreign entities.—Generally, a withholding agent must deduct and withhold a tax equal to 30 percent on any withholdable payment made to a *foreign financial institution* or to a *non-financial foreign entity* (Code Secs. 1471(a) and 1472(a), as added by the Hiring Incentives to Restore Employment (HIRE) Act (P.L. 111-147)).

A *withholdable payment* is any payment of interest (including original issue discount (OID)), dividends, rents, salaries, wages, premiums, annuities, compensations, remunerations, emoluments, and other fixed or determinable annual or periodical gains, profits and income from sources within the United States, including gross proceeds from the sale of any property that can produce interest or dividends from sources within the United States (Code Sec. 1473(1)(A), as added by the 2010 HIRE Act). Items of income connected with a U.S. business under Code Sec. 871(b)(1) or Code Sec. 882(a)(1) are not withholdable payments (Code Sec. 1473(1)(B), as added by the 2010 HIRE Act). The rule for sourcing interest paid by foreign branches of domestic financial institutions under Code Sec. 861(a)(1)(B) does not apply in determining the source of a payment (Code Sec. 1473(1)(C), as added by the 2010 HIRE Act). A *withholding agent*

NEW LAW EXPLAINED

includes any person in whatever capacity having control, receipt, custody, disposal, or payment of any withholdable payment (Code Sec. 1473(4), as added by the 2010 HIRE Act).

Withholdable payments to foreign financial institutions. A withholding agent must deduct and withhold a tax equal to 30 percent on any withholdable payment made to a foreign financial institution, unless specific additional reporting requirements are satisfied (Code Sec. 1471(a), as added by the 2010 HIRE Act).

> **Comment:** Withholding generally applies to payments made after December 31, 2012; however, no amount must be deducted or withheld from any payment under any obligation outstanding on the date that is two years after March 18, 2010 (Act Sec. 501(d)(2) of the 2010 HIRE Act).

The term *financial institution* means any entity that:

(1) accepts deposits in the ordinary course of a banking or similar business,

(2) as a substantial portion of its business, holds financial assets for the account of others, or

(3) is engaged primarily in the business of investing, reinvesting, or trading in securities, partnership interests, commodities, or any interest in such securities, partnership interests, or commodities (Code Sec. 1471(d)(5), as added by the 2010 HIRE Act).

The term *foreign financial institution* means any financial institution that is a foreign entity, but excludes any financial institution organized under the laws of any U.S. possession (Code Sec. 1471(d)(4), as added by the 2010 HIRE Act). A *foreign entity* is any entity that is not a U.S. person (Code Sec. 1473(5), as added by the 2010 HIRE Act).

No withholding is required if an agreement is in effect between the foreign financial institution and the IRS pursuant to which the institution agrees to:

(1) obtain information regarding account holders that is necessary to determine which accounts are U.S. accounts;

(2) comply with verification and due diligence procedures as the IRS requires with regard to the identification of U.S. accounts;

(3) report annually certain information regarding any U.S. account;

(4) deduct and withhold a 30-percent tax on any passthru payment to a recalcitrant account holder or other financial institution not entering into an agreement with the IRS, or a foreign financial institution electing to be withheld upon rather than to withhold regarding a payment allocable to a recalcitrant account holder or foreign financial institution not having an agreement with the IRS;

(5) comply with any requests by the IRS for additional information regarding any U.S. account maintained at the institution; and

(6) attempt to obtain a waiver in any case where any foreign law would prevent the reporting of information required by this provision with respect to any U.S. account and, if a waiver is not obtained within a reasonable period of time, close the account (Code Sec. 1471(b)(1), as added by the 2010 HIRE Act).

¶705

NEW LAW EXPLAINED

The IRS may terminate any agreement if the IRS determines that the foreign financial institution is out of compliance with the terms of the agreement (Code Sec. 1471(b)(1), as added by the 2010 HIRE Act). A foreign financial institution is *deemed* to meet the requirements of an agreement with the IRS if the institution complies with IRS procedures meant to ensure that the institution does not maintain U.S. accounts and complies with IRS rules regarding accounts of other foreign financial institutions maintained by the institution, or the institution is a member of a class of institutions for which the IRS has determined the agreement requirements are not necessary (Code Sec. 1471(b)(2), as added by the 2010 HIRE Act).

A *passthru payment* is any withholdable payment or other payment to the extent it is attributable to a withholdable payment (Code Sec. 1471(d)(7), as added by the 2010 HIRE Act). A *recalcitrant account holder* is any account holder who fails to comply with reasonable requests for information necessary to determine if the account is a U.S. account, fails to provide the name, address and TIN of each specified U.S. person and each substantial U.S. owner of a U.S. owned foreign entity, or fails to provide a waiver of any foreign law preventing the foreign financial institution from reporting required information (Code Sec. 1471(d)(6), as added by the 2010 HIRE Act).

A foreign financial institution that has an agreement with the IRS can elect to have a U.S. withholding agent or foreign financial institution that has entered into an agreement with the IRS withhold on payments made to the electing institution rather than acting as a withholding agent: (1) for payments it makes to other foreign financial institutions that do not have an agreement with the IRS or have elected not to act as a withholding agent, or (2) for payments it makes to account holders that fail to provide the required information (Code Sec. 1471(b)(3), as added by the 2010 HIRE Act). If the election is made, the 30-percent withholding tax applies to any withholdable payment made to the electing institution to the extent that the payment is allocable to accounts held by foreign financial institutions that do not have an agreement with the IRS, or to accounts held by recalcitrant account holders (Code Sec. 1471(b)(3)(B), as added by the 2010 HIRE Act). The electing institution is required to notify the withholding agent of its election, provide necessary information so that the withholding agent can determine the amount of withholding, and the electing institution must waive any rights under a treaty (Code Sec. 1471(b)(3)(C), as added by the 2010 HIRE Act).

A foreign financial institution that is a party to an agreement with the IRS must report the following information regarding each U.S. account maintained by the institution:

(1) The name, address, and TIN of each account holder that is a specified U.S. person.

(2) The name, address, and TIN of each substantial U.S. owner of any account holder that is a U.S. owned foreign entity.

(3) The account number.

(4) The account balance or value as determined at such time and in such manner as the IRS prescribes.

NEW LAW EXPLAINED

(5) The gross receipts and gross withdrawals or payments from the account as determined for such period and in such manner as the IRS prescribes (Code Sec. 1471(c)(1), as added by the 2010 HIRE Act).

Comment: The rule requiring 30 percent withholding on any withholdable payment made to a foreign financial institution that fails to report the required information is not intended to create an alternative to information reporting. It is anticipated that the IRS may require a foreign financial institution to achieve certain reporting levels under its agreement with the IRS, or close accounts. Furthermore, in the case of new accounts, the foreign financial institution may be prohibited from withholding as an alternative to collecting information required under its agreement with the IRS (Joint Committee on Taxation, Technical Explanation of the Hiring Incentives to Restore Employment Act (JCX-4-10)).

With respect to any financial institution, except as otherwise provided by the IRS, the term *financial account* means any depository or custodial account maintained by such financial institution, and any equity or debt interest in such financial institution other than interests that are regularly traded on an established securities market (Code Sec. 1471(d)(2), as added by the 2010 HIRE Act).

A *U. S. account* is any financial account held by one or more specified U.S. persons or U.S. owned foreign entities (Code Sec. 1471(d)(1)(A), as added by the 2010 HIRE Act). Unless the foreign financial institution elects not to have this rule apply, depository accounts are not treated as U.S. accounts if all holders of the account are natural persons and the aggregate value of depository accounts held by each holder of the account maintained by the financial institution is $50,000 or less. As provided by the IRS, financial institutions that are members of the same affiliated group are treated as a single financial institution for purposes of determining whether an account has an aggregate value that does not exceed $50,000 with respect to each account holder (Code Sec. 1471(d)(1)(B), as added by the 2010 HIRE Act). A financial account is not a U.S. account if the account is in a foreign financial institution held by another foreign financial institution that has entered into an agreement with the IRS or is otherwise subject to information reporting requirements that the IRS determines would make the reporting duplicative (Code Sec. 1471(d)(1)(C), as added by the 2010 HIRE Act).

A *specified U.S. person* is any U.S. person except:

(1) a publicly traded corporation or a member of the same expanded affiliated group (as generally defined in Code Sec. 1471(e)(2));

(2) any tax-exempt organization or individual retirement plan;

(3) the United States or a wholly owned agency or instrumentality of the United States;

(4) a state, the District of Columbia, any possession of the United States, or a political subdivision or wholly owned agency of a state, the District of Columbia, or a U.S. possession;

(5) a bank;

(6) a real estate investment trust (REIT);

(7) a regulated investment company (RIC);

NEW LAW EXPLAINED

(8) a common trust fund; and

(9) a trust that is exempt from tax under Code Sec. 664(c)) or is described in Code Sec. 4947(a)(1) (Code Sec. 1473(3), as added by the 2010 HIRE Act).

The term *U.S. owned foreign entity* means any foreign entity that has one or more substantial U.S. owners (Code Sec. 1471(d)(3), as added by the 2010 HIRE Act). A *substantial U.S. owner* is:

(1) with respect to any corporation, any specified U.S. person that owns, directly or indirectly, more than 10 percent of the corporate stock by vote or value;

(2) with respect to any partnership, a specified U.S. person that directly or indirectly owns more than 10 percent of the profits *or* capital interests of the partnership; and

(3) with respect to any trust, any specified U.S. person treated as an owner of any portion of the trust under the grantor trust rules and, as provided by the IRS, any specified U.S. person holding more than 10 percent of the beneficial interests of the trust (Code Sec. 1473(2)(A), as added by the 2010 HIRE Act).

The 10-percent ownership threshold for classifying a *substantial U.S. owner* is reduced to zero percent to the extent the foreign entity is a corporation, partnership, or trust engaged, or holding itself out as being engaged, primarily in the business of investing, reinvesting, or trading in securities, interests in partnerships, commodities, or any interest (including a futures or forward contract or option) in such securities, interests, or commodities (Code Sec. 1473(2)(B), as added by the 2010 HIRE Act).

An *expanded affiliated group* is an affiliated group, as defined by reference to Code Sec. 1504(a), with one or more chains of includible corporations connected through stock ownership with a common parent that is an includible corporation, provided that the following two requirements are met:

(1) the common parent must directly own stock possessing more than 50 percent of the total voting power of at least one of the other includible corporations and have a value equal to more than 50 percent of the total value of stock of the corporation; and

(2) stock meeting the more than 50 percent test in each includible corporation other than the common parent must be owned directly by one or more of the other includible corporations (Code Sec. 1471(e)(2)(A), as added by the 2010 HIRE Act).

The definition of expanded affiliated group does not apply to insurance companies subject to tax under Code Sec. 801 or foreign corporations (Code Sec. 1471(e)(2)(B), as added by the 2010 HIRE Act). A partnership or other non-corporate entity is treated as a member of an expanded affiliated group if the entity is controlled by members of such expanded affiliated group.

> **Comment:** The provisions providing for an agreement between a foreign financial institution and the IRS (Code Sec. 1471(b)) and foreign financial institution reporting requirements (Code Sec. 1471(c)(1)) apply to U.S. accounts maintained by the foreign financial institution and to U.S. accounts maintained by any other financial institution that is a member of the same expanded affiliated group,

NEW LAW EXPLAINED

except as provided by the IRS and excluding a financial institution that enters into its own agreement with the IRS (Code Sec. 1471(e)(1), as added by the 2010 HIRE Act).

Election. As an alternative to the specific foreign financial institution reporting requirements provided in Code Sec. 1471(c)(1), a foreign financial institution may elect to be subject to the same reporting as U.S. financial institutions, as if such foreign financial institution were a U.S. person and as if each holder of an account that is a specified U.S. person or U.S. owned foreign entity is a natural person and citizen of the United States, and provide full Form 1099 reporting under Code Sec. 6041 (information at source), Code Sec. 6042 (returns covering payments of dividends and corporate earnings and profits), Code Sec. 6045 (returns of brokers), and Code Sec. 6049 (returns covering payments of interest) (Code Sec. 1471(c)(2), as added by the 2010 HIRE Act). If the election is made, the foreign financial institution is not required to provide the account balance or value, or the gross receipts and withdrawals from the account (Code Sec. 1471(c)(2)(A), as added by the 2010 HIRE Act).

> **Comment:** The IRS will provide guidance as to the time, manner and conditions for such an election (Code Sec. 1471(c)(2), as added by the 2010 HIRE Act).

Qualified intermediary. Foreign financial institutions that have entered into a qualified intermediary (QI) agreement with the IRS under Code Sec. 1441 are required to meet the requirements of this provision in addition to any other requirements imposed under the QI agreement (Code Sec. 1471(c)(3), as added by the 2010 HIRE Act).

Exceptions. The 30-percent withholding provision for withholdable payments to foreign financial institutions does not apply to any payment if the beneficial owner of the payment is any foreign government or political subdivision of the government, any international organization, any foreign central bank of issue, or any other class of persons identified by the IRS as posing a low risk of tax evasion (Code Sec. 1471(f), as added by the 2010 HIRE Act).

Withholdable payments to non-financial foreign entities. A withholding agent must deduct and withhold a tax equal to 30 percent on any withholdable payment made to a non-financial foreign entity unless the beneficial owner of the payment is a non-financial foreign entity that meets specified requirements (Code Sec. 1472(a), as added by the 2010 HIRE Act). A *non-financial foreign entity* is any foreign entity that is not a financial institution (Code Sec. 1472(d), as added by the 2010 HIRE Act).

> **Comment:** Withholding generally applies to payments made after December 31, 2012, however, no amount must be deducted or withheld from any payment under any obligation outstanding on the date that is two years after March 18, 2010 (Act Sec. 501(d)(2) of the 2010 HIRE Act).

No withholding is required on payments made to a non-financial foreign entity if:

(1) the beneficial owner or payee provides the withholding agent with either a certification that the beneficial owner does not have any substantial U.S. owners, or the name, address, and TIN of each substantial U.S. owner;

(2) the withholding agent does not know, or has no reason to know, that any information provided about substantial U.S. owners is incorrect; and

NEW LAW EXPLAINED

(3) the withholding agent reports the name, address and TIN of any substantial U.S. owners to the IRS as prescribed by the IRS (Code Sec. 1472(b), as added by the 2010 HIRE Act).

Exceptions The 30-percent withholding provision for withholdable payments to non-financial foreign entities does not apply to any payment beneficially owned by:

(1) a publicly traded corporation or a member of an expanded affiliated group of a publicly traded corporation;

(2) any entity organized under the laws of a U.S. possession that is wholly owned by one or more bona fide residents of the possession;

(3) any foreign government or a political subdivision or wholly owned agency of any foreign government;

(4) any international organization;

(5) any foreign central bank of issue; or

(6) any other class of persons identified by the IRS (Code Sec. 1472(c)(1), as added by the 2010 HIRE Act).

In addition, 30-percent withholding for withholdable payments to non-financial foreign entities does not apply to any class of payments identified by the IRS as posing a low risk of tax evasion (Code Sec. 1472(c)(2), as added by the 2010 HIRE Act).

General rules. Some general rules apply with respect to the new withholding and reporting requirements for foreign financial institutions and non-financial foreign entities.

Liability. Every person required to deduct and withhold any tax to enforce reporting on certain foreign accounts is liable for the tax and is indemnified against claims and demands of anyone for the amount of the payments (Code Sec. 1474(a), as added by the 2010 HIRE Act).

Credits and refunds. The determination of whether there is an overpayment of tax deducted and withheld on payments to foreign financial institutions and non-financial foreign entities is made in the same manner as if the tax had been deducted and withheld on nonresident aliens and foreign corporations (Code Sec. 1474(b)(1), as added by the 2010 HIRE Act). Any tax deducted and withheld pursuant to an agreement between a foreign financial institution and the IRS is treated as a tax deducted and withheld by a withholding agent on a withholdable payment made to a foreign financial institution (Code Sec. 1474(e), as added by the 2010 HIRE Act).

> **Comment:** The credit and refund mechanism ensures that the withholding provisions of Code Secs. 1471 and 1472 are consistent with U.S. obligations under existing income tax treaties. A specific procedure need not be followed for achieving treaty benefits. If proof of treaty benefit entitlement is provided prior to a payment, the United States may permit reduced withholding or exemption at the time of payment. Alternatively, withholding may be required at the time of payment and treaty country residents may obtain treaty benefits through the refund process (Joint Committee on Taxation, Technical Explanation of the Hiring Incentives to Restore Employment Act (JCX-4-10)).

NEW LAW EXPLAINED

If a beneficial owner of a payment is a foreign financial institution, the payment is a *specified financial institution payment* (Code Sec. 1474(b)(2)(B), as added by the 2010 HIRE Act). Generally, credits and refunds with respect to specified financial institution payments are not allowed. However, if the foreign financial institution that is the beneficial owner of the payment is entitled to a reduced rate of withholding tax on the payment under an income tax treaty, the beneficial owner may be eligible for a credit or refund of the excess amount withheld over the amount permitted to be withheld under the treaty (Code Sec. 1474(b)(2), as added by the 2010 HIRE Act). No interest is payable with respect to any credit or refund of tax properly withheld on the specified financial institution payment (Code Sec. 1474(b)(2)(A)(i)(II), as added by the 2010 HIRE Act). Furthermore, no credit or refund is allowed unless the beneficial owner provides the IRS with sufficient information regarding whether it is a U.S. owned foreign entity and the identity of any substantial U.S. owners of the entity (Code Sec. 1474(b)(3), as added by the 2010 HIRE Act).

The grace period during which the IRS is not required to pay interest on any overpayment is increased from 45 days to 180 days for overpayments resulting from excess amounts deducted and withheld under the nonresident alien and foreign corporation withholding rules of Code Sec. 1441 and the foreign account withholding rules of Code Secs. 1471 and 1472 (Code Sec. 6611(e)(4), as added by the 2010 HIRE Act). The increased grace period applies to: (1) returns with due dates (excluding extensions) after March 18, 2010, (2) claims for credit or refund of overpayments filed after March 18, 2010, and (3) refunds paid on adjustments initiated by the IRS that are paid after March 18, 2010 (Act Sec. 501(d)(3) of the 2010 HIRE Act).

Confidentiality. No person may use any information obtained under the rules for withholding tax to enforce reporting on certain foreign accounts except for the purpose of meeting withholding requirements or for purposes permitted under Code Sec. 6103. The identity of foreign financial institutions that have entered into an agreement with the IRS, however, is not treated as return information for purposes of Code Sec. 6103 (Code Sec. 1474(c), as added by the 2010 HIRE Act).

IRS guidance. The IRS has authority to prescribe regulations and any other guidance necessary to enforce reporting and withholding on certain foreign accounts (Code Sec. 1474(f), as added by the 2010 HIRE Act). And, the IRS is to provide for the coordination of foreign account withholding rules with other withholding provisions to prevent double withholding (Code Sec. 1474(d), as added by the 2010 HIRE Act).

▶ **Effective date.** The provisions generally apply to payments made after December 31, 2012 (Act Sec. 501(d)(1) of the Hiring Incentives to Restore Employment (HIRE) Act (P.L. 111-147)). However, no amount must be deducted or withheld from any payment under any obligation outstanding on the date that is two years after March 18, 2010, or from the gross proceeds from any disposition of such an obligation (Act Sec. 501(d)(2) of the 2010 HIRE Act). The interest on overpayments provision increasing the grace period from 45 to 180 days during which no interest must be paid by the IRS applies to returns with due dates (excluding extensions) after March 18, 2010, claims for credit or refund of overpayments filed after March 18, 2010, and refunds paid on adjustments initiated by the IRS that are paid after March 18, 2010 (Act Sec. 501(d)(3) of the 2010 HIRE Act).

¶705

NEW LAW EXPLAINED

Law source: Law at ¶6085, ¶6090, ¶6095, ¶6100, ¶6150, ¶6155, ¶6160, ¶6165, and ¶6185. Committee Report at ¶11,120.

— Act Sec. 501(a) of the Hiring Incentives to Restore Employment (HIRE) Act (P.L. 111-147), adding Code Secs 1471, 1472, 1473 and 1474;

— Act Sec. 501(b) adding Code Sec. 6611(e)(4);

— Act Sec. 501(c) amending Code Secs. 6414, 6501(b)(1) and (b)(2), 6513(b)(3) and (c), and 6724(d)(1) and (d)(2);

— Act Sec. 501(d), providing the effective date.

Reporter references: For further information, consult the following CCH reporters.

— Standard Federal Tax Reporter, ¶32,716.01

— Tax Research Consultant, EXPAT: 15,052.05

— Practical Tax Explanation, §37,305

¶710 Disclosure of Information with Respect to Foreign Financial Assets

SUMMARY OF NEW LAW

Individuals holding interests in specified foreign financial assets must attach to their income tax returns certain information with respect to each asset if the aggregate value of all the assets exceeds $50,000. An individual who fails to furnish the required information is subject to a penalty of $10,000. An additional penalty may apply if the failure continues for more than 90 days after a notification by the IRS. The penalty may be avoided if the taxpayer shows a reasonable cause for the failure to comply.

BACKGROUND

U.S. persons who transfer assets to, and hold interests in, foreign bank accounts or foreign entities may be subject to self-reporting requirements under both the Internal Revenue Code (the Code) and the Bank Secrecy Act (the BSA).

The BSA imposes reporting obligations on both financial institutions and account holders. With respect to account holders, a U.S. citizen, resident, or person doing business in the United States is required to keep records and file reports if that person enters into a transaction or maintains an account with a foreign financial agency. A foreign financial agency for this purpose includes financial institutions. Regulations issued under the BSA provide additional guidance regarding the disclosure obligation with respect to foreign accounts. In February 2010, the Treasury Department's Financial Crimes Enforcement Network (FinCEN) issued proposed revisions to the BSA regulations regarding reports of foreign financial accounts. The proposed rules would clarify which persons must file reports of foreign financial accounts and which accounts are reportable. They would also exempt certain persons with signature or

BACKGROUND

other authority over foreign financial accounts from filing reports and would include provisions intended to prevent U.S. persons from avoiding this reporting requirement (NPRM RIN-1506-AB08).

U.S. persons must generally disclose any account in which they have a financial interest or as to which they have signature or other authority on Form TD F 90-22.1, Report of Foreign Bank and Financial Accounts, (the FBAR). The FBAR must be filed by June 30 of the year following the year in which a $10,000 filing threshold is met. The $10,000 threshold is the aggregate value of all foreign financial accounts in which a U.S. person has a financial interest or over which the U.S. person has signature or other authority. In 2008, the IRS revised the FBAR and its accompanying instructions to clarify the filing requirements for U.S. persons holding interests in foreign bank accounts. Subsequently, the IRS requested public comments to help determine the scope and nature of future additional guidance (Notice 2009-62, I.R.B. 2009-35, 260). Although the FBAR is received and processed by the IRS, it is not part of the income tax return and is not filed in the IRS office where the return is filed. As a result, for purposes of the Code, the FBAR is not considered return information, and its distribution to other law enforcement agencies is not limited by the Code Sec. 6103 nondisclosure rules.

Even though the obligation to file an FBAR arises under the BSA, individual taxpayers subject to the FBAR reporting requirements are alerted to this requirement while preparing their income tax returns. Form 1040, Schedule B, Part III (Foreign Accounts and Trusts) includes a question about interests in foreign financial accounts and directs taxpayers to Form TD F 90-22.1 for filing requirements and exceptions. Responding to this question does not discharge the taxpayer's obligations under the BSA and constitutes return information protected from routine disclosure to those charged with enforcing the BSA. In addition, the Form 1040 instructions identify certain types of accounts that are not subject to disclosure, including the exception for the $10,000 combined value of all accounts held by the taxpayer during the year. Other than providing an answer to the question included on Form 1040, Schedule B, taxpayers are not required to disclose information includible on the FBAR on their tax returns.

In general, information reported on an FBAR is available to the IRS and other law enforcement agencies. In contrast, information on income tax returns, including the Schedule B information regarding foreign bank accounts, is not readily available to those within the IRS who are charged with administering FBAR compliance, despite the fact that the federal returns may be the best source of information for this purpose. Thus, the IRS personnel charged with investigating and enforcing the civil penalties under the BSA are not routinely permitted access to Form 1040 information that would support or shed light on the existence of an FBAR violation.

Failure to comply with the FBAR filing requirements is subject to civil and criminal penalties imposed under the BSA. Until 2003, the FinCEN had responsibility for civil penalty enforcement of FBAR, and persons who were more than 180 days delinquent in paying any FBAR penalties were referred for collection action to the Financial Management Service of the Treasury Department, which is responsible for such non-tax collections. In 2003, the civil enforcement of the FBAR was delegated to the IRS.

BACKGROUND

The delegated authority includes the authority to determine and enforce civil penalties, as well as to revise the form and instructions. However, the IRS's collection and enforcement powers to enforce the Code provisions are not available to it in the enforcement of FBAR civil penalties, which remain collectible only in accordance with the procedures for non-tax collections.

In addition to the FBAR, U.S. persons engaged in foreign activities are required to file additional reports with the IRS under numerous Code provisions. For example, Code Sec. 6038 requires ceratin U.S. persons to file an information return with respect to the formation, acquisition or ongoing ownership of certain foreign corporations (Form 5471, Information Return of U.S. Persons with Respect to Certain Foreign Corporations) and with respect to certain interests in a controlled foreign partnership (Form 8865, Return of U.S. Persons with Respect to Certain Foreign Partnerships). U.S. persons that transfer property to a foreign entity are also generally required to file an information return under Code Sec. 6038B (Form 926, Return by a U.S. Transferor of Property to a Foreign Corporation). Code Sec. 6048 requires U.S. persons to file an information return with respect to certain foreign trusts (Form 3520, Annual Return to Report Transactions with Foreign Trusts and Receipt of Certain Foreign Gifts). Failure to comply with the Code information reporting requirements is subject to a variety of sanctions, including imposition of penalties, suspension of the applicable statute of limitations, and disallowance of otherwise permitted tax attributes, deductions or credits.

NEW LAW EXPLAINED

Information disclosure with respect to foreign financial assets required.—Individuals who hold any interest in specified foreign financial assets during the tax year must attach to their tax returns for the year certain information with respect to each asset if the aggregate value of all the assets exceeds $50,000 (or a higher dollar amount prescribed by the Secretary of the Treasury) (Code Sec. 6038D(a), as added by the Hiring Incentives to Restore Employment (HIRE) Act (P.L. 111-147)).

> **Comment:** The Joint Committee Report clarifies that although the nature of the information required to be disclosed is similar to the information disclosed on an FBAR, it is not identical. For example, a beneficiary of a foreign trust who is not within the scope of the FBAR reporting requirements because his interest in the trust is less than 50 percent may nonetheless be required to disclose the interest with his tax return under this provision if the value threshold is met. In addition, nothing in this provision is intended as a substitute for compliance with the FBAR reporting requirements, which remain unchanged (Joint Committee on Taxation, Technical Explanation of the Hiring Incentives to Restore Employment Act (JCX-4-10)).

For purposes of the Code Sec. 6038D reporting requirements, a specified foreign financial asset includes:

• any depository, custodial, or other financial account maintained by a foreign financial institution, and

¶710

NEW LAW EXPLAINED

- any of the following assets that are not held in an account maintained by a financial institution:

  (i) any stock or security issued by a person other than a U.S. person,

  (ii) any financial instrument or contract held for investment that has an issuer or counterparty other than a U.S. person, and

  (iii) any interest in a foreign entity (Code Sec. 6038D(b), as added by the 2010 HIRE Act).

  Comment: For a discussion of the definitions of financial accounts, foreign financial institution, financial institution, and interest in a foreign entity under the new foreign account withholding and reporting rules of Code Secs. 1471 and 1473, see ¶705.

The information required to be disclosed with respect to any asset must include the maximum value of the asset during the tax year (Code Sec. 6038D(c), as added by the 2010 HIRE Act). In addition, for a financial account, the taxpayer must disclose the name and address of the financial institution in which the account is maintained and the number of the account. In the case of any stock or security, the disclosed information must include the name and address of the issuer and such other information as is necessary to identify the class or issue of which the stock or security is a part. In the case of any other instrument, contract, or interest, a taxpayer must provide any information necessary to identify the instrument, contract, or interest along with the names and addresses of all issuers and counterparties with respect to the instrument, contract, or interest.

  Comment: Under these rules, an individual is not required to disclose interests held in a custodial account with a U.S. financial institution or to identify separately any stock, security instrument, contract, or interest in a disclosed foreign financial account.

An individual who fails to furnish the required information with respect to any tax year at the prescribed time and in the prescribed manner is subject to a penalty of $10,000 (Code Sec. 6038D(d), as added by the 2010 HIRE Act). An additional penalty may apply if the Secretary of the Treasury notifies the individual by mail of the failure to disclose and the failure to disclose continues. In such cases, if the failure to disclose the required information continues for more than 90 days after the day on which the notice was mailed, the individual is subject to an additional penalty of $10,000 for each 30-day period (or a fraction thereof) during which the failure continues after the expiration of the 90-day period. The additional penalty with respect to any failure may not exceed $50,000.

  Practice Pointer: The computation of the penalty is similar to the penalty applicable to failures to file reports with respect to certain foreign corporations under Code Sec. 6038. Thus, an individual who is notified of his failure to disclose with respect to a single tax year under this provision and who takes remedial action on the 95th day after the notice is mailed incurs a penalty of $20,000, consisting of the base amount of $10,000 plus $10,000 for the fraction (i.e., the five days) of the 30-day period following the lapse of 90 days after the notice of noncompliance was mailed. An individual who postpones remedial

NEW LAW EXPLAINED

action until the 181st day is subject to the maximum penalty of $50,000, which consists of the base amount of $10,000 plus $30,000 for the three 30-day periods, plus $10,000 for the one fraction (i.e., the single day) of the 30-day period following the lapse of 90 days after the notice was mailed (Joint Committee on Taxation, Technical Explanation of the Hiring Incentives to Restore Employment Act (JCX-4-10)).

Comment: In addition to the penalty under Code Sec. 6038D for failure to disclose the required information for foreign financial assets, a 40-percent accuracy-related penalty is imposed on any understatement of tax attributable to a transaction involving an undisclosed foreign financial asset, see ¶715. In addition, the statute of limitations for omission of gross income attributable to foreign financial assets subject to information reporting is extended to six year, see ¶720.

The Code Sec. 6038D penalties are not imposed on any individual who can show that the failure is due to reasonable cause and not willful neglect (Code Sec. 6038D(g), as added by the 2010 HIRE Act). The fact that a foreign jurisdiction would impose a civil or criminal penalty on the taxpayer (or any other person) for disclosing the required information is not a reasonable cause.

If the Secretary of the Treasury determines that an individual has an interest in one or more specified foreign financial assets, and the individual does not provide sufficient information to demonstrate the aggregate value of such assets, then the aggregate value of the assets is presumed to have exceeded $50,000 (or any higher dollar amount prescribed by the Secretary of the Treasury) for purposes of assessing the Code Sec. 6038D penalties (Code Sec. 6038D(e), as added by the 2010 HIRE Act). The Secretary of the Treasury is also allowed to issue regulations or other guidance that would apply the Code Sec. 6038D reporting obligations to any domestic entity in the same manner as if such entity were an individual if that domestic entity is formed or availed of for purposes of holding, directly or indirectly, specified foreign financial assets (Code Sec. 6038D(f), as added by the 2010 HIRE Act).

In addition, the Secretary of the Treasury is authorized to prescribe regulations and other guidance that may be necessary or appropriate to carry out the purposes of this provision (Code Sec. 6038D(h), as added by the 2010 HIRE Act). Such regulations or other guidance may provide for appropriate exceptions from the application of Code Sec. 6038D, as added by the 2010 HIRE Act, in the case of: (i) classes of assets identified by the Secretary of the Treasury, including any assets with respect to which the Secretary of the Treasury determines that disclosure under this provision would be duplicative of other disclosures, (ii) nonresident aliens, and (iii) bona fide residents of any U.S. possession.

Practical Analysis: Steven Toscher, J.D., and Michel R. Stein, J.D., LL.M., Principals at Hochman, Salkin, Rettig, Toscher & Perez, P.C., of Beverly Hills, California, observe that while the new disclosure provisions of the HIRE Act broaden reporting requirements, they also add duplication and complexity to an already complicated foreign financial account reporting regime.

¶710

NEW LAW EXPLAINED

The FBAR reporting regime, once largely unenforced and historically without much regulatory or other official guidance, has gained much attention recently since civil enforcement was delegated to the IRS in 2003. The new focus has shown gaps in the current reporting regime which the new legislation is attempting to fill.

The HIRE Act broadens the reporting requirements and extends the rules to ownership of foreign assets, such as foreign stocks or securities and interests in foreign entities, not covered by the FBAR reporting regime.

While the threshold reporting requirement amount—$50,000—exceeds the threshold relating to FBARs, the amount is low enough to affect many, if not most, taxpayers with foreign assets. Other significant differences exist. While the FBAR reporting regime covers those having signatory or other authority, the new reporting regime focuses on ownership.

Unfortunately the different reporting regimes will likely create confusion among taxpayers and professionals suggesting that the Congress will need to look at these different regimes and consolidate them in a single foreign asset reporting regime.

▶ **Effective date.** The provision applies to tax years beginning after March 18, 2010 (Act Sec. 511(c) of the Hiring Incentives to Restore Employment (HIRE) Act (P.L. 111-147)).

Law source: Law at ¶6125. Committee Report at ¶11,080.

— Act Sec. 511(a) of the Hiring Incentives to Restore Employment (HIRE) Act (P.L. 111-147), adding Code Sec. 6038D;

— Act Sec. 511(b);

— Act Sec. 511(c), providing the effective date.

Reporter references: For further information, consult the following CCH reporters.

— Standard Federal Tax Reporter, ¶36,555.027

— Tax Research Consultant, FILEBUS: 9,104

— Practical Tax Explanation, § 39,005.15

¶715 Penalty for Underpayments Attributable to Undisclosed Foreign Financial Assets

SUMMARY OF NEW LAW

A 40-percent accuracy-related penalty is imposed for underpayments attributable to transactions involving undisclosed foreign financial assets. Undisclosed foreign financial assets include foreign financial assets that are subject to information reporting under various provisions, but for which the required information was not provided by the taxpayer.

¶715

BACKGROUND

Code Sec. 6662 imposes an accuracy-related penalty equal to 20 percent of the portion of any underpayment of tax attributable to one or more of the following: (i) negligence or disregard of rules or regulations; (ii) any substantial understatement of income tax; (iii) any substantial valuation misstatement; (iv) any substantial overstatement of pension liabilities; and (v) any substantial estate or gift tax valuation understatement (Code Sec. 6662(a) and (b)). The penalty is increased to 40 percent in the case of a gross valuation misstatement (Code Sec. 6662(h)).

The accuracy-related penalty does not apply to any portion of the underpayment to which the fraud penalty under Code Sec. 6663 applies. In addition, the Code Sec. 6662 penalty is generally not applied to any portion of the underpayment attributable to a reportable transaction understatement on which a penalty under Code Sec. 6662A is imposed (Code Sec. 6662(b)). The accuracy-related penalty applies only if a return is filed. However, it is inapplicable where the IRS prepares the taxpayer's return under Code Sec. 6020(b) (Code Sec. 6664(b)).

For purposes of the penalty, the underpayment of tax is generally determined as follows: (i) the correct tax (as calculated by the IRS), less (ii) the amount shown as tax by the taxpayer on the return, less (iii) amounts not so shown but previously assessed (or collected without assessment), plus (iv) the amount of rebates made (abatements, credits, refunds, or other payments previously made) (Code Sec. 6664(a)).

The penalty for a substantial understatement may be reduced to the extent of the portion of the understatement attributable to an item on the return for which the challenged tax treatment (i) is supported by substantial authority, or (ii) is adequately disclosed on the return and there was a reasonable basis for such treatment. The tax treatment is considered to have been adequately disclosed only if all relevant facts are disclosed with the return. Regardless of whether an item would otherwise meet either of these tests, this defense is not available with respect to penalties imposed on understatements arising from tax shelters (Code Sec. 6662(d)(2)(B)).

In addition, if the accuracy-related penalty is asserted, a taxpayer may defend against the penalty by showing that there was a reasonable cause for the underpayment and that the taxpayer acted in good faith (Code Sec. 6664(c)). In the case of reportable transaction understatements, an exception to the Code Sec. 6662A penalty is available if the taxpayer satisfies a higher standard under the reasonable cause and good faith exception (Code Sec. 6664(d)).

A number of reporting requirements with respect to foreign transactions are imposed by the Code. For example, Code Sec. 6038 generally requires every U.S. person (a citizen or resident of the United States, a domestic corporation, domestic partnership, or an estate or trust, other than a foreign estate or trust) that owns a controlling interest in a foreign business entity to furnish certain information about the entity and its subsidiaries. Foreign-controlled corporations (domestic corporations engaged in U.S. business and 25 percent foreign owned) must also furnish information about transactions with corporations in their control group and transactions with related parties during the tax year (Code Sec. 6038A). In addition, a U.S. person who is a 10-percent (or greater) partner in a foreign partnership must report changes to his or her ownership interest in the partnership. The reporting obligation is generally

BACKGROUND

limited to reportable events concerning direct interests in foreign partnerships (Code Sec. 6046A). Furthermore, special reporting rules apply with respect to foreign trusts with a U.S. grantor and foreign trusts that distribute money or property to a U.S. person (Code Sec. 6048).

Failure to comply with various information reporting requirements generally does not, in itself, determine the amount of the penalty imposed on an underpayment of tax. However, such failure to comply may be relevant to (i) establishing negligence under Code Sec. 6662 or fraudulent intent under Code Sec. 6663, (ii) determining whether penalties based on culpability are applicable, or (iii) determining whether certain defenses are available.

NEW LAW EXPLAINED

Penalty imposed for underpayment attributable to undisclosed foreign financial assets.—A 40-percent accuracy-related penalty is imposed for underpayment of tax that is attributable to an undisclosed foreign financial asset understatement (Code Sec. 6662(b)(7) and (j), as added by the Hiring Incentives to Restore Employment (HIRE) Act (P.L. 111-147)). For this purpose, an undisclosed foreign financial asset understatement for any tax year is the portion of the understatement for the year that is attributable to any transaction involving undisclosed foreign financial asset. An undisclosed foreign financial asset includes any asset that is subject to the information reporting requirements of Code Secs. 6038, 6038B, 6046A, 6048 and new Code Sec. 6038D (as added by the 2010 HIRE Act), but for which the required information was not provided by the taxpayer as required under the applicable reporting provisions. For a discussion of the new Code Sec. 6038D reporting requirements, see ¶ 710.

> **Comment:** Thus, a U.S. person who fails to comply with the various self-reporting requirements for a foreign financial asset and engages in a transaction with respect to the asset incurs an accuracy-related penalty on any resulting underpayment that is double the otherwise applicable penalty for substantial understatements or negligence. For example, if a taxpayer fails to disclose amounts held in a foreign financial account, any underpayment of tax related to the transaction that gave rise to the income would be subject to the penalty provision, as would any underpayment related to interest, dividends or other returns accrued on such undisclosed amounts. The new 40-percent penalty is subject to the same defenses that are otherwise available for the Code Sec. 6662 penalties (Joint Committee on Taxation, Technical Explanation of the Hiring Incentives to Restore Employment Act (JCX-4-10)).

> **Caution:** There is a discrepancy between the text of the provision and the explanation provided in the Joint Committee Report (Joint Committee on Taxation, Technical Explanation of the Hiring Incentives to Restore Employment Act (JCX-4-10) regarding the definition of an undisclosed foreign financial asset. While the information reporting requirements with respect to foreign financial assets identified in the provision include, among others, Code Sec. 6038B (see Code Sec. 6662(j)(2), as added by the 2010 HIRE Act), the Joint Committee Report points to Code Sec. 6038A, instead of Code Sec. 6038B.

¶715

NEW LAW EXPLAINED

Practical Analysis: Steven Toscher, J.D., and Michel R. Stein, J.D., LL.M., Principals at Hochman, Salkin, Rettig, Toscher & Perez, P.C., of Beverly Hills, California, observe the new penalty provisions of the HIRE Act are in many respects less draconian than the FBAR penalties, and they give the IRS assessment and collection remedies unavailable with respect to the FBAR penalty. These additional Code penalties will likely create a bias within the IRS to impose these new penalties, rather than the FBAR penalties. It would seem the existing FBAR penalties were more than sufficient to serve as a deterrent to the noncompliant in the wake of the current attention foreign compliance has been afforded by the IRS. Nevertheless, the legislation adds a new layer of penalties under the Code.

Unlike with a typical Internal Revenue Code tax or penalty, which is subject to collection under the Internal Revenue Code's broad administrative collection remedies of liens and levies, the FBAR penalty is not subject to these administrative collection remedies. Remedies available to collect the FBAR penalty are limited to collection through the Financial Management System, which collects nontax debts for the government and in appropriate cases, by law suits filed in federal district court. The HIRE Act penalties will give the IRS the ability to assess and collect these new penalties through its broad administrative powers, including levy and lien.

The new penalties under the HIRE Act are calibrated more toward the understatement of tax and impose a lesser burden of proof and threshold for imposition of the penalty than the willful FBAR penalty. On the other hand, the new penalties are less draconian than the willful FBAR penalty and are not as vulnerable to challenges of excessiveness under the Eight Amendment Excessive Fine Clause.

▶ **Effective date.** The provision applies to tax years beginning after March 18, 2010 (Act Sec. 512(b) of the Hiring Incentives to Restore Employment (HIRE) Act (P.L. 111-147)).

Law source: Law at ¶6170. Committee Report at ¶11,090.

— Act Sec. 512(a) of the Hiring Incentives to Restore Employment (HIRE) Act (P.L. 111-147), adding Code Sec. 6662(b)(7) and (j);

— Act Sec. 512(b), providing the effective date.

Reporter references: For further information, consult the following CCH reporters.

— Standard Federal Tax Reporter, ¶39,651D.01

— Tax Research Consultant, PENALTY: 3,100

— Practical Tax Explanation, § 40,210

¶720 Statute of Limitations for Omission of Income in Connection with Foreign Assets

SUMMARY OF NEW LAW

The statute of limitations for assessments of tax is extended to six years if there is an omission of gross income in excess of $5,000 attributable to a foreign financial asset. The foreign financial asset may or may not be subject to information reporting under new Code Sec. 6038D. The three-year limitations period is suspended for failure to timely provide Code Sec. 6038D information reporting or information returns with respect to passive foreign investment companies.

BACKGROUND

Taxes are generally required to be assessed within three years after a taxpayer's return was filed, whether or not it was timely filed. Returns filed before the due date are deemed filed on the due date. The execution of returns by the IRS, however, does not start the running of the period of limitations (Code Sec. 6501(a) and (b)).

There are a number of exceptions to this general rule (Code Sec. 6501(c)). One such exception applies in the case of a failure to furnish required information to the IRS of certain foreign transfers. Under this exception, the time for assessment of any tax imposed with respect to any event or period to which information of certain foreign transactions required to be reported relates does not expire any earlier than three years after the required information is actually provided to the IRS by the person required to file the return (Code Sec. 6501(c)(8)).

Information reporting subject to this exception includes: reporting by U.S. persons owning controlling interests in certain foreign corporations and partnerships (Code Sec. 6038); reporting by certain foreign-owned corporations of transactions with corporations in their control group and transactions with related parties (Code Sec. 6038A); reporting by U.S. persons of certain transfers of property to foreign entities and persons (Code Sec. 6038B); reporting by U.S. persons of organizations, reorganizations, and acquisitions of stock of foreign corporations (Code Sec. 6046); reporting by U.S. persons of changes in foreign partnership interests (6046A); and (reporting with respect to foreign trusts with a U.S. grantor and foreign trusts distributing money or property to a U.S. person) (Code Sec. 6048). Since such information reporting is generally due with the taxpayer's return, the three-year limitation period commences when a timely and complete return that includes all the required information is filed. Without the inclusion of the required information with the return, the limitation period does not commence until the time the information is provided to the IRS, even though the return has been filed.

A special rule extends the three-year limitations period in the case where there is a substantial omission of income. If a taxpayer omits substantial income on a return, any tax with respect to that return may be assessed and collected within six years of the date on which the return was filed. In the case of income taxes, there is a substantial omission of income if the taxpayer omits from gross income an amount

BACKGROUND

that was properly includible in gross income and that is in excess of 25 percent of the amount of income stated on the return. For this purpose, the gross income of a trade or business means gross receipts, without reduction for the cost of sales or services. An amount is not considered to have been omitted if the item is disclosed on the return in a manner adequate to apprise the IRS of the nature and amount of the item (Code Sec. 6501(e)(1)(A)). There is also a substantial omission of income if a taxpayer omits from gross income an amount properly includible in gross income under Code Sec. 951(a) (regarding inclusion of a controlled foreign corporation's (CFC's) subpart F income by certain U.S. shareholders) (Code Sec. 6501(e)(1)(B)).

Partnerships. A three-year statute of limitations applies to the assessment of tax attributable to partnership items, or to any addition to tax or additional amount imposed as penalties for failure to pay such taxes (Code Sec. 6229(a)). Code Sec. 6229 provides for a number of exceptions to the three-year limitations period. One such exception applies if a partnership omits from gross income an amount that is properly includible in gross income and that is in excess of 25 percent of the amount of gross income stated on the return. In such cases, the limitations period for assessment against the partners is extended to six years (Code Sec. 6229(c)(2)).

Passive foreign investment companies. Any U.S. shareholder of a passive foreign investment company (PFIC) can elect to treat the PFIC as a qualified electing fund (QEF) and be taxed currently on a share of the QEF's income (Code Secs. 1293 and 1295). PFICs must furnish earnings information on a PFIC Annual Information Statement to a shareholder that has made a QEF election under Code Sec. 1295(b) for each PFIC year that ends in a tax year of the shareholder to which the QEF election applies. In order to maintain the QEF election, the shareholders must include some of the information from the statement on Form 8621, Return by a Shareholder of a Passive Foreign Investment Company or Qualified Electing Fund, and retain copies of the statements in their records (Reg. § 1.1295-1(f) and (g)). The IRS is authorized to issue any regulations that are necessary or appropriate to carry out the purposes of the PFIC rules (Code Sec. 1298(f)).

NEW LAW EXPLAINED

Statute of limitations extended for omissions of income attributable to foreign assets and suspended for failure to timely provide foreign asset or PFIC information reporting.—A new exception to the three-year statute of limitations for assessment of tax is added in the case of certain omissions of income attributable to foreign financial assets. Under the new exception, the limitations period is extended to six years if there is an omission of gross income in excess of $5,000 and the omitted gross income is attributable to a foreign financial asset with respect to which:

- information reporting is required under Code Sec. 6038D, or

- would be required if Code Sec. 6038D were applied without regard to the $50,000 aggregate asset value threshold amount and any other exceptions provided by IRS regulations in the case of duplicative disclosure of certain classes of assets (Code

NEW LAW EXPLAINED

Sec. 6501(e)(1)(A), as added by the Hiring Incentives to Restore Employment (HIRE) Act (P.L. 111-147)).

Comment: For a discussion of the disclosure requirements under Code Sec. 6038D with respect to foreign financial assets, including the $50,000 aggregate asset value threshold and other exceptions, see ¶710.

As a result of this extension, any resulting tax deficiency arising from the omission of income in excess of $5,000 attributable to a foreign financial asset may be assessed, or a court proceeding for collection of such tax deficiency may be begun without assessment, at any time within six years after the tax return was filed (Code Sec. 6501(e)(1)(A), as added by the 2010 HIRE Act). The current exception providing for a six-year limitations period for substantial omission of an amount in excess of 25 percent of the all gross income reported on the return remains unchanged. The six-year limitations period for the omission of income attributable to foreign assets and for substantial omission of gross income also applies in the case of such omissions of income by partnerships (Code Sec. 6229(c)(2), as amended by the 2010 HIRE Act).

Comment: The extended statute of limitations applies not only when the omitted income is attributable to a foreign financial asset subject to Code Sec. 6038D reporting, but also in cases where the omitted income is attributable to a foreign financial asset that the taxpayer does not have to report under Code Sec. 6038D either because the asset's value is less than $50,000 or because a duplicative disclosure exception from the Code Sec. 6038D reporting requirements is provided in the regulations. Thus, in the last case, a regulatory provision that alleviates duplicative reporting obligations by providing that a report that complies with another provision may satisfy the taxpayer's obligations under Code Sec. 6038D, does not change the nature of the asset subject to reporting and the assets remains one that is subject to the Code Sec. 6038D requirements for purposes of determining if the six-year statute of limitations applies. In addition, although the Code Sec. 6038D reporting applies generally to individuals, a domestic entity that is formed or availed of to hold foreign financial assets may also be subject to Code Sec. 6038D reporting in the same manner as an individual. Therefore, the six-year limitations period may also apply to such entities (Joint Committee on Taxation, Technical Explanation of the Hiring Incentives to Restore Employment Act (JCX-4-10)). It should be noted that even though the Committee Report provides that, for purposes of the extended limitations period, the application of Code Sec. 6038D is determined without regard to the dollar threshold, the statutory exception for nonresident aliens and any exceptions provided by regulations, the new law extending the limitations period disregards only the dollar threshold and the duplicative disclosure exception of Code Sec. 6038D(h)(1).

The statute of limitations period will be suspended if a taxpayer fails to timely provide information with respect to foreign financial assets required to be reported under Code Sec. 6038D or information with respect to passive foreign investment companies (PFIC) required to be reported pursuant to a Code Sec. 1295(b) election or under Code Sec. 1298(f) (Code Sec. 6501(c)(8), as amended by the 2010 HIRE Act). Thus, the limitations period will not begin to run until the information required by

NEW LAW EXPLAINED

these provisions has been furnished to the IRS. The rule for the suspension of the limitations period in the case of failure to provide required information on foreign transfers is also clarified to provide that such a rule applies to the limitations period for assessment of tax imposed with respect to any return, event or period to which the information required to be reported relates.

> **Comment:** The new six-year statute of limitations applies not only to returns filed after March 18, 2010 on which the taxpayer fails to report income in excess of $5,000 attributable to foreign financial assets, but also to returns filed on or before that date for which the statute of limitations, determined without regard to this change, is still open on March 18, 2010 (Act Sec. 513(d) of the Hiring Incentives to Restore Employment (HIRE) Act (P.L. 111-147)). For example, a 2006 return filed in 2007, on which the taxpayer failed to report more than $5,000 of income attributable to a foreign financial asset and which is otherwise subject to the three-year limitations period, will be subject to the new six-year statute of limitations, instead.

> **Practical Analysis:** Steven Toscher, J.D., and Michel R. Stein, J.D., LL.M., Principals at Hochman, Salkin, Rettig, Toscher & Perez, P.C., of Beverly Hills, California, observe that the new six-year statute of limitations for omission of income gives the IRS a new tool even in situations where only a smaller amount of income (more than $5,000) from foreign assets has been omitted by the taxpayer.
>
> Historically, the extended statute of limitations was reserved for the most egregious situations, such as omissions of income exceeding 25% of reported income. Congress has made a policy decision that foreign compliance presents enforcement obstacles for the IRS justifying increased time to detect noncompliance. The suspension of the statute of limitations indefinitely where the taxpayer has failed to disclose the foreign assets is consistent with legislative changes over the years of indefinitely suspending the statute of limitations where the taxpayer fails to comply with disclosure requirements.

▶ **Effective date.** The amendments apply to returns filed after March 18, 2010 and to returns filed on or before such date if the period specified in Code Sec. 6501 (determined without regard to these amendments) for assessment of such taxes has not expired as of such date (Act Sec. 513(d) of the Hiring Incentives to Restore Employment (HIRE) Act (P.L. 111-147)).

Law source: Law at ¶6135 and ¶6155. Committee Report at ¶11,100.

— Act Sec. 513(a) of the Hiring Incentives to Restore Employment (HIRE) Act (P.L. 111-147), amending Code Secs. 6501(e)(1) and 6229(c)(2);

— Act Sec. 513(b) and (c), amending Code Sec. 6501(c)(8);

— Act Sec. 513(d), providing the effective date.

Reporter references: For further information, consult the following CCH reporters.

— Standard Federal Tax Reporter, ¶38,963.01

— Tax Research Consultant, IRS: 30,150

— Practical Tax Explanation, §39,505.10

¶725 Information Reporting for Passive Foreign Investment Companies

SUMMARY OF NEW LAW

U.S. shareholders of passive foreign investment companies (PFICs) must file an annual information return containing information required by the IRS.

BACKGROUND

A special taxing system applies to U.S. shareholders of foreign corporations that derive a significant amount of their income from investments in passive assets. The rules that affect such passive foreign investment companies (PFICs) are designed to eliminate the benefit of the tax deferral that the U.S. shareholders of these companies could otherwise receive because a foreign corporation is generally exempt from U.S. tax on foreign source income and its U.S. shareholders are generally not taxed until they dispose of their stock or receive a distribution. For this purpose, a PFIC is a foreign corporation if it either derives at least 75 percent of its income from passive investments (income test), or at least 50 percent of the company's average total assets produce passive income or are held for the production of passive income (asset test) (Code Sec. 1297). A number of miscellaneous rules apply for purposes of determining the status of a company as a passive foreign investment company (PFIC) and the interaction between the PFIC rules and other rules applicable to foreign corporations including controlled foreign corporations (CFCs) (Code Sec. 1298).

A U.S. taxpayer's ownership in a PFIC is subject to one of three taxing regimes: the default method for excess distributions from a PFIC, as well as dispositions of PFIC stock; the qualified electing fund (QEF) method; or the mark-to-market method. Under the default method, if a U.S. taxpayer receives an excess distribution on PFIC stock or disposes of the PFIC stock, then gain recognized is considered to be ordinary income earned *pro rata* over the shareholder's holding period of his investment (Code Sec. 1291). If a U.S. shareholder elects for the PFIC to be a treated as a QEF and thereby agrees to provide adequate information to the IRS, the shareholder must includes in income his or her share of the PFIC's earnings and profits, with appropriate basis adjustments for amounts not distributed and for distributions previously included in income (Code Secs. 1293—1295). Any inclusion by a shareholder requires current payment of tax, unless the shareholder elects deferral. Finally, if PFIC stock is marketable, the U.S. shareholder of the PFIC may make a mark-to-market election. If the election is made, the U.S. shareholder will include in gross income for the tax year, as ordinary income, the excess of the fair market value of the PFIC stock over its adjusted basis (Code Sec. 1296). The shareholder's basis in the stock is increased by the amount included in gross income of the shareholder.

Generally, a U.S. person who is a PFIC shareholder must file IRS Form 8621, Return by a Shareholder of a Passive Foreign Investment Company or Qualifying Electing

BACKGROUND

Fund, for each tax year in which that person: (1) recognizes gain on a direct or indirect disposition of PFIC stock; (2) receives certain direct or indirect distributions from a PFIC; or (3) is making a reportable election. Code Sec. 1291(e) includes a general reporting requirement for certain PFIC shareholders that is contingent upon the issuance of IRS regulations. Proposed regulations issued in 1992 have not been finalized and the current IRS form requires reporting only based on one of the three triggering events above.

NEW LAW EXPLAINED

Annual information return is required to be filed by any U.S. shareholder of a PFIC.—Except as otherwise provided by the IRS, each U.S. person who is a shareholder of a passive foreign investment company (PFIC) must file an annual information return containing such information as is required by the IRS (Code Sec. 1298(f), as added by the Hiring Incentives to Restore Employment (HIRE) Act (P.L. 111-147)). A U.S. person who meets the new reporting requirement as a shareholder of a PFIC may also meet the requirements of new Code Sec. 6038D, requiring disclosure of information with respect to foreign financial assets. Regulations are expected to be issued to avoid duplicative reporting (Joint Committee on Taxation, Technical Explanation of the Hiring Incentives to Restore Employment Act (JCX-4-10)).

> **Comment:** For a discussion of the new Code Sec. 6038D reporting requirements with respect to foreign financial assets, see ¶710.

Practical Analysis: Sandra L. Soltis, a Partner at Blackman Kallick of Chicago, Illinois, reports that under new Code Sec. 1298, a U.S. person who is a PFIC shareholder must file an annual report containing information required by the IRS. Since a PFIC shareholder only reports information required by the IRS, Code Sec. 1298(f) does not requires any reporting until the IRS issues guidance. In effect, this provision is contingent upon IRS's instructions.

In addition to new Code Sec. 1298(f), an individual who is a PFIC shareholder can also be required to disclose annual information under new Code Sec. 6038D. This provision requires an individual taxpayer with an interest in a "specified foreign financial asset" to disclose certain information for a tax year if the aggregate value of all such assets exceeds $50,000 (or a higher dollar amount prescribed by the IRS). A "specified foreign financial asset" includes an interest in a PFIC. Unlike Code Sec. 1298(f), Code Sec. 6038D is not contingent upon the issuance of guidance from the IRS. It is effective for tax years beginning after the date of enactment.

Code Sec. 1298(f) applies to all U.S. persons. In contrast, only individuals are subject to Code Sec. 6038D, unless the IRS issues guidance requiring annual information disclosure for domestic entities (e.g., corporations, partnerships, LLCs and trusts) that are formed (or availed of) to hold specified foreign financial assets. It is anticipated that regulations and other guidance will be forthcoming to limit duplicative reporting requirements under different Code sections.

NEW LAW EXPLAINED

▶   **Effective date.** The amendments take effect on March 18, 2010 (Act Sec. 521(c) of the Hiring Incentives to Restore Employment (HIRE) Act (P.L. 111-147)).

Law source: Law at ¶6075 and ¶6080. Committee Report at ¶11,110.

— Act Sec. 521(a) of the Hiring Incentives to Restore Employment (HIRE) Act (P.L. 111-147), redesignating Code Sec. 1298(f) as Code Sec. 1298(g) and adding new Code Sec. 1298(f)

— Act Sec. 521(b), amending Code Sec. 1291(e);

— Act Sec.521(c), providing the effective date.

Reporter references: For further information, consult the following CCH reporters.

— Standard Federal Tax Reporter, ¶31,642.01

— Tax Research Consultant, INTLOUT: 18,200

— Practical Tax Explanation, §39,101

¶730   E-filing of Certain Returns Related to Withholding on Foreign Transfers

SUMMARY OF NEW LAW

The IRS may require financial institutions to file certain returns related to withholding on foreign transfers electronically.

BACKGROUND

The IRS has the authority to prescribe regulations providing standards for determining which returns must be filed on magnetic media (e.g., e-filing) or in other machine-readable form (Code Sec. 6011(e)(1)). In prescribing these regulations, the IRS may not require a person to file returns on magnetic media unless the person is required to file at least 250 returns during the calendar year, and it must take into account (among other relevant factors) the ability of the taxpayer to comply at reasonable cost with the requirements of the regulations (Code Sec. 6011(e)(2)). Notwithstanding the 250-return threshold, the IRS must require partnerships having more than 100 partners to file returns on magnetic media (Code Sec. 6011(e)(2)). No penalty for failure to file correct information returns may be imposed under Code Sec. 6721 solely by reason of a failure to file returns on magnetic media, except to the extent that the failure occurs with respect to more than 250 information returns (more than 100 information returns in the case of a partnership having more than 100 partners) (Code Sec. 6724(c)).

Generally, a withholding agent is required to deduct and withhold 30 percent from certain U.S. source income payments made to nonresident aliens and foreign corporations (Code Secs. 1441 and 1442). The withholding agent is the person having control or custody over payment of an item of income to a foreign person who is subject to withholding (Reg. §1.1441-7(a)(1)). The withholding agent is made liable for the tax,

BACKGROUND

and is also indemnified against the claims and demands of any person for the amount of any payments made in accordance with the nonresident alien and foreign corporation withholding provisions (Code Sec. 1461). Withholding agents are required to file annual returns on Form 1042, Annual Withholding Tax Return for U.S. Source Income of Foreign Persons, on or before March 15 of the year following the year of payment, reporting taxes withheld and paying any taxes still owed (Reg. § 1.1461-1(b)(1)). In addition, the agent must also file Form 1042-S, Foreign Person's U.S. Source Income Subject to Withholding, by March 15 for each foreign recipient to whom payments were made, listing all items of income paid to the foreign person during the previous year (Reg. § 1.1461-1(c)(1)).

For returns filed after December 31, 2010, the IRS must require that individual income tax returns prepared and filed by certain tax return preparers be filed on magnetic media (i.e., electronically) (Code Sec. 6011(e)(3)). Specifically, the IRS must require filing on magnetic media if the individual income tax return is prepared and filed by the preparer who is a "specified tax return preparer" for the calendar year during which the return is filed. A specified tax return preparer, with respect to any calendar year, means any tax return preparer, unless the preparer reasonably expects to file 10 or fewer individual income tax returns during the calendar year.

NEW LAW EXPLAINED

E-filing certain returns related to withholding on foreign transfers.—The IRS is authorized to require a financial institution to electronically file returns with respect to withheld taxes for which the institution is liable as a withholding agent under the nonresident alien and foreign corporation withholding rules (Code Sec. 1461), or under the new foreign account withholding rules (Code Sec. 1474), even though the financial institution is required to file less than 250 returns during the tax year (Code Sec. 6011(e)(4), as added by the Hiring Incentives to Restore Employment (HIRE) Act (P.L. 111-147)). For this purpose, the definition of financial institution is the same as used for purposes of the new foreign account withholding rules and includes any entity that:

- accepts deposits in the ordinary course of a banking or similar business;
- as a substantial portion of its business, holds financial assets for the account of others; or
- is engaged primarily in the business of investing, reinvesting, or trading in securities, partnership interests, commodities, or any interest in such securities, partnership interests, or commodities (Code Sec. 1471(d)(5), as added by the 2010 HIRE Act).

  Comment: For a discussion of the definition of a financial institution and the new foreign account withholding rules, see ¶ 705.

  Comment: In prescribing regulations providing standards for determining which returns must be filed on magnetic media (e.g., electronic filing) or in other machine-readable form, the IRS must still comply with other provisions of Code Sec. 6011(e). For example, it must take into account (among other relevant factors) the ability of the financial institution to comply at reasonable cost with

NEW LAW EXPLAINED

the requirements of the regulations (Code Sec. 6011(e), as amended by the 2010 HIRE Act).

A failure to file penalty may be imposed under Code Sec. 6721 against a financial institution that fails to comply with the electronic filing requirements of Code Sec. 6011(e)(4) (Code Sec. 6724(c), as amended by the 2010 HIRE Act; Joint Committee on Taxation (Technical Explanation of the Hiring Incentives to Restore Employment Act (JCX-4-10)).

▶ **Effective date.** The provision applies to returns the due date for which (determined without regard to extensions) is after March 18, 2010 (Act Sec. 522(c) of the Hiring Incentives to Restore Employment (HIRE) Act (P.L. 111-147)).

Law source: Law at ¶6120 and ¶6185. Committee Report at ¶11,120.

— Act Sec. 522(a) of the Hiring Incentives to Restore Employment (HIRE) Act (P.L. 111-147) adding Code Sec. 6011(e)(4);

— Act Sec. 522(b), amending Code Sec. 6724(c);

— Act Sec. 522(c), providing the effective date.

Reporter references: For further information, consult the following CCH reporters.

— Standard Federal Tax Reporter, ¶32,828.01, ¶35,141.035, ¶40,285.01

— Tax Research Consultant, FILEBUS: 12,302, EXPAT: 15,056, PENALTY: 3,202

— Practical Tax Explanation, § 37,001, § 37,315.05, § 39,150, § 39,225.10

¶735 Foreign Trusts Treated as Having U.S. Beneficiary

SUMMARY OF NEW LAW

For purposes of treating a foreign trust as a grantor trust, there is a rebuttable presumption that the trust has a U.S. beneficiary if a U.S. person transfers property to the trust. An amount is treated as accumulated for a U.S. person even if that person has a contingent interest in the trust. A foreign trust is generally treated as having a U.S. beneficiary if any person has discretion to make a trust distribution, unless none of the recipients are U.S. persons. Finally, if any U.S. person who transfers property to the trust is involved in any agreement that may result in trust income or corpus being paid or accumulated to or for a U.S. person, that agreement will be treated as a term of the trust.

BACKGROUND

A foreign trust is a trust that is not a "United States person." A trust is a U.S. person if (1) a U.S. court is able to exercise primary supervision over administration of the trust, and (2) one or more U.S. persons have the authority to control all substantial decisions of the trust (Code Sec. 7701(a)(30)(E) and (31)(B); Reg. § 301.7701-7). For

BACKGROUND

purposes of the rules governing the income tax treatment of a foreign trust having one or more U.S. beneficiaries, a "U.S. person" is a U.S. citizen or resident, a domestic partnership or corporation, or a non-foreign estate or trust, as well as a nonresident alien individual who elects to be treated as a U.S. resident, and a dual resident individual taxpayer (Code Sec. 7701(a)(30); Reg. § 1.679-1(c)(2)).

If a U.S. person transfers property to a foreign trust that has a U.S. beneficiary for the transferor's tax year, the transferor is treated as the owner of the portion of the trust attributable to the property transferred in that tax year (Code Sec. 679(a)(1)). Because the transferor is treated as the owner, any income received by the trust with respect to the transferred property is generally taxed to the transferor under the grantor trust rules (Code Sec. 671). This rule does not apply if the transfer is due to the transferor's death or is for fair market value, or if the foreign trust is a Code Sec. 501(c)(3) exempt organization or a certain type of employee trust under Code Sec. 6048(a)(3)(B)(ii) (Code Sec. 679(a)(1) and (2); Reg. § 1.679-4).

A trust is treated as having a U.S. beneficiary for the tax year *unless*:

- no part of the trust's income or corpus (property) may be paid or accumulated during the tax year to or for the benefit of a U.S. person, under the terms of the trust; *and*

- no part of the trust's income or corpus could be paid to or for the benefit of a U.S. person if the trust were terminated at any time during the tax year (Code Sec. 679(c)(1); Reg. § 1.679-2).

Income or corpus may be paid or accumulated to or for the benefit of a U.S. person if, either directly or indirectly, income may be distributed to or accumulated for the benefit of a U.S. person, or corpus may be distributed to or held for the future benefit of a U.S. person. This determination is made regardless of whether income or corpus is actually distributed, or whether a U.S. person's interest is contingent on a future event. A person who is neither a named beneficiary nor a member of a beneficiary class defined in the trust instrument is not taken into consideration if the U.S. transferor demonstrates to the IRS's satisfaction that the person's contingent interest in the trust is so remote as to be negligible. This does not apply, however, for persons to whom distributions could be made under a grant of discretion to the trustee or any other person (Reg. § 1.679-2(a)(2)).

Even if a foreign trust is not treated as having a U.S. beneficiary based on the terms of the trust, the trust may still be treated as having a U.S. beneficiary based on other documentation, including:

- all written and oral agreements and understandings related to the trust,

- memoranda or letters of wishes,

- all records that relate to the actual distribution of income and corpus, and

- all other documents that relate to the trust, regardless of their purported legal effect.

BACKGROUND

Other factors to be considered include:

- whether the trust terms allow the trust to be amended to benefit a U.S. person,
- whether applicable law requires payments or accumulations of income or corpus to a U.S. person (even if the trust does not allow such amendment), and
- whether the parties to the trust ignore or are reasonably expected to ignore the trust terms to benefit a U.S. person (Reg. § 1.679-2(a)(4)).

NEW LAW EXPLAINED

Treatment and presumption of foreign trusts as having U.S. beneficiary.—The circumstances under which a foreign trust will be treated as having a United States beneficiary, and thus be treated as a grantor trust, where trust income or corpus may be paid or accumulated to or for the benefit of a U.S. person have been clarified. Specifically the presumption that a foreign trust has a U.S. beneficiary contained in the regulations has been added to the Internal Revenue Code.

Specifically, an amount will be treated as accumulated for the benefit of a U.S. person even if that person's interest in the trust is contingent on a future event (Code Sec. 679(c)(1), as amended by the Hiring Incentives to Restore Employment (HIRE) Act (P.L. 111-147)). Additionally, if any person has the discretion—by authority given in the trust agreement, by power of appointment, or otherwise—of making a distribution from the trust to or for the benefit of any person, the trust will be treated as having a beneficiary who is a U.S. person, *unless* the trust terms specifically identify the class of persons to whom such distributions may be made, and none of those persons are U.S. persons during the tax year (Code Sec. 679(c)(4), as added by the 2010 HIRE Act).

> **Comment:** These provisions are intended to be consistent with existing regulations (Joint Committee on Taxation, Technical Explanation of the Hiring Incentives to Restore Employment Act (JCX-4-10)). See Reg. § 1.679-2(a).

If any U.S. person who directly or indirectly transfers property to the trust is directly or indirectly involved in any agreement or understanding that may result in trust income or corpus being paid or accumulated to or for the benefit of a U.S. person, that agreement or understanding will be treated as a term of the trust (Code Sec. 679(c)(5), as added by the 2010 HIRE Act). The agreement or understanding may be written, oral or otherwise.

> **Comment:** This provision assumes that the transferor is generally directly or indirectly involved with agreements regarding the accumulation or disposition of the trust's income and corpus (Joint Committee on Taxation, Technical Explanation of the Hiring Incentives to Restore Employment Act (JCX-4-10)).

Presumption of U.S. beneficiary. If a U.S. person directly or indirectly transfers property to a foreign trust, the IRS may treat the trust as having a U.S. beneficiary for purposes of applying these tax rules to the transfer, *unless* the U.S. person:

- submits to the IRS any information that the IRS may require regarding the transfer, and
- demonstrates to the IRS's satisfaction that—

NEW LAW EXPLAINED

(i) no part of the trust's income or corpus may be paid or accumulated during the tax year to or for the benefit of a U.S. person under the terms of the trust, *and*

(ii) no part of the trust's income or corpus could be paid to or for the benefit of a U.S. person if the trust were terminated at any time during the tax year (Code Sec. 679(d), as added by the 2010 HIRE Act).

This rule does not apply to a foreign trust that is described in Code Sec. 6048(a)(3)(B)(ii), namely, a trust that is part of an employee benefit plan under Code Secs. 402(b), 404(a)(4), or 404A, or a trust the IRS determines is a Code Sec. 501(c)(3) exempt organization.

> **Practical Analysis:** Michael J. Miller, a partner at Roberts & Holland LLP of New York, New York, comments that, although the new presumption is rebuttable, the need to demonstrate the absence of U.S. beneficiaries "to the satisfaction of the Secretary" is quite intimidating. Consider, for example, a foreign trust that, by its terms, is solely for the benefit of the transferor's five nonresident alien children, but that can be amended under local law to provide for an additional beneficiary, such as the transferor's one U.S. child (for whom other arrangements have been made). If the IRS believes there to be an unwritten understanding that the transferor's U.S. child would be added at a later time, the foreign trust would apparently be deemed to have a U.S. beneficiary, even if there is no evidence to support the existence of any such understanding. Query whether, or in what circumstances, the Secretary's refusal to be satisfied may be considered an abuse of discretion.
>
> On its face, the new flush language at the end of Code Sec. 679(c)(1) provides that an amount "shall" be treated as accumulated for the benefit of a U.S. person even if such person's interest in the trust is contingent on a future event, without regard to the likelihood or remoteness of the contingency. This seemingly absolute directive may be read to conflict with Reg. § 1.679-2(a)(2)(ii), which provides for a contingency to be disregarded if the transferor demonstrates (to the satisfaction of the IRS) that the contingent interest "is so remote as to be negligible." It seems clear, however, that the amendment to Code Sec. 679(c)(1) was not intended to override this rule in the existing regulations. The Joint Committee's Technical Explanation expressly provides that the new provision "is meant to be consistent with existing regulations under section 679."

▶ **Effective date.** No specific effective date is provided by the Act for the provisions which clarify the treatment of (1) amounts accumulated for the benefit of a U.S. person with a contingent interest in the trust, (2) the discretion to identify beneficiaries, and (3) certain agreements and understandings as terms of the trust. These provisions are, therefore, considered effective on March 18, 2010. The provision creating a rebuttable presumption allowing the IRS to treat a foreign trust as having a U.S. beneficiary if a U.S. person directly or indirectly transfers property to the trust applies to transfers of property after March 18, 2010 (Act Sec. 532(b) of the Hiring Incentives to Restore Employment (HIRE) Act (P.L. 111-147)).

NEW LAW EXPLAINED

Law source: Law at ¶6050. Committee Report at ¶11,130 and ¶11,140.

— Act Sec. 531(a) of the Hiring Incentives to Restore Employment (HIRE) Act (P.L. 111-147), amending Code Sec. 679(c)(1);

— Act Sec. 531(b), adding new Code Sec. 679(c)(4);

— Act Sec. 531(c), adding new Code Sec. 679(c)(5);

— Act Sec. 532(a), redesignating Code Sec. 679(d) as Code Sec. 679(e) and adding new Code Sec. 679(d);

— Act Sec. 532(b), providing the effective date.

Reporter references: For further information, consult the following CCH reporters.

— Standard Federal Tax Reporter, ¶24,821.021

— Tax Research Consultant, ESTTRST: 36,254

— Practical Tax Explanation, § 32,801

¶740 Uncompensated Use of Trust Property

SUMMARY OF NEW LAW

The uncompensated use of foreign trust property by a U.S. grantor, U.S. beneficiary, or a U.S. person related to either of them is treated as a distribution by the trust for nongrantor trust income tax purposes. The loan of cash or marketable securities by a foreign trust, or the use of any other property of the trust, to or by any U.S. person is also treated as paid or accumulated for the benefit of a U.S. person, for purposes of applying the grantor trust income tax rules.

BACKGROUND

A foreign trust is a trust that is not a "United States person." A trust is a U.S. person if (1) a U.S. court is able to exercise primary supervision over administration of the trust, and (2) one or more U.S. persons have the authority to control all substantial decisions of the trust (Code Sec. 7701(a)(30)(E) and (31)(B); Reg. § 301.7701-7). Generally, a "U.S. person" is a U.S. citizen or resident, a domestic partnership or corporation, or a nonforeign estate or trust (Code Sec. 7701(a)(30)).

Under the federal income tax rules governing nongrantor trusts, if a foreign trust makes a loan of cash or marketable securities to a U.S. grantor, a U.S. beneficiary, or any U.S. person related to either of them, the loan is treated as a distribution by the trust to the grantor or beneficiary (Code Sec. 643(i)(1)). This rule applies for purposes of determining:

• the distribution deduction for simple trusts (i.e., trusts required by their trust instruments to distribute income currently to beneficiaries) and for complex trusts (i.e., trusts not required to distribute income currently);

BACKGROUND

- the gross income of trust beneficiaries; and
- the treatment of excess trust distributions.

The rule does not apply to loans made to tax-exempt entities (Code Sec. 643(i)(2)(C)). If a foreign trust is treated as making a distribution under the rule, it will not be treated as a simple trust (Code Sec. 643(i)(2)(D)).

If a loan is treated as a distribution under this rule, any subsequent transaction between the trust and the original borrower regarding the loan principal is disregarded for federal tax purposes. Subsequent transactions include complete or partial repayment, satisfaction, cancellation, discharge or otherwise (Code Sec. 643(i)(3)). These rules do not expressly apply to other types of property or transactions.

Foreign trusts and grantor trust rules. If a U.S. person transfers property to a foreign trust that has a U.S. beneficiary for the transferor's tax year, the transferor is treated as the owner of the portion of the trust attributable to the property transferred in that tax year (Code Sec. 679(a)(1)). Because of this treatment, any income received by the trust with respect to the transferred property is generally taxed to the transferor under the grantor trust rules (Code Sec. 671). This treatment does not apply if the transfer is due to the transferor's death, is for fair market value, or if the foreign trust is a Code Sec. 501(c)(3) exempt organization or a certain type of employee benefit trust under Code Sec. 6048(a)(3)(B)(ii) (Code Sec. 679(a)(1) and (2); Reg. § 1.679-4).

A trust is generally treated as having a U.S. beneficiary for the tax year *unless*: (1) no part of the trust's income or corpus (property) may be paid or accumulated during the tax year to or for the benefit of a U.S. person, under the terms of the trust; *and* (2) no part of the trust's income or corpus could be paid to or for the benefit of a U.S. person if the trust were terminated at any time during the tax year (Code Sec. 679(c)(1); Reg. § 1.679-2).

NEW LAW EXPLAINED

Uncompensated use of trust property treated as distribution.—The distribution treatment of foreign trust transactions has been expanded to include the uncompensated use of property by certain United States persons. The treatment of foreign trusts as having a U.S. beneficiary for grantor trust purposes has also been expanded to include loans of cash or marketable securities or the use of any other trust property to or by a U.S. person.

If a foreign trust permits the use of any trust property by a U.S. grantor, a U.S. beneficiary, or any U.S. person related to either of them, the fair market value of the use of such property is treated as a distribution by the trust to the grantor or beneficiary (Code Sec. 643(i)(1), as amended by the Hiring Incentives to Restore Employment (HIRE) Act (P.L. 111-147)). However, this treatment does not apply to the extent that the trust is paid the fair market value of such use within a reasonable time period (Code Sec. 643(i)(2)(E), as added by the 2010 HIRE Act). If distribution treatment does apply to the use of trust property, then the subsequent return of such property is disregarded for federal tax purposes (Code Sec. 643(i)(3), as amended by the 2010 HIRE Act).

NEW LAW EXPLAINED

Comment: Accordingly, certain uncompensated uses of foreign trust property by U.S. persons will factor into the determination of the distribution deduction for simple and complex trusts, the gross income of trust beneficiaries, and the treatment of excess trust distributions.

Application to grantor trusts. Under the rule generally treating a foreign trust as having a U.S. beneficiary for the tax year, thereby causing a U.S. person who transfers property to such trust to be treated as the owner of the portion of the trust attributable to the property under the grantor trust rules, a loan of cash or marketable securities, or the use of any other trust property, directly or indirectly to or by any U.S. person is treated as paid or accumulated for the benefit of a U.S. person. For this treatment to apply, the U.S. person does not need to be a beneficiary under the terms of the trust. However, this treatment does not apply to the extent that the U.S. person repays the loan at a market rate of interest, or pays the fair market value of the use of the property, within a reasonable time period (Code Sec. 679(c)(6), as added by the 2010 HIRE Act).

▶ **Effective date.** These provisions apply to loans made, and uses of property, after March 18, 2010 (Act Sec. 533(e) of the Hiring Incentives to Restore Employment (HIRE) Act (P.L. 111-147)).

Law source: Law at ¶6045 and ¶6050. Committee Report at ¶11,150.

— Act Sec. 533(a) of the Hiring Incentives to Restore Employment (HIRE) Act (P.L. 111-147), amending Code Sec. 643(i)(1);

— Act Sec. 533(b), adding Code Sec. 643(i)(2)(E);

— Act Sec. 533(c), adding Code Sec. 679(c)(6);

— Act Sec. 533(d), amending Code Sec. 643(i)(3);

— Act Sec. 533(e), providing the effective date.

Reporter references: For further information, consult the following CCH reporters.

— Standard Federal Tax Reporter, ¶24,334.043 and ¶24,821.021

— Tax Research Consultant, ESTTRST: 36,254 and INTL: 30,252.05

— Practical Tax Explanation, §32,515 and §32,801

¶745 Reporting Requirement for U.S. Persons Treated as Owners of Foreign Trusts

SUMMARY OF NEW LAW

A U.S. person who is treated as the owner of any portion of a foreign trust under the grantor trust rules must submit any information required by the IRS with respect to the foreign trust.

BACKGROUND

Foreign trusts and certain parties associated with foreign trusts are subject to special reporting rules (Code Sec. 6048). Responsible parties, which include the grantor of an inter vivos trust, the transferor in a reportable event other than transfer by death, and the executor of a decedent's estate, must provide written notice of the reportable event to the IRS. In general, reportable events are:

- the creation of a foreign trust by a U.S. person;

- the direct or indirect transfer of money to a foreign trust by a U.S. person, including a transfer by reason of death; and

- the death of a U.S. citizen or resident if the decedent was treated as the owner of any portion of a foreign trust under the grantor trust rules or if any portion of the foreign trust was included in the gross estate of the decedent (Code Sec. 6048(a)(3)(A)).

The notice of the reportable event is due on or before the 90th day after the reportable event and must contain information that the IRS requires (Code Sec. 6048(a)(1) and (2)). This reporting requirement is generally satisfied by the filing of Form 3520, Annual Return to Report Transactions With Foreign Trusts and Receipt of Certain Foreign Gifts. Many nongratuitous transfers do not have to be reported (Code Sec. 6048(a)(3)(B)).

In addition to responsible parties, certain U.S. beneficiaries of foreign trusts are also subject to reporting requirements. Any U.S. person that receives a direct or indirect distribution from a foreign trust must make a return with respect to the trust that includes the name of the trust, the aggregate amount of distributions received from the trust during the year, and any other information required by the IRS (Code Sec. 6048(c)(1)). This reporting requirement is generally satisfied by the filing of Form 3520, Annual Return to Report Transactions with Foreign Trusts and Receipt of Certain Foreign Gifts.

Finally, any U.S. person that is treated as the owner of any portion of a foreign trust under the grantor trust rules is responsible for ensuring that the trust satisfies certain reporting requirements. In general, such U.S. persons must ensure that the trust: (1) makes a return that sets forth a complete accounting of trust activities and operations for the year, the name of the U.S. agent for the trust, and other information required by the IRS; and (2) provides information, as required by the IRS, to each U.S. person who is treated as the owner of any portion of the trust or who receives a direct or indirect distribution from the trust (Code Sec. 6048(b)(1)). This reporting requirement is generally satisfied by the filing of Form 3520-A, Annual Information Return of Foreign Trust With a U.S. Owner, and by providing copies of the Foreign Grantor Trust Owner Statement and the Foreign Grantor Trust Beneficiary Statement to the U.S. owners and beneficiaries.

NEW LAW EXPLAINED

Reporting expanded for U.S. persons treated as owners of foreign trusts.—Any U.S. person who, at any time during the person's tax year, is treated as the owner of any

NEW LAW EXPLAINED

portion of a foreign trust under the grantor trust rules must submit any information required by the IRS with respect to the foreign trust for that year (Code Sec. 6048(b)(1), as amended by the Hiring Incentives to Restore Employment (HIRE) Act (P.L. 111-147)). This requirement to supply information about the trust applies to tax years beginning after March 18, 2010 (Act Sec. 534(b) of the 2010 HIRE Act).

The new requirement imposed on U.S. persons treated as owners of foreign trusts to supply information about the trust is in addition to the current requirement that such U.S. persons are responsible for ensuring that the foreign trust complies with its own reporting obligations (Joint Committee on Taxation, Technical Explanation of the Hiring Incentives to Restore Employment Act (JCX-4-10)). The current reporting obligations of a foreign trust include making a return for the year and providing certain information to each U.S. person who is treated as the owner of any portion of the trust or who receives a direct or indirect distribution from the trust (Code Sec. 6048(b)(1)(A) and (B)).

> **Comment:** For a discussion of the penalties applicable for the failure to report information or file returns with respect to foreign trusts, see ¶750.

Practical Analysis: Michael J. Miller, a partner at Roberts & Holland LLP of New York, New York, comments that, although Code Sec. 6048(b)(1) purports to make U.S. owners of foreign grantor trusts "responsible to ensure" that the foreign grantor trusts file Form 3520-A, the change in law seems to signal the government's realization that such U.S. owners often have neither the legal authority nor the practical ability to make the trustees cooperate. U.S. owners in this situation sometimes take the proactive step of filing Form 3520-A themselves, based on whatever information is available to them, and disclose that the signature provided is the U.S. owner's, not the trustee's. In other instances, U.S. owners that cannot convince the trustees of the foreign grantor trusts to file Form 3520-A simply do nothing, *e.g.,* because it does not occur to them that they should, or even could, purport to act for the trusts when they clearly are not authorized to do so. Therefore, the imposition of a new reporting obligation on the U.S. owners themselves should enable the IRS to obtain at least some information about foreign grantor trusts with uncooperative trustees.

▶ **Effective date.** The amendment applies to tax years beginning after March 18, 2010 (Act Sec. 534(b) of the Hiring Incentives to Restore Employment (HIRE) Act (P.L. 111-147)).

Law source: Law at ¶6130. Committee Report at ¶11,160.

— Act Sec. 534(a) of the Hiring Incentives to Restore Employment (HIRE) Act (P.L. 111-147), amending Code Sec. 6048(b)(1);

— Act Sec. 534(b), providing the effective date.

Reporter references: For further information, consult the following CCH reporters.

— Standard Federal Tax Reporter, ¶36,004.0765 and ¶39,820.022

— Tax Research Consultant, ESTTRST: 36,258.10 and PENALTY: 3,208.70

— Practical Tax Explanation, § 39,135.15

¶745

¶750 Penalty for Failure to Report Information or File Return Concerning Certain Foreign Trusts

SUMMARY OF NEW LAW

The minimum amount of the penalty for failure to report information or file returns with respect to foreign trusts is increased to $10,000. If the aggregate penalties imposed exceed the maximum amount, which is equal to the gross reportable amount, then the excess must be refunded to the taxpayer.

BACKGROUND

Foreign trusts and certain parties associated with foreign trusts, including U.S. persons creating or making transfers to foreign trusts, certain decedents, U.S. grantors treated as owners of foreign trusts, and U.S. beneficiaries of foreign trusts, are subject to special reporting rules under Code Sec. 6048 (see ¶745). Basically, there are three reporting rules with a penalty imposed for failure to comply with the rules (Code Sec. 6677). In most cases, the penalty imposed when required information is reported late, is incomplete, or is incorrect is equal to 35 percent of the gross reportable amount. If the failure to report persists for more than 90 days after the IRS has mailed notice of such failure to the person required to pay such penalty, an additional penalty is imposed that is equal to $10,000 for each 30-day period (or portion thereof) during which such failure continues after the 90-day period expires.

The gross reportable amount on which the penalty is based and the percentage amount of the penalty depend on the reporting rule that is violated. If a responsible party fails to provide required notice of a reportable event on or before the 90th day after the reportable event, the initial penalty is equal to 35 percent of the gross reportable amount. The gross reportable amount in this case is equal to the gross value of the property involved in the reportable event, as determined on the date of the event (Code Secs. 6048(a) and 6677(c)(1)).

If a U.S. person, who is treated as the owner of a foreign trust under the grantor trust rules, fails to ensure that the trust files a return and provides required information, the initial penalty is equal to just five percent of the gross reportable amount (Code Sec. 6677(b)(2)). The gross reportable amount in this case is equal to the gross value of the portion of the trust's assets at the close of the year that are treated as owned by the U.S. person (Code Secs. 6048(b)(1) and 6677(c)(2)).

If a U.S. beneficiary of a foreign trust fails to file a return with respect to the trust or fails to provide required information, the initial penalty is equal to 35 percent of the gross reportable amount (Code Sec. 6677(a)). The gross reportable amount in this case is equal to the gross amount of the distributions to the U.S. beneficiary (Code Secs. 6048(c) and 6677(c)(3)).

A maximum limit is set on the amount of the penalty for failure provide information with respect to foreign trusts. The penalty imposed cannot exceed the gross reporta-

BACKGROUND

ble amount (Code Sec. 6677(a)). In addition, no penalty will be imposed if the failure to report is due to reasonable cause and not willful neglect (Code Sec. 6677(d)).

NEW LAW EXPLAINED

Minimum penalty increased; maximum penalty modified.—The amount of the penalty for failure to report information or file returns with respect to certain foreign trusts has changed for notices and returns required to be filed after December 31, 2009 (Code Sec. 6677(a), as amended by the Hiring Incentives to Restore Employment (HIRE) Act (P.L. 111-147); Act Sec. 535(b) of the 2010 HIRE Act). The minimum amount of the penalty has been increased and the determination of the maximum amount has been modified.

Minimum amount of penalty. If any notice or return required to be filed under Code Sec. 6048 is not filed on or before the due date or does not include all of the information that is required or includes incorrect information, then the person required to file such notice or return must pay a penalty equal to the *greater* of:

- $10,000 or

- 35 percent of the gross reportable amount (five percent for U.S. persons treated as owners of the trust) (Code Sec. 6677(a), as amended by the 2010 HIRE Act).

    Comment: Prior to this change, the penalty for failure to provide required information or file a return with respect to certain foreign trusts was simply equal to 35 percent of the gross reportable amount (five percent for U.S. persons treated as owners of the trust). With the new minimum amount, the IRS will be able to impose a $10,000 penalty even when there is not enough information to determine the gross reportable amount (Joint Committee on Taxation, Technical Explanation of the Hiring Incentives to Restore Employment Act (JCX-4-10)).

Although the minimum amount of the initial penalty has increased, no change has been made to the additional $10,000 penalty for each 30-day period (or portion thereof) during which the failure to report continues after the 90-day period expires (Joint Committee on Taxation, Technical Explanation of the Hiring Incentives to Restore Employment Act (JCX-4-10)).

Maximum amount of penalty. In addition to the new set minimum amount of the penalty, the determination of the maximum amount of the penalty has changed. In general, the penalty for failure to report information or file returns with respect to certain foreign trusts cannot exceed the gross reportable amount (Code Sec. 6677(a)). Now, when the gross reportable amount with respect to any failure can be determined by the IRS, any subsequent penalty imposed with respect to such failure shall be reduced as necessary to ensure that the aggregate amount of such penalties does not exceed the gross reportable amount. To the extent that the aggregate amount of such penalties already exceeds the gross reportable amount, the IRS must refund the excess to the taxpayer (Code Sec. 6677(a), as amended by the 2010 HIRE Act).

NEW LAW EXPLAINED

▶ **Effective date.** The amendments apply to notices and returns required to be filed after December 31, 2009 (Act Sec. 535(b) of the Hiring Incentives to Restore Employment (HIRE) Act (P.L. 111-147)).

Law source: Law at ¶6175. Committee Report at ¶11,170.

— Act Sec. 535(a) of the Hiring Incentives to Restore Employment (HIRE) Act (P.L. 111-147), amending Code Sec. 6677(a);

— Act Sec. 535(b), providing the effective date.

Reporter references: For further information, consult the following CCH reporters.

— Standard Federal Tax Reporter, ¶39,820.021

— Tax Research Consultant, PENALTY: 3,208.70

— Practical Tax Explanation, §39,135.15

¶755 Substitute Dividends and Dividend Equivalent Payments Received by Foreign Persons

SUMMARY OF NEW LAW

Dividend equivalent payments received by foreign persons are treated as U.S.-source dividends for purposes of Code Secs. 871(a), 881 and 4948(a), and chapters 3 and 4 of subtitle A of the Code. Dividend equivalent payments generally include substitute dividends made pursuant to a securities lending or sale-repurchase transaction and payments made pursuant to notional principal contracts if such substitute dividends and payments are contingent upon, or determined by reference to, the payments of U.S.-source dividends. Any other payments substantially similar to such substitute dividends or notional principal contract payments are also considered dividend equivalents.

BACKGROUND

Nonresident alien individuals and foreign corporations (i.e., foreign persons) are subject to U.S. income tax on their U.S.-source income and income effectively connected with a U.S. trade or business. A foreign person's income effectively connected with a U.S. trade or business is taxed at the regular graduated tax rates in the same manner as if earned by a U.S. person (i.e., a U.S. citizen or resident or a domestic corporation) (Code Secs. 871(b) and 882).

U.S.-source income received by foreign persons that is not effectively connected with a U.S. trade or business is subject to a 30-percent withholding tax, which may be reduced or even eliminated by an income tax treaty (Code Secs. 871(a) and 881). Specifically, the 30-percent (or a lower treaty rate) withholding tax is imposed on a foreign person's fixed or determinable, annual or periodic U.S.-source (FDAP) income, which includes interest, dividends, rents and similar types of investment

BACKGROUND

income that is not effectively connected with a U.S. trade or business. Withholding is generally required on such income without reduction for deductions or credits. The person that makes a payment of U.S.-source income to a foreign person (otherwise known as the withholding agent) must deduct and withhold the 30-percent tax from the payment, unless it establishes that the payee is eligible for an exemption from withholding or a reduced tax treaty rate (Code Sec. 1441).

A number of statutory exemptions from the 30-percent withholding tax are provided for certain types of U.S.-source income received by foreign persons that is not effectively connected with a U.S. trade or business. For example, an exemption applies to U.S.-source portfolio interest, interest on bank deposits, and gains from the sale of property by foreign persons (subject to certain exceptions). Certain dividends are also exempt from withholding. Thus, the portion of any dividend paid by a U.S. corporation that meets the 80-percent foreign business requirement of Code Sec. 861(c)(1) is exempt from the withholding tax (Code Secs. 871(i)(2)(B) and 881(d)). A portion of a dividend that is paid by a foreign corporation and treated as U.S.-source income under the 25-percent source rule of Code Sec. 861(a)(2)(B) is also generally exempt from the withholding tax (Code Secs. 871(i)(2)(D) and 881(d)). In addition, tax is not withheld on interest-related dividends and short-term capital gains dividends received from a mutual fund (regulated investment company or RIC), subject to certain exceptions (Code Secs. 871(k) and 881(e)).

For purposes of determining withholding on FDAP income, IRS regulations provide that substitute interest and dividend payments are treated as having the same source and character as the dividend or interest income for which they substitute (Reg. §§1.871-7(b)(2) and 1.881-2(b)(2)). This transparency rule is intended to eliminate abuse where the substitute payment is characterized in a different manner than the underlying payment. A substitute interest or dividend payment is a payment made to a transferor of a security in a securities lending transaction or sale-repurchase agreement that equals the dividend or interest that the owner of the transferred security would normally receive. A securities lending transaction is a transfer of one or more securities described in Code Sec. 1058(a) (i.e., a tax-free transfer of securities pursuant to an agrement that provides for the return of identical securities to the transferor and for other conditions, whereby no gain or loss is recognized on the initial exchange of the securities and on their subsequent return to the transferor) or a substantially similar transaction. A sale-repurchase transaction is an agreement under which a person transfers a security for cash and simultaneously agrees to receive substantially identical securities from the transferee in the future in exchange for cash (Reg. §§1.861-2(a)(7) and 1.861-3(a)(6)).

> **Comment:** The substitute interest or dividend payment rule is intended to eliminate abuse where the substitute payment is characterized in a different manner than the underlying payment. Thus, substitute dividends paid to a foreign person with respect to stock of a domestic corporation are treated as U.S.-source dividends that are subject to the withholding tax. On the other hand, payments made to foreign persons under a notional principal contract are treated as foreign source income and are not generally subject to the withholding tax (although they may be subject to U.S. tax if the recipient is engaged in a U.S.

BACKGROUND

trade or business to which the payment is effectively connected), even if the payments are calculated by reference, for example, to U.S.-source dividends paid on the underlying reference security. Such dividend equivalent payments made with respect to equity derivative contracts are not, therefore, subject to U.S. withholding tax.

Comment: Unlike substitute interest or dividend payments, payments made pursuant to a notional principal contract (i.e., a derivative), are sourced in accordance with the recipient's residence (Reg. §1.863-7(b)).

In Notice 97-66, 1997-2 CB 328, the IRS provided a withholding mechanism to eliminate excessive withholding that could arise on multiple payments in a chain of substitute dividend payments due to the sourcing rules described provided in the regulations. Specifically, the amount of U.S. withholding tax to be imposed on a foreign-to-foreign payment is the amount of the underlying dividend multiplied by a rate equal to the excess of the rate of U.S. withholding tax that would be applicable to U.S. source dividends paid by a U.S. person directly to the recipient of the substitute payment over the rate of U.S. withholding tax that would be applicable to U.S. source dividends paid by a U.S. person directly to the payer of the substitute payment. This amount may be reduced or eliminated to the extent that the total U.S. tax actually withheld on the underlying dividend and any previous substitute payments is greater than the amount of U.S. withholding tax that would be imposed on U.S. source dividends paid by a U.S. person directly to the payer of the substitute payment. The recipient of a substitute payment may not, however, disregard the form of its transaction to reduce the U.S. withholding tax. Therefore, a recipient of a foreign-to-foreign payment is not entitled to a refund or tax credit against any other U.S. tax liability to reflect the fact that the rate of U.S. withholding tax that would be applicable to a U.S. source dividend paid by a U.S. person directly to the recipient is less than the rate of U.S. withholding tax that would be applicable to a U.S. source dividend paid by a U.S. person directly to the payer of the substitute payment (or any payer of a previous substitute payment or the underlying dividend).

Foreign private foundation. A foreign private foundation is subject to a tax of four percent of its gross investment income derived from the United States. This tax is imposed in lieu of the two-percent tax under Code Sec. 4940, which is imposed on the net investment income of every private foundation exempt from tax under Code Sec. 501 (Code Sec. 4948(a)). For this purpose, gross investment income generally includes gross income from interest, dividends, rents, royalties, payments with respect to securities loan, and payments from similar sources, but excludes such income to the extent it is taken into account in computing the tax imposed by Code Sec. 511 (Code Sec. 4940(c)(2)).

A foreign private foundation is generally exempt from certain excise tax sanctions, rules relating to termination of a private foundation status and other special rules if substantially all of its support, other than gross investment income, is derived from sources outside the United States (Code Sec. 4948(b)). This exemption, however, does not apply if the foreign private foundation engages in certain prohibited transactions. A prohibited transaction for this purpose includes any act or failure to act that would

BACKGROUND

have subjected a domestic private foundation to a penalty under Code Sec. 6684 penalty or termination tax under Code Sec. 507 tax (Code Sec. 4948(c)).

NEW LAW EXPLAINED

Dividend equivalent payments received by foreign persons treated as U.S.-source dividends.—A dividend equivalent payment will be treated as a dividend from sources within the United States for purposes of the taxation of nonresident aliens and foreign corporations on fixed or determinable, annual or periodic (FDAP) income under Code Secs. 871(a) and 881, the taxation of foreign private foundations on U.S. gross investment income under Code Sec. 4948(a), the withholding of tax by a withholding agent on payments of FDAP income to nonresident aliens and foreign corporations, and the taxation and withholding on payments of FDAP income to an account in a foreign financial institution or non-financial foreign entity (Code Sec. 871(l)(1), as added by the Hiring Incentives to Restore Employment (HIRE) Act (P.L. 111-147)). For a discussion of the disclosure and reporting requirements for withholdable payments to an account in a foreign financial institution or non-financial foreign entity, see ¶ 705. A dividend equivalent includes:

- any substitute dividend made pursuant to a securities lending or a sale-repurchase transaction that (directly or indirectly) is contingent upon, or determined by reference to, the payment of a dividend from sources within the United States;

- any payment made pursuant to a specified notional principal contract that (directly or indirectly) is contingent upon, or determined by referenced to, the payment of a dividend from sources within the United States; and

- any other payment determined by the Secretary of the Treasury to be substantially similar to such substitute dividend or such payment made pursuant to a specified notional principal contract (Code Sec. 871(l)(2), as added by the 2010 HIRE Act).

> **Comment:** In determining substitute dividends that are treated as dividend equivalents, the substitute dividend definition in Reg. § 1.861-3(a)(6) is used. In addition, the Joint Committee Report indicates that under the rule for determining substantially similar payments, the Secretary of the Treasury may, for example, conclude that payments under certain forward contracts or other financial contracts that reference stock of U.S. corporations are dividend equivalents (Joint Committee on Taxation, Technical Explanation of the Hiring Incentives to Restore Employment Act (JCX-4-10)). The treatment of dividend equivalents as dividends is intended to prevent the avoidance of tax withholding on dividends by recharacterizing such payments as other types of income exempt from withholding, such as exempt portfolio interest, through the use of derivative transactions or other arrangements. In addition, the new source rule for dividend equivalent payments under notional principal contracts ensures that such payments will be treated as U.S.-source dividends when made with respect to domestic stock. Thus, such payments may no longer escape the withholding tax by being sourced as foreign income based on the recipient's residence.

NEW LAW EXPLAINED

For purposes of the treatment of dividend equivalents as U.S.-source income, a specified notional principal contract is any notional principal contract if:

- in connection with entering into the contract, any long party to the contract transfers the underlying security to any short party to the contract;

- in connection with the termination of the contract, any short party to the contract transfers the underlying security to any long party to the contract;

- the underlying security is not readily tradable on an established securities market;

- in connection with entering into the contract, the underlying security is posted as collateral by any short party to the contract with any long party to the contract; or

- the contract is identified by the Secretary of the Treasury as a specified notional principal contract Code Sec. 871(l)(3)(A), as added by the 2010 HIRE Act).

In the case of payments made after the date that is two years after March 18, 2010, a specified notional principal contract is any notional principal contract, unless the Secretary of the Treasury determines that such a contract is of a type that does not have the potential for tax avoidance (Code Sec. 871(l)(3)(B), as added by the 2010 HIRE Act).

For purposes of the specified principal contract definition, a long party means, with respect to any underlying security of any notional principal contract, any party to the contract that is entitled to receive any payment pursuant to the contract which is contingent upon, or determined by reference to, the payment of a dividend from sources within the United States with respect to the underlying security (Code Sec. 871(l)(4), as added by the 2010 HIRE Act). A short party with respect to any underlying security of any notional principal contract is any party to the contract that is not a long party with respect to the underlying security. Underlying security includes, with respect to any notional principal contract, the security with respect to which the dividend payment referred to in item (2), above (in the dividend equivalent definition) is paid. For this purpose, any index or fixed basket of securities is treated as a single security.

> **Comment:** The Joint Committee Report clarifies that an index or fixed basket of securities that is treated as a single security will be deemed to be regularly traded on an established securities market if every component of such index or fixed basket is a security that is readily tradable on an established securities market. It further clarifies that no inference is intended as to whether the definition of a specified notional principal contract, or any determination under this provision that a transaction does not have the potential for the avoidance of taxes on U.S.-source dividends, is relevant in determining whether an agency relationship exists under general tax principles or whether a foreign party to a contract should be treated as having beneficial tax ownership of the stock giving rise to U.S.-source dividends (Joint Committee on Taxation, Technical Explanation of the Hiring Incentives to Restore Employment Act (JCX-4-10)).

Payments that are treated as U.S.-source dividends under these rules are the gross amounts used in computing any net amounts transferred to or from the taxpayer (Code Sec. 871(l)(5), as added by the 2010 HIRE Act).

NEW LAW EXPLAINED

Example: Under a typical total return swap referencing stock of a domestic corporation, a foreign investor enters into an agreement with a counterparty under which amounts due to each party are based on the returns generated by a notional investment in a specified dollar amount of the stock underlying the swap. The investor agrees for a specified period to pay to the counterparty an amount calculated by reference to a market interest rate (such as the London Interbank Offered Rate (LIBOR)) on the notional amount of the underlying stock and any depreciation in the value of the stock. In return, the counterparty agrees for the specified period to pay the investor any dividends paid on the stock and any appreciation in the value of the stock.

Amounts owed by each party under this swap typically are netted so that only one party makes an actual payment. The rule for determining payments on gross basis treats any dividend-based amount under the swap as a payment even though any actual payment under the swap is a net amount determined in part by other amounts (for example, the interest amount and the amount of any appreciation or depreciation in value of the referenced stock). Accordingly, a counterparty to a total return swap may be obligated to withhold and remit tax on the gross amount of a dividend equivalent even though, as a result of a netting of payments due under the swap, the counterparty is not required to make an actual payment to the foreign investor (Joint Committee on Taxation, Technical Explanation of the Hiring Incentives to Restore Employment Act (JCX-4-10)).

In order to prevent over-withholding in the case of any chain of dividend equivalents, one or more of which is subject to tax on FDAP income under Code Sec. 871(a) or 881, the Secretary of the Treasury may reduce the tax, but only to the extent that the taxpayer can establish that such tax has been paid with respect to another dividend equivalent in such a chain or is not otherwise due, or as the Secretary of the Treasury determines is appropriate to address the role of financial intermediaries in the chain. For purposes of this rule, a dividend is treated as a dividend equivalent (Code Sec. 871(l)(6), as added by the 2010 HIRE Act).

> **Comment:** A chain of dividend equivalents may occur, for example, under transactions similar to those described in Notice 97-66, 1997-2 CB 328.

For purposes of the withholding of tax by a withholding agent on payments of FDAP income to nonresident aliens and foreign corporations, and the taxation and withholding on payments of FDAP income to an account in a foreign financial institution or non-financial foreign entity, each person that is a party to any contract or other arrangement providing for the payment of a dividend equivalent is treated as having control over such a payment (Code Sec. 871(l)(7), as added by the 2010 HIRE Act).

> **Comment:** Based on this rule, the IRS may provide guidance requiring either party to withhold tax on dividend equivalents (Joint Committee on Taxation, Technical Explanation of the Hiring Incentives to Restore Employment Act (JCX-4-10)).

NEW LAW EXPLAINED

Comment: The rules treating dividend equivalents as U.S.-source dividends are not intended to limit the authority of the Secretary of the Treasury (1) to determine the appropriate source of income from financial arrangements (including notional principal contracts) under Code Sec. 863 or 865, or (2) to provide additional guidance addressing the source and characterization of substitute payments made in securities lending and similar transactions (Joint Committee on Taxation, Technical Explanation of the Hiring Incentives to Restore Employment Act (JCX-4-10)).

Practical Analysis: Michael J. Miller, a partner at Roberts & Holland LLP of New York, New York, notes that, from a substantive tax perspective, reversing the netting of payments under the swap, and taxing the long party on the gross amount of the dividend equivalent deemed to have been received, seems reasonable. Requiring the short party to "withhold" more than the amount it is required to pay under the swap, however, seems inappropriate. Moreover, a withholding obligation would logically seem to presuppose custody of some amount from which it is possible to withhold. In practice, it seems likely that most swap transactions to which the new sourcing rule would apply will be terminated before the effective date of new Code Sec. 871(l), e.g., under a change of law provision in standard ISDA documentation. New Code Sec. 871(l) will apply to payments made on or after the date that is 180 days after the date of enactment.

Although the Joint Committee's Technical Explanation states that no inference is intended as to whether the definition of "specified notional principal contract" is relevant in determining whether an agency relationship exists under general tax principles, or whether a foreign long party to a swap should be considered the beneficial owner of the underlying security, it seems clear that the factors included in such definition were chosen with a view towards tax principles of agency and beneficial ownership. Indeed, the underlying rationale for the definition seems to be that the factors enumerated in new Code Sec. 871(l)(3)(A) are highly suggestive of an agency arrangement such that, if even one such factor is present, the long party should in effect be treated as the beneficial owner for dividend withholding purposes. Presumably, the purpose of the caveat in the legislative history is to prevent taxpayers from arguing that an agency relationship cannot exist under common law if none of the enumerated factors in Code Sec. 871(1)(3)(A) are present.

Taxpayers and practitioners are also cautioned to keep in mind that, for payments made more than two years after the date of enactment, the absence of any factors enumerated in Code Sec. 871(1)(3)(A) will not be determinative, because every swap will presumptively become a specified notional principal contract under new Code Sec. 871(1)(3)(B). An exception will apply for any swap that the Secretary determines to be of a type that does not have the potential for tax avoidance, but, as of the date of this writing, it is not possible to predict the scope of any such exception. Accordingly, investors and their tax advisors should be mindful of the need to reexamine any swaps that may still be outstanding when Code Sec. 871(l)(3)(B) takes effect. Care should also be taken to ensure that, where necessary, it will be possible to terminate such swaps (without penalty) at that time.

NEW LAW EXPLAINED

▶ **Effective date.** The provision applies to payments made on or after the date that is 180 days after March 18, 2010, the date of enactment (Act. Sec. 541(b) of the Hiring Incentives to Restore Employment (HIRE) Act (P.L. 111-147)).

Law source: Law at ¶6060. Committee Report at ¶11,180.

— Act Sec. 541(a) of the Hiring Incentives to Restore Employment (HIRE) Act (P.L. 111-147), redesignating Code Sec. 871(l) as Code Sec. 871(m) and adding new Code Sec. 871(l);

— Act Sec. 541(b), providing the effective date.

Reporter references: For further information, consult the following CCH reporters.

— Standard Federal Tax Reporter, ¶27,343.01 and ¶27,484.01

— Tax Research Consultant, INTL: 3,550

— Practical Tax Explanation, § 37,010.15 and § 37,015.15

¶760 Repeal of Certain Foreign Exceptions to Registered Bond Requirements

SUMMARY OF NEW LAW

Exceptions to the registered bond requirements for foreign-targeted obligations are repealed for purposes of the deduction of interest paid on a registered-required obligation, the exclusion from gross income of interest paid on state and local bonds, the exclusion of portfolio income from the withholding of tax from FDAP income paid to nonresident aliens and foreign corporations, the registration-required obligation for United States Treasury bonds, the deduction of losses sustained on registration-required obligations, and the treatment of gain from the sale of a registration-required obligation as ordinary income.

BACKGROUND

The federal tax treatment with respect to an bond obligation, for both issuers and beneficial owners, may depend on whether the obligation is in registered form.

Code Sec. 163 interest deduction. In general, a deduction is allowed for interest paid or accrued on indebtedness (Code Sec. 163). However, no deduction is allowed for interest on a registration-required obligation unless the obligation is in registered form. A registration-required obligation is generally any obligation (including an obligation issued by a governmental entity) except for an obligation issued by a natural person, of the type offered to the public, with a maturity (at issue) of not more than one year, or a "foreign-targeted obligation"). A non-public obligation or short-term obligation is not excepted from the registration requirement if it is of a type determined by regulations to be used frequently in avoiding Federal taxes and is issued after the date such regulations take effect.

BACKGROUND

For this purpose, a foreign-targeted obligation is defined as an obligation: (1) for which there are arrangements reasonably designed to ensure that the obligation will be sold (or resold in connection with the original issue) only to a person who is not a U.S. person; and (2) in the case of an obligation not in registered form, interest on the obligation is payable only outside the United States and its possessions, and on the face of the obligation there is a statement that any U.S. person who holds such obligation will be subject to limitations under the U.S. income tax laws. However, a foreign-targeted obligation is not excepted from the Code Sec. 163(f) registration requirement if it is a type specified in IRS regulations and is issued after the date such regulations take effect.

State and local bonds. Gross income generally does not include interest on a state or local bond (Code Sec. 103). However, this exception is not available unless the bond meets the applicable registration requirements under Code Sec. 149. A book entry bond, for these purposes, is treated as in registered form if the right to the principal of, and stated interest on, the bond may be transferred only through a book entry consistent with IRS regulations. Also, the IRS is required to prescribe regulations as may be necessary to carry out these purposes where there is a nominee or chain of nominees. A registration-required bond, for these purposes, means any bond other than a bond which is not of a type offered to the public, has a maturity (at issue) of not more than one year, or a foreign-targeted obligation.

> **Comment:** Rules similar to those regarding tax-exempt bonds apply, with respect to whether a book entry bond is treated as in registered form and regarding a nominee or chain of nominees (Code Sec. 163(f)(3)).

Portfolio interest exclusion. Payments of U.S. source fixed or determinable annual or periodical (FDAP) income, including interest, dividends, and similar types of investment income, made to nonresident aliens and foreign corporations are subject to U.S. withholding tax at a 30 percent rate if such income is not effectively connected with the conduct of a U.S. trade or business, unless the withholding agent can establish that the beneficial owner of the amount is eligible for an exemption from withholding or a reduced rate of withholding under an income tax treaty (Code Secs. 871, 881, 1441 and 1442). Generally, FDAP income includes interest, dividends, rents, salaries, wages, premiums, annuities, compensation, remunerations, emoluments and any other item of annual or periodical gain, profit or income. U.S.-source portfolio interest is generally not considered fixed or determinable periodic income subject to the flat 30-percent tax. Exempt portfolio interest includes any interest and original issue discount (OID) accrued on an obligation in either bearer or registered form held by the nonresident alien or foreign corporation. Documentation establishing foreign status is required for interest on a registered obligation to qualify as portfolio interest.

> **Comment:** If the IRS determines that the exchange of information agreement between the United States and a foreign country is inadequate to prevent the evasion of U.S. income tax by U.S. persons, the IRS may publish a written statement that the portfolio interest exclusion will not apply from the date the IRS specifies until the date the agreement is adequate to prevent tax evasion (Code Sec. 871(h)(6)(A)).

BACKGROUND

U.S. Treasury obligations. Under Section 3121 of Title 31 of the United States Code every registration-required obligation of the United States Treasury must be in registered form (31 U.S.C. 3121(g)). A similar definition of registration-required obligation is used for this purposes as used under the Code including the foreign-targeted obligation exception. As a result, a foreign-targeted obligation of the Treasury can be in bearer form rather than registered form (see Joint Committee on Taxation, Technical Explanation of the Hiring Incentives to Restore Employment Act (JCX-4-10)).

Excise tax on issuers. Pursuant to Code Sec. 4701, an excise tax is imposed on a person who issues a registration-required obligation which is not in registered form. For purposes of this tax, a registration-required obligation has the same meaning as when used in Code Sec. 163(f) (regarding the Code Sec. 163 interest deduction), except that it does not include an obligation required to be registered under Code Sec. 149(a) (regarding tax-exempt obligations).

Gain and loss. In general, a deduction is allowed for a loss sustained and not compensated for by insurance or otherwise (Code Sec. 165). However, a deduction is not provided for a loss sustained on a registration-required obligation unless the obligation is in registered form or the issuance of the obligation was subject to the excise tax under Code Sec. 4701. Also, if a registration-required obligation is not in registered form, any gain on the sale or other disposition of the obligation is generally treated as ordinary income unless the issuance of the obligation was subject to the excise tax under Code Sec. 4701 (Code Sec. 1287). For these purposes, a registration-required obligation has the same meaning as in Code Sec. 163(f)(2) (regarding the Code Sec. 163 interest deduction), except that the exception for a foreign-targeted obligation does not apply. However, the IRS may provide that rules disallowing a loss deduction or treating gain on the sale of an obligation as ordinary income do not apply with respect to obligations of certain holders.

NEW LAW EXPLAINED

Repeal of certain foreign exceptions to registered bond requirements.—Certain foreign exceptions to registered bond requirements are repealed.

Code Sec. 163 interest deduction. With respect to the Code Sec. 163 interest deduction, foreign-targeted obligations are not excepted from the Code Sec. 163(f)(2) definition of a registration-required obligation. Thus, a deduction for interest is disallowed with respect to any obligation not issued in registered form, unless that obligation is issued by a natural person, of the type offered to the public, or with a maturity (at issue) of not more than one year (Code Sec. 163(f)(2), as amended by the Hiring Incentives to Restore Employment (HIRE) Act (P.L. 111-147)).

> **State Tax Consequences:** Interest on state and local bonds not issued in registered form may also not be deducted. Although most states conform to Code Sec. 163(f), these amendments may affect states that do not conform to the Internal Revenue Code as currently amended. The nonconforming states may continue to allow the exemption and such interest would be subtracted for state

NEW LAW EXPLAINED

income tax purposes. However, because the amendments apply to debt obligations issued after the date that is two years after March 18, 2010, most states will conform by the time the provision takes effect.

State and local bonds. With respect to the provision in Code Sec. 149(a)(1) that interest on a registration-required bond is not exempt from federal income tax unless the bond is in registered form, a registration-required bond means any bond other than a bond which is not of a type offered to the public or has a maturity (at issue) of not more than one year (Code Sec. 149(a)(2), as amended by the 2010 HIRE Act).

Portfolio interest exclusion. An obligation must be in registered form to qualify as portfolio interest which may be excluded U.S.-source portfolio interest for purposes of taxation and withholding with respect to fixed or determinable periodic (FDAP) U.S. source income of nonresident aliens and foreign corporation she flat 30-percent tax (Code Sec. 871(h)(2) and Code Sec. 881(c)(2), as amended by the 2010 HIRE Act). Specifically, interest qualifies as portfolio interest only if it is paid on an obligation that is issued in registered form and either (1) the beneficial owner has provided the withholding agent with a statement certifying that the beneficial owner is not a United States person (on IRS Form W-8), or (2) the IRS has determined that such statement is not required.

> **Comment:** According to the Joint Committee on Taxation, "[i]t is anticipated that the Secretary may exercise its authority under this rule to waive the requirement of collecting Forms W-8 in circumstances in which the Secretary has determined there is a low risk of tax evasion and there are adequate documentation standards within the country of tax residency of the beneficial owner of the obligations in question. Generally, however, as a result of the provision, interest paid to a foreign person on an obligation that is not issued in registered form is subject to U.S. withholding tax at a 30-percent rate, unless the withholding agent can establish that the beneficial owner of the amount is eligible for an exemption from withholding other than the portfolio interest exemption or for a reduced rate of withholding under an income tax treaty." (Joint Committee on Taxation, Technical Explanation of the Hiring Incentives to Restore Employment Act (JCX-4-10)).

U.S. Treasury obligations. The foreign-targeted exception to the definition of a registration-required obligation in Section 3121(g) of Title 31 of the United States Code has been repealed (31 U.S.C. 3121(g), as amended by the 2010 HIRE Act). A foreign-targeted obligation of the Treasury must therefore be in registered form (Joint Committee of Taxation, Technical Explanation of the Hiring Incentives to Restore Employment Act (JCX-4-10)).

Registered form. Rules similar to those of Code Sec. 149(a)(3) (regarding tax-exempt bonds) apply, with respect to whether a book entry bond is treated as in registered form and regarding a nominee or chain of nominees, except that a dematerialized book-entry system or other book entry system specified by the IRS shall be treated as a book-entry system described in Code Sec. 149(a)(3) (Code Sec. 163(f)(3), as amended by the 2010 HIRE Act).

> **Comment:** According to the Joint Committee on Taxation, "[a] debt obligation that is formally in bearer form is treated, for the purposes of Code Sec. 163(f), as

NEW LAW EXPLAINED

held in a book-entry system as long as the debt obligation may be transferred only through a dematerialized book entry system or other book entry system specified by the IRS." (Joint Committee on Taxation, Technical Explanation of the Hiring Incentives to Restore Employment Act (JCX-4-10)).

Excise tax on issuers. The exceptions to the excise tax on issuers of a registration-required obligation which is not in registered form will continue to include an exception for obligations that meet the foreign-targeted requirements. Thus, for purposes of the excise tax, a registration-required obligation does not include an obligation if:

- there are arrangements reasonably designed to ensure that the obligation will be sold (or resold in connection with the original issue) only to a person who is not a United States person;
- interest on the obligation is payable only outside the United States and its possessions; and
- on the face of the obligation there is a statement that any U.S. person who holds the obligation will be subject to limitations under the U.S. income tax laws (Code Sec. 4701(b)(1), as amended by the 2010 HIRE Act).

Gain and loss. For purposes of the registration requirement with respect to deducting losses under Code Sec. 165(j), a registration-required obligation has the same meaning as in Code Sec. 163(f)(2) (regarding the Code Sec. 163 interest deduction). Likewise, with respect to the Code Sec. 1287 treatment of gain on a registration-required obligation not in registered form. The references to foreign-targeted obligations in Code Sec. 163(f)(2)(A)(iv), prior to its being stricken by the 2010 HIRE Act, are stricken.

▶ **Effective date.** The provision applies to obligations issued after the date which is two years after March 18, 2010 (Act Sec. 502(f) of the Hiring Incentives to Restore Employment (HIRE) Act (P.L. 111-147).

Law source: Law at ¶6025, ¶6030, ¶6035, ¶6060, ¶6065, ¶6070, ¶6115, ¶7212. Committee Report at ¶11,070.

— Act Sec. 502(a) of the Hiring Incentives to Restore Employment (HIRE) Act (P.L. 111-147), amending Code Sec. 149(a)(2), Code Sec. 163(f)(2), Code Sec. 165(j)(2)(A), and Code Sec. 1287(b)(1);

— Act Sec. 502(b), amending Code Sec. 871(h)(2), (h)(3)(A), and Code Sec. 881(c)(2);

— Act Sec. 502(c), amending Code Sec. 163(f)(3);

— Act Sec. 502(d), amending 31 U.S.C. §3121(g);

— Act Sec. 502(e), amending Code Sec. 4701(b)(1);

— Act Sec. 502(f), providing the effective date.

Reporter references: For further information, consult the following CCH reporters.

— Standard Federal Tax Reporter, ¶7905.01, ¶9300.01, ¶10,203.01, ¶27,343.046, ¶27,484.024, ¶31,502.01 and ¶33,943.01

— Tax Research Consultant, BUSEXP: 21,204, BUSEXP: 21,206 , BUSEXP: 30,252, SALES: 24,404, SALES: 51,062, EXPAT: 15,154 and INTL: 3,558.20

— Practical Tax Explanation, §3,105, §7,401, §19,301, §19,340 and §37,015.15

— Federal Estate and Gift Tax Reporter, ¶7975.07

¶765 Interest Expense Sourcing for Worldwide Affiliated Groups

SUMMARY OF NEW LAW

Implementation of the elections to allocate interest expense on a worldwide basis and expand a financial institution group of a worldwide affiliated group are delayed for two years. The elections will take effect for tax years beginning after December 31, 2020.

BACKGROUND

A U.S. taxpayer is allowed a credit against U.S. tax liability for taxes paid during the year to a foreign country or U.S. possession. The foreign tax credit is limited to prevent taxpayers from using the credit to reduce U.S. tax liability on U.S. source income (Code Sec. 904). The limit in effect caps the credit at the amount of the U.S. tax that would be paid on foreign source taxable income.

The limitation is the lesser of the foreign tax paid or accrued or:

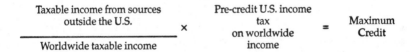

$$\frac{\text{Taxable income from sources outside the U.S.}}{\text{Worldwide taxable income}} \times \begin{array}{c}\text{Pre-credit U.S. income}\\ \text{tax}\\ \text{on worldwide}\\ \text{income}\end{array} = \begin{array}{c}\text{Maximum}\\ \text{Credit}\end{array}$$

The larger the amount of foreign source taxable income is, the larger the foreign tax credit limitation will be. For this reason, the basic planning formula calls for increasing the amount of gross income characterized as foreign source income, while minimizing deductions, such as interest expense, that are allocated to foreign source income.

The interest expense sourcing rules are based on the concept that money is fungible and interest expenses should be attributed to all business activities and property of the taxpayer, regardless of the reason for the loan (Temporary Reg. § 1.861-9T(a)). Interest expense allocations must be based on the asset values of an affiliated group of corporations, rather than the gross income of the group (Temporary Reg. §§ 1.861-8T(c)(2) and 1.861-9T(g)(1)(i)). Domestic members of the group generally are treated as a single corporation (the "one-taxpayer rule") (Code Sec. 864(e)(1); Temporary Reg. § 1.861-11T(c)).

An affiliated group of corporations is generally defined as a group of related corporations, including Code Sec. 936 possession corporations, that are eligible to file a consolidated tax return under Code Sec. 1504, whether or not a consolidated return

BACKGROUND

is filed (Code Sec. 864(e)(5)(A); Temporary Reg. § 1.861-11T(c)). Foreign affiliates and their assets are excluded from the group (Code Sec. 1504(b)(3)). Also excluded from the affiliated group are financial corporations. Financial corporations are corporations that would otherwise be included in the affiliated group for consolidated return purposes and that are certain financial institutions under Code Sec. 581 or Code Sec. 591. Financial corporations also include, to the extent provided in the regulations, bank holding companies, subsidiaries of banks and bank holding companies and savings institutions. Financial corporations are treated as a separate single corporation for interest allocation purposes (i.e., not treated as part of the regular affiliated group for purposes of applying the one-taxpayer rule) (Code Sec. 864(e)(5)(B) and (C); Temporary Reg. § 1.861-11T(d)(4)).

Eliminating foreign affiliates and their assets from the worldwide group can result in the over allocation of U.S. interest expense to foreign source income. For example, the stock of the foreign corporation is treated as a foreign asset of the domestic corporation that produces foreign source dividend income. The U.S. source interest expense can be used to reduce the foreign source income, even though the interest expense of the foreign corporation may have already been taken into account by reducing earnings from which the dividend was paid (see House Committee Report for the American Jobs Creation Act of 2004 (P.L. 108-357) (H.R. Rep. No. 108-548, pt. 1).

To address this, the American Jobs Creation Act of 2004 (P.L. 108-357) allowed an affiliated group to make a one-time election to determine foreign source taxable income of the group, by allocating and apportioning interest expense of the domestic members of the worldwide affiliated group on a worldwide basis, as if all members of the worldwide group were a single corporation (Code Sec. 864(f)).

A group that makes this election will determine the taxable income of the domestic members of the worldwide affiliated group from sources outside of the United States by allocating and apportioning the third-party interest expense of those domestic members to foreign source income in an amount equal to the excess (if any) of:

(1) the worldwide affiliated group's total third-party interest expense multiplied by the ratio which the foreign assets of the worldwide affiliated group bears to the total assets of the worldwide affiliated group; over

(2) the third-party interest expense incurred by foreign members of the group to the extent such interest would be allocated to foreign sources if the provision's principles were applied separately to the foreign members of the group.

Under the election, a U.S. company is not required to allocate U.S. interest expense against foreign source income (preventing double taxation), unless the debt-to-asset ratio is higher in the United States than in foreign countries (House Committee Report for the American Jobs Creation Act of 2004 (P.L. 108-357) (H.R. Rep. No. 108-548, pt. 1)).

A worldwide affiliated group is defined as:

(1) all of the corporations in an affiliated group under Code Sec. 1504(a), including insurance companies, which would otherwise be excluded under Code Sec. 1504(b)(2) and corporations subject to possessions tax credit election, which would otherwise be excluded under Code Sec. 1504(b)(4); plus

BACKGROUND

(2) all controlled foreign corporations that, in the aggregate, meet the consolidated group ownership requirements, either directly or indirectly, and would be members of the affiliated group if foreign corporations were not excluded from the definition of an includible corporation under Code Sec. 1504(b)(3) (i.e., in which at least 80 percent of the vote or value of the stock of such corporation owned by one or more other corporations included in the affiliated group (Code Sec. 864(f)(1)(C), as added by P.L. 108-357).

If an affiliated group makes an election to be treated as a worldwide affiliated group for purposes of interest expense allocations, an election may also be made to include the following in the financial institution subgroup of the worldwide affiliated group (Code Sec. 864(f)(5)):

(1) all corporations that are part of the present-law bank subgroup; and

(2) at the election of the taxpayer, all financial corporations (i.e., any member that derives at least 80 percent of its gross income from financial services income from transactions with unrelated persons).

Implementation of the elections for a worldwide affiliated group to allocate interest expense on a worldwide basis and expand a financial institution group of a world-wide affiliated group was delayed both by the by the Housing Assistance Tax Act of 2008 (P.L. 110-289) and the Worker, Homeownership, and Business Assistance Act of 2009 (P.L. 111-92). The elections will apply to tax years beginning after December 31, 2017 (Code Sec. 864(f)(5)(D) and (6)).

NEW LAW EXPLAINED

Elections to allocate interest on worldwide basis and expand the financial institution group delayed. Implementation of the one-time election for worldwide affiliated groups to allocate interest expense on a worldwide basis is delayed for three years (Code Sec. 864(f)(6), as amended by the Hiring Incentives to Restore Employment (HIRE) Act (P.L. 111-147)). Implementation of the one-time election to expand a financial institution group of a worldwide affiliated group is also delayed for three years (Code Sec. 864(f)(5)(D), as amended by the 2010 HIRE Act). Thus, the election to allocate interest on a worldwide basis must be made by the common parent of the domestic affiliated group for the first tax year beginning after December 31, 2020, in which an affiliated group exists and includes the affiliated group and at least one foreign corporation. The election to expand the financial institution group on a worldwide basis must be made by the common parent of the pre-election worldwide affiliated group for the first tax year beginning after December 31, 2020, in which the affiliated group includes one or more financial corporations.

> **Caution:** Once the election is made, it applies to the tax year and all subsequent tax years, unless revoked with the consent of the IRS (Code Sec. 864(f)(5)(D) and (6), as amended by the 2010 HIRE Act).

> **Comment:** The Congressional Research Service has issued a report discussing the worldwide interest allocation rules and the expansion of the bank subgroup

NEW LAW EXPLAINED

election. The report concludes that the worldwide allocation of interest rule, while losing revenue, is more consistent with the basic objective of the foreign tax credit limit than is the one-taxpayer rule. The report cautions that planning techniques could undermine the objective, and that the rules could contribute to tax distortions. The report also states that the expansion of the subgroup election may not be consistent with the worldwide allocation of interest and that the elections may permit firms to avoid the impact of the interest allocation rules (Congressional Research Service Report for Congress-The Foreign Tax Credit's Interest Allocation Rules, October 30, 2009).

State Tax Consequences: There should be no immediate effect on state taxation of the delay in the effective date of the worldwide interest allocation rules for three years, from taxable years beginning after 2017, until taxable years beginning after 2020. When the rules take effect, those states that have not conformed may require an adjustment to interest on the state income tax return.

Practical Analysis: Sandra L. Soltis, a Partner at Blackman Kallick of Chicago, Illinois, notes that a U.S. taxpayer is taxed on its worldwide income. To prevent double taxation of income earned outside the United States, a U.S. taxpayer can credit its foreign income taxes against its U.S. tax liability.

The amount of foreign tax credits a taxpayer can use in any year is limited to the lesser of the actual foreign income taxes paid on its foreign-source income or the U.S. income tax allocable to the income ("FTC limitation"). This FTC limitation prevents the use of the foreign tax as a credit against income tax on U.S. source income.

The FTC limitation is based on foreign source taxable income; therefore, deductions must be allocated or apportioned between foreign source gross income and U.S. source gross income (Reg. § 1.861-8(a)(2)). Foreign source taxable income is foreign source gross income after directly allocated and apportioned expenses.

The rules for allocating and apportioning interest expense operates on the theory that money is fungible and interest expense is attributable to all activities, regardless of the purpose of a particular debt.

Interest expense is apportioned between foreign and U.S. source income based on the relative average value of the assets in each income group (Reg. §§ 1.861-8T(c)(2) and 1.861-9T(g)(1)(i)). The asset's value may be based on adjusted tax basis or fair market value. Assets are classified as U.S. or foreign source based on the source and type of income it generates or may reasonably be expected to generate.

Although the foreign affiliated members have their own interest expenses, none are apportioned between the domestic group's U.S. and foreign source income. Therefore, the interest allocation rules tend to over allocate a worldwide group's interest expense to foreign source income. This over-allocation will result in a reduction of the FTC limitation of the domestic members of the affiliated group. As a result, the total amount of foreign taxes paid may not be claimed as foreign tax credits due to the lower FTC limitation.

NEW LAW EXPLAINED

The American Jobs Creation Act of 2004 ("AJCA") provided a one-time election to allocate interest expense on a worldwide basis. This one-time election could only be made for the first tax year beginning after 2008. A provision in the Housing Assistance Act of 2008 delayed the effective date of worldwide interest allocation rules for two additional years—until tax years beginning after December 31, 2010. This effective date was again delayed in the Worker, Homeownership and Business Assistance Act of 2009, this time for seven years—to the first tax year beginning after 2017.

Under the Hiring Incentives to Restore Employment Act ("HIRE"), this election was again delayed—this time until tax years beginning after 2020.

Effective date. The provision is effective on March 18, 2010 (Act Sec. 551(b)) of the Hiring Incentives to Restore Employment (HIRE) Act (P.L. 111-147)).

Law source: Law at ¶ 6055. Committee Report at ¶ 11,190.

— Act Sec. 551(a) of the Hiring Incentives to Restore Employment (HIRE) Act (P.L. 111-147), amending Code Sec. 864(f)(5)(D) and Code Sec. 864(f)(6);

— Act Sec. 551(b), providing the effective date.

Reporter references: For further information, consult the following CCH reporters.

— Standard Federal Tax Reporter, ¶ 27,189.041 and ¶ 27,189.0415

— Tax Research Consultant, INTL: 6,108.25, CONSOL: 45,100 and CONSOL: 45,106

— Practical Tax Explanation, § 37,210.10

Code Sections Added, Amended Or Repealed

PATIENT PROTECTION AND AFFORDABLE CARE ACT
HEALTH CARE AND EDUCATION RECONCILIATION ACT OF 2010

[¶ 5001]

≫→ *Caution: The provisions below reflect amendments made by P.L. 111-148 and P.L. 111-152; see ¶ 6001 and following for amendments made by P.L. 111-144 and P.L. 111-147.*

INTRODUCTION.

The Internal Revenue Code provisions amended by the Patient Protection and Affordable Care Act (P.L. 111-148), and the Health Care and Education Reconciliation Act of 2010 (P.L. 111-152) are shown in the following paragraphs. Deleted Code material or the text of the Code Section prior to amendment appears in the amendment notes following each amended Code provision. *Any changed or added material is set out in italics.*

[¶ 5005] CODE SEC. 24. CHILD TAX CREDIT.

* * *

(b) LIMITATIONS.—

* * *

(3) LIMITATION BASED ON AMOUNT OF TAX.—In the case of a taxable year to which section 26(a)(2) does not apply, the credit allowed under subsection (a) for any taxable year shall not exceed the excess of—

(A) the sum of the regular tax liability (as defined in section 26(b)) plus the tax imposed by section 55, over

≫→ *Caution: Code Sec. 24(b)(3)(B), below, was amended by P.L. 111-148. For sunset provision, see P.L. 111-148, §10909(c), in the amendment notes.*

(B) the sum of the credits allowable under this subpart (other than this section and sections 25A(i), 25B, 25D, 30, 30B, and 30D) and section 27 for the taxable year.

* * *

[Committee Reports at ¶ 10,390.]

Amendments

• 2010, Patient Protection and Affordable Care Act (P.L. 111-148)

P.L. 111-148, §10909(b)(2)(A):

Amended Code Sec. 24(b)(3)(B) by striking "23," before "25A(i)". Effective for tax years beginning after 12-31-2009.

P.L. 111-148, §10909(c), provides:

(c) APPLICATION AND EXTENSION OF EGTRRA SUNSET.—Notwithstanding section 901 of the Economic Growth and Tax

Relief Reconciliation Act of 2001, such section shall apply to the amendments made by this section and the amendments made by section 202 of such Act by substituting "December 31, 2011" for "December 31, 2010" in subsection (a)(1) thereof.

[¶5010] CODE SEC. 25. INTEREST ON CERTAIN HOME MORTGAGES.

* * *

(e) SPECIAL RULES AND DEFINITIONS.—For purposes of this section—

(1) CARRYFORWARD OF UNUSED CREDIT.—

* * *

>>>➔ *Caution: Code Sec. 25(e)(1)(C), below, was amended by P.L. 111-148. For sunset provision, see P.L. 111-148, §10909(c), in the amendment notes.*

(C) APPLICABLE TAX LIMIT.—For purposes of this paragraph, the term "applicable tax limit" means—

(i) in the case of a taxable year to which section 26(a)(2) applies, the limitation imposed by section 26(a)(2) for the taxable year reduced by the sum of the credits allowable under this subpart (other than this section and sections 25D, and 1400C), and

(ii) in the case of a taxable year to which section 26(a)(2) does not apply, the limitation imposed by section 26(a)(1) for the taxable year reduced by the sum of the credits allowable under this subpart (other than this section and sections 24, 25A(i), 25B, 25D, 30, 30B, 30D, and 1400C).

* * *

[Committee Reports at ¶10,390.]

Amendments

• **2010, Patient Protection and Affordable Care Act (P.L. 111-148)**

P.L. 111-148, §10909(b)(2)(B):

Amended Code Sec. 25(e)(1)(C) by striking "23," after "other than this section and sections" both places it appears. **Effective** for tax years beginning after 12-31-2009.

P.L. 111-148, §10909(c), provides:

(c) APPLICATION AND EXTENSION OF EGTRRA SUNSET.—Notwithstanding section 901 of the Economic Growth and Tax Relief Reconciliation Act of 2001, such section shall apply to the amendments made by this section and the amendments made by section 202 of such Act by substituting "December 31, 2011" for "December 31, 2010" in subsection (a)(1) thereof.

[¶5015] CODE SEC. 25A. HOPE AND LIFETIME LEARNING CREDITS.

* * *

(i) AMERICAN OPPORTUNITY TAX CREDIT.—In the case of any taxable year beginning in 2009 or 2010—

* * *

(5) CREDIT ALLOWED AGAINST ALTERNATIVE MINIMUM TAX.—In the case of a taxable year to which section 26(a)(2) does not apply, so much of the credit allowed under subsection (a) as is attributable to the Hope Scholarship Credit shall not exceed the excess of—

(A) the sum of the regular tax liability (as defined in section 26(b)) plus the tax imposed by section 55, over

>>>➔ *Caution: Code Sec. 25A(i)(5)(B), below, was amended by P.L. 111-148. For sunset provision, see P.L. 111-148, §10909(c), in the amendment notes.*

(B) the sum of the credits allowable under this subpart (other than this subsection and sections 25D and 30D) and section 27 for the taxable year.

* * *

[Committee Reports at ¶10,390.]

Amendments

• **2010, Patient Protection and Affordable Care Act (P.L. 111-148)**

P.L. 111-148, §10909(b)(2)(C):

Amended Code Sec. 25A(i)(5)(B) by striking "23, 25D," and inserting "25D". **Effective** for tax years beginning after 12-31-2009.

P.L. 111-148, §10909(c), provides:

(c) APPLICATION AND EXTENSION OF EGTRRA SUNSET.—Notwithstanding section 901 of the Economic Growth and Tax Relief Reconciliation Act of 2001, such section shall apply to the amendments made by this section and the amendments made by section 202 of such Act by substituting "December 31, 2011" for "December 31, 2010" in subsection (a)(1) thereof.

[¶5020] CODE SEC. 25B. ELECTIVE DEFERRALS AND IRA CONTRIBUTIONS BY CERTAIN INDIVIDUALS.

* * *

(g) LIMITATION BASED ON AMOUNT OF TAX.—In the case of a taxable year to which section 26(a)(2) does not apply, the credit allowed under subsection (a) for the taxable year shall not exceed the excess of—

(1) the sum of the regular tax liability (as defined in section 26(b)) plus the tax imposed by section 55, over

≫→ *Caution: Code Sec. 25B(g)(2), below, was amended by P.L. 111-148. For sunset provision, see P.L. 111-148, §10909(c), in the amendment notes.*

(2) the sum of the credits allowable under this subpart (other than this section and sections 25A(i), 25D, 30, 30B, and 30D) and section 27 for the taxable year.

[Committee Reports at ¶10,390.]

Amendments

• **2010, Patient Protection and Affordable Care Act (P.L. 111-148)**

P.L. 111-148, §10909(b)(2)(D):

Amended Code Sec. 25B(g)(2) by striking "23," before "25A(i)". **Effective** for tax years beginning after 12-31-2009.

P.L. 111-148, §10909(c), provides:

(c) APPLICATION AND EXTENSION OF EGTRRA SUNSET.—Notwithstanding section 901 of the Economic Growth and Tax

Relief Reconciliation Act of 2001, such section shall apply to the amendments made by this section and the amendments made by section 202 of such Act by substituting "December 31, 2011" for "December 31, 2010" in subsection (a)(1) thereof.

[¶5025] CODE SEC. 26. LIMITATION BASED ON TAX LIABILITY; DEFINITION OF TAX LIABILITY.

(a) LIMITATION BASED ON AMOUNT OF TAX.—

≫→ *Caution: Code Sec. 26(a)(1), below, was amended by P.L. 111-148. For sunset provision, see P.L. 111-148, §10909(c), in the amendment notes.*

(1) IN GENERAL.—The aggregate amount of credits allowed by this subpart (other than sections 24, 25A(i), 25B, 25D, 30, 30B, and 30D) for the taxable year shall not exceed the excess (if any) of—

(A) the taxpayer's regular tax liability for the taxable year, over

(B) the tentative minimum tax for the taxable year (determined without regard to the alternative minimum tax foreign tax credit).

For purposes of subparagraph (B), the taxpayer's tentative minimum tax for any taxable year beginning during 1999 shall be treated as being zero.

* * *

[Committee Reports at ¶10,390.]

Amendments

• **2010, Patient Protection and Affordable Care Act (P.L. 111-148)**

P.L. 111-148, §10909(b)(2)(E):

Amended Code Sec. 26(a)(1) by striking "23," before "24". **Effective** for tax years beginning after 12-31-2009.

P.L. 111-148, §10909(c), provides:

(c) APPLICATION AND EXTENSION OF EGTRRA SUNSET.—Notwithstanding section 901 of the Economic Growth and Tax

Relief Reconciliation Act of 2001, such section shall apply to the amendments made by this section and the amendments made by section 202 of such Act by substituting "December 31, 2011" for "December 31, 2010" in subsection (a)(1) thereof.

[¶5030] CODE SEC. 30. CERTAIN PLUG-IN ELECTRIC VEHICLES.

* * *

(c) APPLICATION WITH OTHER CREDITS.—

* * *

(2) PERSONAL CREDIT.—

* * *

(B) LIMITATION BASED ON AMOUNT OF TAX.—In the case of a taxable year to which section 26(a)(2) does not apply, the credit allowed under subsection (a) for any taxable year (determined after application of paragraph (1)) shall not exceed the excess of—

(i) the sum of the regular tax liability (as defined in section 26(b)) plus the tax imposed by section 55, over

⟫→ *Caution: Code Sec. 30(c)(2)(B)(ii), below, was amended by P.L. 111-148. For sunset provision, see P.L. 111-148, §10909(c), in the amendment notes.*

(ii) the sum of the credits allowable under subpart A (other than this section and sections 25D and 30D) and section 27 for the taxable year.

* * *

[Committee Reports at ¶10,390.]

Amendments

• 2010, Patient Protection and Affordable Care Act (P.L. 111-148)

P.L. 111-148, §10909(b)(2)(F):

Amended Code Sec. 30(c)(2)(B)(ii) by striking "23, 25D," and inserting "25D". **Effective** for tax years beginning after 12-31-2009.

P.L. 111-148, §10909(c), provides:

(c) APPLICATION AND EXTENSION OF EGTRRA SUNSET.—Notwithstanding section 901 of the Economic Growth and Tax Relief Reconciliation Act of 2001, such section shall apply to the amendments made by this section and the amendments made by section 202 of such Act by substituting "December 31, 2011" for "December 31, 2010" in subsection (a)(1) thereof.

[¶5035] CODE SEC. 30B. ALTERNATIVE MOTOR VEHICLE CREDIT.

* * *

(g) APPLICATION WITH OTHER CREDITS.—

* * *

(2) PERSONAL CREDIT.—

* * *

(B) LIMITATION BASED ON AMOUNT OF TAX.—In the case of a taxable year to which section 26(a)(2) does not apply, the credit allowed under subsection (a) for any taxable year (determined after application of paragraph (1)) shall not exceed the excess of—

(i) the sum of the regular tax liability (as defined in section 26(b)) plus the tax imposed by section 55, over

⟫→ *Caution: Code Sec. 30B(g)(2)(B)(ii), below, was amended by P.L. 111-148. For sunset provision, see P.L. 111-148, §10909(c), in the amendment notes.*

(ii) the sum of the credits allowable under subpart A (other than this section and sections 25D, 30, and 30D) and section 27 for the taxable year.

* * *

[Committee Reports at ¶ 10,390.]

Amendments

• **2010, Patient Protection and Affordable Care Act (P.L. 111-148)**

P.L. 111-148, § 10909(b)(2)(G):

Amended Code Sec. 30B(g)(2)(B)(ii) by striking "23," before "25D". **Effective** for tax years beginning after 12-31-2009.

P.L. 111-148, § 10909(c), provides:

(c) Application and Extension of EGTRRA Sunset.—Notwithstanding section 901 of the Economic Growth and Tax Relief Reconciliation Act of 2001, such section shall apply to the amendments made by this section and the amendments made by section 202 of such Act by substituting "December 31, 2011" for "December 31, 2010" in subsection (a)(1) thereof.

[¶ 5040] CODE SEC. 30D. NEW QUALIFIED PLUG-IN ELECTRIC DRIVE MOTOR VEHICLES.

* * *

(c) Application With Other Credits.—

* * *

(2) Personal Credit.—

* * *

(B) Limitation based on amount of tax.—In the case of a taxable year to which section 26(a)(2) does not apply, the credit allowed under subsection (a) for any taxable year (determined after application of paragraph (1)) shall not exceed the excess of—

(i) the sum of the regular tax liability (as defined in section 26(b)) plus the tax imposed by section 55, over

≫→ *Caution: Code Sec. 30D(c)(2)(B)(ii), below, was amended by P.L. 111-148. For sunset provision, see P.L. 111-148, §10909(c), in the amendment notes.*

(ii) the sum of the credits allowable under subpart A (other than this section and *section* 25D) and section 27 for the taxable year.

* * *

[Committee Reports at ¶ 10,390.]

Amendments

• **2010, Patient Protection and Affordable Care Act (P.L. 111-148)**

P.L. 111-148, § 10909(b)(2)(H):

Amended Code Sec. 30D(c)(2)(B)(ii) by striking "sections 23 and" and inserting "section". **Effective** for tax years beginning after 12-31-2009.

P.L. 111-148, § 10909(c), provides:

(c) Application and Extension of EGTRRA Sunset.—Notwithstanding section 901 of the Economic Growth and Tax Relief Reconciliation Act of 2001, such section shall apply to the amendments made by this section and the amendments made by section 202 of such Act by substituting "December 31, 2011" for "December 31, 2010" in subsection (a)(1) thereof.

≫→ *Caution: Code Sec. 36B, below, as added by P.L. 111-148, applies to tax years ending after December 31, 2013.*

[¶ 5045] *CODE SEC. 36B. REFUNDABLE CREDIT FOR COVERAGE UNDER A QUALIFIED HEALTH PLAN.*

(a) In General.—In the case of an applicable taxpayer, there shall be allowed as a credit against the tax imposed by this subtitle for any taxable year an amount equal to the premium assistance credit amount of the taxpayer for the taxable year.

(b) Premium Assistance Credit Amount.—For purposes of this section—

(1) In general.—The term "premium assistance credit amount" means, with respect to any taxable year, the sum of the premium assistance amounts determined under paragraph (2) with respect to all coverage months of the taxpayer occurring during the taxable year.

(2) Premium assistance amount.—The premium assistance amount determined under this subsection with respect to any coverage month is the amount equal to the lesser of—

(A) the monthly premiums for such month for 1 or more qualified health plans offered in the individual market within a State which cover the taxpayer, the taxpayer's spouse, or any dependent

(as defined in section 152) of the taxpayer and which were enrolled in through an Exchange established by the State under 1311 of the Patient Protection and Affordable Care Act, or

(B) the excess (if any) of—

(i) the adjusted monthly premium for such month for the applicable second lowest cost silver plan with respect to the taxpayer, over

(ii) an amount equal to 1/12 of the product of the applicable percentage and the taxpayer's household income for the taxable year.

(3) OTHER TERMS AND RULES RELATING TO PREMIUM ASSISTANCE AMOUNTS.—For purposes of paragraph (2)—

(A) APPLICABLE PERCENTAGE.—

(i) IN GENERAL.—Except as provided in clause (ii), the applicable percentage for any taxable year shall be the percentage such that the applicable percentage for any taxpayer whose household income is within an income tier specified in the following table shall increase, on a sliding scale in a linear manner, from the initial premium percentage to the final premium percentage specified in such table for such income tier:

In the case of household income (expressed as a percent of poverty line) within the following income tier:	The initial premium percentage is—	The final premium percentage is—
Up to 133%	2.0%	2.0%
133% up to 150%	3.0%	4.0%
150% up to 200%	4.0%	6.3%
200% up to 250%	6.3%	8.05%
250% up to 300%	8.05%	9.5%
300% up to 400%	9.5%	9.5%

(ii) INDEXING.—

(I) IN GENERAL.—Subject to subclause (II), in the case of taxable years beginning in any calendar year after 2014, the initial and final applicable percentages under clause (i) (as in effect for the preceding calendar year after application of this clause) shall be adjusted to reflect the excess of the rate of premium growth for the preceding calendar year over the rate of income growth for the preceding calendar year.

(II) ADDITIONAL ADJUSTMENT.—Except as provided in subclause (III), in the case of any calendar year after 2018, the percentages described in subclause (I) shall, in addition to the adjustment under subclause (I), be adjusted to reflect the excess (if any) of the rate of premium growth estimated under subclause (I) for the preceding calendar year over the rate of growth in the consumer price index for the preceding calendar year.

(III) FAILSAFE.—Subclause (II) shall apply for any calendar year only if the aggregate amount of premium tax credits under this section and cost-sharing reductions under section 1402 of the Patient Protection and Affordable Care Act for the preceding calendar year exceeds an amount equal to 0.504 percent of the gross domestic product for the preceding calendar year.

(B) APPLICABLE SECOND LOWEST COST SILVER PLAN.—The applicable second lowest cost silver plan with respect to any applicable taxpayer is the second lowest cost silver plan of the individual market in the rating area in which the taxpayer resides which—

(i) is offered through the same Exchange through which the qualified health plans taken into account under paragraph (2)(A) were offered, and

(ii) provides—

(I) self-only coverage in the case of an applicable taxpayer—

(aa) whose tax for the taxable year is determined under section 1(c) (relating to unmarried individuals other than surviving spouses and heads of households) and who is not allowed a deduction under section 151 for the taxable year with respect to a dependent, or

(bb) *who is not described in item (aa) but who purchases only self-only coverage,* and

(II) family coverage in the case of any other applicable taxpayer.

If a taxpayer files a joint return and no credit is allowed under this section with respect to 1 of the spouses by reason of subsection (e), the taxpayer shall be treated as described in clause (ii)(I) unless a deduction is allowed under section 151 for the taxable year with respect to a dependent other than either spouse and subsection (e) does not apply to the dependent.

(C) ADJUSTED MONTHLY PREMIUM.—The adjusted monthly premium for an applicable second lowest cost silver plan is the monthly premium which would have been charged (for the rating area with respect to which the premiums under paragraph (2)(A) were determined) for the plan if each individual covered under a qualified health plan taken into account under paragraph (2)(A) were covered by such silver plan and the premium was adjusted only for the age of each such individual in the manner allowed under section 2701 of the Public Health Service Act. In the case of a State participating in the wellness discount demonstration project under section 2705(d) of the Public Health Service Act, the adjusted monthly premium shall be determined without regard to any premium discount or rebate under such project.

(D) ADDITIONAL BENEFITS.—If—

(i) a qualified health plan under section 1302(b)(5) of the Patient Protection and Affordable Care Act offers benefits in addition to the essential health benefits required to be provided by the plan, or

(ii) a State requires a qualified health plan under section 1311(d)(3)(B) of such Act to cover benefits in addition to the essential health benefits required to be provided by the plan,

the portion of the premium for the plan properly allocable (under rules prescribed by the Secretary of Health and Human Services) to such additional benefits shall not be taken into account in determining either the monthly premium or the adjusted monthly premium under paragraph (2).

(E) SPECIAL RULE FOR PEDIATRIC DENTAL COVERAGE.—For purposes of determining the amount of any monthly premium, if an individual enrolls in both a qualified health plan and a plan described in section 1311(d)(2)(B)(ii)(I) of the Patient Protection and Affordable Care Act for any plan year, the portion of the premium for the plan described in such section that (under regulations prescribed by the Secretary) is properly allocable to pediatric dental benefits which are included in the essential health benefits required to be provided by a qualified health plan under section 1302(b)(1)(J) of such Act shall be treated as a premium payable for a qualified health plan.

[CCH Explanation at ¶210. Committee Reports at ¶10,360.]

Amendments

• 2010, Health Care and Education Reconciliation Act of 2010 (P.L. 111-152)

P.L. 111-152, §1001(a)(1)(A)-(B):

Amended Code Sec. 36B, as added by section 1401 of the Patient Protection and Affordable Care Act (P.L. 111-148) and amended by section 10105, in clause (i) of subsection (b)(3)(A), by striking "with respect to any taxpayer" and all that follows up to the end period and inserting "for any taxable year shall be the percentage such that the applicable percentage for any taxpayer whose household income is within an income tier specified in the following table shall increase, on a sliding scale in a linear manner, from the initial premium percentage to the final premium percentage specified in such table for such income tier:" and a new table; and by striking clauses (ii) and (iii) of subsection (b)(3)(A) and inserting a new clause (ii). **Effective 3-30-2010.** Prior to amendment, Code Sec. 36B(b)(3)(A) read as follows:

(A) APPLICABLE PERCENTAGE.—

(i) IN GENERAL.—Except as provided in clause (ii), the applicable percentage with respect to any taxpayer for any taxable year is equal to 2.8 percent, increased by the number of percentage points (not greater than 7) which bears the same ratio to 7 percentage points as—

(I) the taxpayer's household income for the taxable year in excess of 100 percent of the poverty line for a family of the size involved, bears to

(II) an amount equal to 200 percent of the poverty line for a family of the size involved.

(ii) SPECIAL RULE FOR TAXPAYERS UNDER 133 PERCENT OF POVERTY LINE.—If a taxpayer's household income for the taxable year equals or exceeds 100 percent, but not more than 133 percent, of the poverty line for a family of the size involved, the taxpayer's applicable percentage shall be 2 percent.

(iii) INDEXING.—In the case of taxable years beginning in any calendar year after 2014, the Secretary shall adjust the initial and final applicable percentages under clause (i), and the 2 percent under clause (ii), for the calendar year to reflect the excess of the rate of premium growth between the preceding calendar year and 2013 over the rate of income growth for such period.

• 2010, Patient Protection and Affordable Care Act (P.L. 111-148)

P.L. 111-148, §10105(a):

Amended Code Sec. 36B(b)(3)(A)(ii), as added by Act Sec. 1401(a), by striking "is in excess of" and inserting "equals or exceeds". **Effective 3-23-2010.**

(c) DEFINITION AND RULES RELATING TO APPLICABLE TAXPAYERS, COVERAGE MONTHS, AND QUALIFIED HEALTH PLAN.—*For purposes of this section—*

(1) APPLICABLE TAXPAYER.—

(A) IN GENERAL.—*The term "applicable taxpayer" means, with respect to any taxable year, a taxpayer whose household income for the taxable year equals or exceeds 100 percent but does not exceed 400 percent of an amount equal to the poverty line for a family of the size involved.*

(B) SPECIAL RULE FOR CERTAIN INDIVIDUALS LAWFULLY PRESENT IN THE UNITED STATES.—*If—*

(i) *a taxpayer has a household income which is not greater than 100 percent of an amount equal to the poverty line for a family of the size involved, and*

(ii) *the taxpayer is an alien lawfully present in the United States, but is not eligible for the medicaid program under title XIX of the Social Security Act by reason of such alien status,*

the taxpayer shall, for purposes of the credit under this section, be treated as an applicable taxpayer with a household income which is equal to 100 percent of the poverty line for a family of the size involved.

(C) MARRIED COUPLES MUST FILE JOINT RETURN.—*If the taxpayer is married (within the meaning of section 7703) at the close of the taxable year, the taxpayer shall be treated as an applicable taxpayer only if the taxpayer and the taxpayer's spouse file a joint return for the taxable year.*

(D) DENIAL OF CREDIT TO DEPENDENTS.—*No credit shall be allowed under this section to any individual with respect to whom a deduction under section 151 is allowable to another taxpayer for a taxable year beginning in the calendar year in which such individual's taxable year begins.*

(2) COVERAGE MONTH.—*For purposes of this subsection—*

(A) IN GENERAL.—*The term "coverage month" means, with respect to an applicable taxpayer, any month if—*

(i) *as of the first day of such month the taxpayer, the taxpayer's spouse, or any dependent of the taxpayer is covered by a qualified health plan described in subsection (b)(2)(A) that was enrolled in through an Exchange established by the State under section 1311 of the Patient Protection and Affordable Care Act, and*

(ii) *the premium for coverage under such plan for such month is paid by the taxpayer (or through advance payment of the credit under subsection (a) under section 1412 of the Patient Protection and Affordable Care Act).*

(B) EXCEPTION FOR MINIMUM ESSENTIAL COVERAGE.—

(i) IN GENERAL.—*The term "coverage month" shall not include any month with respect to an individual if for such month the individual is eligible for minimum essential coverage other than eligibility for coverage described in section 5000A(f)(1)(C) (relating to coverage in the individual market).*

(ii) MINIMUM ESSENTIAL COVERAGE.—*The term "minimum essential coverage" has the meaning given such term by section 5000A(f).*

(C) SPECIAL RULE FOR EMPLOYER-SPONSORED MINIMUM ESSENTIAL COVERAGE.—*For purposes of subparagraph (B)—*

(i) COVERAGE MUST BE AFFORDABLE.—*Except as provided in clause (iii), an employee shall not be treated as eligible for minimum essential coverage if such coverage—*

(I) *consists of an eligible employer-sponsored plan (as defined in section 5000A(f)(2)), and*

(II) *the employee's required contribution (within the meaning of section 5000A(e)(1)(B)) with respect to the plan exceeds 9.5 percent of the applicable taxpayer's household income.*

This clause shall also apply to an individual who is eligible to enroll in the plan by reason of a relationship the individual bears to the employee.

(ii) COVERAGE MUST PROVIDE MINIMUM VALUE.—*Except as provided in clause (iii), an employee shall not be treated as eligible for minimum essential coverage if such coverage consists of an eligible employer-sponsored plan (as defined in section 5000A(f)(2)) and the plan's share of the total allowed costs of benefits provided under the plan is less than 60 percent of such costs.*

(iii) EMPLOYEE OR FAMILY MUST NOT BE COVERED UNDER EMPLOYER PLAN.—*Clauses (i) and (ii) shall not apply if the employee (or any individual described in the last sentence of clause (i)) is covered under the eligible employer-sponsored plan or the grandfathered health plan.*

(iv) INDEXING.—*In the case of plan years beginning in any calendar year after 2014, the Secretary shall adjust the 9.5 percent under clause (i)(II) in the same manner as the percentages are adjusted under subsection (b)(3)(A)(ii).*

⫸→ Caution: Code Sec. 36B(c)(2)(D), below, as added by P.L. 111-148, applies to tax years beginning after December 31, 2013.

(D) EXCEPTION FOR INDIVIDUAL RECEIVING FREE CHOICE VOUCHERS.—*The term "coverage month" shall not include any month in which such individual has a free choice voucher provided under section 10108 of the Patient Protection and Affordable Care Act.*

(3) DEFINITIONS AND OTHER RULES.—

(A) QUALIFIED HEALTH PLAN.—*The term "qualified health plan" has the meaning given such term by section 1301(a) of the Patient Protection and Affordable Care Act, except that such term shall not include a qualified health plan which is a catastrophic plan described in section 1302(e) of such Act.*

(B) GRANDFATHERED HEALTH PLAN.—*The term "grandfathered health plan" has the meaning given such term by section 1251 of the Patient Protection and Affordable Care Act.*

[CCH Explanation at ¶210. Committee Reports at ¶10,360 and ¶10,370.]

Amendments

• **2010, Health Care and Education Reconciliation Act of 2010 (P.L. 111-152)**

P.L. 111-152, §1001(a)(2)(A)-(B):

Amended Code Sec. 36B, as added by section 1401 and amended by section 10105 of the Patient Protection and Affordable Care Act (P.L. 111-148), by striking "9.8 percent" in clauses (i)(II) and (iv) of subsection (c)(2)(C) and inserting "9.5 percent", and by striking "(b)(3)(A)(iii)" in clause (iv) of subsection (c)(2)(C) and inserting "(b)(3)(A)(ii)". **Effective** 3-30-2010.

• **2010, Patient Protection and Affordable Care Act (P.L. 111-148)**

P.L. 111-148, §10105(b):

Amended Code Sec. 36B(c)(1)(A), as added by Act Sec. 1401(a), by inserting "equals or" before "exceeds". **Effective** 3-23-2010.

P.L. 111-148, §10105(c):

Amended Code Sec. 36B(c)(2)(C)(iv), as added by Act Sec. 1401(a), by striking "subsection (b)(3)(A)(ii)" and inserting "subsection (b)(3)(A)(iii)". **Effective** 3-23-2010.

P.L. 111-148, §10108(h)(1):

Amended Code Sec. 36B(c)(2), as added by Act Sec. 1401, by adding at the end a new subparagraph (D). **Effective for** tax years beginning after 12-31-2013.

(d) TERMS RELATING TO INCOME AND FAMILIES.—*For purposes of this section—*

(1) FAMILY SIZE.—*The family size involved with respect to any taxpayer shall be equal to the number of individuals for whom the taxpayer is allowed a deduction under section 151 (relating to allowance of deduction for personal exemptions) for the taxable year.*

(2) HOUSEHOLD INCOME.—

(A) HOUSEHOLD INCOME.—*The term "household income" means, with respect to any taxpayer, an amount equal to the sum of—*

(i) the modified adjusted gross income of the taxpayer, plus

(ii) the aggregate modified adjusted gross incomes of all other individuals who—

(I) *were taken into account in determining the taxpayer's family size under paragraph (1), and*

(II) *were required to file a return of tax imposed by section 1 for the taxable year.*

(B) MODIFIED ADJUSTED GROSS INCOME.—*The term "modified adjusted gross income" means adjusted gross income increased by—*

(i) *any amount excluded from gross income under section 911, and*

(ii) *any amount of interest received or accrued by the taxpayer during the taxable year which is exempt from tax.*

(3) POVERTY LINE.—

(A) IN GENERAL.—*The term "poverty line" has the meaning given that term in section 2110(c)(5) of the Social Security Act (42 U.S.C. 1397jj(c)(5)).*

(B) POVERTY LINE USED.—*In the case of any qualified health plan offered through an Exchange for coverage during a taxable year beginning in a calendar year, the poverty line used shall be the most recently published poverty line as of the 1st day of the regular enrollment period for coverage during such calendar year.*

[CCH Explanation at ¶ 210.]

Amendments

• 2010, Health Care and Education Reconciliation Act of 2010 (P.L. 111-152)

P.L. 111-152, § 1004(a)(1)(A):

Amended Code Sec. 36B(d)(2)(A)(i)-(ii), as added by section 1401 of the Patient Protection and Affordable Care Act (P.L. 111-148), by striking "modified gross" each place it appears and inserting "modified adjusted gross". **Effective** 3-30-2010.

P.L. 111-152, § 1004(a)(2)(A):

Amended Code Sec. 36B(d)(2)(B), as added by section 1401 of the Patient Protection and Affordable Care Act (P.L.

111-148). **Effective** 3-30-2010. Prior to amendment, Code Sec. 36B(d)(2)(B) read as follows:

(B) MODIFIED GROSS INCOME.—The term "modified gross income" means gross income—

(i) decreased by the amount of any deduction allowable under paragraph (1), (3), (4), or (10) of section 62(a),

(ii) increased by the amount of interest received or accrued during the taxable year which is exempt from tax imposed by this chapter, and

(iii) determined without regard to sections 911, 931, and 933.

(e) RULES FOR INDIVIDUALS NOT LAWFULLY PRESENT.—

(1) IN GENERAL.—*If 1 or more individuals for whom a taxpayer is allowed a deduction under section 151 (relating to allowance of deduction for personal exemptions) for the taxable year (including the taxpayer or his spouse) are individuals who are not lawfully present—*

(A) *the aggregate amount of premiums otherwise taken into account under clauses (i) and (ii) of subsection (b)(2)(A) shall be reduced by the portion (if any) of such premiums which is attributable to such individuals, and*

(B) *for purposes of applying this section, the determination as to what percentage a taxpayer's household income bears to the poverty level for a family of the size involved shall be made under one of the following methods:*

(i) *A method under which—*

(I) *the taxpayer's family size is determined by not taking such individuals into account, and*

(II) *the taxpayer's household income is equal to the product of the taxpayer's household income (determined without regard to this subsection) and a fraction—*

(aa) *the numerator of which is the poverty line for the taxpayer's family size determined after application of subclause (I), and*

(bb) *the denominator of which is the poverty line for the taxpayer's family size determined without regard to subclause (I).*

(ii) *A comparable method reaching the same result as the method under clause (i).*

(2) LAWFULLY PRESENT.—*For purposes of this section, an individual shall be treated as lawfully present only if the individual is, and is reasonably expected to be for the entire period of enrollment for*

which the credit under this section is being claimed, a citizen or national of the United States or an alien lawfully present in the United States.

(3) SECRETARIAL AUTHORITY.—The Secretary of Health and Human Services, in consultation with the Secretary, shall prescribe rules setting forth the methods by which calculations of family size and household income are made for purposes of this subsection. Such rules shall be designed to ensure that the least burden is placed on individuals enrolling in qualified health plans through an Exchange and taxpayers eligible for the credit allowable under this section.

(f) RECONCILIATION OF CREDIT AND ADVANCE CREDIT.—

(1) IN GENERAL.—The amount of the credit allowed under this section for any taxable year shall be reduced (but not below zero) by the amount of any advance payment of such credit under section 1412 of the Patient Protection and Affordable Care Act.

(2) EXCESS ADVANCE PAYMENTS.—

(A) IN GENERAL.—If the advance payments to a taxpayer under section 1412 of the Patient Protection and Affordable Care Act for a taxable year exceed the credit allowed by this section (determined without regard to paragraph (1)), the tax imposed by this chapter for the taxable year shall be increased by the amount of such excess.

(B) LIMITATION ON INCREASE WHERE INCOME LESS THAN 400 PERCENT OF POVERTY LINE.—

(i) IN GENERAL.—In the case of an applicable taxpayer whose household income is less than 400 percent of the poverty line for the size of the family involved for the taxable year, the amount of the increase under subparagraph (A) shall in no event exceed $400 ($250 in the case of a taxpayer whose tax is determined under section 1(c) for the taxable year).

(ii) INDEXING OF AMOUNT.—In the case of any calendar year beginning after 2014, each of the dollar amounts under clause (i) shall be increased by an amount equal to—

(I) such dollar amount, multiplied by

(II) the cost-of-living adjustment determined under section 1(f)(3) for the calendar year, determined by substituting "calendar year 2013" for "calendar year 1992" in subparagraph (B) thereof.

If the amount of any increase under clause (i) is not a multiple of $50, such increase shall be rounded to the next lowest multiple of $50.

(3) INFORMATION REQUIREMENT.—Each Exchange (or any person carrying out 1 or more responsibilities of an Exchange under section 1311(f)(3) or 1321(c) of the Patient Protection and Affordable Care Act) shall provide the following information to the Secretary and to the taxpayer with respect to any health plan provided through the Exchange:

(A) The level of coverage described in section 1302(d) of the Patient Protection and Affordable Care Act and the period such coverage was in effect.

(B) The total premium for the coverage without regard to the credit under this section or cost-sharing reductions under section 1402 of such Act.

(C) The aggregate amount of any advance payment of such credit or reductions under section 1412 of such Act.

(D) The name, address, and TIN of the primary insured and the name and TIN of each other individual obtaining coverage under the policy.

(E) Any information provided to the Exchange, including any change of circumstances, necessary to determine eligibility for, and the amount of, such credit.

(F) Information necessary to determine whether a taxpayer has received excess advance payments.

[CCH Explanation at ¶ 210.]

Amendments

• **2010, Health Care and Education Reconciliation Act of 2010 (P.L. 111-152)**

P.L. 111-152, § 1004(c):

Amended Code Sec. 36B(f), as added by section 1401(a) of the Patient Protection and Affordable Care Act (P.L.

111-148), by adding at the end a new paragraph (3). **Effective** 3-30-2010.

(g) REGULATIONS.—*The Secretary shall prescribe such regulations as may be necessary to carry out the provisions of this section, including regulations which provide for—*

(1) the coordination of the credit allowed under this section with the program for advance payment of the credit under section 1412 of the Patient Protection and Affordable Care Act, and

(2) the application of subsection (f) where the filing status of the taxpayer for a taxable year is different from such status used for determining the advance payment of the credit.

[CCH Explanation at ¶ 210. Committee Reports at ¶ 10,030.]

Amendments

• **2010, Patient Protection and Affordable Care Act (P.L. 111-148)**

P.L. 111-148, § 1401(a):

Amended subpart C of part IV of subchapter A of chapter 1 by inserting after Code Sec. 36A a new Code Sec. 36B. **Effective** for tax years ending after 12-31-2013.

[¶ 5050] *CODE SEC. 36C.* ADOPTION EXPENSES.

(a) ALLOWANCE OF CREDIT.—

* * *

⟫→ **Caution:** *Former Code Sec. 23(a)(3) was redesignated as Code Sec. 36C(a)(3), below, and amended by P.L. 111-148. For sunset provision, see P.L. 111-148, §10909(c), in the amendment notes.*

(3) *$13,170* CREDIT FOR ADOPTION OF CHILD WITH SPECIAL NEEDS REGARDLESS OF EXPENSES.—In the case of an adoption of a child with special needs which becomes final during a taxable year, the taxpayer shall be treated as having paid during such year qualified adoption expenses with respect to such adoption in an amount equal to the excess (if any) of *$13,170* over the aggregate qualified adoption expenses actually paid or incurred by the taxpayer with respect to such adoption during such taxable year and all prior taxable years.

[CCH Explanation at ¶ 240. Committee Reports at ¶ 10,390.]

Amendments

• **2010, Patient Protection and Affordable Care Act (P.L. 111-148)**

P.L. 111-148, § 10909(a)(1)(B)(i)-(ii):

Amended Code Sec. 23(a)(3), in the text by striking "$10,000" and inserting "$13,170", and in the heading by striking "$10,000" and inserting "$13,170". **Effective** for tax years beginning after 12-31-2009.

P.L. 111-148, § 10909(b)(1)(A)-(B):

Amended [subpart A of part IV of subchapter A of chapter 1] by redesignating Code Sec. 23, as amended by Act Sec.

10909(a), as Code Sec. 36C, and by moving it before Code Sec. 37 in subpart C of part IV of subchapter A of chapter 1. **Effective** for tax years beginning after 12-31-2009.

P.L. 111-148, § 10909(c), provides:

(c) APPLICATION AND EXTENSION OF EGTRRA SUNSET.—Notwithstanding section 901 of the Economic Growth and Tax Relief Reconciliation Act of 2001, such section shall apply to the amendments made by this section and the amendments made by section 202 of such Act by substituting "December 31, 2011" for "December 31, 2010' ' in subsection (a)(1) thereof.

(b) LIMITATIONS.—

⟫→ **Caution:** *Former Code Sec. 23(b)(1) was amended and redesignated as Code Sec. 36C(b)(1), below, by P.L. 111-148. For sunset provision, see P.L. 111-148, §10909(c), in the amendment notes.*

(1) DOLLAR LIMITATION.—The aggregate amount of qualified adoption expenses which may be taken into account under subsection (a) for all taxable years with respect to the adoption of a child by the taxpayer shall not exceed *$13,170*.

* * *

➤➤➤ *Caution: Former Code Sec. 23(b)(4) was redesignated as Code Sec. 36C(b)(4), below, and stricken by P.L. 111-148. For sunset provision, see P.L. 111-148, §10909(c), in the amendment notes.*

(4) [*Stricken.*]

[CCH Explanation at ¶240. Committee Reports at ¶10,390.]

Amendments

• **2010, Patient Protection and Affordable Care Act (P.L. 111-148)**

P.L. 111-148, 10909(a)(1)(A):

Amended Code Sec. 23(b)(1) by striking "$10,000" and inserting "$13,170". **Effective** for tax years beginning after 12-31-2009.

P.L. 111-148, §10909(b)(1)(A)-(B):

Amended [subpart A of part IV of subchapter A of chapter 1] by redesignating Code Sec. 23, as amended by Act Sec. 10909(a), as Code Sec. 36C, and by moving it before Code Sec. 37 in subpart C of part IV of subchapter A of chapter 1. **Effective** for tax years beginning after 12-31-2009.

P.L. 111-148, 10909(b)(2)(I)(i):

Amended Code Sec. 36C, as so redesignated, by striking paragraph (b)(4). **Effective** for tax years beginning after 12-31-2009. Prior to amendment, Code Sec. 36C(b)(4) read as follows:

(4) LIMITATION BASED ON AMOUNT OF TAX.—In the case of a taxable year to which section 26(a)(2) does not apply, the credit allowed under subsection (a) for any taxable year shall not exceed the excess of—

(A) the sum of the regular tax liability (as defined in section 26(b)) plus the tax imposed by section 55, over

(B) the sum of the credits allowable under this subpart (other than this section and section 25D) and section 27 for the taxable year.

P.L. 111-148, §10909(c), provides:

(c) APPLICATION AND EXTENSION OF EGTRRA SUNSET.—Notwithstanding section 901 of the Economic Growth and Tax Relief Reconciliation Act of 2001, such section shall apply to the amendments made by this section and the amendments made by section 202 of such Act by substituting "December 31, 2011" for "December 31, 2010' ' in subsection (a)(1) thereof.

➤➤➤ *Caution: Former Code Sec. 23(c) was redesignated as Code Sec. 36C(c), below, and stricken by P.L. 111-148. For sunset provision, see P.L. 111-148, §10909(c), in the amendment notes.*

(c) [*Stricken.*]

* * *

[Committee Reports at ¶10,390.]

Amendments

• **2010, Patient Protection and Affordable Care Act (P.L. 111-148)**

P.L. 111-148, §10909(b)(1)(A)-(B):

Amended [subpart A of part IV of subchapter A of chapter 1] by redesignating Code Sec. 23, as amended by Act Sec. 10909(a), as Code Sec. 36C, and by moving it before Code Sec. 37 in subpart C of part IV of subchapter A of chapter 1. **Effective** for tax years beginning after 12-31-2009.

P.L. 111-148, §10909(b)(2)(I)(ii):

Amended Code Sec. 36C, as so redesignated, by striking subsection (c). **Effective** for tax years beginning after 12-31-2009. Prior to amendment, Code Sec. 36C(c) read as follows:

(c) CARRYFORWARDS OF UNUSED CREDIT.—

(1) RULE FOR YEARS IN WHICH ALL PERSONAL CREDITS ALLOWED AGAINST REGULAR AND ALTERNATIVE MINIMUM TAX.—In the case of a taxable year to which section 26(a)(2) applies, if the credit allowable under subsection (a) for any taxable year exceeds the limitation imposed by section 26(a)(2) for such taxable year reduced by the sum of the credits allowable under this subpart (other than this section and sections 25D

and 1400C), such excess shall be carried to the succeeding taxable year and added to the credit allowable under subsection (a) for such taxable year.

(2) RULE FOR OTHER YEARS.—In the case of a taxable year to which section 26(a)(2) does not apply, if the credit allowable under subsection (a) for any taxable year exceeds the limitation imposed by subsection (b)(4) for such taxable year, such excess shall be carried to the succeeding taxable year and added to the credit allowable under subsection (a) for such taxable year.

(3) LIMITATION.—No credit may be carried forward under this subsection to any taxable year following the fifth taxable year after the taxable year in which the credit arose. For purposes of the preceding sentence, credits shall be treated as used on a first-in first-out basis.

P.L. 111-148, §10909(c), provides:

(c) APPLICATION AND EXTENSION OF EGTRRA SUNSET.—Notwithstanding section 901 of the Economic Growth and Tax Relief Reconciliation Act of 2001, such section shall apply to the amendments made by this section and the amendments made by section 202 of such Act by substituting "December 31, 2011" for "December 31, 2010' ' in subsection (a)(1) thereof.

➤➤➤ *Caution: Former Code Sec. 23(h) was amended and redesignated as Code Sec. 36C(h), below, by P.L. 111-148. For sunset provision, see P.L. 111-148, §10909(c), in the amendment notes.*

(h) *ADJUSTMENTS FOR INFLATION.—*

(1) *DOLLAR LIMITATIONS.—In the case of a taxable year beginning after December 31, 2010, each of the dollar amounts in subsections (a)(3) and (b)(1) shall be increased by an amount equal to—*

(A) such dollar amount, multiplied by

(B) the cost-of-living adjustment determined under section 1(f)(3) for the calendar year in which the taxable year begins, determined by substituting "calendar year 2009" for "calendar year 1992" in subparagraph (B) thereof.

If any amount as increased under the preceding sentence is not a multiple of $10, such amount shall be rounded to the nearest multiple of $10.

(2) INCOME LIMITATION.—In the case of a taxable year beginning after December 31, 2002, the dollar amount in subsection (b)(2)(A)(i) shall be increased by an amount equal to—

(A) such dollar amount, multiplied by

(B) the cost-of-living adjustment determined under section 1(f)(3) for the calendar year in which the taxable year begins, determined by substituting "calendar year 2001" for "calendar year 1992" in subparagraph (B) thereof.

If any amount as increased under the preceding sentence is not a multiple of $10, such amount shall be rounded to the nearest multiple of $10.

* * *

[CCH Explanation at ¶240. Committee Reports at ¶10,390.]

Amendments

● **2010, Patient Protection and Affordable Care Act (P.L. 111-148)**

P.L. 111-148, §10909(a)(1)(C):

Amended Code Sec. 23(h). **Effective** for tax years beginning after 12-31-2009. Prior to amendment, Code Sec. 23(h) read as follows:

(h) ADJUSTMENTS FOR INFLATION.—In the case of a taxable year beginning after December 31, 2002, each of the dollar amounts in subsection (a)(3) and paragraphs (1) and (2)(A)(i) of subsection (b) shall be increased by an amount equal to—

(1) such dollar amount, multiplied by

(2) the cost-of-living adjustment determined under section 1(f)(3) for the calendar year in which the taxable year begins, determined by substituting "calendar year 2001" for "calendar year 1992" in subparagraph (B) thereof.

If any amount as increased under the preceding sentence is not a multiple of $10, such amount shall be rounded to the nearest multiple of $10.

P.L. 111-148, §10909(b)(1)(A)-(B):

Amended [subpart A of part IV of subchapter A of chapter 1] by redesignating Code Sec. 23, as amended by Act Sec. 10909(a), as Code Sec. 36C, and by moving it before Code Sec. 37 in subpart C of part IV of subchapter A of chapter 1. **Effective** for tax years beginning after 12-31-2009.

P.L. 111-148, §10909(c), provides:

(c) APPLICATION AND EXTENSION OF EGTRRA SUNSET.—Notwithstanding section 901 of the Economic Growth and Tax Relief Reconciliation Act of 2001, such section shall apply to the amendments made by this section and the amendments made by section 202 of such Act by substituting "December 31, 2011" for "December 31, 2010" in subsection (a)(1) thereof.

[¶5055] CODE SEC. 38. GENERAL BUSINESS CREDIT.

* * *

(b) CURRENT YEAR BUSINESS CREDIT.—For purposes of this subpart, the amount of the current year business credit is the sum of the following credits determined for the taxable year:

* * *

(34) the carbon dioxide sequestration credit determined under section 45Q(a)[,]

(35) the portion of the new qualified plug-in electric drive motor vehicle credit to which section 30D(c)(1) applies, *plus*

(36) *the small employer health insurance credit determined under section 45R.*

[CCH Explanation at ¶310. Committee Reports at ¶10,070.]

Amendments

● **2010, Patient Protection and Affordable Care Act (P.L. 111-148)**

P.L. 111-148, §1421(b):

Amended Code Sec. 38(b) by striking "plus" at the end of paragraph (34), by striking the period at the end of para-

graph (35) and inserting ", plus", and by inserting after paragraph (35) a new paragraph (36). **Effective** for amounts paid or incurred in tax years beginning after 12-31-2009 [effective date changed by Act Sec. 10105(e)(4).—CCH].

(c) LIMITATION BASED ON AMOUNT OF TAX.—

* * *

(4) SPECIAL RULES FOR SPECIFIED CREDITS.—

* * *

(B) SPECIFIED CREDITS.—For purposes of this subsection, the term "specified credits" means—

* * *

(vi) the credit determined under section 45R,

(vii) the credit determined under section 46 to the extent that such credit is attributable to the energy credit determined under section 48,

(viii) the credit determined under section 46 to the extent that such credit is attributable to the rehabilitation credit under section 47, but only with respect to qualified rehabilitation expenditures properly taken into account for periods after December 31, 2007, and

(ix) the credit determined under section 51.

* * *

[CCH Explanation at ¶310. Committee Reports at ¶10,070.]

Amendments

• **2010, Patient Protection and Affordable Care Act (P.L. 111-148)**

P.L. 111-148, §1421(c):

Amended Code Sec. 38(c)(4)(B) by redesignating clauses (vi), (vii), and (viii) as clauses (vii), (viii), and (ix), respec-

tively, and by inserting after clause (v) a new clause (vi). **Effective** for amounts paid or incurred in tax years beginning after 12-31-2009 [effective date changed by Act Sec. 10105(e)(4).—CCH].

[¶5057] CODE SEC. 40. ALCOHOL, etc., USED AS FUEL.

* * *

(b) DEFINITION OF ALCOHOL MIXTURE CREDIT, ALCOHOL CREDIT, AND SMALL ETHANOL PRODUCER CREDIT.—For purposes of this section, and except as provided in subsection (h)—

* * *

(6) CELLULOSIC BIOFUEL PRODUCER CREDIT.—

* * *

(E) CELLULOSIC BIOFUEL.—For purposes of this paragraph—

* * *

(iii) EXCLUSION OF UNPROCESSED FUELS.—The term "cellulosic biofuel" shall not include any fuel if—

(I) more than 4 percent of such fuel (determined by weight) is any combination of water and sediment, or

(II) the ash content of such fuel is more than 1 percent (determined by weight).

* * *

[CCH Explanation at ¶357. Committee Reports at ¶10,430.]

Amendments

• **2010, Health Care and Education Reconciliation Act of 2010 (P.L. 111-152)**

P.L. 111-152, §1408(a):

Amended Code Sec. 40(b)(6)(E), by adding at the end a new clause (iii). **Effective** for fuels sold or used on or after 1-1-2010.

[¶5060] *CODE SEC. 45R. EMPLOYEE HEALTH INSURANCE EXPENSES OF SMALL EMPLOYERS.*

(a) GENERAL RULE.—For purposes of section 38, in the case of an eligible small employer, the small employer health insurance credit determined under this section for any taxable year in the credit period is the amount determined under subsection (b).

(b) HEALTH INSURANCE CREDIT AMOUNT.—Subject to subsection (c), the amount determined under this subsection with respect to any eligible small employer is equal to 50 percent (35 percent in the case of a tax-exempt eligible small employer) of the lesser of—

(1) the aggregate amount of nonelective contributions the employer made on behalf of its employees during the taxable year under the arrangement described in subsection (d)(4) for premiums for qualified health plans offered by the employer to its employees through an Exchange, or

(2) the aggregate amount of nonelective contributions which the employer would have made during the taxable year under the arrangement if each employee taken into account under paragraph (1) had enrolled in a qualified health plan which had a premium equal to the average premium (as determined by the Secretary of Health and Human Services) for the small group market in the rating area in which the employee enrolls for coverage.

(c) PHASEOUT OF CREDIT AMOUNT BASED ON NUMBER OF EMPLOYEES AND AVERAGE WAGES.—The amount of the credit determined under subsection (b) without regard to this subsection shall be reduced (but not below zero) by the sum of the following amounts:

(1) Such amount multiplied by a fraction the numerator of which is the total number of full-time equivalent employees of the employer in excess of 10 and the denominator of which is 15.

(2) Such amount multiplied by a fraction the numerator of which is the average annual wages of the employer in excess of the dollar amount in effect under subsection (d)(3)(B) and the denominator of which is such dollar amount.

(d) ELIGIBLE SMALL EMPLOYER.—For purposes of this section—

(1) IN GENERAL.—The term "eligible small employer" means, with respect to any taxable year, an employer—

(A) which has no more than 25 full-time equivalent employees for the taxable year,

(B) the average annual wages of which do not exceed an amount equal to twice the dollar amount in effect under paragraph (3)(B) for the taxable year, and

(C) which has in effect an arrangement described in paragraph (4).

(2) FULL-TIME EQUIVALENT EMPLOYEES.—

(A) IN GENERAL.—The term "full-time equivalent employees" means a number of employees equal to the number determined by dividing—

(i) the total number of hours of service for which wages were paid by the employer to employees during the taxable year, by

(ii) 2,080.

Such number shall be rounded to the next lowest whole number if not otherwise a whole number.

(B) EXCESS HOURS NOT COUNTED.—If an employee works in excess of 2,080 hours of service during any taxable year, such excess shall not be taken into account under subparagraph (A).

(C) HOURS OF SERVICE.—The Secretary, in consultation with the Secretary of Labor, shall prescribe such regulations, rules, and guidance as may be necessary to determine the hours of service of an employee, including rules for the application of this paragraph to employees who are not compensated on an hourly basis.

(3) AVERAGE ANNUAL WAGES.—

(A) IN GENERAL.—The average annual wages of an eligible small employer for any taxable year is the amount determined by dividing—

(i) the aggregate amount of wages which were paid by the employer to employees during the taxable year, by

(ii) the number of full-time equivalent employees of the employee determined under paragraph (2) for the taxable year.

Such amount shall be rounded to the next lowest multiple of $1,000 if not otherwise such a multiple.

(B) DOLLAR AMOUNT.—For purposes of paragraph (1)(B) and subsection (c)(2)—

(i) 2010, 2011, 2012, AND 2013.—The dollar amount in effect under this paragraph for taxable years beginning in 2010, 2011, 2012, or 2013 is $25,000.

(ii) SUBSEQUENT YEARS.—In the case of a taxable year beginning in a calendar year after 2013, the dollar amount in effect under this paragraph shall be equal to $25,000, multiplied by the cost-of-living adjustment under section 1(f)(3) for the calendar year, determined by substituting "calendar year 2012" for "calendar year 1992" in subparagraph (B) thereof.

(4) CONTRIBUTION ARRANGEMENT.—An arrangement is described in this paragraph if it requires an eligible small employer to make a nonelective contribution on behalf of each employee who enrolls in a qualified health plan offered to employees by the employer through an exchange in an amount equal to a uniform percentage (not less than 50 percent) of the premium cost of the qualified health plan.

(5) SEASONAL WORKER HOURS AND WAGES NOT COUNTED.—For purposes of this subsection—

(A) IN GENERAL.—The number of hours of service worked by, and wages paid to, a seasonal worker of an employer shall not be taken into account in determining the full-time equivalent employees and average annual wages of the employer unless the worker works for the employer on more than 120 days during the taxable year.

(B) DEFINITION OF SEASONAL WORKER.—The term "seasonal worker" means a worker who performs labor or services on a seasonal basis as defined by the Secretary of Labor, including workers covered by section 500.20(s)(1) of title 29, Code of Federal Regulations and retail workers employed exclusively during holiday seasons.

[CCH Explanation at ¶310. Committee Reports at ¶10,360.]

Amendments

• **2010, Patient Protection and Affordable Care Act (P.L. 111-148)**

P.L. 111-148, §10105(e)(1):

Amended Code Sec. 45R(d)(3)(B), as added by Act Sec. 1421(a). **Effective** as if included in the enactment of Act Sec. 1421 [**effective** for amounts paid or incurred in tax years beginning after 12-31-2009 [**effective** date changed by Act Sec. 10105(e)(4).—CCH]]. Prior to amendment, Code Sec, 45R(d)(3)(B) read as follows:

(B) DOLLAR AMOUNT.—For purposes of paragraph (1)(B)—

(i) 2011, 2012, AND 2013.—The dollar amount in effect under this paragraph for taxable years beginning in 2011, 2012, or 2013 is $20,000.

(ii) SUBSEQUENT YEARS.—In the case of a taxable year beginning in a calendar year after 2013, the dollar amount in effect under this paragraph shall be equal to $20,000, multiplied by the cost-of-living adjustment determined under section 1(f)(3) for the calendar year, determined by substituting "calendar year 2012" for "calendar year 1992" in subparagraph (B) thereof.

(e) OTHER RULES AND DEFINITIONS.—For purposes of this section—

(1) EMPLOYEE.—

(A) CERTAIN EMPLOYEES EXCLUDED.—The term "employee" shall not include—

(i) an employee within the meaning of section 401(c)(1),

(ii) any 2-percent shareholder (as defined in section 1372(b)) of an eligible small business which is an S corporation,

(iii) any 5-percent owner (as defined in section 416(i)(1)(B)(i)) of an eligible small business, or

(iv) any individual who bears any of the relationships described in subparagraphs (A) through (G) of section 152(d)(2) to, or is a dependent described in section 152(d)(2)(H) of, an individual described in clause (i), (ii), or (iii).

(B) LEASED EMPLOYEES.—The term "employee" shall include a leased employee within the meaning of section 414(n).

(2) CREDIT PERIOD.—*The term "credit period" means, with respect to any eligible small employer, the 2-consecutive-taxable year period beginning with the 1st taxable year in which the employer (or any predecessor) offers 1 or more qualified health plans to its employees through an Exchange.*

(3) NONELECTIVE CONTRIBUTION.—*The term "nonelective contribution" means an employer contribution other than an employer contribution pursuant to a salary reduction arrangement.*

(4) WAGES.—*The term "wages" has the meaning given such term by section 3121(a) (determined without regard to any dollar limitation contained in such section).*

(5) AGGREGATION AND OTHER RULES MADE APPLICABLE.—

(A) AGGREGATION RULES.—*All employers treated as a single employer under subsection (b), (c), (m), or (o) of section 414 shall be treated as a single employer for purposes of this section.*

(B) OTHER RULES.—*Rules similar to the rules of subsections (c), (d), and (e) of section 52 shall apply.*

(f) CREDIT MADE AVAILABLE TO TAX-EXEMPT ELIGIBLE SMALL EMPLOYERS.—

(1) IN GENERAL.—*In the case of a tax-exempt eligible small employer, there shall be treated as a credit allowable under subpart C (and not allowable under this subpart) the lesser of—*

(A) *the amount of the credit determined under this section with respect to such employer, or*

(B) *the amount of the payroll taxes of the employer during the calendar year in which the taxable year begins.*

(2) TAX-EXEMPT ELIGIBLE SMALL EMPLOYER.—*For purposes of this section, the term "tax-exempt eligible small employer" means an eligible small employer which is any organization described in section 501(c) which is exempt from taxation under section 501(a).*

(3) PAYROLL TAXES.—*For purposes of this subsection—*

(A) IN GENERAL.—*The term "payroll taxes" means—*

(i) *amounts required to be withheld from the employees of the tax-exempt eligible small employer under section 3401(a),*

(ii) *amounts required to be withheld from such employees under section 3101(b), and*

(iii) *amounts of the taxes imposed on the tax-exempt eligible small employer under section 3111(b).*

(B) SPECIAL RULE.—*A rule similar to the rule of section 24(d)(2)(C) shall apply for purposes of subparagraph (A).*

(g) APPLICATION OF SECTION FOR CALENDAR YEARS 2010, 2011, 2012, AND 2013.—*In the case of any taxable year beginning in 2010, 2011, 2012, or 2013, the following modifications to this section shall apply in determining the amount of the credit under subsection (a):*

(1) NO CREDIT PERIOD REQUIRED.—*The credit shall be determined without regard to whether the taxable year is in a credit period and for purposes of applying this section to taxable years beginning after 2013, no credit period shall be treated as beginning with a taxable year beginning before 2014.*

(2) AMOUNT OF CREDIT.—*The amount of the credit determined under subsection (b) shall be determined—*

(A) *by substituting "35 percent (25 percent in the case of a tax-exempt eligible small employer)" for "50 percent (35 percent in the case of a tax-exempt eligible small employer)",*

(B) *by reference to an eligible small employer's nonelective contributions for premiums paid for health insurance coverage (within the meaning of section 9832(b)(1)) of an employee, and*

(C) *by substituting for the average premium determined under subsection (b)(2) the amount the Secretary of Health and Human Services determines is the average premium for the small group market in the State in which the employer is offering health insurance coverage (or for such area within the State as is specified by the Secretary).*

(3) CONTRIBUTION ARRANGEMENT.—An arrangement shall not fail to meet the requirements of subsection (d)(4) solely because it provides for the offering of insurance outside of an Exchange.

[CCH Explanation at ¶310. Committee Reports at ¶10,360.]

Amendments

• 2010, Patient Protection and Affordable Care Act (P.L. 111-148)

P.L. 111-148, §10105(e)(2):

Amended Code Sec. 45R(g), as added by Act Sec. 1421(a), by striking "2011" both places it appears and inserting

"2010, 2011". **Effective** as if included in the enactment of Act Sec. 1421 [**effective** for amounts paid or incurred in tax years beginning after 12-31-2009 [**effective** date changed by Act Sec. 10105(e)(4).—CCH]].

(h) INSURANCE DEFINITIONS.—Any term used in this section which is also used in the Public Health Service Act or subtitle A of title I of the Patient Protection and Affordable Care Act shall have the meaning given such term by such Act or subtitle.

(i) REGULATIONS.—The Secretary shall prescribe such regulations as may be necessary to carry out the provisions of this section, including regulations to prevent the avoidance of the 2-year limit on the credit period through the use of successor entities and the avoidance of the limitations under subsection (c) through the use of multiple entities.

[CCH Explanation at ¶310. Committee Reports at ¶10,070.]

Amendments

• 2010, Patient Protection and Affordable Care Act (P.L. 111-148)

P.L. 111-148, §1421(a):

Amended subpart D of part IV of subchapter A of chapter 1 by inserting after Code Sec. 45Q a new Code Sec. 45R.

Effective for amounts paid or incurred in tax years beginning after 12-31-2009 [**effective** date changed by Act Sec. 10105(e)(4).—CCH].

[¶5065] CODE SEC. 46. AMOUNT OF CREDIT.

(1) the rehabilitation credit,

(2) the energy credit,

(3) the qualifying advanced coal project credit,

(4) the qualifying gasification project credit[,]

(5) the qualifying advanced energy project credit, *and*

(6) the qualifying therapeutic discovery project credit.

[CCH Explanation at ¶355. Committee Reports at ¶10,350.]

Amendments

• 2010, Patient Protection and Affordable Care Act (P.L. 111-148)

P.L. 111-148, §9023(b)(1)-(3):

Amended Code Sec. 46 by adding a comma at the end of paragraph (2), by striking the period at the end of para-

graph (5) and inserting ", and" and by adding at the end a new paragraph (6). **Effective** for amounts paid or incurred after 12-31-2008, in tax years beginning after such date.

[¶5070] *CODE SEC. 48D. QUALIFYING THERAPEUTIC DISCOVERY PROJECT CREDIT.*

(a) IN GENERAL.—For purposes of section 46, the qualifying therapeutic discovery project credit for any taxable year is an amount equal to 50 percent of the qualified investment for such taxable year with respect to any qualifying therapeutic discovery project of an eligible taxpayer.

(b) QUALIFIED INVESTMENT.—

(1) IN GENERAL.—For purposes of subsection (a), the qualified investment for any taxable year is the aggregate amount of the costs paid or incurred in such taxable year for expenses necessary for and directly related to the conduct of a qualifying therapeutic discovery project.

(2) LIMITATION.—*The amount which is treated as qualified investment for all taxable years with respect to any qualifying therapeutic discovery project shall not exceed the amount certified by the Secretary as eligible for the credit under this section.*

(3) EXCLUSIONS.—*The qualified investment for any taxable year with respect to any qualifying therapeutic discovery project shall not take into account any cost—*

(A) *for remuneration for an employee described in section 162(m)(3),*

(B) *for interest expenses,*

(C) *for facility maintenance expenses,*

(D) *which is identified as a service cost under section 1.263A-1(e)(4) of title 26, Code of Federal Regulations, or*

(E) *for any other expense as determined by the Secretary as appropriate to carry out the purposes of this section.*

(4) CERTAIN PROGRESS EXPENDITURE RULES MADE APPLICABLE.—*In the case of costs described in paragraph (1) that are paid for property of a character subject to an allowance for depreciation, rules similar to the rules of subsections (c)(4) and (d) of section 46 (as in effect on the day before the date of the enactment of the Revenue Reconciliation Act of 1990) shall apply for purposes of this section.*

(5) APPLICATION OF SUBSECTION.—*An investment shall be considered a qualified investment under this subsection only if such investment is made in a taxable year beginning in 2009 or 2010.*

(c) DEFINITIONS.—

(1) QUALIFYING THERAPEUTIC DISCOVERY PROJECT.—*The term "qualifying therapeutic discovery project" means a project which is designed—*

(A) *to treat or prevent diseases or conditions by conducting pre-clinical activities, clinical trials, and clinical studies, or carrying out research protocols, for the purpose of securing approval of a product under section 505(b) of the Federal Food, Drug, and Cosmetic Act or section 351(a) of the Public Health Service Act,*

(B) *to diagnose diseases or conditions or to determine molecular factors related to diseases or conditions by developing molecular diagnostics to guide therapeutic decisions, or*

(C) *to develop a product, process, or technology to further the delivery or administration of therapeutics.*

(2) ELIGIBLE TAXPAYER.—

(A) IN GENERAL.—*The term "eligible taxpayer" means a taxpayer which employs not more than 250 employees in all businesses of the taxpayer at the time of the submission of the application under subsection (d)(2).*

(B) AGGREGATION RULES.—*All persons treated as a single employer under subsection (a) or (b) of section 52, or subsection (m) or (o) of section 414, shall be so treated for purposes of this paragraph.*

(3) FACILITY MAINTENANCE EXPENSES.—*The term "facility maintenance expenses" means costs paid or incurred to maintain a facility, including—*

(A) *mortgage or rent payments,*

(B) *insurance payments,*

(C) *utility and maintenance costs, and*

(D) *costs of employment of maintenance personnel.*

(d) QUALIFYING THERAPEUTIC DISCOVERY PROJECT PROGRAM.—

(1) ESTABLISHMENT.—

(A) IN GENERAL.—*Not later than 60 days after the date of the enactment of this section, the Secretary, in consultation with the Secretary of Health and Human Services, shall establish a qualifying therapeutic discovery project program to consider and award certifications for qualified investments eligible for credits under this section to qualifying therapeutic discovery project sponsors.*

(B) LIMITATION.—*The total amount of credits that may be allocated under the program shall not exceed $1,000,000,000 for the 2-year period beginning with 2009.*

(2) CERTIFICATION.—

(A) APPLICATION PERIOD.—*Each applicant for certification under this paragraph shall submit an application containing such information as the Secretary may require during the period beginning on the date the Secretary establishes the program under paragraph (1).*

(B) TIME FOR REVIEW OF APPLICATIONS.—*The Secretary shall take action to approve or deny any application under subparagraph (A) within 30 days of the submission of such application.*

(C) MULTI-YEAR APPLICATIONS.—*An application for certification under subparagraph (A) may include a request for an allocation of credits for more than 1 of the years described in paragraph (1)(B).*

(3) SELECTION CRITERIA.—*In determining the qualifying therapeutic discovery projects with respect to which qualified investments may be certified under this section, the Secretary—*

(A) *shall take into consideration only those projects that show reasonable potential—*

(i) *to result in new therapies—*

(I) *to treat areas of unmet medical need, or*

(II) *to prevent, detect, or treat chronic or acute diseases and conditions,*

(ii) *to reduce long-term health care costs in the United States, or*

(iii) *to significantly advance the goal of curing cancer within the 30-year period beginning on the date the Secretary establishes the program under paragraph (1), and*

(B) *shall take into consideration which projects have the greatest potential—*

(i) *to create and sustain (directly or indirectly) high quality, high-paying jobs in the United States, and*

(ii) *to advance United States competitiveness in the fields of life, biological, and medical sciences.*

(4) DISCLOSURE OF ALLOCATIONS.—*The Secretary shall, upon making a certification under this subsection, publicly disclose the identity of the applicant and the amount of the credit with respect to such applicant.*

(e) SPECIAL RULES.—

(1) BASIS ADJUSTMENT.—*For purposes of this subtitle, if a credit is allowed under this section for an expenditure related to property of a character subject to an allowance for depreciation, the basis of such property shall be reduced by the amount of such credit.*

(2) DENIAL OF DOUBLE BENEFIT.—

(A) BONUS DEPRECIATION.—*A credit shall not be allowed under this section for any investment for which bonus depreciation is allowed under section 168(k), 1400L(b)(1), or 1400N(d)(1).*

(B) DEDUCTIONS.—*No deduction under this subtitle shall be allowed for the portion of the expenses otherwise allowable as a deduction taken into account in determining the credit under this section for the taxable year which is equal to the amount of the credit determined for such taxable year under subsection (a) attributable to such portion. This subparagraph shall not apply to expenses related to property of a character subject to an allowance for depreciation the basis of which is reduced under paragraph (1), or which are described in section 280C(g).*

(C) CREDIT FOR RESEARCH ACTIVITIES.—

(i) IN GENERAL.—*Except as provided in clause (ii), any expenses taken into account under this section for a taxable year shall not be taken into account for purposes of determining the credit allowable under section 41 or 45C for such taxable year.*

(ii) EXPENSES INCLUDED IN DETERMINING BASE PERIOD RESEARCH EXPENSES.—*Any expenses for any taxable year which are qualified research expenses (within the meaning of section 41(b)) shall be taken into account in determining base period research expenses for purposes of applying section 41 to subsequent taxable years.*

(f) COORDINATION WITH DEPARTMENT OF TREASURY GRANTS.—In the case of any investment with respect to which the Secretary makes a grant under section 9023(e) of the Patient Protection and Affordable Care Act of 2009 [sic]—

(1) DENIAL OF CREDIT.—No credit shall be determined under this section with respect to such investment for the taxable year in which such grant is made or any subsequent taxable year.

(2) RECAPTURE OF CREDITS FOR PROGRESS EXPENDITURES MADE BEFORE GRANT.—If a credit was determined under this section with respect to such investment for any taxable year ending before such grant is made—

(A) the tax imposed under subtitle A on the taxpayer for the taxable year in which such grant is made shall be increased by so much of such credit as was allowed under section 38,

(B) the general business carryforwards under section 39 shall be adjusted so as to recapture the portion of such credit which was not so allowed, and

(C) the amount of such grant shall be determined without regard to any reduction in the basis of any property of a character subject to an allowance for depreciation by reason of such credit.

(3) TREATMENT OF GRANTS.—Any such grant shall not be includible in the gross income of the taxpayer.

[CCH Explanation at ¶355. Committee Reports at ¶10,350.]

Amendments

• **2010, Patient Protection and Affordable Care Act (P.L. 111-148)**

P.L. 111-148, §9023(a):

Amended subpart E of part IV of subchapter A of chapter 1 by inserting after Code Sec. 48C a new Code Sec. 48D.

Effective for amounts paid or incurred after 12-31-2008, in tax years beginning after such date.

[¶5075] CODE SEC. 49. AT-RISK RULES.

(a) GENERAL RULE.—

(1) CERTAIN NONRECOURSE FINANCING EXCLUDED FROM CREDIT BASE.—

* * *

(C) CREDIT BASE DEFINED.—For purposes of this paragraph, the term "credit base" means—

* * *

(iv) the basis of any property which is part of a qualifying gasification project under section 48B,

(v) the basis of any property which is part of a qualifying advanced energy project under section 48C, *and*

(vi) the basis of any property to which paragraph (1) of section 48D(e) applies which is part of a qualifying therapeutic discovery project under such section 48D.

* * *

[CCH Explanation at ¶355. Committee Reports at ¶10,350.]

Amendments

• **2010, Patient Protection and Affordable Care Act (P.L. 111-148)**

P.L. 111-148, §9023(c)(1)(A)-(C):

Amended Code Sec. 49(a)(1)(C) by striking "and" at the end of clause (iv), by striking the period at the end of clause

(v) and inserting ", and", and by adding at the end a new clause (vi). Effective for amounts paid or incurred after 12-31-2008, in tax years beginning after such date.

[¶5080] CODE SEC. 56.   ADJUSTMENTS IN COMPUTING ALTERNATIVE MINIMUM TAXABLE INCOME.

* * *

(b) ADJUSTMENTS APPLICABLE TO INDIVIDUALS.—In determining the amount of the alternative minimum taxable income of any taxpayer (other than a corporation), the following treatment shall apply (in lieu of the treatment applicable for purposes of computing the regular tax):

(1) LIMITATION ON DEDUCTIONS.—

* * *

>>>→ *Caution: Code Sec. 56(b)(1)(B), below, as amended by P.L. 111-148, applies to tax years beginning after December 31, 2012.*

(B) MEDICAL EXPENSES.—In determining the amount allowable as a deduction under section 213, subsection (a) of section 213 shall be applied *without regard to subsection (f) of such section.*

* * *

[CCH Explanation at ¶215. Committee Reports at ¶10,280.]

Amendments
• **2010, Patient Protection and Affordable Care Act (P.L. 111-148)**

P.L. 111-148, §9013(c):

Amended Code Sec. 56(b)(1)(B) by striking "by substituting '10 percent' for '7.5 percent'" and inserting "without

regard to subsection (f) of such section". **Effective for tax years beginning after 12-31-2012.**

[¶5083] CODE SEC. 105.   AMOUNTS RECEIVED UNDER ACCIDENT AND HEALTH PLANS.

* * *

(b) AMOUNTS EXPENDED FOR MEDICAL CARE.—Except in the case of amounts attributable to (and not in excess of) deductions allowed under section 213 (relating to medical, etc., expenses) for any prior taxable year, gross income does not include amounts referred to in subsection (a) if such amounts are paid, directly or indirectly, to the taxpayer to reimburse the taxpayer for expenses incurred by him for the medical care (as defined in section 213(d)) of the taxpayer, his spouse, *his dependents* (as defined in section 152, determined without regard to subsections (b)(1), (b)(2), and (d)(1)(B) thereof, *and any child (as defined in section 152(f)(1)) of the taxpayer who as of the end of the taxable year has not attained age 27.* Any child to whom section 152(e) applies shall be treated as a dependent of both parents for purposes of this subsection.

* * *

[CCH Explanation at ¶242. Committee Reports at ¶10,400.]

Amendments
• **2010, Health Care and Education Reconciliation Act of 2010 (P.L. 111-152)**

P.L. 111-152, §1004(d)(1)(A)-(B):

Amended the first sentence of Code Sec. 105(b) by striking "and his dependents" and inserting "his dependents";

and by inserting before the period ", and any child (as defined in section 152(f)(1)) of the taxpayer who as of the end of the taxable year has not attained age 27". **Effective 3-30-2010.**

[¶5085] CODE SEC. 106. CONTRIBUTIONS BY EMPLOYER TO ACCIDENT AND HEALTH PLANS.

* * *

»»→ Caution: *Code Sec. 106(f), below, as added by P.L. 111-148, applies to expenses incurred with respect to tax years beginning after December 31, 2010.*

(f) REIMBURSEMENTS FOR MEDICINE RESTRICTED TO PRESCRIBED DRUGS AND INSULIN.—For purposes of this section and section 105, reimbursement for expenses incurred for a medicine or a drug shall be treated as a reimbursement for medical expenses only if such medicine or drug is a prescribed drug (determined without regard to whether such drug is available without a prescription) or is insulin.

[CCH Explanation at ¶220. Committee Reports at ¶10,180.]
Amendments
• **2010, Patient Protection and Affordable Care Act (P.L. 111-148)**

P.L. 111-148, §9003(c):
Amended Code Sec. 106 by adding at the end a new subsection (f). **Effective** for expenses incurred with respect to tax years beginning after 12-31-2010.

[¶5090] CODE SEC. 108. INCOME FROM DISCHARGE OF INDEBTEDNESS.

* * *

(f) STUDENT LOANS.—

* * *

(4) PAYMENTS UNDER NATIONAL HEALTH SERVICE CORPS LOAN REPAYMENT PROGRAM AND CERTAIN STATE LOAN REPAYMENT PROGRAMS.—In the case of an individual, gross income shall not include any amount received under section 338B(g) of the Public Health Service Act, under a State program described in section 338I of such Act, or under any other State loan repayment or loan forgiveness program that is intended to provide for the increased availability of health care services in underserved or health professional shortage areas (as determined by such State).

* * *

[CCH Explanation at ¶245. Committee Reports at ¶10,380.]
Amendments
• **2010, Patient Protection and Affordable Care Act (P.L. 111-148)**

P.L. 111-148, §10908(a):
Amended Code Sec. 108(f)(4). **Effective** for amounts received by an individual in tax years beginning after 12-31-2008. Prior to amendment, Code Sec. 108(f)(4) read as follows:

(4) PAYMENTS UNDER NATIONAL HEALTH SERVICE CORPS LOAN REPAYMENT PROGRAM AND CERTAIN STATE LOAN REPAYMENT PROGRAMS.—In the case of an individual, gross income shall not include any amount received under section 338B(g) of the Public Health Service Act or under a State program described in section 338I of such Act.

[¶5095] CODE SEC. 125. CAFETERIA PLANS.

* * *

»»→ Caution: *Code Sec. 125(f), below, as amended by P.L. 111-148, applies to tax years beginning after December 31, 2013.*

(f) QUALIFIED BENEFITS DEFINED.—*For purposes of this section—*

(1) IN GENERAL.—The term "qualified benefit"means any benefit which, with the application of subsection (a), is not includible in the gross income of the employee by reason of an express provision of this chapter (other than section 106(b), 117, 127, or 132). Such term includes any group term life insurance which is includible in gross income only because it exceeds the dollar limitation of section 79 and such term includes any other benefit permitted under regulations.

(2) LONG-TERM CARE INSURANCE NOT QUALIFIED.—The term "qualified benefit" shall not include any product which is advertised, marketed, or offered as long-term care insurance.

(3) CERTAIN EXCHANGE-PARTICIPATING QUALIFIED HEALTH PLANS NOT QUALIFIED.—

(A) IN GENERAL.—The term "qualified benefit" shall not include any qualified health plan (as defined in section 1301(a) of the Patient Protection and Affordable Care Act) offered through an Exchange established under section 1311 of such Act.

(B) EXCEPTION FOR EXCHANGE-ELIGIBLE EMPLOYERS.—Subparagraph (A) shall not apply with respect to any employee if such employee's employer is a qualified employer (as defined in section 1312(f)(2) of the Patient Protection and Affordable Care Act) offering the employee the opportunity to enroll through such an Exchange in a qualified health plan in a group market.

* * *

[CCH Explanation at ¶320. Committee Reports at ¶10,120.]

Amendments

• **2010, Patient Protection and Affordable Care Act (P.L. 111-148)**

P.L. 111-148, §1515(a):

Amended Code Sec. 125(f) by adding at the end a new paragraph (3). **Effective** for tax years beginning after 12-31-2013.

P.L. 111-148, §1515(b)(1)-(2):

Amended Code Sec. 125(f) by striking "For purposes of this section, the term" and inserting "For purposes of this section—"

"(1) IN GENERAL.—The term",

and by striking "Such term shall not include" and inserting:

"(2) LONG-TERM CARE INSURANCE NOT QUALIFIED.—The term 'qualified benefit' shall not include".

Effective for tax years beginning after 12-31-2013.

》》→ Caution: *Code Sec. 125(i), below, as added and amended by P.L. 111-148, applies to tax years beginning after December 31, 2012.*

(i) LIMITATION ON HEALTH FLEXIBLE SPENDING ARRANGEMENTS.—

(1) IN GENERAL.—For purposes of this section, if a benefit is provided under a cafeteria plan through employer contributions to a health flexible spending arrangement, such benefit shall not be treated as a qualified benefit unless the cafeteria plan provides that an employee may not elect for any taxable year to have salary reduction contributions in excess of $2,500 made to such arrangement.

(2) ADJUSTMENT FOR INFLATION.—In the case of any taxable year beginning after December 31, 2013, the dollar amount in paragraph (1) shall be increased by an amount equal to—

(A) such amount, multiplied by

(B) the cost-of-living adjustment determined under section 1(f)(3) for the calendar year in which such taxable year begins by substituting "calendar year 2012" for "calendar year 1992" in subparagraph (B) thereof.

If any increase determined under this paragraph is not a multiple of $50, such increase shall be rounded to the next lowest multiple of $50.

[CCH Explanation at ¶325. Committee Reports at ¶10,200.]

Amendments

• **2010, Health Care and Education Reconciliation Act of 2010 (P.L. 111-152)**

P.L. 111-152, §1403(b)(1)-(2):

Amended Code Sec. 125(i)(2), as added by section 9005 of the Patient Protection and Affordable Care Act (P.L. 111-148) and amended by section 10902 of such Act, by striking "December 31, 2011" and inserting "December 31, 2013" in the matter preceding subparagraph (A); and by striking "2010" and inserting "2012" in subparagraph (B). **Effective** 3-30-2010.

• **2010, Patient Protection and Affordable Care Act (P.L. 111-148)**

P.L. 111-148, §9005(a)(1)-(2):

Amended Code Sec. 125 by redesignating subsections (i) and (j) as subsections (j) and (k), respectively, and by inserting after subsection (h) a new subsection (i). **Effective** for tax years beginning after 12-31-2010.

P.L. 111-148, §10902(a):

Amended Code Sec. 125(i), as added by Act Sec. 9005. **Effective** for tax years beginning after 12-31-2012 [effective date changed by P.L. 111-152, §1403(a).—CCH]. Prior to amendment, Code Sec. 125(i) read as follows:

(i) LIMITATION ON HEALTH FLEXIBLE SPENDING ARRANGE-MENTS.—For purposes of this section, if a benefit is provided under a cafeteria plan through employer contributions to a health flexible spending arrangement, such benefit shall not be treated as a qualified benefit unless the cafeteria plan provides that an employee may not elect for any taxable year to have salary reduction contributions in excess of $2,500 made to such arrangement.

>>>→ *Caution: Code Sec. 125(j), below, as added by P.L. 111-148, applies to years beginning after December 31, 2010.*

(j) SIMPLE CAFETERIA PLANS FOR SMALL BUSINESSES.—

(1) IN GENERAL.—An eligible employer maintaining a simple cafeteria plan with respect to which the requirements of this subsection are met for any year shall be treated as meeting any applicable nondiscrimination requirement during such year.

(2) SIMPLE CAFETERIA PLAN.—For purposes of this subsection, the term "simple cafeteria plan" means a cafeteria plan—

(A) which is established and maintained by an eligible employer, and

(B) with respect to which the contribution requirements of paragraph (3), and the eligibility and participation requirements of paragraph (4), are met.

(3) CONTRIBUTION REQUIREMENTS.—

(A) IN GENERAL.—The requirements of this paragraph are met if, under the plan the employer is required, without regard to whether a qualified employee makes any salary reduction contribution, to make a contribution to provide qualified benefits under the plan on behalf of each qualified employee in an amount equal to—

(i) a uniform percentage (not less than 2 percent) of the employee's compensation for the plan year, or

(ii) an amount which is not less than the lesser of—

(I) 6 percent of the employee's compensation for the plan year, or

(II) twice the amount of the salary reduction contributions of each qualified employee.

(B) MATCHING CONTRIBUTIONS ON BEHALF OF HIGHLY COMPENSATED AND KEY EMPLOYEES.—The requirements of subparagraph (A)(ii) shall not be treated as met if, under the plan, the rate of contributions with respect to any salary reduction contribution of a highly compensated or key employee at any rate of contribution is greater than that with respect to an employee who is not a highly compensated or key employee.

(C) ADDITIONAL CONTRIBUTIONS.—Subject to subparagraph (B), nothing in this paragraph shall be treated as prohibiting an employer from making contributions to provide qualified benefits under the plan in addition to contributions required under subparagraph (A).

(D) DEFINITIONS.—For purposes of this paragraph—

(i) SALARY REDUCTION CONTRIBUTION.—The term "salary reduction contribution" means, with respect to a cafeteria plan, any amount which is contributed to the plan at the election of the employee and which is not includible in gross income by reason of this section.

(ii) QUALIFIED EMPLOYEE.—The term "qualified employee" means, with respect to a cafeteria plan, any employee who is not a highly compensated or key employee and who is eligible to participate in the plan.

(iii) HIGHLY COMPENSATED EMPLOYEE.—The term "highly compensated employee" has the meaning given such term by section 414(q).

(iv) KEY EMPLOYEE.—The term "key employee" has the meaning given such term by section 416(i).

(4) MINIMUM ELIGIBILITY AND PARTICIPATION REQUIREMENTS.—

(A) IN GENERAL.—The requirements of this paragraph shall be treated as met with respect to any year if, under the plan—

(i) all employees who had at least 1,000 hours of service for the preceding plan year are eligible to participate, and

(ii) each employee eligible to participate in the plan may, subject to terms and conditions applicable to all participants, elect any benefit available under the plan.

(B) CERTAIN EMPLOYEES MAY BE EXCLUDED.—*For purposes of subparagraph (A)(i), an employer may elect to exclude under the plan employees—*

(i) who have not attained the age of 21 before the close of a plan year,

(ii) who have less than 1 year of service with the employer as of any day during the plan year,

(iii) who are covered under an agreement which the Secretary of Labor finds to be a collective bargaining agreement if there is evidence that the benefits covered under the cafeteria plan were the subject of good faith bargaining between employee representatives and the employer, or

(iv) who are described in section 410(b)(3)(C) (relating to nonresident aliens working outside the United States).

A plan may provide a shorter period of service or younger age for purposes of clause (i) or (ii).

(5) ELIGIBLE EMPLOYER.—*For purposes of this subsection—*

(A) IN GENERAL.—*The term "eligible employer" means, with respect to any year, any employer if such employer employed an average of 100 or fewer employees on business days during either of the 2 preceding years. For purposes of this subparagraph, a year may only be taken into account if the employer was in existence throughout the year.*

(B) EMPLOYERS NOT IN EXISTENCE DURING PRECEDING YEAR.—*If an employer was not in existence throughout the preceding year, the determination under subparagraph (A) shall be based on the average number of employees that it is reasonably expected such employer will employ on business days in the current year.*

(C) GROWING EMPLOYERS RETAIN TREATMENT AS SMALL EMPLOYER.—

(i) IN GENERAL.—If—

(I) an employer was an eligible employer for any year (a "qualified year"), and

(II) such employer establishes a simple cafeteria plan for its employees for such year,

then, notwithstanding the fact the employer fails to meet the requirements of subparagraph (A) for any subsequent year, such employer shall be treated as an eligible employer for such subsequent year with respect to employees (whether or not employees during a qualified year) of any trade or business which was covered by the plan during any qualified year.

(ii) EXCEPTION.—This subparagraph shall cease to apply if the employer employs an average of 200 or more employees on business days during any year preceding any such subsequent year.

(D) SPECIAL RULES.—

(i) PREDECESSORS.—Any reference in this paragraph to an employer shall include a reference to any predecessor of such employer.

(ii) AGGREGATION RULES.—All persons treated as a single employer under subsection (a) or (b) of section 52, or subsection (n) or (o) of section 414, shall be treated as one person.

(6) APPLICABLE NONDISCRIMINATION REQUIREMENT.—*For purposes of this subsection, the term "applicable nondiscrimination requirement" means any requirement under subsection (b) of this section, section 79(d), section 105(h), or paragraph (2), (3), (4), or (8) of section 129(d).*

(7) COMPENSATION.—*The term "compensation" has the meaning given such term by section 414(s).*

[CCH Explanation at ¶330. Committee Reports at ¶10,340.]

Amendments

• 2010, Patient Protection and Affordable Care Act (P.L. 111-148)

P.L. 111-148, §9022(a):

Amended Code Sec. 125, as amended by this Act, by redesignating subsections (j) and (k) as subsections (k) and

(l), respectively, and by inserting after subsection (i) a new subsection (j). **Effective** for years beginning after 12-31-2010.

→→→ *Caution: Former Code Sec. 125(i) was redesignated as Code Sec. 125(j) by P.L. 111-148, §9005(a)(1), applicable to tax years beginning after December 31, 2010, and further redesignated as Code Sec. 125(k), below, by P.L. 111-148, §9022(a), applicable to years beginning after December 31, 2010.*

(k) CROSS REFERENCE.—

For reporting and recordkeeping requirements, see section 6039D.

[Committee Reports at ¶10,200 and ¶10,340.]

Amendments

• 2010, Patient Protection and Affordable Care Act (P.L. 111-148)

P.L. 111-148, §9005(a)(1):

Amended Code Sec. 125 by redesignating subsection (i) as (j). **Effective** for tax years beginning after 12-31-2010.

P.L. 111-148, §9022(a):

Amended Code Sec. 125, as amended by this Act, by redesignating subsection (j) as subsection (k). **Effective** for years beginning after 12-31-2010.

→→→ *Caution: Former Code Sec. 125(j) was redesignated as Code Sec. 125(k) by P.L. 111-148, §9005(a)(1), applicable to tax years beginning after December 31, 2010, and further redesignated as Code Sec. 125(l), below, by P.L. 111-148, §9022(a), applicable to years beginning after December 31, 2010.*

(l) REGULATIONS.—The Secretary shall prescribe such regulations as may be necessary to carry out the provisions of this section.

[Committee Reports at ¶10,200 and ¶10,340.]

Amendments

• 2010, Patient Protection and Affordable Care Act (P.L. 111-148)

P.L. 111-148, §9005(a)(1):

Amended Code Sec. 125 by redesignating subsection (j) as (k). **Effective** for tax years beginning after 12-31-2010.

P.L. 111-148, §9022(a):

Amended Code Sec. 125, as amended by this Act, by redesignating subsection (k) as subsection (l). **Effective** for years beginning after 12-31-2010.

[¶5100] CODE SEC. 137. ADOPTION ASSISTANCE PROGRAMS.

(a) EXCLUSION.—

* * *

→→→ *Caution: Code Sec. 137(a)(2), below, was amended by P.L. 111-148. For sunset provision, see P.L. 111-148, §10909(c), in the amendment notes.*

(2) *$13,170* EXCLUSION FOR ADOPTION OF CHILD WITH SPECIAL NEEDS REGARDLESS OF EXPENSES.—In the case of an adoption of a child with special needs which becomes final during a taxable year, the qualified adoption expenses with respect to such adoption for such year shall be increased by an amount equal to the excess (if any) of *$13,170* over the actual aggregate qualified adoption expenses with respect to such adoption during such taxable year and all prior taxable years.

[CCH Explanation at ¶240. Committee Reports at ¶10,390.]

Amendments

• **2010, Patient Protection and Affordable Care Act (P.L. 111-148)**

P.L. 111-148, §10909(a)(2)(B)(i)-(ii):

Amended Code Sec. 137(a)(2), in the text by striking "$10,000" and inserting "$13,170", and in the heading by striking "$10,000" and inserting "$13,170". **Effective** for tax years beginning after 12-31-2009.

(b) LIMITATIONS.—

P.L. 111-148, §10909(c), provides:

(c) APPLICATION AND EXTENSION OF EGTRRA SUNSET.—Notwithstanding section 901 of the Economic Growth and Tax Relief Reconciliation Act of 2001, such section shall apply to the amendments made by this section and the amendments made by section 202 of such Act by substituting "December 31, 2011" for "December 31, 2010" in subsection (a)(1) thereof.

⋙→ *Caution: Code Sec. 137(b)(1), below, was amended by P.L. 111-148. For sunset provision, see P.L. 111-148, §10909(c), in the amendment notes.*

(1) DOLLAR LIMITATION.—The aggregate of the amounts paid or expenses incurred which may be taken into account under subsection (a) for all taxable years with respect to the adoption of a child by the taxpayer shall not exceed *$13,170*.

* * *

[CCH Explanation at ¶240. Committee Reports at ¶10,390.]

Amendments

• **2010, Patient Protection and Affordable Care Act (P.L. 111-148)**

P.L. 111-148, §10909(a)(2)(A):

Amended Code Sec. 137(b)(1) by striking "$10,000" and inserting "$13,170". **Effective** for tax years beginning after 12-31-2009.

P.L. 111-148, §10909(c), provides:

(c) APPLICATION AND EXTENSION OF EGTRRA SUNSET.—Notwithstanding section 901 of the Economic Growth and Tax Relief Reconciliation Act of 2001, such section shall apply to the amendments made by this section and the amendments made by section 202 of such Act by substituting "December 31, 2011" for "December 31, 2010" in subsection (a)(1) thereof.

⋙→ *Caution: Code Sec. 137(d), below, was amended by P.L. 111-148. For sunset provision, see P.L. 111-148, §10909(c), in the amendment notes.*

(d) QUALIFIED ADOPTION EXPENSES.—For purposes of this section, the term "qualified adoption expenses" has the meaning given such term by *section 36C(d)* (determined without regard to reimbursements under this section).

[Committee Reports at ¶10,390.]

Amendments

• **2010, Patient Protection and Affordable Care Act (P.L. 111-148)**

P.L. 111-148, §10909(b)(2)(J)(i):

Amended Code Sec. 137(d) by striking "section 23(d)" and inserting "section 36C(d)". **Effective** for tax years beginning after 12-31-2009.

P.L. 111-148, §10909(c), provides:

(c) APPLICATION AND EXTENSION OF EGTRRA SUNSET.—Notwithstanding section 901 of the Economic Growth and Tax Relief Reconciliation Act of 2001, such section shall apply to the amendments made by this section and the amendments made by section 202 of such Act by substituting "December 31, 2011" for "December 31, 2010" in subsection (a)(1) thereof.

⋙→ *Caution: Code Sec. 137(e), below, was amended by P.L. 111-148. For sunset provision, see P.L. 111-148, §10909(c), in the amendment notes.*

(e) CERTAIN RULES TO APPLY.—Rules similar to the rules of subsections (e), (f), and (g) of *section 36C* shall apply for purposes of this section.

[Committee Reports at ¶10,390.]

Amendments

• **2010, Patient Protection and Affordable Care Act (P.L. 111-148)**

P.L. 111-148, §10909(b)(2)(J)(ii):

Amended Code Sec. 137(e) by striking "section 23" and inserting "section 36C". **Effective** for tax years beginning after 12-31-2009.

P.L. 111-148, §10909(c), provides:

(c) APPLICATION AND EXTENSION OF EGTRRA SUNSET.—Notwithstanding section 901 of the Economic Growth and Tax Relief Reconciliation Act of 2001, such section shall apply to the amendments made by this section and the amendments made by section 202 of such Act by substituting "December 31, 2011" for "December 31, 2010" in subsection (a)(1) thereof.

>>>→ *Caution: Code Sec. 137(f), below, was amended by P.L. 111-148. For sunset provision, see P.L. 111-148, §10909(c), in the amendment notes.*

(f) ADJUSTMENTS FOR INFLATION.—

(1) DOLLAR LIMITATIONS.—In the case of a taxable year beginning after December 31, 2010, each of the dollar amounts in subsections (a)(2) and (b)(1) shall be increased by an amount equal to—

(A) such dollar amount, multiplied by

(B) the cost-of-living adjustment determined under section 1(f)(3) for the calendar year in which the taxable year begins, determined by substituting "calendar year 2009" for "calendar year 1992" in subparagraph (B) thereof.

If any amount as increased under the preceding sentence is not a multiple of $10, such amount shall be rounded to the nearest multiple of $10.

(2) INCOME LIMITATION.—In the case of a taxable year beginning after December 31, 2002, the dollar amount in subsection (b)(2)(A) shall be increased by an amount equal to—

(A) such dollar amount, multiplied by

(B) the cost-of-living adjustment determined under section 1(f)(3) for the calendar year in which the taxable year begins, determined by substituting "calendar year 2001" for "calendar year 1992" in subparagraph [(B)] thereof.

If any amount as increased under the preceding sentence is not a multiple of $10, such amount shall be rounded to the nearest multiple of $10.

[CCH Explanation at ¶240. Committee Reports at ¶10,390.]

Amendments

● **2010, Patient Protection and Affordable Care Act (P.L. 111-148)**

P.L. 111-148, §10909(a)(2)(C):

Amended Code Sec. 137(f). **Effective** for tax years beginning after 12-31-2009. Prior to amendment, Code Sec. 137(f) read as follows:

(f) ADJUSTMENTS FOR INFLATION.—In the case of a taxable year beginning after December 31, 2002, each of the dollar amounts in subsection (a)(2) and paragraphs (1) and (2)(A) of subsection (b) shall be increased by an amount equal to—

(1) such dollar amount, multiplied by

(2) the cost-of-living adjustment determined under section 1(f)(3) for the calendar year in which the taxable year

begins, determined by substituting "calendar year 2001" for "calendar year 1992" in subparagraph (B) thereof.

If any amount as increased under the preceding sentence is not a multiple of $10, such amount shall be rounded to the nearest multiple of $10.

P.L. 111-148, §10909(c), provides:

(c) APPLICATION AND EXTENSION OF EGTRRA SUNSET.—Notwithstanding section 901 of the Economic Growth and Tax Relief Reconciliation Act of 2001, such section shall apply to the amendments made by this section and the amendments made by section 202 of such Act by substituting "December 31, 2011" for "December 31, 2010" in subsection (a)(1) thereof.

>>>→ *Caution: Code Sec. 139A, below, as amended by P.L. 111-148, applies to tax years beginning after December 31, 2012.*

[¶5105] CODE SEC. 139A. FEDERAL SUBSIDIES FOR PRESCRIPTION DRUG PLANS.

Gross income shall not include any special subsidy payment received under section 1860D-22 of the Social Security Act.

[CCH Explanation at ¶335. Committee Reports at ¶10,270.]

Amendments

● **2010, Patient Protection and Affordable Care Act (P.L. 111-148)**

P.L. 111-148, §9012(a):

Amended Code Sec. 139A by striking the second sentence. **Effective** for tax years beginning after 12-31-2012

[effective date changed by P.L. 111-152, §1407.—CCH]. Prior to being stricken, the second sentence of Code Sec. 139A read as follows:

This section shall not be taken into account for purposes of determining whether any deduction is allowable with respect to any cost taken into account in determining such payment.

[¶5110] *CODE SEC. 139D. INDIAN HEALTH CARE BENEFITS.*

(a) GENERAL RULE.—Except as otherwise provided in this section, gross income does not include the value of any qualified Indian health care benefit.

(b) QUALIFIED INDIAN HEALTH CARE BENEFIT.—*For purposes of this section, the term "qualified Indian health care benefit" means—*

(1) any health service or benefit provided or purchased, directly or indirectly, by the Indian Health Service through a grant to or a contract or compact with an Indian tribe or tribal organization, or through a third-party program funded by the Indian Health Service,

(2) medical care provided or purchased by, or amounts to reimburse for such medical care provided by, an Indian tribe or tribal organization for, or to, a member of an Indian tribe, including a spouse or dependent of such a member,

(3) coverage under accident or health insurance (or an arrangement having the effect of accident or health insurance), or an accident or health plan, provided by an Indian tribe or tribal organization for medical care to a member of an Indian tribe, include a spouse or dependent of such a member, and

(4) any other medical care provided by an Indian tribe or tribal organization that supplements, replaces, or substitutes for a program or service relating to medical care provided by the Federal government to Indian tribes or members of such a tribe.

(c) DEFINITIONS.—*For purposes of this section—*

(1) INDIAN TRIBE.—*The term "Indian tribe" has the meaning given such term by section 45A(c)(6).*

(2) TRIBAL ORGANIZATION.—*The term "tribal organization" has the meaning given such term by section 4(l) of the Indian Self-Determination and Education Assistance Act.*

(3) MEDICAL CARE.—*The term "medical care" has the same meaning as when used in section 213.*

(4) ACCIDENT OR HEALTH INSURANCE; ACCIDENT OR HEALTH PLAN.—*The terms "accident or health insurance" and "accident or health plan" have the same meaning as when used in section 105.*

(5) DEPENDENT.—*The term "dependent" has the meaning given such term by section 152, determined without regard to subsections (b)(1), (b)(2), and (d)(1)(B) thereof.*

(d) DENIAL OF DOUBLE BENEFIT.—*Subsection (a) shall not apply to the amount of any qualified Indian health care benefit which is not includible in gross income of the beneficiary of such benefit under any other provision of this chapter, or to the amount of any such benefit for which a deduction is allowed to such beneficiary under any other provision of this chapter.*

[CCH Explanation at ¶ 250. Committee Reports at ¶ 10,330.]

Amendments

• **2010, Patient Protection and Affordable Care Act (P.L. 111-148)**

P.L. 111-148, § 9021(a):

Amended part III of subchapter B of chapter 1 by inserting after Code Sec. 139C a new Code Sec. 139D. **Effective** for benefits and coverage provided after 3-23-2010. For a special rule, see Act Sec. 9021(d), below.

P.L. 111-148, § 9021(d), provides:

(d) NO INFERENCE.—Nothing in the amendments made by this section shall be construed to create an inference with respect to the exclusion from gross income of—

(1) benefits provided by an Indian tribe or tribal organization that are not within the scope of this section, and

(2) benefits provided prior to the date of the enactment of this Act.

⋙→ *Caution: Code Sec. 139D[E], below, as added by P.L. 111-148, applies to vouchers provided after December 31, 2013.*

[¶ 5115] *CODE SEC. 139D[E]. FREE CHOICE VOUCHERS.*

Gross income shall not include the amount of any free choice voucher provided by an employer under section 10108 of the Patient Protection and Affordable Care Act to the extent that the amount of such voucher does not exceed the amount paid for a qualified health plan (as defined in section 1301 of such Act) by the taxpayer.

[CCH Explanation at ¶315. Committee Reports at ¶10,370.]
Amendments
• 2010, Patient Protection and Affordable Care Act
(P.L. 111-148)

P.L. 111-148, §10108(f)(1):

Amended part III of subchapter B of chapter 1 by inserting after Code Sec. 139C[D] a new Code Sec. 139D[E]. **Effective** for vouchers provided after 12-31-2013.

[¶5120] CODE SEC. 162. TRADE OR BUSINESS EXPENSES.

(a) In General.—There shall be allowed as a deduction all the ordinary and necessary expenses paid or incurred during the taxable year in carrying on any trade or business, including—

(1) a reasonable allowance for salaries or other compensation for personal services actually rendered;

(2) traveling expenses (including amounts expended for meals and lodging other than amounts which are lavish or extravagant under the circumstances) while away from home in the pursuit of a trade or business; and

(3) rentals or other payments required to be made as a condition to the continued use or possession, for purposes of the trade or business, of property to which the taxpayer has not taken or is not taking title or in which he has no equity.

⫸→ *Caution: The last sentence of Code Sec. 162(a), below, as added by P.L. 111-148, applies to vouchers provided after December 31, 2013.*

For purposes of the preceding sentence, the place of residence of a Member of Congress (including any Delegate and Resident Commissioner) within the State, congressional district, or possession which he represents in Congress shall be considered his home, but amounts expended by such Members within each taxable year for living expenses shall not be deductible for income tax purposes in excess of $3,000. For purposes of paragraph (2), the taxpayer shall not be treated as being temporarily away from home during any period of employment if such period exceeds 1 year. The preceding sentence shall not apply to any Federal employee during any period for which such employee is certified by the Attorney General (or the designee thereof) as traveling on behalf of the United States in temporary duty status to investigate or prosecute, or provide support services for the investigation or prosecution of, a Federal crime. *For purposes of paragraph (1), the amount of a free choice voucher provided under section 10108 of the Patient Protection and Affordable Care Act shall be treated as an amount for compensation for personal services actually rendered.*

* * *

[CCH Explanation at ¶315. Committee Reports at ¶10,370.]
Amendments
• 2010, Patient Protection and Affordable Care Act
(P.L. 111-148)

P.L. 111-148, §10108(g)(1):

Amended Code Sec. 162(a) by adding at the end a new sentence. **Effective** for vouchers provided after 12-31-2013.

(l) Special Rules for Health Insurance Costs of Self-Employed Individuals.—

(1) Allowance of Deduction.—In the case of a taxpayer who is an employee within the meaning of section 401(c)(1), there shall be allowed as a deduction under this section an amount equal to the amount paid during the taxable year for insurance which constitutes medical care for—

(A) the taxpayer,

(B) the taxpayer's spouse,

(C) the taxpayer's dependents, and

(D) any child (as defined in section 152(f)(1)) of the taxpayer who as of the end of the taxable year has not attained age 27.

(2) Limitations.—

* * *

(B) Other coverage.—Paragraph (1) shall not apply to any taxpayer for any calendar month for which the taxpayer is eligible to participate in any subsidized health plan maintained by any employer of the taxpayer or of the spouse of, *or any dependent, or individual described in subparagraph (D) of paragraph (1) with respect to*, the taxpayer. The preceding sentence shall be applied separately with respect to—

(i) plans which include coverage for qualified long-term care services (as defined in section 7702B(c)) or are qualified long-term care insurance contracts (as defined in section 7702B(b)), and

(ii) plans which do not include such coverage and are not such contracts.

* * *

[CCH Explanation at ¶242. Committee Reports at ¶10,400.]
Amendments

• **2010, Health Care and Education Reconciliation Act of 2010 (P.L. 111-152)**

P.L. 111-152, §1004(d)(2):

Amended Code Sec. 162(l)(1). **Effective** 3-30-2010. Prior to amendment, Code Sec. 162(l)(1) read as follows:

(1) Allowance of deduction.—

(A) In general.—In the case of an individual who is an employee within the meaning of section 401(c)(1), there shall be allowed as a deduction under this section an amount equal to the applicable percentage of the amount paid during the taxable year for insurance which constitutes medical care for the taxpayer, his spouse, and dependents.

(B) Applicable percentage.—For purposes of subparagraph (A), the applicable percentage shall be determined under the following table:

For taxable years beginning in calendar year—	The applicable percentage is—
1999 through 2001	60
2002	70
2003 and thereafter	100

P.L. 111-152, §1004(d)(3):

Amended Code Sec. 162(l)(2)(B) by inserting ", or any dependent, or individual described in subparagraph (D) of paragraph (1) with respect to," after "spouse of". **Effective** 3-30-2010.

(m) Certain Excessive Employee Remuneration.—

* * *

(6) *Special rule for application to certain health insurance providers.*—

(A) *In general.—No deduction shall be allowed under this chapter—*

(i) *in the case of applicable individual remuneration which is for any disqualified taxable year beginning after December 31, 2012, and which is attributable to services performed by an applicable individual during such taxable year, to the extent that the amount of such remuneration exceeds $500,000, or*

(ii) *in the case of deferred deduction remuneration for any taxable year beginning after December 31, 2012, which is attributable to services performed by an applicable individual during any disqualified taxable year beginning after December 31, 2009, to the extent that the amount of such remuneration exceeds $500,000 reduced (but not below zero) by the sum of—*

(I) *the applicable individual remuneration for such disqualified taxable year, plus*

(II) *the portion of the deferred deduction remuneration for such services which was taken into account under this clause in a preceding taxable year (or which would have been taken into account under this clause in a preceding taxable year if this clause were applied by substituting "December 31, 2009" for "December 31, 2012" in the matter preceding subclause (I)).*

(B) *Disqualified taxable year.—For purposes of this paragraph, the term "disqualified taxable year" means, with respect to any employer, any taxable year for which such employer is a covered health insurance provider.*

(C) *Covered health insurance provider.—For purposes of this paragraph—*

(i) IN GENERAL.—The term "covered health insurance provider" means—

(I) with respect to taxable years beginning after December 31, 2009, and before January 1, 2013, any employer which is a health insurance issuer (as defined in section 9832(b)(2)) and which receives premiums from providing health insurance coverage (as defined in section 9832(b)(1)), and

(II) with respect to taxable years beginning after December 31, 2012, any employer which is a health insurance issuer (as defined in section 9832(b)(2)) and with respect to which not less than 25 percent of the gross premiums received from providing health insurance coverage (as defined in section 9832(b)(1)) is from minimum essential coverage (as defined in section 5000A(f)).

(ii) AGGREGATION RULES.—Two or more persons who are treated as a single employer under subsection (b), (c), (m), or (o) of section 414 shall be treated as a single employer, except that in applying section 1563(a) for purposes of any such subsection, paragraphs (2) and (3) thereof shall be disregarded.

(D) APPLICABLE INDIVIDUAL REMUNERATION.—For purposes of this paragraph, the term "applicable individual remuneration" means, with respect to any applicable individual for any disqualified taxable year, the aggregate amount allowable as a deduction under this chapter for such taxable year (determined without regard to this subsection) for remuneration (as defined in paragraph (4) without regard to subparagraphs (B), (C), and (D) thereof) for services performed by such individual (whether or not during the taxable year). Such term shall not include any deferred deduction remuneration with respect to services performed during the disqualified taxable year.

(E) DEFERRED DEDUCTION REMUNERATION.—For purposes of this paragraph, the term "deferred deduction remuneration" means remuneration which would be applicable individual remuneration for services performed in a disqualified taxable year but for the fact that the deduction under this chapter (determined without regard to this paragraph) for such remuneration is allowable in a subsequent taxable year.

(F) APPLICABLE INDIVIDUAL.—For purposes of this paragraph, the term "applicable individual" means, with respect to any covered health insurance provider for any disqualified taxable year, any individual—

(i) who is an officer, director, or employee in such taxable year, or

(ii) who provides services for or on behalf of such covered health insurance provider during such taxable year.

(G) COORDINATION.—Rules similar to the rules of subparagraphs (F) and (G) of paragraph (4) shall apply for purposes of this paragraph.

(H) REGULATORY AUTHORITY.—The Secretary may prescribe such guidance, rules, or regulations as are necessary to carry out the purposes of this paragraph.

* * *

[CCH Explanation at ¶ 340. Committee Reports at ¶ 10,290.]

Amendments

• 2010, Patient Protection and Affordable Care Act (P.L. 111-148)

P.L. 111-148, § 9014(a):

Amended Code Sec. 162(m) by adding at the end a new subparagraph (6). **Effective** for tax years beginning after 12-31-2009, with respect to services performed after such date.

[¶ 5125] CODE SEC. 164. TAXES.

* * *

(f) Deduction for One-Half of Self-Employment Taxes.—

>>>→ *Caution: Code Sec. 164(f)(1), below, as amended by P.L. 111-148, applies with respect to remuneration received, and tax years beginning, after December 31, 2012.*

(1) In general.—In the case of an individual, in addition to the taxes described in subsection (a), there shall be allowed as a deduction for the taxable year an amount equal to one-half of the taxes imposed by section 1401 *(other than the taxes imposed by section 1401(b)(2))* for such taxable year.

* * *

[CCH Explanation at ¶ 230. Committee Reports at ¶ 10,300.]

Amendments

• **2010, Patient Protection and Affordable Care Act (P.L. 111-148)**

P.L. 111-148, § 9015(b)(2)(A):

Amended Code Sec. 164(f)[(1)] by inserting "(other than the taxes imposed by section 1401(b)(2))" after "section

1401) [sic]". **Effective** with respect to remuneration received, and tax years beginning, after 12-31-2012.

[¶ 5130] CODE SEC. 196. DEDUCTION FOR CERTAIN UNUSED BUSINESS CREDITS.

* * *

(c) Qualified Business Credits.—For purposes of this section, the term "qualified business credits" means—

* * *

(12) the low sulfur diesel fuel production credit determined under section 45H(a),

(13) the new energy efficient home credit determined under section 45L(a), *and*

(14) *the small employer health insurance credit determined under section 45R(a).*

* * *

[CCH Explanation at ¶ 310. Committee Reports at ¶ 10,070.]

Amendments

• **2010, Patient Protection and Affordable Care Act (P.L. 111-148)**

P.L. 111-148, § 1421(d)(2):

Amended Code Sec. 196(c) by striking "and" at the end of paragraph (12), by striking the period at the end of para-

graph (13) and inserting ", and", and by adding at the end a new paragraph (14). **Effective** for amounts paid or incurred in tax years beginning after 12-31-2009 **[effective date changed by Act Sec. 10105(e)(4).—CCH]**.

[¶ 5135] CODE SEC. 213. MEDICAL, DENTAL, ETC., EXPENSES.

>>>→ *Caution: Code Sec. 213(a), below, as amended by P.L. 111-148, applies to tax years beginning after December 31, 2012.*

(a) Allowance of Deduction.—There shall be allowed as a deduction the expenses paid during the taxable year, not compensated for by insurance or otherwise, for medical care of the taxpayer, his spouse, or a dependent (as defined in section 152, determined without regard to subsections (b)(1), (b)(2), and (d)(1)(B) thereof), to the extent that such expenses exceed *10 percent* of adjusted gross income.

* * *

[CCH Explanation at ¶ 215. Committee Reports at ¶ 10,280.]

Amendments

• **2010, Patient Protection and Affordable Care Act (P.L. 111-148)**

P.L. 111-148, § 9013(a):

Amended Code Sec. 213(a) by striking "7.5 percent" and inserting "10 percent". **Effective** for tax years beginning after 12-31-2012.

》》→ *Caution: Code Sec. 213(f), below, as added by P.L. 111-148, applies to tax years beginning after December 31, 2012.*

(f) Special Rule for 2013, 2014, 2015, and 2016.—In the case of any taxable year beginning after December 31, 2012, and ending before January 1, 2017, subsection (a) shall be applied with respect to a taxpayer by substituting "7.5 percent" for "10 percent" if such taxpayer or such taxpayer's spouse has attained age 65 before the close of such taxable year.

[CCH Explanation at ¶ 215. Committee Reports at ¶ 10,280.]

Amendments

• **2010, Patient Protection and Affordable Care Act (P.L. 111-148)**

P.L. 111-148, § 9013(b):

Amended Code Sec. 213 by adding at the end a new subsection (f). **Effective** for tax years beginning after 12-31-2012.

[¶ 5140] CODE SEC. 220. ARCHER MSAs.

* * *

(d) Archer MSA.—For purposes of this section—

* * *

(2) Qualified Medical Expenses.—

》》→ *Caution: Code Sec. 220(d)(2)(A), below, as amended by P.L. 111-148, applies to amounts paid with respect to tax years beginning after December 31, 2010.*

(A) In general.—The term "qualified medical expenses" means, with respect to an account holder, amounts paid by such holder for medical care (as defined in section 213(d)) for such individual, the spouse of such individual, and any dependent (as defined in section 152, determined without regard to subsections (b)(1), (b)(2), and (d)(1)(B) thereof) of such individual, but only to the extent such amounts are not compensated for by insurance or otherwise. *Such term shall include an amount paid for medicine or a drug only if such medicine or drug is a prescribed drug (determined without regard to whether such drug is available without a prescription) or is insulin.*

* * *

[CCH Explanation at ¶ 220. Committee Reports at ¶ 10,180.]

Amendments

• **2010, Patient Protection and Affordable Care Act (P.L. 111-148)**

P.L. 111-148, § 9003(b):

Amended Code Sec. 220(d)(2)(A) by adding at the end a new sentence. **Effective** for amounts paid with respect to tax years beginning after 12-31-2010.

(f) Tax Treatment of Distributions.—

* * *

(4) Additional tax on distributions not used for qualified medical expenses.—

⟫→ *Caution: Code Sec. 220(f)(4)(A), below, as amended by P.L. 111-148, applies to distributions made after December 31, 2010.*

(A) In general.—The tax imposed by this chapter on the account holder for any taxable year in which there is a payment or distribution from an Archer MSA of such holder which is includible in gross income under paragraph (2) shall be increased by *20 percent* of the amount which is so includible.

* * *

[CCH Explanation at ¶ 225. Committee Reports at ¶ 10,190.]

Amendments
• 2010, Patient Protection and Affordable Care Act
(P.L. 111-148)

P.L. 111-148, § 9004(b):

Amended Code Sec. 220(f)(4)(A) by striking "15 percent" and inserting "20 percent". **Effective** for distributions made after 12-31-2010.

[¶ 5145] CODE SEC. 223. HEALTH SAVINGS ACCOUNTS.

* * *

(d) Health Savings Account.—For purposes of this section—

* * *

(2) Qualified medical expenses.—

⟫→ *Caution: Code Sec. 223(d)(2)(A), below, as amended by P.L. 111-148, applies to amounts paid with respect to tax years beginning after December 31, 2010.*

(A) In general.—The term "qualified medical expenses" means, with respect to an account beneficiary, amounts paid by such beneficiary for medical care (as defined in section 213(d)[)]for such individual, the spouse of such individual, and any dependent (as defined in section 152, determined without regard to subsections (b)(1), (b)(2), and (d)(1)(B) thereof) of such individual, but only to the extent such amounts are not compensated for by insurance or otherwise. *Such term shall include an amount paid for medicine or a drug only if such medicine or drug is a prescribed drug (determined without regard to whether such drug is available without a prescription) or is insulin.*

* * *

[CCH Explanation at ¶ 220. Committee Reports at ¶ 10,180.]

Amendments
• 2010, Patient Protection and Affordable Care Act
(P.L. 111-148)

P.L. 111-148, § 9003(a):

Amended Code Sec. 223(d)(2)(A) by adding at the end a new sentence. **Effective** for amounts paid with respect to tax years beginning after 12-31-2010.

(f) Tax Treatment of Distributions.—

* * *

(4) ADDITIONAL TAX ON DISTRIBUTIONS NOT USED FOR QUALIFIED MEDICAL EXPENSES.—

>>>→ *Caution: Code Sec. 223(f)(4)(A), below, as amended by P.L. 111-148, applies to distributions made after December 31, 2010.*

(A) IN GENERAL.—The tax imposed by this chapter on the account beneficiary for any taxable year in which there is a payment or distribution from a health savings account of such beneficiary which is includible in gross income under paragraph (2) shall be increased by *20 percent* of the amount which is so includible.

* * *

[CCH Explanation at ¶225. Committee Reports at ¶10,190.]

Amendments

• 2010, Patient Protection and Affordable Care Act (P.L. 111-148)

P.L. 111-148, §9004(a):

Amended Code Sec. 223(f)(4)(A) by striking "10 percent" and inserting "20 percent". **Effective** for distributions made after 12-31-2010.

[¶5150] CODE SEC. 280C. CERTAIN EXPENSES FOR WHICH CREDITS ARE ALLOWABLE.

* * *

>>>→ *Caution: Code Sec. 280C(g), below, as added by P.L. 111-148, applies to tax years ending after December 31, 2013.*

(g) CREDIT FOR HEALTH INSURANCE PREMIUMS.—*No deduction shall be allowed for the portion of the premiums paid by the taxpayer for coverage of 1 or more individuals under a qualified health plan which is equal to the amount of the credit determined for the taxable year under section 36B(a) with respect to such premiums.*

[CCH Explanation at ¶210. Committee Reports at ¶10,030.]

Amendments

• 2010, Patient Protection and Affordable Care Act (P.L. 111-148)

P.L. 111-148, §1401(b):

Amended Code Sec. 280C by adding at the end a new subsection (g). **Effective** for tax years ending after 12-31-2013.

(h) CREDIT FOR EMPLOYEE HEALTH INSURANCE EXPENSES OF SMALL EMPLOYERS.—*No deduction shall be allowed for that portion of the premiums for qualified health plans (as defined in section 1301(a) of the Patient Protection and Affordable Care Act), or for health insurance coverage in the case of taxable years beginning in 2010, 2011, 2012, or 2013, paid by an employer which is equal to the amount of the credit determined under section 45R(a) with respect to the premiums.*

[CCH Explanation at ¶310. Committee Reports at ¶10,070 and ¶10,360.]

Amendments

• 2010, Patient Protection and Affordable Care Act (P.L. 111-148)

P.L. 111-148, §1421(d)(1):

Amended Code Sec. 280C, as amended by Act Sec. 1401(b), by adding at the end a new subsection (h). **Effective** for amounts paid or incurred in tax years beginning after 12-31-2009 [**effective** date changed by Act Sec. 10105(e)(4).—CCH].

P.L. 111-148, §10105(e)(3):

Amended Code Sec. 280C(h), as added by Act Sec. 1421(d)(1), by striking "2011" and inserting "2010, 2011". **Effective** as if included in the enactment of Act Sec. 1421 [**effective** for amounts paid or incurred in tax years beginning after 12-31-2009 [**effective** date changed by Act Sec. 10105(e)(4).—CCH]].

(g)[(i)] QUALIFYING THERAPEUTIC DISCOVERY PROJECT CREDIT.—

(1) IN GENERAL.—*No deduction shall be allowed for that portion of the qualified investment (as defined in section 48D(b)) otherwise allowable as a deduction for the taxable year which—*

(A) would be qualified research expenses (as defined in section 41(b)), basic research expenses (as defined in section 41(e)(2)), or qualified clinical testing expenses (as defined in section 45C(b)) if the credit under section 41 or section 45C were allowed with respect to such expenses for such taxable year, and

(B) is equal to the amount of the credit determined for such taxable year under section 48D(a), reduced by—

(i) the amount disallowed as a deduction by reason of section 48D(e)(2)(B), and

(ii) the amount of any basis reduction under section 48D(e)(1).

(2) SIMILAR RULE WHERE TAXPAYER CAPITALIZES RATHER THAN DEDUCTS EXPENSES.—*In the case of expenses described in paragraph (1)(A) taken into account in determining the credit under section 48D for the taxable year, if—*

(A) the amount of the portion of the credit determined under such section with respect to such expenses, exceeds

(B) the amount allowable as a deduction for such taxable year for such expenses (determined without regard to paragraph (1)),

the amount chargeable to capital account for the taxable year for such expenses shall be reduced by the amount of such excess.

(3) CONTROLLED GROUPS.—*Paragraph (3) of subsection (b) shall apply for purposes of this subsection.*

[CCH Explanation at ¶355. Committee Reports at ¶10,350.]

Amendments
• **2010, Patient Protection and Affordable Care Act (P.L. 111-148)**

P.L. 111-148, §9023(c)(2):

Amended Code Sec. 280C by adding at the end a new subsection (g)[(i)]. **Effective** for amounts paid or incurred after 12-31-2008, in tax years beginning after such date.

[¶5153] CODE SEC. 401. QUALIFIED PENSION, PROFIT-SHARING, AND STOCK BONUS PLANS.

* * *

(h) MEDICAL, ETC., BENEFITS FOR RETIRED EMPLOYEES AND THEIR SPOUSES AND DEPENDENTS.—Under regulations prescribed by the Secretary, and subject to the provisions of section 420, a pension or annuity plan may provide for the payment of benefits for sickness, accident, hospitalization, and medical expenses of retired employees, their spouses and their dependents, but only if—

(1) such benefits are subordinate to the retirement benefits provided by the plan,

(2) a separate account is established and maintained for such benefits,

(3) the employer's contributions to such separate account are reasonable and ascertainable,

(4) it is impossible, at any time prior to the satisfaction of all liabilities under the plan to provide such benefits, for any part of the corpus or income of such separate account to be (within the taxable year or thereafter) used for, or diverted to, any purpose other than the providing of such benefits,

(5) notwithstanding the provisions of subsection (a)(2), upon the satisfaction of all liabilities under the plan to provide such benefits, any amount remaining in such separate account must, under the terms of the plan, be returned to the employer, and

(6) in the case of an employee who is a key employee, a separate account is established and maintained for such benefits payable to such employee (and his spouse and dependents) and such benefits (to the extent attributable to plan years beginning after March 31, 1984, for which

the employee is a key employee) are only payable to such employee (and his spouse and dependents) from such separate account.

For purposes of paragraph (6), the term "key employee" means any employee, who at any time during the plan year or any preceding plan year during which contributions were made on behalf of such employee, is or was a key employee as defined in section 416(i). In no event shall the requirements of paragraph (1) be treated as met if the aggregate actual contributions for medical benefits, when added to actual contributions for life insurance protection under the plan, exceed 25 percent of the total actual contributions to the plan (other than contributions to fund past service credits) after the date on which the account is established. *For purposes of this subsection, the term "dependent" shall include any individual who is a child (as defined in section 152(f)(1)) of a retired employee who as of the end of the calendar year has not attained age 27.*

* * *

[CCH Explanation at ¶242. Committee Reports at ¶10,400.]
Amendments
• **2010, Health Care and Education Reconciliation Act of 2010 (P.L. 111-152)**

P.L. 111-152, §1004(d)(5):

Amended Code Sec. 401(h) by adding at the end a new sentence. Effective 3-30-2010.

[¶5155] CODE SEC. 501. EXEMPTION FROM TAX ON CORPORATIONS, CERTAIN TRUSTS, ETC.

* * *

(c) LIST OF EXEMPT ORGANIZATIONS.—The following organizations are referred to in subsection (a):

* * *

(9) Voluntary employees' beneficiary associations providing for the payment of life, sick, accident, or other benefits to the members of such association or their dependents or designated beneficiaries, if no part of the net earnings of such association inures (other than through such payments) to the benefit of any private shareholder or individual. *For purposes of providing for the payment of sick and accident benefits to members of such an association and their dependents, the term "dependent" shall include any individual who is a child (as defined in section 152(f)(1)) of a member who as of the end of the calendar year has not attained age 27.*

* * *

(29) *CO-OP* HEALTH INSURANCE ISSUERS.—

(A) IN GENERAL.—*A qualified nonprofit health insurance issuer (within the meaning of section 1322 of the Patient Protection and Affordable Care Act) which has received a loan or grant under the CO-OP program under such section, but only with respect to periods for which the issuer is in compliance with the requirements of such section and any agreement with respect to the loan or grant.*

(B) CONDITIONS FOR EXEMPTION.—*Subparagraph (A) shall apply to an organization only if—*

(i) the organization has given notice to the Secretary, in such manner as the Secretary may by regulations prescribe, that it is applying for recognition of its status under this paragraph,

(ii) except as provided in section 1322(c)(4) of the Patient Protection and Affordable Care Act, no part of the net earnings of which inures to the benefit of any private shareholder or individual,

(iii) no substantial part of the activities of which is carrying on propaganda, or otherwise attempting, to influence legislation, and

(iv) the organization does not participate in, or intervene in (including the publishing or distributing of statements), any political campaign on behalf of (or in opposition to) any candidate for public office.

* * *

[CCH Explanation at ¶242 and ¶435. Committee Reports at ¶10,010 and ¶10,400.]

Amendments

• 2010, Health Care and Education Reconciliation Act of 2010 (P.L. 111-152)

P.L. 111-152, §1004(d)(4):

Amended Code Sec. 501(c)(9) by adding at the end a new sentence. **Effective** 3-30-2010.

• 2010, Patient Protection and Affordable Care Act (P.L. 111-148)

P.L. 111-148, §1322(h)(1):

Amended Code Sec. 501(c) by adding at the end a new paragraph (29). **Effective** 3-23-2010.

(l) GOVERNMENT CORPORATIONS EXEMPT UNDER SUBSECTION (c)(1).—For purposes of subsection (c)(1), the following organizations are described in this subsection:

* * *

(4) *The Patient-Centered Outcomes Research Institute established under section 1181(b) of the Social Security Act.*

* * *

[CCH Explanation at ¶445. Committee Reports at ¶10,150.]

Amendments

• 2010, Patient Protection and Affordable Care Act (P.L. 111-148)

P.L. 111-148, §6301(f):

Amended Code Sec. 501(l) by adding at the end a new paragraph (4). **Effective** 3-23-2010.

(r) ADDITIONAL REQUIREMENTS FOR CERTAIN HOSPITALS.—

(1) IN GENERAL.—*A hospital organization to which this subsection applies shall not be treated as described in subsection (c)(3) unless the organization—*

(A) *meets the community health needs assessment requirements described in paragraph (3),*

(B) *meets the financial assistance policy requirements described in paragraph (4),*

(C) *meets the requirements on charges described in paragraph (5), and*

(D) *meets the billing and collection requirement described in paragraph (6).*

(2) HOSPITAL ORGANIZATIONS TO WHICH SUBSECTION APPLIES.—

(A) IN GENERAL.—*This subsection shall apply to—*

(i) *an organization which operates a facility which is required by a State to be licensed, registered, or similarly recognized as a hospital, and*

(ii) *any other organization which the Secretary determines has the provision of hospital care as its principal function or purpose constituting the basis for its exemption under subsection (c)(3) (determined without regard to this subsection).*

(B) ORGANIZATIONS WITH MORE THAN 1 HOSPITAL FACILITY.—*If a hospital organization operates more than 1 hospital facility—*

(i) *the organization shall meet the requirements of this subsection separately with respect to each such facility, and*

(ii) *the organization shall not be treated as described in subsection (c)(3) with respect to any such facility for which such requirements are not separately met.*

(3) COMMUNITY HEALTH NEEDS ASSESSMENTS.—

(A) IN GENERAL.—*An organization meets the requirements of this paragraph with respect to any taxable year only if the organization—*

(i) *has conducted a community health needs assessment which meets the requirements of subparagraph (B) in such taxable year or in either of the 2 taxable years immediately preceding such taxable year, and*

(ii) *has adopted an implementation strategy to meet the community health needs identified through such assessment.*

Code Sec. 501(r)(3)(A)(ii) ¶5155

(B) COMMUNITY HEALTH NEEDS ASSESSMENT.—*A community health needs assessment meets the requirements of this paragraph if such community health needs assessment—*

(i) *takes into account input from persons who represent the broad interests of the community served by the hospital facility, including those with special knowledge of or expertise in public health, and*

(ii) *is made widely available to the public.*

(4) FINANCIAL ASSISTANCE POLICY.—*An organization meets the requirements of this paragraph if the organization establishes the following policies:*

(A) FINANCIAL ASSISTANCE POLICY.—*A written financial assistance policy which includes—*

(i) *eligibility criteria for financial assistance, and whether such assistance includes free or discounted care,*

(ii) *the basis for calculating amounts charged to patients,*

(iii) *the method for applying for financial assistance,*

(iv) *in the case of an organization which does not have a separate billing and collections policy, the actions the organization may take in the event of non-payment, including collections action and reporting to credit agencies, and*

(v) *measures to widely publicize the policy within the community to be served by the organization.*

(B) POLICY RELATING TO EMERGENCY MEDICAL CARE.—*A written policy requiring the organization to provide, without discrimination, care for emergency medical conditions (within the meaning of section 1867 of the Social Security Act (42 U.S.C. 1395dd)) to individuals regardless of their eligibility under the financial assistance policy described in subparagraph (A).*

(5) LIMITATION ON CHARGES.—*An organization meets the requirements of this paragraph if the organization—*

(A) *limits amounts charged for emergency or other medically necessary care provided to individuals eligible for assistance under the financial assistance policy described in paragraph (4)(A) to not more than the amounts generally billed to individuals who have insurance covering such care, and*

(B) *prohibits the use of gross charges.*

(6) BILLING AND COLLECTION REQUIREMENTS.—*An organization meets the requirement of this paragraph only if the organization does not engage in extraordinary collection actions before the organization has made reasonable efforts to determine whether the individual is eligible for assistance under the financial assistance policy described in paragraph (4)(A).*

(7) REGULATORY AUTHORITY.—*The Secretary shall issue such regulations and guidance as may be necessary to carry out the provisions of this subsection, including guidance relating to what constitutes reasonable efforts to determine the eligibility of a patient under a financial assistance policy for purposes of paragraph (6).*

[CCH Explanation at ¶ 440. Committee Reports at ¶ 10,220.]

Amendments

• **2010, Patient Protection and Affordable Care Act (P.L. 111-148)**

P.L. 111-148, §9007(a):

Amended Code Sec. 501 by redesignating subsection (r) as subsection (s) and by inserting after subsection (q) a new subsection (r). **Effective** for tax years beginning after 3-23-2010. For a special rule, see Act Sec. 9007(f)(2), below.

P.L. 111-148, §9007(f)(2), provides:

(2) COMMUNITY HEALTH NEEDS ASSESSMENT.—The requirements of section 501(r)(3) of the Internal Revenue Code of 1986, as added by subsection (a), shall apply to taxable years beginning after the date which is 2 years after the date of the enactment of this Act.

P.L. 111-148, §10903(a):

Amended Code Sec. 501(r)(5)(A), as added by Act Sec. 9007, by striking "the lowest amounts charged" and inserting "the amounts generally billed". **Effective** for tax years beginning 3-23-2010.

(s) CROSS REFERENCE.—

For nonexemption of Communist-controlled organizations, see section 11(b) of the Internal Security Act of 1950 (64 Stat. 997; 50 U. S. C. 790 (b)).

[Committee Reports at ¶ 10,220.]

Amendments

• **2010, Patient Protection and Affordable Care Act (P.L. 111-148)**

P.L. 111-148, § 9007(a):

Amended Code Sec. 501 by redesignating subsection (r) as subsection (s). **Effective** for tax years beginning 3-23-2010.

[¶ 5160] CODE SEC. 833. TREATMENT OF BLUE CROSS AND BLUE SHIELD ORGANIZATIONS, ETC.

* * *

(c) ORGANIZATIONS TO WHICH SECTION APPLIES.—

* * *

(5) *NONAPPLICATION OF SECTION IN CASE OF LOW MEDICAL LOSS RATIO.—Notwithstanding the preceding paragraphs, this section shall not apply to any organization unless such organization's percentage of total premium revenue expended on reimbursement for clinical services provided to enrollees under its policies during such taxable year (as reported under section 2718 of the Public Health Service Act) is not less than 85 percent.*

[CCH Explanation at ¶ 360. Committee Reports at ¶ 10,310.]

Amendments

• **2010, Patient Protection and Affordable Care Act (P.L. 111-148)**

P.L. 111-148, § 9016(a):

Amended Code Sec. 833(c) by adding at the end a new paragraph (5). **Effective** for tax years beginning after 12-31-2009.

[¶ 5165] CODE SEC. 904. LIMITATION ON CREDIT.

* * *

➤➤➤ *Caution: Code Sec. 904(i), below, was amended by P.L. 111-148. For sunset provision, see P.L. 111-148, § 10909(c), in the amendment notes.*

(i) COORDINATION WITH NONREFUNDABLE PERSONAL CREDITS.—In the case of any taxable year of an individual to which section 26(a)(2) does not apply, for purposes of subsection (a), the tax against which the credit is taken is such tax reduced by the sum of the credits allowable under subpart A of part IV of subchapter A of this chapter (other than sections 24, 25A(i), 25B, 30, 30B, and 30D).

* * *

[Committee Reports at ¶ 10,390.]

Amendments

• **2010, Patient Protection and Affordable Care Act (P.L. 111-148)**

P.L. 111-148, § 10909(b)(2)(K):

Amended Code Sec. 904(i) by striking "23," before "24". **Effective** for tax years beginning after 12-31-2009.

P.L. 111-148, § 10909(c), provides:

(c) APPLICATION AND EXTENSION OF EGTRRA SUNSET.—Notwithstanding section 901 of the Economic Growth and Tax Relief Reconciliation Act of 2001, such section shall apply to the amendments made by this section and the amendments made by section 202 of such Act by substituting "December 31, 2011" for "December 31, 2010" in subsection (a)(1) thereof.

[¶ 5170] CODE SEC. 1016. ADJUSTMENTS TO BASIS.

(a) GENERAL RULE.—Proper adjustment in respect of the property shall in all cases be made—

* * *

≫→ Caution: *Code Sec. 1016(a)(26), below, was amended by P.L. 111-148. For sunset provision, see P.L. 111-148, §10909(c), in the amendment notes.*

(26) to the extent provided in sections 36C(g) and 137(e),

* * *

[Committee Reports at ¶ 10,390.]

Amendments

• **2010, Patient Protection and Affordable Care Act (P.L. 111-148)**

P.L. 111-148, §10909(b)(2)(L):

Amended Code Sec. 1016(a)(26) by striking "23(g)" and inserting "36C(g)". **Effective** for tax years beginning after 12-31-2009.

P.L. 111-148, §10909(c), provides:

(c) APPLICATION AND EXTENSION OF EGTRRA SUNSET.—Notwithstanding section 901 of the Economic Growth and Tax Relief Reconciliation Act of 2001, such section shall apply to the amendments made by this section and the amendments made by section 202 of such Act by substituting "December 31, 2011" for "December 31, 2010" in subsection (a)(1) thereof.

[¶ 5175] CODE SEC. 1400C. FIRST-TIME HOMEBUYER CREDIT FOR DISTRICT OF COLUMBIA.

* * *

(d) CARRYFORWARD OF UNUSED CREDIT.—

* * *

≫→ Caution: *Code Sec. 1400C(d)(2), below, was amended by P.L. 111-148. For sunset provision, see P.L. 111-148, §10909(c), in the amendment notes.*

(2) RULE FOR OTHER YEARS.—In the case of a taxable year to which section 26(a)(2) does not apply, if the credit allowable under subsection (a) exceeds the limitation imposed by section 26(a)(1) for such taxable year reduced by the sum of the credits allowable under subpart A of part IV of subchapter A (other than this section and sections 24, 25A(i), 25B, 25D, 30, and 30B, and 30D), such excess shall be carried to the succeeding taxable year and added to the credit allowable under subsection (a) for such taxable year.

* * *

[Committee Reports at ¶ 10,390.]

Amendments

• **2010, Patient Protection and Affordable Care Act (P.L. 111-148)**

P.L. 111-148, §10909(b)(2)(M):

Amended Code Sec. 1400C(d)[(2)] by striking "23," before "24". **Effective** for tax years beginning after 12-31-2009.

P.L. 111-148, §10909(c), provides:

(c) APPLICATION AND EXTENSION OF EGTRRA SUNSET.—Notwithstanding section 901 of the Economic Growth and Tax Relief Reconciliation Act of 2001, such section shall apply to the amendments made by this section and the amendments made by section 202 of such Act by substituting "December 31, 2011" for "December 31, 2010" in subsection (a)(1) thereof.

[¶ 5180] CODE SEC. 1401. RATE OF TAX.

* * *

≫→ Caution: *Code Sec. 1401(b), below, as amended by P.L. 111-148 and P.L. 111-152, applies with respect to remuneration received, and tax years beginning, after December 31, 2012.*

(b) HOSPITAL INSURANCE.—

(1) IN GENERAL.—In addition to the tax imposed by the preceding subsection, there shall be imposed for each taxable year, on the self-employment income of every individual, a tax equal to the following percent of the amount of the self-employment income for such taxable year:

In the case of a taxable year

Beginning after:	And before:	Percent
December 31, 1983	January 1, 1985	2.60
December 31, 1984	January 1, 1986	2.70
December 31, 1985		2.90

(2) *ADDITIONAL TAX.*—

(A) IN GENERAL.—*In addition to the tax imposed by paragraph (1) and the preceding subsection, there is hereby imposed on every taxpayer (other than a corporation, estate, or trust) for each taxable year beginning after December 31, 2012, a tax equal to 0.9 percent of the self-employment income for such taxable year which is in excess of—*

(i) *in the case of a joint return, $250,000,*

(ii) *in the case of a married taxpayer (as defined in section 7703) filing a separate return, ½ of the dollar amount determined under clause (i), and*

(iii) *in any other case, $200,000.*

(B) COORDINATION WITH FICA.—*The amounts under clause (i), (ii), or (iii) (whichever is applicable) of subparagraph (A) shall be reduced (but not below zero) by the amount of wages taken into account in determining the tax imposed under section 3121(b)(2) with respect to the taxpayer.*

* * *

[CCH Explanation at ¶ 230. Committee Reports at ¶ 10,300.]

Amendments

● **2010, Health Care and Education Reconciliation Act of 2010 (P.L. 111-152)**

P.L. 111-152, § 1402(b)(1)(B)(i)-(ii):

Amended Code Sec. 1401(b)(2), as added by section 9015 of the Patient Protection and Affordable Care Act (P.L. 111-148), and amended by section 10906 of such Act, by striking "and" at the end of clause (i), by redesignating clause (ii) as clause (iii), and by inserting after clause (i) a new clause (ii) in subparagraph (A); by striking "under clauses (i) and (ii)" and inserting "under clause (i), (ii), or (iii) (whichever is applicable)" in subparagraph (B). **Effective** with respect to remuneration received, and tax years beginning after, 12-31-2012.

● **2010, Patient Protection and Affordable Care Act (P.L. 111-148)**

P.L. 111-148, § 9015(b)(1)(A)-(B):

Amended Code Sec. 1401(b) by striking "In addition" and inserting:

"(1) IN GENERAL.—In addition",

and by adding at the end a new paragraph (2). **Effective** with respect to remuneration received, and tax years beginning, after 12-31-2012.

P.L. 111-148, § 10906(b):

Amended Code Sec. 1401(b)(2)(A), as added by Act Sec. 9015(b)(1), by striking "0.5 percent" and inserting "0.9 percent". **Effective** with respect to remuneration received, and tax years beginning, after 12-31-2012.

[¶ 5185] CODE SEC. 1402. DEFINITIONS.

(a) NET EARNINGS FROM SELF-EMPLOYMENT.—The term "net earnings from self-employment" means the gross income derived by an individual from any trade or business carried on by such individual, less the deductions allowed by this subtitle which are attributable to such trade or business, plus his distributive share (whether or not distributed) of income or loss described in section 702(a)(8) from any trade or business carried on by a partnership of which he is a member; except that in computing such gross income and deductions and such distributive share of partnership ordinary income or loss—

* * *

(12) in lieu of the deduction provided by section 164(f) (relating to deduction for one-half of self-employment taxes), there shall be allowed a deduction equal to the product of—

(A) the taxpayer's net earnings from self-employment for the taxable year (determined without regard to this paragraph), and

➤➤➤ *Caution: Code Sec. 1402(a)(12)(B), below, as amended by P.L. 111-148, applies with respect to remuneration received, and tax years beginning, after December 31, 2012.*

(B) one-half of the sum of the rates imposed by subsections (a) and (b) of section 1401 for such year (*determined without regard to the rate imposed under paragraph (2) of section 1401(b)*);

* * *

[CCH Explanation at ¶ 230. Committee Reports at ¶ 10,300.]

Amendments

• 2010, Patient Protection and Affordable Care Act (P.L. 111-148)

P.L. 111-148, § 9015(b)(2)(B):

Amended Code Sec. 1402(a)(12)(B) by inserting "(determined without regard to the rate imposed under paragraph

(2) of section 1401(b))" after "for such year". **Effective with** respect to remuneration received, and for tax years beginning, after 12-31-2012.

≫→ Caution: *Code Sec. 1411, below, as added by P.L. 111-152, applies to tax years beginning after December 31, 2012.*

[¶ 5187] *CODE SEC. 1411. IMPOSITION OF TAX.*

(a) In General.—Except as provided in subsection (e)—

(1) Application to individuals.—In the case of an individual, there is hereby imposed (in addition to any other tax imposed by this subtitle) for each taxable year a tax equal to 3.8 percent of the lesser of—

(A) net investment income for such taxable year, or

(B) the excess (if any) of—

(i) the modified adjusted gross income for such taxable year, over

(ii) the threshold amount.

(2) Application to estates and trusts.—In the case of an estate or trust, there is hereby imposed (in addition to any other tax imposed by this subtitle) for each taxable year a tax of 3.8 percent of the lesser of—

(A) the undistributed net investment income for such taxable year, or

(B) the excess (if any) of—

(i) the adjusted gross income (as defined in section 67(e)) for such taxable year, over

(ii) the dollar amount at which the highest tax bracket in section 1(e) begins for such taxable year.

(b) Threshold Amount.—For purposes of this chapter, the term "threshold amount" means—

(1) in the case of a taxpayer making a joint return under section 6013 or a surviving spouse (as defined in section 2(a)), $250,000,

(2) in the case of a married taxpayer (as defined in section 7703) filing a separate return, ½ of the dollar amount determined under paragraph (1), and

(3) in any other case, $200,000.

(c) Net Investment Income.—For purposes of this chapter—

(1) In general.—The term "net investment income" means the excess (if any) of—

(A) the sum of—

(i) gross income from interest, dividends, annuities, royalties, and rents, other than such income which is derived in the ordinary course of a trade or business not described in paragraph (2),

(ii) other gross income derived from a trade or business described in paragraph (2), and

(iii) net gain (to the extent taken into account in computing taxable income) attributable to the disposition of property other than property held in a trade or business not described in paragraph (2), over

(B) the deductions allowed by this subtitle which are properly allocable to such gross income or net gain.

(2) Trades and businesses to which tax applies.—A trade or business is described in this paragraph if such trade or business is—

(A) a passive activity (within the meaning of section 469) with respect to the taxpayer, or

(B) a trade or business of trading in financial instruments or commodities (as defined in section 475(e)(2)).

(3) INCOME ON INVESTMENT OF WORKING CAPITAL SUBJECT TO TAX.—A rule similar to the rule of section 469(e)(1)(B) shall apply for purposes of this subsection.

(4) EXCEPTION FOR CERTAIN ACTIVE INTERESTS IN PARTNERSHIPS AND S CORPORATIONS.—In the case of a disposition of an interest in a partnership or S corporation—

(A) gain from such disposition shall be taken into account under clause (iii) of paragraph (1)(A) only to the extent of the net gain which would be so taken into account by the transferor if all property of the partnership or S corporation were sold for fair market value immediately before the disposition of such interest, and

(B) a rule similar to the rule of subparagraph (A) shall apply to a loss from such disposition.

(5) EXCEPTION FOR DISTRIBUTIONS FROM QUALIFIED PLANS.—The term "net investment income" shall not include any distribution from a plan or arrangement described in section 401(a), 403(a), 403(b), 408, 408A, or 457(b).

(6) SPECIAL RULE.—Net investment income shall not include any item taken into account in determining self-employment income for such taxable year on which a tax is imposed by section 1401(b).

(d) MODIFIED ADJUSTED GROSS INCOME.—For purposes of this chapter, the term "modified adjusted gross income" means adjusted gross income increased by the excess of—

(1) the amount excluded from gross income under section 911(a)(1), over

(2) the amount of any deductions (taken into account in computing adjusted gross income) or exclusions disallowed under section 911(d)(6) with respect to the amounts described in paragraph (1).

(e) NONAPPLICATION OF SECTION.—This section shall not apply to—

(1) a nonresident alien, or

(2) a trust all of the unexpired interests in which are devoted to one or more of the purposes described in section 170(c)(2)(B).

[CCH Explanation at ¶ 232. Committee Reports at ¶ 10,410.]

Amendments

• 2010, Health Care and Education Reconciliation Act of 2010 (P.L. 111-152)

P.L. 111-152, § 1402(a)(1):

Amended subtitle A by inserting after chapter 2 a new chapter 2A (Code Sec. 1411). **Effective** for tax years beginning after 12-31-2012.

[¶ 5190] CODE SEC. 3101. RATE OF TAX.

* * *

⋙→ *Caution: Code Sec. 3101(b), below, as amended by P.L. 111-148 and P.L. 111-152, applies with respect to remuneration received, and tax years beginning, after December 31, 2012.*

(b) HOSPITAL INSURANCE.—

(1) IN GENERAL.—In addition to the tax imposed by the preceding subsection, there is hereby imposed on the income of every individual a tax equal to 1.45 percent of the wages (as defined in section 3121(a)) received by him with respect to employment (as defined in section 3121(b)).

(2) ADDITIONAL TAX.—In addition to the tax imposed by paragraph (1) and the preceding subsection, there is hereby imposed on every taxpayer (other than a corporation, estate, or trust) a tax equal to 0.9 percent of wages which are received with respect to employment (as defined in section 3121(b)) during any taxable year beginning after December 31, 2012, and which are in excess of—

(A) in the case of a joint return, $250,000,

(B) *in the case of a married taxpayer (as defined in section 7703) filing a separate return, ½ of the dollar amount determined under subparagraph (A), and*

(C) *in any other case, $200,000.*

* * *

[CCH Explanation at ¶230. Committee Reports at ¶10,300.]
Amendments

• **2010, Health Care and Education Reconciliation Act of 2010 (P.L. 111-152)**

P.L. 111-152, §1402(b)(1)(A):

Amended Code Sec. 3101(b)(2), as added by section 9015 of the Patient Protection and Affordable Care Act (P.L. 111-148), and amended by section 10906 of such Act, by striking "and" at the end of subparagraph (A), by redesignating subparagraph (B) as subparagraph (C), and by inserting after subparagraph (A) a new subparagraph (B). **Effective** with respect to remuneration received, and tax years beginning after, 12-31-2012.

• **2010, Patient Protection and Affordable Care Act (P.L. 111-148)**

P.L. 111-148, §9015(a)(1)(A)-(D):

Amended Code Sec. 3101(b) by striking "In addition" and inserting:

"(1) In GENERAL.—In addition",

by striking "the following percentages of the" and inserting "1.45 percent of the", by striking "(as defined in section 3121(b))—"and all that follows and inserting "(as defined in section 3121(b)).", and by adding at the end a new paragraph (2). **Effective** with respect to remuneration received, and tax years beginning, after 12-31-2012. Prior to amendment, Code Sec. 3101(b) read as follows:

(b) HOSPITAL INSURANCE.—In addition to the tax imposed by the preceding subsection, there is hereby imposed on the income of every individual a tax equal to the following percentages of the wages (as defined in section 3121(a)) received by him with respect to employment (as defined in section 3121(b))—

(1) with respect to wages received during the calendar years 1974 through 1977, the rate shall be 0.90 percent;

(2) with respect to wages received during the calendar year 1978, the rate shall be 1.00 percent;

(3) with respect to wages received during the calendar years 1979 and 1980, the rate shall be 1.05 percent;

(4) with respect to wages received during the calendar years 1981 through 1984, the rate shall be 1.30 percent;

(5) with respect to wages received during the calendar year 1985, the rate shall be 1.35 percent; and

(6) with respect to wages received after December 31, 1985, the rate shall be 1.45 percent.

P.L. 111-148, §10906(a):

Amended Code Sec. 3101(b)(2), as added by Act Sec. 9015(a)(1), by striking "0.5 percent" and inserting "0.9 percent". **Effective** with respect to remuneration received, and tax years beginning, after 12-31-2012.

[¶5195] CODE SEC. 3102. DEDUCTION OF TAX FROM WAGES.

* * *

»»→ *Caution: Code Sec. 3102(f), below, as added by P.L. 111-148, applies with respect to remuneration received, and tax years beginning, after December 31, 2012.*

(f) SPECIAL RULES FOR ADDITIONAL TAX.—

(1) IN GENERAL.—*In the case of any tax imposed by section 3101(b)(2), subsection (a) shall only apply to the extent to which the taxpayer receives wages from the employer in excess of $200,000, and the employer may disregard the amount of wages received by such taxpayer's spouse.*

(2) COLLECTION OF AMOUNTS NOT WITHHELD.—*To the extent that the amount of any tax imposed by section 3101(b)(2) is not collected by the employer, such tax shall be paid by the employee.*

(3) TAX PAID BY RECIPIENT.—*If an employer, in violation of this chapter, fails to deduct and withhold the tax imposed by section 3101(b)(2) and thereafter the tax is paid by the employee, the tax so required to be deducted and withheld shall not be collected from the employer, but this paragraph shall in no case relieve the employer from liability for any penalties or additions to tax otherwise applicable in respect of such failure to deduct and withhold.*

[CCH Explanation at ¶230. Committee Reports at ¶10,300.]
Amendments

• **2010, Patient Protection and Affordable Care Act (P.L. 111-148)**

P.L. 111-148, §9015(a)(2):

Amended Code Sec. 3102 by adding at the end a new subsection (f). **Effective** with respect to remuneration received, and tax years beginning, after 12-31-2012.

⬭→ *Caution: Code Sec. 4191, below, as added by P.L. 111-152, applies to sales after December 31, 2012.*

[¶5197] CODE SEC. 4191. MEDICAL DEVICES.

(a) IN GENERAL.—There is hereby imposed on the sale of any taxable medical device by the manufacturer, producer, or importer a tax equal to 2.3 percent of the price for which so sold.

(b) TAXABLE MEDICAL DEVICE.—For purposes of this section—

(1) IN GENERAL.—The term "taxable medical device" means any device (as defined in section 201(h) of the Federal Food, Drug, and Cosmetic Act) intended for humans.

(2) EXEMPTIONS.—Such term shall not include—

(A) eyeglasses,

(B) contact lenses,

(C) hearing aids, and

(D) any other medical device determined by the Secretary to be of a type which is generally purchased by the general public at retail for individual use.

[CCH Explanation at ¶350. Committee Reports at ¶10,420.]
Amendments
• **2010, Health Care and Education Reconciliation Act of 2010 (P.L. 111-152)**

P.L. 111-152, §1405(a)(1):

Amended chapter 32 by inserting after subchapter D a new subchapter E (Code Sec. 4191). **Effective** for sales after 12-31-2012.

[¶5198] CODE SEC. 4221. CERTAIN TAX-FREE SALES.

(a) GENERAL RULE.—Under regulations prescribed by the Secretary, no tax shall be imposed under this chapter (other than under section 4121 or 4081) on the sale by the manufacturer (or under subchapter A or C of chapter 31 on the first retail sale) of an article—

(1) for use by the purchaser for further manufacture, or for resale by the purchaser to a second purchaser for use by such second purchaser in further manufacture,

(2) for export, or for resale by the purchaser to a second purchaser for export,

(3) for use by the purchaser as supplies for vessels or aircraft,

(4) to a State or local government for the exclusive use of a State or local government,

(5) to a nonprofit educational organization for its exclusive use, or

(6) to a qualified blood collector organization (as defined in section 7701(a)(49)) for such organization's exclusive use in the collection, storage, or transportation of blood,

⬭→ *Caution: The last sentence of Code Sec. 4221(a), below, as added by P.L. 111-152, applies to sales after December 31, 2012.*

but only if such exportation or use is to occur before any other use. Paragraphs (4), (5), and (6) shall not apply to the tax imposed by section 4064. In the case of taxes imposed by section 4051 or 4071, paragraphs (4) and (5) shall not apply on and after October 1, 2011. In the case of the tax imposed by section 4131, paragraphs (3), (4), and (5) shall not apply and paragraph (2) shall apply only if the use of the exported vaccine meets such requirements as the Secretary may by regulations prescribe. In the case of taxes imposed by subchapter A of chapter 31, paragraphs (1), (3), (4), and (5) shall not apply. In the case of taxes imposed by subchapter C or D, paragraph (6) shall not apply. *In the case of the tax imposed by section 4191, paragraphs (3), (4), (5), and (6) shall not apply.*

* * *

[CCH Explanation at ¶350. Committee Reports at ¶10,420.]
Amendments

• **2010, Health Care and Education Reconciliation Act of 2010 (P.L. 111-152)**

P.L. 111-152, §1405(b)(1):
Amended Code Sec. 4221(a) by adding at the end a new sentence. **Effective** for sales after 12-31-2012.

[¶5200] *CODE SEC. 4375. HEALTH INSURANCE.*

(a) IMPOSITION OF FEE.—There is hereby imposed on each specified health insurance policy for each policy year ending after September 30, 2012, a fee equal to the product of $2 ($1 in the case of policy years ending during fiscal year 2013) multiplied by the average number of lives covered under the policy.

(b) LIABILITY FOR FEE.—The fee imposed by subsection (a) shall be paid by the issuer of the policy.

(c) SPECIFIED HEALTH INSURANCE POLICY.—For purposes of this section:

(1) IN GENERAL.—Except as otherwise provided in this section, the term "specified health insurance policy" means any accident or health insurance policy (including a policy under a group health plan) issued with respect to individuals residing in the United States.

(2) EXEMPTION FOR CERTAIN POLICIES.—The term "specified health insurance policy" does not include any insurance if substantially all of its coverage is of excepted benefits described in section 9832(c).

(3) TREATMENT OF PREPAID HEALTH COVERAGE ARRANGEMENTS.—

(A) IN GENERAL.—In the case of any arrangement described in subparagraph (B), such arrangement shall be treated as a specified health insurance policy, and the person referred to in such subparagraph shall be treated as the issuer.

(B) DESCRIPTION OF ARRANGEMENTS.—An arrangement is described in this subparagraph if under such arrangement fixed payments or premiums are received as consideration for any person's agreement to provide or arrange for the provision of accident or health coverage to residents of the United States, regardless of how such coverage is provided or arranged to be provided.

(d) ADJUSTMENTS FOR INCREASES IN HEALTH CARE SPENDING.—In the case of any policy year ending in any fiscal year beginning after September 30, 2014, the dollar amount in effect under subsection (a) for such policy year shall be equal to the sum of such dollar amount for policy years ending in the previous fiscal year (determined after the application of this subsection), plus an amount equal to the product of—

(1) such dollar amount for policy years ending in the previous fiscal year, multiplied by

(2) the percentage increase in the projected per capita amount of National Health Expenditures, as most recently published by the Secretary before the beginning of the fiscal year.

(e) TERMINATION.—This section shall not apply to policy years ending after September 30, 2019.

[CCH Explanation at ¶445. Committee Reports at ¶10,150.]
Amendments

• **2010, Patient Protection and Affordable Care Act (P.L. 111-148)**

P.L. 111-148, §6301(e)(2)(A):
Amended chapter 34 by adding at the end a new subchapter B [sic] (Code Secs. 4375-4377). **Effective** 3-23-2010.

[¶5205] *CODE SEC. 4376. SELF-INSURED HEALTH PLANS.*

(a) IMPOSITION OF FEE.—In the case of any applicable self-insured health plan for each plan year ending after September 30, 2012, there is hereby imposed a fee equal to $2 ($1 in the case of plan years ending during fiscal year 2013) multiplied by the average number of lives covered under the plan.

(b) LIABILITY FOR FEE.—

(1) IN GENERAL.—The fee imposed by subsection (a) shall be paid by the plan sponsor.

(2) *PLAN SPONSOR.—For purposes of paragraph (1) the term "plan sponsor" means—*

(A) the employer in the case of a plan established or maintained by a single employer,

(B) the employee organization in the case of a plan established or maintained by an employee organization,

(C) in the case of—

(i) a plan established or maintained by 2 or more employers or jointly by 1 or more employers and 1 or more employee organizations,

(ii) a multiple employer welfare arrangement, or

(iii) a voluntary employees' beneficiary association described in section 501(c)(9), the association, committee, joint board of trustees, or other similar group of representatives of the parties who establish or maintain the plan, or

(D) the cooperative or association described in subsection (c)(2)(F) in the case of a plan established or maintained by such a cooperative or association.

(c) *APPLICABLE SELF-INSURED HEALTH PLAN.—For purposes of this section, the term "applicable self-insured health plan" means any plan for providing accident or health coverage if—*

(1) any portion of such coverage is provided other than through an insurance policy, and

(2) such plan is established or maintained—

(A) by 1 or more employers for the benefit of their employees or former employees,

(B) by 1 or more employee organizations for the benefit of their members or former members,

(C) jointly by 1 or more employers and 1 or more employee organizations for the benefit of employees or former employees,

(D) by a voluntary employees' beneficiary association described in section 501(c)(9),

(E) by any organization described in section 501(c)(6), or

(F) in the case of a plan not described in the preceding subparagraphs, by a multiple employer welfare arrangement (as defined in section 3(40) of [the] Employee Retirement Income Security Act of 1974), a rural electric cooperative (as defined in section 3(40)(B)(iv) of such Act), or a rural telephone cooperative association (as defined in section 3(40)(B)(v) of such Act).

(d) *ADJUSTMENTS FOR INCREASES IN HEALTH CARE SPENDING.—In the case of any plan year ending in any fiscal year beginning after September 30, 2014, the dollar amount in effect under subsection (a) for such plan year shall be equal to the sum of such dollar amount for plan years ending in the previous fiscal year (determined after the application of this subsection), plus an amount equal to the product of—*

(1) such dollar amount for plan years ending in the previous fiscal year, multiplied by

(2) the percentage increase in the projected per capita amount of National Health Expenditures, as most recently published by the Secretary before the beginning of the fiscal year.

(e) *TERMINATION.—This section shall not apply to plan years ending after September 30, 2019.*

[CCH Explanation at ¶445. Committee Reports at ¶10,150.]
Amendments
• **2010, Patient Protection and Affordable Care Act**
(P.L. 111-148)

P.L. 111-148, §6301(e)(2)(A):

Amended chapter 34 by adding at the end a new subchapter B [sic] (Code Secs. 4375-4377). **Effective** 3-23-2010.

[¶5210] *CODE SEC. 4377. DEFINITIONS AND SPECIAL RULES.*

(a) *DEFINITIONS.—For purposes of this subchapter—*

(1) *ACCIDENT AND HEALTH COVERAGE.—The term "accident and health coverage" means any coverage which, if provided by an insurance policy, would cause such policy to be a specified health insurance policy (as defined in section 4375(c)).*

(2) INSURANCE POLICY.—*The term "insurance policy" means any policy or other instrument whereby a contract of insurance is issued, renewed, or extended.*

(3) UNITED STATES.—*The term "United States" includes any possession of the United States.*

(b) TREATMENT OF GOVERNMENTAL ENTITIES.—

(1) IN GENERAL.—*For purposes of this subchapter—*

(A) *the term "person" includes any governmental entity, and*

(B) *notwithstanding any other law or rule of law, governmental entities shall not be exempt from the fees imposed by this subchapter except as provided in paragraph (2).*

(2) TREATMENT OF EXEMPT GOVERNMENTAL PROGRAMS.—*In the case of an exempt governmental program, no fee shall be imposed under section 4375 or section 4376 on any covered life under such program.*

(3) EXEMPT GOVERNMENTAL PROGRAM DEFINED.—*For purposes of this subchapter, the term "exempt governmental program" means—*

(A) *any insurance program established under title XVIII of the Social Security Act,*

(B) *the medical assistance program established by title XIX or XXI of the Social Security Act,*

(C) *any program established by Federal law for providing medical care (other than through insurance policies) to individuals (or the spouses and dependents thereof) by reason of such individuals being members of the Armed Forces of the United States or veterans, and*

(D) *any program established by Federal law for providing medical care (other than through insurance policies) to members of Indian tribes (as defined in section 4(d) of the Indian Health Care Improvement Act).*

(c) TREATMENT AS TAX.—*For purposes of subtitle F, the fees imposed by this subchapter shall be treated as if they were taxes.*

(d) NO COVER OVER TO POSSESSIONS.—*Notwithstanding any other provision of law, no amount collected under this subchapter shall be covered over to any possession of the United States.*

[CCH Explanation at ¶445. Committee Reports at ¶10,150.]

Amendments
• **2010, Patient Protection and Affordable Care Act (P.L. 111-148)**

P.L. 111-148, §6301(e)(2)(A):

Amended chapter 34 by adding at the end a new subchapter B [sic] (Code Secs. 4375-4377). **Effective 3-23-2010.**

[¶5215] CODE SEC. 4958. TAXES ON EXCESS BENEFIT TRANSACTIONS.

* * *

(e) APPLICABLE TAX-EXEMPT ORGANIZATION.—For purposes of this subchapter, the term "applicable tax-exempt organization" means—

(1) any organization which (without regard to any excess benefit) would be described in *paragraph (3), (4), or (29)* of section 501(c) and exempt from tax under section 501(a), and

(2) any organization which was described in paragraph (1) at any time during the 5-year period ending on the date of the transaction.

Such term shall not include a private foundation (as defined in section 509(a)).

* * *

[CCH Explanation at ¶435. Committee Reports at ¶10,010.]
Amendments
• 2010, Patient Protection and Affordable Care Act
(P.L. 111-148)

P.L. 111-148, §1322(h)(3):
Amended Code Sec. 4958(e)(1) by striking "paragraph (3) or (4)" and inserting "paragraph (3), (4), or (29)". Effective 3-23-2010.

[¶5220] CODE SEC. 4959. TAXES ON FAILURES BY HOSPITAL ORGANIZATIONS.

If a hospital organization to which section 501(r) applies fails to meet the requirement of section 501(r)(3) for any taxable year, there is imposed on the organization a tax equal to $50,000.

[CCH Explanation at ¶440. Committee Reports at ¶10,220.]
Amendments
• 2010, Patient Protection and Affordable Care Act
(P.L. 111-148)

P.L. 111-148, §9007(b)(1):
Amended subchapter D of chapter 42 by adding at the end a new Code Sec. 4959. Effective for failures occurring after 3-23-2010.

≫→ *Caution: Code Sec. 4980H, below, as added and amended by P.L. 111-148, applies to months beginning after December 31, 2013.*

[¶5225] CODE SEC. 4980H. SHARED RESPONSIBILITY FOR EMPLOYERS REGARDING HEALTH COVERAGE.

(a) LARGE EMPLOYERS NOT OFFERING HEALTH COVERAGE.—If—

(1) any applicable large employer fails to offer to its full-time employees (and their dependents) the opportunity to enroll in minimum essential coverage under an eligible employer-sponsored plan (as defined in section 5000A(f)(2)) for any month, and

(2) at least one full-time employee of the applicable large employer has been certified to the employer under section 1411 of the Patient Protection and Affordable Care Act as having enrolled for such month in a qualified health plan with respect to which an applicable premium tax credit or cost-sharing reduction is allowed or paid with respect to the employee,

then there is hereby imposed on the employer an assessable payment equal to the product of the applicable payment amount and the number of individuals employed by the employer as full-time employees during such month.

(b) [Stricken.]

[CCH Explanation at ¶305. Committee Reports at ¶10,100.]
Amendments
• 2010, Health Care and Education Reconciliation Act of 2010 (P.L. 111-152)

P.L. 111-152, §1003(d):
Amended Code Sec. 4980H, as added by section 1513 of the Patient Protection and Affordable Care Act (P.L. 111-148) and amended by section 10106 of such Act, and as amended by Act Sec. 1003(a)-(c) of this Act, by striking subsection (b) and redesignating subsections (c), (d), and (e) as subsections (b), (c), and (d), respectively. Effective 3-30-2010. Prior to being stricken, Code Sec. 4980H(b) read as follows:

(b) LARGE EMPLOYERS WITH WAITING PERIODS EXCEEDING 60 DAYS.—

(1) IN GENERAL.—In the case of any applicable large employer which requires an extended waiting period to enroll in any minimum essential coverage under an employer-sponsored plan (as defined in section 5000A(f)(2)), there is

hereby imposed on the employer an assessable payment of $600 for each full-time employee of the employer to whom the extended waiting period applies.

(2) EXTENDED WAITING PERIOD.—The term "extended waiting period" means any waiting period (as defined in section 2701(b)(4) of the Public Health Service Act) which exceeds 60 days.

• 2010, Patient Protection and Affordable Care Act (P.L. 111-148)

P.L. 111-148, §10106(e):
Amended Code Sec. 4980H(b), as added by Act Sec. 1513(a). Effective 3-23-2010. Prior to amendment, Code Sec. 4980H(b) read as follows:

(b) LARGE EMPLOYERS WITH WAITING PERIODS EXCEEDING 30 DAYS.—

(1) IN GENERAL.—In the case of any applicable large employer which requires an extended waiting period to enroll

in any minimum essential coverage under an employer-sponsored plan (as defined in section 5000A(f)(2)), there is hereby imposed on the employer an assessable payment, in the amount specified in paragraph (2), for each full-time employee of the employer to whom the extended waiting period applies.

(2) AMOUNT.—For purposes of paragraph (1), the amount specified in this paragraph for a full-time employee is—

(A) in the case of an extended waiting period which exceeds 30 days but does not exceed 60 days, $400, and

(B) in the case of an extended waiting period which exceeds 60 days, $600.

(3) EXTENDED WAITING PERIOD.—The term "extended waiting period" means any waiting period (as defined in section 2701(b)(4) of the Public Health Service Act) which exceeds 30 days.

(b) LARGE EMPLOYERS OFFERING COVERAGE WITH EMPLOYEES WHO QUALIFY FOR PREMIUM TAX CREDITS OR COST-SHARING REDUCTIONS.—

(1) IN GENERAL.—If—

(A) an applicable large employer offers to its full-time employees (and their dependents) the opportunity to enroll in minimum essential coverage under an eligible employer-sponsored plan (as defined in section 5000A(f)(2)) for any month, and

(B) 1 or more full-time employees of the applicable large employer has been certified to the employer under section 1411 of the Patient Protection and Affordable Care Act as having enrolled for such month in a qualified health plan with respect to which an applicable premium tax credit or cost-sharing reduction is allowed or paid with respect to the employee,

then there is hereby imposed on the employer an assessable payment equal to the product of the number of full-time employees of the applicable large employer described in subparagraph (B) for such month and an amount equal to $\frac{1}{12}$ of $3,000.

(2) OVERALL LIMITATION.—The aggregate amount of tax determined under paragraph (1) with respect to all employees of an applicable large employer for any month shall not exceed the product of the applicable payment amount and the number of individuals employed by the employer as full-time employees during such month.

(3) SPECIAL RULES FOR EMPLOYERS PROVIDING FREE CHOICE VOUCHERS.—No assessable payment shall be imposed under paragraph (1) for any month with respect to any employee to whom the employer provides a free choice voucher under section 10108 of the Patient Protection and Affordable Care Act for such month.

[CCH Explanation at ¶305 and ¶315. Committee Reports at ¶10,100 and ¶10,370.]

Amendments

• **2010, Health Care and Education Reconciliation Act of 2010 (P.L. 111-152)**

P.L. 111-152, §1003(b)(1):

Amended Code Sec. 4980H, as added by section 1513 of the Patient Protection and Affordable Care Act (P.L. 111-148) and amended by section 10106 of such Act, in the flush text following subsection (c)(1)(B), by striking "400 percent of the applicable payment amount" and inserting "an amount equal to ¹/₁₂ of $3,000". **Effective 3-30-2010.**

P.L. 111-152, §1003(d):

Amended Code Sec. 4980H, as added by section 1513 of the Patient Protection and Affordable Care Act (P.L.

111-148) and amended by section 10106 of such Act, and as amended by Act Sec. 1003(a)-(c) of this Act, by redesignating subsection (c) as subsection (b). **Effective 3-30-2010.**

• **2010, Patient Protection and Affordable Care Act (P.L. 111-148)**

P.L. 111-148, §10108(i)(1)(A):

Amended Code Sec. 4980H(c), as added by Act Sec. 1513, by adding at the end a new paragraph (3). **Effective for months beginning after 12-31-2013.**

(c) DEFINITIONS AND SPECIAL RULES.—For purposes of this section—

(1) APPLICABLE PAYMENT AMOUNT.—The term "applicable payment amount" means, with respect to any month, $\frac{1}{12}$ of $2,000.

(2) APPLICABLE LARGE EMPLOYER.—

(A) IN GENERAL.—The term "applicable large employer" means, with respect to a calendar year, an employer who employed an average of at least 50 full-time employees on business days during the preceding calendar year.

(B) EXEMPTION FOR CERTAIN EMPLOYERS.—

(i) IN GENERAL.—An employer shall not be considered to employ more than 50 full-time employees if—

(I) the employer's workforce exceeds 50 full-time employees for 120 days or fewer during the calendar year, and

(II) the employees in excess of 50 employed during such 120-day period were seasonal workers.

(ii) DEFINITION OF SEASONAL WORKERS.—The term "seasonal worker" means a worker who performs labor or services on a seasonal basis as defined by the Secretary of Labor, including workers covered by section 500.20(s)(1) of title 29, Code of Federal Regulations and retail workers employed exclusively during holiday seasons.

(C) RULES FOR DETERMINING EMPLOYER SIZE.—For purposes of this paragraph—

(i) APPLICATION OF AGGREGATION RULE FOR EMPLOYERS.—All persons treated as a single employer under subsection (b), (c), (m), or (o) of section 414 of the Internal Revenue Code of 1986 shall be treated as 1 employer.

(ii) EMPLOYERS NOT IN EXISTENCE IN PRECEDING YEAR.—In the case of an employer which was not in existence throughout the preceding calendar year, the determination of whether such employer is an applicable large employer shall be based on the average number of employees that it is reasonably expected such employer will employ on business days in the current calendar year.

(iii) PREDECESSORS.—Any reference in this subsection to an employer shall include a reference to any predecessor of such employer.

(D) APPLICATION OF EMPLOYER SIZE TO ASSESSABLE PENALTIES.—

(i) IN GENERAL.—The number of individuals employed by an applicable large employer as full-time employees during any month shall be reduced by 30 solely for purposes of calculating—

(I) the assessable payment under subsection (a), or

(II) the overall limitation under subsection (b)(2).

(ii) AGGREGATION.—In the case of persons treated as 1 employer under subparagraph (C)(i), only 1 reduction under subclause (I) or (II) shall be allowed with respect to such persons and such reduction shall be allocated among such persons ratably on the basis of the number of full-time employees employed by each such person.

(E) FULL-TIME EQUIVALENTS TREATED AS FULL-TIME EMPLOYEES.—Solely for purposes of determining whether an employer is an applicable large employer under this paragraph, an employer shall, in addition to the number of full-time employees for any month otherwise determined, include for such month a number of full-time employees determined by dividing the aggregate number of hours of service of employees who are not full-time employees for the month by 120.

(3) APPLICABLE PREMIUM TAX CREDIT AND COST-SHARING REDUCTION.—The term "applicable premium tax credit and cost-sharing reduction" means—

(A) any premium tax credit allowed under section 36B,

(B) any cost-sharing reduction under section 1402 of the Patient Protection and Affordable Care Act, and

(C) any advance payment of such credit or reduction under section 1412 of such Act.

(4) FULL-TIME EMPLOYEE.—

(A) IN GENERAL.—The term "full-time employee" means, with respect to any month, an employee who is employed on average at least 30 hours of service per week.

(B) HOURS OF SERVICE.—The Secretary, in consultation with the Secretary of Labor, shall prescribe such regulations, rules, and guidance as may be necessary to determine the hours of service of an employee, including rules for the application of this paragraph to employees who are not compensated on an hourly basis.

(5) INFLATION ADJUSTMENT.—

(A) IN GENERAL.—*In the case of any calendar year after 2014, each of the dollar amounts in subsection (b) and paragraph (1) shall be increased by an amount equal to the product of—*

(i) *such dollar amount, and*

(ii) *the premium adjustment percentage (as defined in section 1302(c)(4) of the Patient Protection and Affordable Care Act) for the calendar year.*

(B) ROUNDING.—*If the amount of any increase under subparagraph (A) is not a multiple of $10, such increase shall be rounded to the next lowest multiple of $10.*

(6) OTHER DEFINITIONS.—*Any term used in this section which is also used in the Patient Protection and Affordable Care Act shall have the same meaning as when used in such Act.*

(7) TAX NONDEDUCTIBLE.—*For denial of deduction for the tax imposed by this section, see section 275(a)(6).*

[CCH Explanation at ¶ 305.]

Amendments

• **2010, Health Care and Education Reconciliation Act of 2010 (P.L. 111-152)**

P.L. 111-152, § 1003(a):

Amended subsection (d)(2)(D) of Code Sec. 4980H, as added by section 1513 of the Patient Protection and Affordable Care Act (P.L. 111-148) and amended by section 10106 of such Act. **Effective** 3-30-2010. Prior to amendment, Code Sec. 4980H(d)(2)(D) read as follows:

(D) APPLICATION TO CONSTRUCTION INDUSTRY EMPLOYERS.—In the case of any employer the substantial annual gross receipts of which are attributable to the construction industry—

(i) subparagraph (A) shall be applied by substituting "who employed an average of at least 5 full-time employees on business days during the preceding calendar year and whose annual payroll expenses exceed $250,000 for such preceding calendar year" for "who employed an average of at least 50 full-time employees on business days during the preceding calendar year", and

(ii) subparagraph (B) shall be applied by substituting "5" for "50".

P.L. 111-152, § 1003(b)(2):

Amended Code Sec. 4980H, as added by section 1513 of the Patient Protection and Affordable Care Act (P.L. 111-148) and amended by section 10106 of such Act, in subsection (d)(1), by striking "$750" and inserting "$2,000". **Effective** 3-30-2010.

P.L. 111-152, § 1003(b)(3):

Amended Code Sec. 4980H, as added by section 1513 of the Patient Protection and Affordable Care Act (P.L.

111-148) and amended by section 10106 of such Act, in the matter preceding clause (i) of subsection (d)(5)(A), by striking "subsection (b)(2) and (d)(1)" and inserting "subsection (b) and paragraph (1)". **Effective** 3-30-2010.

P.L. 111-152, § 1003(c):

Amended Code Sec. 4980H(d)(2), as added by section 1513 of the Patient Protection and Affordable Care Act (P.L. 111-148) and amended by section 10106 of such Act and as amended by Act Sec. 1003(a), by adding at the end a new subparagraph (E). **Effective** 3-30-2010.

P.L. 111-152, § 1003(d):

Amended Code Sec. 4980H, as added by section 1513 of the Patient Protection and Affordable Care Act (P.L. 111-148) and amended by section 10106 of such Act, and as amended by Act Sec. 1003(a)-(c) of this Act, by redesignating subsection (d) as subsection (c). **Effective** 3-30-2010.

• **2010, Patient Protection and Affordable Care Act (P.L. 111-148)**

P.L. 111-148, § 10106(f)(1):

Amended Code Sec. 4980H(d)(4)(A), as added by Act Sec. 1513(a), by inserting ", with respect to any month," after "means". **Effective** 3-23-2010.

P.L. 111-148, § 10106(f)(2):

Amended Code Sec. 4980H(d)(2), as added by Act Sec. 1513(a), by adding at the end a new subparagraph (D). **Effective** for months beginning after 12-31-2013.

(d) ADMINISTRATION AND PROCEDURE.—

(1) IN GENERAL.—*Any assessable payment provided by this section shall be paid upon notice and demand by the Secretary, and shall be assessed and collected in the same manner as an assessable penalty under subchapter B of chapter 68.*

(2) TIME FOR PAYMENT.—*The Secretary may provide for the payment of any assessable payment provided by this section on an annual, monthly, or other periodic basis as the Secretary may prescribe.*

(3) COORDINATION WITH CREDITS, ETC.—*The Secretary shall prescribe rules, regulations, or guidance for the repayment of any assessable payment (including interest) if such payment is based on the allowance or payment of an applicable premium tax credit or cost-sharing reduction with respect to an employee, such allowance or payment is subsequently disallowed, and the assessable payment would not have been required to be made but for such allowance or payment.*

[CCH Explanation at ¶ 305. Committee Reports at ¶ 10,100.]

Amendments

• **2010, Health Care and Education Reconciliation Act of 2010 (P.L. 111-152)**

P.L. 111-152, § 1003(d):

Amended Code Sec. 4980H, as added by section 1513 of the Patient Protection and Affordable Care Act (P.L. 111-148) and amended by section 10106 of such Act, and as amended by Act Sec. 1003(a)-(c) of this Act, by redesignating subsection (e) as subsection (d). **Effective** 3-30-2010.

• **2010, Patient Protection and Affordable Care Act (P.L. 111-148)**

P.L. 111-148, § 1513(a):

Amended chapter 43 by adding at the end a new Code Sec. 4980H. **Effective** for months beginning after 12-31-2013.

»»→ Caution: *Code Sec. 4980I, below, as added and amended by P.L. 111-148 , applies to tax years beginning after December 31, 2017.*

[¶ 5230] *CODE SEC. 4980I. EXCISE TAX ON HIGH COST EMPLOYER-SPONSORED HEALTH COVERAGE.*

(a) *IMPOSITION OF TAX.—If—*

(1) *an employee is covered under any applicable employer-sponsored coverage of an employer at any time during a taxable period, and*

(2) *there is any excess benefit with respect to the coverage,*

there is hereby imposed a tax equal to 40 percent of the excess benefit.

(b) *EXCESS BENEFIT.—For purposes of this section—*

(1) *IN GENERAL.—The term "excess benefit" means, with respect to any applicable employer-sponsored coverage made available by an employer to an employee during any taxable period, the sum of the excess amounts determined under paragraph (2) for months during the taxable period.*

(2) *MONTHLY EXCESS AMOUNT.—The excess amount determined under this paragraph for any month is the excess (if any) of—*

(A) *the aggregate cost of the applicable employer-sponsored coverage of the employee for the month, over*

(B) *an amount equal to ¹⁄₁₂ of the annual limitation under paragraph (3) for the calendar year in which the month occurs.*

(3) *ANNUAL LIMITATION.—For purposes of this subsection—*

(A) *IN GENERAL.—The annual limitation under this paragraph for any calendar year is the dollar limit determined under subparagraph (C) for the calendar year.*

(B) *APPLICABLE ANNUAL LIMITATION.—*

(i) *IN GENERAL.—Except as provided in clause (ii), the annual limitation which applies for any month shall be determined on the basis of the type of coverage (as determined under subsection (f)(1)) provided to the employee by the employer as of the beginning of the month.*

(ii) *MULTIEMPLOYER PLAN COVERAGE.—Any coverage provided under a multiemployer plan (as defined in section 414(f)) shall be treated as coverage other than self-only coverage.*

(C) *APPLICABLE DOLLAR LIMIT.—*

(i) *2018.—In the case of 2018, the dollar limit under this subparagraph is—*

(I) *in the case of an employee with self-only coverage, $10,200 multiplied by the health cost adjustment percentage (determined by only taking into account self-only coverage), and*

(II) *in the case of an employee with coverage other than self-only coverage, $27,500 multiplied by the health cost adjustment percentage (determined by only taking into account coverage other than self-only coverage).*

(ii) *HEALTH COST ADJUSTMENT PERCENTAGE.—For purposes of clause (i), the health cost adjustment percentage is equal to 100 percent plus the excess (if any) of—*

(I) *the percentage by which the per employee cost for providing coverage under the Blue Cross/Blue Shield standard benefit option under the Federal Employees Health Benefits Plan for plan year 2018 (determined by using the benefit package for such coverage in 2010) exceeds such cost for plan year 2010, over*

(II) *55 percent.*

(iii) AGE AND GENDER ADJUSTMENT.—

(I) IN GENERAL.—*The amount determined under subclause (I) or (II) of clause (i), whichever is applicable, for any taxable period shall be increased by the amount determined under subclause (II).*

(II) AMOUNT DETERMINED.—*The amount determined under this subclause is an amount equal to the excess (if any) of—*

(aa) *the premium cost of the Blue Cross/Blue Shield standard benefit option under the Federal Employees Health Benefits Plan for the type of coverage provided such individual in such taxable period if priced for the age and gender characteristics of all employees of the individual's employer, over*

(bb) *that premium cost for the provision of such coverage under such option in such taxable period if priced for the age and gender characteristics of the national workforce.*

(iv) EXCEPTION FOR CERTAIN INDIVIDUALS.—*In the case of an individual who is a qualified retiree or who participates in a plan sponsored by an employer the majority of whose employees covered by the plan are engaged in a high-risk profession or employed to repair or install electrical or telecommunications lines—*

(I) *the dollar amount in clause (i)(I) shall be increased by $1,650, and*

(II) *the dollar amount in clause (i)(II) shall be increased by $3,450,*

(v) SUBSEQUENT YEARS.—*In the case of any calendar year after 2018, each of the dollar amounts under clauses (i) (after the application of clause (ii)) and (iv) shall be increased to the amount equal to such amount as in effect for the calendar year preceding such year, increased by an amount equal to the product of—*

(I) *such amount as so in effect, multiplied by*

(II) *the cost-of-living adjustment determined under section 1(f)(3) for such year (determined by substituting the calendar year that is 2 years before such year for "1992" in subparagraph (B) thereof), increased by 1 percentage point in the case of determinations for calendar years beginning before 2020.*

If any amount determined under this clause is not a multiple of $50, such amount shall be rounded to the nearest multiple of $50.

(D) [Stricken.]

[CCH Explanation at ¶ 345.]

Amendments

• **2010, Health Care and Education Reconciliation Act of 2010 (P.L. 111-152)**

P.L. 111-152, § 1401(a)(1)(A)-(B):

Amended Code Sec. 4980I, as added by section 9001 of the Patient Protection and Affordable Care Act (P.L. 111-148), and amended by section 10901 of such Act, by striking "The annual" in subsection (b)(3)(B) and inserting:

"(i) IN GENERAL.—Except as provided in clause (ii), the annual";

and by adding at the end a new clause (ii). **Effective** 3-30-2010.

P.L. 111-152, § 1401(a)(2)(A)-(E):

Amended Code Sec. 4980I, as added by section 9001 of the Patient Protection and Affordable Care Act (P.L. 111-148)

and amended by section 10901 of such Act, by striking "Except as provided in subparagraph (D)—"in subsection (b)(3)(C); by striking "2013" in clause (i) of subsection (b)(3)(C) each place it appears in the heading and the text and inserting "2018"; by striking "$8,500" in subclause (I) and inserting "$10,200 multiplied by the health cost adjustment percentage (determined by only taking into account self-only coverage)"; and by striking "$23,000" in subclause (II) and inserting "$27,500 multiplied by the health cost adjustment percentage (determined by only taking into account coverage other than self-only coverage)"; by redesignating clauses (ii) and (iii) of subsection (b)(3)(C) as clauses (iv) and (v), respectively, and by inserting after clause (i) new clauses (ii) and (iii); in clause (iv) of subsection (b)(3)(C), as redesignated by Act Sec. 1401(a)(2)(C), by inserting "covered by the plan" after "whose employees"; and by striking subclauses (I) and (II) and inserting new subclauses (I) and (II); in clause (v) of subsection (b)(3)(C), as redesignated by Act Sec. 1401(a)(2)(C), by striking "2013" and inserting "2018"; by striking "clauses (i) and (ii)" and inserting "clauses (i) (after the application of clause (ii)) and (iv)"; and by inserting "in the case of determinations for calendar years beginning before 2020" after "1 percentage point" in subclause (II) thereof. **Effective** 3-30-2010. Prior to amendment, Code Sec. 4980I(b)(3)(C) read as follows:

(C) APPLICABLE DOLLAR LIMIT.—Except as provided in subparagraph (D)—

(i) 2013.—In the case of 2013, the dollar limit under this subparagraph is—

(I) in the case of an employee with self-only coverage, $8,500, and

(II) in the case of an employee with coverage other than self-only coverage, $23,000.

(ii) EXCEPTION FOR CERTAIN INDIVIDUALS.—In the case of an individual who is a qualified retiree or who participates in a plan sponsored by an employer the majority of whose employees are engaged in a high-risk profession or employed to repair or install electrical or telecommunications lines—

(I) the dollar amount in clause (i)(I) (determined after the application of subparagraph (D)) shall be increased by $1,350, and

(II) the dollar amount in clause (i)(II) (determined after the application of subparagraph (D)) shall be increased by $3,000.

(iii) SUBSEQUENT YEARS.—In the case of any calendar year after 2013, each of the dollar amounts under clauses (i) and (ii) shall be increased to the amount equal to such amount as in effect for the calendar year preceding such year, increased by an amount equal to the product of—

(I) such amount as so in effect, multiplied by

(II) the cost-of-living adjustment determined under section 1(f)(3) for such year (determined by substituting the

calendar year that is 2 years before such year for "1992" in subparagraph (B) thereof), increased by 1 percentage point.

If any amount determined under this clause is not a multiple of $50, such amount shall be rounded to the nearest multiple of $50.

P.L. 111-152, § 1401(a)(3):

Amended Code Sec. 4980I, as added by section 9001 of the Patient Protection and Affordable Care Act (P.L. 111-148) and amended by section 10901 of such Act, by striking subparagraph (D) of subsection (b)(3). **Effective** 3-30-2010. Prior to being stricken, Code Sec. 4980I(b)(3)(D) read as follows:

(D) TRANSITION RULE FOR STATES WITH HIGHEST COVERAGE COSTS.—

(i) IN GENERAL.—If an employee is a resident of a high cost State on the first day of any month beginning in 2013, 2014, or 2015, the annual limitation under this paragraph for such month with respect to such employee shall be an amount equal to the applicable percentage of the annual limitation (determined without regard to this subparagraph or subparagraph (C)(ii)).

(ii) APPLICABLE PERCENTAGE.—The applicable percentage is 120 percent for 2013, 110 percent for 2014, and 105 percent for 2015.

(iii) HIGH COST STATE.—The term "high cost State" means each of the 17 States which the Secretary of Health and Human Services, in consultation with the Secretary, estimates had the highest average cost during 2012 for employer-sponsored coverage under health plans. The Secretary's estimate shall be made on the basis of aggregate premiums paid in the State for such health plans, determined using the most recent data available as of August 31, 2012.

(c) LIABILITY TO PAY TAX.—

(1) IN GENERAL.—Each coverage provider shall pay the tax imposed by subsection (a) on its applicable share of the excess benefit with respect to an employee for any taxable period.

(2) COVERAGE PROVIDER.—For purposes of this subsection, the term "coverage provider" means each of the following:

(A) HEALTH INSURANCE COVERAGE.—If the applicable employer-sponsored coverage consists of coverage under a group health plan which provides health insurance coverage, the health insurance issuer.

(B) HSA AND MSA CONTRIBUTIONS.—If the applicable employer-sponsored coverage consists of coverage under an arrangement under which the employer makes contributions described in subsection (b) or (d) of section 106, the employer.

(C) OTHER COVERAGE.—In the case of any other applicable employer-sponsored coverage, the person that administers the plan benefits.

(3) APPLICABLE SHARE.—For purposes of this subsection, a coverage provider's applicable share of an excess benefit for any taxable period is the amount which bears the same ratio to the amount of such excess benefit as—

(A) the cost of the applicable employer-sponsored coverage provided by the provider to the employee during such period, bears to

(B) the aggregate cost of all applicable employer-sponsored coverage provided to the employee by all coverage providers during such period.

(4) RESPONSIBILITY TO CALCULATE TAX AND APPLICABLE SHARES.—

(A) IN GENERAL.—Each employer shall—

(i) *calculate for each taxable period the amount of the excess benefit subject to the tax imposed by subsection (a) and the applicable share of such excess benefit for each coverage provider, and*

(ii) *notify, at such time and in such manner as the Secretary may prescribe, the Secretary and each coverage provider of the amount so determined for the provider.*

(B) SPECIAL RULE FOR MULTIEMPLOYER PLANS.—*In the case of applicable employer-sponsored coverage made available to employees through a multiemployer plan (as defined in section 414(f)), the plan sponsor shall make the calculations, and provide the notice, required under subparagraph (A).*

(d) APPLICABLE EMPLOYER-SPONSORED COVERAGE; COST.—*For purposes of this section—*

(1) APPLICABLE EMPLOYER-SPONSORED COVERAGE.—

(A) IN GENERAL.—*The term "applicable employer-sponsored coverage" means, with respect to any employee, coverage under any group health plan made available to the employee by an employer which is excludable from the employee's gross income under section 106, or would be so excludable if it were employer-provided coverage (within the meaning of such section 106).*

(B) EXCEPTIONS.—*The term "applicable employer-sponsored coverage" shall not include—*

(i) *any coverage (whether through insurance or otherwise) described in section 9832(c)(1) (other than subparagraph (G) thereof) or for long-term care, or*

(ii) *any coverage under a separate policy, certificate, or contract of insurance which provides benefits substantially all of which are for treatment of the mouth (including any organ or structure within the mouth) or for treatment of the eye, or*

(iii) *any coverage described in section 9832(c)(3) the payment for which is not excludable from gross income and for which a deduction under section 162(l) is not allowable.*

(C) COVERAGE INCLUDES EMPLOYEE PAID PORTION.—*Coverage shall be treated as applicable employer-sponsored coverage without regard to whether the employer or employee pays for the coverage.*

(D) SELF-EMPLOYED INDIVIDUAL.—*In the case of an individual who is an employee within the meaning of section 401(c)(1), coverage under any group health plan providing health insurance coverage shall be treated as applicable employer-sponsored coverage if a deduction is allowable under section 162(l) with respect to all or any portion of the cost of the coverage.*

(E) GOVERNMENTAL PLANS INCLUDED.—*Applicable employer-sponsored coverage shall include coverage under any group health plan established and maintained primarily for its civilian employees by the Government of the United States, by the government of any State or political subdivision thereof, or by any agency or instrumentality of any such government.*

(2) DETERMINATION OF COST.—

(A) IN GENERAL.—*The cost of applicable employer-sponsored coverage shall be determined under rules similar to the rules of section 4980B(f)(4), except that in determining such cost, any portion of the cost of such coverage which is attributable to the tax imposed under this section shall not be taken into account and the amount of such cost shall be calculated separately for self-only coverage and other coverage. In the case of applicable employer-sponsored coverage which provides coverage to retired employees, the plan may elect to treat a retired employee who has not attained the age of 65 and a retired employee who has attained the age of 65 as similarly situated beneficiaries.*

(B) HEALTH FSAS.—*In the case of applicable employer-sponsored coverage consisting of coverage under a flexible spending arrangement (as defined in section 106(c)(2)), the cost of the coverage shall be equal to the sum of—*

(i) *the amount of employer contributions under any salary reduction election under the arrangement, plus*

(ii) *the amount determined under subparagraph (A) with respect to any reimbursement under the arrangement in excess of the contributions described in clause (i).*

(C) ARCHER MSAS AND HSAS.—In the case of applicable employer-sponsored coverage consisting of coverage under an arrangement under which the employer makes contributions described in subsection (b) or (d) of section 106, the cost of the coverage shall be equal to the amount of employer contributions under the arrangement.

(D) ALLOCATION ON A MONTHLY BASIS.—If cost is determined on other than a monthly basis, the cost shall be allocated to months in a taxable period on such basis as the Secretary may prescribe.

(3) EMPLOYEE.—The term "employee" includes any former employee, surviving spouse, or other primary insured individual.

[CCH Explanation at ¶ 345.]

Amendments

• 2010, Health Care and Education Reconciliation Act of 2010 (P.L. 111-152)

P.L. 111-152, § 1401(a)(4)-(5):

Amended Code Sec. 4980I, as added by section 9001 of the Patient Protection and Affordable Care Act (P.L. 111-148), and amended by section 10901 of such Act, by redesignating clause (ii) as clause (iii) in subsection (d)(1)(B), and by inserting after clause (i) a new clause (ii); and by adding at the end of subsection (d) a new paragraph (3). **Effective** 3-30-2010.

• 2010, Patient Protection and Affordable Care Act (P.L. 111-148)

P.L. 111-148, § 10901(b):

Amended Code Sec. 4980I(d)(1)(B)(i), as added by Act Sec. 9001, by striking "section 9832(c)(1)(A)" and inserting "section 9832(c)(1) (other than subparagraph (G) thereof)". **Effective** for tax years beginning after 12-31-2017 **[effective date changed by P.L. 111-152, § 1401(b)(2).—CCH].**

(e) PENALTY FOR FAILURE TO PROPERLY CALCULATE EXCESS BENEFIT.—

(1) IN GENERAL.—If, for any taxable period, the tax imposed by subsection (a) exceeds the tax determined under such subsection with respect to the total excess benefit calculated by the employer or plan sponsor under subsection (c)(4)—

(A) each coverage provider shall pay the tax on its applicable share (determined in the same manner as under subsection (c)(4)) of the excess, but no penalty shall be imposed on the provider with respect to such amount, and

(B) the employer or plan sponsor shall, in addition to any tax imposed by subsection (a), pay a penalty in an amount equal to such excess, plus interest at the underpayment rate determined under section 6621 for the period beginning on the due date for the payment of tax imposed by subsection (a) to which the excess relates and ending on the date of payment of the penalty.

(2) LIMITATIONS ON PENALTY.—

(A) PENALTY NOT TO APPLY WHERE FAILURE NOT DISCOVERED EXERCISING REASONABLE DILIGENCE.— No penalty shall be imposed by paragraph (1)(B) on any failure to properly calculate the excess benefit during any period for which it is established to the satisfaction of the Secretary that the employer or plan sponsor neither knew, nor exercising reasonable diligence would have known, that such failure existed.

(B) PENALTY NOT TO APPLY TO FAILURES CORRECTED WITHIN 30 DAYS.—No penalty shall be imposed by paragraph (1)(B) on any such failure if—

(i) such failure was due to reasonable cause and not to willful neglect, and

(ii) such failure is corrected during the 30-day period beginning on the 1st date that the employer knew, or exercising reasonable diligence would have known, that such failure existed.

(C) WAIVER BY SECRETARY.—In the case of any such failure which is due to reasonable cause and not to willful neglect, the Secretary may waive part or all of the penalty imposed by paragraph (1), to the extent that the payment of such penalty would be excessive or otherwise inequitable relative to the failure involved.

(f) OTHER DEFINITIONS AND SPECIAL RULES.—For purposes of this section—

(1) COVERAGE DETERMINATIONS.—

(A) IN GENERAL.—Except as provided in subparagraph (B), an employee shall be treated as having self-only coverage with respect to any applicable employer-sponsored coverage of an employer.

(B) *MINIMUM ESSENTIAL COVERAGE.—An employee shall be treated as having coverage other than self-only coverage only if the employee is enrolled in coverage other than self-only coverage in a group health plan which provides minimum essential coverage (as defined in section 5000A(f)) to the employee and at least one other beneficiary, and the benefits provided under such minimum essential coverage do not vary based on whether any individual covered under such coverage is the employee or another beneficiary.*

(2) *QUALIFIED RETIREE.—The term "qualified retiree" means any individual who—*

(A) *is receiving coverage by reason of being a retiree,*

(B) *has attained age 55, and*

(C) *is not entitled to benefits or eligible for enrollment under the Medicare program under title XVIII of the Social Security Act.*

(3) *EMPLOYEES ENGAGED IN HIGH-RISK PROFESSION.—The term "employees engaged in a high-risk profession" means law enforcement officers (as such term is defined in section 1204 of the Omnibus Crime Control and Safe Streets Act of 1968), employees in fire protection activities (as such term is defined in section 3(y) of the Fair Labor Standards Act of 1938), individuals who provide out-of-hospital emergency medical care (including emergency medical technicians, paramedics, and first-responders), individuals whose primary work is longshore work (as defined in section 258(b) of the Immigration and Nationality Act (8 U.S.C. 1288(b)), determined without regard to paragraph (2) thereof), and individuals engaged in the construction, mining, agriculture (not including food processing), forestry, and fishing industries. Such term includes an employee who is retired from a high-risk profession described in the preceding sentence, if such employee satisfied the requirements of such sentence for a period of not less than 20 years during the employee's employment.*

(4) *GROUP HEALTH PLAN.—The term "group health plan" has the meaning given such term by section 5000(b)(1).*

(5) *HEALTH INSURANCE COVERAGE; HEALTH INSURANCE ISSUER.—*

(A) *HEALTH INSURANCE COVERAGE.—The term "health insurance coverage" has the meaning given such term by section 9832(b)(1) (applied without regard to subparagraph (B) thereof, except as provided by the Secretary in regulations).*

(B) *HEALTH INSURANCE ISSUER.—The term "health insurance issuer" has the meaning given such term by section 9832(b)(2).*

(6) *PERSON THAT ADMINISTERS THE PLAN BENEFITS.—The term "person that administers the plan benefits" shall include the plan sponsor if the plan sponsor administers benefits under the plan.*

(7) *PLAN SPONSOR.—The term "plan sponsor" has the meaning given such term in section 3(16)(B) of the Employee Retirement Income Security Act of 1974.*

(8) *TAXABLE PERIOD.—The term "taxable period" means the calendar year or such shorter period as the Secretary may prescribe. The Secretary may have different taxable periods for employers of varying sizes.*

(9) *AGGREGATION RULES.—All employers treated as a single employer under subsection (b), (c), (m), or (o) of section 414 shall be treated as a single employer.*

(10) *DENIAL OF DEDUCTION.—For denial of a deduction for the tax imposed by this section, see section 275(a)(6).*

[CCH Explanation at ¶345.]

Amendments

• **2010, Patient Protection and Affordable Care Act (P.L. 111-148)**

P.L. 111-148, §10901(a):

Amended Code Sec. 4980I(f)(3), as added by Act Sec. 9001, by inserting "individuals whose primary work is long-shore work (as defined in section 258(b) of the Immigration and Nationality Act (8 U.S.C. 1288(b)), determined without regard to paragraph (2) thereof)," before "and individuals engaged in the construction, mining". **Effective** for tax years beginning after 12-31-2017 [**effective** date changed by P.L. 111-152, §1401(b)(2).—CCH].

(g) REGULATIONS.—The Secretary shall prescribe such regulations as may be necessary to carry out this section.

[CCH Explanation at ¶345. Committee Reports at ¶10,160.]

Amendments

• **2010, Patient Protection and Affordable Care Act (P.L. 111-148)**

P.L. 111-148, §9001(a):

Amended chapter 43, as amended by Act Sec. 1513, by adding at the end a new Code Sec. 4980I. **Effective** for tax years beginning after 12-31-2017 [**effective** date changed by P.L. 111-152, §1401(b)(1).—CCH].

>>> *Caution: Code Sec. 5000A, below, as added by P.L. 111-148, applies to tax years ending after December 31, 2013.*

[¶5235] *CODE SEC. 5000A. REQUIREMENT TO MAINTAIN MINIMUM ESSENTIAL COVERAGE.*

(a) REQUIREMENT TO MAINTAIN MINIMUM ESSENTIAL COVERAGE.—An applicable individual shall for each month beginning after 2013 ensure that the individual, and any dependent of the individual who is an applicable individual, is covered under minimum essential coverage for such month.

(b) SHARED RESPONSIBILITY PAYMENT.—

(1) IN GENERAL.—If a taxpayer who is an applicable individual, or an applicable individual for whom the taxpayer is liable under paragraph (3), fails to meet the requirement of subsection (a) for 1 or more months, then, except as provided in subsection (e), there is hereby imposed on the taxpayer a penalty with respect to such failures in the amount determined under subsection (c).

(2) INCLUSION WITH RETURN.—Any penalty imposed by this section with respect to any month shall be included with a taxpayer's return under chapter 1 for the taxable year which includes such month.

(3) PAYMENT OF PENALTY.—If an individual with respect to whom a penalty is imposed by this section for any month—

(A) is a dependent (as defined in section 152) of another taxpayer for the other taxpayer's taxable year including such month, such other taxpayer shall be liable for such penalty, or

(B) files a joint return for the taxable year including such month, such individual and the spouse of such individual shall be jointly liable for such penalty.

[CCH Explanation at ¶205.]

Amendments

• **2010, Patient Protection and Affordable Care Act (P.L. 111-148)**

P.L. 111-148, §10106(b)(1):

Amended Code Sec. 5000A(b)(1), as added by Act Sec. 1501(b). **Effective** 3-23-2010. Prior to amendment, Code Sec. 5000A(b)(1) read as follows:

(1) IN GENERAL.—If an applicable individual fails to meet the requirement of subsection (a) for 1 or more months during any calendar year beginning after 2013, then, except as provided in subsection (d), there is hereby imposed a penalty with respect to the individual in the amount determined under subsection (c).

(c) AMOUNT OF PENALTY.—

(1) IN GENERAL.—The amount of the penalty imposed by this section on any taxpayer for any taxable year with respect to failures described in subsection (b)(1) shall be equal to the lesser of—

(A) the sum of the monthly penalty amounts determined under paragraph (2) for months in the taxable year during which 1 or more such failures occurred, or

(B) an amount equal to the national average premium for qualified health plans which have a bronze level of coverage, provide coverage for the applicable family size involved, and are offered through Exchanges for plan years beginning in the calendar year with or within which the taxable year ends.

(2) MONTHLY PENALTY AMOUNTS.—*For purposes of paragraph (1)(A), the monthly penalty amount with respect to any taxpayer for any month during which any failure described in subsection (b)(1) occurred is an amount equal to ¹⁄₁₂ of the greater of the following amounts:*

(A) FLAT DOLLAR AMOUNT.—*An amount equal to the lesser of—*

(i) *the sum of the applicable dollar amounts for all individuals with respect to whom such failure occurred during such month, or*

(ii) *300 percent of the applicable dollar amount (determined without regard to paragraph (3)(C)) for the calendar year with or within which the taxable year ends.*

(B) PERCENTAGE OF INCOME.—*An amount equal to the following percentage of the excess of the taxpayer's household income for the taxable year over the amount of gross income specified in section 6012(a)(1) with respect to the taxpayer for the taxable year:*

(i) *1.0 percent for taxable years beginning in 2014.*

(ii) *2.0 percent for taxable years beginning in 2015.*

(iii) *2.5 percent for taxable years beginning after 2015.*

(3) APPLICABLE DOLLAR AMOUNT.—*For purposes of paragraph (1)—*

(A) IN GENERAL.—*Except as provided in subparagraphs (B) and (C), the applicable dollar amount is $695.*

(B) PHASE IN.—*The applicable dollar amount is $95 for 2014 and $325 for 2015.*

(C) SPECIAL RULE FOR INDIVIDUALS UNDER AGE 18.—*If an applicable individual has not attained the age of 18 as of the beginning of a month, the applicable dollar amount with respect to such individual for the month shall be equal to one-half of the applicable dollar amount for the calendar year in which the month occurs.*

(D) INDEXING OF AMOUNT.—*In the case of any calendar year beginning after 2016, the applicable dollar amount shall be equal to $695, increased by an amount equal to—*

(i) *$695, multiplied by*

(ii) *the cost-of-living adjustment determined under section 1(f)(3) for the calendar year, determined by substituting "calendar year 2015" for "calendar year 1992" in subparagraph (B) thereof.*

If the amount of any increase under clause (i) is not a multiple of $50, such increase shall be rounded to the next lowest multiple of $50.

(4) TERMS RELATING TO INCOME AND FAMILIES.—*For purposes of this section—*

(A) FAMILY SIZE.—*The family size involved with respect to any taxpayer shall be equal to the number of individuals for whom the taxpayer is allowed a deduction under section 151 (relating to allowance of deduction for personal exemptions) for the taxable year.*

(B) HOUSEHOLD INCOME.—*The term "household income" means, with respect to any taxpayer for any taxable year, an amount equal to the sum of—*

(i) *the modified adjusted gross income of the taxpayer, plus*

(ii) *the aggregate modified adjusted gross incomes of all other individuals who—*

(I) *were taken into account in determining the taxpayer's family size under paragraph (1), and*

(II) *were required to file a return of tax imposed by section 1 for the taxable year.*

(C) MODIFIED ADJUSTED GROSS INCOME.—*The term "modified adjusted gross income" means adjusted gross income increased by—*

(i) *any amount excluded from gross income under section 911, and*

(ii) *any amount of interest received or accrued by the taxpayer during the taxable year which is exempt from tax.*

(D) *[Stricken.]*

[CCH Explanation at ¶205.]

Amendments

- **2010, Health Care and Education Reconciliation Act of 2010 (P.L. 111-152)**

P.L. 111-152, §1002(a)(1)(A)-(D):

Amended Code Sec. 5000A(c), as added by section 1501(b) of the Patient Protection and Affordable Care Act (P.L. 111-148) and amended by section 10106, in the matter preceding clause (i) of paragraph (2)(B) by inserting "the excess of" before "the taxpayer's household income"; and inserting "for the taxable year over the amount of gross income specified in section 6012(a)(1) with respect to the taxpayer" before "for the taxable year"; by striking "0.5" and inserting "1.0" in clause (i) of paragraph (2)(B); by striking "1.0" and inserting "2.0" in clause (ii) of paragraph (2)(B); and by striking "2.0" and inserting "2.5" in clause (iii) of paragraph (2)(B). **Effective** 3-30-2010.

P.L. 111-152, §1002(a)(2)(A)-(C):

Amended Code Sec. 5000A(c), as added by section 1501(b) of the Patient Protection and Affordable Care Act (P.L. 111-148) and amended by section 10106, by striking "$750" and inserting "$695" in subparagraph (A) of paragraph (3); by striking "$495" and inserting "$325" in subparagraph (B) of paragraph (3); and in the matter preceding clause (i) of subparagraph (D) by striking "$750" and inserting "$695"; and by striking "$750" and inserting "$695" in clause (i) of subparagraph (D). **Effective** 3-30-2010.

P.L. 111-152, §1002(b)(1):

Amended Code Sec. 5000A, as added by section 1501(b) of the Patient Protection and Affordable Care Act (P.L. 111-148) and amended by section 10106, by striking subsection (c)(4)(D). **Effective** 3-30-2010. Prior to being stricken, Code Sec. 5000A(c)(4)(D) read as follows:

(D) POVERTY LINE.—

(i) IN GENERAL.—The term "poverty line" has the meaning given that term in section 2110(c)(5) of the Social Security Act (42 U.S.C. 1397jj(c)(5)).

(ii) POVERTY LINE USED.—In the case of any taxable year ending with or within a calendar year, the poverty line used shall be the most recently published poverty line as of the 1st day of such calendar year.

P.L. 111-152, §1004(a)(1)(C):

Amended Code Sec. 5000A(c)(4)[(B)](i)-(ii), as added by section 1501(b) of the Patient Protection and Affordable Care

Act (P.L. 111-148), by striking "modified gross" each place it appears and inserting "modified adjusted gross". **Effective** 3-30-2010.

P.L. 111-152, §1004(a)(2)(B):

Amended Code Sec. 5000A(c)(4)(C), as added by section 1501(b) of the Patient Protection and Affordable Care Act (P.L. 111-148). **Effective** 3-30-2010. Prior to amendment, Code Sec. 5000A(c)(4)(C) read as follows:

(C) MODIFIED GROSS INCOME.—The term "modified gross income" means gross income—

(i) decreased by the amount of any deduction allowable under paragraph (1), (3), (4), or (10) of section 62(a),

(ii) increased by the amount of interest received or accrued during the taxable year which is exempt from tax imposed by this chapter, and

(iii) determined without regard to sections 911, 931, and 933.

- **2010, Patient Protection and Affordable Care Act (P.L. 111-148)**

P.L. 111-148, §10106(b)(2):

Amended Code Sec. 5000A(c)(1)-(2), as added by this Act. **Effective** 3-23-2010. Prior to amendment, Code Sec. 5000A(c)(1)-(2) read as follows:

(1) IN GENERAL.—The penalty determined under this subsection for any month with respect to any individual is an amount equal to ¹⁄₁₂ of the applicable dollar amount for the calendar year.

(2) DOLLAR LIMITATION.—The amount of the penalty imposed by this section on any taxpayer for any taxable year with respect to all individuals for whom the taxpayer is liable under subsection (b)(3) shall not exceed an amount equal to 300 percent [of] the applicable dollar amount (determined without regard to paragraph (3)(C)) for the calendar year with or within which the taxable year ends.

P.L. 111-148, §10106(b)(3):

Amended Code Sec. 5000A(c)(3)[(B)], as added by Act Sec. 1501(b), by striking "$350" and inserting "$495". **Effective** 3-23-2010.

(d) APPLICABLE INDIVIDUAL.—*For purposes of this section—*

(1) IN GENERAL.—*The term "applicable individual" means, with respect to any month, an individual other than an individual described in paragraph (2), (3), or (4).*

(2) RELIGIOUS EXEMPTIONS.—

(A) RELIGIOUS CONSCIENCE EXEMPTION.—*Such term shall not include any individual for any month if such individual has in effect an exemption under section 1311(d)(4)(H) of the Patient Protection and Affordable Care Act which certifies that such individual is—*

(i) a member of a recognized religious sect or division thereof which is described in section 1402(g)(1), and

(ii) an adherent of established tenets or teachings of such sect or division as described in such section.

(B) HEALTH CARE SHARING MINISTRY.—

(i) IN GENERAL.—*Such term shall not include any individual for any month if such individual is a member of a health care sharing ministry for the month.*

(ii) HEALTH CARE SHARING MINISTRY.—*The term "health care sharing ministry" means an organization—*

(I) which is described in section 501(c)(3) and is exempt from taxation under section 501(a),

(II) members of which share a common set of ethical or religious beliefs and share medical expenses among members in accordance with those beliefs and without regard to the State in which a member resides or is employed,

(III) members of which retain membership even after they develop a medical condition,

(IV) which (or a predecessor of which) has been in existence at all times since December 31, 1999, and medical expenses of its members have been shared continuously and without interruption since at least December 31, 1999, and

(V) which conducts an annual audit which is performed by an independent certified public accounting firm in accordance with generally accepted accounting principles and which is made available to the public upon request.

(3) INDIVIDUALS NOT LAWFULLY PRESENT.—*Such term shall not include an individual for any month if for the month the individual is not a citizen or national of the United States or an alien lawfully present in the United States.*

(4) INCARCERATED INDIVIDUALS.—*Such term shall not include an individual for any month if for the month the individual is incarcerated, other than incarceration pending the disposition of charges.*

[CCH Explanation at ¶ 205.]

Amendments

• **2010, Patient Protection and Affordable Care Act (P.L. 111-148)**

P.L. 111-148, § 10106(c):

Amended Code Sec. 5000A(d)(2)(A), as added by Act Sec. 1501(b). **Effective** 3-23-2010. Prior to amendment, Code Sec. 5000A(d)(2)(A) read as follows:

(A) RELIGIOUS CONSCIENCE EXEMPTION.—Such term shall not include any individual for any month if such individual has in effect an exemption under section 1311(d)(4)(H) of the Patient Protection and Affordable Care Act which certifies that such individual is a member of a recognized religious sect or division thereof described in section 1402(g)(1) and an adherent of established tenets or teachings of such sect or division as described in such section.

(e) EXEMPTIONS.—*No penalty shall be imposed under subsection (a) with respect to—*

(1) INDIVIDUALS WHO CANNOT AFFORD COVERAGE.—

(A) IN GENERAL.—*Any applicable individual for any month if the applicable individual's required contribution (determined on an annual basis) for coverage for the month exceeds 8 percent of such individual's household income for the taxable year described in section 1412(b)(1)(B) of the Patient Protection and Affordable Care Act. For purposes of applying this subparagraph, the taxpayer's household income shall be increased by any exclusion from gross income for any portion of the required contribution made through a salary reduction arrangement.*

(B) REQUIRED CONTRIBUTION.—*For purposes of this paragraph, the term "required contribution" means—*

(i) in the case of an individual eligible to purchase minimum essential coverage consisting of coverage through an eligible-employer-sponsored plan, the portion of the annual premium which would be paid by the individual (without regard to whether paid through salary reduction or otherwise) for self-only coverage, or

(ii) in the case of an individual eligible only to purchase minimum essential coverage described in subsection (f)(1)(C), the annual premium for the lowest cost bronze plan available in the individual market through the Exchange in the State in the rating area in which the individual resides (without regard to whether the individual purchased a qualified health plan through the Exchange), reduced by the amount of the credit allowable under section 36B for the taxable year (determined as if the individual was covered by a qualified health plan offered through the Exchange for the entire taxable year).

(C) SPECIAL RULES FOR INDIVIDUALS RELATED TO EMPLOYEES.—*For purposes of subparagraph (B)(i), if an applicable individual is eligible for minimum essential coverage through an employer by*

reason of a relationship to an employee, the determination under subparagraph (A) shall be made by reference to required contribution of the employee.

(D) INDEXING.—*In the case of plan years beginning in any calendar year after 2014, subparagraph (A) shall be applied by substituting for "8 percent" the percentage the Secretary of Health and Human Services determines reflects the excess of the rate of premium growth between the preceding calendar year and 2013 over the rate of income growth for such period.*

(2) TAXPAYERS WITH INCOME BELOW FILING THRESHOLD.—*Any applicable individual for any month during a calendar year if the individual's household income for the taxable year described in section 1412(b)(1)(B) of the Patient Protection and Affordable Care Act is less than the amount of gross income specified in section 6012(a)(1) with respect to the taxpayer.*

(3) MEMBERS OF INDIAN TRIBES.—*Any applicable individual for any month during which the individual is a member of an Indian tribe (as defined in section 45A(c)(6)).*

(4) MONTHS DURING SHORT COVERAGE GAPS.—

(A) IN GENERAL.—*Any month the last day of which occurred during a period in which the applicable individual was not covered by minimum essential coverage for a continuous period of less than 3 months.*

(B) SPECIAL RULES.—*For purposes of applying this paragraph—*

(i) *the length of a continuous period shall be determined without regard to the calendar years in which months in such period occur,*

(ii) *if a continuous period is greater than the period allowed under subparagraph (A), no exception shall be provided under this paragraph for any month in the period, and*

(iii) *if there is more than 1 continuous period described in subparagraph (A) covering months in a calendar year, the exception provided by this paragraph shall only apply to months in the first of such periods.*

The Secretary shall prescribe rules for the collection of the penalty imposed by this section in cases where continuous periods include months in more than 1 taxable year.

(5) HARDSHIPS.—*Any applicable individual who for any month is determined by the Secretary of Health and Human Services under section 1311(d)(4)(H) to have suffered a hardship with respect to the capability to obtain coverage under a qualified health plan.*

[CCH Explanation at ¶ 205.]

Amendments

• 2010, Health Care and Education Reconciliation Act of 2010 (P.L. 111-152)

P.L. 111-152, § 1002(b)(2)(A)-(B):

Amended Code Sec. 5000A(e)(2), as added by section 1501(b) of the Patient Protection and Affordable Care Act (P.L. 111-148) and amended by section 10106, by striking "UNDER 100 PERCENT OF POVERTY LINE" and inserting "BELOW FILING THRESHOLD" [in the heading]; and by striking all that follows "less than" and inserting "the amount of gross income specified in section 6012(a)(1) with respect to the taxpayer.". **Effective** 3-30-2010. Prior to being stricken, all that followed "less than" in Code Sec. 5000A(e)(2) read as follows:

100 percent of the poverty line for the size of the family involved (determined in the same manner as under subsection (b)(4)).

• 2010, Patient Protection and Affordable Care Act (P.L. 111-148)

P.L. 111-148, § 10106(d):

Amended Code Sec. 5000A(e)(1)(C), as added by Act Sec. 1501(b). **Effective** 3-23-2010. Prior to amendment, Code Sec. 5000A(e)(1)(C) read as follows:

(C) SPECIAL RULES FOR INDIVIDUALS RELATED TO EMPLOYEES.— For purposes of subparagraph (B)(i), if an applicable individual is eligible for minimum essential coverage through an employer by reason of a relationship to an employee, the determination shall be made by reference to the affordability of the coverage to the employee.

(f) MINIMUM ESSENTIAL COVERAGE.—*For purposes of this section—*

(1) IN GENERAL.—*The term "minimum essential coverage" means any of the following:*

(A) GOVERNMENT SPONSORED PROGRAMS.—*Coverage under—*

(i) *the Medicare program under part A of title XVIII of the Social Security Act,*

(ii) the Medicaid program under title XIX of the Social Security Act,

(iii) the CHIP program under title XXI of the Social Security Act,

(iv) the TRICARE for Life program,

(v) the veteran's health care program under chapter 17 of title 38, United States Code, or

(vi) a health plan under section 2504(e) of title 22, United States Code (relating to Peace Corps volunteers).

(B) EMPLOYER-SPONSORED PLAN.—Coverage under an eligible employer-sponsored plan.

(C) PLANS IN THE INDIVIDUAL MARKET.—Coverage under a health plan offered in the individual market within a State.

(D) GRANDFATHERED HEALTH PLAN.—Coverage under a grandfathered health plan.

(E) OTHER COVERAGE.—Such other health benefits coverage, such as a State health benefits risk pool, as the Secretary of Health and Human Services, in coordination with the Secretary, recognizes for purposes of this subsection.

(2) ELIGIBLE EMPLOYER-SPONSORED PLAN.—The term "eligible employer-sponsored plan" means, with respect to any employee, a group health plan or group health insurance coverage offered by an employer to the employee which is—

(A) a governmental plan (within the meaning of section 2791(d)(8) of the Public Health Service Act), or

(B) any other plan or coverage offered in the small or large group market within a State.

Such term shall include a grandfathered health plan described in paragraph (1)(D) offered in a group market.

(3) EXCEPTED BENEFITS NOT TREATED AS MINIMUM ESSENTIAL COVERAGE.—The term "minimum essential coverage" shall not include health insurance coverage which consists of coverage of excepted benefits—

(A) described in paragraph (1) of subsection (c) of section 2791 of the Public Health Service Act; or

(B) described in paragraph (2), (3), or (4) of such subsection if the benefits are provided under a separate policy, certificate, or contract of insurance.

(4) INDIVIDUALS RESIDING OUTSIDE UNITED STATES OR RESIDENTS OF TERRITORIES.—Any applicable individual shall be treated as having minimum essential coverage for any month—

(A) if such month occurs during any period described in subparagraph (A) or (B) of section 911(d)(1) which is applicable to the individual, or

(B) if such individual is a bona fide resident of any possession of the United States (as determined under section 937(a)) for such month.

(5) INSURANCE-RELATED TERMS.—Any term used in this section which is also used in title I of the Patient Protection and Affordable Care Act shall have the same meaning as when used in such title.

(g) ADMINISTRATION AND PROCEDURE.—

(1) IN GENERAL.—The penalty provided by this section shall be paid upon notice and demand by the Secretary, and except as provided in paragraph (2), shall be assessed and collected in the same manner as an assessable penalty under subchapter B of chapter 68.

(2) SPECIAL RULES.—Notwithstanding any other provision of law—

(A) WAIVER OF CRIMINAL PENALTIES.—In the case of any failure by a taxpayer to timely pay any penalty imposed by this section, such taxpayer shall not be subject to any criminal prosecution or penalty with respect to such failure.

(B) LIMITATIONS ON LIENS AND LEVIES.—The Secretary shall not—

(i) file notice of lien with respect to any property of a taxpayer by reason of any failure to pay the penalty imposed by this section, or

(ii) levy on any such property with respect to such failure.

[CCH Explanation at ¶ 205. Committee Reports at ¶ 10,080.]

Amendments

• **2010, Patient Protection and Affordable Care Act (P.L. 111-148)**

P.L. 111-148, § 1501(b):

Amended subtitle D by adding at the end a new chapter 48 (Code Sec. 5000A). **Effective** for tax years ending after 12-31-2013.

>>>→ *Caution: Code Sec. 5000B, below, as added by P.L. 111-148, applies to services performed on or after July 1, 2010.*

[¶ 5240] CODE SEC. 5000B. IMPOSITION OF TAX ON INDOOR TANNING SERVICES.

(a) IN GENERAL.—There is hereby imposed on any indoor tanning service a tax equal to 10 percent of the amount paid for such service (determined without regard to this section), whether paid by insurance or otherwise.

(b) INDOOR TANNING SERVICE.—For purposes of this section—

(1) IN GENERAL.—The term "indoor tanning service" means a service employing any electronic product designed to incorporate 1 or more ultraviolet lamps and intended for the irradiation of an individual by ultraviolet radiation, with wavelengths in air between 200 and 400 nanometers, to induce skin tanning.

(2) EXCLUSION OF PHOTOTHERAPY SERVICES.—Such term does not include any phototherapy service performed by a licensed medical professional.

(c) PAYMENT OF TAX.—

(1) IN GENERAL.—The tax imposed by this section shall be paid by the individual on whom the service is performed.

(2) COLLECTION.—Every person receiving a payment for services on which a tax is imposed under subsection (a) shall collect the amount of the tax from the individual on whom the service is performed and remit such tax quarterly to the Secretary at such time and in such manner as provided by the Secretary.

(3) SECONDARY LIABILITY.—Where any tax imposed by subsection (a) is not paid at the time payments for indoor tanning services are made, then to the extent that such tax is not collected, such tax shall be paid by the person who performs the service.

[CCH Explanation at ¶ 235. Committee Reports at ¶ 10,320.]

Amendments

• **2010, Patient Protection and Affordable Care Act (P.L. 111-148)**

P.L. 111-148, § 10907(b):

Amended subtitle D, as amended by this Act, by adding at the end a new Chapter 49 (Code Sec. 5000B). **Effective** for services performed on or after 7-1-2010.

P.L. 111-148, § 10907(a), provides:

(a) IN GENERAL.—The provisions of, and amendments made by, section 9017 of this Act are hereby deemed null, void, and of no effect.

P.L. 111-148, § 9017(a), provided:

(a) IN GENERAL.—Subtitle D of the Internal Revenue Code of 1986, as amended by this Act, is amended by adding at the end the following new chapter [Code Sec. 5000B]:

SEC. 5000B. IMPOSITION OF TAX ON ELECTIVE COSMETIC MEDICAL PROCEDURES.

(a) IN GENERAL.—There is hereby imposed on any cosmetic surgery and medical procedure a tax equal to 5 percent of the amount paid for such procedure (determined without regard to this section), whether paid by insurance or otherwise.

(b) COSMETIC SURGERY AND MEDICAL PROCEDURE.—For purposes of this section, the term "cosmetic surgery and medical procedure" means any cosmetic surgery (as defined in section 213(d)(9)(B)) or other similar procedure which—

(1) is performed by a licensed medical professional, and

(2) is not necessary to ameliorate a deformity arising from, or directly related to, a congenital abnormality, a personal injury resulting from an accident or trauma, or disfiguring disease.

* * *

(c) PAYMENT OF TAX.—

(1) IN GENERAL.—The tax imposed by this section shall be paid by the individual on whom the procedure is performed.

(2) COLLECTION.—Every person receiving a payment for procedures on which a tax is imposed under subsection (a) shall collect the amount of the tax from the individual on whom the procedure is performed and remit such tax quar-terly to the Secretary at such time and in such manner as provided by the Secretary.

(3) SECONDARY LIABILITY.—Where any tax imposed by sub-section (a) is not paid at the time payments for cosmetic surgery and medical procedures are made, then to the ex-tent that such tax is not collected, such tax shall be paid by the person who performs the procedure.

[¶5245] CODE SEC. 6033. RETURNS BY EXEMPT ORGANIZATIONS.

* * *

(b) CERTAIN ORGANIZATIONS DESCRIBED IN SECTION 501(c)(3).—Every organization described in section 501(c)(3) which is subject to the requirements of subsection (a) shall furnish annually information, at such time and in such manner as the Secretary may by forms or regulations prescribe, setting forth—

* * *

(10) the respective amounts (if any) of the taxes imposed on the organization, or any organization manager of the organization, during the taxable year under any of the following provisions (and the respective amounts (if any) of reimbursements paid by the organization during the taxable year with respect to taxes imposed on any such organization manager under any of such provisions):

* * *

(B) section 4912 (relating to tax on disqualifying lobbying expenditures of certain organizations),

(C) section 4955 (relating to taxes on political expenditures of section 501(c)(3) organiza-tions), except to the extent that, by reason of section 4962, the taxes imposed under such section are not required to be paid or are credited or refunded, *and*

(D) section 4959 (relating to taxes on failures by hospital organizations),

* * *

(14) such information as the Secretary may require with respect to disaster relief activities, including the amount and use of qualified contributions to which section 1400S(a) applies,

(15) in the case of an organization to which the requirements of section 501(r) apply for the taxable year—

(A) a description of how the organization is addressing the needs identified in each community health needs assessment conducted under section 501(r)(3) and a description of any such needs that are not being addressed together with the reasons why such needs are not being addressed, and

(B) the audited financial statements of such organization (or, in the case of an organization the financial statements of which are included in a consolidated financial statement with other organiza-tions, such consolidated financial statement).

(16) such other information for purposes of carrying out the internal revenue laws as the Secretary may require.

* * *

[CCH Explanation at ¶440. Committee Reports at ¶10,220.]

Amendments

• 2010, Patient Protection and Affordable Care Act (P.L. 111-148)

P.L. 111-148, § 9007(d)(1):

Amended Code Sec. 6033(b) by striking "and" at the end of paragraph (14), by redesignating paragraph (15) as para-graph (16), and by inserting after paragraph (14) a new paragraph (15). **Effective** for tax years beginning after 3-23-2010.

P.L. 111-148, § 9007(d)(2):

Amended Code Sec. 6033(b)(10) by striking "and" at the end of subparagraph (B), by inserting "and" at the end of subparagraph (C), and by adding at the end a new subpara-graph (D). **Effective** for tax years beginning after 3-23-2010.

(m) ADDITIONAL INFORMATION REQUIRED FROM CO-OP INSURERS.—An organization described in section 501(c)(29) shall include on the return required under subsection (a) the following information:

(1) The amount of the reserves required by each State in which the organization is licensed to issue qualified health plans.

(2) The amount of reserves on hand.

[CCH Explanation at ¶435. Committee Reports at ¶10,010.]

Amendments

• **2010, Patient Protection and Affordable Care Act (P.L. 111-148)**

P.L. 111-148, §1322(h)(2):

Amended Code Sec. 6033 by redesignating subsection (m) as subsection (n) and by inserting after subsection (l) a new subsection (m). **Effective** 3-23-2010.

(n) CROSS REFERENCE.—

* * *

Amendments

• **2010, Patient Protection and Affordable Care Act (P.L. 111-148)**

P.L. 111-148, §1322(h)(2):

Amended Code Sec. 6033 by redesignating subsection (m) as subsection (n). **Effective** 3-23-2010.

[¶5250] CODE SEC. 6041. INFORMATION AT SOURCE.

»»→ *Caution: Code Sec. 6041(a), below, as amended by P.L. 111-148, applies to payments made after December 31, 2011.*

(a) PAYMENTS OF $600 OR MORE.—All persons engaged in a trade or business and making payment in the course of such trade or business to another person, of rent, salaries, wages, *amounts in consideration for property,* premiums, annuities, compensations, remunerations, emoluments, or other *gross proceeds,* fixed or determinable gains, profits, and income (other than payments to which section 6042(a)(1), 6044(a)(1), 6047(e)[d], 6049(a), or 6050N(a) applies, and other than payments with respect to which a statement is required under the authority of section 6042(a)(2), 6044(a)(2), or 6045), of $600 or more in any taxable year, or, in the case of such payments made by the United States, the officers or employees of the United States having information as to such payments and required to make returns in regard thereto by the regulations hereinafter provided for, shall render a true and accurate return to the Secretary, under such regulations and in such form and manner and to such extent as may be prescribed by the Secretary, setting forth the amount of such *gross proceeds,* gains, profits, and income, and the name and address of the recipient of such payment.

* * *

[CCH Explanation at ¶420. Committee Reports at ¶10,210.]

Amendments

• **2010, Patient Protection and Affordable Care Act (P.L. 111-148)**

P.L. 111-148, §9006(b)(1)-(3):

Amended Code Sec. 6041(a) by inserting "amounts in consideration for property," after "wages,", by inserting "gross proceeds," after "emoluments, or other", and by inserting "gross proceeds," after "setting forth the amount of such". **Effective** for payments made after 12-31-2011.

»»→ *Caution: Code Sec. 6041(h), below, as added by P.L. 111-148, applies to payments made after December 31, 2011.*

(h) APPLICATION TO CORPORATIONS.—*Notwithstanding any regulation prescribed by the Secretary before the date of the enactment of this subsection, for purposes of this section the term "person" includes any corporation that is not an organization exempt from tax under section 501(a).*

[CCH Explanation at ¶ 420. Committee Reports at ¶ 10,210.]

Amendments

• 2010, Patient Protection and Affordable Care Act
(P.L. 111-148)

P.L. 111-148, § 9006(a):

Amended Code Sec. 6041 by adding at the end a new subsection (h). **Effective** for payments made after 12-31-2011.

⋙→ *Caution: Code Sec. 6041(i), below, as added by P.L. 111-148, applies to payments made after December 31, 2011.*

(i) REGULATIONS.—*The Secretary may prescribe such regulations and other guidance as may be appropriate or necessary to carry out the purposes of this section, including rules to prevent duplicative reporting of transactions.*

[CCH Explanation at ¶ 420. Committee Reports at ¶ 10,210.]

Amendments

• 2010, Patient Protection and Affordable Care Act
(P.L. 111-148)

P.L. 111-148, § 9006(a):

Amended Code Sec. 6041 by adding at the end a new subsection (i). **Effective** for payments made after 12-31-2011.

[¶ 5255] CODE SEC. 6051. RECEIPTS FOR EMPLOYEES.

(a) REQUIREMENT.—Every person required to deduct and withhold from an employee a tax under section 3101 or 3402, or who would have been required to deduct and withhold a tax under section 3402 (determined without regard to subsection (n)) if the employee had claimed no more than one withholding exemption, or every employer engaged in a trade or business who pays remuneration for services performed by an employee, including the cash value of such remuneration paid in any medium other than cash, shall furnish to each such employee in respect of the remuneration paid by such person to such employee during the calendar year, on or before January 31 of the succeeding year, or, if his employment is terminated before the close of such calendar year, within 30 days after the date of receipt of a written request from the employee if such 30-day period ends before January 31, a written statement showing the following:

* * *

(12) the amount contributed to any health savings account (as defined in section 223(d)) of such employee or such employee's spouse,

(13) the total amount of deferrals for the year under a nonqualified deferred compensation plan (within the meaning of section 409A(d)), *and*

⋙→ *Caution: Code Sec. 6051(a)(14), below, as added by P.L. 111-148, applies to tax years beginning after December 31, 2010.*

(14) the aggregate cost (determined under rules similar to the rules of section 4980B(f)(4)) of applicable employer-sponsored coverage (as defined in section 4980I(d)(1)), except that this paragraph shall not apply to—

(A) coverage to which paragraphs (11) and (12) apply, or

(B) the amount of any salary reduction contributions to a flexible spending arrangement (within the meaning of section 125).

* * *

[CCH Explanation at ¶405. Committee Reports at ¶10,170.]

Amendments

• **2010, Patient Protection and Affordable Care Act (P.L. 111-148)**

P.L. 111-148, §9002(a):

Amended Code Sec. 6051(a) by striking "and" at the end of paragraph (12), by striking the period at the end of paragraph (13) and inserting ", and", and by adding after paragraph (13) a new paragraph (14). **Effective** for tax years beginning after 12-31-2010.

⋙→ *Caution: Code Sec. 6055, below, as added by P.L. 111-148, applies to calendar years beginning after 2013.*

[¶5260] *CODE SEC. 6055. REPORTING OF HEALTH INSURANCE COVERAGE.*

(a) *IN GENERAL.—Every person who provides minimum essential coverage to an individual during a calendar year shall, at such time as the Secretary may prescribe, make a return described in subsection (b).*

(b) *FORM AND MANNER OF RETURN.—*

(1) *IN GENERAL.—A return is described in this subsection if such return—*

(A) *is in such form as the Secretary may prescribe, and*

(B) *contains—*

(i) *the name, address and TIN of the primary insured and the name and TIN of each other individual obtaining coverage under the policy,*

(ii) *the dates during which such individual was covered under minimum essential coverage during the calendar year,*

(iii) *in the case of minimum essential coverage which consists of health insurance coverage, information concerning—*

(I) *whether or not the coverage is a qualified health plan offered through an Exchange established under section 1311 of the Patient Protection and Affordable Care Act, and*

(II) *in the case of a qualified health plan, the amount (if any) of any advance payment under section 1412 of the Patient Protection and Affordable Care Act of any cost-sharing reduction under section 1402 of such Act or of any premium tax credit under section 36B with respect to such coverage, and*

(iv) *such other information as the Secretary may require.*

(2) *INFORMATION RELATING TO EMPLOYER-PROVIDED COVERAGE.—If minimum essential coverage provided to an individual under subsection (a) consists of health insurance coverage of a health insurance issuer provided through a group health plan of an employer, a return described in this subsection shall include—*

(A) *the name, address, and employer identification number of the employer maintaining the plan,*

(B) *the portion of the premium (if any) required to be paid by the employer, and*

(C) *if the health insurance coverage is a qualified health plan in the small group market offered through an Exchange, such other information as the Secretary may require for administration of the credit under section 45R (relating to credit for employee health insurance expenses of small employers).*

(c) *STATEMENTS TO BE FURNISHED TO INDIVIDUALS WITH RESPECT TO WHOM INFORMATION IS REPORTED.—*

(1) *IN GENERAL.—Every person required to make a return under subsection (a) shall furnish to each individual whose name is required to be set forth in such return a written statement showing—*

(A) *the name and address of the person required to make such return and the phone number of the information contact for such person, and*

(B) *the information required to be shown on the return with respect to such individual.*

(2) TIME FOR FURNISHING STATEMENTS.—*The written statement required under paragraph (1) shall be furnished on or before January 31 of the year following the calendar year for which the return under subsection (a) was required to be made.*

(d) COVERAGE PROVIDED BY GOVERNMENTAL UNITS.—*In the case of coverage provided by any governmental unit or any agency or instrumentality thereof, the officer or employee who enters into the agreement to provide such coverage (or the person appropriately designated for purposes of this section) shall make the returns and statements required by this section.*

(e) MINIMUM ESSENTIAL COVERAGE.—*For purposes of this section, the term "minimum essential coverage" has the meaning given such term by section 5000A(f).*

[CCH Explanation at ¶410. Committee Reports at ¶10,090.]
Amendments
• **2010, Patient Protection and Affordable Care Act (P.L. 111-148)**

P.L. 111-148, §1502(a):

Amended part III of subchapter A of chapter 61 by inserting after subpart C a new subpart D (Code Sec. 6055). **Effective** for calendar years beginning after 2013.

>>→ *Caution: Code Sec. 6056, below, as added and amended by P.L. 111-148, applies to periods beginning after December 31, 2013.*

[¶5265] CODE SEC. 6056. CERTAIN EMPLOYERS REQUIRED TO REPORT ON HEALTH INSURANCE COVERAGE.

(a) IN GENERAL.—*Every applicable large employer required to meet the requirements of section 4980H with respect to its full-time employees during a calendar year and every offering employer shall, at such time as the Secretary may prescribe, make a return described in subsection (b).*

[CCH Explanation at ¶415.]
Amendments
• **2010, Patient Protection and Affordable Care Act (P.L. 111-148)**

P.L. 111-148, §10108(j)(1):

Amended Code Sec. 6056(a), as added by Act Sec. 1514, by inserting "and every offering employer" before "shall". **Effective** for periods beginning after 12-31-2013.

P.L. 111-148, §10108(j)(3)(A):

Amended the heading of Code Sec. 6056, as added by Act Sec. 1514, by striking "LARGE" and inserting "CERTAIN". **Effective** for periods beginning after 12-31-2013.

(b) FORM AND MANNER OF RETURN.—*A return is described in this subsection if such return—*

(1) *is in such form as the Secretary may prescribe, and*

(2) *contains—*

(A) *the name, date, and employer identification number of the employer,*

(B) *a certification as to whether the employer offers to its full-time employees (and their dependents) the opportunity to enroll in minimum essential coverage under an eligible employer-sponsored plan (as defined in section 5000A(f)(2)),*

(C) *if the employer certifies that the employer did offer to its full-time employees (and their dependents) the opportunity to so enroll—*

(i) *in the case of an applicable large employer, the length of any waiting period (as defined in section 2701(b)(4) of the Public Health Service Act) with respect to such coverage,*

(ii) *the months during the calendar year for which coverage under the plan was available,*

(iii) *the monthly premium for the lowest cost option in each of the enrollment categories under the plan,*

(iv) *the employer's share of the total allowed costs of benefits provided under the plan, and*

(v) in the case of an offering employer, the option for which the employer pays the largest portion of the cost of the plan and the portion of the cost paid by the employer in each of the enrollment categories under such option,

(D) the number of full-time employees for each month during the calendar year,

(E) the name, address, and TIN of each full-time employee during the calendar year and the months (if any) during which such employee (and any dependents) were covered under any such health benefits plans, and

(F) such other information as the Secretary may require.

The Secretary shall have the authority to review the accuracy of the information provided under this subsection, including the applicable large employer's share under paragraph (2)(C)(iv).

[CCH Explanation at ¶ 415.]

Amendments

• **2010, Patient Protection and Affordable Care Act (P.L. 111-148)**

P.L. 111-148, § 10106(g):

Amended Code Sec. 6056(b), as added by Act Sec. 1514(a), by adding at the end a new flush sentence. **Effective** 3-23-2010.

P.L. 111-148, § 10108(j)(3)(B)(i)–(v):

Amended Code Sec. 6056(b)(2)(C) by inserting "in the case of an applicable large employer," before "the length" in clause (i); by striking "and" at the end of clause (iii); by striking "applicable large employer" in clause (iv) and inserting "employer"; by inserting "and" at the end of clause (iv); and by inserting at the end a new clause (v). **Effective** for periods beginning after 12-31-2013.

(c) STATEMENTS TO BE FURNISHED TO INDIVIDUALS WITH RESPECT TO WHOM INFORMATION IS REPORTED.—

(1) IN GENERAL.—Every person required to make a return under subsection (a) shall furnish to each full-time employee whose name is required to be set forth in such return under subsection (b)(2)(E) a written statement showing—

(A) the name and address of the person required to make such return and the phone number of the information contact for such person, and

(B) the information required to be shown on the return with respect to such individual.

(2) TIME FOR FURNISHING STATEMENTS.—The written statement required under paragraph (1) shall be furnished on or before January 31 of the year following the calendar year for which the return under subsection (a) was required to be made.

(d) COORDINATION WITH OTHER REQUIREMENTS.—To the maximum extent feasible, the Secretary may provide that—

(1) any return or statement required to be provided under this section may be provided as part of any return or statement required under section 6051 or 6055, and

(2) in the case of an applicable large employer or offering employer offering health insurance coverage of a health insurance issuer, the employer may enter into an agreement with the issuer to include information required under this section with the return and statement required to be provided by the issuer under section 6055.

[CCH Explanation at ¶ 415.]

Amendments

• **2010, Patient Protection and Affordable Care Act (P.L. 111-148)**

P.L. 111-148, § 10108(j)(3)(C):

Amended Code Sec. 6056(d)(2) by inserting "or offering employer" after "applicable large employer". **Effective** for periods beginning after 12-31-2013.

(e) COVERAGE PROVIDED BY GOVERNMENTAL UNITS.—In the case of any applicable large employer or offering employer which is a governmental unit or any agency or instrumentality thereof, the person appropriately designated for purposes of this section shall make the returns and statements required by this section.

[CCH Explanation at ¶415.]

Amendments

• 2010, Patient Protection and Affordable Care Act (P.L. 111-148)

P.L. 111-148, §10108(j)(3)(D):

Amended Code Sec. 6056(e) by inserting "or offering employer" after "applicable large employer". **Effective for** periods beginning after 12-31-2013.

(f) DEFINITIONS.—For purposes of this section—

(1) OFFERING EMPLOYER.—

(A) IN GENERAL.—The term "offering employer" means any offering employer (as defined in section 10108(b) of the Patient Protection and Affordable Care Act) if the required contribution (within the meaning of section 5000A(e)(1)(B)(i)) of any employee exceeds 8 percent of the wages (as defined in section 3121(a)) paid to such employee by such employer.

(B) INDEXING.—In the case of any calendar year beginning after 2014, the 8 percent under subparagraph (A) shall be adjusted for the calendar year to reflect the rate of premium growth between the preceding calendar year and 2013 over the rate of income growth for such period.

(2) OTHER DEFINITIONS.—Any term used in this section which is also used in section 4980H shall have the meaning given such term by section 4980H.

[CCH Explanation at ¶415. Committee Reports at ¶10,110.]

Amendments

• 2010, Patient Protection and Affordable Care Act (P.L. 111-148)

P.L. 111-148, §1514(a):

Amended subpart D of part III of subchapter A of chapter 61, as added by Act Sec. 1502, by inserting after Code Sec. 6055 a new Code Sec. 6056. **Effective** for periods beginning after 12-31-2013.

P.L. 111-148, §10108(j)(2):

Amended Code Sec. 6056(f), as added by Act Sec. 1514. **Effective** for periods beginning after 12-31-2013. **Prior to** amendment, Code Sec. 6056(f) read as follows:

(f) DEFINITIONS.—For purposes of this section, any term used in this section which is also used in section 4980H shall have the meaning given such term by section 4980H.

[¶5270] CODE SEC. 6103. CONFIDENTIALITY AND DISCLOSURE OF RETURNS AND RETURN INFORMATION.

(a) GENERAL RULE.—Returns and return information shall be confidential, and except as authorized by this title—

* * *

(3) no other person (or officer or employee thereof) who has or had access to returns or return information under subsection (e)(1)(D)(iii), paragraph (6), (10), (12), (16), (19), *(20), or (21)* of subsection (l), paragraph (2) or (4)(B) of subsection (m), or subsection (n),

shall disclose any return or return information obtained by him in any manner in connection with his service as such an officer or an employee or otherwise or under the provisions of this section. For purposes of this subsection, the term "officer or employee" includes a former officer or employee.

* * *

[CCH Explanation at ¶425. Committee Reports at ¶10,050.]

Amendments

• 2010, Patient Protection and Affordable Care Act (P.L. 111-148)

P.L. 111-148, §1414(b):

Amended Code Sec. 6103(a)(3) by striking "or (20)" and inserting "(20), or (21)". **Effective** 3-23-2010.

(l) DISCLOSURE OF RETURNS AND RETURN INFORMATION FOR PURPOSES OTHER THAN TAX ADMINISTRATION.—

* * *

(20) DISCLOSURE OF RETURN INFORMATION TO CARRY OUT MEDICARE PART B PREMIUM SUBSIDY ADJUSTMENT *AND PART D BASE BENEFICIARY PREMIUM INCREASE*.—

(A) IN GENERAL.—The Secretary shall, upon written request from the Commissioner of Social Security, disclose to officers, employees, and contractors of the Social Security Administration return information of a taxpayer whose premium (according to the records of the Secretary) may be subject to adjustment under section 1839(i) *or increase under section 1860D–13(a)(7)* of the Social Security Act. Such return information shall be limited to—

(i) taxpayer identity information with respect to such taxpayer,

(ii) the filing status of such taxpayer,

(iii) the adjusted gross income of such taxpayer,

(iv) the amounts excluded from such taxpayer's gross income under sections 135 and 911 to the extent such information is available,

(v) the interest received or accrued during the taxable year which is exempt from the tax imposed by chapter 1 to the extent such information is available,

(vi) the amounts excluded from such taxpayer's gross income by sections 931 and 933 to the extent such information is available,

(vii) such other information relating to the liability of the taxpayer as is prescribed by the Secretary by regulation as might indicate in the case of a taxpayer who is an individual described in subsection (i)(4)(B)(iii) of section 1839 of the Social Security Act that the amount of the premium of the taxpayer under such section may be subject to adjustment under subsection (i) of such section *or increase under section 1860D–13(a)(7) of such Act* and the amount of such adjustment, and

(viii) the taxable year with respect to which the preceding information relates.

(B) RESTRICTION ON USE OF DISCLOSED INFORMATION.—

(i) IN GENERAL.—Return information disclosed under subparagraph (A) may be used by officers, employees, and contractors of the Social Security Administration only for the purposes of, and to the extent necessary in, establishing the appropriate amount of any premium adjustment under such section 1839(i) *or increase under such section 1860D-13(a)(7) or for the purpose of resolving taxpayer appeals with respect to any such premium adjustment or increase.*

(ii) DISCLOSURE TO OTHER AGENCIES.—Officers, employees, and contractors of the Social Security Administration may disclose—

(I) the taxpayer identity information and the amount of the premium subsidy adjustment or premium increase with respect to a taxpayer described in subparagraph (A) to officers, employees, and contractors of the Centers for Medicare and Medicaid Services, to the extent that such disclosure is necessary for the collection of the premium subsidy amount or the increased premium amount,

(II) the taxpayer identity information and the amount of the premium subsidy adjustment or the increased premium amount with respect to a taxpayer described in subparagraph (A) to officers and employees of the Office of Personnel Management and the Railroad Retirement Board, to the extent that such disclosure is necessary for the collection of the premium subsidy amount or the increased premium amount,

(III) return information with respect to a taxpayer described in subparagraph (A) to officers and employees of the Department of Health and Human Services to the extent necessary to resolve administrative appeals of such premium subsidy adjustment or increased premium, and

(IV) return information with respect to a taxpayer described in subparagraph (A) to officers and employees of the Department of Justice for use in judicial proceedings to the extent necessary to carry out the purposes described in clause (i).

(21) DISCLOSURE OF RETURN INFORMATION TO CARRY OUT ELIGIBILITY REQUIREMENTS FOR CERTAIN PROGRAMS.—

(A) IN GENERAL.—The Secretary, upon written request from the Secretary of Health and Human Services, shall disclose to officers, employees, and contractors of the Department of Health and Human Services return information of any taxpayer whose income is relevant in determining any premium tax credit under section 36B or any cost-sharing reduction under section 1402 of the Patient Protection and Affordable Care Act or eligibility for participation in a State medicaid program under title XIX of the Social Security Act, a State's children's health insurance program under title XXI of the Social Security Act, or a basic health program under section 1331 of Patient Protection and Affordable Care Act. Such return information shall be limited to—

(i) taxpayer identity information with respect to such taxpayer,

(ii) the filing status of such taxpayer,

(iii) the number of individuals for whom a deduction is allowed under section 151 with respect to the taxpayer (including the taxpayer and the taxpayer's spouse),

(iv) the modified adjusted gross income (as defined in section 36B) of such taxpayer and each of the other individuals included under clause (iii) who are required to file a return of tax imposed by chapter 1 for the taxable year,

(v) such other information as is prescribed by the Secretary by regulation as might indicate whether the taxpayer is eligible for such credit or reduction (and the amount thereof), and

(vi) the taxable year with respect to which the preceding information relates or, if applicable, the fact that such information is not available.

(B) INFORMATION TO EXCHANGE AND STATE AGENCIES.—The Secretary of Health and Human Services may disclose to an Exchange established under the Patient Protection and Affordable Care Act or its contractors, or to a State agency administering a State program described in subparagraph (A) or its contractors, any inconsistency between the information provided by the Exchange or State agency to the Secretary and the information provided to the Secretary under subparagraph (A).

(C) RESTRICTION ON USE OF DISCLOSED INFORMATION.—Return information disclosed under subparagraph (A) or (B) may be used by officers, employees, and contractors of the Department of Health and Human Services, an Exchange, or a State agency only for the purposes of, and to the extent necessary in—

(i) establishing eligibility for participation in the Exchange, and verifying the appropriate amount of, any credit or reduction described in subparagraph (A),

(ii) determining eligibility for participation in the State programs described in subparagraph (A).

* * *

[CCH Explanation at ¶425 and ¶430. Committee Reports at ¶10,050 and ¶10,140.]

Amendments

• 2010, Health Care and Education Reconciliation Act of 2010 (P.L. 111-152)

P.L. 111-152, §1004(a)(1)(B):

Amended Code Sec. 6103(l)(21)(A)(iv), as added by section 1414 of the Patient Protection and Affordable Care Act (P.L. 111-148), by striking "modified gross" and inserting "modified adjusted gross". **Effective** 3-30-2010.

• 2010, Patient Protection and Affordable Care Act (P.L. 111-148)

P.L. 111-148, §1414(a)(1):

Amended Code Sec. 6103(l) by adding at the end a new paragraph (21). **Effective** 3-23-2010.

(p) PROCEDURE AND RECORDKEEPING.—

P.L. 111-148, §3308(b)(2)(A)-(C):

Amended Code Sec. 6103(l)(20), in the heading, by inserting "AND PART D BASE BENEFICIARY PREMIUM INCREASE" after "PART B PREMIUM SUBSIDY ADJUSTMENT"; in subparagraph (A), in the matter preceding clause (i), by inserting "or increase under section 1860D–13(a)(7)" after "1839(i)"; and in clause (vii), by inserting "or increase under section 1860D–13(a)(7) of such Act" after "subsection (i) of such section"; and in subparagraph (B), by striking "Return information" and inserting "(i) IN GENERAL.—Return information"; by inserting "or increase under such section 1860D–13(a)(7)" before the period at the end; and, as amended by Act Sec. 3308(b)(2)(C)(i), by inserting "or for the purpose of resolving taxpayer appeals with respect to any such premium adjustment or increase" before the period at the end; and by adding at the end a new clause (ii). **Effective** 3-23-2010.

* * *

(4) SAFEGUARDS.—Any Federal agency described in subsection (h)(2), (h)(5), (i)(1), (2), (3), (5), or (7), (j)(1), (2), or (5), (k)(8) or (10), (l)(1), (2), (3), (5), (10), (11), (13), (14), or (17) or (o)(1)(A), the Government Accountability Office, the Congressional Budget Office, or any agency, body, or commission described in subsection (d), (i)(3)(B)(i) or 7(A)(ii), or (l)(6), (7), (8), (9), (12), (15), or (16), any appropriate State officer (as defined in section 6104(c)), or any other person described in subsection (l)(10), (16), (18), (19), or (20), *or any entity described in subsection (l)(21)*, shall, as a condition for receiving returns or return information—

* * *

(F) upon completion of use of such returns or return information—

(i) in the case of an agency, body, or commission described in subsection (d), (i)(3)(B)(i), or (l)(6), (7), (8), (9), or (16), any appropriate State officer (as defined in section 6104(c)), or any other person described in subsection (l)(10), (16), (18), (19), or (20) return to the Secretary such returns or return information (along with any copies made there-from) or make such returns or return information undisclosable in any manner and furnish a written report to the Secretary describing such manner,

(ii) in the case of an agency described in subsections (h)(2), (h)(5), (i)(1), (2), (3), (5) or (7), (j)(1), (2), or (5), (k)(8) or (10), (l)(1), (2), (3), (5), (10), (11), (12), (13), (14), (15), or (17) or (o)(1)(A) *or any entity described in subsection (l)(21)*, the Government Accountability Office, or the Congressional Budget Office, either—

(I) return to the Secretary such returns or return information (along with any copies made therefrom),

(II) otherwise make such returns or return information undisclosable, or

(III) to the extent not so returned or made undisclosable, ensure that the conditions of subparagraphs (A), (B), (C), (D), and (E) of this paragraph continue to be met with respect to such returns or return information, and

(iii) in the case of the Department of Health and Human Services for purposes of subsection (m)(6), destroy all such return information upon completion of its use in providing the notification for which the information was obtained, so as to make such information undisclosable;

except that the conditions of subparagraphs (A), (B), (C), (D), and (E) shall cease to apply with respect to any return or return information if, and to the extent that, such return or return information is disclosed in the course of any judicial or administrative proceeding and made a part of the public record thereof. If the Secretary determines that any such agency, body, or commission, including an agency, an appropriate State officer (as defined in subsection (l)(10), (16), (18), (19), or (20), *or any entity described in subsection (l)(21)*, or the Government Accountability Office or the Congressional Budget Office, has failed to, or does not, meet the requirements of this paragraph, he may, after any proceedings for review established under paragraph (7), take such actions as are necessary to ensure such requirements are met, including refusing to disclose returns or return information to such agency, body, or commission, including an agency, an appropriate State officer (as defined in section 6104(c)), or any other person described in subsection (l)(10), (16), (18), (19), or (20), *or any entity described in subsection (l)(21)*, or the Government Accountability Office or the Congressional Budget Office, until he determines that such requirements have been or will be met. In the case of any agency which receives any mailing address under paragraph (2), (4), (6), or (7) of subsection (m) and which discloses any such mailing address to any agent or which receives any information under paragraph (6)(A), (10), (12)(B), or (16) of subsection (l) and which discloses any such information to any agent, or any person including an agent described in subsection (l)(10) or (16), this paragraph shall apply to such agency and each such agent or other person (except that, in the case of an agent, or any person including an agent described in subsection (l)(10) or (16), any report to the Secretary or other action with respect to the Secretary shall be made or taken through such agency). For purposes of applying this paragraph in any case to which subsection (m)(6) applies, the term "return information" includes related blood donor records (as defined in section 1141(h)(2) of the Social Security Act).

* * *

[CCH Explanation at ¶ 425. Committee Reports at ¶ 10,050.]

Amendments

• **2010, Patient Protection and Affordable Care Act (P.L. 111-148)**

P.L. 111-148, § 1414(c)(1)-(3):

Amended Code Sec. 6103(p)(4) by inserting ", or any entity described in subsection (l)(21)," after "or (20)" in the matter preceding subparagraph (A), by inserting "or any entity described in subsection (l)(21)," after "or (o)(1)(A)" in subparagraph (F)(ii), and by inserting "or any entity described in subsection (l)(21)," after "or (20)," both places it appears in the matter after subparagraph (F). **Effective** 3-23-2010.

[¶ 5275] CODE SEC. 6211. DEFINITION OF A DEFICIENCY.

* * *

(b) RULES FOR APPLICATION OF SUBSECTION (a).—For purposes of this section—

* * *

(4) For purposes of subsection (a)—

➤➤➤ *Caution: Code Sec. 6211(b)(4)(A), below, was amended by P.L. 111-148. For sunset provision, see P.L. 111-148, § 10909(c), in the amendment notes.*

(A) any excess of the sum of the credits allowable under sections 24(d), 25A by reason of subsection (i)(6) thereof, 32, 34, 35, 36, 36A, *36B, 36C,* 53(e), 168(k)(4), 6428, and 6431 over the tax imposed by subtitle A (determined without regard to such credits), and

(B) any excess of the sum of such credits as shown by the taxpayer on his return over the amount shown as the tax by the taxpayer on such return (determined without regard to such credits),

[CCH Explanation at ¶ 210. Committee Reports at ¶ 10,390.]

Amendments

• **2010, Patient Protection and Affordable Care Act (P.L. 111-148)**

P.L. 111-148, § 10105(d):

Amended Act Sec. 1401(d) by adding at the end a new Act Sec. 1401(d)(3), which amends Code Sec. 6211(b)(4)(A) by inserting "36B," after "36A,". **Effective** 3-23-2010.

P.L. 111-148, § 10909(b)(2)(N):

Amended Code Sec. 6211(b)(4)(A) by inserting "36C," before "53(e)". **Effective** for tax years beginning after 12-31-2009.

P.L. 111-148, § 10909(c), provides:

(c) APPLICATION AND EXTENSION OF EGTRRA SUNSET.—Notwithstanding section 901 of the Economic Growth and Tax Relief Reconciliation Act of 2001, such section shall apply to the amendments made by this section and the amendments made by section 202 of such Act by substituting "December 31, 2011" for "December 31, 2010" in subsection (a)(1) thereof.

[¶ 5276] CODE SEC. 6416. CERTAIN TAXES ON SALES AND SERVICES.

* * *

(b) SPECIAL CASES IN WHICH TAX PAYMENTS CONSIDERED OVERPAYMENTS.—Under regulations prescribed by the Secretary, credit or refund (without interest) shall be allowed or made in respect of the overpayments determined under the following paragraphs:

* * *

(2) SPECIFIED USES AND RESALES.—The tax paid under chapter 32 (or under subsection (a) or (d) of section 4041 in respect of sales or under section 4051) in respect of any article shall be deemed to be an overpayment if such article was, by any person—

(A) exported;

(B) used or sold for use as supplies for vessels or aircraft;

(C) sold to a State or local government for the exclusive use of a State or local government;

(D) sold to a nonprofit educational organization for its exclusive use;

(E) sold to a qualified blood collector organization (as defined in section 7701(a)(49)) for such organization's exclusive use in the collection, storage, or transportation of blood;

(F) in the case of any tire taxable under section 4071(a), sold to any person for use as described in section 4221(e)(3); or

(G) in the case of gasoline, used or sold for use in the production of special fuels referred to in section 4041.

≫→ *Caution: The last sentence of Code Sec. 6416(b)(2), below, as added by P.L. 111-152, applies to sales after December 31, 2012.*

Subparagraphs (C), (D), and (E) shall not apply in the case of any tax paid under section 4064. This paragraph shall not apply in the case of any tax imposed under section 4041(a)(1) or 4081 on diesel fuel or kerosene and any tax paid under section 4121. In the case of the tax imposed by section 4131, subparagraphs (B), (C), (D), and (E) shall not apply and subparagraph (A) shall apply only if the use of the exported vaccine meets such requirements as the Secretary may by regulations prescribe. Subparagraphs (C) and (D) shall not apply in the case of any tax imposed on gasoline under section 4081 if the requirements of subsection (a)(4) are not met. In the case of taxes imposed by subchapter C or D of chapter 32, subparagraph (E) shall not apply. *In the case of the tax imposed by section 4191, subparagraphs (B), (C), (D), and (E) shall not apply.*

* * *

[CCH Explanation at ¶350. Committee Reports at ¶10,420.]

Amendments

• **2010, Health Care and Education Reconciliation Act of 2010 (P.L. 111-152)**

P.L. 111-152, §1405(b)(2):

Amended Code Sec. 6416(b)(2), by adding at the end a new sentence. Effective for sales after 12-31-2012.

[¶5277] CODE SEC. 6654. FAILURE BY INDIVIDUAL TO PAY ESTIMATED INCOME TAX.

≫→ *Caution: Code Sec. 6654(a), below, as amended by P.L. 111-152, applies to tax years beginning after December 31, 2012.*

(a) ADDITION TO THE TAX.—Except as otherwise provided in this section, in the case of any underpayment of estimated tax by an individual, there shall be added to the tax under chapter 1[,] *the tax under chapter 2, and the tax under chapter 2A* for the taxable year an amount determined by applying—

(1) the underpayment rate established under section 6621,

(2) to the amount of the underpayment,

(3) for the period of the underpayment.

* * *

[CCH Explanation at ¶232. Committee Reports at ¶10,410.]

Amendments

• **2010, Health Care and Education Reconciliation Act of 2010 (P.L. 111-152)**

P.L. 111-152, §1402(a)(2)(A):

Amended Code Sec. 6654(a) by striking "and the tax under chapter 2" and inserting "the tax under chapter 2, and the tax under chapter 2A". Effective for tax years beginning after 12-31-2012.

(f) TAX COMPUTED AFTER APPLICATION OF CREDITS AGAINST TAX.—For purposes of this section, the term "tax" means—

(1) the tax imposed by chapter 1 (other than any increase in such tax by reason of section 143(m)), plus

>>>→ *Caution: Code Sec. 6654(f)(2)-(4), below, as amended by P.L. 111-152, applies to tax years beginning after December 31, 2012.*

(2) the tax imposed by chapter 2, *plus*

(3) *the taxes imposed by chapter 2A, minus*

(4) the credits against tax provided by part IV of subchapter A of chapter 1, other than the credit against tax provided by section 31 (relating to tax withheld on wages).

* * *

[CCH Explanation at ¶ 232. Committee Reports at ¶ 10,410.]

Amendments

• **2010, Health Care and Education Reconciliation Act of 2010 (P.L. 111-152)**

P.L. 111-152, § 1402(a)(2)(B)(i)-(ii):

Amended Code Sec. 6654(f) by striking "minus" at the end of paragraph (2) and inserting "plus"; and by redesig-

nating paragraph (3) as paragraph (4) and inserting after paragraph (2) a new paragraph (3). **Effective** for tax years beginning after 12-31-2012.

>>>→ *Caution: Code Sec. 6654(m), below, as added by P.L. 111-152, applies with respect to remuneration received, and tax years beginning after, December 31, 2012.*

(m) SPECIAL RULE FOR MEDICARE TAX.—For purposes of this section, the tax imposed under section 3101(b)(2) (to the extent not withheld) shall be treated as a tax imposed under chapter 2.

[CCH Explanation at ¶ 230. Committee Reports at ¶ 10,410.]

Amendments

• **2010, Health Care and Education Reconciliation Act of 2010 (P.L. 111-152)**

P.L. 111-152, § 1402(b)(2):

Amended Code Sec. 6654 by redesignating subsection (m) as subsection (n) and by inserting after subsection (l) a new

subsection (m). **Effective** with respect to remuneration received, and tax years beginning after, 12-31-2012.

>>>→ *Caution: Former Code Sec. 6654(m) was redesignated by P.L. 111-152 as Code Sec. 6654(n), below, applicable with respect to remuneration received, and tax years beginning after, December 31, 2012.*

(n) REGULATIONS.—The Secretary shall prescribe such regulations as may be necessary to carry out the purposes of this section.

[CCH Explanation at ¶ 230. Committee Reports at ¶ 10,410.]

Amendments

• **2010, Health Care and Education Reconciliation Act of 2010 (P.L. 111-152)**

P.L. 111-152, § 1402(b)(2):

Amended Code Sec. 6654 by redesignating subsection (m) as subsection (n). **Effective** with respect to remuneration received, and tax years beginning after, 12-31-2012.

>>>→ *Caution: The text of Code Sec. 6662, below, highlights only the amendments made by P.L. 111-152. For the version of Code Sec. 6662, as amended by P.L. 111-147, please see ¶ 6170.*

[¶ 5278] CODE SEC. 6662. IMPOSITION OF ACCURACY-RELATED PENALTY ON UNDERPAYMENTS.

* * *

(b) PORTION OF UNDERPAYMENT TO WHICH SECTION APPLIES.—This section shall apply to the portion of any underpayment which is attributable to 1 or more of the following:

(1) Negligence or disregard of rules or regulations.

(2) Any substantial understatement of income tax.

(3) Any substantial valuation misstatement under chapter 1.

(4) Any substantial overstatement of pension liabilities.

(5) Any substantial estate or gift tax valuation understatement.

(6) *Any disallowance of claimed tax benefits by reason of a transaction lacking economic substance (within the meaning of section 7701(o)) or failing to meet the requirements of any similar rule of law.*

(7) Any undisclosed foreign financial asset understatement.

This section shall not apply to any portion of an underpayment on which a penalty is imposed under section 6663. Except as provided in paragraph (1) or (2)(B) of section 6662A(e), this section shall not apply to the portion of any underpayment which is attributable to a reportable transaction understatement on which a penalty is imposed under section 6662A.

* * *

[CCH Explanation at ¶343. Committee Reports at ¶10,440.]

Amendments

• **2010, Health Care and Education Reconciliation Act of 2010 (P.L. 111-152)**

P.L. 111-152, §1409(b)(1):

Amended Code Sec. 6662(b) by inserting after paragraph (5) a new paragraph (6). **Effective** for underpayments attributable to transactions entered into after 3-30-2010.

(i) INCREASE IN PENALTY IN CASE OF NONDISCLOSED NONECONOMIC SUBSTANCE TRANSACTIONS.—

(1) IN GENERAL.—*In the case of any portion of an underpayment which is attributable to one or more nondisclosed noneconomic substance transactions, subsection (a) shall be applied with respect to such portion by substituting "40 percent" for "20 percent".*

(2) NONDISCLOSED NONECONOMIC SUBSTANCE TRANSACTIONS.—*For purposes of this subsection, the term "nondisclosed noneconomic substance transaction" means any portion of a transaction described in subsection (b)(6) with respect to which the relevant facts affecting the tax treatment are not adequately disclosed in the return nor in a statement attached to the return.*

(3) SPECIAL RULE FOR AMENDED RETURNS.—*In no event shall any amendment or supplement to a return of tax be taken into account for purposes of this subsection if the amendment or supplement is filed after the earlier of the date the taxpayer is first contacted by the Secretary regarding the examination of the return or such other date as is specified by the Secretary.*

[CCH Explanation at ¶343. Committee Reports at ¶10,440.]

Amendments

• **2010, Health Care and Education Reconciliation Act of 2010 (P.L. 111-152)**

P.L. 111-152, §1409(b)(2):

Amended Code Sec. 6662 by adding at the end a new subsection (i). **Effective** for underpayments attributable to transactions entered into after 3-30-2010.

[¶5279] CODE SEC. 6662A. IMPOSITION OF ACCURACY-RELATED PENALTY ON UNDERSTATEMENTS WITH RESPECT TO REPORTABLE TRANSACTIONS.

* * *

(e) SPECIAL RULES.—

* * *

(2) COORDINATION WITH OTHER PENALTIES.—

* * *

(B) Coordination with *certain increased underpayment penalties.*—This section shall not apply to any portion of an understatement on which a penalty is imposed under section 6662 if the rate of the penalty is determined under *subsections* [sic] *(h) or (i) of section 6662.*

* * *

[CCH Explanation at ¶ 343. Committee Reports at ¶ 10,440.]

Amendments

• **2010, Health Care and Education Reconciliation Act of 2010 (P.L. 111-152)**

P.L. 111-152, § 1409(b)(3)(A)-(B):

Amended Code Sec. 6662A(e)(2)(B) by striking "section 6662(h)" and inserting "subsections [sic] (h) or (i) of section

6662"; and by striking "GROSS VALUATION MISSTATEMENT PENALTY" in the heading and inserting "CERTAIN INCREASED UNDERPAYMENT PENALTIES". **Effective** for underpayments attributable to transactions entered into after 3-30-2010.

[¶ 5279A] CODE SEC 6664. DEFINITIONS AND SPECIAL RULES.

* * *

(c) Reasonable Cause Exception for Underpayments.—

* * *

(2) Exception.—Paragraph (1) shall not apply to any portion of an underpayment which is attributable to one or more transactions described in section 6662(b)(6).

(3) Special rule for certain valuation overstatements.—In the case of any underpayment attributable to a substantial or gross valuation over statement under chapter 1 with respect to charitable deduction property, paragraph (1) shall not apply. The preceding sentence shall not apply to a substantial valuation overstatement under chapter 1 if—

(A) the claimed value of the property was based on a qualified appraisal made by a qualified appraiser, and

(B) in addition to obtaining such appraisal, the taxpayer made a good faith investigation of the value of the contributed property.

(4) Definitions.—For purposes of this subsection—

(A) Charitable deduction property.—The term "charitable deduction property" means any property contributed by the taxpayer in a contribution for which a deduction was claimed under section 170. For purposes of *paragraph (3)*, such term shall not include any securities for which (as of the date of the contribution) market quotations are readily available on an established securities market.

* * *

[CCH Explanation at ¶ 343. Committee Reports at ¶ 10,440.]

Amendments

• **2010, Health Care and Education Reconciliation Act of 2010 (P.L. 111-152)**

P.L. 111-152, § 1409(c)(1)(A)-(C):

Amended Code Sec. 6664(c) by redesignating paragraphs (2) and (3) as paragraphs (3) and (4), respectively; by strik-

ing "paragraph (2)" in paragraph (4)(A), as so redesignated, and inserting "paragraph (3)"; and by inserting after paragraph (1) a new paragraph (2). **Effective** for underpayments attributable to transactions entered into after 3-30-2010.

(d) Reasonable Cause Exception for Reportable Transaction Understatements.—

* * *

(2) Exception.—Paragraph (1) shall not apply to any portion of a reportable transaction understatement which is attributable to one or more transactions described in section 6662(b)(6).

(3) Special rules.—Paragraph (1) shall not apply to any reportable transaction understatement unless—

(A) the relevant facts affecting the tax treatment of the item are adequately disclosed in accordance with the regulations prescribed under section 6011,

(B) there is or was substantial authority for such treatment, and

(C) the taxpayer reasonably believed that such treatment was more likely than not the proper treatment.

A taxpayer failing to adequately disclose in accordance with section 6011 shall be treated as meeting the requirements of subparagraph (A) if the penalty for such failure was rescinded under section 6707A(d).

(4) RULES RELATING TO REASONABLE BELIEF.—For purposes of *paragraph (3)(C)—*

* * *

[CCH Explanation at ¶ 343. Committee Reports at ¶ 10,440.]

Amendments

• **2010, Health Care and Education Reconciliation Act of 2010 (P.L. 111-152)**

P.L. 111-152, § 1409(c)(2)(A)-(C):

Amended Code Sec. 6664(d) by redesignating paragraphs (2) and (3) as paragraphs (3) and (4), respectively; by strik-ing "paragraph (2)(C)" in paragraph (4), as so redesignated, and inserting "paragraph (3)(C)"; and by inserting after paragraph (1) a new paragraph (2). **Effective** for understatements attributable to transactions entered into after 3-30-2010.

[¶ 5279C] CODE SEC. 6676. ERRONEOUS CLAIM FOR REFUND OR CREDIT.

* * *

(c) NONECONOMIC SUBSTANCE TRANSACTIONS TREATED AS LACKING REASONABLE BASIS.—*For purposes of this section, any excessive amount which is attributable to any transaction described in section 6662(b)(6) shall not be treated as having a reasonable basis.*

[CCH Explanation at ¶ 343. Committee Reports at ¶ 10,440.]

Amendments

• **2010, Health Care and Education Reconciliation Act of 2010 (P.L. 111-152)**

P.L. 111-152, § 1409(d):

Amended Code Sec. 6676 by redesignating subsection (c) as subsection (d) and inserting after subsection (b) a new subsection (c). **Effective** for refunds and credits attributable to transactions entered into after 3-30-2010.

(d) COORDINATION WITH OTHER PENALTIES.—This section shall not apply to any portion of the excessive amount of a claim for refund or credit which is subject to a penalty imposed under part II of subchapter A of chapter 68.

[Committee Reports at ¶ 10,440.]

Amendments

• **2010, Health Care and Education Reconciliation Act of 2010 (P.L. 111-152)**

P.L. 111-152, § 1409(d):

Amended Code Sec. 6676 by redesignating subsection (c) as subsection (d). **Effective** for refunds and credits attributable to transactions entered into after 3-30-2010.

⨠⨠➔ *Caution: The text of Code Sec. 6724, below, highlights only the amendments made by P.L. 111-148. For the version of Code Sec. 6724, as amended by P.L. 111-147, please see ¶ 6185.*

[¶ 5280] CODE SEC. 6724. WAIVER; DEFINITIONS AND SPECIAL RULES.

* * *

(d) DEFINITIONS.—For purposes of this part—

(1) INFORMATION RETURN.—The term "information return" means—

* * *

(B) any return required by—

* * *

(xxii) section 6039(a) (relating to returns required with respect to certain options),

(xxiii) section 6050W (relating to returns to payments made in settlement of payment card transactions),

≫→ *Caution: Code Sec. 6724(d)(1)(B)(xxiv), below, as added by P.L. 111-148, applies to calendar years beginning after 2013.*

(xxiv) *section 6055 (relating to returns relating to information regarding health insurance coverage), or*

≫→ *Caution: Code Sec. 6724(d)(1)(B)(xxv), below, as added and amended by P.L. 111-148, applies to periods beginning after December 31, 2013.*

(xxv) *section 6056 (relating to returns relating to certain employers required to report on health insurance coverage), and*

* * *

(2) PAYEE STATEMENT.—The term "payee statement" means any statement required to be furnished under—

* * *

(EE) section 6050U (relating to charges or payments for qualified long-term care insurance contracts under combined arrangements),

(FF) section 6050W(c) (relating to returns relating to payments made in settlement of payment card transactions),

≫→ *Caution: Code Sec. 6724(d)(2)(GG), below, as added by P.L. 111-148, applies to calendar years beginning after 2013.*

(GG) *section 6055(c) (relating to statements relating to information regarding health insurance coverage), or*

≫→ *Caution: Code Sec. 6724(d)(2)(HH), below, as added and amended by P.L. 111-148, applies to periods beginning after December 31, 2013.*

(HH) *section 6056(c) (relating to statements relating to certain employers required to report on health insurance coverage).*

* * *

[CCH Explanation at ¶410 and ¶415. Committee Reports at ¶10,090 and ¶10,110.]

Amendments

• 2010, Patient Protection and Affordable Care Act (P.L. 111-148)

P.L. 111-148, §1502(b)(1):

Amended Code Sec. 6724(d)(1)(B) by striking "or" at the end of clause (xxii), by striking "and" at the end of clause (xxiii) and inserting "or", and by inserting after clause (xxiii) a new clause (xxiv). **Effective** for calendar years beginning after 2013.

P.L. 111-148, §1502(b)(2):

Amended Code Sec. 6724(d)(2) by striking "or" at the end of subparagraph (EE), by striking the period at the end of subparagraph (FF) and inserting ", or" and by inserting after subparagraph (FF) a new subparagraph (GG). **Effective** for calendar years beginning after 2013.

P.L. 111-148, §1514(b)(1):

Amended Code Sec. 6724(d)(1)(B), as amended by Act Sec. 1502(b)(1), by striking "or" at the end of clause (xxiii),

by striking "and" at the end of clause (xxiv) and inserting "or", and by inserting after clause (xxiv) a new clause (xxv). **Effective** for periods beginning after 12-31-2013.

P.L. 111-148, §1514(b)(2):

Amended Code Sec. 6724(d)(2), as amended by Act Sec. 1502(b)(2), by striking "or" at the end of subparagraph (FF), by striking the period at the end of subparagraph (GG) and inserting ", or" and by inserting after subparagraph (GG) a new subparagraph (HH). **Effective** for periods beginning after 12-31-2013.

P.L. 111-148, §10108(j)(3)(E):

Amended Code Sec. 6724(d)(1)(B)(xxv), as added by Act Sec. 1514(b)(1), by striking "large" and inserting "certain". **Effective** for periods beginning after 12-31-2013.

P.L. 111-148, §10108(j)(3)(F):

Amended Code Sec. 6724(d)(2)(HH), as added by Act Sec. 1514(b)(2), by striking "large" and inserting "certain". **Effective** for periods beginning after 12-31-2013.

[¶5285] CODE SEC. 7213. UNAUTHORIZED DISCLOSURE OF INFORMATION.

(a) RETURNS AND RETURN INFORMATION.—

* * *

(2) STATE AND OTHER EMPLOYEES.—It shall be unlawful for any person (not described in paragraph (1)) willfully to disclose to any person, except as authorized in this title, any return or return information (as defined in section 6103(b)) acquired by him or another person under subsection (d), (i)(3)(B)(i) or (7)(A)(ii), (l)(6), (7), (8), (9), (10), (12), (15), (16), (19), *(20), or (21)* or (m)(2), (4), (5), (6), or (7) of section 6103 or under section 6104(c). Any violation of this paragraph shall be a felony punishable by a fine in any amount not exceeding $5,000, or imprisonment of not more than 5 years, or both, together with the costs of prosecution.

* * *

[CCH Explanation at ¶425. Committee Reports at ¶10,050.]

Amendments

• **2010, Patient Protection and Affordable Care Act (P.L. 111-148)**

P.L. 111-148, §1414(d):

Amended Code Sec. 7213(a)(2) by striking "or (20)" and inserting "(20), or (21)". **Effective** 3-23-2010.

[¶5287] CODE SEC. 7701. DEFINITIONS.

* * *

(o) CLARIFICATION OF ECONOMIC SUBSTANCE DOCTRINE.—

(1) APPLICATION OF DOCTRINE.—*In the case of any transaction to which the economic substance doctrine is relevant, such transaction shall be treated as having economic substance only if—*

(A) the transaction changes in a meaningful way (apart from Federal income tax effects) the taxpayer's economic position, and

(B) the taxpayer has a substantial purpose (apart from Federal income tax effects) for entering into such transaction.

(2) SPECIAL RULE WHERE TAXPAYER RELIES ON PROFIT POTENTIAL.—

(A) IN GENERAL.—*The potential for profit of a transaction shall be taken into account in determining whether the requirements of subparagraphs (A) and (B) of paragraph (1) are met with respect to the transaction only if the present value of the reasonably expected pre-tax profit from the transaction is substantial in relation to the present value of the expected net tax benefits that would be allowed if the transaction were respected.*

(B) TREATMENT OF FEES AND FOREIGN TAXES.—*Fees and other transaction expenses shall be taken into account as expenses in determining pre-tax profit under subparagraph (A). The Secretary shall issue regulations requiring foreign taxes to be treated as expenses in determining pre-tax profit in appropriate cases.*

(3) STATE AND LOCAL TAX BENEFITS.—*For purposes of paragraph (1), any State or local income tax effect which is related to a Federal income tax effect shall be treated in the same manner as a Federal income tax effect.*

(4) FINANCIAL ACCOUNTING BENEFITS.—*For purposes of paragraph (1)(B), achieving a financial accounting benefit shall not be taken into account as a purpose for entering into a transaction if the origin of such financial accounting benefit is a reduction of Federal income tax.*

(5) DEFINITIONS AND SPECIAL RULES.—*For purposes of this subsection—*

(A) ECONOMIC SUBSTANCE DOCTRINE.—*The term "economic substance doctrine" means the common law doctrine under which tax benefits under subtitle A with respect to a transaction are not allowable if the transaction does not have economic substance or lacks a business purpose.*

(B) EXCEPTION FOR PERSONAL TRANSACTIONS OF INDIVIDUALS.—*In the case of an individual, paragraph (1) shall apply only to transactions entered into in connection with a trade or business or an activity engaged in for the production of income.*

(C) DETERMINATION OF APPLICATION OF DOCTRINE NOT AFFECTED.—*The determination of whether the economic substance doctrine is relevant to a transaction shall be made in the same manner as if this subsection had never been enacted.*

(D) TRANSACTION.—*The term "transaction" includes a series of transactions.*

[CCH Explanation at ¶342. Committee Reports at ¶10,440.]

Amendments

• **2010, Health Care and Education Reconciliation Act of 2010 (P.L. 111-152)**

P.L. 111-152, §1409(a):

Amended Code Sec. 7701 by redesignating subsection (o) as subsection (p) and by inserting after subsection (n) a new

(p) CROSS REFERENCES.—

subsection (o). **Effective** for transactions entered into after 3-30-2010.

* * *

[CCH Explanation at ¶342. Committee Reports at ¶10,440.]

Amendments

• **2010, Health Care and Education Reconciliation Act of 2010 (P.L. 111-152)**

P.L. 111-152, §1409(a):

Amended Code Sec. 7701 by redesignating subsection (o) as subsection (p). **Effective** for transactions entered into after 3-30-2010.

[¶5290] CODE SEC. 9511. PATIENT-CENTERED OUTCOMES RESEARCH TRUST FUND.

(a) CREATION OF TRUST FUND.—*There is established in the Treasury of the United States a trust fund to be known as the "Patient-Centered Outcomes Research Trust Fund" (hereafter in this section referred to as the "PCORTF"), consisting of such amounts as may be appropriated or credited to such Trust Fund as provided in this section and section 9602(b).*

(b) TRANSFERS TO FUND.—

(1) APPROPRIATION.—*There are hereby appropriated to the Trust Fund the following:*

(A) *For fiscal year 2010, $10,000,000.*

(B) *For fiscal year 2011, $50,000,000.*

(C) *For fiscal year 2012, $150,000,000.*

(D) *For fiscal year 2013—*

(i) *an amount equivalent to the net revenues received in the Treasury from the fees imposed under subchapter B of chapter 34 (relating to fees on health insurance and self-insured plans) for such fiscal year; and*

(ii) *$150,000,000.*

(E) *For each of fiscal years 2014, 2015, 2016, 2017, 2018, and 2019—*

(i) *an amount equivalent to the net revenues received in the Treasury from the fees imposed under subchapter B of chapter 34 (relating to fees on health insurance and self-insured plans) for such fiscal year; and*

(ii) *$150,000,000.*

The amounts appropriated under subparagraphs (A), (B), (C), (D)(ii), and (E)(ii) shall be transferred from the general fund of the Treasury, from funds not otherwise appropriated.

(2) TRUST FUND TRANSFERS.—*In addition to the amounts appropriated under paragraph (1), there shall be credited to the PCORTF the amounts transferred under section 1183 of the Social Security Act.*

(3) LIMITATION ON TRANSFERS TO PCORTF.—*No amount may be appropriated or transferred to the PCORTF on and after the date of any expenditure from the PCORTF which is not an expenditure permitted under this section. The determination of whether an expenditure is so permitted shall be made without regard to—*

(A) any provision of law which is not contained or referenced in this chapter or in a revenue Act, and

(B) whether such provision of law is a subsequently enacted provision or directly or indirectly seeks to waive the application of this paragraph.

(c) TRUSTEE.—*The Secretary of the Treasury shall be a trustee of the PCORTF.*

(d) EXPENDITURES FROM FUND.—

(1) AMOUNTS AVAILABLE TO THE PATIENT-CENTERED OUTCOMES RESEARCH INSTITUTE.—*Subject to paragraph (2), amounts in the PCORTF are available, without further appropriation, to the Patient-Centered Outcomes Research Institute established under section 1181(b) of the Social Security Act for carrying out part D of title XI of the Social Security Act (as in effect on the date of enactment of such Act).*

(2) TRANSFER OF FUNDS.—

(A) IN GENERAL.—*The trustee of the PCORTF shall provide for the transfer from the PCORTF of 20 percent of the amounts appropriated or credited to the PCORTF for each of fiscal years 2011 through 2019 to the Secretary of Health and Human Services to carry out section 937 of the Public Health Service Act.*

(B) AVAILABILITY.—*Amounts transferred under subparagraph (A) shall remain available until expended.*

(C) REQUIREMENTS.—*Of the amounts transferred under subparagraph (A) with respect to a fiscal year, the Secretary of Health and Human Services shall distribute—*

(i) 80 percent to the Office of Communication and Knowledge Transfer of the Agency for Healthcare Research and Quality (or any other relevant office designated by Agency for Healthcare Research and Quality) to carry out the activities described in section 937 of the Public Health Service Act; and

(ii) 20 percent to the Secretary to carry out the activities described in such section 937.

(e) NET REVENUES.—*For purposes of this section, the term "net revenues" means the amount estimated by the Secretary of the Treasury based on the excess of—*

(1) the fees received in the Treasury under subchapter B of chapter 34, over

(2) the decrease in the tax imposed by chapter 1 resulting from the fees imposed by such subchapter.

(f) TERMINATION.—*No amounts shall be available for expenditure from the PCORTF after September 30, 2019, and any amounts in such Trust Fund after such date shall be transferred to the general fund of the Treasury.*

[CCH Explanation at ¶445. Committee Reports at ¶10,150.]
Amendments
• **2010, Patient Protection and Affordable Care Act (P.L. 111-148)**

P.L. 111-148, §6301(e)(1)(A):
Amended subchapter A of chapter 98 by adding at the end a new Code Sec. 9511. **Effective** 3-23-2010.

[¶5295] *CODE SEC. 9815. ADDITIONAL MARKET REFORMS.*

(a) GENERAL RULE.—*Except as provided in subsection (b)—*

(1) the provisions of part A of title XXVII of the Public Health Service Act (as amended by the Patient Protection and Affordable Care Act) shall apply to group health plans, and health insurance issuers providing health insurance coverage in connection with group health plans, as if included in this subchapter; and

(2) *to the extent that any provision of this subchapter conflicts with a provision of such part A with respect to group health plans, or health insurance issuers providing health insurance coverage in connection with group health plans, the provisions of such part A shall apply.*

(b) EXCEPTION.—*Notwithstanding subsection (a), the provisions of sections 2716 and 2718 of title XXVII of the Public Health Service Act (as amended by the Patient Protection and Affordable Care Act) shall not apply with respect to self-insured group health plans, and the provisions of this subchapter shall continue to apply to such plans as if such sections of the Public Health Service Act (as so amended) had not been enacted.*

[CCH Explanation at ¶455.]
Amendments
• **2010, Patient Protection and Affordable Care Act (P.L. 111-148)**

P.L. 111-148, §1563(f) (as redesignated by P.L. 111-148, §10107(b)):

Amended subchapter B of chapter 100 by adding at the end a new Code Sec. 9815. Effective 3-23-2010.

HIRING INCENTIVES TO RESTORE EMPLOYMENT ACT

[¶ 6001]

≫→ *Caution: The provisions below reflect amendments made by P.L. 111-144 and P.L. 111-147; see ¶5001 and following for amendments made by P.L. 111-148 and P.L. 152.*

INTRODUCTION.

The Internal Revenue Code provisions amended by the Hiring Incentives to Restore Employment Act (P.L. 111-147) and the Temporary Extension Act of 2010 (P.L. 111-144) are shown in the following paragraphs. Deleted Code material or the text of the Code Section prior to amendment appears in the amendment notes following each amended Code provision. *Any changed or added material is set out in italics.*

[¶ 6005] CODE SEC. 35. HEALTH INSURANCE COSTS OF ELIGIBLE INDIVIDUALS.

* * *

(g) SPECIAL RULES.—

* * *

(9) COBRA PREMIUM ASSISTANCE.—In the case of an assistance eligible individual who receives premium reduction for COBRA continuation coverage under *section 3001(a) of title III of division B of the American Recovery and Reinvestment Act of 2009* for any month during the taxable year, such individual shall not be treated as an eligible individual, a certified individual, or a qualifying family member for purposes of this section or section 7527 with respect to such month.

* * *

[CCH Explanation at ¶ 615. Committee Reports at ¶ 11,030.]

Amendments

• **2010, Temporary Extension Act of 2010 (P.L. 111-144)**

P.L. 111-144, §3(b)(5)(A):

Amended Code Sec. 35(g)(9) by striking "section 3002(a) of the Health Insurance Assistance for the Unemployed Act of 2009" and inserting "section 3001(a) of title III of division B of the American Recovery and Reinvestment Act of 2009". Effective as if included in the provision of section 3001 of division B of the American Recovery and Reinvestment Act of 2009 to which it relates [effective for tax years ending after 2-17-2009.—CCH].

[¶ 6010] CODE SEC. 51. AMOUNT OF CREDIT.

* * *

(c) WAGES DEFINED.—For purposes of this subpart—

* * *

(5) *COORDINATION WITH PAYROLL TAX FORGIVENESS.—The term "wages" shall not include any amount paid or incurred to a qualified individual (as defined in section 3111(d)(3)) during the 1-year period beginning on the hiring date of such individual by a qualified employer (as defined in section 3111(d)) unless such qualified employer makes an election not to have section 3111(d) apply.*

* * *

[CCH Explanation at ¶ 605. Committee Reports at ¶ 11,010.]

Amendments

• **2010, Hiring Incentives to Restore Employment Act (P.L. 111-147)**

P.L. 111-147, §101(b):

Amended Code Sec. 51(c) by adding at the end a new paragraph (5). Effective for wages paid after 3-18-2010.

[¶6015] CODE SEC. 54F. QUALIFIED SCHOOL CONSTRUCTION BONDS.

* * *

(d) ALLOCATION OF LIMITATION.—

(1) ALLOCATION AMONG STATES.—Except as provided in paragraph (2)(C), the limitation applicable under subsection (c) for any calendar year shall be allocated by the Secretary among the States in proportion to the respective amounts each such State is eligible to receive under section 1124 of the Elementary and Secondary Education Act of 1965 (20 U.S.C. 6333) for the most recent fiscal year ending before such calendar year. The limitation amount allocated to a State under the preceding sentence shall be allocated *by the State education agency (or such other agency as is authorized under State law to make such allocation)* to issuers within such State.

* * *

[CCH Explanation at ¶625. Committee Reports at ¶11,040.]

Amendments

• 2010, Hiring Incentives to Restore Employment Act (P.L. 111-147)

P.L. 111-147, §301(b)(1):

Amended the second sentence of Code Sec. 54F(d)(1) by striking "by the State" and inserting "by the State education agency (or such other agency as is authorized under State law to make such allocation)". **Effective** as if included in section 1521 of the American Recovery and Reinvestment Tax Act of 2009 [**effective** for obligations issued after 2-17-2009.—CCH].

(e) CARRYOVER OF UNUSED LIMITATION.—If for any calendar year—

(1) the amount allocated under subsection (d) to any State, exceeds

(2) the amount of bonds issued during such year which are designated under subsection (a) pursuant to such allocation,

the limitation amount under such subsection for such State for the following calendar year shall be increased by the amount of such excess. A similar rule shall apply to the amounts allocated under *paragraphs (2) and (4) of subsection (d).*

Amendments

• 2010, Hiring Incentives to Restore Employment Act (P.L. 111-147)

P.L. 111-147, §301(b)(2):

Amended the second sentence of Code Sec. 54F(e) by striking "subsection (d)(4)" and inserting "paragraphs (2) and (4) of subsection (d)". **Effective** as if included in section 1521 of the American Recovery and Reinvestment Tax Act of 2009 [**effective** for obligations issued after 2-17-2009.—CCH].

[¶6020] CODE SEC. 139C. COBRA PREMIUM ASSISTANCE.

In the case of an assistance eligible individual (as defined in *section 3001 of title III of division B of the American Recovery and Reinvestment Act of 2009*), gross income does not include any premium reduction provided under subsection (a) of such section.

[CCH Explanation at ¶615. Committee Reports at ¶11,030.]

Amendments

• 2010, Temporary Extension Act of 2010 (P.L. 111-144)

P.L. 111-144, §3(b)(5)(B):

Amended Code Sec. 139C by striking "section 3002 of the Health Insurance Assistance for the Unemployed Act of 2009" and inserting "section 3001 of title III of division B of the American Recovery and Reinvestment Act of 2009". **Effective** as if included in the provision of section 3001 of division B of the American Recovery and Reinvestment Act of 2009 to which it relates [**effective** for tax years ending after 2-17-2009.—CCH].

[¶6025] CODE SEC. 149. BONDS MUST BE REGISTERED TO BE TAX EXEMPT; OTHER REQUIREMENTS.

(a) BONDS MUST BE REGISTERED TO BE TAX EXEMPT.—

* * *

(2) REGISTRATION-REQUIRED BOND.—For purposes of paragraph (1), the term "registration-required bond" means any bond other than a bond which—

(A) is not of a type offered to the public, *or*

(B) has a maturity (at issue) of not more than 1 year.

≫→ *Caution: Code Sec. 149(a)(2)(C), below, was stricken by P.L. 111-147, applicable to obligations issued after the date which is 2 years after March 18, 2010.*

(C) is described in section 163(f)(2)(B).

* * *

[CCH Explanation at ¶ 760.]

Amendments

• **2010, Hiring Incentives to Restore Employment Act (P.L. 111-147)**

P.L. 111-147, § 502(a)(2)(A):

Amended Code Sec. 149(a)(2) by inserting "or" at the end of subparagraph (A), by striking ", or" at the end of subpar-

agraph (B) and inserting a period, and by striking subparagraph (C). **Effective** for obligations issued after the date which is 2 years after 3-18-2010. Prior to being stricken, Code Sec. 149(a)(2)(C) read as follows:

(C) is described in section 163(f)(2)(B).

[¶ 6030] CODE SEC. 163. INTEREST.

* * *

(f) DENIAL OF DEDUCTION FOR INTEREST ON CERTAIN OBLIGATIONS NOT IN REGISTERED FORM.—

* * *

(2) REGISTRATION-REQUIRED OBLIGATION.—For purposes of this section—

(A) IN GENERAL.—The term "registration-required obligation" means any obligation (including any obligation issued by a governmental entity) other than an obligation which—

(i) is issued by a natural person,

(ii) is not of a type offered to the public, *or*

(iii) has a maturity (at issue) of not more than 1 year.

≫→ *Caution: Code Sec. 163(f)(2)(A)(iv), below, was stricken by P.L. 111-147, applicable to obligations issued after the date which is 2 years after March 18, 2010.*

(iv) is described in subparagraph (B).

≫→ *Caution: Code Sec. 163(f)(2)(B), below, was stricken by P.L. 111-147, applicable to obligations issued after the date which is 2 years after March 18, 2010.*

(B) CERTAIN OBLIGATIONS NOT INCLUDED.—An obligation is described in this subparagraph if—

(i) there are arrangements reasonably designed to ensure that such obligation will be sold (or resold in connection with the original issue) only to a person who is not a United States person, and

(ii) in the case of an obligation not in registered form—

(I) interest on such obligation is payable only outside the United States and its possessions, and

(II) on the face of such obligation there is a statement that any United States person who holds such obligation will be subject to limitations under the United States income tax laws.

≫→ *Caution: Former Code Sec. 163(f)(2)(C) was redesignated as Code Sec. 163(f)(2)(B), below, and amended by P.L. 111-147, applicable to obligations issued after the date which is 2 years after March 18, 2010.*

(B) AUTHORITY TO INCLUDE OTHER OBLIGATIONS.—Clauses (ii) and (iii) of subparagraph (A) shall not apply to any obligation if—

(i) such obligation is of a type which the Secretary has determined by regulations to be used frequently in avoiding Federal taxes, and

(ii) such obligation is issued after the date on which the regulations referred to in clause (i) take effect.

»»→ Caution: *Code Sec. 163(f)(3), below, as amended by P.L. 111-147, applies to obligations issued after the date which is 2 years after March 18, 2010.*

(3) BOOK ENTRIES PERMITTED, ETC.—For purposes of this subsection, rules similar to the rules of section 149(a)(3) shall apply, *except that a dematerialized book entry system or other book entry system specified by the Secretary shall be treated as a book entry system described in such section.*

[CCH Explanation at ¶ 760. Committee Reports at ¶ 11,070.]

Amendments

• **2010, Hiring Incentives to Restore Employment Act (P.L. 111-147)**

P.L. 111-147, § 502(a)(1):

Amended Code Sec. 163(f)(2) by striking subparagraph (B) and by redesignating subparagraph (C) as subparagraph (B). **Effective** for obligations issued after the date which is 2 years after 3-18-2010. Prior to being stricken, Code Sec. 163(f)(2)(B) read as follows:

(B) CERTAIN OBLIGATIONS NOT INCLUDED.—An obligation is described in this subparagraph if—

(i) there are arrangements reasonably designed to ensure that such obligation will be sold (or resold in connection with the original issue) only to a person who is not a United States person, and

(ii) in the case of an obligation not in registered form—

(I) interest on such obligation is payable only outside the United States and its possessions, and

(II) on the face of such obligation there is a statement that any United States person who holds such obligation will be subject to limitations under the United States income tax laws.

P.L. 111-147, § 502(a)(2)(B):

Amended Code Sec. 163(f)(2)(A) by inserting "or" at the end of clause (ii), by striking ", or" at the end of clause (iii)

and inserting a period, and by striking clause (iv). **Effective** for obligations issued after the date which is 2 years after 3-18-2010. Prior to being stricken, Code Sec. 163(f)(2)(A)(iv) read as follows:

(iv) is described in subparagraph (B).

P.L. 111-147, § 502(a)(2)(C)(i)-(ii):

Amended Code Sec. 163(f)(2)(B), as redesignated by Act Sec. 502(a)(1), by striking ", and subparagraph (B)," following "of subparagraph (A)" in the matter preceding clause (i), and by amending clause (i). **Effective** for obligations issued after the date which is 2 years after 3-18-2010. Prior to amendment, Code Sec. 163(f)(2)(B)(i) read as follows:

(i) in the case of—

(I) subparagraph (A), such obligation is of a type which the Secretary has determined by regulations to be used frequently in avoiding Federal taxes, or

(II) subparagraph (B), such obligation is of a type specified by the Secretary in regulations, and

P.L. 111-147, § 502(c):

Amended Code Sec. 163(f)(3) by inserting ", except that a dematerialized book entry system or other book entry system specified by the Secretary shall be treated as a book entry system described in such section" before the period at the end. **Effective** for obligations issued after the date which is 2 years after 3-18-2010.

[¶ 6035] CODE SEC. 165. LOSSES.

* * *

(j) DENIAL OF DEDUCTION FOR LOSSES ON CERTAIN OBLIGATIONS NOT IN REGISTERED FORM.—

* * *

(2) DEFINITIONS.—For purposes of this subsection—

»»→ Caution: *Code Sec. 165(j)(2)(A), below, as amended by P.L. 111-147, applies to obligations issued after the date which is 2 years after March 18, 2010.*

(A) REGISTRATION-REQUIRED OBLIGATION.—The term "registration-required obligation" has the meaning given to such term by section 163(f)(2).

* * *

[CCH Explanation at ¶ 760.]

Amendments

• **2010, Hiring Incentives to Restore Employment Act (P.L. 111-147)**

P.L. 111-147, § 502(a)(2)(D):

Amended Code Sec. 165(j)(2)(A) by striking "except that clause (iv) of subparagraph (A), and subparagraph (B), of

such section shall not apply" following "section 163(f)(2)". **Effective** for obligations issued after the date which is 2 years after 3-18-2010.

[¶6040] CODE SEC. 179. ELECTION TO EXPENSE CERTAIN DEPRECIABLE BUSINESS ASSETS.

* * *

(b) LIMITATIONS.—

(1) DOLLAR LIMITATION.—The aggregate cost which may be taken into account under subsection (a) for any taxable year shall not exceed $25,000 (*$250,000 in the case of taxable years beginning after 2007 and before 2011*).

(2) REDUCTION IN LIMITATION.—The limitation under paragraph (1) for any taxable year shall be reduced (but not below zero) by the amount by which the cost of section 179 property placed in service during such taxable year exceeds $200,000 (*$800,000 in the case of taxable years beginning after 2007 and before 2011*).

* * *

(5) LIMITATION ON COST TAKEN INTO ACCOUNT FOR CERTAIN PASSENGER VEHICLES.—

* * *

(7) [*Stricken.*]

* * *

[CCH Explanation at ¶610. Committee Reports at ¶11,030.]

Amendments

• **2010, Hiring Incentives to Restore Employment Act (P.L. 111-147)**

P.L. 111-147, §201(a)(1)-(4):

Amended Code Sec. 179(b) by striking "($125,000 in the case of taxable years beginning after 2006 and before 2011)" in paragraph (1) and inserting "($250,000 in the case of taxable years beginning after 2007 and before 2011)", by striking "($500,000 in the case of taxable years beginning after 2006 and before 2011)" in paragraph (2) and inserting "($800,000 in the case of taxable years beginning after 2007 and before 2011)", by striking paragraphs (5) and (7), and by redesignating paragraph (6) as paragraph (5). **Effective for** tax years beginning after 12-31-2009. Prior to being stricken, Code Sec. 179(b)(5) and (7) read as follows:

(5) INFLATION ADJUSTMENTS.—

(A) IN GENERAL.—In the case of any taxable year beginning in a calendar year after 2007 and before 2011, the $125,000 and $500,000 amounts in paragraphs (1) and (2) shall each be increased by an amount equal to—

(i) such dollar amount, multiplied by

(ii) the cost-of-living adjustment determined under section 1(f)(3) for the calendar year in which the taxable year

begins, by substituting "calendar year 2006" for "calendar year 1992" in subparagraph (B) thereof.

(B) ROUNDING.—

(i) DOLLAR LIMITATION.—If the amount in paragraph (1) as increased under subparagraph (A) is not a multiple of $1,000, such amount shall be rounded to the nearest multiple of $1,000.

(ii) PHASEOUT AMOUNT.—If the amount in paragraph (2) as increased under subparagraph (A) is not a multiple of $10,000, such amount shall be rounded to the nearest multiple of $10,000.

* * *

(7) INCREASE IN LIMITATIONS FOR 2008, AND [sic] 2009.—In the case of any taxable year beginning in 2008, or [sic] 2009—

(A) the dollar limitation under paragraph (1) shall be $250,000,

(B) the dollar limitation under paragraph (2) shall be $800,000, and

(C) the amounts described in subparagraphs (A) and (B) shall not be adjusted under paragraph (5).

[¶6045] CODE SEC. 643. DEFINITIONS APPLICABLE TO SUBPARTS A, B, C, AND D.

* * *

(i) LOANS FROM FOREIGN TRUSTS.—For purposes of subparts B, C, and D—

(1) GENERAL RULE.—Except as provided in regulations, if a foreign trust makes a loan of cash or marketable securities (*or permits the use of any other trust property) directly or indirectly to or by*—

(A) any grantor or beneficiary of such trust who is a United States person, or

(B) any United States person not described in subparagraph (A) who is related to such grantor or beneficiary,

the amount of such loan (*or the fair market value of the use of such property*) shall be treated as a distribution by such trust to such grantor or beneficiary (as the case may be).

(2) DEFINITIONS AND SPECIAL RULES.—For purposes of this subsection—

* * *

(E) EXCEPTION FOR COMPENSATED USE OF PROPERTY.—In the case of the use of any trust property other than a loan of cash or marketable securities, paragraph (1) shall not apply to the extent that the trust is paid the fair market value of such use within a reasonable period of time of such use.

(3) SUBSEQUENT TRANSACTIONS.—If any loan *(or use of property)* is taken into account under paragraph (1), any subsequent transaction between the trust and the original borrower regarding the principal of the loan (by way of complete or partial repayment, satisfaction, cancellation, discharge, or otherwise) *or the return of such property* shall be disregarded for purposes of this title.

[CCH Explanation at ¶ 740. Committee Reports at ¶ 11,150.]

Amendments

• **2010, Hiring Incentives to Restore Employment Act (P.L. 111-147)**

P.L. 111-147, § 533(a)(1)-(2):

Amended Code Sec. 643(i)(1) by striking "directly or indirectly to" and inserting "(or permits the use of any other trust property) directly or indirectly to or by", and by inserting "(or the fair market value of the use of such property)" after "the amount of such loan". **Effective** for loans made, and uses of property, after 3-18-2010.

P.L. 111-147, § 533(b):

Amended Code Sec. 643(i)(2) by adding at the end a new subparagraph (E). **Effective** for loans made, and uses of property, after 3-18-2010.

P.L. 111-147, § 533(d)(1)-(3):

Amended Code Sec. 643(i)(3) by inserting "(or use of property)" after "If any loan", by inserting "or the return of such property" before "shall be disregarded", and by striking "REGARDING LOAN PRINCIPAL" following "SUBSEQUENT TRANSACTIONS" in the heading thereof. **Effective** for loans made, and uses of property, after 3-18-2010.

[¶ 6050] CODE SEC. 679. FOREIGN TRUSTS HAVING ONE OR MORE UNITED STATES BENEFICIARIES.

* * *

(c) TRUSTS TREATED AS HAVING A UNITED STATES BENEFICIARY.—

(1) IN GENERAL.—For purposes of this section, a trust shall be treated as having a United States beneficiary for the taxable year unless—

(A) under the terms of the trust, no part of the income or corpus of the trust may be paid or accumulated during the taxable year to or for the benefit of a United States person, and

(B) if the trust were terminated at any time during the taxable year, no part of the income or corpus of such trust could be paid to or for the benefit of a United States person.

For purposes of subparagraph (A), an amount shall be treated as accumulated for the benefit of a United States person even if the United States person's interest in the trust is contingent on a future event.

* * *

(4) SPECIAL RULE IN CASE OF DISCRETION TO IDENTIFY BENEFICIARIES.—For purposes of paragraph (1)(A), if any person has the discretion (by authority given in the trust agreement, by power of appointment, or otherwise) of making a distribution from the trust to, or for the benefit of, any person, such trust shall be treated as having a beneficiary who is a United States person unless—

(A) the terms of the trust specifically identify the class of persons to whom such distributions may be made, and

(B) none of those persons are United States persons during the taxable year.

(5) CERTAIN AGREEMENTS AND UNDERSTANDINGS TREATED AS TERMS OF THE TRUST.—For purposes of paragraph (1)(A), if any United States person who directly or indirectly transfers property to the trust is directly or indirectly involved in any agreement or understanding (whether written, oral, or otherwise) that may result in the income or corpus of the trust being paid or accumulated to or for the benefit of a United States person, such agreement or understanding shall be treated as a term of the trust.

(6) *Uncompensated Use Of Trust Property Treated As A Payment.*—*For purposes of this subsection, a loan of cash or marketable securities (or the use of any other trust property) directly or indirectly to or by any United States person (whether or not a beneficiary under the terms of the trust) shall be treated as paid or accumulated for the benefit of a United States person. The preceding sentence shall not apply to the extent that the United States person repays the loan at a market rate of interest (or pays the fair market value of the use of such property) within a reasonable period of time.*

[CCH Explanation at ¶735 and 740. Committee Reports at ¶11,130 and 11,150.]

Amendments

• **2010, Hiring Incentives to Restore Employment Act (P.L. 111-147)**

P.L. 111-147, §531(a):

Amended Code Sec. 679(c)(1) by adding at the end a new sentence. **Effective** 3-18-2010.

P.L. 111-147, §531(b):

Amended Code Sec. 679(c) by adding at the end a new paragraph (4). **Effective** 3-18-2010.

P.L. 111-147, §531(c):

Amended Code Sec. 679(c), as amended by Act Sec. 531(b), by adding at the end a new paragraph (5). **Effective** on 3-18-2010.

P.L. 111-147, §533(c):

Amended Code Sec. 679(c), as amended by this Act, by adding at the end a new paragraph (6). **Effective** for loans made, and uses of property, after 3-18-2010.

(d) *Presumption That Foreign Trust Has United States Beneficiary.*—*If a United States person directly or indirectly transfers property to a foreign trust (other than a trust described in section 6048(a)(3)(B)(ii)), the Secretary may treat such trust as having a United States beneficiary for purposes of applying this section to such transfer unless such person—*

(1) *submits such information to the Secretary as the Secretary may require with respect to such transfer, and*

(2) *demonstrates to the satisfaction of the Secretary that such trust satisfies the requirements of subparagraphs (A) and (B) of subsection (c)(1).*

[CCH Explanation at ¶735. Committee Reports at ¶11,140.]

Amendments

• **2010, Hiring Incentives to Restore Employment Act (P.L. 111-147)**

P.L. 111-147, §532(a):

Amended Code Sec. 679 by redesignating subsection (d) as subsection (e) and inserting after subsection (c) a new

subsection (d). **Effective** for transfers of property after 3-18-2010.

(e) *Regulations.*—The Secretary shall prescribe such regulations as may be necessary or appropriate to carry out the purposes of this section.

Amendments

• **2010, Hiring Incentives to Restore Employment Act (P.L. 111-147)**

P.L. 111-147, §532(a):

Amended Code Sec. 679 by redesignating subsection (d) as subsection (e). **Effective** for transfers of property after 3-18-2010.

[¶6055] CODE SEC. 864. DEFINITIONS AND SPECIAL RULES.

* * *

(f) *Election To Allocate Interest, Etc. on Worldwide Basis.*—For purposes of this subchapter, at the election of the worldwide affiliated group—

* * *

(5) *Election To Expand Financial Institution Group Of Worldwide Group.*—

* * *

(D) *Election.*—An election under this paragraph with respect to any financial institution group may be made only by the common parent of the pre-election worldwide affiliated group and may be made only for the first taxable year beginning after *December 31, 2020,* in which such affiliated group includes 1 or more financial corporations. Such an election, once made, shall apply to all financial corporations which are members of the electing financial institution group for such taxable year and all subsequent years unless revoked with the consent of the Secretary.

* * *

(6) ELECTION.—An election to have this subsection apply with respect to any worldwide affiliated group may be made only by the common parent of the domestic affiliated group referred to in paragraph (1)(C) and may be made only for the first taxable year beginning after *December 31, 2020,* in which a worldwide affiliated group exists which includes such affiliated group and at least 1 foreign corporation. Such an election, once made, shall apply to such common parent and all other corporations which are members of such worldwide affiliated group for such taxable year and all subsequent years unless revoked with the consent of the Secretary.

* * *

[CCH Explanation at ¶ 765. Committee Reports at ¶ 11,190.]
Amendments
• 2010, Hiring Incentives to Restore Employment Act (P.L. 111-147)

P.L. 111-147, § 551(a):

Amended Code Sec. 864(f)(5)(D) and (6) by striking "December 31, 2017" and inserting "December 31, 2020". **Effective** 3-18-2010.

[¶ 6060] CODE SEC. 871. TAX ON NONRESIDENT ALIEN INDIVIDUALS.
* * *

(h) REPEAL OF TAX ON INTEREST OF NONRESIDENT ALIEN INDIVIDUALS RECEIVED FROM CERTAIN PORTFOLIO DEBT INVESTMENTS.—

* * *

⋙→ *Caution: Code Sec. 871(h)(2), below, as amended by P.L. 111-147, applies to obligations issued after the date which is 2 years after March 18, 2010.*

(2) PORTFOLIO INTEREST.—*For purposes of this subsection, the term "portfolio interest" means any interest (including original issue discount) which—*

(A) *would be subject to tax under subsection (a) but for this subsection, and*

(B) *is paid on an obligation—*

(i) *which is in registered form, and*

(ii) *with respect to which—*

(I) *the United States person who would otherwise be required to deduct and withhold tax from such interest under section 1441(a) receives a statement (which meets the requirements of paragraph (5)) that the beneficial owner of the obligation is not a United States person, or*

(II) *the Secretary has determined that such a statement is not required in order to carry out the purposes of this subsection.*

(3) PORTFOLIO INTEREST NOT TO INCLUDE INTEREST RECEIVED BY 10-PERCENT SHAREHOLDERS.—For purposes of this subsection—

⋙→ *Caution: Code Sec. 871(h)(3)(A), below, as amended by P.L. 111-147, applies to obligations issued after the date which is 2 years after March 18, 2010.*

(A) IN GENERAL.—The term "portfolio interest" shall not include any interest described in paragraph (2) which is received by a 10-percent shareholder.

* * *

[CCH Explanation at ¶760. Committee Reports at ¶11,070.]

Amendments

• **2010, Hiring Incentives to Restore Employment Act (P.L. 111-147)**

P.L. 111-147, §502(b)(1):

Amended Code Sec. 871(h)(2). **Effective** for obligations issued after the date which is 2 years after 3-18-2010. Prior to amendment, Code Sec. 871(h)(2) read as follows:

(2) PORTFOLIO INTEREST.—For purposes of this subsection, the term "portfolio interest" means any interest (including original issue discount) which would be subject to tax under subsection (a) but for this subsection and which is described in any of the following subparagraphs:

(A) CERTAIN OBLIGATIONS WHICH ARE NOT REGISTERED.—Interest which is paid on any obligation which—

(i) is not in registered form, and

(ii) is described in section 163(f)(2)(B).

(B) CERTAIN REGISTERED OBLIGATIONS.—Interest which is paid on an obligation—

(i) which is in registered form, and

(ii) with respect to which the United States person who would otherwise be required to deduct and withhold tax from such interest under section 1441(a) receives a statement (which meets the requirements of paragraph (5)) that the beneficial owner of the obligation is not a United States person.

P.L. 111-147, §502(b)(2)(A):

Amended Code Sec. 871(h)(3)(A) by striking "subparagraph (A) or (B) of" following "any interest described in". **Effective** for obligations issued after the date which is 2 years after 3-18-2010.

⟫→ *Caution: Code Sec. 871(l), below, as added by P.L. 111-147, applies to payments made on or after the date that is 180 days after March 18, 2010.*

(l) TREATMENT OF DIVIDEND EQUIVALENT PAYMENTS.—

(1) IN GENERAL.—For purposes of subsection (a), sections 881 and 4948(a), and chapters 3 and 4, a dividend equivalent shall be treated as a dividend from sources within the United States.

(2) DIVIDEND EQUIVALENT.—For purposes of this subsection, the term "dividend equivalent" means—

(A) any substitute dividend made pursuant to a securities lending or a sale-repurchase transaction that (directly or indirectly) is contingent upon, or determined by reference to, the payment of a dividend from sources within the United States,

(B) any payment made pursuant to a specified notional principal contract that (directly or indirectly) is contingent upon, or determined by reference to, the payment of a dividend from sources within the United States, and

(C) any other payment determined by the Secretary to be substantially similar to a payment described in subparagraph (A) or (B).

(3) SPECIFIED NOTIONAL PRINCIPAL CONTRACT.—For purposes of this subsection, the term "specified notional principal contract" means—

(A) any notional principal contract if—

(i) in connection with entering into such contract, any long party to the contract transfers the underlying security to any short party to the contract,

(ii) in connection with the termination of such contract, any short party to the contract transfers the underlying security to any long party to the contract,

(iii) the underlying security is not readily tradable on an established securities market,

(iv) in connection with entering into such contract, the underlying security is posted as collateral by any short party to the contract with any long party to the contract, or

(v) such contract is identified by the Secretary as a specified notional principal contract,

(B) in the case of payments made after the date which is 2 years after the date of the enactment of this subsection, any notional principal contract unless the Secretary determines that such contract is of a type which does not have the potential for tax avoidance.

(4) DEFINITIONS.—For purposes of paragraph (3)(A)—

(A) LONG PARTY.—The term "long party" means, with respect to any underlying security of any notional principal contract, any party to the contract which is entitled to receive any payment pursuant to such contract which is contingent upon, or determined by reference to, the payment of a dividend from sources within the United States with respect to such underlying security.

(B) *Short party.*—The term "short party" means, with respect to any underlying security of any notional principal contract, any party to the contract which is not a long party with respect to such underlying security.

(C) *Underlying security.*—The term "underlying security" means, with respect to any notional principal contract, the security with respect to which the dividend referred to in paragraph (2)(B) is paid. For purposes of this paragraph, any index or fixed basket of securities shall be treated as a single security.

(5) *Payments determined on gross basis.*—For purposes of this subsection, the term "payment" includes any gross amount which is used in computing any net amount which is transferred to or from the taxpayer.

(6) *Prevention of over-withholding.*—In the case of any chain of dividend equivalents one or more of which is subject to tax under subsection (a) or section 881, the Secretary may reduce such tax, but only to the extent that the taxpayer can establish that such tax has been paid with respect to another dividend equivalent in such chain, or is not otherwise due, or as the Secretary determines is appropriate to address the role of financial intermediaries in such chain. For purposes of this paragraph, a dividend shall be treated as a dividend equivalent.

(7) *Coordination with chapters 3 and 4.*—For purposes of chapters 3 and 4, each person that is a party to any contract or other arrangement that provides for the payment of a dividend equivalent shall be treated as having control of such payment.

[CCH Explanation at ¶ 755.]

Amendments

• 2010, Hiring Incentives to Restore Employment Act (P.L. 111-147)

P.L. 111-147, § 541(a):

Amended Code Sec. 871 by redesignating subsection (l) as subsection (m) and by inserting after subsection (k) a new subsection (l). **Effective** for payments made on or after the date that is 180 days after 3-18-2010.

≫→ *Caution: Former Code Sec. 871(l) was redesignated as Code Sec. 871(m), below, by P.L. 111-147, applicable to payments made on or after the date that is 180 days after March 18, 2010.*

(m) Cross References.—

* * *

Amendments

• 2010, Hiring Incentives to Restore Employment Act (P.L. 111-147)

P.L. 111-147, § 541(a):

Amended Code Sec. 871 by redesignating subsection (l) as subsection (m). **Effective** for payments made on or after the date that is 180 days after 3-18-2010.

[¶ 6065] CODE SEC. 881. TAX ON INCOME OF FOREIGN CORPORATIONS NOT CONNECTED WITH UNITED STATES BUSINESS.

* * *

(c) Repeal of Tax on Interest of Foreign Corporations Received From Certain Portfolio Debt Investments.—

* * *

≫→ *Caution: Code Sec. 881(c)(2), below, as amended by P.L. 111-147, applies to obligations issued after the date which is 2 years after March 18, 2010.*

(2) *Portfolio interest.*—For purposes of this subsection, the term "portfolio interest" means any interest (including original issue discount) which—

(A) would be subject to tax under subsection (a) but for this subsection, and

(B) is paid on an obligation—

(i) which is in registered form, and

(ii) with respect to which—

(I) the person who would otherwise be required to deduct and withhold tax from such interest under section 1442(a) receives a statement which meets the requirements of section 871(h)(5) that the beneficial owner of the obligation is not a United States person, or

(II) the Secretary has determined that such a statement is not required in order to carry out the purposes of this subsection.

* * *

[CCH Explanation at ¶760.]

Amendments

• 2010, Hiring Incentives to Restore Employment Act (P.L. 111-147)

P.L. 111-147, §502(b)(2)(B):

Amended Code Sec. 881(c)(2). **Effective** for obligations issued after the date which is 2 years after 3-18-2010. Prior to amendment, Code Sec. 881(c)(2) read as follows:

(2) PORTFOLIO INTEREST.—For purposes of this subsection, the term "portfolio interest" means any interest (including original issue discount) which would be subject to tax under subsection (a) but for this subsection and which is described in any of the following subparagraphs:

(A) CERTAIN OBLIGATIONS WHICH ARE NOT REGISTERED.—Interest which is paid on any obligation which is described in section 871(h)(2)(A).

(B) CERTAIN REGISTERED OBLIGATIONS.—Interest which is paid on an obligation—

(i) which is in registered form, and

(ii) with respect to which the person who would otherwise be required to deduct and withhold tax from such interest under section 1442(a) receives a statement which meets the requirements of section 871(h)(5) that the beneficial owner of the obligation is not a United States person.

[¶6070] CODE SEC. 1287. DENIAL OF CAPITAL GAIN TREATMENT FOR GAINS ON CERTAIN OBLIGATIONS NOT IN REGISTERED FORM.

* * *

(b) DEFINITIONS.—For purposes of subsection (a)—

»»→ *Caution: Code Sec. 1287(b)(1), below, as amended by P.L. 111-147, applies to obligations issued after the date which is 2 years after March 18, 2010.*

(1) REGISTRATION-REQUIRED OBLIGATION.—The term "registration-required obligation" has the meaning given to such term by section 163(f)(2).

* * *

[CCH Explanation at ¶760.]

Amendments

• 2010, Hiring Incentives to Restore Employment Act (P.L. 111-147)

P.L. 111-147, §502(a)(2)(D):

Amended Code Sec. 1287(b)(1) by striking "except that clause (iv) of subparagraph (A), and subparagraph (B), of

such section shall not apply" following "section 163(f)(2)". **Effective** for obligations issued after the date which is 2 years after 3-18-2010.

[¶6075] CODE SEC. 1291. INTEREST ON TAX DEFERRAL.

* * *

(e) CERTAIN BASIS, ETC., RULES MADE APPLICABLE.—Except to the extent inconsistent with the regulations prescribed under subsection (f), rules similar to the rules of subsections (c) *and (d)* of section 1246 (as in effect on the day before the date of the enactment of the American Jobs Creation Act of 2004) shall apply for purposes of this section.

* * *

[CCH Explanation at ¶725.]
Amendments

• **2010, Hiring Incentives to Restore Employment Act (P.L. 111-147)**

P.L. 111-147, § 521(b):

Amended Code Sec. 1291(e) by striking ", (d), and (f)" and inserting "and (d)". **Effective** 3-18-2010.

[¶6080] CODE SEC. 1298. SPECIAL RULES.

* * *

(f) Reporting Requirement.—Except as otherwise provided by the Secretary, each United States person who is a shareholder of a passive foreign investment company shall file an annual report containing such information as the Secretary may require.

[CCH Explanation at ¶725. Committee Reports at ¶11,110.]
Amendments

• **2010, Hiring Incentives to Restore Employment Act (P.L. 111-147)**

P.L. 111-147, § 521(a):

Amended Code Sec. 1298 by redesignating subsection (f) as subsection (g) and by inserting after subsection (e) a new subsection (f). **Effective** 3-18-2010.

*(g) Regulations.—*The Secretary shall prescribe such regulations as may be necessary or appropriate to carry out the purposes of this part.
Amendments

• **2010, Hiring Incentives to Restore Employment Act (P.L. 111-147)**

P.L. 111-147, § 521(a):

Amended Code Sec. 1298 by redesignating subsection (f) as subsection (g). **Effective** 3-18-2010.

⨠→ *Caution: Code Sec. 1471, below, as added by P.L. 111-147, applies generally to payments made after December 31, 2012.*

[¶6085] *CODE SEC. 1471. WITHHOLDABLE PAYMENTS TO FOREIGN FINANCIAL INSTITUTIONS.*

(a) In General.—In the case of any withholdable payment to a foreign financial institution which does not meet the requirements of subsection (b), the withholding agent with respect to such payment shall deduct and withhold from such payment a tax equal to 30 percent of the amount of such payment.

(b) Reporting Requirements, etc.—

(1) In general.—The requirements of this subsection are met with respect to any foreign financial institution if an agreement is in effect between such institution and the Secretary under which such institution agrees—

(A) to obtain such information regarding each holder of each account maintained by such institution as is necessary to determine which (if any) of such accounts are United States accounts,

(B) to comply with such verification and due diligence procedures as the Secretary may require with respect to the identification of United States accounts,

(C) in the case of any United States account maintained by such institution, to report on an annual basis the information described in subsection (c) with respect to such account,

(D) to deduct and withhold a tax equal to 30 percent of—

(i) any passthru payment which is made by such institution to a recalcitrant account holder or another foreign financial institution which does not meet the requirements of this subsection, and

(ii) *in the case of any passthru payment which is made by such institution to a foreign financial institution which has in effect an election under paragraph (3) with respect to such payment, so much of such payment as is allocable to accounts held by recalcitrant account holders or foreign financial institutions which do not meet the requirements of this subsection,*

(E) *to comply with requests by the Secretary for additional information with respect to any United States account maintained by such institution, and*

(F) *in any case in which any foreign law would (but for a waiver described in clause (i)) prevent the reporting of any information referred to in this subsection or subsection (c) with respect to any United States account maintained by such institution—*

(i) *to attempt to obtain a valid and effective waiver of such law from each holder of such account, and*

(ii) *if a waiver described in clause (i) is not obtained from each such holder within a reasonable period of time, to close such account.*

Any agreement entered into under this subsection may be terminated by the Secretary upon a determination by the Secretary that the foreign financial institution is out of compliance with such agreement.

(2) FINANCIAL INSTITUTIONS DEEMED TO MEET REQUIREMENTS IN CERTAIN CASES.—*A foreign financial institution may be treated by the Secretary as meeting the requirements of this subsection if—*

(A) *such institution—*

(i) *complies with such procedures as the Secretary may prescribe to ensure that such institution does not maintain United States accounts, and*

(ii) *meets such other requirements as the Secretary may prescribe with respect to accounts of other foreign financial institutions maintained by such institution, or*

(B) *such institution is a member of a class of institutions with respect to which the Secretary has determined that the application of this section is not necessary to carry out the purposes of this section.*

(3) ELECTION TO BE WITHHELD UPON RATHER THAN WITHHOLD ON PAYMENTS TO RECALCITRANT ACCOUNT HOLDERS AND NONPARTICIPATING FOREIGN FINANCIAL INSTITUTIONS.—*In the case of a foreign financial institution which meets the requirements of this subsection and such other requirements as the Secretary may provide and which elects the application of this paragraph—*

(A) *the requirements of paragraph (1)(D) shall not apply,*

(B) *the withholding tax imposed under subsection (a) shall apply with respect to any withholdable payment to such institution to the extent such payment is allocable to accounts held by recalcitrant account holders or foreign financial institutions which do not meet the requirements of this subsection, and*

(C) *the agreement described in paragraph (1) shall—*

(i) *require such institution to notify the withholding agent with respect to each such payment of the institution's election under this paragraph and such other information as may be necessary for the withholding agent to determine the appropriate amount to deduct and withhold from such payment, and*

(ii) *include a waiver of any right under any treaty of the United States with respect to any amount deducted and withheld pursuant to an election under this paragraph.*

To the extent provided by the Secretary, the election under this paragraph may be made with respect to certain classes or types of accounts of the foreign financial institution.

(c) INFORMATION REQUIRED TO BE REPORTED ON UNITED STATES ACCOUNTS.—

(1) IN GENERAL.—*The agreement described in subsection (b) shall require the foreign financial institution to report the following with respect to each United States account maintained by such institution:*

(A) *The name, address, and TIN of each account holder which is a specified United States person and, in the case of any account holder which is a United States owned foreign entity, the name, address, and TIN of each substantial United States owner of such entity.*

(B) *The account number.*

(C) *The account balance or value (determined at such time and in such manner as the Secretary may provide).*

(D) *Except to the extent provided by the Secretary, the gross receipts and gross withdrawals or payments from the account (determined for such period and in such manner as the Secretary may provide).*

(2) ELECTION TO BE SUBJECT TO SAME REPORTING AS UNITED STATES FINANCIAL INSTITUTIONS.—*In the case of a foreign financial institution which elects the application of this paragraph—*

(A) *subparagraphs (C) and (D) of paragraph (1) shall not apply, and*

(B) *the agreement described in subsection (b) shall require such foreign financial institution to report such information with respect to each United States account maintained by such institution as such institution would be required to report under sections 6041, 6042, 6045, and 6049 if—*

(i) *such institution were a United States person, and*

(ii) *each holder of such account which is a specified United States person or United States owned foreign entity were a natural person and citizen of the United States.*

An election under this paragraph shall be made at such time, in such manner, and subject to such conditions as the Secretary may provide.

(3) SEPARATE REQUIREMENTS FOR QUALIFIED INTERMEDIARIES.—*In the case of a foreign financial institution which is treated as a qualified intermediary by the Secretary for purposes of section 1441 and the regulations issued thereunder, the requirements of this section shall be in addition to any reporting or other requirements imposed by the Secretary for purposes of such treatment.*

(d) DEFINITIONS.—*For purposes of this section—*

(1) UNITED STATES ACCOUNT.—

(A) IN GENERAL.—*The term "United States account" means any financial account which is held by one or more specified United States persons or United States owned foreign entities.*

(B) EXCEPTION FOR CERTAIN ACCOUNTS HELD BY INDIVIDUALS.—*Unless the foreign financial institution elects to not have this subparagraph apply, such term shall not include any depository account maintained by such financial institution if—*

(i) *each holder of such account is a natural person, and*

(ii) *with respect to each holder of such account, the aggregate value of all depository accounts held (in whole or in part) by such holder and maintained by the same financial institution which maintains such account does not exceed $50,000.*

To the extent provided by the Secretary, financial institutions which are members of the same expanded affiliated group shall be treated for purposes of clause (ii) as a single financial institution.

(C) ELIMINATION OF DUPLICATIVE REPORTING REQUIREMENTS.—*Such term shall not include any financial account in a foreign financial institution if—*

(i) *such account is held by another financial institution which meets the requirements of subsection (b), or*

(ii) *the holder of such account is otherwise subject to information reporting requirements which the Secretary determines would make the reporting required by this section with respect to United States accounts duplicative.*

(2) FINANCIAL ACCOUNT.—*Except as otherwise provided by the Secretary, the term "financial account" means, with respect to any financial institution—*

(A) *any depository account maintained by such financial institution,*

(B) *any custodial account maintained by such financial institution, and*

(C) *any equity or debt interest in such financial institution (other than interests which are regularly traded on an established securities market).*

Any equity or debt interest which constitutes a financial account under subparagraph (C) with respect to any financial institution shall be treated for purposes of this section as maintained by such financial institution.

(3) UNITED STATES OWNED FOREIGN ENTITY.—The term "United States owned foreign entity" means any foreign entity which has one or more substantial United States owners.

(4) FOREIGN FINANCIAL INSTITUTION.—The term "foreign financial institution" means any financial institution which is a foreign entity. Except as otherwise provided by the Secretary, such term shall not include a financial institution which is organized under the laws of any possession of the United States.

(5) FINANCIAL INSTITUTION.—Except as otherwise provided by the Secretary, the term "financial institution" means any entity that—

(A) accepts deposits in the ordinary course of a banking or similar business,

(B) as a substantial portion of its business, holds financial assets for the account of others, or

(C) is engaged (or holding itself out as being engaged) primarily in the business of investing, reinvesting, or trading in securities (as defined in section 475(c)(2) without regard to the last sentence thereof), partnership interests, commodities (as defined in section 475(e)(2)), or any interest (including a futures or forward contract or option) in such securities, partnership interests, or commodities.

(6) RECALCITRANT ACCOUNT HOLDER.—The term "recalcitrant account holder" means any account holder which—

(A) fails to comply with reasonable requests for the information referred to in subsection (b)(1)(A) or (c)(1)(A), or

(B) fails to provide a waiver described in subsection (b)(1)(F) upon request.

(7) PASSTHRU PAYMENT.—The term "passthru payment" means any withholdable payment or other payment to the extent attributable to a withholdable payment.

(e) AFFILIATED GROUPS.—

(1) IN GENERAL.—The requirements of subsections (b) and (c)(1) shall apply—

(A) with respect to United States accounts maintained by the foreign financial institution, and

(B) except as otherwise provided by the Secretary, with respect to United States accounts maintained by each other foreign financial institution (other than any foreign financial institution which meets the requirements of subsection (b)) which is a member of the same expanded affiliated group as such foreign financial institution.

(2) EXPANDED AFFILIATED GROUP.—For purposes of this section, the term "expanded affiliated group" means an affiliated group as defined in section 1504(a), determined—

(A) by substituting "more than 50 percent" for "at least 80 percent" each place it appears, and

(B) without regard to paragraphs (2) and (3) of section 1504(b).

A partnership or any other entity (other than a corporation) shall be treated as a member of an expanded affiliated group if such entity is controlled (within the meaning of section 954(d)(3)) by members of such group (including any entity treated as a member of such group by reason of this sentence).

(f) EXCEPTION FOR CERTAIN PAYMENTS.—Subsection (a) shall not apply to any payment to the extent that the beneficial owner of such payment is—

(1) any foreign government, any political subdivision of a foreign government, or any wholly owned agency or instrumentality of any one or more of the foregoing,

(2) any international organization or any wholly owned agency or instrumentality thereof,

(3) any foreign central bank of issue, or

(4) any other class of persons identified by the Secretary for purposes of this subsection as posing a low risk of tax evasion.

[CCH Explanation at ¶705. Committee Reports at ¶11,060.]

Amendments

• **2010, Hiring Incentives to Restore Employment Act (P.L. 111-147)**

P.L. 111-147, §501(a):

Amended [subtitle A of] the Internal Revenue Code of 1986 by inserting after chapter 3 a new chapter 4 (Code Secs. 1471-1474). Effective generally for payments made after 12-31-2012. For a special rule, see Act Sec. 501(d)(2), below.

P.L. 111-147, §501(d)(2), provides:

(2) GRANDFATHERED TREATMENT OF OUTSTANDING OBLIGATIONS.—The amendments made by this section shall not require any amount to be deducted or withheld from any payment under any obligation outstanding on the date which is 2 years after the date of the enactment of this Act or from the gross proceeds from any disposition of such an obligation.

»»→ Caution: *Code Sec. 1472, below, as added by P.L. 111-147, applies generally to payments made after December 31, 2012.*

[¶6090] CODE SEC. 1472. WITHHOLDABLE PAYMENTS TO OTHER FOREIGN ENTITIES.

(a) IN GENERAL.—In the case of any withholdable payment to a non-financial foreign entity, if—

(1) the beneficial owner of such payment is such entity or any other non-financial foreign entity, and

(2) the requirements of subsection (b) are not met with respect to such beneficial owner,

then the withholding agent with respect to such payment shall deduct and withhold from such payment a tax equal to 30 percent of the amount of such payment.

(b) REQUIREMENTS FOR WAIVER OF WITHHOLDING.—The requirements of this subsection are met with respect to the beneficial owner of a payment if—

(1) such beneficial owner or the payee provides the withholding agent with either—

(A) a certification that such beneficial owner does not have any substantial United States owners, or

(B) the name, address, and TIN of each substantial United States owner of such beneficial owner,

(2) the withholding agent does not know, or have reason to know, that any information provided under paragraph (1) is incorrect, and

(3) the withholding agent reports the information provided under paragraph (1)(B) to the Secretary in such manner as the Secretary may provide.

(c) EXCEPTIONS.—Subsection (a) shall not apply to—

(1) except as otherwise provided by the Secretary, any payment beneficially owned by—

(A) any corporation the stock of which is regularly traded on an established securities market,

(B) any corporation which is a member of the same expanded affiliated group (as defined in section 1471(e)(2) without regard to the last sentence thereof) as a corporation described in subparagraph (A),

(C) any entity which is organized under the laws of a possession of the United States and which is wholly owned by one or more bona fide residents (as defined in section 937(a)) of such possession,

(D) any foreign government, any political subdivision of a foreign government, or any wholly owned agency or instrumentality of any one or more of the foregoing,

(E) any international organization or any wholly owned agency or instrumentality thereof,

(F) any foreign central bank of issue, or

(G) any other class of persons identified by the Secretary for purposes of this subsection, and

(2) any class of payments identified by the Secretary for purposes of this subsection as posing a low risk of tax evasion.

(d) NON-FINANCIAL FOREIGN ENTITY.—For purposes of this section, the term "non-financial foreign entity" means any foreign entity which is not a financial institution (as defined in section 1471(d)(5)).

[CCH Explanation at ¶705. Committee Reports at ¶11,060.]

Amendments

• 2010, Hiring Incentives to Restore Employment Act (P.L. 111-147)

P.L. 111-147, § 501(a):

Amended [subtitle A of] the Internal Revenue Code of 1986 by inserting after chapter 3 a new chapter 4 (Code Secs. 1471-1474). **Effective** generally for payments made after 12-31-2012. For a special rule, see Act Sec. 501(d)(2), below.

P.L. 111-147, § 501(d)(2), provides:

(2) GRANDFATHERED TREATMENT OF OUTSTANDING OBLIGA-TIONS.—The amendments made by this section shall not require any amount to be deducted or withheld from any payment under any obligation outstanding on the date which is 2 years after the date of the enactment of this Act or from the gross proceeds from any disposition of such an obligation.

≫→ *Caution: Code Sec. 1473, below, as added by P.L. 111-147, applies generally to payments made after December 31, 2012.*

[¶ 6095] CODE SEC. 1473. DEFINITIONS.

For purposes of this chapter—

(1) WITHHOLDABLE PAYMENT.—Except as otherwise provided by the Secretary—

    (A) IN GENERAL.—The term "withholdable payment" means—

        (i) any payment of interest (including any original issue discount), dividends, rents, salaries, wages, premiums, annuities, compensations, remunerations, emoluments, and other fixed or determinable annual or periodical gains, profits, and income, if such payment is from sources within the United States, and

        (ii) any gross proceeds from the sale or other disposition of any property of a type which can produce interest or dividends from sources within the United States.

    (B) EXCEPTION FOR INCOME CONNECTED WITH UNITED STATES BUSINESS.—Such term shall not include any item of income which is taken into account under section 871(b)(1) or 882(a)(1) for the taxable year.

    (C) SPECIAL RULE FOR SOURCING INTEREST PAID BY FOREIGN BRANCHES OF DOMESTIC FINANCIAL INSTITUTIONS.—Subparagraph (B) of section 861(a)(1) shall not apply.

(2) SUBSTANTIAL UNITED STATES OWNER.—

    (A) IN GENERAL.—The term "substantial United States owner" means—

        (i) with respect to any corporation, any specified United States person which owns, directly or indirectly, more than 10 percent of the stock of such corporation (by vote or value),

        (ii) with respect to any partnership, any specified United States person which owns, directly or indirectly, more than 10 percent of the profits interests or capital interests in such partnership, and

        (iii) in the case of a trust—

            (I) any specified United States person treated as an owner of any portion of such trust under subpart E of part I of subchapter J of chapter 1, and

            (II) to the extent provided by the Secretary in regulations or other guidance, any specified United States person which holds, directly or indirectly, more than 10 percent of the beneficial interests of such trust.

    (B) SPECIAL RULE FOR INVESTMENT VEHICLES.—In the case of any financial institution described in section 1471(d)(5)(C), clauses (i), (ii), and (iii) of subparagraph (A) shall be applied by substituting "0 percent" for "10 percent".

(3) SPECIFIED UNITED STATES PERSON.—Except as otherwise provided by the Secretary, the term "specified United States person" means any United States person other than—

    (A) any corporation the stock of which is regularly traded on an established securities market,

    (B) any corporation which is a member of the same expanded affiliated group (as defined in section 1471(e)(2) without regard to the last sentence thereof) as a corporation the stock of which is regularly traded on an established securities market,

    (C) any organization exempt from taxation under section 501(a) or an individual retirement plan,

    (D) the United States or any wholly owned agency or instrumentality thereof,

(E) any State, the District of Columbia, any possession of the United States, any political subdivision of any of the foregoing, or any wholly owned agency or instrumentality of any one or more of the foregoing,

(F) any bank (as defined in section 581),

(G) any real estate investment trust (as defined in section 856),

(H) any regulated investment company (as defined in section 851),

(I) any common trust fund (as defined in section 584(a)), and

(J) any trust which—

(i) is exempt from tax under section 664(c), or

(ii) is described in section 4947(a)(1).

(4) WITHHOLDING AGENT.—The term "withholding agent" means all persons, in whatever capacity acting, having the control, receipt, custody, disposal, or payment of any withholdable payment.

(5) FOREIGN ENTITY.—The term "foreign entity" means any entity which is not a United States person.

[CCH Explanation at ¶705. Committee Reports at ¶11,060.]

Amendments

• 2010, Hiring Incentives to Restore Employment Act (P.L. 111-147)

P.L. 111-147, §501(a):

Amended [subtitle A of] the Internal Revenue Code of 1986 by inserting after chapter 3 a new chapter 4 (Code Secs. 1471-1474). **Effective** generally for payments made after 12-31-2012. For a special rule, see Act Sec. 501(d)(2), below.

P.L. 111-147, §501(d)(2), provides:

(2) GRANDFATHERED TREATMENT OF OUTSTANDING OBLIGATIONS.—The amendments made by this section shall not require any amount to be deducted or withheld from any payment under any obligation outstanding on the date which is 2 years after the date of the enactment of this Act or from the gross proceeds from any disposition of such an obligation.

➤➤➤ *Caution: Code Sec. 1474, below, as added by P.L. 111-147, applies generally to payments made after December 31, 2012.*

[¶6100] CODE SEC. 1474. SPECIAL RULES.

(a) LIABILITY FOR WITHHELD TAX.—Every person required to deduct and withhold any tax under this chapter is hereby made liable for such tax and is hereby indemnified against the claims and demands of any person for the amount of any payments made in accordance with the provisions of this chapter.

(b) CREDITS AND REFUNDS.—

(1) IN GENERAL.—Except as provided in paragraph (2), the determination of whether any tax deducted and withheld under this chapter results in an overpayment by the beneficial owner of the payment to which such tax is attributable shall be made as if such tax had been deducted and withheld under subchapter A of chapter 3.

(2) SPECIAL RULE WHERE FOREIGN FINANCIAL INSTITUTION IS BENEFICIAL OWNER OF PAYMENT.—

(A) IN GENERAL.—In the case of any tax properly deducted and withheld under section 1471 from a specified financial institution payment—

(i) if the foreign financial institution referred to in subparagraph (B) with respect to such payment is entitled to a reduced rate of tax with respect to such payment by reason of any treaty obligation of the United States—

(I) the amount of any credit or refund with respect to such tax shall not exceed the amount of credit or refund attributable to such reduction in rate, and

(II) no interest shall be allowed or paid with respect to such credit or refund, and

(ii) if such foreign financial institution is not so entitled, no credit or refund shall be allowed or paid with respect to such tax.

(B) SPECIFIED FINANCIAL INSTITUTION PAYMENT.—The term "specified financial institution payment" means any payment if the beneficial owner of such payment is a foreign financial institution.

(3) REQUIREMENT TO IDENTIFY SUBSTANTIAL UNITED STATES OWNERS.—No credit or refund shall be allowed or paid with respect to any tax properly deducted and withheld under this chapter unless the

beneficial owner of the payment provides the Secretary such information as the Secretary may require to determine whether such beneficial owner is a United States owned foreign entity (as defined in section 1471(d)(3)) and the identity of any substantial United States owners of such entity.

(c) CONFIDENTIALITY OF INFORMATION.—

(1) IN GENERAL.—For purposes of this chapter, rules similar to the rules of section 3406(f) shall apply.

(2) DISCLOSURE OF LIST OF PARTICIPATING FOREIGN FINANCIAL INSTITUTIONS PERMITTED.—The identity of a foreign financial institution which meets the requirements of section 1471(b) shall not be treated as return information for purposes of section 6103.

(d) COORDINATION WITH OTHER WITHHOLDING PROVISIONS.—The Secretary shall provide for the coordination of this chapter with other withholding provisions under this title, including providing for the proper crediting of amounts deducted and withheld under this chapter against amounts required to be deducted and withheld under such other provisions.

(e) TREATMENT OF WITHHOLDING UNDER AGREEMENTS.—Any tax deducted and withheld pursuant to an agreement described in section 1471(b) shall be treated for purposes of this title as a tax deducted and withheld by a withholding agent under section 1471(a).

(f) REGULATIONS.—The Secretary shall prescribe such regulations or other guidance as may be necessary or appropriate to carry out the purposes of, and prevent the avoidance of, this chapter.

[CCH Explanation at ¶705. Committee Reports at ¶11,060.]

Amendments

• 2010, Hiring Incentives to Restore Employment Act (P.L. 111-147)

P.L. 111-147, §501(a):

Amended [subtitle A of] the Internal Revenue Code of 1986 by inserting after chapter 3 a new chapter 4 (Code Secs. 1471-1474). **Effective** generally for payments made after 12-31-2012. For a special rule, see Act Sec. 501(d)(2), below.

P.L. 111-147, §501(d)(2), provides:

(2) GRANDFATHERED TREATMENT OF OUTSTANDING OBLIGATIONS.—The amendments made by this section shall not require any amount to be deducted or withheld from any payment under any obligation outstanding on the date which is 2 years after the date of the enactment of this Act or from the gross proceeds from any disposition of such an obligation.

[¶6105] CODE SEC. 3111. RATE OF TAX.

* * *

(d) SPECIAL EXEMPTION FOR CERTAIN INDIVIDUALS HIRED IN 2010.—

(1) IN GENERAL.—Subsection (a) shall not apply to wages paid by a qualified employer with respect to employment during the period beginning on the day after the date of the enactment of this subsection and ending on December 31, 2010, of any qualified individual for services performed—

(A) in a trade or business of such qualified employer, or

(B) in the case of a qualified employer exempt from tax under section 501(a), in furtherance of the activities related to the purpose or function constituting the basis of the employer's exemption under section 501.

(2) QUALIFIED EMPLOYER.—For purposes of this subsection—

(A) IN GENERAL.—The term "qualified employer" means any employer other than the United States, any State, or any political subdivision thereof, or any instrumentality of the foregoing.

(B) TREATMENT OF EMPLOYEES OF POSTSECONDARY EDUCATIONAL INSTITUTIONS.—Notwithstanding subparagraph (A), the term "qualified employer" includes any employer which is a public institution of higher education (as defined in section 101(b) of the Higher Education Act of 1965).

(3) QUALIFIED INDIVIDUAL.—For purposes of this subsection, the term "qualified individual" means any individual who—

(A) begins employment with a qualified employer after February 3, 2010, and before January 1, 2011,

(B) certifies by signed affidavit, under penalties of perjury, that such individual has not been employed for more than 40 hours during the 60-day period ending on the date such individual begins such employment,

(C) is not employed by the qualified employer to replace another employee of such employer unless such other employee separated from employment voluntarily or for cause, and

(D) is not an individual described in section 51(i)(1) (applied by substituting "qualified employer" for "taxpayer" each place it appears).

(4) ELECTION.—A qualified employer may elect to have this subsection not apply. Such election shall be made in such manner as the Secretary may require.

(5) SPECIAL RULE FOR FIRST CALENDAR QUARTER OF 2010.—

(A) NONAPPLICATION OF EXEMPTION DURING FIRST QUARTER.—Paragraph (1) shall not apply with respect to wages paid during the first calendar quarter of 2010.

(B) CREDITING OF FIRST QUARTER EXEMPTION DURING SECOND QUARTER.—The amount by which the tax imposed under subsection (a) would (but for subparagraph (A)) have been reduced with respect to wages paid by a qualified employer during the first calendar quarter of 2010 shall be treated as a payment against the tax imposed under subsection (a) with respect to the qualified employer for the second calendar quarter of 2010 which is made on the date that such tax is due.

[CCH Explanation at ¶ 605. Committee Reports at ¶ 11,010.]
Amendments
• 2010, Hiring Incentives to Restore Employment Act (P.L. 111-147)

P.L. 111-147, § 101(a):

Amended Code Sec. 3111 by adding at the end a new subsection (d). Effective for wages paid after 3-18-2010.

[¶ 6110] CODE SEC. 3221. RATE OF TAX.

* * *

(c) SPECIAL RATE FOR CERTAIN INDIVIDUALS HIRED IN 2010.—

(1) IN GENERAL.—In the case of compensation paid by a qualified employer during the period beginning on the day after the date of the enactment of this subsection and ending on December 31, 2010, with respect to having a qualified individual in the employer's employ for services rendered to such qualified employer, the applicable percentage under subsection (a) shall be equal to the rate of tax in effect under section 3111(b) for the calendar year.

(2) QUALIFIED EMPLOYER.—The term "qualified employer" means any employer other than the United States, any State, or any political subdivision thereof, or any instrumentality of the foregoing.

(3) QUALIFIED INDIVIDUAL.—For purposes of this subsection, the term "qualified individual" means any individual who—

(A) begins employment with a qualified employer after February 3, 2010, and before January 1, 2011,

(B) certifies by signed affidavit, under penalties of perjury, that such individual has not been employed for more than 40 hours during the 60-day period ending on the date such individual begins such employment,

(C) is not employed by the qualified employer to replace another employee of such employer unless such other employee separated from employment voluntarily or for cause, and

(D) is not an individual described in section 51(i)(1) (applied by substituting "qualified employer" for "taxpayer" each place it appears).

(4) ELECTION.—A qualified employer may elect to have this subsection not apply. Such election shall be made in such manner as the Secretary may require.

(5) Special rule for first calendar quarter of 2010.—

(A) Nonapplication of exemption during first quarter.—Paragraph (1) shall not apply with respect to compensation paid during the first calendar quarter of 2010.

(B) Crediting of first quarter exemption during second quarter.—The amount by which the tax imposed under subsection (a) would (but for subparagraph (A)) have been reduced with respect to compensation paid by a qualified employer during the first calendar quarter of 2010 shall be treated as a payment against the tax imposed under subsection (a) with respect to the qualified employer for the second calendar quarter of 2010 which is made on the date that such tax is due.

[CCH Explanation at ¶ 605.]

Amendments

• **2010, Hiring Incentives to Restore Employment Act (P.L. 111-147)**

P.L. 111-147, § 101(d)(1):

Amended Code Sec. 3221 by redesignating subsection (c) as subsection (d) and by inserting after subsection (b) a new subsection (c). **Effective** for compensation paid after 3-18-2010.

(d) Cross Reference.—

For application of different contribution bases with respect to the taxes imposed by subsections (a) and (b), see section 3231(e)(2).

Amendments

• **2010, Hiring Incentives to Restore Employment Act (P.L. 111-147)**

P.L. 111-147, § 101(d)(1):

Amended Code Sec. 3221 by redesignating subsection (c) as subsection (d). **Effective** for compensation paid after 3-18-2010.

[¶ 6115] CODE SEC. 4701. TAX ON ISSUER OF REGISTRATION-REQUIRED OBLIGATION NOT IN REGISTERED FORM.

* * *

(b) Definitions.—For purposes of this section—

⋙→ *Caution: Code Sec. 4701(b)(1), below, as amended by P.L. 111-147, applies to obligations issued after the date which is 2 years after March 18, 2010.*

(1) Registration-required obligation.—

(A) In general.—The term "registration-required obligation" has the same meaning as when used in section 163(f), except that such term shall not include any obligation which—

(i) is required to be registered under section 149(a), or

(ii) is described in subparagraph (B).

(B) Certain obligations not included.—An obligation is described in this subparagraph if—

(i) there are arrangements reasonably designed to ensure that such obligation will be sold (or resold in connection with the original issue) only to a person who is not a United States person,

(ii) interest on such obligation is payable only outside the United States and its possessions, and

(iii) on the face of such obligation there is a statement that any United States person who holds such obligation will be subject to limitations under the United States income tax laws.

* * *

[CCH Explanation at ¶760. Committee Reports at ¶11,070.]

Amendments

• **2010, Hiring Incentives to Restore Employment Act (P.L. 111-147)**

P.L. 111-147, §502(e):

Amended Code Sec. 4701(b)(1). **Effective** for obligations issued after the date which is 2 years after 3-18-2010. Prior to amendment, Code Sec. 4701(b)(1) read as follows:

(1) REGISTRATION-REQUIRED OBLIGATION.—The term "registration-required obligation" has the same meaning as when used in section 163(f), except that such term shall not include any obligation required to be registered under section 149(a).

[¶6120] CODE SEC. 6011. GENERAL REQUIREMENT OF RETURN, STATEMENT, OR LIST.

* * *

(e) REGULATIONS REQUIRING RETURNS ON MAGNETIC MEDIA, ETC.—

* * *

(4) SPECIAL RULE FOR RETURNS FILED BY FINANCIAL INSTITUTIONS WITH RESPECT TO WITHHOLDING ON FOREIGN TRANSFERS.—The numerical limitation under paragraph (2)(A) shall not apply to any return filed by a financial institution (as defined in section 1471(d)(5)) with respect to tax for which such institution is made liable under section 1461 or 1474(a).

[CCH Explanation at ¶730. Committee Reports at ¶11,120.]

Amendments

• **2010, Hiring Incentives to Restore Employment Act (P.L. 111-147)**

P.L. 111-147, §522(a):

Amended Code Sec. 6011(e) by adding at the end a new paragraph (4). **Effective** for returns the due date for which (determined without regard to extensions) is after 3-18-2010.

[¶6125] CODE SEC. 6038D. INFORMATION WITH RESPECT TO FOREIGN FINANCIAL ASSETS.

(a) IN GENERAL.—Any individual who, during any taxable year, holds any interest in a specified foreign financial asset shall attach to such person's return of tax imposed by subtitle A for such taxable year the information described in subsection (c) with respect to each such asset if the aggregate value of all such assets exceeds $50,000 (or such higher dollar amount as the Secretary may prescribe).

(b) SPECIFIED FOREIGN FINANCIAL ASSETS.—For purposes of this section, the term "specified foreign financial asset" means—

(1) any financial account (as defined in section 1471(d)(2)) maintained by a foreign financial institution (as defined in section 1471(d)(4)), and

(2) any of the following assets which are not held in an account maintained by a financial institution (as defined in section 1471(d)(5))—

(A) any stock or security issued by a person other than a United States person,

(B) any financial instrument or contract held for investment that has an issuer or counterparty which is other than a United States person, and

(C) any interest in a foreign entity (as defined in section 1473).

(c) REQUIRED INFORMATION.—The information described in this subsection with respect to any asset is:

(1) In the case of any account, the name and address of the financial institution in which such account is maintained and the number of such account.

(2) In the case of any stock or security, the name and address of the issuer and such information as is necessary to identify the class or issue of which such stock or security is a part.

(3) In the case of any other instrument, contract, or interest—

(A) such information as is necessary to identify such instrument, contract, or interest, and

(B) *the names and addresses of all issuers and counterparties with respect to such instrument, contract, or interest.*

(4) *The maximum value of the asset during the taxable year.*

(d) PENALTY FOR FAILURE TO DISCLOSE.—

(1) IN GENERAL.—*If any individual fails to furnish the information described in subsection (c) with respect to any taxable year at the time and in the manner described in subsection (a), such person shall pay a penalty of $10,000.*

(2) INCREASE IN PENALTY WHERE FAILURE CONTINUES AFTER NOTIFICATION.—*If any failure described in paragraph (1) continues for more than 90 days after the day on which the Secretary mails notice of such failure to the individual, such individual shall pay a penalty (in addition to the penalties under paragraph (1)) of $10,000 for each 30-day period (or fraction thereof) during which such failure continues after the expiration of such 90-day period. The penalty imposed under this paragraph with respect to any failure shall not exceed $50,000.*

(e) PRESUMPTION THAT VALUE OF SPECIFIED FOREIGN FINANCIAL ASSETS EXCEEDS DOLLAR THRESHOLD.— *If—*

(1) *the Secretary determines that an individual has an interest in one or more specified foreign financial assets, and*

(2) *such individual does not provide sufficient information to demonstrate the aggregate value of such assets,*

then the aggregate value of such assets shall be treated as being in excess of $50,000 (or such higher dollar amount as the Secretary prescribes for purposes of subsection (a)) for purposes of assessing the penalties imposed under this section.

(f) APPLICATION TO CERTAIN ENTITIES.—*To the extent provided by the Secretary in regulations or other guidance, the provisions of this section shall apply to any domestic entity which is formed or availed of for purposes of holding, directly or indirectly, specified foreign financial assets, in the same manner as if such entity were an individual.*

(g) REASONABLE CAUSE EXCEPTION.—*No penalty shall be imposed by this section on any failure which is shown to be due to reasonable cause and not due to willful neglect. The fact that a foreign jurisdiction would impose a civil or criminal penalty on the taxpayer (or any other person) for disclosing the required information is not reasonable cause.*

(h) REGULATIONS.—*The Secretary shall prescribe such regulations or other guidance as may be necessary or appropriate to carry out the purposes of this section, including regulations or other guidance which provide appropriate exceptions from the application of this section in the case of—*

(1) *classes of assets identified by the Secretary, including any assets with respect to which the Secretary determines that disclosure under this section would be duplicative of other disclosures,*

(2) *nonresident aliens, and*

(3) *bona fide residents of any possession of the United States.*

[CCH Explanation at ¶710. Committee Reports at ¶11,080.]
Amendments
• **2010, Hiring Incentives to Restore Employment Act (P.L. 111-147)**

P.L. 111-147, § 511(a):

Amended subpart A of part III of subchapter A of chapter 61 by inserting after Code Sec. 6038C a new Code Sec. 6038D. **Effective** for tax years beginning after 3-18-2010.

[¶ 6130] CODE SEC. 6048. INFORMATION WITH RESPECT TO CERTAIN FOREIGN TRUSTS.

* * *

(b) UNITED STATES OWNER OF FOREIGN TRUST.—

(1) IN GENERAL.—If, at any time during any taxable year of a United States person, such person is treated as the owner of any portion of a foreign trust under the rules of subpart E of part I of subchapter J of chapter 1, such person *shall submit such information as the Secretary may prescribe with respect to such trust for such year and* shall be responsible to ensure that—

(A) such trust makes a return for such year which sets forth a full and complete accounting of all trust activities and operations for the year, the name of the United States agent for such trust, and such other information as the Secretary may prescribe, and

(B) such trust furnishes such information as the Secretary may prescribe to each United States person (i) who is treated as the owner of any portion of such trust or (ii) who receives (directly or indirectly) any distribution from the trust.

* * *

[CCH Explanation at ¶ 745. Committee Reports at ¶ 11,160.]

Amendments

• **2010, Hiring Incentives to Restore Employment Act (P.L. 111-147)**

P.L. 111-147, § 534(a):

Amended Code Sec. 6048(b)(1) by inserting "shall submit such information as the Secretary may prescribe with re-

spect to such trust for such year and" before "shall be responsible to ensure". **Effective** for tax years beginning after 3-18-2010.

[¶ 6135] CODE SEC. 6229. PERIOD OF LIMITATIONS FOR MAKING ASSESSMENTS.

* * *

(c) SPECIAL RULE IN CASE OF FRAUD, ETC.—

* * *

(2) SUBSTANTIAL OMISSION OF INCOME.—If any partnership omits from gross income an amount properly includible therein *and such amount is described in clause (i) or (ii) of section 6501(e)(1)(A),* subsection (a) shall be applied by substituting "6 years" for "3 years".

* * *

[CCH Explanation at ¶ 720.]

Amendments

• **2010, Hiring Incentives to Restore Employment Act (P.L. 111-147)**

P.L. 111-147, § 513(a)(2)(B):

Amended Code Sec. 6229(c)(2) by striking "which is in excess of 25 percent of the amount of gross income stated in its return" and inserting "and such amount is described in clause (i) or (ii) of section 6501(e)(1)(A)". For the **effective** date, see Act Sec. 513(d), below.

P.L. 111-147, § 513(d), provides:

(d) EFFECTIVE DATE.—The amendments made by this section shall apply to—

(1) returns filed after the date of the enactment of this Act; and

(2) returns filed on or before such date if the period specified in section 6501 of the Internal Revenue Code of 1986 (determined without regard to such amendments) for assessment of such taxes has not expired as of such date.

⋙→ *Caution: Code Sec. 6414, below, as amended by P.L. 111-147, applies generally to payments made after December 31, 2012.*

[¶ 6140] CODE SEC. 6414. INCOME TAX WITHHELD.

In the case of an overpayment of tax imposed by chapter 24, or by chapter 3 *or 4*, refund or credit shall be made to the employer or to the withholding agent, as the case may be, only to the extent that the amount of such overpayment was not deducted and withheld by the employer or withholding agent.

[CCH Explanation at ¶705.]

Amendments

• **2010, Hiring Incentives to Restore Employment Act (P.L. 111-147)**

P.L. 111-147, §501(c)(1):

Amended Code Sec. 6414 by inserting "or 4" after "chapter 3". **Effective** generally for payments made after 12-31-2012. For a special rule, see Act Sec. 501(d)(2), below.

P.L. 111-147, §501(d)(2), provides:

(2) GRANDFATHERED TREATMENT OF OUTSTANDING OBLIGATIONS.—The amendments made by this section shall not require any amount to be deducted or withheld from any payment under any obligation outstanding on the date which is 2 years after the date of the enactment of this Act or from the gross proceeds from any disposition of such an obligation.

[¶6145] CODE SEC. 6431. CREDIT FOR QUALIFIED BONDS ALLOWED TO ISSUER.

* * *

(f) *APPLICATION OF SECTION TO CERTAIN QUALIFIED TAX CREDIT BONDS.—*

(1) *IN GENERAL.—In the case of any specified tax credit bond—*

(A) *such bond shall be treated as a qualified bond for purposes of this section,*

(B) *subsection (a) shall be applied without regard to the requirement that the qualified bond be issued before January 1, 2011,*

(C) *the amount of the payment determined under subsection (b) with respect to any interest payment due under such bond shall be equal to the lesser of—*

(i) *the amount of interest payable under such bond on such date, or*

(ii) *the amount of interest which would have been payable under such bond on such date if such interest were determined at the applicable credit rate determined under section 54A(b)(3),*

(D) *interest on any such bond shall be includible in gross income for purposes of this title,*

(E) *no credit shall be allowed under section 54A with respect to such bond,*

(F) *any payment made under subsection (b) shall not be includible as income for purposes of this title, and*

(G) *the deduction otherwise allowed under this title to the issuer of such bond with respect to interest paid under such bond shall be reduced by the amount of the payment made under this section with respect to such interest.*

(2) *SPECIAL RULE FOR NEW CLEAN RENEWABLE ENERGY BONDS AND QUALIFIED ENERGY CONSERVATION BONDS.—In the case of any specified tax credit bond described in clause (i) or (ii) of paragraph (3)(A), the amount determined under paragraph (1)(C)(ii) shall be 70 percent of the amount so determined without regard to this paragraph and sections 54C(b) and 54D(b).*

(3) *SPECIFIED TAX CREDIT BOND.—For purposes of this subsection, the term "specified tax credit bond" means any qualified tax credit bond (as defined in section 54A(d)) if—*

(A) *such bond is—*

(i) *a new clean renewable energy bond (as defined in section 54C),*

(ii) *a qualified energy conservation bond (as defined in section 54D),*

(iii) *a qualified zone academy bond (as defined in section 54E), or*

(iv) *a qualified school construction bond (as defined in section 54F), and*

(B) *the issuer of such bond makes an irrevocable election to have this subsection apply.*

[CCH Explanation at ¶620. Committee Reports at ¶11,040.]

Amendments

• **2010, Hiring Incentives to Restore Employment Act (P.L. 111-147)**

P.L. 111-147, §301(a):

Amended Code Sec. 6431 by adding at the end a new subsection (f). **Effective** for bonds issued after 3-18-2010.

[¶ 6150] CODE SEC. 6432. COBRA PREMIUM ASSISTANCE.

(a) IN GENERAL.—The person to whom premiums are payable under COBRA continuation coverage shall be reimbursed as provided in subsection (c) for the amount of premiums not paid by assistance eligible individuals by reason of *section 3001(a) of title III of division B of the American Recovery and Reinvestment Act of 2009.*

* * *

[CCH Explanation at ¶ 615.]

Amendments

• **2010, Temporary Extension Act of 2010 (P.L. 111-144)**

P.L. 111-144, § 3(b)(5)(C)(i):

Amended Code Sec. 6432(a) by striking "section 3002(a) of the Health Insurance Assistance for the Unemployed Act

of 2009" and inserting "section 3001(a) of title III of division B of the American Recovery and Reinvestment Act of 2009". **Effective** as if included in the provision of section 3001 of division B of the American Recovery and Reinvestment Act of 2009 to which it relates [**effective** generally for premiums for a period of coverage beginning on or after 2-17-2009.— CCH].

(c) METHOD OF REIMBURSEMENT.—Except as otherwise provided by the Secretary—

* * *

(3) REIMBURSEMENT CONTINGENT ON PAYMENT OF REMAINING PREMIUM.—No reimbursement may be made under this section to a person with respect to any assistance eligible individual until after the reduced premium required under *section 3001(a)(1)(A) of title III of division B of the American Recovery and Reinvestment Act of 2009* with respect to such individual has been received.

* * *

[CCH Explanation at ¶ 615.]

Amendments

• **2010, Temporary Extension Act of 2010 (P.L. 111-144)**

P.L. 111-144, § 3(b)(5)(C)(ii):

Amended Code Sec. 6432(c)(3) by striking "section 3002(a)(1)(A) of such Act" and inserting "section

3001(a)(1)(A) of title III of division B of the American Recovery and Reinvestment Act of 2009". **Effective** as if included in the provision of section 3001 of division B of the American Recovery and Reinvestment Act of 2009 to which it relates [**effective** generally for premiums for a period of coverage beginning on or after 2-17-2009.—CCH].

(e) EMPLOYER DETERMINATION OF QUALIFYING EVENT AS INVOLUNTARY TERMINATION.—*For purposes of this section, in any case in which—*

(1) based on a reasonable interpretation of section 3001(a)(3)(C) of division B of the American Recovery and Reinvestment Act of 2009 and administrative guidance thereunder, an employer determines that the qualifying event with respect to COBRA continuation coverage for an individual was involuntary termination of a covered employee's employment, and

(2) the employer maintains supporting documentation of the determination, including an attestation by the employer of involuntary termination with respect to the covered employee,

the qualifying event for the individual shall be deemed to be involuntary termination of the covered employee's employment.

[CCH Explanation at ¶ 615.]

Amendments

• **2010, Temporary Extension Act of 2010 (P.L. 111-144)**

P.L. 111-144, § 3(b)(5)(C)(iii):

Amended Code Sec. 6432 by redesignating subsections (e) and (f) as subsections (f) and (g), respectively, and inserting

after subsection (d) a new subsection (e). **Effective** as if included in the provision of section 3001 of division B of the American Recovery and Reinvestment Act of 2009 to which it relates [**effective** generally for premiums for a period of coverage beginning on or after 2-17-2009.—CCH].

(f) REPORTING.—Each person entitled to reimbursement under subsection (a) for any period shall submit such reports (at such time and in such manner) as the Secretary may require, including—

* * *

Amendments

• **2010, Temporary Extension Act of 2010 (P.L. 111-144)**

P.L. 111-144, § 3(b)(5)(C)(iii):

Amended Code Sec. 6432 by redesignating subsection (e) as subsection (f). Effective as if included in the provision of

section 3001 of division B of the American Recovery and Reinvestment Act of 2009 to which it relates [effective generally for premiums for a period of coverage beginning on or after 2-17-2009.—CCH].

(g) REGULATIONS.—The Secretary shall issue such regulations or other guidance as may be necessary or appropriate to carry out this section, including—

* * *

Amendments

• **2010, Temporary Extension Act of 2010 (P.L. 111-144)**

P.L. 111-144, § 3(b)(5)(C)(iii):

Amended Code Sec. 6432 by redesignating subsection (f) as subsection (g). Effective as if included in the provision of

section 3001 of division B of the American Recovery and Reinvestment Act of 2009 to which it relates [effective generally for premiums for a period of coverage beginning on or after 2-17-2009.—CCH].

[¶ 6155] CODE SEC. 6501. LIMITATIONS ON ASSESSMENT AND COLLECTION.

(b) TIME RETURN DEEMED FILED.—

>>>→ *Caution: Code Sec. 6501(b)(1)-(2), below, as amended by P.L. 111-147, applies generally to payments made after December 31, 2012.*

(1) EARLY RETURN.—For purposes of this section, a return of tax imposed by this title, except tax imposed by chapter 3, 4, 21, or 24, filed before the last day prescribed by law or by regulations promulgated pursuant to law for the filing thereof, shall be considered as filed on such last day.

(2) RETURN OF CERTAIN EMPLOYMENT *AND WITHHOLDING TAXES.*—For purposes of this section, if a return of tax imposed by chapter 3, 4, 21 or 24 for any period ending with or within a calendar year is filed before April 15 of the succeeding calendar year, such return shall be considered filed on April 15 of such calendar year.

* * *

[CCH Explanation at ¶ 705.]

Amendments

• **2010, Hiring Incentives to Restore Employment Act (P.L. 111-147)**

P.L. 111-147, § 501(c)(2):

Amended Code Sec. 6501(b)(1) by inserting "4," after "chapter 3,". Effective generally for payments made after 12-31-2012. For a special rule, see Act Sec. 501(d)(2), below.

P.L. 111-147, § 501(c)(3)(A)-(B):

Amended Code Sec. 6501(b)(2) by inserting "4," after "chapter 3," in the text thereof, and by striking "TAXES AND TAX IMPOSED BY CHAPTER 3" in the heading thereof and in-

serting "AND WITHHOLDING TAXES". Effective generally for payments made after 12-31-2012. For a special rule, see Act Sec. 501(d)(2), below.

P.L. 111-147, § 501(d)(2), provides:

(2) GRANDFATHERED TREATMENT OF OUTSTANDING OBLIGATIONS.—The amendments made by this section shall not require any amount to be deducted or withheld from any payment under any obligation outstanding on the date which is 2 years after the date of the enactment of this Act or from the gross proceeds from any disposition of such an obligation.

(c) EXCEPTIONS.—

* * *

(8) FAILURE TO NOTIFY SECRETARY OF CERTAIN FOREIGN TRANSFERS.—In the case of any information which is required to be reported to the Secretary *pursuant to an election under section 1295(b) or* under section *1298(f),* 6038, 6038A, 6038B, *6038D,* 6046, 6046A, or 6048, the time for assessment of any tax imposed by this title with respect to any *tax return, event,* or period to which such information relates shall not expire before the date which is 3 years after the date on which the Secretary is furnished the information required to be reported under such section.

* * *

[CCH Explanation at ¶720. Committee Reports at ¶11,100.]

<table>
<tr><td colspan="2" align="center">Amendments</td></tr>
</table>

• **2010, Hiring Incentives to Restore Employment Act (P.L. 111-147)**

P.L. 111-147, § 513(b)(1)-(3):

Amended Code Sec. 6501(c)(8) by inserting "pursuant to an election under section 1295(b) or" before "under section 6038", by inserting "1298(f)," before "6038", and by inserting "6038D," after "6038B,". For the **effective** date, see Act Sec. 513(d), below.

P.L. 111-147, § 513(c):

Amended Code Sec. 6501(c)(8) by striking "event" and inserting "tax return, event,". For the **effective** date, see Act Sec. 513(d), below.

P.L. 111-147, § 513(d), provides:

(d) EFFECTIVE DATE.—The amendments made by this section shall apply to—

(1) returns filed after the date of the enactment of this Act; and

(2) returns filed on or before such date if the period specified in section 6501 of the Internal Revenue Code of 1986 (determined without regard to such amendments) for assessment of such taxes has not expired as of such date.

(e) SUBSTANTIAL OMISSION OF ITEMS.—Except as otherwise provided in subsection (c)—

(1) INCOME TAXES.—In the case of any tax imposed by subtitle A—

(A) GENERAL RULE.—If the taxpayer omits from gross income an amount properly includible therein and—

(i) such amount is in excess of 25 percent of the amount of gross income stated in the return, or

(ii) such amount—

(I) is attributable to one or more assets with respect to which information is required to be reported under section 6038D (or would be so required if such section were applied without regard to the dollar threshold specified in subsection (a) thereof and without regard to any exceptions provided pursuant to subsection (h)(1) thereof), and

(II) is in excess of $5,000,

the tax may be assessed, or a proceeding in court for collection of such tax may be begun without assessment, at any time within 6 years after the return was filed.

(B) DETERMINATION OF GROSS INCOME.—For purposes of subparagraph (A)—

(i) In the case of a trade or business, the term "gross income" means the total of the amounts received or accrued from the sale of goods or services (if such amounts are required to be shown on the return) prior to diminution by the cost of such sales or services; and

(ii) In determining the amount omitted from gross income, there shall not be taken into account any amount which is omitted from gross income stated in the return if such amount is disclosed in the return, or in a statement attached to the return, in a manner adequate to apprise the Secretary of the nature and amount of such item.

(C) CONSTRUCTIVE DIVIDENDS.—If the taxpayer omits from gross income an amount properly includible therein under section 951(a), the tax may be assessed, or a proceeding in court for the collection of such tax may be done without assessing, at any time within 6 years after the return was filed.

* * *

[CCH Explanation at ¶720. Committee Reports at ¶11,100.]

<table>
<tr><td colspan="2" align="center">Amendments</td></tr>
</table>

• **2010, Hiring Incentives to Restore Employment Act (P.L. 111-147)**

P.L. 111-147, § 513(a)(1):

Amended Code Sec. 6501(e)(1) by redesignating subparagraphs (A) and (B) as subparagraphs (B) and (C), respectively, and by inserting before subparagraph (B) (as so redesignated) a new subparagraph (A). For the **effective** date, see Act Sec. 513(d), below.

P.L. 111-147, § 513(a)(2)(A):

Amended Code Sec. 6501(e)(1)(B), as redesignated by Act Sec. 513(a)(1), by striking all that precedes clause (i) and inserting "(B) DETERMINATION OF GROSS INCOME.—For purposes of subparagraph (A)—". For the **effective** date, see Act Sec. 513(d), below. Prior to being stricken, all that precedes clause (i) of Code Sec. 6501(e)(1)(B) read as follows:

(B) GENERAL RULE.—If the taxpayer omits from gross income an amount properly includible therein which is in excess of 25 percent of the amount of gross income stated in the return, the tax may be assessed, or a proceeding in court for the collection of such tax may be begun without assessment, at any time within 6 years after the return was filed. For purposes of this subparagraph—

P.L. 111-147, §513(d), provides:

(d) Effective date.—The amendments made by this section shall apply to—

(1) returns filed after the date of the enactment of this Act; and

(2) returns filed on or before such date if the period specified in section 6501 of the Internal Revenue Code of 1986 (determined without regard to such amendments) for assessment of such taxes has not expired as of such date.

[¶6160] CODE SEC. 6513. TIME RETURN DEEMED FILED AND TAX CONSIDERED PAID.

* * *

(b) Prepaid Income Tax.—For purposes of section 6511 or 6512—

* * *

»»→ Caution: *Code Sec. 6513(b)(3), below, as amended by P.L. 111-147, applies generally to payments made after December 31, 2012.*

(3) Any tax withheld at the source under chapter 3 *or 4* shall, in respect of the recipient of the income, be deemed to have been paid by such recipient on the last day prescribed for filing the return under section 6012 for the taxable year (determined without regard to any extension of time for filing) with respect to which such tax is allowable as a credit under section 1462 *or 1474(b)*. For this purpose, any exemption granted under section 6012 from the requirement of filing a return shall be disregarded.

* * *

[CCH Explanation at ¶705.]

Amendments

• **2010, Hiring Incentives to Restore Employment Act (P.L. 111-147)**

P.L. 111-147, §501(c)(4)(A)-(B):

Amended Code Sec. 6513(b)(3) by inserting "or 4" after "chapter 3", and by inserting "or 1474(b)" after "section 1462". **Effective** generally for payments made after 12-31-2012. For a special rule, see Act Sec. 501(d)(2), below.

P.L. 111-147, §501(d)(2), provides:

(2) Grandfathered treatment of outstanding obligations.—The amendments made by this section shall not require any amount to be deducted or withheld from any payment under any obligation outstanding on the date which is 2 years after the date of the enactment of this Act or from the gross proceeds from any disposition of such an obligation.

»»→ Caution: *Code Sec. 6513(c), below, as amended by P.L. 111-147, applies generally to payments made after December 31, 2012.*

(c) Return and Payment of Social Security Taxes and Income Tax Withholding.—Notwithstanding subsection (a), for purposes of section 6511 with respect to any tax imposed by chapter 3, 4, 21, or 24—

(1) If a return for any period ending with or within a calendar year is filed before April 15 of the succeeding calendar year, such return shall be considered filed on April 15 of such succeeding calendar year; and

(2) If a tax with respect to remuneration or other amount paid during any period ending with or within a calendar year is paid before April 15 of the succeeding calendar year, such tax shall be considered paid on April 15 of such succeeding calendar year.

[CCH Explanation at ¶705.]

Amendments

• **2010, Hiring Incentives to Restore Employment Act (P.L. 111-147)**

P.L. 111-147, §501(c)(5):

Amended Code Sec. 6513(c) by inserting "4," after "chapter 3,". **Effective** generally for payments made after 12-31-2012. For a special rule, see Act Sec. 501(d)(2), below.

P.L. 111-147, §501(d)(2), provides:

(2) Grandfathered treatment of outstanding obligations.—The amendments made by this section shall not require any amount to be deducted or withheld from any payment under any obligation outstanding on the date which is 2 years after the date of the enactment of this Act or from the gross proceeds from any disposition of such an obligation.

[¶6165] CODE SEC. 6611. INTEREST ON OVERPAYMENTS.

* * *

(e) DISALLOWANCE OF INTEREST ON CERTAIN OVERPAYMENTS.—

* * *

(4) CERTAIN WITHHOLDING TAXES.—In the case of any overpayment resulting from tax deducted and withheld under chapter 3 or 4, paragraphs (1), (2), and (3) shall be applied by substituting "180 days" for "45 days" each place it appears.

[CCH Explanation at ¶705.]

Amendments

• **2010, Hiring Incentives to Restore Employment Act (P.L. 111-147)**

P.L. 111-147, §501(b):

Amended Code Sec. 6611(e) by adding at the end a new paragraph (4). For the **effective** date, see Act Sec. 501(d)(3), below.

P.L. 111-147, §501(d)(3), provides:

(3) INTEREST ON OVERPAYMENTS.—The amendment made by subsection (b) shall apply—

(A) in the case of such amendment's application to paragraph (1) of section 6611(e) of the Internal Revenue Code of

1986, to returns the due date for which (determined without regard to extensions) is after the date of the enactment of this Act,

(B) in the case of such amendment's application to paragraph (2) of such section, to claims for credit or refund of any overpayment filed after the date of the enactment of this Act (regardless of the taxable period to which such refund relates), and

(C) in the case of such amendment's application to paragraph (3) of such section, to refunds paid after the date of the enactment of this Act (regardless of the taxable period to which such refund relates).

⟫⟩→ *Caution: The text of Code Sec. 6662, below, highlights only the amendments made by P.L. 111-147. For the version of Code Sec. 6662, as amended by P.L. 111-152, please see ¶5278.*

[¶6170] CODE SEC. 6662. IMPOSITION OF ACCURACY-RELATED PENALTY ON UNDERPAYMENTS.

* * *

(b) PORTION OF UNDERPAYMENT TO WHICH SECTION APPLIES.—This section shall apply to the portion of any underpayment which is attributable to 1 or more of the following:

* * *

(7)[(6)] Any undisclosed foreign financial asset understatement.

* * *

[CCH Explanation at ¶715. Committee Reports at ¶11,090.]

Amendments

• **2010, Hiring Incentives to Restore Employment Act (P.L. 111-147)**

P.L. 111-147, §512(a)(1):

Amended Code Sec. 6662, as amended by this Act, in subsection (b) by inserting after paragraph (6)[(5)] a new

paragraph (7)[(6)]. **Effective** for tax years beginning after 3-18-2010.

(j)[(i)] UNDISCLOSED FOREIGN FINANCIAL ASSET UNDERSTATEMENT.—

(1) IN GENERAL.—For purposes of this section, the term "undisclosed foreign financial asset understatement" means, for any taxable year, the portion of the understatement for such taxable year which is attributable to any transaction involving an undisclosed foreign financial asset.

(2) UNDISCLOSED FOREIGN FINANCIAL ASSET.—For purposes of this subsection, the term "undisclosed foreign financial asset" means, with respect to any taxable year, any asset with respect to which information was required to be provided under section 6038, 6038B, 6038D, 6046A, or 6048 for such taxable year but was not provided by the taxpayer as required under the provisions of those sections.

(3) INCREASE IN PENALTY FOR UNDISCLOSED FOREIGN FINANCIAL ASSET UNDERSTATEMENTS.—In the case of any portion of an underpayment which is attributable to any undisclosed foreign financial asset

understatement, subsection (a) shall be applied with respect to such portion by substituting "40 percent" for "20 percent".

[CCH Explanation at ¶715.]

Amendments

• 2010, Hiring Incentives to Restore Employment Act (P.L. 111-147)

P.L. 111-147, §512(a)(2):

Amended Code Sec. 6662, as amended by this Act, by adding at the end a new subsection (j)[(i)]. **Effective** for tax years beginning after 3-18-2010.

[¶6175] CODE SEC. 6677. FAILURE TO FILE INFORMATION WITH RESPECT TO CERTAIN FOREIGN TRUSTS.

(a) CIVIL PENALTY.—In addition to any criminal penalty provided by law, if any notice or return required to be filed by section 6048—

(1) is not filed on or before the time provided in such section, or

(2) does not include all the information required pursuant to such section or includes incorrect information,

the person required to file such notice or return shall pay a penalty equal to *the greater of $10,000 or 35* percent of the gross reportable amount. If any failure described in the preceding sentence continues for more than 90 days after the day on which the Secretary mails notice of such failure to the person required to pay such penalty, such person shall pay a penalty (in addition to the amount determined under the preceding sentence) of $10,000 for each 30-day period (or fraction thereof) during which such failure continues after the expiration of such 90-day period. *At such time as the gross reportable amount with respect to any failure can be determined by the Secretary, any subsequent penalty imposed under this subsection with respect to such failure shall be reduced as necessary to assure that the aggregate amount of such penalties do not exceed the gross reportable amount (and to the extent that such aggregate amount already exceeds the gross reportable amount the Secretary shall refund such excess to the taxpayer).*

[CCH Explanation at ¶750. Committee Reports at ¶11,170.]

Amendments

• 2010, Hiring Incentives to Restore Employment Act (P.L. 111-147)

P.L. 111-147, §535(a)(1)-(2):

Amended Code Sec. 6677(a) by inserting "the greater of $10,000 or" before "35 percent", and by striking the last

sentence and inserting a new sentence. **Effective** for notices and returns required to be filed after 12-31-2009. Prior to being stricken, the last sentence of Code Sec. 6677(a) read as follows:

In no event shall the penalty under this subsection with respect to any failure exceed the gross reportable amount.

[¶6180] CODE SEC. 6720C. PENALTY FOR FAILURE TO NOTIFY HEALTH PLAN OF CESSATION OF ELIGIBILITY FOR COBRA PREMIUM ASSISTANCE.

(a) IN GENERAL.—Any person required to notify a group health plan under *section 3001(a)(2)(C) of title III of division B of the American Recovery and Reinvestment Act of 2009* who fails to make such a notification at such time and in such manner as the Secretary of Labor may require shall pay a penalty of 110 percent of the premium reduction provided under such section after termination of eligibility under such subsection.

* * *

[CCH Explanation at ¶615.]

Amendments

• 2010, Temporary Extension Act of 2010 (P.L. 111-144)

P.L. 111-144, §3(b)(5)(D):

Amended Code Sec. 6720C(a) by striking "section 3002(a)(2)(C) of the Health Insurance Assistance for the

Unemployed Act of 2009" and inserting "section 3001(a)(2)(C) of title III of division B of the American Recovery and Reinvestment Act of 2009". **Effective** as if included in the provision of section 3001 of division B of the American Recovery and Reinvestment Act of 2009 to which it relates [effective for failures occurring after 2-17-2009.—CCH].

>>→ *Caution: The text of Code Sec. 6724, below, highlights only the amendments made by P.L. 111-147. For the version of Code Sec. 6724, as amended by P.L. 111-148, please see ¶5280.*

[¶6185] CODE SEC. 6724. WAIVER; DEFINITIONS AND SPECIAL RULES.

* * *

(c) SPECIAL RULE FOR FAILURE TO MEET MAGNETIC MEDIA REQUIREMENTS.—No penalty shall be imposed under section 6721 solely by reason of any failure to comply with the requirements of the regulations prescribed under section 6011(e)(2), except to the extent that such a failure occurs with respect to more than 250 information returns (more than 100 information returns in the case of a partnership having more than 100 partners) *or with respect to a return described in section 6011(e)(4).*

Amendments

• 2010, Hiring Incentives to Restore Employment Act (P.L. 111-147)

P.L. 111-147, § 522(b):

Amended Code Sec. 6724(c) by inserting "or with respect to a return described in section 6011(e)(4)" before the end

period. **Effective** for returns the due date for which (determined without regard to extensions) is after 3-18-2010.

(d) DEFINITIONS.—For purposes of this part—

(1) INFORMATION RETURN.—The term "information return" means—

* * *

>>→ *Caution: The last sentence of Code Sec. 6724(d)(1), below, as amended by P.L. 111-147, applies generally to payments made after December 31, 2012.*

Such term also includes any form, statement, or schedule required to be filed with the Secretary *under chapter 4 or* with respect to any amount from which tax was required to be deducted and withheld under chapter 3 (or from which tax would be required to be so deducted and withheld but for an exemption under this title or any treaty obligation of the United States).

(2) PAYEE STATEMENT.—The term "payee statement" means any statement required to be furnished under—

* * *

>>→ *Caution: The last sentence of Code Sec. 6724(d)(2), below, as amended by P.L. 111-147, applies generally to payments made after December 31, 2012.*

Such term also includes any form, statement, or schedule required to be furnished to the recipient of any amount from which tax was required to be deducted and withheld under chapter 3 *or 4* (or from which tax would be required to be so deducted and withheld but for an exemption under this title or any treaty obligation of the United States).

* * *

[CCH Explanation at ¶705.]

Amendments

• 2010, Hiring Incentives to Restore Employment Act (P.L. 111-147)

P.L. 111-147, § 501(c)(6):

Amended Code Sec. 6724(d)(1) by inserting "under chapter 4 or" after "filed with the Secretary" in the last sentence thereof. **Effective** generally for payments made after 12-31-2012. For a special rule, see Act Sec. 501(d)(2), below.

P.L. 111-147, § 501(c)(7):

Amended [the last sentence of] Code Sec. 6724(d)(2) by inserting "or 4" after "chapter 3". **Effective** generally for

payments made after 12-31-2012. For a special rule, see Act Sec. 501(d)(2), below.

P.L. 111-147, § 501(d)(2), provides:

(2) GRANDFATHERED TREATMENT OF OUTSTANDING OBLIGATIONS.—The amendments made by this section shall not require any amount to be deducted or withheld from any payment under any obligation outstanding on the date which is 2 years after the date of the enactment of this Act or from the gross proceeds from any disposition of such an obligation.

[¶6190] CODE SEC. 9502. AIRPORT AND AIRWAY TRUST FUND.

(a) CREATION OF TRUST FUND.—There is established in the Treasury of the United States a trust fund to be known as the "Airport and Airway Trust Fund", consisting of such amounts as may be appropriated, credited, or paid into the Airport and Airway Trust Fund as provided in this section, *section 9503(c)(5)*, or section 9602(b).

* * *

Amendments	transfers relating to amounts paid and credits allowed after 3-18-2010.
• 2010, Hiring Incentives to Restore Employment Act (P.L. 111-147)	

P.L. 111-147, § 444(b)(1):

Amended Code Sec. 9502(a) by striking "section 9503(c)(7)" and inserting "section 9503(c)(5)". **Effective** for

[¶ 6195] CODE SEC. 9503. HIGHWAY TRUST FUND.

* * *

(b) TRANSFER TO HIGHWAY TRUST FUND OF AMOUNTS EQUIVALENT TO CERTAIN TAXES AND PENALTIES.—

* * *

(4) CERTAIN TAXES NOT TRANSFERRED TO HIGHWAY TRUST FUND.—For purposes of paragraphs (1) and (2), there shall not be taken into account the taxes imposed by—

* * *

(D) in the case of gasoline and special motor fuels used as described in *paragraph (3)(D) or (4)(B)* of subsection (c), section 4041 or 4081 with respect to so much of the rate of tax as exceeds—

(i) 11.5 cents per gallon with respect to taxes imposed before October 1, 2001,

(ii) 13 cents per gallon with respect to taxes imposed after September 30, 2001, and before October 1, 2003, and

(iii) 13.5 cents per gallon with respect to taxes imposed after September 30, 2003, and before October 1, 2005.

* * *

(6) LIMITATION ON TRANSFERS TO HIGHWAY TRUST FUND.—

* * *

(B) EXCEPTION FOR PRIOR OBLIGATIONS.—Subparagraph (A) shall not apply to any expenditure to liquidate any contract entered into (or for any amount otherwise obligated) before *December 31, 2010 (January 1, 2011*, in the case of expenditures for administrative expenses), in accordance with the provisions of this section.

Amendments	**Effective** for transfers relating to amounts paid and credits allowed after 3-18-2010.
• 2010, Hiring Incentives to Restore Employment Act (P.L. 111-147)	
	P.L. 111-147, § 445(a)(3):
P.L. 111-147, § 444(b)(2):	Amended Code Sec. 9503(b)(6)(B) by striking "September 30, 2009 (October 1, 2009" and inserting "December 31, 2010 (January 1, 2011". **Effective** 9-30-2009.
Amended Code Sec. 9503(b)(4)(D) by striking "paragraph (4)(D) or (5)(B)" and inserting "paragraph (3)(D) or (4)(B)".	

(c) EXPENDITURES FROM HIGHWAY TRUST FUND.—

(1) FEDERAL-AID HIGHWAY PROGRAM.—Except as provided in subsection (e), amounts in the Highway Trust Fund shall be available, as provided by appropriation Acts, for making expenditures before *December 31, 2010 (January 1, 2011*, in the case of expenditures for administrative expenses), to meet those obligations of the United States heretofore or hereafter incurred which are authorized to be paid out of the Highway Trust Fund *under the Surface Transportation Extension Act of 2010 or any other provision of law which was referred to in this paragraph before the date of the enactment of such Act (as such Act and provisions of law are in effect on the date of the enactment of such Act).*

(2) FLOOR STOCKS REFUNDS.—The Secretary shall pay from time to time from the Highway Trust Fund into the general fund of the Treasury amounts equivalent to the floor stocks refunds made before July 1, 2012, under section 6412(a). *The amounts payable from the Highway Trust Fund*

under the preceding sentence shall be determined by taking into account only the portion of the taxes which are deposited into the Highway Trust Fund.

(3) TRANSFERS FROM THE TRUST FUND FOR MOTORBOAT FUEL TAXES.—

* * *

(4) TRANSFERS FROM THE TRUST FUND FOR SMALL-ENGINE FUEL TAXES.—

* * *

(5) TRANSFERS FROM THE TRUST FUND FOR CERTAIN AVIATION FUEL TAXES.—The Secretary shall pay at least monthly from the Highway Trust Fund into the Airport and Airway Trust Fund amounts (as determined by the Secretary) equivalent to the taxes received on or after October 1, 2005, and before October 1, 2011, under section 4081 with respect to so much of the rate of tax as does not exceed—

* * *

Amendments

• **2010, Hiring Incentives to Restore Employment Act (P.L. 111-147)**

P.L. 111-147, § 444(a):

Amended Code Sec. 9503(c) by striking paragraph (2) and by redesignating paragraphs (3), (4), (5), and (6) as paragraphs (2), (3), (4), and (5), respectively. **Effective** for transfers relating to amounts paid and credits allowed after 3-18-2010. Prior to being stricken, Code Sec. 9503(c)(2) read as follows:

(2) TRANSFERS FROM HIGHWAY TRUST FUND FOR CERTAIN REPAYMENTS AND CREDITS.—

(A) IN GENERAL.—The Secretary shall pay from time to time from the Highway Trust Fund into the general fund of the Treasury amounts equivalent to—

(i) the amounts paid before July 1, 2012, under—

(I) section 6420 (relating to amounts paid in respect of gasoline used on farms),

(II) section 6421 (relating to amounts paid in respect of gasoline used for certain nonhighway purposes or by local transit systems), and

(III) section 6427 (relating to fuels not used for taxable purposes), on the basis of claims filed for periods ending before October 1, 2011, and

(ii) the credits allowed under section 34 (relating to credit for certain uses of fuel) with respect to fuel used before October 1, 2011.

The amounts payable from the Highway Trust Fund under this subparagraph or paragraph (3) shall be determined by taking into account only the portion of the taxes which are deposited into the Highway Trust Fund. Clauses (i)(III) and (ii) shall not apply to claims under section 6427(e).

(e) ESTABLISHMENT OF MASS TRANSIT ACCOUNT.—

(B) TRANSFERS BASED ON ESTIMATES.—Transfers under subparagraph (A) shall be made on the basis of estimates by the Secretary, and proper adjustments shall be made in amounts subsequently transferred to the extent prior estimates were in excess or less than the amounts required to be transferred.

(C) EXCEPTION FOR USE IN AIRCRAFT AND MOTORBOATS.—This paragraph shall not apply to amounts estimated by the Secretary as attributable to use of gasoline and special fuels in motorboats or in aircraft.

P.L. 111-147, § 444(b)(3):

Amended Code Sec. 9503(c)(2), as redesignated by Act Sec. 444(a), by adding at the end a new sentence. **Effective** for transfers relating to amounts paid and credits allowed after 3-18-2010.

P.L. 111-147, § 445(a)(1)(A)-(B):

Amended Code Sec. 9503(c)(1) by striking "September 30, 2009 (October 1, 2009" and inserting "December 31, 2010 (January 1, 2011"; and by striking "under" and all that follows and inserting "under the Surface Transportation Extension Act of 2010 or any other provision of law which was referred to in this paragraph before the date of the enactment of such Act (as such Act and provisions of law are in effect on the date of the enactment of such Act).". **Effective** 9-30-2009. Prior to being stricken, all that followed "under" in Code Sec. 9503(c)(1) read as follows:

the first Continuing Appropriations Resolution for Fiscal Year 2010 enacted into law or any other provision of law which was referred to in this paragraph before the date of the enactment of such Continuing Appropriations Resolution (as such Resolution and provisions of law are in effect on the date of the enactment of the last amendment to such Resolution).

(1) CREATION OF ACCOUNT.—There is established in the Highway Trust Fund a separate account to be known as the "Mass Transit Account" consisting of such amounts as may be transferred or credited to the Mass Transit Account as provided in *this section* or section 9602(b).

* * *

(3) EXPENDITURES FROM ACCOUNT.—Amounts in the Mass Transit Account shall be available, as provided by appropriation Acts, for making capital or capital related expenditures (including capital expenditures for new projects) before *January 1, 2011, in accordance with the Surface Transportation Extension Act of 2010 or any other provision of law which was referred to in this paragraph before the date of the enactment of such Act (as such Act and provisions of law are in effect on the date of the enactment of such Act).*

* * *

(5) PORTION OF CERTAIN TRANSFERS TO BE MADE FROM ACCOUNT.—

(A) IN GENERAL.—Transfers under paragraphs *(2) and (3)* of subsection (c) shall be borne by the Highway Account and the Mass Transit Account in proportion to the respective revenues transferred under this section to the Highway Account (after the application of paragraph (2)) and the Mass Transit Account.

* * *

Amendments

● **2010, Hiring Incentives to Restore Employment Act (P.L. 111-147)**

P.L. 111-147, § 442(b):

Amended Code Sec. 9503(e)(1) by striking "this subsection" and inserting "this section". **Effective** 3-18-2010.

P.L. 111-147, § 444(b)(4):

Amended Code Sec. 9503(e)(5)(A) by striking "(2), (3), and (4)" and inserting "(2) and (3)". **Effective** for transfers relating to amounts paid and credits allowed after 3-18-2010.

P.L. 111-147, § 445(a)(2)(A)-(B):

Amended Code Sec. 9503(e)(3) by striking "October 1, 2009" and inserting "January 1, 2011"; and by striking "in accordance with" and all that follows and inserting "in accordance with the Surface Transportation Extension Act of 2010 or any other provision of law which was referred to in this paragraph before the date of the enactment of such Act (as such Act and provisions of law are in effect on the date of the enactment of such Act).". **Effective** 9-30-2009. Prior to being stricken, all that followed "in accordance with" in Code Sec. 9503(e)(3) read as follows:

the first Continuing Appropriations Resolution for Fiscal Year 2010 enacted into law or any other provision of law which was referred to in this paragraph before the date of the enactment of such Continuing Appropriations Resolution (as such Resolution and provisions of law are in effect on the date of the enactment of the last amendment to such Resolution).

(f) DETERMINATION OF TRUST FUND BALANCES AFTER SEPTEMBER 30, 1998.—

(1) IN GENERAL.—For purposes of determining the balances of the Highway Trust Fund and the Mass Transit Account after September 30, *1998, the opening balance* of the Highway Trust Fund (other than the Mass Transit Account) on October 1, 1998, shall be $8,000,000,000.

The Secretary shall cancel obligations held by the Highway Trust Fund to reflect the reduction in the balance under this paragraph.

(2) *RESTORATION OF FOREGONE INTEREST.—Out of money in the Treasury not otherwise appropriated, there is hereby appropriated—*

(A) *$14,700,000,000 to the Highway Account (as defined in subsection (e)(5)(B)) in the Highway Trust Fund; and*

(B) *$4,800,000,000 to the Mass Transit Account in the Highway Trust Fund.*

(4)[(3)] *TREATMENT OF APPROPRIATED AMOUNTS.—Any amount appropriated under this subsection to the Highway Trust Fund shall remain available without fiscal year limitation.*

Amendments

● **2010, Hiring Incentives to Restore Employment Act (P.L. 111-147)**

P.L. 111-147, § 441(a):

Amended Code Sec. 9503(f)(1) by striking subparagraph (B). **Effective** 3-18-2010. Prior to being stricken, Code Sec. 9503(f)(1)(B) read as follows:

(B) notwithstanding section 9602(b), obligations held by such Fund after September 30, 1998, shall be obligations of the United States which are not interest-bearing.

P.L. 111-147, § 441(b)(1)-(2):

Amended Code Sec. 9503(f)(1), as amended by Act Sec. 441(1)[(a)], by striking ", and" at the end of subparagraph (A) and inserting a period; and by striking "1998" in the matter preceding subparagraph (A) and all that follows through "the opening balance" and inserting "1998, the opening balance". **Effective** 3-18-2010. Prior to amendment, Code Sec. 9503(f)(1) read as follows:

(1) IN GENERAL.—For purposes of determining the balances of the Highway Trust Fund and the Mass Transit Account after September 30, 1998—

(A) the opening balance of the Highway Trust Fund (other than the Mass Transit Account) on October 1, 1998, shall be $8,000,000,000, and

The Secretary shall cancel obligations held by the Highway Trust Fund to reflect the reduction in the balance under this paragraph.

P.L. 111-147, § 442(a):

Amended Code Sec. 9503(f)(2). **Effective** 3-18-2010. Prior to amendment, Code Sec. 9503(f)(2) read as follows:

(2) INCREASE IN FUND BALANCE.—Out of money in the Treasury not otherwise appropriated, there is hereby appropriated (without fiscal year limitation) to the Highway Trust Fund $7,000,000,000.

P.L. 111-147, § 443(a):

Amended Code Sec. 9503(f), as amended by this Act, by adding at the end a new paragraph (4)[(3)]. **Effective** 3-18-2010.

[¶6200] CODE SEC. 9504. SPORT FISH RESTORATION AND BOATING TRUST FUND.

(a) CREATION OF TRUST FUND.—There is hereby established in the Treasury of the United States a trust fund to be known as the "Sport Fish Restoration and Boating Trust Fund". Such Trust Fund shall consist of such amounts as may be appropriated, credited, or paid to it as provided in this section, *section 9503(c)(3), section 9503(c)(4), or section 9602(b).*

<table>
<tr><td colspan="2" align="center">Amendments</td></tr>
<tr><td>• 2010, Hiring Incentives to Restore Employment Act (P.L. 111-147)</td><td>9503(c)(3), section 9503(c)(4)". **Effective** for transfers relating to amounts paid and credits allowed after 3-18-2010.</td></tr>
</table>

P.L. 111-147, §444(b)(5):

Amended Code Sec. 9504(a) by striking "section 9503(c)(4), section 9503(c)(5)" and inserting "section

(b) SPORT FISH RESTORATION AND BOATING TRUST FUND.—

* * *

(2) EXPENDITURES FROM TRUST FUND.—Amounts in the Sport Fish Restoration and Boating Trust Fund shall be available, as provided by appropriation Acts, for making expenditures—

(A) to carry out the purposes of the Dingell-Johnson Sport Fish Restoration Act *(as in effect on the date of the enactment of the Surface Transportation Extension Act of 2010),*

(B) to carry out the purposes of section 7404(d) of the Transportation Equity Act for the 21st Century *(as in effect on the date of the enactment of the Surface Transportation Extension Act of 2010), and*

(C) to carry out the purposes of the Coastal Wetlands Planning Protection and Restoration Act *(as in effect on the date of the enactment of the Surface Transportation Extension Act of 2010).*

Amounts transferred to such account under *section 9503(c)(4)* may be used only for making expenditures described in subparagraph (C) of this paragraph.

* * *

Amendments

• 2010, Hiring Incentives to Restore Employment Act (P.L. 111-147)

P.L. 111-147, §444(b)(6):

Amended Code Sec. 9504(b)(2) by striking "section 9503(c)(5)" and inserting "section 9503(c)(4)". **Effective** for transfers relating to amounts paid and credits allowed after 3-18-2010.

P.L. 111-147, §445(b)(1)(A)-(C):

Amended Code Sec. 9504(b)(2) by striking "(as in effect" in subparagraph (A) and all that follows in such subparagraph and inserting "(as in effect on the date of the enactment of the Surface Transportation Extension Act of 2010),", by striking "(as in effect" in subparagraph (B) and all that follows in such subparagraph and inserting "(as in effect on the date of the enactment of the Surface Transportation Extension Act of 2010), and", and by striking "(as in effect" in subparagraph (C) and all that follows in such subparagraph and inserting "(as in effect on the date of the enactment of the Surface Transportation Extension Act of 2010).". **Effective** 9-30-2009. Prior to amendment, Code Sec. 9504(b)(2)(A)-(C) read as follows:

(2) EXPENDITURES FROM TRUST FUND.—Amounts in the Sport Fish Restoration and Boating Trust Fund shall be available, as provided by appropriation Acts, for making expenditures—

(A) to carry out the purposes of the Dingell-Johnson Sport Fish Restoration Act (as in effect on the date of the enactment of the last amendment to the first Continuing Appropriations Resolution for Fiscal Year 2010),

(B) to carry out the purposes of section 7404(d) of the Transportation Equity Act for the 21st Century (as in effect on the date of the enactment of the last amendment to the first Continuing Appropriations Resolution for Fiscal Year 2010), and

(C) to carry out the purposes of the Coastal Wetlands Planning Protection and Restoration Act (as in effect on the date of the enactment of the last amendment to the first Continuing Appropriations Resolution for Fiscal Year 2010).

Amounts transferred to such account under section 9503(c)(5) may be used only for making expenditures described in subparagraph (C) of this paragraph.

(d) LIMITATION ON TRANSFERS TO TRUST FUND.—

* * *

(2) EXCEPTION FOR PRIOR OBLIGATIONS.—Paragraph (1) shall not apply to any expenditure to liquidate any contract entered into (or for any amount otherwise obligated) before *January 1, 2011,* in accordance with the provisions of this section.

(e) CROSS REFERENCE.—

For provision transferring motorboat fuels taxes to Sport Fish Restoration and Boating Trust Fund, see *[section] 9503(c)(3)*.

Act Sections Not Amending Code Sections

PATIENT PROTECTION AND AFFORDABLE CARE ACT

[¶7003] ACT SEC. 1. SHORT TITLE; TABLE OF CONTENTS.

(a) SHORT TITLE.—This Act may be cited as the "Patient Protection and Affordable Care Act".

* * *

TITLE I—QUALITY, AFFORDABLE HEALTH CARE FOR ALL AMERICANS

* * *

Subtitle D—Available Coverage Choices for All Americans

* * *

PART V—REINSURANCE AND RISK ADJUSTMENT

[¶7006] ACT SEC. 1341. TRANSITIONAL REINSURANCE PROGRAM FOR INDIVIDUAL MARKET IN EACH STATE.

* * *

(c) APPLICABLE REINSURANCE ENTITY.—For purposes of this section—

(1) IN GENERAL.—The term "applicable reinsurance entity" means a not-for-profit organization—

(A) the purpose of which is to help stabilize premiums for coverage in the individual market in a State during the first 3 years of operation of an Exchange for such markets within the State when the risk of adverse selection related to new rating rules and market changes is greatest; and

(B) the duties of which shall be to carry out the reinsurance program under this section by coordinating the funding and operation of the risk-spreading mechanisms designed to implement the reinsurance program.

(2) STATE DISCRETION.—A State may have more than 1 applicable reinsurance entity to carry out the reinsurance program under this section within the State and 2 or more States may enter into agreements to provide for an applicable reinsurance entity to carry out such program in all such States.

(3) ENTITIES ARE TAX-EXEMPT.—An applicable reinsurance entity established under this section shall be exempt from taxation under chapter 1 of the Internal Revenue Code of 1986. The preceding sentence shall not apply to the tax imposed by section 511 such Code (relating to tax on unrelated business taxable income of an exempt organization).

[Note: The title of Act Sec. 1341 and the text of Act Sec. 1341(c)(1)(A), as reproduced above, reflect amendments made by Act Sec. 10104(r). See ¶7042.]

* * *

[CCH Explanation at ¶435. Committee Report at ¶10,020.]

Subtitle E—Affordable Coverage Choices for All Americans

PART I—PREMIUM TAX CREDITS AND COST-SHARING REDUCTIONS

Subpart A—Premium Tax Credits and Cost-sharing Reductions

[¶7009] ACT SEC. 1401. REFUNDABLE TAX CREDIT PROVIDING PREMIUM ASSISTANCE FOR COVERAGE UNDER A QUALIFIED HEALTH PLAN.

* * *

(c) STUDY ON AFFORDABLE COVERAGE.—

(1) STUDY AND REPORT.—

(A) IN GENERAL.—Not later than 5 years after the date of the enactment of this Act, the Comptroller General shall conduct a study on the affordability of health insurance coverage, including—

(i) the impact of the tax credit for qualified health insurance coverage of individuals under section 36B of the Internal Revenue Code of 1986 and the tax credit for employee health insurance expenses of small employers under section 45R of such Code on maintaining and expanding the health insurance coverage of individuals;

(ii) the availability of affordable health benefits plans, including a study of whether the percentage of household income used for purposes of section 36B(c)(2)(C) of the Internal Revenue Code of 1986 (as added by this section) is the appropriate level for determining whether employer-provided coverage is affordable for an employee and whether such level may be lowered without significantly increasing the costs to the Federal Government and reducing employer-provided coverage; and

(iii) the ability of individuals to maintain essential health benefits coverage (as defined in section 5000A(f) of the Internal Revenue Code of 1986).

(B) REPORT.—The Comptroller General shall submit to the appropriate committees of Congress a report on the study conducted under subparagraph (A), together with legislative recommendations relating to the matters studied under such subparagraph.

(2) APPROPRIATE COMMITTEES OF CONGRESS.—In this subsection, the term "appropriate committees of Congress" means the Committee on Ways and Means, the Committee on Education and Labor, and the Committee on Energy and Commerce of the House of Representatives and the Committee on Finance and the Committee on Health, Education, Labor and Pensions of the Senate.

* * *

[CCH Explanation at ¶210. Committee Report at ¶10,030.]

Subpart B—Eligibility Determinations
* * *

[¶7012] ACT SEC. 1414. DISCLOSURES TO CARRY OUT ELIGIBILITY REQUIREMENTS FOR CERTAIN PROGRAMS.

(a) DISCLOSURE OF TAXPAYER RETURN INFORMATION AND SOCIAL SECURITY NUMBERS.—
* * *

(2) SOCIAL SECURITY NUMBERS.—Section 205(c)(2)(C) of the Social Security Act is amended by adding at the end the following new clause:

"(x) The Secretary of Health and Human Services, and the Exchanges established under section 1311 of the Patient Protection and Affordable Care Act, are authorized to collect and use the names and social security account numbers of individuals as required to administer the provisions of, and the amendments made by, the [sic]such Act.".

* * *

[CCH Explanation at ¶ 425. Committee Report at ¶ 10,050.]

Subtitle F—Shared Responsibility for Health Care

PART I—INDIVIDUAL RESPONSIBILITY
* * *

[¶ 7015] ACT SEC. 1502. REPORTING OF HEALTH INSURANCE COVERAGE.
* * *

(c) NOTIFICATION OF NONENROLLMENT.—Not later than June 30 of each year, the Secretary of the Treasury, acting through the Internal Revenue Service and in consultation with the Secretary of Health and Human Services, shall send a notification to each individual who files an individual income tax return and who is not enrolled in minimum essential coverage (as defined in section 5000A of the Internal Revenue Code of 1986). Such notification shall contain information on the services available through the Exchange operating in the State in which such individual resides.
* * *

[CCH Explanation at ¶ 410. Committee Report at ¶ 10,090.]

PART II—EMPLOYER RESPONSIBILITIES
* * *

[¶ 7018] ACT SEC. 1513. SHARED RESPONSIBILITY FOR EMPLOYERS.
* * *

(c) STUDY AND REPORT OF EFFECT OF TAX ON WORKERS' WAGES.—

(1) IN GENERAL.—The Secretary of Labor shall conduct a study to determine whether employees' wages are reduced by reason of the application of the assessable payments under section 4980H of the Internal Revenue Code of 1986 (as added by the amendments made by this section). The Secretary shall make such determination on the basis of the National Compensation Survey published by the Bureau of Labor Statistics.

(2) REPORT.—The Secretary shall report the results of the study under paragraph (1) to the Committee on Ways and Means of the House of Representatives and to the Committee on Finance of the Senate.
* * *

[CCH Explanation at ¶ 305. Committee Report at ¶ 10,100.]

TITLE VI—TRANSPARENCY AND PROGRAM INTEGRITY
* * *

Subtitle D—Patient-Centered Outcomes Research

[¶ 7021] ACT SEC. 6301. PATIENT-CENTERED OUTCOMES RESEARCH.

(a) IN GENERAL.—Title XI of the Social Security Act (42 U.S.C. 1301 et seq.) is amended by adding at the end the following new part:

"PART D—COMPARATIVE CLINICAL EFFECTIVENESS RESEARCH

"COMPARATIVE CLINICAL EFFECTIVENESS RESEARCH

"SEC. 1181. (a) DEFINITIONS.—In this section:

"(1) BOARD.—The term 'Board' means the Board of Governors established under subsection (f).

"(2) COMPARATIVE CLINICAL EFFECTIVENESS RESEARCH; RESEARCH.—

"(A) IN GENERAL.—The terms 'comparative clinical effectiveness research' and 'research' mean research evaluating and comparing health outcomes and the clinical effectiveness, risks, and benefits of 2 or more medical treatments, services, and items described in subparagraph (B).

"(B) MEDICAL TREATMENTS, SERVICES, AND ITEMS DESCRIBED.—The medical treatments, services, and items described in this subparagraph are health care interventions, protocols for treatment, care management, and delivery, procedures, medical devices, diagnostic tools, pharmaceuticals (including drugs and biologicals), integrative health practices, and any other strategies or items being used in the treatment, management, and diagnosis of, or prevention of illness or injury in, individuals.

"(3) CONFLICT OF INTEREST.—The term 'conflict of interest' means an association, including a financial or personal association, that have [sic] the potential to bias or have the appearance of biasing an individual's decisions in matters related to the Institute or the conduct of activities under this section.

"(4) REAL CONFLICT OF INTEREST.—The term 'real conflict of interest' means any instance where a member of the Board, the methodology committee established under subsection (d)(6), or an advisory panel appointed under subsection (d)(4), or a close relative of such member, has received or could receive either of the following:

"(A) A direct financial benefit of any amount deriving from the result or findings of a study conducted under this section.

"(B) A financial benefit from individuals or companies that own or manufacture medical treatments, services, or items to be studied under this section that in the aggregate exceeds $10,000 per year. For purposes of the preceding sentence, a financial benefit includes honoraria, fees, stock, or other financial benefit and the current value of the member or close relative's already existing stock holdings, in addition to any direct financial benefit deriving from the results or findings of a study conducted under this section.

"(b) PATIENT-CENTERED OUTCOMES RESEARCH INSTITUTE.—

"(1) ESTABLISHMENT.—There is authorized to be established a nonprofit corporation, to be known as the 'Patient-Centered Outcomes Research Institute' (referred to in this section as the 'Institute') which is neither an agency nor establishment of the United States Government.

"(2) APPLICATION OF PROVISIONS.—The Institute shall be subject to the provisions of this section, and, to the extent consistent with this section, to the District of Columbia Nonprofit Corporation Act.

"(3) FUNDING OF COMPARATIVE CLINICAL EFFECTIVENESS RESEARCH.—For fiscal year 2010 and each subsequent fiscal year, amounts in the Patient-Centered Outcomes Research Trust Fund (referred to in this section as the 'PCORTF') under section 9511 of the Internal Revenue Code of 1986 shall be available, without further appropriation, to the Institute to carry out this section.

"(c) PURPOSE.—The purpose of the Institute is to assist patients, clinicians, purchasers, and policy-makers in making informed health decisions by advancing the quality and relevance of evidence concerning the manner in which diseases, disorders, and other health conditions can effectively and appropriately be prevented, diagnosed, treated, monitored, and managed through research and evidence synthesis that considers variations in patient subpopulations, and the dissemination of research findings with respect to the relative health outcomes, clinical effectiveness, and appropriateness of the medical treatments, services, and items described in subsection (a)(2)(B).

"(d) DUTIES.—

"(1) IDENTIFYING RESEARCH PRIORITIES AND ESTABLISHING RESEARCH PROJECT AGENDA.—

"(A) IDENTIFYING RESEARCH PRIORITIES.—The Institute shall identify national priorities for research, taking into account factors of disease incidence, prevalence, and burden in the United States (with emphasis on chronic conditions), gaps in evidence in terms of clinical outcomes, practice variations and health disparities in terms of delivery and outcomes of care, the potential for new evidence to improve patient health, well-being, and the quality of care, the effect on national expenditures associated with a health care treatment, strategy, or health conditions, as well as patient needs, outcomes, and preferences, the relevance to patients and clinicians in making informed health decisions, and priorities in the National Strategy for quality care established under section 399H of the Public Health Service Act that are consistent with this section.

"(B) ESTABLISHING RESEARCH PROJECT AGENDA.—The Institute shall establish and update a research project agenda for research to address the priorities identified under subparagraph (A), taking into consideration the types of research that might address each priority and the relative value (determined based on the cost of conducting research compared to the potential usefulness of the information produced by research) associated with the different types of research, and such other factors as the Institute determines appropriate.

"(2) CARRYING OUT RESEARCH PROJECT AGENDA.—

"(A) RESEARCH.—The Institute shall carry out the research project agenda established under paragraph (1)(B) in accordance with the methodological standards adopted under paragraph (9) using methods, including the following:

"(i) Systematic reviews and assessments of existing and future research and evidence including original research conducted subsequent to the date of the enactment of this section.

"(ii) Primary research, such as randomized clinical trials, molecularly informed trials, and observational studies.

"(iii) Any other methodologies recommended by the methodology committee established under paragraph (6) that are adopted by the Board under paragraph (9).

"(B) CONTRACTS FOR THE MANAGEMENT OF FUNDING AND CONDUCT OF RESEARCH.—

"(i) CONTRACTS.—

"(I) IN GENERAL.—In accordance with the research project agenda established under paragraph (1)(B), the Institute shall enter into contracts for the management of funding and conduct of research in accordance with the following:

"(aa) Appropriate agencies and instrumentalities of the Federal Government.

"(bb) Appropriate academic research, private sector research, or study-conducting entities.

"(II) PREFERENCE.—In entering into contracts under subclause (I), the Institute shall give preference to the Agency for Healthcare Research and Quality and the National Institutes of Health, but only if the research to be conducted or managed under such contract is authorized by the governing statutes of such Agency or Institutes.

"(ii) CONDITIONS FOR CONTRACTS.—A contract entered into under this subparagraph shall require that the agency, instrumentality, or other entity—

"(I) abide by the transparency and conflicts of interest requirements under subsection (h) that apply to the Institute with respect to the research managed or conducted under such contract;

"(II) comply with the methodological standards adopted under paragraph (9) with respect to such research;

"(III) consult with the expert advisory panels for clinical trials and rare disease appointed under clauses (ii) and (iii), respectively, of paragraph (4)(A);

"(IV) subject to clause (iv), permit a researcher who conducts original research under the contract for the agency, instrumentality, or other entity to have such research published in a peer-reviewed journal or other publication;

"(V) have appropriate processes in place to manage data privacy and meet ethical standards for the research;

"(VI) comply with the requirements of the Institute for making the information available to the public under paragraph (8); and

"(VII) comply with other terms and conditions determined necessary by the Institute to carry out the research agenda adopted under paragraph (2).

"(iii) COVERAGE OF COPAYMENTS OR COINSURANCE.—A contract entered into under this subparagraph may allow for the coverage of copayments or coinsurance, or allow for other appropriate measures, to the extent that such coverage or other measures are necessary to preserve the validity of a research project, such as in the case where the research project must be blinded.

"(iv) REQUIREMENTS FOR PUBLICATION OF RESEARCH.—Any research published under clause (ii)(IV) shall be within the bounds of and entirely consistent with the evidence and findings produced under the contract with the Institute under this subparagraph. If the Institute determines that those requirements are not met, the Institute shall not enter into another contract with the agency, instrumentality, or entity which managed or conducted such research for a period determined appropriate by the Institute (but not less than 5 years).

"(C) REVIEW AND UPDATE OF EVIDENCE.—The Institute shall review and update evidence on a periodic basis as appropriate.

"(D) TAKING INTO ACCOUNT POTENTIAL DIFFERENCES.—Research shall be designed, as appropriate, to take into account the potential for differences in the effectiveness of health care treatments, services, and items as used with various subpopulations, such as racial and ethnic minorities, women, age, and groups of individuals with different comorbidities, genetic and molecular sub-types, or quality of life preferences and include members of such subpopulations as subjects in the research as feasible and appropriate.

"(E) DIFFERENCES IN TREATMENT MODALITIES.—Research shall be designed, as appropriate, to take into account different characteristics of treatment modalities that may affect research outcomes, such as the phase of the treatment modality in the innovation cycle and the impact of the skill of the operator of the treatment modality.

"(3) DATA COLLECTION.—

"(A) IN GENERAL.—The Secretary shall, with appropriate safeguards for privacy, make available to the Institute such data collected by the Centers for Medicare & Medicaid Services under the programs under titles XVIII, XIX, and XXI, as well as provide access to the data networks developed under section 937(f) of the Public Health Service Act, as the Institute and its contractors may require to carry out this section. The Institute may also request and obtain data from Federal, State, or private entities, including data from clinical databases and registries.

"(B) USE OF DATA.—The Institute shall only use data provided to the Institute under subparagraph (A) in accordance with laws and regulations governing the release and use of such data, including applicable confidentiality and privacy standards.

"(4) APPOINTING EXPERT ADVISORY PANELS.—

"(A) APPOINTMENT.—

"(i) IN GENERAL.—The Institute may appoint permanent or ad hoc expert advisory panels as determined appropriate to assist in identifying research priorities and establishing the research project agenda under paragraph (1) and for other purposes.

"(ii) EXPERT ADVISORY PANELS FOR CLINICAL TRIALS.—The Institute shall appoint expert advisory panels in carrying out randomized clinical trials under the research project agenda under paragraph (2)(A)(ii). Such expert advisory panels shal' advise the Institute and the agency, instrumentality, or entity conducting the research on the research question involved and the research design or protocol, including important patient subgroups and other parameters of the research. Such panels shall be available as a resource for technical questions that may arise during the conduct of such research.

"(iii) EXPERT ADVISORY PANE⌐ FOR RARE ⌐ISEASE —⌐n the case of a research study for rare disease, the Institute shall appoint an expert advisory panel for purposes of assisting in the design of the research study and determining the relative value and feasibility of conducting the research study.

"(B) COMPOSITION.—An expert advisory panel appointed under subparagraph (A) shall include representatives of practicing and research clinicians, patients, and experts in scientific and health services research, health services delivery, and evidence-based medicine who have experience in the relevant topic, and as appropriate, experts in integrative health and primary prevention strategies. The Institute may include a technical expert of each manufacturer or each medical technology that is included under the relevant topic, project, or category for which the panel is established.

"(5) SUPPORTING PATIENT AND CONSUMER REPRESENTATIVES.—The Institute shall provide support and resources to help patient and consumer representatives effectively participate on the Board and expert advisory panels appointed by the Institute under paragraph (4).

"(6) ESTABLISHING METHODOLOGY COMMITTEE.—

"(A) IN GENERAL.—The Institute shall establish a standing methodology committee to carry out the functions described in subparagraph (C).

"(B) APPOINTMENT AND COMPOSITION.—The methodology committee established under subparagraph (A) shall be composed of not more than 15 members appointed by the Comptroller General of the United States. Members appointed to the methodology committee shall be experts in their scientific field, such as health services research, clinical research, comparative clinical effectiveness research, biostatistics, genomics, and research methodologies. Stakeholders with such expertise may be appointed to the methodology committee. In addition to the members appointed under the first sentence, the Directors of the National Institutes of Health and the Agency for Healthcare Research and Quality (or their designees) shall each be included as members of the methodology committee.

"(C) FUNCTIONS.—Subject to subparagraph (D), the methodology committee shall work to develop and improve the science and methods of comparative clinical effectiveness research by, not later than 18 months after the establishment of the Institute, directly or through subcontract, developing and periodically updating the following:

"(i) Methodological standards for research. Such methodological standards shall provide specific criteria for internal validity, generalizability, feasibility, and timeliness of research and for health outcomes measures, risk adjustment, and other relevant aspects of research and assessment with respect to the design of research. Any methodological standards developed and updated under this subclause shall be scientifically based and include methods by which new information, data, or advances in technology are considered and incorporated into ongoing research projects by the Institute, as appropriate. The process for developing and updating such standards shall include input from relevant experts, stakeholders, and decisionmakers, and shall provide opportunities for public comment. Such standards shall also include methods by which patient subpopulations can be accounted for and evaluated in different types of research. As appropriate, such standards shall build on existing work on methodological standards for defined categories of health interventions and for each of the major categories of comparative clinical effectiveness research methods (determined as of the date of enactment of the Patient Protection and Affordable Care Act).

"(ii) A translation table that is designed to provide guidance and act as a reference for the Board to determine research methods that are most likely to address each specific research question.

"(D) CONSULTATION AND CONDUCT OF EXAMINATIONS.—The methodology committee may consult and contract with the Institute of Medicine of the National Academies and academic, nonprofit, or other private and governmental entities with relevant expertise to carry out activities described in subparagraph (C) and may consult with relevant stakeholders to carry out such activities.

"(E) REPORTS.—The methodology committee shall submit reports to the Board on the committee's performance of the functions described in subparagraph (C). Reports shall contain recommendations for the Institute to adopt methodological standards developed and updated by the methodology committee as well as other actions deemed necessary to comply with such methodological standards.

"(7) PROVIDING FOR A PEER-REVIEW PROCESS FOR PRIMARY RESEARCH.—

"(A) IN GENERAL.—The Institute shall ensure that there is a process for peer review of primary research described in subparagraph (A)(ii) of paragraph (2) that is conducted under such paragraph. Under such process—

"(i) evidence from such primary research shall be reviewed to assess scientific integrity and adherence to methodological standards adopted under paragraph (9); and

"(ii) a list of the names of individuals contributing to any peer-review process during the preceding year or years shall be made public and included in annual reports in accordance with paragraph (10)(D).

"(B) COMPOSITION.—Such peer-review process shall be designed in a manner so as to avoid bias and conflicts of interest on the part of the reviewers and shall be composed of experts in the scientific field relevant to the research under review.

"(C) USE OF EXISTING PROCESSES.—

"(i) PROCESSES OF ANOTHER ENTITY.—In the case where the Institute enters into a contract or other agreement with another entity for the conduct or management of research under this section, the Institute may utilize the peer-review process of such entity if such process meets the requirements under subparagraphs (A) and (B).

"(ii) PROCESSES OF APPROPRIATE MEDICAL JOURNALS.—The Institute may utilize the peer-review process of appropriate medical journals if such process meets the requirements under subparagraphs (A) and (B).

"(8) RELEASE OF RESEARCH FINDINGS.—

"(A) IN GENERAL.—The Institute shall, not later than 90 days after the conduct or receipt of research findings under this part, make such research findings available to clinicians, patients, and the general public. The Institute shall ensure that the research findings—

"(i) convey the findings of research in a manner that is comprehensible and useful to patients and providers in making health care decisions;

"(ii) fully convey findings and discuss considerations specific to certain subpopulations, risk factors, and comorbidities, as appropriate;

"(iii) include limitations of the research and what further research may be needed as appropriate;

"(iv) not be construed as mandates for practice guidelines, coverage recommendations, payment, or policy recommendations; and

"(v) not include any data which would violate the privacy of research participants or any confidentiality agreements made with respect to the use of data under this section.

"(B) DEFINITION OF RESEARCH FINDINGS.—In this paragraph, the term 'research findings' means the results of a study or assessment.

"(9) ADOPTION.—Subject to subsection (h)(1), the Institute shall adopt the national priorities identified under paragraph (1)(A), the research project agenda established under paragraph (1)(B), the methodological standards developed and updated by the methodology committee under paragraph (6)(C)(i), and any peer-review process provided under paragraph (7) by majority vote. In the case where the Institute does not adopt such processes in accordance with the preceding sentence, the processes shall be referred to the appropriate staff or entity within the Institute (or, in the case of the methodological standards, the methodology committee) for further review.

"(10) ANNUAL REPORTS.—The Institute shall submit an annual report to Congress and the President, and shall make the annual report available to the public. Such report shall contain—

"(A) a description of the activities conducted under this section, research priorities identified under paragraph (1)(A) and methodological standards developed and updated by the methodology committee under paragraph (6)(C)(i) that are adopted under paragraph (9) during the preceding year;

"(B) the research project agenda and budget of the Institute for the following year;

"(C) any administrative activities conducted by the Institute during the preceding year;

"(D) the names of individuals contributing to any peer-review process under paragraph (7), without identifying them with a particular research project; and

"(E) any other relevant information (including information on the membership of the Board, expert advisory panels, methodology committee, and the executive staff of the Institute, any conflicts of interest with respect to these individuals, and any bylaws adopted by the Board during the preceding year).

"(e) ADMINISTRATION.—

"(1) IN GENERAL.—Subject to paragraph (2), the Board shall carry out the duties of the Institute.

"(2) NONDELEGABLE DUTIES.—The activities described in subsections (d)(1) and (d)(9) are nondelegable.

"(f) Board of Governors.—

"(1) In general.—The Institute shall have a Board of Governors, which shall consist of the following members:

"(A) The Director of Agency for Healthcare Research and Quality (or the Director's designee).

"(B) The Director of the National Institutes of Health (or the Director's designee).

"(C) Seventeen members appointed, not later than 6 months after the date of enactment of this section, by the Comptroller General of the United States as follows:

"(i) 3 members representing patients and health care consumers.

"(ii) 5 members representing physicians and providers, including at least 1 surgeon, nurse, State-licensed integrative health care practitioner, and representative of a hospital.

"(iii) 3 members representing private payers, of whom at least 1 member shall represent health insurance issuers and at least 1 member shall represent employers who self-insure employee benefits.

"(iv) 3 members representing pharmaceutical, device, and diagnostic manufacturers or developers.

"(v) 1 member representing quality improvement or independent health service researchers.

"(vi) 2 members representing the Federal Government or the States, including at least 1 member representing a Federal health program or agency.

"(2) Qualifications.—The Board shall represent a broad range of perspectives and collectively have scientific expertise in clinical health sciences research, including epidemiology, decisions sciences, health economics, and statistics. In appointing the Board, the Comptroller General of the United States shall consider and disclose any conflicts of interest in accordance with subsection (h)(4)(B). Members of the Board shall be recused from relevant Institute activities in the case where the member (or an immediate family member of such member) has a real conflict of interest directly related to the research project or the matter that could affect or be affected by such participation.

"(3) Terms; vacancies.—A member of the Board shall be appointed for a term of 6 years, except with respect to the members first appointed, whose terms of appointment shall be staggered evenly over 2-year increments. No individual shall be appointed to the Board for more than 2 terms. Vacancies shall be filled in the same manner as the original appointment was made.

"(4) Chairperson and vice-chairperson.—The Comptroller General of the United States shall designate a Chairperson and Vice Chairperson of the Board from among the members of the Board. Such members shall serve as Chairperson or Vice Chairperson for a period of 3 years.

"(5) Compensation.—Each member of the Board who is not an officer or employee of the Federal Government shall be entitled to compensation (equivalent to the rate provided for level IV of the Executive Schedule under section 5315 of title 5, United States Code) and expenses incurred while performing the duties of the Board. An officer or employee of the Federal government who is a member of the Board shall be exempt from compensation.

"(6) Director and staff; experts and consultants.—The Board may employ and fix the compensation of an Executive Director and such other personnel as may be necessary to carry out the duties of the Institute and may seek such assistance and support of, or contract with, experts and consultants that may be necessary for the performance of the duties of the Institute.

"(7) MEETINGS AND HEARINGS.—The Board shall meet and hold hearings at the call of the Chairperson or a majority of its members. Meetings not solely concerning matters of personnel shall be advertised at least 7 days in advance and open to the public. A majority of the Board members shall constitute a quorum, but a lesser number of members may meet and hold hearings.

"(g) FINANCIAL AND GOVERNMENTAL OVERSIGHT.—

"(1) CONTRACT FOR AUDIT.—The Institute shall provide for the conduct of financial audits of the Institute on an annual basis by a private entity with expertise in conducting financial audits.

"(2) REVIEW AND ANNUAL REPORTS.—

"(A) REVIEW.—The Comptroller General of the United States shall review the following:

"(i) Not less frequently than on an annual basis, the financial audits conducted under paragraph (1).

"(ii) Not less frequently than every 5 years, the processes established by the Institute, including the research priorities and the conduct of research projects, in order to determine whether information produced by such research projects is objective and credible, is produced in a manner consistent with the requirements under this section, and is developed through a transparent process.

"(iii) Not less frequently than every 5 years, the dissemination and training activities and data networks established under section 937 of the Public Health Service Act, including the methods and products used to disseminate research, the types of training conducted and supported, and the types and functions of the data networks established, in order to determine whether the activities and data are produced in a manner consistent with the requirements under such section.

"(iv) Not less frequently than every 5 years, the overall effectiveness of activities conducted under this section and the dissemination, training, and capacity building activities conducted under section 937 of the Public Health Service Act. Such review shall include an analysis of the extent to which research findings are used by health care decision-makers, the effect of the dissemination of such findings on reducing practice variation and disparities in health care, and the effect of the research conducted and disseminated on innovation and the health care economy of the United States.

"(v) Not later than 8 years after the date of enactment of this section, the adequacy and use of the funding for the Institute and the activities conducted under section 937 of the Public Health Service Act, including a determination as to whether, based on the utilization of research findings by public and private payers, funding sources for the Patient-Centered Outcomes Research Trust Fund under section 9511 of the Internal Revenue Code of 1986 are appropriate and whether such sources of funding should be continued or adjusted.

"(B) ANNUAL REPORTS.—Not later than April 1 of each year, the Comptroller General of the United States shall submit to Congress a report containing the results of the review conducted under subparagraph (A) with respect to the preceding year (or years, if applicable), together with recommendations for such legislation and administrative action as the Comptroller General determines appropriate.

"(h) ENSURING TRANSPARENCY, CREDIBILITY, AND ACCESS.—The Institute shall establish procedures to ensure that the following requirements for ensuring transparency, credibility, and access are met:

"(1) PUBLIC COMMENT PERIODS.—The Institute shall provide for a public comment period of not less than 45 days and not more than 60 days prior to the adoption under subsection (d)(9) of the national priorities identified under subsection (d)(1)(A), the research project agenda established under subsection (d)(1)(B), the methodological standards developed and updated by the methodology committee under subsection (d)(6)(C)(i), and the peer-review process provided under paragraph (7), and after the release of draft findings with respect to systematic reviews of existing research and evidence.

"(2) ADDITIONAL FORUMS.—The Institute shall support forums to increase public awareness and obtain and incorporate public input and feedback through media (such as an Internet website) on research priorities, research findings, and other duties, activities, or processes the Institute determines appropriate.

"(3) PUBLIC AVAILABILITY.—The Institute shall make available to the public and disclose through the official public Internet website of the Institute the following:

"(A) Information contained in research findings as specified in subsection (d)(9).

"(B) The process and methods for the conduct of research, including the identity of the entity and the investigators conducing [sic] such research and any conflicts of interests of such parties, any direct or indirect links the entity has to industry, and research protocols, including measures taken, methods of research and analysis, research results, and such other information the Institute determines appropriate) concurrent with the release of research findings.

"(C) Notice of public comment periods under paragraph (1), including deadlines for public comments.

"(D) Subsequent comments received during each of the public comment periods.

"(E) In accordance with applicable laws and processes and as the Institute determines appropriate, proceedings of the Institute.

"(4) DISCLOSURE OF CONFLICTS OF INTEREST.—

"(A) IN GENERAL.—A conflict of interest shall be disclosed in the following manner:

"(i) By the Institute in appointing members to an expert advisory panel under subsection (d)(4), in selecting individuals to contribute to any peer-review process under subsection (d)(7), and for employment as executive staff of the Institute.

"(ii) By the Comptroller General in appointing members of the methodology committee under subsection (d)(6);

"(iii) By the Institute in the annual report under subsection (d)(10), except that, in the case of individuals contributing to any such peer review process, such description shall be in a manner such that those individuals cannot be identified with a particular research project.

"(B) MANNER OF DISCLOSURE.—Conflicts of interest shall be disclosed as described in subparagraph (A) as soon as practicable on the Internet web site of the Institute and of the Government Accountability Office. The information disclosed under the preceding sentence shall include the type, nature, and magnitude of the interests of the individual involved, except to the extent that the individual recuses himself or herself from participating in the consideration of or any other activity with respect to the study as to which the potential conflict exists.

"(i) RULES.—The Institute, its Board or staff, shall be prohibited from accepting gifts, bequeaths, or donations of services or property. In addition, the Institute shall be prohibited from establishing a corporation or generating revenues from activities other than as provided under this section.

"(j) RULES OF CONSTRUCTION.—

"(1) COVERAGE.—Nothing in this section shall be construed—

"(A) to permit the Institute to mandate coverage, reimbursement, or other policies for any public or private payer; or

"(B) as preventing the Secretary from covering the routine costs of clinical care received by an individual entitled to, or enrolled for, benefits under title XVIII, XIX, or XXI in the case where such individual is participating in a clinical trial and such costs would otherwise be covered under such title with respect to the beneficiary.".

* * *

[CCH Explanation at ¶445. Committee Report at ¶10,150.]

TITLE VIII—CLASS ACT
* * *

[¶7024] ACT SEC. 8002. ESTABLISHMENT OF NATIONAL VOLUNTARY INSURANCE PROGRAM FOR PURCHASING COMMUNITY LIVING ASSISTANCE SERVICES AND SUPPORT.

(a) ESTABLISHMENT OF CLASS PROGRAM.—

(1) IN GENERAL.—The Public Health Service Act (42 U.S.C. 201 et seq.), as amended by section 4302(a), is amended by adding at the end the following:

"TITLE XXXII—COMMUNITY LIVING ASSISTANCE SERVICES AND SUPPORTS

"SEC. 3201. PURPOSE.

"The purpose of this title is to establish a national voluntary insurance program for purchasing community living assistance services and supports in order to—

"(1) provide individuals with functional limitations with tools that will allow them to maintain their personal and financial independence and live in the community through a new financing strategy for community living assistance services and supports;

"(2) establish an infrastructure that will help address the Nation's community living assistance services and supports needs;

"(3) alleviate burdens on family caregivers; and

"(4) address institutional bias by providing a financing mechanism that supports personal choice and independence to live in the community.

"SEC. 3202. DEFINITIONS.

"In this title:

"(1) ACTIVE ENROLLEE.—The term 'active enrollee' means an individual who is enrolled in the CLASS program in accordance with section 3204 and who has paid any premiums due to maintain such enrollment.

"(2) ACTIVELY EMPLOYED.—The term 'actively employed' means an individual who—

"(A) is reporting for work at the individual's usual place of employment or at another location to which the individual is required to travel because of the individual's employment (or in the case of an individual who is a member of the uniformed services, is on active duty and is physically able to perform the duties of the individual's position); and

"(B) is able to perform all the usual and customary duties of the individual's employment on the individual's regular work schedule.

"(3) ACTIVITIES OF DAILY LIVING.—The term 'activities of daily living' means each of the following activities specified in section 7702B(c)(2)(B) of the Internal Revenue Code of 1986:

"(A) Eating.

"(B) Toileting.

"(C) Transferring.

"(D) Bathing.

"(E) Dressing.

"(F) Continence.

"(4) CLASS PROGRAM.—The term 'CLASS program' means the program established under this title.

"(5) ELIGIBILITY ASSESSMENT SYSTEM.—The term 'Eligibility Assessment System' means the entity established by the Secretary under section 3205(a)(2) to make functional eligibility determinations for the CLASS program.

"(6) ELIGIBLE BENEFICIARY.—

"(A) IN GENERAL.—The term 'eligible beneficiary' means any individual who is an active enrollee in the CLASS program and, as of the date described in subparagraph (B)—

"(i) has paid premiums for enrollment in such program for at least 60 months;

"(ii) has earned, with respect to at least 3 calendar years that occur during the first 60 months for which the individual has paid premiums for enrollment in the program, at least an amount equal to the amount of wages and self-employment income which an individual must have in order to be credited with a quarter of coverage under section 213(d) of the Social Security Act for the year; and

"(iii) has paid premiums for enrollment in such program for at least 24 consecutive months, if a lapse in premium payments of more than 3 months has occurred during the period that begins on the date of the individual's enrollment and ends on the date of such determination.

"(B) DATE DESCRIBED.—For purposes of subparagraph (A), the date described in this subparagraph is the date on which the individual is determined to have a functional limitation described in section 3203(a)(1)(C) that is expected to last for a continuous period of more than 90 days.

"(C) REGULATIONS.—The Secretary shall promulgate regulations specifying exceptions to the minimum earnings requirements under subparagraph (A)(ii) for purposes of being considered an eligible beneficiary for certain populations.

"(7) HOSPITAL; NURSING FACILITY; INTERMEDIATE CARE FACILITY FOR THE MENTALLY RETARDED; INSTITUTION FOR MENTAL DISEASES.—The terms 'hospital', 'nursing facility', 'intermediate care facility for the mentally retarded', and 'institution for mental diseases' have the meanings given such terms for purposes of Medicaid.

"(8) CLASS INDEPENDENCE ADVISORY COUNCIL.—The term 'CLASS Independence Advisory Council' or 'Council' means the Advisory Council established under section 3207 to advise the Secretary.

"(9) CLASS INDEPENDENCE BENEFIT PLAN.—The term 'CLASS Independence Benefit Plan' means the benefit plan developed and designated by the Secretary in accordance with section 3203.

"(10) CLASS INDEPENDENCE FUND.—The term 'CLASS Independence Fund' or 'Fund' means the fund established under section 3206.

"(11) MEDICAID.—The term 'Medicaid' means the program established under title XIX of the Social Security Act (42 U.S.C. 1396 et seq.).

"(12) POVERTY LINE.—The term 'poverty line' has the meaning given that term in section 2110(c)(5) of the Social Security Act (42 U.S.C. 1397jj(c)(5)).

"(13) PROTECTION AND ADVOCACY SYSTEM.—The term 'Protection and Advocacy System' means the system for each State established under section 143 of the Developmental Disabilities Assistance and Bill of Rights Act of 2000 (42 U.S.C. 15043).

"SEC. 3203. CLASS INDEPENDENCE BENEFIT PLAN.

"(a) Process for development.—

"(1) In general.—The Secretary, in consultation with appropriate actuaries and other experts, shall develop at least 3 actuarially sound benefit plans as alternatives for consideration for designation by the Secretary as the CLASS Independence Benefit Plan under which eligible beneficiaries shall receive benefits under this title. Each of the plan alternatives developed shall be designed to provide eligible beneficiaries with the benefits described in section 3205 consistent with the following requirements:

"(A) Premiums.—

"(i) In general.—Beginning with the first year of the CLASS program, and for each year thereafter, subject to clauses (ii) and (iii), the Secretary shall establish all premiums to be paid by enrollees for the year based on an actuarial analysis of the 75-year costs of the program that ensures solvency throughout such 75-year period.

"(ii) Nominal premium for poorest individuals and full-time students.—

"(I) In general.—The monthly premium for enrollment in the CLASS program shall not exceed the applicable dollar amount per month determined under subclause (II) for—

"(aa) any individual whose income does not exceed the poverty line; and

"(bb) any individual who has not attained age 22, and is actively employed during any period in which the individual is a full-time student (as determined by the Secretary).

"(II) Applicable dollar amount.—The applicable dollar amount described in this subclause is the amount equal to $5, increased by the percentage increase in the consumer price index for all urban consumers (U.S. city average) for each year occurring after 2009 and before such year.

"(iii) Class independence fund reserves.—At such time as the CLASS program has been in operation for 10 years, the Secretary shall establish all premiums to be paid by enrollees for the year based on an actuarial analysis that accumulated reserves in the CLASS Independence Fund would not decrease in that year. At such time as the Secretary determines the CLASS program demonstrates a sustained ability to finance expected yearly expenses with expected yearly premiums and interest credited to the CLASS Independence Fund, the Secretary may decrease the required amount of CLASS Independence Fund reserves.

"(B) Vesting period.—A 5-year vesting period for eligibility for benefits.

"(C) Benefit triggers.—A benefit trigger for provision of benefits that requires a determination that an individual has a functional limitation, as certified by a licensed health care practitioner, described in any of the following clauses that is expected to last for a continuous period of more than 90 days:

"(i) The individual is determined to be unable to perform at least the minimum number (which may be 2 or 3) of activities of daily living as are required under the plan for the provision of benefits without substantial assistance (as defined by the Secretary) from another individual.

"(ii) The individual requires substantial supervision to protect the individual from threats to health and safety due to substantial cognitive impairment.

"(iii) The individual has a level of functional limitation similar (as determined under regulations prescribed by the Secretary) to the level of functional limitation described in clause (i) or (ii).

"(D) Cash benefit.—Payment of a cash benefit that satisfies the following requirements:

"(i) MINIMUM REQUIRED AMOUNT.—The benefit amount provides an eligible beneficiary with not less than an average of $50 per day (as determined based on the reasonably expected distribution of beneficiaries receiving benefits at various benefit levels).

"(ii) AMOUNT SCALED TO FUNCTIONAL ABILITY.—The benefit amount is varied based on a scale of functional ability, with not less than 2, and not more than 6, benefit level amounts.

"(iii) DAILY OR WEEKLY.—The benefit is paid on a daily or weekly basis.

"(iv) NO LIFETIME OR AGGREGATE LIMIT.—The benefit is not subject to any lifetime or aggregate limit.

"(E) COORDINATION WITH SUPPLEMENTAL COVERAGE OBTAINED THROUGH THE EXCHANGE.—The benefits allow for coordination with any supplemental coverage purchased through an Exchange established under section 1311 of the Patient Protection and Affordable Care Act.

"(2) REVIEW AND RECOMMENDATION BY THE CLASS INDEPENDENCE ADVISORY COUNCIL.—The CLASS Independence Advisory Council shall—

"(A) evaluate the alternative benefit plans developed under paragraph (1); and

"(B) recommend for designation as the CLASS Independence Benefit Plan for offering to the public the plan that the Council determines best balances price and benefits to meet enrollees' needs in an actuarially sound manner, while optimizing the probability of the long-term sustainability of the CLASS program.

"(3) DESIGNATION BY THE SECRETARY.—Not later than October 1, 2012, the Secretary, taking into consideration the recommendation of the CLASS Independence Advisory Council under paragraph (2)(B), shall designate a benefit plan as the CLASS Independence Benefit Plan. The Secretary shall publish such designation, along with details of the plan and the reasons for the selection by the Secretary, in a final rule that allows for a period of public comment.

"(b) ADDITIONAL PREMIUM REQUIREMENTS.—

"(1) ADJUSTMENT OF PREMIUMS.—

"(A) IN GENERAL.—Except as provided in subparagraphs (B), (C), (D), and (E), the amount of the monthly premium determined for an individual upon such individual's enrollment in the CLASS program shall remain the same for as long as the individual is an active enrollee in the program.

"(B) RECALCULATED PREMIUM IF REQUIRED FOR PROGRAM SOLVENCY.—

"(i) IN GENERAL.—Subject to clause (ii), if the Secretary determines, based on the most recent report of the Board of Trustees of the CLASS Independence Fund, the advice of the CLASS Independence Advisory Council, and the annual report of the Inspector General of the Department of Health and Human Services, and waste, fraud, and abuse, or such other information as the Secretary determines appropriate, that the monthly premiums and income to the CLASS Independence Fund for a year are projected to be insufficient with respect to the 20-year period that begins with that year, the Secretary shall adjust the monthly premiums for individuals enrolled in the CLASS program as necessary (but maintaining a nominal premium for enrollees whose income is below the poverty line or who are full-time students actively employed).

"(ii) EXEMPTION FROM INCREASE.—Any increase in a monthly premium imposed as result of a determination described in clause (i) shall not apply with respect to the monthly premium of any active enrollee who—

"(I) has attained age 65;

"(II) has paid premiums for enrollment in the program for at least 20 years; and

"(III) is not actively employed.

"(C) RECALCULATED PREMIUM IF REENROLLMENT [SIC] AFTER MORE THAN A 3-MONTH LAPSE.—

"(i) IN GENERAL.—The reenrollment of an individual after a 90-day period during which the individual failed to pay the monthly premium required to maintain the individual's enrollment in the CLASS program shall be treated as an initial enrollment for purposes of age-adjusting the premium for enrollment in the program.

"(ii) CREDIT FOR PRIOR MONTHS IF REENROLLED WITHIN 5 YEARS.—An individual who reenrolls in the CLASS program after such a 90-day period and before the end of the 5-year period that begins with the first month for which the individual failed to pay the monthly premium required to maintain the individual's enrollment in the program shall be—

"(I) credited with any months of paid premiums that accrued prior to the individual's lapse in enrollment; and

"(II) notwithstanding the total amount of any such credited months, required to satisfy section 3202(6)(A)(ii) before being eligible to receive benefits.

"(D) NO LONGER STATUS AS A FULL-TIME STUDENT.—An individual subject to a nominal premium on the basis of being described in subsection (a)(1)(A)(ii)(I)(bb) who ceases to be described in that subsection, beginning with the first month following the month in which the individual ceases to be so described, shall be subject to the same monthly premium as the monthly premium that applies to an individual of the same age who first enrolls in the program under the most similar circumstances as the individual (such as the first year of eligibility for enrollment in the program or in a subsequent year).

"(E) PENALTY FOR REENOLLMENT AFTER 5-YEAR LAPSE.—In the case of an individual who reenrolls in the CLASS program after the end of the 5-year period described in subparagraph (C)(ii), the monthly premium required for the individual shall be the age-adjusted premium that would be applicable to an initially enrolling individual who is the same age as the reenrolling individual, increased by the greater of—

"(i) an amount that the Secretary determines is actuarially sound for each month that occurs during the period that begins with the first month for which the individual failed to pay the monthly premium required to maintain the individual's enrollment in the CLASS program and ends with the month preceding the month in which the reenrollment is effective; or

"(ii) 1 percent of the applicable age-adjusted premium for each such month occurring in such period.

"(2) ADMINISTRATIVE EXPENSES.—In determining the monthly premiums for the CLASS program the Secretary may factor in costs for administering the program, not to exceed for any year in which the program is in effect under this title, an amount equal to 3 percent of all premiums paid during the year.

"(3) NO UNDERWRITING REQUIREMENTS.—No underwriting (other than on the basis of age in accordance with subparagraphs (D) and (E) of paragraph (1)) shall be used to—

"(A) determine the monthly premium for enrollment in the CLASS program; or

"(B) prevent an individual from enrolling in the program.

"(c) SELF-ATTESTATION AND VERIFICATION OF INCOME.—The Secretary shall establish procedures to—

"(1) permit an individual who is eligible for the nominal premium required under subsection (a)(1)(A)(ii), as part of their automatic enrollment in the CLASS program, to self-attest that their income does not exceed the poverty line or that their status as a full-time student who is actively employed;

"(2) verify, using procedures similar to the procedures used by the Commissioner of Social Security under section 1631(e)(1)(B)(ii) of the Social Security Act and consistent with the requirements applicable to the conveyance of data and information under section 1942 of such Act, the validity of such self-attestation; and

"(3) require an individual to confirm, on at least an annual basis, that their income does not exceed the poverty line or that they continue to maintain such status.

"SEC. 3204. ENROLLMENT AND DISENROLLMENT REQUIREMENTS.

"(a) AUTOMATIC ENROLLMENT.—

"(1) IN GENERAL.—Subject to paragraph (2), the Secretary, in coordination with the Secretary of the Treasury, shall establish procedures under which each individual described in subsection (c) may be automatically enrolled in the CLASS program by an employer of such individual in the same manner as an employer may elect to automatically enroll employees in a plan under section 401(k), 403(b), or 457 of the Internal Revenue Code of 1986.

"(2) ALTERNATIVE ENROLLMENT PROCEDURES.—The procedures established under paragraph (1) shall provide for an alternative enrollment process for an individual described in subsection (c) in the case of such an individual—

"(A) who is self-employed;

"(B) who has more than 1 employer; or

"(C) whose employer does not elect to participate in the automatic enrollment process established by the Secretary.

"(3) ADMINISTRATION.—

"(A) IN GENERAL.—The Secretary and the Secretary of the Treasury shall, by regulation, establish procedures to ensure that an individual is not automatically enrolled in the CLASS program by more than 1 employer.

"(B) FORM.—Enrollment in the CLASS program shall be made in such manner as the Secretary may prescribe in order to ensure ease of administration.

"(b) ELECTION TO OPT-OUT.—An individual described in subsection (c) may elect to waive enrollment in the CLASS program at any time in such form and manner as the Secretary and the Secretary of the Treasury shall prescribe.

"(c) INDIVIDUAL DESCRIBED.—For purposes of enrolling in the CLASS program, an individual described in this paragraph is an individual—

"(1) who has attained age 18;

"(2) who—

"(A) receives wages on which there is imposed a tax under section 3201(a) of the Internal Revenue Code of 1986; or

"(B) derives self-employment income on which there is imposed a tax under section 1401(a) of the Internal Revenue Code of 1986;

"(3) who is actively employed; and

"(4) who is not—

"(A) a patient in a hospital or nursing facility, an intermediate care facility for the mentally retarded, or an institution for mental diseases and receiving medical assistance under Medicaid; or

"(B) confined in a jail, prison, other penal institution or correctional facility, or by court order pursuant to conviction of a criminal offense or in connection with a verdict or finding described in section 202(x)(1)(A)(ii) of the Social Security Act (42 U.S.C. 402(x)(1)(A)(ii)).

"(d) RULE OF CONSTRUCTION.—Nothing in this title shall be construed as requiring an active enrollee to continue to satisfy subparagraph (B) or (C) of subsection (c)(1) in order to maintain enrollment in the CLASS program.

"(e) PAYMENT.—

"(1) PAYROLL DEDUCTION.—An amount equal to the monthly premium for the enrollment in the CLASS program of an individual shall be deducted from the wages or self-employment income of such individual in accordance with such procedures as the Secretary, in coordination with the Secretary of the Treasury, shall establish for employers who elect to deduct and withhold such premiums on behalf of enrolled employees.

"(2) ALTERNATIVE PAYMENT MECHANISM.—The Secretary, in coordination with the Secretary of the Treasury, shall establish alternative procedures for the payment of monthly premiums by an individual enrolled in the CLASS program—

"(A) who does not have an employer who elects to deduct and withhold premiums in accordance with subparagraph (A); or

"(B) who does not earn wages or derive self-employment income.

"(f) TRANSFER OF PREMIUMS COLLECTED.—

"(1) IN GENERAL.—During each calendar year the Secretary of the Treasury shall deposit into the CLASS Independence Fund a total amount equal, in the aggregate, to 100 percent of the premiums collected during that year.

"(2) TRANSFERS BASED ON ESTIMATES.—The amount deposited pursuant to paragraph (1) shall be transferred in at least monthly payments to the CLASS Independence Fund on the basis of estimates by the Secretary and certified to the Secretary of the Treasury of the amounts collected in accordance with subparagraphs (A) and (B) of paragraph (5). Proper adjustments shall be made in amounts subsequently transferred to the Fund to the extent prior estimates were in excess of, or were less than, actual amounts collected.

"(g) OTHER ENROLLMENT AND DISENROLLMENT OPPORTUNITIES.—The Secretary, in coordination with the Secretary of the Treasury, shall establish procedures under which—

"(1) an individual who, in the year of the individual's initial eligibility to enroll in the CLASS program, has elected to waive enrollment in the program, is eligible to elect to enroll in the program, in such form and manner as the Secretaries shall establish, only during an open enrollment period established by the Secretaries that is specific to the individual and that may not occur more frequently than biennially after the date on which the individual first elected to waive enrollment in the program; and

"(2) an individual shall only be permitted to disenroll from the program (other than for nonpayment of premiums) during an annual disenrollment period established by the Secretaries and in such form and manner as the Secretaries shall establish.

"SEC. 3205. BENEFITS.

"(a) DETERMINATION OF ELIGIBILITY.—

"(1) APPLICATION FOR RECEIPT OF BENEFITS.—The Secretary shall establish procedures under which an active enrollee shall apply for receipt of benefits under the CLASS Independence Benefit Plan.

"(2) ELIGIBILITY ASSESSMENTS.—

"(A) IN GENERAL.—Not later than January 1, 2012, the Secretary shall—

"(i) establish an Eligibility Assessment System (other than a service with which the Commissioner of Social Security has entered into an agreement, with respect to any State, to make disability determinations for purposes of title II or XVI of the Social Security Act) to provide for eligibility assessments of active enrollees who apply for receipt of benefits;

"(ii) enter into an agreement with the Protection and Advocacy System for each State to provide advocacy services in accordance with subsection (d); and

"(iii) enter into an agreement with public and private entities to provide advice and assistance counseling in accordance with subsection (e).

"(B) REGULATIONS.—The Secretary shall promulgate regulations to develop an expedited nationally equitable eligibility determination process, as certified by a licensed health care practitioner, an appeals process, and a redetermination process, as certified by a licensed health care practitioner, including whether an active enrollee is eligible for a cash benefit under the program and if so, the amount of the cash benefit (in accordance [with] the sliding scale established under the plan).

"(C) Presumptive eligibility for certain institutionalized enrollees planning to discharge.—An active enrollee shall be deemed presumptively eligible if the enrollee—

"(i) has applied for, and attests is eligible for, the maximum cash benefit available under the sliding scale established under the CLASS Independence Benefit Plan;

"(ii) is a patient in a hospital (but only if the hospitalization is for long-term care), nursing facility, intermediate care facility for the mentally retarded, or an institution for mental diseases; and

"(iii) is in the process of, or about to begin the process of, planning to discharge from the hospital, facility, or institution, or within 60 days from the date of discharge from the hospital, facility, or institution.

"(D) Appeals.—The Secretary shall establish procedures under which an applicant for benefits under the CLASS Independence Benefit Plan shall be guaranteed the right to appeal an adverse determination.

"(b) Benefits.—An eligible beneficiary shall receive the following benefits under the CLASS Independence Benefit Plan:

"(1) Cash benefit.—A cash benefit established by the Secretary in accordance with the requirements of section 3203(a)(1)(D) that—

"(A) the first year in which beneficiaries receive the benefits under the plan, is not less than the average dollar amount specified in clause (i) of such section; and

"(B) for any subsequent year, is not less than the average per day dollar limit applicable under this subparagraph for the preceding year, increased by the percentage increase in the consumer price index for all urban consumers (U.S. city average) over the previous year.

"(2) Advocacy services.—Advocacy services in accordance with subsection (d).

"(3) Advice and assistance counseling.—Advice and assistance counseling in accordance with subsection (e).

"(4) Administrative expenses.—Advocacy services and advise [sic] and assistance counseling services under paragraphs (2) and (3) of this subsection shall be included as administrative expenses under section 3203(b)(3).

"(c) Payment of Benefits.—

"(1) Life independence account.—

"(A) In general.—The Secretary shall establish procedures for administering the provision of benefits to eligible beneficiaries under the CLASS Independence Benefit Plan, including the payment of the cash benefit for the beneficiary into a Life Independence Account established by the Secretary on behalf of each eligible beneficiary.

"(B) Use of cash benefits.—Cash benefits paid into a Life Independence Account of an eligible beneficiary shall be used to purchase nonmedical services and supports that the beneficiary needs to maintain his or her independence at home or in another residential setting of their choice in the community, including (but not limited to) home modifications, assistive technology, accessible transportation, homemaker services, respite care, personal assistance services, home care aides, and nursing support. Nothing in the preceding sentence shall prevent an eligible beneficiary from using cash benefits paid into a Life Independence Account for obtaining assistance with decision making concerning medical care, including the right to accept or refuse medical or surgical treatment and the right to formulate advance directives or other written instructions recognized under State law, such as a living will or durable power of attorney for health care, in the case that an injury or illness causes the individual to be unable to make health care decisions.

"(C) ELECTRONIC MANAGEMENT OF FUNDS.—The Secretary shall establish procedures for—

"(i) crediting an account established on behalf of a beneficiary with the beneficiary's cash daily benefit;

"(ii) allowing the beneficiary to access such account through debit cards; and

"(iii) accounting for withdrawals by the beneficiary from such account.

"(D) PRIMARY PAYOR RULES FOR BENEFICIARIES WHO ARE ENROLLED IN MEDICAID.—In the case of an eligible beneficiary who is enrolled in Medicaid, the following payment rules shall apply:

"(i) INSTITUTIONALIZED BENEFICIARY.—If the beneficiary is a patient in a hospital, nursing facility, intermediate care facility for the mentally retarded, or an institution for mental diseases, the beneficiary shall retain an amount equal to 5 percent of the beneficiary's daily or weekly cash benefit (as applicable) (which shall be in addition to the amount of the beneficiary's personal needs allowance provided under Medicaid), and the remainder of such benefit shall be applied toward the facility's cost of providing the beneficiary's care, and Medicaid shall provide secondary coverage for such care.

"(ii) BENEFICIARIES RECEIVING HOME AND COMMUNITY-BASED SERVICES.—

"(I) 50 PERCENT OF BENEFIT RETAINED BY BENEFICIARY.—Subject to subclause (II), if a beneficiary is receiving medical assistance under Medicaid for home and community based services, the beneficiary shall retain an amount equal to 50 percent of the beneficiary's daily or weekly cash benefit (as applicable), and the remainder of the daily or weekly cash benefit shall be applied toward the cost to the State of providing such assistance (and shall not be used to claim Federal matching funds under Medicaid), and Medicaid shall provide secondary coverage for the remainder of any costs incurred in providing such assistance.

"(II) REQUIREMENT FOR STATE OFFSET.—A State shall be paid the remainder of a beneficiary's daily or weekly cash benefit under subclause (I) only if the State home and community-based waiver under section 1115 of the Social Security Act (42 U.S.C. 1315) or subsection (c) or (d) of section 1915 of such Act (42 U.S.C. 1396n), or the State plan amendment under subsection (i) of such section does not include a waiver of the requirements of section 1902(a)(1) of the Social Security Act (relating to statewideness) or of section 1902(a)(10)(B) of such Act (relating to comparability) and the State offers at a minimum case management services, personal care services, habilitation services, and respite care under such a waiver or State plan amendment.

"(III) DEFINITION OF HOME AND COMMUNITY-BASED SERVICES.—In this clause, the term 'home and community-based services' means any services which may be offered under a home and community-based waiver authorized for a State under section 1115 of the Social Security Act (42 U.S.C. 1315) or subsection (c) or (d) of section 1915 of such Act (42 U.S.C. 1396n) or under a State plan amendment under subsection (i) of such section.

"(iii) BENEFICIARIES ENROLLED IN PROGRAMS OF ALL-INCLUSIVE CARE FOR THE ELDERLY (PACE)

"(I) IN GENERAL.—Subject to subclause (II), if a beneficiary is receiving medical assistance under Medicaid for PACE program services under section 1934 of the Social Security Act (42 U.S.C. 1396u-4), the beneficiary shall retain an amount equal to 50 percent of the beneficiary's daily or weekly cash benefit (as applicable), and the remainder of the daily or weekly cash benefit shall be applied toward the cost to the State of providing such assistance (and shall not be used to claim Federal matching funds under Medicaid), and Medicaid shall provide secondary coverage for the remainder of any costs incurred in providing such assistance.

"(II) INSTITUTIONALIZED RECIPIENTS OF PACE PROGRAM SERVICES.—If a beneficiary receiving assistance under Medicaid for PACE program services is a patient in a hospital, nursing facility, intermediate care facility for the mentally retarded, or an institution for mental diseases, the beneficiary shall be treated as in [sic] institutionalized beneficiary under clause (i).

"(2) AUTHORIZED REPRESENTATIVES.—

"(A) IN GENERAL.—The Secretary shall establish procedures to allow access to a beneficiary's cash benefits by an authorized representative of the eligible beneficiary on whose behalf such benefits are paid.

"(B) QUALITY ASSURANCE AND PROTECTION AGAINST FRAUD AND ABUSE.—The procedures established under subparagraph (A) shall ensure that authorized representatives of eligible beneficiaries comply with standards of conduct established by the Secretary, including standards requiring that such representatives provide quality services on behalf of such beneficiaries, do not have conflicts of interest, and do not misuse benefits paid on behalf of such beneficiaries or otherwise engage in fraud or abuse.

"(3) COMMENCEMENT OF BENEFITS.—Benefits shall be paid to, or on behalf of, an eligible beneficiary beginning with the first month in which an application for such benefits is approved.

"(4) ROLLOVER OPTION FOR LUMP-SUM PAYMENT.—An eligible beneficiary may elect to—

"(A) defer payment of their daily or weekly benefit and to rollover any such deferred benefits from month-to-month, but not from year-to-year; and

"(B) receive a lump-sum payment of such deferred benefits in an amount that may not exceed the lesser of—

"(i) the total amount of the accrued deferred benefits; or

"(ii) the applicable annual benefit.

"(5) PERIOD FOR DETERMINATION OF ANNUAL BENEFITS.—

"(A) IN GENERAL.—The applicable period for determining with respect to an eligible beneficiary the applicable annual benefit and the amount of any accrued deferred benefits is the 12-month period that commences with the first month in which the beneficiary began to receive such benefits, and each 12-month period thereafter.

"(B) INCLUSION OF INCREASED BENEFITS.—The Secretary shall establish procedures under which cash benefits paid to an eligible beneficiary that increase or decrease as a result of a change in the functional status of the beneficiary before the end of a 12-month benefit period shall be included in the determination of the applicable annual benefit paid to the eligible beneficiary.

"(C) RECOUPMENT OF UNPAID, ACCRUED BENEFITS.—

"(i) IN GENERAL.—The Secretary, in coordination with the Secretary of the Treasury, shall recoup any accrued benefits in the event of—

"(I) the death of a beneficiary; or

"(II) the failure of a beneficiary to elect under paragraph (4)(B) to receive such benefits as a lump-sum payment before the end of the 12-month period in which such benefits accrued.

"(ii) PAYMENT INTO CLASS INDEPENDENCE FUND.—Any benefits recouped in accordance with clause (i) shall be paid into the CLASS Independence Fund and used in accordance with section 3206.

"(6) REQUIREMENT TO RECERTIFY ELIGIBILITY FOR RECEIPT OF BENEFITS.—An eligible beneficiary shall periodically, as determined by the Secretary—

"(A) recertify by submission of medical evidence the beneficiary's continued eligibility for receipt of benefits; and

"(B) submit records of expenditures attributable to the aggregate cash benefit received by the beneficiary during the preceding year.

"(7) SUPPLEMENT, NOT SUPPLANT OTHER HEALTH CARE BENEFITS.—Subject to the Medicaid payment rules under paragraph (1)(D), benefits received by an eligible beneficiary shall supplement, but not supplant, other health care benefits for which the beneficiary is eligible under Medicaid or any other Federally funded program that provides health care benefits or assistance.

"(d) ADVOCACY SERVICES.—An agreement entered into under subsection (a)(2)(A)(ii) shall require the Protection and Advocacy System for the State to—

"(1) assign, as needed, an advocacy counselor to each eligible beneficiary that is covered by such agreement and who shall provide an eligible beneficiary with—

"(A) information regarding how to access the appeals process established for the program;

"(B) assistance with respect to the annual recertification and notification required under subsection (c)(6); and

"(C) such other assistance with obtaining services as the Secretary, by regulation, shall require; and

"(2) ensure that the System and such counselors comply with the requirements of subsection (h).

"(e) ADVICE AND ASSISTANCE COUNSELING.—An agreement entered into under subsection (a)(2)(A)(iii) shall require the entity to assign, as requested by an eligible beneficiary that is covered by such agreement, an advice and assistance counselor who shall provide an eligible beneficiary with information regarding—

"(1) accessing and coordinating long-term services and supports in the most integrated setting;

"(2) possible eligibility for other benefits and services;

"(3) development of a service and support plan;

"(4) information about programs established under the Assistive Technology Act of 1998 and the services offered under such programs;

"(5) available assistance with decision making concerning medical care, including the right to accept or refuse medical or surgical treatment and the right to formulate advance directives or other written instructions recognized under State law, such as a living will or durable power of attorney for health care, in the case that an injury or illness causes the individual to be unable to make health care decisions; and

"(6) such other services as the Secretary, by regulation, may require.

"(f) NO EFFECT ON ELIGIBILITY FOR OTHER BENEFITS.—Benefits paid to an eligible beneficiary under the CLASS program shall be disregarded for purposes of determining or continuing the beneficiary's eligibility for receipt of benefits under any other Federal, State, or locally funded assistance program, including benefits paid under titles II, XVI, XVIII, XIX, or XXI of the Social Security Act (42 U.S.C. 401 et seq., 1381 et seq., 1395 et seq., 1396 et seq., 1397aa et seq.), under the laws administered by the Secretary of Veterans Affairs, under low-income housing assistance programs, or under the supplemental nutrition assistance program established under the Food and Nutrition Act of 2008 (7 U.S.C. 2011 et seq.).

"(g) RULE OF CONSTRUCTION.—Nothing in this title shall be construed as prohibiting benefits paid under the CLASS Independence Benefit Plan from being used to compensate a family caregiver for providing community living assistance services and supports to an eligible beneficiary.

"(h) PROTECTION AGAINST CONFLICT OF INTERESTS.—The Secretary shall establish procedures to ensure that the Eligibility Assessment System, the Protection and Advocacy System for a State, advocacy counselors for eligible beneficiaries, and any other entities that provide services to active enrollees and eligible beneficiaries under the CLASS program comply with the following:

"(1) If the entity provides counseling or planning services, such services are provided in a manner that fosters the best interests of the active enrollee or beneficiary.

"(2) The entity has established operating procedures that are designed to avoid or minimize conflicts of interest between the entity and an active enrollee or beneficiary.

"(3) The entity provides information about all services and options available to the active enrollee or beneficiary, to the best of its knowledge, including services available through other entities or providers.

"(4) The entity assists the active enrollee or beneficiary to access desired services, regardless of the provider.

"(5) The entity reports the number of active enrollees and beneficiaries provided with assistance by age, disability, and whether such enrollees and beneficiaries received services from the entity or another entity.

"(6) If the entity provides counseling or planning services, the entity ensures that an active enrollee or beneficiary is informed of any financial interest that the entity has in a service provider.

"(7) The entity provides an active enrollee or beneficiary with a list of available service providers that can meet the needs of the active enrollee or beneficiary.

"SEC. 3206. CLASS INDEPENDENCE FUND.

"(a) ESTABLISHMENT OF CLASS INDEPENDENCE FUND.—There is established in the Treasury of the United States a trust fund to be known as the 'CLASS Independence Fund'. The Secretary of the Treasury shall serve as Managing Trustee of such Fund. The Fund shall consist of all amounts derived from payments into the Fund under sections 3204(f) and 3205(c)(5)(C)(ii), and remaining after investment of such amounts under subsection (b), including additional amounts derived as income from such investments. The amounts held in the Fund are appropriated and shall remain available without fiscal year limitation—

"(1) to be held for investment on behalf of individuals enrolled in the CLASS program;

"(2) to pay the administrative expenses related to the Fund and to investment under subsection (b); and

"(3) to pay cash benefits to eligible beneficiaries under the CLASS Independence Benefit Plan.

"(b) INVESTMENT OF FUND BALANCE.—The Secretary of the Treasury shall invest and manage the CLASS Independence Fund in the same manner, and to the same extent, as the Federal Supplementary Medical Insurance Trust Fund may be invested and managed under subsections (c), (d), and (e) of section 1841(d) of the Social Security Act (42 U.S.C. 1395t).

"(c) BOARD OF TRUSTEES.—

"(1) IN GENERAL.—With respect to the CLASS Independence Fund, there is hereby created a body to be known as the Board of Trustees of the CLASS Independence Fund (hereinafter in this section referred to as the 'Board of Trustees') composed of the Secretary of the Treasury, the Secretary of Labor, and the Secretary of Health and Human Services, all ex officio, and of two members of the public (both of whom may not be from the same political party), who shall be nominated by the President for a term of 4 years and subject to confirmation by the Senate. A member of the Board of Trustees serving as a member of the public and nominated and confirmed to fill a vacancy occurring during a term shall be nominated and confirmed only for the remainder of such term. An individual nominated and confirmed as a member of the public may serve in such position after the expiration of such member's term until the earlier of the time at which the member's successor takes office or the time at which a report of the Board is first issued under paragraph (2) after the expiration of the member's term. The Secretary of the Treasury shall be the Managing Trustee of the Board of Trustees. The Board of Trustees shall meet not less frequently than once each calendar year. A person serving on the Board of Trustees shall not be considered to be a fiduciary and shall not be personally liable for actions taken in such capacity with respect to the Trust Fund.

"(2) DUTIES.—

"(A) IN GENERAL.—It shall be the duty of the Board of Trustees to do the following:

"(i) Hold the CLASS Independence Fund.

"(ii) Report to the Congress not later than the first day of April of each year on the operation and status of the CLASS Independence Fund during the preceding fiscal year and on its expected operation and status during the current fiscal year and the next 2 fiscal years.

"(iii) Report immediately to the Congress whenever the Board is of the opinion that the amount of the CLASS Independence Fund is not actuarially sound in regards to the projection under section 3203(b)(1)(B)(i).

"(iv) Review the general policies followed in managing the CLASS Independence Fund, and recommend changes in such policies, including necessary changes in the provisions of law which govern the way in which the CLASS Independence Fund is to be managed.

"(B) REPORT.—The report provided for in subparagraph (A)(ii) shall—

"(i) include—

"(I) a statement of the assets of, and the disbursements made from, the CLASS Independence Fund during the preceding fiscal year;

"(II) an estimate of the expected income to, and disbursements to be made from, the CLASS Independence Fund during the current fiscal year and each of the next 2 fiscal years;

"(III) a statement of the actuarial status of the CLASS Independence Fund for the current fiscal year, each of the next 2 fiscal years, and as projected over the 75-year period beginning with the current fiscal year; and

"(IV) an actuarial opinion by the Chief Actuary of the Centers for Medicare & Medicaid Services certifying that the techniques and methodologies used are generally accepted within the actuarial profession and that the assumptions and cost estimates used are reasonable; and

"(ii) be printed as a House document of the session of the Congress to which the report is made.

"(C) RECOMMENDATIONS.—If the Board of Trustees determines that enrollment trends and expected future benefit claims on the CLASS Independence Fund are not actuarially sound in regards to the projection under section 3203(b)(1)(B)(i) and are unlikely to be resolved with reasonable premium increases or through other means, the Board of Trustees shall include in the report provided for in subparagraph (A)(ii) recommendations for such legislative action as the Board of Trustees determine to be appropriate, including whether to adjust monthly premiums or impose a temporary moratorium on new enrollments.

"SEC. 3207. CLASS INDEPENDENCE ADVISORY COUNCIL.

"(a) ESTABLISHMENT.—There is hereby created an Advisory Committee to be known as the 'CLASS Independence Advisory Council'.

"(b) MEMBERSHIP.—

"(1) IN GENERAL.—The CLASS Independence Advisory Council shall be composed of not more than 15 individuals, not otherwise in the employ of the United States—

"(A) who shall be appointed by the President without regard to the civil service laws and regulations; and

"(B) a majority of whom shall be representatives of individuals who participate or are likely to participate in the CLASS program, and shall include representatives of older and younger workers, individuals with disabilities, family caregivers of individuals who require services and supports to maintain their independence at home or in another residential setting of their choice in the community, individuals with expertise in long-term care or disability insurance, actuarial science, economics, and other relevant disciplines, as determined by the Secretary.

"(2) TERMS.—

"(A) IN GENERAL.—The members of the CLASS Independence Advisory Council shall serve overlapping terms of 3 years (unless appointed to fill a vacancy occurring prior to the expiration of a term, in which case the individual shall serve for the remainder of the term).

"(B) LIMITATION.—A member shall not be eligible to serve for more than 2 consecutive terms.

"(3) CHAIR.—The President shall, from time to time, appoint one of the members of the CLASS Independence Advisory Council to serve as the Chair.

"(c) DUTIES.—The CLASS Independence Advisory Council shall advise the Secretary on matters of general policy in the administration of the CLASS program established under this title and in the formulation of regulations under this title including with respect to—

"(1) the development of the CLASS Independence Benefit Plan under section 3203;

"(2) the determination of monthly premiums under such plan; and

"(3) the financial solvency of the program.

"(d) APPLICATION OF FACA.—The Federal Advisory Committee Act (5 U.S.C. App.), other than section 14 of that Act, shall apply to the CLASS Independence Advisory Council.

"(e) AUTHORIZATION OF APPROPRIATIONS.—

"(1) IN GENERAL.—There are authorized to be appropriated to the CLASS Independence Advisory Council to carry out its duties under this section, such sums as may be necessary for fiscal year 2011 and for each fiscal year thereafter.

"(2) AVAILABILITY.—Any sums appropriated under the authorization contained in this section shall remain available, without fiscal year limitation, until expended.

"SEC. 3208. SOLVENCY AND FISCAL INDEPENDENCE; REGULATIONS; ANNUAL REPORT.

"(a) SOLVENCY.—The Secretary shall regularly consult with the Board of Trustees of the CLASS Independence Fund and the CLASS Independence Advisory Council, for purposes of ensuring that enrollees premiums are adequate to ensure the financial solvency of the CLASS program, both with respect to fiscal years occurring in the near-term and fiscal years occurring over 20- and 75-year periods, taking into account the projections required for such periods under subsections (a)(1)(A)(i) and (b)(1)(B)(i) of section 3202.

"(b) NO TAXPAYER FUNDS USED TO PAY BENEFITS.—No taxpayer funds shall be used for payment of benefits under a CLASS Independent Benefit Plan. For purposes of this subsection, the term 'taxpayer funds' means any Federal funds from a source other than premiums deposited by CLASS program participants in the CLASS Independence Fund and any associated interest earnings.

"(c) REGULATIONS.—The Secretary shall promulgate such regulations as are necessary to carry out the CLASS program in accordance with this title. Such regulations shall include provisions to prevent fraud and abuse under the program.

"(d) ANNUAL REPORT.—Beginning January 1, 2014, the Secretary shall submit an annual report to Congress on the CLASS program. Each report shall include the following:

"(1) The total number of enrollees in the program.

"(2) The total number of eligible beneficiaries during the fiscal year.

"(3) The total amount of cash benefits provided during the fiscal year.

"(4) A description of instances of fraud or abuse identified during the fiscal year.

"(5) Recommendations for such administrative or legislative action as the Secretary determines is necessary to improve the program, ensure the solvency of the program, or to prevent the occurrence of fraud or abuse.

"SEC. 3209. INSPECTOR GENERAL'S REPORT.

"The Inspector General of the Department of Health and Human Services shall submit an annual report to the Secretary and Congress relating to the overall progress of the CLASS program and of the existence of waste, fraud, and abuse in the CLASS program. Each such report shall include findings in the following areas:

"(1) The eligibility determination process.

"(2) The provision of cash benefits.

"(3) Quality assurance and protection against waste, fraud, and abuse.

"(4) Recouping of unpaid and accrued benefits.

"SEC. 3210. TAX TREATMENT OF PROGRAM.

"The CLASS program shall be treated for purposes of the Internal Revenue Code of 1986 in the same manner as a qualified long-term care insurance contract for qualified long-term care services.".

* * *

[CCH Explanation at ¶450.]

TITLE IX—REVENUE PROVISIONS

Subtitle A—Revenue Offset Provisions

* * *

[¶7027] ACT SEC. 9007. ADDITIONAL REQUIREMENTS FOR CHARITABLE HOSPITALS.

* * *

(c) MANDATORY REVIEW OF TAX EXEMPTION FOR HOSPITALS.—The Secretary of the Treasury or the Secretary's delegate shall review at least once every 3 years the community benefit activities of each hospital organization to which section 501(r) of the Internal Revenue Code of 1986 (as added by this section) applies.

* * *

(e) REPORTS.—

(1) REPORT ON LEVELS OF CHARITY CARE.—The Secretary of the Treasury, in consultation with the Secretary of Health and Human Services, shall submit to the Committees on Ways and Means, Education and Labor, and Energy and Commerce of the House of Representatives and to the Committees on Finance and Health, Education, Labor, and Pensions of the Senate an annual report on the following:

(A) Information with respect to private tax-exempt, taxable, and government-owned hospitals regarding—

(i) levels of charity care provided,

(ii) bad debt expenses,

(iii) unreimbursed costs for services provided with respect to means-tested government programs, and

(iv) unreimbursed costs for services provided with respect to non-means tested government programs.

(B) Information with respect to private tax-exempt hospitals regarding costs incurred for community benefit activities.

(2) REPORT ON TRENDS.—

(A) STUDY.—The Secretary of the Treasury, in consultation with the Secretary of Health and Human Services, shall conduct a study on trends in the information required to be reported under paragraph (1).

(B) REPORT.—Not later than 5 years after the date of the enactment of this Act, the Secretary of the Treasury, in consultation with the Secretary of Health and Human Services, shall submit a report on the study conducted under subparagraph (A) to the Committees on Ways and Means, Education and Labor, and Energy and Commerce of the House of Representatives and to the Committees on Finance and Health, Education, Labor, and Pensions of the Senate.

* * *

[CCH Explanation at ¶440. Committee Report at ¶10,220.]

[¶7030] ACT SEC. 9008. IMPOSITION OF ANNUAL FEE ON BRANDED PRESCRIPTION PHARMACEUTICAL MANUFACTURERS AND IMPORTERS.

(a) IMPOSITION OF FEE.—

(1) IN GENERAL.—Each covered entity engaged in the business of manufacturing or importing branded prescription drugs shall pay to the Secretary of the Treasury not later than the annual payment date of each calendar year beginning after 2009 a fee in an amount determined under subsection (b).

(2) ANNUAL PAYMENT DATE.—For purposes of this section, the term "annual payment date" means with respect to any calendar year the date determined by the Secretary, but in no event later than September 30 of such calendar year.

(b) DETERMINATION OF FEE AMOUNT.—

(1) IN GENERAL.—With respect to each covered entity, the fee under this section for any calendar year shall be equal to an amount that bears the same ratio to $2,300,000,000 as—

(A) the covered entity's branded prescription drug sales taken into account during the preceding calendar year, bear to

(B) the aggregate branded prescription drug sales of all covered entities taken into account during such preceding calendar year.

(2) SALES TAKEN INTO ACCOUNT.—For purposes of paragraph (1), the branded prescription drug sales taken into account during any calendar year with respect to any covered entity shall be determined in accordance with the following table:

With respect to a covered entity's aggregate branded prescription drug sales during the calendar year that are:	The percentage of such sales taken into account is:
Not more than $5,000,000	0 percent
More than $5,000,000 but not more than $125,000,000.	10 percent
More than $125,000,000 but not more than $225,000,000.	40 percent
More than $225,000,000 but not more than $400,000,000.	75 percent
More than $400,000,000	100 percent.

(3) SECRETARIAL DETERMINATION.—The Secretary of the Treasury shall calculate the amount of each covered entity's fee for any calendar year under paragraph (1). In calculating such amount, the Secretary of the Treasury shall determine such covered entity's branded prescription drug sales on the basis of reports submitted under subsection (g) and through the use of any other source of information available to the Secretary of the Treasury.

(c) TRANSFER OF FEES TO MEDICARE PART B TRUST FUND.—There is hereby appropriated to the Federal Supplementary Medical Insurance Trust Fund established under section 1841 of the Social Security Act an amount equal to the fees received by the Secretary of the Treasury under subsection (a).

(d) COVERED ENTITY.—

(1) IN GENERAL.—For purposes of this section, the term "covered entity" means any manufacturer or importer with gross receipts from branded prescription drug sales.

(2) CONTROLLED GROUPS.—

(A) IN GENERAL.—For purposes of this subsection, all persons treated as a single employer under subsection (a) or (b) of section 52 of the Internal Revenue Code of 1986 or subsection (m) or (o) of section 414 of such Code shall be treated as a single covered entity.

(B) INCLUSION OF FOREIGN CORPORATIONS.—For purposes of subparagraph (A), in applying subsections (a) and (b) of section 52 of such Code to this section, section 1563 of such Code shall be applied without regard to subsection (b)(2)(C) thereof.

(e) BRANDED PRESCRIPTION DRUG SALES.—For purposes of this section—

(1) IN GENERAL.—The term "branded prescription drug sales" means sales of branded prescription drugs to any specified government program or pursuant to coverage under any such program.

(2) BRANDED PRESCRIPTION DRUGS.—

(A) IN GENERAL.—The term "branded prescription drug" means—

(i) any prescription drug the application for which was submitted under section 505(b) of the Federal Food, Drug, and Cosmetic Act (21 U.S.C. 355(b)), or

(ii) any biological product the license for which was submitted under section 351(a) of the Public Health Service Act (42 U.S.C. 262(a)).

(B) PRESCRIPTION DRUG.—For purposes of subparagraph (A)(i), the term "prescription drug" means any drug which is subject to section 503(b) of the Federal Food, Drug, and Cosmetic Act (21 U.S.C. 353(b)).

(3) EXCLUSION OF ORPHAN DRUG SALES.—The term "branded prescription drug sales" shall not include sales of any drug or biological product with respect to which a credit was allowed for any taxable year under section 45C of the Internal Revenue Code of 1986. The preceding sentence shall not apply with respect to any such drug or biological product after the date on which such drug or biological product is approved by the Food and Drug Administration for marketing for any indication other than the treatment of the rare disease or condition with respect to which such credit was allowed.

(4) SPECIFIED GOVERNMENT PROGRAM.—The term "specified government program" means—

(A) the Medicare Part D program under part D of title XVIII of the Social Security Act,

(B) the Medicare Part B program under part B of title XVIII of the Social Security Act,

(C) the Medicaid program under title XIX of the Social Security Act,

(D) any program under which branded prescription drugs are procured by the Department of Veterans Affairs,

(E) any program under which branded prescription drugs are procured by the Department of Defense, or

(F) the TRICARE retail pharmacy program under section 1074g of title 10, United States Code.

(f) TAX TREATMENT OF FEES.—The fees imposed by this section—

(1) for purposes of subtitle F of the Internal Revenue Code of 1986, shall be treated as excise taxes with respect to which only civil actions for refund under procedures of such subtitle shall apply, and

(2) for purposes of section 275 of such Code, shall be considered to be a tax described in section 275(a)(6).

(g) REPORTING REQUIREMENT.—Not later than the date determined by the Secretary of the Treasury following the end of any calendar year, the Secretary of Health and Human Services, the Secretary of Veterans Affairs, and the Secretary of Defense shall report to the Secretary of the Treasury, in such manner as the Secretary of the Treasury prescribes, the total branded prescription drug sales for each covered entity with respect to each specified government program under such Secretary's jurisdiction using the following methodology:

(1) MEDICARE PART D PROGRAM.—The Secretary of Health and Human Services shall report, for each covered entity and for each branded prescription drug of the covered entity covered by the Medicare Part D program, the product of—

(A) the per-unit ingredient cost, as reported to the Secretary of Health and Human Services by prescription drug plans and Medicare Advantage prescription drug plans, minus any per-unit rebate, discount, or other price concession provided by the covered entity, as reported to the Secretary of Health and Human Services by the prescription drug plans and Medicare Advantage prescription drug plans, and

(B) the number of units of the branded prescription drug paid for under the Medicare Part D program.

(2) MEDICARE PART B PROGRAM.—The Secretary of Health and Human Services shall report, for each covered entity and for each branded prescription drug of the covered entity covered by the Medicare Part B program under section 1862(a) of the Social Security Act, the product of—

(A) the per-unit average sales price (as defined in section 1847A(c) of the Social Security Act) or the per-unit Part B payment rate for a separately paid branded prescription drug without a reported average sales price, and

(B) the number of units of the branded prescription drug paid for under the Medicare Part B program.

The Centers for Medicare and Medicaid Services shall establish a process for determining the units and the allocated price for purposes of this section for those branded prescription drugs that are not separately payable or for which National Drug Codes are not reported.

(3) MEDICAID PROGRAM.—The Secretary of Health and Human Services shall report, for each covered entity and for each branded prescription drug of the covered entity covered under the Medicaid program, the product of—

(A) the per-unit ingredient cost paid to pharmacies by States for the branded prescription drug dispensed to Medicaid beneficiaries, minus any per-unit rebate paid by the covered entity under section 1927 of the Social Security Act and any State supplemental rebate, and

(B) the number of units of the branded prescription drug paid for under the Medicaid program.

(4) DEPARTMENT OF VETERANS AFFAIRS PROGRAMS.—The Secretary of Veterans Affairs shall report, for each covered entity and for each branded prescription drug of the covered entity, the total amount paid for each such branded prescription drug procured by the Department of Veterans Affairs for its beneficiaries.

(5) DEPARTMENT OF DEFENSE PROGRAMS AND TRICARE.—The Secretary of Defense shall report, for each covered entity and for each branded prescription drug of the covered entity, the sum of—

(A) the total amount paid for each such branded prescription drug procured by the Department of Defense for its beneficiaries, and

(B) for each such branded prescription drug dispensed under the TRICARE retail pharmacy program, the product of—

(i) the per-unit ingredient cost, minus any per-unit rebate paid by the covered entity, and

(ii) the number of units of the branded prescription drug dispensed under such program.

(h) SECRETARY.—For purposes of this section, the term "Secretary" includes the Secretary's delegate.

(i) GUIDANCE.—The Secretary of the Treasury shall publish guidance necessary to carry out the purposes of this section.

(j) APPLICATION OF SECTION.—This section shall apply to any branded prescription drug sales after December 31, 2008.

(k) Conforming Amendment.—Section 1841(a) of the Social Security Act is amended by inserting "or section 9008(c) of the Patient Protection and Affordable Care Act of 2009" after "this part".

[Note: The text of Act Sec. 9008, as reproduced above, does not reflect amendments made by Act Sec. 1404 of the Health Care and Education Reconciliation Act of 2010. See ¶7106.]

[CCH Explanation at ¶350. Committee Report at ¶10,230.]

[¶7033] ACT SEC. 9009. IMPOSITION OF ANNUAL FEE ON MEDICAL DEVICE MANUFACTURERS AND IMPORTERS.

(a) Imposition of Fee.—

(1) In General.—Each covered entity engaged in the business of manufacturing or importing medical devices shall pay to the Secretary not later than the annual payment date of each calendar year beginning after 2010 a fee in an amount determined under subsection (b).

(2) Annual payment date.—For purposes of this section, the term "annual payment date" means with respect to any calendar year the date determined by the Secretary, but in no event later than September 30 of such calendar year.

(b) Determination of Fee Amount.—

(1) In General.—With respect to each covered entity, the fee under this section for any calendar year shall be equal to an amount that bears the same ratio to $2,000,000,000 ($3,000,000,000 after 2017) as—

(A) the covered entity's gross receipts from medical device sales taken into account during the preceding calendar year, bear to

(B) the aggregate gross receipts of all covered entities from medical device sales taken into account during such preceding calendar year.

(2) Gross receipts from sales taken into account.—For purposes of paragraph (1), the gross receipts from medical device sales taken into account during any calendar year with respect to any covered entity shall be determined in accordance with the following table:

With respect to a covered entity's aggregate gross receipts from medical device sales during the calendar year that are:	The percentage of gross receipts taken into account is:
Not more than $5,000,000	0 percent
More than $5,000,000 but not more than $25,000,000.	50 percent
More than $25,000,000	100 percent.

(3) Secretarial determination.—The Secretary shall calculate the amount of each covered entity's fee for any calendar year under paragraph (1). In calculating such amount, the Secretary shall determine such covered entity's gross receipts from medical device sales on the basis of reports submitted by the covered entity under subsection (f) and through the use of any other source of information available to the Secretary.

(c) Covered Entity.—

(1) In General.—For purposes of this section, the term "covered entity" means any manufacturer or importer with gross receipts from medical device sales.

(2) Controlled groups.—

(A) In General.—For purposes of this subsection, all persons treated as a single employer under subsection (a) or (b) of section 52 of the Internal Revenue Code of 1986 or subsection (m) or (o) of section 414 of such Code shall be treated as a single covered entity.

(B) Inclusion of foreign corporations.—For purposes of subparagraph (A), in applying subsections (a) and (b) of section 52 of such Code to this section, section 1563 of such Code shall be applied without regard to subsection (b)(2)(C) thereof.

(d) Medical Device Sales.—For purposes of this section—

(1) In General.—The term "medical device sales" means sales for use in the United States of any medical device, other than the sales of a medical device that—

(A) has been classified in class II under section 513 of the Federal Food, Drug, and Cosmetic Act (21 U.S.C. 360c) and is primarily sold to consumers at retail for not more than $100 per unit, or

(B) has been classified in class I under such section.

(2) UNITED STATES.—For purposes of paragraph (1), the term "United States" means the several States, the District of Columbia, the Commonwealth of Puerto Rico, and the possessions of the United States.

(3) MEDICAL DEVICE.—For purposes of paragraph (1), the term "medical device" means any device (as defined in section 201(h) of the Federal Food, Drug, and Cosmetic Act (21 U.S.C. 321(h))) intended for humans.

(e) TAX TREATMENT OF FEES.—The fees imposed by this section—

(1) for purposes of subtitle F of the Internal Revenue Code of 1986, shall be treated as excise taxes with respect to which only civil actions for refund under procedures of such subtitle shall apply, and

(2) for purposes of section 275 of such Code, shall be considered to be a tax described in section 275(a)(6).

(f) REPORTING REQUIREMENT.—

(1) IN GENERAL.—Not later than the date determined by the Secretary following the end of any calendar year, each covered entity shall report to the Secretary, in such manner as the Secretary prescribes, the gross receipts from medical device sales of such covered entity during such calendar year.

(2) PENALTY FOR FAILURE TO REPORT.—

(A) IN GENERAL.—In the case of any failure to make a report containing the information required by paragraph (1) on the date prescribed therefor (determined with regard to any extension of time for filing), unless it is shown that such failure is due to reasonable cause, there shall be paid by the covered entity failing to file such report, an amount equal to—

(i) $10,000, plus

(ii) the lesser of—

(I) an amount equal to $1,000, multiplied by the number of days during which such failure continues, or

(II) the amount of the fee imposed by this section for which such report was required.

(B) TREATMENT OF PENALTY.—The penalty imposed under subparagraph (A)—

(i) shall be treated as a penalty for purposes of subtitle F of the Internal Revenue Code of 1986,

(ii) shall be paid on notice and demand by the Secretary and in the same manner as tax under such Code, and

(iii) with respect to which only civil actions for refund under procedures of such subtitle F shall apply.

(g) SECRETARY.—For purposes of this section, the term "Secretary" means the Secretary of the Treasury or the Secretary's delegate.

(h) GUIDANCE.—The Secretary shall publish guidance necessary to carry out the purposes of this section, including identification of medical devices described in subsection (d)(1)(A) and with respect to the treatment of gross receipts from sales of medical devices to another covered entity or to another entity by reason of the application of subsection (c)(2).

(i) APPLICATION OF SECTION.—This section shall apply to any medical device sales after December 31, 2009.

[Note: The text of Act Sec. 9009, as reproduced above, reflects amendments made by Act Sec. 10904. See ¶7048. It was subsequently repealed by Act Sec. 1405 of the Health Care and Education Reconciliation Act of 2010. See ¶7109.]

[CCH Explanation at ¶350. Committee Report at ¶10,240.]

[¶7036] ACT SEC. 9010. IMPOSITION OF ANNUAL FEE ON HEALTH INSURANCE PROVIDERS.

(a) IMPOSITION OF FEE.—

(1) IN GENERAL.—Each covered entity engaged in the business of providing health insurance shall pay to the Secretary not later than the annual payment date of each calendar year beginning after 2010 a fee in an amount determined under subsection (b).

(2) ANNUAL PAYMENT DATE.—For purposes of this section, the term "annual payment date" means with respect to any calendar year the date determined by the Secretary, but in no event later than September 30 of such calendar year.

(b) DETERMINATION OF FEE AMOUNT.—

(1) IN GENERAL.—With respect to each covered entity, the fee under this section for any calendar year shall be equal to an amount that bears the same ratio to the applicable amount as—

(A) the covered entity's net premiums written with respect to health insurance for any United States health risk that are taken into account during the preceding calendar year, bears to

(B) the aggregate net premiums written with respect to such health insurance of all covered entities that are taken into account during such preceding calendar year.

(2) AMOUNTS TAKEN INTO ACCOUNT.—For purposes of paragraph (1), the net premiums written with respect to health insurance for any United States health risk that are taken into account during any calendar year with respect to any covered entity shall be determined in accordance with the following table:

"With respect to a covered entity's net premiums written during the calendar year that are:	The percentage of net premiums written that are taken into account is:
Not more than $25,000,000	0 percent
More than $25,000,000 but not more than $50,000,000.	50 percent
More than $50,000,000	100 percent.

(3) SECRETARIAL DETERMINATION.—The Secretary shall calculate the amount of each covered entity's fee for any calendar year under paragraph (1). In calculating such amount, the Secretary shall determine such covered entity's net premiums written with respect to any United States health risk on the basis of reports submitted by the covered entity under subsection (g) and through the use of any other source of information available to the Secretary.

(c) COVERED ENTITY.—

(1) IN GENERAL.—For purposes of this section, the term "covered entity" means any entity which provides health insurance for any United States health risk.

(2) EXCLUSION.—Such term does not include—

(A) any employer to the extent that such employer self-insures its employees' health risks,

(B) any governmental entity,

(C) any entity—

(i)(I) which is incorporated as, is a wholly owned subsidiary of, or is a wholly owned affiliate of, a nonprofit corporation under a State law, or

(II) which is described in section 501(c)(4) of the Internal Revenue Code of 1986 and the activities of which consist of providing commercial-type insurance (within the meaning of section 501(m) of such Code),

(ii) the premium rate increases of which are regulated by a State authority,

(iii) which, as of the date of the enactment of this section, acts as the insurer of last resort in the State and is subject to State guarantee issue requirements, and

(iv) for which the medical loss ratio (determined in a manner consistent with the determination of such ratio under section 2718(b)(1)(A) of the Public Health Service Act) with respect to the individual insurance market for such entity for the calendar year is not less than 100 percent,

(D) any entity—

(i)(I) which is incorporated as a nonprofit corporation under a State law, or

(II) which is described in section 501(c)(4) of the Internal Revenue Code of 1986 and the activities of which consist of providing commercial-type insurance (within the meaning of section 501(m) of such Code), and

(ii) for which the medical loss ratio (as so determined)—

(I) with respect to each of the individual, small group, and large group insurance markets for such entity for the calendar year is not less than 90 percent, and

(II) with respect to all such markets for such entity for the calendar year is not less than 92 percent, or

(E) any entity—

(i) which is a mutual insurance company,

(ii) which for the period reported on the 2008 Accident and Health Policy Experience Exhibit of the National Association of Insurance Commissioners had—

(I) a market share of the insured population of a State of at least 40 but not more than 60 percent, and

(II) with respect to all markets described in subparagraph (D)(ii)(I), a medical loss ratio of not less than 90 percent, and

(iii) with respect to annual payment dates in calendar years after 2011, for which the medical loss ratio (determined in a manner consistent with the determination of such ratio under section 2718(b)(1)(A) of the Public Health Service Act) with respect to all such markets for such entity for the preceding calendar year is not less than 89 percent (except that with respect to such annual payment date for 2012, the calculation under 2718(b)(1)(B)(ii) of such Act is determined by reference to the previous year, and with respect to such annual payment date for 2013, such calculation is determined by reference to the average for the previous 2 years).

(3) CONTROLLED GROUPS.—

(A) IN GENERAL.—For purposes of this subsection, all persons treated as a single employer under subsection (a) or (b) of section 52 of the Internal Revenue Code of 1986 or subsection (m) or (o) of section 414 of such Code shall be treated as a single covered entity (or employer for purposes of paragraph (2)).

(B) INCLUSION OF FOREIGN CORPORATIONS.—For purposes of subparagraph (A), in applying subsections (a) and (b) of section 52 of such Code to this section, section 1563 of such Code shall be applied without regard to subsection (b)(2)(C) thereof.

If any entity described in subparagraph (C)(i)(I), (D)(i)(I) or (E)(i) of paragraph (2) is treated as a covered entity by reason of the application of the preceding sentence, the net premiums written with respect to health insurance for any United States health risk of such entity shall not be taken into account for purposes of this section.

(d) UNITED STATES HEALTH RISK.—For purposes of this section, the term "United States health risk" means the health risk of any individual who is—

(1) a United States citizen,

(2) a resident of the United States (within the meaning of section 7701(b)(1)(A) of the Internal Revenue Code of 1986), or

(3) located in the United States, with respect to the period such individual is so located.

(e) APPLICABLE AMOUNT.—For purposes of subsection (b)(1), the applicable amount shall be determined in accordance with the following table:

"Calendar year	Applicable amount
2011	$2,000,000,000
2012	$4,000,000,000
2013	$7,000,000,000
2014, 2015 and 2016	$9,000,000,000
2017 and thereafter	$10,000,000,000.".

(f) TAX TREATMENT OF FEES.—The fees imposed by this section—

(1) for purposes of subtitle F of the Internal Revenue Code of 1986, shall be treated as excise taxes with respect to which only civil actions for refund under procedures of such subtitle shall apply, and

(2) for purposes of section 275 of such Code shall be considered to be a tax described in section 275(a)(6).

(g) REPORTING REQUIREMENT.—

(1) IN GENERAL.—Not later than the date determined by the Secretary following the end of any calendar year, each covered entity shall report to the Secretary, in such manner as the Secretary prescribes, the covered entity's net premiums written with respect to health insurance for any United States health risk for such calendar year.

(2) PENALTY FOR FAILURE TO REPORT.—

(A) IN GENERAL.—In the case of any failure to make a report containing the information required by paragraph (1) on the date prescribed therefor (determined with regard to any extension of time for filing), unless it is shown that such failure is due to reasonable cause, there shall be paid by the covered entity failing to file such report, an amount equal to—

(i) $10,000, plus

(ii) the lesser of—

(I) an amount equal to $1,000, multiplied by the number of days during which such failure continues, or

(II) the amount of the fee imposed by this section for which such report was required.

(B) TREATMENT OF PENALTY.—The penalty imposed under subparagraph (A)—

(i) shall be treated as a penalty for purposes of subtitle F of the Internal Revenue Code of 1986,

(ii) shall be paid on notice and demand by the Secretary and in the same manner as tax under such Code, and

(iii) with respect to which only civil actions for refund under procedures of such subtitle F shall apply.

(h) ADDITIONAL DEFINITIONS.—For purposes of this section—

(1) SECRETARY.—The term "Secretary" means the Secretary of the Treasury or the Secretary's delegate.

(2) UNITED STATES.—The term "United States" means the several States, the District of Columbia, the Commonwealth of Puerto Rico, and the possessions of the United States.

(3) HEALTH INSURANCE.—The term "health insurance" shall not include—

(A) any insurance coverage described in paragraph (1)(A) or (3) of section 9832(c) of the Internal Revenue Code of 1986,

(B) any insurance for long-term care, or

(C) "any medicare supplemental health insurance (as defined in section 1882(g)(1) of the Social Security Act).".

(i) GUIDANCE.—The Secretary shall publish guidance necessary to carry out the purposes of this section and shall prescribe such regulations as are necessary or appropriate to prevent avoidance of the purposes of this section, including inappropriate actions taken to qualify as an exempt entity under subsection (c)(2).

(j) APPLICATION OF SECTION.—This section shall apply to any net premiums written after December 31, 2009, with respect to health insurance for any United States health risk.

* * *

[Note: The text of Act Sec. 9010, as reproduced above, reflects amendments made by Act Sec. 10905. See ¶7051. It does not reflect amendments made by Act Sec. 1406 of the Health Care and Education Reconciliation Act of 2010. See ¶7112]

[CCH Explanation at ¶350. Committee Report at ¶10,250.]

Subtitle B—Other Provisions

[¶7039] ACT SEC. 9021. EXCLUSION OF HEALTH BENEFITS PROVIDED BY INDIAN TRIBAL GOVERNMENTS.

* * *

(d) NO INFERENCE.—Nothing in the amendments made by this section shall be construed to create an inference with respect to the exclusion from gross income of—

(1) benefits provided by an Indian tribe or tribal organization that are not within the scope of this section, and

(2) benefits provided prior to the date of the enactment of this Act.

* * *

[CCH Explanation at ¶250. Committee Report at ¶10,330.]

TITLE X—STRENGTHENING QUALITY, AFFORDABLE HEALTH CARE FOR ALL AMERICANS

Subtitle A—Provisions Relating to Title I

* * *

[¶7042] ACT SEC. 10104. AMENDMENTS TO SUBTITLE D.

* * *

(r) Section 1341 of this Act is amended—

(1) in the section heading, by striking **"AND SMALL GROUP MARKETS"** and inserting **"MARKET"**;

* * *

(3) in subsection (c)(1)(A), by striking "and small group markets" and inserting "market".

* * *

[CCH Explanation at ¶435.]

[¶7045] ACT SEC. 10108. FREE CHOICE VOUCHERS.

(a) IN GENERAL.—An offering employer shall provide free choice vouchers to each qualified employee of such employer.

(b) OFFERING EMPLOYER.—For purposes of this section, the term "offering employer" means any employer who—

(1) offers minimum essential coverage to its employees consisting of coverage through an eligible employer-sponsored plan; and

(2) pays any portion of the costs of such plan.

(c) QUALIFIED EMPLOYEE.—For purposes of this section—

(1) IN GENERAL.—The term "qualified employee" means, with respect to any plan year of an offering employer, any employee—

(A) whose required contribution (as determined under section 5000A(e)(1)(B)) for minimum essential coverage through an eligible employer-sponsored plan—

(i) exceeds 8 percent of such employee's household income for the taxable year described in section 1412(b)(1)(B) which ends with or within in [sic] the plan year; and

(ii) does not exceed 9.8 percent of such employee's household income for such taxable year;

(B) whose household income for such taxable year is not greater than 400 percent of the poverty line for a family of the size involved; and

(C) who does not participate in a health plan offered by the offering employer.

(2) INDEXING.—In the case of any calendar year beginning after 2014, the Secretary shall adjust the 8 percent under paragraph (1)(A)(i) and 9.8 percent under paragraph (1)(A)(ii) for the calendar year to reflect the rate of premium growth between the preceding calendar year and 2013 over the rate of income growth for such period.

(d) FREE CHOICE VOUCHER.—

(1) AMOUNT.—

(A) IN GENERAL.—The amount of any free choice voucher provided under subsection (a) shall be equal to the monthly portion of the cost of the eligible employer-sponsored plan which would have been paid by the employer if the employee were covered under the plan with respect to which the employer pays the largest portion of the cost of the plan. Such amount shall be equal to the amount the employer would pay for an employee with self-only coverage unless such employee elects family coverage (in which case such amount shall be the amount the employer would pay for family coverage).

(B) DETERMINATION OF COST.—The cost of any health plan shall be determined under the rules similar to the rules of section 2204 of the Public Health Service Act, except that such amount shall be adjusted for age and category of enrollment in accordance with regulations established by the Secretary.

(2) USE OF VOUCHERS.—An Exchange shall credit the amount of any free choice voucher provided under subsection (a) to the monthly premium of any qualified health plan in the Exchange in which the qualified employee is enrolled and the offering employer shall pay any amounts so credited to the Exchange.

(3) PAYMENT OF EXCESS AMOUNTS.—If the amount of the free choice voucher exceeds the amount of the premium of the qualified health plan in which the qualified employee is enrolled for such month, such excess shall be paid to the employee.

(e) OTHER DEFINITIONS.—Any term used in this section which is also used in section 5000A of the Internal Revenue Code of 1986 shall have the meaning given such term under such section 5000A.

* * *

(i) COORDINATION WITH EMPLOYER RESPONSIBILITIES.—

* * *

(2) NOTIFICATION REQUIREMENT.—Section 18B(a)(3) of the Fair Labor Standards Act of 1938, as added by section 1512, is amended—

(A) by inserting "and the employer does not offer a free choice voucher" after "Exchange"; and

(B) by striking "will lose" and inserting "may lose".

* * *

[CCH Explanation at ¶210 and ¶315. Committee Report at ¶10,370.]

Subtitle H—Provisions Relating to Title IX
* * *

[¶7048] ACT SEC. 10904. MODIFICATION OF ANNUAL FEE ON MEDICAL DEVICE MANUFACTURERS AND IMPORTERS.

(a) IN GENERAL.—Section 9009 of this Act is amended—

(1) by striking "2009" in subsection (a)(1) and inserting "2010",

(2) by inserting "($3,000,000,000 after 2017)" after "$2,000,000,000", and

(3) by striking "2008" in subsection (i) and inserting "2009".

(b) EFFECTIVE DATE.—The amendments made by this section shall take effect as if included in the enactment of section 9009.

[CCH Explanation at ¶350.]

[¶7051] ACT SEC. 10905. MODIFICATION OF ANNUAL FEE ON HEALTH INSURANCE PROVIDERS.

(a) DETERMINATION OF FEE AMOUNT.—Subsection (b) of section 9010 of this Act is amended to read as follows:

"(b) DETERMINATION OF FEE AMOUNT.—

"(1) IN GENERAL.—With respect to each covered entity, the fee under this section for any calendar year shall be equal to an amount that bears the same ratio to the applicable amount as—

"(A) the covered entity's net premiums written with respect to health insurance for any United States health risk that are taken into account during the preceding calendar year, bears to

"(B) the aggregate net premiums written with respect to such health insurance of all covered entities that are taken into account during such preceding calendar year.

"(2) AMOUNTS TAKEN INTO ACCOUNT.—For purposes of paragraph (1), the net premiums written with respect to health insurance for any United States health risk that are taken into account during any calendar year with respect to any covered entity shall be determined in accordance with the following table:

"With respect to a covered entity's net premiums written during the calendar year that are:	The percentage of net premiums written that are taken into account is:
Not more than $25,000,000	0 percent
More than $25,000,000 but not more than $50,000,000.	50 percent
More than $50,000,000	100 percent.

"(3) SECRETARIAL DETERMINATION.—The Secretary shall calculate the amount of each covered entity's fee for any calendar year under paragraph (1). In calculating such amount, the Secretary shall determine such covered entity's net premiums written with respect to any United States health risk on the basis of reports submitted by the covered entity under subsection (g) and through the use of any other source of information available to the Secretary.".

(b) APPLICABLE AMOUNT.—Subsection (e) of section 9010 of this Act is amended to read as follows:

"(e) APPLICABLE AMOUNT.—For purposes of subsection (b)(1), the applicable amount shall be determined in accordance with the following table:

"Calendar year	Applicable amount
2011	$2,000,000,000
2012	$4,000,000,000
2013	$7,000,000,000

"Calendar year	Applicable amount
2014, 2015 and 2016	$9,000,000,000
2017 and thereafter	$10,000,000,000.".

(c) EXEMPTION FROM ANNUAL FEE ON HEALTH INSURANCE FOR CERTAIN NONPROFIT ENTITIES.—Section 9010(c)(2) of this Act is amended by striking "or" at the end of subparagraph (A), by striking the period at the end of subparagraph (B) and inserting a comma, and by adding at the end the following new subparagraphs:

"(C) any entity—

"(i) (I) which is incorporated as, is a wholly owned subsidiary of, or is a wholly owned affiliate of, a nonprofit corporation under a State law, or

"(II) which is described in section 501(c)(4) of the Internal Revenue Code of 1986 and the activities of which consist of providing commercial-type insurance (within the meaning of section 501(m) of such Code),

"(ii) the premium rate increases of which are regulated by a State authority,

"(iii) which, as of the date of the enactment of this section, acts as the insurer of last resort in the State and is subject to State guarantee issue requirements, and

"(iv) for which the medical loss ratio (determined in a manner consistent with the determination of such ratio under section 2718(b)(1)(A) of the Public Health Service Act) with respect to the individual insurance market for such entity for the calendar year is not less than 100 percent,

"(D) any entity—

"(i) (I) which is incorporated as a nonprofit corporation under a State law, or

"(II) which is described in section 501(c)(4) of the Internal Revenue Code of 1986 and the activities of which consist of providing commercial-type insurance (within the meaning of section 501(m) of such Code), and

"(ii) for which the medical loss ratio (as so determined)—

"(I) with respect to each of the individual, small group, and large group insurance markets for such entity for the calendar year is not less than 90 percent, and

"(II) with respect to all such markets for such entity for the calendar year is not less than 92 percent, or

"(E) any entity—

"(i) which is a mutual insurance company,

"(ii) which for the period reported on the 2008 Accident and Health Policy Experience Exhibit of the National Association of Insurance Commissioners had—

"(I) a market share of the insured population of a State of at least 40 but not more than 60 percent, and

"(II) with respect to all markets described in subparagraph (D)(ii)(I), a medical loss ratio of not less than 90 percent, and

"(iii) with respect to annual payment dates in calendar years after 2011, for which the medical loss ratio (determined in a manner consistent with the determination of such ratio under section 2718(b)(1)(A) of the Public Health Service Act) with respect to all such markets for such entity for the preceding calendar year is not less than 89 percent (except that with respect to such annual payment date for 2012, the calculation under [section] 2718(b)(1)(B)(ii) of such Act is determined by reference to the previous year, and with respect to such annual payment date for 2013, such calculation is determined by reference to the average for the previous 2 years).".

(d) CERTAIN INSURANCE EXEMPTED FROM FEE.—Paragraph (3) of section 9010(h) of this Act is amended to read as follows:

"(3) HEALTH INSURANCE.—The term 'health insurance' shall not include—

"(A) any insurance coverage described in paragraph (1)(A) or (3) of section 9832(c) of the Internal Revenue Code of 1986,

"(B) any insurance for long-term care, or

"(C) any medicare supplemental health insurance (as defined in section 1882(g)(1) of the Social Security Act).".

(e) ANTI-AVOIDANCE GUIDANCE.—Subsection (i) of section 9010 of this Act is amended by inserting "and shall prescribe such regulations as are necessary or appropriate to prevent avoidance of the purposes of this section, including inappropriate actions taken to qualify as an exempt entity under subsection (c)(2)" after "section".

(f) CONFORMING AMENDMENTS.—

(1) Section 9010(a)(1) of this Act is amended by striking "2009" and inserting "2010".

(2) Section 9010(c)(2)(B) of this Act is amended by striking "(except" and all that follows through "1323)".

(3) Section 9010(c)(3) of this Act is amended by adding at the end the following new sentence: "If any entity described in subparagraph (C)(i)(I), (D)(i)(I), or (E)(i) of paragraph (2) is treated as a covered entity by reason of the application of the preceding sentence, the net premiums written with respect to health insurance for any United States health risk of such entity shall not be taken into account for purposes of this section.".

(4) Section 9010(g)(1) of this Act is amended by striking "and third party administration agreement fees".

(5) Section 9010(j) of this Act is amended—

(A) by striking "2008" and inserting "2009", and

(B) by striking ", and any third party administration agreement fees received after such date".

(g) EFFECTIVE DATE.—The amendments made by this section shall take effect as if included in the enactment of section 9010.

* * *

[CCH Explanation at ¶350.]

[¶7054] ACT SEC. 10909. EXPANSION OF ADOPTION CREDIT AND ADOPTION ASSISTANCE PROGRAMS.

* * *

(c) APPLICATION AND EXTENSION OF EGTRRA SUNSET.—Notwithstanding section 901 of the Economic Growth and Tax Relief Reconciliation Act of 2001, such section shall apply to the amendments made by this section and the amendments made by section 202 of such Act by substituting "December 31, 2011" for "December 31, 2010" in subsection (a)(1) thereof.

(d) EFFECTIVE DATE.—The amendments made by this section shall apply to taxable years beginning after December 31, 2009.

[CCH Explanation at ¶240. Committee Report at ¶10,390.]

HEALTH CARE AND EDUCATION RECONCILIATION ACT OF 2010

[¶7103] ACT SEC. 1. SHORT TITLE; TABLE OF CONTENTS.

(a) SHORT TITLE.—This Act may be cited as the "Health Care and Education Reconciliation Act of 2010".

* * *

TITLE I—COVERAGE, MEDICARE, MEDICAID, AND REVENUES
* * *

Subtitle E—Provisions Relating to Revenue
* * *

[¶7106] ACT SEC. 1404. BRAND NAME PHARMACEUTICALS.

(a) IN GENERAL.—Section 9008 of the Patient Protection and Affordable Care Act is amended—

(1) in subsection (a)(1), by striking "2009" and inserting "2010";

(2) in subsection (b)—

(A) by striking "$2,300,000,000" in paragraph (1) and inserting "the applicable amount"; and

(B) by adding at the end the following new paragraph:

"(4) APPLICABLE AMOUNT.—For purposes of paragraph (1), the applicable amount shall be determined in accordance with the following table:

"Calendar year	Applicable amount
2011	.$2,500,000,000
2012	.$2,800,000,000
2013	.$2,800,000,000
2014	.$3,000,000,000
2015	.$3,000,000,000
2016	.$3,000,000,000
2017	.$4,000,000,000
2018	.$4,100,000,000
2019 and thereafter	$2,800,000,000.";

(3) in subsection (d), by adding at the end the following new paragraph:

"(3) JOINT AND SEVERAL LIABILITY.—If more than one person is liable for payment of the fee under subsection (a) with respect to a single covered entity by reason of the application of paragraph (2), all such persons shall be jointly and severally liable for payment of such fee."; and

(4) by striking subsection (j) and inserting the following new subsection:

"(j) EFFECTIVE DATE.—This section shall apply to calendar years beginning after December 31, 2010.".

(b) EFFECTIVE DATE.—The amendments made by this section shall take effect as if included in section 9008 of the Patient Protection and Affordable Care Act.

[CCH Explanation at ¶350.]

[¶7109] ACT SEC. 1405. EXCISE TAX ON MEDICAL DEVICE MANUFACTURERS.
* * *

(d) REPEAL OF SECTION 9009 OF THE PATIENT PROTECTION AND AFFORDABLE CARE ACT.—Section 9009 of the Patient Protection and Affordable Care Act, as amended by section 10904 of such Act, is repealed effective as of the date of enactment of that Act.

[Note: The text of Act Sec. 9009 of the Patient Protection and Affordable Care Act, prior to repeal, can be found at ¶7033.]

[CCH Explanation at ¶ 350. Committee Report at ¶ 10,420.]

[¶ 7112] ACT SEC. 1406. HEALTH INSURANCE PROVIDERS.

(a) IN GENERAL.—Section 9010 of the Patient Protection and Affordable Care Act, as amended by section 10905 of such Act, is amended—

(1) in subsection (a)(1), by striking "2010" and inserting "2013";

(2) in subsection (b)(2)—

(A) by striking "For purposes of paragraph (1), the net premiums" and inserting "For purposes of paragraph (1)—

"(A) IN GENERAL.—The net premiums"; and

(B) by adding at the end the following subparagraph:

"(B) PARTIAL EXCLUSION FOR CERTAIN EXEMPT ACTIVITIES.—After the application of subparagraph (A), only 50 percent of the remaining net premiums written with respect to health insurance for any United States health risk that are attributable to the activities (other than activities of an unrelated trade or business as defined in section 513 of the Internal Revenue Code of 1986) of any covered entity qualifying under paragraph (3), (4), (26), or (29) of section 501(c) of such Code and exempt from tax under section 501(a) of such Code shall be taken into account.";

(3) in subsection (c)—

(A) by inserting "during the calendar year in which the fee under this section is due" in paragraph (1) after "risk";

(B) in paragraph (2), by striking subparagraphs (C), (D), and (E) and inserting the following new subparagraphs:

"(C) any entity—

"(i) which is incorporated as a nonprofit corporation under a State law,

"(ii) no part of the net earnings of which inures to the benefit of any private shareholder or individual, no substantial part of the activities of which is carrying on propaganda, or otherwise attempting, to influence legislation (except as otherwise provided in section 501(h) of the Internal Revenue Code of 1986), and which does not participate in, or intervene in (including the publishing or distributing of statements), any political campaign on behalf of (or in opposition to) any candidate for public office, and

"(iii) more than 80 percent of the gross revenues of which is received from government programs that target low-income, elderly, or disabled populations under titles XVIII, XIX, and XXI of the Social Security Act, and

"(D) any entity which is described in section 501(c)(9) of such Code and which is established by an entity (other than by an employer or employers) for purposes of providing health care benefits.";

(C) in paragraph (3)(A), by striking "subparagraph (C)(i)(I), (D)(i)(I), or (E)(i)" and inserting "subparagraph (C) or (D)"; and

(D) by adding at the end the following new paragraph:

"(4) JOINT AND SEVERAL LIABILITY.—If more than one person is liable for payment of the fee under subsection (a) with respect to a single covered entity by reason of the application of paragraph (3), all such persons shall be jointly and severally liable for payment of such fee.";

(4) by striking subsection (e) and inserting the following:

"(e) APPLICABLE AMOUNT.—For purposes of subsection (b)(1)—

"(1) YEARS BEFORE 2019.—In the case of calendar years beginning before 2019, the applicable amount shall be determined in accordance with the following table:

"Calendar year	Applicable amount
2014	$8,000,000,000
2015	$11,300,000,000
2016	$11,300,000,000
2017	$13,900,000,000
2018	$14,300,000,000.

"(2) YEARS AFTER 2018.—In the case of any calendar year beginning after 2018, the applicable amount shall be the applicable amount for the preceding calendar year increased by the rate of premium growth (within the meaning of section 36B(b)(3)(A)(ii) of the Internal Revenue Code of 1986) for such preceding calendar year.";

(5) in subsection (g), by adding at the end the following new paragraphs:

"(3) ACCURACY-RELATED PENALTY.—

"(A) IN GENERAL.—In the case of any understatement of a covered entity's net premiums written with respect to health insurance for any United States health risk for any calendar year, there shall be paid by the covered entity making such understatement, an amount equal to the excess of—

"(i) the amount of the covered entity's fee under this section for the calendar year the Secretary determines should have been paid in the absence of any such understatement, over

"(ii) the amount of such fee the Secretary determined based on such understatement.

"(B) UNDERSTATEMENT.—For purposes of this paragraph, an understatement of a covered entity's net premiums written with respect to health insurance for any United States health risk for any calendar year is the difference between the amount of such net premiums written as reported on the return filed by the covered entity under paragraph (1) and the amount of such net premiums written that should have been reported on such return.

"(C) TREATMENT OF PENALTY.—The penalty imposed under subparagraph (A) shall be subject to the provisions of subtitle F of the Internal Revenue Code of 1986 that apply to assessable penalties imposed under chapter 68 of such Code.

"(4) TREATMENT OF INFORMATION.—Section 6103 of the Internal Revenue Code of 1986 shall not apply to any information reported under this subsection."; and

(6) by striking subsection (j) and inserting the following new subsection:

"(j) EFFECTIVE DATE.—This section shall apply to calendar years beginning after December 31, 2013.".

(b) EFFECTIVE DATE.—The amendments made by this section shall take effect as if included in section 9010 of the Patient Protection and Affordable Care Act.

• • *PATIENT PROTECTION AND AFFORDABLE CARE ACT, ACT SEC. 9010 AS AMENDED*———————————————————————————————————————

ACT SEC. 9010. IMPOSITION OF ANNUAL FEE ON HEALTH INSURANCE PROVIDERS.

(a) IMPOSITION OF FEE—

(1) IN GENERAL—Each covered entity engaged in the business of providing health insurance shall pay to the Secretary not later than the annual payment date of each calendar year beginning after *2013* a fee in an amount determined under subsection (b).

* * *

(b) DETERMINATION OF FEE AMOUNT—

* * *

(2) AMOUNTS TAKEN INTO ACCOUNT.—*For purposes of paragraph (1)*—

(A) IN GENERAL.—The net premiums written with respect to health insurance for any United States health risk that are taken into account during any calendar year with respect to any covered entity shall be determined in accordance with the following table:

* * *

(B) PARTIAL EXCLUSION FOR CERTAIN EXEMPT ACTIVITIES.—After the application of subparagraph (A), only 50 percent of the remaining net premiums written with respect to health insurance for any United States health risk that are attributable to the activities (other than activities of an unrelated trade or business as defined in section 513 of the Internal Revenue Code of 1986) of any covered entity qualifying under paragraph (3), (4), (26), or (29) of section 501(c) of such Code and exempt from tax under section 501(a) of such Code shall be taken into account.

• • PATIENT PROTECTION AND AFFORDABLE CARE ACT, ACT SEC. 9010 AS AMENDED

* * *

(c) COVERED ENTITY.—

(1) IN GENERAL.—For purposes of this section, the term "covered entity" means any entity which provides health insurance for any United States health risk *during the calendar year in which the fee under this section is due.*

(2) EXCLUSION.—Such term does not include—

* * *

(C) any entity—

(i) which is incorporated as a nonprofit corporation under a State law,

(ii) no part of the net earnings of which inures to the benefit of any private shareholder or individual, no substantial part of the activities of which is carrying on propaganda, or otherwise attempting, to influence legislation (except as otherwise provided in section 501(h) of the Internal Revenue Code of 1986), and which does not participate in, or intervene in (including the publishing or distributing of statements), any political campaign on behalf of (or in opposition to) any candidate for public office, and

(iii) more than 80 percent of the gross revenues of which is received from government programs that target low-income, elderly, or disabled populations under titles XVIII, XIX, and XXI of the Social Security Act, and

(D) any entity which is described in section 501(c)(9) of such Code and which is established by an entity (other than by an employer or employers) for purposes of providing health care benefits.

(3) CONTROLLED GROUPS.—

* * *

If any entity described in *subparagraph (C) or (D)* of paragraph (2) is treated as a covered entity by reason of the application of the preceding sentence, the net premiums written with respect to health insurance for any United States health risk of such entity shall not be taken into account for purposes of this section.

(4) JOINT AND SEVERAL LIABILITY.—If more than one person is liable for payment of the fee under subsection (a) with respect to a single covered entity by reason of the application of paragraph (3), all such persons shall be jointly and severally liable for payment of such fee.

* * *

(e) APPLICABLE AMOUNT.—For purposes of subsection (b)(1)—

(1) YEARS BEFORE 2019.—In the case of calendar years beginning before 2019, the applicable amount shall be determined in accordance with the following table:

"Calendar year	Applicable amount
2014	$8,000,000,000
2015	$11,300,000,000
2016	$11,300,000,000
2017	$13,900,000,000
2018	$14,300,000,000.

(2) YEARS AFTER 2018.—In the case of any calendar year beginning after 2018, the applicable amount shall be the applicable amount for the preceding calendar year increased by the rate of premium growth (within the meaning of section 36B(b)(3)(A)(ii) of the Internal Revenue Code of 1986) for such preceding calendar year.

* * *

(g) REPORTING REQUIREMENT.—

* * *

(3) ACCURACY-RELATED PENALTY.—

• • *PATIENT PROTECTION AND AFFORDABLE CARE ACT, ACT SEC. 9010 AS AMENDED*

(A) IN GENERAL.—In the case of any understatement of a covered entity's net premiums written with respect to health insurance for any United States health risk for any calendar year, there shall be paid by the covered entity making such understatement, an amount equal to the excess of—

(i) the amount of the covered entity's fee under this section for the calendar year the Secretary determines should have been paid in the absence of any such understatement, over

(ii) the amount of such fee the Secretary determined based on such understatement.

(B) UNDERSTATEMENT.—For purposes of this paragraph, an understatement of a covered entity's net premiums written with respect to health insurance for any United States health risk for any calendar year is the difference between the amount of such net premiums written as reported on the return filed by the covered entity under paragraph (1) and the amount of such net premiums written that should have been reported on such return.

(C) TREATMENT OF PENALTY.—The penalty imposed under subparagraph (A) shall be subject to the provisions of subtitle F of the Internal Revenue Code of 1986 that apply to assessable penalties imposed under chapter 68 of such Code.

(4) TREATMENT OF INFORMATION.—Section 6103 of the Internal Revenue Code of 1986 shall not apply to any information reported under this subsection.

* * *

(j) EFFECTIVE DATE.—This section shall apply to calendar years beginning after December 31, 2013.

* * *

[CCH Explanation at ¶ 350.]

[¶ 7115] ACT SEC. 1410. TIME FOR PAYMENT OF CORPORATE ESTIMATED TAXES.

The percentage under paragraph (1) of section 202(b) of the Corporate Estimated Tax Shift Act of 2009 in effect on the date of the enactment of this Act is increased by 15.75 percentage points.

[CCH Explanation at ¶ 630. Committee Report at ¶ 10,450.]

HIRING INCENTIVES TO RESTORE EMPLOYMENT ACT

[¶7203] ACT SEC. 1. SHORT TITLE; AMENDMENT OF 1986 CODE.

(a) SHORT TITLE.—This Act may be cited as the "Hiring Incentives to Restore Employment Act".

(b) AMENDMENT OF 1986 CODE.—Except as otherwise expressly provided, whenever in this Act an amendment or repeal is expressed in terms of an amendment to, or repeal of, a section or other provision, the reference shall be considered to be made to a section or other provision of the Internal Revenue Code of 1986.

* * *

TITLE I—INCENTIVES FOR HIRING AND RETAINING UNEMPLOYED WORKERS

[¶7206] ACT SEC. 101. PAYROLL TAX FORGIVENESS FOR HIRING UNEMPLOYED WORKERS.

* * *

(c) TRANSFERS TO FEDERAL OLD-AGE AND SURVIVORS INSURANCE TRUST FUND.—There are hereby appropriated to the Federal Old-Age and Survivors Trust Fund and the Federal Disability Insurance Trust Fund established under section 201 of the Social Security Act (42 U.S.C. 401) amounts equal to the reduction in revenues to the Treasury by reason of the amendments made by subsection (a). Amounts appropriated by the preceding sentence shall be transferred from the general fund at such times and in such manner as to replicate to the extent possible the transfers which would have occurred to such Trust Fund had such amendments not been enacted.

(d) APPLICATION TO RAILROAD RETIREMENT TAXES

* * *

(2) TRANSFERS TO SOCIAL SECURITY EQUIVALENT BENEFIT ACCOUNT.—There are hereby appropriated to the Social Security Equivalent Benefit Account established under section 15A(a) of the Railroad Retirement Act of 1974 (45 U.S.C. 231n-1(a)) amounts equal to the reduction in revenues to the Treasury by reason of the amendments made by paragraph (1). Amounts appropriated by the preceding sentence shall be transferred from the general fund at such times and in such manner as to replicate to the extent possible the transfers which would have occurred to such Account had such amendments not been enacted.

(e) EFFECTIVE DATES.—

(1) IN GENERAL.—Except as provided in paragraph (2), the amendments made by this subsection shall apply to wages paid after the date of the enactment of this Act.

(2) RAILROAD RETIREMENT TAXES.—The amendments made by subsection (d) shall apply to compensation paid after the date of the enactment of this Act.

[CCH Explanation at ¶605. Committee Reports at ¶11,010.]

[¶7209] ACT SEC. 102. BUSINESS CREDIT FOR RETENTION OF CERTAIN NEWLY HIRED INDIVIDUALS IN 2010.

(a) IN GENERAL.—In the case of any taxable year ending after the date of the enactment of this Act, the current year business credit determined under section 38(b) of the Internal Revenue Code of 1986 for such taxable year shall be increased, with respect to each retained worker with respect to which subsection (b)(2) is first satisfied during such taxable year, by the lesser of—

(1) $1,000, or

(2) 6.2 percent of the wages (as defined in section 3401(a)) paid by the taxpayer to such retained worker during the 52 consecutive week period referred to in subsection (b)(2).

(b) RETAINED WORKER.—For purposes of this section, the term "retained worker" means any qualified individual (as defined in section 3111(d)(3) or section 3221(c)(3) of the Internal Revenue Code of 1986)—

(1) who was employed by the taxpayer on any date during the taxable year,

(2) who was so employed by the taxpayer for a period of not less than 52 consecutive weeks, and

(3) whose wages (as defined in section 3401(a)) for such employment during the last 26 weeks of such period equaled at least 80 percent of such wages for the first 26 weeks of such period.

(c) LIMITATION ON CARRYBACKS.—No portion of the unused business credit under section 38 of the Internal Revenue Code of 1986 for any taxable year which is attributable to the increase in the current year business credit under this section may be carried to a taxable year beginning before the date of the enactment of this section.

(d) TREATMENT OF POSSESSIONS.—

(1) PAYMENTS TO POSSESSIONS.—

(A) MIRROR CODE POSSESSIONS.—The Secretary of the Treasury shall pay to each possession of the United States with a mirror code tax system amounts equal to the loss to that possession by reason of the application of this section (other than this subsection). Such amounts shall be determined by the Secretary of the Treasury based on information provided by the government of the respective possessions.

(B) OTHER POSSESSIONS.—The Secretary of the Treasury shall pay to each possession of the United States which does not have a mirror code tax system amounts estimated by the Secretary of the Treasury as being equal to the aggregate benefits that would have been provided to residents of such possession by reason of the application of this section (other than this subsection) if a mirror code tax system had been in effect in such possession. The preceding sentence shall not apply with respect to any possession of the United States unless such possession has a plan, which has been approved by the Secretary of the Treasury, under which such possession will promptly distribute such payments to the residents of such possession.

(2) COORDINATION WITH CREDIT ALLOWED AGAINST UNITED STATES INCOME TAXES.—No increase in the credit determined under section 38(b) of the Internal Revenue Code of 1986 against United States income taxes for any taxable year determined under subsection (a) shall be taken into account with respect to any person—

(A) to whom a credit is allowed against taxes imposed by the possession by reason of this section for such taxable year, or

(B) who is eligible for a payment under a plan described in paragraph (1)(B) with respect to such taxable year.

(3) DEFINITIONS AND SPECIAL RULES.—

(A) POSSESSION OF THE UNITED STATES.—For purposes of this subsection, the term "possession of the United States" includes the Commonwealth of Puerto Rico and the Commonwealth of the Northern Mariana Islands.

(B) MIRROR CODE TAX SYSTEM.—For purposes of this subsection, the term "mirror code tax system" means, with respect to any possession of the United States, the income tax system of such possession if the income tax liability of the residents of such possession under such system is determined by reference to the income tax laws of the United States as if such possession were the United States.

(C) TREATMENT OF PAYMENTS.—For purposes of section 1324(b)(2) of title 31, United States Code, rules similar to the rules of section 1001(b)(3)(C) of the American Recovery and Reinvestment Tax Act of 2009 shall apply.

* * *

[CCH Explanation at ¶605. Committee Reports at ¶11,020.]

TITLE V—OFFSET PROVISIONS

Subtitle A—Foreign Account Tax Compliance
* * *

[¶7212] ACT SEC. 502. REPEAL OF CERTAIN FOREIGN EXCEPTIONS TO REGISTERED BOND REQUIREMENTS.
* * *

(d) Repeal of Exception to Requirement That Treasury Obligations Be in Registered Form.—

(1) In general.—Subsection (g) of section 3121 of title 31, United States Code, is amended by striking paragraph (2) and by redesignating paragraphs (3) and (4) as paragraphs (2) and (3), respectively.

(2) Conforming amendments.—Paragraph (1) of section 3121(g) of such title is amended—

(A) by adding "or" at the end of subparagraph (A),

(B) by striking "; or" at the end of subparagraph (B) and inserting a period, and

(C) by striking subparagraph (C).
* * *

[CCH Explanation at ¶760. Committee Reports at ¶11,070.]

Subtitle C—Budgetary Provisions
* * *

[¶7215] ACT SEC. 561. TIME FOR PAYMENT OF CORPORATE ESTIMATED TAXES.
Notwithstanding section 6655 of the Internal Revenue Code of 1986, in the case of a corporation with assets of not less than $1,000,000,000 (determined as of the end of the preceding taxable year)—

(1) the percentage under paragraph (1) of section 202(b) of the Corporate Estimated Tax Shift Act of 2009 in effect on the date of the enactment of this Act is increased by 23 percentage points,

(2) the amount of any required installment of corporate estimated tax which is otherwise due in July, August, or September of 2015 shall be 121.5 percent of such amount,

(3) the amount of any required installment of corporate estimated tax which is otherwise due in July, August, or September of 2019 shall be 106.5 percent of such amount, and

(4) the amount of the next required installment after an installment referred to in paragraph (2) or (3) shall be appropriately reduced to reflect the amount of the increase by reason of such paragraph.

[CCH Explanation at ¶630.]

[¶7218] ACT SEC. 562. PAYGO COMPLIANCE.
The budgetary effects of this Act, for purposes of complying with the Statutory Pay-As-You-Go-Act of 2010, shall be determined by reference to the latest statement titled "Budgetary Effects of PAYGO Legislation" for this Act, jointly submitted for printing in the Congressional Record by the Chairman of the House and Senate Budget Committees, provided that such statement has been submitted prior to the vote on passage in the House acting first on this conference report or amendments between the Houses.

TEMPORARY EXTENSION ACT OF 2010

[¶ 7303] ACT SEC. 1. SHORT TITLE.

This Act may be cited as the "Temporary Extension Act of 2010".

* * *

[¶ 7306] ACT SEC. 3. EXTENSION AND IMPROVEMENT OF PREMIUM ASSISTANCE FOR COBRA BENEFITS.

(a) EXTENSION OF ELIGIBILITY PERIOD.—Subsection (a)(3)(A) of section 3001 of division B of the American Recovery and Reinvestment Act of 2009 (Public Law 111-5) is amended by striking "February 28, 2010" and inserting "March 31, 2010".

• • *AMERICAN RECOVERY AND REINVESTMENT ACT OF 2009 DIVISION B ACT SEC. 3001(a)(3)(A) [as amended by P.L. 111-118, §1010(a)] AS AMENDED*————————

ACT SEC. 3001. PREMIUM ASSISTANCE FOR COBRA BENEFITS.

(a) PREMIUM ASSISTANCE FOR COBRA CONTINUATION COVERAGE FOR INDIVIDUALS AND THEIR FAMILIES.—

* * *

(3) ASSISTANCE ELIGIBLE INDIVIDUAL.—For purposes of this section, the term "assistance eligible individual" means any qualified beneficiary if—

(A) such qualified beneficiary is eligible for COBRA continuation coverage related to a qualifying event occurring during the period that begins with September 1, 2008, and ends with *March 31, 2010,*

* * *

(b) CLARIFICATIONS RELATING TO SECTION 3001 OF ARRA.—

(1) CLARIFICATION REGARDING COBRA CONTINUATION RESULTING FROM REDUCTIONS IN HOURS.— Subsection (a) of section 3001 of division B of the American Recovery and Reinvestment Act of 2009 (Public Law 111-5) is amended—

(A) in paragraph (3)(C), by inserting before the period at the end the following: "or consists of a reduction of hours followed by such an involuntary termination of employment during such period (as described in paragraph (17)(C))"; and

• • *AMERICAN RECOVERY AND REINVESTMENT ACT OF 2009 DIVISION B ACT SEC. 3001(a)(3)(C) AS AMENDED*————————

ACT SEC. 3001. PREMIUM ASSISTANCE FOR COBRA BENEFITS.

(a) PREMIUM ASSISTANCE FOR COBRA CONTINUATION COVERAGE FOR INDIVIDUALS AND THEIR FAMILIES.—

* * *

(3) ASSISTANCE ELIGIBLE INDIVIDUAL.—For purposes of this section, the term "assistance eligible individual" means any qualified beneficiary if—

* * *

(C) the qualifying event with respect to the COBRA continuation coverage consists of the involuntary termination of the covered employee's employment and occurred during such period *or consists of a reduction of hours followed by such an involuntary termination of employment during such period (as described in paragraph (17)(C)).*

* * *

(B) by adding at the end the following:

"(17) SPECIAL RULES IN CASE OF INDIVIDUALS LOSING COVERAGE BECAUSE OF A REDUCTION OF HOURS.—

"(A) NEW ELECTION PERIOD.—

"(i) IN GENERAL.—For the purposes of the COBRA continuation provisions, in the case of an individual described in subparagraph (C) who did not make (or who made and discontinued) an election of COBRA continuation coverage on the basis of the reduction of hours of employment, the involuntary termination of employment of such individual on or after the date of the enactment of this paragraph shall be treated as a qualifying event.

"(ii) COUNTING COBRA DURATION PERIOD FROM PREVIOUS QUALIFYING EVENT.—In any case of an individual referred to in clause (i), the period of such individual's continuation coverage shall be determined as though the qualifying event were the reduction of hours of employment.

"(iii) CONSTRUCTION.—Nothing in this paragraph shall be construed as requiring an individual referred to in clause (i) to make a payment for COBRA continuation coverage between the reduction of hours and the involuntary termination of employment.

"(iv) PREEXISTING CONDITIONS.—With respect to an individual referred to in clause (i) who elects COBRA continuation coverage pursuant to such clause, rules similar to the rules in paragraph (4)(C) shall apply.

"(B) NOTICES.—In the case of an individual described in subparagraph (C), the administrator of the group health plan (or other entity) involved shall provide, during the 60-day period beginning on the date of such individual's involuntary termination of employment, an additional notification described in paragraph (7)(A), including information on the provisions of this paragraph. Rules similar to the rules of paragraph (7) shall apply with respect to such notification.

"(C) INDIVIDUALS DESCRIBED.—Individuals described in this subparagraph are individuals who are assistance eligible individuals on the basis of a qualifying event consisting of a reduction of hours occurring during the period described in paragraph (3)(A) followed by an involuntary termination of employment insofar as such involuntary termination of employment occurred on or after the date of the enactment of this paragraph.".

(2) CODIFICATION OF CURRENT INTERPRETATION.—Subsection (a)(16) of such section is amended—

(A) by striking clause (ii) of subparagraph (A) and inserting the following:

"(ii) such individual pays, the amount of such premium, after the application of paragraph (1)(A), by the latest of—

"(I) 60 days after the date of the enactment of this paragraph,

"(II) 30 days after the date of provision of the notification required under subparagraph (D)(ii), or

"(III) the end of the period described in section 4980B(f)(2)(B)(iii) of the Internal Revenue Code of 1986."; and

• • *AMERICAN RECOVERY AND REINVESTMENT ACT OF 2009 DIVISION B ACT SEC. 3001(a)(16)(A)(ii) [as added by P.L. 111-118, §1010(c)] PRIOR TO AMENDMENT—*

ACT SEC. 3001. PREMIUM ASSISTANCE FOR COBRA BENEFITS.

(a) PREMIUM ASSISTANCE FOR COBRA CONTINUATION COVERAGE FOR INDIVIDUALS AND THEIR FAMILIES.—

* * *

(16) RULES RELATED TO 2009 EXTENSION.—

(A) ELECTION TO PAY PREMIUMS RETROACTIVELY AND MAINTAIN COBRA COVERAGE.—In the case of any premium for a period of coverage during an assistance eligible individual's transition period, such individual shall be treated for purposes of any COBRA continuation provision as having timely paid the amount of such premium if—

* * *

(ii) such individual pays, not later than 60 days after the date of the enactment of this paragraph (or, if later, 30 days after the date of provision of the notification

• • *AMERICAN RECOVERY AND REINVESTMENT ACT OF 2009 DIVISION B ACT SEC. 3001(a)(16)(A)(ii) [as added by P.L. 111-118, §1010(c)] PRIOR TO AMENDMENT——*

required under subparagraph (D)(ii)), the amount of such premium, after the application of paragraph (1)(A).

(B) by striking subclause (I) of subparagraph (C)(i), and inserting the following:

"(I) such assistance eligible individual experienced an involuntary termination that was a qualifying event prior to the date of enactment of the Department of Defense Appropriations Act, 2010; and".

• • *AMERICAN RECOVERY AND REINVESTMENT ACT OF 2009 DIVISION B ACT SEC. 3001(a)(16)(C)(i)(I) [as added by P.L. 111-118, §1010(c)] PRIOR TO AMENDMENT—*

ACT SEC. 3001. PREMIUM ASSISTANCE FOR COBRA BENEFITS.

(a) PREMIUM ASSISTANCE FOR COBRA CONTINUATION COVERAGE FOR INDIVIDUALS AND THEIR FAMILIES.—

* * *

(16) RULES RELATED TO 2009 EXTENSION.—

* * *

(C) TRANSITION PERIOD.—

* * *

(i) IN GENERAL.—For purposes of this paragraph, the term "transition period" means, with respect to any assistance eligible individual, any period of coverage if—

(I) such period begins before the date of the enactment of this paragraph, and

* * *

---

(3) CLARIFICATION OF PERIOD OF ASSISTANCE.—Subsection (a)(2)(A)(ii)(I) of such section is amended by striking "of the first month".

• • *AMERICAN RECOVERY AND REINVESTMENT ACT OF 2009 DIVISION B ACT SEC. 3001(a)(2)(A)(ii)(I) [as amended by P.L. 111-118, §1010(b)] PRIOR TO AMENDMENT—*

ACT SEC. 3001. PREMIUM ASSISTANCE FOR COBRA BENEFITS.

(a) CONTINUATION COVERAGE FOR INDIVIDUALS AND THEIR FAMILIES.—

* * *

(2) LIMITATION OF PERIOD OF PREMIUM ASSISTANCE.—

(A) IN GENERAL.—Paragraph (1)(A) shall not apply with respect to any assistance eligible individual for months of coverage beginning on or after the earlier of—

* * *

(ii) the earliest of—

(I) the date which is 15 months after the first day of the first month that paragraph (1)(A) applies with respect to such individual,

* * *

---

(4) ENFORCEMENT.—Subsection (a)(5) of such section is amended by adding at the end the following: "In addition to civil actions that may be brought to enforce applicable provisions of such Act or other laws, the appropriate Secretary or an affected individual may bring a civil action to

enforce such determinations and for appropriate relief. In addition, such Secretary may assess a penalty against a plan sponsor or health insurance issuer of not more than $110 per day for each failure to comply with such determination of such Secretary after 10 days after the date of the plan sponsor's or issuer's receipt of the determination.".

• • *AMERICAN RECOVERY AND REINVESTMENT ACT OF 2009 DIVISION B ACT SEC. 3001(a)(5) AS AMENDED*————————————————————————————

ACT SEC. 3001. PREMIUM ASSISTANCE FOR COBRA BENEFITS.

(a) PREMIUM ASSISTANCE FOR COBRA CONTINUATION COVERAGE FOR INDIVIDUALS AND THEIR FAMILIES.—

* * *

(5) EXPEDITED REVIEW OF DENIALS OF PREMIUM ASSISTANCE.—In any case in which an individual requests treatment as an assistance eligible individual and is denied such treatment by the group health plan, the Secretary of Labor (or the Secretary of Health and Human Services in connection with COBRA continuation coverage which is provided other than pursuant to part 6 of subtitle B of title I of the Employee Retirement Income Security Act of 1974), in consultation with the Secretary of the Treasury, shall provide for expedited review of such denial. An individual shall be entitled to such review upon application to such Secretary in such form and manner as shall be provided by such Secretary. Such Secretary shall make a determination regarding such individual's eligibility within 15 business days after receipt of such individual's application for review under this paragraph. Either Secretary's determination upon review of the denial shall be de novo and shall be the final determination of such Secretary. A reviewing court shall grant deference to such Secretary's determination. The provisions of this paragraph, paragraphs (1) through (4), and paragraph (7) shall be treated as provisions of title I of the Employee Retirement Income Security Act of 1974 for purposes of part 5 of subtitle B of such title. *In addition to civil actions that may be brought to enforce applicable provisions of such Act or other laws, the appropriate Secretary or an affected individual may bring a civil action to enforce such determinations and for appropriate relief. In addition, such Secretary may assess a penalty against a plan sponsor or health insurance issuer of not more than $110 per day for each failure to comply with such determination of such Secretary after 10 days after the date of the plan sponsor's or issuer's receipt of the determination.*

* * *

——

* * *

(c) EFFECTIVE DATE.—The amendments made by this section shall take effect as if included in the provisions of section 3001 of division B of the American Recovery and Reinvestment Act of 2009 to which they relate, except that—

(1) the amendments made by subsection (b)(1) shall apply to periods of coverage beginning after the date of the enactment of this Act;

(2) the amendments made by subsection (b)(2) shall take effect as if included in the amendments made by section 1010 of division B of the Department of Defense Appropriations Act, 2010; and

(3) the amendments made by subsections (b)(3) and (b)(4) shall take effect on the date of the enactment of this Act.

* * *

[CCH Explanation at ¶ 615.]

HAITI EARTHQUAKE RELIEF

[¶7350] ACT SEC. 1. ACCELERATION OF INCOME TAX BENEFITS FOR CHARITABLE CASH CONTRIBUTIONS FOR RELIEF OF VICTIMS OF EARTHQUAKE IN HAITI.

(a) IN GENERAL.—For purposes of section 170 of the Internal Revenue Code of 1986, a taxpayer may treat any contribution described in subsection (b) made after January 11, 2010, and before March 1, 2010, as if such contribution was made on December 31, 2009, and not in 2010.

(b) CONTRIBUTION DESCRIBED.—A contribution is described in this subsection if such contribution is a cash contribution made for the relief of victims in areas affected by the earthquake in Haiti on January 12, 2010, for which a charitable contribution deduction is allowable under section 170 of the Internal Revenue Code of 1986.

(c) RECORDKEEPING.—In the case of a contribution described in subsection (b), a telephone bill showing the name of the donee organization, the date of the contribution, and the amount of the contribution shall be treated as meeting the recordkeeping requirements of section 170(f)(17) of the Internal Revenue Code of 1986.

(d) PAYGO.—All applicable provisions in this section are designated as an emergency for purposes of pay-as-you-go principles.

[CCH Explanation at ¶635. Committee Reports at ¶12,001, ¶12,005 and ¶12,010.]

Committee Reports

Patient Protection and Affordable Care Act
Health Care and Education Reconciliation Act of 2010

¶10,001 Introduction

The Patient Protection and Affordable Care Act (P.L. 111-148) was passed by Congress on March 21, 2010, and signed by the President on March 23, 2010. The Joint Committee on Taxation produced a Technical Explanation of certain revenue provisions of the bill on March 21, 2010 (JCX-18-10). This report explains the intent of Congress regarding the provisions of the Act. There was no conference report issued for this Act. The Technical Explanation from the Joint Committee on Taxation is included in this section to aid the reader's understanding, but may not be cited as the official Conference Committee Report accompanying the Act. At the end of each section, references are provided to the corresponding CCH explanation and the Internal Revenue Code provisions. Subscribers to the electronic version can link from these references to the corresponding material. *The pertinent sections of the Technical Explanation relating to the Patient Protection and Affordable Care Act (P.L. 111-148) appear in Act Section order beginning at ¶10,010.*

The Technical Explanation includes provisions related to the Health Care and Education Reconciliation Act of 2010 (P.L. 111-152), an amendment in the nature of a substitute to H.R. 4872, the Reconciliation Act of 2010, as amended. *The pertinent sections of the Technical Explanation relating to the Health Care and Education Reconciliation Act of 2010 appear in Act Section order beginning at ¶10,400.*

¶10,005 Background

The "Patient Protection and Affordable Care Act" (P.L. 111-148) was introduced in the House of Representatives on September 17, 2009. The House agreed by a vote of 416 to zero on motion to suspend the rules and pass the bill on October 8, 2009, on which date the bill was read in the Senate. On December 24, 2009, the Senate passed the bill with an amendment and an amendment to the title by a vote of 60 to 30. On March 21, 2010, the House agreed to the Senate amendments by a vote of 219-212. The bill was then signed by the President on March 22, 2010, and on March 23, 2010, the bill became Public Law No. 111-148.

The "Health Care and Education Reconciliation Act of 2010" (P.L. 111-152) was introduced in the House on March 17, 2010, as H.R. 4872. The bill was passed by the House on March 21, 2010, by a vote of 220 to 211. On March 25, 2010, the Senate voted to pass the bill by a margin of 56 to 43. On that date the bill was sent back to the House, where it was passed by a vote of 220 to 207. The bill was signed by the President on March 30, 2010, and on March 31, 2010, the bill became Public Law No. 111-152.

References are to the following report:

• The Joint Committee on Taxation, *Technical Explanation of the Revenue Provisions of the "Reconciliation Act of 2010," as amended, in combination with the "Patient Protection and Affordable Care Act,"* March 21, 2010, is referred to as Joint Committee on Taxation (J.C.T. REP. NO. JCX-18-10).

[¶10,010] Act Sec. 1322. Tax exemption for certain member-run health insurance issuers[2]

Joint Committee on Taxation (J.C.T. REP. NO. JCX-18-10)

[Code Sec. 6033]

Present Law

In general

Although present law provides that certain limited categories of organizations that offer insurance may qualify for exemption from Federal income tax, present law generally does not provide tax-exempt status for newly established, member-run nonprofit health insurers that are established and funded pursuant to the Consumer Oriented, Not-for-Profit Health Plan program created under the bill and described below.

Taxation of insurance companies

Taxation of stock and mutual companies providing health insurance

Present law provides special rules for determining the taxable income of insurance companies (subchapter L of the Code). Both mutual insurance companies and stock insurance companies are subject to Federal income tax under these rules. Separate sets of rules apply to life insurance companies and to property and casualty insurance companies. Insurance companies are subject to Federal income tax at regular corporate income tax rates.

An insurance company that provides health insurance is subject to Federal income tax as either a life insurance company or as a property and casualty insurance company, depending on its mix of lines of business and on the resulting portion of its reserves that are treated as life insurance reserves. For Federal income tax purposes, an insurance company is treated as a life insurance company if the sum of its (1) life insurance reserves and (2) unearned premiums and unpaid losses on noncancellable life, accident or health contracts not included in life insurance reserves, comprise more than 50 percent of its total reserves.[3]

Life insurance companies

A life insurance company, whether stock or mutual, is taxed at regular corporate rates on its life insurance company taxable income (LICTI). LICTI is life insurance gross income reduced by life insurance deductions.[4] An alternative tax applies if a company has a net capital gain for the taxable year, if such tax is less than the tax that would otherwise apply. Life insurance gross income is the sum of (1) premiums, (2) decreases in reserves, and (3) other amounts generally includible by a taxpayer in gross income. Methods for determining reserves for Federal income tax purposes generally are based on reserves prescribed by the National Association of Insurance Commissioners for purposes of financial reporting under State regulatory rules.

Because deductible reserves might be viewed as being funded proportionately out of taxable and tax-exempt income, the net increase and net decrease in reserves are computed by reducing the ending balance of the reserve items by a portion of tax-exempt interest (known as a proration rule).[5] Similarly, a life insurance company is allowed a dividends-received deduction for intercorporate dividends from nonaffiliates only in proportion to the company's share of such dividends.[6]

---

[2] Section 1322 of the Senate amendment as amended by section 10104.

[3] Sec. 816(a).

[4] Sec. 801.

[5] Secs. 807(b)(2)(B) and (b)(1)(B).

[6] Secs. 805(a)(4), 812. Fully deductible dividends from affiliates are excluded from the application of this proration formula (so long as such dividends are not themselves distributions from tax-exempt interest or from dividend income that would not be fully deductible if received directly by the taxpayer). In addition, the proration rule includes in prorated amounts the increase for the taxable year in policy cash values of life insurance policies and annuity and endowment contracts owned by the company (the inside buildup on which is not taxed).

Property and casualty insurance companies

The taxable income of a property and casualty insurance company is determined as the sum of the amount earned from underwriting income and from investment income (as well as gains and other income items), reduced by allowable deductions.[7] For this purpose, underwriting income and investment income are computed on the basis of the underwriting and investment exhibit of the annual statement approved by the National Association of Insurance Commissioners.[8]

Underwriting income means premiums earned during the taxable year less losses incurred and expenses incurred.[9] Losses incurred include certain unpaid losses (reported losses that have not been paid, estimates of losses incurred but not reported, resisted claims, and unpaid loss adjustment expenses). Present law limits the deduction for unpaid losses to the amount of discounted unpaid losses, which are discounted using prescribed discount periods and a prescribed interest rate, to take account partially of the time value of money.[10] Any net decrease in the amount of unpaid losses results in income inclusion, and the amount included is computed on a discounted basis.

In calculating its reserve for losses incurred, a proration rule requires that a property and casualty insurance company must reduce the amount of losses incurred by 15 percent of (1) the insurer's tax-exempt interest, (2) the deductible portion of dividends received (with special rules for dividends from affiliates), and (3) the increase for the taxable year in the cash value of life insurance, endowment, or annuity contracts the company owns (sec. 832(b)(5)). This rule reflects the fact that reserves are generally funded in part from tax-exempt interest, from wholly or

partially deductible dividends, or from other untaxed amounts.

Tax exemption for certain organizations

In general

Section 501(a) generally provides for exemption from Federal income tax for certain organizations. These organizations include: (1) qualified pension, profit sharing, and stock bonus plans described in section 401(a); (2) religious and apostolic organizations described in section 501(d); and (3) organizations described in section 501(c). Sections 501(c) describes 28 different categories of exempt organizations, including: charitable organizations (section 501(c)(3)); social welfare organizations (section 501(c)(4)); labor, agricultural, and horticultural organizations (section 501(c)(5)); professional associations (section 501(c)(6)); and social clubs (section 501(c)(7)).[11]

Insurance organizations described in section 501(c)

Although most organizations that engage principally in insurance activities are not exempt from Federal income tax, certain organizations that engage in insurance activities are described in section 501(c) and exempt from tax under section 501(a). Section 501(c)(8), for example, describes certain fraternal beneficiary societies, orders, or associations operating under the lodge system or for the exclusive benefit of their members that provide for the payment of life, sick, accident, or other benefits to the members or their dependents. Section 501(c)(9) describes certain voluntary employees' beneficiary societies that provide for the payment of life, sick, accident, or other benefits to the members of the association or their dependents or designated

---

[7] Sec. 832.

[8] Sec. 832(b)(1)(A).

[9] Sec. 832(b)(3). In determining premiums earned, the company deducts from gross premiums the increase in unearned premiums for the year (sec. 832(b)(4)(B)). The company is required to reduce the deduction for increases in unearned premiums by 20 percent, reflecting the matching of deferred expenses to deferred income.

[10] Sec. 846.

[11] Certain organizations that operate on a cooperative basis are taxed under special rules set forth in Subchapter T of the Code. The two principal criteria for determining whether an entity is operating on a cooperative basis are: (1) ownership of the cooperative by persons who patronize the cooperative (e.g., the farmer members of a cooperative formed to market the farmers' produce); and (2) return of earnings to patrons in proportion to their patronage. In general, cooperative members are those who participate in the management of the cooperative and who share in pa-

tronage capital. For Federal income tax purposes, a cooperative that is taxed under the Subchapter T rules generally computes its income as if it were a taxable corporation, with one exception — the cooperative may deduct from its taxable income distributions of patronage dividends. In general, patronage dividends are the profits of the cooperative that are rebated to its patrons pursuant to a preexisting obligation of the cooperative to do so. Certain farmers' cooperatives described in section 521 are authorized to deduct not only patronage dividends from patronage sources, but also dividends on capital stock and certain distributions to patrons from nonpatronage sources.

Separate from the Subchapter T rules, the Code provides tax exemption for certain cooperatives. Section 501(c)(12), for example, provides that certain rural electric and telephone cooperative are exempt from tax under section 501(a), provided that 85 percent or more of the cooperative's income consists of amounts collected from members for the sole purpose of meeting losses or expenses, and certain other requirements are met.

beneficiaries. Section 501(c)(12)(A) describes certain benevolent life insurance associations of a purely local character. Section 501(c)(15) describes certain small non-life insurance companies with annual gross receipts of no more than $600,000 ($150,000 in the case of a mutual insurance company). Section 501(c)(26) describes certain membership organizations established to provide health insurance to certain high-risk individuals.[12] Section 501(c)(27) describes certain organizations established to provide workmen's compensation insurance.

Certain section 501(c)(3) organizations

Certain health maintenance organizations (HMOs) have been held to qualify for tax exemption as charitable organizations described in section 501(c)(3). In *Sound Health Association v. Commissioner*,[13] the Tax Court held that a staff model HMO qualified as a charitable organization. A staff model HMO generally employs its own physicians and staff and serves its subscribers at its own facilities. The court concluded that the HMO satisfied the section 501(c)(3) community benefit standard, as its membership was open to almost all members of the community. Although membership was limited to persons who had the money to pay the fixed premiums, the court held that this was not disqualifying, because the HMO had a subsidized premium program for persons of lesser means to be funded through donations and Medicare and Medicaid payments. The HMO also operated an emergency room open to all persons regardless of income. The court rejected the government's contention that the HMO conferred primarily a private benefit to its subscribers, stating that when the potential membership is such a broad segment of the community, benefit to the membership is benefit to the community.

In *Geisinger Health Plan v. Commissioner*,[14] the court applied the section 501(c)(3) community benefit standard to an individual practice association (IPA) model HMO. In the IPA model, health care generally is provided by physicians practicing independently in their own offices, with the IPA usually contracting on behalf of the physicians with the HMO. Reversing a Tax Court decision, the court held that the HMO did not

qualify as charitable, because the community benefit standard requires that an HMO be an actual provider of health care rather than merely an arranger or deliverer of health care, which is how the court viewed the IPA model in that case.

More recently, in *IHC Health Plans, Inc. v. Commissioner*,[15] the court ruled that three affiliated HMOs did not operate primarily for the benefit of the community they served. The organizations in the case did not provide health care directly, but provided group insurance that could be used at both affiliated and non-affiliated providers. The court found that the organizations primarily performed a risk-bearing function and provided virtually no free or below-cost health care services. In denying charitable status, the court held that a health-care provider must make its services available to all in the community plus provide additional community or public benefits.[16] The benefit must either further the function of government-funded institutions or provide a service that would not likely be provided within the community but for the subsidy. Further, the additional public benefit conferred must be sufficient to give rise to a strong inference that the public benefit is the primary purpose for which the organization operates.[17]

Certain organizations providing commercial-type insurance

Section 501(m) provides that an organization may not be exempt from tax under section 501(c)(3) (generally, charitable organizations) or section 501(c)(4) (social welfare organizations) unless no substantial part of its activities consists of providing commercial-type insurance. For this purpose, commercial-type insurance excludes, among other things: (1) insurance provided at substantially below cost to a class of charitable recipients; and (2) incidental health insurance provided by an HMO of a kind customarily provided by such organizations.

When section 501(m) was enacted in 1986, the following reasons for the provision were stated: "The committee is concerned that exempt charitable and social welfare organizations that engaged in insurance activities are engaged in an

---

[12] When section 501(c)(26) was enacted in 1996, the House Ways and Means Committee, in reporting out the bill, stated as its reasons for change: "The Committee believes that eliminating the uncertainty concerning the eligibility of certain State health insurance risk pools for tax-exempt status will assist States in providing medical care coverage for their uninsured high-risk residents." H.R. Rep. No. 104-496, Part I, "Health Coverage Availability and Affordability Act of 1996," 104th Cong., 2d Sess., March 25, 1996, 124. *See also* Joint Committee on Taxation, *General Explanation of Tax Leg-*

islation Enacted in the 104th Congress, JCS-12-96, December 18, 1996, 351.

[13] 71 T.C. 158 (1978), *acq.* 1981-2 C.B. 2.

[14] 985 F.2d 1210 (3rd Cir. 1993), *rev'g* T.C. Memo. 1991-649.

[15] 325 F.3d 1188 (10th Cir. 2003).

[16] *Ibid.* at 1198.

[17] *Ibid.*

activity whose nature and scope is so inherently commercial that tax exempt status is inappropriate. The committee believes that the tax-exempt status of organizations engaged in insurance activities provides an unfair competitive advantage to these organizations. The committee further believes that the provision of insurance to the general public at a price sufficient to cover the costs of insurance generally constitutes an activity that is commercial. In addition, the availability of tax-exempt status . . . has allowed some large insurance entities to compete directly with commercial insurance companies. For example, the Blue Cross/Blue Shield organizations historically have been treated as tax-exempt organizations described in sections 501(c)(3) or (4). This group of organizations is now among the largest health care insurers in the United States. Other tax-exempt charitable and social welfare organizations engaged in insurance activities also have a competitive advantage over commercial insurers who do not have tax-exempt status . . . ."[18]

Unrelated business income tax

Most organizations that are exempt from tax under section 501(a) are subject to the unrelated business income tax rules of sections 511 through 515. The unrelated business income tax generally applies to income derived from a trade or business regularly carried on by the organization that is not substantially related to the performance of the organization's tax-exempt functions. Certain types of income are specifically exempt from the unrelated business income tax, such as dividends, interest, royalties, and certain rents, unless derived from debt-financed property or from certain 50-percent controlled subsidiaries.

Explanation of Provision

In general

The provision authorizes $6 billion in funding for, and instructs the Secretary of Health and Human Services ("HHS") to establish, the Consumer Operated and Oriented Plan (the "program") to foster the creation of qualified nonprofit health insurance issuers to offer qualified health plans in the individual and small group markets in the States in which the issuers are licensed to offer such plans. Federal funds are to be distributed as loans to assist with start-up costs and grants to assist in meeting State solvency requirements.

Under the provision, the Secretary of HHS must require any person receiving a loan or grant under the program to enter into an agreement with the Secretary of HHS requiring the recipient of funds to meet and continue to meet any requirement under the provision for being treated as a qualified nonprofit health insurance issuer, and any requirements to receive the loan or grant. The provision also requires that the agreement prohibit the use of loan or grant funds for carrying on propaganda or otherwise attempting to influence legislation or for marketing.

If the Secretary of HHS determines that a grant or loan recipient failed to meet the requirements described in the preceding paragraph, and failed to correct such failure within a reasonable period from when the person first knew (or reasonably should have known) of such failure, then such person must repay the Secretary of HHS an amount equal to 110 percent of the aggregate amount of the loans and grants received under the program, plus interest on such amount for the period during which the loans or grants were outstanding. The Secretary of HHS must notify the Secretary of the Treasury of any determination of a failure that results in the termination of the grantee's Federal tax-exempt status.

Qualified nonprofit health insurance issuers

The provision defines a qualified nonprofit health insurance issuer as an organization that meets the following requirements:

1. The organization is organized as a nonprofit, member corporation under State law;

2. Substantially all of its activities consist of the issuance of qualified health plans in the individual and small group markets in each State in which it is licensed to issue such plans;

3. None of the organization, a related entity, or a predecessor of either was a health insurance issuer as of July 16, 2009;

4. The organization is not sponsored by a State or local government, any political subdivision thereof, or any instrumentality of such government or political subdivision;

5. Governance of the organization is subject to a majority vote of its members;

---

[18] H.R. Rep. No. 99-426, "Tax Reform Act of 1985," Report of the Committee on Ways and Means, 99th Cong., 1st Sess., December 7, 1985, 664. *See also* Joint Committee on Taxation, *General Explanation of the Tax Reform Act of 1986*, JCS-10-87, May 4, 1987, 584.

6. The organization's governing documents incorporate ethics and conflict of interest standards protecting against insurance industry involvement and interference;

7. The organization must operate with a strong consumer focus, including timeliness, responsiveness, and accountability to its members, in accordance with regulations to be promulgated by the Secretary of HHS;

8. Any profits made must be used to lower premiums, improve benefits, or for other programs intended to improve the quality of health care delivered to its members;

9. The organization meets all other requirements that other issuers of qualified health plans are required to meet in any State in which it offers a qualified health plan, including solvency and licensure requirements, rules on payments to providers, rules on network adequacy, rate and form filing rules, and any applicable State premium assessments. Additionally, the organization must coordinate with certain other State insurance reforms under the bill; and

10. The organization does not offer a health plan in a State until that State has in effect (or the Secretary of HHS has implemented for the State), the market reforms required by part A of title XXVII of the Public Health Service Act ("PHSA"), as amended by the bill.

Tax exemption for qualified nonprofit health insurance issuers

An organization receiving a grant or loan under the program qualifies for exemption from

Federal income tax under section 501(a) of the Code with respect to periods during which the organization is in compliance with the above-described requirements of the program and with the terms of any program grant or loan agreement to which such organization is a party. Such organizations also are subject to organizational and operational requirements applicable to certain section 501(c) organizations, including the prohibitions on private inurement and political activities, the limitation on lobbying activities, taxation of excess benefit transactions (section 4958), and taxation of unrelated business taxable income under section 511.

Program participants are required to file an application for exempt status with the IRS in such manner as the Secretary of the Treasury may require, and are subject to annual information reporting requirements. In addition, such an organization is required to disclose on its annual information return the amount of reserves required by each State in which it operates and the amount of reserves on hand.

Effective Date

The provision is effective on date of enactment.

[Law at ¶ 5155].

[¶ 10,020] Act Sec. 1341. Tax exemption for entities established pursuant to transitional reinsurance program for individual market in each state[19]

Joint Committee on Taxation (J.C.T. REP. No. JCX-18-10)

[Act Sec. 1341]

Present Law

Although present law provides that certain limited categories of organizations that offer insurance may qualify for exemption from Federal income tax, present law does not provide tax-exempt status for transitional nonprofit reinsurance entities created under the Senate bill and described below.

Explanation of Provision

In general, issuers of health benefit plans that are offered in the individual market would be required to contribute to a temporary reinsurance program for individual policies that is administered by a nonprofit reinsurance entity. Such contributions would begin January 1, 2014, and continue for a 36-month period. The provision requires each State, no later than January 1,

---

[19] Section 1341 of the Senate amendment as amended by section 10104.

2014, to adopt a reinsurance program based on a model regulation and to establish (or enter into a contract with) one or more applicable reinsurance entities to carry out the reinsurance program under the provision. For purposes of the provision, an applicable reinsurance entity is a not-for-profit organization (1) the purpose of which is to help stabilize premiums for coverage in the individual market in a State during the first three years of operation of an exchange for such markets within the State, and (2) the duties of which are to carry out the reinsurance program under the provision by coordinating the funding and operation of the risk-spreading mechanisms designed to implement the reinsurance program. A State may have more than one applicable reinsurance entity to carry out the

reinsurance program in the State, and two or more States may enter into agreements to allow a reinsurer to operate the reinsurance program in those States.

An applicable reinsurance entity established under the provision is exempt from Federal income tax. Notwithstanding an applicable reinsurance entity's tax-exempt status, it is subject to tax on unrelated business taxable income under section 511 as if such entity were described in section 511(a)(2).

Effective Date

The provision is effective on the date of enactment.

[Law at ¶7006. CCH Explanation at ¶435.]

[¶10,030] Act Secs. 1401, 1411 and 1412. Refundable tax credit providing premium assistance for coverage under a qualified health plan[20]

Joint Committee on Taxation (J.C.T. REP. NO. JCX-18-10)

[New Code Sec. 36B]

Present Law

Currently there is no tax credit that is generally available to low or middle income individuals or families for the purchase of health insurance. Some individuals may be eligible for health coverage through State Medicaid programs which consider income, assets, and family circumstances. However, these Medicaid programs are not in the Code.

Health coverage tax credit

Certain individuals are eligible for the health coverage tax credit ("HCTC"). The HCTC is a refundable tax credit equal to 80 percent of the cost of qualified health coverage paid by an eligible individual. In general, eligible individuals are individuals who receive a trade adjustment allowance (and individuals who would be eligible to receive such an allowance but for the fact that they have not exhausted their regular unemployment benefits), individuals eligible for the alternative trade adjustment assistance program, and individuals over age 55 who receive pension benefits from the Pension Benefit Guaranty Corporation. The HCTC is available for "qualified health insurance," which includes certain employer-based insurance, certain State-

based insurance, and in some cases, insurance purchased in the individual market.

The credit is available on an advance basis through a program established and administered by the Treasury Department. The credit generally is delivered as follows: the eligible individual sends his or her portion of the premium to the Treasury, and the Treasury then pays the full premium (the individual's portion and the amount of the refundable tax credit) to the insurer. Alternatively, an eligible individual is also permitted to pay the entire premium during the year and claim the credit on his or her income tax return.

Individuals entitled to Medicare and certain other governmental health programs, covered under certain employer-subsidized health plans, or with certain other specified health coverage are not eligible for the credit.

COBRA continuation coverage premium reduction

The Consolidated Omnibus Reconciliation Act of 1985 ("COBRA")[21] requires that a group health plan must offer continuation coverage to qualified beneficiaries in the case of a qualifying event (such as a loss of employment). A plan may require payment of a premium for any pe-

---

[20] Sections 1401, 1411 and 1412 of the Senate amendment, as amended by sections 10104, 10105, 10107, are further amended by section 1001 of the Reconciliation bill.

[21] Pub. L. No. 99-272.

riod of continuation coverage. The amount of such premium generally may not exceed 102 percent of the "applicable premium" for such period and the premium must be payable, at the election of the payor, in monthly installments.

Section 3001 of the American Recovery and Reinvestment Act of 2009,[22] as amended by the Department of Defense Appropriations Act, 2010,[23] and the Temporary Extension Act of 2010[24] provides that, for a period not exceeding 15 months, an assistance eligible individual is treated as having paid any premium required for COBRA continuation coverage under a group health plan if the individual pays 35 percent of the premium. Thus, if the assistance eligible individual pays 35 percent of the premium, the group health plan must treat the individual as having paid the full premium required for COBRA continuation coverage, and the individual is entitled to a subsidy for 65 percent of the premium. An assistance eligible individual generally is any qualified beneficiary who elects COBRA continuation coverage and the qualifying event with respect to the covered employee for that qualified beneficiary is a loss of group health plan coverage on account of an involuntary termination of the covered employee's employment (for other than gross misconduct).[25] In addition, the qualifying event must occur during the period beginning September 1, 2008, and ending March 31, 2010.

The COBRA continuation coverage subsidy also applies to temporary continuation coverage elected under the Federal Employees Health Benefits Program and to continuation health coverage under State programs that provide coverage comparable to continuation coverage. The subsidy is generally delivered by requiring employers to pay the subsidized portion of the premium for assistance eligible individuals. The employer then treats the payment of the subsidized portion as a payment of employment taxes and offsets its employment tax liability by the amount of the subsidy. To the extent that the aggregate amount of the subsidy for all assistance eligible individuals for which the employer is entitled to a credit for a quarter exceeds the employer's employment tax liability for the

quarter, the employer can request a tax refund or can claim the credit against future employment tax liability.

There is an income limit on the entitlement to the COBRA continuation coverage subsidy. Taxpayers with modified adjusted gross income exceeding $145,000 (or $290,000 for joint filers), must repay any subsidy received by them, their spouse, or their dependant, during the taxable year. For taxpayers with modified adjusted gross incomes between $125,000 and $145,000 (or $250,000 and $290,000 for joint filers), the amount of the subsidy that must be repaid is reduced proportionately. The subsidy is also conditioned on the individual not being eligible for certain other health coverage. To the extent that an eligible individual receives a subsidy during a taxable year to which the individual was not entitled due to income or being eligible for other health coverage, the subsidy overpayment is repaid on the individual's income tax return as additional tax. However, in contrast to the HCTC, the subsidy for COBRA continuation coverage may only be claimed through the employer and cannot be claimed at the end of the year on an individual tax return.

Explanation of Provision

Premium assistance credit

The provision creates a refundable tax credit (the "premium assistance credit") for eligible individuals and families who purchase health insurance through an exchange.[26] The premium assistance credit, which is refundable and payable in advance directly to the insurer, subsidizes the purchase of certain health insurance plans through an exchange.

Under the provision, an eligible individual enrolls in a plan offered through an exchange and reports his or her income to the exchange. Based on the information provided to the exchange, the individual receives a premium assistance credit based on income and the Treasury pays the premium assistance credit amount directly to the insurance plan in which the individual is enrolled. The individual then pays to the plan in which he or she is enrolled the dollar

---

[22] Pub. L. No. 111-5.

[23] Pub. L. No. 111-118.

[24] Pub. L. No. 111-144.

[25] TEA expanded eligibility for the COBRA subsidy to include individuals who experience a loss of coverage on account of a reduction in hours of employment followed by the involuntary termination of employment of the covered employee. For an individual entitled to COBRA because of a reduction in hours and who is then subsequently involunta-

rily terminated from employment, the termination is considered a qualifying event for purposes of the COBRA subsidy, as long as the termination occurs during the period beginning on the date following TEA's date of enactment and ending on March 31, 2010.

[26] Individuals enrolled in multi-state plans, pursuant to section 1334 of the Senate amendment, are also eligible for the credit.

difference between the premium tax credit amount and the total premium charged for the plan.[27] Individuals who fail to pay all or part of the remaining premium amount are given a mandatory three-month grace period prior to an involuntary termination of their participation in the plan. For employed individuals who purchase health insurance through a State exchange, the premium payments are made through payroll deductions. Initial eligibility for the premium assistance credit is based on the individual's income for the tax year ending two years prior to the enrollment period. Individuals (or couples) who experience a change in marital status or other household circumstance, experience a decrease in income of more than 20 percent, or receive unemployment insurance, may update eligibility information or request a redetermination of their tax credit eligibility.

The premium assistance credit is available for individuals (single or joint filers) with household incomes between 100 and 400 percent of the Federal poverty level ("FPL") for the family size involved who do not received health insurance through an employer or a spouse's employer.[28] Household income is defined as the sum of: (1) the taxpayer's modified adjusted gross income, plus (2) the aggregate modified adjusted gross incomes of all other individuals taken into account in determining that taxpayer's family size (but only if such individuals are required to file a tax return for the taxable year). Modified adjusted gross income is defined as adjusted gross income increased by: (1) the amount (if any) normally excluded by section 911 (the exclusion from gross income for citizens or residents living abroad), plus (2) any tax-exempt interest received or accrued during the tax year. To be eligible for the premium assistance credit, taxpayers who are married (within the meaning of section 7703) must file a joint return. Individuals who are listed as dependants on a return are ineligible for the premium assistance credit.

As described in Table 1 below, premium assistance credits are available on a sliding scale basis for individuals and families with household incomes between 100 and 400 percent of FPL to help offset the cost of private health insurance premiums. The premium assistance credit amount is determined by the Secretary of HHS based on the percentage of income the cost of premiums represents, rising from two percent of income for those at 100 percent of FPL for the family size involved to 9.5 percent of income for those at 400 percent of FPL for the family size involved. Beginning in 2014, the percentages of income are indexed to the excess of premium growth over income growth for the preceding calendar year (in order to hold steady the share of premiums that enrollees at a given poverty level pay over time). Beginning in 2018, if the aggregate amount of premium assistance credits and cost-sharing reductions[29] exceeds 0.504 percent of the gross domestic product for that year, the percentage of income is also adjusted to reflect the excess (if any) of premium growth over the rate of growth in the consumer price index for the preceding calendar year. For purposes of calculating household size, individuals who are in the country illegally are not included. Individuals who are listed as dependants on a return are ineligible for the premium assistance credit.

Premium assistance credits, or any amounts that are attributable to them, cannot be used to pay for abortions for which federal funding is prohibited. Premium assistance credits are not available for months in which an individual has a free choice voucher (as defined in section 10108 of the Senate amendment).

The low income premium credit phase-out

The premium assistance credit increases, on a sliding scale in a linear manner, as shown in the table below.

Household Income (expressed as a percent of poverty line)	Initial Premium (percentage)	Final Premium (percentage)
100% through 133%	2.0	3.0
133% through 150%	3.0	4.0

[27] Although the credit is generally payable in advance directly to the insurer, individuals may elect to purchase health insurance out-of-pocket and apply to the IRS for the credit at the end of the taxable year. The amount of the reduction in premium is required to be included with each bill sent to the individual.

[28] Individuals who are lawfully present in the United States but are not eligible for Medicaid because of their immigration status are treated as having a household income equal to 100 percent of FPL (and thus eligible for the premium assistance credit) as long as their household income does not actually exceed 100 percent of FPL.

[29] As described in section 1402 of the Senate amendment.

Household Income (expressed as a percent of poverty line)	Initial Premium (percentage)	Final Premium (percentage)
150% through 200%	4.0	6.3
200% through 250%	6.3	8.05
250% through 300%	8.05	9.5
300% through 400%	9.5	9.5

The premium assistance credit amount is tied to the cost of the second lowest-cost silver plan (adjusted for age) which: (1) is in the rating area where the individual resides, (2) is offered through an exchange in the area in which the individual resides, and (3) provides self-only coverage in the case of an individual who purchases self-only coverage, or family coverage in the case of any other individual. If the plan in which the individual enrolls offers benefits in addition to essential health benefits,[30] even if the State in which the individual resides requires such additional benefits, the portion of the premium that is allocable to those additional benefits is disregarded in determining the premium assistance credit amount.[31] Premium assistance credits may be used for any plan purchased through an exchange, including bronze, silver, gold and platinum level plans and, for those eligible,[32] catastrophic plans.

Minimum essential coverage and employer offer of health insurance coverage

Generally, if an employee is offered minimum essential coverage[33] in the group market, including employer-provided health insurance coverage, the individual is ineligible for the premium tax credit for health insurance purchased through a State exchange.

If an employee is offered unaffordable coverage by his or her employer or the plan's share of provided benefits is less than 60 percent, the employee can be eligible for the premium tax credit, but only if the employee declines to enroll in the coverage and satisfies the conditions for receiving a tax credit through an exchange. Unaffordable is defined as coverage with a premium required to be paid by the employee that is 9.5 percent or more of the employee's household

income, based on the type of coverage applicable (e.g., individual or family coverage).[34] The percentage of income that is considered unaffordable is indexed in the same manner as the percentage of income is indexed for purposes of determining eligibility for the credit (as discussed above). The Secretary of the Treasury is informed of the name and employer identification number of every employer that has one or more employees receiving a premium tax credit.

No later than five years after the date of the enactment of the provision the Comptroller General must conduct a study of whether the percentage of household income used for purposes of determining whether coverage is affordable is the appropriate level, and whether such level can be lowered without significantly increasing the costs to the Federal Government and reducing employer-provided health coverage. The Secretary reports the results of such study to the appropriate committees of Congress, including any recommendations for legislative changes.

Procedures for determining eligibility

For purposes of the premium assistance credit, exchange participants must provide information from their tax return from two years prior during the open enrollment period for coverage during the next calendar year. For example, if an individual applies for a premium assistance credit for 2014, the individual must provide a tax return from 2012 during the 2103 open enrollment period. The Internal Revenue Service ("IRS") is authorized to disclose to HHS limited tax return information to verify a taxpayer's income based on the most recent return information available to establish eligibility for the premium tax credit. Existing privacy and safeguard requirements apply. Individuals who do not qualify for the premium tax credit on the

---

[30] As defined in section 1302(b) of the Senate amendment.

[31] A similar rule applies to additional benefits that are offered in multi-State plans, under section 1334 of the Senate amendment.

[32] Those eligible to purchase catastrophic plans either must have not reached the age of 30 before the beginning of the plan year, or have certification or an affordability or

hardship exemption from the individual responsibility payment, as described in new sections 5000A(e)(1) and 5000A(e)(5), respectively.

[33] As defined in section 5000A(f) of the Senate amendment.

[34] The 9.5 percent amount is indexed for calendar years beginning after 2014.

basis of their prior year income may apply for the premium tax credit based on specified changes in circumstances. For individuals and families who did not file a tax return in the prior tax year, the Secretary of HHS will establish alternative income documentation that may be provided to determine income eligibility for the premium tax credit.

The Secretary of HHS must establish a program for determining whether or not individuals are eligible to: (1) enroll in an exchange-offered health plan; (2) claim a premium assistance credit; and (3) establish that their coverage under an employer-sponsored plan is unaffordable. The program must provide for the following: (1) the details of an individual's application process; (2) the details of how public entities are to make determinations of individuals' eligibility; (3) procedures for deeming individuals to be eligible; and, (4) procedures for allowing individuals with limited English proficiency to have proper access to exchanges.

In applying for enrollment in an exchange-offered health plan, an individual applicant is required to provide individually identifiable information, including name, address, date of birth, and citizenship or immigration status. In the case of an individual claiming a premium assistance credit, the individual is required to submit to the exchange income and family size information and information regarding changes in marital or family status or income. Personal information provided to the exchange is submitted to the Secretary of HHS. In turn, the Secretary of HHS submits the applicable information to the Social Security Commissioner, Homeland Security Secretary, and Treasury Secretary for verification purposes. The Secretary of HHS is notified of the results following verification, and notifies the exchange of such results. The provision specifies actions to be undertaken if inconsistencies are found. The Secretary of HHS, in consultation with the Social Security Commissioner, the Secretary of Homeland Security, and the Treasury Secretary must establish procedures for appealing determinations resulting from the verification process, and redetermining eligibility on a periodic basis.

An employer must be notified if one of its employees is determined to be eligible for a premium assistance credit because the employer does not provide minimal essential coverage through an employer-sponsored plan, or the employer does offer such coverage but it is not affordable. The notice must include information about the employer's potential liability for payments under section 4980H and that terminating or discriminating against an employee because he or she received a credit or subsidy is in violation of the Fair Labor Standards Act.[35] An employer is generally not entitled to information about its employees who qualify for the premium assistance credit. Employers may, however, be notified of the name of the employee and whether his or her income is above or below the threshold used to measure the affordability of the employer's health insurance coverage.

Personal information submitted for verification may be used only to the extent necessary for verification purposes and may not be disclosed to anyone not identified in this provision. Any person, who submits false information due to negligence or disregard of any rule, and without reasonable cause, is subject to a civil penalty of not more than $25,000. Any person who intentionally provides false information will be fined not more than $250,000. Any person who knowingly and willfully uses or discloses confidential applicant information will be fined not more than $25,000. Any fines imposed by this provision may not be collected through a lien or levy against property, and the section does not impose any criminal liability.

The provision requires the Secretary of HHS, in consultation with the Secretaries of the Treasury and Labor, to conduct a study to ensure that the procedures necessary to administer the determination of individuals' eligibility to participate in an exchange, to receive premium assistance credits, and to obtain an individual responsibility exemption, adequately protect employees' rights of privacy and employers' rights to due process. The results of the study must be reported by January 1, 2013, to the appropriate committees of Congress.

Reconciliation

If the premium assistance received through an advance payment exceeds the amount of credit to which the taxpayer is entitled, the excess advance payment is treated as an increase in tax. For persons whose household income is below 400% of the FPL, the amount of the increase in tax is limited to $400. If the premium assistance received through an advance payment is less than the amount of the credit to which the taxpayer is entitled, the shortfall is treated as a reduction in tax.

[35] Pub. L. No. 75-718.

The eligibility for and amount of premium assistance is determined in advance of the coverage year, on the basis of household income and family size from two years prior, and the monthly premiums for qualified health plans in the individual market in which the taxpayer, spouse and any dependent enroll in an exchange. Any advance premium assistance is paid during the year for which coverage is provided by the exchange. In the subsequent year, the amount of advance premium assistance is required to be reconciled with the allowable refundable credit for the year of coverage. Generally, this would be accomplished on the tax return filed for the year of coverage, based on that year's actual household income, family size, and premiums. Any adjustment to tax resulting from the difference between the advance premium assistance and the allowable refundable tax credit would be assessed as additional tax or a reduction in tax on the tax return.

Separately, the provision requires that the exchange, or any person with whom it contracts to administer the insurance program, must report to the Secretary with respect to any taxpayer's participation in the health plan offered by the Exchange. The information to be reported is information necessary to determine whether a person has received excess advance payments, identifying information about the taxpayer (such as name, taxpayer identification number, months of coverage) and any other person covered by that policy; the level of coverage purchased by the taxpayer; the total premium charged for the coverage, as well as the aggregate advance payments credited to that taxpayer; and information provided to the Exchange for the purpose of establishing eligibility for the program, including changes of circumstances of the taxpayer since first purchasing the coverage. Finally, the party submitting the report must provide a copy to the taxpayer whose information is the subject of the report.

Effective Date

The provision is effective for taxable years ending after December 31, 2013.

[Law at ¶5045, ¶5150, and ¶7009. CCH Explanation at ¶210.]

[¶10,040] Act Secs. 1402, 1411 and 1412. Reduced cost-sharing for individuals enrolling in qualified health plans[36]

Joint Committee on Taxation (J.C.T. Rep. No. JCX-18-10)

[Act Secs. 1402, 1411 and 1412]

Present Law

Currently there is no tax credit that is generally available to low or middle income individuals or families for the purchase of health insurance. Some individuals may be eligible for health coverage through State Medicaid programs which consider income, assets, and family circumstances. However, these Medicaid programs are not in the Code.

Health coverage tax credit

Certain individuals are eligible for the HCTC. The HCTC is a refundable tax credit equal to 80 percent of the cost of qualified health coverage paid by an eligible individual. In general, eligible individuals are individuals who receive a trade adjustment allowance (and individuals who would be eligible to receive such an allowance but for the fact that they have not exhausted their regular unemployment benefits), individuals eligible for the alternative trade adjustment assistance program, and individuals over age 55 who receive pension benefits from the Pension Benefit Guaranty Corporation. The HCTC is available for "qualified health insurance," which includes certain employer-based insurance, certain State-based insurance, and in some cases, insurance purchased in the individual market.

The credit is available on an advance basis through a program established and administered by the Treasury Department. The credit generally is delivered as follows: the eligible individual sends his or her portion of the premium to the Treasury, and the Treasury then pays the full premium (the individual's portion and the amount of the refundable tax credit) to the insurer. Alternatively, an eligible individual is also permitted to pay the entire premium during the year and claim the credit on his or her income tax return.

---

[36] Sections 1401, 1411 and 1412 of the Senate amendment, as amended by section 10104, is further amended by section 1001 of the Reconciliation bill.

Individuals entitled to Medicare and certain other governmental health programs, covered under certain employer-subsidized health plans, or with certain other specified health coverage are not eligible for the credit.

COBRA continuation coverage premium reduction

COBRA[37] requires that a group health plan must offer continuation coverage to qualified beneficiaries in the case of a qualifying event (such as a loss of employment). A plan may require payment of a premium for any period of continuation coverage. The amount of such premium generally may not exceed 102 percent of the "applicable premium" for such period and the premium must be payable, at the election of the payor, in monthly installments.

Section 3001 of the American Recovery and Reinvestment Act of 2009,[38] as amended by the Department of Defense Appropriations Act, 2010,[39] and the Temporary Extension Act of 2010[40] provides that, for a period not exceeding 15 months, an assistance eligible individual is treated as having paid any premium required for COBRA continuation coverage under a group health plan if the individual pays 35 percent of the premium. Thus, if the assistance eligible individual pays 35 percent of the premium, the group health plan must treat the individual as having paid the full premium required for COBRA continuation coverage, and the individual is entitled to a subsidy for 65 percent of the premium. An assistance eligible individual generally is any qualified beneficiary who elects COBRA continuation coverage and the qualifying event with respect to the covered employee for that qualified beneficiary is a loss of group health plan coverage on account of an involuntary termination of the covered employee's employment (for other than gross misconduct).[41] In addition, the qualifying event must occur during the period beginning September 1, 2008, and ending March 31, 2010.

The COBRA continuation coverage subsidy also applies to temporary continuation coverage elected under the Federal Employees Health Benefits Program and to continuation health coverage under State programs that provide coverage comparable to continuation coverage. The subsidy is generally delivered by requiring employers to pay the subsidized portion of the premium for assistance eligible individuals. The employer then treats the payment of the subsidized portion as a payment of employment taxes and offsets its employment tax liability by the amount of the subsidy. To the extent that the aggregate amount of the subsidy for all assistance eligible individuals for which the employer is entitled to a credit for a quarter exceeds the employer's employment tax liability for the quarter, the employer can request a tax refund or can claim the credit against future employment tax liability.

There is an income limit on the entitlement to the COBRA continuation coverage subsidy. Taxpayers with modified adjusted gross income exceeding $145,000 (or $290,000 for joint filers), must repay any subsidy received by them, their spouse, or their dependant, during the taxable year. For taxpayers with modified adjusted gross incomes between $125,000 and $145,000 (or $250,000 and $290,000 for joint filers), the amount of the subsidy that must be repaid is reduced proportionately. The subsidy is also conditioned on the individual not being eligible for certain other health coverage. To the extent that an eligible individual receives a subsidy during a taxable year to which the individual was not entitled due to income or being eligible for other health coverage, the subsidy overpayment is repaid on the individual's income tax return as additional tax. However, in contrast to the HCTC, the subsidy for COBRA continuation coverage may only be claimed through the employer and cannot be claimed at the end of the year on an individual tax return.

Explanation of Provision

Cost-sharing subsidy

A cost-sharing subsidy is provided to reduce annual out-of-pocket cost-sharing for individuals and households between 100 and 400 percent FPL (for the family size involved). The reductions are made in reference to the dollar cap on annual deductibles for high deductable health plans in section 223(c)(2)(A)(ii) (currently $5,000 for self-only coverage and $10,000 for family coverage). For individuals with house-

---

[37] Pub. L. No. 99-272.

[38] Pub. L. No. 111-5.

[39] Pub. L. No. 111-118.

[40] Pub. L. No. 111-144.

[41] TEA expanded eligibility for the COBRA subsidy to include individuals who experience a loss of coverage on account of a reduction in hours of employment followed by the involuntary termination of employment of the covered employee. For an individual entitled to COBRA because of a reduction in hours and who is then subsequently involuntarily terminated from employment, the termination is considered a qualifying event for purposes of the COBRA subsidy, as long as the termination occurs during the period beginning on the date following TEA's date of enactment and ending on March 31, 2010.

hold income of more than 100 but not more than 200 percent of FPL, the out-of-pocket limit is reduced by two-thirds. For those between 201 and 300 percent of FPL by one-half, and for those between 301 and 400 percent of FPL by one-third.

The cost-sharing subsidy that is provided must buy out any difference in cost-sharing between the qualified health insurance purchased and the actuarial values specified below. For individuals between 100 and 150 percent of FPL (for the family size involved), the subsidy must bring the value of the plan to not more than 94 percent actuarial value. For those between 150 and 200 percent of FPL, the subsidy must bring the value of the plan to not more than 87 percent actuarial value. For those between 201 and 250 percent of FPL, the subsidy must bring the value of the plan to not more than 73 percent actuarial value. For those between 251 and 400 percent of FPL, the subsidy must bring the value of the plan to not more than 70 percent actuarial value. The determination of cost-sharing subsidies will be made based on data from the same taxable year as is used for determining advance credits under section 1412 of the Senate amendment (and not the taxable year used for determining premium assistance credits under section 36B). The amount received by an insurer as a cost-sharing subsidy on behalf of an individual, as well as any out-of-pocket spending by the individual, counts towards the out-of-pocket limit. Individuals enrolled in multi-state plans, pursuant to section 1334 of the Senate amendment, are eligible for the subsidy.

In addition to adjusting actuarial values, plans must further reduce cost-sharing for low-income individuals as specified below. For individuals between 100 and 150 percent of FPL (for the family size involved) the plan's share of the total allowed cost of benefits provided under the plan must be 94 percent. For those between 151 and 200 percent of FPL, the plan's share must be 87 percent, and for those between 201 and 250 percent of FPL the plan's share must be 73 percent.

The cost-sharing subsidy is available only for those months in which an individual receives an affordability credit under new section 36B.[42]

As with the premium assistance credit, if the plan in which the individual enrolls offers benefits in addition to essential health benefits,[43] even if the State in which the individual resides requires such additional benefits, the reduction in cost-sharing does not apply to the additional benefits. In addition, individuals enrolled in both a qualified health plan and a pediatric dental plan may not receive a cost-sharing subsidy for the pediatric dental benefits that are included in the essential health benefits required to be provided by the qualified health plan. Cost-sharing subsidies, and any amounts that are attributable to them, cannot be used to pay for abortions for which federal funding is prohibited.

The Secretary of HHS must establish a program for determining whether individuals are eligible to claim a cost-sharing credit. The program must provide for the following: (1) the details of an individual's application process; (2) the details of how public entities are to make determinations of individuals' eligibility; (3) procedures for deeming individuals to be eligible; and, (4) procedures for allowing individuals with limited English proficiency proper access to exchanges.

In applying for enrollment, an individual claiming a cost-sharing subsidy is required to submit to the exchange income and family size information and information regarding changes in marital or family status or income. Personal information provided to the exchange is submitted to the Secretary of HHS. In turn, the Secretary of HHS submits the applicable information to the Social Security Commissioner, Homeland Security Secretary, and Treasury Secretary for verification purposes. The Secretary of HHS is notified of the results following verification, and notifies the exchange of such results. The provision specifies actions to be undertaken if inconsistencies are found. The Secretary of HHS, in consultation with the Treasury Secretary, Homeland Security Secretary, and Social Security Commissioner, must establish procedures for appealing determinations resulting from the verification process, and redetermining eligibility on a periodic basis.

The Secretary notifies the plan that the individual is eligible and the plan reduces the cost-sharing by reducing the out-of-pocket limit under the provision. The plan notifies the Secretary of cost-sharing reductions and the Secretary makes periodic and timely payments to the plan equal to the value of the reductions in cost-sharing. The provision authorizes the Secretary to establish a capitated payment system with appropriate risk adjustments.

An employer must be notified if one of its employees is determined to be eligible for a cost-sharing subsidy. The notice must include information about the employer's potential liability

---

[42] Section 1401 of the Senate amendment.

[43] As defined in section 1302(b) of the Senate amendment.

for payments under section 4980H and explicit notice that hiring, terminating, or otherwise discriminating against an employee because he or she received a credit or subsidy is in violation of the Fair Labor Standards Act.[44] An employer is generally not entitled to information about its employees who qualify for the premium assistance credit or the cost-sharing subsidy. Employers may, however, be notified of the name of an employee and whether his or her income is above or below the threshold used to measure the affordability of the employer's health insurance coverage.

The Secretary of the Treasury is informed of the name and employer identification number of every employer that has one or more employee receiving a cost-sharing subsidy.

The provision implements special rules for Indians (as defined by the Indian Health Care Improvement Act) and undocumented aliens.

The provision prohibits cost-sharing reductions for individuals who are not lawfully present in the United States, and such individuals are not taken into account in determining the family size involved.

The provision defines any term used in this section that is also used by section 36B as having the same meaning as defined by the latter. The provision also denies subsidies to dependents, with respect to whom a deduction under section 151 is allowable to another taxpayer for a taxable year beginning in the calendar year in which the individual's taxable year begins. Further, the provision does not permit a subsidy for any month that is not treated as a coverage month.

Effective Date

The provision is effective on date of enactment.

[CCH Explanation at ¶ 520.]

[¶ 10,050] Act Sec. 1414. Disclosures to carry out eligibility requirements for certain programs[45]

Joint Committee on Taxation (J.C.T. Rep. No. JCX-18-10)

[Code Sec. 6103]

Present Law

Section 6103 provides that returns and return information are confidential and may not be disclosed by the IRS, other Federal employees, State employees, and certain others having access to such information except as provided in the Internal Revenue Code. Section 6103 contains a number of exceptions to the general rule of nondisclosure that authorize disclosure in specifically identified circumstances. For example, section 6103 provides for the disclosure of certain return information for purposes of establishing the appropriate amount of any Medicare Part B premium subsidy adjustment.

Section 6103(p)(4) requires, as a condition of receiving returns and return information, that Federal and State agencies (and certain other recipients) provide safeguards as prescribed by the Secretary of the Treasury by regulation to be necessary or appropriate to protect the confidentiality of returns or return information. Unauthorized disclosure of a return or return information is a felony punishable by a fine not exceeding

$5,000 or imprisonment of not more than five years, or both, together with the costs of prosecution.[46] The unauthorized inspection of a return or return information is punishable by a fine not exceeding $1,000 or imprisonment of not more than one year, or both, together with the costs of prosecution.[47] An action for civil damages also may be brought for unauthorized disclosure or inspection.[48]

Explanation of Provision

Individuals will submit income information to an exchange as part of an application process in order to claim the cost-sharing reduction and the tax credit on an advance basis. The Department of HHS serves as the centralized verification agency for information submitted by individuals to the exchanges with respect to the reduction and the tax credit to the extent provided on an advance basis. The IRS is permitted to substantiate the accuracy of income information that has been provided to HHS for eligibility determination.

Specifically, upon written request of the Secretary of HHS, the IRS is permitted to disclose

---

[44] Pub. Law No. 75-718.

[45] Section 1414 of the Senate amendment is amended by section 1004 of the Reconciliation bill.

[46] Sec. 7213.

[47] Sec. 7213A.

[48] Sec. 7431.

the following return information of any taxpayer whose income is relevant in determining the amount of the tax credit or cost-sharing reduction, or eligibility for participation in the specified State health subsidy programs (i.e., a State Medicaid program under title XIX of the Social Security Act, a State's children's health insurance program under title XXI of such Act, or a basic health program under section 2228 of such Act): (1) taxpayer identity; (2) the filing status of such taxpayer; (3) the modified adjusted gross income (as defined in new sec. 36B of the Code) of such taxpayer, the taxpayer's spouse and of any dependants who are required to file a tax return; (4) such other information as is prescribed by Treasury regulation as might indicate whether such taxpayer is eligible for the credit or subsidy (and the amount thereof); and (5) the taxable year with respect to which the preceding information relates, or if applicable, the fact that such information is not available. HHS is permitted to disclose to an exchange or its contractors, or to the State agency administering the health subsidy programs referenced above (and their contractors) any inconsistency between the information submitted and IRS records.

The disclosed return information may be used only for the purposes of, and only to the extent necessary in, establishing eligibility for participation in the exchange, verifying the appropriate amount of the tax credit, and cost-sharing subsidy, or eligibility for the specified State health subsidy programs.

Recipients of the confidential return information are subject to the safeguard protections and civil and criminal penalties for unauthorized disclosure and inspection. Special rules apply to the disclosure of return information to contractors.

The IRS is required to make an accounting for all disclosures.

Effective Date

The provision is effective on date of enactment.

[Law at ¶5270 and ¶5285. CCH Explanation at ¶425.]

[¶10,060] Act Sec. 1415. Premium tax credit and cost-sharing reduction payments disregarded for federal and federally assisted programs

Joint Committee on Taxation (J.C.T. REP. No. JCX-18-10)

[Act Sec. 1415]

Present Law

There is no tax credit that is generally available to low or middle income individuals or families for the purchase of health insurance.

Explanation of Provision

Any premium assistance tax credits and cost-sharing subsidies provided to an individual under the Senate amendment are disregarded for purposes of determining that individual's eligibility for benefits or assistance, or the amount or extent of benefits and assistance, under any Federal program or under any State or local pro-

gram financed in whole or in part with Federal funds. Specifically, any amount of premium tax credit provided to an individual is not counted as income, and cannot be taken into account as resources for the month of receipt and the following two months. Any cost sharing subsidy provided on the individual's behalf is treated as made to the health plan in which the individual is enrolled and not to the individual.

Effective Date
The provision is effective on date of enactment.

[CCH Explanation at ¶210.]

[¶10,070] Act Sec. 1421. Small business tax credit[49]

Joint Committee on Taxation (J.C.T. Rep. No. JCX-18-10)

[New Code Sec. 45R]

Present Law

The Code does not provide a tax credit for employers that provide health coverage for their employees. The cost to an employer of providing health coverage for its employees is generally deductible as an ordinary and necessary business expense for employee compensation.[50] In addition, the value of employer-provided health insurance is not subject to employer-paid Federal Insurance Contributions Act ("FICA") tax.

The Code generally provides that employees are not taxed on the value of employer-provided health coverage under an accident or health plan.[51] That is, these benefits are excluded from gross income. In addition, medical care provided under an accident or health plan for employees, their spouses, and their dependents generally is excluded from gross income.[52] Active employees participating in a cafeteria plan may be able to pay their share of premiums on a pre-tax basis through salary reduction.[53] Such salary reduction contributions are treated as employer contributions and thus also are excluded from gross income.

Explanation of Provisions

Small business employers eligible for the credit

Under the provision, a tax credit is provided for a qualified small employer for nonelective contributions to purchase health insurance for its employees. A qualified small business employer for this purpose generally is an employer with no more than 25 full-time equivalent employees ("FTEs") employed during the employer's taxable year, and whose employees have annual full-time equivalent wages that average no more than $50,000. However, the full amount of the credit is available only to an employer with 10 or fewer FTEs and whose employees have average annual fulltime equivalent wages from the employer of less than $25,000. These wage limits are indexed to the Consumer Price Index for Urban

Consumers ("CPI-U") for years beginning in 2014.

Under the provision, an employer's FTEs are calculated by dividing the total hours worked by all employees during the employer's tax year by 2080. For this purpose, the maximum number of hours that are counted for any single employee is 2080 (rounded down to the nearest whole number). Wages are defined in the same manner as under section 3121(a) (as determined for purposes of FICA taxes but without regard to the dollar limit for covered wages) and the average wage is determined by dividing the total wages paid by the small employer by the number of FTEs (rounded down to the nearest $1,000).

The number of hours of service worked by, and wages paid to, a seasonal worker of an employer is not taken into account in determining the full-time equivalent employees and average annual wages of the employer unless the worker works for the employer on more than 120 days during the taxable year. For purposes of the credit the term 'seasonal worker' means a worker who performs labor or services on a seasonal basis as defined by the Secretary of Labor, including workers covered by 29 CFR sec. 500.20(s)(1) and retail workers employed exclusively during holiday seasons.

The contributions must be provided under an arrangement that requires the eligible small employer to make a nonelective contribution on behalf of each employee who enrolls in certain defined qualifying health insurance offered to employees by the employer equal to a uniform percentage (not less than 50 percent) of the premium cost of the qualifying health plan.

The credit is only available to offset actual tax liability and is claimed on the employer's tax return. The credit is not payable in advance to the taxpayer or refundable. Thus, the employer must pay the employees' premiums during the year and claim the credit at the end of the year on its income tax return. The credit is a general

---

[49] Section 1421 of the Senate amendment is amended by section 10105 of the Senate amendment.

[50] Sec. 162. However, see special rules in sections 419 and 419A for the deductibility of contributions to welfare benefit plans with respect to medical benefits for employees and their dependents.

[51] Sec 106.
[52] Sec. 105(b).
[53] Sec. 125.

business credit, and can be carried back for one year and carried forward for 20 years. The credit is available for tax liability under the alternative minimum tax.

Years the credit is available

Under the provision, the credit is initially available for any taxable year beginning in 2010, 2011, 2012, or 2013. Qualifying health insurance for claiming the credit for this first phase of the credit is health insurance coverage within the meaning of section 9832, which is generally health insurance coverage purchased from an insurance company licensed under State law.

For taxable years beginning in years after 2013, the credit is only available to a qualified small employer that purchases health insurance coverage for its employees through a State exchange and is only available for a maximum coverage period of two consecutive taxable years beginning with the first year in which the employer or any predecessor first offers one or more qualified plans to its employees through an exchange.[54]

The maximum two-year coverage period does not take into account any taxable years beginning in years before 2014. Thus a qualified small employer could potentially qualify for this credit for six taxable years, four years under the first phase and two years under the second phase.

Calculation of credit amount

The credit is equal to the applicable percentage of the small business employer's contribution to the health insurance premium for each covered employee. Only nonelective contributions by the employer are taken into account in calculating the credit. Therefore, any amount contributed pursuant to a salary reduction arrangement under a cafeteria plan within the meaning of section 125 is not treated as an employer contribution for purposes of this credit. The credit is equal to the lesser of the following two amounts multiplied an applicable tax credit percentage: (1) the amount of contributions the employer made on behalf of the employees during the taxable year for the qualifying health coverage and (2) the amount of contributions that the employer would have made during the taxable year if each employee had enrolled in coverage with a small business benchmark premium. To calculate such contributions under the second of these two amounts, the benchmark

premium is multiplied by the number of employees enrolled in coverage and then multiplied by the uniform percentage that applies for calculating the level of coverage selected by the employer. As discussed above, this tax credit is only available if this uniform percentage is at least 50 percent.

For the first phase of the credit (any taxable years beginning in 2010, 2011, 2012, or 2013), the applicable tax credit percentage is 35 percent. The benchmark premium is the average total premium cost in the small group market for employer-sponsored coverage in the employer's State. The premium and the benchmark premium vary based on the type of coverage provided to the employee (i.e., single, adult with child, family or two adults).

For taxable years beginning in years after 2013, the applicable tax credit percentage is 50 percent. The benchmark premium is the average total premium cost in the small group market for employer-sponsored coverage in the employer's State. The premium and the benchmark premium vary based on the type of coverage being provided to the employee (e.g. single or family).

The credit is reduced for employers with more than 10 FTEs but not more than 25 FTEs. The credit is also reduced for an employer for whom the average wages per employee is between $25,000 and $50,000. The amount of this reduction is equal to the amount of the credit (determined before any reduction) multiplied by a fraction, the numerator of which is the average annual wages of the employer in excess of $25,000 and the denominator is $25,000. For an employer with more than 10 FTEs, the percentage is reduced in proportion to the number of FTEs in excess of 10. For an employer with both more than 10 FTEs and average annual wages in excess of $25,000, the reduction is the sum of the amount of the two reductions.

Tax exempt organizations as qualified small employers

Any organization described in section 501(c) which is exempt under section 501(a) that otherwise qualifies for the small business tax credit is eligible to receive the credit. However, for tax-exempt organizations, the applicable percentage for the credit during the first phase of the credit (any taxable year beginning in 2010, 2011, 2012, or 2013) is limited to 25 percent and the applicable percentage for the credit during the second

---

[54] Sec. 1301 of the Senate amendment provides the requirements for a qualified health plan purchased through the exchange.

phase (taxable years beginning in years after 2013) is limited to 35 percent. The small business tax credit is otherwise calculated in the same manner for tax-exempt organizations that are qualified small employers as the tax credit is calculated for all other qualified small employers. Tax-exempt organizations are eligible to apply the tax credit against the organization's liability as an employer for payroll taxes for the taxable year to the extent of: (1) the amount of income tax withheld from its employees under section 3401(a); (2) the amount of hospital insurance tax withheld from its employees under section 3101(b); (3) and the amount of the hospital tax imposed on the organization under section 3111(b). However, the organization is not eligible for a credit in excess of the amount of these payroll taxes.

Special rules

The employer is entitled to a deduction under section 162 equal to the amount of the employer contribution minus the dollar amount of the credit. For example, if a qualified small employer pays 100 percent of the cost of its employees' health insurance coverage and the tax credit under this provision is 50 percent of that cost, the employer is able to claim a section 162 deduction for the other 50 percent of the premium cost.

The employer is determined by applying the employer aggregations rules in section 414(b), (c), and (m). In addition, the definition of employee includes a leased employee within the meaning of section 414(n).[55]

Self-employed individuals, including partners and sole proprietors, two percent shareholders of an S Corporation, and five percent owners of the employer (within the meaning of section 416(i)(1)(B)(i)) are not treated as employees for purposes of this credit. Any employee with respect to a self employed individual is not an employee of the employer for purposes of this credit if the employee is not performing services in the trade or business of the employer. Thus, the credit is not available for a domestic employee of a sole proprietor of a business. There is also a special rule to prevent sole proprietorships from receiving the credit for the owner and their family members. Thus, no credit is available for any contribution to the purchase of health insurance for these individuals and the individual is not taken into account in determining the number of FTEs or average full-time equivalent wages.

The Secretary of is directed to prescribe such regulations as may be necessary to carry out the provisions of new section 45R, including regulations to prevent the avoidance of the two-year limit on the credit period for the second phase of the credit through the use of successor entities and the use of the limit on the number of employees and the amount of average wages through the use of multiple entities. The Secretary of Treasury, in consultation with the Secretary of Labor, is directed to prescribe such regulations, rules, and guidance as may be necessary to determine the hours of service of an employee for purposes of determining FTEs, including rules for the employees who are not compensated on an hourly basis.

Effective Date

The provision is effective for taxable years beginning after December 31, 2009.

[Law at ¶5055, ¶5060, ¶5130 and ¶5150. CCH Explanation at ¶310.]

---

[55] Section 414(b) provides that, for specified employee benefit purposes, all employees of all corporations which are members of a controlled group of corporations are treated as employed by a single employer. There is a similar rule in section 414(c) under which all employees of trades or businesses (whether or not incorporated) which are under common are treated under regulations as employed by a single employer, and, in section 414(m), under which employees of an affiliated service group (as defined in that section) are treated as employed by a single employer. Section 414(n) provides that leased employees, as defined in that section, are treated as employees of the service recipient for specified purposes. Section 414(o) authorizes the Treasury to issue regulations to prevent avoidance of the certain requirement under section 414(m) and 414(n).

[¶ 10,080] Act Sec. 1501. Excise tax on individuals without essential health benefits coverage[56]

Joint Committee on Taxation (J.C.T. Rep. No. JCX-18-10)

[New Code Sec. 5000A]

Present Law

Federal law does not require individuals to have health insurance. Only the Commonwealth of Massachusetts, through its statewide program, requires that individuals have health insurance (although this policy has been considered in other states, such as California, Maryland, Maine, and Washington). All adult residents of Massachusetts are required to have health insurance that meets "minimum creditable coverage" standards if it is deemed "affordable" at their income level under a schedule set by the board of the Commonwealth Health Insurance Connector Authority ("Connector"). Individuals report their insurance status on State income tax forms. Individuals can file hardship exemptions from the mandate; persons for whom there are no affordable insurance options available are not subject to the requirement for insurance coverage.

For taxable year 2007, an individual without insurance and who was not exempt from the requirement did not qualify under Massachusetts law for a State income tax personal exemption. For taxable years beginning on or after January 1, 2008, a penalty is levied for each month an individual is without insurance. The penalty consists of an amount up to 50 percent of the lowest premium available to the individual through the Connector. The penalty is reported and paid by the individual with the individual's Massachusetts State income tax return at the same time and in the same manner as State income taxes. Failure to pay the penalty results in the same interest and penalties as apply to unpaid income tax.

Explanation of Provision

Personal responsibility requirement

Beginning January, 2014, non-exempt U.S. citizens and legal residents are required to maintain minimum essential coverage. Minimum essential coverage includes government sponsored programs, eligible employer-sponsored plans, plans in the individual market, grandfathered group health plans and other coverage as recognized by the Secretary of HHS in coordination with the Secretary of the Treasury. Government sponsored programs include Medicare, Medicaid, Children's Health Insurance Program, coverage for members of the U.S. military,[57] veterans health care,[58] and health care for Peace Corps volunteers.[59] Eligible employer-sponsored plans include: governmental plans,[60] church plans,[61] grandfathered plans and other group health plans offered in the small or large group market within a State. Minimum essential coverage does not include coverage that consists of certain HIPAA excepted benefits.[62] Other HIPAA excepted benefits that do not constitute minimum essential coverage if offered under a separate policy, certificate or contract of insurance include long term care, limited scope dental and vision benefits, coverage for a disease or specified illness, hospital indemnity or other fixed indemnity insurance or Medicare supplemental health insurance.[63]

Individuals are exempt from the requirement for months they are incarcerated, not legally present in the United States or maintain religious exemptions. Those who are exempt from the requirement due to religious reasons must be members of a recognized religious sect exempting them from self employment taxes[64]

---

[56] Section 1501 of the Senate amendment, as amended by section 10106, is further amended by section 1002 of the Reconciliation bill.

[57] 10 U.S.C. 55 and 38 U.S.C. 1781.

[58] 38 U.S.C. 17.

[59] 22 U.S.C. 2504(e).

[60] ERISA Sec. 3(32), U.S.C. 5: Chapter 89, except a plan described in paragraph (1)(A).

[61] ERISA sec. 3(33).

[62] U.S.C. 42 sec. 300gg-91(c)(1). HIPAA excepted benefits include: (1) coverage only for accident, or disability income

insurance; (2) coverage issued as a supplement to liability insurance; (3) liability insurance, including general liability insurance and automobile liability insurance; (4) workers' compensation or similar insurance; (5) automobile medical payment insurance; (6) credit-only insurance; (7) coverage for on-site medical clinics; and (8) other similar insurance coverage, specified in regulations, under which benefits for medical care are secondary or incidental to other insurance benefits.

[63] 42 U.S.C. 300gg-91(c)(2-4).

[64] Sec. 1402(g)(1).

and adhere to tenets of the sect. Individuals residing[65] outside of the United States are deemed to maintain minimum essential coverage. If an individual is a dependent[66] of another taxpayer, the other taxpayer is liable for any penalty payment with respect to the individual.

Penalty

Individuals who fail to maintain minimum essential coverage in 2016 are subject to a penalty equal to the greater of: (1) 2.5 percent of household income in excess of the taxpayer's household income for the taxable year over the threshold amount of income required for income tax return filing for that taxpayer under section 6012(a)(1);[67] or (2) $695 per uninsured adult in the household. The fee for an uninsured individual under age 18 is one-half of the adult fee for an adult. The total household penalty may not exceed 300 percent of the per adult penalty ($2,085). The total annual household payment may not exceed the national average annual premium for bronze level health plan offered through the Exchange that year for the household size.

This per adult annual penalty is phased in as follows: $95 for 2014; $325 for 2015; and $695 in 2016. For years after 2016, the $695 amount is indexed to CPI-U, rounded to the next lowest $50. The percentage of income is phased in as follows: one percent for 2014; two percent in 2015; and 2.5 percent beginning after 2015. If a taxpayer files a joint return, the individual and spouse are jointly liable for any penalty payment.

The penalty applies to any period the individual does not maintain minimum essential coverage and is determined monthly. The penalty is assessed through the Code and accounted for as an additional amount of Federal tax owed. However, it is not subject to the enforcement provisions of subtitle F of the Code.[68] The use of liens and seizures otherwise authorized for collection of taxes does not apply to the collection of this penalty. Non-compliance with the personal responsibility requirement to have health coverage is not subject to criminal or civil penalties under the Code and interest does not accrue for failure to pay such assessments in a timely manner.

Individuals who cannot afford coverage because their required contribution for employer-sponsored coverage or the lowest cost bronze plan in the local Exchange exceeds eight percent of household income for the year are exempt from the penalty.[69] In years after 2014, the eight percent exemption is increased by the amount by which premium growth exceeds income growth. If self-only coverage is affordable to an employee, but family coverage is unaffordable, the employee is subject to the mandate penalty if the employee does not maintain minimum essential coverage. However, any individual eligible for employer coverage due to a relationship with an employee (e.g. spouse or child of employee) is exempt from the penalty if that individual does not maintain minimum essential coverage because family coverage is not affordable[70] (i.e., exceeds eight percent of household income). Taxpayers with income below the income tax filing threshold[71] shall also be exempt from the penalty for failure to maintain minimum essential coverage. All members of Indian tribes[72] are exempt from the penalty.

No penalty is assessed for individuals who do not maintain health insurance for a period of

---

[65] Sec. 911(d)(1).

[66] Sec. 152.

[67] Generally, in 2010, the filing threshold is $9,350 for a single person or a married person filing separately and is $18,700 for married filing jointly. IR-2009-93, Oct. 15, 2009.

[68] IRS authority to assess and collect taxes is generally provided in subtitle F, "Procedure and Administration" in the Code. That subtitle establishes the rules governing both how taxpayers are required to report information to the IRS and pay their taxes as well as their rights. It also establishes the duties and authority of the IRS to enforce the Code, including civil and criminal penalties.

[69] In the case of an individual participating in a salary reduction arrangement, the taxpayer's household income is increased by any exclusion from gross income for any portion of the required contribution to the premium. The required contribution to the premium is the individual contribution to coverage through an employer or in the purchase of a bronze plan through the Exchange.

[70] For example, if an employee with a family is offered self-only coverage costing five percent of income and family coverage costing 10 percent of income, the employee is not eligible for the tax credit in the Exchange because self-only coverage costs less than 9.5 percent of household income. The employee is not exempt from the individual responsibility penalty on the grounds of an affordability exemption because the self-only plan costs less than eight percent of income. Although family coverage costs more than 9.5 percent of income, the family does not qualify for a tax credit regardless of whether the employee purchases self-only coverage or does not purchase self-only coverage through the employer. However, if the family of the employee does not maintain minimum essential benefits coverage, the employee's family is exempt from the individual mandate penalty because while self-only coverage is affordable to the employee, family coverage is not considered affordable.

[71] Generally, in 2010, the filing threshold is $9,350 for a single person or a married person filing separately and is $18,700 for married filing jointly. IR-2009-93, Oct. 15, 2009.

[72] Tribal membership is defined in section 45A(c)(6).

three months or less during the taxable year. If an individual exceeds the three month maximum during the taxable year, the penalty for the full duration of the gap during the year is applied. If there are multiple gaps in coverage during a calendar year, the exemption from penalty applies only to the first such gap in coverage. The Secretary of the Treasury shall provide rules when a coverage gap includes months in multiple calendar years. Individuals may also apply to the Secretary of HHS for a hardship exemption due to hardship in obtaining coverage.[73] Residents of the possessions[74] of the United States are treated as being covered by acceptable coverage.

Family size is the number of individuals for whom the taxpayer is allowed a personal exemption. Household income is the sum of the modified adjusted gross incomes of the taxpayer and all individuals accounted for in the family size required to file a tax return for that year. Modified adjusted gross income means adjusted gross income increased by all tax-exempt interest and foreign earned income.[75]

Effective Date

The provision is effective for taxable years beginning after December 31, 2013.

[Law at ¶ 5235. CCH Explanation at ¶ 205.]

[¶ 10,090] Act Sec. 1502. Reporting of health insurance coverage

Joint Committee on Taxation (J.C.T. Rep. No. JCX-18-10)

[Code Sec. 6724(d) and New Code Sec. 6055]

Present Law

Insurer reporting of health insurance coverage

No provision.

Penalties for failure to comply with information reporting requirements

Present law imposes a variety of information reporting requirements on participants in certain transactions.[76] These requirements are intended to assist taxpayers in preparing their income tax returns and help the IRS determine whether such returns are correct and complete. Failure to comply with the information reporting requirements may result in penalties, including: a penalty for failure to file the information return,[77] a penalty for failure to furnish payee statements,[78] and a penalty for failure to comply with various other reporting requirements.[79]

The penalty for failure to file an information return generally is $50 for each return for which such failure occurs. The total penalty imposed on a person for all failures during a calendar year cannot exceed $250,000. Additionally, special rules apply to reduce the per-failure and maximum penalty where the failure is corrected within a specified period.

The penalty for failure to provide a correct payee statement is $50 for each statement with respect to which such failure occurs, with the total penalty for a calendar year not to exceed $100,000. Special rules apply that increase the per-statement and total penalties where there is intentional disregard of the requirement to furnish a payee statement.

Explanation of Provision

Under the provision, insurers (including employers who self-insure) that provide minimum essential coverage[80] to any individual during a calendar year must report certain health insurance coverage information to both the covered individual and to the IRS. In the case of coverage provided by a governmental unit, or any agency or instrumentality thereof, the reporting requirement applies to the person or employee who enters into the agreement to provide the health insurance coverage (or their designee).

The information required to be reported includes: (1) the name, address, and taxpayer identification number of the primary insured, and the name and taxpayer identification number of each other individual obtaining coverage under

---

[73] Sec. 1311(d)(4)(H).

[74] Sec. 937(a).

[75] Sec. 911.

[76] Secs. 6031 through 6060.

[77] Sec. 6721.

[78] Sec. 6722.

[79] Sec. 6723. The penalty for failure to comply timely with a specified information reporting requirement is $50 per failure, not to exceed $100,000 for a calendar year.

[80] As defined in section 5000A of the Senate amendment, as amended by section 10106, as further amended by section 1002 of the Reconciliation bill.

the policy; (2) the dates during which the individual was covered under the policy during the calendar year; (3) whether the coverage is a qualified health plan offered through an exchange; (4) the amount of any premium tax credit or cost-sharing reduction received by the individual with respect to such coverage; and (5) such other information as the Secretary may require.

To the extent health insurance coverage is through an employer-provided group health plan, the insurer is also required to report the name, address and employer identification number of the employer, the portion of the premium, if any, required to be paid by the employer, and any other information the Secretary may require to administer the new tax credit for eligible small employers.

The insurer is required to report the above information, along with the name, address and contact information of the reporting insurer, to the covered individual on or before January 31 of the year following the calendar year for which the information is required to be reported to the IRS.

The provision amends the information reporting provisions of the Code to provide that an insurer who fails to comply with these new reporting requirements is subject to the penalties for failure to file an information return and failure to furnish payee statements, respectively.

The IRS is required, not later than June 30 of each year, in consultation with the Secretary of HHS, to provide annual notice to each individual who files an income tax return and who fails to enroll in minimum essential coverage. The notice is required to include information on the services available through the exchange operating in the individual's State of residence.

Effective Date

The provision is effective for calendar years beginning after 2013.

[Law at ¶ 5235, ¶ 5260, ¶ 5280 and ¶ 7015. CCH Explanation at ¶ 410.]

[¶ 10,100] Act Sec. 1513. Shared responsibility for employers[81]

Joint Committee on Taxation (J.C.T. REP. NO. JCX-18-10)

[New Code Sec. 4980H]

Present Law

Currently, there is no Federal requirement that employers offer health insurance coverage to employees or their families. However, as with other compensation, the cost of employer-provided health coverage is a deductible business expense under section 162 of the Code.[82] In addition, employer-provided health insurance coverage is generally not included in an employee's gross income.[83]

Employees participating in a cafeteria plan may be able to pay the portion of premiums for health insurance coverage not otherwise paid for by their employers on a pre-tax basis through salary reduction.[84] Such salary reduction contributions are treated as employer contributions for purposes of the Code, and are thus excluded from gross income.

One way that employers can offer employer-provided health insurance coverage for purposes of the tax exclusion is to offer to reimburse employees for the premiums for health insurance purchased by employees in the individual health insurance market. The payment or reimbursement of employees' substantiated individual health insurance premiums is excludible from employees' gross income.[85] This reimbursement for individual health insurance premiums can also be paid through salary reduction under a cafeteria plan.[86] However, this offer to reimburse individual health insurance premiums constitutes a group health plan

The Employee Retirement Income Security Act of 1974 ("ERISA")[87] preempts State law relating to certain employee benefit plans, including employer-sponsored health plans. While ERISA specifically provides that its preemption rule does not exempt or relieve any person from

---

[81] Section 1513 of the Senate amendment, as amended by section 10106, is further amended by section 1003 of the Reconciliation bill.

[82] Sec. 162. However see special rules in sections 419 and 419A for the deductibility of contributions to welfare benefit plans with respect to medical benefits for employees and their dependents.

[83] Sec. 106.

[84] Sec. 125.

[85] Rev. Rul. 61-146 (1961-2 CB 25).

[86] Proposed Treas. Reg. sec.1.125-1(m).

[87] Pub. L. 93-406

any State law which regulates insurance, ERISA also provides that an employee benefit plan is not deemed to be engaged in the business of insurance for purposes of any State law regulating insurance companies or insurance contracts. As a result of this ERISA preemption, self-insured employer-sponsored health plans need not provide benefits that are mandated under State insurance law.

While ERISA does not require an employer to offer health benefits, it does require compliance if an employer chooses to offer health benefits, such as compliance with plan fiduciary standards, reporting and disclosure requirements, and procedures for appealing denied benefit claims. There are other Federal requirements for health plans which include, for example, rules for health care continuation coverage.[88] The Code imposes an excise tax on group health plans that fail to meet these other requirements.[89] The excise tax generally is equal to $100 per day per failure during the period of noncompliance and is imposed on the employer sponsoring the plan.

Under Medicaid, States may establish "premium assistance" programs, which pay a Medicaid beneficiary's share of premiums for employer-sponsored health coverage. Besides being available to the beneficiary through his or her employer, the coverage must be comprehensive and cost-effective for the State. An individual's enrollment in an employer plan is considered cost-effective if paying the premiums, deductibles, coinsurance and other cost-sharing obligations of the employer plan is less expensive than the State's expected cost of directly providing Medicaid-covered services. States are also required to provide coverage for those Medicaid-covered services that are not included in the private plans. A 2007 analysis showed that 12 States had Medicaid premium assistance programs as authorized under current law.

Explanation of Provision

An applicable large employer that does not offer coverage for all its full-time employees, offers minimum essential coverage that is unaffordable, or offers minimum essential coverage that consists of a plan under which the plan's share of the total allowed cost of benefits is less than 60 percent, is required to pay a penalty if any full-time employee is certified to the employer as having purchased health insurance through a state exchange with respect to which a tax credit or cost-sharing reduction is allowed or paid to the employee.

Applicable large employer

An employer is an applicable large employer with respect to any calendar year if it employed an average of at least 50 full-time employees during the preceding calendar year. For purposes of the provision, "employer" includes any predecessor employer. An employer is not treated as employing more than 50 full-time employees if the employer's workforce exceeds 50 full-time employees for 120 days or fewer during the calendar year and the employees that cause the employer's workforce to exceed 50 full-time employees are seasonal workers. A seasonal worker is a worker who performs labor or services on a seasonal basis (as defined by the Secretary of Labor), including retail workers employed exclusively during the holiday season and workers whose employment is, ordinarily, the kind exclusively performed at certain seasons or periods of the year and which, from its nature, may not be continuous or carried on throughout the year.[90]

In counting the number of employees for purposes of determining whether an employer is an applicable large employer, a full-time employee (meaning, for any month, an employee working an average of at least 30 hours or more each week) is counted as one employee and all other employees are counted on a pro-rated basis in accordance with regulations prescribed by the Secretary. The number of full-time equivalent employees that must be taken into account for purposes of determining whether the employer exceeds the threshold is equal to the aggregate number of hours worked by non-full-time employees for the month, divided by 120 (or such other number based on an average of 30 hours of service each week as the Secretary may prescribe in regulations).

The Secretary, in consultation with the Secretary of Labor, is directed to issue, as necessary, rules, regulations and guidance to determine an employee's hours of service, including rules that

---

[88] These rules were added to ERISA and the Code by the Consolidated Omnibus Budget Reconciliation Act of 1985 (Pub. L. No. 99-272).

[89] Sec. 4980B.

[90] Section 500.20(s)(1) of title 29, Code of Federal Regulations. Under section 5000.20(s)(1), a worker who moves from one seasonal activity to another, while employed in agriculture or performing agricultural labor, is employed on a seasonal basis even though he may continue to be employed during a major portion of the year.

apply to employees who are not compensated on an hourly basis.

The aggregation rules of section 414(b), (c), (m), and (o) apply in determining whether an employer is an applicable large employer. The determination of whether an employer that was not in existence during the preceding calendar year is an applicable large employer is made based on the average number of employees that it is reasonably expected to employ on business days in the current calendar year.

Penalty for employers not offering coverage

An applicable large employer who fails to offer its full-time employees and their dependents the opportunity to enroll in minimum essential coverage under an employer-sponsored plan for any month is subject to a penalty if at least one of its full-time employees is certified to the employer as having enrolled in health insurance coverage purchased through a State exchange with respect to which a premium tax credit or cost-sharing reduction is allowed or paid to such employee or employees. The penalty for any month is an excise tax equal to the number of full-time employees over a 30-employee threshold during the applicable month (regardless of how many employees are receiving a premium tax credit or cost-sharing reduction) multiplied by one-twelfth of $2,000. In the case of persons treated as a single employer under the provision, the 30-employee reduction in full-time employees is made from the total number of full-time employees employed by such persons (i.e., only one 30-person reduction is permitted per controlled group of employers) and is allocated among such persons in relation to the number of full-time employees employed by each such person.

For example, in 2014, Employer A fails to offer minimum essential coverage and has 100 full-time employees, ten of whom receive a tax credit for the year for enrolling in a State exchange-offered plan. For each employee over the 30-employee threshold, the employer owes $2,000, for a total penalty of $140,000 ($2,000 multiplied by 70 ((100-30)). This penalty is assessed on a monthly basis.

For calendar years after 2014, the $2,000 dollar amount is increased by the percentage (if any) by which the average per capita premium for health insurance coverage in the United States for the preceding calendar year (as estimated by the Secretary of HHS no later than October 1 of the preceding calendar year) exceeds the average per capita premium for 2013

(as determined by the Secretary of HHS), rounded down to the nearest $10.

Penalty for employees receiving premium credits

An applicable large employer who offers, for any month, its full-time employees and their dependents the opportunity to enroll in minimum essential coverage under an employer-sponsored plan is subject to a penalty if any full-time employee is certified to the employer as having enrolled in health insurance coverage purchased through a State exchange with respect to which a premium tax credit or cost-sharing reduction is allowed or paid to such employee or employees.

The penalty is an excise tax that is imposed for each employee who receives a premium tax credit or cost-sharing reduction for health insurance purchased through a State exchange. For each full-time employee receiving a premium tax credit or cost-sharing subsidy through a State exchange for any month, the employer is required to pay an amount equal to one-twelfth of $3,000. The penalty for each employer for any month is capped at an amount equal to the number of full-time employees during the month (regardless of how many employees are receiving a premium tax credit or cost-sharing reduction) in excess of 30, multiplied by one-twelfth of $2,000. In the case of persons treated as a single employer under the provision, the 30-employee reduction in full-time employees for purposes of calculating the maximum penalty is made from the total number of full-time employees employed by such persons (i.e., only one 30-person reduction is permitted per controlled group of employers) and is allocated among such persons in relation to the number of full-time employees employed by each such person.

For example, in 2014, Employer A offers health coverage and has 100 full-time employees, 20 of whom receive a tax credit for the year for enrolling in a State exchange offered plan. For each employee receiving a tax credit, the employer owes $3,000, for a total penalty of $60,000. The maximum penalty for this employer is capped at the amount of the penalty that it would have been assessed for a failure to provide coverage, or $140,000 ($2,000 multiplied by 70 ((100-30)). Since the calculated penalty of $60,000 is less than the maximum amount, Employer A pays the $60,000 calculated penalty. This penalty is assessed on a monthly basis.

For calendar years after 2014, the $3,000 and $2,000 dollar amounts are increased by the percentage (if any) by which the average per capita premium for health insurance coverage in the United States for the preceding calendar year (as estimated by the Secretary of HHS no later than October 1 of the preceding calendar year) exceeds the average per capita premium for 2013 (as determined by the Secretary of HHS), rounded down to the nearest $10.

Time for payment, deductibility of excise taxes, restrictions on assessment

The excise taxes imposed under this provision are payable on an annual, monthly or other periodic basis as the Secretary of Treasury may prescribe. The excise taxes imposed under this provision for employees receiving premium tax credits are not deductible under section 162 as a business expense. The restrictions on assessment under section 6213 are not applicable to the excise taxes imposed under the provision.

Employer offer of health insurance coverage

Under the provision, as under current law, an employer is not required to offer health insurance coverage. If an employee is offered health insurance coverage by his or her employer and chooses to enroll in the coverage, the employer-provided portion of the coverage is excluded from gross income. The tax treatment is the same whether the employer offers coverage outside of a State exchange or the employer offers a coverage option through a State exchange.

Definition of coverage

As a general matter, if an employee is offered affordable minimum essential coverage under an employer-sponsored plan, the individual is ineligible for a premium tax credit and cost sharing reductions for health insurance purchased through a State exchange.

Unaffordable coverage

If an employee is offered minimum essential coverage by their employer that is either unaffordable or that consists of a plan under which the plan's share of the total allowed cost of benefits is less than 60 percent, however, the employee is eligible for a premium tax credit and cost sharing reductions, but only if the employee declines to enroll in the coverage and purchases coverage through the exchange instead. Unaffordable is defined as coverage with a premium required to be paid by the employee that is more than 9.5 percent of the employee's household income (as defined for purposes of the premium tax credits provided under the Senate amendment). This percentage of the employee's income is indexed to the per capita growth in premiums for the insured market as determined by the

Secretary of HHS. The employee must seek an affordability waiver from the State exchange and provide information as to family income and the lowest cost employer option offered to them. The State exchange then provides the waiver to the employee. The employer penalty applies for any employee(s) receiving an affordability waiver.

For purposes of determining if coverage is unaffordable, required salary reduction contributions are treated as payments required to be made by the employee. However, if an employee is reimbursed by the employer for any portion of the premium for health insurance coverage purchased through the exchange, including any reimbursement through salary reduction contributions under a cafeteria plan, the coverage is employer-provided and the employee is not eligible for premium tax credits or cost-sharing reductions. Thus, an individual is not permitted to purchase coverage through the exchange, apply for the premium tax credit, and pay for the individual's portion of the premium using salary reduction contributions under the cafeteria plan of the individual's employer.

An employer must be notified if one of its employees is determined to be eligible for a premium assistance credit or a cost-sharing reduction because the employer does not provide minimal essential coverage through an employer-sponsored plan, or the employer does offer such coverage but it is not affordable or the plan's share of the total allowed cost of benefits is less than 60 percent. The notice must include information about the employer's potential liability for payments under section 4980H. The employer must also receive notification of the appeals process established for employers notified of potential liability for payments under section 4980H. An employer is generally not entitled to information about its employees who qualify for the premium assistance credit or cost-sharing reductions; however, the appeals process must provide an employer the opportunity to access the data used to make the determination of an employee's eligibility for a premium assistance credit or cost-sharing reduction, to the extent allowable by law.

The Secretary is required to prescribe rules, regulations or guidance for the repayment of any assessable payment (including interest) if the payment is based on the allowance or payment of a premium tax credit or cost-sharing reduction with respect to an employee that is subsequently disallowed and with respect to which the assessable payment would not have been required to have been made in the absence of the allowance or payment.

Effect of medicaid enrollment

A Medicaid-eligible individual can always choose to leave the employer's coverage and enroll in Medicaid, and an employer is not required to pay a penalty for any employees enrolled in Medicaid.

Study and reporting on employer responsibility requirements

The Secretary of Labor is required to study whether employee wages are reduced by reason of the application of the employer responsibility requirements, using the National Compensation Survey published by the Bureau of Labor Statistics. The Secretary of Labor is to report the results of this study to the Committee on Ways and Means of the House of Representatives and the Committee on Finance of the Senate.

Effective Date

The provision is effective for months beginning after December 31, 2013.

[Law at ¶ 5225 and ¶ 7018. CCH Explanation at ¶ 305.]

[¶ 10,110] Act Sec. 1514. Reporting of employer health insurance coverage

Joint Committee on Taxation (J.C.T. REP. No. JCX-18-10)

[Code Sec. 6274(d) and New Code Sec. 6056]

Present Law

Employer reporting of health insurance coverage

No provision.

Penalties for failure to comply with information reporting requirements

Present law imposes a variety of information reporting requirements on participants in certain transactions.[91] These requirements are intended to assist taxpayers in preparing their income tax returns and help the IRS determine whether such returns are correct and complete. Failure to comply with the information reporting requirements may result in penalties, including: a penalty for failure to file the information return,[92] a penalty for failure to furnish payee statements,[93] and a penalty for failure to comply with various other reporting requirements.[94]

The penalty for failure to file an information return generally is $50 for each return for which such failure occurs. The total penalty imposed on a person for all failures during a calendar year cannot exceed $250,000. Additionally, special rules apply to reduce the per-failure and maximum penalty where the failure is corrected within a specified period.

The penalty for failure to provide a correct payee statement is $50 for each statement with respect to which such failure occurs, with the total penalty for a calendar year not to exceed $100,000. Special rules apply that increase the per-statement and total penalties where there is intentional disregard of the requirement to furnish a payee statement.

Explanation of Provision

Under the provision, each applicable large employer subject to the employer responsibility provisions of new section 4980H and each "offering employer" must report certain health insurance coverage information to both its full-time employees and to the IRS. An offering employer is any employer who offers minimum essential coverage[95] to its employees under an eligible employer-sponsored plan and who pays any portion of the costs of such plan, but only if the required employer contribution of any employee exceeds eight percent of the wages paid by the employer to the employee. In the case of years after 2014, the eight percent is indexed to reflect the rate of premium growth over income growth between 2013 and the preceding calendar year. In the case of coverage provided by a governmental unit, or any agency or instrumentality thereof, the reporting requirement applies to the person or employee appropriately designated for

---

[91] Secs. 6031 through 6060.

[92] Sec. 6721.

[93] Sec. 6722.

[94] Sec. 6723. The penalty for failure to comply timely with a specified information reporting requirement is $50 per failure, not to exceed $100,000 for a calendar year.

[95] As defined in section 5000A of the Senate amendment, as amended by section 10106, as further amended by section 1002 of the Reconciliation bill.

purposes of making the returns and statements required by the provision.

The information required to be reported includes: (1) the name, address and employer identification number of the employer; (2) a certification as to whether the employer offers its full-time employees and their dependents the opportunity to enroll in minimum essential coverage under an eligible employer-sponsored plan; (3) the number of full-time employees of the employer for each month during the calendar year; (4) the name, address and taxpayer identification number of each full-time employee employed by the employer during the calendar year and the number of months, if any, during which the employee (and any dependents) was covered under a plan sponsored by the employer during the calendar year; and (5) such other information as the Secretary may require.

Employers who offer the opportunity to enroll in minimum essential coverage must also report: (1) in the case of an applicable large employer, the length of any waiting period with respect to such coverage; (2) the months during the calendar year during which the coverage was available; (3) the monthly premium for the lowest cost option in each of the enrollment categories under the plan; (4) the employer's share of the total allowed costs of benefits under the plan; and (5), in the case of an offering employer, the option for which the employer pays the largest position of the cost of the plan and the portion of the cost paid by the employer in each of the enrollment categories under each option.

The employer is required to report to each full-time employee the above information required to be reported with respect to that employee, along with the name, address and contact information of the reporting employer, on or before January 31 of the year following the calendar year for which the information is required to be reported to the IRS.

The provision amends the information reporting provisions of the Code to provide that an employer who fails to comply with these new reporting requirements is subject to the penalties for failure to file an information return and failure to furnish payee statements, respectively.

To the maximum extent feasible, the Secretary may provide that any information return or payee statement required to be provided under the provision may be provided as part of any return or statement required under new sections 6051[96] or 6055[97] and, in the case of an applicable large employer or offering employer offering health insurance coverage of a health insurance issuer, the employer may enter into an agreement with the issuer to include the information required by the provision with the information return and payee statement required under new section 6055.

The Secretary has the authority, in coordination with the Secretary of Labor, to review the accuracy of the information reported by the employer, including the employer's share of the total allowed costs of benefits under the plan.

Effective Date

The provision is effective for periods beginning after December 31, 2013.

[Law at ¶5265 and ¶5280. CCH Explanation at ¶415.]

[¶10,120] Act Sec. 1515. Offering of qualified health plans through cafeteria plans

Joint Committee on Taxation (J.C.T. Rep. No. JCX-18-10)

[Code Sec. 125]

Present Law

Currently, there is no Federal requirement that employers offer health insurance coverage to employees or their families. However, as with other compensation, the cost of employer-provided health coverage is a deductible business expense under section 162 of the Code.[98] In addition, employer-provided health insurance coverage is generally not included in an employee's gross income.[99]

---

[96] For additional information on new section 6051, see the explanation of section 9002 of the Senate amendment, "Inclusion of Employer-Sponsored Health Coverage on W-2."

[97] For additional information on new section 6055, see the explanation of section 1502 of the Senate amendment, "Reporting of Health Insurance Coverage."

[98] Sec. 162. However see special rules in sections 419 and 419A for the deductibility of contributions to welfare benefit plans with respect to medical benefits for employees and their dependents.

[99] Sec. 106.

Definition of a cafeteria plan

If an employee receives a qualified benefit (as defined below) based on the employee's election between the qualified benefit and a taxable benefit under a cafeteria plan, the qualified benefit generally is not includable in gross income.[100] However, if a plan offering an employee an election between taxable benefits (including cash) and nontaxable qualified benefits does not meet the requirements for being a cafeteria plan, the election between taxable and nontaxable benefits results in gross income to the employee, regardless of what benefit is elected and when the election is made.[101] A cafeteria plan is a separate written plan under which all participants are employees, and participants are permitted to choose among at least one permitted taxable benefit (for example, current cash compensation) and at least one qualified benefit. Finally, a cafeteria plan must not provide for deferral of compensation, except as specifically permitted in sections 125(d)(2)(B), (C), or (D).

Qualified benefits

Qualified benefits under a cafeteria plan are generally employer-provided benefits that are not includable in gross income under an express provision of the Code. Examples of qualified benefits include employer-provided health insurance coverage, group term life insurance coverage not in excess of $50,000, and benefits under a dependent care assistance program. In order to be excludable, any qualified benefit elected under a cafeteria plan must independently satisfy any requirements under the Code section that provides the exclusion. However, some employer-provided benefits that are not includable in gross income under an express provision of the Code are explicitly not allowed in a cafeteria plan. These benefits are generally referred to as nonqualified benefits. Examples of nonqualified benefits include scholarships[102]; employer-provided meals and lodging;[103] educational assistance;[104] and fringe benefits.[105] A plan offering any nonqualified benefit is not a cafeteria plan.[106]

Payment of Health Insurance Premiums Through a Cafeteria Plan

Employees participating in a cafeteria plan may be able to pay the portion of premiums for health insurance coverage not otherwise paid for by their employers on a pre-tax basis through salary reduction.[107] Such salary reduction contributions are treated as employer contributions for purposes of the Code, and are thus excluded from gross income.

One way that employers can offer employer-provided health insurance coverage for purposes of the tax exclusion is to offer to reimburse employees for the premiums for health insurance purchased by employees in the individual health insurance market. The payment or reimbursement of employees' substantiated individual health insurance premiums is excludible from employees' gross income.[108] This reimbursement for individual health insurance premiums can also be paid for through salary reduction under a cafeteria plan.[109] This offer to reimburse individual health insurance premiums constitutes a group health plan.

Explanation of Provision

Under the provision, reimbursement (or direct payment) for the premiums for coverage under any qualified health plan (as defined in section 1301(a) of the the Senate amendment) offered through an Exchange established under section 1311 of the Senate amendment is a qualified benefit under a cafeteria plan if the employer is a qualified employer. Under section 1312(f)(2) of the Senate amendment, a qualified employer is generally a small employer that elects to make all its full-time employees eligible for one or more qualified plans offered in the small group market through an Exchange.[110] Otherwise, reimbursement (or direct payment) for the premiums for coverage under any qualified health plan offered through an Exchange is not a qualified benefit under a cafeteria plan. Thus, an employer that is not a qualified employer cannot offer to reimburse an employee for

---

[100] Sec. 125(a).
[101] Proposed Treas. Reg. sec. 1.125-1(b).
[102] Sec. 117.
[103] Sec. 119.
[104] Sec.127.
[105] Sec. 132.
[106] Proposed Treas. Reg. sec. 1.125-1(q). Long-term care services, contributions to Archer Medical Savings Accounts, group term life insurance for an employee's spouse, child or dependent, and elective deferrals to section 403(b) plans are also nonqualified benefits.

[107] Sec. 125.
[108] Rev. Rul. 61-146 (1961-2 CB 25).
[109] Proposed Treas. Reg. sec.1.125-1(m).
[110] Beginning in 2017, each State may allow issuers of health insurance coverage in the large group market in a state to offer qualified plans in the large group market. In that event, a qualified employer includes a small employer that elects to make all its full-time employees eligible for one or more qualified plans offered in the large group market through an Exchange.

the premium for a qualified plan that the employee purchases through the individual market in an Exchange as a health insurance coverage option under its cafeteria plan.

Effective Date

This provision applies to taxable years beginning after December 31, 2013.

[¶10,130] Act Sec. 1562. Conforming amendments

Joint Committee on Taxation (J.C.T. Rep. No. JCX-18-10)

[New Code Sec. 9815]

Present Law

The Health Insurance Portability and Accountability Act of 1996 ("HIPAA")[111] imposes a number of requirements with respect to group health coverage that are designed to provide protections to health plan participants. These protections include limitations on exclusions from coverage based on pre-existing conditions; the prohibition of discrimination on the basis of health status; guaranteed renewability in multiemployer plans and certain employer welfare arrangements; standards relating to benefits for mother and newborns; parity in the application of certain limits to mental health benefits; and coverage of dependent students on medically necessary leave of absence. The requirements are enforced through the Code, ERISA,[112] and PHSA.[113] The HIPAA requirements in the Code are in chapter 100 of Subtitle K, Group Health Plan Requirements.

A group health plan is defined as a plan (including a self-insured plan) of, or contributed to by, an employer (including a self-employed person) or employee organization to provide health care (directly or otherwise) to the employees, former employees, the employer, others associated or formerly associated with the employer in a business relationship, or their families.[114]

The Code imposes an excise tax on group health plans which fail to meet the HIPAA requirements.[115] The excise tax is equal to $100 per day during the period of noncompliance and is generally imposed on the employer sponsoring the plan if the plan fails to meet the require-

[Law at ¶5095. CCH Explanation at ¶320.]

ments. The maximum tax that can be imposed during a taxable year cannot exceed the lesser of: (1) 10 percent of the employer's group health plan expenses for the prior year; or (2) $500,000. No tax is imposed if the Secretary of the Treasury determines that the employer did not know, and in exercising reasonable diligence would not have known, that the failure existed.

Explanation of Provision

The provision adds new Code section 9815 which provides that the provisions of part A of title XXVII of the PHSA (as amended by the Senate amendment) apply to group health plans, and health insurance issuers providing health insurance coverage in connection with group health plans, as if included in the HIPAA provisions of the Code. To the extent that any HIPAA provision of the Code conflicts with a provision of part A of title XXVII of the PHSA with respect to group health plans, or health insurance issuers providing health insurance coverage in connection with group health plans, the provisions of such part A generally apply.

The provisions of part A of title XXVII of the PHSA added by section 1001 of the Senate amendment that are incorporated by reference in new section 9815 include the following: section 2711 (No lifetime or annual limits); section 2712 (Prohibition on rescissions); section 2713 (Coverage of preventive health services); section 2714 (Extension of dependent coverage); section 2715 (Development and utilization of uniform explanation of coverage documents and standardized definitions); section 2716 (Prohibition of discrimination based on salary); section 2717 (Ensuring the quality of care); section 2718 (Bringing down

---

[111] Pub. L. No. 104-191.

[112] Pub. L. No. 93-406.

[113] 42 U.S.C. 6A.

[114] The requirements do not apply to any governmental plan or any group health plan that has fewer than two participants who are current employees.

[115] Sec. 4980D.

the cost of health care coverage); and section 2719 (Appeals process). These new sections of the PHSA, which relate to individual and group market reforms, are effective six months after the date of enactment.

The provisions of part A of title XXVII of the PHSA added by section 1201 of the Senate amendment that are incorporated by reference in new section 9815 include the following: section 2704 (Prohibition of preexisting condition exclusions or other discrimination based on health status); section 2701 (Fair health insurance premiums); section 2702 (Guaranteed availability of coverage) section 2703 (Guaranteed renewability of coverage); section 2705 (Prohibiting discrimination against individual participants and beneficiaries based on health status); section 2706 (Non-discrimination in health care); section 2707 (Comprehensive health insurance coverage); and section 2708 (Prohibition on excessive waiting periods). These new sections of the PHSA, which

relate to general health insurance reforms, are effective for plan years beginning on or after January 1, 2014.

New section 9815 specifies that section 2716 (Prohibition of discrimination based on salary) and 2718 (Bringing down the cost of health coverage) of title XXVII of the PHSA (as amended by the Senate amendment) do not apply under the Code provisions of HIPAA with respect to self-insured group health plans.

As a result of incorporating these HIPAA provision by reference, the excise tax that applies in the event of a violation of present law HIPAA requirements also applies in the event of a violation of these new requirements.

Effective Date

This provision is effective on the date of enactment.

[Law at ¶5295. CCH Explanation at ¶455.]

[¶10,140] Act Sec. 3308(b)(2). Disclosures to carry out the reduction of Medicare Part D subsidies for high income beneficiaries

Joint Committee on Taxation (J.C.T. Rep. No. JCX-18-10)

[Code Sec. 6103]

Present Law

Section 6103 provides that returns and return information are confidential and may not be disclosed by the IRS, other Federal employees, State employees, and certain others having access to such information except as provided in the Code. Section 6103 contains a number of exceptions to the general rule of nondisclosure that authorize disclosure in specifically identified circumstances. For example, section 6103 provides for the disclosure of certain return information for purposes of establishing the appropriate amount of any Medicare Part B premium subsidy adjustment.

Specifically, upon written request from the Commissioner of Social Security, the IRS may disclose the following limited return information of a taxpayer whose premium, according to the records of the Secretary, may be subject to adjustment under section 1839(i) of the Social Security Act (relating to Medicare Part B):

• Taxpayer identity information with respect to such taxpayer;

• The filing status of the taxpayer;

• The adjusted gross income of such taxpayer;

• The amounts excluded from such taxpayer's gross income under sections 135 and 911 to the extent such information is available;

• The interest received or accrued during the taxable year which is exempt from the tax imposed by chapter 1 to the extent such information is available;

• The amounts excluded from such taxpayer's gross income by sections 931 and 933 to the extent such information is available;

• Such other information relating to the liability of the taxpayer as is prescribed by the Secretary by regulation as might indicate that the amount of the premium of the taxpayer may be subject to an adjustment and the amount of such adjustment; and

• The taxable year with respect to which the preceding information relates.

This return information may be used by officers, employees, and contractors of the Social Security Administration only for the purposes of, and to the extent necessary in, establishing the appropriate amount of any Medicare Part B premium subsidy adjustment.

Section 6103(p)(4) requires, as a condition of receiving returns and return information, that Federal and State agencies (and certain other recipients) provide safeguards as prescribed by the Secretary by regulation to be necessary or appropriate to protect the confidentiality of returns or return information. Unauthorized disclosure of a return or return information is a felony punishable by a fine not exceeding $5,000 or imprisonment of not more than five years, or both, together with the costs of prosecution.[116] The unauthorized inspection of a return or return information is punishable by a fine not exceeding $1,000 or imprisonment of not more than one year, or both, together with the costs of prosecution.[117] An action for civil damages also may be brought for unauthorized disclosure or inspection.[118]

Explanation of Provision

Upon written request from the Commissioner of Social Security, the IRS may disclose the following limited return information of a taxpayer whose Medicare Part D premium subsidy, according to the records of the Secretary, may be subject to adjustment:

• Taxpayer identity information with respect to such taxpayer;

• The filing status of the taxpayer;

• The adjusted gross income of such taxpayer;

• The amounts excluded from such taxpayer's gross income under sections 135 and 911 to the extent such information is available;

• The interest received or accrued during the taxable year which is exempt from the tax imposed by chapter 1 to the extent such information is available;

• The amounts excluded from such taxpayer's gross income by sections 931 and 933 to the extent such information is available;

• Such other information relating to the liability of the taxpayer as is prescribed by the

Secretary by regulation as might indicate that the amount of the Part D premium of the taxpayer may be subject to an adjustment and the amount of such adjustment; and

• The taxable year with respect to which the preceding information relates.

This return information may be used by officers, employees, and contractors of the Social Security Administration only for the purposes of, and to the extent necessary in, establishing the appropriate amount of any Medicare Part D premium subsidy adjustment.

For purposes of both the Medicare Part B premium subsidy adjustment and the Medicare Part D premium subsidy adjustment, the provision provides that the Social Security Administration may redisclose only taxpayer identity and the amount of premium subsidy adjustment to officers and employees and contractors of the Centers for Medicare and Medicaid Services, and officers and employees of the Office of Personnel Management and the Railroad Retirement Board. This redisclosure is permitted only to the extent necessary for the collection of the premium subsidy amount from the taxpayers under the jurisdiction of the respective agencies.

Further, the Social Security Administration may redisclose the return information received under this provision to officers and employees of the Department of HHS to the extent necessary to resolve administrative appeals of the Part B and Part D subsidy adjustments and to officers and employees of the Department of Justice to the extent necessary for use in judicial proceedings related to establishing and collecting the appropriate amount of any Medicare Part B or Medicare Part D premium subsidy adjustments.

Effective Date

The provision is effective on date of enactment.

[Law at ¶5270. CCH Explanation at ¶430.]

---

[116] Sec. 7213.
[117] Sec. 7213A.

[118] Sec. 7431.

[¶10,150] Act Sec. 6301. Patient-centered outcomes research trust fund; financing for trust fund

Joint Committee on Taxation (J.C.T. Rep. No. JCX-18-10)

[New Code Secs. 4375, 4376, 4377 and 9511]

Present Law

No provision.

Explanation of Provision

Patient-Centered Outcomes Research Trust Fund

Under new section 9511, there is established in the Treasury of the United States a trust fund, the Patient Centered Outcomes Research Trust Fund ("PCORTF"), to carry out the provisions in the Senate amendment relating to comparative effectiveness research. The PCORTF is funded in part from fees imposed on health plans under new sections 4375 through 4377.

Fee on insured and self-insured health plans

Insured plans

Under new section 4375, a fee is imposed on each specified health insurance policy. The fee is equal to two dollars (one dollar in the case of policy years ending during fiscal year 2013) multiplied by the average number of lives covered under the policy. For any policy year beginning after September 30, 2014, the dollar amount is equal to the sum of: (1) the dollar amount for policy years ending in the preceding fiscal year, plus (2) an amount equal to the product of (A) the dollar amount for policy years ending in the preceding fiscal year, multiplied by (B) the percentage increase in the projected per capita amount of National Health Expenditures, as most recently published by the Secretary before the beginning of the fiscal year. The issuer of the policy is liable for payment of the fee. A specified health insurance policy includes any accident or health insurance policy[119] issued with respect to individuals residing in the United States.[120] An arrangement under which fixed

payments of premiums are received as consideration for a person's agreement to provide, or arrange for the provision of, accident or health coverage to residents of the United States, regardless of how such coverage is provided or arranged to be provided, is treated as a specified health insurance policy. The person agreeing to provide or arrange for the provision of coverage is treated as the issuer.

Self-insured plans

In the case of an applicable self-insured health plan, new Code section 4376 imposes a fee equal to two dollars (one dollar in the case of policy years ending during fiscal year 2013) multiplied by the average number of lives covered under the plan. For any policy year beginning after September 30, 2014, the dollar amount is equal to the sum of: (1) the dollar amount for policy years ending in the preceding fiscal year, plus (2) an amount equal to the product of (A) the dollar amount for policy years ending in the preceding fiscal year, multiplied by (B) the percentage increase in the projected per capita amount of National Health Expenditures, as most recently published by the Secretary before the beginning of the fiscal year. The plan sponsor is liable for payment of the fee. For purposes of the provision, the plan sponsor is: the employer in the case of a plan established or maintained by a single employer or the employee organization in the case of a plan established or maintained by an employee organization. In the case of: (1) a plan established or maintained by two or more employers or jointly by one of more employers and one or more employee organizations, (2) a multiple employer welfare arrangement, or (3) a voluntary employees' beneficiary association described in Code section 501(c)(9) ("VEBA"), the plan sponsor is the association, committee, joint board of trustees, or other similar group of representatives of the parties who establish or maintain the plan. In the case of a rural electric cooperative or a rural telephone

---

[119] A specified health insurance policy does not include insurance if substantially all of the coverage provided under such policy consists of excepted benefits described in section 9832(c). Examples of excepted benefits described in section 9832(c) are coverage for only accident, or disability insurance, or any combination thereof; liability insurance, including general liability insurance and automobile liability insurance; workers' compensation or similar insurance; automobile medical payment insurance; coverage for on-site

medical clinics; limited scope dental or vision benefits; benefits for long term care, nursing home care, community based care, or any combination thereof; coverage only for a specified disease or illness; hospital indemnity or other fixed indemnity insurance; and Medicare supplemental coverage.

[120] Under the provision, the United States includes any possession of the United States.

cooperative, the plan sponsor is the cooperative or association.

Under the provision, an applicable self-insured health plan is any plan providing accident or health coverage if any portion of such coverage is provided other than through an insurance policy and such plan is established or maintained: (1) by one or more employers for the benefit of their employees or former employees, (2) by one or more employee organizations for the benefit of their members or former members, (3) jointly by one or more employers and one or more employee organizations for the benefit of employees or former employees, (4) by a VEBA, (5) by any organization described in section 501(c)(6) of the Code, or (6) in the case of a plan not previously described, by a multiple employer welfare arrangement (as defined in section 3(40) of ERISA), a rural electric cooperative (as defined in section 3(40)(B)(iv) of ERISA), or a rural telephone cooperative association (as defined in section 3(40)(B)(v) of ERISA).

Other special rules

Governmental entities are generally not exempt from the fees imposed under the provision.

There is an exception for exempt governmental programs including, Medicare, Medicaid, SCHIP, and any program established by Federal law for proving medical care (other than through insurance policies) to members of the Armed Forces, veterans, or members of Indian tribes.

No amount collected from the fee on health insurance and self-insured plans is covered over to any possession of the United States. For purposes of the Code's procedure and administration rules, the fee imposed under the provision is treated as a tax. The fees imposed under new sections 4375 and 4376 do not apply to plan years ending after September 31, 2019.

Effective Date

The fee on health insurance and self-insured plans is effective with respect to policies and plans for portions of policy or plan years beginning on or after October 1, 2012.

[Law at ¶5155, ¶5200, ¶5205, ¶5210, ¶5290 and ¶7021. CCH Explanation at ¶445.]

[¶10,160] Act Sec. 9001. Excise tax on high cost employer-sponsored health coverage[121]

Joint Committee on Taxation (J.C.T. REP. No. JCX-18-10)

[New Code Sec. 4980I]

Present Law

Taxation of insurance companies

Current law provides special rules for determining the taxable income of insurance companies (subchapter L of the Code). Separate sets of rules apply to life insurance companies and to property and casualty insurance companies. Insurance companies generally are subject to Federal income tax at regular corporate income tax rates.

An insurance company that provides health insurance is subject to Federal income tax as either a life insurance company or as a property insurance company, depending on its mix of lines of business and on the resulting portion of its reserves that are treated as life insurance reserves. For Federal income tax purposes, an insurance company is treated as a life insurance

company if the sum of its (1) life insurance reserves and (2) unearned premiums and unpaid losses on noncancellable life, accident or health contracts not included in life insurance reserves, comprise more than 50 percent of its total reserves.[122]

Some insurance providers may be exempt from Federal income tax under section 501(a) if specific requirements are satisfied. Section 501(c)(8), for example, describes certain fraternal beneficiary societies, orders, or associations operating under the lodge system or for the exclusive benefit of their members that provide for the payment of life, sick, accident, or other benefits to the members or their dependents. Section 501(c)(9) describes certain voluntary employees' beneficiary associations that provide for the payment of life, sick, accident, or other benefits to the members of the association or their dependents or designated beneficiaries. Section

---

[121] Section 9001 of the Senate amendment, as amended by section 10901, is further amended by section 1401 of the Reconciliation bill.

[122] Sec. 816(a).

501(c)(12)(A) describes certain benevolent life insurance associations of a purely local character. Section 501(c)(15) describes certain small non-life insurance companies with annual gross receipts of no more than $600,000 ($150,000 in the case of a mutual insurance company). Section 501(c)(26) describes certain membership organizations established to provide health insurance to certain high-risk individuals. Section 501(c)(27) describes certain organizations established to provide workmen's compensation insurance. A health maintenance organization that is tax-exempt under section 501(c)(3) or (4) is not treated as providing prohibited[123] commercial-type insurance, in the case of incidental health insurance provided by the health maintenance organization that is of a kind customarily provided by such organizations.

Treatment of employer-sponsored health coverage

As with other compensation, the cost of employer-provided health coverage is a deductible business expense under section 162.[124] Employer-provided health insurance coverage is generally not included in an employee's gross income.

In addition, employees participating in a cafeteria plan may be able to pay the portion of premiums for health insurance coverage not otherwise paid for by their employers on a pre-tax basis through salary reduction.[125] Such salary reduction contributions are treated as employer contributions for Federal income purposes, and are thus excluded from gross income.

Employers may agree to reimburse medical expenses of their employees (and their spouses and dependents), not covered by a health insurance plan, through flexible spending arrangements which allow reimbursement not in excess of a specified dollar amount (either elected by an employee under a cafeteria plan or otherwise specified by the employer). Reimbursements under these arrangements are also excludible from gross income as employer-provided health coverage.

A flexible spending arrangement for medical expenses under a cafeteria plan ("Health FSA") is an unfunded arrangement under which employees are given the option to reduce their current cash compensation and instead have the amount made available for use in reimbursing the employee for his or her medical expenses.[126] Health FSAs that are funded on a salary reduction basis are subject to the requirements for cafeteria plans, including a requirement that amounts remaining under a Health FSA at the end of a plan year must be forfeited by the employee (referred to as the "use-it-or-lose-it rule").[127]

Alternatively, the employer may specify a dollar amount that is available for medical expense reimbursement. These arrangements are commonly called Health Reimbursement Arrangements ("HRAs"). Some of the rules applicable to HRAs and Health FSAs are similar (e.g., the amounts in the arrangements can only be used to reimburse medical expenses and not for other purposes), but the rules are not identical. In particular, HRAs cannot be funded on a salary reduction basis and the use-it-or-lose-it rule does not apply. Thus, amounts remaining at the end of the year may be carried forward to be used to reimburse medical expenses in following years.[128]

Current law provides that individuals with a high deductible health plan (and generally no other health plan) may establish and make tax-deductible contributions to a health savings account ("HSA"). An HSA is subject to a condition that the individual is covered under a high deductible health plan (purchased either through the individual market or through an employer). Subject to certain limitations,[129] contributions made to an HSA by an employer, including contributions made through a cafeteria plan through salary reduction, are excluded from income (and

---

[123] Sec. 501(m).

[124] Sec. 162. However see special rules in section 419 and 419A for the deductibility of contributions to welfare benefit plans with respect to medical benefits for employees and their dependents.

[125] Sec. 125.

[126] Sec. 125. Prop. Treas. Reg. sec. 1.125-5 provides rules for Health FSAs. There is a similar type of flexible spending arrangement for dependent care expenses.

[127] Sec. 125(d)(2). A cafeteria plan is permitted to allow a grace period not to exceed two and one-half months immediately following the end of the plan year during which unused amounts may be used. Notice 2005-42, 2005-1 C.B. 1204.

[128] Guidance with respect to HRAs, including the interaction of FSAs and HRAs in the case of an individual covered under both, is provided in Notice 2002-45, 2002-2 C.B. 93.

[129] For 2010, the maximum aggregate annual contribution that can be made to an HSA is $3,050 in the case of self-only coverage and $6,150 in the case of family coverage. The annual contribution limits are increased for individuals who have attained age 55 by the end of the taxable year (referred to as "catch-up contributions"). In the case of policyholders and covered spouses who are age 55 or older, the HSA annual contribution limit is greater than the otherwise applicable limit by $1,000 in 2009 and thereafter. Contributions, including catch-up contributions, cannot be made once an individual is enrolled in Medicare.

from wages for payroll tax purposes). Contributions made by individuals are deductible for income tax purposes, regardless of whether the individuals itemize. Like an HSA, an Archer MSA is a tax-exempt trust or custodial account to which tax-deductible contributions may be made by individuals with a high deductible health plan; however, only self-employed individuals and employees of small employers are eligible to have an Archer MSA. Archer MSAs provide tax benefits similar to, but generally not as favorable as, those provided by HSAs for individuals covered by high deductible health plans.[130]

ERISA[131] preempts State law relating to certain employee benefit plans, including employer-sponsored health plans. While ERISA specifically provides that its preemption rule does not exempt or relieve any person from any State law which regulates insurance, ERISA also provides that an employee benefit plan is not deemed to be engaged in the business of insurance for purposes of any State law regulating insurance companies or insurance contracts. As a result of this ERISA preemption, self-insured employer-sponsored health plans need not provide benefits that are mandated under State insurance law.

While ERISA does not require an employer to offer health benefits, it does require compliance if an employer chooses to offer health benefits, such as compliance with plan fiduciary standards, reporting and disclosure requirements, and procedures for appealing denied benefit claims. ERISA was amended (as well as the PHSA and the Code) by COBRA[132] and HIPAA,[133] which added other Federal requirements for health plans, including rules for health care continuation coverage, limitations on exclusions from coverage based on preexisting conditions, and a few benefit requirements such as minimum hospital stay requirements for mothers following the birth of a child.

COBRA requires that a group health plan offer continuation coverage to qualified beneficiaries in the case of a qualifying event (such as a loss of employment).[134] A plan may require payment of a premium for any period of continuation coverage. The amount of such premium generally may not exceed 102 percent of the "applicable premium" for such period and the premium must be payable, at the election of the payor, in monthly installments. The applicable premium for any period of continuation coverage means the cost to the plan for such period of coverage for similarly situated non-COBRA beneficiaries with respect to whom a qualifying event has not occurred, and is determined without regard to whether the cost is paid by the employer or employee. There are special rules for determining the applicable premium in the case of self-insured plans. Under the special rules for self-insured plans, the applicable premium generally is equal to a reasonable estimate of the cost of providing coverage for similarly situated beneficiaries which is determined on an actuarial basis and takes into account such other factors as the Secretary of Treasury may prescribe in regulations.

Current law imposes an excise tax on group health plans that fail to meet HIPAA and COBRA requirements.[135] The excise tax generally is equal to $100 per day per failure during the period of noncompliance and is imposed on the employer sponsoring the plan.

Deduction for health insurance costs of self-employed individuals

Under current law, self-employed individuals may deduct the cost of health insurance for themselves and their spouses and dependents.[136] The deduction is not available for any month in which the self-employed individual is eligible to participate in an employer-subsidized health plan. Moreover, the deduction may not exceed the individual's earned income from self-employment. The deduction applies only to the cost of insurance (i.e., it does not apply to out-of-pocket expenses that are not reimbursed by insurance). The deduction does not apply for self-employment tax purposes. For purposes of the deduction, a more-than-two-percent-shareholder-employee of an S corporation is treated the same as a self-employed individual. Thus,

---

[130] In addition to being limited to self-employed individuals and employees of small employers, the definition of a high deductible health plan for an Archer MSA differs from that for an HSA. After 2007, no new contributions can be made to Archer MSAs except by or on behalf of individuals who previously had made Archer MSA contributions and employees who are employed by a participating employer.

[131] Pub. L. No. 93-406.

[132] Pub. L. No. 99-272.

[133] Pub. L. No. 104-191.

[134] A group health plan is defined as a plan (including a self-insured plan) of, or contributed to by, an employer (including a self-employed person) or employee organization to provide health care (directly or otherwise) to the employees, former employees, the employer, others associated or formerly associated with the employer in a business relationship, or their families. The COBRA requirements are enforced through the Code, ERISA, and the PHSA.

[135] Secs. 4980B and 4980D.

[136] Sec. 162(l).

the exclusion for employer provided health care coverage does not apply to such individuals, but they are entitled to the deduction for health insurance costs as if they were self-employed.

Deductibility of excise taxes

In general, excise taxes may be deductible under section 162 of the Code if such taxes are paid or incurred in carrying on a trade or business, and are not within the scope of the disallowance of deductions for certain taxes enumerated in section 275 of the Code.

Explanation of Provision

The provision imposes an excise tax on insurers if the aggregate value of employer-sponsored health insurance coverage for an employee (including, for purposes of the provision, any former employee, surviving spouse and any other primary insured individual) exceeds a threshold amount. The tax is equal to 40 percent of the aggregate value that exceeds the threshold amount. For 2018, the threshold amount is $10,200 for individual coverage and $27,500 for family coverage, multiplied by the health cost adjustment percentage (as defined below) and increased by the age and gender adjusted excess premium amount (as defined below).

The health cost adjustment percentage is designed to increase the thresholds in the event that the actual growth in the cost of U.S. health care between 2010 and 2018 exceeds the projected growth for that period. The health cost adjustment percentage is equal to 100 percent plus the excess, if any, of (1) the percentage by which the per employee cost of coverage under the Blue Cross/Blue Shield standard benefit option under the Federal Employees Health Benefits Plan ("standard FEHBP coverage")[137] for plan year 2018 (as determined using the benefit package for standard FEHBP coverage for plan year 2010) exceeds the per employee cost of standard FEHBP coverage for plan year 2010; over (2) 55 percent. In 2019, the threshold amounts, after application of the health cost adjustment percentage in 2018, if any, are indexed to the CPI-U, as determined by the Department of Labor, plus one percentage point, rounded to the nearest $50. In 2020 and thereafter, the threshold amounts are indexed to the CPI-U as determined by the Department of Labor, rounded to the nearest $50.

For each employee (other than for certain retirees and employees in high risk professions, whose thresholds are adjusted under rules described below), the age and gender adjusted excess premium amount is equal to the excess, if any, of (1) the premium cost of standard FEHBP coverage for the type of coverage provided to the individual if priced for the age and gender characteristics of all employees of the individual's employer over (2) the premium cost, determined under procedures proscribed by the Secretary, for that coverage if priced for the age and gender characteristics of the national workforce.

For example, if the growth in the cost of health care during the period between 2010 and 2018, calculated by reference to the growth in the per employee cost of standard FEHBP coverage during that period (holding benefits under the standard FEBHP plan constant during the period) is 57 percent, the threshold amounts for 2013 will be $10,200 for individual coverage and $27,500 for family coverage, multiplied by 102 percent (100 percent plus the excess of 57 percent over 55 percent), or $10,404 for individual coverage and $28,050 for family coverage. In 2019, the new threshold amounts of $10,404 for individual coverage and $28,050 for family coverage are indexed for CPI-U, plus one percentage point, rounded to the nearest $50. Beginning in 2020, the threshold amounts are indexed to the CPI-U, rounded to the nearest $50.

The new threshold amounts (as indexed) are then increased for any employee by the age and gender adjusted excess premium amount, if any. For an employee with individual coverage in 2019, if standard FEHBP coverage priced for the age and gender characteristics of the workforce of the employee's employer is $11,400 and the Secretary estimates that the premium cost for individual standard FEHBP coverage priced for the age and gender characteristics of the national workforce is $10,500, the threshold for that employee is increased by $900 ($11,400 less $10,500) to $11,304 ($10,404 plus $900).

The excise tax is imposed pro rata on the issuers of the insurance. In the case of a self-insured group health plan, a Health FSA or an HRA, the excise tax is paid by the entity that administers benefits under the plan or arrangement ("plan administrator"). Where the em-

---

[137] For purposes of determining the health cost adjustment percentage in 2018 and the age and gender adjusted excess premium amount in any year, in the event the standard Blue Cross/Blue Shield option is not available under the Federal Employees Health Benefit Plan for such year,

the Secretary will determine the health cost adjustment percentage by reference to a substantially similar option available under the Federal Employees Health Benefit Plan for that year.

ployer acts as plan administrator to a self-insured group health plan, a Health FSA or an HRA, the excise tax is paid by the employer. Where an employer contributes to an HSA or an Archer MSA, the employer is responsible for payment of the excise tax, as the insurer.

Employer-sponsored health insurance coverage is health coverage under any group health plan offered by an employer to an employee without regard to whether the employer provides the coverage (and thus the coverage is excludable from the employee's gross income) or the employee pays for the coverage with after-tax dollars. Employer-sponsored health insurance coverage includes coverage under any group health plan established and maintained primarily for the civilian employees of the Federal government or any of its agencies or instrumentalities and, except as provided below, of any State government or political subdivision thereof or by any of agencies or instrumentalities of such government or subdivision.

Employer-sponsored health insurance coverage includes both fully-insured and self-insured health coverage excludable from the employee's gross income, including, in the self-insured context, on-site medical clinics that offer more than a de minimis amount of medical care to employees and executive physical programs. In the case of a self-employed individual, employer-sponsored health insurance coverage is coverage for any portion of which a deduction is allowable to the self-employed individual under section 162(l).

In determining the amount by which the value of employer-sponsored health insurance coverage exceeds the threshold amount, the aggregate value of all employer-sponsored health insurance coverage is taken into account, including coverage in the form of reimbursements under a Health FSA or an HRA, contributions to an HSA or Archer MSA, and, except as provided below, other supplementary health insurance coverage. The value of employer-sponsored coverage for long term care and the following benefits described in section 9832(c)(1) that are excepted from the portability, access and renewability requirements of HIPAA are not taken into account in the determination of whether the value of health coverage exceeds the threshold amount: (1) coverage only for accident or disability income insurance, or any combination of these coverages; (2) coverage issued as a supplement to liability insurance; (3) liability insurance, including general liability insurance and automobile liability insurance; (4) workers' compensation or similar insurance; (5) automobile medical payment insurance; (5) credit-only in-

surance; and (6) other similar insurance coverage, specified in regulations, under which benefits for medical care are secondary or incidental to other insurance benefits.

The value of employer-sponsored health insurance coverage does not include the value of independent, noncoordinated coverage described in section 9832(c)(3) as excepted from the portability, access and renewability requirements of HIPAA if that coverage is purchased exclusively by the employee with after-tax dollars (or, in the case of a self-employed individual, for which a deduction under section 162(l) is not allowable). The value of employer-sponsored health insurance coverage does include the value of such coverage if any portion of the coverage is employer-provided (or, in the case of a self-employed individual, if a deduction is allowable for any portion of the payment for the coverage). Coverage described in section 9832(c)(3) is coverage only for a specified disease or illness or for hospital or other fixed indemnity health coverage. Fixed indemnity health coverage pays fixed dollar amounts based on the occurrence of qualifying events, including but not limited to the diagnosis of a specific disease, an accidental injury or a hospitalization, provided that the coverage is not coordinated with other health coverage.

Finally, the value of employer-sponsored health insurance coverage does not include any coverage under a separate policy, certificate, or contract of insurance which provides benefits substantially all of which are for treatment of the mouth (including any organ or structure within the mouth) or for treatment of the eye.

Calculation and proration of excise tax and reporting requirements

Applicable threshold

In general, the individual threshold applies to any employee covered by employer-sponsored health insurance coverage. The family threshold applies to an employee only if such individual and at least one other beneficiary are enrolled in coverage other than self-only coverage under an employer-sponsored health insurance plan that provides minimum essential coverage (as determined for purposes of the individual responsibility requirements) and under which the benefits provided do not vary based on whether the covered individual is the employee or other beneficiary.

For all employees covered by a multiemployer plan, the family threshold applies regardless of whether the individual maintains individual or family coverage under the plan.

For purposes of the provision, a multiemployer plan is an employee health benefit plan to which more than one employer is required to contribute, which is maintained pursuant to one or more collective bargaining agreements between one or more employee organizations and more than one employer.

Amount of applicable premium

Under the provision, the aggregate value of all employer-sponsored health insurance coverage, including any supplementary health insurance coverage not excluded from the value of employer-sponsored health insurance, is generally calculated in the same manner as the applicable premiums for the taxable year for the employee determined under the rules for COBRA continuation coverage, but without regard to the excise tax. If the plan provides for the same COBRA continuation coverage premium for both individual coverage and family coverage, the plan is required to calculate separate individual and family premiums for this purpose. In determining the coverage value for retirees, employers may elect to treat pre-65 retirees together with post-65 retirees.

Value of coverage in the form of Health FSA reimbursements

In the case of a Health FSA from which reimbursements are limited to the amount of the salary reduction, the value of employer-sponsored health insurance coverage is equal to the dollar amount of the aggregate salary reduction contributions for the year. To the extent that the Health FSA provides for employer contributions in excess of the amount of the employee's salary reduction, the value of the coverage generally is determined in the same manner as the applicable premium for COBRA continuation coverage. If the plan provides for the same COBRA continuation coverage premium for both individual coverage and family coverage, the plan is required to calculate separate individual and family premiums for this purpose.

Amount subject to the excise tax and reporting requirement

The amount subject to the excise tax on high cost employer-sponsored health insurance coverage for each employee is the sum of the aggregate premiums for health insurance coverage, the amount of any salary reduction contributions

to a Health FSA for the taxable year, and the dollar amount of employer contributions to an HSA or an Archer MSA, minus the dollar amount of the threshold. The aggregate premiums for health insurance coverage include all employer-sponsored health insurance coverage including coverage for any supplementary health insurance coverage. The applicable premium for health coverage provided through an HRA is also included in this aggregate amount.

Under a separate rule,[138] an employer is required to disclose the aggregate premiums for health insurance coverage for each employee on his or her annual Form W-2.

Under the provision, the excise tax is allocated pro rata among the insurers, with each insurer responsible for payment of the excise tax on an amount equal to the amount subject to the total excise tax multiplied by a fraction, the numerator of which is the amount of employer-sponsored health insurance coverage provided by that insurer to the employee and the denominator of which is the aggregate value of all employer-sponsored health insurance coverage provided to the employee. In the case of a self-insured group health plan, a Health FSA or an HRA, the excise tax is allocated to the plan administrator. If an employer contributes to an HSA or an Archer MSA, the employer is responsible for payment of the excise tax, as the insurer. The employer is responsible for calculating the amount subject to the excise tax allocable to each insurer and plan administrator and for reporting these amounts to each insurer, plan administrator and the Secretary, in such form and at such time as the Secretary may prescribe. Each insurer and plan administrator is then responsible for calculating, reporting and paying the excise tax to the IRS on such forms and at such time as the Secretary may prescribe.

For example, if in 2018 an employee elects family coverage under a fully-insured health care policy covering major medical and dental with a value of $31,000, the health cost adjustment percentage for that year is 100 percent, and the age and gender adjusted excess premium amount for the employee is $600, the amount subject to the excise tax is $2,900 ($31,000 less the threshold of $28,100 ($27,500 multiplied by 100 percent and increased by $600)). The employer reports $2,900 as taxable to the insurer, which calculates and remits the excise tax to the IRS.

---

[138] See the explanation of section 9002 of the Senate amendment, "Inclusion of Cost of Employer Sponsored Health Coverage on W-2."

Alternatively, if in 2018 an employee elects family coverage under a fully-insured major medical policy with a value of $28,500 and contributes $2,500 to a Health FSA, the employee has an aggregate health insurance coverage value of $31,000. If the health cost adjustment percentage for that year is 100 percent and the age and gender adjusted excess premium amount for the employee is $600, the amount subject to the excise tax is $2,900 ($31,000 less the threshold of $28,100 ($27,500 multiplied by 100 percent and increased by $600)). The employer reports $2,666 ($2,900 × $28,500/$31,000) as taxable to the major medical insurer which then calculates and remits the excise tax to the IRS. If the employer uses a third-party administrator for the Health FSA, the employer reports $234 ($2,900 × $2,500/$31,000) to the administrator and the administrator calculates and remits the excise tax to the IRS. If the employer is acting as the plan administrator of the Health FSA, the employer is responsible for calculating and remitting the excise tax on the $234 to the IRS.

Penalty for Underreporting Liability for Tax to Insurers

If the employer reports to insurers, plan administrators and the IRS a lower amount of insurance cost subject to the excise tax than required, the employer is subject to a penalty equal to the sum of any additional excise tax that each such insurer and administrator would have owed if the employer had reported correctly and interest attributable to that additional excise tax as determined under Code section 6621 from the date that the tax was otherwise due to the date paid by the employer. This may occur, for example, if the employer undervalues the aggregate premium and thereby lowers the amount subject to the excise tax for all insurers and plan administrators (including the employer, when acting as plan administrator of a self-insured plan).

The penalty will not apply if it is established to the satisfaction of the Secretary that the employer neither knew, nor exercising reasonable diligence would have known, that the failure existed. In addition, no penalty will be imposed on any failure corrected within the 30-day period beginning on the first date that the employer knew, or exercising reasonable diligence, would have known, that the failure existed, so long as the failure is due to reasonable cause and not to willful neglect. All or part of the penalty may be waived by the Secretary in the case of any failure due to reasonable cause and not to willful neglect, to the extent that the payment of the penalty would be excessive or otherwise inequitable relative to the failure involved.

The penalty is in addition to the amount of excise tax owed, which may not be waived.

Increased Thresholds for Certain Retirees and Individuals in High-Risk Professions

The threshold amounts are increased for an individual who has attained age of 55 who is non-Medicare eligible and receiving employer-sponsored retiree health coverage or who is covered by a plan sponsored by an employer the majority of whose employees covered by the plan are engaged in a high risk profession or employed to repair or install electrical and telecommunications lines. For these individuals, the threshold amount in 2018 is increased by (1) $1,650 for individual coverage or $3,450 for family coverage and (2) the age and gender adjusted excess premium amount (as defined above). In 2019, the additional $1,650 and $3,450 amounts are indexed to the CPI-U, plus one percentage point, rounded to the nearest $50. In 2020 and thereafter, the additional threshold amounts are indexed to the CPI-U, rounded to the nearest $50.

For purposes of this rule, employees considered to be engaged in a high risk profession are law enforcement officers, employees who engage in fire protection activities, individuals who provide out-of-hospital emergency medical care (including emergency medical technicians, paramedics, and first-responders), individuals whose primary work is longshore work, and individuals engaged in the construction, mining, agriculture (not including food processing), forestry, and fishing industries. A retiree with at least 20 years of employment in a high risk profession is also eligible for the increased threshold.

Under this provision, an individual's threshold cannot be increased by more than $1,650 for individual coverage or $3,450 for family coverage (indexed as described above) and the age and gender adjusted excess premium amount, even if the individual would qualify for an increased threshold both on account of his or her status as a retiree over age 55 and as a participant in a plan that covers employees in a high risk profession.

Deductibility of Excise Tax

Under the provision, the amount of the excise tax imposed is not deductible for Federal income tax purposes.

Regulatory Authority

The Secretary is directed to prescribe such regulations as may be necessary to carry out the provision.

Effective Date

The provision is effective for taxable years beginning after December 31, 2017.

[Law at ¶5230. CCH Explanation at ¶345.]

[¶10,170] Act Sec. 9002. Inclusion of cost of employer-sponsored health coverage on W-2

Joint Committee on Taxation (J.C.T. REP. NO. JCX-18-10)

[Code Sec. 6051]

Present Law

In many cases, an employer pays for all or a portion of its employees' health insurance coverage as an employee benefit. This benefit often includes premiums for major medical, dental, and other supplementary health insurance coverage. Under present law, the value of employer-provided health coverage is not required to be reported to the IRS or any other Federal agency. The value of the employer contribution to health coverage is excludible from an employee's income.[139]

Under current law, every employer is required to furnish each employee and the Federal government with a statement of compensation information, including wages, paid by the employer to the employee, and the taxes withheld from such wages during the calendar year. The statement, made on the Form W-2, must be provided to each employee by January 31 of the succeeding year. There is no requirement that the employer report the total value of employer-sponsored health insurance coverage on the Form W-2,[140] although some employers voluntarily report the amount of salary reduction under a cafeteria plan resulting in tax-free employee benefits in box 14.

Explanation of Provision

Under the provision, an employer is required to disclose on each employee's annual Form W-2 the value of the employee's health insurance coverage sponsored by the employer.

If an employee enrolls in employer-sponsored health insurance coverage under multiple plans, the employer must disclose the aggregate value of all such health coverage (excluding the value of a health flexible spending arrangement). For example, if an employee enrolls in employer-sponsored health insurance coverage under a major medical plan, a dental plan, and a vision plan, the employer is required to report the total value of the combination of all of these health related insurance policies. For this purpose, employers generally use the same value for all similarly situated employees receiving the same category of coverage (such as single or family health insurance coverage).

To determine the value of employer-sponsored health insurance coverage, the employer calculates the applicable premiums for the taxable year for the employee under the rules for COBRA continuation coverage under section 4980B(f)(4) (and accompanying Treasury regulations), including the special rule for self-insured plans. The value that the employer is required to report is the portion of the aggregate premium. If the plan provides for the same COBRA continuation coverage premium for both individual coverage and family coverage, the plan would be required to calculate separate individual and family premiums for this purpose.

Effective Date

The provision is effective for taxable years beginning after December 31, 2010.

[Law at ¶5255. CCH Explanation at ¶405.]

---

[139] Sec. 106.

[140] Any portion of employer sponsored coverage that is paid for by the employee with after-tax contributions is included as wages on the W-2 Form.

[¶10,180] Act Sec. 9003. Distributions for medicine qualified only if for prescribed drug or insulin

Joint Committee on Taxation (J.C.T. REP. NO. JCX-18-10)

[Code Secs. 105, 106, 220 and 223]

Present Law

Individual deduction for medical expenses

Expenses for medical care, not compensated for by insurance or otherwise, are deductible by an individual under the rules relating to itemized deductions to the extent the expenses exceed 7.5 percent of adjusted gross income ("AGI").[141] Medical care generally is defined broadly as amounts paid for diagnoses, cure, mitigation, treatment or prevention of disease, or for the purpose of affecting any structure of the body.[142] However, any amount paid during a taxable year for medicine or drugs is explicitly deductible as a medical expense only if the medicine or drug is a prescribed drug or is insulin.[143] Thus, any amount paid for medicine available without a prescription ("over-the-counter medicine") is not deductible as a medical expense, including any medicine recommended by a physician.[144]

Exclusion for employer-provided health care

The Code generally provides that employees are not taxed on (that is, may exclude from gross income) the value of employer-provided health coverage under an accident or health plan.[145] In addition, any reimbursements under an accident or health plan for medical care expenses for employees, their spouses, and their dependents generally are excluded from gross income.[146] An employer may agree to reimburse expenses for medical care of its employees (and their spouses and dependents), not covered by a

health insurance plan, through a flexible spending arrangement ("FSA") which allows reimbursement not in excess of a specified dollar amount. Such dollar amount is either elected by an employee under a cafeteria plan ("Health FSA") or otherwise specified by the employer under an HRA. Reimbursements under these arrangements are also excludible from gross income as employer-provided health coverage. The general definition of medical care without the explicit limitation on medicine applies for purposes of the exclusion for employer-provided health coverage and medical care.[147] Thus, under an HRA or under a Health FSA, amounts paid for prescription and over-the-counter medicine are treated as medical expenses, and reimbursements for such amounts are excludible from gross income.

Medical savings arrangements

Present law provides that individuals with a high deductible health plan (and generally no other health plan) purchased either through the individual market or through an employer may establish and make tax-deductible contributions to a health savings account ("HSA").[148] Subject to certain limitations,[149] contributions made to an HSA by an employer, including contributions made through a cafeteria plan through salary reduction, are excluded from income (and from wages for payroll tax purposes). Contributions made by individuals are deductible for income tax purposes, regardless of whether the individuals itemize. Distributions from an HSA that are used for qualified medical expenses are excludible from gross income.[150] The general definition of medical care without the explicit limitation on medicine also applies for purposes of this exclu-

---

[141] Sec. 213(a).

[142] Sec. 213(d). There are certain limitations on the general definition including a rule that cosmetic surgery or similar procedures are generally not medical care.

[143] Sec. 213(b).

[144] Rev. Rul. 2003-58, 2003-1 CB 959.

[145] Sec 106.

[146] Sec. 105(b).

[147] Sec. 105(b) provides that reimbursements for medical care within the meaning of section 213(d) pursuant to employer-provided health coverage are excludible from gross income. The definition of medical care in section 213(d) does not include the prescription drug limitation in section 213(b).

[148] Sec. 223.

[149] For 2009, the maximum aggregate annual contribution that can be made to an HSA is $3,000 in the case of self-only coverage and $5,950 in the case of family coverage ($3,050 and $6,150 for 2010). The annual contribution limits are increased for individuals who have attained age 55 by the end of the taxable year (referred to as "catch-up contributions"). In the case of policyholders and covered spouses who are age 55 or older, the HSA annual contribution limit is greater than the otherwise applicable limit by $1,000 in 2009 and thereafter. Contributions, including catch-up contributions, cannot be made once an individual is enrolled in Medicare.

[150] Sec. 223(f).

sion.[151] Similar rules apply for another type of medical savings arrangement called an Archer MSA.[152] Thus, a distribution from a HSA or an Archer MSA used to purchase over-the-counter medicine also is excludible as an amount used for qualified medical expenses.

Explanation of Provision

Under the provision, with respect to medicines, the definition of medical expense for purposes of employer-provided health coverage (including HRAs and Health FSAs), HSAs, and Archer MSAs, is conformed to the definition for purposes of the itemized deduction for medical expenses, except that prescribed drug is deter-

mined without regard to whither the drug is available without a prescription. Thus, under the provision, the cost of over-the-counter medicines may not be reimbursed with excludible income through a Health FSA, HRA, HSA, or Archer MSA, unless the medicine is prescribed by a physician.

Effective Date

The provision is effective for expenses incurred after December 31, 2010.

[Law at ¶ 5085, ¶ 5140, and ¶ 5145. CCH Explanation at ¶ 220.]

[¶ 10,190] Act Sec. 9004. Increase in additional tax on distributions from HSAs not used for medical expenses

Joint Committee on Taxation (J.C.T. REP. No. JCX-18-10)

[Code Secs. 220 and 223]

Present Law

Health savings account

Present law provides that individuals with a high deductible health plan (and generally no other health plan) may establish and make tax-deductible contributions to a health savings account ("HSA").[153] An HSA is a tax-exempt account held by a trustee or custodian for the benefit of the individual. An HSA is subject to a condition that the individual is covered under a high deductible health plan (purchased either through the individual market or through an employer). The decision to create and fund an HSA is made on an individual-by-individual basis and does not require any action on the part of the employer.

Subject to certain limitations, contributions made to an HSA by an employer, including contributions made through a cafeteria plan through salary reduction, are excluded from income (and from wages for payroll tax purposes). Contributions made by individuals are deductible for income tax purposes, regardless of whether the

individuals itemize their deductions on their tax return (rather than claiming the standard deduction). Income from investments made in HSAs is not taxable and the overall income is not taxable upon disbursement for medical expenses.

For 2010, the maximum aggregate annual contribution that can be made to an HSA is $3,050 in the case of self-only coverage and $6,150 in the case of family coverage. The annual contribution limits are increased for individuals who have attained age 55 by the end of the taxable year (referred to as "catch-up contributions"). In the case of policyholders and covered spouses who are age 55 or older, the HSA annual contribution limit is greater than the otherwise applicable limit by $1,000 in 2010 and thereafter. Contributions, including catch-up contributions, cannot be made once an individual is enrolled in Medicare.

A high deductible health plan is a health plan that has an annual deductible that is at least $1,200 for self-only coverage or $2,400 for family coverage for 2010 and that limits the sum of the annual deductible and other payments that the individual must make with respect to covered

---

[151] Sec. 223(d)(2).

[152] Sec. 220.

[153] An individual with other coverage in addition to a high deductible health plan is still eligible for an HSA if such other coverage is "permitted insurance" or "permitted coverage." Permitted insurance is: (1) insurance if substantially all of the coverage provided under such insurance relates to (a) liabilities incurred under worker's compensation law, (b) tort liabilities, (c) liabilities relating to ownership or use of property (e.g., auto insurance), or (d) such

other similar liabilities as the Secretary may prescribe by regulations; (2) insurance for a specified disease or illness; and (3) insurance that provides a fixed payment for hospitalization. Permitted coverage is coverage (whether provided through insurance or otherwise) for accidents, disability, dental care, vision care, or long-term care. With respect to coverage for years beginning after December 31, 2006, certain coverage under a Health FSA is disregarded in determining eligibility for an HSA.

benefits to no more than $5,950 in the case of self-only coverage and $11,900 in the case of family coverage for 2010.

Distributions from an HSA that are used for qualified medical expenses are excludible from gross income. Distributions from an HSA that are not used for qualified medical expenses are includible in gross income. An additional 10 percent tax is added for all HSA disbursements not made for qualified medical expenses. The additional 10-percent tax does not apply, however, if the distribution is made after death, disability, or attainment of age of Medicare eligibility (currently, age 65). Unlike reimbursements from a flexible spending arrangement or health reimbursement arrangement, distributions from an HSA are not required to be substantiated by the employer or a third party for the distributions to be excludible from income.

As in the case of individual retirement arrangements,[154] the individual is the beneficial owner of his or her HSA, and thus the individual is required to maintain books and records with respect to the expense and claim the exclusion for a distribution from the HSA on their tax return. The determination of whether the distribution is for a qualified medical expense is subject to individual self-reporting and IRS enforcement.

Archer medical savings account

An Archer MSA is also a tax-exempt trust or custodial account to which tax-deductible contributions may be made by individuals with a high deductible health plan.[155] Archer MSAs provide tax benefits similar to, but generally not as favorable as, those provided by HSAs for individuals covered by high deductible health plans. The main differences include: (1) only self-employed individuals and employees of small employers are eligible to have an Archer MSA; (2) for Archer MSA purposes, a high deductible health plan is a health plan with (a) an annual deductible for 2010 of at least $2,000 and no more than $3,000 in the case of self-only coverage and at least $4,050 and no more than $6,050 in the case of family coverage and (b) maximum out-of-pocket expenses for 2010 of no more than $4,050 in the case of self-only coverage and no more than $7,400 in the case of family coverage; and (3) the additional tax on distributions not used for medical expenses is 15 percent rather than 10 percent. After 2007, no new contributions can be made to Archer MSAs except by or on behalf of individuals who previously had made Archer MSA contributions and employees who are employed by a participating employer.

Explanation of Provision

The additional tax on distributions from an HSA or an Archer MSA that are not used for qualified medical expenses is increased to 20 percent of the disbursed amount.

Effective Date

The change is effective for disbursements made during tax years starting after December 31, 2010.

[Law at ¶ 5140 and ¶ 5145. CCH Explanation at ¶ 225.]

[¶ 10,200] Act Sec. 9005. Limitation on health flexible spending arrangements under cafeteria plans[156]

Joint Committee on Taxation (J.C.T. REP. NO. JCX-18-10)

[Code Sec. 125]

Present law

Exclusion from income for employer-provided health coverage

The Code generally provides that the value of employer-provided health coverage under an accident or health plan is excludible from gross income.[157] In addition, any reimbursements under an accident or health plan for medical care expenses for employees, their spouses, and their dependents generally are excluded from gross

---

[154] Sec. 408.

[155] Sec. 220.

[156] Section 9005 of the Senate amendment, as amended by section 10902, is further amended by section 1403 of the Reconciliation bill.

[157] Sec. 106. Health coverage provided to active members of the uniformed services, military retirees, and their depen-

dents are excludable under section 134. That section provides an exclusion for "qualified military benefits," defined as benefits received by reason of status or service as a member of the uniformed services and which were excludable from gross income on September 9, 1986, under any provision of law, regulation, or administrative practice then in effect.

income.[158] The exclusion applies both to health coverage in the case in which an employer absorbs the cost of employees' medical expenses not covered by insurance (i.e., a self-insured plan) as well as in the case in which the employer purchases health insurance coverage for its employees. There is no limit on the amount of employer-provided health coverage that is excludable. A similar rule excludes employer-provided health insurance coverage from the employees' wages for payroll tax purposes.[159]

Employers may also provide health coverage in the form of an agreement to reimburse medical expenses of their employees (and their spouses and dependents), not reimbursed by a health insurance plan, through flexible spending arrangements which allow reimbursement for medical care not in excess of a specified dollar amount (either elected by an employee under a cafeteria plan or otherwise specified by the employer). Health coverage provided in the form of one of these arrangements is also excludible from gross income as employer-provided health coverage under an accident or health plan.[160]

Qualified benefits

Qualified benefits under a cafeteria plan are generally employer-provided benefits that are not includable in gross income under an express provision of the Code. Examples of qualified benefits include employer-provided health coverage, group term life insurance coverage not in excess of 50,000, and benefits under a dependent care assistance program. In order to be excludable, any qualified benefit elected under a cafeteria plan must independently satisfy any requirements under the Code section that provides the exclusion. However, some employer-provided benefits that are not includable in gross income under an express provision of the Code are explicitly not allowed in a cafeteria plan. These benefits are generally referred to as nonqualified benefits. Examples of nonqualified benefits include scholarships;[161] employer-provided meals and lodging;[162] educational assistance;[163]

and fringe benefits.[164] A plan offering any nonqualified benefit is not a cafeteria plan.[165]

Flexible spending arrangement under a cafeteria plan

A flexible spending arrangement for medical expenses under a cafeteria plan ("Health FSA") is health coverage in the form of an unfunded arrangement under which employees are given the option to reduce their current cash compensation and instead have the amount of the salary reduction contributions made available for use in reimbursing the employee for his or her medical expenses.[166] Health FSAs are subject to the general requirements for cafeteria plans, including a requirement that amounts remaining under a Health FSA at the end of a plan year must be forfeited by the employee (referred to as the "use-it-or-lose-it rule").[167] A Health FSA is permitted to allow a grace period not to exceed two and one-half months immediately following the end of the plan year during which unused amounts may be used.[168] A Health FSA can also include employer flex-credits which are non-elective employer contributions that the employer makes for every employee eligible to participate in the employer's cafeteria plan, to be used only for one or more tax excludible qualified benefits (but not as cash or a taxable benefit).[169]

A flexible spending arrangement including a Health FSA (under a cafeteria plan) is generally distinguishable from other employer-provided health coverage by the relationship between the value of the coverage for a year and the maximum amount of reimbursement reasonably available during the same period. A flexible spending arrangement for health coverage generally is defined as a benefit program which provides employees with coverage under which specific incurred medical care expenses may be reimbursed (subject to reimbursement maximums and other conditions) and the maximum amount of reimbursement reasonably available

---

[158] Sec. 105(b).

[159] Secs. 3121(a)(2), and 3306(a)(2). See also section 3231(e)(1) for a similar rule with respect to compensation for purposes of Railroad Retirement Tax.

[160] Sec. 106.

[161] Sec. 117.

[162] Sec. 119.

[163] Sec.127.

[164] Sec. 132.

[165] Proposed Treas. Reg. sec. 1.125-1(q). Long-term care services, contributions to Archer Medical Savings Accounts,

group term life insurance for an employee's spouse, child or dependent, and elective deferrals to section 403(b) plans are also nonqualified benefits.

[166] Sec. 125 and proposed Treas. Reg. sec. 1.125-5.

[167] Sec. 125(d)(2) and proposed Treas. Reg. sec. 1.125-5(c).

[168] Notice 2005-42, 2005-1 C.B. 1204 and proposed Treas. Reg. sec. 1.125-1(e).

[169] Proposed Treas. Reg. sec. 1-125-5(b).

is less than 500 percent of the value of such coverage.[170]

Health reimbursement arrangement

Rather than offering a Health FSA through a cafeteria plan, an employer may specify a dollar amount that is available for medical expense reimbursement. These arrangements are commonly called HRAs. Some of the rules applicable to HRAs and Health FSAs are similar (e.g., the amounts in the arrangements can only be used to reimburse medical expenses and not for other purposes), but the rules are not identical. In particular, HRAs cannot be funded on a salary reduction basis and the use-it-or-lose-it rule does not apply. Thus, amounts remaining at the end of the year may be carried forward to be used to reimburse medical expenses in following years.[171]

Explanation of Provision

Under the provision, in order for a Health FSA to be a qualified benefit under a cafeteria plan, the maximum amount available for reimbursement of incurred medical expenses of an employee, the employee's dependents, and any other eligible beneficiaries with respect to the employee, under the Health FSA for a plan year (or other 12-month coverage period) must not exceed 2500.[172] The 2,500 limitation is indexed to CPI-U, with any increase that is not a multiple of 50 rounded to the next lowest multiple of 50 for years beginning after December 31, 2013.

A cafeteria plan that does not include this limitation on the maximum amount available for reimbursement under any FSA is not a cafeteria plan within the meaning of section 125. Thus, when an employee is given the option under a cafeteria plan maintained by an employer to reduce his or her current cash compensation and instead have the amount of the salary reduction be made available for use in reimbursing the employee for his or her medical expenses under a Health FSA, the amount of the reduction in cash compensation pursuant to a salary reduction election must be limited to 2,500 for a plan year.

It is intended that regulations would require all cafeteria plans of an employer to be aggregated for purposes of applying this limit. The employer for this purpose is determined after applying the employer aggregation rules in section 414(b), (c), (m), and (o).[173] In the event of a plan year or coverage period that is less than 12 months, it is intended that the limit be required to be prorated.

The provision does not limit the amount permitted to be available for reimbursement under employer-provided health coverage offered through an HRA, including a flexible spending arrangement within the meaning of section 106(c)(2), that is not part of a cafeteria plan.

Effective Date

The provision is effective for taxable year beginning after December 31, 2012.

Law at ¶ 5095. CCH Explanation at ¶ 325.

---

[170] Sec. 106(c)(2) and proposed Treas. Reg. sec. 1.125-5(a).

[171] Guidance with respect to HRAs, including the interaction of FSAs and HRAs in the case of an individual covered under both, is provided in Notice 2002-45, 2002-2 C.B. 93.

[172] The provision does not change the present law treatment as described in proposed Treas. Reg. sec. 1.125-5 for dependent care flexible spending arrangements or adoption assistance flexible spending arrangements.

[173] Section 414(b) provides that, for specified employee benefit purposes, all employees of all corporations which are members of a controlled group of corporations are treated as employed by a single employer. There is a similar rule in section 414(c) under which all employees of trades or businesses (whether or not incorporated) which are under common control are treated under regulations as employed by a single employer, and, in section 414(m), under which employees of an affiliated service group (as defined in that section) are treated as employed by a single employer. Section 414(o) authorizes the Treasury to issue regulations to prevent avoidance of the requirements under section 414(m). Section 125(g)(4) applies this rule to cafeteria plans.

[¶10,210] Act Sec. 9006. Require information reporting on payments to corporations[238]

Joint Committee on Taxation (J.C.T. REP. NO. JCX-18-10)

[Code Sec. 6041]

Present Law

Present law imposes a variety of information reporting requirements on participants in certain transactions.[239] These requirements are intended to assist taxpayers in preparing their income tax returns and to help the IRS determine whether such returns are correct and complete.

The primary provision governing information reporting by payors requires an information return by every person engaged in a trade or business who makes payments aggregating $600 or more in any taxable year to a single payee in the course of that payor's trade or business.[240] Payments subject to reporting include fixed or determinable income or compensation, but do not include payments for goods or certain enumerated types of payments that are subject to other specific reporting requirements.[241] The payor is required to provide the recipient of the payment with an annual statement showing the aggregate payments made and contact information for the payor.[242] The regulations generally except from reporting, payments to corporations, exempt organizations, governmental entities, international organizations, or retirement plans.[243]

However, the following types of payments to corporations must be reported: Medical and healthcare payments;[244] fish purchases for cash;[245] attorney's fees;[246] gross proceeds paid to an attorney;[247] substitute payments in lieu of dividends or tax-exempt interest;[248] and payments by a Federal executive agency for services.[249]

Failure to comply with the information reporting requirements results in penalties, which may include a penalty for failure to file the information return,[250] and a penalty for failure to furnish payee statements[251] or failure to comply with other various reporting requirements.[252]

Detailed rules are provided for the reporting of various types of investment income, including interest, dividends, and gross proceeds from brokered transactions (such as a sale of stock).[253] In general, the requirement to file Form 1099 applies with respect to amounts paid to U.S. persons and is linked to the backup withholding rules of section 3406. Thus, a payor of interest, dividends or gross proceeds generally must request that a U.S. payee (other than certain exempt recipients) furnish a Form W-9 providing that person's name and taxpayer identification

---

[238] This description is based upon the discussion at page 334 in S. Report 111-89, final Committee Report of the Senate Finance Committee on "America's Healthy Future Act of 2009," published October 21, 2009.

[239] Secs. 6031 through 6060.

[240] Sec. 6041(a). The information return is generally submitted electronically as a Form-1099 or Form-1096, although certain payments to beneficiaries or employees may require use of Forms W-3 or W-2, respectively. Treas. Reg. sec. 1.6041-1(a)(2).

[241] Sec. 6041(a) requires reporting as to "other fixed or determinable gains, profits, and income (other than payments to which section 6042(a)(1), 6044(a)(1), 6047(c), 6049(a) or 6050N(a) applies and other than payments with respect to which a statement is required under authority of section 6042(a), 6044(a)(2) or 6045)[.]" These excepted payments include most interest, royalties, and dividends.

[242] Sec. 6041(d).

[243] Treas. Reg. sec. 1.6041-3(p). Certain for-profit health provider corporations are not covered by this general exception, including those organizations providing billing services for such companies.

[244] Sec. 6050T.

[245] Sec. 6050R.

[246] Sec. 6045(f)(1) and (2); Treas. Reg. secs. 1.6041-1(d)(2) and 1.6045-5(d)(5).

[247] Ibid.

[248] Sec. 6045(d).

[249] Sec. 6041(d)(3).

[250] Sec. 6721. The penalty for the failure to file an information return generally is $50 for each return for which such failure occurs. The total penalty imposed on a person for all failures during a calendar year cannot exceed $250,000. Additionally, special rules apply to reduce the per-failure and maximum penalty where the failure is corrected within a specified period.

[251] Sec. 6722. The penalty for failure to provide a correct payee statement is $50 for each statement with respect to which such failure occurs, with the total penalty for a calendar year not to exceed $100,000. Special rules apply that increase the per-statement and total penalties where there is intentional disregard of the requirement to furnish a payee statement.

[252] Sec. 6723. The penalty for failure to timely comply with a specified information reporting requirement is $50 per failure, not to exceed $100,000 for a calendar year.

[253] Secs. 6042 (dividends), 6045 (broker reporting) and 6049 (interest) and the Treasury regulations thereunder.

number.[254] That information is then used to complete the Form 1099.

Explanation of Provision

Under the provision, a business is required to file an information return for all payments aggregating $600 or more in a calendar year to a single payee (other than a payee that is a tax-exempt corporation), notwithstanding any regulation promulgated under section 6041 prior to the date of enactment. The payments to be reported include gross proceeds paid in considera-tion for property or services. However, the provision does not override specific provisions elsewhere in the Code that except certain payments from reporting, such as securities or broker transactions as defined under section 6045(a) and the regulations thereunder.

Effective Date

The provision is effective for payments made after December 31, 2011.

[Law at ¶5250. CCH Explanation at ¶420.]

[¶10,220] Act Sec. 9007. Additional requirements for charitable hospitals[174]

Joint Committee on Taxation (J.C.T. REP. NO. JCX-18-10)

[Code Secs. 501(c) and 6033 and New Code Sec. 4959]

Present Law

Tax exemption

Charitable organizations, i.e., organizations described in section 501(c)(3), generally are exempt from Federal income tax, are eligible to receive tax deductible contributions,[175] have access to tax-exempt financing through State and local governments (described in more detail below),[176] and generally are exempt from State and local taxes. A charitable organization must operate primarily in pursuit of one or more tax-exempt purposes constituting the basis of its tax exemption.[177] The Code specifies such purposes as religious, charitable, scientific, educational, literary, testing for public safety, to foster international amateur sports competition, or for the prevention of cruelty to children or animals. In general, an organization is organized and operated for charitable purposes if it provides relief for the poor and distressed or the underprivileged.[178]

The Code does not provide a per se exemption for hospitals. Rather, a hospital qualifies for exemption if it is organized and operated for a charitable purpose and otherwise meets the requirements of section 501(c)(3).[179] The promotion of health has been recognized by the IRS as a charitable purpose that is beneficial to the community as a whole.[180] It includes not only the establishment or maintenance of charitable hospitals, but clinics, homes for the aged, and other providers of health care.

Since 1969, the IRS has applied a "community benefit" standard for determining whether a hospital is charitable.[181] According to Revenue Ruling 69-545, community benefit can include, for example: maintaining an emergency room open to all persons regardless of ability to pay; having an independent board of trustees composed of representatives of the community; operating with an open medical staff policy, with privileges available to all qualifying physicians; providing charity care; and utilizing surplus funds to improve the quality of patient care, expand facilities, and advance medical training, education and research. Beginning in 2009, hospitals generally are required to submit information on community benefit on their annual information returns filed with the IRS.[182] Present law does not include sanctions short of revoca-

---

[254] See Treas. Reg. sec. 31.3406(h)-3.

[174] Section 9007 of the Senate amendment is amended by section 10903 of the Senate amendment.

[175] Sec. 170.

[176] Sec. 145.

[177] Treas. Reg. sec. 1.501(c)(3)-1(c)(1).

[178] Treas. Reg. sec. 1.501(c)(3)-1(d)(2).

[179] Although nonprofit hospitals generally are recognized as tax-exempt by virtue of being "charitable" organizations, some might qualify for exemption as educational or scientific organizations because they are organized and operated primarily for medical education and research purposes.

[180] Rev. Rul. 69-545, 1969-2 C.B. 117; see also Restatement (Second) of Trusts secs. 368, 372 (1959); see Bruce R. Hopkins, *The Law of Tax-Exempt Organizations*, sec. 6.3 (8th ed. 2003) (discussing various forms of health-care providers that may qualify for exemption under section 501(c)(3)).

[181] Rev. Rul. 69-545, 1969-2 C.B. 117. From 1956 until 1969, the IRS applied a "financial ability" standard, requiring that a charitable hospital be "operated to the extent of its financial ability for those not able to pay for the services rendered and not exclusively for those who are able and expected to pay." Rev. Rul. 56-185, 1956-1 C.B. 202.

[182] IRS Form 990, Schedule H.

tion of tax-exempt status for hospitals that fail to satisfy the community benefit standard.

Although section 501(c)(3) hospitals generally are exempt from Federal tax on their net income, such organizations are subject to the unrelated business income tax on income derived from a trade or business regularly carried on by the organization that is not substantially related to the performance of the organization's tax-exempt functions.[183] In general, interest, rents, royalties, and annuities are excluded from the unrelated business income of tax-exempt organizations.[184]

Charitable contributions

In general, a deduction is permitted for charitable contributions, including charitable contributions to tax-exempt hospitals, subject to certain limitations that depend on the type of taxpayer, the property contributed, and the donee organization. The amount of deduction generally equals the fair market value of the contributed property on the date of the contribution. Charitable deductions are provided for income, estate, and gift tax purposes.[185]

Tax-exempt financing

In addition to issuing tax-exempt bonds for government operations and services, State and local governments may issue tax-exempt bonds to finance the activities of charitable organizations described in section 501(c)(3). Because interest income on tax-exempt bonds is excluded from gross income, investors generally are willing to accept a lower pre-tax rate of return on such bonds than they might otherwise accept on a taxable investment. This, in turn, lowers the cost of capital for the users of such financing. Both capital expenditures and limited working capital expenditures of charitable organizations described in section 501(c)(3) generally may be financed with tax-exempt bonds. Private, nonprofit hospitals frequently are the beneficiaries of this type of financing.

Bonds issued by State and local governments may be classified as either governmental bonds or private activity bonds. Governmental bonds are bonds the proceeds of which are primarily used to finance governmental functions or which are repaid with governmental funds. Private activity bonds are bonds in which the State or local government serves as a conduit providing financing to nongovernmental persons (e.g., private businesses or individuals). For these purposes, the term "nongovernmental person" generally includes the Federal government and all other individuals and entities other than States or local governments, including section 501(c)(3) organizations. The exclusion from income for interest on State and local bonds does not apply to private activity bonds, unless the bonds are issued for certain permitted purposes ("qualified private activity bonds") and other Code requirements are met.

Reporting and disclosure requirements

Exempt organizations are required to file an annual information return, stating specifically the items of gross income, receipts, disbursements, and such other information as the Secretary may prescribe.[186] Section 501(c)(3) organizations that are classified as public charities must file Form 990 (Return of Organization Exempt From Income Tax),[187] including Schedule A, which requests information specific to section 501(c)(3) organizations. Additionally, an organization that operates at least one facility that is, or is required to be, licensed, registered, or similarly recognized by a state s a hospital must complete Schedule H (Form 990), which requests information regarding charity care, community benefits, bad debt expense, and certain management company and joint venture arrangements of a hospital.

An organization described in section 501(c) or (d) generally is also required to make available for public inspection for a period of three years a copy of its annual information return (Form 990) and exemption application materials.[188] This requirement is satisfied if the organization has made the annual return and exemption application widely available (e.g., by posting such information on its website).[189]

---

[183] Secs. 511-514.

[184] Sec. 512(b).

[185] Secs. 170, 2055, and 2522, respectively.

[186] Sec. 6033(a). An organization that has not received a determination of its tax-exempt status, but that claims tax-exempt status under section 501(a), is subject to the same annual reporting requirements and exceptions as organizations that have received a tax-exemption determination.

[187] Social welfare organizations, labor organizations, agricultural organizations, horticultural organizations, and business leagues are subject to the generally applicable Form 990, Form 990-EZ, and Form 990-T annual filing requirements.

[188] Sec. 6104(d).

[189] Sec. 6104(d)(4); Treas. Reg. sec. 301.6104(d)-2(b).

Explanation of Provision

Additional requirements for section 501(c)(3) hospitals[190]

In general

The provision establishes new requirements applicable to section 501(c)(3) hospitals. The new requirements are in addition to, and not in lieu of, the requirements otherwise applicable to an organization described in section 501(c)(3). The requirements generally apply to any section 501(c)(3) organization that operates at least one hospital facility. For purposes of the provision, a hospital facility generally includes: (1) any facility that is, or is required to be, licensed, registered, or similarly recognized by a State as a hospital; and (2) any other facility or organization the Secretary of the Treasury (the "Secretary"), in consultation with the Secretary of HHS and after public comment, determines has the provision of hospital care as its principal purpose. To qualify for tax exemption under section 501(c)(3), an organization subject to the provision is required to comply with the following requirements with respect to each hospital facility operated by such organization.

Community health needs assessment

Each hospital facility is required to conduct a community health needs assessment at least once every three taxable years and adopt an implementation strategy to meet the community needs identified through such assessment. The assessment may be based on current information collected by a public health agency or non-profit organizations and may be conducted together with one or more other organizations, including related organizations. The assessment process must take into account input from persons who represent the broad interests of the community served by the hospital facility, including those with special knowledge or expertise of public health issues. The hospital must disclose in its annual information report to the IRS (i.e., Form 990 and related schedules) how it is addressing the needs identified in the assessment and, if all identified needs are not addressed, the reasons why (e.g., lack of financial or human resources). Each hospital facility is required to make the assessment widely available. Failure to complete a community health needs assessment in any applicable three-year period results in a penalty on the organization of up to $50,000. For example, if a facility does not complete a community

health needs assessment in taxable years one, two or three, it is subject to the penalty in year three. If it then fails to complete a community health needs assessment in year four, it is subject to another penalty in year four (for failing to satisfy the requirement during the three-year period beginning with taxable year two and ending with taxable year four). An organization that fails to disclose how it is meeting needs identified in the assessment is subject to existing incomplete return penalties.[191]

Financial assistance policy

Each hospital facility is required to adopt, implement, and widely publicize a written financial assistance policy. The financial assistance policy must indicate the eligibility criteria for financial assistance and whether such assistance includes free or discounted care. For those eligible for discounted care, the policy must indicate the basis for calculating the amounts that will be billed to such patients. The policy must also indicate how to apply for such assistance. If a hospital does not have a separate billing and collections policy, the financial assistance policy must also indicate what actions the hospital may take in the event of non-response or non-payment, including collections action and reporting to credit rating agencies. Each hospital facility also is required to adopt and implement a policy to provide emergency medical treatment to individuals. The policy must prevent discrimination in the provision of emergency medical treatment, including denial of service, against those eligible for financial assistance under the facility's financial assistance policy or those eligible for government assistance.

Limitation on charges

Each hospital facility is permitted to bill for emergency or other medically necessary care provided to individuals who qualify for financial assistance under the facility's financial assistance policy no more than the amounts generally billed to individuals who have insurance covering such care. A hospital facility may not use gross charges (i.e., "chargemaster" rates) when billing individuals who qualify for financial assistance. It is intended that amounts billed to those who qualify for financial assistance may be based on either the best, or an average of the three best, negotiated commercial rates, or Medicare rates.

---

[190] No inference is intended regarding whether an organization satisfies the present law community benefit standard.

[191] Sec. 6652.

Collection processes

Under the provision, a hospital facility (or its affiliates) may not undertake extraordinary collection actions (even if otherwise permitted by law) against an individual without first making reasonable efforts to determine whether the individual is eligible for assistance under the hospital's financial assistance policy. Such extraordinary collection actions include lawsuits, liens on residences, arrests, body attachments, or other similar collection processes. The Secretary is directed to issue guidance concerning what constitutes reasonable efforts to determine eligibility. It is intended that for this purpose, "reasonable efforts" includes notification by the hospital of its financial assistance policy upon admission and in written and oral communications with the patient regarding the patient's bill, including invoices and telephone calls, before collection action or reporting to credit rating agencies is initiated.

Reporting and disclosure requirements

The provision includes new reporting and disclosure requirements. Under the provision, the Secretary or the Secretary's delegate is required to review information about a hospital's community benefit activities (currently reported on Form 990, Schedule H) at least once every three years. The provision also requires each organization to which the provision applies to file with its annual information return (i.e., Form 990) a copy of its audited financial statements (or, in the case of an organization the financial statements of which are included in a consolidated financial statement with other organizations, such consolidated financial statements).

The provision requires the Secretary, in consultation with the Secretary of HHS, to submit annually a report to Congress with information regarding the levels of charity care, bad debt expenses, unreimbursed costs of means-tested government programs, and unreimbursed costs of non-means tested government programs incurred by private tax-exempt, taxable, and governmental hospitals, as well as the costs incurred by private tax-exempt hospitals for community benefit activities. In addition, the Secretary, in consultation with the Secretary of HHS, must conduct a study of the trends in these amounts, and submit a report on such study to Congress not later than five years from date of enactment.

Effective Date

Except as provided below, the provision is effective for taxable years beginning after the date of enactment. The community health needs assessment requirement is effective for taxable years beginning after the date which is two years after the date of enactment.[192] The excise tax on failures to satisfy the community health needs assessment requirement is effective for failures occurring after the date of enactment.

[**Law at ¶5155, ¶5220, ¶5245 and ¶7027. CCH Explanation at ¶440.**]

[¶10,230] Act Sec. 9008. Imposition of annual fee on branded prescription pharmaceutical manufacturers and importers[193]

Joint Committee on Taxation (J.C.T. REP. NO. JCX-18-10)

[Act Sec. 9008]

Present Law

There are two Medicare trust funds under present law, the Hospital Insurance ("HI") fund and the Supplementary Medical Insurance ("SMI") fund.[194] The HI trust fund is primarily funded through payroll tax on covered earnings. Employers and employees each pay 1.45 percent of wages, while self-employed workers pay 2.9 percent of a portion of their net earnings from self-employment. Other HI trust fund revenue sources include a portion of the Federal income taxes paid on Social Security benefits, and interest paid on the U.S. Treasury securities held in the HI trust fund. For the SMI trust fund, transfers from the general fund of the Treasury represent the largest source of revenue, but additional revenues include monthly premiums paid by beneficiaries, and interest paid on the

---

[192] For example, assume the date of enactment is April 1, 2010. A calendar year taxpayer would test whether it meets the community health needs assessment requirement in the taxable year ending December 31, 2013. To avoid the penalty, the taxpayer must have satisfied the community health needs assessment requirements in 2011, 2012, or 2013.

[193] Section 9008 of the Senate amendment is amended by section 1404 of the Reconciliation bill.

[194] See 2009 Annual Report of the Boards of Trustees of the Federal Hospital Insurance and Federal Supplementary Medical Insurance Trust Funds, available at http://www.cms.hhs.gov/ReportsTrustFunds/downloads/tr2009.pdf.

U.S. Treasury securities held in the SMI trust fund.

Present law does not impose a fee creditable to the Medicare trust funds on companies that manufacture or import prescription drugs for sale in the United States.

Explanation of Provision

The provision imposes a fee on each covered entity engaged in the business of manufacturing or importing branded prescription drugs for sale to any specified government program or pursuant to coverage under any such program for each calendar year beginning after 2010. Fees collected under the provision are credited to the Medicare Part B trust fund.

The aggregate annual fee for all covered entities is the applicable amount. The applicable amount is $2.5 billion for calendar year 2011, $2.8 billion for calendar years 2012 and 2013, $3 billion for calendar years 2014 through 2016, $4 billion for calendar year 2017, $4.1 billion for calendar year 2018, and $2.8 billion for calendar year 2019 and thereafter.

The aggregate fee is apportioned among the covered entities each year based on such entity's relative share of branded prescription drug sales taken into account during the previous calendar year. The Secretary of the Treasury will establish an annual payment date that will be no later than September 30 of each calendar year.

The Secretary of the Treasury will calculate the amount of each covered entity's fee for each calendar year by determining the relative market share for each covered entity. A covered entity's relative market share for a calendar year is the covered entity's branded prescription drug sales taken into account during the preceding calendar year as a percentage of the aggregate branded prescription drug sales of all covered entities taken into account during the preceding calendar year. The branded prescription drug sales taken into account during any calendar year with respect to any covered entity is: (1) zero percent of sales not more than $5 million, (2) 10 percent of sales over $5 million but not more than $125 million, (3) 40 percent of sales over $125 million but not more than $225 million, (4) 75 percent of sales over $225 million but not more than $400 million, and (5) 100 percent of sales over $400 million.

For purposes of the provision, a covered entity is any manufacturer or importer with gross receipts from branded prescription drug sales. All persons treated as a single employer under section 52(a) or (b) or under section 414(m) or 414(o) will be treated as a single covered entity for purposes of the provision. In applying the single employer rules under 52(a) and (b), foreign corporations will not be excluded. If more than one person is liable for payment of the fee imposed by this provision, all such persons are jointly and severally liable for payment of such fee. It is anticipated that the Secretary may require each covered entity to identify each member of the group that is treated as a single covered entity under the provision.

Under the provision, branded prescription drug sales are sales of branded prescriptions drugs made to any specified government program or pursuant to coverage under any such program. The term branded prescription drugs includes any drug which is subject to section 503(b) of the Federal Food, Drug, and Cosmetic Act and for which an application was submitted under section 505(b) of such Act, and any biological product for which an application was submitted under section 351(a) of such Act. Branded prescription drug sales, as defined under the provision, does not include sales of any drug or biological product with respect to which an orphan drug tax credit was allowed for any taxable year under section 45C. The exception for orphan drug sales does not apply to any drug or biological product after such drug or biological product is approved by the Food and Drug Administration for marketing for any indication other than the rare disease or condition with respect to which the section 45C credit was allowed.

Specified government programs under the provision include: (1) the Medicare Part D program under part D of title XVIII of the Social Security Act; (2) the Medicare Part B program under part B of title XVIII of the Social Security Act; (3) the Medicaid program under title XIX of the Social Security Act; (4) any program under which branded prescription drugs are procured by the Department of Veterans Affairs; (5) any program under which branded prescription drugs are procured by the Department of Defense; or (6) the TRICARE retail pharmacy program under section 1074g of title 10, United States Code.

The Secretary of HHS, the Secretary of Veterans Affairs, and the Secretary of Defense will report to the Secretary of the Treasury, at a time and in such a manner as the Secretary of the Treasury prescribes, the total branded prescription drug sales for each covered entity with respect to each specified government program under such Secretary's jurisdiction. The provision includes specific information to be included in the reports by the respective Secretaries for each specified government program.

The fees imposed under the provision are treated as excise taxes with respect to which only civil actions for refunds under the provisions of subtitle F will apply. Thus, the fees may be assessed and collected using the procedures in subtitle F without regard to the restrictions on assessment in section 6213.

The Secretary of the Treasury has authority to publish guidance as necessary to carry out the purposes of this provision. It is anticipated that the Secretary of the Treasury will publish guidance related to the determination of the fee under this section. For example, the Secretary may publish initial determinations, allow a notice and comment period, and then provide notice and demand for payment of the fee. It is also anticipated that the Secretary of the Treasury will provide guidance as to the determination of the fee in situations involving mergers, acquisitions, business divisions, bankruptcy, or any other situations where guidance is necessary to account for sales taken into account for determining the fee for any calendar year.

The fees imposed under the provision are not deductible for U.S. income tax purposes.

Effective Date

The provision is effective for calendar years beginning after December 31, 2010.

[Law at ¶ 7030. CCH Explanation at ¶ 350.]

[¶ 10,240] Act Sec. 9009. Imposition of annual fee on medical device manufacturers and importers[195]

Joint Committee on Taxation (J.C.T. Rep. No. JCX-18-10)

[Act Sec. 9009]

Repeal

The provision imposing an annual fee on manufactures and importers of medical devices is repealed.

Effective Date

The repeal is effective as of the date of enactment of the Senate amendment.

[Law at ¶ 7033. CCH Explanation at ¶ 350.]

[¶ 10,250] Act Sec. 9010. Imposition of annual fee on health insurance providers[196]

Joint Committee on Taxation (J.C.T. Rep. No. JCX-18-10)

[Act Sec. 9010]

Present Law

Present law provides special rules for determining the taxable income of insurance companies (subchapter L of the Code). Separate sets of rules apply to life insurance companies and to property and casualty insurance companies. Insurance companies are subject to Federal income tax at regular corporate income tax rates.

An insurance company that provides health insurance is subject to Federal income tax as either a life insurance company or as a property insurance company, depending on its mix of lines of business and on the resulting portion of its reserves that are treated as life insurance reserves. For Federal income tax purposes, an insurance company is treated as a life insurance company if the sum of its (1) life insurance reserves and (2) unearned premiums and unpaid losses on noncancellable life, accident or health contracts not included in life insurance reserves, comprise more than 50 percent of its total reserves.[197]

Some insurance providers may be exempt from Federal income tax under section 501(a) if specific requirements are satisfied. Section 501(c)(8), for example, describes certain fraternal beneficiary societies, orders, or associations operating under the lodge system or for the exclusive benefit of their members that provide for the payment of life, sick, accident, or other benefits

---

[195] Section 9009 of the Senate amendment is repealed by section 1405(d) of the Reconciliation bill.

[196] Section 9010 of the Senate amendment, as amended by section 10905, is further amended by section 1406 of the Reconciliation bill.

[197] Sec. 816(a).

to the members or their dependents. Section 501(c)(9) describes certain voluntary employees' beneficiary associations that provide for the payment of life, sick, accident, or other benefits to the members of the association or their dependents or designated beneficiaries. Section 501(c)(12)(A) describes certain benevolent life insurance associations of a purely local character. Section 501(c)(15) describes certain small non-life insurance companies with annual gross receipts of no more than $600,000 ($150,000 in the case of a mutual insurance company). Section 501(c)(26) describes certain membership organizations established to provide health insurance to certain high-risk individuals. Section 501(c)(27) describes certain organizations established to provide workmen's compensation insurance.

An excise tax applies to premiums paid to foreign insurers and reinsurers covering U.S. risks.[198] The excise tax is imposed on a gross basis at the rate of one percent on reinsurance and life insurance premiums, and at the rate of four percent on property and casualty insurance premiums. The excise tax does not apply to premiums that are effectively connected with the conduct of a U.S. trade or business or that are exempted from the excise tax under an applicable income tax treaty. The excise tax paid by one party cannot be credited if, for example, the risk is reinsured with a second party in a transaction that is also subject to the excise tax.

IRS authority to assess and collect taxes is generally provided in subtitle F of the Code (secs. 6001 -7874), relating to procedure and administration. That subtitle establishes the rules governing both how taxpayers are required to report information to the IRS and to pay their taxes, as well as their rights. It also establishes the duties and authority of the IRS to enforce the Federal tax law, and sets forth rules relating to judicial proceedings involving Federal tax.

Explanation of Provision

Under the provision, an annual fee applies to any covered entity engaged in the business of providing health insurance with respect to United States health risks. The fee applies for calendar years beginning after 2013. The aggregate annual fee for all covered entities is the applicable amount. The applicable amount is $8 billion for calendar year 2014, $11.3 billion for calendar years 2015 and 2016, $13.9 billion for calendar year 2017, and $14.3 billion for calendar year 2018. For calendar years after 2018, the applicable amount is indexed to the rate of premium growth.

The annual payment date for a calendar year is determined by the Secretary of the Treasury, but in no event may be later than September 30 of that year.

Under the provision, the aggregate annual fee is apportioned among the providers based on a ratio designed to reflect relative market share of U.S. health insurance business. For each covered entity, the fee for a calendar year is an amount that bears the same ratio to the applicable amount as (1) the covered entity's net premiums written during the preceding calendar year with respect to health insurance for any United States health risk, bears to (2) the aggregate net written premiums of all covered entities during such preceding calendar year with respect to such health insurance.

The provision requires the Secretary of the Treasury to calculate the amount of each covered entity's fee for the calendar year, determining the covered entity's net written premiums for the preceding calendar year with respect to health insurance for any United States health risk on the basis of reports submitted by the covered entity and through the use of any other source of information available to the Treasury Department. It is intended that the Treasury Department be able to rely on published aggregate annual statement data to the extent necessary, and may use annual statement data and filed annual statements that are publicly available to verify or supplement the reports submitted by covered entities.

Net written premiums is intended to mean premiums written, including reinsurance premiums written, reduced by reinsurance ceded, and reduced by ceding commissions. Net written premiums do not include amounts arising under arrangements that are not treated as insurance (i.e., in the absence of sufficient risk shifting and risk distribution for the arrangement to constitute insurance).[199]

The amount of net premiums written that are taken into account for purposes of determining a covered entity's market share is subject to dollar thresholds. A covered entity's net premiums written during the calendar year that are not more $25 million are not taken into account for this purpose. With respect to a covered entity's net premiums written during the calendar year that are more than $25 million but not more than $50 million, 50 percent are taken into account, and 100 percent of net premiums written in excess of $50 million are taken into account.

---

[198] Secs. 4371-4374.

[199] See *Helvering v. Le Gierse*, 312 U.S. 531 (1941).

After application of the above dollar thresholds, a special rule provides an exclusion, for purposes of determining an otherwise covered entity's market share, of 50 percent of net premiums written that are attributable to the exempt activities[200] of a health insurance organization that is exempt from Federal income tax[201] by reason of being described in section 501(c)(3) (generally, a public charity), section 501(c)(4) (generally, a social welfare organization), section 501(c)(26) (generally, a high-risk health insurance pool), or section 501(c)(29) (a consumer operated and oriented plan ("CO-OP") health insurance issuer).

A covered entity generally is an entity that provides health insurance with respect to United States health risks during the calendar year in which the fee under this section is due. Thus for example, an insurance company subject to tax under part I or II of subchapter L, an organization exempt from tax under section 501(a), a foreign insurer that provides health insurance with respect to United States health risks, or an insurer that provides health insurance with respect to United States health risks under Medicare Advantage, Medicare Part D, or Medicaid, is a covered entity under the provision except as provided in specific exceptions.

Specific exceptions are provided to the definition of a covered entity. A covered entity does not include an employer to the extent that the employer self-insures the health risks of its employees. For example, a manufacturer that enters into a self-insurance arrangement with respect to the health risks of its employees is not treated as a covered entity. As a further example, an insurer that sells health insurance and that also enters into a self-insurance arrangement with respect to the health risks of its own employees is treated as a covered entity with respect to its health insurance business, but is not treated as a covered entity to the extent of the self-insurance of its own employees' health risks.

A covered entity does not include any governmental entity. For this purpose, it is intended that a governmental entity includes a county organized health system entity that is an independent public agency organized as a nonprofit under State law and that contracts with a State to administer State Medicaid benefits through local care providers or HMOs.

A covered entity does not include an entity that (1) qualifies as nonprofit under applicable State law, (2) meets the private inurement and limitation on lobbying provisions described in section 501(c)(3), and (3) receives more than 80 percent of its gross revenue from government programs that target low-income, elderly, or disabled populations (including Medicare, Medicaid, the State Children's Health Insurance Plan ("SCHIP"), and dual-eligible plans).

A covered entity does not include an organization that qualifies as a VEBA under section 501(c)(9) that is established by an entity other than the employer (i.e., a union) for the purpose of providing health care benefits. This exclusion does not apply to multi-employer welfare arrangements ("MEWAs").

For purposes of the provision, all persons treated as a single employer under section 52(a) or (b) or section 414(m) or (o) are treated as a single covered entity (or as a single employer, for purposes of the rule relating to employers that self-insure the health risks of employees), and otherwise applicable exclusion of foreign corporations under those rules is disregarded. However, the exceptions to the definition of a covered entity are applied on a separate entity basis, not taking into account this rule. If more than one person is liable for payment of the fee by reason of being treated as a single covered entity, all such persons are jointly and severally liable for payment of the fee.

A United States heath risk means the health risk of an individual who is a U.S. citizen, is a U.S. resident within the meaning of section 7701(b)(1)(A) (whether or not located in the United States), or is located in the United States, with respect to the period that the individual is located there. In general, it is intended that risks in the following lines of business reported on the annual statement as prescribed by the National Association of Insurance Commissioners and as filed with the insurance commissioners of the States in which insurers are licensed to do business constitute health risks for this purpose: comprehensive (hospital and medical), vision, dental, Federal Employees Health Benefit plan, title XVIII Medicare, title XIX Medicaid, and other health.

---

[200] The exempt activities for this purpose are activities other than activities of an unrelated trade or business defined in section 513 of the Code.

[201] Section 501(m) of the Code provides that an organization described in section 501(c)(3) or (4) is exempt from Federal income tax only if no substantial part of its activities consists of providing commercial-type insurance. Thus, an organization otherwise described in section 501(c)(3) or (4) that is taxable (under the Federal income tax rules) by reason of section 501(m) is not eligible for the 50-percent exclusion under the insurance fee.

For purposes of the provision, health insurance does not include coverage only for accident, or disability income insurance, or a combination thereof. Health insurance does not include coverage only for a specified disease or illness, nor does health insurance include hospital indemnity or other fixed indemnity insurance. Health insurance does not include any insurance for long-term care or any Medicare supplemental health insurance (as defined in section 1882(g)(1) of the Social Security Act).

For purposes of procedure and administration under the rules of Subtitle F of the Code, the fee under this provision is treated as an excise tax with respect to which only civil actions for refund under Subtitle F apply. The Secretary of the Treasury may redetermine the amount of a covered entity's fee under the provision for any calendar year for which the statute of limitations remains open.

For purposes of section 275, relating to the nondeductibility of specified taxes, the fee is considered to be a nondeductible tax described in section 275(a)(6).

A reporting rule applies under the provision. A covered entity is required to report to the Secretary of the Treasury the amount of its net premiums written during any calendar year with respect to health insurance for any United States health risk.

A penalty applies for failure to report, unless it is shown that the failure is due to reasonable cause. The amount of the penalty is $10,000 plus the lesser of (1) $1,000 per day while the failure continues, or (2) the amount of the fee imposed for which the report was required. The penalty is treated as a penalty for purposes of subtitle F of the Code, must be paid on notice and demand by the Treasury Department and in the same manner as tax, and with respect to which only civil actions for refund under procedures of subtitle F. The reported information is not treated as taxpayer information under section 6103.

An accuracy-related penalty applies in the case of any understatement of a covered entity's net premiums written. For this purpose, an understatement is the difference between the amount of net premiums written as reported on the return filed by the covered entity and the amount of net premiums written that should have been reported on the return. The penalty is equal to the amount of the fee that should have been paid in the absence of an understatement over the amount of the fee determined based on the understatement. The accuracy-related penalty is subject to the provisions of subtitle F of the Code that apply to assessable penalties imposed under Chapter 68.

The provision provides authority for the Secretary of the Treasury to publish guidance necessary to carry out the purposes of the provision and to prescribe regulations necessary or appropriate to prevent avoidance of the purposes of the provision, including inappropriate actions taken to qualify as an exempt entity under the provision.

Effective Date

The annual fee is required to be paid in each calendar year beginning after December 31, 2013. The fee under the provision is determined with respect to net premiums written after December 31, 2012, with respect to health insurance for any United States health risk.

[Law at ¶7036. CCH Explanation at ¶350.]

[¶10,260] Act Sec. 9011. Study and report of effect on veterans health care

Joint Committee on Taxation (J.C.T. REP. No. JCX-18-10)

[Act Sec. 9011]

Present Law

No provision.

Explanation of Provision

The provision requires the Secretary of Veterans Affairs to conduct a study on the effect (if any) of the fees assessed on manufacturers and importers of branded prescription drugs, manufacturers and importers of medical devices, and health insurance providers on (1) the cost of medical care provided to veterans and (2) veterans' access to branded prescription drugs and medical devices.

The Secretary of Veterans Affairs will report the results of the study to the Committee on Ways and Means of the House of Representatives and to the Committee on Finance of the Senate no later than December 31, 2012.

Effective Date

The provision is effective on the date of enactment.

[CCH Explanation at ¶350.]

[¶10,270] Act Sec. 9012. Repeal business deduction for federal subsidies for certain retiree prescription drug plans[202]

Joint Committee on Taxation (J.C.T. REP. NO. JCX-18-10)

[Code Sec. 139A]

Present Law

In general

Sponsors[203] of qualified retiree prescription drug plans are eligible for subsidy payments from the Secretary of HHS with respect to a portion of each qualified covered retiree's gross covered prescription drug costs ("qualified retiree prescription drug plan subsidy").[204] A qualified retiree prescription drug plan is employment-based retiree health coverage[205] that has an actuarial value at least as great as the Medicare Part D standard plan for the risk pool and that meets certain other disclosure and recordkeeping requirements.[206] These qualified retiree prescription drug plan subsidies are excludable from the plan sponsor's gross income for the purposes of regular income tax and alternative minimum tax (including the adjustment for adjusted current earnings).[207]

Subsidy amounts

For each qualifying covered retiree enrolled for a coverage year in a qualified retiree prescription drug plan, the qualified retiree prescription drug plan subsidy is equal to 28 percent of the portion of the allowable retiree costs paid by the plan sponsor on behalf of the retiree that exceed the cost threshold but do not exceed the cost limit. A "qualifying covered retiree" is an individual who is eligible for Medicare but not enrolled in either a Medicare Part D prescription drug plan or a Medicare Advantage-Prescription Drug plan, but who is covered under a qualified retiree prescription drug plan. In general, allowable retiree costs are, with respect to prescription drug costs under a qualified retiree prescription drug plan, the part of the actual costs paid by the plan sponsor on behalf of a qualifying covered retiree under the plan.[208] Both the threshold and limit are indexed to the percentage increase in Medicare per capita prescription drug costs; the cost threshold was $250 in 2006 ($310 in 2010) and the cost limit was $5,000 in 2006 ($6,300 in 2010).[209]

Expenses relating to tax-exempt income

In general, no deduction is allowed under any provision of the Code for any expense or amount which would otherwise be allowable as a deduction if such expense or amount is allocable to a class or classes of exempt income.[210] Thus, expenses or amount paid or incurred with respect to the subsidies excluded from income under section 139A would generally not be deductible. However, a provision under section 139A specifies that the exclusion of the qualified retiree prescription drug plan subsidy from income is not taken into account in determining whether any deduction is allowable with respect to covered retiree prescription drug expenses

---

[202] Section 9012 of the Senate amendment is amended by section 1407 of the Reconciliation bill.

[203] The identity of the plan sponsor is determined in accordance with section 16(B) of ERISA, except that for cases where a plan is maintained jointly by one employer and an employee organization, and the employer is the primary source of financing, the employer is the plan sponsor.

[204] Sec. 1860D-22 of the Social Security Act (SSA), 42 USC Sec. 1395w-132.

[205] Employment-based retiree health coverage is health insurance coverage or other coverage of health care costs (whether provided by voluntary insurance coverage or pursuant to statutory or contractual obligation) for Medicare Part D eligible individuals (their spouses and dependents) under group health plans based on their status as retired participants in such plans. For purposes of the subsidy, group health plans generally include employee welfare benefit plans (as defined in section 607(1) of ERISA) that provide medical care (as defined in section 213(d)), Federal and State governmental plans, collectively bargained plans, and church plans.

[206] In addition to meeting the actuarial value standard, the plan sponsor must also maintain and provide the Secretary of HHS access to records that meet the Secretary of HHS's requirements for purposes of audits and other oversight activities necessary to ensure the adequacy of prescription drug coverage and the accuracy of payments made to eligible individuals under the plan. In addition, the plan sponsor must disclose to the Secretary of HHS whether the plan meets the actuarial equivalence requirement and if it does not, must disclose to retirees the limitations of their ability to enroll in Medicare Part D and that non-creditable coverage enrollment is subject to penalties such as fees for late enrollment. 42 U.S.C. 1395w-132(a)(2).

[207] Sec. 139A.

[208] For purposes of calculating allowable retiree costs, actual costs paid are net of discounts, chargebacks, and average percentage rebates, and exclude administrative costs.

[209] http://www.cms.hhs.gov/MedicareAdvtgSpecRateStats/Downloads/Announcement2010.pdf. Retrieved on March 19, 2010.

[210] Sec. 265(a) and Treas. Reg. sec. 1.265-1(a).

that are taken into account in determining the subsidy payment. Therefore, under present law, a taxpayer may claim a business deduction for covered retiree prescription drug expenses incurred notwithstanding that the taxpayer excludes from income qualified retiree prescription drug plan subsidies allocable to such expenses.

Explanation of Provision

The provision eliminates the rule that the exclusion for subsidy payments is not taken into account for purposes of determining whether a deduction is allowable with respect to retiree prescription drug expenses. Thus, under the provision, the amount otherwise allowable as a deduction for retiree prescription drug expenses is reduced by the amount of the excludable subsidy payments received.

For example, assume a company receives a subsidy of $28 with respect to eligible drug expenses of $100. The $28 is excludable from income under section 139A, and the amount otherwise allowable as a deduction is reduced by the $28. Thus, if the company otherwise meets the requirements of section 162 with respect to its eligible drug expenses, it would be entitled to an ordinary business expense deduction of $72.

Effective Date

The provision is effective for taxable years beginning after December 31, 2012.

[Law at ¶ 5105. CCH Explanation at ¶ 335.]

[¶ 10,280] Act Sec. 9013. Modify the itemized deduction for medical expenses

Joint Committee on Taxation (J.C.T. REP. NO. JCX-18-10)

[Code Sec. 213]

Present Law

Regular income tax.

For regular income tax purposes, individuals are allowed an itemized deduction for unreimbursed medical expenses, but only to the extent that such expenses exceed 7.5 percent of AGI.[211]

This deduction is available both to insured and uninsured individuals; thus, for example, an individual with employer-provided health insurance (or certain other forms of tax-subsidized health benefits) may also claim the itemized deduction for the individual's medical expenses not covered by that insurance if the 7.5 percent AGI threshold is met. The medical deduction encompasses health insurance premiums to the extent they have not been excluded from taxable income through the employer exclusion or self-insured deduction.

Alternative minimum tax.

For purposes of the alternative minimum tax ("AMT"), medical expenses are deductible only to the extent that they exceed 10 percent of AGI.

Explanation of Provision

This provision increases the threshold for the itemized deduction for unreimbursed medical expenses from 7.5 percent of AGI to 10 percent of AGI for regular income tax purposes. However, for the years 2013, 2014, 2015 and 2016, if either the taxpayer or the taxpayer's spouse turns 65 before the end of the taxable year, the increased threshold does not apply and the threshold remains at 7.5 percent of AGI. The provision does not change the AMT treatment of the itemized deduction for medical expenses.

Effective Date

The provision is effective for taxable years beginning after December 31, 2012.

[Law at ¶ 5080 and ¶ 5135. CCH Explanation at ¶ 215.]

---

[211] Sec. 213.

[¶10,290] Act Sec. 9014. Limitation on deduction for remuneration paid by health insurance providers

Joint Committee on Taxation (J.C.T. Rep. No. JCX-18-10)

[Code Sec. 162]

Present Law

An employer generally may deduct reasonable compensation for personal services as an ordinary and necessary business expense. Section 162(m) provides explicit limitations on the deductibility of compensation expenses in the case of corporate employers.

Section 162(m)

In general

The otherwise allowable deduction for compensation paid or accrued with respect to a covered employee of a publicly held corporation[212] is limited to no more than $1 million per year.[213] The deduction limitation applies when the deduction would otherwise be taken. Thus, for example, in the case of compensation resulting from a transfer of property in connection with the performance of services, such compensation is taken into account in applying the deduction limitation for the year for which the compensation is deductible under section 83 (i.e., generally the year in which the employee's right to the property is no longer subject to a substantial risk of forfeiture).

Covered employees

Section 162(m) defines a covered employee as (1) the chief executive officer of the corporation (or an individual acting in such capacity) as of the close of the taxable year and (2) the four most highly compensated officers for the taxable year (other than the chief executive officer). Treasury regulations under section 162(m) provide that whether an employee is the chief executive officer or among the four most highly compensated officers should be determined pursuant to the executive compensation disclosure rules promulgated under the Securities Exchange Act of 1934 ("Exchange Act").

In 2006, the Securities and Exchange Commission amended certain rules relating to executive compensation, including which executive officers' compensation must be disclosed under the Exchange Act. Under the new rules, such officers consist of (1) the principal executive officer (or an individual acting in such capacity), (2) the principal financial officer (or an individual acting in such capacity), and (3) the three most highly compensated executive officers, other than the principal executive officer or financial officer. In response to the Securities and Exchange Commission's new disclosure rules, the IRS issued updated guidance on identifying which employees are covered by section 162(m).[214]

Remuneration subject to the limit

Unless specifically excluded, the deduction limitation applies to all remuneration for services, including cash and the cash value of all remuneration (including benefits) paid in a medium other than cash. If an individual is a covered employee for a taxable year, the deduction limitation applies to all compensation not explicitly excluded from the deduction limitation, regardless of whether the compensation is for services as a covered employee and regardless of when the compensation was earned. The $1 million cap is reduced by excess parachute payments (as defined in sec. 280G, discussed below) that are not deductible by the corporation.

Certain types of compensation are not subject to the deduction limit and are not taken into account in determining whether other compensation exceeds $1 million. The following types of compensation are not taken into account: (1) remuneration payable on a commission basis; (2) remuneration payable solely on account of the attainment of one or more performance goals if certain outside director and shareholder approval requirements are met ("performance-based compensation"); (3) payments to a tax-qualified retirement plan (including salary reduction contributions); (4) amounts that are excludable from the executive's gross income (such as employer-provided health benefits and mis-

---

[212] A corporation is treated as publicly held if it has a class of common equity securities that is required to be registered under section 12 of the Securities Exchange Act of 1934.

[213] Sec. 162(m). This deduction limitation applies for purposes of the regular income tax and the alternative minimum tax.

[214] Notice 2007-49, 2007-25 I.R.B. 1429.

cellaneous fringe benefits[215]); and (5) any remuneration payable under a written binding contract which was in effect on February 17, 1993.

Remuneration does not include compensation for which a deduction is allowable after a covered employee ceases to be a covered employee. Thus, the deduction limitation often does not apply to deferred compensation that is otherwise subject to the deduction limitation (e.g., is not performance-based compensation) because the payment of compensation is deferred until after termination of employment.

Executive compensation of employers participating in the Troubled Assets Relief Program

In general

Under section 162(m)(5), the deduction limit is reduced to $500,000 in the case of otherwise deductible compensation of a covered executive for any applicable taxable year of an applicable employer.

An applicable employer means any employer from which one or more troubled assets are acquired under the "troubled assets relief program" ("TARP") established by the Emergency Stabilization Act of 2008[216] ("EESA") if the aggregate amount of the assets so acquired for all taxable years (including assets acquired through a direct purchase by the Treasury Department, within the meaning of section 113(c) of Title I of EESA) exceeds $300,000,000. However, such term does not include any employer from which troubled assets are acquired by the Treasury Department solely through direct purchases (within the meaning of section 113(c) of Title I of EESA). For example, if a firm sells $250,000,000 in assets through an auction system managed by the Treasury Department, and $100,000,000 to the Treasury Department in direct purchases, then the firm is an applicable employer. Conversely, if all $350,000,000 in sales take the form of direct purchases, then the firm would not be an applicable employer.

Unlike section 162(m), an applicable employer under this provision is not limited to publicly held corporations (or even limited to corporations). For example, an applicable employer could be a partnership if the partnership is an employer from which a troubled asset is acquired. The aggregation rules of section 414(b) and (c) apply in determining whether an employer is an applicable employer. However,

these rules are applied disregarding the rules for brother-sister controlled groups and combined groups in sections 1563(a)(2) and (3). Thus, this aggregation rule only applies to parent-subsidiary controlled groups. A similar controlled group rule applies for trades and businesses under common control.

The result of this aggregation rule is that all corporations in the same controlled group are treated as a single employer for purposes of identifying the covered executives of that employer and all compensation from all members of the controlled group are taken into account for purposes of applying the $500,000 deduction limit. Further, all sales of assets under the TARP from all members of the controlled group are considered in determining whether such sales exceed $300,000,000.

An applicable taxable year with respect to an applicable employer means the first taxable year which includes any portion of the period during which the authorities for the TARP established under EESA are in effect (the "authorities period") if the aggregate amount of troubled assets acquired from the employer under that authority during the taxable year (when added to the aggregate amount so acquired for all preceding taxable years) exceeds $300,000,000, and includes any subsequent taxable year which includes any portion of the authorities period.

A special rule applies in the case of compensation that relates to services that a covered executive performs during an applicable taxable year but that is not deductible until a later year ("deferred deduction executive remuneration"), such as nonqualified deferred compensation. Under the special rule, the unused portion (if any) of the $500,000 limit for the applicable tax year is carried forward until the year in which the compensation is otherwise deductible, and the remaining unused limit is then applied to the compensation.

For example, assume a covered executive is paid $400,000 in cash salary by an applicable employer in 2008 (assuming 2008 is an applicable taxable year) and the covered executive earns $100,000 in nonqualified deferred compensation (along with the right to future earnings credits) payable in 2020. Assume further that the $100,000 has grown to $300,000 in 2020. The full $400,000 in cash salary is deductible under the $500,000 limit in 2008. In 2020, the applicable employer's deduction with respect to the $300,000 will be limited to $100,000 (the lesser of

[215] Sec. 132.

[216] Pub. L. No. 110-343.

the $300,000 in deductible compensation before considering the special limitation, and $500,000 less $400,000, which represents the unused portion of the $500,000 limit from 2008).

Deferred deduction executive remuneration that is properly deductible in an applicable taxable year (before application of the limitation under the provision) but is attributable to services performed in a prior applicable taxable year is subject to the special rule described above and is not double-counted. For example, assume the same facts as above, except that the nonqualified deferred compensation is deferred until 2009 and that 2009 is an applicable taxable year. The employer's deduction for the nonqualified deferred compensation for 2009 would be limited to $100,000 (as in the example above). The limit that would apply under the provision for executive remuneration that is in a form other than deferred deduction executive remuneration and that is otherwise deductible for 2009 is $500,000. For example, if the covered executive is paid $500,000 in cash compensation for 2009, all $500,000 of that cash compensation would be deductible in 2009 under the provision.

Covered executive

The term covered executive means any individual who is the chief executive officer or the chief financial officer of an applicable employer, or an individual acting in that capacity, at any time during a portion of the taxable year that includes the authorities period. It also includes any employee who is one of the three highest compensated officers of the applicable employer for the applicable taxable year (other than the chief executive officer or the chief financial officer and only taking into account employees employed during any portion of the taxable year that includes the authorities period).[217]

Executive remuneration

The provision generally incorporates the present law definition of applicable employee remuneration. However, the present law exceptions for remuneration payable on commission and performance-based compensation do not apply for purposes of the $500,000 limit. In addition, the $500,000 limit only applies to executive remuneration which is attributable to services performed by a covered executive during an ap-

plicable taxable year. For example, assume the same facts as in the example above, except that the covered executive also receives in 2008 a payment of $300,000 in nonqualified deferred compensation that was attributable to services performed in 2006. Such payment is not treated as executive remuneration for purposes of the $500,000 limit.

Taxation of insurance companies

Present law provides special rules for determining the taxable income of insurance companies (subchapter L of the Code). Separate sets of rules apply to life insurance companies and to property and casualty insurance companies. Insurance companies are subject to Federal income tax at regular corporate income tax rates. An insurance company generally may deduct compensation paid in the course of its trade or business.

Explanation of Provision

Under the provision, no deduction is allowed for remuneration which is attributable to services performed by an applicable individual for a covered health insurance provider during an applicable taxable year to the extent that such remuneration exceeds $500,000. As under section 162(m)(5) for remuneration from TARP participants, the exceptions for performance based remuneration, commissions, or remuneration under existing binding contracts do not apply. This $500,000 deduction limitation applies without regard to whether such remuneration is paid during the taxable year or a subsequent taxable year. In applying this rule, rules similar to those in section 162(m)(5)(A)(ii) apply. Thus in the case of remuneration that relates to services that an applicable individual performs during a taxable year but that is not deductible until a later year, such as nonqualified deferred compensation, the unused portion (if any) of the $500,000 limit for the year is carried forward until the year in which the compensation is otherwise deductible, and the remaining unused limit is then applied to the compensation.

In determining whether the remuneration of an applicable individual for a year exceeds $500,000, all remuneration from all members of any controlled group of corporations (within the meaning of section 414(b)), other businesses

---

[217] The determination of the three highest compensated officers is made on the basis of the shareholder disclosure rules for compensation under the Exchange Act, except to the extent that the shareholder disclosure rules are inconsistent with the provision. Such shareholder disclosure rules are applied without regard to whether those rules actually apply to the employer under the Exchange Act. If an em-

ployee is a covered executive with respect to an applicable employer for any applicable taxable year, the employee will be treated as a covered executive for all subsequent applicable taxable years (and will be treated as a covered executive for purposes of any subsequent taxable year for purposes of the special rule for deferred deduction executive remuneration).

under common control (within the meaning of section 414(c)), or affiliated service group (within the meaning of sections 414(m) and (o)) are aggregated.

Covered health insurance provider and applicable taxable year

An insurance provider is a covered health insurance provider if at least 25 percent of the insurance provider's gross premium income from health business is derived from health insurance plans that meet the minimum creditable coverage requirements in the bill ("covered health insurance provider"). A taxable year is an applicable taxable year for an insurance provider if an insurance provider is a covered insurance provider for any portion of the taxable year. Employers with self-insured plans are excluded from the definition of covered health insurance provider.

Applicable individual

Applicable individuals include all officers, employees, directors, and other workers or service providers (such as consultants) performing services for or on behalf of a covered health insurance provider. Thus, in contrast to the general rules under section 162(m) and the special rules executive compensation of employers participating in the TARP program, the limitation on the deductibility of remuneration from a covered health insurance provided is not limited to a small group of officers and covered executives but generally applies to remuneration of all employees and service providers. If an individual is an applicable individual with respect to a covered health insurance provider for any taxable year, the individual is treated as an applicable individual for all subsequent taxable years (and is treated as an applicable individual for purposes of any subsequent taxable year for purposes of the special rule for deferred remuneration).

Effective Date

The provision is effective for remuneration paid in taxable years beginning after 2012 with respect to services performed after 2009.

[Law at ¶ 5120. CCH Explanation at ¶ 340.]

[¶ 10,300] Act Sec. 9015. Additional hospital insurance tax on high income taxpayers[218]

Joint Committee on Taxation (J.C.T. REP. No. JCX-18-10)

[New Code Secs. 1401 and 3101]

Present Law

Federal Insurance Contributions Act tax

The Federal Insurance Contributions Act imposes tax on employers based on the amount of wages paid to an employee during the year. The tax imposed is composed of two parts: (1) the old age, survivors, and disability insurance ("OASDI") tax equal to 6.2 percent of covered wages up to the taxable wage base ($106,800 in 2010); and (2) the HI tax amount equal to 1.45 percent of covered wages. Generally, covered wages means all remuneration for employment, including the cash value of all remuneration (including benefits) paid in any medium other than cash. Certain exceptions from covered wages are also provided. In addition to the tax on employers, each employee is subject to FICA taxes equal to the amount of tax imposed on the employer.

The employee portion of the FICA tax generally must be withheld and remitted to the Federal government by the employer.[219] The employer generally is liable for the amount of this tax whether or not the employer withholds the amount from the employee's wages.[220] In the event that the employer fails to withhold from an employee, the employee generally is not liable to the IRS for the amount of the tax. However, if the employer pays its liability for the amount of the tax not withheld, the employer generally has a right to collect that amount from the employee. Further, if the employer deducts and pays the tax the employer is indemnified against the claims and demands of any person for the amount of any payment of the tax made by the employer.[221]

---

[218] Section 9015 of the Senate bill is amended by section 10906 of the Senate bill.

[219] Sec. 3102(a).

[220] Sec. 3102(b).

[221] Ibid.

Self-Employment Contributions Act tax

As a parallel to FICA taxes, the Self-Employment Contributions Act ("SECA") imposes taxes on the net income from self employment of self employed individuals. The rate of the OASDI portion of SECA taxes is equal to the combined employee and employer OASDI FICA tax rates and applies to self employment income up to the FICA taxable wage base. Similarly, the rate of the HI portion is the same as the combined employer and employee HI rates and there is no cap on the amount of self employment income to which the rate applies.[222]

For purposes of computing net earnings from self employment, taxpayers are permitted a deduction equal to the product of the taxpayer's earnings (determined without regard to this deduction) and one-half of the sum of the rates for OASDI (12.4 percent) and HI (2.9 percent), i.e., 7.65 percent of net earnings. This deduction reflects the fact that the FICA rates apply to an employee's wages, which do not include FICA taxes paid by the employer, whereas the self-employed individual's net earnings are economically equivalent to an employee's wages plus the employer share of FICA taxes.

Explanation of Provision

Additional HI tax on employee portion of HI tax

Calculation of additional tax

The employee portion of the HI tax is increased by an additional tax of 0.9 percent on wages[223] received in excess of the threshold amount. However, unlike the general 1.45 percent HI tax on wages, this additional tax is on the combined wages of the employee and the employee's spouse, in the case of a joint return. The threshold amount is $250,000 in the case of a joint return or surviving spouse, $125,000 in the case of a married individual filing a separate return, and $200,000 in any other case.

Liability for the additional HI tax on wages

As under present law, the employer is required to withhold the additional HI tax on wages but is liable for the tax if the employer fails to withhold the amount of the tax from wages, or collect the tax from the employee if the employer fails to withhold. However, in determining the employer's requirement to withhold and liability for the tax, only wages that the employee receives from the employer in excess of $200,000 for a year are taken into account and the employer must disregard the amount of wages received by the employee's spouse. Thus, the employer is only required to withhold on wages in excess of $200,000 for the year, even though the tax may apply to a portion of the employee's wages at or below $200,000, if the employee's spouse also has wages for the year, they are filing a joint return, and their total combined wages for the year exceed $250,000.

For example, if a taxpayer's spouse has wages in excess of $250,000 and the taxpayer has wages of $100,000, the employer of the taxpayer is not required to withhold any portion of the additional tax, even though the combined wages of the taxpayer and the taxpayer's spouse are over the $250,000 threshold. In this instance, the employer of the taxpayer's spouse is obligated to withhold the additional 0.9-percent HI tax with respect to the $50,000 above the threshold with respect to the wages of $250,000 for the taxpayer's spouse.

In contrast to the employee portion of the general HI tax of 1.45 percent of wages for which the employee generally has no direct liability to the IRS to pay the tax, the employee is also liable for this additional 0.9-percent HI tax to the extent the tax is not withheld by the employer. The amount of this tax not withheld by an employer must also be taken into account in determining a taxpayer's liability for estimated tax.

Additional HI for self-employed individuals

This same additional HI tax applies to the HI portion of SECA tax on self-employment income in excess of the threshold amount. Thus, an additional tax of 0.9 percent is imposed on every self-employed individual on self-employment income[224] in excess of the threshold amount.

As in the case of the additional HI tax on wages, the threshold amount for the additional SECA HI tax is $250,000 in the case of a joint return or surviving spouse, $125,000 in the case of a married individual filing a separate return, and $200,000 in any other case. The threshold

---

[222] For purposes of computing net earnings from self employment, taxpayers are permitted a deduction equal to the product of the taxpayer's earnings (determined without regard to this deduction) and one-half of the sum of the rates for OASDI (12.4 percent) and HI (2.9 percent), i.e., 7.65 percent of net earnings. This deduction reflects the fact that the FICA rates apply to an employee's wages, which do not include FICA taxes paid by the employer, whereas the self-employed individual's net earnings are economically equivalent to an employee's wages plus the employer share of FICA taxes.

[223] Sec. 3121(a).

[224] Sec. 1402(b).

amount is reduced (but not below zero) by the amount of wages taken into account in determining the FICA tax with respect to the taxpayer. No deduction is allowed under section 164(f) for the additional SECA tax, and the deduction under 1402(a)(12) is determined without regard to the additional SECA tax rate.

Effective Date

The provision applies to remuneration received and taxable years beginning after December 31, 2012.

[Law at ¶ 5125, ¶ 5180, ¶ 5185, ¶ 5190 and ¶ 5195. CCH Explanation at ¶ 230.]

[¶ 10,310] Act Sec. 9016. Modification of section 833 treatment of certain health organizations

Joint Committee on Taxation (J.C.T. REP. NO. JCX-18-10)

[Code Sec. 833]

Present Law

A property and casualty insurance company is subject to tax on its taxable income, generally defined as its gross income less allowable deductions (sec. 832). For this purpose, gross income includes underwriting income and investment income, as well as other items. Underwriting income is the premiums earned on insurance contracts during the year, less losses incurred and expenses incurred. The amount of losses incurred is determined by taking into account the discounted unpaid losses. Premiums earned during the year is determined taking into account a 20-percent reduction in the otherwise allowable deduction, intended to represent the allocable portion of expenses incurred in generating the unearned premiums (sec. 832(b)(4)(B)).

Present law provides that an organization described in sections 501(c)(3) and (4) of the Code is exempt from tax only if no substantial part of its activities consists of providing commercial-type insurance (sec. 501(m)). When this rule was enacted in 1986,[225] special rules were provided under section 833 for Blue Cross and Blue Shield organizations providing health insurance that (1) were in existence on August 16, 1986; (2) were determined at any time to be tax-exempt under a determination that had not been revoked; and (3) were tax-exempt for the last taxable year beginning before January 1, 1987 (when the present-law rule became effective), provided that no material change occurred in the structure or operations of the organizations after August 16, 1986, and before the close of 1986 or any subsequent taxable year. Any other organization is eligible for section 833 treatment if it

meets six requirements set forth in section 833(c): (1) substantially all of its activities involve providing health insurance; (2) at least 10 percent of its health insurance is provided to individuals and small groups (not taking into account Medicare supplemental coverage); (3) it provides continuous full-year open enrollment for individuals and small groups; (4) for individuals, it provides full coverage of pre-existing conditions of high-risk individuals and coverage without regard to age, income, or employment of individuals under age 65; (5) at least 35 percent of its premiums are community rated; and (6) no part of its net earnings inures to the benefit of any private shareholder or individual.

Section 833 provides a deduction with respect to health business of such organizations. The deduction is equal to 25 percent of the sum of (1) claims incurred, and liabilities incurred under cost-plus contracts, for the taxable year, and (2) expenses incurred in connection with administration, adjustment, or settlement of claims or in connection with administration of cost-plus contracts during the taxable year, to the extent this sum exceeds the adjusted surplus at the beginning of the taxable year. Only health-related items are taken into account.

Section 833 provides an exception for such an organization from the application of the 20-percent reduction in the deduction for increases in unearned premiums that applies generally to property and casualty companies.

Section 833 provides that such an organization is taxable as a stock property and casualty insurer under the Federal income tax rules applicable to property and casualty insurers.

---

[225] See H. Rep. 99-426, Tax Reform Act of 1985, (December 7, 1985) at 664. The Committee stated, "[T]he availability of tax-exempt status under [then-]present law has allowed some large insurance entities to compete directly with commercial insurance companies. For example, the Blue Cross/ Blue Shield organizations historically have been treated as tax-exempt organizations described in sections 501(c)(3) or (4). This group of organizations is now among the largest health care insurers in the United States." See also Joint Committee on Taxation, General Explanation of the Tax Reform Act of 1986, JCS-10-87 (May 4, 1987) at 583-592.

Explanation of Provision

The provision limits eligibility for the rules of section 833 to those organizations meeting a medical loss ratio standard of 85 percent for the taxable year. Thus, under the provision, an organization that does not meet the 85-percent standard is not allowed the 25-percent deduction and the exception from the 20-percent reduction in the unearned premium reserve deduction under section 833.

For this purpose, an organization's medical loss ratio is determined as the percentage of total premium revenue expended on reimbursement for clinical services that are provided to enrollees under the organization's policies during the taxable year, as reported under section 2718 of the PHSA.

It is intended that the medical loss ratio under this provision be determined on an organization-by-organization basis, not on an affiliated or other group basis, and that Treasury Department guidance be promulgated promptly to carry out the purposes of the provision.

Effective Date

The provision is effective for taxable years beginning after December 31, 2009.

[Law at ¶5160. CCH Explanation at ¶360.]

[¶10,320] Act Sec. 9017. Excise tax on indoor tanning services[226]

Joint Committee on Taxation (J.C.T. Rep. No. JCX-18-10)

[New Code Sec. 5000B]

Present Law

There is no tax on indoor tanning services under present law.

Explanation of Provision

In general

The provision imposes a tax on each individual on whom indoor tanning services are performed. The tax is equal to 10 percent of the amount paid for indoor tanning services.

For purposes of the provision, indoor tanning services are services employing any electronic product designed to induce skin tanning and which incorporate one or more ultraviolet lamps and intended for the irradiation of an individual by ultraviolet radiation, with wavelengths in air between 200 and 400 nanometers. Indoor tanning services do not include any phototherapy service performed by a licensed medical professional.

Payment of tax

The tax is paid by the individual on whom the indoor tanning services are performed. The tax is collected by each person receiving a payment for tanning services on which a tax is imposed. If the tax is not paid by the person receiving the indoor tanning services at the time the payment for the service is received, the person performing the procedure pays the tax.

Payment of the tax is remitted quarterly to the Secretary by the person collecting the tax. The Secretary is given discretion over the manner of the payment.

Effective Date

The provision applies to services performed on or after July 1, 2010.

[Law at ¶5240. CCH Explanation at ¶235.]

---

[226] Section 9017 of the Senate amendment, as amended by section 10907.

[¶10,330] Act Sec. 9021. Exclusion of health benefits provided by Indian tribal governments

Joint Committee on Taxation (J.C.T. REP. No. JCX-18-10)

[New Code Sec. 139D]

Present Law

Present law generally provides that gross income includes all income from whatever source derived.[227] Exclusions from income are provided, however, for certain health care benefits.

Exclusion from income for employer-provided health coverage

Employees generally are not taxed on (that is, may "exclude" from gross income) the value of employer-provided health coverage under an accident or health plan.[228] In addition, any reimbursements under an accident or health plan for medical care expenses for employees, their spouses, and their dependents generally are excluded from gross income.[229] As with cash or other compensation, the amount paid by employers for employer-provided health coverage is a deductible business expense. Unlike other forms of compensation, however, if an employer contributes to a plan providing health coverage for employees (and the employees' spouses and dependents), the value of the coverage and all benefits (including reimbursements) in the form of medical care under the plan are excludable from the employees' income for income tax purposes.[230] The exclusion applies both to health coverage in the case in which an employer absorbs the cost of employees' medical expenses not covered by insurance (i.e., a self-insured plan) as well as in the case in which the employer purchases health insurance coverage for its employees. There is no limit on the amount of employer-provided health coverage that is excludable.

In addition, employees participating in a cafeteria plan may be able to pay the portion of premiums for health insurance coverage not otherwise paid for by their employers on a pre-tax basis through salary reduction.[231] Such salary reduction contributions are treated as employer contributions and thus also are excluded from gross income.

Employers may agree to reimburse medical expenses of their employees (and their spouses and dependents), not covered by a health insurance plan, through flexible spending arrangements which allow reimbursement not in excess of a specified dollar amount (either elected by an employee under a cafeteria plan or otherwise specified by the employer). Reimbursements under these arrangements are also excludible from gross income as employer-provided health coverage.

The general welfare exclusion

Under the general welfare exclusion doctrine, certain payments made to individuals are excluded from gross income. The exclusion has been interpreted to cover payments by governmental units under legislatively provided social benefit programs for the promotion of the general welfare.[232]

---

[227] Sec. 61.

[228] Sec 106.

[229] Sec. 105(b).

[230] Secs. 104, 105, 106, 125. A similar rule excludes employer provided health insurance coverage and reimbursements for medical expenses from the employees' wages for payroll tax purposes under sections 3121(a)(2), and 3306(a)(2). Health coverage provided to active members of the uniformed services, military retirees, and their dependents are excludable under section 134. That section provides an exclusion for "qualified military benefits," defined as benefits received by reason of status or service as a member of the uniformed services and which were excludable from gross income on September 9, 1986, under any provision of law, regulation, or administrative practice then in effect.

[231] Sec. 125.

[232] See, e.g., Rev. Rul. 78-170, 1978-1 C.B. 24 (government payments to assist low-income persons with utility costs are not income); Rev. Rul. 76-395, 1976-2 C.B. 16, 17 (government grants to assist low-income city inhabitants to refurbish homes are not income); Rev. Rul. 76-144, 1976-1 C.B. 17 (government grants to persons eligible for relief under the Disaster Relief Act of 1974 are not income); Rev. Rul. 74-153, 1974-1 C.B. 20 (government payments to assist adoptive parents with support and maintenance of adoptive children are not income); Rev. Rul. 74-205, 1974-1 C.B. 20 (replacement housing payments received by individuals under the Housing and Urban Development Act of 1968 are not includible in gross income; Gen. Couns. Mem. 34506 (May 26, 1971) (federal mortgage assistance payments excluded from income under general welfare exception); Rev. Rul. 57-102, 1957-1 C.B. 26 (government benefits paid to blind persons are not income). The courts have also acknowledged the existence of this doctrine. See, e.g., *Bailey v. Commissioner*, 88 T.C. 1293, 1299-1301 (1987) (new building façade paid for by urban renewal agency on taxpayer's property under facade grant program not considered payments under general welfare doctrine because awarded without regard to any need

The general welfare exclusion generally applies if the payments: (1) are made from a governmental fund, (2) are for the promotion of general welfare (on the basis of the need of the recipient), and (3) do not represent compensation for services.[233] A representative of the IRS recently expressed the view that the general welfare exclusion does not apply to persons with significant income or assets, and that any such extension would represent a departure from well-established administrative practice.[234] The representative further expressed the view that application of the general welfare exclusion to an Indian tribal government providing coverage or benefits to tribal members is dependent upon the structure and administration of the particular program.[235]

Explanation of Provision

The provision allows an exclusion from gross income for the value of specified Indian tribe health care benefits. The exclusion applies to the value of: (1) health services or benefits provided or purchased by the Indian Health Service ("IHS"), either directly or indirectly, through a grant to or a contract or compact with an Indian tribe or tribal organization or through programs of third parties funded by the IHS;[236] (2) medical care (in the form of provided or purchased medical care services, accident or health insurance or an arrangement having the same effect, or amounts paid directly or indirectly, to reimburse the member for expenses incurred for medical care) provided by an Indian tribe or tribal organization to a member of an Indian tribe, including the member's spouse or dependents;[237] (3) accident or health plan coverage (or an arrangement having the same effect) provided by an Indian tribe or tribal organization for medical care to a member of an Indian tribe, including the member's spouse or dependents; and (4) any other medical care provided by an Indian tribe or tribal organization that supplements, replaces, or substitutes for the programs and services provided by the Federal government to Indian tribes or Indians.

This provision does not apply to any amount which is deducted or excluded from gross income under another provision of the Code.

No change made by the provision is intended to create an inference with respect to the exclusion from gross income of benefits provided prior to the date of enactment. Additionally, no inference is intended with respect to the tax treatment of other benefits provided by an

---

(Footnote Continued)

of the recipients); *Graff v. Commissioner*, 74 TC 743, 753-754 (1980) (court acknowledged that rental subsidies under Housing Act were excludable under general welfare doctrine but found that payments at issue made by HUD on taxpayer landlord's behalf were taxable income to him), *affd. per curiam* 673 F.2d 784 (5th Cir. 1982).

[233] See Rev. Rul. 98-19, 1998-1 C.B. 840 (excluding relocation payments made by local governments to those whose homes were damaged by floods). Recent guidance as to whether the need of the recipient (taken into account under the second requirement of the general welfare exclusion) must be based solely on financial means or whether the need can be based on a variety of other considerations including health, educational background, or employment status, has been mixed. Chief Couns. Adv. 200021036 (May 25, 2000) (excluding state adoption assistant payments made to individuals adopting special needs children without regard to financial means of parents; the children were considered to be the recipients); Priv. Ltr. Rul. 200632005 (April 13, 2006) (excluding payments made by Tribe to members based on multiple factors of need pursuant to housing assistance program); Chief Couns. Adv. 200648027 (Jul 25, 2006) (excluding subsidy payments based on financial need of recipient made by state to certain participants in state health insurance program to reduce cost of health insurance premiums).

[234] Testimony of Sarah H. Ingram, Commissioner, Tax Exempt and Government Entities, Internal Revenue Service, before the Senate Committee on Indian Affairs, *Oversight Hearing to Examine the Federal Tax Treatment of Health Care Benefits Provided by Tribal Governments to Their Citizens*, September 17, 2009.

[235] *Ibid.*

[236] The term "Indian tribe" means any Indian tribe, band, nation, pueblo, or other organized group or community, including any Alaska Native village, or regional or village corporation, as defined by, or established pursuant to, the Alaska Native Claims Settlement Act (43 U.S.C. 1601 et. seq.), which is recognized as eligible for the special programs and services provided by the United States to Indians because of their status as Indians. The term "tribal organization" has the same meaning as such term in section 4(l) of the Indian Self-Determination and Education Assistance Act (25 U.S.C. 450b(1)).

[237] The terms "accident or health insurance" and "accident or health plan" have the same meaning as when used in section 105. The term "medical care" is the same as the definition under section 213. For purposes of the provision, dependents are determined under section 152, but without regard to subsections (b)(1), (b)(2), and (d)(1)(B). Section 152(b)(1) generally provides that if an individual is a dependent of another taxpayer during a taxable year such individual is treated as having no dependents for such taxable year. Section 152(b)(2) provides that a married individual filing a joint return with his or her spouse is not treated as a dependent of a taxpayer. Section 152(d)(1)(B) provides that a "qualifying relative" (i.e., a relative that qualifies as a dependent) does not include a person whose gross income for the calendar year in which the taxable year begins equals or exceeds the exempt amount (as defined under section 151).

Indian tribe or tribal organization not covered by this provision.

Effective Date

The provision applies to benefits and coverage provided after the date of enactment.

[Law at ¶ 5110 and ¶ 7039. CCH Explanation at ¶ 250.]

[¶ 10,340] Act Sec. 9022. Establishment of SIMPLE cafeteria plans for small businesses

Joint Committee on Taxation (J.C.T. REP. NO. JCX-18-10)

[Code Sec. 125]

Present Law

Definition of a cafeteria plan

If an employee receives a qualified benefit (as defined below) based on the employee's election between the qualified benefit and a taxable benefit under a cafeteria plan, the qualified benefit generally is not includable in gross income.[255] However, if a plan offering an employee an election between taxable benefits (including cash) and nontaxable qualified benefits does not meet the requirements for being a cafeteria plan, the election between taxable and nontaxable benefits results in gross income to the employee, regardless of what benefit is elected and when the election is made.[256] A cafeteria plan is a separate written plan under which all participants are employees, and participants are permitted to choose among at least one permitted taxable benefit (for example, current cash compensation) and at least one qualified benefit. Finally, a cafeteria plan must not provide for deferral of compensation, except as specifically permitted in sections 125(d)(2)(B), (C), or (D).

Qualified benefits

Qualified benefits under a cafeteria plan are generally employer-provided benefits that are not includable in gross income under an express provision of the Code. Examples of qualified benefits include employer-provided health insurance coverage, group term life insurance coverage not in excess of $50,000, and benefits under a dependent care assistance program. In order to be excludable, any qualified benefit elected under a cafeteria plan must independently sat-

isfy any requirements under the Code section that provides the exclusion. However, some employer-provided benefits that are not includable in gross income under an express provision of the Code are explicitly not allowed in a cafeteria plan. These benefits are generally referred to as nonqualified benefits. Examples of nonqualified benefits include scholarships;[257] employer-provided meals and lodging;[258] educational assistance;[259] and fringe benefits.[260] A plan offering any nonqualified benefit is not a cafeteria plan.[261]

Employer contributions through salary reduction

Employees electing a qualified benefit through salary reduction are electing to forego salary and instead to receive a benefit that is excludible from gross income because it is provided by employer contributions. Section 125 provides that the employee is treated as receiving the qualified benefit from the employer in lieu of the taxable benefit. For example, active employees participating in a cafeteria plan may be able to pay their share of premiums for employer-provided health insurance on a pre-tax basis through salary reduction.[262]

Nondiscrimination requirements

Cafeteria plans and certain qualified benefits (including group term life insurance, self-insured medical reimbursement plans, and dependent care assistance programs) are subject to nondiscrimination requirements to prevent discrimination in favor of highly compensated individuals generally as to eligibility for benefits and as to actual contributions and benefits provided.

---

[255] Sec. 125(a).

[256] Proposed Treas. Reg. sec. 1.125-1(b).

[257] Sec. 117.

[258] Sec. 119.

[259] Sec.127.

[260] Sec. 132.

[261] Proposed Treas. Reg. sec. 1.125-1(q). Long-term care services, contributions to Archer Medical Savings Accounts, group term life insurance for an employee's spouse, child or dependent, and elective deferrals to section 403(b) plans are also nonqualified benefits.

[262] Sec. 125.

There are also rules to prevent the provision of disproportionate benefits to key employees (within the meaning of section 416(i)) through a cafeteria plan.[263] Although the basic purpose of each of the nondiscrimination rules is the same, the specific rules for satisfying the relevant nondiscrimination requirements, including the definition of highly compensated individual,[264] vary for cafeteria plans generally and for each qualified benefit. An employer maintaining a cafeteria plan in which any highly compensated individual participates must make sure that both the cafeteria plan and each qualified benefit satisfies the relevant nondiscrimination requirements, as a failure to satisfy the nondiscrimination rules generally results in a loss of the tax exclusion by the highly compensated individuals.

Explanation of Provision

Under the provision, an eligible small employer is provided with a safe harbor from the nondiscrimination requirements for cafeteria plans as well as from the nondiscrimination requirements for specified qualified benefits offered under a cafeteria plan, including group term life insurance, benefits under a self insured medical expense reimbursement plan, and benefits under a dependent care assistance program. Under the safe harbor, a cafeteria plan and the specified qualified benefits are treated as meeting the specified qualified benefits are treated as meeting the specified cafeteria plan nondiscrimination rules if the cafeteria plan satisfies minimum eligibility and participation requirements and minimum contribution requirements.

Eligibility requirement

The eligibility requirement is met only if all employees (other than excludable employees) are eligible to participate, and each employee eligible to participate is able to elect any benefit available under the plan (subject to the terms and conditions applicable to all participants). However, a cafeteria plan will not fail to satisfy this eligibility requirement merely because the plan excludes employees who (1) have not attained the age of 21 (or a younger age provided in the plan) before the close of a plan year, (2) have fewer than 1,000 hours of service for the preceding plan year, (3) have not completed one year of service with the employer as of any day during the plan year, (4) are covered under an agreement that the Secretary of Labor finds to be a collective bargaining agreement if there is evidence that the benefits covered under the cafeteria plan were the subject of good faith bargaining between employee representatives and the employer, or (5) are described in section 410(b)(3)(C) (relating to nonresident aliens working outside the United States). An employer may have a shorter age and service requirement but only if such shorter service or younger age applies to all employees.

Minimum contribution requirement

The minimum contribution requirement is met if the employer provides a minimum contribution for each nonhighly compensated employee (employee who is not a highly compensated employee[265] or a key employee (within the meaning of section 416(i))) in addition to any salary reduction contributions made by the employee. The minimum must be available for application toward the cost of any qualified benefit (other than a taxable benefit) offered under the plan. The minimum contribution is permitted to be calculated under either the nonelective contribution method or the matching contribution method, but the same method must be used for calculating the minimum contribution for all nonhighly compensated employees.

---

[263] A key employee generally is an employee who, at any time during the year is (1) a five-percent owner of the employer, or (2) a one-percent owner with compensation of more than $150,000 (not indexed for inflation), or (3) an officer with compensation more than $160,000 (for 2010). A special rule limits the number of officers treated as key employees. If the employer is a corporation, a five-percent owner is a person who owns more than five percent of the outstanding stock or stock possessing more than five percent of the total combined voting power of all stock. If the employer is not a corporation, a five-percent owner is a person who owns more than five percent of the capital or profits interest. A one-percent owner is determined by substituting one percent for five percent in the preceding definitions. For purposes of determining employee ownership in the employer, certain attribution rules apply.

[264] For cafeteria plan purposes, a "highly compensated individual" is (1) an officer, (2) a five-percent shareholder, (3) an individual who is highly compensated, or (4) the spouse or dependent of any of the preceding categories. A "highly compensated participant" is a participant who falls

in any of those categories. "Highly compensated" is not defined for this purpose. Under section 105(h), a self-insured medical expense reimbursement plan must not discriminate in favor of a "highly compensated individual," defined as (1) one of the five highest paid officers, (2) a 10-percent shareholder, or (3) an individual among the highest paid 25 percent of all employees. Under section 129 for a dependent care assistance program, eligibility for benefits, and the benefits and contributions provided, generally must not discriminate in favor of highly compensated employees within the meaning of section 414(q).

[265] Section 414(q) generally defines a highly compensated employee as an employee (1) who was a five-percent owner during the year or the preceding year, or (2) who had compensation of $110,000 (for 2010) or more for the preceding year. An employer may elect to limit the employees treated as highly compensated employees based upon their compensation in the preceding year to the highest paid 20 percent of employees in the preceding year. Five-percent owner is defined by cross-reference to the definition of key employee in section 416(i).

The minimum contribution under the nonelective contribution method is an amount equal to a uniform percentage (not less than two percent) of each eligible employee's compensation for the plan year, determined without regard to whether the employees makes any salary reduction contribution under the cafeteria plan. The minimum matching contribution is the lesser of 100 percent of the amount of the salary reduction contribution elected to be made by the employee for the plan year or (2) six percent of the employee's compensation for the plan year. Compensation for purposes of this minimum contribution requirement is compensation with the meaning of section 414(s).

A simple cafeteria plan is permitted to provide for the matching contributions in addition to the minimum required but only if matching contributions with respect to salary reduction contributions for any highly compensated employee or key employee are not made at a greater rate than the matching contributions for any nonhighly compensated employee. Nothing in this provision prohibits an employer from providing qualified benefits under the plan in addition to the required contributions.

Eligible employer

An eligible small employer under the provision is, with respect to any year, an employer who employed an average of 100 or fewer employees on business days during either of the two preceding years. For purposes of the provision, a year may only be taken into account if the employer was in existence throughout the year. If an employer was not in existence throughout the preceding year, the determination is based on the average number of employees that it is reasonably expected such employer will employ on business days in the current year. If an employer was an eligible employer for any year and maintained a simple cafeteria plan for its employees for such year, then, for each subsequent year during which the employer continues, without interruption, to maintain the cafeteria plan, the employer is deemed to be an eligible small employer until the employer employs an average of 200 or more employees on business days during any year preceding any such subsequent year.

The determination of whether an employer is an eligible small employer is determined by applying the controlled group rules of sections 52(a) and (b) under which all members of the controlled group are treated as a single employer. In addition, the definition of employee includes leased employees within the meaning of sections 414(n) and (o).[266]

Effective Date

The provision is effective for taxable years beginning after December 31, 2010.

[Law at ¶ 5095. CCH Explanation at ¶ 330.]

[¶10,350] Act Sec. 9023. Investment credit for qualifying therapeutic discovery projects

Joint Committee on Taxation (J.C.T. Rep. No. JCX-18-10)

[New Code Sec. 48D]

Present Law

Present law provides for a research credit equal to 20 percent (14 percent in the case of the alternative simplified credit) of the amount by which the taxpayer's qualified research expenses for a taxable year exceed its base amount for that year.[267] Thus, the research credit is generally available with respect to incremental increases in qualified research.

A 20-percent research tax credit is also available with respect to the excess of (1) 100 percent of corporate cash expenses (including grants or contributions) paid for basic research conducted by universities (and certain nonprofit scientific research organizations) over (2) the sum of (a)

---

[266] Section 52(b) provides that, for specified purposes, all employees of all corporations which are members of a controlled group of corporations are treated as employed by a single employer. However, section 52(b) provides certain modifications to the control group rules including substituting 50 percent ownership for 80 percent ownership as the measure of control. There is a similar rule in section 52(c) under which all employees of trades or businesses (whether or not incorporated) which are under common control are treated under regulations as employed by a single employer. Section 414(n) provides rules for specified purposes when leased employees are treated as employed by the service recipient and section 414(o) authorizes the Treasury to issue regulations to prevent avoidance of the requirements of section 414(n).

[267] Sec. 41.

the greater of two minimum basic research floors plus (b) an amount reflecting any decrease in nonresearch giving to universities by the corporation as compared to such giving during a fixed-base period, as adjusted for inflation. This separate credit computation is commonly referred to as the "university basic research credit."[268]

Finally, a research credit is available for a taxpayer's expenditures on research undertaken by an energy research consortium. This separate credit computation is commonly referred to as the "energy research credit." Unlike the other research credits, the energy research credit applies to all qualified expenditures, not just those in excess of a base amount.

The research credit, including the university basic research credit and the energy research credit, expired for amounts paid or incurred after December 31, 2009.[269]

Qualified research expenses eligible for the research tax credit consist of: (1) in-house expenses of the taxpayer for wages and supplies attributable to qualified research; (2) certain time-sharing costs for computer use in qualified research; and (3) 65 percent of amounts paid or incurred by the taxpayer to certain other persons for qualified research conducted on the taxpayer's behalf (so-called contract research expenses).[270] Notwithstanding the limitation for contract research expenses, qualified research expenses include 100 percent of amounts paid or incurred by the taxpayer to an eligible small business, university, or Federal laboratory for qualified energy research.

Present law also provides a 50-percent credit[271] for expenses related to human clinical testing of drugs for the treatment of certain rare diseases and conditions, generally those that afflict less than 200,000 persons in the United States. Qualifying expenses are those paid or incurred by the taxpayer after the date on which the drug is designated as a potential treatment for a rare disease or disorder by the Food and Drug Administration ("FDA") in accordance

with section 526 of the Federal Food, Drug, and Cosmetic Act.

Present law does not provide a credit specifically designed to encourage investment in new therapies relating to diseases.

Explanation of Provision

In general

The provision establishes a 50 percent nonrefundable investment tax credit for qualified investments in qualifying therapeutic discovery projects. The provision allocates $1 billion during the two-year period 2009 through 2010 for the program. The Secretary, in consultation with the Secretary of HHS, will award certifications for qualified investments. The credit is available only to companies having 250 or fewer employees.[272]

A "qualifying therapeutic discovery project" is a project which is designed to develop a product, process, or therapy to diagnose, treat, or prevent diseases and afflictions by: (1) conducting pre-clinical activities, clinical trials, clinical studies, and research protocols, or (2) by developing technology or products designed to diagnose diseases and conditions, including molecular and companion drugs and diagnostics, or to further the delivery or administration of therapeutics.

The qualified investment for any taxable year is the aggregate amount of the costs paid or incurred in such year for expenses necessary for and directly related to the conduct of a qualifying therapeutic discovery project. The qualified investment for any taxable year with respect to any qualifying therapeutic discovery project does not include any cost for: (1) remuneration for an employee described in section 162(m)(3), (2) interest expense, (3) facility maintenance expenses, (4) a service cost identified under Treas. Reg. Sec. 1.263A-1(e)(4), or (5) any other expenditure as determined by the Secretary as appropriate to carry out the purposes of the provision.

---

[268] Sec. 41(e).

[269] Sec. 41(h).

[270] Under a special rule, 75 percent of amounts paid to a research consortium for qualified research are treated as qualified research expenses eligible for the research credit (rather than 65 percent under the general rule of section 41(b)(3) governing contract research expenses) if (1) such research consortium is a tax-exempt organization that is described in section 501(c)(3) (other than a private foundation) or section 501(c)(6) and is organized and operated

primarily to conduct scientific research, and (2) such qualified research is conducted by the consortium on behalf of the taxpayer and one or more persons not related to the taxpayer. Sec. 41(b)(3)(C).

[271] Sec. 45C.

[272] The number of employees is determined taking into account all businesses of the taxpayer at the time it submits an application, and is determined taking into account the rules for determining a single employer under section 52(a) or (b) or section 414(m) or (o).

Companies must apply to the Secretary to obtain certification for qualifying investments.[273] The Secretary, in determining qualifying projects, will consider only those projects that show reasonable potential to: (1) result in new therapies to treat areas of unmet medical need or to prevent, detect, or treat chronic or acute disease and conditions, (2) reduce long-term health care costs in the United States, or (3) significantly advance the goal of curing cancer within a 30-year period. Additionally, the Secretary will take into consideration which projects would have the greatest potential to: (1) create and sustain (directly or indirectly) high quality, high paying jobs in the United States, and (2) advance the United States' competitiveness in the fields of life, biological, and medical sciences.

Qualified therapeutic discovery project expenditures do not qualify for the research credit, orphan drug credit, or bonus depreciation.[274] If a credit is allowed for an expenditure related to property subject to depreciation, the basis of the property is reduced by the amount of the credit. Additionally, expenditures taken into account in determining the credit are nondeductible to the extent of the credit claimed that is attributable to such expenditures.

Election to receive grant in lieu of tax credit

Taxpayers may elect to receive credits that have been allocated to them in the form of Trea-sury grants equal to 50 percent of the qualifying investment. Any such grant is not includible in the taxpayer's gross income.

In making grants under this section, the Secretary of the Treasury is to apply rules similar to the rules of section 50. In applying such rules, if an investment ceases to be a qualified investment, the Secretary of the Treasury shall provide for the recapture of the appropriate percentage of the grant amount in such manner as the Secretary of the Treasury determines appropriate. The Secretary of the Treasury shall not make any grant under this section to: (1) any Federal, State, or local government (or any political subdivision, agency, or instrumentality thereof),(2) any organization described in section 501(c) and exempt from tax under section 501(a), (3) any entity referred to in paragraph (4) of section 54(j), or (4) any partnership or other pass-thru entity any partner (or other holder of an equity or profits interest) of which is described in paragraph (1), (2) or (3).

Effective Date

The provision applies to expenditures paid or incurred after December 31, 2008, in taxable years beginning after December 31, 2008.

[Law at ¶5065, ¶5070, ¶5075 and ¶5150. CCH Explanation at ¶355.]

[¶10,360] Act Sec. 10105. Study of geographic variation in application of FPL

Joint Committee on Taxation (J.C.T. Rep. No. JCX-18-10)

[Act Sec. 10105]

Present Law

No provision.

Explanation of Provision

The Secretary of HHS is instructed to conduct a study on the feasibility and implication of adjusting the application of the FPL under the provisions enacted in the bill for different geographical areas so as to reflect disparities in the cost of living among different areas in the United States, including the territories. If the Secretary deems such an adjustment feasible, then the study should include a methodology for implementing the adjustment. The Secretary is required to report the results of the study to Congress no later than January 1, 2013. The provision requires that special attention be paid to the impact of disparities between the poverty levels and the cost of living in the territories and the impact of this disparity on the expansion of health coverage in the territories. The territories are the Commonwealth of Puerto Rico, the U.S. Virgin Islands, Guam, the Commonwealth of the

---

[273] The Secretary must take action to approve or deny an application within 30 days of the submission of such application.

[274] Any expenses for the taxable year that are qualified research expenses under section 41(b) are taken into account in determining base period research expenses for purposes of computing the research credit under section 41 for subsequent taxable years.

Northern Mariana Islands and any other territory or possession of the United States.

Effective Date

The provision is effective on date of enactment.

[¶10,370] Act Sec. 10108. Free choice vouchers

Joint Committee on Taxation (J.C.T. Rep. No. JCX-18-10)

[Code Sec. 139D]

Present Law

No provision.

Explanation of Provision

Provision of vouchers

Employers offering minimum essential coverage through an eligible employer-sponsored plan and paying a portion of that coverage must provide qualified employees with a voucher whose value can be applied to purchase of a health plan through the Exchange. Qualified employees are employees whose required contribution for employer sponsored minimum essential coverage exceeds eight percent, but does not exceed 9.5 percent of the employee's household income for the taxable year and the employee's total household income does not exceed 400 percent of the poverty line for the family. In addition, the employee must not participate in the employer's health plan.

The value of the voucher is equal to the dollar value of the employer contribution to the employer offered health plan. If multiple plans are offered by the employer, the value of the voucher is the dollar amount that would be paid if the employee chose the plan for which the employer would pay the largest percentage of the premium cost.[275] The value of the voucher is for self-only coverage unless the individual purchases family coverage in the Exchange. Under the provision, for purposes of calculating the dollar value of the employer contribution, the premium for any health plan is determined under the rules of section 2204 of PHSA, except that the amount is adjusted for age and category

[Law at ¶5045, ¶5150 and ¶5275. CCH Explanation at ¶210.]

of enrollment in accordance with regulations established by the Secretary.

In the case of years after 2014, the eight percent and the 9.5 percent are indexed to the excess of premium growth over income growth for the preceding calendar year.

Use of vouchers

Vouchers can be used in the Exchange towards the monthly premium of any qualified health plan in the Exchange. The value of the voucher to the extent it is used for the purchase of a health plan is not includable in gross income. If the value of the voucher exceeds the premium of the health plan chosen by the employee, the employee is paid the excess value of the voucher. The excess amount received by the employee is includible in the employee's gross income.

If an individual receives a voucher the individual is disqualified from receiving any tax credit or cost sharing credit for the purchase of a plan in the Exchange. Similarly, if any employee receives a free choice voucher, the employer is not assessed a shared responsibility payment on behalf of that employee.[276]

Definition of terms

The terms used for this provision have the same meaning as any term used in the provision for the requirement to maintain minimum essential coverage (section 1501 of the Senate amendment and new section 5000A). Thus for example, the terms "household income," "poverty line," "required contribution," and "eligible employer-sponsored plan" have the same meaning for both provisions. Thus, the required contribution

---

[275] For example, if an employer offering the same plans for $200 and $300 offers a flat $180 contribution for all plans, a contribution of 90 percent for the $200 plan and a contribution of 60 percent for the $300 plan, and the value of the voucher would equal the value of the contribution to the $200 since it received a 90 percent contribution, a value of $180. However, if the firm offers a $150 contribution to the $200 plan (75 percent) and a $200 contribution to the $300 plan (67 percent), the value of the voucher is based on the

plan receiving the greater percentage paid by the employer and would be $150. If a firm offers health plans with monthly premiums of $200 and $300 and provides a payment of 60 percent of any plan purchased, the value of the voucher will be 60 percent the higher premium plan, in this case, 60 percent of $300 or $180.

[276] Section 1513 of the Senate amendment and new section 4980H.

includes the amount of any salary reduction contribution.

Effective Date

The provision is effective after December 31, 2013.

[Law at ¶5045, ¶5115, ¶5120 and ¶7045. CCH Explanation at ¶315.]

[¶10,380] Act Sec. 10908. Exclusion for assistance provided to participants in state student loan repayment programs for certain health professionals

Joint Committee on Taxation (J.C.T. REP. No. JCX-18-10)

[Code Sec. 108(f)(4)]

Present Law

Gross income generally includes the discharge of indebtedness of the taxpayer. Under an exception to this general rule, gross income does not include any amount from the forgiveness (in whole or in part) of certain student loans, provided that the forgiveness is contingent on the student's working for a certain period of time in certain professions for any of a broad class of employers.

Student loans eligible for this special rule must be made to an individual to assist the individual in attending an educational institution that normally maintains a regular faculty and curriculum and normally has a regularly enrolled body of students in attendance at the place where its education activities are regularly carried on. Loan proceeds may be used not only for tuition and required fees, but also to cover room and board expenses. The loan must be made by (1) the United States (or an instrumentality or agency thereof), (2) a State (or any political subdivision thereof), (3) certain tax-exempt public benefit corporations that control a State, county, or municipal hospital and whose employees have been deemed to be public employees under State law, or (4) an educational organization that originally received the funds from which the loan was made from the United States, a State, or a tax-exempt public benefit corporation.

In addition, an individual's gross income does not include amounts from the forgiveness of loans made by educational organizations (and certain tax-exempt organizations in the case of refinancing loans) out of private, nongovern-

mental funds if the proceeds of such loans are used to pay costs of attendance at an educational institution or to refinance any outstanding student loans (not just loans made by educational organizations) and the student is not employed by the lender organization. In the case of such loans made or refinanced by educational organizations (or refinancing loans made by certain tax-exempt organizations), cancellation of the student loan must be contingent upon the student working in an occupation or area with unmet needs and such work must be performed for, or under the direction of, a tax-exempt charitable organization or a governmental entity.

Finally, an individual's gross income does not include any loan repayment amount received under the National Health Service Corps loan repayment program or certain State loan repayment programs.

Explanation of Provision

The provision modifies the gross income exclusion for amounts received under the National Health Service Corps loan repayment program or certain State loan repayment programs to include any amount received by an individual under any State loan repayment or loan forgiveness program that is intended to provide for the increased availability of health care services in underserved or health professional shortage areas (as determined by the State).

Effective Date

The provision is effective for amounts received by an individual in taxable years beginning after December 31, 2008.

[Law at ¶5090. CCH Explanation at ¶245.]

[¶10,390] Act Sec. 10909. Expansion of adoption credit and the exclusion from gross income for employer-provided adoption assistance

Joint Committee on Taxation (J.C.T. REP. NO. JCX-18-10)

[Code Secs. 23 and 137]

Present Law

Tax credit

Non-special needs adoptions

Generally a nonrefundable tax credit is allowed for qualified adoption expenses paid or incurred by a taxpayer subject to the maximum credit. The maximum credit is $12,170 per eligible child for taxable years beginning in 2010. An eligible child is an individual who: (1) has not attained age 18; or (2) is physically or mentally incapable of caring for himself or herself. The maximum credit is applied per child rather than per year. Therefore, while qualified adoption expenses may be incurred in one or more taxable years, the tax credit per adoption of an eligible child may not exceed the maximum credit.

Special needs adoptions

In the case of a special needs adoption finalized during a taxable year, the taxpayer may claim as an adoption credit the amount of the maximum credit minus the aggregate qualified adoption expenses with respect to that adoption for all prior taxable years. A special needs child is an eligible child who is a citizen or resident of the United States whom a State has determined: (1) cannot or should not be returned to the home of the birth parents; and (2) has a specific factor or condition (such as the child's ethnic background, age, or membership in a minority or sibling group, or the presence of factors such as medical conditions, or physical, mental, or emotional handicaps) because of which the child cannot be placed with adoptive parents without adoption assistance.

Qualified adoption expenses

Qualified adoption expenses are reasonable and necessary adoption fees, court costs, attorneys fees, and other expenses that are: (1) directly related to, and the principal purpose of which is for, the legal adoption of an eligible child by the taxpayer; (2) not incurred in violation of State or Federal law, or in carrying out

any surrogate parenting arrangement; (3) not for the adoption of the child of the taxpayer's spouse; and (4) not reimbursed (e.g., by an employer).

Phase-out for higher-income individuals

The adoption credit is phased out ratably for taxpayers with modified adjusted gross income between $182,520 and $222,520 for taxable years beginning in 2010. Under present law, modified adjusted gross income is the sum of the taxpayer's adjusted gross income plus amounts excluded from income under sections 911, 931, and 933 (relating to the exclusion of income of U.S. citizens or residents living abroad; residents of Guam, American Samoa, and the Northern Mariana Islands; and residents of Puerto Rico, respectively).

EGTRRA sunset[277]

For taxable years after 2010, the adoption credit will be reduced to a maximum credit of $6,000 for special needs adoptions and no tax credit for non-special needs adoptions. Also, the credit phase-out range will revert to the pre-EGTRRA levels (i.e., a ratable phase-out between modified adjusted gross income between $75,000 and $115,000). Finally, the adoption credit will be allowed only to the extent the individual's regular income tax liability exceeds the individual's tentative minimum tax, determined without regard to the minimum foreign tax credit.

Exclusion for employer-provided adoption assistance

An exclusion from the gross income of an employee is allowed for qualified adoption expenses paid or reimbursed by an employer under an adoption assistance program. For 2010, the maximum exclusion is $12,170. Also for 2010, the exclusion is phased out ratably for taxpayers with modified adjusted gross income between $182,520 and $222,520. Modified adjusted gross income is the sum of the taxpayer's adjusted gross income plus amounts excluded from income under Code sections 911, 931, and 933 (relating to the exclusion of income of U.S. citi-

---

[277] "EGTRRA" refers to the Economic Growth and Tax Relief Reconciliation Act of 2001.

zens or residents living abroad; residents of Guam, American Samoa, and the Northern Mariana Islands; and residents of Puerto Rico, respectively). For purposes of this exclusion, modified adjusted gross income also includes all employer payments and reimbursements for adoption expenses whether or not they are taxable to the employee.

Adoption expenses paid or reimbursed by the employer under an adoption assistance program are not eligible for the adoption credit. A taxpayer may be eligible for the adoption credit (with respect to qualified adoption expenses he or she incurs) and also for the exclusion (with respect to different qualified adoption expenses paid or reimbursed by his or her employer).

Because of the EGTRRA sunset, the exclusion for employer-provided adoption assistance does not apply to amounts paid or incurred after December 31, 2010.

Explanation of Provision

Tax credit

For 2010, the maximum credit is increased to $13,170 per eligible child (a $1,000 increase). This increase applies to both non-special needs adop-

tions and special needs adoptions. Also, the adoption credit is made refundable.

The new dollar limit and phase-out of the adoption credit are adjusted for inflation in taxable years beginning after December 31, 2010.

The EGTRRA sunset is delayed for one year (i.e., the sunset becomes effective for taxable years beginning after December 31, 2011).

Adoption assistance program

The maximum exclusion is increased to $13,170 per eligible child (a $1,000 increase).

The new dollar limit and income limitations of the employer-provided adoption assistance exclusion are adjusted for inflation in taxable years beginning after December 31, 2010.

The EGTRRA sunset is delayed for one year (i.e., the sunset becomes effective for taxable years beginning after December 31, 2011).

Effective Date

The provisions generally are effective for taxable years beginning after December 31, 2009.

[Law at ¶ 5050, ¶ 5100 and ¶ 7054. CCH Explanation at ¶ 240.]

[¶10,400] Act Sec. 1004. Adult dependents

Joint Committee on Taxation (J.C.T. REP. No. JCX-18-10)

[Code Secs. 105, 162, 401 and 501]

Present Law

Definition of dependent for exclusion for employer-provided health coverage

The Code generally provides that employees are not taxed on (that is, may "exclude" from gross income) the value of employer-provided health coverage under an accident or health plan.[278] This exclusion applies to coverage for personal injuries or sickness for employees (including retirees), their spouses and their dependents.[279] In addition, any reimbursements under an accident or health plan for medical care expenses for employees (including retirees), their spouses, and their dependents (as defined in section 152) generally are excluded from gross income.[280] Section 152 defines a dependent as a qualifying child or qualifying relative.

Under section 152(c), a child generally is a qualifying child of a taxpayer if the child satis-

fies each of five tests for the taxable year: (1) the child has the same principal place of abode as the taxpayer for more than one-half of the taxable year; (2) the child has a specified relationship to the taxpayer; (3) the child has not yet attained a specified age; (4) the child has not provided over one-half of their own support for the calendar year in which the taxable year of the taxpayer begins; and (5) the qualifying child has not filed a joint return (other than for a claim of refund) with their spouse for the taxable year beginning in the calendar year in which the taxable year of the taxpayer begins. A tie-breaking rule applies if more than one taxpayer claims a child as a qualifying child. The specified relationship is that the child is the taxpayer's son, daughter, stepson, stepdaughter, brother, sister, stepbrother, stepsister, or a descendant of any such individual. With respect to the specified age, a child must be under age 19 (or under age 24 in the case of a full-time student). However, no age limit applies with respect to individuals

---

[278] Sec 106.
[279] Treas. Reg. sec. 1.106-1.

[280] Sec. 105(b).

who are totally and permanently disabled within the meaning of section 22(e)(3) at any time during the calendar year. Other rules may apply.

Under section 152(d), a qualifying relative means an individual that satisfies four tests for the taxable year: (1) the individual bears a specified relationship to the taxpayer; (2) the individual's gross income for the calendar year in which such taxable year begins is less than the exemption amount under section 151(d); (3) the taxpayer provides more than one-half the individual's support for the calendar year in which the taxable year begins; and (4) the individual is not a qualifying child of the taxpayer or any other taxpayer for any taxable year beginning in the calendar year in which such taxable year begins. The specified relationship test for qualifying relative is satisfied if that individual is the taxpayer's: (1) child or descendant of a child; (2) brother, sister, stepbrother or stepsister; (3) father, mother or ancestor of either; (4) stepfather or stepmother; (5) niece or nephew; (6) aunt or uncle; (7) in-law; or (8) certain other individuals, who for the taxable year of the taxpayer, have the same principal place of abode as the taxpayer and are members of the taxpayer's household.[281]

Employers may agree to reimburse medical expenses of their employees (and their spouses and dependents), not covered by a health insurance plan, through flexible spending arrangements which allow reimbursement not in excess of a specified dollar amount (either elected by an employee under a cafeteria plan or otherwise specified by the employer). Reimbursements under these arrangements are also excludible from gross income as employer-provided health coverage. The same definition of dependents applies for purposes of flexible spending arrangements.

Deduction for health insurance premiums of self-employed individuals

Under present law, self-employed individuals may deduct the cost of health insurance for themselves and their spouses and dependents. The deduction is not available for any month in which the self-employed individual is eligible to participate in an employer-subsidized health plan. Moreover, the deduction may not exceed the individual's self-employment income. The deduction applies only to the cost of insurance (i.e., it does not apply to out-of-pocket expenses

that are not reimbursed by insurance). The deduction does not apply for self-employment tax purposes. For purposes of the deduction, a more than two percent shareholder-employee of an S corporation is treated the same as a self-employed individual. Thus, the exclusion for employer-provided health care coverage does not apply to such individuals, but they are entitled to the deduction for health insurance costs as if they were self-employed.

Voluntary Employees' Beneficiary Associations

A VEBA is a tax-exempt entity that is a part of a plan for providing life, sick or accident benefits to its members or their dependents or designated beneficiaries.[282] No part of the net earnings of the association inures (other than through the payment of life, sick, accident or other benefits) to the benefit of any private shareholder or individual. A VEBA may be funded with employer contributions or employee contributions or a combination of employer contributions and employee contributions. The same definition of dependent applies for purposes of receipt of medical benefits through a VEBA.

Qualified plans providing retiree health benefits

A qualified pension or annuity plan can establish and maintain a separate account to provide for the payment of sickness, accident, hospitalization, and medical expenses for retired employees, their spouses and their dependents ("401(h) account"). An employer's contributions to a 401(h) account must be reasonable and ascertainable, and retiree health benefits must be subordinate to the retirement benefits provided by the plan. In addition, it must be impossible, at any time prior to the satisfaction of all retiree health liabilities under the plan, for any part of the corpus or income of the 401(h) account to be (within the taxable year or thereafter) used for, or diverted to, any purpose other than providing retiree health benefits and, upon satisfaction of all retiree health liabilities, the plan must provide that any amount remaining in the 401(h) account be returned to the employer.

Explanation of Provision

The provision amends sections 105(b) to extend the general exclusion for reimbursements

---

[281] Generally, same-sex partners do not qualify as dependents under section 152. In addition, same-sex partners are not recognized as spouses for purposes of the Code. Defense of Marriage Act, Pub. L. No. 104-199.

[282] Secs. 419(e) and 501(c)(9).

for medical care expenses under an employer-provided accident or health plan to any child of an employee who has not attained age 27 as of the end of the taxable year. This change is also intended to apply to the exclusion for employer-proved coverage under an accident or health plan for injuries or sickness for such a child. A parallel change is made for VEBAs and 401(h) accounts.

The provision similarly amends section 162(l) to permit self-employed individuals to take a deduction for any child of the taxpayer who has not attained age 27 as of the end of the taxable year.

For purposes of the provision, "child" means an individual who is a son, daughter, stepson, stepdaughter or eligible foster child of the taxpayer.[283] An eligible foster child means an individual who is placed with the taxpayer by an authorized placement agency or by judgment, decree, or other order of any court of competent jurisdiction.

Effective Date

The provision is effective as of the date of enactment.

[Law at ¶5083, ¶5120, ¶5153 and ¶5155. CCH Explanation at ¶242.]

[¶10,410] Act Sec.1402. Unearned income Medicare contribution

Joint Committee on Taxation (J.C.T. REP. No. JCX-18-10)
[New Code Sec. 1411]

Present Law

Social security benefits and certain Medicare benefits are financed primarily by payroll taxes on covered wages. FICA imposes tax on employers based on the amount of wages paid to an employee during the year. The tax imposed is composed of two parts: (1) the OASDI tax equal to 6.2 percent of covered wages up to the taxable wage base ($106,800 in 2010); and (2) the Medicare hospital insurance ("HI") tax amount equal to 1.45 percent of covered wages. In addition to the tax on employers, each employee is subject to FICA taxes equal to the amount of tax imposed on the employer. The employee level tax generally must be withheld and remitted to the Federal government by the employer.

As a parallel to FICA taxes, SECA imposes taxes on the net income from self employment of self employed individuals. The rate of the OASDI portion of SECA taxes is equal to the combined employee and employer OASDI FICA tax rates and applies to self employment income up to the FICA taxable wage base. Similarly, the rate of the HI portion is the same as the combined employer and employee HI rates and there is no cap on the amount of self employment income to which the rate applies.[284]

Explanation of Provision

In general

In the case of an individual, estate, or trust an unearned income Medicare contribution tax is imposed.

In the case of an individual, the tax is the 3.8 percent of the lesser of net investment income or the excess of modified adjusted gross income over the threshold amount.

The threshold amount is $250,000 in the case of a joint return or surviving spouse, $125,000 in the case of a married individual filing a separate return, and $200,000 in any other case.

Modified adjusted gross income is adjusted gross income increased by the amount excluded from income as foreign earned income under section 911(a)(1) (net of the deductions and exclusions disallowed with respect to the foreign earned income).

In the case of an estate or trust, the tax is 3.8 percent of the lesser of undistributed net investment income or the excess of adjusted gross income (as defined in section 67(e)) over the dollar amount at which the highest income tax bracket applicable to an estate or trust begins.

---

[283] Sec. 152(f)(1). Under section 152(f)(1), a legally adopted child of the taxpayer or an individual who is lawfully placed with the taxpayer for legal adoption by the taxpayer is treated as a child of the taxpayer by blood.

[284] For purposes of computing net earnings from self employment, taxpayers are permitted a deduction equal to the product of the taxpayer's earnings (determined without regard to this deduction) and one-half of the sum of the

rates for OASDI (12.4 percent) and HI (2.9 percent), i.e., 7.65 percent of net earnings. This deduction reflects the fact that the FICA rates apply to an employee's wages, which do not include FICA taxes paid by the employer, whereas the self-employed individual's net earnings are economically equivalent to an employee's wages plus the employer share of FICA taxes.

The tax does not apply to a non-resident alien or to a trust all the unexpired interests in which are devoted to charitable purposes. The tax also does not apply to a trust that is exempt from tax under section 501 or a charitable remainder trust exempt from tax under section 664.

The tax is subject to the individual estimated tax provisions. The tax is not deductible in computing any tax imposed by subtitle A of the Internal Revenue Code (relating to income taxes).

Net investment income

Net investment income is investment income reduced by the deductions properly allocable to such income.

Investment income is the sum of (i) gross income from interest, dividends, annuities, royalties, and rents (other than income derived from any trade or business to which the tax does not apply), (ii) other gross income derived from any business to which the tax applies, and (iii) net gain (to the extent taken into account in computing taxable income) attributable to the disposition of property other than property held in a trade or business to which the tax does not apply.[285]

In the case of a trade or business, the tax applies if the trade or business is a passive activity with respect to the taxpayer or the trade or business consists of trading financial instruments or commodities (as defined in section 475(e)(2)). The tax does not apply to other trades or businesses conducted by a sole proprietor, partnership, or S corporation.

In the case of the disposition of a partnership interest or stock in an S corporation, gain or loss is taken into account only to the extent gain or loss would be taken into account by the partner or shareholder if the entity had sold all its properties for fair market value immediately before the disposition. Thus, only net gain or loss attributable to property held by the entity which is not property attributable to an active trade or business is taken into account.[286]

Income, gain, or loss on working capital is not treated as derived from a trade or business. Investment income does not include distributions from a qualified retirement plan or amounts subject to SECA tax.

Effective Date

The provision applies to taxable years beginning after December 31, 2012.

[Law at ¶ 5187. CCH Explanation at ¶ 232.]

[¶ 10,420] Act Sec. 1405. Excise tax on medical device manufacturers[287]

Joint Committee on Taxation (J.C.T. Rep. No. JCX-18-10)

[New Code Sec. 4191]

Present Law

Chapter 32 imposes excise taxes on sales by manufacturers of certain products. Terms and procedures related to the imposition, payment, and reporting of these excise taxes are included in various provisions within the Code.

Certain sales are exempt from the excise tax imposed on manufacturers. Exempt sales include sales (1) for use by the purchaser for further manufacture, or for resale to a second purchaser in further manufacture, (2) for export or for resale to a second purchaser for export, (3) for use

by the purchaser as supplies for vessels or aircraft, (4) to a State or local government for the exclusive use of a State or local government, (5) to a nonprofit educational organization for its exclusive use, or (6) to a qualified blood collector organization for such organization's exclusive use in the collection, storage, or transportation of blood.[288] If an article is sold free of tax for resale to a second purchaser for further manufacture or for export, the exemption will not apply unless, within the six-month period beginning on the date of sale by the manufacturer, the manufacturer receives proof that the article has been exported or resold for the use in further manu-

---

[285] Gross income does not include items, such as interest on tax-exempt bonds, veterans' benefits, and excluded gain from the sale of a principal residence, which are excluded from gross income under the income tax.

[286] For this purpose, a business of trading financial instruments or commodities is not treated as an active trade or business.

[287] The excise tax on medical devices as imposed by this provision replaces the annual fee on medical device manufacturers and importers under section 9009 of the Senate amendment.

[288] Sec. 4221(a).

facturing.[289] In general, the exemptions will not apply unless the manufacturer, the first purchaser, and the second purchaser are registered with the Secretary of the Treasury.

The lease of an article is generally considered to be a sale of such article.[290] Special rules apply for the imposition of tax to each lease payment. Rules are also imposed that treat the use of articles subject to tax by manufacturers, producers, or importers of such articles, as sales for the purpose of imposition of certain excise taxes.[291]

There are also rules for determining the price of an article on which excise tax is imposed.[292] These rules provide for: (1) the inclusion of containers, packaging, and certain transportation charges in the price, (2) determining a constructive sales price if an article is sold for less than the fair market price, and (3) determining the tax due in the case of partial payments or installment sales.

A credit or refund is generally allowed for overpayments of manufacturers excise taxes.[293] Overpayments may occur when tax-paid articles are sold for export and for certain specified uses and resales, when there are price adjustments, and where tax paid articles are subject to further manufacture. Generally, no credit or refund of any overpayment of tax is allowed or made unless the person who paid the tax establishes one of four prerequisites: (1) the tax was not included in the price of the article or otherwise collected from the person who purchased the article; (2) the tax was repaid to the ultimate purchaser of the article; (3) for overpayments due to specified uses and resales, the tax has been repaid to the ultimate vendor or the person has obtained the written consent of such ultimate vendor; or (4) the person has filed with the Secretary of the Treasury the written consent of the ultimate purchaser of the article to the allowance of the credit or making of the refund.[294]

Explanation of Provision

Under the provision, a tax equal to 2.3 percent of the sale price is imposed on the sale of any taxable medical device by the manufacturer, producer, or importer of such device. A taxable medical device is any device, defined in section 201(h) of the Federal Food, Drug, and Cosmetic Act,[295] intended for humans. The excise tax does not apply to eyeglasses, contact lenses, hearing aids, and any other medical device determined by the Secretary to be of a type that is generally purchased by the general public at retail for individual use. The Secretary may determine that a specific medical device is exempt under the provision if the device is generally sold at retail establishments (including over the internet) to individuals for their personal use. The exemption for such items is not limited by device class as defined in section 513 of the Federal Food, Drug, and Cosmetic Act. For example, items purchased by the general public at retail for individual use could include Class I items such as certain bandages and tipped applicators, Class II items such as certain pregnancy test kits and diabetes testing supplies, and Class III items such as certain denture adhesives and snake bite kits. Such items would only be exempt if they are generally designed and sold for individual use. It is anticipated that the Secretary will publish a list of medical device classifications[296] that are of a type generally purchased by the general public at retail for individual use.

The present law manufacturers excise tax exemptions for further manufacture and for export apply to tax imposed under this provision; however exemptions for use as supplies for vessels or aircraft, and for sales to State or local governments, nonprofit educational organizations, and qualified blood collector organizations are not applicable.

The provision repeals section 9009 of the Senate amendment (relating to an annual fee on medical device manufacturers and importers).

Effective Date

The provision applies to sales after December 31, 2012.

---

[289] Sec. 4221(b).

[290] Sec. 4217(a).

[291] Sec. 4218.

[292] Sec. 4216.

[293] Sec. 6416.

[294] Sec. 6416(a).

[295] 21 U.S.C. 321. Section 201(h) defines device as an instrument, apparatus, implement, machine, contrivance, implant, in vitro reagent, or other similar or related article, including any component, part, or accessory, which is (1) recognized in the official National Formulary, or the United States Pharmacopeia, or any supplement to them, (2) intended for use in the diagnosis of disease or other conditions, or in the cure, mitigation, treatment, or prevention of disease, in man or other animals, or (3) intended to affect the structure or any function of the body of man or other animals, and which does not achieve its primary intended purposes through chemical action within or on the body of man or other animals and which is not dependent upon being metabolized for the achievement of its primary intended purposes.

[296] Medical device classifications are found in Title 21 of the Code of Federal Regulations, Parts 862-892.

The repeal of section 9009 of the Senate amendment is effective on the date of enactment of the Senate amendment.

[Law at ¶5197 and ¶7109. CCH Explanation at ¶350.]

[¶10,430] Act Sec. 1408. Elimination of unintended application of cellulosic biofuel producer credit

Joint Committee on Taxation (J.C.T. Rep. No. JCX-18-10)

[Code Sec. 40]

Present Law

The "cellulosic biofuel producer credit" is a nonrefundable income tax credit for each gallon of qualified cellulosic fuel production of the producer for the taxable year. The amount of the credit is generally $1.01 per gallon.[297]

"Qualified cellulosic biofuel production" is any cellulosic biofuel which is produced by the taxpayer and which is: (1) sold by the taxpayer to another person (a) for use by such other person in the production of a qualified cellulosic biofuel mixture in such person's trade or business (other than casual off-farm production), (b) for use by such other person as a fuel in a trade or business, or (c) who sells such cellusic biofuel at retail to another person and places such cellulosic biofuel in the fuel tank of such other person; or (2) used by the producer for any purpose described in (1)(a), (b), or (c).

"Cellulosic biofuel" means any liquid fuel that (1) is produced in the United States and used as fuel in the United States, (2) is derived from any lignocellulosic or hemicellulosic matter that is available on a renewable or recurring basis, and (3) meets the registration requirements for fuels and fuel additives established by the Environmental Protection Agency ("EPA") under section 211 of the Clean Air Act. The cellulosic biofuel producer credit cannot be claimed unless the taxpayer is registered by the IRS as a producer of cellulosic biofuel.

Cellulosic biofuel eligible for the section 40 credit is precluded from qualifying as biodiesel, renewable diesel, or alternative fuel for purposes of the applicable income tax credit, excise tax credit, or payment provisions relating to those fuels.[298]

Because it is a credit under section 40(a), the cellulosic biofuel producer credit is part of the general business credits in section 38. However, the credit can only be carried forward three taxable years after the termination of the credit. The credit is also allowable against the alternative minimum tax. Under section 87, the credit is included in gross income. The cellulosic biofuel producer credit terminates on December 31, 2012.

The kraft process for making paper produces a byproduct called black liquor, which has been used for decades by paper manufacturers as a fuel in the papermaking process. Black liquor is composed of water, lignin and the spent chemicals used to break down the wood. The amount of the biomass in black liquor varies. The portion of the black liquor that is not consumed as a fuel source for the paper mills is recycled back into the papermaking process. Black liquor has ash content (mineral and other inorganic matter) significantly above that of other fuels.

In an informal Chief Counsel Advice ("CCA"), the IRS has concluded that black liquor is a liquid fuel from biomass and may qualify for the cellulosic biofuel producer credit, as well as the refundable alternative fuel mixture credit.[299] A taxpayer cannot claim both the alternative fuel mixture credit and the cellulosic biofuel producer credit. The alternative fuel credits and payment provisions expired December 31, 2009.

---

[297] In the case of cellulosic biofuel that is alcohol, the $1.01 credit amount is reduced by the credit amount of the alcohol mixture credit, and for ethanol, the credit amount for small ethanol producers, as in effect at the time the cellulosic biofuel fuel is produced.

[298] See secs. 40A(d)(1), 40A(f)(3), and 6426(h).

[299] IRS C.C.A. 200941011, 2009 W.L. 3239569 (June 30, 2009). The Code provides for a tax credit of 50 cents for each gallon of alternative fuel used to produce an alternative fuel mixture that is used or sold for use as a fuel. (sec. 6426(e)).

Under Notice 2006-92, an alternative fuel mixture is a mixture of alternative fuel and a taxable fuel (such as diesel) that contains at least 0.1 percent taxable fuel. Liquid fuel derived from biomass is an alternative fuel (sec. 6426(d)(2)(G)). Diesel fuel has been added to black liquor to qualify for the alternative mixture credit and the mixture is burned in a recovery boiler as fuel. Persons that have an alternative fuel mixture credit amount in excess of their taxable fuel excise tax liability may make a claim for payment from the Treasury in the amount of the excess.

Explanation of Provision

The provision modifies the cellulosic biofuel producer credit to exclude fuels with significant water, sediment, or ash content, such as black liquor. Consequently, credits will cease to be available for these fuels. Specifically, the provision excludes from the definition of cellulosic biofuel any fuels that (1) are more than four percent (determined by weight) water and sediment in any combination, or (2) have an ash content of more than one percent (determined by weight). Water content (including both free water and water in solution with dissolved solids) is determined by distillation, using for example ASTM method D95 or a similar method

suitable to the specific fuel being tested. Sediment consists of solid particles that are dispersed in the liquid fuel and is determined by centrifuge or extraction using, for example, ASTM method D1796 or D473 or similar method that reports sediment content in weight percent. Ash is the residue remaining after combustion of the sample using a specified method, such as ASTM D3174 or a similar method suitable for the fuel being tested.

Effective Date

The provision is effective for fuels sold or used on or after January 1, 2010.

[Law at ¶ 5057. CCH Explanation at ¶ 357.]

[¶ 10,440] Act Sec. 1409. Codification of economic substance doctrine and imposition of penalties

Joint Committee on Taxation (J.C.T. REP. NO. JCX-18-10)

[Code Secs. 6662, 6662A, 6664, 6676 and 7701]

Present Law

In general

The Code provides detailed rules specifying the computation of taxable income, including the amount, timing, source, and character of items of income, gain, loss, and deduction. These rules permit both taxpayers and the government to compute taxable income with reasonable accuracy and predictability. Taxpayers generally may plan their transactions in reliance on these rules to determine the Federal income tax consequences arising from the transactions.

In addition to the statutory provisions, courts have developed several doctrines that can be applied to deny the tax benefits of a tax-motivated transaction, notwithstanding that the transaction may satisfy the literal requirements of a specific tax provision. These common-law

doctrines are not entirely distinguishable, and their application to a given set of facts is often blurred by the courts, the IRS, and litigants. Although these doctrines serve an important role in the administration of the tax system, they can be seen as at odds with an objective, "rule-based" system of taxation.

One common-law doctrine applied over the years is the "economic substance" doctrine. In general, this doctrine denies tax benefits arising from transactions that do not result in a meaningful change to the taxpayer's economic position other than a purported reduction in Federal income tax.[300]

Economic substance doctrine

Courts generally deny claimed tax benefits if the transaction that gives rise to those benefits lacks economic substance independent of U.S. Federal income tax considerations—notwithstanding that the purported activity actually oc-

---

[300] *See, e.g., ACM Partnership v. Commissioner,* 157 F.3d 231 (3d Cir. 1998), *aff'g* 73 T.C.M. (CCH) 2189 (1997), *cert. denied* 526 U.S. 1017 (1999); *Klamath Strategic Investment Fund, LLC v. United States,* 472 F. Supp. 2d 885 (E.D. Texas 2007), *aff'd* 568 F.3d 537 (5th Cir. 2009); *Coltec Industries, Inc. v. United States,* 454 F.3d 1340 (Fed. Cir. 2006), *vacating and remanding* 62 Fed. Cl. 716 (2004) (slip opinion at 123-124, 128); *cert. denied,* 127 S. Ct. 1261 (Mem.) (2007).

Closely related doctrines also applied by the courts (sometimes interchangeable with the economic substance doctrine) include the "sham transaction doctrine" and the "business purpose doctrine." *See, e.g., Knetsch v. United States,* 364 U.S. 361 (1960) (denying interest deductions on a "sham transaction" that lacked "commercial economic substance"). Certain "substance over form" cases involving tax-

indifferent parties, in which courts have found that the substance of the transaction did not comport with the form asserted by the taxpayer, have also involved examination of whether the change in economic position that occurred, if any, was consistent with the form asserted, and whether the claimed business purpose supported the particular tax benefits that were claimed. *See, e.g., TIFD III-E, Inc. v. United States,* 459 F.3d 220 (2d Cir. 2006); *BB&T Corporation v. United States,* 2007-1 USTC P 50,130 (M.D.N.C. 2007), *aff'd* 523 F.3d 461 (4th Cir. 2008). Although the Second Circuit found for the government in *TIFD III-E, Inc.,* on remand to consider issues under section 704(e), the District Court found for the taxpayer. See, *TIFD III-E Inc. v. United States,* No. 3:01-cv-01839, 2009 WL 3208650 (D. Conn. Oct. 23, 2009).

curred. The Tax Court has described the doctrine as follows:

> The tax law . . . requires that the intended transactions have economic substance separate and distinct from economic benefit achieved solely by tax reduction. The doctrine of economic substance becomes applicable, and a judicial remedy is warranted, where a taxpayer seeks to claim tax benefits, unintended by Congress, by means of transactions that serve no economic purpose other than tax savings.[301]

Business purpose doctrine

A common law doctrine that often is considered together with the economic substance doctrine is the business purpose doctrine. The business purpose doctrine involves an inquiry into the subjective motives of the taxpayer - that is, whether the taxpayer intended the transaction to serve some useful non-tax purpose. In making this determination, some courts have bifurcated a transaction in which activities with non-tax objectives have been combined with unrelated activities having only tax-avoidance objectives, in order to disallow the tax benefits of the overall transaction.[302]

Application by the courts

Elements of the doctrine

There is a lack of uniformity regarding the proper application of the economic substance

doctrine.[303] Some courts apply a conjunctive test that requires a taxpayer to establish the presence of both economic substance (i.e., the objective component) and business purpose (i.e., the subjective component) in order for the transaction to survive judicial scrutiny.[304] A narrower approach used by some courts is to conclude that either a business purpose or economic substance is sufficient to respect the transaction.[305] A third approach regards economic substance and business purpose as "simply more precise factors to consider" in determining whether a transaction has any practical economic effects other than the creation of tax benefits.[306]

One decision by the Court of Federal Claims questioned the continuing viability of the doctrine. That court also stated that "the use of the 'economic substance' doctrine to trump 'mere compliance with the Code' would violate the separation of powers" though that court also found that the particular transaction at issue in the case did not lack economic substance. The Court of Appeals for the Federal Circuit ("Federal Circuit Court") overruled the Court of Federal Claims decision, reiterating the viability of the economic substance doctrine and concluding that the transaction in question violated that doctrine.[307] The Federal Circuit Court stated that "[w]hile the doctrine may well also apply if the taxpayer's sole subjective motivation is tax avoidance even if the transaction has economic substance, [footnote omitted], a lack of economic substance is sufficient to disqualify the transac-

[301] *ACM Partnership v. Commissioner*, 73 T.C.M. at 2215.

[302] See, *ACM Partnership v. Commissioner*, 157 F.3d at 256 n.48.

[303] "The casebooks are glutted with [economic substance] tests. Many such tests proliferate because they give the comforting illusion of consistency and precision. They often obscure rather than clarify." *Collins v. Commissioner*, 857 F.2d 1383, 1386 (9th Cir. 1988).

[304] See, e.g., *Pasternak v. Commissioner*, 990 F.2d 893, 898 (6th Cir. 1993) ("The threshold question is whether the transaction has economic substance. If the answer is yes, the question becomes whether the taxpayer was motivated by profit to participate in the transaction."). *See also, Klamath Strategic Investment Fund v. United States*, 568 F. 3d 537, (5th Cir. 2009) (even if taxpayers may have had a profit motive, a transaction was disregarded where it did not in fact have any realistic possibility of profit and funding was never at risk).

[305] See, e.g., *Rice's Toyota World v. Commissioner*, 752 F.2d 89, 91-92 (4th Cir. 1985) ("To treat a transaction as a sham, the court must find that the taxpayer was motivated by no business purposes other than obtaining tax benefits in entering the transaction, and, second, that the transaction has no economic substance because no reasonable possibility of a profit exists."); *IES Industries v. United States*, 253 F.3d 350, 358 (8th Cir. 2001) ("In determining whether a transaction is

a sham for tax purposes [under the Eighth Circuit test], a transaction will be characterized as a sham if it is not motivated by any economic purpose outside of tax considerations (the business purpose test), and if it is without economic substance because no real potential for profit exists (the economic substance test)."). As noted earlier, the economic substance doctrine and the sham transaction doctrine are similar and sometimes are applied interchangeably. For a more detailed discussion of the sham transaction doctrine, see, e.g., Joint Committee on Taxation, *Study of Present-Law Penalty and Interest Provisions as Required by Section 3801 of the Internal Revenue Service Restructuring and Reform Act of 1998 (including Provisions Relating to Corporate Tax Shelters)* (JCS-3-99) at 182.

[306] See, e.g., *ACM Partnership v. Commissioner*, 157 F.3d at 247; *James v. Commissioner*, 899 F.2d 905, 908 (10th Cir. 1995); *Sacks v. Commissioner*, 69 F.3d 982, 985 (9th Cir. 1995) ("Instead, the consideration of business purpose and economic substance are simply more precise factors to consider . . . We have repeatedly and carefully noted that this formulation cannot be used as a 'rigid two-step analysis'.")

[307] *Coltec Industries, Inc. v. United States*, 62 Fed. Cl. 716 (2004) (slip opinion at 123-124, 128); *vacated and remanded*, 454 F.3d 1340 (Fed. Cir. 2006), *cert. denied*, 127 S. Ct. 1261 (Mem.) (2007).

tion without proof that the taxpayer's sole motive is tax avoidance."[308]

Nontax economic benefits

There also is a lack of uniformity regarding the type of non-tax economic benefit a taxpayer must establish in order to demonstrate that a transaction has economic substance. Some courts have denied tax benefits on the grounds that a stated business benefit of a particular structure was not in fact obtained by that structure.[309] Several courts have denied tax benefits on the grounds that the subject transactions lacked profit potential.[310] In addition, some courts have applied the economic substance doctrine to disallow tax benefits in transactions in which a taxpayer was exposed to risk and the transaction had a profit potential, but the court concluded that the economic risks and profit potential were insignificant when compared to the tax benefits.[311] Under this analysis, the taxpayer's profit potential must be more than nominal. Conversely, other courts view the application of the economic substance doctrine as requiring an objective determination of whether a "reasonable possibility of profit" from the transaction existed apart from the tax benefits.[312] In these cases, in assessing whether a reasonable possibility of profit exists, it may be sufficient if there is a nominal amount of pre-tax profit as measured against expected tax benefits.

Financial accounting benefits

In determining whether a taxpayer had a valid business purpose for entering into a transaction, at least two courts have concluded that financial accounting benefits arising from tax savings do not qualify as a non-tax business purpose.[313] However, based on court decisions that recognize the importance of financial accounting treatment, taxpayers have asserted that financial accounting benefits arising from tax savings can satisfy the business purpose test.[314]

Tax-indifferent parties

A number of cases have involved transactions structured to allocate income for Federal tax purposes to a tax-indifferent party, with a corresponding deduction, or favorable basis result, to a taxable person. The income allocated to the tax-indifferent party for tax purposes was structured to exceed any actual economic income to be received by the tax indifferent party from the transaction. Courts have sometimes concluded that this particular type of transaction did not satisfy the economic substance doctrine.[315] In other cases, courts have indicated that

---

[308] The Federal Circuit Court stated that "when the taxpayer claims a deduction, it is the taxpayer who bears the burden of proving that the transaction has economic substance." The Federal Circuit Court quoted a decision of its predecessor court, stating that "*Gregory v. Helvering* requires that a taxpayer carry an unusually heavy burden when he attempts to demonstrate that Congress intended to give favorable tax treatment to the kind of transaction that would never occur absent the motive of tax avoidance." The Court also stated that "while the taxpayer's subjective motivation may be pertinent to the existence of a tax avoidance purpose, all courts have looked to the objective reality of a transaction in assessing its economic substance." *Coltec Industries, Inc. v. United States*, 454 F.3d at 1355, 1356.

[309] See, e.g., *Coltec Industries v. United States*, 454 F.3d 1340 (Fed. Cir. 2006). The court analyzed the transfer to a subsidiary of a note purporting to provide high stock basis in exchange for a purported assumption of liabilities, and held these transactions unnecessary to accomplish any business purpose of using a subsidiary to manage asbestos liabilities. The court also held that the purported business purpose of adding a barrier to veilpiercing claims by third parties was not accomplished by the transaction. 454 F.3d at 1358-1360 (Fed. Cir. 2006).

[310] See, e.g., *Knetsch*, 364 U.S. at 361; *Goldstein v. Commissioner*, 364 F.2d 734 (2d Cir. 1966) (holding that an unprofitable, leveraged acquisition of Treasury bills, and accompanying prepaid interest deduction, lacked economic substance).

[311] See, e.g., *Goldstein v. Commissioner*, 364 F.2d at 739-40 (disallowing deduction even though taxpayer had a possibility of small gain or loss by owning Treasury bills); *Sheldon*

v. Commissioner, 94 T.C. 738, 768 (1990) (stating that "potential for gain . . . is infinitesimally nominal and vastly insignificant when considered in comparison with the claimed deductions").

[312] See, e.g., *Rice's Toyota World v. Commissioner*, 752 F. 2d 89, 94 (4th Cir. 1985) (the economic substance inquiry requires an objective determination of whether a reasonable possibility of profit from the transaction existed apart from tax benefits); *Compaq Computer Corp. v. Commissioner*, 277 F.3d 778, 781 (5th Cir. 2001) (applied the same test, citing *Rice's Toyota World*); *IES Industries v. United States*, 253 F.3d 350, 354 (8th Cir. 2001); *Wells Fargo & Company v. United States*, No. 06-628T, 2010 WL 94544, at *57-58 (Fed. Cl. Jan. 8, 2010).

[313] See *American Electric Power, Inc. v. United States*, 136 F. Supp. 2d 762, 791-92 (S.D. Ohio 2001), aff'd, 326 F.3d.737 (6th Cir. 2003) and *Wells Fargo & Company v. United States*, No. 06-628T, 2010 WL 94544, at *59 (Fed. Cl. Jan. 8, 2010).

[314] See, e.g., Joint Committee on Taxation, *Report of Investigation of Enron Corporation and Related Entities Regarding Federal Tax and Compensation Issues, and Policy Recommendations* (JSC-3-03) February, 2003 ("Enron Report"), Volume III at C-93, 289. Enron Corporation relied on Frank Lyon Co. v. United States, 435 U.S. 561, 577-78 (1978), and Newman v. Commissioner, 902 F.2d 159, 163 (2d Cir. 1990), to argue that financial accounting benefits arising from tax savings constitute a good business purpose.

[315] See, e.g., *ACM Partnership v. Commissioner*, 157 F.3d 231 (3d Cir. 1998), aff'g 73 T.C.M. (CCH) 2189 (1997), cert. denied 526 U.S. 1017 (1999).

---

the substance of a transaction did not support the form of income allocations asserted by the taxpayer and have questioned whether asserted business purpose or other standards were met.[316]

Penalty regime

General accuracy-related penalty

An accuracy-related penalty under section 6662 applies to the portion of any underpayment that is attributable to (1) negligence, (2) any substantial understatement of income tax, (3) any substantial valuation misstatement, (4) any substantial overstatement of pension liabilities, or (5) any substantial estate or gift tax valuation understatement. If the correct income tax liability exceeds that reported by the taxpayer by the greater of 10 percent of the correct tax or $5,000 (or, in the case of corporations, by the lesser of (a) 10 percent of the correct tax (or $10,000 if greater) or (b) $10 million), then a substantial understatement exists and a penalty may be imposed equal to 20 percent of the underpayment of tax attributable to the understatement.[317] The section 6662 penalty is increased to 40 percent in the case of gross valuation misstatements as defined in section 6662(h). Except in the case of tax shelters,[318] the amount of any understatement is reduced by any portion attributable to an item if (1) the treatment of the item is supported by substantial authority, or (2) facts relevant to the tax treatment of the item were adequately disclosed and there was a reasonable basis for its tax treatment. The Treasury Secretary may prescribe a list of positions which the Secretary believes do not meet the requirements for substantial authority under this provision.

The section 6662 penalty generally is abated (even with respect to tax shelters) in cases in which the taxpayer can demonstrate that there was "reasonable cause" for the underpayment and that the taxpayer acted in good faith.[319] The relevant regulations for a tax shelter provide that reasonable cause exists where the taxpayer "reasonably relies in good faith on an opinion based on a professional tax advisor's analysis of the pertinent facts and authorities [that] . . . unambiguously concludes that there is a greater than 50-percent likelihood that the tax treatment of the item will be upheld if challenged" by the IRS.[320] For transactions other than tax shelters, the relevant regulations provide a facts and circumstances test, the most important factor generally being the extent of the taxpayer's effort to assess the proper tax liability. If a taxpayer relies on an opinion, reliance is not reasonable if the taxpayer knows or should have known that the advisor lacked knowledge in the relevant aspects of Federal tax law, or if the taxpayer fails to disclose a fact that it knows or should have known is relevant. Certain additional requirements apply with respect to the advice.[321]

Listed transactions and reportable avoidance transactions

In general

A separate accuracy-related penalty under section 6662A applies to any "listed transaction" and to any other "reportable transaction" that is not a listed transaction, if a significant purpose of such transaction is the avoidance or evasion of Federal income tax[322] (hereinafter referred to as a "reportable avoidance transaction"). The penalty rate and defenses available to avoid the penalty vary depending on whether the transaction was adequately disclosed.

Both listed transactions and other reportable transactions are allowed to be described by the Treasury department under section 6011 as

---

[316] See, e.g., *TIFD III-E, Inc. v. United States*, 459 F.3d 220 (2d Cir. 2006). Although the Second Circuit found for the government in *TIFD III-E, Inc.*, on remand to consider issues under section 704(e), the District Court found for the taxpayer. See, *TIFD III-E Inc. v. United States*, No. 3:01-cv-01839, 2009 WL 3208650 (Oct. 23, 2009).

[317] Sec. 6662.

[318] A tax shelter is defined for this purpose as a partnership or other entity, an investment plan or arrangement, or any other plan or arrangement if a significant purpose of such partnership, other entity, plan, or arrangement is the avoidance or evasion of Federal income tax. Sec. 6662(d)(2)(C).

[319] Sec. 6664(c).

[320] Treas. Reg. sec. 1.6662-4(g)(4)(i)(B); Treas. Reg. sec. 1.6664-4(c).

[321] See Treas. Reg. Sec. 1.6664-4(c). In addition to the requirements applicable to taxpayers under the regulations,

advisors may be subject to potential penalties under section 6694 (applicable to return preparers), and to monetary penalties and other sanctions under Circular 230 (which provides rules governing persons practicing before the IRS). Under Circular 230, if a transaction is a "covered transaction" (a term that includes listed transactions and certain non-listed reportable transactions) a "more likely than not" confidence level is required for written tax advice that may be relied upon by a taxpayer for the purpose of avoiding penalties, and certain other standards must also be met. Treasury Dept. Circular 230 (Rev. 4-2008) Sec. 10.35. For other tax advice, Circular 230 generally requires a lower "realistic possibility" confidence level or a "non-frivolous" confidence level coupled with advising the client of any opportunity to avoid the accuracy related penalty under section 6662 by adequate disclosure. Treasury Dept. Circular 230 (Rev. 4-2008) Sec. 10.34.

[322] Sec. 6662A(b)(2).

transactions that must be reported, and section 6707A(c) imposes a penalty for failure adequately to report such transactions under section 6011. A reportable transaction is defined as one that the Treasury Secretary determines is required to be disclosed because it is determined to have a potential for tax avoidance or evasion.[323] A listed transaction is defined as a reportable transaction which is the same as, or substantially similar to, a transaction specifically identified by the Secretary as a tax avoidance transaction for purposes of the reporting disclosure requirements.[324]

Disclosed transactions

In general, a 20-percent accuracy-related penalty is imposed on any understatement attributable to an adequately disclosed listed transaction or reportable avoidance transaction.[325] The only exception to the penalty is if the taxpayer satisfies a more stringent reasonable cause and good faith exception (hereinafter referred to as the "strengthened reasonable cause exception"), which is described below. The strengthened reasonable cause exception is available only if the relevant facts affecting the tax treatment were adequately disclosed, there is or was substantial authority for the claimed tax treatment, and the taxpayer reasonably believed that the claimed tax treatment was more likely than not the proper treatment. A "reasonable belief" must be based on the facts and law as they exist at the time that the return in question is filed, and not take into account the possibility that a return would not be audited. Moreover, reliance on professional advice may support a "reasonable belief" only in certain circumstances.[326]

Undisclosed transactions

If the taxpayer does not adequately disclose the transaction, the strengthened reasonable cause exception is not available (i.e., a strict liability penalty generally applies), and the taxpayer is subject to an increased penalty equal to 30 percent of the understatement.[327] However, a taxpayer will be treated as having adequately disclosed a transaction for this purpose if the IRS

Commissioner has separately rescinded the separate penalty under section 6707A for failure to disclose a reportable transaction.[328] The IRS Commissioner is authorized to do this only if the failure does not relate to a listed transaction and only if rescinding the penalty would promote compliance and effective tax administration.[329]

A public entity that is required to pay a penalty for an undisclosed listed or reportable transaction must disclose the imposition of the penalty in reports to the SEC for such periods as the Secretary specifies. The disclosure to the SEC applies without regard to whether the taxpayer determines the amount of the penalty to be material to the reports in which the penalty must appear, and any failure to disclose such penalty in the reports is treated as a failure to disclose a listed transaction. A taxpayer must disclose a penalty in reports to the SEC once the taxpayer has exhausted its administrative and judicial remedies with respect to the penalty (or if earlier, when paid).[330]

Determination of the understatement amount

The penalty is applied to the amount of any understatement attributable to the listed or reportable avoidance transaction without regard to other items on the tax return. For purposes of this provision, the amount of the understatement is determined as the sum of: (1) the product of the highest corporate or individual tax rate (as appropriate) and the increase in taxable income resulting from the difference between the taxpayer's treatment of the item and the proper treatment of the item (without regard to other items on the tax return);[331] and (2) the amount of any decrease in the aggregate amount of credits which results from a difference between the taxpayer's treatment of an item and the proper tax treatment of such item.

Except as provided in regulations, a taxpayer's treatment of an item will not take into account any amendment or supplement to a return if the amendment or supplement is filed after the earlier of when the taxpayer is first contacted regarding an examination of the return

---

[323] Sec. 6707A(c)(1).

[324] Sec. 6707A(c)(2).

[325] Sec. 6662A(a).

[326] Section 6664(d)(3)(B) does not allow a reasonable belief to be based on a "disqualified opinion" or on an opinion from a "disqualified tax advisor."

[327] Sec. 6662A(c).

[328] Sec. 6664(d).

[329] Sec. 6707A(d).

[330] Sec. 6707A(e).

[331] For this purpose, any reduction in the excess of deductions allowed for the taxable year over gross income for such year, and any reduction in the amount of capital losses which would (without regard to section 1211) be allowed for such year, will be treated as an increase in taxable income. Sec. 6662A(b).

or such other date as specified by the Secretary.[332]

Strengthened reasonable cause exception

A penalty is not imposed under section 6662A with respect to any portion of an understatement if it is shown that there was reasonable cause for such portion and the taxpayer acted in good faith. Such a showing requires: (1) adequate disclosure of the facts affecting the transaction in accordance with the regulations under section 6011;[333] (2) that there is or was substantial authority for such treatment; and (3) that the taxpayer reasonably believed that such treatment was more likely than not the proper treatment. For this purpose, a taxpayer will be treated as having a reasonable belief with respect to the tax treatment of an item only if such belief: (1) is based on the facts and law that exist at the time the tax return (that includes the item) is filed; and (2) relates solely to the taxpayer's chances of success on the merits and does not take into account the possibility that (a) a return will not be audited, (b) the treatment will not be raised on audit, or (c) the treatment will be resolved through settlement if raised.[334]

A taxpayer may (but is not required to) rely on an opinion of a tax advisor in establishing its reasonable belief with respect to the tax treatment of the item. However, a taxpayer may not rely on an opinion of a tax advisor for this purpose if the opinion (1) is provided by a "disqualified tax advisor" or (2) is a "disqualified opinion."

Disqualified tax advisor

A disqualified tax advisor is any advisor who: (1) is a material advisor[335] and who participates in the organization, management, promotion, or sale of the transaction or is related (within the meaning of section 267(b) or 707(b)(1)) to any person who so participates; (2) is compensated directly or indirectly[336] by a ma-

terial advisor with respect to the transaction; (3) has a fee arrangement with respect to the transaction that is contingent on all or part of the intended tax benefits from the transaction being sustained; or (4) as determined under regulations prescribed by the Secretary, has a disqualifying financial interest with respect to the transaction.

A material advisor is considered as participating in the "organization" of a transaction if the advisor performs acts relating to the development of the transaction. This may include, for example, preparing documents: (1) establishing a structure used in connection with the transaction (such as a partnership agreement); (2) describing the transaction (such as an offering memorandum or other statement describing the transaction); or (3) relating to the registration of the transaction with any Federal, state, or local government body.[337] Participation in the "management" of a transaction means involvement in the decision-making process regarding any business activity with respect to the transaction. Participation in the "promotion or sale" of a transaction means involvement in the marketing or solicitation of the transaction to others. Thus, an advisor who provides information about the transaction to a potential participant is involved in the promotion or sale of a transaction, as is any advisor who recommends the transaction to a potential participant.

Disqualified opinion

An opinion may not be relied upon if the opinion: (1) is based on unreasonable factual or legal assumptions (including assumptions as to future events); (2) unreasonably relies upon representations, statements, finding or agreements of the taxpayer or any other person; (3) does not identify and consider all relevant facts; or (4) fails to meet any other requirement prescribed by the Secretary.

---

[332] Sec. 6662A(e)(3).

[333] See the previous discussion regarding the penalty for failing to disclose a reportable transaction.

[334] Sec. 6664(d).

[335] The term "material advisor" means any person who provides any material aid, assistance, or advice with respect to organizing, managing, promoting, selling, implementing, or carrying out any reportable transaction, and who derives gross income in excess of $50,000 in the case of a reportable transaction substantially all of the tax benefits from which are provided to natural persons ($250,000 in any other case). Sec. 6111(b)(1).

[336] This situation could arise, for example, when an advisor has an arrangement or understanding (oral or written) with an organizer, manager, or promoter of a reportable transaction that such party will recommend or refer poten-

tial participants to the advisor for an opinion regarding the tax treatment of the transaction.

[337] An advisor should not be treated as participating in the organization of a transaction if the advisor's only involvement with respect to the organization of the transaction is the rendering of an opinion regarding the tax consequences of such transaction. However, such an advisor may be a "disqualified tax advisor" with respect to the transaction if the advisor participates in the management, promotion, or sale of the transaction (or if the advisor is compensated by a material advisor, has a fee arrangement that is contingent on the tax benefits of the transaction, or as determined by the Secretary, has a continuing financial interest with respect to the transaction). See Notice 2005-12, 2005-1 C.B. 494 regarding disqualified compensation arrangements.

Coordination with other penalties

Any understatement upon which a penalty is imposed under section 6662A is not subject to the accuracy related penalty for underpayments under section 6662.[338] However, that understatement is included for purposes of determining whether any understatement (as defined in sec. 6662(d)(2)) is a substantial understatement under section 6662(d)(1).[339] Thus, in the case of an understatement (as defined in sec. 6662(d)(2)), the amount of the understatement (determined without regard to section 6662A(e)(1)(A)) is increased by the aggregate amount of reportable transaction understatements for purposes of determining whether the understatement is a substantial understatement. The section 6662(a) penalty applies only to the excess of the amount of the substantial understatement (if any) after section 6662A(e)(1)(A) is applied over the aggregate amount of reportable transaction understatements.[340] Accordingly, every understatement is penalized, but only under one penalty provision.

The penalty imposed under section 6662A does not apply to any portion of an understatement to which a fraud penalty applies under section 6663 or to which the 40-percent penalty for gross valuation misstatements under section 6662(h) applies.[341]

Erroneous claim for refund or credit

If a claim for refund or credit with respect to income tax (other than a claim relating to the earned income tax credit) is made for an excessive amount, unless it is shown that the claim for such excessive amount has a reasonable basis, the person making such claim is subject to a penalty in an amount equal to 20 percent of the excessive amount.[342]

The term "excessive amount" means the amount by which the amount of the claim for refund for any taxable year exceeds the amount of such claim allowable for the taxable year.

This penalty does not apply to any portion of the excessive amount of a claim for refund or credit which is subject to a penalty imposed under the accuracy related or fraud penalty provisions (including the general accuracy related penalty, or the penalty with respect to listed and reportable transactions, described above).

Explanation of Provision

The provision clarifies and enhances the application of the economic substance doctrine. Under the provision, new section 7701(o) provides that in the case of any transaction[343] to which the economic substance doctrine is relevant, such transaction is treated as having economic substance only if (1) the transaction changes in a meaningful way (apart from Federal income tax effects) the taxpayer's economic position, and (2) the taxpayer has a substantial purpose (apart from Federal income tax effects) for entering into such transaction. The provision provides a uniform definition of economic substance, but does not alter the flexibility of the courts in other respects.

The determination of whether the economic substance doctrine is relevant to a transaction is made in the same manner as if the provision had never been enacted. Thus, the provision does not change present law standards in determining when to utilize an economic substance analysis.[344]

The provision is not intended to alter the tax treatment of certain basic business transactions that, under longstanding judicial and administrative practice are respected, merely because the choice between meaningful economic alternatives is largely or entirely based on comparative tax advantages. Among[345] these basic transactions are (1) the choice between capitalizing a

---

[338] Sec. 6662(b) (flush language). In addition, section 6662(b) provides that section 6662 does not apply to any portion of an underpayment on which a fraud penalty is imposed under section 6663.

[339] Sec. 6662A(e)(1).

[340] Sec. 6662(d)(2)(A) (flush language)

[341] Sec. 6662A(e)(2).

[342] Sec. 6676.

[343] The term "transaction" includes a series of transactions.

[344] If the realization of the tax benefits of a transaction is consistent with the Congressional purpose or plan that the tax benefits were designed by Congress to effectuate, it is not intended that such tax benefits be disallowed. See, e.g., Treas. Reg. sec. 1.269-2, stating that characteristic of circumstances in which an amount otherwise constituting a deduction, credit, or other allowance is not available are those in which the effect of the deduction, credit, or other allowance would be to distort the liability of the particular taxpayer when the essential nature of the transaction or situation is examined in the light of the basic purpose or plan which the deduction, credit, or other allowance was designed by Congress to effectuate. Thus, for example, it is not intended that a tax credit (e.g., section 42 (low-income housing credit), section 45 (production tax credit), section 45D (new markets tax credit), section 47 (rehabilitation credit), section 48 (energy credit), etc.) be disallowed in a transaction pursuant to which, in form and substance, a taxpayer makes the type of investment or undertakes the type of activity that the credit was intended to encourage.

[345] The examples are illustrative and not exclusive.

business enterprise with debt or equity;[346] (2) a U.S. person's choice between utilizing a foreign corporation or a domestic corporation to make a foreign investment;[347] (3) the choice to enter a transaction or series of transactions that constitute a corporate organization or reorganization under subchapter C;[348] and (4) the choice to utilize a related-party entity in a transaction, provided that the arm's length standard of section 482 and other applicable concepts are satisfied.[349] Leasing transactions, like all other types of transactions, will continue to be analyzed in light of all the facts and circumstances.[350] As under present law, whether a particular transaction meets the requirements for specific treatment under any of these provisions is a question of facts and circumstances. Also, the fact that a transaction meets the requirements for specific treatment under any provision of the Code is not determinative of whether a transaction or series of transactions of which it is a part has economic substance.[351]

The provision does not alter the court's ability to aggregate, disaggregate, or otherwise recharacterize a transaction when applying the doctrine. For example, the provision reiterates the present-law ability of the courts to bifurcate a transaction in which independent activities with

non-tax objectives are combined with an unrelated item having only tax-avoidance objectives in order to disallow those tax-motivated benefits.[352]

Conjunctive analysis

The provision clarifies that the economic substance doctrine involves a conjunctive analysis - there must be an inquiry regarding the objective effects of the transaction on the taxpayer's economic position as well as an inquiry regarding the taxpayer's subjective motives for engaging in the transaction. Under the provision, a transaction must satisfy both tests, i.e., the transaction must change in a meaningful way (apart from Federal income tax effects) the taxpayer's economic position and the taxpayer must have a substantial non-Federal-income-tax purpose for entering into such transaction, in order for a transaction to be treated as having economic substance. This clarification eliminates the disparity that exists among the Federal circuit courts regarding the application of the doctrine, and modifies its application in those circuits in which either a change in economic position or a non-tax business purpose (without having both) is sufficient to satisfy the economic substance doctrine.[353]

---

[346] See, e.g., John Kelley Co. v. Commissioner, 326 U.S. 521 (1946) (respecting debt characterization in one case and not in the other, based on all the facts and circumstances).

[347] See, e.g., Sam Siegel v. Commissioner, 45. T.C. 566 (1966), acq. 1966-2 C.B. 3. But see Commissioner v. Bollinger, 485 U.S. 340 (1988) (agency principles applied to title-holding corporation under the facts and circumstances).

[348] See, e.g., Rev. Proc. 2010-3 2010-1 I.R.B. 110, Secs. 3.01(38), (39),(40,) and (42) (IRS will not rule on certain matters relating to incorporations or reorganizations unless there is a "significant issue"); compare Gregory v. Helvering. 293 U.S. 465 (1935).

[349] See, e.g., National Carbide v. Commissioner, 336 U.S. 422 (1949), Moline Properties v. Commissioner, 319 U.S. 435 (1943); compare, e.g. Aiken Industries, Inc. v. Commissioner, 56 T.C. 925 (1971), acq., 1972-2 C.B. 1; Commissioner v. Bollinger, 485 U.S. 340 (1988); see also sec. 7701(l).

[350] See, e.g., Frank Lyon Co. v. Commissioner, 435 U.S. 561 (1978); Hilton v. Commissioner, 74 T.C. 305, aff'd, 671 F. 2d 316 (9th Cir. 1982), cert. denied, 459 U.S. 907 (1982); Coltec Industries v. United States, 454 F.3d 1340 (Fed. Cir. 2006), cert. denied, 127 S. Ct. 1261 (Mem) (2007); BB&T Corporation v. United States, 2007-1 USTC P 50,130 (M.D.N.C. 2007), aff'd, 523 F.3d 461 (4th Cir. 2008); Wells Fargo & Company v. United States, No. 06-628T, 2010 WL 94544, at *60 (Fed. Cl. Jan. 8, 2010) (distinguishing leasing case Consolidated Edison Company of New York, No. 06-305T, 2009 WL 3418533 (Fed. Cl. Oct. 21, 2009) by observing that "considerations of economic substance are factually specific to the transaction involved").

[351] As examples of cases in which courts have found that a transaction does not meet the requirements for the treat-

ment claimed by the taxpayer under the Code, or does not have economic substance, see e.g., BB&T Corporation v. United States, 2007-1 USTC P 50,130 (M.D.N.C. 2007) aff'd, 523 F.3d 461 (4th Cir. 2008); Tribune Company and Subsidiaries v. Commissioner, 125 T.C. 110 (2005); H.J. Heinz Company and Subsidiaries v. United States, 76 Fed. Cl. 570 (2007); Coltec Industries, Inc. v. United States, 454 F.3d 1340 (Fed. Cir. 2006), cert. denied 127 S. Ct. 1261 (Mem.) (2007); Long Term Capital Holdings LP v. United States, 330 F. Supp. 2d 122 (D. Conn. 2004), aff'd, 150 Fed. Appx. 40 (2d Cir. 2005); Klamath Strategic Investment Fund, LLC v. United States, 472 F. Supp. 2d 885 (E.D. Texas 2007); aff'd, 568 F. 3d 537 (5th Cir. 2009); Santa Monica Pictures LLC v. Commissioner, 89 T.C.M. 1157 (2005).

[352] See, e.g., Coltec Industries, Inc. v. United States, 454 F.3d 1340 (Fed. Cir. 2006), cert. denied 127 S. Ct. 1261 (Mem.) (2007) ("the first asserted business purpose focuses on the wrong transaction—the creation of Garrison as a separate subsidiary to manage asbestos liabilities. . . . [W]e must focus on the transaction that gave the taxpayer a high basis in the stock and thus gave rise to the alleged benefit upon sale . . . ") 454 F.3d 1340, 1358 (Fed. Cir. 2006). See also ACM Partnership v. Commissioner, 157 F.3d at 256 n.48; Minnesota Tea Co. v. Helvering, 302 U.S. 609, 613 (1938) ("A given result at the end of a straight path is not made a different result because reached by following a devious path.").

[353] The provision defines "economic substance doctrine" as the common law doctrine under which tax benefits under subtitle A with respect to a transaction are not allowable if the transaction does not have economic substance or lacks a business purpose. Thus, the definition includes any doctrine that denies tax benefits for lack of economic substance, for lack of business purpose, or for lack of both.

Non-Federal-income-tax business purpose

Under the provision, a taxpayer's non-Federal-income-tax purpose[354] for entering into a transaction (the second prong in the analysis) must be "substantial." For purposes of this analysis, any State or local income tax effect which is related to a Federal income tax effect is treated in the same manner as a Federal income tax effect. Also, a purpose of achieving a favorable accounting treatment for financial reporting purposes is not taken into account as a non-Federal-income-tax purpose if the origin of the financial accounting benefit is a reduction of Federal income tax.[355]

Profit potential

Under the provision, a taxpayer may rely on factors other than profit potential to demonstrate that a transaction results in a meaningful change in the taxpayer's economic position or that the taxpayer has a substantial non-Federal-income-tax purpose for entering into such transaction. The provision does not require or establish a minimum return that will satisfy the profit potential test. However, if a taxpayer relies on a profit potential, the present value of the reasonably expected pre-tax profit must be substantial in relation to the present value of the expected net tax benefits that would be allowed if the transaction were respected.[356] Fees and other transaction expenses are taken into account as expenses in determining pre-tax profit. In addition, the Secretary is to issue regulations requiring foreign taxes to be treated as expenses in determining pre-tax profit in appropriate cases.[357]

Personal transactions of individuals

In the case of an individual, the provision applies only to transactions entered into in connection with a trade or business or an activity engaged in for the production of income.

Other rules

No inference is intended as to the proper application of the economic substance doctrine under present law. The provision is not intended to alter or supplant any other rule of law, including any common-law doctrine or provision of the Code or regulations or other guidance thereunder; and it is intended the provision be construed as being additive to any such other rule of law.

As with other provisions in the Code, the Secretary has general authority to prescribe rules and regulations necessary for the enforcement of the provision.[358]

Penalty for underpayments and understatements attributable to transactions lacking economic substance

The provision imposes a new strict liability penalty under section 6662 for an underpayment attributable to any disallowance of claimed tax benefits by reason of a transaction lacking economic substance, as defined in new section 7701(o), or failing to meet the requirements of any similar rule of law.[359] The penalty rate is 20 percent (increased to 40 percent if the taxpayer does not adequately disclose the relevant facts affecting the tax treatment in the return or a

---

[354] See, e.g., Treas. Reg. sec. 1.269-2(b) (stating that a distortion of tax liability indicating the principal purpose of tax evasion or avoidance might be evidenced by the fact that "the transaction was not undertaken for reasons germane to the conduct of the business of the taxpayer"). Similarly, in *ACM Partnership v. Commissioner*, 73 T.C.M. (CCH) 2189 (1997), the court stated:

Key to [the determination of whether a transaction has economic substance] is that the transaction must be rationally related to a useful nontax purpose that is plausible in light of the taxpayer's conduct and useful in light of the taxpayer's economic situation and intentions. Both the utility of the stated purpose and the rationality of the means chosen to effectuate it must be evaluated in accordance with commercial practices in the relevant industry. A rational relationship between purpose and means ordinarily will not be found unless there was a reasonable expectation that the nontax benefits would be at least commensurate with the transaction costs. [citations omitted]

[355] Claiming that a financial accounting benefit constitutes a substantial non-tax purpose fails to consider the origin of the accounting benefit (i.e., reduction of taxes) and significantly diminishes the purpose for having a substantial non-tax purpose requirement. *See, e.g., American Electric Power, Inc. v. United States*, 136 F. Supp. 2d 762, 791-92 (S.D. Ohio 2001) ("AEP's intended use of the cash flows gener-

ated by the [corporate-owned life insurance] plan is irrelevant to the subjective prong of the economic substance analysis. If a legitimate business purpose for the use of the tax savings 'were sufficient to breathe substance into a transaction whose only purpose was to reduce taxes, [then] every sham tax-shelter device might succeed,'") (citing *Winn-Dixie v. Commissioner*, 113 T.C. 254, 287 (1999)); aff'd, 326 F3d 737 (6th Cir. 2003).

[356] See, e.g., *Rice's Toyota World v. Commissioner*, 752 F.2d at 94 (the economic substance inquiry requires an objective determination of whether a reasonable possibility of profit from the transaction existed apart from tax benefits); *Compaq Computer Corp. v. Commissioner*, 277 F.3d at 781 (applied the same test, citing *Rice's Toyota World*); *IES Industries v. United States*, 253 F.3d at 354 (the application of the objective economic substance test involves determining whether there was a "reasonable possibility of profit . . . apart from tax benefits.").

[357] There is no intention to restrict the ability of the courts to consider the appropriate treatment of foreign taxes in particular cases, as under present law.

[358] Sec. 7805(a).

[359] It is intended that the penalty would apply to a transaction the tax benefits of which are disallowed as a result of the application of the similar factors and analysis that is

statement attached to the return). An amended return or supplement to a return is not taken into account if filed after the taxpayer has been contacted for audit or such other date as is specified by the Secretary. No exceptions (including the reasonable cause rules) to the penalty are available. Thus, under the provision, outside opinions or in-house analysis would not protect a taxpayer from imposition of a penalty if it is determined that the transaction lacks economic substance or fails to meet the requirements of any similar rule of law. Similarly, a claim for refund or credit that is excessive under section 6676 due to a claim that is lacking in economic substance or failing to meet the requirements of any similar rule of law is subject to the 20 percent penalty under that section, and the reasonable basis exception is not available.

The penalty does not apply to any portion of an underpayment on which a fraud penalty is imposed.[360] The new 40-percent penalty for nondisclosed transactions is added to the penalties to which section 6662A will not also apply.[361]

As described above, under the provision, the reasonable cause and good faith exception of present law section 6664(c)(1) does not apply to any portion of an underpayment which is attributable to a transaction lacking economic substance, as defined in section 7701(o), or failing to meet the requirements of any similar rule of law. Likewise, the reasonable cause and good faith exception of present law section 6664(d)(1) does not apply to any portion of a reportable transaction understatement which is attributable to a transaction lacking economic substance, as defined in section 7701(o), or failing to meet the requirements of any similar rule of law.

Effective Date

The provision applies to transactions entered into after the date of enactment and to underpayments, understatements, and refunds and credits attributable to transactions entered into after the date of enactment.

[Law at ¶ 5278, ¶ 5279, ¶ 5279A, ¶ 5279C and ¶ 5287. CCH Explanation at ¶ 342 and ¶ 343.]

[¶ 10,450] Act Sec. 1410. Time for payment of corporate estimated taxes

Joint Committee on Taxation (J.C.T. REP. NO. JCX-18-10)

[Code Sec. 6655]

Present Law

In general, corporations are required to make quarterly estimated tax payments of their income tax liability.[362] For a corporation whose taxable year is a calendar year, these estimated tax payments must be made by April 15, June 15, September 15, and December 15. In the case of a corporation with assets of at least $1 billion (determined as of the end of the preceding taxable year), payments due in July, August, or September, 2014, are increased to 157.75 percent of the payment otherwise due and the next required payment is reduced accordingly.[363]

Explanation of Provision

The provision increases the required payment of estimated tax otherwise due in July, August, or September, 2014, by 15.75 percentage points.

Effective Date

The provision is effective on the date of enactment of the bill.

[Law at ¶ 7115. CCH Explanation at ¶ 630.]

(Footnote Continued)

required under the provision for an economic substance analysis, even if a different term is used to describe the doctrine.

[360] As under present law, the penalties under section 6662 (including the new penalty) do not apply to any portion of an underpayment on which a fraud penalty is imposed.

[361] As revised by the provision, new section 6662A(e)(2)(b) provides that section 6662A will not apply to

any portion of an understatement due to gross valuation misstatement under section 6662(h) or nondisclosed noneconomic substance transactions under new section 6662(i).

[362] Sec. 6655.

[363] The Hiring Incentives to Restore Employment ("HIRE") Act, Sec.561; Pub. L. No. 111-124, Sec. 4; Pub. L. No. 111-92, Sec. 18; Pub. L. No. 111-42, Sec. 202(b)(1).

Committee Reports

Hiring Incentives to Restore Employment Act

¶11,001 Introduction

The Hiring Incentives to Restore Employment Act (P.L. 111-147) was passed by Congress on March 17, 2010, and signed by the President on March 18, 2010. The Joint Committee on Taxation produced a Technical Explanation of the Senate Bill on February 23, 2010 (JCX-4-10). This report explains the intent of Congress regarding the provisions of the Act. There was no conference report issued for this Act. The Technical Explanation from the Joint Committee on Taxation is included in this section to aid the reader's understanding, but may not be cited as the official Conference Committee Report accompanying the 2010 Act. At the end of each section, references are provided to the corresponding CCH explanations and the Internal Revenue Code provisions. Subscribers to the electronic version can link from these references to the corresponding material. *The pertinent sections of the Technical Explanation appear in Act Section order beginning at ¶11,010*

¶11,005 Background

The "Hiring Incentives to Restore Employment Act" was introduced in the House of Representatives on June 12, 2009 as H.R. 2847, "An Act making appropriations for the Departments of Commerce and Justice, and Science, and Related Agencies for the fiscal year ending September 30, 2010, and for other purposes." After several exchanges between House and Senate, the bill was considered by the Senate. The Senate agreed to Amendment 3310 on February 24, 2010, in the nature of a substitute, by a vote of 62 to 34, and renamed the bill as the "Hiring Incentives to Restore Employment Act." H.R. 2847, as thus amended, was considered by the House and on March 4, 2010, the House agreed to the Senate amendment to the House amendment to the Senate amendment, with an amendment, by a vote of 217 to 201. On March 17, 2010, the Senate passed the bill as amended by a vote of 68 to 29. On March 18, 2010, the President signed the Act into law.

References are to the following report:

• The Joint Committee on Taxation, Technical Explanation of Senate Amendment 3310, the "Hiring Incentives to Restore Employment Act," as prepared on February 23, 2010, is referred to as Joint Committee on Taxation (J.C.T. Rep. No. JCX-4-10).)

[¶11,010] Act Sec. 101. Payroll tax forgiveness for hiring unemployed workers

Joint Committee on Taxation (J.C.T. REP. NO. JCX-4-10)

New Code Sec. 3111

Present Law

In general

Social security benefits and certain Medicare benefits are financed primarily by payroll taxes on wages.

Federal Insurance Contributions Act ("FICA") tax

The FICA tax applies to employers based on the amount of covered wages paid to an employee during the year. Generally, covered wages means all remuneration for employment, including the cash value of all remuneration (including benefits) paid in any medium other than cash. Certain exceptions from covered wages are also provided. The tax imposed is composed of two parts: (1) the old age, survivors, and disability insurance ("OASDI") tax equal to 6.2 percent of covered wages up to the taxable wage base ($106,800 in 2010); and (2) the Medicare hospital insurance ("HI") tax amount equal to 1.45 percent of covered wages. In addition to the tax on employers, each employee is subject to FICA taxes equal to the amount of tax imposed on the employer (the "employee portion"). The employee portion generally must be withheld and remitted to the Federal government by the employer.

Self-Employment Contributions Act ("SECA") tax

As a parallel to FICA taxes, the SECA tax applies to the net income from self employment of self-employed individuals. The rate of the OASDI portion of SECA taxes is equal to the combined employee and employer OASDI FICA tax rates and applies to self-employment income up to the FICA taxable wage base. Similarly, the rate of the HI portion is the same as the com-

bined employer and employee HI rates and there is no cap on the amount of self-employment income to which the rate applies.[2]

Explanation of Provision

In general

The bill provides relief from the employer share of OASDI taxes on wages paid by a qualified employer with respect to certain employment. The provision applies to wages paid beginning on the day after enactment and ending on December 31, 2010. Covered employment is limited to service performed by a qualified individual: (1) in a trade or business of a qualified employer; or (2) in furtherance of the activities related to the purpose or function constituting the basis of the employer's exemption under sec. 501 (in the case of a qualified employer that is exempt from tax under sec. 501(a)).

Qualified employer

A qualified employer is any employer other than the United States, any State, any local government, or any instrumentality of the foregoing. Notwithstanding the forgoing, a qualified employer includes any employer that is a public higher education institution (as defined in sec. 101(b) of the Higher Education Act of 1965).

Qualified individual

A qualified individual is any individual who: (1) begins work for a qualified employer after February 3, 2010 and before January 1, 2011; (2) certifies by signed affidavit (under penalties of perjury) that he or she was employed for a total of 40 hours or less during the 60-day period ending on the date such employment begins; (3) is not employed to replace another employee of the employer unless such employee separated from employment voluntarily or for cause;[3] and

---

[2] For purposes of computing net earnings from self employment, taxpayers are permitted a deduction equal to the product of the taxpayer's earnings (determined without regard to this deduction) and one-half of the sum of the rates for OASDI tax (12.4 percent) and HI tax (2.9 percent), i.e., 7.65 percent of net earnings. This deduction reflects the fact that the FICA rates apply to an employee's wages, which do not include FICA taxes paid by the employer, whereas the self-employed individual's net earnings are economically equivalent to an employee's wages plus the employer share of FICA taxes.

[3] It is intended that an employer may qualify for the credit when it hires an otherwise qualified individual to replace an individual whose employment was terminated, for cause or due to other facts and circumstances. For example, an employer may qualify for the credit with respect to wages paid pursuant to the reopening of a factory which had been previously closed due to lack of demand for the product being produced (i.e., the employer may qualify by rehiring qualified individuals who had in the past worked for the employer but were terminated when the factory was closed or by hiring qualified individuals who had not previ-

(4) is not a related party (as defined under rules similar to sec. 51(i)) of the employer).

Employer election

A qualified employer may elect to not have payroll tax forgiveness apply. The election is made in the manner required by the Secretary of the Treasury.

Coordination with work opportunity tax credit

Under the provision, a qualified employer may not receive the work opportunity tax credit on any wages paid to a qualified individual during the one-year period beginning on the hiring date of such individual, if those wages qualify the employer for payroll tax forgiveness under this provision unless the employer makes an election not to have payroll tax forgiveness apply with respect to that individual.

Social Security trust funds

The Federal Old-Age and Survivors Trust Fund and the Federal Disability Insurance Trust Fund will receive transfers from the General Fund of the United States Treasury equal to any reduction in payroll taxes attributable to the payroll tax forgiveness provided under the provision. The amounts will be transferred from the General Fund at such times and in such a manner as to replicate to the extent possible the transfers which would have occurred to the Trust Funds had the provision not been enacted.

Effective Date

The provision applies to wages paid after the date of enactment.

[Law at ¶6010, ¶6105, ¶6110 and ¶7206. CCH Explanation at ¶205.]

[¶11,020] Act Sec. 102. Business credit for retention of certain newly hired individuals in 2010

Joint Committee on Taxation (J.C.T. REP. NO. JCX-4-10)

[Code Sec. 38(b)]

Present Law

Present law does not provide a tax credit specifically for the retention of new employees.

However, present law provides for a general business credit consisting of various business tax credits.[4] The general business credit, to the extent it exceeds the relevant tax liability for the taxable year, may be carried back one year (but, in the case of a new credit, not to a taxable year before that credit is first allowable) and carried forward 20 years.[5]

Explanation of Provision

Under the provision an employer's general business credit is increased by $1,000 for each retained worker that satisfies a minimum employment period. Generally, a retained worker is an individual who is a qualified individual as defined under the payroll tax forgiveness provi-

sion, above (new Code sec. 3111(d)). However, the credit is available only with respect to such an individual, if the individual: (1) is employed by the employer on any date during the taxable year; (2) continues to be employed by the employer for a period of not less than 52 consecutive weeks; and (3) receives wages for such employment during the last 26 weeks of such period that are least 80-percent of such wages during the first 26 weeks of such period.

The portion of the general business credit attributable to the retention credit may not be carried back to a taxable year that begins prior to the date of enactment of this provision.

Effective Date

The provision is effective for taxable years ending after the date of enactment.

[Law at ¶7209. CCH Explanation at ¶205.]

(Footnote Continued)

ously worked for the employer). In contrast, an employer who terminates the employment of an individual not for cause, but rather to claim the credit with respect to the hiring of the same or another individual is not eligible for the credit under this rule.

[4] Sec. 38.
[5] Sec. 39.

[¶11,030] Act Sec. 201. Increase in expensing of certain depreciable business assets

Joint Committee on Taxation (J.C.T. Rep. No. JCX-4-10)

[Code Sec. 179]

Present Law

A taxpayer that satisfies limitations on annual investment may elect under section 179 to deduct (or "expense") the cost of qualifying property, rather than to recover such costs through depreciation deductions.[6] For taxable years beginning in 2009, the maximum amount that a taxpayer may expense is $250,000 of the cost of qualifying property placed in service for the taxable year. The $250,000 amount is reduced (but not below zero) by the amount by which the cost of qualifying property placed in service during the taxable year exceeds $800,000.[7] For taxable years beginning in 2010, the maximum amount that a taxpayer may expense is $125,000 of the cost of qualifying property placed in service for the taxable year. The $125,000 amount is reduced (but not below zero) by the amount by which the cost of qualifying property placed in service during the taxable year exceeds $500,000. The $125,000 and $500,000 amounts are indexed for inflation. In general, qualifying property is defined as depreciable tangible personal property that is purchased for use in the active conduct of a trade or business. Off-the-shelf computer software placed in service in taxable years beginning before 2011 is treated as qualifying property.

The amount eligible to be expensed for a taxable year may not exceed the taxable income for a taxable year that is derived from the active conduct of a trade or business (determined without regard to this provision). Any amount that is not allowed as a deduction because of the taxable income limitation may be carried forward to succeeding taxable years (subject to similar limitations). No general business credit under sec-tion 38 is allowed with respect to any amount for which a deduction is allowed under section 179. An expensing election is made under rules prescribed by the Secretary.[8] An election under section 179 generally is revocable only with prior consent of the Secretary.[9]

For taxable years beginning in 2011 and thereafter, a taxpayer with a sufficiently small amount of annual investment may elect to deduct up to $25,000 of the cost of qualifying property placed in service for the taxable year. The $25,000 amount is reduced (but not below zero) by the amount by which the cost of qualifying property placed in service during the taxable year exceeds $200,000. The $25,000 and $200,000 amounts are not indexed. In general, qualifying property is defined as depreciable tangible personal property that is purchased for use in the active conduct of a trade or business (not including off-the-shelf computer software).

Explanation of Provision

The provision increases for one year the amount a taxpayer may deduct under section 179. The provision provides that the maximum amount a taxpayer may expense, for taxable years beginning after 2009 and before 2011, is $250,000 of the cost of qualifying property placed in service for the taxable year. The $250,000 amount is reduced (but not below zero) by the amount by which the cost of qualifying property placed in service during the taxable year exceeds $800,000.

Effective Date

The provision is effective for taxable years beginning after December 31, 2009.

[Law at ¶6040. CCH Explanation at ¶210.]

---

[6] Additional section 179 incentives are provided with respect to qualified property meeting applicable requirements that is used by a business in an empowerment zone (sec. 1397A), a renewal community (sec. 1400J), or the Gulf Opportunity Zone (sec. 1400N(e)).

[7] The temporary $250,000 and $800,000 amounts were enacted in the Economic Stimulus Act of 2008, Pub. L. No. 110-185, and extended for taxable years beginning in 2009 by the American Recovery and Reinvestment Act of 2009, Pub. L. No. 111-5.

[8] Sec. 179(c)(1). Under Treas. Reg. sec. 1.179-5, applicable to property placed in service in taxable years beginning after 2002 and before 2008, a taxpayer is permitted to make or revoke an election under section 179 without the consent of the Commissioner on an amended Federal tax return for that taxable year. This amended return must be filed within the time prescribed by law for filing an amended return for the taxable year. T.D. 9209, July 12, 2005.

[9] Section 179(c)(2) provides that with respect to any taxable year beginning after 2002 and before 2011, a taxpayer may revoke its section 179 election with respect to any property, and such revocation, once made, is irrevocable.

[¶11,040] Act Sec. 301. Refundable credit for certain qualified tax credit bonds

Joint Committee on Taxation (J.C.T. Rep. No. JCX-4-10)

[Code Secs. 54F and 6431]

Present Law

Build America Bonds

Section 54AA, added to the Code by the American Recovery and Reinvestment Act of 2009 ("ARRA"),[10] permits an issuer to elect to have an otherwise tax-exempt bond, issued prior to January 1, 2011, treated as a "build America bond."[11] In general, build America bonds are taxable governmental bonds, the interest on which is subsidized by the Federal government by means of a tax credit to the holder ("tax-credit build America bonds") or, in the case of certain qualified bonds, a direct payment to the issuer ("direct-pay build America bonds").

Definition and general requirements

A build America bond is any obligation (other than a private activity bond) if the interest on such obligation would be (but for section 54AA) excludable from gross income under section 103, and the issuer makes an irrevocable election to have the rules in section 54AA apply.[12] In determining if an obligation would be tax-exempt under section 103, the credit (or the payment discussed below for direct-pay build America bonds) is not treated as a Federal guarantee.[13] Further, for purposes of the restrictions on arbitrage in section 148, the yield on a tax-credit build America bond is determined without regard to the credit;[14] the yield on a direct-pay build America bond is reduced by the payment made pursuant to section 6431.[15] A build America bond does not include any bond if the issue price has more than a de minimis amount of premium over the stated principal amount of the bond.[16]

Treatment of holders of tax-credit build America bonds

The holder of a tax-credit build America bond accrues a tax credit in the amount of 35 percent of the interest paid on the interest payment dates of the bond during the calendar year.[17] The interest payment date is any date on which the holder of record of the build America bond is entitled to a payment of interest under such bond.[18] The sum of the accrued credits is allowed against regular and alternative minimum tax; unused credit may be carried forward to succeeding taxable years.[19] The credit, as well as the interest paid by the issuer, is included in gross income, and the credit may be stripped under rules similar to those provided in section 54A regarding qualified tax credit bonds.[20] Rules similar to those that apply for S corporations, partnerships and regulated investment companies with respect to qualified tax credit bonds also apply to the credit.[21]

Special rules for direct-pay build America bonds

Under the special rule for qualified bonds, in lieu of the tax credit to the holder, the issuer is allowed a credit equal to 35 percent of each interest payment made under such bond.[22] A "qualified bond," that is, a direct-pay build America bond, is any build America bond issued as part of an issue if 100 percent of the excess of available project proceeds of such issue over the amounts in a reasonably required reserve with respect to such issue are to be used for capital

---

[10] Pub. L. No. 111-5.

[11] Sec. 54AA.

[12] Sec. 54AA(d). Subject to updated IRS reporting forms or procedures, an issuer of build America bonds makes the election required by 54AA on its books and records on or before the issue date of such bonds. Notice 2009-26, 2009-16 I.R.B. 833.

[13] Sec. 54AA(d)(2)(A). Section 149(b) provides that section 103(a) shall not apply to any State or local bond if such bond is federally guaranteed.

[14] Sec. 54AA(d)(2)(B).

[15] Sec. 6431(c).

[16] Sec. 54AA(d)(2)(C).

[17] Sec. 54AA(a) and (b). Original issue discount ("OID") is not treated as a payment of interest for purposes of determining the credit under the provision. OID is the excess of an obligation's stated redemption price at maturity over the obligation's issue price (sec. 1273(a)).

[18] Sec. 54AA(e).

[19] Sec. 54AA(c).

[20] Sec. 54AA(f).

[21] Ibid.

[22] Sec. 54AA(g)(1). OID is not treated as a payment of interest for purposes of calculating the refundable credit under the provision.

expenditures.[23] Direct-pay build America bonds also must be issued before January 1, 2011. The issuer must make an irrevocable election to have the special rule for qualified bonds apply.[24]

The payment by the Secretary is to be made contemporaneously with the interest payment made by the issuer, and may be made either in advance or as reimbursement.[25] In lieu of payment to the issuer, the payment may be made to a person making interest payments on behalf of the issuer.[26]

Qualified Tax Credit Bonds

Qualified tax credit bonds include qualified forestry conservation bonds, new clean renewable energy bonds ("New CREBs"), qualified energy conservation bonds ("QECs"), qualified zone academy bonds issued after the date of enactment of the Tax Extenders and Alternative Minimum Tax Relief Act of 2008 ("QZABs"), and qualified school construction bonds ("QSCBs").[27] Qualified tax credit bonds generally are not interest-bearing obligations. Rather, the taxpayer holding a qualified tax credit bond on a credit allowance date is entitled to a tax credit.[28] The annual amount of the credit is determined by multiplying the bond's applicable credit rate by the outstanding face amount of the bond.[29] The credit rate for an issue of qualified tax credit bonds is determined by the Secretary and is estimated to be a rate that permits issuance of the qualified tax credit bonds without discount and interest cost to the qualified issuer.[30] The Secretary determines credit rates for tax credit bonds based on general assumptions about credit quality of the class of potential eligible issuers and such other factors as the Secretary deems appropriate. The Secretary may determine credit rates based on general credit market yield indices and credit ratings.[31] The credit accrues quarterly,[32] is includible in gross income (as if it were an interest payment on the bond),[33] and can be claimed against regular income tax liability and alternative minimum tax liability.[34] Unused credits may be carried forward to succeeding taxable years.[35] In addition, under regulations prescribed by the Secretary, credits may be stripped.[36]

Qualified tax credit bonds are subject to a maximum maturity limitation. The maximum maturity is the term which the Secretary estimates will result in the present value of the obligation to repay the principal on a qualified tax credit bond being equal to 50 percent of the face amount of such bond.[37] The discount rate used to determine the present value amount is the average annual interest rate of tax-exempt obligations having a term of 10 years or more which are issued during the month the qualified tax credit bonds are issued.

For qualified tax credit bonds, 100 percent of the available project proceeds must be used within the three-year period that begins on the date of issuance.[38] Available project proceeds are the sum of (1) the excess of the proceeds from the sale of the bond issue over issuance costs (not to exceed two percent) and (2) any investment earnings on such sale proceeds.[39] To the extent less than 100 percent of the available project proceeds are used to finance qualified projects during the three-year spending period, bonds will continue to qualify as qualified tax credit bonds if unspent proceeds are used within 90 days from the end of such three-year period to redeem bonds. The three-year spending period

---

[23] Sec. 54AA(g). Under Treas. Reg. sec. 150-1(b), capital expenditure means any cost of a type that is properly chargeable to capital account (or would be so chargeable with a proper election or with the application of the definition of placed in service under Treas. Reg. sec. 1.150-2(c)) under general Federal income tax principles. For purposes of applying the "general Federal income tax principles" standard, an issuer should generally be treated as if it were a corporation subject to taxation under subchapter C of chapter 1 of the Code. An example of a capital expenditure would include expenditures made for the purchase of fiber-optic cable to provide municipal broadband service.

[24] Sec. 54AA(g)(2)(B). Subject to updated IRS reporting forms or procedures, an issuer of direct-pay build America bonds makes the election required by 54AA(g)(2)(B) on its books and records on or before the issue date of such bonds. Notice 2009-26, 2009-16 I.R.B. 833.

[25] Sec. 6431.

[26] Sec. 6431(b).

[27] Sec. 54A(d).

[28] Sec 54A(a).

[29] Sec. 54A(b)(2).

[30] Sec. 54A(b)(3). However, for New CREBs and QECs, the applicable credit rate is 70 percent of the otherwise applicable rate.

[31] See Internal Revenue Service, Notice 2009-15, *Credit Rates on Tax Credit Bonds*, 2009-6 I.R.B. 1 (January 22, 2009). Given the differences in credit quality and other characteristics of individual issuers, the Secretary cannot set credit rates in a manner that will allow each issuer to issue tax credit bonds at par.

[32] Sec. 54(A)(b)(1).

[33] Sec. 54A(f).

[34] Sec. 54A(c).

[35] Ibid.

[36] Sec. 54A(i).

[37] Sec. 54A(d)(5).

[38] Sec. 54A(d)(2).

[39] Sec. 54A(e)(4).

may be extended by the Secretary upon the qualified issuer's request demonstrating that the failure to satisfy the three-year requirement is due to reasonable cause and the projects will continue to proceed with due diligence.

Qualified tax credit bonds also are subject to the arbitrage requirements of section 148 that apply to traditional tax-exempt bonds.[40] Principles under section 148 and the regulations thereunder apply for purposes of determining the yield restriction and arbitrage rebate requirements applicable to qualified tax credit bonds. However, available project proceeds invested during the three-year spending period are not subject to the arbitrage restrictions (i.e., yield restriction and rebate requirements). In addition, amounts invested in a reserve fund are not subject to the arbitrage restrictions to the extent: (1) such fund is funded at a rate not more rapid than equal annual installments; (2) such fund is funded in a manner reasonably expected to result in an amount not greater than an amount necessary to repay the issue; and (3) the yield on such fund is not greater than the average annual interest rate of tax-exempt obligations having a term of 10 years or more that are issued during the month the qualified tax credit bonds are issued.

Issuers of qualified tax credit bonds are required to report issuance to the IRS in a manner similar to the information returns required for tax-exempt bonds.[41] In addition, issuers of qualified tax credit bonds are required to certify that applicable State and local law requirements governing conflicts of interest are satisfied with respect to an issue, and if the Secretary prescribes additional conflicts of interest rules governing the appropriate Members of Congress, Federal, State, and local officials, and their spouses, the issuer must certify compliance with such additional rules with respect to an issue.[42]

New CREBs

A New CREB is any bond issued as part of an issue if: (1) 100 percent of the available project proceeds of such issue are to be used for capital expenditures incurred by governmental bodies, public power providers, or cooperative electric companies for one or more qualified renewable energy facilities; (2) the bond is issued by a qualified issuer; and (3) the issuer designates such bond as a New CREB.[43] Qualified renewable energy facilities are facilities that: (1) qualify for the tax credit under section 45 (other than Indian coal and refined coal production facilities), without regard to the placed-in-service date requirements of that section; and (2) are owned by a public power provider, governmental body, or cooperative electric company.[44]

The term "qualified issuers" includes: (1) public power providers; (2) a governmental body; (3) cooperative electric companies; (4) a not-for-profit electric utility that has received a loan or guarantee under the Rural Electrification Act;[45] and (5) clean renewable energy bond lenders.[46] The term "public power provider" means a State utility with a service obligation, as such terms are defined in section 217 of the Federal Power Act[47] (as in effect on the date of the enactment of this paragraph).[48] A "governmental body" means any State or Indian tribal government, or any political subdivision thereof.[49] The term "cooperative electric company" means a mutual or cooperative electric company (described in section 501(c)(12) or section 1381(a)(2)(C)).[50] A clean renewable energy bond lender means a cooperative that is owned by, or has outstanding loans to, 100 or more cooperative electric companies and is in existence on February 1, 2002 (including any affiliated entity which is controlled by such lender).[51]

There is a national limitation for New CREBs of $2.4 billion.[52] No more than one third of the national limit may be allocated to projects of public power providers, governmental bodies,

---

[40] Sec. 54A(d)(4).

[41] Sec. 54A(d)(3).

[42] Sec. 54A(d)(6).

[43] Sec. 54C(a).

[44] Sec. 54C(d)(1).

[45] Pub. L. No. 74-605.

[46] Sec. 54C(d)(6).

[47] 16 U.S.C. 791a et seq.

[48] Sec. 54C(d)(2).

[49] Sec. 54C(d)(3).

[50] Sec. 54C(d)(4). A mutual or cooperative electric company can be tax exempt under section 501(c)(12) only if 85 percent or more of its income consists of amounts collected from members for the sole purpose of meeting losses and expenses (the "85-percent income test"). Certain types of income, e.g., income from qualified pole rentals, are not taken into account for purposes of the 85-percent income test. Sec. 501(c)(12)(C).

[51] Sec. 54C(d)(5).

[52] Section 54C(c)(4) increases the original $800 million allocation by $1.6 billion for a total of $2.4 billion.

or cooperative electric companies.[53] Allocations to governmental bodies and cooperative electric companies may be made in the manner the Secretary determines appropriate. Allocations to projects of public power providers shall be made, to the extent practicable, in such manner that the amount allocated to each such project bears the same ratio to the cost of such project as the maximum allocation limitation to projects of public power providers bears to the cost of all such projects.[54]

As with other qualified tax credit bonds, a taxpayer holding New CREBs on a credit allowance date is entitled to a tax credit. However, the credit rate on New CREBs is set by the Secretary at a rate that is 70 percent of the rate that would permit issuance of such bonds without discount and interest cost to the issuer.[55]

QECs

A QEC is any bond issued as part of an issue if: (1) 100 percent of the available project proceeds of such issue are to be used for one or more qualified conservation purposes; (2) the bond is issued by a State or local government, and (3) the issuer designates such bond as a QEC.[56]

The term "qualified conservation purpose" means:

1. Capital expenditures incurred for purposes of reducing energy consumption in publicly owned buildings by at least 20 percent; implementing green community programs (including the use of loans, grants, or other repayment mechanisms to implement such programs);[57] rural development involving the production of electricity from renewable energy resources; or any facility eligible for the production tax credit under section 45 (other than Indian coal and refined coal production facilities);[58]

2. Expenditures with respect to facilities or grants that support research in: (a) development of cellulosic ethanol or other nonfossil fuels; (b) technologies for the capture and sequestration of carbon dioxide produced

through the use of fossil fuels; (c) increasing the efficiency of existing technologies for producing nonfossil fuels; (d) automobile battery technologies and other technologies to reduce fossil fuel consumption in transportation; or (e) technologies to reduce energy use in buildings;[59]

3. Mass commuting facilities and related facilities that reduce the consumption of energy, including expenditures to reduce pollution from vehicles used for mass commuting;[60]

4. Demonstration projects designed to promote the commercialization of: (a) green building technology; (b) conversion of agricultural waste for use in the production of fuel or otherwise; (c) advanced battery manufacturing technologies; (d) technologies to reduce peak use of electricity; or (e) technologies for the capture and sequestration of carbon dioxide emitted from combusting fossil fuels in order to produce electricity;[61] and

5. Public education campaigns to promote energy efficiency (other than movies, concerts, and other events held primarily for entertainment purposes).[62]

There is a national limitation on QECs of $3.2 billion.[63] Allocations of QECs are made to the States with sub-allocations to large local governments.[64] Allocations are made to the States according to their respective populations, reduced by any sub-allocations to large local governments (defined below) within the States. Sub-allocations to large local governments shall be an amount of the national QEC limitation that bears the same ratio to the amount of such limitation that otherwise would be allocated to the State in which such large local government is located as the population of such large local government bears to the population of such State. The term "large local government" means any municipality or county if such municipality or county has a population of 100,000 or more. Indian tribal governments also are treated as large local governments for these purposes (without regard to population).

---

[53] Secs. 54C(c)(2) and (c)(4).
[54] Sec. 54C(c)(3).
[55] Sec. 54C(b).
[56] Sec. 54D(a).
[57] For example, States may issue QECs to finance retrofits of existing private buildings through loans and/or grants to individual homeowners or businesses, or through other repayment mechanisms. Other repayment mechanisms can include periodic fees assessed on a government bill or utility bill that approximates the energy savings of energy efficiency or conservation retrofits. Retrofits can include heat-

ing, cooling, lighting, water-saving, storm water-reducing, or other efficiency measures.
[58] Sec. 54D(f)(1)(A).
[59] Sec. 54D(f)(1)(B).
[60] Sec. 54D(f)(1)(C).
[61] Sec. 54D(f)(1)(D).
[62] Sec. 54D(f)(1)(E).
[63] Sec. 54D(d).
[64] Sec. 54D(e).

Each State or large local government receiving an allocation of QECs may further allocate issuance authority to issuers within such State or large local government. However, any allocations to issuers within the State or large local government shall be made in a manner that results in not less than 70 percent of the allocation of QECs to such State or large local government being used to designate bonds that are not private activity bonds (i.e., the bond cannot meet the private business tests or the private loan test of section 141).[65]

As with other qualified tax credit bonds, the taxpayer holding QECs on a credit allowance date is entitled to a tax credit. However, the credit rate on the bonds is set by the Secretary at a rate that is 70 percent of the rate that would permit issuance of such bonds without discount and interest cost to the issuer.[66]

QZABs

A QZAB is any bond issued as part of an issue if: (1) 100 percent of the available project proceeds of such issue are to be used for a qualified purpose with respect to a qualified zone academy established by an eligible local education agency; (2) the bond is issued by a State or local government within the jurisdiction of which such academy is located; (3) the issuer designates such bond as a QZAB and certifies that (a) the private business contribution requirement will be met and (b) it has the written approval of the eligible local education agency for such bond issuance.[67]

A "qualified purpose" is: (1) rehabilitating or repairing the public school facility in which the qualified zone academy is established; (2) providing equipment for use at such academy; (3) developing course materials for education to be provided at such academy; and (4) training teachers and other school personnel in such academy.[68]

A public school (or academic program within a public school) is a "qualified zone academy" if: (1) the public school or program provides education and training below the college level; (2) the public school or program is designed in cooperation with business to enhance the academic curriculum, increase graduation and employment rates, and better prepare students for the rigors of college and the workforce; (3) students in such public school or program will be subject to the same academic standards and assessments as other students educated by the eligible local education agency; (4) the comprehensive education plan of such public school or program is approved by the eligible local education agency; and (5) either (a) the public school is located in an empowerment zone or enterprise community designated under the Code, or (b) it is reasonably expected that at least 35 percent of the students at the school will be eligible for free or reduced-cost lunches under the school lunch program established under the National School Lunch Act.[69]

In general, the private business contribution requirement is met where private entities have promised to contribute to the qualified zone academy certain equipment, technical assistance or training, employee services, or other property or services with a present value (as of the date of the issue) equal to at least 10 percent of the bond proceeds.[70]

There is a national QZAB limitation for each calendar year. For 2009 and 2010, the limitation is $1.4 billion.[71] The limitation is allocated by the Secretary among the States on the basis of their respective populations of individuals below the poverty line; each State education agency then make an allocation of its shares of the national limitation to qualified zone academies in the State.[72] Unused limitation may be carried only to the first two years following the unused limitation year.[73] For this purpose, a limitation amount shall be treated as used on a first-in first-out basis.

QSCBs

In general

QSCBs must meet three requirements: (1) 100 percent of the available project proceeds of the bond issue must be used for the construction, rehabilitation, or repair of a public school facility or for the acquisition of land on which such a bond-financed facility is to be constructed; (2) the bond must be issued by a State or local government within the jurisdiction of which

---

[65] Sec. 54D(e)(3). In the case of any bond used for the purpose of providing grants, loans or other repayment mechanisms for capital expenditures to implement green community programs, such bond shall not be treated as a private activity bond for purposes of determining whether this requirement is met. Sec. 54D(e)(4).

[66] Sec. 54D(b).

[67] Sec. 54E(a).

[68] Sec. 54E(d)(3).

[69] Sec. 54E(d)(1); Pub. L. No. 79-396.

[70] Sec. 54E(b).

[71] Sec. 54E(c)(1).

[72] Sec. 54E(c)(2).

[73] Sec. 54E(c)(4).

such school is located; and (3) the issuer must designate such bonds as a QSCB.[74]

National limitation

There is a national limitation on qualified school construction bonds of $11 billion for calendar years 2009 and 2010, respectively.[75]

Allocation to the States

The national limitation is tentatively allocated among the States in proportion to respective amounts each such State is eligible to receive under section 1124 of the Elementary and Secondary Education Act of 1965[76] for the most recent fiscal year ending before such calendar year. Forty percent of the limitation is then allocated among the largest school districts, and the amount each State is allocated under the tentative allocation formula is then reduced by the amount received by any local large educational agency within the State.[77] The limitation amount allocated to a State is allocated by the State to issuers within such State.

For allocation purposes, a "State" includes the District of Columbia and any possession of the United States. The provision provides a special rule for allocation for possessions of the United States other than Puerto Rico under the national limitation for States.[78] Under this special rule, an allocation to a possession other than Puerto Rico is made on the basis of the respective populations of individuals below the poverty line (as defined by the Office of Management and Budget) rather than respective populations of children aged five through seventeen. This special allocation reduces the State allocation share of the national limitation otherwise available for allocation among the States. Under another special rule, the Secretary of the Interior may allocate $200 million of school construction bonds for 2009 and 2010, respectively, to Indian schools.[79] This special allocation for Indian schools is to be used for purposes of the construction, rehabilitation, and repair of schools funded by the Bureau of Indian Affairs. For purposes of such allocations Indian tribal governments are qualified issuers. The special allocation for Indian schools does not reduce the State allocation share of the national limitation otherwise available for allocation among the States.

If an amount allocated under this allocation to the States is unused for a calendar year it may be carried forward by the State to the next calendar year.[80]

Allocation to large school districts

Forty percent of the national limitation is allocated among large local educational agencies in proportion to the respective amounts each agency received under section 1124 of the Elementary and Secondary Education Act of 1965 for the most recent fiscal year ending before such calendar year.[81] With respect to a calendar year, the term large local educational agency means any local educational agency if such agency is: (1) among the 100 local educational agencies with the largest numbers of children aged five through 17 from families living below the poverty level, or (2) one of not more than 25 local educational agencies (other than in (1), immediately above) that the Secretary of Education determines are in particular need of assistance, based on a low level of resources for school construction, a high level of enrollment growth, or other such factors as the Secretary of Education deems appropriate. If any amount allocated to large local educational agency is unused for a calendar year the agency may reallocate such amount to the State in which the agency is located.

Explanation of Provision

For bonds originally issued after the date of enactment, the provision allows an issuer of New CREBS, QECs, QZABs, or QSCBs to make an irrevocable election on or before the issue date of such bonds to receive a payment under section 6431 in lieu of providing a tax credit to the holder of the bonds.[82] The payment to the issuer on each payment date is equal to (1) in the case of a bond issued by a qualified small issuer, 65 percent of the amount of interest payable on such bond by such issuer with respect to such date, and (2) in the case of a bond issued by any other person, 45 percent of the amount of interest payable on such bond by such issuer with respect to such date. Thus, the amount of the payment to the issuer is a function of the market-determined interest rate on the bond and not a rate set by the Secretary. For purposes of the provision, a "qualified small issuer" means, with

---

[74] Sec. 54F(a).

[75] Sec. 54F(c).

[76] Pub. L. No. 89-10.

[77] Sec. 54F(d).

[78] Sec. 54F(d)(3).

[79] Sec. 54F(d)(4).

[80] Sec. 54F(e).

[81] Sec. 54F(d)(2).

[82] It is anticipated that the election procedure will be similar to the procedure for making the election required under sec. 54AA(g) for a direct-pay build America bond. See Notice 2009-26, 2009-16 I.R.B. 833.

respect to any calendar year, any issuer that is not reasonably expected to issue tax-exempt bonds (other than private activity bonds), New CREBS, QECs, QZABs, and QSCBs during such calendar year that have an aggregate face amount exceeding $30 million.[83] Bonds for which the election is made count against the national limitation in the same way that they would if no election were made.

Interest paid to the holder of the bond is includible in the holder's gross income. The payment made to the issuer under section 6431 is not includible in the issuer's income, and the issuer's deduction for interest paid on the bond is reduced by the amount paid to the issuer under section 6431.

The provision also adds a technical correction relating to QSCBs. The technical correction provides first that the limitation amount allo-

cated to a State is to be allocated to issuers within such State by the State education agency (or such other agency as is authorized under State law to make such allocation). In addition, the technical correction provides that the rule in section 54F(e), permitting the carryover of unused QSCB limitation by a State or Indian tribal government, shall also apply to the 40 percent of QSCB limitation that is allocated among the largest school districts.

Effective Date

The provision is effective for bonds issued after the date of enactment. The technical correction is effective as if it were included in section 1521 of ARRA.

[Law at ¶6015 and ¶6145. CCH Explanation at ¶220 and ¶225.]

[¶11,050] Act Secs. 441–445 Revenue provisions relating to the highway trust fund

Joint Committee on Taxation (J.C.T. REP. NO. JCX-4-10)

[Code Secs. 9503 and 9504]

Present Law

Extension of expenditure authority

The Highway Trust Fund was established in 1956. It is divided into two accounts, a Highway Account and a Mass Transit Account, each of which is the funding source for specific transportation programs. The Highway Trust Fund is funded by taxes on motor fuels (gasoline, kerosene, diesel fuel, and certain alternative fuels), a tax on heavy vehicle tires, a retail sales tax on certain trucks, trailers and tractors, and an annual use tax for heavy highway vehicles. The current expenditure authority for the Highway Trust Fund generally expires on March 1, 2010.[84]

The Sport Fish Restoration and Boating Trust Fund is the funding source for certain coastal wetlands preservation, recreational boating safety, sport fish restoration and other programs. The current expenditure authority for the Sport Fish Restoration and Boating Trust Fund generally expires on March 1, 2010.

Crediting of interest

With respect to trust funds established by the Code, the Code requires that the Secretary invest the balances not needed to meet current withdrawals in interest-bearing obligations of the United States. The interest is credited to the respective Trust Fund.[85] However, as of September 30, 1998, the ability of the Highway Trust Fund to earn interest on its unexpended balances was terminated.[86]

Transfers from the Highway Trust Fund to the General Fund for certain payments and credits

Under present law, revenues from the highway excise taxes generally are dedicated to the Highway Trust Fund. However, under section 9503(c)(2) of the Code, certain transfers are made from the Highway Trust Fund into the General Fund, relating to amounts paid in respect of gasoline used on farms, amounts paid in respect of gasoline used for certain nonhighway purposes or by local transit systems, amounts relat-

---

[83] It is anticipated that rules similar to section 265(b)(3)(E) will apply in determining whether the $30 million limitation is satisfied. It is further anticipated that in the case of any composite, pooled or other conduit financing issue, the proceeds of which are used directly or indirectly to make or finance loans to one or more ultimate borrowers, the $30

million limitation will be applied at the borrower level. Cf. sec. 265(b)(3)(G).

[84] Pub. L. No. 111-118, Division B, sec. 1008 (2009).
[85] Sec. 9602(b).
[86] Sec. 9503(f)(2).

ing to fuels not used for taxable purposes, and income tax credits for certain uses of fuels.

Explanation of Provision

Extension of expenditure authority

The provision extends expenditure authority for the Highway Trust Fund through December 31, 2010. It also extends the expenditure authority for the Sport Fish Restoration and Boating Trust Fund through December 31, 2010.

Crediting of interest

Restoration of forgone interest

The provision transfers $19.5 billion to the Highway Trust Fund, of that amount $14.7 billion is appropriated to the Highway Account of the Highway Trust Fund and $4.8 billion is appropriated to the Mass Transit Account. The amounts appropriated pursuant to this provision remain available without fiscal year limitation.

Repeal of provision prohibiting the crediting of interest

The provision repeals the requirement that obligations held by the Highway Trust Fund not be interest-bearing. The provision permits amounts in the Trust Fund to be invested in interest-bearing obligations of the United States and have the interest be credited to, and form a part of, the Highway Trust Fund. Thus, the Highway Trust Fund will accrue interest under the provision.

Termination of transfers from the Highway Trust Fund for certain repayments and credits

The provision repeals section 9503(c)(2), eliminating the requirement that the Highway Trust Fund reimburse the General Fund for credits and payments related to nontaxable uses.

Effective Date

The provisions are generally effective on the date of enactment. The expenditure authority provisions are effective September 30, 2009. The provision terminating transfers from the Highway Trust Fund is effective for transfers relating to amounts paid and credits allowed after the date of enactment.

[Law at ¶ 6190, ¶ 6195 and ¶ 6200.]

[¶ 11,060] Act Sec. 501. Reporting on certain foreign accounts

Joint Committee on Taxation (J.C.T. REP. NO. JCX-4-10)

[New Code Secs. 1471, 1472, 1473 and 1474 and Code Sec. 6611]

Present Law

Withholding on payments to foreign persons

Payments of U.S.-source fixed or determinable annual or periodical ("FDAP") income, including interest, dividends, and similar types of investment income, that are made to foreign persons are subject to U.S. withholding tax at a 30-percent rate, unless the withholding agent can establish that the beneficial owner of the amount is eligible for an exemption from withholding or a reduced rate of withholding under an income tax treaty.[87] The term "FDAP income" includes all items of gross income,[88] except gains on sales of property (including market discount on bonds and option premiums).[89]

Interest is derived from U.S. sources if it is paid by the United States or any agency or instrumentality thereof, a State or any political subdivision thereof, or the District of Columbia. Interest is also from U.S. sources if it is paid by a resident or a domestic corporation on a bond, note, or other interest-bearing obligation.[90] Dividend income is sourced by reference to the

---

[87] Secs. 871, 881, 1441, 1442; Treas. Reg. sec. 1.1441-1(b). For purposes of the withholding tax rules applicable to payments to nonresident alien individuals and foreign corporations, a withholding agent is defined broadly to include any U.S. or foreign person that has the control, receipt, custody, disposal, or payment of an item of income of a foreign person subject to withholding. Treas. Reg. sec. 1.1441-7(a).

[88] Although technically insurance premiums paid to a foreign insurer or reinsurer are FDAP income, they are exempt from withholding under Treas. Reg. sec.

1.1441-2(a)(7) if the insurance contract is subject to the excise tax under section 4371.

[89] Treas. Reg. sec. 1.1441-2(b)(1)(i), -2(b)(2). However, gain on a sale or exchange of section 306 stock of a domestic corporation is FDAP income to the extent section 306(a) treats the gain as ordinary income. Treas. Reg. sec. 1.306-3(h).

[90] Sec. 861(a)(1); Treas. Reg. sec. 1.861-2(a)(1). Interest paid by the U.S. branch of a foreign corporation is also treated as U.S.-source interest under section 884(f)(1).

payor's place of incorporation.[91] Thus, dividends paid by a domestic corporation are generally treated as entirely U.S.-source income. Similarly, dividends paid by a foreign corporation are generally treated as entirely foreign-source income. Rental income is sourced by reference to the location or place of use of the leased property.[92] The nationality or the country of residence of the lessor or lessee does not affect the source of rental income. Rental income from property located or used in the United States (or from any interest in such property) is U.S.-source income, regardless of whether the property is real or personal, intangible or tangible. Royalties are sourced in the place of use (or the privilege of use) of the property for which the royalties are paid.[93] This source rule applies to royalties for the use of either tangible or intangible property, including patents, copyrights, secret processes, formulas, goodwill, trademarks, trade names, and franchises.

The principal statutory exemptions from the 30-percent withholding tax apply to interest on bank deposits, portfolio interest, and gains derived from the sale of property. Since 1984, the United States has not imposed withholding tax on portfolio interest received by a nonresident individual or foreign corporation from sources within the United States.[94] Portfolio interest includes, generally, any interest (including original issue discount) other than interest received by a 10-percent shareholder,[95] certain contingent interest,[96] interest received by a controlled foreign corporation from a related person,[97] and interest received by a bank on an extension of credit made pursuant to a loan agreement entered into in the ordinary course of its trade or business.[98]

In the case of interest paid on a debt obligation that is in registered form,[99] the portfolio interest exemption is available only to the extent that the U.S. person otherwise required to withhold tax (the "withholding agent") has received a statement made by the beneficial owner of the obligation (or a securities clearing organization, bank, or other financial institution that holds customers' securities in the ordinary course of its trade or business) that the beneficial owner is not a U.S. person.[100]

Interest on deposits with foreign branches of domestic banks and domestic savings and loan associations is not treated as U.S.-source income and is thus exempt from U.S. withholding tax (regardless of whether the recipient is a U.S. or foreign person).[101] In addition, interest on bank deposits, deposits with domestic savings and loan associations, and certain amounts held by insurance companies are not subject to the U.S. withholding tax when paid to a foreign person, unless the interest is effectively connected with a

---

[91] Secs. 861(a)(2), 862(a)(2).

[92] Sec. 861(a)(4).

[93] Ibid.

[94] Secs. 871(h), 881(c). Congress believed that the imposition of a withholding tax on portfolio interest paid on debt obligations issued by U.S. persons might impair the ability of domestic corporations to raise capital in the Eurobond market (i.e., the global market for U.S. dollar-denominated debt obligations). Congress also anticipated that repeal of the withholding tax on portfolio interest would allow the Treasury Department direct access to the Eurobond market. See Joint Committee on Taxation, *General Explanation of the Revenue Provisions of the Deficit Reduction Act of 1984* (JCS-41-84), December 31, 1984, pp. 391-92.

[95] Sec. 871(h)(3). A 10-percent shareholder includes any person who owns 10 percent or more of the total combined voting power of all classes of stock of the corporation (in the case of a corporate obligor), or 10 percent or more of the capital or profits interest of the partnership (in the case of a partnership obligor). The attribution rules of section 318 apply for this purpose, with certain modifications.

[96] Sec. 871(h)(4). Contingent interest generally includes any interest if the amount of such interest is determined by reference to any receipts, sales, or other cash flow of the debtor or a related person; any income or profits of the debtor or a related person; any change in value of any property of the debtor or a related person; any dividend, partnership distributions, or similar payments made by the debtor or a related person; and any other type of contingent interest identified by Treasury regulation. Certain exceptions also apply.

[97] Sec. 881(c)(3)(C). A related person includes, among other things, an individual owning more than 50 percent of the stock of the corporation by value, a corporation that is a member of the same controlled group (defined using a 50-percent common ownership test), a partnership if the same persons own more than 50 percent in value of the stock of the corporation and more than 50 percent of the capital interests in the partnership, any U.S. shareholder (as defined in section 951(b) and generally including any U.S. person who owns 10 percent or more of the voting stock of the corporation), and certain persons related to such a U.S. shareholder.

[98] Sec. 881(c)(3)(A).

[99] An obligation is treated as in registered form if: (1) it is registered as to both principal and interest with the issuer (or its agent) and transfer of the obligation may be effected only by surrender of the old instrument and either the reissuance by the issuer of the old instrument to the new holder or the issuance by the issuer of a new instrument to the new holder; (2) the right to principal and stated interest on the obligation may be transferred only through a book entry system maintained by the issuer or its agent; or (3) the obligation is registered as to both principal and interest with the issuer or its agent and may be transferred through both of the foregoing methods. Treas. Reg. sec. 5f.103-1(c).

[100] Sec. 871(h)(2)(B), (5); Treas. Reg. sec. 1.871-14(e). This certification of non-U.S. ownership most commonly is made on an IRS Form W-8. This certification is not valid if the Secretary determines that statements from the person making the certification do not meet certain requirements.

[101] Sec. 861(a)(1)(B); Treas. Reg. sec. 1.1441-1(b)(4)(iii).

U.S. trade or business of the recipient.[102] Similarly, interest and original issue discount on certain short-term obligations is also exempt from U.S. withholding tax when paid to a foreign person.[103] Additionally, there is no information reporting with respect to payments of such amounts.[104]

Gains derived from the sale of property by a nonresident alien individual or foreign corporation generally are exempt from U.S. tax, unless they are or are treated as effectively connected with the conduct of a U.S. trade or business. Gains derived by a nonresident alien individual generally are subject to U.S. taxation only if the individual is present in the United States for 183 days or more during the taxable year.[105] Foreign corporations are subject to tax with respect to certain gains on disposal of timber, coal, or domestic iron ore and certain gains from contingent payments made in connection with sales or exchanges of patents, copyrights, goodwill, trademarks, and similar intangible property.[106] Gain from the disposition of certain U.S. real property interests (which include interests in U.S. real property holding corporations) are treated as effectively connected with a U.S. trade or business.[107] Special rules apply in the case of interests in real estate investment trusts or interests in regulated investment companies that are or which would be, if not for certain exceptions, U.S. real property holding corporations.[108] Most gains realized by foreign investors on the sale of portfolio investment securities thus are exempt from U.S. taxation.

The 30-percent withholding tax may be reduced or eliminated by a tax treaty between the United States and the country in which the recipient of income otherwise subject to withholding is resident. Most U.S. income tax treaties provide a zero rate of withholding tax on interest payments (other than certain interest the amount of which is determined by reference to certain income items or other amounts of the debtor or a related person). Most U.S. income tax treaties also reduce the rate of withholding on dividends to 15 percent (in the case of portfolio dividends) and to five percent (in the case of "direct investment" dividends paid to a 10 percent-or-greater shareholder).[109] For royalties, the U.S. withholding rate is typically reduced to five percent or to zero. In each case, the reduced withholding rate is available only to a beneficial owner who is treated as a resident of the treaty country within the meaning of the treaty and satisfies all other treaty requirements including any applicable limitation on benefits provisions of the treaty.

Refund or credits of taxes withheld from foreign persons

A withholding agent that makes payments of U.S.-source amounts to a foreign person is required to report those payments, including any amounts of U.S. tax withheld, to the IRS on IRS Forms 1042 and 1042-S by March 15 of the calendar year following the year in which the payment is made.[110] To the extent that the withholding agent deducts and withholds an amount, the withheld tax is credited to the recip-

---

[102] Secs. 871(i)(2)(A), 881(d); Treas. Reg. sec. 1.1441-1(b)(4)(ii). If the bank deposit interest is effectively connected with a U.S. trade or business, it is subject to regular U.S. income tax rather than withholding tax.

[103] Secs. 871(g)(1)(B), 881(a)(3); Treas. Reg. sec. 1.1441-1(b)(4)(iv).

[104] Treas. Reg. sec. 1.1461-1(c)(2)(ii)(A), (B). However, Treasury regulations require a bank to report interest if the recipient is a resident of Canada and the deposit is maintained at an office in the United States. Treas. Reg. secs. 1.6049-4(b)(5), 1.6049-8. This reporting is required to comply with the obligations of the United States under the U.S.-Canada income tax treaty. T.D. 8664, 1996-1 C.B. 292. In 2001, the IRS and the Treasury Department issued proposed regulations that would require annual reporting to the IRS of U.S. bank deposit interest paid to any foreign individual. 66 Fed. Reg. 3925 (Jan. 17, 2001). The 2001 proposed regulations were withdrawn in 2002 and replaced with proposed regulations that would require reporting with respect to payments made only to residents of certain specified countries (Australia, Denmark, Finland, France, Germany, Greece, Ireland, Italy, the Netherlands, New Zealand, Norway, Portugal, Spain, Sweden, and the United Kingdom). 67 Fed. Reg. 50,386 (Aug. 2, 2002). The proposed regulations have not been finalized.

[105] Sec. 871(a)(2). In most cases, however, an individual satisfying this presence test will be treated as a U.S. resident under section 7701(b)(3), and thus will be subject to full residence-based U.S. income taxation.

[106] Secs. 881(a), 631(b), (c).

[107] Sec. 897. Section 1445 imposes withholding requirements with respect to such dispositions.

[108] See Sec. 897(h).

[109] A number of recent U.S. income tax treaties eliminate withholding tax on dividends paid to a majority (typically 80-percent or greater) shareholder, including the present treaties with Australia, Belgium, Denmark, Finland, Germany, Japan, Mexico, the Netherlands, Sweden, and the United Kingdom.

[110] Treas. Reg. sec. 1.1461-1(b), (c). IRS Form 1042, "Annual Withholding Tax Return for U.S. Source Income of Foreign Persons," is the IRS form on which a withholding agent reports a summary of the total U.S.-source income paid and withholding tax withheld on foreign persons for the year. IRS Form 1042-S, "Foreign Person's U.S. Source Income Subject to Withholding," is the IRS form on which a withholding agent reports, to the foreign person and the IRS, a foreign person's U.S.-source income that is subject to reporting.

ient of the income.[111] If the agent withholds more than is required, and results in an overpayment of tax, the excess may be refunded to the recipient of the income upon filing of a timely claim for refund.

Payment of tax

The date an amount is paid is relevant for determining the limitations period in which to claim a refund, the amount of refund available,[112] and the period for which interest may accrue on any overpayment.[113] An amount that is withheld, paid or credited as an estimate or deposit of tax generally does not count as the payment of tax until applied to a specific tax liability. To the extent that amounts previously withheld, paid or credited as an estimate or deposit of tax are applied to the tax liability for a year, they are deemed to have been paid as of the last day prescribed for payment of the tax, for both the recipient of the income[114] and the withholding agent.[115] Amounts that are refunded, credited to other periods, or offset against other liabilities are not considered as paid for this purpose.[116] Any amount that was previously paid but has been credited to a later year is considered credited on the last day prescribed for the payment of tax.[117]

Interest on overpayments

The IRS is generally required to pay interest to a taxpayer whenever there is an overpayment of tax.[118] An overpayment of tax exists whenever more than the correct amount of tax is paid as of the last date prescribed for the payment of the tax. The last date prescribed for the payment of the income tax is the original due date of the return.[119] However, no interest is required to be paid by the IRS if it refunds or credits the amount due within 45 days of the filing of the return.[120] Notwithstanding these general rules, if a required return on which the payment should have been reported is either not filed, or is filed late, no interest on the overpayment accrues for any period prior to the filing of the return.[121]

Different interest rates are provided for the payment of interest depending upon the type of taxpayer, whether the interest relates to an underpayment or overpayment, and the size of the underpayment or overpayment. Interest on both underpayments and overpayments is compounded daily.[122] A special net interest rate of zero applies in situations where interest is both payable and allowable on offsetting amounts of overpayment and underpayment.[123] For individuals, interest on both underpayments and overpayments accrues at a rate equal to the short term applicable Federal rate ("AFR") plus three percentage points.[124] Interest on corporate overpayments generally accrues at a rate equal to the short term AFR plus two percentage points, unless the overpayment exceeds $10,000 in which case interest accrues at a rate equal to the short term AFR plus one-half percentage point.

Period of overpayment

If the overpayment is to be refunded to the taxpayer, interest accrues on the overpayment from the later of the due date of the return or the date the payment is made until a date that is not more than 30 days before the date of the refund check.[125] If the overpayment is to be credited or offset against some other liability, interest will accrue until the date it is so credited or offset.

A payment is not considered made by the taxpayer earlier than the time the taxpayer files a return showing the liability. However, in *MNOPF Trustees, Ltd. v. United States*,[126] the Federal Circuit held that overpayment interest accrued on the taxes unnecessarily withheld from the date that the withholdings were paid to the Service, because MNOPF was a tax-exempt organization, and, therefore, was not required to file tax returns. As a result, the court rejected arguments by the government that interest commenced no earlier than the filing of the refund claims. The court reasoned that sections 6611(d) and 6513(b)(3) did not apply because those sections only relate to taxable income and the tax-

---

[111] Sec. 1462.
[112] See secs. 6511(a) (prescribing the period within which a claim must be filed) and 6511(b)(2) (limiting the amount that can be recovered if a claim is not filed within three years of filing a return). If a return is not filed, a claim for refund of any tax paid must be filed within two years of payment.
[113] Ses. 6611(b)(2), (d).
[114] Sec. 6513(b)(3).
[115] Sec. 6513(c)(2).
[116] Sec. 6513(d).
[117] Sec. 6513(d).

[118] Sec. 6611.
[119] Sec. 6601(b).
[120] Sec. 6611(e).
[121] Sec. 6611(b)(3).
[122] Sec. 6622.
[123] Sec. 6621(d).
[124] Sec. 6621.
[125] Sec. 6611(b)(2).
[126] 123 F.3d 1460, 1465 (Fed. Cir. 1997).

payer was exempt from Federal taxation. Instead, the court held that the organization's overpayment was deemed paid, pursuant to section 6611(b)(2), on the date the withholding agent filed the returns reporting the withheld taxes.

No interest accrues on an overpayment if the IRS makes the refund within 45 days of the later of the filing or the due date of the return showing the refund. If the IRS fails to make the refund within such 45-day period, interest is required to be paid for the entire period of the overpayment. For example, an individual taxpayer files his return on April 15, properly showing a refund due of $10,000. If the IRS pays the refund within 45 days, no interest on the overpayment will be required. However, if the IRS does not pay the refund until the 46th day, interest will be required from April 15.

Certification of foreign status and reporting by U.S. withholding agents

The U.S. withholding tax rules are administered through a system of self-certification. Thus, a nonresident investor seeking to obtain withholding tax relief for U.S.-source investment income typically must provide a certification, on IRS Form W-8 to the withholding agent to establish foreign status and eligibility for an exemption or reduced rate. Provision of the IRS Form W-8 also establishes an exemption from the rules that apply to many U.S. persons governing information reporting on IRS Form 1099 and backup withholding (discussed below).[127]

There are four relevant types of IRS Forms W-8.[128] Three of these forms are designed to be provided to the withholding agent by the beneficial owner of a payment of U.S.-source income:[129] (1) the IRS Form W-8BEN, which is provided by a beneficial owner of U.S.-source non-effectively-connected income; (2) the IRS Form W-8ECI, which is provided by a beneficial owner of U.S.-source effectively-connected income;[130] and (3) the IRS Form W-8EXP, which is provided by a beneficial owner of U.S.-source income that is an exempt organization or foreign government.[131] Each of these forms requires that the beneficial owner provide its name and address and certify that the beneficial owner is not a U.S. person. The IRS Form W-8BEN also includes a certification of eligibility for treaty benefits (for completion where applicable). All certifications on IRS Forms W-8 are made under penalties of perjury.

The fourth type of IRS Form W-8 is the IRS Form W-8IMY, which is provided by a payee that receives a payment of U.S.-source income as an intermediary for the beneficial owner of that income. The intermediary's IRS Form W-8IMY must be accompanied by an IRS Form W-8BEN, W-8EXP, or W-8ECI, as applicable,[132] furnished by the beneficial owner, unless the intermediary is a qualified intermediary ("QI"), a withholding foreign partnership, or a withholding foreign trust. The rules applicable to qualified intermediaries are discussed below. A withholding foreign partnership or trust is a foreign partnership or trust that has entered into an agreement with the IRS to collect appropriate IRS Forms W-8 from its partners or beneficiaries and act as a U.S. withholding agent with respect to those persons.[133]

Information reporting and backup withholding with respect to U.S. persons

Every person engaged in a trade or business must file with the IRS an information return on IRS Form 1099 (or, for wages or other compensation, on IRS Form W-2) for payments of certain amounts totaling at least $600 that it makes to another person in the course of its trade or business.[134] Detailed rules are provided for the reporting of various types of investment income, including interest, dividends, and gross proceeds

---

[127] See Treas. Reg. sec. 1.1441-1(b)(5).

[128] A fifth type of IRS Form W-8, the W-8CE, is filed to provide the payor with notice of a taxpayer's expatriation.

[129] The United States imposes tax on the beneficial owner of income, not its formal recipient. For example, if a U.S. citizen owns securities that are held in "street" name at a brokerage firm, that U.S. citizen (and not the brokerage firm nominee) is treated as the beneficial owner of the securities. A corporation (and not its shareholders) ordinarily is treated as the beneficial owner of the corporation's income. Similarly, a foreign complex trust ordinarily is treated as the beneficial owner of income that it receives, and a U.S. beneficiary or grantor is not subject to tax on that income unless and until he receives a distribution.

[130] The IRS Form W-8ECI requires that the beneficial owner specify the items of income to which the form is intended to apply and certify that those amounts are effec-

tively connected with the conduct of a trade or business in the United States and includible in the beneficial owner's gross income for the taxable year.

[131] The IRS Form W-8EXP requires that the beneficial owner certify as to its qualification as a foreign government, an international organization, a foreign central bank of issue or a foreign tax-exempt organization, in each case meeting certain requirements.

[132] In limited cases, the intermediary may furnish documentary evidence, other than the IRS Form W-8, of the status of the beneficial owner.

[133] Rev. Proc. 2003-64, 2003-32 I.R.B. 306 (July 10, 2003), provides procedures for qualification as a withholding foreign partnership or withholding foreign trust in addition to providing model withholding agreements.

[134] Sec. 6041; Treas. Reg. secs. 1.6041-1, 1.6041-2.

from brokered transactions (such as a sale of stock).[135] In general, the requirement to file IRS Form 1099 applies with respect to amounts paid to U.S. persons and is linked to the backup withholding rules of section 3406. Thus, to avoid backup withholding, a U.S. payee (other than exempt recipients, including corporations and financial institutions) of interest, dividends, or gross proceeds generally must furnish to the payor an IRS Form W-9 providing that person's name and taxpayer identification number.[136] That information is then used to complete the IRS Form 1099.

If an IRS Form W-9 is not provided by a U.S. payee (other than payees exempt from reporting), the payor is required to impose a backup withholding tax of 28 percent of the gross amount of the payment.[137] The backup withholding tax may be credited by the payee against regular income tax liability.[138] This combination of reporting and backup withholding is designed to ensure that U.S. persons not exempt from reporting pay tax with respect to investment income, either by providing the IRS with the information that it needs to audit payment of the tax or, in the absence of such information, requiring collection of the tax on payment.

As described above, amounts paid to foreign persons are generally exempt from information reporting on IRS Form 1099. Foreign persons are subject to a separate information reporting requirement linked to the nonresident withholding provisions of chapter 3 of the Code.

In the case of U.S. source investment income, the information reporting, backup withholding and nonresident withholding rules apply broadly to any financial institution or other payor, including foreign financial institutions.[139] As a practical matter, however, these reporting and withholding requirements are difficult to enforce with respect to foreign financial institutions, unless these institutions have some connection to the United States, e.g., the institution is a foreign subsidiary of a U.S. financial institution, or the foreign financial institution is doing business in the United States. Moreover, to the extent that these rules apply to foreign financial institutions, the rules may also be modified by QI agreements between the institutions and the IRS, as described below.

The qualified intermediary program

A QI is defined as a foreign financial institution or a foreign clearing organization, other than a U.S. branch or U.S. office of such institution or organization, or a foreign branch of a U.S. financial institution that has entered into a withholding and reporting agreement (a "QI agreement") with the IRS.[140]

A foreign financial institution that becomes a QI is not required to forward beneficial ownership information with respect to its customers to a U.S. financial institution or other withholding agent of U.S.-source investment-type income to establish the customer's eligibility for an exemption from, or reduced rate of, U.S. withholding tax.[141] Instead, the QI is permitted to establish for itself the eligibility of its customers for an exemption or reduced rate, based on an IRS Form W-8 or W-9, or other specified documentary evidence, and information as to residence obtained under the know-your-customer rules to which the QI is subject in its home jurisdiction as approved by the IRS or as specified in the QI agreement.[142] The QI certifies as to eligibility on behalf of its customers, and provides withholding rate pool information to the U.S. withholding agent as to the portion of each payment that

---

[135] See secs. 6042 (dividends), 6045 (broker reporting), 6049 (interest), and the corresponding Treasury regulations.

[136] See Treas. Reg. secs. 31.3406(d)-1, 31.3406(h)-3.

[137] Sec. 3406(a)(1).

[138] Sec. 3406(h)(10).

[139] See Treas. Reg. secs. 1.1441-7(a) (definition of withholding agent includes foreign persons), 31.3406(a)-2 (payor for backup withholding purposes means the person (the payor) required to file information returns for payments of interest, dividends, and gross proceeds (and other amounts)), 1.6049-4(a)(2) (definition of payor for interest reporting purposes does not exclude foreign persons), 1.6042-3(b)(2) (payor for dividend reporting purposes has the same meaning as for interest reporting purposes), 1.6045-1(a)(1) (brokers required to report include foreign persons). But see Treas. Reg. secs. 1.6049-5(b) (exception for interest from sources outside the U.S. paid outside the U.S. by a non-U.S. payor or a non-U.S. middleman), 1.6045-1(g)(1)(i) (exception for sales effected at an office outside the U.S. by a non-U.S. payor or a non-U.S. middle-

man), 1.6042-3(b)(1)(iv) (exceptions for distributions from sources outside the U.S. by a non-U.S. payor or a non-U.S. middleman).

[140] The definition also includes: a foreign branch or office of a U.S. financial institution or U.S. clearing organization; a foreign corporation for purposes of presenting income tax treaty claims on behalf of its shareholders; and any other person acceptable to the IRS, in each case that such person has entered into a withholding agreement with the IRS. Treas. Reg. sec. 1.1441-1(e)(5)(ii).

[141] U.S. withholding agents are allowed to rely on a QI's IRS Form W-8IMY without any underlying beneficial owner documentation. By contrast, nonqualified intermediaries are required both to provide an IRS Form W-8IMY to a U.S. withholding agent and to forward with that document IRS Forms W-8 or W-9 or other specified documentation for each beneficial owner.

[142] See Rev. Proc. 2000-12, 2000-1 C.B. 387, QI agreement secs. 2.12, 5.03, 6.01.

qualifies for an exemption or reduced rate of withholding.

The IRS has published a model QI agreement for foreign financial institutions.[143] A prospective QI must submit an application to the IRS providing specified information, and any additional information and documentation requested by the IRS. The application must establish to the IRS's satisfaction that the applicant has adequate resources and procedures to comply with the terms of the QI agreement.

Before entering into a QI agreement that provides for the use of documentary evidence obtained under a country's know-your-customer rules, the IRS must receive (1) that country's know-your-customer practices and procedures for opening accounts and (2) responses to 18 related items.[144] If the IRS has already received this information, a particular prospective QI need not submit it again. The IRS has received such information and has approved know-your-customer rules in 59 countries.

A foreign financial institution or other eligible person becomes a QI by entering into an agreement with the IRS. Under the agreement, the financial institution acts as a QI only for accounts that the financial institution has designated as QI accounts. A QI is not required to act as a QI for all of its accounts; however, if a QI designates an account as one for which it will act as a QI, it must act as a QI for all payments made to that account.

The model QI agreement describes in detail the QI's withholding and reporting obligations. Certain key aspects of the model agreement are described below.[145]

Withholding and reporting responsibilities

As a technical matter, all QIs are withholding agents for purposes of the nonresident withholding and reporting rules, and payors (who are required to withhold and report) for purposes of the backup withholding and IRS Form 1099 information reporting rules. However, under the QI agreement, a QI may choose not to assume primary responsibility for nonresident withholding. In that case, the QI is not required to withhold on payments made to non-U.S. customers, or to report those payments on IRS Form 1042-S. Instead, the QI must provide a U.S. withholding agent with an IRS Form W-8IMY that certifies as to the status of its (unnamed) non-U.S. account holders and withholding rate pool information.

Similarly, a QI may choose not to assume primary responsibility for IRS Form 1099 reporting and backup withholding. In that case, the QI is not required to backup withhold on payments made to U.S. customers or to file IRS Forms 1099. Instead, the QI must provide a U.S. payor with an IRS Form W-9 for each of its U.S. non-exempt recipient account holders (i.e., account holders that are U.S. persons not generally exempt from IRS Form 1099 reporting and backup withholding).[146]

A QI may elect to assume primary nonresident withholding and reporting responsibility, primary backup withholding and IRS Form 1099 reporting responsibility, or both.[147] A QI that assumes such responsibility is subject to all of the related obligations imposed by the Code on U.S. withholding agents or payors. The QI must also provide the U.S. withholding agent (or U.S. payor) additional information about the withholding rates to enable the withholding agent to appropriately withhold and report on payments made through the QI. These rates can be supplied with respect to withholding rate pools that aggregate payments of a single type of income (e.g., interest or dividends) that is subject to a single rate of withholding.

---

[143] Rev. Proc. 2000-12, 2000-1 C.B. 387, *supplemented by* Announcement 2000-50, 2000-1 C.B. 998, and *modified by* Rev. Proc. 2003-64, 2003-2 C.B. 306, and Rev. Proc. 2005-77, 2005-2 C.B. 1176. The QI agreement applies only to foreign financial institutions, foreign clearing organizations, and foreign branches or offices of U.S. financial institutions or U.S. clearing organizations. However, the principles of the QI agreement may be used to conclude agreements with other persons defined as QIs.

[144] See Rev. Proc. 2000-12, 2000-1 C.B. 387, sec. 3.02.

[145] Additional detail can be found in Joint Committee on Taxation, *Selected Issues Relating to Tax Compliance with Respect to Offshore Accounts and Entities* (JCX-65-08), July 23, 2008.

[146] Regardless of whether a QI assumes primary Form 1099 reporting and backup withholding responsibility, the QI is responsible for IRS Form 1099 reporting and backup

withholding on certain reportable payments that are not reportable amounts. See Rev. Proc. 2000-12, 2001-1 C.B. 387, QI agreement secs. 2.43 (defining reportable amount), 2.44 (defining reportable payment), 3.05, 8.04. The reporting responsibility differs depending on whether the QI is a U.S. payor or a non-U.S. payor. Examples of payments for which the QI assumes primary IRS Form 1099 reporting and backup withholding responsibility include certain broker proceeds from the sale of certain assets owned by a U.S. non-exempt recipient and payments of certain foreign-source income to a U.S. non-exempt recipient if such income is paid in the United States or to an account maintained in the United States.

[147] To the extent that a QI assumes primary responsibility for an account, it must do so for all payments made by the withholding agent to that account. See Rev. Proc. 2000-12, QI agreement sec. 3.

If a U.S. non-exempt recipient has not provided an IRS Form W-9, the QI must disclose the name, address, and taxpayer identification number ("TIN") (if available) to the withholding agent (and the withholding agent must apply backup withholding). However, no such disclosure is necessary if the QI is, under local law, prohibited from making the disclosure and the QI has followed certain procedural requirements (including providing for backup withholding, as described further below).

Documentation of account holders

A QI agrees to use its best efforts to obtain documentation regarding the status of their account holders in accordance with the terms of its QI agreement.[148] A QI must apply presumption rules[149] unless a payment can be reliably associated with valid documentation from the account holder. The QI agrees to adhere to the know-your-customer rules set forth in the QI agreement with respect to the account holder from whom the evidence is obtained.

A QI may treat an account holder as a foreign beneficial owner of an amount if the account holder provides a valid IRS Form W-8 (other than an IRS Form W-8IMY) or valid documentary evidence that supports the account holder's status as a foreign person.[150] With such documentation, a QI generally may treat an account holder as entitled to a reduced rate of withholding if all the requirements for the reduced rate are met and the documentation supports entitlement to a reduced rate. A QI may not reduce the rate of withholding if the QI knows that the account holder is not the beneficial owner of a payment to the account.

If a foreign account holder is the beneficial owner of a payment, then a QI may shield the account holder's identity from U.S. custodians and the IRS. If a foreign account holder is not the beneficial owner of a payment (for example, because the account holder is a nominee), the account holder must provide the QI with an IRS Form W-8IMY for itself along with specific information about each beneficial owner to which the payment relates. A QI that receives this information may shield the account holder's identity from a U.S. custodian, but not from the IRS.[151]

In general, if an account holder is a U.S. person, the account holder must provide the QI with an IRS Form W-9 or appropriate documentary evidence that supports the account holder's status as a U.S. person. However, if a QI does not have sufficient documentation to determine whether an account holder is a U.S. or foreign person, the QI must apply presumption rules detailed in the QI agreement. These presumption rules may not be used to grant a reduced rate of nonresident withholding; instead they merely determine whether a payment should be subject to full nonresident withholding (at a 30-percent rate), subject to backup withholding (at a 28-percent rate), or treated as exempt from backup withholding.

In general, under the QI agreement presumptions, U.S.-source investment income that is paid outside the United States to an offshore account is presumed to be paid to an undocumented foreign account holder. A QI must treat such a payment as subject to withholding at a 30-percent rate and report the payment to an unknown account holder on IRS Form 1042-S. However, most U.S.-source deposit interest and interest or original issue discount on short-term obligations that is paid outside the United States to an offshore account is presumed made to an undocumented U.S. non-exempt recipient account holder and thus is subject to backup withholding at a 28-percent rate.[152] Importantly, both foreign-source income and broker proceeds are presumed to be paid to a U.S. exempt recipient (and thus are exempt from both nonresident and backup withholding) when such amounts are paid outside the United States to an offshore account.

---

[148] See Rev. Proc. 2000-12, QI agreement sec. 5.

[149] The QI agreement contains its own presumption rules. See Rev. Proc. 2000-12, QI agreement sec. 5.13(C). An amount subject to withholding that is paid outside the United States to an account maintained outside the United States is presumed made to an undocumented foreign account holder (i.e., subject to 30-percent withholding). Payments of U.S. source deposit interest and certain other U.S. source interest and original issue discount paid outside of the United States to an offshore account is presumed made to an undocumented U.S. non-exempt account holder (i.e., subject to backup withholding). For payments of foreign source income, broker proceeds and certain other amounts, the QI can assume such payments are made to an exempt recipient if the amounts are paid outside the United States to an account maintained outside the United States.

[150] Documentary evidence is any documentation obtained under know-your-customer rules per the QI agreement, evidence sufficient to establish a reduced rate of withholding under Treas. Reg. sec. 1.1441-6, and evidence sufficient to establish status for purposes of chapter 61 under Treas. Reg. 1.6049-5(c). See Rev. Proc. 2000-12, QI agreement sec. 2.12.

[151] This rule restricts one of the principal benefits of the QI regime, nondisclosure of account holders, to financial institutions that have assumed the documentation and other obligations associated with QI status.

[152] These amounts are statutorily exempt from nonresident withholding when paid to non-U.S. persons.

QI information return requirements

A QI must file IRS Form 1042 by March 15 of the year following any calendar year in which the QI acts as a QI. A QI is not required to file IRS Forms 1042-S for amounts paid to each separate account holder, but instead files a separate IRS Form 1042-S for each type of reporting pool.[153] A QI must file separate IRS Forms 1042-S for amounts paid to certain types of account holders, including: (1) other QIs which receive amounts subject to foreign withholding; (2) each foreign account holder of a nonqualified intermediary or other flow-through entity to the extent that the QI can reliably associate such amounts with valid documentation; and (3) unknown recipients of amounts subject to withholding paid through a nonqualified intermediary or other flow-through entity to the extent the QI cannot reliably associate such amounts with valid documentation. The IRS Form 1042 must also include an attachment setting forth the aggregate amounts of reportable payments paid to U.S. non-exempt recipient account holders, and the number of such account holders, whose identity is prohibited by foreign law (including by contract) from disclosure.[154]

A QI has specified IRS Form 1099[155] filing requirements including: (1) filing an aggregate IRS Form 1099 for each type of reportable amount paid to U.S. non-exempt recipient account holders whose identities are prohibited by law from being disclosed; (2) filing an aggregate IRS Form 1099 for reportable payments other than reportable amounts[156] paid to U.S. non-exempt recipient account holders whose identities are prohibited by law from being disclosed; (3) filing separate IRS Forms 1099 for reportable amounts paid to U.S. non-exempt recipient account holders for whom the QI has not provided an IRS Form W-9 or identifying information to a withholding agent; (4) filing separate IRS Forms 1099 for reportable payments other than reportable amounts paid to U.S. non-exempt recipient account holders; (5) filing separate IRS Forms 1099 for reportable amounts paid to U.S. non-exempt recipient account holders for which the QI has assumed primary IRS Form 1099 report-ing and backup withholding responsibility; and (6) filing separate IRS Forms 1099 for reportable payments to an account holder that is a U.S. person if the QI has applied backup withholding and the amount was not otherwise reported on an IRS Form 1099.

Foreign law prohibition of disclosure

The QI agreement includes procedures to address situations in which foreign law (including by contract) prohibits the QI from disclosing the identities of U.S. non-exempt recipients (such as individuals). Separate procedures are provided for accounts established with a QI prior to January 1, 2001, and for accounts established on or after January 1, 2001.

Accounts established prior to January 1, 2001.–For accounts established prior to January 1, 2001, if the QI knows that the account holder is a U.S. non-exempt recipient, the QI must (1) request from the account holder the authority to disclose its name, address, TIN (if available), and reportable payments; (2) request from the account holder the authority to sell any assets that generate, or could generate, reportable payments; or (3) request that the account holder disclose itself by mandating the QI to provide an IRS Form W-9 completed by the account holder. The QI must make these requests at least two times during each calendar year and in a manner consistent with the QI's normal communications with the account holder (or at the time and in the manner that the QI is authorized to communicate with the account holder). Until the QI receives a waiver on all prohibitions against disclosure, authorization to sell all assets that generate, or could generate, reportable payments, or a mandate from the account holder to provide an IRS Form W-9, the QI must backup withhold on all reportable payments paid to the account holder and report those payments on IRS Form 1099 or, in certain cases, provide another withholding agent with all of the information required for that withholding agent to backup withhold and report the payments on IRS Form 1099.

---

[153] A reporting pool consists of income that falls within a particular withholding rate and within a particular income code, exemption code, and recipient code as determined on IRS Form 1042-S.

[154] For undisclosed accounts, QIs must separately report each type of reportable payment (determined by reference to the types of income reported on IRS Forms 1099) and the number of undisclosed account holders receiving such payments.

[155] If the QI is required to file IRS Forms 1099, it must file the appropriate form for the type of income paid (e.g., IRS Form 1099-DIV for dividends, IRS Form 1099-INT for interest, and IRS Form 1099-B for broker proceeds).

[156] The term reportable amount generally includes those amounts that would be reported on IRS Form 1042-S if the amount were paid to a foreign account holder. The term reportable payment generally refers to amounts subject to backup withholding, but it has a different meaning depending upon the status of the QI as a U.S. or non-U.S. payor.

Accounts established on or after January 1, 2001.–For any account established by a U.S. non-exempt recipient on or after January 1, 2001, the QI must (1) request from the account holder the authority to disclose its name, address, TIN (if available), and reportable payments; (2) request from the account holder, prior to opening the account, the authority to exclude from the account holder's account any assets that generate, or could generate, reportable payments; or (3) request that the account holder disclose itself by mandating the QI to transfer an IRS Form W-9 completed by the account holder.

If a QI is authorized to disclose the account holder's name, address, TIN, and reportable amounts, it must obtain a valid IRS Form W-9 from the account holder, and, to the extent the QI does not have primary IRS Form 1099 and backup withholding responsibility, provide the IRS Form W-9 to the appropriate withholding agent promptly after obtaining the form. If an IRS Form W-9 is not obtained, the QI must provide the account holder's name, address, and TIN (if available) to the withholding agents from whom the QI receives reportable amounts on behalf of the account holder, together with the withholding rate applicable to the account holder. If a QI is not authorized to disclose an account holder's name, address, TIN (if available), and reportable amounts, but is authorized to exclude from the account holder's account any assets that generate, or could generate, reportable payments, the QI must follow procedures designed to ensure that it will not hold any assets that generate, or could generate, reportable payments in the account holder's account.[157]

External audit procedures

The IRS generally does not audit a QI with respect to withholding and reporting obligations covered by a QI agreement if an approved external auditor conducts an audit of the QI. An external audit must be performed in the second and fifth full calendar years in which the QI agreement is in effect. In general, the IRS must receive the external auditor's report by June 30 of the year following the year being audited.

Requirements for the external audit are provided in the QI agreement. In general, the QI must permit the external auditor to have access to all relevant records of the QI, including information regarding specific account holders. In addition, the QI must permit the IRS to communicate directly with the external auditor, review the audit procedures followed by the external auditor, and examine the external auditor's work papers and reports.

In addition to the external audit requirements set forth in the QI agreement, the IRS has issued further guidance (the "QI audit guidance") for an external auditor engaged by a QI to verify the QI's compliance with the QI agreement.[158] An external auditor must conduct its audit in accordance with the procedures described in the QI agreement. However, the QI audit guidance is intended to assist the external auditor in understanding and applying those procedures. The QI audit guidance does not amend, modify, or interpret the QI agreement.

Term of a QI agreement

A QI agreement expires on December 31 of the fifth full calendar year after the year in which the QI agreement first takes effect, although it may be renewed. Either the IRS or the QI may terminate the QI agreement prior to its expiration by delivering a notice of termination to the other party. However, the IRS generally does not terminate a QI agreement unless there is a significant change in circumstances or an event of default occurs, and the IRS determines that the change in circumstance or event of default warrants termination. In the event that an event of default occurs, a QI is given an opportunity to cure it within a specified time.

Know-your-customer due diligence requirements

United States

The U.S. know-your-customer rules[159] require financial institutions[160] to develop and maintain a written customer identification program and anti-money laundering policies and procedures. Additionally, financial institutions

---

[157] Under both of these procedures, if the QI is a non-U.S. payor, a U.S. non-exempt recipient may effectively avoid disclosure and backup withholding by investing in assets that generate solely non-reportable payments such as foreign source income (such as bonds issued by a foreign government) paid outside of the United States.

[158] Rev. Proc. 2002-55, 2002-2 C.B. 435.

[159] The U.S. know-your-customer rules are primarily found in the Bank Secrecy Act of 1970 and in Title III, The

International Money Laundering Abatement and Anti-Terrorist Financing Act of 2001 of the USA PATRIOT Act.

[160] The term financial institution is broadly defined under 31 U.S.C. sec. 5312(a)(2) or (c)(1) and includes U.S. banks and agencies or branches of foreign banks doing business in the United States, insurance companies, credit unions, brokers and dealers in securities or commodities, money services businesses, and certain casinos.

must perform customer due diligence. The due diligence requirements are enhanced where the account or the financial institution has a higher risk profile.[161]

A customer identification program at a minimum requires the financial institution to collect the name, date of birth (for individuals), address,[162] and identification number[163] for new customers. In fulfilling their customer due diligence requirements, financial institutions are required to verify enough customer information to enable the financial institution to form a "reasonable belief that it knows the true identity of each customer."[164]

In many cases the know-your-customer rules do not require financial institutions to look through an entity to determine its ultimate ownership.[165] However, based on the financial institution's risk assessment, the financial institution may need to obtain information about individuals with authority or control over such an account in order to verify the identity of the customer.[166] A financial institution's customer due diligence must include gathering sufficient information on a business entity and its owners for the financial institution to understand and assess the risks of the account relationship.[167]

Enhanced due diligence is required if customers are deemed to be of higher risk, and is mandated for certain types of accounts including foreign correspondent accounts, private banking accounts, and accounts for politically exposed persons. Private banking accounts are considered to be of significant risk and enhanced due diligence requires identification of nominal and beneficial owners for these accounts.[168]

Financial institutions must maintain records for a minimum of five years after the account is closed or becomes dormant. They are required to monitor accounts including the frequency, size and ultimate destinations of transfers and must update customer due diligence and enhanced due diligence when there are significant changes to the customer's profile (for example, volume of transaction activity, risk level, or account type).

European Union Third Money Laundering Directive

The European Union ("EU") Third Money Laundering Directive[169] is also applicable to a broad range of persons including credit institutions and financial institutions as well as to persons acting in the exercise of certain professional activities.[170] It requires systems, adequate policies and procedures for customer due diligence, reporting, record keeping, internal controls, risk assessment, risk management, compliance management, and communication. Required customer due diligence measures go further than the know-your-customer rules in the United States in requiring identification and verification of the beneficial owner and an understanding of the ownership and control structure of the customer in addition to the basic customer identification program and customer due diligence requirements.

A beneficial owner is defined as the natural person who ultimately owns or controls the customer and/or the natural person on whose behalf a transaction or activity is being conducted. For corporations, beneficial owner includes: (1) the natural person or persons who ultimately

---

[161] Relevant risks include the types of accounts held at the financial institution, the methods available for opening accounts, the types of customer identification information available, and the size, location, and customer base of the financial institution. 31 C.F.R. sec. 103.121(b)(2).

[162] For a person other than an individual the address is the principal place of business, local office, or other physical location. 31 C.F.R. sec. 103.121(b)(2)(i)(3)(iii).

[163] For a U.S. person the identification number is the TIN. For a non-U.S. person the identification number could be a TIN, passport number, alien identification number, or number and country of issuance of any other government-issued document evidencing nationality or residence and bearing a photograph or similar safeguard. 31 C.F.R. sec. 103.121(b)(2)(i)(4).

[164] See 31 C.F.R. sec. 103.121(b)(2).

[165] For example, a financial institution is not "required to look through trust, escrow, or similar accounts to verify the identities of beneficiaries and instead will only be required to verify the identity of the named accountholder." See 68 Fed. Reg. 25,090, 25,094 (May 9, 2003).

[166] See 31 C.F.R. sec. 103.121(b)(2)(ii)(C).

[167] In order to assess the risk of the account relationship, a financial institution may need to ascertain the type of business, the purpose of the account, the source of the account funds, and the source of the wealth of the owner or beneficial owner of the entity.

[168] 31 C.F.R. sec. 103.178. A private banking account is an account that (1) requires a minimum deposit of not less than 1 million dollars; (2) is established for the benefit of one or more non-U.S. persons who are direct or beneficial owners of the account; and (3) is administered or managed by an officer, employee or agent of the financial institution. Beneficial owner for these purposes is defined as an individual who has a level of control over, or entitlement to the funds or assets in the account. 31 C.F.R. secs. 103.175(b), 103.175(o).

[169] Directive 2005/60/EC of the European Parliament and of the Council, October 26, 2005 ("EU Third Money Laundering Directive").

[170] The directive applies to auditors, accountants, tax advisors, notaries, legal professionals, real estate agents, certain persons trading in goods (cash transactions in excess of EUR 15,000), and casinos.

owns or controls a legal entity through direct or indirect ownership or control over a sufficient percentage (25 percent plus one share) of the shares or voting rights in that legal entity; and 2) the natural person or persons who otherwise exercises control over the management of the legal entity.[171] For foundations, trusts, and like entities that administer and distribute funds, beneficial owner includes: (1) in cases in which future beneficiaries are determined, a natural person who is the beneficiary of 25 percent or more of the property; (2) in cases in which future beneficiaries have yet to be determined, the class of person in whose main interest the legal arrangement is set up or operates; and (3) natural person who exercises control over 25 percent or more of the property.[172] Under the EU Third Money Laundering Directive, EU member states generally must require identification of the customer and any beneficial owners before the establishment of a business relationship.[173]

The EU Third Money Laundering Directive requires ongoing account monitoring including scrutiny of transactions throughout the course of relationship to ensure that the transactions conducted are consistent with the customer and the business risk profile. It requires documents and other information to be updated and requires performance of customer due diligence procedures at appropriate times (such as a change in account signatories or change in the use of an account) for existing customers on a risk sensitive basis. Records must be maintained for up to five years after the customer relationship has ended.

Explanation of Provision

The provision adds a new chapter 4 to the Code that provides for withholding taxes to enforce new reporting requirements on specified foreign accounts owned by specified United States persons or by United States owned foreign entities. The provision establishes rules for withholdable payments to foreign financial institutions and for withholdable payments to other foreign entities.

Withholdable payments to foreign financial institutions

The provision requires a withholding agent to deduct and withhold a tax equal to 30 percent on any withholdable payment made to a foreign financial institution if the foreign financial insti-

tution does not meet certain requirements. Specifically, withholding is generally not required if an agreement is in effect between the foreign financial institution and the Secretary of the Treasury (the "Secretary") under which the institution agrees to:

1. Obtain information regarding each holder of each account maintained by the institution as is necessary to determine which accounts are United States accounts;

2. Comply with verification and due diligence procedures as the Secretary requires with respect to the identification of United States accounts;

3. Report annually certain information with respect to any United States account maintained by such institution;

4. Deduct and withhold 30 percent from any passthru payment that is made to a (1) recalcitrant account holder or another financial institution that does not enter into an agreement with the Secretary, or (2) foreign financial institution that has elected to be withheld upon rather than to withhold with respect to the portion of the payment that is allocable to recalcitrant account holders or to foreign financial institutions that do not have an agreement with the Secretary.

5. Comply with requests by the Secretary for additional information with respect to any United States account maintained by such institution; and

6. Attempt to obtain a waiver in any case in which any foreign law would (but for a waiver) prevent the reporting of information required by the provision with respect to any United States account maintained by such institution, and if a waiver is not obtained from each account holder within a reasonable period of time, to close the account.

If the Secretary determines that the foreign financial institution is out of compliance with the agreement, the agreement may be terminated by the Secretary. The provision applies with respect to United States accounts maintained by the foreign financial institution and, except as provided by the Secretary, to United States accounts maintained by each other financial institution that is a member of the same expanded affiliated group (other than any foreign financial institution that

---

[171] EU Third Money Laundering Directive Art. 3(6)(a). Inquiries into beneficial ownership generally may stop at the level of any owner that is a company listed on a regulated market.

[172] EU Third Money Laundering Directive Art. 3(6)(b).
[173] EU Third Money Laundering Directive Art. 9.

also enters into an agreement with the Secretary).

It is expected that in complying with the requirements of this provision, the foreign financial institution and the other members of the same expanded affiliated group comply with know-your-customer, anti-money laundering, anti-corruption, or other similar rules to which they are subject, as well as with such procedures and rules as the Secretary may prescribe, both with respect to due diligence by the foreign financial institution and verification by or on behalf of the IRS to ensure the accuracy of the information, documentation, or certification obtained to determine if the account is a United States account. The Secretary may use existing know-your-customer, anti-money laundering, anti-corruption, and other regulatory requirements as a basis in crafting due diligence and verification procedures in jurisdictions where those requirements provide reasonable assurance that the foreign financial institution is in compliance with the requirements of this provision.

The provision allowing for withholding on payments made to an account holder that fails to provide the information required under this provision is not intended to create an alternative to information reporting. It is anticipated that the Secretary may require, under the terms of the agreement, that the foreign financial institution achieve certain levels of reporting and make reasonable attempts to acquire the information necessary to comply with the requirements of this section or to close accounts where necessary to meet the purposes of this provision. It is anticipated that the Secretary may also require, under the terms of the agreement that, in the case of new accounts, the foreign financial institution may not withhold as an alternative to collecting the required information.

A foreign financial institution may be deemed, by the Secretary, to meet the requirements of this provision if: (1) the institution complies with procedures prescribed by the Secretary to ensure that the institution does not maintain United States accounts, and meets other requirements as the Secretary may prescribe with respect to accounts of other foreign financial institutions, or (2) the institution is a member of a class of institutions for which the Secretary has determined that the requirements are not necessary to carry out the purposes of this provision. For instance, it is anticipated that the Secretary may provide rules that would permit certain classes of widely held collective investment vehicles, and to the limited extent necessary to implement these rules, the entities providing administration, distribution and payment services on behalf of those vehicles, to be deemed to meet the requirements of this provision. It is anticipated that a foreign financial institution that has an agreement with the Secretary may meet the requirements under this provision with respect to certain members of its expanded affiliated group if the affiliated foreign financial institution complies with procedures prescribed by the Secretary and does not maintain United States accounts. Additionally, the Secretary may identify classes of institutions that are deemed to meet the requirements of this provision if such institutions are subject to similar due diligence and reporting requirements under other provisions in the Code. Such institutions may include certain controlled foreign corporations owned by U.S. financial institutions and certain U.S. branches of foreign financial institutions that are treated as U.S. payors under present law.

Under the provision, a foreign financial institution may elect to have a U.S. withholding agent or a foreign financial institution that has entered into an agreement with the Secretary withhold on payments made to the electing foreign financial institution rather than acting as a withholding agent for the payments it makes to other foreign financial institutions that either do not enter into agreements with the Secretary or that themselves have elected not to act as a withholding agent, or for payments it makes to account holders that fail to provide required information. If the election under this provision is made, the withholding tax will apply with respect to any payment made to the electing foreign financial institution to the extent the payment is allocable to accounts held by foreign financial institutions that do not enter into an agreement with the Secretary or to payments made to recalcitrant account holders.

A payment may be allocable to accounts held by a recalcitrant account holder or a foreign financial institution that does not meet the requirements of this section either as a result of such person holding an account directly with the electing foreign financial institution, or in relation to an indirect account held through other foreign financial institutions that either do not enter into an agreement with the Secretary or are themselves electing foreign financial institutions.

The electing foreign financial institution must notify the withholding agent of its election and must provide information necessary for the withholding agent to determine the appropriate amount of withholding. The information may include information regarding the amount of any payment that is attributable to a withholdable payment and information regarding the amount of any payment that is allocable to recalcitrant account holders or to foreign financial institutions that have not entered into agreements with the Secretary. Additionally, the electing foreign financial institution must waive any right under a treaty with respect to an amount deducted and withheld pursuant to the election. To the extent provided by the Secretary, the election may be made with respect to certain classes or types of accounts.

A foreign financial institution meets the annual information reporting requirements under the provision by reporting the following information:

1. The name, address, and TIN of each account holder that is a specified United States person;

2. The name, address, and TIN of each substantial United States owner of any account holder that is a United States owned foreign entity;

3. The account number;

4. The account balance or value (determined at such time and in such manner as the Secretary provides); and

5. Except to the extent provided by the Secretary, the gross receipts and gross withdrawals or payments from the account (determined for such period and in such manner as the Secretary may provide).

This information is required with respect to each United States account maintained by the foreign financial institution and, except as provided by the Secretary, each United States account maintained by each other foreign financial institution that is a member of the same expanded affiliated group (other than any foreign financial institution that also enters into an agreement with the Secretary).

Alternatively, a foreign financial institution may make an election and report under sections 6041 (information at source), 6042 (returns regarding payments of dividends and corporate earnings and profits), 6045 (returns of brokers), and 6049 (returns regarding payments of interest), as if such foreign financial institution were a U.S. person (i.e., elect to provide full IRS Form 1099 reporting under these sections). Under this election, the foreign financial institution reports on each account holder that is a specified United States person or United States owned foreign entity as if the holder of the account were a natural person and citizen of the United States. As a result, both U.S.- and foreign-source amounts (including gross proceeds) are subject

to reporting under this election regardless of whether the amounts are paid inside or outside the United States. If a foreign financial institution makes this election, the institution is also required to report the following information with respect to each United States account maintained by the institution: (1) the name, address, and TIN of each account holder that is a specified United States person; (2) the name, address, and TIN of each substantial United States owner of any account holder that is a United States owned foreign entity; and (3) the account number. This election can be made by a foreign financial institution even if other members of its expanded affiliated group do not make the election. The Secretary has authority to specify the time and manner of the election and to provide other conditions for meeting the reporting requirements of the election.

Foreign financial institutions that have entered into QI or similar agreements with the Secretary, under section 1441 and the regulations thereunder, are required to meet the requirements of this provision in addition to any other requirements imposed under the QI or similar agreement.

Under the provision, a United States account is any financial account held by one or more specified United States persons or United States owned foreign entities. Depository accounts are not treated as United States accounts for these purposes if (1) each holder of the account is a natural person and (2) the aggregate value of all depository accounts held (in whole or in part) by each holder of the account maintained by the financial institution does not exceed $50,000. A foreign financial institution may, however, elect to include all depository accounts held by U.S. individuals as United States accounts. To the extent provided by the Secretary, financial institutions that are members of the same expanded affiliated group may be treated as a single financial institution for purposes of determining the aggregate value of depository accounts maintained at the financial institution.

In addition, a financial account is not a United States account if the account is held by a foreign financial institution that has entered into an agreement with the Secretary or is otherwise subject to information reporting requirements that the Secretary determines would make the reporting duplicative. It is anticipated that the Secretary may exclude certain financial accounts held by bona fide residents of any possession of the United States maintained by a financial institution organized under the laws of the possession if the Secretary determines that such reporting is not necessary to carry out the purposes of this provision.

Except as otherwise provided by the Secretary, a financial account is any depository or custodial account maintained by a foreign financial institution and, any equity or debt interest in a foreign financial institution (other than interests that are regularly traded on an established securities market). Any equity or debt interest that is treated as a financial account with respect to any financial institution is treated for purposes of this provision as maintained by the financial institution. It is anticipated that the Secretary may determine that certain short-term obligations, or short-term deposits, pose a low risk of U.S. tax evasion and thus, may not treat such obligations or deposits as financial accounts for purposes of this provision.

A United States owned foreign entity is any foreign entity that has one or more substantial United States owners. A foreign entity is any entity that is not a U.S. person.

A foreign financial institution is any financial institution that is a foreign entity, and except as provided by the Secretary, does not include a financial institution organized under the laws of any possession of the United States. The Secretary may exercise its authority to issue guidance that it deems necessary to prevent financial institutions organized under the laws of U.S. possessions from being used as intermediaries in arrangements under which U.S. tax avoidance or evasion is facilitated.

Except as otherwise provided by the Secretary, a financial institution for purposes of this provision is any entity that (1) accepts deposits in the ordinary course of a banking or similar business; (2) as a substantial portion of its business, holds financial assets for the account of others; or (3) is engaged (or holding itself out as being engaged) primarily in the business of investing, reinvesting, or trading in securities,[174] interests in partnerships, commodities,[175] or any interest (including a futures or forward contract or option) in such securities, partnership interests, or commodities. Accordingly, the term financial institution may include among other entities, investment vehicles such as hedge funds and private equity funds. Additionally, the Secretary may provide exceptions for certain classes of institutions. Such exceptions may include entities such as certain holding companies, research and development subsidiaries, or financing sub-

sidiaries within an affiliated group of non-financial operating companies. It is anticipated that the Secretary may prescribe special rules addressing the circumstances in which certain categories of companies, such as certain insurance companies, are financial institutions, or the circumstances in which certain contracts or policies, for example annuity contracts or cash value life insurance contracts, are financial accounts or United States accounts for these purposes.

For purposes of this provision, a recalcitrant account holder is any account holder that (1) fails to comply with reasonable requests for information necessary to determine if the account is a United States account; (2) fails to provide the name, address, and TIN of each specified United States person and each substantial United States owner of a United States owned foreign entity; or (3) fails to provide a waiver of any foreign law that would prevent the foreign financial institution from reporting any information required under this provision.

A passthru payment is any withholdable payment or other payment to the extent it is attributable to a withholdable payment.

The reporting requirements apply with respect to United States accounts maintained by a foreign financial institution and, except as otherwise provided by the Secretary, with respect to United States accounts maintained by each other foreign financial institution that is a member of the same expanded affiliated group as such foreign financial institution. An expanded affiliated group for these purposes is an affiliated group as defined in section 1504(a) except that "more than 50 percent" is substituted for "at least 80 percent" each place it appears in that section, and is determined without regard to paragraphs (2) and (3) of section 1504(b). A partnership or any other entity that is not a corporation is treated as a member of an expanded affiliated group if such entity is controlled by members of such group.[176]

This provision does not apply with respect to a payment to the extent that the beneficial owner of such payment is (1) a foreign government, a political subdivision of a foreign government, or a wholly owned agency of any foreign government or political subdivision; (2) an international organization or any wholly owned agency or instrumentality thereof; (3) a foreign central bank of issue; or (4) any other class of

---

[174] As defined in section 475(c)(2), without regard to the last sentence thereof.

[175] As defined in section 475(e)(2).

[176] Control for these purposes has the same meaning as control for purposes of section 954(d)(3).

persons identified by the Secretary as posing a low risk of U.S. tax evasion.

Under the provision, a withholding agent includes any person, in whatever capacity, having the control, receipt, custody, disposal, or payment of any withholdable payment.

Except as provided by the Secretary, a withholdable payment is any payment of interest (including any original issue discount), dividends, rents, salaries, wages, premiums, annuities, compensations, remunerations, emoluments, and other fixed or determinable annual or periodical gains, profits, and income from sources within the United States. The term also includes any gross proceeds from the sale or other disposition of any property that could produce interest or dividends from sources within the United States, including dividend equivalent payments treated as dividends from sources in the United States pursuant to section 541 of the Act. Any item of income effectively connected with the conduct of a trade or business within the United States that is taken into account under sections 871(b)(1) or 882(a)(2) is not treated as a withholdable payment for purposes of the provision. In determining the source of a payment, section 861(a)(1)(B) (the rule for sourcing interest paid by foreign branches of domestic financial institutions) does not apply. The Secretary may determine that certain payments made with respect to short-term debt or short-term deposits, including gross proceeds paid pose little risk of United States tax evasion and may be excluded from withholdable payments for purposes of this provision.

A substantial United States owner is: (1) with respect to any corporation, any specified U.S. person that directly or indirectly owns more than 10 percent of the stock (by vote or value) of such corporation; (2) with respect to any partnership, a specified United States person that directly or indirectly owns more than 10 percent of the profits or capital interests of such partnership; and (3) with respect to any trust, any specified United States person treated as an owner of any portion of such trust under the grantor trust rules,[177] or to the extent provided by the Secretary, any specified United States person that holds, directly or indirectly, more than 10 percent of the beneficial interests of the trust. To the extent the foreign entity is a corporation or part-

nership engaged (or holding itself out as being engaged) primarily in the business of investing, reinvesting, or trading in securities, interests in partnerships, commodities, or any interest (including a futures or forward contract or option) in such securities, interests or commodities, the 10-percent threshold is reduced to zero percent. In determining whether an entity is a United States owned foreign entity (and whether any person is a substantial United States owner of such entity), only specified United States persons are considered.

Except as otherwise provided by the Secretary, a specified United States person is any U.S. person other than (1) a publicly traded corporation or a member of the same expanded affiliated group as a publicly traded corporation, (2) any tax-exempt organization or individual retirement plan, (3) the United States or a wholly owned agency or instrumentality of the United States, (4) a State, the District of Columbia, any possession of the United States, or a political subdivision or wholly owned agency of a State, the District of Columbia, or a possession of the United States, (5) a bank,[178] (6) a real estate investment trust,[179] (7) a regulated investment company,[180] (8) a common trust fund,[181] and (9) a trust that is exempt from tax under section 664(c)[182] or is described in section 4947(a)(1).[183]

Withholdable payments to other foreign entities

The provision requires a withholding agent to deduct and withhold a tax equal to 30 percent of any withholdable payment made to a non-financial foreign entity if the beneficial owner of such payment is a non-financial foreign entity that does not meet specified requirements.

A non-financial foreign entity is any foreign entity that is not a financial institution under the provision. A non-financial foreign entity meets the requirements of the provision (i.e., payments made to such entity will not be subject to the imposition of 30-percent withholding tax) if the payee or the beneficial owner of the payment provides the withholding agent with either a certification that the foreign entity does not have a substantial United States owner, or provides the withholding agent with the name, address, and TIN of each substantial United States owner. Additionally, the withholding agent must not

---

[177] Subpart E of Part I of subchapter J of chapter 1.

[178] As defined in section 581.

[179] As defined in section 856.

[180] As defined in section 851.

[181] As defined in section 584(a).

[182] This includes charitable remainder annuity trusts and charitable remainder unitrusts.

[183] This includes certain charitable trusts not exempt under section 501(a).

know or have reason to know that the certification or information provided regarding substantial United States owners is incorrect, and the withholding agent must report the name, address, and TIN of each substantial United States owner to the Secretary.

The provision does not apply to any payment beneficially owned by a publicly traded corporation or a member of an expanded affiliated group of a publicly traded corporation (defined as above but without the inclusion of partnerships or other non-corporate entities). Publicly traded corporations (and their affiliates) receiving payments directly from U.S. withholding agents may present a lower risk of U.S. tax evasion than other non-financial foreign entities. The provision also does not apply to any payment beneficially owned by any: (1) entity that is organized under the laws of a possession of the United States and that is wholly owned by one or more bona fide residents of the possession; (2) foreign government, political subdivision of a foreign government, or wholly owned agency or instrumentality of any foreign government or political subdivision of a foreign government; (3) international organization or any wholly owned agency or instrumentality of an international organization; (4) foreign central bank of issue; (5) any other class of persons identified by the Secretary for purposes of the provision; or (6) class of payments identified by the Secretary as posing a low risk of U.S. tax evasion. It is anticipated that the Secretary may exclude certain payments made for goods, services, or the use of property if the payment is made pursuant to an arm's length transaction in the ordinary course of the payor's trade or business.

It is expected that the Secretary will provide coordinating rules for application of the withholding provisions applicable to foreign financial institutions and to foreign entities that are non-financial foreign entities under this provision.

Credits and refunds

In general, the determination of whether an overpayment of tax deducted and withheld under the provision results in an overpayment by the beneficial owner of the payment is made in the same manner as if the tax had been deducted and withheld under subchapter A of chapter 3 (withholding tax on nonresident aliens

and foreign corporations). An amount of tax required to be withheld by a foreign financial institution under its agreement with the Secretary is treated the same as if it were required to be withheld on a withholdable payment made to a foreign financial institution that does not enter into an agreement with the Secretary. Under the provision, if a beneficial owner of a payment is entitled under an income tax treaty to a reduced rate of withholding tax on the payment, that beneficial owner may be eligible for a credit or refund of the excess of the amount withheld under the provision over the amount permitted to be withheld under the treaty. Similarly, if a payment is of an amount not otherwise subject to U.S. tax (because, for instance, the payment represents gross proceeds from the sale of stock or is interest eligible for the portfolio interest exemption), the beneficial owner of the payment generally is eligible for a credit or refund of the full amount of the tax withheld.

The Secretary has the authority to administer credit and refund procedures which may include requirements for taxpayers claiming credits or refunds of amounts withheld from payments to which the provision applies to supply appropriate documentation establishing that they are the beneficial owners of the payments from which tax was withheld, and that, in circumstances in which treaty benefits are being claimed, they are eligible for treaty benefits. No credit or refund is allowed with respect to tax properly deducted and withheld unless the beneficial owner of the payment provides the Secretary with such information as the Secretary may require to determine whether the beneficial owner of the payment is a United States owned foreign entity and the identity of any substantial United States owners of such entity. It is intended that any such guidance provided by the Secretary under this provision, including documentation and requirements to provide information, be consistent with existing income tax treaties.

If tax is withheld under the provision, this credit and refund mechanism ensures that the provisions are consistent with U.S. obligations under existing income tax treaties. U.S. income tax treaties do not require the United States and its treaty partners to follow a specific procedure for providing treaty benefits.[184] For example, in cases in which proof of entitlement to treaty

---

[184] See, for example, the Commentaries on the OECD Model Tax Convention on Income and on Capital, which make clear that individual countries are free to establish procedures for providing any reduced tax rates agreed to by treaty partners. These procedures can include both relief at

source and/or full withholding at domestic rates, followed by a refund. See, e.g., Commentary 26.2 to Article 1.

A number of Articles of the Convention limit the right of a State to tax income derived from its territory. As noted in paragraph 19 of the Commen-

benefits is demonstrated in advance of payment, the United States may permit reduced withholding or exemption at the time of payment. Alternatively, the United States may require withholding at the relevant statutory rate at the time of payment and allow treaty country residents to obtain treaty benefits through a refund process. The credit and refund mechanism ensures that residents of treaty partners continue to obtain treaty benefits in the event tax is withheld under the provision.

A special rule applies with respect to any tax properly deducted and withheld from a specified financial institution payment, which is defined as any payment with respect to which a foreign financial institution is the beneficial owner. Credits and refunds with respect to specified financial institution payments generally are not allowed. However, refunds and credits are allowed if, with respect to the payment, the foreign financial institution is entitled to an exemption or a reduced rate of tax by reason of any treaty obligation of the United States. In such a case, the foreign financial institution is entitled to an exemption or a reduced rate of tax only to the extent provided under the treaty. In no event will interest be allowed or paid with respect to any credit or refund of tax properly withheld on a specified financial institution payment.

Under the provision, the grace period for which the government is not required to pay interest on an overpayment is increased from 45 days to 180 days for overpayments resulting from excess amounts deducted and withheld under chapters 3 or 4 of the Code. The increased grace period applies to refunds of withheld taxes with respect to (1) returns due after the date of enactment, (2) claims for refund filed after date of enactment and (3) IRS-initiated adjustments if the refunds are paid after the date of enactment. It is anticipated that the Secretary may specify the proper form and information required for a claim for refund under section 6611(e)(2) and may provide that a purported claim that does not include such information is not considered filed.

General provisions

Every person required to deduct and withhold any tax under the provision is liable for such tax and is indemnified against claims and demands of any person for the amount of payments made in accordance with the provision.

No person may use information under the provision except for the purpose of meeting any requirements under the provision or for purposes permitted under section 6103. However, the identity of foreign financial institutions that have entered into an agreement with the Secretary is not treated as return information for purposes of section 6103.

The Secretary is expected to provide for the coordination of withholding under this provision with other withholding provisions of the Code, including providing for the proper crediting of amounts deducted and withheld under this provision against amounts required to be deducted and withheld under other provisions of the Code. The Secretary may provide further coordinating rules to prevent double withholding, including in situations involving tiered U.S. withholding agents.

The provision makes several conforming amendments to other provisions in the Code. The provision grants authority to the Secretary to prescribe regulations necessary and appropriate to carry out the purposes of the provision, and to prevent the avoidance of this provision.

Effective Date

The provision generally applies to payments made after December 31, 2012. The provision, however, does not require any amount to be deducted or withheld from any payment under any obligation outstanding on the date that is two years after the date of enactment, or from the gross proceeds from any disposition of such an obligation. It is anticipated that the Secretary may provide guidance as to the application of the material modification rules under section 1001 in determining whether an obligation is

---

(Footnote Continued)

tary on Article 10 as concerns the taxation of dividends, the Convention does not settle procedural questions and each State is free to use the procedure provided in its domestic law in order to apply the limits provided by the Convention. A State can therefore automatically limit the tax that it levies in accordance with the relevant provisions of the Convention, subject to possible prior verification of treaty entitlement, or it can impose the tax provided

for under its domestic law and subsequently refund the part of that tax that exceeds the amount that it can levy under the provisions of the Convention.

Ibid. While Commentary 26.2 notes that a refund mechanism is not the preferred approach, the bill establishes such a mechanism for beneficial owners in certain circumstances. This approach serves to address, in part, observed difficulties in identifying U.S. persons who inappropriately seek treaty benefits to which they are not entitled.

considered to be outstanding on the date that is two years after the date of enactment.

The interest provisions increasing the grace period for which the government is not required to pay interest on an overpayment from 45 to 180 days apply to: (1) returns with due dates after the date of enactment; (2) claims for credit or refund of overpayment filed after the date of enactment; and (3) refunds paid on adjustments initiated by the Secretary paid after the date of enactment.

[**Law at** ¶6085, ¶6090, ¶6095, ¶6100, ¶6140, ¶6155, ¶6160, ¶6165 **and** ¶6185. **CCH Explanation at** ¶305.]

[¶11,070] Act Sec. 502. Repeal of certain foreign exceptions to registered bond requirements

Joint Committee on Taxation (J.C.T. Rep. No. JCX-4-10)

[Code Secs. 149, 163, 165, 871, 881, 1287, and 4701.]

Present Law

Registration-required obligations and treatment of bonds not issued in registered form

In general, a taxpayer may deduct all interest paid or accrued within the taxable year on indebtedness.[185] For registration-required obligations, a deduction for interest is allowed only if the obligation is in registered form. Generally, an obligation is treated as issued in registered form if the issuer or its agent maintains a registration of the identity of the owner of the obligation and the obligation can be transferred only through this registration system.[186] A registration-required obligation is any obligation other than one that: (1) is made by a natural person; (2) matures in one year or less; (3) is not of a type offered to the public; or (4) is a foreign targeted obligation.[187]

In applying this requirement, the IRS has adopted a flexible approach that recognizes that a debt obligation that is formally in bearer (i.e., not in registered) form is nonetheless "in registered form" for these purposes where there are arrangements that preclude individual investors from obtaining definitive bearer securities or that permit such securities to be issued only upon the occurrence of an extraordinary event.[188]

A foreign targeted obligation (to which the registration requirement does not apply) is any obligation satisfying the following requirements: (1) there are arrangements reasonably designed to ensure that such obligation will be sold (or resold in connection with the original issue) only to a person who is not a United States person; (2) interest is payable only outside the United States and its possessions; and (3) the face of the obligation contains a statement that any United States person who holds this obligation will be subject to limitations under the U.S. income tax laws.[189]

In addition to the denial of an interest deduction, interest on a State or local bond that is a registration-required obligation will not qualify for the applicable tax exemption if the bond is not in registered form.[190] Also, an excise tax is imposed on the issuer of any registration-required obligation that is not in registered

---

[185] Sec. 163(a).

[186] An obligation is treated as in registered form if (1) it is registered as to both principal and interest with the issuer (or its agent) and transfer of the obligation may be effected only by surrender of the old instrument and either the reissuance by the issuer of the old instrument to the new holder or the issuance by the issuer of a new instrument to the new holder, (2) the right to principal and stated interest on the obligation may be transferred only through a book entry system maintained by the issuer or its agent, or (3) the obligation is registered as to both principal and interest with the issuer or its agent and may be transferred through both of the foregoing methods. Treas. Reg. sec. 5f.103-1(c).

[187] Sec. 163(f)(2)(A). The registration requirement is intended to preserve liquidity while reducing opportunities for noncompliant taxpayers to conceal income and property from the reach of the income, estate and gift taxes. See Joint Committee on Taxation, *General Explanation of the Revenue*

Provisions of the Tax Equity and Fiscal Responsibility Act of 1982 (JCS-38-82), December 31, 1982, p. 190.

[188] Priv. Ltr. Rul. 1993-43-018 (1993); Priv. Ltr. Rul. 1993-43-019 (1993); Priv. Ltr. Rul. 1996-13-002 (1996). The IRS held that the registration requirement may be satisfied by "dematerialized book-entry systems" developed in some foreign countries, even if, under such a system, a holder is entitled to receive a physical certificate, tradable as a bearer instrument, in the event the clearing organization maintaining the system goes out of existence, because "cessation of operation of the book-entry system would be an extraordinary event." Notice 2006-99, 2006-2 C.B. 907.

[189] Sec. 163(f)(2)(B).

[190] Sec. 103(b)(3). For the purposes of this section, registration-required obligation is any obligation other than one that: (1) is not of a type offered to the public; (2) matures in one year or less; or (3) is a foreign targeted obligation.

form.[191] The excise tax is equal to one percent of the principal amount of the obligation multiplied by the number of calendar years (or portions thereof) during the period beginning on the date of issuance of the obligation and ending on the date of maturity.

Moreover, any gain realized by the beneficial owner of a registration-required obligation that is not in registered form on the sale or other disposition of the obligation is treated as ordinary income (rather than capital gain), unless the issuer of the obligation was subject to the excise tax described above.[192] Finally, deductions for losses realized by beneficial owners of registration-required obligations that are not in a registered form are disallowed.[193] For the purposes of ordinary income treatment and denial of deduction for losses, a registration-required obligation is any obligation other than one that: (1) is made by a natural person; (2) matures in one year or less; or (3) is not of a type offered to the public.

Treatment as portfolio interest

Payments of U.S.-source "fixed or determinable annual or periodical" income, including interest, dividends, and similar types of investment income, that are made to foreign persons are subject to U.S. withholding tax at a 30-percent rate, unless the withholding agent can establish that the beneficial owner of the amount is eligible for an exemption from withholding or a reduced rate of withholding under an income tax treaty.[194] In 1984, the Congress repealed the 30-percent tax on portfolio interest received by a nonresident individual or foreign corporation from sources within the United States.[195]

The term "portfolio interest" means any interest (including original issue discount) that is (1) paid on an obligation that is in registered form and for which the beneficial owner has provided to the U.S. withholding agent a statement certifying that the beneficial owner is not a U.S. person, or (2) paid on an obligation that is not in registered form and that meets the foreign targeting requirements of section 163(f)(2)(B).[196] Portfolio interest, however, does not include interest received by a 10-percent shareholder,[197] certain contingent interest,[198] interest received by a controlled foreign corporation from a related person,[199] or interest received by a bank on an extension of credit made pursuant to a loan agreement entered into in the ordinary course of its trade or business.[200]

Requirement that U.S. Treasury obligations be in registered form

Under title 31 of the United States Code, every "registration-required obligation" of the U.S. Treasury must be in registered form.[201] For this purpose, a foreign targeted obligation is excluded from the definition of a registration-required obligation.[202] Thus, a foreign targeted obligation of the Treasury can be in bearer (rather than registered) form.

---

[191] Sec. 4701.

[192] Sec. 1287.

[193] Sec. 165(j).

[194] Secs. 871, 881; Treas. Reg. sec. 1.1441-1(b). Generally, the determination by a withholding agent of the U.S. or foreign status of a payee and of its other relevant characteristics (e.g., as a beneficial owner or intermediary, or as an individual, corporation, or flow-through entity) is made on the basis of a withholding certificate that is a Form W-8 or a Form 8233 (indicating foreign status of the payee or beneficial owner) or a Form W-9 (indicating U.S. status of the payee).

[195] Secs. 871(h) and 881(c). Congress believed that the imposition of a withholding tax on portfolio interest paid on debt obligations issued by U.S. persons might impair the ability of U.S. corporations to raise capital in the Eurobond market (i.e., the global market for U.S. dollar-denominated debt obligations). Congress also anticipated that repeal of the withholding tax on portfolio interest would allow the U.S. Treasury Department direct access to the Eurobond market. See Joint Committee on Taxation, *General Explanation of the Revenue Provisions of the Deficit Reduction Act of 1984* (JCS-41-84), December 31, 1984, pp. 391-92.

[196] In repealing the 30-percent tax on portfolio interest, under the Deficit Reduction Act of 1984, Congress expressed concern about potential compliance problems in connection with obligations issued in bearer form. Given the foreign targeted exception to the registration requirement under section 163(f)(2)(A), U.S. persons intent on evading U.S. tax on interest income might attempt to buy U.S. bearer obligations overseas, claiming to be foreign persons. These persons might then claim the statutory exemption from withholding tax for the interest paid on the obligations and fail to declare the interest income on their U.S. tax returns, without concern that their ownership of the obligations would come to the attention of the IRS. Because of these concerns, Congress expanded the Treasury's authority to require registration of obligations deigned to be sold to foreign persons. See Joint Committee on Taxation, *General Explanation of the Revenue Provisions of the Deficit Reduction Act of 1984* (JCS-41-84), December 31, 1984, p. 393.

[197] Sec. 871(h)(3).

[198] Sec. 871(h)(4).

[199] Sec. 881(c)(3)(C).

[200] Sec. 881(c)(3)(A).

[201] 31 U.S.C. sec. 3121(g)(3). For purposes of title 31 of the United States Code, registration-required obligation is defined as any obligation except: (1) an obligation not of a type offered to the public; (2) an obligation having a maturity (at issue) of not more than one year; or (3) a foreign targeted obligation.

[202] 31 U.S.C. sec. 3121(g)(2).

Explanation of Provision

Repeal of the foreign targeted obligation exception to the registration requirement

The provision repeals the foreign targeted obligation exception to the denial of a deduction for interest on bonds not issued in registered form. Thus, under the provision, a deduction for interest is disallowed with respect to any obligation not issued in registered form, unless that obligation (1) is issued by a natural person, (2) matures in one year or less, or (3) is not of a type offered to the public.

Also, the provision repeals the foreign targeted obligation exception to the denial of the tax exemption on interest on State and local bonds not issued in registered form. Therefore, under the provision, interest paid on State and local bonds not issued in registered form will not qualify for tax exemption unless that obligation (1) is not of a type offered to the public, or (2) matures in one year or less.

The bill preserves the ordinary income treatment under present law of any gain realized by the beneficial owner from the sale or other disposition of a registration-required obligation that is not in registered form. Similarly, the bill does not change the present law rule disallowing deductions for losses realized by a beneficial owner of a registration-required obligation that is not in a registered form.

Preservation of exception to the registration requirement for excise tax purposes

Under the provision, the foreign targeted obligation exception is available with respect to the excise tax applicable to issuers of registration-required obligations that are not in registered form. Thus, the excise tax applies with respect to any obligation that is not in registered form unless the obligation (1) is issued by a natural person, (2) matures in one year or less, (3) is not of a type offered to the public, or (4) is a foreign targeted obligation.

Repeal of treatment as portfolio interest

The provision repeals the treatment as portfolio interest of interest paid on bonds that are not issued in registered form but meet the foreign targeting requirements of section 163(f)(2)(B). Under the provision, interest qualifies as portfolio interest only if it is paid on an obligation that is issued in registered form and either (1) the beneficial owner has provided the

withholding agent with a statement certifying that the beneficial owner is not a United States person (on IRS Form W-8), or (2) the Secretary has determined that such statement is not required in order to carry out the purposes of the subsection. It is anticipated that the Secretary may exercise its authority under this rule to waive the requirement of collecting Forms W-8 in circumstances in which the Secretary has determined there is a low risk of tax evasion and there are adequate documentation standards within the country of tax residency of the beneficial owner of the obligations in question. Generally, however, as a result of the provision, interest paid to a foreign person on an obligation that is not issued in registered form is subject to U.S. withholding tax at a 30-percent rate, unless the withholding agent can establish that the beneficial owner of the amount is eligible for an exemption from withholding other than the portfolio interest exemption or for a reduced rate of withholding under an income tax treaty.

Dematerialized book-entry systems treated as registered form

The provision provides that a debt obligation held through a dematerialized book entry system, or other book entry system specified by the Secretary, is treated, for purposes of section 163(f), as held through a book entry system for the purpose of treating the obligation as in registered form.[203] A debt obligation that is formally in bearer form is treated, for the purposes of section 163(f), as held in a book-entry system as long as the debt obligation may be transferred only through a dematerialized book entry system or other book entry system specified by the Secretary.

Repeal of exception to requirement that Treasury obligations be in registered form

The provision includes a conforming change to title 31 of the United States Code that repeals the foreign targeted exception to the definition of a registration-required obligation. Thus, a foreign targeted obligation of the Treasury must be in registered form.

Effective Date

The provision applies to debt obligations issued after the date which is two years after the date of enactment.

[Law at ¶6025, ¶6030, ¶6035, ¶6060, ¶6065, ¶6070, ¶6115 and ¶7212. CCH Explanation at ¶360.]

---

[203] By reason of cross references, this rule will also apply to sections 165(j), 312(m), 871(h), 881(c), 1287 and 4701.

[¶11,080] Act Sec. 511. Disclosure of information with respect to foreign financial assets

Joint Committee on Taxation (J.C.T. REP. No. JCX-4-10)

[New Code Sec. 6038D]

Present Law

U.S. persons who transfer assets to, and hold interests in, foreign bank accounts or foreign entities may be subject to self-reporting requirements under both Title 26 (the Internal Revenue Code) and Title 31 (the Bank Secrecy Act) of the United States Code.

Since its enactment, the Bank Secrecy Act has been expanded beyond its original focus on large currency transactions, while retaining its broad purpose of obtaining self-reporting of information with "a high degree of usefulness in criminal, tax, or regulatory investigations or proceedings."[204] As the reporting regime has expanded,[205] reporting obligations have been imposed on both financial institutions and account holders. With respect to account holders, a U.S. citizen, resident, or person doing business in the United States is required to keep records and file reports, as specified by the Secretary, when that person enters into a transaction or maintains an account with a foreign financial agency.[206] Regulations promulgated pursuant to broad regulatory authority granted to the Secretary in the Bank Secrecy Act[207] provide additional guidance regarding the disclosure obligation with respect to foreign accounts. The Bank Secrecy Act specifies only that such disclosure contain the following information "in the way and to the extent the Secretary prescribes": (1) the identity and address of participants in a transaction or relationship; (2) the legal capacity in which a participant is acting; (3) the identity of real parties in interest; and (4) a description of the transaction.

Treasury Department Form TD F 90-22.1, "Report of Foreign Bank and Financial Accounts," (the "FBAR") must be filed by June 30 of the year following the year in which the $10,000 filing threshold is met.[208] The FBAR is filed with the Treasury Department at the IRS Detroit Computing Center. Failure to file the FBAR is subject to both criminal[209] and civil penalties.[210] Since 2004, the civil sanctions have included penalties not to exceed (1) $10,000 for failures that are not willful and (2) the greater of $100,000 or 50 percent of the balance in the account for willful failures. Although the FBAR is received and processed by the IRS, it is neither part of the income tax return filed with the IRS nor filed in the same office as that return. As a result, for purposes of Title 26, the FBAR is not considered "return information," and its distribution to other law enforcement agencies is not limited by the nondisclosure rules of Title 26.[211]

Although the obligation to file an FBAR arises under Title 31, individual taxpayers subject to the FBAR reporting requirements are alerted to this requirement in the preparation of annual Federal income tax returns. Part III ("Foreign Accounts and Trusts") of Schedule B of the 2008 IRS Form 1040 includes the question, "At any time during 2008, did you have an interest in or signatory or any other authority over a financial account in a foreign country, such as a bank account, securities account, or other financial account?" and directs taxpayers to "See page B-2 for exceptions and filing requirements for Form TD F 90-22.1." The Form 1040 instructions advise individuals who answer "yes" to this question to identify the foreign country or countries in

---

[204] 31 U.S.C. sec. 5311.

[205] See e.g., Title III of the USA PATRIOT Act, Pub. L. No. 107-56 (October 26, 2001) (sections 351 through 366 amended the Bank Secrecy Act as part of a series of reforms directed at international financing of terrorism).

[206] 31 U.S.C. sec. 5314. The term "agency" in the Bank Secrecy Act includes financial institutions.

[207] 31 U.S.C. sec. 5314(a) provides: "Considering the need to avoid impeding or controlling the export or import of monetary instruments and the need to avoid burdening unreasonably a person making a transaction with a foreign financial agency, the Secretary of the Treasury shall require a resident or citizen of the United States or a person in, and doing business in, the United States, to keep records, file reports, or keep records and file reports, when the resident,

citizen, or person makes a transaction or maintains a relation for any person with a foreign financial agency."

[208] 31 C.F.R. sec. 103.27(c). The $10,000 threshold is the aggregate value of all foreign financial accounts in which a U.S. person has a financial interest in or over which the U.S. person has signature or other authority.

[209] 31 U.S.C. sec. 5322 (failure to file is punishable by a fine up to $250,000 and imprisonment for five years, which may double if the violation occurs in conjunction with certain other violations).

[210] 31 U.S.C. sec. 5321(a)(5).

[211] Section 6103 bars disclosure of return information, unless permitted by an exception.

which such accounts are located.[212] Responding to this question does not discharge one's obligations under Title 31 and constitutes "return information" protected from routine disclosure to those charged with enforcing Title 31. In addition, the Form 1040 instructions identify certain types of accounts that are not subject to disclosure, including those instances in which the combined value of all accounts held by the taxpayer did not exceed $10,000 at any point during the relevant tax year.

The FBAR requires disclosure of any account in which the filer has a financial interest or as to which the filer has signature or other authority (in which case the filer must identify the owner of the account). The Treasury Department and the IRS revised the FBAR and its accompanying instructions in October, 2008, to clarify the filing requirements for U.S. persons holding interests in foreign bank accounts.[213] For example, the terminology has been updated to reflect new types of financial transactions. For example, "financial account" now specifies that debit or prepaid credit cards are financial accounts,[214] and the definition of "signature or other authority" now encompasses the ability to indirectly exercise this authority, even in the absence of written instructions.[215] The revised instructions also provide that foreign individuals doing business in the United States may be required to file an FBAR.[216] In August, 2009, the IRS requested public comments to help determine the scope and nature of future additional guidance.[217]

The revised instructions explain the basis for reporting other information in more detail, and provide that (1) all foreign persons with an interest in the account must be identified (including foreign identification numbers for each), (2) the

---

[212] 31 C.F.R. sec. 103.24.

[213] Treasury Department Form TD F 90-22.1, Report of Foreign Bank and Financial Accounts, and its instructions states:

A financial interest in a bank, securities, or other financial account in a foreign country means an interest described in one of the following three paragraphs: 1. A United States person has a financial interest in each account for which such person is the owner of record or has legal title, whether the account is maintained for his or her own benefit or for the benefit of others including non-United States persons. 2. A United States person has a financial interest in each bank, securities, or other financial account in a foreign country for which the owner of record or holder of legal title is: (a) a person acting as an agent, nominee, attorney, or in some other capacity on behalf of the U.S. person; (b) a corporation in which the United States person owns directly or indirectly more than 50 percent of the total value of shares of stock or more than 50 percent of the voting power for all shares of stock; (c) a partnership in which the United States person owns an interest in more than 50 percent of the profits (distributive share of income, taking into account any special allocation agreement) or more than 50 percent of the capital of the partnership; or (d) a trust in which the United States person either has a present beneficial interest, either directly or indirectly, in more than 50 percent of the assets or from which such person receives more than 50 percent of the current income. 3. A United States person has a financial interest in each bank, securities, or other financial account in a foreign country for which the owner of record or holder of legal title is a trust, or a person acting on behalf of a trust, that was established by such United States person and for which a trust protector has been appointed. A trust protector is a person who is responsible for monitoring the activities of a trustee, with the authority to influence the decisions of the trustee or to replace, or recommend the replacement of, the trustee. Correspondent or "nostro" accounts (international interbank transfer accounts) maintained by banks that are used solely for the purpose of bank-to-bank settlement need not be reported on this form, but are subject to other Bank Secrecy Act filing requirements. This exception is intended to encompass those accounts utilized for bank-to-bank settlement purposes only.

[214] See Chief Counsel Advice 200603026 (January 20, 2006) for a discussion of whether payment card accounts constitute financial accounts.

[215] According to the instructions to the FBAR, a person has "signature authority" over an account "if such person can control the disposition of money or other property in it by delivery of a document containing his or her signature (or his or her signature and that of one or more other persons) to the bank or other person with whom the account is maintained." "Other authority" exists in a person "who can exercise comparable power over an account by communication to the bank or other person with whom the account is maintained, either directly or through an agent, nominee, attorney, or in some other capacity on behalf of the US person, either orally or by some other means."

[216] Although the revised instructions currently track the language of the statute in stating that a person in or doing business in the United States is within its purview, and thus merely clarify what has long been required, the IRS announced that pending publication of guidance on the scope of the statute, people could rely on the earlier, unrevised instructions to determine whether they are required to file a FBAR. Announcement 2009-51, 2009-25 I.R.B. 1105. Subsequently, the IRS announced that persons with only signature authority over a foreign financial account as well as for signatories or owners of financial interest in a foreign commingled fund have until June 30, 2010 to file an FBAR for the 2008 and earlier calendar years with respect to those accounts. Notice 2009-62, 2009-35 I.R.B. 260.

[217] Notice 2009-62, 2009-35 I.R.B. 260, specifically requested comments concerning: (1) when a person having only signature authority or having an interest in a commingled fund should be relieved of filing an FBAR; (2) the circumstances under which the FBAR filing exceptions for officers and employees of banks and some publicly traded domestic corporations should be expanded; (3) when an interest in a foreign entity should be subject to FBAR reporting; and (4) whether the passive asset and passive income thresholds are appropriate and should apply conjunctively.

highest value held in the account at any point in the year must be disclosed, (3) corporate employees with signature authority but no financial interest are generally required to disclose the signature authority, unless the corporate Chief Financial Officer ("CFO") (or in the case of an employee of a subsidiary, the parent company's CFO) certifies that the account will be reported on the corporate filing and (4) any amended or delinquent filing should be identified as such, and accompanied by an explanatory statement.

In addition to the FBAR requirements under Title 31, there are additional reports required by the Code to be filed with the IRS by U.S. persons engaged in foreign activities, directly or indirectly, through a foreign business entity. Upon the formation, acquisition or ongoing ownership of certain foreign corporations, U.S. persons that are officers, directors, or shareholders must file a Form 5471, "Information Return of U.S. Persons with Respect to Certain Foreign Corporations."[218] Similarly, an IRS Form 8865, "Return of U.S. Persons with Respect to Certain Foreign Partnerships," must be filed with respect to certain interests in a controlled foreign partnership; an IRS Form 3520, "Annual Return to Report Transactions with Foreign Trusts and Receipt of Certain Foreign Gifts," must be filed with respect to certain foreign trusts; and an IRS Form 8858, "Information Return of U.S. Persons With Respect To Foreign Disregarded Entities" must be filed with respect to a foreign disregarded entity.[219] To the extent that the U.S. person engages in such foreign activities indirectly through a foreign business entity, other self-reporting requirements may apply. In addition, a U.S. person that capitalizes a foreign entity generally is required to file an IRS Form 926, "Return by a U.S. Transferor of Property to a Foreign Corporation."[220]

With the exception of the questions included on Form 1040, Schedule B, there is no requirement to disclose the information includible on FBAR on an individual tax return.

FBAR enforcement responsibility

Until 2003, the Financial Crimes and Enforcement Network ("FinCEN"), an agency of the Department of the Treasury, had responsibility for civil penalty enforcement of FBAR.[221] As a result, persons who were more than 180 days delinquent in paying any FBAR penalties were referred for collection action to the Financial Management Service of the Treasury Department, which is responsible for such non-tax collections.[222] Continued nonpayment resulted in a referral to the Department of Justice for institution of court proceedings against the delinquent person. In 2003, the Secretary delegated civil enforcement to the IRS.[223] This change reflected the fact that a major purpose of the FBAR was to identify potential tax evasion, and therefore was not closely aligned with FinCEN's core mission.[224] The authority delegated to the IRS in 2003 included the authority to determine and enforce civil penalties,[225] as well as to revise the form and instructions. However, the collection and enforcement powers available to enforce the Internal Revenue Code under Title 26 are not available to the IRS in the enforcement of FBAR civil penalties, which remain collectible only in accord with the procedures for non-tax collections described above.

In general, information reported on an FBAR is available to the IRS and other law enforcement agencies. In contrast, information on income tax returns-including the Schedule B information regarding foreign bank accounts-is not readily available to those within the IRS who are charged with administering FBAR compliance, despite the fact that Federal returns and return information may be the best source of information for this purpose.

---

[218] Secs. 6038, 6046.

[219] Form 8858 is used to satisfy reporting requirements of sections 6011, 6012, 6031, 6038, and related regulations.

[220] Sec. 6038B. The filing of this form may also be required upon future contributions to the foreign corporation.

[221] Treas. Directive 15-14 (December 1, 1992), in which the Secretary delegated to the IRS authority to investigate violations of the Bank Secrecy Act. If the IRS Criminal Investigation Division declines to pursue a possible criminal case, it is to refer the matter to FinCEN for civil enforcement.

[222] 31 U.S.C. sec. 3711(g).

[223] 31 C.F.R. sec. 103.56(g). Memorandum of Agreement and Delegation of Authority for Enforcement of FBAR Requirements (April 2, 2003); News Release, Internal Revenue Service, IR-2003-48 (April 10, 2003).

[224] Secretary of the Treasury, "A Report to Congress in Accordance with sec. 361(b) of the Uniting and Strengthening America by Providing Appropriate Tools Required to Intercept and Obstruct Terrorism Act of 2001 (USA Patriot Act)" (April 24, 2003).

[225] A penalty may be assessed before the end of the six-year period beginning on the date of the transaction with respect to which the penalty is assessed. 31 U.S.C. sec. 5321(b)(1). A civil action for collection may be commenced within two years of the later of the date of assessment and the date a judgment becomes final in any related criminal action. 31 U.S.C. sec. 5321(b)(2).

The nondisclosure constraints on IRS personnel who examine income tax liability (i.e., Form 1040 reporting) generally preclude the sharing of tax return information with any other IRS personnel or Treasury officials, except for tax administration purposes.[226] Tax administration is defined as "the administration, management, conduct, direction, and supervision of the execution and application of the internal revenue laws or related statutes" and does not necessarily include administration of Title 31.[227] Because Title 31 includes enforcement of non-tax provisions of the Bank Secrecy Act, Title 31 is not, per se, a "related statute," for purposes of finding that a disclosure of such information would be for tax administration purposes. As a result, IRS personnel charged with investigating and enforcing the civil penalties under Title 31 are not routinely permitted access to Form 1040 information that would support or shed light on the existence of an FBAR violation. Instead, there must be a determination, in writing, that the FBAR violation was in furtherance of a Title 26 violation in order to support a finding that the statutes are "related statutes" for purposes of authorizing the disclosure. The effect of this prerequisite is to subsume the bank account information reported on Form 1040 under the scope of "return information" and therefore, the protection from disclosure provided under Title 26.[228]

Penalties

Failure to comply with the FBAR filing requirements is subject to penalties imposed under Title 31 of the United States Code, and may be both civil and criminal. Since the initial enactment of the Bank Secrecy Act, a willful failure to comply with the FBAR reporting requirement has been subject to a civil penalty. In 2004, the available penalties were expanded to include a reduced penalty for a non-willful failure to file.[229] Willful failure to file an FBAR may be subject to penalties in amounts not to exceed the greater of $100,000 or 50 percent of the amount in the account at the time of the violation.[230] A

non-willful, but negligent, failure to file is subject to a penalty of $10,000 for each negligent violation.[231] The penalty may be waived if (1) there is reasonable cause for the failure to report and (2) the amount of the transaction or balance in the account was properly reported. In addition, serious violations are subject to criminal prosecution, potentially resulting in both monetary penalties and imprisonment. Civil and criminal sanctions are not mutually exclusive.

Failure to comply with information returns required by the Internal Revenue Code is subject to a variety of sanctions, including (1) suspension of the applicable statute of limitations,[232] (2) disallowance of otherwise permitted tax attributes, deductions or credits,[233] and (3) imposition of penalties. For most information returns, the failure to file penalty is $50 per return, up to a maximum of $250,000 per taxpayer.[234] Failures to disclose control of any foreign business entity,[235] foreign parties with 25-percent ownership interest in a domestic company,[236] domestic officers and 10-percent owners of a foreign corporation,[237] or change in ownership of a foreign partnership[238] are subject to penalties of $10,000, plus $10,000 for every 30 days the failure to file persists longer than 90 days after the taxpayer is informed of the failure. A failure to report a transfer to a foreign corporation is subject to a penalty equal to 10 percent of the value of the transfer, but is capped at $10,000 if the failure is not willful.[239] Failure to report the creation of a foreign trust is subject to a 35 percent penalty on the reportable amount (or five percent for a Form 3520-A report), plus $10,000 for every 30 days the failure to file persists after 90 days from the date on which the taxpayer is informed of the failure to file. The penalty is capped at the gross reportable amount.[240]

Explanation of Provision

The provision requires individual taxpayers with an interest in a "specified foreign financial asset" during the taxable year to attach a disclo-

---

[226] Sec. 6103(h)(1). In essence, section 6103(h)(1) authorizes officers and employees of both the Treasury Department and IRS to have access to return information on the basis of a "need to know" in order to perform a tax administration function.

[227] Sec. 6103(b)(4).

[228] Internal Revenue Manual, paragraphs 4.26.14.2 and 4.26.14.2.1.

[229] American Jobs Creation Act of 2004, Pub. L. No. 108-357, sec. 821(b), 118 Stat. 1418. This provision is codified in 31 U.S.C. sec. 5321(a)(5).

[230] 31 U.S.C. sec. 5321(a)(5)(C).

[231] 31 U.S.C. sec. 5321(a)(5)(B)(i), (ii).

[232] Sec. 6501(c)(8).

[233] Secs. 1295, 6038.

[234] Sec. 6721.

[235] Sec. 6038.

[236] Sec. 6038A.

[237] Sec. 6046.

[238] Sec. 6046A.

[239] Sec. 6038B.

[240] Sec. 6048.

sure statement to their income tax return for any year in which the aggregate value of all such assets is greater than $50,000. Although the nature of the information required is similar to the information disclosed on an FBAR, it is not identical. For example, a beneficiary of a foreign trust who is not within the scope of the FBAR reporting requirements because his interest in the trust is less than 50 percent may nonetheless be required to disclose the interest in the trust with his tax return under this provision if the value of his interest in the trust together with the value of other specified foreign financial assets exceeds the aggregate value threshold. Nothing in this provision is intended as a substitute for compliance with the FBAR reporting requirements, which are unchanged by this provision.

"Specified foreign financial assets" are depository or custodial accounts at foreign financial institutions and, to the extent not held in an account at a financial institution, (1) stocks or securities issued by foreign persons, (2) any other financial instrument or contract held for investment that is issued by or has a counterparty that is not a U.S. person, and (3) any interest in a foreign entity. The information to be included on the statement includes identifying information for each asset and its maximum value during the taxable year. For an account, the name and address of the institution at which the account is maintained and the account number are required. For a stock or security, the name and address of the issuer, and any other information necessary to identify the stock or security and terms of its issuance must be provided. For all other instruments or contracts, or interests in foreign entities, the information necessary to identify the nature of the instrument, contract or interest must be provided, along with the names and addresses of all foreign issuers and counterparties. An individual is not required under this provision to disclose interests that are held in a custodial account with a U.S. financial institution nor is an individual required to identify separately any stock, security instrument, contract, or interest in a foreign financial account disclosed under the provision. In addition, the provision permits the Secretary to issue regulations that would apply the reporting obligations to a domestic entity in the same manner as if such entity were an individual if that domestic entity is formed or availed of to hold such interests, directly or indirectly.

Individuals who fail to make the required disclosures are subject to a penalty of $10,000 for the taxable year. An additional penalty may apply if the Secretary notifies an individual by mail of the failure to disclose and the failure to disclose continues. If the failure continues beyond 90 days following the mailing, the penalty increases by $10,000 for each 30 day period (or a fraction thereof), up to a maximum penalty of $50,000 for one taxable period. The computation of the penalty is similar to that applicable to failures to file reports with respect to certain foreign corporations under section 6038. Thus, an individual who is notified of his failure to disclose with respect to a single taxable year under this provision and who takes remedial action on the 95th day after such notice is mailed incurs a penalty of $20,000 comprising the base amount of $10,000, plus $10,000 for the fraction (i.e., the five days) of a 30-day period following the lapse of 90 days after the notice of noncompliance was mailed. An individual who postpones remedial action until the 181st day is subject to the maximum penalty of $50,000: the base amount of $10,000, plus $30,000 for the three 30-day periods, plus $10,000 for the one fraction (i.e., the single day) of a 30-day period following the lapse of 90 days after the notice of noncompliance was mailed.

No penalty is imposed under the provision against an individual who can establish that the failure was due to reasonable cause and not willful neglect. Foreign law prohibitions against disclosure of the required information cannot be relied upon to establish reasonable cause.

To the extent the Secretary determines that the individual has an interest in one or more foreign financial assets but the individual does not provide enough information to enable the Secretary to determine the aggregate value thereof, the aggregate value of such identified foreign financial assets will be presumed to have exceeded $50,000 for purposes of assessing the penalty.

The provision also grants authority to promulgate regulations necessary to carry out the intent. Such regulations may include exceptions for nonresident aliens and classes of assets identified by the Secretary, including those assets which the Secretary determines are subject to reporting requirements under other provisions of the Code. In particular, regulatory exceptions to avoid duplicative reporting requirements are anticipated.

Effective Date

The provision is effective for taxable years beginning after the date of enactment.

[Law at ¶6125. CCH Explanation at ¶310.]

[¶11,090] Act Sec. 512. Penalties for underpayments attributable to undisclosed foreign financial assets

Joint Committee on Taxation (J.C.T. REP. NO. JCX-4-10)

[Code Sec. 6662]

Present Law

The Code imposes penalties equal to 20 percent of the portion of any underpayments that are attributable to any of the following five grounds: (1) negligence or disregard of rules or regulations; (2) any substantial understatement[241] of income tax; (3) any substantial valuation misstatement; (4) any substantial overstatement of pension liabilities; and (5) any substantial estate or gift tax valuation understatement. With the exception of a penalty based on negligence or disregard of rules or regulations, these penalties are commonly referred to as accuracy-related penalties, because the imposition of the penalty does not require an inquiry into the culpability of the taxpayer. If the penalty is asserted, a taxpayer may defend against the penalty by demonstrating that (1) there was "reasonable cause" for the underpayment and (2) the taxpayer acted in good faith.[242] Regulations provide that reasonable cause exists in cases in which the taxpayer "reasonably relies in good faith on the opinion of a professional tax advisor, if the opinion is based on the tax advisor's analysis of the pertinent facts and authorities . . . and unambiguously states that the tax advisor concludes that there is a greater than 50-percent likelihood that the tax treatment of the item will be upheld if challenged" by the IRS.[243]

A penalty for a substantial understatement may be reduced to the extent of the portion of the understatement attributable to an item on the return for which the challenged tax treatment (1) is supported by substantial authority or (2) is adequately disclosed on the return and there was

a reasonable basis for such treatment. The tax treatment is considered to have been adequately disclosed only if all relevant facts are disclosed with the return. Regardless of whether an item would otherwise meet either of these tests, this defense is not available with respect to penalties imposed on understatements arising from tax shelters.[244] The Secretary may prescribe a list of positions which the Secretary believes do not meet the requirements for substantial authority under this provision.

Under present law, failure to comply with the various information reporting requirements generally does not, in itself, determine the amount of the penalty imposed on an underpayment of tax. However, such failure to comply may be relevant to (1) establishing negligence under section 6662 or fraudulent intent,[245] (2) determining whether penalties based on culpability are applicable or (3) determining whether certain defenses are available.

In the context of transactions that are subject to the "reportable transaction" disclosure regime,[246] a separate accuracy-related penalty may apply.[247] That penalty applies to "listed transactions" and other "reportable transactions" that have a significant tax avoidance purpose (a "reportable avoidance transaction"). The penalty rate and defenses available to avoid the section 6662A penalty vary, based on the adequacy of disclosure. In general, a 20-percent accuracy-related penalty is imposed on any understatement attributable to an adequately disclosed listed transaction or reportable avoidance transaction.[248] An exception is available if the taxpayer satisfies a higher standard under the reasonable cause and good faith exception. This higher stan-

---

[241] If the correct income tax liability exceeds that reported by the taxpayer by the greater of 10 percent of the correct tax or $5,000 (or, in the case of corporations, by the lesser of (1) 10 percent of the correct tax (or, if greater, $10,000) or (2) $10 million), then a substantial understatement exists.

[242] Sec. 6664(c).

[243] Treas. Reg. secs. 1.6662-4(g)(4)(i)(B), 1.6664-4(c).

[244] A tax shelter is defined for this purpose as a partnership or other entity, an investment plan or arrangement, or any other plan or arrangement if a significant purpose of such partnership, other entity, plan, or arrangement is the avoidance or evasion of Federal income tax. Sec. 6662(d)(2)(C).

[245] Section 6663 imposes a penalty of 75 percent on that portion of the understatement attributable to fraud. If the

government proves that such understatement was attributable to fraud, there is a rebuttable presumption that any other understatement is attributable to fraud.

[246] Secs. 6011 through 6112 require taxpayers and their advisers to disclose certain transactions determined to have the potential for tax avoidance. All such transactions are referred to as "reportable transactions," and include within that class of transactions, those that are "listed," that is, the subject of published guidance in which the Secretary announces his intent to challenge such transactions.

[247] Sec. 6662A.

[248] Sec. 6662A(a).

dard requires the taxpayer to demonstrate that there was (1) adequate disclosure of the relevant facts affecting the treatment on the taxpayer's return, (2) substantial authority for the treatment on the taxpayer's return, and (3) a reasonable belief that the treatment on the taxpayer's return was more likely than not the proper treatment.[249] If the transaction is not adequately disclosed, the reasonable cause exception is not available and the taxpayer is subject to a penalty equal to 30 percent of the understatement.[250]

Explanation of Provision

The provision adds a new accuracy related penalty to section 6662. The new provision, which is subject to the same defenses as are otherwise available under section 6662, imposes a 40-percent penalty on any understatement attributable to an undisclosed foreign financial asset. The term "undisclosed foreign financial asset" includes all assets subject to certain information reporting requirements[251] for which the required information was not provided by the taxpayer as required under the applicable report-

ing provisions. An understatement is attributable to an undisclosed foreign financial asset if it is attributable to any transaction involving such asset. Thus, a U.S. person who fails to comply with the various self-reporting requirements for a foreign financial asset and engages in a transaction with respect to that asset incurs a penalty on any resulting underpayment that is double the otherwise applicable penalty for substantial understatements or negligence. For example, if a taxpayer fails to disclose amounts held in a foreign financial account, any underpayment of tax related to the transaction that gave rise to the income would be subject to the penalty provision, as would any underpayment related to interest, dividends or other returns accrued on such undisclosed amounts.

Effective Date

The provision is effective for taxable years beginning after the date of enactment.

[Law at ¶ 6170. CCH Explanation at ¶ 315.]

[¶ 11,100] Act Sec. 513. Modification of statute of limitations for significant omission of income in connection with foreign assets

Joint Committee on Taxation (J.C.T. Rep. No. JCX-4-10)

[Code Secs. 6229 and 6501]

Present Law

Taxes are generally required to be assessed within three years after a taxpayer's return was filed, whether or not it was timely filed.[252] Of the exceptions to this general rule, only section 6501(c)(8) is specifically targeted at the identification of, and collection of information about, cross-border transactions. Under this exception, the limitation period for assessment of any tax imposed under the Code with respect to any event or period to which information about certain cross-border transactions required to be reported relates does not expire any earlier than three years after the required information is actually provided to the Secretary by the person

required to file the return.[253] In general, such information reporting is due with the taxpayer's return; thus, the three-year limitation period commences when a timely and complete (including all information reporting) return is filed. Without the inclusion of the information reporting with the return, the limitation period does not commence until such time as the information reports are subsequently provided to the Secretary, even though the return has been filed.

In the case of a false or fraudulent return filed with the intent to evade tax, or if the taxpayer fails to file a required return, the tax may be assessed, or a proceeding in court for collection of such tax may be begun without assessment, at any time.[254] The limitation period also

---

[249] Sec. 6664(d).

[250] Sec. 6662A(c).

[251] The information reporting requirements identified include sections 6038, 6038A, new 6038D, 6046A, and 6048.

[252] Sec. 6501(a). Returns that are filed before the date they are due are deemed filed on the due date. See sec. 6501(b)(1) and (2).

[253] Required information reporting subject to this three-year rule is reporting under sections 6038 (certain foreign

corporations and partnerships), 6038A (certain foreign-owned corporations), 6038B (certain transfers to foreign persons), 6046 (organizations, reorganizations, and acquisitions of stock of foreign corporations), 6046A (interests in foreign partnerships), and 6048 (certain foreign trusts).

[254] Sec. 6501(c).

may be extended by taxpayer consent.[255] If a taxpayer engages in a listed transaction but fails to include any of the information required under section 6011 on any return or statement for a taxable year, the limitation period with respect to such transaction will not expire before the date which is one year after the earlier of (1) the date on which the Secretary is provided the information so required, or (2) the date that a "material advisor" (as defined in section 6111) makes its section 6112(a) list available for inspection pursuant to a request by the Secretary under section 6112(b)(1)(A).[256]

A special rule is provided where there is a substantial omission of income. If a taxpayer omits substantial income on a return, any tax with respect to that return may be assessed and collected within six years of the date on which the return was filed. In the case of income taxes, "substantial" means at least 25 percent of the amount that was properly includible in gross income; for estate and gift taxes, it means 25 percent of a gross estate or total gifts. For this purpose, the gross income of a trade or business means gross receipts, without reduction for the cost of sales or services.[257] An amount is not considered to have been omitted if the item properly includible in income is disclosed on the return.[258]

In addition to the exceptions described, there are also circumstances under which the three-year limitation period is suspended. For example, service of an administrative summons triggers the suspension either (1) beginning six months after service (in the case of John Doe summonses)[259] or (2) when a proceeding to quash a summons is initiated by a taxpayer named in a summons to a third-party record-keeper. Judicial proceedings initiated by the government to enforce a summons generally do not suspend the limitation period.

Explanation of Provision

The provision authorizes a new six-year limitations period for assessment of tax on understatements of income attributable to foreign financial assets. The present exception that provides a six-year period for substantial omission of an amount equal to 25 percent of the gross income reported on the return is not changed.

The new exception applies if there is an omission of gross income in excess of $5,000 and the omitted gross income is attributable to an asset with respect to which information reports are required under section 6038D, as applied without regard to the dollar threshold, the statutory exception for nonresident aliens and any exceptions provided by regulation. If a domestic entity is formed or availed of to hold foreign financial assets and is subject to the reporting requirements of section 6038D in the same manner as an individual, the six-year limitations period may also apply to that entity. The Secretary is permitted to assess the resulting deficiency at any time within six years of the filing of the income tax return.

In providing that the applicability of section 6038D information reporting requirements is to be determined without regard to the statutory or regulatory exceptions, the statute ensures that the longer limitation period applies to omissions of income with respect to transactions involving foreign assets owned by individuals. Thus, a regulatory provision that alleviates duplicative reporting obligations by providing that a report that complies with another provision of the Code may satisfy one's obligations under new section 6038D does not change the nature of the asset subject to reporting. The asset remains one that is subject to the requirements of section 6038D for purposes of determining whether the exception to the three-year statute of limitations applies.

The provision also suspends the limitations period for assessment if a taxpayer fails to provide timely information returns required with respect to passive foreign investment corporations[260] and the new self-reporting of foreign financial assets. The limitations period will not begin to run until the information required by those provisions has been furnished to the Secretary. The provision also clarifies that the extension is not limited to adjustments to income related to the information required to be reported by one of the enumerated sections.

Effective Date

The provision applies to returns filed after the date of enactment as well as for any other return for which the assessment period specified in section 6501 has not yet expired as of the date of enactment.

[Law at ¶6135 and ¶6155. CCH Explanation at ¶320.]

---

[255] Sec. 6501(c)(4).

[256] Sec. 6501(c)(10).

[257] Sec. 6501(e)(1)(A)(i).

[258] Sec. 6501(e)(1)(A)(ii) provides that, in determining whether an amount was omitted, any amounts that are disclosed in the return or in a statement attached to the return in a manner adequate to apprise the Secretary of the nature and amount of such item are not taken into account.

[259] Sec. 7609(e)(2).

[260] Sec. 1295(b), (f).

[¶11,110] Act Sec. 521. Reporting of activities with respect to passive foreign investment companies

Joint Committee on Taxation (J.C.T. REP. NO. JCX-4-10)

[Code Sec. 1298]

Present Law

In general, active foreign business income derived by a foreign corporation with U.S. owners is not subject to current U.S. taxation until the corporation makes a dividend distribution to those owners. Certain rules, however, restrict the benefit of deferral of U.S. tax on income derived through foreign corporations. One such regime applies to U.S. persons who own stock of passive foreign investment companies ("PFICs"). A PFIC generally is defined as any foreign corporation if 75 percent or more of its gross income for the taxable year consists of passive income, or 50 percent or more of its assets consist of assets that produce, or are held for the production of, passive income.[261] Various sets of income inclusion rules apply to U.S. persons that are shareholders in a PFIC, regardless of their percentage ownership in the company. One set of rules applies to PFICs under which U.S. shareholders pay tax on certain income or gain realized through the companies, plus an interest charge intended to eliminate the benefit of deferral.[262] A second set of rules applies to PFICs that are "qualified electing funds" ("QEF"), under which electing U.S. shareholders currently include in gross income their respective shares of the company's earnings, with a separate election to defer payment of tax, subject to an interest charge, on income not currently received.[263] A third set of rules applies to marketable PFIC stock, under which electing U.S. shareholders currently take into account as income (or loss) the difference between the fair market value of the stock as of the close of the taxable year and their adjusted basis in such stock (subject to certain limitations), often referred to as "marking to market."[264]

In general, a U.S. person that is a direct or indirect shareholder of a PFIC must file IRS Form 8621, "Return by a Shareholder of a Passive Foreign Investment Company or Qualifying Electing Fund" for each tax year in which that U.S. person (1) recognizes gain on a direct or indirect disposition of PFIC stock, (2) receives certain direct or indirect distributions from a PFIC, or (3) is making a reportable election.[265] The Code includes a general reporting requirement for certain PFIC shareholders which is contingent upon the issuance of regulations.[266] Although Treasury issued proposed regulations in 1992 requiring U.S. persons to file annually Form 8621 for each PFIC of which the person is a shareholder during the taxable year, such regulations have not been finalized and current IRS Form 8621 requires reporting only based on one of the triggering events described above.[267]

Explanation of Provision

The provision requires that, unless otherwise provided by the Secretary, each U.S. person who is a shareholder of a PFIC must file an annual information return containing such information as the Secretary may require. A person that meets the reporting requirements of this provision may, however, also meet the reporting requirements of section 511 of the bill and new section 6038D of the Code requiring disclosure of information with respect to foreign financial assets. It is anticipated that the Secretary will exercise regulatory authority under this provision or new section 6038D to avoid duplicative reporting.

Effective Date

The provision is effective on the date of enactment.

[Law at ¶6075 and ¶6080. CCH Explanation at ¶325.]

---

[261] Sec. 1297.

[262] Sec. 1291.

[263] Secs. 1293-1295.

[264] Sec. 1296.

[265] See Instructions to IRS Form 8621. According to the form, reportable elections include the following: (i) an election to treat the PFIC as a QEF; (ii) an election to recognize gain on the deemed sale of a PFIC interest on the first day of the PFIC's tax year as a QEF; (iii) an election to treat an amount equal to the shareholder's post-1986 earnings and profits of a CFC as an excess distribution on the first day of a PFIC's tax year as a QEF that is also a controlled foreign

corporation under section 957(a); (iv) an election to extend the time for payment of the shareholder's tax on the undistributed earnings and profits of a QEF; (v) an election to treat as an excess distribution the gain recognized on the deemed sale of the shareholder's interest in the PFIC, or to treat such shareholder's share of the PFIC's post-1986 earnings and profits as an excess distribution, on the last day of its last tax year as a PFIC under section 1297(a) if eligible; or (vi) an election to mark-to-market the PFIC stock that is marketable within the meaning of section 1296(e).

[266] Sec. 1291(e) by reference to sec. 1246(f).

[267] Prop. Treas. Reg. sec. 1.1291-1(i).

[¶11,120] Act Sec. 522. Secretary permitted to require financial institutions to file certain returns related to withholding on foreign transfers electronically

Joint Committee on Taxation (J.C.T. Rep. No. JCX-4-10)

[Code Sec. 6011]

Present Law

Withholding responsibility

A withholding agent is any person required to withhold U.S. income tax under sections 1441, 1442, 1443, or 1461. For purposes of these sections, a withholding agent is any person, whether a U.S. or a foreign person, that has the control, receipt, custody, disposal, or payment of an item of income of a foreign person subject to withholding.[268] A withholding agent is personally liable for the tax required to be withheld.[269]

Reporting liability of a withholding agent

Every withholding agent must file an annual return with the IRS on Form 1042, "Annual Withholding Tax Return for U.S. Source Income of Foreign Persons," reporting all taxes withheld during the preceding year and remitting any taxes still owing for such preceding year.[270] IRS Form 1042 must be filed on or before March 15 of the year following the year of the payment. The form must be filled even though no tax has been withheld from income paid during the year.[271] A withholding agent must also file an information return, IRS Form 1042-S, which is entitled "Foreign Person's U.S. Source Income Subject to Withholding," on or before March 15 of the year succeeding the year of payment. IRS Form 1042-S requires the withholding agent to provide all items of income specified in section 1441(b) paid during the previous year to foreign persons.[272] IRS Form 1042-S must be filed for each

foreign recipient to whom payments were made during the preceding year,[273] even if no tax was required to have been withheld. A copy of IRS Form 1042-S must be sent to the payee.

IRS's authority to require electronic filing

The Internal Revenue Service Restructuring and Reform Act of 1998 ("RRA 1998")[274] states that it is a congressional policy to promote the paperless filing of Federal tax returns. Section 2001(a) of RRA 1998 set a goal for the IRS to have at least 80 percent of all Federal tax and information returns filed electronically by 2007. Section 2001(b) of RRA 1998 requires the IRS to establish a 10-year strategic plan to eliminate barriers to electronic filing.

The Secretary has limited authority to issue regulations specifying which returns must be filed electronically. First, in general, such regulations can only apply to persons required to file at least 250 returns during the year.[275] Second, the Secretary is prohibited from requiring that income tax returns of individuals, estates, and trusts be submitted in any format other than paper (although these returns may be filed electronically by choice). Third, the Secretary, in determining which returns must be filed on magnetic media, must take into account relevant factors, including the ability of a taxpayer to comply with magnetic media filing at reasonable cost.[276] Finally, a failure to comply with the regulations mandating electronic filing cannot in itself support a penalty for failure to file an

---

[268] Treas. Reg. sec. 1.1441-7(a)(1).

[269] Sec. 1461.

[270] Treas. Reg. sec.1.1461-1(b)(1).

[271] Ibid.

[272] Treas. Reg. sec. 1.1461-1(c)(1). IRS Form 1042-S filings provide information important for the Secretary's purposes in properly effecting refund claims and in meeting IRS's obligations under exchange of information agreements with various treaty partners. Also, the IRS has the ability to validate electronically filed Form 1042-S upon such filing, thereby serving to better ensure the reliability of information included in such filings.

[273] Ibid. If payments are made to a nominee or representative of a foreign payee, Form 1042-S must also be sent to

the beneficial owner of such payments, if known to the withholding agent.

[274] Pub. L. No. 105-206 (1998).

[275] Partnerships with more than 100 partners are required to file electronically. Sec. 6011(e)(2). For returns filed after 12/31/2010, under the recently enacted Worker, Homeownership, and Business Act of 2009, any individual tax return, including any return of the tax imposed by subtitle A on individuals, estates, or trusts, prepared by a tax return preparer, is required to be filed electronically unless the tax return preparer reasonably expects to file ten or fewer tax returns during such calendar year. Sec. 6011(e)(3).

[276] Sec. 6011(e).

information return, with certain exceptions for corporations and partnerships.[277]

Accordingly, the Secretary requires corporations and tax-exempt organizations that have assets of $10 million or more and file at least 250 returns during a calendar year, including income tax, information, excise tax, and employment tax returns, to file electronically their Form IRS 1120/1120-S income tax returns and IRS Form 990 information returns for tax years ending on or after December 31, 2006. Private foundations and charitable trusts that file at least 250 returns during a calendar year are required to file electronically their IRS Form 990-PF information returns for tax years ending on or after December 31, 2006, regardless of their asset size. Taxpayers can request waivers of the electronic filing requirement if they cannot meet that requirement due to technological constraints, or if compliance with the requirement would result in undue financial burden.

Explanation of Provision

The provision provides an exception to the general annual 250 returns threshold and per-

mits the Secretary to issue regulations to require filing on magnetic media for any return filed by a "financial institution"[278] with respect to any taxes withheld by the "financial institution" for which it is personally liable.[279] Under the provision, the Secretary is authorized to require a financial institution to electronically file returns with respect to any taxes withheld by the financial institution even though such financial institution would be required to file less than 250 returns during the year.

The provision also makes a conforming amendment to section 6724, permitting assertion of a failure to file penalty under section 6721 against a financial institution that fails to comply with the electronic filing requirements.

Effective Date

The provision applies to returns the due date for which (determined without regard to extensions) is after the date of enactment.

[Law at ¶ 6120 and ¶ 6185. CCH Explanation at ¶ 330.]

[¶ 11,130] Act Sec. 531. Clarifications with respect to foreign trusts which are treated as having a United States beneficiary

Joint Committee on Taxation (J.C.T. Rep. No. JCX-4-10)

[Code Sec. 679]

Present Law

Under the grantor trust rules, a U.S. person that directly or indirectly transfers property to a foreign trust[280] is generally treated as the owner of the portion of the trust comprising the transferred property for any taxable year in which there is a U.S. beneficiary of any portion of the trust.[281] This treatment generally does not apply to transfers by reason of death, or to transfers of property to the trust in exchange for at least the fair market value of the transferred property.[282] A trust is treated as having a U.S. beneficiary for

the taxable year unless (1) under the terms of the trust, no part of the income or corpus of the trust may be paid or accumulated during the taxable year to or for the benefit of a U.S. person, and (2) if the trust were terminated at any time during the taxable year, no part of the income or corpus of the trust could be paid to or for the benefit of a U.S. person.[283]

Regulations under section 679 employ a broad approach in determining whether a foreign trust is treated as having a U.S. beneficiary. The determination of whether the trust has a U.S. beneficiary is made for each taxable year of

---

[277] Sec. 6724(c). If a corporation fails to comply with the electronic filing requirements for more than 250 returns that it is required to file, it may be subject to the penalty for failure to file information returns under section 6721. For partnerships, the penalty may only be imposed if the failure extends to more than 100 returns.

[278] See section 1471(d)(5) in section 101 of the bill.

[279] The "financial institution" is personally liable for any tax withheld in accordance with section 1461 and the proposed section 1474(a) under section 101 of the bill.

[280] A trust is a foreign trust if it is not a U.S. person. Sec. 7701(a)(31)(B). A trust is a U.S. person if (1) a U.S. court is

able to exercise primary supervision over the administration of the trust, and (2) one or more U.S. persons have the authority to control all substantial decisions of the trust. Sec. 7701(a)(30)(E).

[281] Sec. 679(a)(1). This rule does not apply to transfers to trusts established to fund certain deferred compensation plan trusts or to trusts exempt from tax under section 501(c)(3).

[282] Sec. 679(a)(2).

[283] Sec. 679(c)(1).

the transferor. The default rule under the statute and regulations is that a trust has a U.S. beneficiary unless during the U.S. transferor's taxable year the trust meets the two requirements as stated above. Income or corpus may be paid or accumulated to or for the benefit of a U.S. person if, directly or indirectly, income may be distributed to or accumulated for the benefit of a U.S. person, or corpus of the trust may be distributed to or held for the future benefit of a U.S. person.[284] The determination is made without regard to whether income or corpus is actually distributed, and without regard to whether a U.S. person's interest in the trust income or corpus is contingent on a future event. A person who is not a named beneficiary and is not a member of a class of beneficiaries will not be taken into account if the transferor can show that the person's contingent interest in the trust is so remote as to be negligible.[285] In considering whether a foreign trust has a U.S. beneficiary under the terms of the trust, the trust instrument must be read together with other relevant factors including (1) all written and oral agreements and understandings related to the trust, (2) memoranda or letters of wishes, (3) all records that relate to the actual distribution of income and corpus, and (4) all other documents that relate to the trust, whether or not of any purported legal effect.[286] Other factors taken into account in determining whether a foreign trust is deemed to have a U.S. beneficiary include whether (1) the terms of the trust allow the trust to be amended to benefit a U.S. person, (2) the trust instrument does not allow such an amendment, but the law applicable to the foreign trust may require payments or accumulations of income or corpus to a U.S. person, or (3) the parties to the trust ignore the terms of the trust, or it reasonably expected that they will do so to benefit a U.S. person.[287]

If a foreign trust that was not treated as a grantor trust acquires a U.S. beneficiary and is treated as a grantor trust under section 679 for the taxable year, the transferor is taxable on the trust's undistributed net income[288] computed at the end of the preceding taxable year.[289] Any additional amount included in the transferor's gross income as a result of this provision is subject to the interest charge rules of section 668.[290]

Explanation of Provision

In determining whether, under section 679, a foreign trust has a U.S. beneficiary, the provision clarifies that an amount is treated as accumulated for the benefit of a U.S. person even if the U.S. person's interest in the trust is contingent on a future event. Under the provision, if any person has the discretion (by authority given in the trust agreement, by power of appointment, or otherwise) to make a distribution from the trust to, or for the benefit of, any person, the trust is treated as having a U.S. beneficiary unless (1) the terms of the trust specifically identify the class of persons to whom such distributions may be made, and (2) none of those persons is a U.S. person during the taxable year. The provision is meant to be consistent with existing regulations under section 679.

The provision clarifies that if any U.S. person who directly or indirectly transfers property to the trust is directly or indirectly involved in any agreement or understanding (whether written, oral, or otherwise) that may result in the income or corpus of the trust being paid or accumulated to or for the benefit of a U.S. person, such agreement or understanding is treated as a term of the trust. It is assumed for these purposes that a transferor of property to the trust is generally directly or indirectly involved with agreements regarding the accumulation or disposition of the income and corpus of the trust.

Effective Date

The provision is effective on the date of enactment.

[Law at ¶6050. CCH Explanation at ¶335.]

---

[284] Treas. Reg. sec. 1.679-2(a)(2)(i).
[285] Treas. Reg. sec. 1.679-2(a)(2)(ii).
[286] Treas. Reg. sec. 1.679-2(a)(4)(i).
[287] Treas. Reg. sec. 1.679-2(a)(4)(ii).

[288] Undistributed net income is defined in section 665(a).
[289] Sec. 679(b).
[290] Treas. Reg. sec. 1.679-2(c)(1).

[¶11,140] Act Sec. 532. Presumption that foreign trust has United States beneficiary

Joint Committee on Taxation (J.C.T. REP. NO. JCX-4-10)

[Code Sec. 679]

Present Law

Under the grantor trust rules, a U.S. person that directly or indirectly transfers property to a foreign trust[291] is generally treated as the owner of the portion of the trust comprising that property for any taxable year in which there is a U.S. beneficiary of any portion of the trust.[292] This treatment generally does not apply to transfers by reason of death, or to transfers of property to the trust in exchange for at least the fair market value of the transferred property.[293] A trust is treated as having a U.S. beneficiary for the taxable year unless (1) under the terms of the trust, no part of the income or corpus of the trust may be paid or accumulated during the taxable year to or for the benefit of a U.S. person, and (2) if the trust were terminated at any time during the taxable year, no part of the income or corpus of the trust could be paid to or for the benefit of a U.S. person.[294]

Section 6048 imposes various reporting obligations on foreign trusts and persons creating, making transfers to, or receiving distributions

from such trusts. Within 90 days after a U.S. person transfers property to a foreign trust, the transferor must provide written notice of the transfer to the Secretary.[295]

Explanation of Provision

Under the provision, if a U.S. person directly or indirectly transfers property to a foreign trust,[296] the Secretary may treat the trust as having a U.S. beneficiary for purposes of section 679 unless such U.S. person submits information as required by the Secretary and demonstrates to the satisfaction of the Secretary that (1) under the terms of the trust, no part of the income or corpus of the trust may be paid or accumulated during the taxable year to or for the benefit of a U.S. person, and (2) if the trust were terminated during the taxable year, no part of the income or corpus of the trust could be paid to or for the benefit of a U.S. person.

Effective Date

The provision applies to transfers of property after the date of enactment.

[Law at ¶6050. CCH Explanation at ¶335.]

[¶11,150] Act Sec. 533. Uncompensated use of trust property

Joint Committee on Taxation (J.C.T. REP. NO. JCX-4-10)

[Code Secs. 643 and 679]

Present Law

Under section 643(i), a loan of cash or marketable securities made by a foreign trust to any U.S. grantor, U.S. beneficiary, or any other U.S. person who is related to a U.S. grantor or U.S. beneficiary generally is treated as a distribution by the foreign trust to such grantor or beneficiary. This rule applies for purposes of determining if the foreign trust is a simple or complex

trust, computing the distribution deduction for the trust, determining the amount of gross income of the beneficiaries, and computing any accumulation distribution. Loans to tax-exempt entities are excluded from this rule.[297] A trust treated under this rule as making a distribution is not treated as a simple trust for the year of the distribution.[298] This rule does not apply for purposes of determining if a trust has a U.S. beneficiary under section 679.

---

[291] A trust is a foreign trust if it is not a U.S. person. Sec. 7701(a)(31)(B). A trust is a U.S. person if (1) a U.S. court is able to exercise primary supervision over the administration of the trust and (2) one or more U.S. persons have the authority to control all substantial decisions of the trust. Sec. 7701(a)(30)(E).

[292] Sec. 679(a)(1). This rule does not apply to transfers to trusts established to fund certain deferred compensation plan trusts or to trusts exempt from tax under section 501(c)(3).

[293] Sec. 679(a)(2).

[294] Sec. 679(c)(1).

[295] Sec. 6048(a).

[296] A foreign trust for this purpose does not include deferred compensation and charitable trusts described in section 6048(a)(3)(B)(ii).

[297] Sec. 643(i)(2)(C).

[298] Sec. 643(i)(2)(D).

A subsequent repayment, satisfaction, or cancellation of a loan treated as a distribution under section 643(i) is disregarded for tax purposes.[299] This section applies a broad set of related party rules that treat a loan of cash or marketable securities to a spouse, sibling, ancestor, descendant of the grantor or beneficiary, other trusts in which the grantor or beneficiary has an interest, and corporations or partnerships controlled by the beneficiary or grantor or by family members of the beneficiary or grantor, as a distribution to the related grantor or beneficiary.[300]

Explanation of Provision

The provision expands section 643(i) to provide that any use of trust property by the U.S. grantor, U.S. beneficiary or any U.S. person related to a U.S. grantor or U.S. beneficiary is treated as a distribution of the fair market value of the use of the property to the U.S. grantor or U.S. beneficiary. The use of property is not treated as a distribution to the extent that the trust is paid the fair market value for the use of the property within a reasonable period of time. A subsequent return of property treated as a distribution under section 643(i) is disregarded for tax purposes.

For purposes of determining whether a foreign trust has a U.S. beneficiary under section 679, a loan of cash or marketable securities or the use of any other trust property by a U.S. person is treated as a payment from the trust to the U.S. person in the amount of the loan or the fair market value of the use of the property. A loan or use of property is not treated as a payment to the extent that the U.S. person repays the loan at a market rate of interest or pays the fair market value for the use of the trust property within a reasonable period of time.

Effective Date

The provision applies to loans made and uses of property after the date of enactment.

[Law at ¶ 6045 and ¶ 6050. CCH Explanation at ¶ 340.]

[¶ 11,160] Act Sec. 534. Reporting requirement of United States owners of foreign trusts

Joint Committee on Taxation (J.C.T. REP. NO. JCX-4-10)

[Code Sec. 6048]

Present Law

Section 6048 imposes various reporting obligations on foreign trusts and persons creating, making transfers to, or receiving distributions from such trusts. If a U.S. person is treated as the owner of any portion of a foreign trust under the rules of subpart E of part I of subchapter J of chapter 1 (grantor trust provisions), the U.S. person is responsible for ensuring that the trust files an information return for the year and that the trust provides other information as the Secretary may require to each U.S. person who (1) is treated as the owner of any portion of the trust, or (2) receives (directly or indirectly) any distribution from the trust.[301]

Explanation of Provision

The provision requires a U.S. person that is treated as an owner of any portion of a foreign trust under the rules of subpart E of part I of subchapter J of chapter 1 (grantor trust provisions) to provide information as the Secretary may require with respect to the trust, in addition to ensuring that the trust complies with its reporting obligations.

Effective Date

The provision applies to taxable years beginning after the date of enactment.

[Law at ¶ 6130. CCH Explanation at ¶ 345.]

---

[299] Sec. 643(i)(3).

[300] Section 643(i)(2)(B) treats a person as a related person if the relationship between such person would result in a disallowance of losses under sections 267 or 707(b), broad-ened to include the spouses of members of the family described in such sections.

[301] Sec. 6048(b)(1).

[¶11,170] Act Sec. 535. Minimum penalty with respect to failure to report on certain foreign trusts

Joint Committee on Taxation (J.C.T. REP. NO. JCX-4-10)

[Code Sec. 6677]

Present Law

Minimum penalty with respect to failure to report on certain foreign trusts

Section 6048 imposes various reporting obligations on foreign trusts and persons creating, making transfers to, or receiving distributions from such trusts. Generally, a trust is a foreign trust unless a U.S. court is able to exercise primary supervision over the trust's administration and a U.S. trustee has authority to control all substantial decisions of the trust.[302] If a U.S. person creates or transfers property to a foreign trust, the U.S. person generally must report this event and certain other information by the due date for the U.S. person's tax return, including extensions, for the tax year in which the creation of the trust or the transfer occurs.[303] Similar rules apply in the case of the death of a U.S. citizen or resident if the decedent was treated as the owner of any portion of a foreign trust under the grantor trust rules or if any portion of a foreign trust was included in the decedent's gross estate. If a U.S. person directly or indirectly receives a distribution from a foreign trust, the U.S. person generally must report the distribution by the due date for the U.S. person's tax return, including extensions, for the tax year during which the distribution is received.[304] If a U.S. person is the owner of any portion of a foreign grantor trust at any time during the year, the person is responsible for causing an information return to be filed for the trust, which must, among other things, give the name of a U.S. agent for the trust.[305]

If a notice or return required under the rules just described is not filed when due or is filed without all required information, the person required to file is generally subject to a penalty based on the "gross reportable amount."[306] The gross reportable amount is (1) the value of property transferred to the foreign trust if the delinquency is failure to file notice of the creation of or a transfer to a foreign trust; (2) the value (on the last day of the year) of the portion of a grantor trust owned by a U.S. person who fails to cause an annual return to be filed for the trust; and (3) the amount distributed to a distributee who fails to report distributions.[307] The initial penalty is 35 percent of the gross reportable amount in cases (1) and (3) and five percent in case (2).[308] If the return is more than 90 days late, additional penalties are imposed of $10,000 for every 30 days the delinquency continues, except that the aggregate of the penalties may not exceed the gross reportable amount.[309]

Maximum penalty with respect to failure to report on certain foreign trusts

In no event may the penalties imposed with respect to any failure to report under section 6048 exceed the gross reportable amount.[310]

Explanation of Provision

Increase of the minimum penalty with respect to failure to report on certain foreign trusts

Under the provision, the initial penalty for failing to report under section 6048 is the greater of $10,000 or 35 percent of the gross reportable amount in cases (1) and (3) and the greater of $10,000 or five percent of the gross reportable amount in case (2). Thus, an initial penalty of $10,000 may be imposed even where the Secretary has insufficient information to determine the gross reportable amount. The additional $10,000 penalty for every additional 30 days of delinquency continues to apply.

Amendment to the maximum penalty with respect to failure to report on certain foreign trusts

The provision provides that the penalties with respect to failure to report on certain foreign trusts may exceed the gross reportable amount. However, to the extent that a taxpayer provides sufficient information for the Secretary to determine that the aggregate amount of the penalties exceeds the gross reportable amount,

---

[302] Sec. 7701(a)(30)(E), (31)(B). In addition, for purposes of section 6048, the IRS can classify a trust as foreign if it "has substantial activities, or holds substantial property, outside the United States." Sec. 6048(d)(2).

[303] Sec. 6048(a).

[304] Sec. 6048(c).

[305] Sec. 6048(b).

[306] Sec. 6677(a).

[307] Sec. 6677(c).

[308] Sec. 6677(b).

[309] Sec. 6677(a).

[310] Ibid.

the Secretary is required to refund such excess to the taxpayer.

[Law at ¶ 6175. CCH Explanation at ¶ 350.]

Effective Date

The provision applies to notices and returns required to be filed after December 31, 2009.

[¶ 11,180] Act Sec. 541. Substitute dividends and dividend equivalent payments received by foreign persons treated as dividends

Joint Committee on Taxation (J.C.T. Rep. No. JCX-4-10)

[Code Sec. 871]

Present Law

Payments of U.S.-source "fixed or determinable annual or periodical" income, including interest, dividends, and similar types of investment income, made to foreign persons are generally subject to U.S. tax, collected by withholding, at a 30-percent rate, unless the withholding agent can establish that the beneficial owner of the amount is eligible for an exemption from withholding or a reduced rate of withholding under an income tax treaty.[311] Dividends paid by a domestic corporation are generally U.S.-source[312] and therefore potentially subject to withholding tax when paid to foreign persons.

The source of notional principal contract income generally is determined by reference to the residence of the recipient of the income.[313] Consequently, a foreign person's income related to a notional principal contract that references stock of a domestic corporation, including any amount attributable to, or calculated by reference to, dividends paid on the stock, generally is foreign source and is therefore not subject to U.S. withholding tax.

In contrast, a substitute dividend payment made to the transferor of stock in a securities lending transaction or a sale-repurchase transaction is sourced in the same manner as actual dividends paid on the transferred stock.[314] Accordingly, because dividends paid with respect to the stock of a U.S. company are generally U.S. source, if a foreign person lends stock of a U.S. company to another person (or sells the stock to the other person and later repurchases the stock in a transaction treated as a loan for U.S. federal income tax purposes) and receives substitute dividend payments from that other person, the substitute dividend payments are U.S. source and are generally subject to U.S. withholding tax.[315] In 1997, the Treasury and IRS issued Notice 97-66 to address concerns that the sourcing rule just described (and the accompanying character rule) could cause the total U.S. withholding tax imposed in a series of securities lending or sale-repurchase transactions to be excessive.[316] In that Notice, the Treasury and IRS also stated that they intended to propose new regulations to provide detailed guidance on how substitute dividend payments made by one foreign person

---

[311] Secs. 871, 881, 1441, 1442; Treas. Reg. sec. 1.1441-1(b). For purposes of the withholding tax rules applicable to payments to nonresident alien individuals and foreign corporations, a withholding agent is defined broadly to include any U.S. or foreign person that has the control, receipt, custody, disposal, or payment of an item of income of a foreign person subject to withholding. Treas. Reg. sec. 1.1441-7(a).

[312] Sec. 861(a)(2).

[313] Treas. Reg. sec. 1.863-7(b)(1). A notional principal contract is a financial instrument that provides for the payment of amounts by one party to another at specified intervals calculated by reference to a specified index upon a notional principal amount in exchange for specified consideration or a promise to pay similar amounts. Treas. Reg. sec. 1.446-3(c)(1).

[314] Treas. Reg. sec. 1.861-3(a)(6). This regulation defines a substitute dividend payment as a payment, made to the transferor of a security in a securities lending transaction or a sale-repurchase transaction, of an amount equivalent to a dividend distribution which the owner of the transferred security is entitled to receive during the term of the transaction.

[315] For purposes of the imposition of the 30-percent withholding tax, substitute dividend payments (and substitute interest payments) received by a foreign person under a securities lending or sale-repurchase transaction have the same character as dividend (and interest) income received in respect of the transferred security. Treas. Reg. secs. 1.871-7(b)(2), 1.881-2(b)(2).

[316] Notice 97-66, 1997-2 C.B. 328 (December 1, 1997).

to another foreign person were to be treated. To date, no regulations have been proposed.[317]

Explanation of Provision

The provision treats a dividend equivalent as a dividend from U.S. sources for certain purposes, including the U.S. withholding tax rules applicable to foreign persons.

A dividend equivalent is any substitute dividend made pursuant to a securities lending or a sale-repurchase transaction that (directly or indirectly) is contingent upon, or determined by reference to, the payment of a dividend from sources within the United States or any payment made under a specified notional principal contract that directly or indirectly is contingent upon, or determined by reference to, the payment of a dividend from sources within the United States. A dividend equivalent also includes any other payment that the Secretary determines is substantially similar to a payment described in the immediately preceding sentence. Under this rule, for example, the Secretary may conclude that payments under certain forward contracts or other financial contracts that reference stock of U.S. corporations are dividend equivalents.

A specified notional principal contract is any notional principal contract that has any one of the following five characteristics: (1) in connection with entering into the contract, any long party to the contract transfers the underlying security to any short party to the contract; (2) in connection with the termination of the contract, any short party to the contract transfers the underlying security to any long party to the contract; (3) the underlying security is not readily tradable on an established securities market; (4) in connection with entering into the contract, any short party to the contract posts the underlying security as collateral with any long party to the contract; or (5) the Secretary identifies the contract as a specified notional principal contract.[318] For purposes of these characteristics, for any underlying security of any notional principal contract (1) a long party is any party to the contract that is entitled to receive any payment under the contract that is contingent upon or determined by reference to the payment of a

U.S.-source dividend on the underlying security, and (2) a short party is any party to the contract that is not a long party in respect of the underlying security. An underlying security in a notional principal contract is the security with respect to which the dividend equivalent is paid. For these purposes, any index or fixed basket of securities is treated as a single security. In applying this rule, it is intended that such a security will be deemed to be regularly traded on an established securities market if every component of such index or fixed basket is a security that is readily tradable on an established securities market.

For payments made more than two years after the provision's date of enactment, a specified notional principal contract also includes any notional principal contract unless the Secretary determines that the contract is of a type that does not have the potential for tax avoidance.

No inference is intended as to whether the definition of specified notional principal contract, or any determination under this provision that a transaction does not have the potential for the avoidance of taxes on U.S.-source dividends (or, in the case of a debt instrument, U.S.-source interest), is relevant in determining whether an agency relationship exists under general tax principles or whether a foreign party to a contract should be treated as having beneficial tax ownership of the stock giving rise to U.S.-source dividends.

The payments that are treated as U.S.-source dividends under the provision are the gross amounts that are used in computing any net amounts transferred to or from the taxpayer. The example of a "total return swap" referencing stock of a domestic corporation (an example of a notional principal contract to which the provision generally applies), illustrates the consequences of this rule. Under a typical total return swap, a foreign investor enters into an agreement with a counterparty under which amounts due to each party are based on the returns generated by a notional investment in a specified dollar amount of the stock underlying the swap. The investor agrees for a specified period to pay to the counterparty (1) an amount calculated by

---

[317] There is evidence that some taxpayers have taken the position that Notice 97-66 sanctions the elimination of withholding tax in certain situations. See United States Senate, Permanent Subcommittee on Investigations, Committee on Homeland Security and Governmental Affairs, *Dividend Tax Abuse: How Offshore Entities Dodge Taxes on U.S. Stock Dividends*, Staff Report, September 11, 2008, pp. 18-20, 22-23, 40, 47, 52. In the Obama administration's fiscal year 2010 budget, the Treasury Department has announced that, to address the avoidance of U.S. withholding tax through the use of securities lending transactions, it plans to revoke

Notice 97-66 and issue guidance that eliminates the benefits of those transactions but minimizes over-withholding. Department of the Treasury, General Explanations of the Administration's Fiscal Year 2010 Revenue Proposals, May 2009, p. 37.

[318] Any notional principal contract identified by the Secretary as a specified notional principal contract will be subject to the provision's general effective date described below.

reference to a market interest rate (such as the London Interbank Offered Rate ("LIBOR")) on the notional amount of the underlying stock and (2) any depreciation in the value of the stock. In return, the counterparty agrees for the specified period to pay the investor (1) any dividends paid on the stock and (2) any appreciation in the value of the stock. Amounts owed by each party under this swap typically are netted so that only one party makes an actual payment. The provision treats any dividend-based amount under the swap as a payment even though any actual payment under the swap is a net amount determined in part by other amounts (for example, the interest amount and the amount of any appreciation or depreciation in value of the referenced stock). Accordingly, a counterparty to a total return swap may be obligated to withhold and remit tax on the gross amount of a dividend equivalent even though, as a result of a netting of payments due under the swap, the counterparty is not required to make an actual payment to the foreign investor.

If there is a chain of dividend equivalents (under, for example, transactions similar to those described in Notice 97-66), and one or more of the dividend equivalents is subject to tax under the provision or under section 881, the Secretary may reduce that tax, but only to the extent that the taxpayer either establishes that the tax has been paid on another dividend equivalent in the chain, or that such tax is not otherwise due, or as the Secretary determines is appropriate to address the role of financial intermediaries in such chain. An actual dividend is treated as a dividend equivalent for purposes of this rule.

For purposes of chapter 3 (withholding of tax on nonresident aliens and foreign corporations) and chapter 4 (taxes to enforce reporting on certain foreign accounts), each person that is a party to a contract or other arrangement that provides for the payment of a dividend equivalent is treated as having control of the payment. Accordingly, Treasury may provide guidance requiring either party to withhold tax on dividend equivalents.

The rule treating dividend equivalents as U.S.-source dividends is not intended to limit the authority of the Secretary (1) to determine the appropriate source of income from financial arrangements (including notional principal contracts) under present law section 863 or 865 or (2) to provide additional guidance addressing the source and characterization of substitute payments made in securities lending and similar transactions.

Effective Date

The provision applies to payments made on or after the date that is 180 days after the date of enactment.

[Law at ¶ 6060. CCH Explanation at ¶ 355.]

[¶11,190] Act Sec. 551. Delay in application of worldwide allocation of interest

Joint Committee on Taxation (J.C.T. Rep. No. JCX-4-10)

[Code Sec. 864(f)]

Present Law

In general

To compute the foreign tax credit limitation, a taxpayer must determine the amount of its taxable income from foreign sources. Thus, the taxpayer must allocate and apportion deductions between items of U.S.-source gross income, on the one hand, and items of foreign-source gross income, on the other.

In the case of interest expense, the rules generally are based on the approach that money is fungible and that interest expense is properly attributable to all business activities and property of a taxpayer, regardless of any specific purpose for incurring an obligation on which interest is paid.[319] For interest allocation purposes, all members of an affiliated group of corporations generally are treated as a single corporation (the so-called "one-taxpayer rule") and allocation must be made on the basis of assets rather than gross income. The term "affiliated group" in this context generally is defined by reference to the rules for determining whether corporations are eligible to file consolidated returns.

For consolidation purposes, the term "affiliated group" means one or more chains of includible corporations connected through stock ownership with a common parent corporation that is an includible corporation, but only if: (1)

---

[319] However, exceptions to the fungibility principle are provided in particular cases, some of which are described below.

the common parent owns directly stock possessing at least 80 percent of the total voting power and at least 80 percent of the total value of at least one other includible corporation; and (2) stock meeting the same voting power and value standards with respect to each includible corporation (excluding the common parent) is directly owned by one or more other includible corporations.

Generally, the term "includible corporation" means any domestic corporation except certain corporations exempt from tax under section 501 (for example, corporations organized and operated exclusively for charitable or educational purposes), certain life insurance companies, corporations electing application of the possession tax credit, regulated investment companies, real estate investment trusts, and domestic international sales corporations. A foreign corporation generally is not an includible corporation.

Subject to exceptions, the consolidated return and interest allocation definitions of affiliation generally are consistent with each other.[320] For example, both definitions generally exclude all foreign corporations from the affiliated group. Thus, while debt generally is considered fungible among the assets of a group of domestic affiliated corporations, the same rules do not apply as between the domestic and foreign members of a group with the same degree of common control as the domestic affiliated group.

Banks, savings institutions, and other financial affiliates

The affiliated group for interest allocation purposes generally excludes what are referred to in the Treasury regulations as "financial corporations."[321] A financial corporation includes any corporation, otherwise a member of the affiliated group for consolidation purposes, that is a financial institution (described in section 581 or section 591), the business of which is predominantly with persons other than related persons or their customers, and which is required by State or Federal law to be operated separately from any other entity that is not a financial institution.[322] The category of financial corporations also includes, to the extent provided in regulations, bank holding companies (including financial holding companies), subsidiaries of banks and bank holding companies (including financial holding companies), and savings institutions predominantly engaged in the active conduct of a banking, financing, or similar business.[323]

A financial corporation is not treated as a member of the regular affiliated group for purposes of applying the one-taxpayer rule to other non-financial members of that group. Instead, all such financial corporations that would be so affiliated are treated as a separate single corporation for interest allocation purposes.

Worldwide interest allocation

In general

The American Jobs Creation Act of 2004 ("AJCA")[324] modified the interest expense allocation rules described above (which generally apply for purposes of computing the foreign tax credit limitation) by providing a one-time election (the "worldwide affiliated group election") under which the taxable income of the domestic members of an affiliated group from sources outside the United States generally is determined by allocating and apportioning interest expense of the domestic members of a worldwide affiliated group on a worldwide-group basis (i.e., as if all members of the worldwide group were a single corporation). If a group makes this election, the taxable income of the domestic members of a worldwide affiliated group from sources outside the United States is determined by allocating and apportioning the third-party interest expense of those domestic members to foreign-source income in an amount equal to the excess (if any) of (1) the worldwide affiliated group's worldwide third-party interest expense multiplied by the ratio that the foreign assets of the worldwide affiliated group bears to the total assets of the worldwide affiliated group,[325] over (2) the third-party interest expense incurred by foreign members of the group to the extent such interest would be allocated to foreign sources if the principles of worldwide interest allocation were applied separately to the foreign members of the group.[326]

For purposes of the new elective rules based on worldwide fungibility, the worldwide affili-

---

[320] One such exception is that the affiliated group for interest allocation purposes includes section 936 corporations (certain electing domestic corporations that have income from the active conduct of a trade or business in Puerto Rico or another U.S. possession) that are excluded from the consolidated group.

[321] Treas. Reg. sec. 1.861-11T(d)(4).

[322] Sec. 864(e)(5)(C).

[323] Sec. 864(e)(5)(D).

[324] Pub. L. No. 108-357, sec. 401.

[325] For purposes of determining the assets of the worldwide affiliated group, neither stock in corporations within the group nor indebtedness (including receivables) between members of the group is taken into account.

[326] Although the interest expense of a foreign subsidiary is taken into account for purposes of allocating the interest expense of the domestic members of the electing worldwide affiliated group for foreign tax credit limitation purposes, the interest expense incurred by a foreign subsidiary is not deductible on a U.S. return.

ated group means all corporations in an affiliated group as well as all controlled foreign corporations that, in the aggregate, either directly or indirectly,[327] would be members of such an affiliated group if section 1504(b)(3) did not apply (i.e., in which at least 80 percent of the vote and value of the stock of such corporations is owned by one or more other corporations included in the affiliated group). Thus, if an affiliated group makes this election, the taxable income from sources outside the United States of domestic group members generally is determined by allocating and apportioning interest expense of the domestic members of the worldwide affiliated group as if all of the interest expense and assets of 80-percent or greater owned domestic corporations (i.e., corporations that are part of the affiliated group, as modified to include insurance companies) and certain controlled foreign corporations were attributable to a single corporation.

Financial institution group election

Taxpayers are allowed to apply the bank group rules to exclude certain financial institutions from the affiliated group for interest allocation purposes under the worldwide fungibility approach. The rules also provide a one-time "financial institution group" election that expands the bank group. At the election of the common parent of the pre-election worldwide affiliated group, the interest expense allocation rules are applied separately to a subgroup of the worldwide affiliated group that consists of (1) all corporations that are part of the bank group, and (2) all "financial corporations." For this purpose, a corporation is a financial corporation if at least 80 percent of its gross income is financial services income (as described in section 904(d)(2)(C)(i) and the regulations thereunder) that is derived from transactions with unrelated persons.[328] For these purposes, items of income or gain from a transaction or series of transactions are disregarded if a principal purpose for the transaction or transactions is to qualify any corporation as a financial corporation.

In addition, anti-abuse rules are provided under which certain transfers from one member of a financial institution group to a member of the worldwide affiliated group outside of the financial institution group are treated as reducing the amount of indebtedness of the separate financial institution group. Regulatory authority is provided with respect to the election to provide for the direct allocation of interest expense in circumstances in which such allocation is appropriate to carry out the purposes of these rules, to prevent assets or interest expense from being taken into account more than once, or to address changes in members of any group (through acquisitions or otherwise) treated as affiliated under these rules.

Effective date of worldwide interest allocation

The common parent of the domestic affiliated group must make the worldwide affiliated group election. It must be made for the first taxable year beginning after December 31, 2017, in which a worldwide affiliated group exists that includes at least one foreign corporation that meets the requirements for inclusion in a worldwide affiliated group.[329] The common parent of the pre-election worldwide affiliated group must make the election for the first taxable year beginning after December 31, 2017, in which a worldwide affiliated group includes a financial corporation. Once either election is made, it applies to the common parent and all other members of the worldwide affiliated group or to all members of the financial institution group, as applicable, for the taxable year for which the election is made and all subsequent taxable years, unless revoked with the consent of the Secretary of the Treasury.

Explanation of Provision

The provision delays the effective date of the worldwide interest allocation rules for two year, until taxable years beginning after December 31, 2019. The required dates for making the worldwide affiliated group election and the financial institution group election are changed accordingly.

Effective Date

The provision is effective on the date of enactment.

[Law at ¶6055. CCH Explanation at ¶630.]

---

[327] Indirect ownership is determined under the rules of section 958(a)(2) or through applying rules similar to those of section 958(a)(2) to stock owned directly or indirectly by domestic partnerships, trusts, or estates.

[328] See Treas. Reg. sec. 1.904-4(e)(2).

[329] As originally enacted under AJCA, the worldwide interest allocation rules were effective for taxable years beginning after December 31, 2008. However, the Housing and Economic Recovery Act of 2008 delayed the implementation of the worldwide interest allocation rules for two years, until taxable years beginning after December 31, 2010. Pub. L. No. 110-289, sec. 3093. The implementation of the worldwide interest allocation rules was further delayed by seven years, until taxable years beginning after December 31, 2017, by the Worker, Homeownership, and Business Assistance Act of 2009. Pub. L. No. 111-92, sec. 15.

Committee Reports

Charitable Contributions for Haiti Earthquake Relief

¶12,001 Introduction

Legislation was signed by the President on January 22, 2010, after unanimous passage in the House and Senate, that allows calendar-year taxpayers to claim a charitable deduction on their 2009 returns for qualified contributions made after January 11, 2010, and before March 1, 2010, to help Haiti recover from the devastating earthquake that occurred on January 12, 2010 (P.L. 111-126). The Joint Committee on Taxation produced a Technical Explanation of the House Bill on January 20, 2010 (JCX-2-10). This report explains the intent of Congress regarding the provisions of the Act. There was no conference report issued for this Act. The Technical Explanation from the Joint Committee on Taxation is included in this section to aid the reader's understanding, but may not be cited as the official Conference Committee Report accompanying the 2010 Act. At the end of each section, references are provided to the corresponding CCH explanations and the Internal Revenue Code provisions. Subscribers to the electronic version can link from these references to the corresponding material. *The pertinent sections of the Technical Explanation appear in Act Section order beginning at ¶12,010*

¶12,005 Background

Legislation was signed by the President on January 22, 2010, after unanimous passage in the House and Senate, that allows calendar-year taxpayers to claim a charitable deduction on their 2009 returns for qualified contributions made after January 11, 2010, and before March 1, 2010, to help Haiti recover from the devastating earthquake that occurred on January 12, 2010 (P.L. 111-126).

References are to the following report

• The Joint Committee on Taxation, "Technical Explanation of H.R. 4462: A Bill to Accelerate the Income Tax Benefits for Charitable Cash Contributions for the Relief of Victims of the Earthquake in Haiti," as signed by the President on January 22, 2010, after unanimous passage in the House and Senate, is referred to as Joint Committee on Taxation (J.C.T. REP. NO. JCX-2-10).

[¶12,010] Act Sec. 1. Technical Explanation of H.R. 4462: A Bill to Accelerate the Income Tax Benefits for Charitable Cash Contributions for the Relief of Victims of the Earthquake in Haiti

Joint Committee on Taxation (J.C.T. REP. NO. JCX-2-10)

[Act Sec. 1]

Present Law

In general, under present law, taxpayers may claim an income tax deduction for charitable contributions. The charitable deduction generally is available for the taxable year in which the contribution is made. For taxpayers whose taxable year is the calendar year, the tax benefit of a charitable contribution made in January or February often is not realized until the following calendar year when the tax return is filed.

A donor who claims a charitable deduction for a charitable contribution of money, regardless of amount, must maintain as a record of the contribution a bank record or a written communication from the donee showing the name of the donee organization, the date of the contribution, and the amount of the contribution.[1] In addition to the foregoing recordkeeping requirements, substantiation requirements apply in the case of charitable contributions with a value of $250 or more. No charitable deduction is allowed for any contribution of $250 or more unless the taxpayer substantiates the contribution by a contemporaneous written acknowledgment of the contribution by the donee organization.

Explanation of Provision

The provision permits taxpayers to treat charitable contributions of cash made after January 11, 2010, and before March 1, 2010, as contributions made on December 31, 2009, if such contributions were for the purpose of providing relief to victims in areas affected by the earthquake in Haiti that occurred on January 12, 2010. Thus, the effect of the provision is to give calendar-year taxpayers who make Haitian earthquake-related charitable contributions of cash after January 11, 2010, and before March 1, 2010, the opportunity to accelerate their tax benefit. Under the provision, such taxpayers may realize the tax benefit of such contributions by taking a deduction on their 2009 tax return.

The provision also clarifies the recordkeeping requirement for monetary contributions eligible for the accelerated income tax benefits described above. With respect to such contributions, a telephone bill will also satisfy the recordkeeping requirement if it shows the name of the donee organization, the date of the contribution, and the amount of the contribution. Thus, for example, in the case of a charitable contribution made by text message and chargeable to a telephone or wireless account, a bill from the telecommunications company containing the relevant information will satisfy the recordkeeping requirement.

Effective Date

The provision is effective on the date of enactment.

[Law at ¶7350. CCH Explanation at ¶235.]

---

[1] Sec. 170(f)(17).

¶20,001 Effective Dates

Patient Protection and Affordable Care Act, as amended by the 2010 Reconciliation Act

This CCH-prepared table presents the general effective dates for major law provisions added, amended or repealed by the Patient Protection and Affordable Care Act (PPACA) (P.L. 111-148), enacted March 23, 2010, as amended by the Health Care and Education Reconciliation Act of 2010 (RECON) (P.L. 111-152), enacted March 30, 2010. Entries are listed in Code Section order.

Code Sec.	Act Sec.	Act Provision Subject	Effective Date
23	10909(b)(1)(A)—PPAC	Expansion of Adoption Credit and Adoption Assistance Programs—Credit Made Refundable—Credit Moved to Subpart Relating to Refundable Credits	Tax years beginning after December 31, 2009
23(a)(3)	10909(a)(1)(B)(i)-(ii)—PPAC	Expansion of Adoption Credit and Adoption Assistance Programs—Increase in Dollar Limitation—Adoption Credit—Child With Special Needs	Tax years beginning after December 31, 2009
23(b)(1)	10909(a)(1)(A)—PPAC	Expansion of Adoption Credit and Adoption Assistance Programs—Increase in Dollar Limitation—Adoption Credit	Tax years beginning after December 31, 2009
23(h)	10909(a)(1)(C)—PPAC	Expansion of Adoption Credit and Adoption Assistance Programs—Increase in Dollar Limitation—Adoption Credit—Conforming Amendment to Inflation Adjustment	Tax years beginning after December 31, 2009
24(b)(3)(B)	10909(b)(2)(A)—PPAC	Expansion of Adoption Credit and Adoption Assistance Programs—Credit Made Refundable—Conforming Amendments	Tax years beginning after December 31, 2009
25(e)(1)(C)	10909(b)(2)(B)—PPAC	Expansion of Adoption Credit and Adoption Assistance Programs—Credit Made Refundable—Conforming Amendments	Tax years beginning after December 31, 2009
25A(i)(5)(B)	10909(b)(2)(C)—PPAC	Expansion of Adoption Credit and Adoption Assistance Programs—Credit Made Refundable—Conforming Amendments	Tax years beginning after December 31, 2009
25B(g)(2)	10909(b)(2)(D)—PPAC	Expansion of Adoption Credit and Adoption Assistance Programs—Credit Made Refundable—Conforming Amendments	Tax years beginning after December 31, 2009
26(a)(1)	10909(b)(2)(E)—PPAC	Expansion of Adoption Credit and Adoption Assistance Programs—Credit Made Refundable—Conforming Amendments	Tax years beginning after December 31, 2009

Code Sec.	Act Sec.	Act Provision Subject	Effective Date
30(c)(2)(B)(ii)	10909(b)(2)(F)—PPAC	Expansion of Adoption Credit and Adoption Assistance Programs—Credit Made Refundable—Conforming Amendments	Tax years beginning after December 31, 2009
30B(g)(2)(B)(ii)	10909(b)(2)(G)—PPAC	Expansion of Adoption Credit and Adoption Assistance Programs—Credit Made Refundable—Conforming Amendments	Tax years beginning after December 31, 2009
30D(c)(2)(B)(ii)	10909(b)(2)(H)—PPAC	Expansion of Adoption Credit and Adoption Assistance Programs—Credit Made Refundable—Conforming Amendments	Tax years beginning after December 31, 2009
36B	1401(a)—PPAC	Refundable Tax Credit Providing Premium Assistance for Coverage Under a Qualified Health Plan	Tax years ending after December 31, 2013
36B(b)(3)(A)	1001(a)(1)(A)-(B)—RECON	Affordability—Premium Tax Credits	March 30, 2010
36B(b)(3)(A)(ii)	10105(a)—PPAC	Amendments to Subtitle E	March 23, 2010
36B(c)(1)(A)	10105(b)—PPAC	Amendments to Subtitle E	March 23, 2010
36B(c)(2)(C)	1001(a)(2)(A)-(B)—RECON	Affordability—Premium Tax Credits	March 30, 2010
36B(c)(2)(C)(iv)	10105(c)—PPAC	Amendments to Subtitle E	March 23, 2010
36B(c)(2)(D)	10108(h)(1)—PPAC	Free Choice Vouchers—Voucher Taken Into Account in Determining Premium Credit	Tax years beginning after December 31, 2013
36B(d)(2)(B)	1004(a)(2)(A)—RECON	Income Definitions—Modified Adjusted Gross Income—Definition	March 30, 2010
36B(d)(2)(A)(i)-(ii)	1004(a)(1)(A)—RECON	Income Definitions—Modified Adjusted Gross Income	March 30, 2010
36B(f)(3)	1004(c)—RECON	Income Definitions—No Excess Payments	March 30, 2010
36C	10909(b)(1)(A)—PPAC	Expansion of Adoption Credit and Adoption Assistance Programs—Credit Made Refundable—Credit Moved to Subpart Relating to Refundable Credits	Tax years beginning after December 31, 2009
36C	10909(b)(1)(B)—PPAC	Expansion of Adoption Credit and Adoption Assistance Programs—Credit Made Refundable—Credit Moved to Subpart Relating to Refundable Credits	Tax years beginning after December 31, 2009
36C)(b)-(c)	10909(b)(2)(I)(i)-(ii)—PPAC	Expansion of Adoption Credit and Adoption Assistance Programs—Credit Made Refundable—Conforming Amendments	Tax years beginning after December 31, 2009
38(b)(34)-(36)	1421(b)—PPAC	Credit for Employee Health Insurance Expenses of Small Businesses—Credit to be Part of General Business Credit	Amounts paid or incurred in tax years beginning after December 31, 2009
38(c)(4)(B)(vi)-(ix)	1421(c)—PPAC	Credit for Employee Health Insurance Expenses of Small Businesses—Credit Allowed Against Alternative Minimum Tax	Credits determined under Code Sec. 45R in tax years beginning after December 31, 2009, and to carrybacks of such credits

¶20,001

Code Sec.	Act Sec.	Act Provision Subject	Effective Date
40(b)(6)(E)(iii)	1408(a)—RECON	Elimination of Unintended Application of Cellulosic Biofuel Producer Credit	Fuels sold or used on or after January 1, 2010
45R	1421(a)—PPAC	Credit for Employee Health Insurance Expenses of Small Businesses	Amounts paid or incurred in tax years beginning after December 31, 2009
45R(d)(3)(B)	10105(e)(1)—PPAC	Amendments to Subtitle E	Amounts paid or incurred in tax years beginning after December 31, 2010
45R(g)	10105(e)(2)—PPAC	Amendments to Subtitle E	Amounts paid or incurred in tax years beginning after December 31, 2010
46(2)	9023(b)(1)-(3)—PPAC	Qualifying Therapeutic Discovery Project Credit—Inclusion as Part of Investment Credit	Amounts paid or incurred after December 31, 2008, in tax years beginning after such date
48D	9023(a)—PPAC	Qualifying Therapeutic Discovery Project Credit	Amounts paid or incurred after December 31, 2008, in tax years beginning after such date
49(a)(1)(C)(iv)-(vi)	9023(c)(1)(A)-(C)—PPAC	Qualifying Therapeutic Discovery Project Credit—Conforming Amendments	Amounts paid or incurred after December 31, 2008, in tax years beginning after such date
56(b)(1)(B)	9013(c)—PPAC	Modification of Itemized Deduction for Medical Expenses—Conforming Amendment	Tax years beginning after December 31, 2012
105(b)	1004(d)(1)(A)-(B)—RECON	Income Definitions—Adult Dependents—Exclusion of Amounts Expended for Medical Care	March 30, 2010
106(f)	9003(c)—PPAC	Distributions for Medicine Qualified Only If for Prescribed Drug or Insulin—Health Flexible Spending Arrangements and Health Reimbursement Arrangements	Expenses incurred with respect to tax years beginning after December 31, 2010
108(f)(4)	10908(a)—PPAC	Exclusion for Assistance Provided to Participants in State Student Loan Repayment Programs for Certain Health Professionals	Amounts received by an individual in tax years beginning after December 31, 2008
125(f)	1515(b)(1)-(2)—PPAC	Offering of Exchange-Participating Qualified Health Plans Through Cafeteria Plans—Conforming Amendments	Tax years beginning after December 31, 2013
125(f)(3)	1515(a)—PPAC	Offering of Exchange-Participating Qualified Health Plans Through Cafeteria Plans	Tax years beginning after December 31, 2013
125(i)	10902(a)—PPAC	Inflation Adjustment of Limitation on Health Flexible Spending Arrangements Under Cafeteria Plans	Tax years beginning after December 31, 2012

Code Sec.	Act Sec.	Act Provision Subject	Effective Date
125(i)(2)	1403(b)(1)-(2)—RECON	Delay of Limitation on Health Flexible Spending Arrangements Under Cafeteria Plans—Inflation Adjustment	March 30, 2010
125(i)-(k)	9005(a)(1)-(2)—PPAC	Limitation on Health Flexible Spending Arrangements Under Cafeteria Plans	Tax years beginning after December 31, 2010
125(j)-(l)	9022(a)(i)-(ii)—PPAC	Establishment of Simple Cafeteria Plans for Small Business	Tax years beginning after December 31, 2010
137	10909(b)(2)(J)(i)-(ii)—PPAC	Expansion of Adoption Credit and Adoption Assistance Programs—Credit Made Refundable—Conforming Amendments	Tax years beginning after December 31, 2009
137(a)(2)	10909(b)(2)—PPAC	Expansion of Adoption Credit and Adoption Assistance Programs—Increase in Dollar Limitation—Adoption Assistance Programs—Child With Special Needs	Tax years beginning after December 31, 2009
137(b)(1)	10909(a)(2)(A)—PPAC	Expansion of Adoption Credit and Adoption Assistance Programs—Increase in Dollar Limitation—Adoption Assistance Programs	Tax years beginning after December 31, 2009
137(f)	10909(a)(2)(C)—PPAC	Expansion of Adoption Credit and Adoption Assistance Programs—Increase in Dollar Limitation—Adoption Assistance Programs—Conforming Amendment to Inflation Adjustment	Tax years beginning after December 31, 2009
139A	9012(a)—PPAC	Elimination of Deduction for Expenses Allocable to Medicare Part D Subsidy	Tax years beginning after December 31, 2012
139D	10108(f)(1)—PPAC	Free Choice Vouchers—Exclusion From Income for Employee	Vouchers provided after December 31, 2013
139D[E]	9021(a)—PPAC	Exclusion of Health Benefits Provided by Indian Tribal Governments	Benefits and coverage provided after March 23, 2010
162(a)	10108(g)(1)—PPAC	Free Choice Vouchers—Deduction Allowed to Employer	Vouchers provided after December 31, 2013
162(l)(1)	1004(d)(2)—RECON	Income Definitions—Adult Dependents—Self-Employed Health Insurance Deduction	March 30, 2010
162(l)(2)(B)	1004(d)(3)—RECON	Income Definitions—Adult Dependents—Conforming Amendments	March 30, 2010
162(m)(6)	9014(a)—PPAC	Limitation on Excessive Remuneration Paid by Certain Health Insurance Providers	Tax years beginning after December 31, 2009, with respect to services performed after such date
164(f)	9015(b)(2)(A)—PPAC	Additional Hospital Insurance Tax on High-Income Taxpayers—SECA—No Deduction for Additional Tax	Remuneration received, and tax years beginning after December 31, 2012
196(c)(12)-(14)	1421(d)(2)—PPAC	Credit for Employee Health Insurance Expenses of Small Businesses—Disallowance of Deduction for Certain Expenses for Which Credit Allowed—Deduction for Expiring Credits	Amounts paid or incurred in tax years beginning after December 31, 2009

¶20,001

Code Sec.	Act Sec.	Act Provision Subject	Effective Date
213(a)	9013(a)—PPAC	Modification of Itemized Deduction for Medical Expenses	Tax years beginning after December 31, 2012
213(f)	9013(b)—PPAC	Modification of Itemized Deduction for Medical Expenses—Temporary Waiver of Increase for Certain Seniors	Tax years beginning after December 31, 2012
220(d)(2)(A)	9003(b)—PPAC	Distributions for Medicine Qualified Only If for Prescribed Drug or Insulin—Archer MSAs	Amounts paid with respect to tax years beginning after December 31, 2010
220(f)(4)(A)	9004(b)—PPAC	Increase in Additional Tax on Distributions From HSAs and Archer MSAs Not Used for Qualified Medical Expenses—Archer MSAs	Distributions made after December 31, 2010
223(d)(2)(A)	9003(a)—PPAC	Distributions for Medicine Qualified Only If for Prescribed Drug or Insulin—HSAs	Amounts paid with respect to tax years beginning after December 31, 2010
223(f)(4)(A)	9004(a)—PPAC	Increase in Additional Tax on Distributions From HSAs and Archer MSAs Not Used for Qualified Medical Expenses—HSAs	Distributions made after December 31, 2010
280C(g)	9023(c)(2)—PPAC	Qualifying Therapeutic Discovery Project Credit—Conforming Amendments	Amounts paid or incurred after December 31, 2008, in tax years beginning after such date
280C(g)[i]	1401(b)—PPAC	Refundable Tax Credit Providing Premium Assistance for Coverage Under a Qualified Health Plan—Disallowance of Deduction	Tax years ending after December 31, 2013
280C(h)	1421(d)(1)—PPAC	Credit for Employee Health Insurance Expenses of Small Businesses—Disallowance of Deduction for Certain Expenses for Which Credit Allowed	Amounts paid or incurred in tax years beginning after December 31, 2009
280C(h)	10105(e)(3)—PPAC	Amendments to Subtitle E	Amounts paid or incurred in tax years beginning after December 31, 2010
401(h)	1004(d)(5)—RECON	Income Definitions—Adult Dependents—Medical and Other Benefits for Retired Employees	March 30, 2010
501(c)(9)	1004(d)(4)—RECON	Income Definitions—Adult Dependents—Sick and Accident Benefits Provided to Members of a Voluntary Employees' Beneficiary Association and Their Dependents	March 30, 2010
501(c)(29)	1322(h)(1)—PPAC	Federal Program to Assist Establishment and Operation of Nonprofit, Member-Run Health Insurance Issuers—Tax Exemption for Qualified Nonprofit Health Insurance Issuer	March 23, 2010

Code Sec.	Act Sec.	Act Provision Subject	Effective Date
501(l)(4)	6301(f)—PPAC	Patient-Centered Outcomes Research—Tax-Exempt Status for the Patient-Centered Outcomes Research Institute	March 23, 2010
501(r)(5)(A)	10903(a)—PPAC	Modification of Limitation on Charges by Charitable Hospitals	Tax years beginning after March 23, 2010
501(r)-(s)	9007(a)—PPAC	Additional Requirements for Charitable Hospitals—Requirements to Qualify as Section 501(c)(3) Charitable Hospital Organization	Tax years beginning after March 23, 2010
833(c)(5)	9016(a)—PPAC	Modification of Section 833 Treatment of Certain Health Organizations	Tax years beginning after December 31, 2009
904(i)	10909(b)(2)(K)—PPAC	Expansion of Adoption Credit and Adoption Assistance Programs—Credit Made Refundable—Conforming Amendments	Tax years beginning after December 31, 2009
1016(a)(26)	10909(b)(2)(L)—PPAC	Expansion of Adoption Credit and Adoption Assistance Programs—Credit Made Refundable—Conforming Amendments	Tax years beginning after December 31, 2009
1400C(d)	10909(b)(2)(M)—PPAC	Expansion of Adoption Credit and Adoption Assistance Programs—Credit Made Refundable—Conforming Amendments	Tax years beginning after December 31, 2009
1401(b)	9015(b)(1)(A)-(B)—PPAC	Additional Hospital Insurance Tax on High-Income Taxpayers—SECA	Remuneration received, and tax years beginning after December 31, 2012
1401(b)(2)(A)	10906(b)—PPAC	Modifications to Additional Hospital Insurance Tax on High-Income Taxpayers—SECA	Remuneration received, and tax years beginning after December 31, 2012
1401(b)(2)(A)-(B)	1402(b)(1)(B)(i)-(ii)—RECON	Medicare Tax—Earned Income—Threshold—SECA	Remuneration received, and tax years beginning after, December 31, 2012
1402(a)(12)(B)	9015(b)(2)(B)—PPAC	Additional Hospital Insurance Tax on High-Income Taxpayers—SECA—No Deduction for Additional Tax—Deduction for Net Earnings From Self-Employment	Remuneration received, and tax years beginning after December 31, 2012
1411	1402(a)(1)—RECON	Medicare Tax—Investment Income	Tax years beginning after December 31, 2012
3101(b)	9015(a)(1)(A)-(D)—PPAC	Additional Hospital Insurance Tax on High-Income Taxpayers—FICA	Remuneration received, and tax years beginning after December 31, 2012
3101(b)(2)	10906(a)—PPAC	Modifications to Additional Hospital Insurance Tax on High-Income Taxpayers—FICA	Remuneration received, and tax years beginning after December 31, 2012
3101(b)(2)(A)-(C)	1402(b)(1)(A)—RECON	Medicare Tax—Earned Income—Threshold—FICA	Remuneration received, and tax years beginning after, December 31, 2012

Code Sec.	Act Sec.	Act Provision Subject	Effective Date
3102(f)	9015(a)(1)(A)—PPAC	Additional Hospital Insurance Tax on High-Income Taxpayers—FICA—Collection of Tax	Remuneration received, and tax years beginning after December 31, 2012
4191	1405(a)(1)—RECON	Excise Tax on Medical Device Manufacturers	Sales after December 31, 2012
4221(a)	1405(b)(1)—RECON	Excise Tax on Medical Device Manufacturers—Certain Exemptions Not to Apply	Sales after December 31, 2012
4375-4377	6301(e)(2)(A)—PPAC	Patient-Centered Outcomes Research—Patient Centered Outcomes Research Trust Fund; Financing for Trust Fund—Financing for Fund From Fees on Insured and Self-Insured Health Plans	March 23, 2010
4958(e)(1)	1322(h)(3)—PPAC	Federal Program to Assist Establishment and Operation of Nonprofit, Member-Run Health Insurance Issuers—Tax Exemption for Qualified Nonprofit Health Insurance Issuer—Appllication of Tax on Excess Benefit Transactions	March 23, 2010
4959	9007(b)(1)—PPAC	Additional Requirements for Charitable Hospitals—Excise Tax for Failures to Meet Hospital Exemption Requirements	Failures occurring after March 23, 2010
4980H	1513(a)—PPAC	Shared Responsibilities for Employers	Months beginning after December 31, 2013
4980H(b)	10106(e)—PPAC	Amendments to Subtitle F	March 23, 2010
4980H(b)-(e)	1003(d)—RECON	Employer Responsibility—Eliminating Waiting Period Assessment	March 30, 2010
4980H(c)(1)	1003(b)(1)—RECON	Employer Responsibility—Applicable Payment Amount	March 30, 2010
4980H(c)(3)	10108(i)(1)(A)—PPAC	Free Choice Vouchers—Coordination With Employer Responsibilities—Shared Responsibility Penalty	Months beginning after December 31, 2013
4980H(d)(1)	1003(b)(2)—RECON	Employer Responsibility—Applicable Payment Amount	March 30, 2010
4980H(d)(2)(D)	1003(a)—RECON	Employer Responsibility—Payment Calculation	March 30, 2010
4980H(d)(2)(D)	10106(f)(2)—PPAC	Amendments to Subtitle F	Months beginning after December 31, 2013
4980H(d)(2)(E)	1003(c)—RECON	Employer Responsibility—Counting Part-Time Workers in Setting the Threshold for Employer Responsibility	March 30, 2010
4980H(d)(4)(A)	10106(f)(1)—PPAC	Amendments to Subtitle F	March 30, 2010
4980H(d)(5)(A)	1003(b)(3)—RECON	Employer Responsibility—Applicable Payment Amount	March 30, 2010
4980I	9001(a)—PPAC	Excise Tax on High Cost Employer-Sponsored Health Coverage	Tax years beginning after December 31, 2017
4980I(b)(3)(B)-(D)	1401(a)(1)-(3)—RECON	High-Cost Plan Excise Tax	March 30, 2010
4980I(d)	1401(a)(5)—RECON	High-Cost Plan Excise Tax	March 30, 2010
4980I(d)(1)(B)	1401(a)(4)—RECON	High-Cost Plan Excise Tax	March 30, 2010

Code Sec.	Act Sec.	Act Provision Subject	Effective Date
4980I(d)(1)(B)(i)	10901(b)—PPAC	Modifications to Excise Tax on High Cost Employer-Sponsored Health Coverage—Exemption From High-Cost Insurance Tax Includes Certain Additional Excepted Benefits	Tax years beginning after December 31, 2017
4980I(f)(3)	10901(a)—PPAC	Modifications to Excise Tax on High Cost Employer-Sponsored Health Coverage—Longshore Workers Treated as Employees Engaged in High-Risk Professions	Tax years beginning after December 31, 2017
5000A	1501(b)—PPAC	Requirement to Maintain Minimum Essential Coverage	Tax years ending after December 31, 2013
5000A(b)(1)	10106(b)(1)—PPAC	Amendments to Subtitle F	March 23, 2010
5000A(c)(1)-(2)	10106(b)(2)—PPAC	Amendments to Subtitle F	March 23, 2010
5000A(c)(2)-(3)	1002(a)(1)-(2)—RECON	Individual Responsibility—Amounts	March 30, 2010
5000A(c)(3)[B]	10106(b)(3)—PPAC	Amendments to Subtitle F	March 23, 2010
5000A(c)(4)(C)	1004(a)(2)(B)—RECON	Income Definitions—Modified Adjusted Gross Income—Definition	March 30, 2010
5000A(c)(4)(D)	1002(b)(1)—RECON	Individual Responsibility—Threshold	March 30, 2010
5000A(c)(4)[(B)](i)-(ii)	1004(a)(1)(C)—RECON	Income Definitions—Modified Adjusted Gross Income	March 30, 2010
5000A(d)(2)(A)	10106(c)—PPAC	Amendments to Subtitle F	March 23, 2010
5000A(e)(1)(C)	10106(d)—PPAC	Amendments to Subtitle F	March 23, 2010
5000A(e)(2)	1002(b)(2)(A)-(B)—RECON	Individual Responsibility—Threshold	March 30, 2010
5000B	10907(b)—PPAC	Excise Tax on Indoor Tanning Services in Lieu of Elective Cosmetic Medical Procedures—Excise Tax on Indoor Tanning Services	Services performed on or after July 1, 2010
6033(b)(10)(B)-(D)	9007(d)(2)—PPAC	Additional Requirements for Charitable Hospitals—Additional Reporting Requirements—Taxes	Tax years beginning after March 23, 2010
6033(b)(14)-(16)	9007(d)(1)—PPAC	Additional Requirements for Charitable Hospitals—Additional Reporting Requirements—Community Health Needs Assessments and Audited Financial Statements	Tax years beginning after March 23, 2010
6033(m)-(n)	1322(h)(2)—PPAC	Federal Program to Assist Establishment and Operation of Nonprofit, Member-Run Health Insurance Issuers—Tax Exemption for Qualified Nonprofit Health Insurance Issuer—Additional Reporting Requirement	March 23, 2010
6041(a)	9006(b)(1)-(3)—PPAC	Expansion of Information Reporting Requirements—Payments for Property and Other Gross Proceeds	Payments made after December 31, 2011
6041(h)-(i)	9006(a)—PPAC	Expansion of Information Reporting Requirements	Payments made after December 31, 2011
6051(a)(12)-(14)	9002(a)—PPAC	Inclusion of Cost of Employer-Sponsored Health Coverage on W-2	Tax years beginning after December 31, 2010
6055	1502(a)—PPAC	Reporting of Health Coverage	Calendar years beginning after 2013
6056	1514(a)—PPAC	Reporting of Employer Health Insurance Coverage	Periods beginning after December 31, 2013

¶20,001

Code Sec.	Act Sec.	Act Provision Subject	Effective Date
6056	10108(j)(3)(A)—PPAC	Free Choice Vouchers—Employer Reporting—Conforming Amendments	Periods beginning after December 31, 2013
6056(a)	10108(j)(1)—PPAC	Free Choice Vouchers—Employer Reporting	Periods beginning after December 31, 2013
6056(b)	10106(g)—PPAC	Amendments to Subtitle F	March 23, 2010
6056(b)(2)(C)	10108(j)(3)(B)(i)-(v)—PPAC	Free Choice Vouchers—Employer Reporting—Conforming Amendments	Periods beginning after December 31, 2013
6056(d)(2)	10108(j)(3)(C)—PPAC	Free Choice Vouchers—Employer Reporting—Conforming Amendments	Periods beginning after December 31, 2013
6056(e)	10108(j)(3)(D)—PPAC	Free Choice Vouchers—Employer Reporting—Conforming Amendments	Periods beginning after December 31, 2013
6056(f)	10108(j)(2)—PPAC	Free Choice Vouchers—Employer Reporting—Offering Employers	Periods beginning after December 31, 2013
6103(a)(3)	1414(b)—PPAC	Disclosures to Carry Out Eligibility Requirements for Certain Programs—Confidentiality and Disclosure	March 23, 2010
6103(l)(20)	3308(b)(2)(A)-(C)—PPAC	Reducing Part D Premium Subsidy for High-Income Beneficiaries—Conforming Amendments—Internal Revenue Code	March 23, 2010
6103(l)(21)	1414(a)(1)—PPAC	Disclosures to Carry Out Eligibility Requirements for Certain Programs—Disclosure of Taxpayer Return Information and Social Security Numbers—Taxpayer Return Information	March 23, 2010
6103(l)(21)(A)(iv)	1004(a)(1)(B)—RECON	Income Definitions—Modified Adjusted Gross Income	March 30, 2010
6103(p)(4)	1414(c)(1)-(3)—PPAC	Disclosures to Carry Out Eligibility Requirements for Certain Programs—Procedures and Recordkeeping Related to Disclosures	March 23, 2010
6211(b)(4)(A)	10105(d)—PPAC	Amendments to Subtitle E	March 23, 2010
6211(b)(4)(A)	10909(b)(2)(N)—PPAC	Expansion of Adoption Credit and Adoption Assistance Programs—Credit Made Refundable—Conforming Amendments	Tax years beginning after December 31, 2009
6416(b)(2)	1405(b)(2)—RECON	Excise Tax on Medical Device Manufacturers—Certain Exemptions Not to Apply	Sales after December 31, 2012
6654(a)	1402(a)(2)(A)—RECON	Medicare Tax—Investment Income—Estimated Taxes	Tax years beginning after December 31, 2012
6654(f)(2)-(4)	1402(a)(2)(B)(i)-(ii)—RECON	Medicare Tax—Investment Income—Estimated Taxes	Tax years beginning after December 31, 2012
6654(m)-(n)	1402(b)(2)—RECON	Medicare Tax—Earned Income—Estimated Taxes	Remuneration received, and tax years beginning after, December 31, 2012
6662(b)(6)	1409(b)(1)—RECON	Codification of Economic Substance Doctrine and Penalties—Penalty for Underpayments Attributable to Transactions Lacking Economic Substance	Underpayments attributable to transactions entered into after March 30, 2010

Code Sec.	Act Sec.	Act Provision Subject	Effective Date
6662(i)	1409(b)(2)—RECON	Codification of Economic Substance Doctrine and Penalties—Penalty for Underpayments Attributable to Transactions Lacking Economic Substance—Increased Penalty for Nondisclosed Transactions	Underpayments attributable to transactions entered into after March 30, 2010
6662A(e)(2)(B)	1409(b)(3)(A)-(B)—RECON	Codification of Economic Substance Doctrine and Penalties—Penalty for Underpayments Attributable to Transactions Lacking Economic Substance—Conforming Amendment	Underpayments attributable to transactions entered into after March 30, 2010
6664(c)((2)-(4)	1409(c)(1)(A)-(C)—RECON	Codification of Economic Substance Doctrine and Penalties—Reasonable Cause Exception not Applicable to Noneconomic Substance Transactions—Reasonable Cause Exception for Underpayments	Underpayments attributable to transactions entered into after March 30, 2010
6664(d)(2)-(4)	1409(c)(2)(A)-(C)—RECON	Codification of Economic Substance Doctrine and Penalties—Reasonable Cause Exception not Applicable to Noneconomic Substance Transactions—Reasonable Cause Exception for Reportable Transaction Understatements	Understatements attributable to transactions entered into after March 30, 2010
6676(c)-(d)	1409(d)—RECON	Codification of Economic Substance Doctrine and Penalties—Application of Penalty for Erroneous Claim for Refund or Credit to Noneconomic Substance Transactions	Refunds and credits attributable to transactions entered into after March 30, 2010
6724(d)(1)(B)(xii)-(xiv)	1502(b)(1)—PPAC	Reporting of Health Coverage—Assessable Penalties	Calendar years beginning after 2013
6724(d)(1)(B)(xxiii)-(xxv)	1514(b)(1)—PPAC	Reporting of Employer Health Insurance Coverage—Assessable Penalties	Periods beginning after December 31, 2013
6724(d)(1)(B)(xxv)	10108(j)(3)(E)—PPAC	Free Choice Vouchers—Employer Reporting—Conforming Amendments	Periods beginning after December 31, 2013
6724(d)(2)(EE)-(GG)	1502(b)(2)—PPAC	Reporting of Health Coverage—Assessable Penalties	Calendar years beginning after 2013
6724(d)(2)(FF)-(HH)	1514(b)(2)—PPAC	Reporting of Employer Health Insurance Coverage—Assessable Penalties	Periods beginning after December 31, 2013
6724(d)(2)(HH)	10108(j)(3)(F)—PPAC	Free Choice Vouchers—Employer Reporting—Conforming Amendments	Periods beginning after December 31, 2013
7213(a)(2)	1414(d)—PPAC	Disclosures to Carry Out Eligibility Requirements for Certain Programs—Unauthorized Disclosure or Inspection	March 23, 2010
7701(o)-(p)	1409(a)—RECON	Codification of Economic Substance Doctrine and Penalties	Transactions entered into after March 30, 2010
9511	6301(e)(1)—PPAC	Patient-Centered Outcomes Research—Patient Centered Outcomes Research Trust Fund; Financing for Trust Fund—Establishment of Trust Fund	March 23, 2010
9815	1562(f)—PPAC	Conforming Amendments—Technical Amendment to the Internal Revenue Code of 1986	March 23, 2010

¶20,001

¶20,005 Effective Dates

Hiring Incentives to Restore Employment Act

This CCH-prepared table presents the general effective dates for major law provisions added, amended or repealed by the Hiring Incentives to Restore Employment Act (P.L. 111-147), enacted March 18, 2010. Entries are listed in Code Section order.

Code Sec.	Act Sec.	Act Provision Subject	Effective Date
51(c)(5)	101(b)	Payroll Tax Forgiveness for Hiring Unemployed Workers—Coordination With Work Opportunity Credit	Wages paid after March 18, 2010
54F(d)(1)	301(b)(1)	Issuer Allowed Refundable Credit for Certain Qualified Tax Credit Bonds—Technical Corrections Relating to Qualified School Construction Bonds	Obligations issued after February 17, 2009
54F(e)	301(b)(2)	Issuer Allowed Refundable Credit for Certain Qualified Tax Credit Bonds—Technical Corrections Relating to Qualified School Construction Bonds	Obligations issued after February 17, 2009
149(a)(2)(A)-(C)	502(a)(2)(A)	Repeal of Certain Foreign Exceptions to Registered Bond Requirements—Repeal of Exception to Denial of Deduction for Interest on Non-Registered Bonds—Conforming Amendments	Obligations issued after the date which is 2 years after March 18, 2010
163(f)(2)(A)(ii)-(iv)	502(a)(2)(B)	Repeal of Certain Foreign Exceptions to Registered Bond Requirements—Repeal of Exception to Denial of Deduction for Interest on Non-Registered Bonds—Conforming Amendments	Obligations issued after the date which is 2 years after March 18, 2010
163(f)(2)(B)	502(a)(2)(C)(i)-(ii)	Repeal of Certain Foreign Exceptions to Registered Bond Requirements—Repeal of Exception to Denial of Deduction for Interest on Non-Registered Bonds—Conforming Amendments	Obligations issued after the date which is 2 years after March 18, 2010
163(f)(2)(B)-(C)	502(a)(1)	Repeal of Certain Foreign Exceptions to Registered Bond Requirements—Repeal of Exception to Denial of Deduction for Interest on Non-Registered Bonds	Obligations issued after the date which is 2 years after March 18, 2010
163(f)(3)	502(c)	Repeal of Certain Foreign Exceptions to Registered Bond Requirements—Dematerialized Book Entry Systems Treated as Registered Form	Obligations issued after the date which is 2 years after March 18, 2010

Code Sec.	Act Sec.	Act Provision Subject	Effective Date
165(j)(2)(A)	502(a)(2)(D)	Repeal of Certain Foreign Exceptions to Registered Bond Requirements—Repeal of Exception to Denial of Deduction for Interest on Non-Registered Bonds—Conforming Amendments	Obligations issued after the date which is 2 years after March 18, 2010
179(b)	201(a)(1)-(4)	Increase in Expensing of Certain Depreciable Business Assets	Tax years beginning after December 31, 2009
643(i)(1)	533(a)(1)-(2)	Uncompensated Use of Trust Property	Loans made, and the uses of property, after March 18, 2010
643(i)(2)(E)	533(b)	Uncompensated Use of Trust Property—Exception for Compensated Use	Loans made, and the uses of property, after March 18, 2010
643(i)(3)	533(d)(1)-(3)	Uncompensated Use of Trust Property—Conforming Amendments	Loans made, and the uses of property, after March 18, 2010
679(c)(1)	531(a)	Clarifications with Respect to Foreign Trusts Which are Treated as Having a United States Beneficiary	March 18, 2010
679(c)(4)	531(b)	Clarifications with Respect to Foreign Trusts Which are Treated as Having a United States Beneficiary—Clarification Regarding Discretion to Identify Beneficiaries	March 18, 2010
679(c)(5)	531(c)	Clarifications with Respect to Foreign Trusts Which are Treated as Having a United States Beneficiary—Clarification that Certain Agreements and Understandings are Terms of the Trust	March 18, 2010
679(c)(6)	533(c)	Uncompensated Use of Trust Property—Application of Grantor Trusts	Loans made, and the uses of property, after March 18, 2010
679(d)-(e)	532(a)	Presumption that Foreign Trust has United States Beneficiary	Transfers of property after March 18, 2010
864(f)(5)-(6)	551(a)	Delay in Application of Worldwide Allocation of Interest	March 18, 2010
871(h)(2)	502(b)(1)	Repeal of Certain Foreign Exceptions to Registered Bond Requirements—Repeal of Treatment as Portfolio Debt	Obligations issued after the date which is 2 years after March 18, 2010
871(h)(3)(A)	502(b)(2)(A)	Repeal of Certain Foreign Exceptions to Registered Bond Requirements—Repeal of Treatment as Portfolio Debt—Conforming Amendments	Obligations issued after the date which is 2 years after March 18, 2010
871(l)-(m)	541(a)	Substitute Dividends and Dividend Equivalent Payments Received by Foreign Persons Treated as Dividends	Payments made on or after the date that is 180 days after March 18, 2010
881(c)(2)	502(b)(2)(B)	Repeal of Certain Foreign Exceptions to Registered Bond Requirements—Repeal of Treatment as Portfolio Debt—Conforming Amendments	Obligations issued after the date which is 2 years after March 18, 2010

¶20,005

Code Sec.	Act Sec.	Act Provision Subject	Effective Date
1287(b)(1)	502(a)(2)(D)	Repeal of Certain Foreign Exceptions to Registered Bond Requirements—Repeal of Exception to Denial of Deduction for Interest on Non-Registered Bonds—Conforming Amendments	Obligations issued after the date which is 2 years after March 18, 2010
1291(e)	521(b)	Reporting of Activities with Respect to Passive Foreign Investment Companies—Conforming Amendment	March 18, 2010
1298(f)-(g)	521(a)	Reporting of Activities with Respect to Passive Foreign Investment Companies	March 18, 2010
1471-1474	501(a)	Reporting on Certain Foreign Accounts	Payments made after December 31, 2012
3111(d)	101(a)	Payroll Tax Forgiveness for Hiring Unemployed Workers	Wages paid after March 18, 2010
3221(c)-(d)	101(d)(1)	Payroll Tax Forgiveness for Hiring Unemployed Workers—Application to Railroad Retirement Taxes	Compensation paid after March 18, 2010
4701(b)(1)	502(e)	Repeal of Certain Foreign Exceptions to Registered Bond Requirements—Preservation of Exception for Excise Tax Purposes	Obligations issued after the date which is 2 years after March 18, 2010
6011(e)(4)	522(a)	Secretary Permitted to Require Financial Institutions to File Certain Returns Related to Withholding on Foreign Transfers Electronically	Returns the due date for which (determined without regard to extensions) is after March 18, 2010
6038D	511(a)	Disclosure of Information With Respect to Foreign Financial Assets	Tax years beginning after March 18, 2010
6048(b)(1)	534(a)	Reporting Requirement of United States Owners of Foreign Trusts	Tax years beginning after March 18, 2010
6229(c)(2)	513(a)(2)(B)	Modification of Statute of Limitations for Significant Omission of Income in Connection with Foreign Assets—Extension of Statute of Limitations—Conforming Amendments	Returns filed after March 18, 2010 and returns filed on or before such date if the period specified in IRC Sec. 6501 for assessment of such taxes has not expired as of such date
6414	501(c)(1)	Reporting on Certain Foreign Accounts—Conforming Amendments	Payments made after December 31, 2012
6431(f)	301(a)	Issuer Allowed Refundable Credit for Certain Qualified Tax Credit Bonds—Credit Allowed	Bonds issued after March 18, 2010
6501(b)(1)	501(c)(2)	Reporting on Certain Foreign Accounts—Conforming Amendments	Payments made after December 31, 2012
6501(b)(2)	501(c)(3)(A)-(B)	Reporting on Certain Foreign Accounts—Conforming Amendments	Payments made after December 31, 2012

¶20,005

Code Sec.	Act Sec.	Act Provision Subject	Effective Date
6501(c)(8)	513(b)(1)-(3)	Modification of Statute of Limitations for Significant Omission of Income in Connection with Foreign Assets—Additional Reports to Extended Period	Returns filed after March 18, 2010 and returns filed on or before such date if the period specified in IRC Sec. 6501 for assessment of such taxes has not expired as of such date
6501(c)(8)	513(c)	Modification of Statute of Limitations for Significant Omission of Income in Connection with Foreign Assets—Clarifications Related to Failure to Disclose Foreign Transfers	Returns filed after March 18, 2010 and returns filed on or before such date if the period specified in IRC Sec. 6501 for assessment of such taxes has not expired as of such date
6501(e)(1)(A)-(C)	513(a)(1)	Modification of Statute of Limitations for Significant Omission of Income in Connection with Foreign Assets—Extension of Statute of Limitations	Returns filed after March 18, 2010 and returns filed on or before such date if the period specified in IRC Sec. 6501 for assessment of such taxes has not expired as of such date
6501(e)(1)(B)	513(a)(2)(A)	Modification of Statute of Limitations for Significant Omission of Income in Connection with Foreign Assets—Extension of Statute of Limitations—Conforming Amendments	Returns filed after March 18, 2010 and returns filed on or before such date if the period specified in IRC Sec. 6501 for assessment of such taxes has not expired as of such date
6513(b)(3)	501(c)(4)(A)-(B)	Reporting on Certain Foreign Accounts—Conforming Amendments	Payments made after December 31, 2012
6513(c)	501(c)(5)	Reporting on Certain Foreign Accounts—Conforming Amendments	Payments made after December 31, 2012

¶20,005

Code Sec.	Act Sec.	Act Provision Subject	Effective Date
6611(e)(4)	501(b)	Reporting on Certain Foreign Accounts—Special Rule for Interest on Overpayments	Returns, the due date for which (determined without regard to extensions) is after March 18, 2010 (for amendment's application to 6611(e)(1)); claims for credit or refund of any overpayment filed after March 18, 2010 (for amendment's application to 6611(e)(2)); and refunds paid after March 18, 2010 (for amendment's application to 6611(e)(3)).
6662(b)(7)	512(a)(1)	Penalties for Underpayments Attributable to Undisclosed Foreign Financial Assets	Tax years beginning after March 18, 2010
6662(j)	512(a)(2)	Penalties for Underpayments Attributable to Undisclosed Foreign Financial Assets	Tax years beginning after March 18, 2010
6677(a)	535(a)(1)-(2)	Minimum Penalty with Respect to Failure to Report on Certain Foreign Trusts	Notices and returns required to be filed after December 31, 2009
6724(c)	522(b)	Secretary Permitted to Require Financial Institutions to File Certain Returns Related to Withholding on Foreign Transfers Electronically—Conforming Amendment	Returns the due date for which (determined without regard to extensions) is after March 18, 2010
6724(d)(1)	501(c)(6)	Reporting on Certain Foreign Accounts—Conforming Amendments	Payments made after December 31, 2012
6724(d)(2)	501(c)(7)	Reporting on Certain Foreign Accounts—Conforming Amendments	Payments made after December 31, 2012
9502(a)	444(b)(1)	Termination of Transfers from Highway Trust Fund for Certain Repayments and Credits—Conforming Amendments	Transfers relating to amounts paid and credits allowed after March 18, 2010
9503(b)(4)(D)	444(b)(2)	Termination of Transfers from Highway Trust Fund for Certain Repayments and Credits—Conforming Amendments	Transfers relating to amounts paid and credits allowed after March 18, 2010
9503(b)(6)(B)	445(a)(3)	Extension of Authority for Expenditures—Highways Trust Fund—Exception to Limitation on Transfers	September 30, 2009
9503(c)(1)	445(a)(1)(A)-(B)	Extension of Authority for Expenditures—Highways Trust Fund—Highway Account	September 30, 2009
9503(c)(2)	444(b)(3)	Termination of Transfers from Highway Trust Fund for Certain Repayments and Credits—Conforming Amendments	Transfers relating to amounts paid and credits allowed after March 18, 2010

¶20,005

Code Sec.	Act Sec.	Act Provision Subject	Effective Date
9503(c)(2)-(6)	444(a)	Termination of Transfers from Highway Trust Fund for Certain Repayments and Credits	Transfers relating to amounts paid and credits allowed after March 18, 2010
9503(e)(1)	442(b)	Restoration of Certain Foregone Interest to Highway Trust Fund—Conforming Amendment	March 18, 2010
9503(e)(3)	445(a)(2)(A)-(B)	Extension of Authority for Expenditures—Highways Trust Fund—Mass Transit Account	September 30, 2009
9503(e)(5)(A)	444(b)(4)	Termination of Transfers from Highway Trust Fund for Certain Repayments and Credits—Conforming Amendments	Transfers relating to amounts paid and credits allowed after March 18, 2010
9503(f)(1)	441(b)(1)-(2)	Repeal of Provision Prohibiting the Crediting of Interest to the Highway Trust Fund—Conforming Amendments	March 18, 2010
9503(f)(1)(B)	441(a)	Repeal of Provision Prohibiting the Crediting of Interest to the Highway Trust Fund	March 18, 2010
9503(f)(2)	442(a)	Restoration of Certain Foregone Interest to Highway Trust Fund	March 18, 2010
9503(f)(4)	443(a)	Treatment of Certain Amounts Appropriated to Highway Trust Fund	March 18, 2010
9504(a)	444(b)(5)	Termination of Transfers from Highway Trust Fund for Certain Repayments and Credits—Conforming Amendments	Transfers relating to amounts paid and credits allowed after March 18, 2010
9504(b)(2)	444(b)(6)	Termination of Transfers from Highway Trust Fund for Certain Repayments and Credits—Conforming Amendments	Transfers relating to amounts paid and credits allowed after March 18, 2010
9504(b)(2)	445(b)(1)(A)-(C)	Extension of Authority for Expenditures—Sport Fish Restoration and Boating Trust Fund	September 30, 2009
9504(d)(2)	445(b)(2)	Extension of Authority for Expenditures—Sport Fish Restoration and Boating Trust Fund—Exception to Limitation on Transfers	September 30, 2009
9504(e)	444(b)(7)	Termination of Transfers from Highway Trust Fund for Certain Repayments and Credits—Conforming Amendments	Transfers relating to amounts paid and credits allowed after March 18, 2010
. . .	101(c)	Payroll Tax Forgiveness for Hiring Unemployed Workers—Transfers to Federal Old-Age and Survivors Insurance Trust Fund	March 18, 2010
. . .	511(b)	Disclosure of Information With Respect to Foreign Financial Assets—Clerical Amendment	March 18, 2010

¶20,005

¶20,010 Effective Dates

Temporary Extension Act of 2010

This CCH-prepared table presents the general effective dates for major law provisions added, amended or repealed by the Temporary Extension Act of 2010 (P.L. 111-144), enacted March 2, 2010. Entries are listed in Code Section order.

Code Sec.	Act Sec.	Act Provision Subject	Effective Date
35(g)(9)	3(b)(5)(A)	Extension and Improvement of Premium Assistance for COBRA Benefits—Clarifications Relating to Section 3001 of ARRA—Amendments Relating to Section 3001	Tax years ending after March 2, 2010
139C	3(b)(5)(B)	Extension and Improvement of Premium Assistance for COBRA Benefits—Clarifications Relating to Section 3001 of ARRA—Amendments Relating to Section 3001	Tax years ending after March 2, 2010
6432(a)	3(b)(5)(C)(i)	Extension and Improvement of Premium Assistance for COBRA Benefits—Clarifications Relating to Section 3001 of ARRA—Amendments Relating to Section 3001	Premium for a period of coverage beginning on or after March 2, 2010, generally
6432(c)(3)	3(b)(5)(C)(ii)	Extension and Improvement of Premium Assistance for COBRA Benefits—Clarifications Relating to Section 3001 of ARRA—Amendments Relating to Section 3001	Premium for a period of coverage beginning on or after March 2, 2010, generally
6432(e)-(g)	3(b)(5)(C)(iii)	Extension and Improvement of Premium Assistance for COBRA Benefits—Clarifications Relating to Section 3001 of ARRA—Amendments Relating to Section 3001	Premium for a period of coverage beginning on or after March 2, 2010, generally
6720C(a)	3(b)(5)(D)	Extension and Improvement of Premium Assistance for COBRA Benefits—Clarifications Relating to Section 3001 of ARRA—Amendments Relating to Section 3001	Failures occurring after March 2, 2010

¶25,001 Code Section to Explanation Table

¶25,005 Code Sections Added, Amended or Repealed

The list below notes all the Code Sections or subsections of the Internal Revenue Code that were added, amended or repealed by the Patient Protection and Affordable Health Care Act (P.L. 111-148), enacted March 23, 2010, the Health Care and Education Reconciliation Act of 2010 (P.L. 111-152), enacted March 30, 2010, the Hiring Incentives to Restore Employment Act (P.L. 111-147), enacted March 18, 2010, and the Temporary Extension Act of 2010 (P.L. 111-144), enacted March 2, 2010. The first column indicates the Code Section added, amended or repealed, and the second column indicates the Act Section.

Patient Protection and Affordable Health Care Act

Code Sec.	Act Sec.	Code Sec.	Act Sec.
23	10909(b)(1)(A)-(B)	137(a)(2)	10909(a)(2)(B)(i)-(ii)
23(a)(3)	10909(a)(2)(B)(i)-(ii)	137(b)(1)	10909(a)(2)(A)
23(b)(1)	10909(a)(1)(A)	137(d)-(e)	10909(b)(2)(J)(i)-(ii)
23(h)	10909(a)(1)(C)	137(f)	10909(a)(2)(C)
24(b)(3)(B)	10909(b)(2)(A)	139A	9012(a)
25(e)(1)(C)	10909(b)(2)(B)	139D[139E]	9021(a)
25A(i)(5)(B)	10909(b)(2)(C)	139D	10108(f)(1)
25B(g)(2)	10909(b)(2)(D)	162(a)	10108(g)(1)
26(a)(1)	10909(b)(2)(E)	162(m)(6)	9014(a)
30(c)(2)(B)(ii)	10909(b)(2)(F)	164(f)[(1)]	9015(b)(2)(A)
30B(g)(2)(B)(ii)	10909(b)(2)(G)	196(c)(12)-(14)	1421(d)(2)
30D(c)(2)(B)(ii)	10909(b)(2)(H)	213(a)	9013(a)
36B	1401(a)	213(f)	9013(b)
36B(b)(3)(A)(ii)	10105(a)	220(d)(2)(A)	9003(b)
36B(c)(1)(A)	10105(b)	220(f)(4)(A)	9004(b)
36B(c)(2)(C)(iv)	10105(c)	223(d)(2)(A)	9003(a)
36B(c)(2)(D)	10108(h)(1)	223(f)(4)(A)	9004(a)
36C	10909(b)(1)(A)-(B)	280C(g)	1401(b)
36C	10909(b)(2)(I)(i)-(ii)	280C(g)[(i)]	9023(c)(2)
38(b)(34)-(36)	1421(b)	280C(h)	1421(d)(1)
38(c)(4)(B)(vi)-(ix)	1421(c)	280C(h)	10105(e)(3)
45R	1421(a)	501(c)(29)	1322(h)(1)
45R(d)(3)(B)	10105(e)(1)	501(l)(4)	6301(f)
45R(g)	10105(e)(2)	501(r)(5)(A)	10903(a)
46	9023(b)(1)-(3)	501(r)-(s)	9007(a)
48D	9023(a)	833(c)(5)	9016(a)
49(a)(1)(C)(iv)-(vi)	9023(c)(1)(A)-(C)	904(i)	10909(b)(2)(K)
56(b)(1)(B)	9013(c)	1016(a)(26)	10909(b)(2)(L)
106(f)	9003(c)	1400C(d)[(2)]	10909(b)(2)(M)
108(f)(4)	10908(a)	1401(b)	9015(b)(1)(A)-(B)
125(f)	1515(b)(1)-(2)	1401(b)(2)(A)	10906(b)
125(f)(3)	1515(a)	1402(a)(12)(B)	9015(b)(2)(B)
125(i)	10902(a)	3101(b)	9015(a)(1)(A)-(D)
125(i)-(k)	9005(a)(1)-(2)	3101(b)(2)	10906(a)
125(j)-(l)	9022(a)	3102(f)	9015(a)(2)

Code Sec.	Act Sec.	Code Sec.	Act Sec.
4375-4377	6301(e)(2)(A)	6055	1502(a)
4958(e)(1)	1322(h)(3)	6056	1514(a)
4959	9007(b)(1)	6056	10108(j)(3)(A)
4980H	1513(a)	6056(a)	10108(j)(1)
4980H(b)	10106(e)	6056(b)	10106(g)
4980H(c)(3)	10108(i)(1)(A)	6056(b)(2)(C)	10108(j)(3)(B)(i)-(v)
4980H(d)(2)(D)	10106(f)(2)	6056(d)(2)	10108(j)(3)(C)
4980H(d)(4)(A)	10106(f)(1)	6056(e)	10108(j)(3)(D)
4980I	9001(a)	6056(f)	10108(j)(2)
4980I(d)(1)(B)(i)	10901(b)	6103(a)(3)	1414(b)
4980I(f)(3)	10901(a)	6103(l)(20)	3308(b)(2)(A)-(C)
5000A	1501(b)	6103(l)(21)	1414(a)(1)
5000A(b)(1)	10106(b)(1)	6103(p)(4)	1414(c)(1)-(3)
5000A(c)(1)-(2)	10106(b)(2)	6211(b)(4)(A)	10105(d)
5000A(c)(3)[(B)]	10106(b)(3)	6211(b)(4)(A)	10909(b)(2)(N)
5000A(d)(2)(A)	10106(c)	6724(d)(1)(B)(xxii)-	
5000A(e)(1)(C)	10106(d)	(xxiv)	1502(b)(1)
5000B	9017(a)	6724(d)(1)(B)(xxiii)-	
5000B	10907(a)	(xxv)	1514(b)(1)
5000B	10907(b)	6724(d)(1)(B)(xxv)	10108(j)(3)(E)
6033(b)(10)(B)-(D)	9007(d)(2)	6724(d)(2)(EE)-(GG)	1502(b)(2)
6033(b)(14)-(16)	9007(d)(1)	6724(d)(2)(FF)-(HH)	1514(b)(2)
6033(m)-(n)	1322(h)(2)	6724(d)(2)(HH)	10108(j)(3)(F)
6041(a)	9006(b)(1)-(3)	7213(a)(2)	1414(d)
6041(h)-(i)	9006(a)	9511	6301(e)(1)(A)
6051(a)(12)-(14)	9002(a)	9815	1562(f)

Health Care and Education Reconciliation Act of 2010

Code Sec.	Act Sec.	Code Sec.	Act Sec.
36B(b)(3)(A)	1001(a)(1)(A)-(B)	4980H(d)(2)(E)	1003(c)
36B(c)(2)(C)	1001(a)(2)(A)-(B)	4980H(d)(5)(A)	1003(b)(3)
36B(d)(2)(A)(i)-(ii)	1004(a)(1)(A)	4980I(b)(3)(B)-(D)	1401(a)(1)-(3)
36B(d)(2)(B)	1004(a)(2)(A)	4980I(d)	1401(a)(4)-(5)
36B(f)(3)	1004(c)	5000A(c)(2)-(3)	1002(a)(1)-(2)
40(b)(6)(E)(iii)	1408(a)	5000A(c)(4)(C)	1004(a)(2)(B)
105(b)	1004(d)(1)(A)-(B)	5000A(c)(4)(D)	1002(b)(1)
125(i)(2)	1403(b)(1)-(2)	5000A(c)(4)[(B)](i)-(ii)	1004(a)(1)(C)
162(l)(1)	1004(d)(2)	5000A(e)(2)	1002(b)(2)(A)-(B)
162(l)(2)(B)	1004(d)(3)	6103(l)(21)(A)(iv)	1004(a)(1)(B)
401(h)	1004(d)(5)	6416(b)(2)	1405(b)(2)
501(c)(9)	1004(d)(4)	6654(a)	1402(a)(2)(A)
1401(b)(2)(A)-(B)	1402(b)(1)(B)(i)-(ii)	6654(f)(2)-(4)	1402(a)(2)(B)(i)-(ii)
1411	1402(a)(1)	6654(m)-(n)	1402(b)(2)
3101(b)(2)(A)-(C)	1402(b)(1)(A)	6662(b)(6)	1409(b)(1)
4191	1405(a)(1)	6662(i)	1409(b)(2)
4221(a)	1405(b)(1)	6662A(e)(2)	1409(b)(3)(A)-(B)
4980H(b)-(e)	1003(d)	6664(c)(2)-(4)	1409(c)(1)(A)-(C)
4980H(c)(1)	1003(b)(1)	6664(d)(2)-(4)	1409(c)(2)(A)-(C)
4980H(d)(1)	1003(b)(2)	6676(c)-(d)	1409(d)
4980H(d)(2)(D)	1003(a)	7701(o)-(p)	1409(a)

¶25,005

Hiring Incentives to Restore Employment Act

Code Sec.	Act Sec.	Code Sec.	Act Sec.
51(c)(5)	101(b)	6431(f)	301(a)
54F(d)(1)	301(b)(1)	6501(b)(1)	501(c)(2)
54F(e)	301(b)(2)	6501(b)(2)	501(c)(3)(A)-(B)
149(a)(2)(A)-(C)	502(a)(2)(A)	6501(c)(8)	513(b)(1)-(3)
163(f)(2)(A)(ii)-(iv)	502(a)(2)(B)	6501(c)(8)	513(c)
163(f)(2)(B)	502(a)(2)(C)(i)-(ii)	6501(e)(1)(A)-(C)	513(a)(1)
163(f)(2)(B)-(C)	502(a)(1)	6501(e)(1)(B)	513(a)(2)(A)
163(f)(3)	502(c)	6513(b)(3)	501(c)(4)(A)-(B)
165(j)(2)(A)	502(a)(2)(D)	6513(c)	501(c)(5)
179(b)	201(a)(1)-(4)	6611(e)(4)	501(b)
643(i)(1)	533(a)(1)-(2)	6662(b)(7)[(6)]	512(a)(1)
643(i)(2)(E)	533(b)	6662(j)[(i)]	512(a)(2)
643(i)(3)	533(d)(1)-(3)	6677(a)	535(a)(1)-(2)
679(c)(1)	531(a)	6724(c)	522(b)
679(c)(4)	531(b)	6724(d)(1)	501(c)(6)
679(c)(5)	531(c)	6724(d)(2)	501(c)(7)
679(c)(6)	533(c)	9502(a)	444(b)(1)
679(d)-(e)	532(a)	9503(b)(4)(D)	444(b)(2)
864(f)(5)-(6)	551(a)	9503(b)(6)(B)	445(a)(3)
871(h)(2)	502(b)(1)	9503(c)(1)	445(a)(1)(A)-(B)
871(h)(3)(A)	502(b)(2)(A)	9503(c)(2)	444(b)(3)
871(l)-(m)	541(a)	9503(c)(2)-(6)	444(a)
881(c)(2)	502(b)(2)(B)	9503(e)(1)	442(b)
1287(b)(1)	502(a)(2)(D)	9503(e)(3)	445(a)(2)(A)-(B)
1291(e)	521(b)	9503(e)(5)(A)	444(b)(4)
1298(f)-(g)	521(a)	9503(f)(1)	441(b)(1)-(2)
1471-1474	501(a)	9503(f)(1)(B)	441(a)
3111(d)	101(a)	9503(f)(2)	442(a)
3221(c)-(d)	101(d)(1)	9503(f)(4)[(3)]	443(a)
4701(b)(1)	502(e)	9504(a)	444(b)(5)
6011(e)(4)	522(a)	9504(b)(2)	444(b)(6)
6038D	511(a)	9504(b)(2)	445(b)(1)(A)-(C)
6048(b)(1)	534(a)	9504(d)(2)	445(b)(2)
6229(c)(2)	513(a)(2)(B)	9504(e)	444(b)(7)
6414	501(c)(1)		

Temporary Extension Act of 2010

Code Sec.	Act Sec.	Code Sec.	Act Sec.
35(g)(9)	3(b)(5)(A)	6432(e)-(g)	3(b)(5)(C)(iii)
139C	3(b)(5)(B)	6720C(a)	3(b)(5)(D)
6432(a)	3(b)(5)(C)(i)		
6432(c)(3)	3(b)(5)(C)(ii)		

¶25,010 Table of Amendments to Other Acts

Patient Protection and Affordable Care Act

Amended Act Sec.	H.R. 3590 Sec.	Par. (¶)	Amended Act Sec.	H.R. 3590 Sec.	Par. (¶)
			Fair Labor Standards Act of 1938		
The Social Security Act			18B(a)(3)	10108(i)(2)	¶7045
1181	6301(a)	¶7021			
1841(a)	9008(k)	¶7030			
The Public Health Service Act					
3201 - 3210	8002(a)	¶7024			

Health Care and Education Reconciliation Act of 2010

Amended Act Sec.	H.R. 4872 Sec.	Par. (¶)	Amended Act Sec.	H.R. 4872 Sec.	Par. (¶)
			9009	1405	7033
Patient Protection and Affordable Care Act			9010	1406	7036
9008	1404	7030			

Hiring Incentives to Restore Employment Act

Amended Act Sec.	H.R. 2847 Sec.	Par. (¶)	Amended Act Sec.	H.R. 2847 Sec.	Par. (¶)
			502(d)(2)	3121(g)(1)	¶7212
Title 31, United States Code					
502(d)(1)	3121(g)	¶7212			

Temporary Extension Act of 2010

Amended Act Sec.	Act Sec.	Par. (¶)	Amended Act Sec.	Act Sec.	Par. (¶)
			3001(a)(17)	3(b)(1)(B)	¶7306
American Recovery and Reinvestment Act of 2009, Division B			3001(a)(16)	3(b)(2)	¶7306
			3001(a)(2)(A)(ii)(I)	3(b)(3)	¶7306
3001(a)(3)(A)	3(a)	¶7306	3001(a)(5)	3(b)(4)	¶7306
3001(a)(3)(C)	3(b)(1)(A)	¶7306			

¶25,015 Table of Act Sections Not Amending Internal Revenue Code Sections

Patient Protection and Affordable Care Act

Health Care and Education Reconciliation Act of 2010

Hiring Incentives to Restore Employment Act

Temporary Extension Act of 2010

Haiti Earthquake Relief

Paragraph

¶25,020 Act Sections Amending Code Sections

Patient Protection and Affordable Care Act

Act Sec.	Code Sec.	Act Sec.	Code Sec.
1322(h)(1)	501(c)(29)	9013(a)	213(a)
1322(h)(2)	6033(m)-(n)	9013(b)	213(f)
1322(h)(3)	4958(e)(1)	9013(c)	56(b)(1)(B)
1401(a)	36B	9014(a)	162(m)(6)
1401(b)	280C(g)	9015(a)(1)(A)-(D)	3101(b)
1421(a)	45R	9015(a)(2)	3102(f)
1421(b)	38(b)(34)-(36)	9015(b)(1)(A)-(B)	1401(b)
1421(c)	38(c)(4)(B)(vi)-(ix)	9015(b)(2)(A)	164(f)[(1)]
1421(d)(1)	280C(h)	9015(b)(2)(B)	1402(a)(12)(B)
1421(d)(2)	196(c)(12)-(14)	9016(a)	833(c)(5)
1414(a)(1)	6103(l)(21)	9017(a)	5000B
1414(b)	6103(a)(3)	9021(a)	139D
1414(c)(1)-(3)	6103(p)(4)	9022(a)	125(j)-(l)
1414(d)	7213(a)(2)	9023(a)	48D
1501(b)	5000A	9023(b)(1)-(3)	46
1502(a)	6055	9023(c)(1)(A)-(C)	49(a)(1)(C)(iv)-(vi)
	6724(d)(1)(B)(xxii)-	9023(c)(2)	280C(g)[(i)]
1502(b)(1)	(xxiv)	10105(a)	36B(b)(3)(A)(ii)
1502(b)(2)	6724(d)(2)(EE)-(GG)	10105(b)	36B(c)(1)(A)
1513(a)	4980H	10105(c)	36B(c)(2)(C)(iv)
1514(a)	6056	10105(d)	6211(b)(4)(A)
	6724(d)(1)(B)(xxiii)-	10105(e)(1)	45R(d)(3)(B)
1514(b)(1)	(xxv)	10105(e)(2)	45R(g)
1514(b)(2)	6724(d)(2)(FF)-(HH)	10105(e)(3)	280C(h)
1515(a)	125(f)(3)	10106(b)(1)	5000A(b)(1)
1515(b)(1)-(2)	125(f)	10106(b)(2)	5000A(c)(1)-(2)
1562(f)	9815	10106(b)(3)	5000A(c)(3)[(B)]
3308(b)(2)(A)-(C)	6103(l)(20)	10106(c)	5000A(d)(2)(A)
6301(e)(1)(A)	9511	10106(d)	5000A(e)(1)(C)
6301(e)(2)(A)	4375-4377	10106(e)	4980H(b)
6301(f)	501(l)(4)	10106(f)(1)	4980H(d)(4)(A)
9001(a)	4980I	10106(f)(2)	4980H(d)(2)(D)
9002(a)	6051(a)(12)-(14)	10106(g)	6056(b)
9003(a)	223(d)(2)(A)	10108(f)(1)	139D[139E]
9003(b)	220(d)(2)(A)	10108(g)(1)	162(a)
9003(c)	106(f)	10108(h)(1)	36B(c)(2)(D)
9004(a)	223(f)(4)(A)	10108(i)(1)(A)	4980H(c)(3)
9004(b)	220(f)(4)(A)	10108(j)(1)	6056(a)
9005(a)(1)-(2)	125(i)-(k)	10108(j)(2)	6056(f)
9006(a)	6041(h)-(i)	10108(j)(3)(A)	6056
9006(b)(1)-(3)	6041(a)	10108(j)(3)(B)(i)-(v)	6056(b)(2)(C)
9007(a)	501(r)-(s)	10108(j)(3)(C)	6056(d)(2)
9007(b)(1)	4959	10108(j)(3)(D)	6056(e)
9007(d)(1)	6033(b)(14)-(16)	10108(j)(3)(E)	6724(d)(1)(B)(xxv)
9007(d)(2)	6033(b)(10)(B)-(D)	10108(j)(3)(F)	6724(d)(2)(HH)
9012(a)	139A	10901(a)	4980I(f)(3)

Act Sec.	Code Sec.	Act Sec.	Code Sec.
10901(b)	4980I(d)(1)(B)(i)	10909(b)(1)(A)-(B)	36C
10902(a)	125(i)	10909(b)(2)(A)	24(b)(3)(B)
10903(a)	501(r)(5)(A)	10909(b)(2)(B)	25(e)(1)(C)
10906(a)	3101(b)(2)	10909(b)(2)(C)	25A(i)(5)(B)
10906(b)	1401(b)(2)(A)	10909(b)(2)(D)	25B(g)(2)
10907(a)	5000B	10909(b)(2)(E)	26(a)(1)
10907(b)	5000B	10909(b)(2)(F)	30(c)(2)(B)(ii)
10908(a)	108(f)(4)	10909(b)(2)(G)	30B(g)(2)(B)(ii)
10909(a)(1)(A)	23(b)(1)	10909(b)(2)(H)	30D(c)(2)(B)(ii)
10909(a)(1)(C)	23(h)	10909(b)(2)(I)(i)-(ii)	36C
10909(a)(2)(A)	137(b)(1)	10909(b)(2)(J)(i)-(ii)	137(d)-(e)
10909(a)(2)(B)(i)-(ii)	23(a)(3)	10909(b)(2)(K)	904(i)
10909(a)(2)(B)(i)-(ii)	137(a)(2)	10909(b)(2)(L)	1016(a)(26)
10909(a)(2)(C)	137(f)	10909(b)(2)(M)	1400C(d)[(2)]
10909(b)(1)(A)-(B)	23	10909(b)(2)(N)	6211(b)(4)(A)

Health Care and Education Reconciliation Act of 2010

Act Sec.	Code Sec.	Act Sec.	Code Sec.
1001(a)(1)(A)-(B)	36B(b)(3)(A)	1004(d)(5)	401(h)
1001(a)(2)(A)-(B)	36B(c)(2)(C)	1401(a)(1)-(3)	4980I(b)(3)(B)-(D)
1002(a)(1)-(2)	5000A(c)(2)-(3)	1401(a)(4)-(5)	4980I(d)
1002(b)(1)	5000A(c)(4)(D)	1402(a)(1)	1411
1002(b)(2)(A)-(B)	5000A(e)(2)	1402(a)(2)(A)	6654(a)
1003(a)	4980H(d)(2)(D)	1402(a)(2)(B)(i)-(ii)	6654(f)(2)-(4)
1003(b)(1)	4980H(c)(1)	1402(b)(1)(A)	3101(b)(2)(A)-(C)
1003(b)(2)	4980H(d)(1)	1402(b)(1)(B)(i)-(ii)	1401(b)(2)(A)-(B)
1003(b)(3)	4980H(d)(5)(A)	1402(b)(2)	6654(m)-(n)
1003(c)	4980H(d)(2)(E)	1403(b)(1)-(2)	125(i)(2)
1003(d)	4980H(b)-(e)	1405(a)(1)	4191
1004(a)(1)(A)	36B(d)(2)(A)(i)-(ii)	1405(b)(1)	4221(a)
1004(a)(1)(B)	6103(l)(21)(A)(iv)	1405(b)(2)	6416(b)(2)
1004(a)(1)(C)	5000A(c)(4)[(B)](i)-(ii)	1408(a)	40(b)(6)(E)(iii)
1004(a)(2)(A)	36B(d)(2)(B)	1409(a)	7701(o)-(p)
1004(a)(2)(B)	5000A(c)(4)(C)	1409(b)(1)	6662(b)(6)
1004(c)	36B(f)(3)	1409(b)(2)	6662(i)
1004(d)(1)(A)-(B)	105(b)	1409(b)(3)(A)-(B)	6662A(e)(2)
1004(d)(2)	162(l)(1)	1409(c)(1)(A)-(C)	6664(c)(2)-(4)
1004(d)(3)	162(l)(2)(B)	1409(c)(2)(A)-(C)	6664(d)(2)-(4)
1004(d)(4)	501(c)(9)	1409(d)	6676(c)-(d)

Hiring Incentives to Restore Employment Act

Act Sec.	Code Sec.	Act Sec.	Code Sec.
101(a)	3111(d)	442(a)	9503(f)(2)
101(b)	51(c)(5)	442(b)	9503(e)(1)
101(d)(1)	3221(c)-(d)	443(a)	9503(f)(4)[(3)]
201(a)(1)-(4)	179(b)	444(a)	9503(c)(2)-(6)
301(a)	6431(f)	444(b)(1)	9502(a)
301(b)(1)	54F(d)(1)	444(b)(2)	9503(b)(4)(D)
301(b)(2)	54F(e)	444(b)(3)	9503(c)(2)
441(a)	9503(f)(1)(B)	444(b)(4)	9503(e)(5)(A)
441(b)(1)-(2)	9503(f)(1)	444(b)(5)	9504(a)

Act Sec.	Code Sec.
444(b)(6)	9504(b)(2)
444(b)(7)	9504(e)
445(a)(1)(A)-(B)	9503(c)(1)
445(a)(2)(A)-(B)	9503(e)(3)
445(a)(3)	9503(b)(6)(B)
445(b)(1)(A)-(C)	9504(b)(2)
445(b)(2)	9504(d)(2)
501(a)	1471-1474
501(b)	6611(e)(4)
501(c)(1)	6414
501(c)(2)	6501(b)(1)
501(c)(3)(A)-(B)	6501(b)(2)
501(c)(4)(A)-(B)	6513(b)(3)
501(c)(5)	6513(c)
501(c)(6)	6724(d)(1)
501(c)(7)	6724(d)(2)
502(a)(1)	163(f)(2)(B)-(C)
502(a)(2)(A)	149(a)(2)(A)-(C)
502(a)(2)(B)	163(f)(2)(A)(ii)-(iv)
502(a)(2)(C)(i)-(ii)	163(f)(2)(B)
502(a)(2)(D)	165(j)(2)(A)
502(a)(2)(D)	1287(b)(1)
502(b)(1)	871(h)(2)
502(b)(2)(A)	871(h)(3)(A)
502(b)(2)(B)	881(c)(2)
502(c)	163(f)(3)

Act Sec.	Code Sec.
502(e)	4701(b)(1)
511(a)	6038D
512(a)(1)	6662(b)(7)[(6)]
512(a)(2)	6662(j)[(i)]
513(a)(1)	6501(e)(1)(A)-(C)
513(a)(2)(A)	6501(e)(1)(B)
513(a)(2)(B)	6229(c)(2)
513(b)(1)-(3)	6501(c)(8)
513(c)	6501(c)(8)
521(a)	1298(f)-(g)
521(b)	1291(e)
522(a)	6011(e)(4)
522(b)	6724(c)
531(a)	679(c)(1)
531(b)	679(c)(4)
531(c)	679(c)(5)
532(a)	679(d)-(e)
533(a)(1)-(2)	643(i)(1)
533(b)	643(i)(2)(E)
533(c)	679(c)(6)
533(d)(1)-(3)	643(i)(3)
534(a)	6048(b)(1)
535(a)(1)-(2)	6677(a)
541(a)	871(l)-(m)
551(a)	864(f)(5)-(6)

Temporary Extension Act of 2010

Act Sec.	Code Sec.
3(b)(5)(A)	35(g)(9)
3(b)(5)(B)	139C
3(b)(5)(C)(i)	6432(a)
3(b)(5)(C)(ii)	6432(c)(3)

Act Sec.	Code Sec.
3(b)(5)(C)(iii)	6432(e)-(g)
3(b)(5)(D)	6720C(a)

¶27,001 Client Letters

¶27,005 CLIENT LETTER #1

Re: Dealing with Health Care Reform's New Tax Laws

Dear Client:

Now that Congress has passed landmark health care reform package, much work needs to be done in dealing with new requirements. While the end result of the legislative process is necessarily health care related, the tax law plays a major role in its implementation. From the tax credits and subsidies used to expand health coverage, to the many penalties, fees and surtaxes designed to pay for it, the Tax Code is front and center.

Two new laws

Health care reform is actually made up of two new laws: the Patient Protection and Affordable Care Act of 2010 and the Health Care and Education Reconciliation Act of 2010. The Patient Protection Act was crafted largely in the Senate and sets out the general framework of health care reform. The Reconciliation Act was prepared in the House to modify the Patient Protection Act, especially in the areas of tax credits and cost sharing for individuals to help make coverage more affordable. Common features to both laws are delayed effective dates for many of the provisions, which make strategic planning all that more important.

New taxes and penalties

Viewing the historic health care reform package from the context of the Tax Code, many new taxes and penalties stand out immediately above the rest. Initially, we would advise taking particular note of the following highlights:

- Individuals who earn more than $200,000 for the year ($250,000 for married couples) will be paying an additional 0.9 percent in Hospital Insurance (Medicare) tax, starting in 2013;

- Individuals whose adjusted gross income for the year exceed $200,000 ($250,000 for joint filers), whether from wages or otherwise, will also be paying an additional 3.8 percent Medicare tax on net investment income, starting in 2013;

- Employers with 50 or more employees generally will be required to provide a minimum level of health insurance for their employees or pay a penalty per employee, starting in 2014;

- Small employers with no more than 25 employees are entitled to up to a 35 percent tax credit on the cost of providing health insurance for employees, starting immediately in 2010;

- Most individuals will be required to obtain health insurance or be subject to a penalty tax starting in 2014;

- Tax credits to subsidize the cost of health insurance premiums will be available to individuals earning up to 400 percent of the poverty level, starting in 2014;

- Health flexible savings arrangement (FSA) dollars will be limited to prescription medications with some exceptions after 2010, along with placing a $2,500 annual cap on expenses covered under health FSAs, starting in 2013.
- A 40 percent excise tax will be imposed on high-cost, "Cadillac" employer-sponsored health coverage, starting in 2018;
- Fees will be imposed on the pharmaceutical industry and health insurance providers , starting in 2011 and 2014, respectively;
- An excise tax will be imposed on medical device manufacturers after 2012; and
- Limits on tax-subsidized medical expenses will be imposed by raising the itemized medical expense deduction floor for regular tax purposes from 7.5 percent to 10 percent, generally starting in 2013.

Tax incentives

Among a handful of tax incentives provided under the new health-care reform package, two are particularly notable at this time: (1) the ability of parents to cover adult children up to age 27 under their tax-qualified employer-provided health plans, starting immediately on or after March 23, 2010; and (2) the unveiling of a simplified cafeteria plan specifically tailored to small businesses, starting in 2011.

Exchanges

The health care reform package requires each state to establish an exchange by 2014 to help individuals and qualified employers obtain coverage. Coverage will be offered at various levels. Qualified individuals may be eligible for premium assistance tax credits, cost-sharing or vouchers to help pay for coverage through an insurance exchange. An individual's income whether or not coverage is provided by his or her employer will all be taken into account when determining if the individual qualifies for a premium assistance tax credit, cost-sharing or voucher.

IRS guidance

Over the course of the next few months, the IRS and other federal agencies will be filling in details on how to comply with all the provisions under the massive health care reform package. The IRS is expected to issue guidance soon on the provisions with effective dates in 2010 and 2011. This office will be staying on top of all developments, with an eye toward how to best maximize results under the new law for our clients. We are prepared to advise our clients on all compliance rules and tax-reduction opportunities that undoubtedly will arise. In the meantime, if you have any questions about the new law, please do not hesitate to call our office.

Sincerely yours,

¶27,010 CLIENT LETTER #2

Re: Patient Protection and Affordable Care Act: Individuals

Dear Client:

The Patient Protection and Affordable Care (PPAC) Act, as amended by the Health Care and Education Reconciliation Act of 2010 (Reconciliation Act), was enacted to provide quality, affordable health care for all Americans. Although the primary thrust of the PPAC Act is health insurance reform, the tax law plays a key role in implementing that goal. Individuals both receive benefits and are subject to responsibilities under the PPAC Act. The following are highlights of the tax provisions of the PPAC Act that affect individuals. Several of these provisions take effect in 2010, but others are not effective until later years.

Penalty for failing to carry health insurance. Beginning in 2014, the PPAC Act imposes a penalty on "applicable individuals" who fail to ensure that they and their dependents have minimum essential health coverage by obtaining insurance either from a private insurer or through one of the new American Health Benefit Exchanges (AHBEs) to be established by each state by January 1, 2014. This penalty is also called a "shared responsibility payment." The penalty is equal to the lesser of the sum of the monthly penalty amounts for the tax year, or the amount of the national average premium for qualified health plans that offer a specified minimum level of coverage; provide coverage for families the size of the taxpayer's family; and are offered through AHBEs.

The nonprofit AHBEs are responsible for certifying that an "applicable individual" is exempt from the penalty because no affordable qualified health plan is available through the individual's AHBE or employer, or because the individual meets the requirements for any other exemption from the penalty.

Medical benefits for children under age 27. The exclusion from gross income for reimbursements made under an employer-provided accident or health insurance plan for medical care expenses of an employee, employee's spouse, or employee's dependents, is extended to apply to any child of the employee who is not age 27 as of the end of the tax year. The child does not have to be a dependent of the employee for this exclusion to apply. Therefore, the exclusion applies even if the child provides more than one-half of his or her own support, earns more income than the exemption amount, or does not live with the parents. The provision is effective on the date of enactment of the 2010 Reconciliation Act.

Health insurance premium assistance refundable credit. Those individuals who cannot afford coverage may be eligible for a refundable health insurance premium assistance credit (PAC). For those purchasing coverage within an AHBE, an advanceable and refundable PAC can limit the out-of-pocket expense for silver health plan premiums. Those purchasing silver-level coverage may also qualify for cost-sharing subsidies to help pay for deductibles, copayments, etc.

The PAC operates on a sliding scale that begins at two percent of income for taxpayers at 100 percent of the federal poverty level (FPL) and phases out at 9.5 percent of income for those at 300-400 percent of the FPL. This credit applies to tax years ending after December 31, 2013.

Free choice voucher. Under the PPAC Act, individuals who cannot afford the plans provided by their employers may be eligible for a free choice voucher to help them purchase insurance through their state's AHBE. If the amount of the free choice voucher exceeds the amount of the premium of the qualified health plan in which the qualified employee is enrolled for the month, the excess is paid to the employee. The amount of any free choice voucher provided is excluded from the employee's gross income to the extent that the amount of the voucher does not exceed the amount paid for a qualified health plan. This exclusion applies to vouchers issued after December 31, 2013.

Itemized deduction for medical expenses. The PPAC Act increases the threshold for the itemized deduction for unreimbursed medical expenses from 7.5% to 10% of adjusted gross income (AGI) for tax years beginning after December 31, 2012. A temporary waiver of the increased threshold applies to tax years beginning after 2012 and before 2017 for individuals who are age 65 and older before the close of the tax year.

Distributions and reimbursements limited to prescribed medicines and insulin. The definition of qualified medical expense for purposes of Health Savings Accounts, Archer Medical Savings Accounts, Health Flexible Spending Arrangements, Health Reimbursement Arrangements, and other accident and health plans does not include any amounts paid for over-the counter medications. This applies to distributions from such accounts after December 31, 2010.

Reduction of Part D premium subsidy for high-income beneficiaries. Starting in 2011, the Medicare portion or premium subsidy amount has been reduced for certain beneficiaries of the Voluntary Prescription Drug Benefit Program under Medicare Part D whose modified adjusted gross income (AGI) exceeds the thresholds used under Part B. The PPAC provides the Social Security Administration with access to certain Internal Revenue Service information about taxpayers which helps in determining these reductions. This information-sharing provision is considered effective on March 23, 2010.

Additional tax on HSA and Archer MSA distributions. The PPAC Act increases the additional tax on distributions made from HSAs not used for qualified medical expenses from 10 percent to 20 percent of the amount includible in gross income. Similarly, the additional tax on distributions made from Archer MSAs not used for qualified medical expenses is increased from 15 percent to 20 percent of the amount includible in gross income. These provisions apply to distributions made after December 31, 2010.

Health FSAs offered in cafeteria plans. For tax years beginning after December 31, 2012, a Health FSA is not a qualified benefit under a cafeteria plan unless the plan provides for a $2,500 maximum salary reduction contribution to the FSA. If the plan does allow salary reductions in excess of $2,500, then an employee is subject to tax on Health FSA distributions.

Additional hospital insurance (Medicare) taxes for high-income taxpayers. In addition to the 1.45 percent employee portion of the hospital and hospital service insurance (HI) tax imposed on wages, 0.9 percent tax will be imposed on individuals who receive wages or self-employment income in excess of $200,000 ($250,000 for married joint filers, and $125,000 for married separate filers). These excess wages are subject to a total HI rate (combined employer and employee portions) of 3.8 percent. If the additional HI tax is not withheld by the employer, the employee is responsible for paying the tax. This additional HI tax does not qualify for the one-half of self-employment taxes above-the-line deduction from income. These provisions apply with respect to remuneration received, and tax years beginning, after December 31, 2012.

Medicare tax on unearned income. The 2010 Reconciliation Act imposes a 3.8 percent unearned income Medicare contribution tax on the lesser of an individual's net investment income, or any excess of modified AGI for the tax year over a threshold amount. The unearned income Medicare contribution tax is subject to the failure to pay estimated tax penalty. The new Medicare tax applies to tax years beginning after December 31, 2012.

Excise tax on tanning salons. The PPAC Act adds a 10 percent excise tax on the cost of "indoor tanning services." The excise tax is imposed on the full amount of the charge for the service and is imposed regardless of who pays the ultimate cost of the service, whether insurance or otherwise. Although the tax is imposed on the patron of the tanning salon, the salon owner is required to collect the taxes and remit them to the IRS on a quarterly basis. This provision applies to tanning services performed on or after July 1, 2010.

Expansion of adoption credit and adoption assistance programs. The adoption credit for qualified adoption expenses for each eligible child has been increased by $1,000 to $13,170, and is made refundable. These amounts are still indexed for inflation. An employee's gross income does not include amounts paid or expenses incurred by an employer for the employee's qualified adoption expenses pursuant to an adoption assistance program. The adoption credit and adoption assistance program amendments apply to tax years beginning after December 31, 2009. In addition, the previous sunset provision, which would have reduced the amount of the credit and exclusion allowable to previous levels, is extended through December 31, 2011.

Gross income exclusion for repayments under state loan programs for health care professionals. In addition to repayments under the National Health Service Corps Loan Program and state repayment programs under the Public Health Service Act, the PPAC Act excludes from gross income those repayments under other state loan repayment or forgiveness programs that are intended to provide for the increased availability of health care services in underserved or health professional shortage areas (as determined by the state). This incentive is available for amounts received by health care professionals in tax years beginning after 2008.

Qualified health care benefits of Indian tribe members. Qualified health care benefits provided after March 23, 2010 to the member of an Indian tribe, the member's spouse, or the member's dependents are excluded from the recipient's gross income. To deny a double tax benefit, this exclusion does not apply to the amount of a qualified Indian health care benefit that ls not includible in the gross income of the beneficiary under another tax law provision. Similarly, the exclusion does not apply to the amount of a qualified benefit for which the beneficiary may claim a deduction under another provision.

If you have any questions regarding these health care provisions, please call our office at your earliest convenience.

Sincerely yours,

¶27,010

¶27,015 CLIENT LETTER #3

Re: Patient Protection and Affordable Care Act: Businesses

Dear Client:

The Patient Protection and Affordable Care (PPAC) Act, as amended by the Health Care and Education Reconciliation Act of 2010 (Reconciliation Act), was enacted to provide quality, affordable health care for all Americans. Although the primary thrust of the PPAC Act is health insurance reform, the tax law provides a key role in achieving that goal. Employers have many responsibilities to help achieve health insurance reform. These range from providing greater health insurance coverage and helping to pay for that coverage, to providing the information necessary to enforce the requirements of the new legislation. Health insurance providers also have many new requirements imposed by the legislation, including taxes, fees, reporting obligations and limits on executive compensation. The following are highlights of the tax provisions of the PPAC Act relating to businesses.

Shared responsibility assessable payment imposed on certain large employers. Beginning after December 31, 2013, an assessable payment will be imposed on an applicable large employer that

1. fails to offer to its full-time employees (and their dependents) the opportunity to enroll in minimum essential coverage under an eligible employer-sponsored plan for any month, and

2. has at least one full-time employee who has been certified as having enrolled for that month in a state exchange offered plan with respect to which an applicable premium tax credit or cost-sharing reduction is allowed or paid for the employee.

The assessable payment is equal to $166.67 (adjusted for inflation) times the number of full-time employees for the month.

Additional hospital insurance tax on high-income taxpayers. In addition to the 1.45 percent employee portion of the hospital service insurance tax (HT) imposed on wages, 0.9 percent (HT) will be imposed on every taxpayer who receives wages in excess of $200,000 ($250,000 in the case of a joint return, $125,000 in the case of a married taxpayer filing separately). This provision applies to wages paid after 2012.

Credit for employee health expenses of eligible small employers. For tax years beginning after 2009, an eligible small employer may claim a tax credit if it makes nonelective contributions that pay for at least one-half of the cost of health insurance premiums for the coverage of participating employees.

Free choice vouchers. An employer who offers minimum essential coverage to its employees consisting of coverage through an eligible employer-sponsored plan and pays any portion of the plan's costs shall provide free-choice vouchers to its qualified employees. Qualified employees are those who do not participate in a health plan offered by the employer and meet other requirements. The free-choice voucher amount is generally equal to the monthly portion of the cost of the eligible employer-sponsored plan that would have been paid by the employer if the employee were covered under the plan.

Exchange-participating qualified health plans offered through cafeteria plans. A cafeteria plan may not provide a health plan that is offered through the American

Health Benefit Exchange unless the employer is a qualified employer for purposes of the Exchange.

Limitation of FSAs offered as part of cafeteria plans. For tax years beginning after December 31, 2012, a health flexible spending arrangement (FSA) will not be a qualified benefit under a cafeteria plan unless the plan provides for a $2,500 maximum salary reduction contribution to the FSA. Any excess contributions are subject to tax at the time of the distribution.

Distributions and reimbursements limited to prescribed medicines and insulin. The definition of qualified medical expense for purposes of Health Savings Accounts, Archer Medical Savings Accounts, Health Flexible Spending Arrangements, Health Reimbursement Arrangements, and other accident and health plans does not include any amounts paid for over-the counter medications. This applies to distributions from such accounts after December 31, 2010.

Small employers can provide simple cafeteria plans. In tax years beginning after December 31, 2010, certain small employers' cafeteria plans may qualify as "simple" cafeteria plans under which the applicable nondiscrimination requirements of a classic cafeteria plan are treated as satisfied.

Deduction repealed for expenses allocable to Medicare Part D subsidy. The provision that allows an employer to disregard the value of any qualified retiree prescription drug plan subsidy in calculating the employer's business deduction for retiree prescription drug costs is repealed for tax years beginning after December 31, 2012.

New limitations on employee remuneration. An individual's remuneration for services in excess of $500,000 is not deductible by certain covered health insurance providers for tax years beginning after December 31, 2009.

Excise tax on high cost employer-sponsored health coverage. A 40 percent excise tax will be imposed on insurers starting in 2018 to the extent that the aggregate value of employer-sponsored coverage for an employee exceeds a threshold amount. The tax is not deductible for federal income tax purposes.

Annual fee imposed on drug manufacturers and importers and U.S. health insurance providers; excise tax on sales of medical devices. New annual fees apply to manufacturers and importers for U.S. sales of branded prescription drugs beginning in 2011. New annual fees are also imposed on the net premium written by certain health insurance providers beginning in 2014. A new excise tax is imposed on sales of certain medical devices after December 31, 2012.

Credit for investment in qualifying therapeutic discovery project. A tax credit is allowed for 50 percent of an eligible taxpayer's qualified investment for the tax year with respect to any qualifying therapeutic discovery project. This credit is part of the investment credit. An eligible taxpayer is one that has no more than 250 employees.

Excise tax on patrons of indoor tanning salons. A 10 percent excise tax is added to the cost of indoor tanning services performed on or after July 1, 2010.

New disclosure requirements for employers. For tax years beginning after December 31, 2010, employers are required to disclose the total cost of certain health

¶27,015

insurance coverage provided to the employee on the employee's Form W-2 regardless of whether the employee or the employer pays for the coverage.

Information reporting required for health insurance coverage. Every employer who provides minimum essential coverage to an individual during a calendar year is required to file a return reporting such coverage.

Reporting requirements for large employers. Large employers that are subject to the new rules for shared responsibility regarding healthcare coverage, and certain employers that offer minimum essential coverage to their employees through an eligible plan are required to file a return reporting such coverage.

Information reporting of payments to corporations. The general information reporting requirement exception for payments to corporations is eliminated. Therefore, if the total of all payments made by a payer in the course of its trade or business to a corporation equals $600 or more in any tax year, the payer must file the appropriate information return.

This is just a brief summary of highlights of the healthcare legislation. The details of the new provisions including definitions, calculations, procedures and exceptions are too numerous to include in this letter. It is expected that the IRS will issue guidance in the near future. In the meantime, please call our office if you wish to discuss how this may affect you. We will be happy to answer any questions you might have.

Sincerely yours,

¶27,020 CLIENT LETTER #4

Re: HIRE Act: Incentives to Hire and Retain the Unemployed

Dear Client:

In an effort to confront high unemployment, the Hiring Incentives to Restore Employment (HIRE) Act provides incentives for hiring and retaining unemployed workers. Under the HIRE Act, a qualified employer's 6.2 percent share of OASDI Social Security tax liability is forgiven for new hires, and a general business credit is allowed for each retained worker that satisfies a minimum employment period.

Payroll Tax Forgiveness for Hiring Unemployed Workers. The HIRE Act provides relief from the employer share of OASDI taxes on wages paid by a qualified employer with respect to certain covered employment. Covered employment is limited to service performed by a qualified individual in a trade or business of a qualified employer, or in the furtherance of the activities related to the purpose or function constituting the basis of the employer's exemption under Code Sec. 501. This provision applies to wages paid beginning on the day after enactment and ending on December 31, 2010.

Although a qualified employer does not include the United States, any State, any local government, or any instrumentality thereof, a qualified employer may include a public higher education institution.

A qualified individual is any individual who:

1. begins work for a qualified employer after February 3, 2010, and before January 1, 2011;
2. certifies by signed affidavit (under penalties of perjury) that he or she was employed for a total of 40 hours or less during the 60-day period ending on the date such employment begins;
3. is not employed to replace another employee of the employer unless such employee separated from employment voluntarily or for cause; and
4. is not a related party.

Employers who qualify for the OASDI forgiveness in the first quarter of 2010 will receive the benefit through a credit toward general second quarter 2010 OASDI liability; they can't simply stop paying the 6.2 percent OASDI tax immediately on wages paid to new hires. After the first quarter, however, the employer does not pay the 6.2 percent tax as wages are paid.

A qualified employer may not receive the work opportunity tax credit on wages paid to an individual during the one-year period beginning on the hire date for the same wages used to qualify for the forgiveness of payroll tax. However, an employer may elect to not have payroll tax forgiveness apply.

Business Credit for Retention of Certain Newly Hired Individuals. Under the HIRE Act, an employer's general business credit is increased by the lesser of $1,000 or 6.2 percent of salary for each retained worker that satisfies a minimum employment period. Generally, a retained worker is an individual who is a qualified individual as defined for purposes of the provision for payroll tax forgiveness. However, the credit is available only with respect to such individual, if the individual:

1. is employed by the employer on any date during the tax year;
2. continues to be employed by the employer for a period of not less than 52 consecutive weeks; and
3. receives wages for such employment during the last 26 weeks of such period that are at least 80-percent of such wages during the first 26 weeks of such period.

Therefore, an employer will qualify for the full $1,000 credit for each new hire with a salary over the 52 retention period of at least $16,129. An employer that hires some part-time new employees, in addition to full-time employees, is entitled to the full $1,000 credit, if, of course, the part-time or full-time employee decides to stay for 52 weeks.

Because payroll taxes are deductible as an ordinary and necessary business expense, employers may have a correspondingly smaller business expense deduction on their 2010 tax returns. By combining the benefit of the business credit for new hires with the forgiveness incentive, employers in the highest brackets will realize a net tax benefit of just over four percent of wages paid to qualified new employees, up to the $106,800 social security maximum wage base. Therefore, for the maximum $6,621.60 tax forgiveness for a new hire, a net benefit of approximately $4,304 would be realized.

If you have any questions regarding the hiring incentives under the HIRE Act, please call our office at your earliest convenience.

Sincerely yours,

¶27,025 CLIENT LETTER #5

Re: HIRE Act: Extension of Increased Code Sec. 179 Expensing

Dear Client:

Congress has passed the Hiring Incentives to Restore Employment (HIRE) Act, which, as an incentive for business investment in capital and equipment, includes a provision extending for one year previous increases in the maximum amount that a business taxpayer may deduct for the cost of such investment under Code Sec. 179. This provision extends prior law increases in the limitation on expense deductions for new equipment placed in service during the tax year. More specifically, the HIRE Act extends the available expense deduction limitation under Code Sec. 179 of $250,000, and the phase-out amount of $800,000, through tax years beginning in 2010. Bonus depreciation is not extended.

Because these extensions are temporary and generally apply only to tax years beginning in 2010, new purchases should be made and placed in service accordingly. The expense deduction of $250,000 will drop to $25,000 for qualifying assets placed in service after 2010. Similarly, in 2011, the phase-out amount is scheduled to be reduced to $200,000.

If you have any questions about how this development applies to you, or about any other aspects of this legislation, please contact our office at your convenience.

Sincerely yours,

¶27,030 CLIENT LETTER #6

Re: HIRE Act: Foreign Account Tax Compliance Requirements

Dear Client:

The Hiring Incentives to Restore Employment (HIRE) Act imposes additional reporting and disclosure requirements for taxpayers with any interest in a "specified foreign financial asset" if the aggregate value of all such assets exceeds $50,000. These reporting requirements apply to any domestic entity which holds "specified foreign financial assets" directly or indirectly, as if the entity were an individual taxpayer.

For purposes of the additional reporting and disclosure requirements, a specified foreign financial asset is:

- any financial account maintained by a foreign financial institution;
- any of the following assets which are not held in an account maintained by a financial institution:
  - any stock or security issued by a person other than a U.S. person;
  - any financial instrument or contract held for investment that has an issuer or countertparty which is other than a U.S. person; and
  - any interest in a foreign entity.

The required information varies depending on the type of specified foreign financial asset. Therefore, taxpayers with an interest in:

- foreign bank accounts must provide the name and address of the financial institution where the account is maintained, and the account number;
- foreign-issued stocks and securities must provide the name and address of the issuer, and all pertinent information that allows the class or issue of such stock or security to be identified; and
- foreign instruments, contracts, or entities must provide the names and addresses of all foreign issuers and counterparties, the maximum value of the asset during the tax year, and all pertinent information required to identify the foreign asset.

The HIRE Act also requires a withholding agent to deduct and withhold a tax equal to 30 percent on any withholdable payment made to a foreign financial institution if the foreign financial institution does not meet certain requirements. There are exceptions and special rules in situations where there is an agreement in effect between the financial institution and the Secretary of the Treasury.

A withholding agent includes any person, in whatever capacity, having the control, receipt, custody, disposal, or payment of any payment of interest (including OID), dividends, rents, salaries, wages, premiums, annuities, compensations, remunerations, emoluments, and other fixed or determinable annual or periodic gains, profits, and income from sources within the United States.

A foreign financial institution may make an election and report as if the foreign financial institution were a U.S. person. The withholding payments provision generally applies to payments made after December 31, 2012.

The penalty for failing to disclose the required information in a timely manner is $10,000. If the failure to disclose continues for more than 90 days after the IRS notifies the taxpayer of a failure to report, the taxpayer must pay an additional $10,000 for each 30-day period (or fraction thereof) during which such failure continues after the expiration of the 90-day period. The maximum penalty is $50,000. However, no penalty is imposed if the failure to disclose is due to reasonable cause, and not due to willful neglect. In addition, the penalties have increased from 20 percent to 40 percent for any portion of an underpayment attributable to understatement.

Because of the substantial penalties associated with these new requirements, it is important that you have a complete understanding of your obligations if you have an interest in a specified foreign financial asset. Please call our office for more information.

Sincerely yours,

¶27,035 CLIENT LETTER #7

Re: HIRE Act: Hiring Incentives to Restore Employment Act

Dear Client:

To help jumpstart business hiring and spending, Congress has passed, and President Obama has signed, the Hiring Incentives to Restore Employment (HIRE) Act (H.R. 2847). The HIRE Act provides for payroll tax forgiveness and an employer tax credit of up to $1,000 for qualified new hires. The HIRE Act also extends enhanced Code Sec. 179 small business expensing and makes some enhancements to tax credit bonds. These measures are paid for, in part, by comprehensive reforms to the reporting and disclosure of accounts in foreign financial institutions, a further delay in implementation of worldwide allocation of interest and an acceleration of certain corporate estimated income tax payments. The HIRE Act is expected to be the first of several targeted jobs bills to be passed by Congress in 2010.

Hiring incentives. The HIRE Act provides qualified employers with temporary payroll tax forgiveness of the employer's 6.2 percent share of Social Security payroll taxes on wages paid to new hires who had been previously unemployed. Payroll tax forgiveness is effective for qualified employees on wages earned for work after March 18, 2010 and on or before December 31, 2010. A qualified employee must begin work any time after February 3, 2010 and before January 1, 2011. The employer generally must be a private sector for-profit or tax-exempt employer (with some limited exceptions).

The newly hired worker must not have been employed for more than 40 hours during the 60-day period ending on the date that the individual begins employment. Additionally, the newly hired employee cannot displace a worker who is currently on the employer's payroll unless the worker voluntarily separated from employment or was separated from employment for cause. Newly hired individuals who are related to the employer or who own (directly or indirectly) more than 50 percent of the business are ineligible. A qualified individual may be hired for any number of hours, full-time or part-time, since the benefits to the employer are tied only to 6.2 percent of any salary paid.

The HIRE Act requires that individuals certify they have not been employed for more than 40 hours during the 60-day period ending on the date they begin employment. The IRS is expected to issue guidance on the certification requirement.

Let's take a look at an example.

ABC Co. hires Jean on January 25, 2010 as a full-time employee working 40 hours each week. ABC hires Luis on February 15, 2010 as a full-time employee working 40 hours each week. ABC hires Sam on March 1, 2010 as a full-time employee working 40 hours each week. Jean, Luis and Sam all certify that they had not been employed for more than 40 hours during the 60-day period ending on the date that they began employment with ABC Co. However, Jean is not a qualified employee for purposes of payroll tax forgiveness under the HIRE Act because her hire date is before February 4, 2010. Luis and Sam are qualified employees for purpose of payroll tax forgiveness because their hire dates are after February 3, 2010.

Keep in mind that the HIRE Act's payroll tax forgiveness applies only to the employer's share of Social Security taxes. Employers remain liable for Medicare payroll taxes. The worker also must pay his or her share of Social Security taxes as well as federal income taxes.

The HIRE Act also provides that the direct payroll tax holiday will not apply to wages paid during the first calendar quarter of 2010. Instead, whatever tax holiday amount would have been allowed for first quarter 2010 will instead be credited against the employer's general OASDI liability for the second quarter of 2010. Beginning for any new-hire wages paid starting April 1, an employer takes direct OASDI forgiveness into account in depositing payroll taxes under the regular deposit rule applicable to that employer.

Retained worker business credit. Under the HIRE Act, employers that hire new workers who qualify for payroll tax forgiveness may also be eligible for a tax credit for each qualified employee. For the employer to be entitled to this new credit, the qualified employee must be retained on the employer's payroll for 52 consecutive weeks. The business credit under Code Sec. 38 will be increased, with respect to each qualified retained worker, by the lesser of $1,000 or 6.2 percent of wages paid by the taxpayer to the qualified retained worker during the 52 week period.

A qualified retained worker must be paid an amount equal to at least 80 percent of his first 26 weeks of wages during the last 26 weeks of the 52-week qualifying period. The HIRE Act excludes wages earned by a domestic worker or an individual eligible for the foreign earned income exclusion. The HIRE Act also includes carryback rules for the credit.

If you have any questions about payroll tax forgiveness or the retained worker business credit, please contact our office for more details.

Expensing. Under Code Sec. 179, businesses can elect to recover all or part of the cost of qualifying property, up to a limit, by deducting it in the year it is placed in service. Before the HIRE Act, Code Sec. 179 expensing for 2010 was limited to $125,000 with a $500,000 cap (both amounts adjusted for inflation). The HIRE Act raises the dollar limit to $250,000 and the cap to $800,000 (the same amounts in place in 2009). Under the HIRE Act, write-offs can be taken under phaseout rules until qualified purchases reach $1,050,000. The HIRE Act applies to qualified purchases made in tax years beginning after December 31, 2009 and before January 1, 2011. The HIRE Act also provides that off-the-shelf computer software, a popular business purchase, is Code Sec. 179 property.

Tax credit bonds. The American Recovery and Reinvestment Act of 2009 (2009 Recovery Act) created the new Build America Bond program, which authorizes state and local governments to issue Build America Bonds. These are taxable bonds issued in 2009 and 2010 to finance any capital expenditures for which state and local governments could issue tax-exempt governmental bonds. At the election of the state or local government, the U.S. Treasury will make a direct payment to the issuer in an amount equal to 35 percent of the interest payment on Build America Bonds. This feature is designed to provide a federal subsidy for a larger portion of the borrowing costs of state and local governments than traditional tax-exempt bonds.

The HIRE Act allows issuers of existing tax credit bonds to treat bonds issued after March 18, 2010 as Build America Bonds. Consequently, issuers would qualify for the direct subsidy under Build America Bonds. Some of the tax credit bonds that may qualify include renewable energy bonds, qualified energy conservation bonds, qualified zone academy bonds, and qualified school construction bonds.

Foreign accounts. The Bank Secrecy Act requires taxpayers to report if they have a financial interest in, signature authority or other authority over one or more accounts in a foreign country, and the value of the account exceeds $10,000 at any time during the calendar year. The Bank Secrecy Act does not prohibit taxpayers from owning a foreign bank account. It just requires reporting and disclosure. The rules apply to all citizens and residents of the U.S. as well as domestic corporations, estates, partnerships, and trusts.

The HIRE Act imposes additional reporting and disclosure requirements on taxpayers and financial institutions. Generally, individuals with accounts in foreign financial institutions must disclose on their federal tax returns the name of the financial institution, the account number and the maximum value of the asset during the tax year. The aggregate value of the foreign financial assets must exceed $50,000 for the disclosure requirements to apply. The HIRE Act provides penalties for failing to disclose. The penalties range from a low of $10,000 to a high of $50,000. A 40 percent penalty will apply to the portion of any underpayment attributable to an undisclosed foreign financial asset.

Foreign financial institutions will also be subject to heightened reporting requirements. Generally, foreign financial institutions will be required, among other things, to report the name, address and tax identification number (TIN) of each account holder who is a specified U.S. person. The HIRE Act also will require withholding agents—starting after 2012—to withhold 30 percent of certain payments to foreign financial institutions that do not agree to the new reporting requirements.

Along with the heightened reporting and disclosure measures, the HIRE Act also increases the statute of limitations to six years for failure to report certain offshore transactions and income. The HIRE Act also clarifies when a foreign trust is considered to have a U.S. beneficiary and addresses the treatment of substitute dividends and dividend equivalent payments.

The foreign account compliance measures in the HIRE Act are very complex. The IRS is expected to issue guidance on the measures. Please contact our office if you have any questions about the foreign account compliance provisions in the HIRE Act.

Worldwide allocation of interest. Qualified taxpayers may elect to take advantage of a rule for allocating interest expense between U.S. sources and foreign sources for purposes of determining a taxpayer's foreign tax credit limitation. Implementation of worldwide allocation of interest was enacted in 2004 but has been delayed several times. The HIRE Act further delays implementation to tax years beginning after 2020.

Corporate estimated income taxes. Generally, a corporation is required to make quarterly estimated payments of income tax during its tax year. The HIRE Act increases the estimated payment required to be made by corporations with assets of $1 billion or more in July, August or September of 2014, 2015 and 2019 with proportional reductions for the respective subsequent installment periods.

Pending legislation. Congress continues to debate several other bills designed to stimulate economic growth. Pending bills include a package of extenders. These are popular but temporary tax breaks, which generally expired at the end of 2009.

¶27,035

Congress is also debating an extension of COBRA premium assistance, which provides a subsidy to qualified individuals to help offset the cost of COBRA continuation coverage. Also waiting for passage in Congress is an extension of the federal estate tax, which expired for decedents dying after December 31, 2009. Several retirement and pension bills are also pending. Additionally, Congress has to approve a fiscal year (FY) 2011 budget for the IRS. The Obama administration has asked Congress to increase the IRS's funding for enforcement, compliance and customer service. Finally, Congress is also expected to act shortly on health care reform. At least initially, a new health care law will introduce a new level of complexity for many individuals and businesses alike. Health care reform, if enacted, is expected to be implemented over several years.

If you have any questions about the HIRE Act or pending legislation, please contact our office.

Sincerely yours,

Topical Index

References are to paragraph (¶) numbers

References are to paragraph (¶) numbers

References are to paragraph (¶) numbers

PAT